Virtues and Fallacies of VAT

Virtues and Fallacies of VAT

An Evaluation after 50 Years

Edited by

Robert F. van Brederode

Wolters Kluwer

Published by:
Kluwer Law International B.V.
PO Box 316
2400 AH Alphen aan den Rijn
The Netherlands
E-mail: international-sales@wolterskluwer.com
Website: lrus.wolterskluwer.com

Sold and distributed by:
Wolters Kluwer Legal & Regulatory U.S.
7201 McKinney Circle
Frederick, MD 21704
United States of America
E-mail: customer.service@wolterskluwer.com

ISBN 978-94-035-2423-8

e-Book: ISBN 978-94-035-2424-5
web-PDF: ISBN 978-94-035-2425-2

In memory of our colleague and friend, Richard M. Bird, who passed shortly after we finalized this book. He will be deeply missed.

Editor

Robert F. van Brederode (LL.M., Utrecht University, 1985; PhD, Amsterdam University, 1993) is the Managing Partner of BrederodeTax, LLC, a niche consulting firm, and an independent researcher. He is a former PwC partner and served as Professor of Taxation at the Erasmus University, School of Economics, and as adjunct professor at New York University, School of Law, Graduate Tax Program. His most recent books are *Ethics and Taxation* (Springer, 2020), *VAT and Financial Services: Comparative Law and Economic Perspectives* (Springer, 2017 with Richard Krever), and *Legal Interpretation of Tax Law* (Kluwer Law International, 2nd revised and extended ed., 2017 with Richard Krever).

Contributors

Christian Amand has a law degree from the University of Louvain (1977). He has gained extensive experience in VAT, first as tax adviser with KPMG and later as a lawyer with Loyens & Loeff, and Xirius. He has been involved in the preparation of 7 preliminary ruling before the Court of Justice of the European Union.

He has chaired the indirect taxation subgroup of the Confédération Fiscale Européenne (CFE-Tax Advisers Europe) from 2008 to 2012. He is currently involved with the "EU VAT Forum" at the European Commission which is developing an ongoing dialogue between national VAT Authorities, the business community, and VAT advisers to find practical solutions within the current framework of EU VAT legislation.

Aleksandra Bal is a VAT and technology specialist. She works in the software and information services industry, leading the development of digital solutions and software for tax professionals. She holds a PhD in International Taxation (Leiden University), an Executive MBA (Rotterdam School of Management), LL.M. International Tax Law (Maastricht University), MSc Tax Management (Maastricht University), B.Sc. Business Administration (University of Frankfurt (Oder)) and Mag. iur. in Polish and German law (University of Poznan / University of Frankfurt (Oder)). Aleksandra has published nearly 70 tax journal articles and is a frequent speaker at tax conferences and seminars. Her latest book *Taxation, Virtual Currency and Blockchain* (Wolters Kluwer, 2018) is the first to examine this topic from a comparative perspective.

Jeroen Bijl is an Assistant Professor at Leiden University (the Netherlands) where he leads the VAT section of the Tax Law Faculty. He studied tax law at Groningen University and obtained his PhD from Tilburg University. The topic of his thesis was the EU VAT treatment of vouchers in the context of promotional activities. He has also been a VAT practitioner for over 20 years, currently working for EY (Amsterdam). He also serves as a part time judge at the Court of Appeals in the Hague. Jeroen regularly publishes about VAT in both Dutch and international journals.

Richard M. Bird (1938-2021) was Professor Emeritus of Economics, Rotman School of Management, and Senior Fellow of the Institute for Municipal Governance and Finance, Munk School of Global Affairs, University of Toronto. He served as a Visiting Professor in the United States, the Netherlands, Australia, Japan, and India and a consultant to many national and international organizations, and published extensively on taxation and fiscal issues, particularly in developing countries. His most recent books were *Fiscal Decentralization and Local Finance in Developing Countries: Development from Below* (Edward Elgar, 2018) and *Financing Infrastructure: Who Should Pay?* (McGill-Queens University Press, 2017).

Chris Evans is a Professor of Taxation at UNSW Sydney and an Extraordinary Professor at the University of Pretoria, South Africa. He is also an International Research Fellow at Oxford University and a Visiting Professor at various other world class institutions. In a former life he held senior positions in the UK's (then) Inland Revenue and in a boutique international tax consultancy in London. He holds a PhD from UNSW Sydney, Masters in Education and in International Politics from Leeds University and Leicester University, and an Honours in Economics from London University. He specializes in comparative taxation, CGT and personal and corporate taxation, and in tax administration, particularly tax compliance and the tax compliance burden. Chris has served on many governmental and professional body committees and working parties in Australia and overseas and has conducted significant tax related research and consultancies for bodies such as the World Bank and other international agencies and firms.

Pierre-Pascal Gendron is Professor of Economics and Program Coordinator, Bachelor of Commerce – International Business, Faculty of Business and International Development Institute, Humber Institute of Technology & Advanced Learning, in Toronto, Canada. He has been a Visiting Professor at the Fiscal Affairs Department of the IMF and at the Centro de Investigaciones Socioeconómicas, Universidad Autonóma de Coahuila, Saltillo, Mexico. He has served as a tax policy consultant to national and international organizations in many countries, and has published extensively on taxation, especially in a developing country context. His influential book, *The VAT in Developing and Transitional Countries*, co-authored with Richard Bird, received its paperback release by Cambridge University Press in 2011.

Charlène Herbain is a Lecturer at the Catholic University of Louvain-la-Neuve (Belgium). Previously, she held an academic position at the University of Luxembourg (Luxembourg). After working as a tax lawyer in some of Luxembourg major law firms, she recently joined the public sector. Her PhD thesis, "VAT Neutrality" (published by Larcier) received a very honorable mention from the jury of the IFA Maurice Lauré Prize in June 2015. She published numerous journal articles and 4 books. Her latest book is *Taxe sur la valeur ajoutée, Droit belge et européen* (Larcier, Bruxelles, 2020).

Benedikt Hoffmann is a German qualified lawyer specialized in corporate tax law and tax disputes with a focus on VAT. He practises in the Munich office of an international law firm.

Catalina Hoyos-Jiménez is a tax lawyer with more than 20 years' experience in international and local tax law. As senior tax partner, she leads the tax litigation, transfer pricing, tax planning, tax consultancy and tax compliance groups of Godoy-Hoyos Goh) in Colombia. In addition, she serves as Professor of Tax Law at the Universidad del Rosario. Catalina holds a JD from Universidad del Rosario, is a PhD Candidate of Salamanca University, and attended the Comparative Tax Policy and Administration program of Harvard Kennedy School, 2018; the Blockchain Program of MIT, 2018; the FinTech Program of Oxford Said Business School, 2018 and the innovation of IESE Business School. She holds several specialization studies in Local and International Tax Law (Universidad del Rosario, Universidad Austral, Universidad de Santiago de Compostela). She currently attends the LL.M. in International Dispute Resolution of Queen Mary University of London.
She has been the President of the Colombian Institute of Tax Law; member of the board of directors of IFA Colombia; and honorary member of the Colombian Institute of Tax Law. She is a member of the list of arbitrators to the Bogota and Caracas Chambers of Commerce and member of the board of Tribute (tribute-arbitration.org).

Kathryn James teaches and researches in taxation law and policy at the Monash Law School, Australia. She has expertise in the value added tax (VAT) and her research is focused on the interplay between taxation and questions of distributive justice. Kathryn is an Australian Research Council, Discovery Early Career Research Fellow from December 2019 to December 2024 for a project that examines "Whether Australia Can and Should Reform the Goods and Services Tax" (DE190100346). The project builds upon her research to date that has focused on explaining the rapid global rise of the VAT/GST. This research formed the basis of her book *The Rise of the Value-Added Tax* (Cambridge University Press, 2015). Kathryn holds a PhD in Taxation Law, a first class Honours in Law and a Bachelor of Arts.

Christian Knotzer, M.Sc. (WU), B.Sc., is a research and teaching associate at the WU Vienna University of Economics and Business, Institute for Austrian and International Tax Law. He holds a Master's in Taxation and Accounting from WU Vienna and a Bachelor's in Business, Economics and Social Sciences from the University of Vienna. He is currently pursuing a doctoral degree in Business Law at WU Vienna.

Richard Krever is a Professor at the University of Western Australia Law School, Perth and an International Fellow at the Centre for Business Taxation at the University of Oxford, Oxford. He has previously held tax law drafting, design and interpretation roles with the IMF, World Bank, Australian Treasury and Australian Taxation Office and provided tax law design and drafting assistance on behalf of international organizations in many Asian, African, Caribbean, South American, Pacific and eastern European nations. Professor Krever was made a Member of the Order of Australia in recognition of his contributions to tax academia in Australia.

Yoshihiro Masui (LL.B. University of Tokyo, 1987; ITP/LL.M. Harvard University, 1992) is Professor of Law at the University of Tokyo. He has been a member of the Tax Commission of the Japanese Government since 2013 and was a Member of the Permanent Scientific Committee of the IFA (1999-2009). His monograph *Taxation of Corporate Groups* (University of Tokyo Press, 2002, in Japanese) won the Institute of Tax Research and Literature Award.

Madeleine Merkx (1982) studied tax law at Tilburg University (2000-2004) where she obtained her PhD in 2011 on the subject of place of establishment and place of residence in EU VAT. She is currently working as a Partner at the Tax Research Center of BDO in the Netherlands and as an endowed Professor of Indirect Taxes specialized in VAT at Erasmus University, Rotterdam. She is also a Deputy Judge at the District Court of Noord-Holland.

Sacchidananda Mukherjee is an Associate Professor at the National Institute of Public Finance and Policy (NIPFP), New Delhi. NIPFP is one of the premiere think tanks in Asia working on public finance and fiscal policy issues. His areas of research include public finance and fiscal policy in general and design and implementation of Goods and Services Tax (GST), Value Added Tax (VAT), tax reforms, revenue mobilization in particular. He is engaged in policy research for the federal and provincial governments in India for more than a decade on issues related to Performance Assessment of Tax Administration, Restructuring and Reorganization of Tax Administration, Tax Compliance Behavior, Revenue Potential Estimation, Tax and Non-Tax Revenue Mobilization etc. He has a Ph.D. in Economics from the University of Madras (Madras School of Economics), Chennai. His recent co-authored book on *Evolution of Goods and Services Tax in India* is published by the Cambridge University Press in April 2019.

Marius van Oordt holds a PhD in Tax Policy from the University of Pretoria. His research focus is on indirect taxes in developing countries and he has published on this topic in well-recognized journals. He occupies a permanent position at the African Tax Institute (ATI) in the Economics Department of the University of Pretoria in South Africa and is an external expert of the Fiscal Affairs Department of the International Monetary Fund. He is also a member of the United Nations Subcommittee on Extractive Industries Taxation. He has provided advice on the indirect tax policies Ethiopia, Kenya, Malawi, Rwanda, and South Africa.

Sebastian Pfeiffer is a judge at the Austrian Federal Fiscal Court and an external lecturer at the WU Vienna University of Economics and Business. Before that he was a VAT expert at the Austrian Ministry of Finance and a research and teaching associate at the Institute of Austrian and International Tax Law at WU. For his doctoral thesis

VAT Grouping from a European Perspective (Amsterdam: IBFD, 2015), he was awarded the Maurice Lauré prize by the International Fiscal Association in 2014.

Nicholas Shatalow received a JD with specialization in Taxation Law from Osgoode Hall Law School in 2019. He is currently an LL.M. Candidate (Business Law) at the University of Toronto Faculty of Law.

Karoline Spies is Full Professor and holds a chair in tax law at the Institute for Austrian and International Tax Law at WU. Prior to that she was a (post-)doctoral researcher at the same Institute for more than eight years (2010-2018) and has also gained international experience by conducting research stays at various institutions (e.g., Singapore Management University, and the CJEU). Since 2019, Karoline has been a member of the VAT Expert Group at the European Commission, where she contributes to the discussions on potential reforms of the EU VAT system. Karoline is also actively involved at an international tax consultancy company in Austria. Her main area of research is EU tax law in the field of direct and indirect tax law. She has received a number or prestigious awards for her research (most significantly the European Academic Tax Thesis Award and the Maurice Lauré Prize).

Bettina Spilker is a Professor of Tax Law at the University of Vienna. Bettina focuses her research on VAT, procedural tax law and the impact of digitalisation on tax law. She is also qualified as German lawyer and practised in a local law firm in Munich.

Simon Thang is a lawyer and principal of the tax law firm Thang Tax Law in Toronto, Canada. Simon's practice focuses on Goods and Services Tax, Harmonized Sales Tax, Provincial Sales Tax, customs law, and all other Canadian indirect taxes. In addition to advising on indirect tax matters, Simon represents clients in appeals and litigation. Simon has taught consumption tax at Osgoode Hall Law School and frequently writes and presents on related topics. Simon graduated from Osgoode Hall Law School and from the London School of Economics and Political Science, where he received an LL.M. in Taxation.

Christopher Thompson is a Director with EY's EMEIA Financial Services Organisation, where he leads the Belgian Indirect Tax practice. Within this role, he focusses on VAT issues faced by insurers, banks and asset managers. He holds a law degree from the Catholic University of Louvain-la-Neuve (Belgium), a Master in Tax Law from the University of Antwerp (Belgium) and a Postgraduate Diploma in EU Law from King's College, London (UK).

David White is an adjunct research associate of Victoria University of Wellington's Centre for Accounting, Governance and Taxation Research. In this research centre, he has, among other things, been a lead organizer of the New Zealand GST 20th anniversary conference in 2006, the New Zealand GST Project (2005-2012) and co-organizer of a review of the New Zealand tax system (2009-2010). He was a member of the New Zealand tax system review group, many of whose recommendations, including a tax mix shift from income tax to GST, were implemented in 2010, in the largest New Zealand tax package in nearly 25 years. David has been a Research Fellow at the Institute for Fiscal Studies, London, from 2006 to 2010, (when he was a commentator on VAT and Excises for the Mirrlees Review, which sought to identify the characteristics of a good tax system in any open developed economy in the 21st century), a Visiting Fellow at the Urban-Brookings Tax Policy Center, Washington DC (2012) and a Visiting Associate Professor at the Faculty of Law at the National University of Singapore (2016). David has worked as a diplomat in the New Zealand Ministry of Foreign Affairs (1976-1983), a commercial lawyer (1983-1987), a tax policy analyst in the New Zealand Treasury (1987-2000) and a teacher and researcher of tax at Victoria University of Wellington (2000-2018). David has degrees from Victoria University of Wellington (LL.B. Hons), the London School of Economics and Political Science (LL.M.) and the University of Sydney (SJD).

Yan Xu is Scientia Associate Professor of Tax Law in the Business School at the University of New South Wales in Australia, and Adjunct Associate Professor in the Faculty of Law at the University of Hong Kong. She was awarded Fulbright Senior Research Scholar 2014-2015 and has held a number of international academic scholarships at institutions which include Columbia University and the University of Cambridge. She has published in a range of international journals, secured several competitive government grants, presented papers at high-level international conferences, and made presentations on invitation from prominent international bodies, including the Australian Commonwealth Treasury. She is often invited to act as referee for highly ranked law journals and academic books. Her research interests include comparative tax law and policy, international taxation, history of tax law, VAT, and environment taxation.

Summary of Contents

Table of Contents

List of Figures

List of Tables

List of Abbreviations

AED	Additional Excise Duty (India)
AG	Advocate-General (EU)
ALS	Arm's length standard
ANTS	A New Tax System (Australia)
APA	Advance pricing arrangement
AR	Actual Revenue
ATF	Aviation Turbine Fuel
ATO	Australian Tax Office
AUD	Australian dollar
BCD	Basic Customs Duty (India)
BEPS	Base-erosion and profits shifting
BFH	Bundesfinanzhof (Germany)
BMF	Bundesministerium der Finanzen (Ministry of Finance, Germany)
BTA	Border Tax Adjustment
B2B	Business to business
B2C	Business to Consumer
B2G	Business to Government
B2V	Business Tax to VAT (China)
BverfG	BundesverfassungsGericht (Germany)
CAD	Canadian dollar
CASE	Center for Social and Economic Research
CBR	Cross-border rulings (EU)
CCC	Community Customs Code
CenVAT	Central VAT (India)
Cf.	Confer (Latin: compare)

CGA	Code general des impôts (France)
CGST	Central Goods and Services Tax (India)
Ch.	Chapter
CIAT	Centro Interamericano de Administraciones Tributarias (Inter-American Center of Tax Administrations)
CJEU	Court of Justice of the European Union
COP	Colombian Pesos
CPR	Current Policy Revenue
CRA	Canada Revenue Agency
CST	Central Sales Tax (India)
C2C	Consumer to consumer
CT	Consumption Tax (Japan)
CTD	Commercial Tax departments (India)
CUP	Comparable uncontrolled price
CVD	Countervailing duty
DC	District of Colombia de
DIAN	Directión de Impuestos y Aduanas Nacionales (Directorate of National Taxes and Customs-Colombia)
Div.	Division
DST	Digital services tax
EAC	East African Community
EC	European Community
ECE	Ethiopian Commodity Exchange
ECLI	European Case Law Identifier
ECSC	European Coal and Steel Community
ECSFM	Empowered Committee of State Finance Ministers (India)
Ed.	Editor
Eds.	Editors
EEC	European Economic Community
e.g.	*exempli gratia* (Latin: for example)
et al	*et alii* (Latin: and others)
etc.	*et cetera* (Latin: and so forth)
EU	European Union
EUR	Euro
EWB	E-Way Bill (India)
EWHC	England and Wales High Court
FAD	Fiscal Affairs Department (of the IMF)
FCAFC	Federal Court of Australia Full Court
FCT	Federal Commissioner of Taxation (Australia)
FE	Fixed establishment
FG	Finanzgericht

FTA	Forum of Tax Administration
GATT	General Agreement on Tariffs and Trade
GCC	Gulf Cooperation Council
GDP	Gross Domestic Product
GST	Goods and Services Tax
GSTA	Goods and Services Tax Ruling (Australia)
GTA	Goods Transport Agency (India)
HMRC	Her Majesty's Revenue and Customs (UK)
HSD	High Speed Diesel (India)
HST	Harmonised sales tax
IBFD	International Bureau of Fiscal Documentation
ICT	Information, Computer and Telecommunication
Ibid	Ibidem (Latin: at the same place)
ICC	International Chamber of Commerce
ID	Identification
I.e.	Id est (Latin: that is)
IGST	Integrated Goods and Services Tax (India)
IMF	International Monetary Fund
Inc.	Incorporate
INR	Indian Rupee
IP	Internet protocol
ITC	Input tax credit
ITR	Implicit Tax Rate (on consumption)
Jo.	Juncto (Latin: in conjunction with)
JPN	Japanese Yen
KPMG	Klynveld Peat Marwick Goerdeler
KSA	Kingdom of Saudi Arabia
KTF	Kelkar Task Force Report on Indirect Taxation (India)
LBT	Local Body Tax (India)
LLC	Limited Liability Company
MA	Massachusetts
MLE	Multiple location enterprises
MNE	Multinational enterprise
MODVAT	Modified Value Added Tax (India)
MOF	Ministry of Finance
MSP	Multi-sided Platforms
MwStR	Mehrwertsteuer Recht
n.	Note
NBER	National Bureau of Economic Research
No.	Number

OECC	Organisation for European Economic Cooperation
OECD	Organisation of Economic Coordination and Development
OECD Plus	OECD countries and selected other economies
OJ	Official Journal (EU)
p.	Page
PE	Permanent establishment
PwC	PricewaterhouseCoopers
QRPM	Quarterly Return Monthly Payment (India)
QST	Quebec sales tax
RA-GAP	Revenue Administration Gap
REC	Regional Economic Communities
RCM	Reverse Charge Mechanism
RITC	reduced input tax credit (Australia)
RPM	Resale price method
Rs.	Indian Rupee
RST	Retail Sales Tax
RUT	Registro único tributario (Single Tax Register-Colombia)
SaaS	Software as a Service
SACU	Southern African Customs Union
SAD	Special Additional Duty (India)
SADC	Southern African Development Community
SED	Special Excise Duty (India)
SICAV	Société d'investissement à Capital Variable
SME	Small and Medium-sized Enterprises
SSI	Small Scale Industries (India)
STA	State Taxation Administration (China)
STC	Simons' Tax Cases
SWD	Staff Working Document
TADAT	Tax Administration Diagnostic Assessment Tool
TCC	Tax Court Cases
TFEU	Treaty on the Functioning of the European Union
TIEA	Tax Information Exchange Agreement
TINXSYS	Tax Information Exchange System (India)
TRM	Tasa Representativa del mercado (official exchange rate-Colombia)
TVA	Taxe sur la Valeur Ajoutée (Tax on Value Added, France)
TWG	Tax Working Group)New Zealand)
UAE	United Arab Emirates
UCC	Union Customs Code
UED	Union Excise Duties (India)

UK	United Kingdom
UKUT	United Kingdom Upper Tribunal
UN	United Nations
US	United States
USD	United States dollar
UStAE	Umsatzsteueranwendungserlass (VAT Application Decree, Germany)
UStG	Umsatzsteuergesetz (Austria and Germany)
UT	Union Territories (India)
v.	versus
VAT	Value Added Tax
VFA	(GCC) VAT Framework Agreement
VPN	Virtual Private Network
VRR	VAT Revenue Ratio
VTTL	VAT Total Tax Liability
VUW TWG	Victoria University of Wellington Tax Working Group (New Zealand)
VwGH	Verwaltungsgerichtshof (Austria)
WCO	World Customs Organization
WTO	World Trade Organization

Preface

VAT is in operation for just over 50 years, starting with Denmark in 1967, France and Germany in 1968, the Netherlands in 1969, and from there, we have witnessed a remarkable global proliferation. It is time to evaluate, to reflect on what works and what does not work or not so well; in what respect is VAT successful, and where does it fail.

This book is divided into 2 parts. We start with a number of chapters covering technical topics that are particularly relevant for measuring the success of VAT, followed by 6 country reports, which share the experience in respectively New Zealand as the birthplace of the modern VAT; Japan which operated a consumption tax without the requirement of a tax invoice; China where VAT operates in a transitional economy; Colombia a developing country representing Latin America; Ethiopia a developing country representing the African continent; and India as the most recent developing economy to introduce a VAT at the federal level.

Countries contemplating on imposing a general consumption tax should certainly consider VAT on the basis of its merits while accepting the existence of some fallacies. The aim of policymakers should be to design and implement a consumption tax, whether the VAT or another type, that is as good as it can be from a technical and political perspective. We trust that this book can be a guide to tax policy development in the area of general consumption taxation and support realizing that goal.

This book is current with literature and case law through December 2020.

Robert F. van Brederode
Cary, NC, USA

CHAPTER 1

Introduction: VAT Does Well, but Does It Do Well Enough?

Robert F. van Brederode

The value added tax (VAT) is a fiscal success story since its introduction in the second half of the 20th century. The first state to introduce a VAT was Michigan in 1953, based on Thomas Adams' theoretical model of a business income type VAT;[1] the consumption type VAT model, developed by Carl Friedrich von Siemens,[2] was adopted in Europe.[3] France introduced VAT gradually, starting with the manufacturing stage at first in 1948, extending it to include the wholesale stage in 1954, and applying it in full per 1968, a year after Denmark which introduced a VAT to all stages of the supply chain in 1967. The European Union (EU) and its predecessor the European Economic Community (EEC) deserve credit for the initial spread of VAT. It was pertinent to

1. Thomas S. Adams, *Fundamental Problems of Federal Income Taxation* 35(4) Q. J. Econ. 527 (1921).
2. Carl F. von Siemens, *Veredelte Umsatzsteuer* (Siemensstadt 1920, 2nd ed., 1921).
3. The difference between a consumption type VAT and income type VAT can be explained as follows. Under the consumption type VAT, all tax paid on purchases for use in the production process is immediately and fully recoverable. In other words, business procurement can be expensed. As a result, capital investment is not penalized through an additional tax burden, and the tax does not favor any method of production over another since substituting labor for capital or vice versa does not influence the total tax burden incurred by a firm. If we ignore economic relations with foreign countries and exemptions, gross national income (Y) is the sum of total consumption (C) and total investments (I), or $Y = C + I$. When we deduct the value of investments, we find the value of consumption, or $Y - I = C$. For this reason, the tax is referred to as consumption type VAT because the tax base equals total private consumption expenditure.

   If the expensing of capital investment is replaced by a system of depreciation *pro rata temporis* (D), the character of the VAT changes accordingly from a consumption type into an income type. The VAT basically mimics the approach under corporate income taxes where capital goods are to be written off over their life cycle as the value of these goods depreciates, by allowing only part of the purchase to be treated as a deductible input in computing value added. Again, ignoring foreign economic relations, the net national product or income is the sum of all domestic income, or $Y - D = C + I - D = Y_{net}$.

replace the cascading turnover taxes, imposed at the time in all founding Member States but France, with a tax that would be neutral to cross-border transactions within the newly created common market. Because of the cascading effect, turnover taxes do not allow for the exact calculations of Border Tax Adjustments (BTA) as the tax burden depends on the length of the supply chain. Thus, by default, BTAs under a turnover tax regime are estimates of the average domestic tax burden on a specific product. It was feared that Member States might use the BTAs protectionistically, i.e., subsidizing exports[4] and penalizing imports.[5] VAT solves that problem as the credit system prevents cascading and the tax burden will always be equal to the statutory rate applied to the price of a product. For that reason, the adoption of VAT was made mandatory in the EU which, in turn, triggered the proliferation of VAT in Europe at a pace equal to the expansion of the EU to presently 27 Member States.[6] At the same time, other European trade partners of the EU, such as Switzerland and Norway, followed suit. The European experience proved to be contagious and many other countries, including mostly Francophone African countries and Latin American based their VAT on the European model, often referred to as the "traditional VAT." In 1986 New Zealand transformed the traditional VAT as it tried to eliminate several fallacies of the European model. Although structurally quite similar to the traditional VAT, New Zealand created a new model, often referred to as the "Modern VAT," mitigating many of the negative aspect of the traditional European VAT, and which became the model for modern VAT law. It was adopted to significant extent in Australia, South Africa, Singapore, Canada, and beyond as VAT policy experts of international organizations such as the International Monetary Fund (IMF) and the World Bank promoted it strongly, based on its simplified compliance and administrative requirements and improved economic performance. The traditional VAT and Modern VAT are the two dominant models of VAT applied around the world. Close to 170 countries apply a form of VAT. In Table 1.1, we provide an overview of VAT's proliferation from the 1960s to the present.

4. Refund > true average domestic tax burden in export country of the exported product.
5. Import tax > true average domestic tax burden in import country of imported product.
6. The EU had 6 founding Member States, Belgium, France, Germany, Italy, Luxembourg, and the Netherlands. In 1973 Denmark, Ireland and the UK joined, followed by Greece in 1981 and Spain and Portugal in 1986. Austria, Finland, and Sweden acceded in 1995. The year 2004 saw membership of Malta, Cyprus, the Czech Republic, Estonia, Hungary, Latvia, Lithuania, Poland, Slovakia, and Slovenia with Bulgaria and Romania following in 2007 and Croatia in 2013. The UK seceded from the EU in 2020.

*Table 1.1 The Global Proliferation of VAT**

1960-1969	Brazil, Denmark, France, Germany, Ivory Coast, Madagascar, the Netherlands, Nicaragua, Sweden, Uruguay.
1970-1979	Argentina, Austria, Belgium, Bolivia, Chili, Colombia, Costa Rica, Ecuador, Honduras, Ireland, Israel, Italy, Luxembourg, Nicaragua, Norway, Panama, UK.
1980-1989	Dominican Rep., Greece, Guatemala, Haiti, Hungary, Indonesia, Japan, Jordan, Malawi, Mexico, Morocco, New Zealand, Niger, Philippines, Portugal, Senegal, Spain, Taiwan, Tunisia, Turkey.
1990-1999	Albania, Algeria, Antigua & Barbuda, Armenia, Azerbaijan, Bangladesh, Barbados, Belarus, Benin, Bulgaria, Burkina Faso, Cambodia, Cameroon, Canada, China, Congo Rep., Croatia, Cyprus, Czech Rep., Egypt, El Salvador, Estonia, Fiji, Finland, Gabon, Georgia, Ghana, Guinea, Iceland, Jamaica, Kazakhstan, Kenya, Korea, Kyrgyzstan, Latvia, Liechtenstein, Lithuania, Mali, Malta, Mauritania, Mauritius, Moldova, Mongolia, Mozambique, Nepal, Nigeria, Pakistan, Palestinian Terr., Papua New Guinea, Paraguay, Peru, Poland, Romania, Russia, Samoa, Singapore, Slovak Rep., Slovenia, South-Africa, Sri Lanka, Switzerland, Tajikistan, Tanzania, Thailand, Trinidad & Tobago, Turkmenistan, Uganda, Ukraine, Uzbekistan, Vanuatu, Venezuela, Vietnam, Zambia.
2000-2009	Australia, Bosnia & Herzegovina, Botswana, Chad, Equatorial Guinea, Ethiopia, Guyana, India, Kosovo, Lebanon, Namibia, N. Macedonia, Rwanda, Serbia, Sudan, Togo, Zimbabwe.
2010-2019	Andorra, Angola, Bahamas, Bahrain, Congo Dem. Rep., Isle of Man, Jersey, Lao PDR, Maldives, Montenegro, Saudi Arabia, Saint Lucia, Swaziland, UAE.

* This list consists of 153 countries and is not fully complete as well over 160 countries currently apply VAT.

Initially, with few exceptions, VAT was introduced exclusively in Europe and Latin America. In the first three decennia of its proliferation, the growth of VAT was gradual from 10 countries increasing with 17, and then with 20. The time period 1990-1999 is VAT's "Golden Age" with about 73 countries joining, and since it has returned to its original growth pattern, adding between 10-20 countries each decennium. Only a few countries are left without a VAT, including the world's largest economy, the United States. In terms of proliferation, VAT is clearly a success.

Michael Gove at the time (2019) a candidate to replace Theresa May as UK's prime minister suggested in his economic plan that, if elected, he would replace the 20% VAT with a low rate and simpler sales tax once Britain left the EU.[7] That is a remarkable statement given the general enthusiasm for the VAT in Europe, and the successful global proliferation of VAT. Repealing a VAT is an exceptional occurrence and, moreover, in most cases VAT was reintroduced at a later date. I am aware of only

7. Michael Gove, *Scrapping VAT and Introducing a Lower, Simpler Sales Tax Will Help Britain to Prosper*. Op-Ed, Daily Telegraph (June 8, 2019).

6 instances. South Vietnam repealed the VAT in 1971 during war times but, after the 1976 reunification with the North, VAT was reintroduced in 1999. Grenada introduced VAT in 1986, dismantled it gradually, and reintroduced VAT in 2010. Ghana introduced VAT effectively in March of 1995, repealed it within three months due to implementation failures[8]—restoring the previous indirect taxes—and then reintroduced VAT in 1998.[9] Belize introduced the tax in 1996, removed it in 1999 to reintroduce it in 2006. Zambia replaced VAT with an all stage sales tax, i.e., a gross receipts tax, as of January 2020.[10] At the subnational level, British Columbia replaced its RST with VAT (Goods and Services Tax (GST)) on July 1, 2010 but returned to RST after a referendum per April 1, 2013.[11] Its extensive proliferation and the few instances of repeal demonstrate the strength of VAT as well as its attraction, matching—it has been claimed—the power of seduction of the notorious temptress Mata Hari: "many are tempted, many succumb, some tremble at the brink, while others leave only to return, eventually, the attraction appears irresistible."[12]

Mr. Gove is the first European politician ever to make such a daunting policy proposal and he was quickly and strongly criticized for it.[13] On the other side of the Atlantic, Andrew Yang, an American entrepreneur and former candidate in the 2020 Democrat party presidential primary race, suggested to introduce a federal VAT in the Unites States (US) to fund a form of universal basic income of USD 1,000 for all adult citizens.[14] The contrast between the two policy proposals, i.e., introducing a federal VAT in a country that has retail sales taxes at the subnational level versus replacing

8. *See* Seth E. Terkper, *VAT in Ghana: Why It Failed* 12(23) Tax N. Int'l 1801 (1996); Joseph R.A. Ayee, *Policy Management in Africa: The Case of Value Added Tax* 2(8/9) Afr. J. Public Admin, & Mgmt 51 (1997); George O. Assibey-Mensah, *The Value Added Tax in Ghana* 19(2) Pub. Budg. & Fin. 76 (1999); Emmanuel Owusu-Afriyie, *An Assessment of the Impact of Tax Reforms on the Tax System of Ghana*, Monetary Policy Analysis and Financial Stability Department, Bank of Ghana Working Paper WP/BOG-2009-1 (2009).
9. *See* Seth E. Terkper, *Ghana: Scope of New VAT Laws* 10(1) Int'l VAT Monitor (1999); Seth E. Terkper, *Ghana Reintroduces VAT: Lessons Learned and Progress After a Year* 20(11) Tax N. Int'l 1253 (2000); Philip D. Osei, *Political Liberalisation and the Implementation of Value Added Tax in Ghana* 38(2) J. Mod. Afr. Stud. 255 (2000).
10. *Cabinet Approves Sales Tax, Abolishes VAT, Lusaka Times* (April 2, 2019). The article includes the full government statement.
11. For background and comments, *see* George M. Abbott, *The Precarious Politics of Shifting Direction: The Introduction of a Harmonized Sales Tax in British Columbia and Ontario* 186 BC Studies 125 (2015); John Richards, *British Columbia's Unharmonized Referendum: The Problem with Plebiscitary Democracy* 60(1) Can. Tax J. 103 (2012); David D. Robertson, *Comparing the Introduction of the HST in British Columbia and Ontario: Lessons from the Political Trenches* 60(1) Can. Tax J. 113 (2012).
12. Ben Terra and Julie Kajus, *A Guide to the European VAT Directives*. Vol. 1: Introduction to European VAT, Preface at vii (IBFD, 2020).
13. *See* Victor Cramer, *Waving Goodbye to VAT?* Bloomberg online, Daily Tax Report: International (June 20, 2019); Tim Worstall, *University Expansion Wasn't A Good Idea—Gove VAT and Sales Tax Edition*, Continental Telegraph (June 9, 2019).
14. www.yang2020.com/policies/value-added-tax. For a financial analysis as to the feasibility of the proposal, *see* Kyle Pomerleau, *Does Andrew Yang's "Freedom Dividend" Proposal Add Up?* Tax Foundation (July 29, 2019).

VAT with a sales tax,[15] is intriguing and should ignite a renewed academic debate on the pros and cons of each tax and, in particular, whether the orthodox view of the superiority of the traditional invoice-credit method VAT is correct in the current socio-economic circumstances.

The view that VAT is the superior consumption tax is almost axiomatic and supported by a large body of academic journal articles, all mimicking the same arguments. To our knowledge, only a few journal articles since VAT was introduced in the EU, over half a century ago, have put forward critical notes on VAT.[16] This book's aim is to evaluate VAT based on over 50 years of experience with its intricacies, to reflect on what works and what does not work or not so well; in what respect is VAT successful, and where does it fail to some degree. Countries contemplating on imposing a general consumption tax, should certainly consider VAT on the basis of its merits; accepting the existence of some fallacies for the simple reason that perfection may be a desired quality in taxation, it is also realistically unobtainable. But we can design a VAT that is as good as it can be from a technical and political perspective. I trust that this book can be a guide to realize that objective.

This book is divided into 2 parts. We start with a number of chapters covering technical topics that are particularly relevant for measuring the success of VAT, followed by 6 country reports, which share the experience in respectively New Zealand as the birthplace of the modern VAT; Japan which operated a consumption tax without the requirement of a tax invoice; China where VAT operates in a transitional economy; Colombia a developing country representing Latin America; Ethiopia a developing country representing the African continent; and India as the most recent developing economy to introduce a VAT at the federal level.

Revenue generation is an important objective of almost all taxes and prima facie VAT seems to be an obvious success in that respect. Gendron, in Chapter 2, surveys the topic of VAT revenue performance, starting by positioning the revenue objective of VAT among other possible objectives. He then reviews the various revenue performance measurements, illustrated with detailed examples of country data examples, before he moves on to the often-neglected issue of the proper coordination between VAT, excise, trade and other indirect taxes. Last but certainly not least, Gendron reviews the limitations of revenue performance indicators and justifies more advanced performance measures.

One of the strengths of VAT, which has led to its wide following, is economic neutrality. Where VAT is able to remove the tax burden completely from businesses through the credit system and shift the tax incidence to final consumers, VAT

15. Introducing a federal VAT in the US is not a new idea and Yang is far from the first to suggest it, *see* Alan Schenk, *Prior U.S. Flirtations With VAT* in *The VAT Reader: What a Federal Consumption Tax Would Mean for America* 52 (Tax Analysts, 2011).
16. Graeme Cooper and Richard Vann, *A Few Myths About the GST* 23 UNSW L. J. 252 (2000); Mario Leccisotti & Mauro Marè *On the Presumed Technical Superiority of VAT,* 9 Austl. Tax F. 259 (1992); Graeme Cooper, *The Discrete Charm of the VAT*, Legal Studies Research Paper No. 07/65, Sydney Law School (November 2007), available at http://ssrn.com/abstract=1027512 (2007); Robert F. van Brederode and Sebastian Pfeiffer, *VAT's Superiority: Is the Emperor Dressed Like Adam?* 26(4) Int'l VAT Monitor 226 (2015).

realizes—at least in theory—economic neutrality in terms of business organization, consumption choices, and investment choices. Amand takes a dive into neutrality in Chapter 3. He disagrees with the common notion that neutrality in VAT is an expression of the principle of equal treatment, because they present many differences. Although they may sometimes cover the same situations, neutrality is an economic concept, intended to prevent distortions, while equality is a legal concept aimed at realizing equal treatment of those who are in comparable situations. Neutrality and the absence of distortion of competition have been the key objective of the European VAT. Neutrality is realized by levying a tax strictly proportional to the price of goods and services at retail level, notwithstanding that the tax is applied through the whole process of production and distribution. Although neutrality is an underlying principle of VAT, it does not by or in itself create protected rights, contrary to equality and non-discrimination that do provide rights protected by the courts. Equality and the closely related concept of non-discrimination are fundamental principles of law protected by the courts. As principles, neutrality and equality do not prevent distortions of competition, non-taxation, double taxation, and delocalization driven by market forces and consecutive to VAT exemptions. This observation highlights, according to Amand, the importance of well-informed political decisions.

Two of the main issues affecting neutrality negatively are rate variation and exemptions. Chapter 4 deals with the former and it explains and evaluates the arguments for rate variation. In Europe, where VAT replaced existing turnover taxes characterized by a multiple rate structure that had a dissimilar impact across economic sectors, it was essential for policy makers to win the buy-in from the business sector, i.e., overcoming their natural resistance to change, by replicating the impact of the former turnover taxes. In addition, there was a political need to address the perceived regressivity of VAT. The VAT is regressive in that lower income groups pay a higher percentage of their income to the tax. This is true on an annual assessment of income, but if we take a life-cycle approach to income, recognizing that savings constitute postponed consumption, VAT is close to proportional, except for the very rich and the systemically poor with no prospect of social-economic advancement.[17] Regressivity can be addressed by applying lower rates to goods and services primarily purchased by lower income groups, and increased rates to goods and services primarily used by higher income groups. But that is not a simple exercise to undertake as there are few goods and services exclusively used by particular income groups. Lower rates in essence may have an opposite result to their intent; instead of mitigating regressivity, it may actually enhance it. Rate variation can also be used to encourage (through lower rates) or discourage (through standard or higher rates) the purchase of merit and demerit goods and services respectively, and for the purpose of economic stimulus in times of financial and economic crisis. However, rate variation triggers substitution effects where consumers will try to replace standard rated goods and services with similar lower taxed products and services. Rate variation leads to classification issues between similar products, resulting in dead weight losses caused by reclassification

17. *See* Robert F. van Brederode, *VAT's Regressivity: Empirical Truth or Political Correctness* 18(2) Int'l VAT Monitor 86 (2007) and further sources referred there.

efforts either by businesses or tax administrations and subsequent litigation to arrive at the preferred outcome. Practical difficulties also arise in determining the applicable tax rate when supplies are packaged. The chapter illustrates the complexity of classification and composite supplies with cases from the UK, Germany, and the Netherlands. Moreover, rate variation leads to an increase of compliance costs for businesses and administrative costs for tax agencies. The conclusion is that the VAT is not a suitable vehicle for realizing social policy.

Exemptions are dealt with by Knotzer and Pfeiffer in Chapter 5. The starting position is the consensus view that exemptions constitute a fallacy of VAT. They explain the inaccuracy of the term "exemption" as used in VAT as no full relief of tax is realized, list the economic distortions triggered by exemptions, and classify exemptions based on serving policy objectives or their objective/subjective character. Section 5.01[D] of this chapter takes a closer look at the rationale for exemptions, such as combatting the perceived regressivity of VAT, creating an incentive for merit goods, and avoiding technical difficulties, and provide a cost/benefit analysis of the pros and cons of exemptions, concluding that the distortive effects of exemptions outweigh the benefits. Section 5.02 provides a comprehensive treatise of the many exemptions applied under the EU VAT system and explains their historic roots for the further purpose of comparing the EU policy regarding exemptions with that of modern VATs, exemplified by short overviews of exemptions applied in Australia and the countries of the Gulf Cooperation Council (GCC). In their conclusions, Knotzer and Pfeiffer point to the relatively low VAT Revenue Ratio (VRR) of the EU in part caused by exemptions. Apart from economic distortions, exemptions create dead weight losses in terms of administrative and compliance difficulties and the high number of disputes between tax administrations and taxpayers as demonstrated by the case load of the Court of Justice of the EU (CJEU).

The benefits of VAT come at a cost for businesses required to collect the tax and comply with all reporting requirements. Evans and Krever, in Chapter 6, recognize the difficulty in accurately defining these costs. They distinguish between a number of monetary, social, psychological, and non-monetary components and point to the problem of entanglement with other business costs, which complicates identification and estimation of compliance costs. The chapter provides an overview of the research into tax compliance costs generally and of the VAT more particularly, explaining how and where the research has taken place and what the research has shown. Three major conclusions have emerged from the studies: compliance costs are high and significant; compliance costs are regressive; and compliance costs are not reducing over time. Next, the key drivers of the VAT compliance burden are identified: the technical, structural, and compliance complexity of the tax system; legislative change, regardless of whether intended to provide relief or protect the tax base; and, ironically, choice or options offered to taxpayers for the purpose of creating a more equitable tax system. Options to mitigate the compliance burden are extensively discussed. Concessional measures in VAT regimes, particularly multiple rates, exemptions, and zero-rating, generate significant compliance costs for businesses, particularly small businesses with far less capacity to use economies of scale to absorb compliance costs. VAT laws can be changed to accommodate small enterprises, for example, by introducing a high registration threshold, by clarifying definitions of supplies located on the borderline of different rate categories and exemptions, or by other simplification measures, such as cash accounting or margin schemes. However, the authors conclude that in practice simplification regimes intended to offset the additional costs resulting from primary drivers of compliance burdens such as multiple rates or exempt inputs may add new layers of complexity and compliance burdens to the VAT system.

Changes in administrative practice may also contribute to a reduction of the compliance costs. The authors mention in particular: streamlining and automating the registration process; reduction of the reporting frequency; expediting the refund process and paying interest on delayed refunds; improving the audit process; improving tax agency support of and guidance to taxpayers; enhancing the use of technology.

Finally, the chapter addresses issues related to globalization and the growth of internet sales using offshore platforms. The digital economy creates new compliance issues and also offers new solutions. However, the source of compliance burdens lies in determining the base in the first place, particularly making judgments about the character of supplies in systems with multiple borderlines between concessionally-taxed and ordinary supplies.

Collecting taxes for the government is in itself, at least in my opinion,[18] a tax in natura, and it would be reasonable to compensate enterprises financially for the compliance costs they incur by acting as unpaid tax collectors by allowing them to withhold a small part of the tax they collect. Evans and Krever do not mention this option, probably because it has never been applied in any VAT system, but it is more common under the US sales tax system in the form of discounts for timely filing and remittance.[19] It seems worthwhile to examine whether this would also be a fruitful policy to implement in VAT, not only on fairness grounds but as a powerful compliance incentive.

In the post-COVID-19 environment, policy makers in many countries will be searching for revenues. Due to the political difficulty of creating new taxes or raising existing ones significantly, the focus may well shift to improving the yield of existing or reformed taxes. Gendron and Bird in Chapter 7 explore VAT revenue efficiency and its relationship with the VAT gap, providing a justification for the use of VAT gaps, discussing the different versions of the gap and outlining the main approaches to measurement, including two widely accepted top-down approaches (the EU and IMF) and bottom-up approaches generally. Broadly, top-down approaches calculate the potential revenue of a jurisdiction in a given year and compare to actual revenue to arrive at the VAT-gap. Bottom-up approaches start with data produced by the tax

18. Robert F. van Brederode, *The Morality of Coerced Tax Collection* 9(1) J. Acct., Ethics & Pub. Policy 1 (2008).

19. Twenty-seven states allow a discount varying from 0.25% in Nevada to 5% in New York for filing return and remitting sales tax timely. Higher discount rates are paired with a maximum dollar amount per month, or quarter or year. In some states, the vendor discount varies by the amount paid, which could be a tool to allow small businesses a higher discount to account for the regressive nature of compliance costs. The rationale for discounts is not compensation for compliance cost but to create an incentive for compliance; nevertheless, in effect, the practice rewards enterprises for tax collection and the receipts reduce actual compliance costs. Source: taxadmin.org/assets/docs/Research/Rates/vendors.pdf (accessed November 11, 2020).

administration during its operations and apply a variety of numerical and statistical methods and simulations to make gap estimations. Bottom-up have the advantage of offering insights in taxpayer behavior, but are more labor intensive, and require strong IT systems which may be a challenge for the tax agencies in some countries. Next, Gendron and Bird turn to the interpretation and limitations of VAT gap estimates, presenting some cross-country estimates calculated under different approaches. Finally, they consider some implications of VAT (and other tax) gap estimates for developing countries in the context of consumption tax reform for revenue mobilization, including a brief look at some political economy challenges to the use of VAT gap estimates. They conclude that VAT gap estimations provide useful insights into potential improvements in existing VAT systems or potential new ones and are, therefore, a useful tool for policymakers, but we need to arrive at a common methodology to produce VAT gap estimates. Many countries will need assistance to develop the required inputs for that purpose. Further development of bottom-up approaches is recommended as well as further in-depth research and analysis of the politics and political economy of VAT gaps and tax gaps in general.

Brederode, in Chapter 8, focusses on whether VAT is less susceptible to fraud than similar consumption taxes, in particular the retail sales tax (RST). This is relevant because one of the main arguments for choosing VAT is its strength in compliance enforcement. Related advantages attributed to VAT are the creation of an auditable paper trail of invoices, which Brederode confirms under the caveat that such a trail exist in any modern developed economy, regardless of whether a VAT or other or no consumption tax is imposed, either by legal requirement or business practice; a fractioned collection system, which the author shows through flow charts to be a misleading term as no actual collection takes place in the supply chain prior to the retail stage due to the input-tax credit system; and finally that VAT has a lesser risk of retail stage fraud compared to in particular the retail sales tax as VAT does not depend for collection on the weakest link in the supply chain, i.e., the large number of small, mostly family-owned businesses. Based of VAT gap studies from several jurisdictions and fraud data from the state of California this widely held assumption cannot be confirmed. Brederode defends the premise that the retail sector has changed since the first implementation of VAT, not only in the US but also in Europe and other developed economies, and with that the far majority, about 90%, of retail sales are currently generated by a small number of large retail chains that are evidently not prone to fraudulent activities. On the other hand, VAT by introducing tax charges along the full supply chain has created opportunity for fraud in stages prior to the retail stage and the size of this fraud appears to be much larger than the fraud committed at the retail stage. He concludes that from a fraud risk perspective a benchmark RST and its equivalent, the reverse charge VAT, are feasible alternatives for the credit-invoice VAT.

He also points out that the measures to counter VAT fraud do not address the underlying problem that fraud is enabled by the design of VAT, i.e., the introduction of a tax charge in the supply chain prior to the retail sale. In other words, these measures react to the symptoms but do not combat the disease. Moreover, these countermeasures are burdensome and costly from a compliance perspective and could lead to information gathering by governments that poses a danger to civil liberties. For that reason, he argues for a cost/benefits analysis before measures to combat fraud are introduced.

VAT is considered to be an indirect tax on private consumption, using the expenditure made for consumption as a proxy for the consumption itself. A direct expenditure tax is feasible and has been proposed by Kaldor[20] as an alternative for the personal income tax, calculating annual consumption on the basis of the Haig-Simons theorem[21] as C = Y-S, i.e., consumption is income minus saving, but has not been imposed anywhere. The reference point for an indirect consumption tax is the supply by a seller of goods and services to a consumer. The tax base is the expenditure made for, or the consumer market price of, a certain purchase. That is a practical approach, but adjustments are required if at some point in time after the conclusion of the transaction, an event occurs that changes the liability of the supplier. The need to revisit transactions finds balance in the requirements of legal certainty and faithfulness to the transactional nature of the VAT. Despite the importance of the topic of VAT adjustments at a policy and practical level, Chapter 9 of this volume by James and Spies contains the first comprehensive treatise of the topic as a whole. The chapter is divided in 3 parts. The first part, section 9.02, contextualizes VAT adjustments and provides a typology of adjustments that commonly arise in VAT systems. The second part, section 9.03, explores the VAT design issues that arise in dealing with such events and emphasizes the importance of domestic context in shaping jurisdictional responses to VAT adjustments. The last part, sections 9.04-9.06, contains a comparative analysis of the treatment in Australia and in the EU. The analysis shows how the common challenge of being both faithful to the predictive nature of the VAT and trying to capture relevant subsequent variations gives rise to broadly similar policy responses but with important variations influenced by the respective local and regional contexts.

Chapters 10 and 11 are related to Chapter 9 in that they deal with specific adjustments situations. Chapter 10, also by James and Spies, is dedicated to adjustments necessitated by intercompany transfer pricing. Comparatively, little work has been undertaken on the relationship between the VAT and transfer pricing despite the topic giving rise to a number of complex and important issues and potentially involving significant revenue risks. This chapter addresses that gap. Tax liability for both corporate income taxes and VAT depends on value ascribed to transactions, but that value is generally ascertained through different methods with different underlying purposes which can amplify revenue and compliance risks. For corporate tax, the starting point is the fiction of an arm's length price, an "objective" or criteria-based standard; for VAT, the starting point is the reality of the price agreed upon between

20. Nicholas Kaldor, *An Expenditure Tax* (George Allen & Unwin, 1955). His idea was that expenditure constitutes a better measure of the ability to pay than income. A progressive expenditure would be less of a disincentive to work than a progressive income tax while yielding the same revenue. Today, most countries combine a progressive income tax with an effectively proportional VAT.

21. Robert M. Haig, *The Concept of Income-Economic and Legal Aspects*, in *The Federal Income Tax* 1-28 (Robert M. Haig, ed., Columbia University Press, 1921); and Henry C. Simons, *Personal Income Taxation: The Definition of Income as a Problem of Fiscal Policy* (University of Chicago Press, 1938).

parties, or the consideration actually received by the supplier, a "subjective" standard. Where the goal of corporate income tax is to allocate profits among jurisdictions, VAT aims at taxing private consumption expenditure in the destination country. Regardless of those differences, the authors posit that increasingly there are points of overlap between the VAT and transfer pricing, which require a principled and considered policy response. To do this appropriately, effectively, and fairly, jurisdictions need to legislate, administer, and coordinate their responses. The authors provide a comparative overview of the approaches taken in Australia and the EU in regard of corporate income tax, customs duties, and VAT, outlining the relationship between them.

The dynamic between the three tax bases is a complicated one due to opposing interests. This is particularly the case with customs duties and income taxes as VAT is only a concern in the context of transfer pricing adjustments to businesses that are not allowed full input tax recovery. The tax authorities of the exporting country prefer a higher transfer price, so that more taxable income accrues to the exporting entity, while for income tax purposes the importing state prefers a lower price, reducing deductible cost and increasing the taxable margin of the importing entity. Within the importing country, the income tax authority, preferring a lower price, represents an opposite interest to that of the Customs authority which will always seek to establish a higher import value to increase duty revenue. The taxpayer would normally prefer a lower customs value but for income taxes its position is ambivalent and will depend on the actual tax rates in the exporting and importing country, trying to shift more income to the country with the lowest corporate income tax rate. Without careful coordination and exchange of information these opposite interests could easily lead to a lose/lose situation for either the Treasury or the taxpayer. The issue of the potential interaction between the three bases is likely to arise when an adjustment is made for the purposes of one tax giving rise to the question of whether this should have any effect on another tax. The answer is not straightforward due to the different starting point of the taxes, i.e., objective versus subjective price, and the use of different valuation methods. The authors pay particular attention to the question whether a transfer pricing adjustment should affect the VAT liability and discuss the four theoretical outcomes that may result as a consequence thereof. There exist, however, no universal consensus as to which approach should be the preferred one, as demonstrated in the final sections of the chapter where the authors provide an overview of the approaches taken in Australia and the EU respectively. They conclude that there is in some instances overlap between VAT and transfer pricing triggering the need for coordinate administration of VAT, customs, and income tax. On the other hand, it makes sense to keep the two areas separate given the different purpose of the VAT and the income tax and manner in which they operate as well as to insulate VAT from the gaming that seems to be a permanent feature in transfer pricing.

Bijl, in Chapter 11, deals with discounts provided through the issuance of vouchers. A voucher is a financial instrument other than cash (legal tender) to which the issuer has assigned a monetary value. Vouchers, generally, have a fixed value and can only be used to acquire non-cashable credits on purchases of certain goods or services and generally at a limited number or outlets or on-line. He starts by discussing the various types of vouchers and the different scenarios under which they can be redeemed and provides a theoretical model on how they should be treated for VAT purposes. The final section of the chapter contains a comparative law analysis of the VAT treatment of vouchers under various scenarios in the EU, Australia, New Zealand, and South Africa. As long as transactions remain within the ring of taxable businesses, there is no rationale for any adjustments as the VAT does not adhere due to the credit system. Issues arise, particularly, when discounts through a cash back coupon are given by manufacturers to private consumers. Bijl is critical of the CJEU that allows the cash back to be applied as a reduction of the sales price of the supply by the manufacturer to the retailer or wholesaler on grounds of preserving the neutrality of VAT.[22] Indeed, this is an artificial legal construction with no footing in reality. Bijl proposes to treat the cash back coupon as a third-party partial payment of the retailer price. The manufacturer would then be perceived as the part recipient of the supply and allowed to deduct VAT included in the cash back amount. I agree with the first part of the analysis that the cash back is a third-party payment. However, in my mind, the last part is as fictional as the CJEU's approach and, moreover, redundant. If a cash back is a third-party partial payment of the consumer price, then *ipso facto* the consumer price has not changed, and the government, contrary to the CJEU's reasoning that it received too much VAT in relation to what the consumer paid, collected exactly the correct amount relative to the consumption expenditure made for the supply; that part of the price was paid by someone else than the consumer is irrelevant for the levying of VAT. Cash back coupons constitute a promotional cost, and the CJEU decided wrongly in *Elida Gibbs* that such coupons effected a reduction of the transaction price of the supply made by manufacturer to the wholesaler. That finding is divorced from reality: the manufacturer received exactly the contractual price, and no reduction was ever given to the wholesaler, neither legally nor economically. Thus, there is no reason for any adjustment of VAT throughout the supply chain because there is no tax incidence as long as supplies are made within the ring of taxable persons (B2B). In effect, the CJEU in *Elida Gibbs* provides for a subsidy of the promotional costs in order of the VAT amount included in the cash back coupon.

The concept of fixed establishment (FE) is an EU phenomenon and plays an important role in proper tax jurisdiction allocation in case of cross-border service transactions with the common market. Although the fixed establishment is used as a term in the EU legislation, there exists no legislative definition, and the concept is solely developed through the case law of the CJEU. Bal, in Chapter 12, starts with providing context by explaining the purpose of legislative provisions that mention the fixed establishment to better understand its role. She focuses on the place of supply rules (tax jurisdiction rules) and the impact of the existence of a FE on the reverse charge mechanism. Next, she analyzes the most important CJEU cases and the criteria developed by the Court to determine whether a FE exists. This is followed by a comparison of the concept of FE, used in VAT, with that of PE, used for income taxes. Her approach is to contrast each building stone of the PE concept as laid down in the OECD Model Convention with the criteria developed by the CJEU for the existence of

22. CJEU, 24 October 1996, Case C-317/94, *Elida Gibbs Ltd v. Commissioners of Customs and Excise*, ECLI:EU:C:1996:400.

a FE, which results in a very insightful section. Separately, Bal discusses the VAT implications of cross-border transactions between head offices and FEs, which belong to the same legal entity, including the situation where the FE is part of a VAT group, which is treated for VAT purposes as a separate entity. Another fascinating aspect of foreign FEs is the impact they may have on the input-VAT credits of the head office, especially when the latter is partially exempt. The chapter ends with a view at the future of the FE concept. Bal wonders whether the requirement of human resources will be abandoned by the CJEU; the VAT will follow the PE concept insofar as treating the FE always as a separate entity for tax purposes; the concepts of PE and FE will be aligned at some future time.

Holding companies play an important role in multinational conglomerates and may serve the purpose of asset holding only, the so-called pure holding, or may have more active oversight roles. The VAT regime for holdings in the EU is largely created by the CJEU as there is no specific legislative provision in the VAT Directive dedicated to holdings. However, from a theoretical perspective, the treatment of holdings is quite straightforward. VAT is aimed at taxing only consumption expenditures and not productive expenditures. Even in case of a pure holding without any taxable output, its inputs do not qualify as private consumption. Thus, tax relief by allowing holdings to register and deduct input VAT should be provided for. That is not the case in the EU as explained by Herbain and Thompson in Chapter 13, who compare different types of holdings from the perspective of the legal requirements to qualify as taxable person and the right to input tax credits. It seems to me that the CJEU has dug itself in a hole by not including the underlying objective of VAT to tax only private consumption while interpreting the VAT Directive. Indeed, I would say, that the Directive does not help arriving at the correct solution. It defines as taxable person "*any person who ... carries out ... any economic activity*,"[23] and further defines economic activity as any activity of producers, traders, service providers, including mining and agricultural activities and activities of the professions as well as the exploitation of tangible or intangible property. For the CJEU a pure holding company equates a private investor[24] and dividends are not consideration for a supply,[25] reasons to deny holdings the right to deduct input tax. The first argument, however, ignores the context in which the holding operates, i.e., as part of and with a function in a large conglomerate of firms. The comparison with a private investor is simply flawed. The second argument has no bearing for determining the status of taxable person but serves only to decide whether a supply is taxable. The absence of taxable output should not automatically disqualify a holding company for applying input tax credits. In my opinion, *Polysar* was wrongfully decided and in all its subsequent rulings the CJEU seems trying to mitigate the negative consequences of its initial decision. Better were for the Court to overturn

23. Article 9 of Council Directive 2006/1112/EC of 28 November 2006 on the common system of value added tax, OJ L 347 of 11 December 2006 (Corrigendum OJ L335 of 20 December 2007).
24. CJEU, 20 June 1991, Case C-60/90, *Polysar Investments Netherlands v. Inspecteur der Invoerrechten en Accijnzen*, ECLI:EU:C:1991:268.
25. *See*, e.g., CJEU, 14 November 2000, Case C-142/99, *Floridienne SA and Berginvest SA v. Belgian State*, ECLI:EU:C:2000:623, and CJEU, 27 September 2001, Case C-16/00, *Cibo Participations SA v. Directeur régional des impôts du NordPas-de-Calais*, ECLI:EU:C:2001:495.

its earlier ruling and apply a standard for input VAT recovery in line with the legal character of VAT as a tax on private consumptive expenditures: as long as expenditure do not constitute private consumption, input tax credits should be allowed.

VAT is a tax on final consumption which is enabled by providing intermediate businesses relief from the tax paid on their inputs, either as a credit against output-VAT collected, or as a refund. For the proper effectiveness of VAT, it is crucial that those refunds are paid out without any delay, otherwise the tax becomes a cost either as such (if a refund is not granted) or in terms of negative cash flow (if refunds are delayed). Van Oordt, in Chapter 14, perceives the inherent necessity of the VAT collection system to grant refunds of excess input-VAT as one of its major weaknesses, especially in developing countries. This chapter asks and answers four questions.

One, should developing countries with a VAT consider an alternative broad-based consumption tax that does not require refunds? He addresses this question by comparing the VAT with the only feasible alternative, the retail sales tax (RST) as to tax base, compliance considerations, tax administration, and the risk of evasion. For developing countries, he concludes that VAT would be the better option. The solution for refund challenges, therefore, needs to be found within the VAT system.

Two, what policy options can be recommended to decrease VAT refund claims? Refunds are caused by exports, domestic zero-rated supplies, and the timing difference between capital investments and the occurrence of sufficient output to offset the input-VAT. As most capital investment in less developed countries is imported and, thus, subject to customs verification, he discusses the pros and cons of introducing a VAT deferral, i.e., a postponed accounting regime for these imports.

Three, what administrative options can improve developing countries' VAT refund practices? Van Oordt points out that governments often, but erroneously, consider VAT remitted before the retail stage as revenue. Instead, revenue is the tax amount that remains after all refunds have been paid. He suggests creating a VAT forecasting and monitoring system to estimate and set aside the amount of VAT that needs to be refunded, which he prefers over offsetting VAT refund claims against other tax debt or the issuing of tradable bonds.

And four, why should developing countries prioritize the prompt payment of VAT refunds? The reason to prioritize payment of refunds is that it encourages investments, both in the short term and in the long term and, thus, will harm the local economy and the general welfare. Moreover, non-payment of refunds may ignite a cycle of decreasing future tax revenues.

It has become trite to assert that the digitization of commerce has posed enormous challenges for tax systems around the world. Similarly, there is no longer anything contentious in stating that tax rules and principles that are premised on physical presence have been revealed by e-commerce to be inadequate. This is most apparent in the current calls to overhaul or even abandon aspects of the international income tax system, namely the concept of using permanent establishment to allocate taxing jurisdiction. Chapter 15, prepared by Thang and Shatalow, is dedicated to the topic of digital cross-border transactions.

The VAT has not been immune to the challenges of e-commerce. Although these challenges are less existential than those faced in the income tax context, they are nonetheless significant. E-commerce allows non-residents with no physical presence in a jurisdiction to access that jurisdiction's markets while potentially avoiding its VAT registration obligations. Although it has previously been suggested that destination-based VATs are particularly susceptible to the threat of e-commerce, Thang and Shatalow contend that the destination principle is ultimately a virtue for VAT regimes in the e-commerce context. This virtue results from the fact that a destination-based VAT gives jurisdictions a less mobile tax base than an origin-based VAT would. That said, many VAT systems do not perfectly embody the destination principle. To the extent that these VAT systems rely upon nexus rules for non-residents, they will face the same challenges present in the income tax context. Even when VAT regimes embody the destination principle, e-commerce presents difficult questions about administrative compliance: who will collect the tax? And what happens in the case of non-remittance? One of VAT's most remarkable virtues—convergence on the destination principle despite the absence of legal treaties—may also prove to be one of its main weaknesses: there is no legal mechanism specifically for enforcing VAT collection rules on sellers located outside the consumption jurisdiction. While it has been noted that existing model treaties and agreements could be applied to VAT, it is not clear how widely available these mechanisms are under existing agreements negotiated to address direct tax. They also rely on mutual cooperation and are therefore vulnerable to imbalances in incentives. The OECD has long hoped for a technical solution to these problems, but such a solution has not materialized. The authors, however, that a market solution may have emerged. Specifically, marketplace facilitators may be convenient VAT-collection agents in respect of e-commerce supplies made by non-residents, although this approach is not without its challenges.

Other potential challenges should not be ignored. The destination principle is premised on rules which determine a single *situs* of consumption. This may become more difficult to apply consistently as the lines between various types of electronic supplies become blurred. Finally, multi-sided platforms expose that a transactional VAT is not well-suited to tax forms of consumption that do not give rise to expenditures or, in other words, are not related to consideration. The VAT may in fact be less structurally capable in taxing the likes of Google, Facebook, and Apple than the income tax.

VAT is charged on the consideration received for a supply of goods and services. As long as pricing occurs under arm's length conditions, determining the size of the consideration is a matter between the parties involved. There exists no reason to correct a discounted price agreed between independent contractual parties. In case a supply is made free of charge, there is no consideration and, thus, the tax base for calculating VAT is absent, and no VAT is due. In other words, they fall outside the scope of VAT because supplies free of charge do not fulfil the legal definition of a taxable supply, which is a supply made for consideration. Are supplies free of charge or below cost price a problem for the proper functioning of VAT? The theoretical correct answer is mostly no. As long as there is no measure of private consumption which remains untaxed or undertaxed, the rationale of VAT is satisfied. No justification arises to restrict the corresponding input tax credits, or increase the sales price, or artificially create a self or deemed supply, leading to a VAT burden of the supplier contrary to the stated purpose of VAT to tax consumption and not production expenditure. This is recognized in modern VAT systems, such as Australia, but not by the EU. Corrections are only needed in case such supplies benefit the owners or the employees of the enterprise, because then, indeed, private consumption would escape the VAT. Merkx, in Chapter 16, provides an extensive treatise on the EU rules and relevant CJEU jurisprudence in regard of supplies free of charge and below cost price. The issue in the EU is, in my mind, the erroneous position of the CJEU in its cornerstone *Hong Kong* case[26] that consumption takes place when the chain of transactions comes to an end, which is when the final consumer is reached who cannot pass on the tax. In the absence of consideration, the supplier of free of charge supplies is now considered to occupy the final phase of the transaction chain and must, like a final consumer, so is the reasoning, bear the VAT. Thus, the supplier is denied the right to deduct the corresponding input tax. This reasoning of the Court is, in my assessment, based on a misunderstanding of which consequences logically derive from the objective of the VAT. As a tax on private consumption, production inputs should be relieved from the tax. Thus, the context in which procurement is made, should be decisive for the right to deduct input VAT, not whether consideration is received or the amount thereof. Discounts serve to attract customers or boost sales; donations to charities are aimed at producing a positive image or improve the profile of the company in the community it serves. Regardless of the presence of some degree of altruism, commercial objectives are the main motivator, even if goods are purchased for the purpose of gifting. Spilker and Hoffmann in Chapter 17 address the same topic but more narrowly, focused on donations in kind to charities in the context of supporting the objectives of the EU green policy. They compare the EU level rules with the practices in Germany and France, both EU Member States, and the UK and Australia, the latter a representative of modern VAT jurisdictions and, theoretically correct, applying no restrictions on input tax deductions for supplies free of charge or below cost price.

The second part of this book is focused on the experience with VAT of particular countries.

New Zealand is generally credited for launching the so-called Modern VAT and has become the benchmark for countries contemplating on introducing a VAT or modifying an existing general consumption tax system. Evaluating the New Zealand experience is, therefore, crucial for the development of future indirect tax policy and White takes on this task in Chapter 18. New Zealand has sustained a broad-base, uniform-rate approach to GST design for 35 years now, with what has been characterized as a second-generation VAT. While this approach has endured, it continues to be contested, especially in relation to the tax treatment of food and basic necessities. For some, the comprehensive, uniform-rate approach in the GST is a "virtue" and for others it is a "fallacy." This chapter examines the latest OECD data on the performance of the GST, especially in an economic crisis. It draws comparisons between the performance of this tax with the first-generation VAT of the United Kingdom and a fellow second-generation GST in Australia. It examines the findings of 3 New Zealand

26. CJEU, 1 April 1982, Case C-89/81, *Hong Kong*, ECLI:EU:C:1982:121.

tax reviews held over the last twenty years about the New Zealand GST base and rate and of the latest reviews of the United Kingdom VAT and the Australian GST. Finally, it reports the latest research on the distributive effects of the New Zealand GST. While the New Zealand GST is not perfect and regularly requires maintenance, it seems clear that New Zealand should retain its broad-base, uniform-rate design. It is a less costly way of raising revenue and other government instruments can be used to achieve distributional, wellbeing and other objectives.

For some 30 years, Japan applied a unique consumption tax system, a form of credit-subtraction VAT, characterized by a broad base, a single rate, the absence of a tax invoice requirement, and with one of the highest VAT Revenue Ratios. Masui, in Chapter 19, starts with a historical overview of the political decision-making process to explain why Japan introduced its Consumption Tax and why it decided to modify it into a multi-rate, credit-invoice method VAT. He explains how the Japanese consumption tax works in practice, i.e., how a business calculates its tax liabilities from its accounts by subtracting total inputs from total outputs and apply the tax rate to the difference, and the special rules for exempt sales, the registration threshold, the simplified filing scheme to accommodate small traders, and the administration of the tax. Under the consumption tax, a business can also subtract inputs from exempt sellers, which goes beyond the objective of a VAT of relieving businesses from the tax and prevent cascading; it essentially constitutes an unwarranted subsidy. This is a main weakness of the Japanese consumption tax, according to Masui. The Japanese consumption tax has been a success and, interestingly, the absence of a tax invoice did not negatively influence compliance enforcement. The political need for a reduced rate, which a subtraction type of VAT cannot sustain, ended the Japanese experiment in that in modified its consumption tax into a credit-invoice VAT. Likely, in the not-so-distant future, Japan will face the same issues as other jurisdictions with the application of a multiple VAT system as discussed in Chapter 4 and summarized above.

The significant growth of international trade in services poses challenges to the VAT. The destination principle, the widely endorsed principle that achieves neutrality in cross-border supplies, requires removal of VAT from exported supplies to allow room for full imposition of the tax in the place where final consumption occurs. However, the rapid digitalization of the economy makes the implementation of the principle difficult in cross-border trade in services, in particular with respect to the determination of the place in which final consumption takes place. Xu in Chapter 20 considers this—identifying the place of taxation—and the separate challenge of collecting tax where the supplier is out of the jurisdiction and the customers are unregistered persons, using the Chinese experience to illustrate the difficulties and possible solutions to these problems. She argues that place of taxation rules and collection mechanisms must be both clear and practical, taking into consideration that the ultimate purpose of the destination principle is to achieve trade neutrality.

Hoyos-Jiménez in Chapter 21 describes the development over the years from first implementation to the present of the VAT in Colombia, a Latin-American developing country. It serves as a good example of the political complexities of tax reform where she explains the design flaws of the Colombian VAT and the many attempts at improving its effectiveness and fairness. She provides an overview of the current structure of the VAT and points out where the Colombian VAT fails the theoretical benchmark. Important areas for improvement are the neutrality of Colombian VAT where not all imports and exports are treated equally, resulting in economic distortions; the taxation of investments by not allowing input tax credits for capital assets; and the negative cashflows for many businesses due to the withholding obligations. Hoyos-Jiménez declares herself a proponent of abolishing the multi-rate system and moving the Colombian VAT to a single VAT rate, because the rationale for reduced rates, found in the regressivity of VAT, has no basis in reality as higher income groups seem to benefit more from reduced rates than the lowest income groups that are the stated beneficiaries, a notion that echoes some of the findings in Chapter 4.

Mukherjee, in Chapter 22, shares India's experience of introducing VAT at the federal level in a developing economy. India is a federal state with significant autonomy at the sub-national and provincial level. The introduction of the GST in India since 1 July 2017 is the result of a journey that started 3 decades ago. India embraced the concept of VAT in 1986 by introducing the Modified VAT (MODVAT) to replace Union Excise Duties (UEDs) on manufacturing. Given the Constitutional assignment of taxation power to different governments, the fiscal autonomy enjoyed by the sub-national governments, and the complexities involved in bringing consensus among sub-national governments, the evolution of Indian GST provides an interesting example of reforms in indirect taxes for scholars interested in public finance, especially in the case of federal countries. Building consensus for a destination based dual VAT system between federal, state, and provincial governments with quite diverse political and economic interests is a great achievement in the history of fiscal federalism.

Reforms initiated since the late eighties in indirect taxes helped in sequencing big tax reforms like GST in India and also helped in accommodating political-economy dimensions as well as acceptability aspects of the tax reform. The chapter captures the policy evolution of the concept of GST in India since late 1980s. Indian GST is unique for its structure, design and administrative framework and three years' experience of GST shows that India needs to travel a long path ahead in indirect tax reforms to address emerging challenges of the present system.

The VAT of Ethiopia has some strengths, such as a single rate which is generally preferred for countries with limited administrative capacities, and a high registration threshold providing protection to small businesses from high compliance costs. An important weakness lies in the absence of legal definitions of crucial concepts within VAT, which runs the risk of making the application of VAT arbitrary. Van Oordt, in Chapter 23, evaluates Ethiopia's VAT system from a macro-economic perspective. Ethiopia's economy is characterized by excess capacity due to insufficient capital and unutilized labor with low levels of demand. In Ethiopia, supply does not create demand, and that calls for special remedies. To mobilize the excess capacity investments are needed, and Van Oordt argues how VAT can be an effective instrument for this purpose. To increase effective demand in the Ethiopian context, tax policies should in theory redistribute profits to wages which, in turn, would lead to increased investment. VAT has the most revenue potential but as a tax on consumption would decrease the share of wages in national income. Although using VAT may have the appearance of being counterproductive, Van Oordt argues that VAT can be designed to tackle the problems facing an economy characterized by excess capacity, low demand, a small export sector, and foreign exchange shortages, such as Ethiopia. He discusses the pros and cons of increasing the VAT rate, abolishing the zero rate on indirect exports, changing administrative processes such as registration and refunds (*see also* Chapter 15 by the same author) that tighten financial constraint for businesses, and removing certain exemptions. Unintuitively, some exemptions may enhance economic growth, but those are rare. He convincingly shows that under circumstances exemptions for goods and services purchased by high-propensity consumers may generate the desired economic effects. In addition, he provides a list of exempt items that have a negative growth effect and should, thus, be taxed. He concludes that VATs need to be better aligned with the objective that taxes support economic growth and remove supply side and financial constraints to investment.

Indeed, VAT is a success story in terms of application, now by almost 170 countries. However, we must keep in mind that a best-selling music album, while obviously a commercial success, does not necessarily contain the best quality music. In the same sense can the successful proliferation of VAT not serve as proof of its inherent quality. This book describes and evaluates VAT's virtues and fallacies and, unsurprisingly, VAT has both. The main strength of VAT is its capacity to generate revenue. That virtue should not be disregarded as raising revenue to fund the cost of the public sector is the main or secondary purpose of all taxes. The main purpose of some taxes may be external to revenue raising, such as environmental taxes that seem to primarily serve to change consumptive behavior, but the classical taxes are focused on revenue. Consumption taxes have an advantage as revenue raisers due to their inherent, basic simplicity. But they are not the right tool to accomplish secondary policy objectives such as the redistribution of income. VAT is a revenue raising workhorse and any attempt to make it into a show jumper, steeple chaser, racehorse, or dressage horse must simply fail, because it does not correspond to the nature of the animal. That simple truth has not prevented lawmakers from trying to use it for other policy objectives; to their defense, often under pressure from influential lobby groups. It is generally recognized that VAT is not an adequate vehicle to realize objectives outside revenue generation and multiple rates, exemptions and other exceptions only complicate the tax, without realizing their objective,[27] and lead to increasing deadweight losses in the form of compliance and administrative costs. Increased complexity also leads to a rise in mistakes and classification disputes between tax agencies and taxpayers. A policymaker once told me during a conversation that tax avoidance schemes set up by (partially) exempt entities to mitigate or reduce the burden of non-deductible input-VAT were unethical. However, it is the other way around: exemptions (without credit) violate the purpose of VAT to only tax private consumption and provide relief to businesses. Back in 1957, Maurice Lauré[28] already declared exemptions to be the cancer of a VAT system; thus, from that perspective, killing the

27. *See* Chapter 4 of this book and Rita de la Feria and Michael Walpole, *The Impact of Public Perception on General Consumption Taxes* 67/5 British Tax Rev. 637 (2020).
28. Maurice Lauré, *Au Secours de la TVA* (PUF, 1957).

"cancer" through tax planning might actually be meritorious and restore the ethical balance.

The many problems and areas of complexity of VAT occur mostly within the ring of businesses transactions where VAT should be irrelevant as the VAT targets private consumption expenditure and not business expenditure. VAT is charged on every transaction in the supply chain but provides relief to businesses through the input tax deduction mechanism. Thus, while the VAT moves along the supply and distribution chain it does not generate any revenue until it leaves the ring of taxable business transactions. Money is simply pumped around when buyers pay VAT to sellers, the sellers remit that VAT to the tax authority which then returns the VAT to the buyers in the form of a credit or actual refund. All these transactions must be administered and supervised by businesses and tax authorities without any raising of revenue in real terms. Those observations raise the obvious question whether the credit invoice VAT is truly the most rational way to tax private consumption. VAT may continue its worldwide spread but counties contemplating the introduction of a general consumption tax should also consider whether alternative taxes are available, such as a well-designed retail sales tax, that avoids the problems encountered with VAT and would be efficient, manageable, and administrable given the stage of development of their economy. If VAT is chosen, policymakers should intimate themselves with the design features to ensure that distortions are minimal, and efficiency is optimal. An important philosophical consideration for policymakers and constituents to make in that context, which should have an impact on the choice of type of consumption tax and the design thereof, is how much government supervision and information gathering is desirable from the perspective of protecting individual privacy and retaining a free society.

PART I Technical Topics

CHAPTER 2

Revenue Performance

Pierre-Pascal Gendron

§2.01 INTRODUCTION

Revenue mobilization, in the best of circumstances, remains a challenge everywhere but especially in developing countries. The value-added tax (VAT) is a very important part of the solution to this revenue mobilization challenge: it is the mainstay of revenue systems in many countries, particularly developing and less developed countries, and an important source of revenue in over 160 countries around the world.[1] Countries have adopted VATs for many reasons. The principal reason is simply that it is a major revenue producer. In contrast to alternatives or complementary policies such as income taxes, selective excise taxes, or import duties, a broad-based consumption tax like VAT is a relatively efficient way to raise significant amounts of revenue from an economic perspective because it is less distorting and hence less likely to discourage investment, saving, labour supply decisions, and growth. Finally, because consumption is a more stable revenue base than other tax bases, VAT revenues generally should grow more or less at the same rate as the entire economy, unlike other taxes and notably those on business income, whose revenues usually expand more rapidly when the economy grows but tend to contract more rapidly when growth slows down.

Revenue raising is the only objective a VAT can achieve well. Yet, many countries, developed and developing, have used and still use VAT to fulfil a host of non-revenue objectives. This practice undermines the revenue performance of VAT as well as its economic neutrality. Of course, as many economic characteristics of countries and economic conditions can affect revenue performance, there are several methods to calculate and evaluate revenue performance. This chapter focuses on the various approaches to the measurement and assessment of revenue performance and

1. *See* Richard M. Bird, *VAT During and After the Pandemic*, 99 Tax Notes International 6 (28 September 2020).

the interpretation of performance indicators. It is important to note at the outset that the notion of VAT performance is broader than just VAT revenue productivity. Performance assessment includes revenue productivity, of course, but it also considers productivity in relation to other macroeconomic indicators such as consumption, imports, and GDP. Although VAT incidence and burden distribution are important elements of performance, they deserve their own separate inquiry and will be set aside in this chapter.

Given the breadth of the performance area and space limitations, this chapter is very selective and does not aim at surveying the entire field of VAT performance assessment. It focuses on the main data and methods that can be used to assess revenue performance and deepen one's understanding of an actual VAT in action.

Section 2.02 presents the case for focusing on the revenue objective only. Section 2.03 describes the methodologies and data commonly used to assess and measure revenue performance and provides examples of data presentation. Section 2.04 explores the additional revenue that can arise from the proper coordination of VAT with other indirect taxes and discusses the transition to the assessment of performance relative to potential revenue. Section 2.05 concludes.

§2.02 REVENUE: NOTHING ELSE MATTERS TO VAT

This section reviews the multiple objectives that have weighted down on the VAT in actual practice and the possible outcomes of this situation. It argues that, in a normative sense, the production of revenue should be the only objective of a VAT. Yet, field experience shows that the VAT is used, or thought to be used, to achieve multiple non-revenue objectives, including:[2]

- Income redistribution and equity;
- Formalization of the informal economy;
- Investment promotion;
- Price control or management;
- Protection of domestic industry; and
- Promotion of competitiveness.

Despite the almost total absence of prima facie evidence that the VAT can achieve those objectives, numerous developing countries have attempted to use the VAT to achieve some or all of the above. In many of those cases, the trigger has been the weakness of other policy instruments (e.g., direct taxation, government expenditures, trade policies, institutional quality) to achieve such goals. So, the problems spill over beyond VAT and are really wide-ranging governance problems.[3]

The desire to achieve those objectives explains, in large part, the proliferation of exemptions, reduced rates, and other concessions provided through VAT systems. A

2. The list of issues and experience draw on Pierre-Pascal Gendron, *Real VATs vs. the Good VAT: Reflections from a Decade of Technical Assistance*, 32 Austl. Tax F. 257 (2017).
3. For a discussion in the context of Africa, *see* Mick Moore, Wilson Prichard, and Odd-Helge Fjeldstad, *Taxing Africa: Coercion, Reform and Development* (Zed Books, 2018).

vast sum of field experience suggests that the VAT, despite those departures from good design, fail to achieve those objectives.[4] Moreover, the departures from sound design come at a significant revenue loss, even though the individual impacts of such departures are difficult to measure empirically, especially in developing countries. Good tax policy design (broad base, single rate, few or no exemptions, relatively high registration threshold), competent tax administration, and revenue performance are self-reinforcing. The remainder of the chapter will proceed under the assumption that the sole purpose of the VAT is to mobilize revenue. This leaves non-revenue objectives to other policy instruments.

§2.03 METHODOLOGIES AND MEASUREMENT OF PERFORMANCE

This section explores the various methodologies that are used to measure and assess revenue performance. Those include, without being limited to: relative contribution analysis, C-efficiency analysis, macro analysis, econometric and statistical analysis, revenue forecasting, and micro analysis.

[A] Relative Contribution Analysis

This first and necessary step to the performance assessment requires a positioning of VAT revenue relative to GDP and other sources of tax revenues. GDP is especially important since the tax ratio (tax revenue to GDP) is used heavily as a first-line measure of the relative contribution of different taxes. Table 2.1 shows an example of contribution analysis. It is ideal to compile and present revenue contribution data for several years (at least five, but the more the better) to allow for cyclical swings, structural breaks (e.g., major policy changes) and other impacts. Detailed revenue data usually come from the Ministry of Finance, including published government budgets. Table 2.1 is suggestive of the level of disaggregation required for a good contribution analysis. The general rule argues for as much disaggregation as possible. One benefit of this approach is the identification of revenue-unproductive or nuisance taxes that would be good candidates for elimination or consolidation.

Given the focus on VAT, it is helpful to further disaggregate VAT revenue between collections on imports and collections that originate from the domestic economy. One of the reasons is that relative compliance on the collection on imported goods should be strong, all else equal. Table 2.2 draws on the figures of Table 2.1 to provide that further breakdown of VAT revenues and shows the relative revenue contributions of the trade (imports, as opposed to exports, in a destination-based VAT) and domestic sectors.

4. For a cross-section of the more comprehensive works in this literature, *see* Sijbren Cnossen, *Modernizing VATs in Africa* (Oxford University Press, 2019); Richard M. Bird and Pierre-Pascal Gendron, *The VAT in Developing and Transitional Countries* (Cambridge University Press, 2007 [2011]); and Liam Ebrill, Michael Keen, Jean-Paul Bodin, and Victoria Summers, *The Modern VAT* (International Monetary Fund, 2001).

Table 2.1 Sample Revenue Contribution Analysis for a Country

Revenue (million local currency units)	2012	2013	2014	2015	2016	2017	2018	2019
Tax revenue	79,598	89,085	100,959	111,409	118,334	126,510	135,890	142,896
Income taxes	31,242	33,197	39,243	43,060	43,949	46,128	51,183	54,500
Company income tax	15,812	17,032	20,502	21,239	22,951	25,997	28,933	30,297
Withholding tax	2,755	2,852	3,322	4,977	4,843	4,932	4,351	4,310
Personal income tax	12,674	13,314	15,419	16,845	16,155	15,199	17,900	19,894
Consumption tax, imports	0	14	0	0	0	0	0	0
Value-added and excise taxes	37,102	44,672	48,363	53,047	56,849	61,659	65,709	68,807
Value-added tax	23,975	23,216	27,044	31,103	34,077	34,317	37,307	35,374
Excise tax	13,103	21,422	21,293	21,891	22,744	27,271	28,234	33,330
Miscellaneous	23	34	26	53	28	71	168	103
Other customs tax	267	192	187	230	222	224	241	291
Other domestic tax	2,768	2,942	3,434	3,945	4,413	5,086	4,900	5,271
Taxes on international trade and transactions	8,218	8,068	9,732	11,126	12,901	13,412	13,856	14,027
Import duties	6,602	6,804	8,302	9,864	11,561	11,866	12,167	12,357
Export duties	9	8	7	10	9	14	14	12
Travel tax	1,144	1,255	1,423	1,253	1,331	1,532	1,676	1,658
Other levies	464	0	0	0	0	0	0	0
Non-tax revenue	3,350	5,805	6,917	9,507	11,895	9,985	9,836	18,814
In percent of tax revenue								
Total	100.0	100.0	100.0	100.0	100.0	100.0	100.0	100.0
Income taxes	39.2	37.3	38.9	38.7	37.1	36.5	37.7	38.1
Value-added tax	30.1	26.1	26.8	27.9	28.8	27.1	27.5	24.8
Excise tax	16.5	24.0	21.1	19.6	19.2	21.6	20.8	23.3
Import duties	8.3	7.6	8.2	8.9	9.8	9.4	9.0	8.6
Other	5.9	5.0	5.0	4.9	5.1	5.5	5.1	5.1
In percent of GDP								
Tax revenue	20.3	21.6	21.9	21.2	20.3	20.6	21.4	21.9
Of which:								
Income taxes	8.0	8.0	8.5	8.2	7.5	7.5	8.1	8.3
Value-added tax	6.1	5.6	5.9	5.9	5.8	5.6	5.9	5.4
Excise tax	3.3	5.2	4.6	4.2	3.9	4.4	4.4	5.1
Import duties	1.7	1.6	1.8	1.9	2.0	1.9	1.9	1.9
Non-tax revenue	0.9	1.4	1.5	1.8	2.0	1.6	1.5	2.9
GDP (nominal, million local currency units)	391,505	413,114	460,072	525,672	582,657	614,130	635,262	653,836

Source: Author's anonymized compilation based on own field work.

Table 2.2 Value-Added Tax Revenue – Imports Versus Domestic

	2012	2013	2014	2015	2016	2017	2018	2019
VAT revenues (million local currency units)	23,975	23,216	27,044	31,103	34,077	34,317	37,307	35,374
Imports	14,385	13,930	17,579	19,595	19,765	18,874	22,384	21,932
Domestic	9,590	9,286	9,466	11,508	14,312	15,443	14,923	13,442
In percent of VAT revenues	100.0	100.0	100.0	100.0	100.0	100.0	100.0	100.0
Imports	60.0	60.0	65.0	63.0	58.0	55.0	60.0	62.0
Domestic	40.0	40.0	35.0	37.0	42.0	45.0	40.0	38.0
In percent of GDP	6.1	5.6	5.9	5.9	5.8	5.6	5.9	5.4
Imports	3.7	3.4	3.8	3.7	3.4	3.1	3.5	3.4
Domestic	2.4	2.2	2.1	2.2	2.5	2.5	2.3	2.1

Source: Author's anonymized compilation based on own field work.

A different but illuminating relative contribution analysis involves the comparison across countries or regional economic communities (RECs) of the contribution of various indirect taxes (VAT, excises and similar taxes, trade taxes, customs fees, others) to GDP and total tax revenues. Table 2.3 presents such data, in selected years, for African countries that belong to the Southern African Development Community (SADC) and the East African Community (EAC).

Exhibits such as Table 2.3 can become imposing, especially if one wishes to consider all RECs in Africa, in which case the table would spread over three pages. In such cases, charts are more practical and less time consuming to prepare. As an alternative or complement to large tables, charts perform better. For example, Figure 2.1 illustrates the relative importance of VAT revenues by region in terms of the usual measures of VAT revenue as a percentage of revenue and GDP, and total tax revenue as a percentage of GDP. The data show interesting patterns. VAT tends to be a relatively important component of revenue systems not only in regions with relatively low overall tax revenue mobilization (Sub-Saharan Africa, Latin America, and the Caribbean) but also in revenues with high overall tax ratios (Europe and Central Asia). North America is an outlier with strong revenue mobilization and a very low weight for VAT in total tax revenues, largely because the United States does not have a VAT, although Canada does.

Table 2.3 Revenue from VAT, Excises and Import Duties, Selected African Countries and Years

RECs and Countries	Total tax as % GDP	% GDP				% Total tax revenue				Year of data
		Total indirect	VAT	Excise and other	Trade taxes	Total indirect	VAT	Excise and other	Trade taxes	
Southern African Development Community										
SACU										
Botswana	25.8	14.7	3.9	10.8		57.0	15.1	41.9		2014
Lesotho	34.3	24.4	6.2	18.2		71.1	18.1	53.0		2017
Namibia	29.5	16.7	7.7	9.0		56.6	26.1	30.5		2016
South Africa	26.3	10.6	7.0	2.6	1.0	40.3	26.6	9.9	3.8	2016
Swaziland (now Eswatini)	29.0	23.4	4.2	19.2		80.7	14.5	66.2		2012
Other										
Congo, Democratic Republic	7.2	5.0	2.4	0.1	2.5	69.4	33.3	1.4	34.7	2010
Madagascar	10.9	8.2	5.3	1.2	1.7	75.2	48.6	11.0	15.6	2016
Malawi	17.3	8.9	4.8	2.6	1.5	51.4	27.7	15.0	8.7	2017
Mauritius	18.1	13.6	8.0	5.3	0.3	75.1	44.2	29.3	1.6	2016
Mozambique	20.1	10.9	7.0	2.1	1.8	54.2	34.8	10.4	9.0	2016
Seychelles	31.6	20.0	10.6	7.5	1.9	63.2	33.5	23.7	6.0	2016
Zambia	14.9	6.6	3.7	2.0	0.9	44.2	24.8	13.4	6.0	2016
Zimbabwe	24.5	15.5	6.2	3.8	5.5	63.2	25.3	15.5	22.4	2012
East African Community										
Burundi	12.9	9.2	5.0	2.9	1.3	71.3	38.8	22.4	10.1	2013
Kenya	16.3	8.2	4.1	2.5	1.6	50.3	25.2	15.3	9.8	2015
Rwanda	13.3	7.9	4.4	2.4	1.1	59.4	33.1	18.0	8.3	2017
Tanzania	12.1	7.7	3.4	3.0	1.3	63.6	28.1	24.8	10.7	2017
Uganda	12.9	8.5	4.1	2.9	1.5	65.9	31.8	22.5	11.6	2016

Source: Cnossen, *supra* n. 4, Table 6.1, at 63.

Figure 2.1 VAT as a Source of Revenue, Regional Comparison, 2019

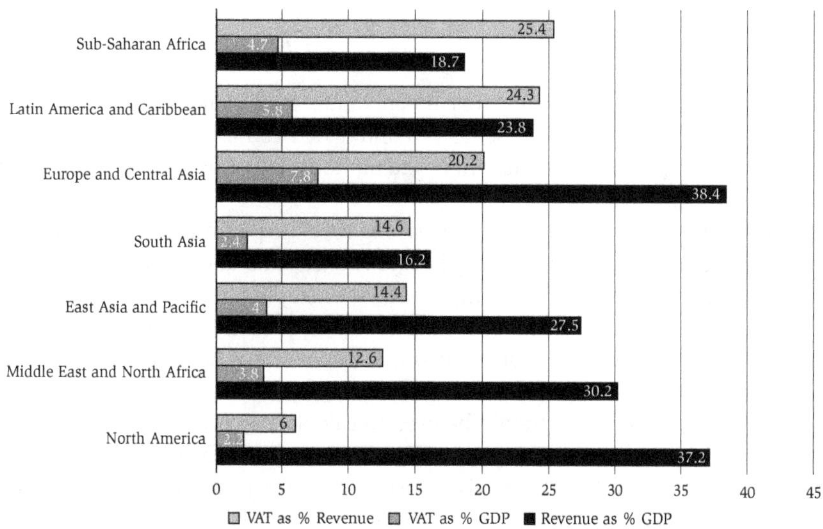

Source: Bird, *supra* n. 1, Figure 1, at 7.

[B] C-Efficiency Ratio Analysis

Individual contribution analyses are absolutely necessary exercises but can become time-consuming and difficult to use if one wishes replicate them for multiple countries to compare VAT revenue efficiency across countries. Under the intellectual leadership of the Fiscal Affairs Department (FAD) of the International Monetary Fund (IMF), a new performance measure was born just over 20 years ago: the C-efficiency (or collection efficiency) ratio, or *C-efficiency* in short.[5] In order to derive the ratio, write VAT revenue (denoted by *V*) as a percentage of GDP (*Y*) as:

$$(1) \qquad \frac{V}{Y} = \tau_s E^C \left(\frac{C}{Y}\right)$$

where τ_s denotes the standard VAT rate, *C* denotes consumption (valued at VAT-exclusive prices), and E^C denotes C-efficiency.

5. *See* Ebrill et al., *supra* n. 4, and Michael Keen, *The Anatomy of VAT*, 66 Nat'l Tax J. 423 (2013). The discussion that follows draws more closely on the latter.

Further define C-efficiency as:

$$(2) \qquad E^C \equiv \frac{V}{\tau_s C}$$

The C-efficiency ratio compares the revenue an actual VAT raises with the revenue it would raise if perfectly enforced and levied at a uniform rate (equal to the standard rate) on all consumption with no exemptions. Equation (2) shows the ratio as it is calculated empirically.

C-efficiency close to 100% suggests strong revenue performance while one close to zero suggests a very poor performance. A few caveats about the measure are in order. First, the taxation of business inputs due to exemptions and cascading, although economically inefficient, will boost the numerator of Equation (2). Second, the practice of not paying VAT refunds will also boost the numerator of Equation (2) since gross collections will be larger than true net revenues (i.e., net of refunds). Net revenues, as opposed to gross collections, should be used to calculate V in Equation (2). For those reasons, C-efficiencies above 1.0 are possible although rare. Nevertheless, C-efficiency is easy to calculate and the analysis is useful to provide a quick and convenient comparison between countries. More importantly, it should always invite further data collection and analysis. Consumption data are available from expenditure-based GDP series in the national accounts published by statistical agencies. Tax rate data is available in the VAT law and on websites of tax or revenue administrations.

The VAT-Revenue-Ratio (VRR) – in the OECD's terminology – is essentially another name for C-efficiency but measured a bit differently as the ratio of actual VAT revenue to the potential revenue if the standard VAT rate were applied to final (including public) consumption in the national accounts, less actual VAT revenue.[6]

The Fiscal Affairs Department of the IMF compiles and maintains C-efficiency data for a wide range of countries and regions. Regional groups include Australia and New Zealand, Baltic States, Caribbean, Central America, Central Asia, Eastern Africa, Eastern Asia, Eastern Europe, Melanesia, Micronesia, Middle Africa, Middle East, Northern Africa, Northern America, Northern Europe, Polynesia, South America, South-Eastern Asia, Southern Africa, Southern Asia, Southern Europe, Western Africa, Western Asia, and Western Europe. Together those regions account for a total of 214 jurisdictions, an unwieldy number to present data in tabular form.

Suppose, for example, that one were interested in comparing C-efficiency data between Baltic States and Eastern European Countries over the period 2010-2018. Table 2.4 shows the annual C-efficiency ratios over the period and additional information such as the income group, region, and country group to which each individual country belongs. The numbers exhibit a fairly wide dispersion. Figure 2 illustrates, using a standard bar chart, the C-efficiency ratios for Baltic States and Eastern European countries in 2018, organized in decreasing order and omitting countries with no estimates (with 'na' or blanks for all years).

6. *See* Hannah Simon and Michelle Harding, *What Drives Consumption Tax Revenues? Disentangling Policy and Macroeconomic Drivers*, OECD Taxation Working Paper No. 47 (OECD, 2020).

Table 2.4 C-Efficiency in Baltic States and Eastern Europe, 2010-2018

Countries				C-efficiency								
	Income group	Region	Country groups	2010	2011	2012	2013	2014	2015	2016	2017	2018
Belarus	Upper middle income	Eastern Europe	CIS				0.744	0.748	0.677	0.752	0.713	0.720
Bosnia and Herzegovina	Upper middle income	Eastern Europe					1.238	1.254	1.352	1.311	1.357	1.385
Bulgaria	Upper middle income	Eastern Europe	EU	0.655	0.629	0.668	0.664	0.638	0.644	0.678	0.667	0.678
Croatia	High income: nonOECD	Eastern Europe	EU	0.763	0.739	0.744	0.723	0.732	0.770	0.791	0.817	0.839
Czech Republic	High income: OECD	Eastern Europe	EU	0.535	0.564	0.585	0.568	0.584	0.587	0.632	0.625	0.612
Estonia	High income: OECD	Baltic States	EU	0.670	0.680	0.698	0.663	0.698	0.729	0.723	0.745	0.754
Hungary	High income: OECD	Eastern Europe	EU	0.529	0.524	0.527	0.522	0.561	0.630	0.568	0.579	0.586
Kosovo	Lower middle income	Eastern Europe		na	na	na	na	na	na	na	na	na
Latvia	High income: nonOECD	Baltic States	EU	0.628	0.541	0.616	0.498	0.559	0.525	0.551	0.546	0.574
Lithuania	High income: nonOECD	Baltic States	EU	0.479	0.503	0.490	0.496	0.569	0.512	0.513	0.529	0.526
Macedonia (FYR)	Upper middle income	Eastern Europe					0.542	0.586	0.529	0.572	0.587	0.566
Moldova	Lower middle income	Eastern Europe	CIS				0.528	0.570	0.584	0.492	0.517	0.539
Montenegro	Upper middle income	Eastern Europe		na	na	na	na	na	na	na	na	na
Poland	High income: OECD	Eastern Europe	EU	0.477	0.483	0.432	0.425	0.436	0.438	0.455	0.495	0.523
Romania	Upper middle income	Eastern Europe	EU	0.554	0.518	0.506	0.562	0.467	0.499	0.452	0.455	0.448
Russia	High income: nonOECD	Eastern Europe	CIS				0.470	0.428	0.453	0.474	0.488	0.535
Serbia	Upper middle income	Eastern Europe		na	na	na	na	na	na	na	na	na
Slovak Republic	High income: OECD	Eastern Europe	EU	0.468	0.496	0.440	0.472	0.494	0.523	0.496	0.514	0.519
Slovenia	High income: OECD	Eastern Europe	EU	0.592	0.596	0.585	0.634	0.592	0.592	0.585	0.594	0.687
Ukraine	Lower middle income	Eastern Europe	CIS				0.534	0.538	0.577	0.655	0.689	0.663

Source: Author's tabulation based on data supplied by the International Monetary Fund, December 2020.

Figure 2.2 C-Efficiency in Baltic States and Eastern Europe, 2018

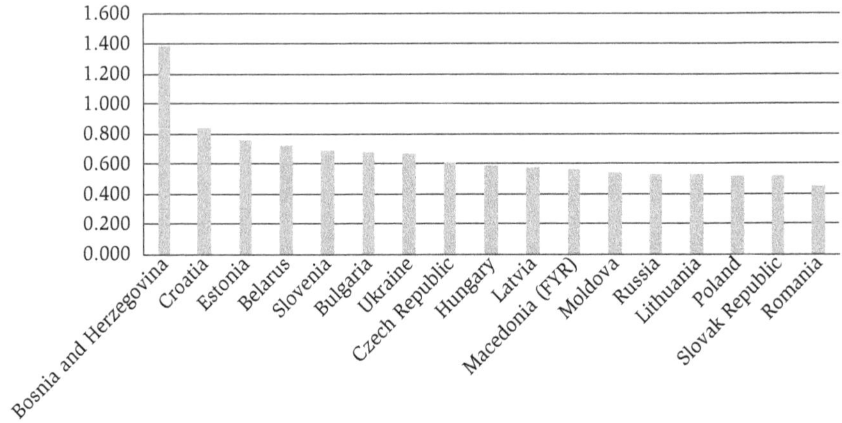

Source: Author's chart based on data supplied by the International Monetary Fund, December 2020.

Figure 2.3 C-Efficiency in Baltic States and Eastern Europe, 2013-2018

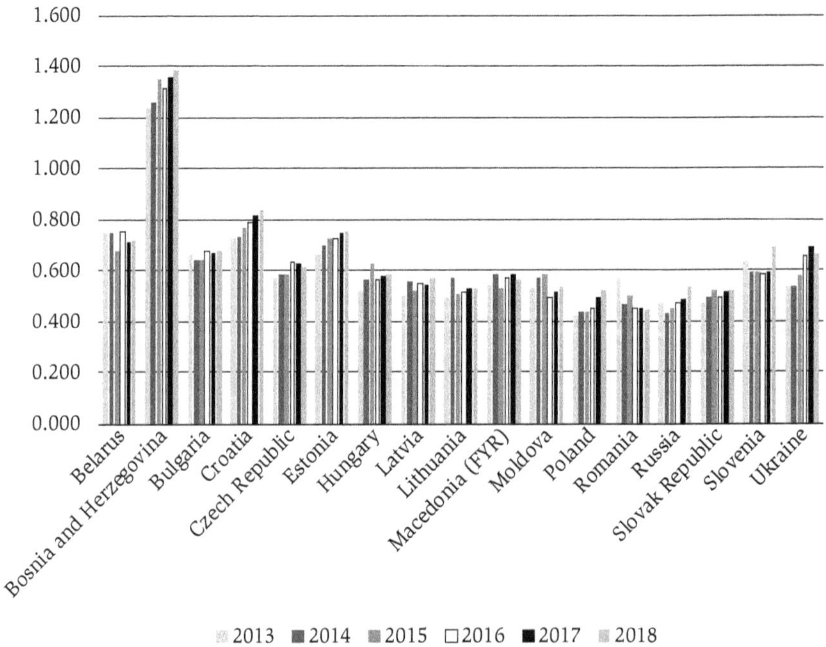

Source: Author's chart based on data supplied by the International Monetary Fund, December 2020.

Figure 2.4 shows C-efficiency averages by region of the world in 2017. The figures are arithmetic averages and the number of countries per region varies. Some bars reflect the influence of outliers. For example, South-Eastern Asia contains a very high value for Maldives which distorts the average.

Figure 2.4 C-Efficiency Averages by Region, 2017

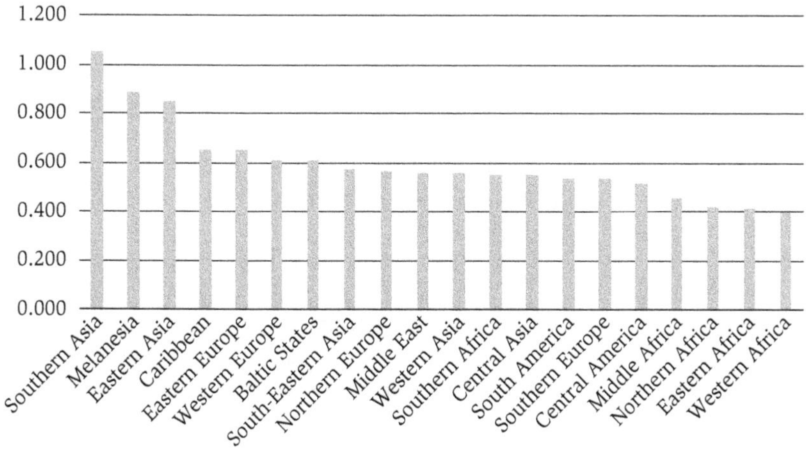

Source: Author's chart based on data supplied by the International Monetary Fund, December 2020.

[C] Macro Analysis

VAT performance depends on the economic and sectoral structure of the economy. In other words, it depends on the size, composition, and allocation of value-added throughout the economy. An analysis of macroeconomic variables can, therefore, support the performance assessment of VAT collection. The standard macro analyses conducted to evaluate VAT performance typically rely on the following set of easy-to-compute indicators:[7]

VAT revenues to GDP. VAT tax ratio as presented in Part A of this section.

VAT revenues to total tax revenues. VAT tax revenue ratio as presented in Part A.

VAT revenues to consumption. Ratio of VAT revenues to consumption (*C*) from the national accounts. It provides a rough estimate of the average effective VAT rate assuming a C-efficiency of 1.0 (*see* Equation (2) above). This ratio can be split between household consumption and government consumption under the rationale that VAT reaches a lower fraction of government consumption.

7. For further discussion of macro performance indicators, *see* International Monetary Fund, *Tax Policy Assessment Framework*, VAT Module, available at https://www.imf.org/en/Data/TPAF (last accessed 29 January 2021).

VAT buoyancy. The ratio equals (Percent change in VAT revenue) / (Percent change in GDP). The ratio tracks the total response of VAT revenues to changes in national income and to discretionary changes in tax policy over time.

VAT elasticity. Elasticity of VAT revenue with respect to gross income or household expenditure. The ratio measures the responsiveness of VAT revenues to changes in gross income or expenditures. Ratio equals (Percent change in VAT revenue) / (Percent change in gross income or household expenditures).[8]

Import VAT revenues to imports. The ratio equals (Import VAT revenues) / imports. Given that VAT is a strong tax handle on imported goods, it makes the most sense to calculate this ratio as (Goods imports VAT revenues) / (Imports of goods).

Sectoral composition of GDP. The sectoral composition of GDP equals (Value-added by sector) / (Total value-added), ideally calculated as a vector of ratios, with one ratio for each sector. It is an important performance indicator given that VAT in practice reaches some sectors more easily or comprehensively than others. Knowledge of the sectoral composition of GDP may provide an indication of the revenue impact of sectoral VAT exemptions and zero-rating, and individual zero-rated or exempt supplies.

VAT tax expenditures. Revenue foregone from tax expenditures implemented through the VAT system. Tax expenditures provide revenue foregone estimates from VAT exemptions, domestic zero rating, and other concessions that depart from the benchmark VAT system.[9]

Table 2.5 shows a selection of macroeconomic and VAT indicators for Latin-American countries for selected years.[10] It is helpful to define some new variable labels: *ConHous/GDP* and *ConGov/GDP* stand for the ratio of household consumption to GDP and government consumption to GDP; VAT/Tot stands for VAT collections over total revenue; and *Tot/GDP* stands for total tax collections to GDP. Figure 2.5 draws on the data of Table 2.5 and illustrates a plot of the VAT revenue to GDP ratio on GDP per capita. The chart also shows a regression line fitted through the scatter plot (a method that belongs to Part D).

8. *See* Jean Acheson, Yota Deli, Edgar Morgenroth, Derek Lambert, and Martin Murphy, *VAT Revenue Elasticities: An Analytical Approach*, ESRI Working Paper No. 596 (The Economic and Social Research Institute, 2018).
9. Tax expenditures reflect the cost of certain policies in terms of revenue foregone or revenue gain, depending on the situation. For an example of VAT tax expenditure estimates, *see* Pierre-Pascal Gendron, *Canada's GST at 21: A Tax Expenditure View of Reform*, 1 World J. of VAT/GST Law 125 (2012). For an explanation of the methodologies, *see* Christopher Heady and Mario Mansour, *Tax Expenditure Reporting and Its Use in Fiscal Management: A Guide for Developing Economies*. How-to Note No. 19/2 (International Monetary Fund, 2019).
10. Santiago Díaz de Sarralde Miguez, *Value Added Tax: Revenue, Efficiency, Tax Expenditures and Inefficiencies in Latin America*. Working Paper 5, Tax Studies & Research Directorate (Inter-American Center of Tax Administrations, 2017).

Table 2.5 Latin America – Tax Collection, Taxes, GDP and Final Expenditure

Country	Year	GDPpc	ConHous/GDP	ConGov/GDP	ConTotal/GDP	Rate	VAT/Con	VAT/GDP	VAT/Tot	Tot/GDP
Ar	2015	20.472	65,8	18,2	84,0	21	9,7	7,4	23,1	32,0
Bo	2013	6.303	60,2	13,8	74,0	14,94	11,8	7,8	28,7	27,1
Ch	2015	23.682	64,4	13,4	77,8	19	12,2	8,4	40,2	21,0
Co	2015	13.833	63,8	18,0	81,8	16	6,8	5,2	25,5	20,4
CR	2014	15.050	65,1	17,8	82,9	13	6,1	4,7	21,5	22,1
Ec	2014	11.417	58,9	14,0	72,9	12	9,5	6,3	31,3	20,2
ES	2013	8.111	92,7	11,6	104,2	13	7,2	7,0	38,6	18,1
Gu	2015	7.759	85,0	10,4	95,3	12	5,3	4,8	39,7	12,0
Mx	2015	18.463	68,4	12,5	80,9	16	5,0	3,9	25,1	15,5
Ni	2013	4.712	85,4	7,0	92,4	15	7,2	6,2	29,0	21,5
Pan	2012	18.448	54,0	10,6	64,6	7	4,8	3,0	17,0	17,5
Par	2015	9.040	69,6	12,8	82,4	10	9,1	6,9	36,8	18,7
Pe	2015	12.389	65,5	13,0	78,5	16	9,7	7,0	39,7	17,5
DR	2015	15.019	71,0	11,8	82,7	16	6,2	4,9	35,3	13,8
Ur	2014	20.680	72,4	14,8	87,2	22	12,1	9,4	29,2	32,3
Md		13.692	69,5	13,3	82,8	14,9	8,2	6,2	30,7	20,6

Source: Díaz de Sarralde Miguez, *supra* n. 10, Table 1, at 10.

Figure 2.5 Latin America – VAT/GDP (y) and GDP per Capita (x), Selected Years

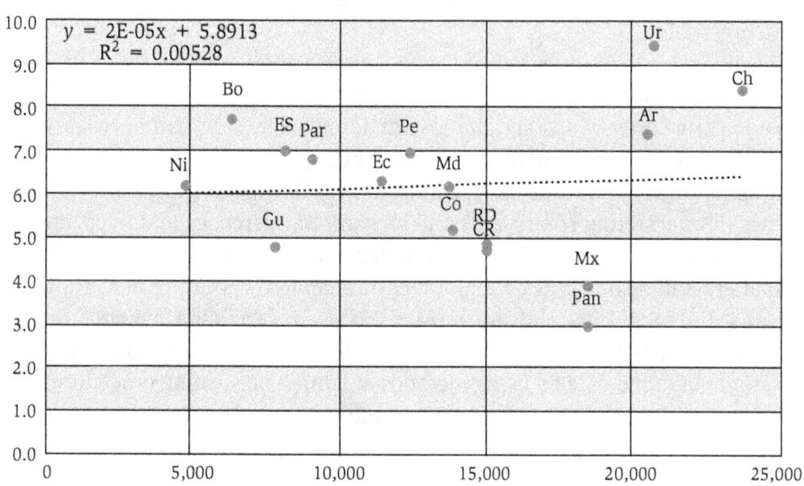

Source: Díaz de Sarralde Miguez, *supra* n. 10, Graph 1, at 11.

While macro indicators and the analyses like those presented above provide useful and necessary starting points to understand revenue performance in a macro sense, they do not provide insight on the reasons for poor (perceived or real) revenue performance. Governments (and their outside technical advisers) seeking to uncover the reasons for poor performance would supplement that knowledge by accessing the much more detailed data from tax or revenue administrations. Analysts without such access would need to push the analysis further by using statistical and econometric methods.

[D] Econometric and Statistical Analysis

As noted in the previous section, VAT performance and revenue productivity depend on a host of variables. The econometric (statistical) analysis of such relationships can shed light on the direction of the impacts of particular variables and the strength of the impacts. In the VAT literature, those relationships have usually been tested outside the context of structural economic models, often using C-efficiency as a dependent variable and a host of other variables as independent variables. In parallel to the formalization of C-efficiency, early estimation work was performed by the IMF.[11] Those largely ad hoc models produce correlations (or associations) between variables as opposed to causal relationships. This is an absolutely fundamental point to remember when interpreting the results described next.

An econometric analysis for 34 African countries provides a good example of recent estimates of the impact of various variables on C-efficiency.[12] The C-efficiency ratio is used as the measure of VAT performance and plays the role of dependent variable of the model. Indicators of economic development, VAT structure, and administration and compliance enter the model as independent variables. Table 2.6 describes the independent variables and the expected sign of the relationship with the dependent variable.

Results from the regression of C-efficiency on the variables listed in Table 2.6 produces coefficients with the expected signs in all cases except for one dummy variable for *some exemptions* and the ease of doing business.[13] Ordinary least-squares regressions cannot, on a stand-alone basis, address potential problems with the model such as simultaneity and, especially, endogeneity. The analyst must therefore exercise great care in interpreting coefficients and be wary of inferences and over-interpreting the results. The combination of microeconomic and macroeconomic variables complicates matters and also brings potential measurement errors in the mix. Nonetheless, the results are suggestive and are most valuable in providing avenues for further research and data exploration. When the data allow it, the analyst should extract more information out of the data by using methods and inference testing procedures that are more advanced than ordinary least squares and the typical t and F tests.

11. Ebrill et al., *supra* n. 4, at Chapter 4.
12. Cnossen, *supra* n. 4, at Chapter 6. The data come from various tables contained in the book. For additional background with additional analyses, *see* Sijbren Cnossen, *Mobilizing VAT Revenues in African Countries*, 22 Int'l Tax & Pub. Fin. 1077 (2015).
13. *See* Cnossen, *supra* n. 4, at Chapter 6 for details about the values of coefficients, measures of statistical significance, sample size, and other statistical information surrounding the estimates.

Table 2.6 Independent Variables to Explain VAT Performance

Economic Development	VAT Structure	Administration and Compliance
Per-capita income, a measure of the stage of economic development and potentially administrative effectiveness (+)	Standard VAT rate, also a measure of compliance pressure since higher rate strengthens the incentive to evade the tax (-)	Primary school completion rate, a proxy for ease of taxpayer compliance and self-assessment (+)
Share of agricultural value-added in GDP, a proxy for the size of the informal sector not directly subject to VAT, except for taxable inputs (-)	Age of VAT, since experience is gained over time in administering and complying with the VAT (+)	Ease of doing business, following the assumption that it includes the ease with which VAT obligations can be discharged (+)
Openness, the ratio of imports or trade (imports + exports) to GDP, since imports of goods are an easy tax handle to collect VAT up front through Customs (+)	Extent of non-standard exemptions which, like reduced rates, depress VAT performance (-)	Government effectiveness, a measure of tax enforcement (+)
	Level of VAT registration threshold, which may reduce revenue by excluding small trader margins, and/or improve administration by focusing on large traders (+/-)	Control of corruption, with corruption being a proxy for the lack of tax enforcement (+)

Source: Cnossen, *supra* n. 4, at 71, with author's minor restatements.

More recent work on consumption tax revenue performance has focused squarely on macroeconomic and policy variables. This fits in the tradition of analytical work by ministries of finance, central banks, and international organizations. In one recent study,[14] the authors conducted a comprehensive review and time-series analysis of consumption tax and VAT revenues in OECD countries before and after the economic crisis of 2007-09. Variables of interest include the VAT-revenue-ratio (VRR),[15] the implicit tax rate on consumption (ITR), defined as the ratio of consumption tax revenues to the conceptual tax base (consumption), and – interestingly – the share of government consumption to total consumption. The study includes several detailed and enlightening data appendices.

The authors set to identify how economic downturns affect consumption tax revenues. Their first major finding is that the economic crisis of 2007-09 altered consumption patterns by shifting consumption towards public consumption and

14. Simon and Harding, *supra* n. 6.
15. *See* the description of VRR in the text below Equation (2) above.

consumption of necessities, two outcomes that undermined the efficiency of VAT systems as measured by the VRR. This conclusion follows from the fact that public consumption and some necessities are not subject to VAT at the standard rate in many EU countries. Note that the conclusion would have been exactly the same using C-efficiency. Second, the authors conclude that the changes in consumption patterns have not been reversed since and that consumption revenues are now less robust to economic shocks, especially for countries with low VRRs and a smaller share of consumption subject to the standard VAT rate. These findings illustrate the macro risk of *shotgun* tax policy during the COVID-19 pandemic which consisted in reducing VAT rates in some countries.

[E] Revenue Forecasting

The forecasting of VAT revenues using explicit econometric forecasting methods constitutes a hybrid of the macro and econometric approaches presented above. The performance assessment component will come out of the comparison between forecast revenues and actual revenues, going back (backcasting) or forward in time (forecasting). Ministries of finance (and their tax policy units, when they exist) normally conduct this type of work for policy and budgeting purposes, and to understand the impact of various cyclical factors and shocks.

Forecasting methods for tax revenues, including VAT, form an established body of knowledge and techniques.[16] While it is impossible to outline the details of those approaches due to space limitations – they consider the entire macro-economy and all taxes – the main elements of VAT revenue forecasting are worth describing.[17] Statistical agencies, central banks, and tax administrations publish or produce the data necessary to use those methods.

Revenue forecasting begins with the estimation of the VAT base to establish a benchmark. Three approaches are used: aggregate approach, sectoral approach, or input-output approach. Under the aggregate approach, national accounts data are used, beginning with GDP accounts and making adjustments to estimate an aggregate VAT base using expenditure-based and income-based GDP components. The sectoral approach proceeds by adding the value-added generated by each sector of the economy and making adjustments to arrive at the VAT base. Finally, the input-output approach begins with the economy's input-output tables (nowadays, more likely to be supply and use tables) and uses the equivalence between VAT and a retail sales tax levied on the final selling price of goods and services. The method focuses on domestic consumption and its final demand components, after making a number of adjustments. In practice, the input-output (supply and use) method is used the most because of its

16. The classic source very likely remains the book by Glenn Jenkins, Chun-Yan Kuo, and Gangadhar Shukla, *Tax Analysis and Revenue Forecasting: Issues and Approaches*, Harvard Institute for International Development, Harvard University (June 2000). A more compact overview is provided in the presentation by Rajul Awashti, *Forecasting Tax Revenues: An Overview*, Webinar for Parliamentary Budget Offices, Global Tax Team, Europe and Central Asia Lead, World Bank Group (April 2017).
17. For analytical details of each approach, *see* Jenkins et al., *supra* n. 16, at Chapter 8.

greater disaggregation, accuracy and flexibility: it can be used to measure the potential VAT base, assess tax incidence, and simulate the impact of tax policy changes.

The outputs of those analyses are combined with macro-economic data. Statistical methods (including macro-economic models and time-series methods) and micro-simulation methods (using data from VAT returns and tax administration operations) are then used to forecast future revenues or simulate the impact of policy changes on revenues.[18]

[F] Micro Analysis: Drilling Down the VAT Code

Low C-efficiency and poor macro VAT revenue indicators are often simply symptoms of structural problems in the VAT itself. Establishing the causes requires additional work. In the ideal case where the analyst is on staff at the Ministry of Finance, for example, access to revenue models and data as well as data from the tax or revenue administration and all other sources provides a key to the answers. Using analyses to disentangle the impact of policy decision from the impacts of compliance on revenues, the analyst can drill down to the causes of poor revenue performance. This is the subject of Chapter 7 in this volume.

For the outside analyst without the luxury of access to internal government data, drilling down to the causes of poor performance requires assembling data on the possible causes of poor performance.[19] Examples of pertinent information include, but are not restricted to:

- presence of non-standard exemptions such as basic foodstuffs, drugs, medical supplies, agricultural inputs, passenger transportation, public utilities, petroleum products, newspapers and printed materials, industrial machinery and equipment, extra-territorial exemptions for activities in free zones, exemptions under tax incentives and special investment codes, and any other goods and services not part of standard exemptions;[20]
- presence of VAT rates other than the standard rate, including zero-rate on domestic consumption, reduced rates, and higher rates;
- VAT exemptions and waivers at import;
- differential taxation of services or non-enumeration of services as taxable supplies;
- VAT registration threshold that are either too low (the usual case) or too high.[21]

18. For details on most of those methods, *see* Jenkins et al., *supra* n. 16, at Chapter 5.
19. Cnossen, *supra* n. 4, does an exemplary job at this task in the context of all African countries. This section draws on his approach and adds the author's preferences.
20. Standard exemptions refer to the ones found in EU VATs: out-of-scope supplies, activities in the public interest, difficult-to-tax activities (financial services and insurance, sales and rental of residential property, etc.), and administratively difficult-to-tax sectors (small businesses and farmers). *See* discussion in Cnossen, *supra* n. 4, at Chapters 9-10.
21. Gendron, *supra* n. 2, contains an analysis and example of the threshold-setting decision with actual taxpayer segmentation data.

The data sources to compile this information include: VAT code and VAT regulations of the country or countries of interest, websites of tax administrations or revenue authorities, website of the Ministry of Finance and central bank for research reports, publicly available reports from the tax practices of accounting and advisory services firms, and so on.[22] If the statistical agency produces a household expenditure survey, the analyst could attempt to quantify the revenue impact of some exclusions in the sample, as well as assess VAT incidence by quintile or decile of household expenditure and household income.

The case study method fits nicely with micro analysis of VAT when it focuses on a single country because it attaches highly relevant information to the facts and figures. The method is cumbersome to use to conduct cross-country comparisons, but it can shed a lot of light on the situation of an individual country.[23]

§2.04 MOVING TOWARDS POTENTIAL REVENUE

This section first explores another source of poor VAT performance that is external to the VAT: the improper coordination of VAT with other indirect taxes. It then turns to the transition from explaining poor performance to assessing the potential performance of a VAT and identifying corrective actions.

[A] Coordination of Indirect Taxes

The proper coordination of indirect taxes (VAT, excises and import duties or tariffs) is rarely mentioned in discussions of VAT performance but it matters for VAT performance, and in fact it may matter a lot. Since VAT, excises and import duties, when applicable, are imposed for different reasons, the taxes exert a cumulative impact on gross-of-tax prices to the consumer.[24] Gross prices are therefore calculated as follows, depending on the origin of the goods. For domestically produced goods, the excise applies to the ex-factory (manufacturing) price. The VAT applies to the price inclusive of excise tax. For imported goods, import duties apply to the CIF value of the goods. Excises then apply to the duty-inclusive value of the goods. Finally, the VAT applies to the duty and excise-inclusive value of the goods as calculated at the previous step.

Three phenomena cause VAT revenue loss in practice: tax substitution, discriminatory protection, and programming errors in the tariff. Tax substitution occurs when

22. For example, PwC, *VAT in Africa: Navigating Africa's VAT Landscape*, 2020 Africa VAT Guide, PwC Global; and EY, *Strategically Managing Indirect Taxes in Latin America*, EY Global (2017), and International Bureau of Fiscal Documentation (IBFD) publications and tax summaries.
23. For two examples of case studies of Ukraine, *see* Richard M. Bird and Pierre-Pascal Gendron, *Is VAT the Best Way to Impose a General Consumption Tax in Developing Countries?* in Special Report: *Some Fiscal Parameters of the Investment Climate in Select Countries of Eurasia* (International Tax and Investment Center, June 2007), and Bird and Gendron, *Is VAT the Best Way to Impose a General Consumption Tax in Developing Countries?* 60 Bul. Int'l Taxation 287 (2006). The latter study contains more details and comparative cross-country data.
24. For a clear discussion of the rationale for excises and their implications for the coordination between indirect taxes, *see* Sijbren Cnossen, *The Role and Rationale for Excise Taxes in ASEAN Countries*, 59 Bul. Int'l Fiscal Doc. 503 (2005).

the authorities replace a tax by another. For example, some countries will not subject some fuels to a VAT because it is already subject to excise, or vice versa. If, for example, a good is subject to excise but not VAT, the VAT revenue loss is calculated by multiplying the VAT rate by the ex-factory price including the excise tax. Discriminatory protection is observed when a country exempts domestic production from excises (or imposes a lower rate) while comparable imported goods are subject to excise tax at the statutory rate. The VAT revenue loss is equal to the VAT rate times the excise tax amount foregone on domestic production. Finally, customs administrations sometimes make mistakes in programming the tariff by improperly coordinating indirect taxes as described above. Depending on import volumes, those mistakes can cause significant revenue losses. Field experience has shown that such programming errors are frequent and almost always result in revenue loss. For many developing countries and island states, imports are a critically important tax handle for all indirect taxes and especially VAT. Full taxation at customs is a powerful tool to ensure compliance and protect revenues.[25]

There is anecdotal evidence that excise tax burdens, especially but not exclusively in developing countries, are too low and this clearly results in significant foregone revenues. Recent research on excises shows that excise tax rates are substantially below their economically efficient levels.[26] The research concludes that in developing countries, in particular, excise revenues could increase by a factor of three. These conclusions reinforce the importance of proper coordination of indirect taxes and the potential for additional VAT revenues from raising excise tax rates on a host of commodities, including traditional 'bads' (tobacco products, alcoholic beverages, games of chance), new 'bads' (sugar-sweetened beverages, plastics, fats), transportation (fuels, motor vehicles, roads, waterways, and airways), and income-elastic goods and services such as telecommunication services and luxury goods. This is an area that requires much more research attention and policy action.

[B] Actual Versus Potential Performance

This chapter shows that VAT performance can be examined from many different angles. Yet, one limitation of all those approaches should be obvious: there is no point of reference for performance. What is good? A C-efficiency over 0.7? Over 0.8? What is bad? A C-efficiency below 0.4? Below 0.3? It would be a typical answer for an economist to say it depends. It would be a rarer answer by an economist to say I do not know. Based on the above review, it depends and we do not know. The central question is: What do we compare observed performance to?

25. For an empirical analysis of the role of customs on VAT compliance, *see* Peter Morrow, Michael Smart, and Artur Swistak, *VAT Compliance, Trade and Institutions*, CESifo Working Paper No. 7780 (August 2019).
26. Sijbren Cnossen, *Excise Taxation for Domestic Revenue Mobilization*, CESifo Working Papers 8442 (July 2020). In addition to revenue estimates, the paper provides an up-to-date discussion of excise design and administration.

Even without an immediate answer, the due diligence of thorough analyses along the lines suggested above is necessary discipline to understand a particular VAT in its context or to compare VATs. Breaking out of the limitations requires a methodology to assess the revenue a VAT could potentially produce if certain conditions are met. In other words, we would like to compare actual revenue performance to potential performance to understand the reasons why actual performance is lower than potential performance to inform corrective actions. This work, known by the name of VAT gap analysis, requires a decomposition of C-efficiency into two components: one that depends on policy decisions, and one that depends on compliance. Again, this is the subject of Chapter 7 in this volume.

§2.05 CONCLUSION

A thorough analysis of revenue performance on a punctual basis and over time is a necessary step to understand a country's VAT or conduct cross-country comparisons. The methods presented above are, for the most part, necessary and complementary. Aside from the econometric and revenue forecasting approaches, none require specific knowledge beyond government statistics and electronic data manipulation using standard tools such as Microsoft Excel.

The obvious limitation of the outcomes of performance assessment analyses is the absence of a relative internal benchmark against which to evaluate performance. VAT gap analysis can provide an internal benchmark by providing an estimate of potential revenue against which to compare actual revenue.

CHAPTER 3

Neutrality Versus Equality

Christian Amand

§3.01 INTRODUCTION

Neutrality and equality seem to be close to one another. In the European Union (EU), neutrality has been described as the 'equivalent in the field of VAT' to the 'principle of equal treatment'.[1] However, neutrality and equality present major differences. Before Courts in the EU, neutrality is only considered as a 'principle of interpretation'[2] of the VAT system while the prohibition of discrimination may trigger the invalidation of a legal provision of national or even EU law. The thesis of this chapter is that VAT-neutrality and equality are not of the same nature.[3]

Neutrality is an economic concept. Internal (economic) neutrality is realized when the VAT does not unduly influence the optimal allocation of resources. International neutrality means equal treatment of the supplies of goods and services irrespective of the country in which they are produced. Neutrality is exclusively driven by the legislature and intends to eliminate any distortion of competition caused by legislation during the process of production and of commercialization prior to the retail stage. Neutrality is vertical, i.e., it follows the whole process of production and commercialization until the final consumer.

1. Friederike Grube, *Neutrality and Input Tax Deductibility* 17 Austl. GST J. 8, 9 (2017); Antonio Victoria-Sanchez, *The European Court of Justice and VAT: The European Commission's Perspective* in *CJEU – Recent Developments in Value Added Tax 2014*, 17 (Michael Lang et al., eds., Linde Verlag, 2015).
2. CJEU, 19 July 2012, Case C-44/11, *Deutsche Bank*, ECLI:EU:C:2012:484 paragraph 45; CJEU, 2 July 2020, Case C-231/19, *Blackrock Investment Management (UK)*, ECLI:EU:C:2020:513, paragraph 51.
3. This is the opposite thread than the one developed in a previous article published by the author in 2013: *VAT Neutrality: A Principle of EU Law or a Principle of the VAT System?* 2 (3) W. J. VAT/GST L. 163 (2013).

Equality is a legal concept that, through the closely related concept of non-discrimination, requires to treat equally those who are in comparable situations. Non-discrimination creates rights that receive protection by the courts. Equality is horizontal i.e., it is appreciated at one specific stage of production, even when the regulations allow distortions of competition at the retailer's level.

Legal provisions that create a lack of neutrality in a tax system may be compatible with the principle of equality.

Neutrality and equality may sometimes cover identical situations. In addition, the text of the VAT Directive/national rules specifically sometimes refers to distortions of competition (linked to neutrality) while most of the time they do not. In the European Union, this is made complex by: (i) the superposition of supra-national and national rules, (ii) the fact that some EU rules that have not been implemented in a national legal system may be invoked directly by EU citizens before Courts and others not, (iii) the numerous exceptions and the fact that the system itself justifies them by the fact that it is not achieved, and (iv) the various meanings of the neutrality principle, which does not grant rights protected by the courts, except when an obligation of absence of distortion of competition is expressly provided for by a legal provision.

This chapter deals with (1) the economic concept of neutrality and the absence of distortion of competition as driving forces of the emergence of the VAT in Europe, (2) the legal concepts of equality and non-discrimination (3) the EU case law about the distortion of competition and the discriminations that are one of the consequences of the lack of neutrality, (4) the structural deflection of neutrality in Europe, its origin and possible alternative and extension, (5) recent OECD views on neutrality, (6) ways to promote neutrality, (7) political consequences of the distinction neutrality/equality.

§3.02 NEUTRALITY AND DISTORTIONS OF COMPETITION

The so-called VAT is a single general tax on consumption of goods and services pursuant to an exchange or the introduction of goods into a territory. It is exactly proportional to the price (whatever its expression). It is collected at every stage of the production and distribution chain up to and including the retail stage, regardless of the number of transactions and where they are located. Due to the mechanism of deduction of the tax supported on the various production factors, VAT is neutral on the allocation of all types of resources and technologies and, normally, it does not influence business decisions, the place of production, the technology used or the distribution process. Neutrality has been, and is still, the economic objective that has guided the progressive emergence of this tax. Internal neutrality intends to allow an optimal use of resources. External neutrality intends to attribute the tax to the country of effective consumption and to avoid trade protectionism. Lawmakers only create neutrality artificially; it cannot be established through the self-regulation of the market[4] or by courts.

4. Borbála Kolozs, *Neutrality in VAT* in *Value Added Tax and Direct Taxation, Similarities and Differences* 203 (Michael Lang et al., eds, IBFD, 2009).

The concept of neutrality is linked to the origin of the VAT in Europe and it is the driving force in the emergence of an efficient tax system.

[A] Germany (1919)

In 1916, the German Reich introduced a Stamp duty (*Warenumsatzstempel*) on all commercial transactions. In 1918, it was replaced by the *Umsatzsteuer* or turnover tax that remained in force with some changes in 1934 and 1951 until the introduction of VAT on January 1, 1968. The *Umsatzsteuer* concerned every transaction of goods and services and it was imposed at every stage of the production and the distribution chain. Assuming forward shifting of the tax, tax accumulation occurred at every stage where the tax was levied on a sales price including the tax paid at the previous stage of the supply chain. This created an incentive for vertical integration as the final retail price of goods and services would be lower when produced by integrated businesses, avoiding the tax on the integrated stages, compared to non-integrated businesses.

In 1919, Carl Friedrich von Siemens suggested the adoption of a *veredelte umsatzsteuer* (improved turnover tax) on the sales, under deduction of totality of the purchases subject to the tax.[5] Although the German Parliament examined the tax proposal, it was never adopted. The suggestion of Siemens would be examined again after France introduced the *Taxe sur la Valeur Ajoutée* in 1954.

[B] France (1954)

France introduced a Stamp duty in 1917, which was replaced by a turnover tax in 1920. Like in Germany, this system favourized concentration and it was purposely intending to eliminate useless intermediaries. It proved necessary to exempt small businesses, but this led to the difficulty of accurately defining what a small business is.[6] This was the origin of a tumultuous series of changes until 1954.

[1] Inspiration from United States

In 1930, Carl S. Shoup, then a young professor at the University of Columbia, observed also the negative impact of the cumulative character of the French Sales Tax.[7] He made proposals to improve the Direct Tax System in United States[8] and tried to implement his ideas in Japan in 1949. Shoup's ideas inspired French Civil servants who were trying to find ways to improve the French economy and its productivity. In 1952, Maurice Lauré suggested to deduct from the tax due by the producers on each sales transaction the

5. Carl Friedrich von Siemens, *Veredelte umsatzsteuer* (Siemenstadt, 1921).
6. Georges Egret, *La TVA* (PUF, 1978), 10.
7. Carl Shoup, *The Sales Tax in France* (Columbia University Press, 1930).
8. The Business Activities Tax introduced in 1953 in Michigan is based on the Shoup studies, *see* Clarence W. Lock, Donovan J. Rau, and Howard D. Hamilton, *The Michigan Value-Added-Tax* 8(4) Nat'l Tax J. 357 (1955) and Clara K. Sullivan, *The Tax on Value Added*, XII, 298-311 (Columbia University Press, 1965).

amount of the tax supported on all the costs.[9] He recognized the negative economic impact tax planning could have, including artificial delocalizations, demonstrated by the example of Ernest Solvay, the inventor of a process to produce soda on the base of salt instead of ash-kelp, who decided to locate his new business in Belgium instead of France due to the French tax on salt (*la gabelle*).

[2] WTO Rules (1947) and the ECSC Dispute (1953)

Lauré faced resolute opposition from the French tax authorities, but circumstances turned out to be in his favour.

First, during the negotiations on the GATT Agreement of 1947[10] the question arose of whether the existing *Taxe à la production* was indeed an indirect tax and not a direct tax. This may explain the political pressure as from 1948 to transform the tax on production into a truly indirect tax by introducing a deduction mechanism that ensured a greater neutrality of the tax on the production process.

Second, from February to May 1953, the 'steel provisions' of the Treaty on the European Coal and Steel Community (ECSC) entered into force. At that time, the question was whether and, if so, how in a common market, i.e., under conditions of free trade, the procedure laid down by Articles III and XVI of the GATT Agreement of 1947 should be implemented. Those provisions allowed, in respect of cross-border supplies of goods, for compensation of indirect taxes at the border, along with the prohibition of such compensation for direct taxes. Germany, where the rate of turnover tax was 5%, was opposed to the border compensation for indirect taxes, whereas France, where the *taxe à la production* was imposed at the rate of 15%, was (of course) in favour of the compensation system. German steel producers were of the opinion that all general taxes, both direct and indirect taxes, should be considered as 'location costs' affecting competition in the common market. In their view, limiting the compensation to indirect taxes was arbitrary.[11] The dispute was settled on the basis of the Tinbergen Report, drawn up by a group of experts commissioned by the High Authority of the ECSC to elucidate the underlying economic aspects of the dispute. The experts pronounced in favour of maintaining the compensation at the border for the turnover tax on the final transactions because the compensation concerned only a few products.[12]

9. Maurice Lauré, *La Taxe sur la Valeur Ajoutée* (Recueil Sirey, 1952).
10. Alain Frenkel, *La Genèse de la Taxe sur la Valeur Ajoutée* (Unpublished thesis, University of Paris II, 1976), 275.
11. Maria Dolores Schulte, *The Economic Theory of the Destination Principle and the Origin Principle* in *Comparison and Harmonization of Public Revenue Systems, Especially of Fiscal Systems*, Congrès de Luxembourg, September 1963, XIX Session. The dispute may explain the importance of the origin principle in respect of intra-Community transactions, which is still under discussion today, *inter alia*, in the Commission's *Green Paper on the future of VAT in the European Union* of 1 December 2010, COM(2010)695.
12. European Coal and Steel Community, High Authority – *Report on the Problem Raised by the Different Turnover Tax Systems Applied within the Common Market (Tinbergen Report)*, Luxembourg, 1953.

Lauré proposal to transform the *taxe à la production* (Tax on production) into a *taxe sur la valeur ajoutée* (Value added tax) was adopted by the French Parliament on 10 April 1954.

In a book published in 1957 evaluating the first years of experience with VAT in France, Lauré denounced 'the cancer of VAT', i.e., the fact that VAT exemptions tend to proliferate under pressure of businesses engaged in exempt transactions.[13]

[C] The OECC Works (1954-1957)

In the framework of the Marshall plan, which was aimed at the reconstruction of Europe after World War II, the United States found it difficult to deal with the large number of European governments. They convoked the Conference of Sixteen (Conference for European Economic Co-operation)[14] that decided to create the Organisation for European Economic Co-operation (OEEC) which came into existence on 16 April 1948. The OEEC (which evolved into the OECD in 1961) was a permanent organization to continue the work on a joint recovery programme and, in particular, to supervise the distribution of US aid.[15] It functioned on the basis of the principles of promoting co-operation between the participating countries and their national programmes for the reconstruction of Europe, developing intra-European trade by reducing tariffs and other barriers to the expansion of trade, studying the feasibility of creating a customs union or free-trade area, studying multi-lateralization of payments, and achieving conditions for better utilization of labour.

In September 1954, after the introduction of the TVA in France, the OEEC set up a working group, the *Agence Européenne de la Productivité* (European Agency for Productivity) that published in November 1957 a report on turnover taxes[16] prepared by Charles Campet.[17] This report contained three parts:

(1) A theoretical analysis of various turnover tax systems.
(2) An economic analyse of these systems in the light of an increase of the productivity.
(3) A detailed description of the turnover tax systems applicable at that time in most European countries, including Spain, the United Kingdom, Greece, and Turkey.

---

13. Maurice Lauré, *Au secours de la TVA* (PUF, 1957).
14. For the position of the United States as regards cooperation between the European countries and the different views of the United Kingdom (in favour of cooperation) and the continental countries (in favour of integration), *see* Pierre Wigny, *Historique* in *Les Novelles*: *Droit des Communautés Européennes* 3 (Walter J. Ganshof van der Meersch, ed., Larcier, 1969), 4 and the references mentioned there.
15. The OEEC was the economic counterpart of the NATO.
16. Agence Européenne de productivité de l'Organisation Européenne de Coopération Economique, *Le Régime Fiscal du Chiffre d'Affaires et son incidence sur la productivité (The Regime of Turnover Tax and its Effect on Productivity)*, Project No. 315 (November 1957).
17. Charles Campet is also a reporter of the ABC reports (1962), and later, as the Head of Division of the Directorate General Competition of the European Commission, he is in charge of drafting the First and Second VAT Directives.

The report describes in detail all the possible systems:

- Multiple Stage Tax;
- Multiple Special Taxes;
- Single General taxes: retail, wholesale, production, or raw materials; and
- A Value Added Tax, but simple, by opposition to the French TVA.

The Agency criticized the cumulative turnover taxes and in particular the German turnover tax.[18] The German tax favoured vertical integration and hampered specialization of companies. It did not tax products in the same manner at consumer's level. It was an obstacle to international trade because of the difficulty of determining the correct amount of border tax adjustments, and it penalized investments. This report demonstrated the weakness of specific measures that were aimed at limiting the negative impact of cumulative turnover taxes, such as grouping (Organschaft).

It described with details the positives and negatives of each of the various types of single general taxes: retail, wholesale, production, or raw materials. When the tax collection happens close of the consumer, the distortions are limited. This single tax can be collected at one stage or at various stages. When collected at various stages, the pressure on a single stage is reduced and the fraud is limited. Multi-stage collection requires compensation at borders. And the most efficient system at that time was the French TVA, even if it was much too complex.

The Agency recommended general and national measures, in particular, the introduction of non-cumulative taxes and taxes that were neutral on production (a general tax on retail transactions, a purchase tax, or a general Value Added Tax on goods and services).

[D] The Treaty of Rome (1957)

The principle of neutrality of consumption taxes is enshrined in Articles 95-99 of the Treaty, in the chapter related to competition, together with dumping (Article 91) and State Aid (Articles 92-94). Indeed, consumption taxes have a direct impact on the prices and therefore on the free movement of goods, persons, services, and capital:

- Article 95 (now Article 110 TFEU) intended to guarantee the complete neutrality of internal taxation as regards competition between domestic products and imported products. [19] It consists in the prohibition of existing discriminatory or protective provisions. Article 95 supplements the abolition of customs duties and charges having equivalent effect. Its aim is to ensure free movement of goods between the member states in normal conditions of competition by the elimination of all forms of protection which result from the application of internal taxation which discriminates against products from other Member States.

18. Campet's view seems to summarize the analysis of German academics, in particular, the analysis of Professor Günther Schmölders, *Organische Steuerreform* (Valhen Verlag, 1953).
19. CJEU, 27 February 1980, Case 168/78, *Commission v. France*, ECLI:EU:C:1980:51, paragraph 4.

- Articles 96-98 put in place a transitional system of lump sum refunds of national taxes at the time of export and lump sum taxation at the time of import.
- The authors of the Treaty knew in advance that the system of Articles 96-98 would never function properly. Therefore, they inserted Article 99 (now the amended Article 113 TFEU) inviting the European Commission to propose a neutral consumption tax system that at that time did not exist. Of course, contrary to a negative provision such as Article 95 of the Treaty of Rome (now Article 110 TFEU), it took some time to develop and introduce a mechanism of a single multistage consumption tax compatible with an internal market.

[E] The First and the Second VAT Directives (1967)

The solution to neutrality on the intra-community trade was the VAT because its fundamental principle is the full deduction of the tax incurred in the production chain. This allows for the objective and exact determination of border tax adjustments, i.e., the amount of the tax to refund at the time of export and the tax to impose at the time of import. The preliminary report to the introduction of a VAT system opposed to any kind of VAT exemption.[20] This explains why the proposal of Second VAT Directive[21] considers that operations regarding immovable property, insurance[22] and banking should also be taxed.

However, for Belgium and Italy, the introduction of VAT at the retail stage caused an increase of the number of taxable persons to be administered by the tax authorities. In addition, these countries also faced the problem of having to educate large groups of taxable persons and tax inspectors. Those circumstances explain why, in its initial Proposal for the First Directive,[23] the European Commission came up with a compromise between, on the one hand, Belgium and Italy and, on the other hand, France and mainly Germany. The Commission's initial proposal was to allow Member States to replace the cumulative taxes applicable at that time (except in France) by a facultative single-stage tax or to introduce, immediately or at a later stage, a tax based on the principles of the French VAT.

This proposal was not welcomed by the European Parliament. It recommended that the VAT system should be adopted immediately. Therefore, the Parliament

20. Commission, *General Report of Sub-groups A, B and C, set up to examine the different possibilities for harmonization value added taxes*, 3310/IV/62-F (European Commission, January 1962), 96 and 97.
21. Commission *'Proposal for a Second Council Directive for the harmonization among Member States of turnover tax legislation, concerning the form and the methods of application of the common system of taxation on value added'* COM (65) 144 final, Supplement to Bulletin of the European Economic Community No. 5 – 1965, 17.
22. Insurance services should also have been subject to VAT, but they have never been listed as such because they were topic for a discussion that never ended in an agreement.
23. Proposal of 5 November 1962 for a [First] Directive for the harmonization amongst Member States of turnover tax legislation, IV/COM(62)217 of 31 October 1962, Bulletin of the European Economic Community No. 12 – 1962.

suggested to give Member States the freedom to exempt supplies made by retailers, because in the economic and legal environment of that time these supplies could only be supplied by retailers and, therefore, exemptions would have no impact on the national neutrality, international trade, or the principle of equality. This is how the VAT exemptions came to be in the EU VAT system. The details of the VAT exemptions were left to member States. [24] This is why today, the Court of Justice is missing any national explanation on distinctions such as immovable property, credit, etc. The Parliament certainly never anticipated that their proposal would allow for the continuance of exemptions until today and it did not envisage the distortive consequences on the internal market that would arise much later.

The endless negotiations on the First and Second VAT Directives were a painful experience for the negotiators at that time. An external breakthrough occurred on 16 June 1966 when what is now the Court of Justice of the European Union (CJEU) declared in *Lütticke* that Article 95 of the Treaty had direct effect. Consequently, many German businesses considered that Article 97 of the Treaty should also have direct effect, since it essentially implemented Article 95. They lodged more than 300,000 complaints about the German turnover tax and tens of thousands legal proceedings challenging the validity of the tax.[25] On 20 December 1966, the German Constitutional Court decided that the German Parliament was required to adopt, within two years, a tax system that was less discriminatory than the cumulative turnover tax system that existed at that time.[26]

The EU Council adopted the First and Second Directives on 11 April 1967 and new legislation based on the Directives was adopted in Germany on 29 May 1967. The new legislation entered into force in Germany on 1 January 1968. The President of the CJEU, Robert Lecourt, later qualified the adoption of the First and Second VAT Directives as *Un progrès communautaire résultait ainsi de l'oeuvre du juge* (a Community progress resulting from judicial decisions).

[F] The Sixth VAT Directive (1977)

[1] Priority to Own Resources

The adoption of the Sixth VAT Directive was necessitated by the fact that, under Article 4 of the Council Decision of 24 April 1970, part of the European Union's own resources

24. Article 3 as amended by the European Parliament – *Report of the Committee for the internal market on the Proposal of the Commission to the Council (Doc 121, 1962-1963) concerning a Directive on the harmonization of the legislations of the Member States on turnover taxes ('Deringer Report')* (European Parliament, Documents Session 1963-1964, Document 56, 20 August 1963).
25. CJEU, 16 June 1966, Case 57/65, *Alfons Lütticke GmbH v. Hauptzollamt Saarlouis*, ECLI:EU: C:1966:34. For a detailed description of this landmark event in the history of taxation, *see* Léontin-Jean Constantinesco, *L'applicabilité directe dans le droit de la CEE*, Bruylant, 2006, 101 to 115. *See also* Robert Lecourt, *L'Europe des juges*, 57 (Bruylant [1976], 2008); and Paul Farmer and Richard Lyall, *EC Tax Law* 80 (Clarendon Press, 1994).
26. Judgment of the First Chamber of the German Constitutional Court, 20 December 1966 – 1 BvR 320/57, 70/63, *Allphasenumsatzsteuer*.

is determined on the basis of a percentage of a uniform assessment base of VAT. Therefore, the basis of assessment of VAT had to be determined in a uniform manner in all Member States. But this change had little impact on the intra-community trade. Neutrality – whatever its meaning- was not an objective of the Sixth VAT Directive and the existing VAT exemptions applicable in most of the Member States at that time have been introduced without impact assessment. The only uniform thing was the taxable base for the purposes of the EU's own resources.

During the plenary session of the European Parliament on 20 April 1977, Harry Notenboom declared on behalf of the Budget Commission that the text of the Sixth Directive, which the Council had agreed to adopt, required a more detailed examination. He added that the Council had given precedence to the Own Resources and had neglected the aspect of tax harmonization, which could result in distortions of competition.[27] On that occasion, he invited the European Commission to submit, as soon as possible, a proposal for a Seventh Directive aimed at enhancing the neutrality aspects of the tax.[28]

[2] Introduction of the VAT Exemptions in the European Directive

From the published explanatory documents and from the archives that are public since 2007, there is no indication that the list of VAT exemptions contained in the Sixth VAT Directive have been drafted on the base of economic assessment, even though financial services and immovable property have been subject to detailed independent studies. According to the explanatory memorandum of the Sixth VAT Directive:[29]

> The list of exemptions has been drawn up having regard (i) to the exemptions already existing in the various Member States, and (ii) the need to keep the number of exemptions as small as possible. This need reflects a concern to keep exceptions to the minimum in a general system of taxation of consumption, but also reflects a desire to avoid the inconveniences which such exemptions cause, mainly by reason of the fact that, unless the transaction exempted forms part of an international trading operation, taxes paid on inputs will not be deductible. The exemptions provided for within the territory of a country are based on a variety of grounds. The exemptions set out in section A[30] are those already existing in the majority of the Member States. They relate to the postal services (a), to medical services (b), (c), (d), (e) and (f), to welfare services (g), to educational services (h) and (i), to physical recreation (j), and to bodies providing services of a social, cultural or educational nature (k).

27. *Debates of the European Parliament*, Report of the sessions from 18 to 22 April 1977, *OJ* 216, Enclosures, p 180. An example is the option to tax financial services that has been implemented only in a few Member States in order to maintain some existing structures at that time and that now allows to outsource major financial services in all the EU.
28. This should not be confused with, 'Proposal for a seventh Council Directive on the harmonization of the laws of the Member States relating to turnover taxes – common system of value added tax to be applied to works of art, collectors' items, antiques and used goods' COM (77) 735 final, OJ C 26/2, but its scope was restricted to the treatment of second-hand goods. This proposal was withdrawn on 11 November 1987.
29. Commission des Communautés Européennes, *supplément* 11/73.
30. Currently Article 132 of Directive 2006/112/EC.

> The other exemptions, which are set out in section B, relate to specific fields, such as insurance, provision of credit and dealings in currency and on the stock exchange, where they are justified for reasons of general policy common to all the Member States.

By comparing the text of the German Turnover tax Act of 16 October 1934 (modified by the laws of 19 September 1950 and 28 June 1951) with the text of the exemptions in the EU VAT Directive, it is clear that they have been inspired by the German exemptions for social security, public bodies, youth work and education, charities, artists, postal and telegraph services, financial transactions, transactions involving buildings subject to other taxes, gambling, insurance, etc.[31] In addition to the social motives reflected in the political priorities in Germany at the beginning of 1930s, these exemptions were probably based on the necessity to limit the negative consequences of the cumulative turnover taxes, as well as the crucial importance to determine the turnover[32] under the turnover taxes existing at that time.

According to French literature, the current list of VAT exemptions for the financial sector is derived from the list of services that were exempt from the *Taxe sur les Activités Financières* (Tax on Financial Services) which applied in France between 1968 and 1978. That tax was similar to the Insurance Premium Tax but applied to specific banking transactions.[33]

The reason for the special treatment of the public bodies is found in the archives of the negotiation of the Sixth VAT Directive. The French delegation feared that traditional activities of public bodies would be subject to VAT. Consequently, the price paid by the users of these services would increase and local authorities would be subject to tax inspection (!), an operation which would be difficult both technically and politically.[34] The situation of the VAT status of public bodies is interesting. It has been subject to a study for the European Commission suggesting that an extension of the VAT to this sector would allow for a reduction of the VAT rate with 5% points in all Member States. The reaction of subnational governments through Brussels' lobby groups[35] has been uncommon by comparison to similar reports. The consequence has been that the excellent efforts of the European Commission[36] have been stopped, 'by highest level decision', without any discussion.

---

31. Similar provisions existed also in the existing turnover taxes legislation in the Netherlands and in Luxembourg which had adopted the German Turnover Taxes in the years 1940s.
32. For example, the determination of the taxable base on the granting of credit and gambling was impossible in a turnover tax system while it does not present difficulties in a VAT/GST system.
33. For references, *see* Christian Amand and Veronique Lenoir, *Pro Rata Deduction of VAT by Financial Institutions – Gross Margin or Interest?* 17(1) Int'l VAT Monitor 17 (2006).
34. Historical archives of the Sixth VAT Directive, folder 12, Working Document T/373/74 (fin).
35. Council of European Municipalities and Regions, *VAT and Tax Exemptions on Public Bodies: No Taxation Without Representation*, CEMR draft response to the European Commission consultation on the review of existing VAT legislation on public bodies and tax exemptions in the public interest (April 2014), https://ccre.org/img/uploads/piecesjointe/filename/CEMR_response_to_VAT_consultation_EN.pdf (accessed on 16 February 2021).
36. Copenhagen Economics and KPMG, *VAT in the Public Sector and Exemptions in the Public Interest* (2013), https://ec.europa.eu/taxation_customs/sites/taxation/files/resources/documents/common/publications/studies/vat_public_sector_exemptions_en.pdf (accessed on 16 February 2021).

[3] *Subsequent Justifications of VAT Exemptions*

Overtime, additional explanations were given for what Rita de la Feria calls 'merit exemptions':[37]

- Vertical equity: VAT weights more heavily on poorer households. So, applying exemptions to key products would limit the impact of the tax on those households.
- Positive externalities: concessions are likely to increase the consumption of merit goods and services.
- Increase of employment.

Although it is generally accepted that VAT is regressive, this is not confirmed by recent economic studies.[38]

For politicians, neutrality is acceptable as far as it reduces distortions of competition with other countries or benefits some categories of business and persons, i.e., it creates jobs. Distortion of competition is immediately understood and promoted by persons more familiar with corporate taxes than with VAT.

[4] *Distortions of Competition in the Text of the Directive*

According to the VAT Directive, Member States are obliged to implement the Directive in such a way that the national provisions do not lead to distortion of competition, i.e., violation of neutrality, but without reference to the principle of neutrality:

- taxation of transactions by public authorities;[39]
- derogation to self-supplies treated as self-supplied services and assimilation to supply of services;[40]
- threshold applicable to distance sales of goods;[41]
- prevent double taxation or non-taxation of services with third countries;[42]
- open market value at the time of importation of goods;[43]

---

37. Rita de la Feria, *EU VAT Principles as Interpretative Aids to EU VAT Rules: The Inherent Paradox*, Oxford University Center for Business Taxation WP 16/03, p. 4, at https://jean-monnet-chair-eu-tax-policy-administration.webnode.gr/_files/200000035-57c0f58bfc/VAT%20Rita%20De%20la%20Feria.pdf (accessed on 16 February 2021).
38. Alastair Thomas, *Reassessing the Regressivity of the VAT*, OECD Taxation Working Papers 2020, n° 29, https://www.oecd-ilibrary.org/taxation/reassessing-the-regressivity-of-the-vat_b76ced82-en (accessed on 16 February 2021); *see also* Rita de la Feria and Michael Walpole, T*he Impact of Public Perception on General Consumption Taxes* [2020] 67/5 British Tax Rev. 637; and Chapter 4.03[B] of this volume.
39. Article 13(1) second al. of the Directive 2006/112/EC.
40. Articles 26(2) and 27 of the Directive 2006/112/EC.
41. Article 34(2) of the Directive 2006/112/CE.
42. Article 59 of the Directive 2006/112/EC.
43. Article 72 of the Directive 2006/112/EC.

- possible distortive consequences of provisions destined to limit the distortive consequence of VAT exemptions (i.e., independent group of persons);[44]
- fund raising activities by VAT exempt organizations;[45]
- optional VAT exemptions;[46]
- limitation of VAT exemptions;[47]
- importation of goods by European institutions and by international institutions[48] and supplies to these organizations;
- restrictions of the right of deduction[49] and adjustment of the right of deduction;[50]
- measures to prevent distortions of competition regarding second-hand means of transport.[51]

[G] Treaty on the Functioning of the European Union (1 December 2009)

Article 99 of the Treaty of Rome is the legal base on which the European Commission was requested to submit proposals of measures necessary to ensure the establishment and the functioning of the internal market. This article has been modified by the Treaty on the Functioning of the European Union that entered into force on December 1, 2009 and it is now Article 113 of the TFEU. The Commission is now requested to submit proposals in order 'to avoid distortions of competition', i.e., to improve the neutrality of the VAT system. It is questionable whether the importance of this obligation to take on the causes of distortions of competition has been fully perceived.

[H] Economic Appreciation

From an economic perspective, a tax should be neutral in respect of 1) labour and capital, 2) choices for consumers and 3) different allocations of resources. In general, it should not distort the free play of market. Neutrality amounts to the opposite of tax subsidy or tax incentives.

Some authors observed that the current management of VAT comes at a cost to businesses and, therefore, would not be neutral.[52] In addition, there is no synchronization between VAT liability, VAT deduction and VAT collection and this causes a financial cost. Indeed, the cost of management of the VAT, creates differences in consumer prices and it influences the process of production and distribution.

44. Article 132(1)(f) of the Directive 2006/112/EC.
45. Article 132(1)(o) of the Directive 2006/112/EC.
46. Article 133 of the Directive 2006/112/EC.
47. Article 134 of the Directive 2006/112/CE.
48. Articles 143(f)a, 145(2) and 151 of the Directive 2006/112/CE.
49. Article 177 of the Directive 2006/112/CE.
50. Article 191 of the Directive 2006/112/CE.
51. Articles 342 and 343 of the Directive 2006/112/EC.
52. Charlène Herbain, *VAT Neutrality* (Larcier, 2015). On the cost of tax compliance, *see* Chapter 6 of this volume.

§3.03 EQUALITY AND NON-DISCRIMINATION

Equality requires that similar situations shall not be treated differently unless differentiation is objectively justified[53] and that different situations must not be treated in the same way unless such treatment is objectively justified.[54] Equality is one of the fundamental principles of community law.[55]

In *Compass Contract Services,* the Court of Justice considered that:

> According to settled case-law, a breach of the principle of equal treatment as a result of different treatment presupposes that the situations concerned are comparable, having regard to all the elements which characterise them.[56] The elements which characterise various situations, and hence their comparability, must in particular be determined and assessed in the light of the subject matter of the provisions in question and of the aim they pursue, whilst account must be taken for that purpose of the principles and objectives of the field to which the measure at issue relates.[57]

In *Marks & Spencer,* the Court considered that 'the general principle of equal treatment, the infringement of which may be established, in matters relating to tax, by discrimination affecting traders who are not necessarily in competition with each other but are nevertheless in a similar situation in other respects'.[58] While the neutrality can only be envisaged among competing economic operators, the principle of equal treatment affects operators who are not necessarily competitors, but who are in comparable situations in other aspect.[59]

The principle of equal treatment is essential to the process of European integration. It is one of the main principles – if not the main principle – driving this process

53. CJEU, 19 October 1977, Case 124/76, *Moulins et Huileries de Pont-à-Mousson,* ECLI:EU:C:1977:161; CJEU, 5 March 1980, Case 265/78, *Ferwerda,* ECLI:EU:C:1980:66.
54. CJEU, 16 December 2008, Case C-127/07, *Société Arcelor Atlantique et Lorraine,* ECLI:EU:C:2008:728.
55. The general principles of European Union law are general principles of law which are applied by the European Court of Justice and the national courts of the member states when determining the lawfulness of legislative and administrative measures within the European Union. General principles of European Union law may be derived from common legal principles in the various EU member states, or general principles found in international law or European Union law. Among others the European Court of Justice has recognised fundamental rights, proportionality, legal certainty, equality before the law and subsidiarity as general principles of European Union law. General principles of law should be distinguished from rules of law as principles are more general and open-ended in the sense that they need to be honed to be applied to specific cases with correct results (Wikipedia quoting Jan H. Jans et al., *Europeanisation of Public Law* (1st ed.) Europa Law Publishing, 1st ed., 2007, 418).
56. *Société Arcelor Atlantique et Lorraine supra* n. 55, paragraph 25.
57. CJEU, 14 June 2017, Case C-38/16, *Compass Contract Services,* ECLI:EU:C:2017:454, paragraph 25; *see,* to that effect, *Arcelor Atlantique et Lorraine, supra* n. 54, paragraph 26; CJEU, 7 March 2017, Case C-390/15, *RPO,* EU:C:2017:174, paragraph 42.
58. CJEU, 10 April 2008, Case C-309/06, *Marks & Spencer,* ECLI:EU:C:2008:211, paragraph 54.
59. Javier Sánchez Gallardo and Amparo Sanchis Sierra, *ECJ Case-Law on VAT* (Manual Francis Lefebvre, 2019), 67.

forward. Equal treatment between States and the prohibition to discriminate on grounds of nationality are indeed cornerstones of the European project.[60]

The creation of a common market requires by itself equal legal conditions.[61] Freedom of circulation of goods, persons, services and capital can only be effective if the citizens of this common market are treated equally. Equality is another way to express the concept of non-discrimination. Equality before the law is the democratic base of the Member States of such Common Market.

The principle of equal treatment is a general principle of Union Law.[62] The validity of provisions of the VAT Directive themselves can be challenged for infringement of the principle of equal treatment.[63]

Non-discrimination is a negative, but limited and operative form of the concept of equality. Non- discrimination intends to correct disorders caused by certain types of inequalities.

In *Roders and others*, the Court of Justice considered that: 'According to the settled case-law of the Court, which has interpreted the concept of similarity widely, in order to determine whether products are similar it is necessary to consider whether they have similar characteristics and meet the same needs from the point of view of consumers, the test being not whether they are strictly identical but whether their use is similar and comparable.'[64]

The different treatment of identical or comparable situations does not offend the principle if the difference in treatment is objectively justified and proportionate.[65]

§3.04 DISTORTION OF COMPETITION VERSUS DISCRIMINATION OF THE CASE LAW OF THE COURT OF JUSTICE OF THE EUROPEAN UNION

Neutrality means absence of distortion of competition at retailer level and in the chain of production. Competition is influenced by various factors in the chain of production and of commercialization. One of these factors is taxes, including the VAT. Neutrality

60. Elise Muir, *The Essence of the Fundamental Right to Equal Treatment: Back to the Origins*, 20(6) *German Law J.* 817 (2019).
61. Rémy Hernu, *Le principe d'égalité et le principe de non-discrimination dans la jurisprudence de la CJUE*, Titre VII [en ligne], April 2020, n° 4, available at https://www.conseil-constitutionnel.fr/publications/titre-vii/le-principe-d-egalite-et-le-principe-de-non-discrimination-dans-la-jurisprudence-de-la-cjue.
62. Francis Lefebvre, *Union Européenne 2008-2009* (Memento Pratique) n° 156; CJEU, 21 June 1958, Case C-8/57, *Groupement des hauts fourneaux et aciéries belges*, ECLI:EU:C:1958:9; *Ferwerda*, *supra* n. 53.
63. *See* Conclusion AG Jääskinen, 27 November 2012, in Case C-480/10, *Commission v. Sweden*, ECLI:EU:C:2012:751, referring to CJEU, 23 April 2009, Case C-460/07, *Puffer*, ECLI:EU:C:2009:254; *BlackRock*, *supra* n. 2, paragraph 51.
64. CJEU, 11 August 1995, Case C-367/93 to C-377/93, *Roders and Others*, ECLI:EU:C:1995:261, paragraph 27, referring to CJEU, 4 March 1986, Case 106/84, *Commission v. Denmark*, ECLI:EU:C:1986:99, paragraph 12.
65. Koen Lenaerts, *L'égalité de traitement en droit communautaire* (1-2) Cahiers de droit européen 3, 10 (1991); Karol P.E. Lasok, *EU Value Added Tax Law* (Edward Elgar Publishing, 2020), 98.

is the official objective of the EU VAT. It is mentioned in Article 1 of the First VAT Directive and of the current VAT Directive, as well as in the preambles of these Directives. Therefore, it is not surprising that by the end of 2020 neutrality has been referred to in more than 460 VAT cases before the Court of Justice of the EU. For practitioners and scholars from other countries, the application of the neutrality principle in the EU may be confusing: 'it is reduced by inconsistencies and is unpredictable in its outworking. It is subject to judicial abuse and manipulations; it is Delphic in its evolutions.'[66]

After a detailed analyse of more than 140 CJEU cases, M.E. van Hilten concluded that while the Court always refers to 'the' neutrality, in fact neutrality is a broad concept, which has different meanings depending on the context. There is no single fiscal neutrality, but one for the competition, and another one for the interpretation of VAT exemptions.[67]

Giorgio Beretta has summarized the issue as follows:

> Although not part of primary EU law,[68] the principle of neutrality is undoubtfully the leading principle of the EU VAT (...). Indeed, the principle of fiscal neutrality has inspired the purposive construction of the EU VAT system in several matters, such as the treatment of 'taxable persons', the notion of 'taxable transactions', the determination of the 'taxable amount', the scope of the 'tax exemptions', the extend of the 'right of deduct', as well the possibility to apply different tax rates. The CJEU has also maintained that double taxation constitutes an infringement of the principle of fiscal neutrality. Nevertheless, the VAT Directive, by itself, does not explain the exact meaning of the term 'neutrality'. Scholars mostly agree that neutrality has at least two dimensions, which reflect its external and internal orientation. Based on such understanding, the concept can further be divided into external and internal neutrality. External neutrality related to the international aspect of levying EU VAT. It mandates a neutral functioning of the tax frontiers, by prescribing, on the one hand, that the tax on foreign products shall not exceed that levied internally on comparable domestic products, and by requiring, on the other hand, a refund on exported products of the same amount of tax that was levied domestically (...). Internal neutrality, instead, relates to the domestic aspects of levying EU VAT. From such a perspective, it can be grossly divided into legal and economic neutrality. Legal neutrality is tightly clinched to the normative character of the EU VAT, which requires that tax being applied equally to similar products and its amount reflecting a set percentage of the retail price. Economic neutrality, instead, demands that levying of VAT shall not interfere with the optimal allocation of overall wealth, but rather it is a means to promote growth in the overall economy. (...) The principle of neutrality is also used for interpreting EU VAT provisions and, in particular exemptions. (...) However, the principle of

66. Gordon Brysland, *Fiscal Neutrality, Foreign ghost in our GST Machine? Where Policy Meets Reality*, paper of a conference organized by the University of Sydney on 25 and 26 March 2019 at the occasion of the 20th Anniversary of the GST in Australia, https://www.business.unsw.edu.au/News-Events-Site/Events-Site/Documents/Gordon-Brysland-Fiscal-neutrality_paper.pdf (accessed on 16 February 2021).
67. Mariken E. van Hilten, *Over Neutraliteit van de Omzetbelasting en Het Hellend Vlak van de Uitzonderingen* (Kluwer, 2010); and Giorgio Beretta, *European VAT and the Sharing Economy* (Kluwer Law International, 2019) 62.
68. If it would be a part of the primary law, such as the general principle of non-discrimination, it would prevail over the text of the EU Directives.

> neutrality is not absolute. Rather, it must be traded off with other interpretative principles, notably with those which demand strict, contextual, or uniform interpretation of exemptions. As such, the principle of neutrality cannot serve to extend the scope of an exemption in the absence of a clear provision in that effect.[69]

According to Ad van Doesum, the CJEU considers neutrality as the reflection in the field of VAT of the general principle of equal treatment. It forms a special manifestation of an overall EU law principle. It is applicable in respect of similar services and goods which are in competition with each other. Its scope is limited in the sense that infringement of the principle of fiscal neutrality may be envisaged only between competing traders. Therefore, the general principle of equal treatment merely serves as a *lex generalis* in the field of VAT. In the context of EU VAT law, this general principle of equal treatment can be applied only in similar situations.[70] Neutrality and its corollary, the principle of VAT uniformity, preclude similar goods from being treated differently for VAT purposes.[71]

For Lasok, at different times, neutrality has been said to be (or been treated as) distinct from the principle of equal treatment, to encompass, or to be a reflection of, the principle of equal treatment in the area of VAT, and to encompass the principles of VAT uniformity and the elimination of distortions of competition. Insofar as it encompasses the principle of equal treatment, it differs in certain respects from that principle both in terms of its content and in term of its effect.[72]

In the present chapter, it is argued that according to the EU Directives as interpreted by the Court of Justice, although the principle of neutrality has a broad scope, it has only legal consequences when it corresponds to the narrow scope of the 'EU principle of equal treatment', i.e., non-discrimination, but only at a comparable level of distribution or production. This thesis is based on the CJEU case-law about distortion of competition and VAT exemptions.

[A] Lack of Clarity in the Distinctions Neutrality Versus Equality in the Case Law of the Court of Justice of the EU

First, by 2020, the Court of Justice has dealt with the concept of neutrality in more than 460 of the 1,000 cases on VAT.[73]

---

69. Giorgio Beretta, *supra* n. 67, 62.
70. Ad van Doesum et al., *Fundamentals of EU VAT Law* (Wolters Kluwer, 2020), 41 and 42.
71. Rita de la Feria, *VAT: A New Dawn for the Principle of Fiscal Neutrality?* (Oxford University Centre for Business Taxation, PP 11/04), https://core.ac.uk/download/pdf/288286521.pdf (accessed on 16 February 2021).
72. Karol P.E. Lasok, *EU Value Added Tax Law, supra* n. 65, 107.
73. At first glance, the little importance given to neutrality by the Court of Justice may be surprising, but one should keep in mind the methods of interpretation before the CJEU: Text, context, objective and 'effet utile'. Since neutrality is the objective of the VAT Directives, it is normal that it is referred to when the parties deal with the objective of the Directive. This is probably also why the Court of Justice considers neutrality as one of the particular interpretation methods of the VAT, *see Deutsche Bank, supra* n. 2, paragraph 45; CJEU, 15 November 2012, Case C-174/11, *Zimmerman*, ECLI:EU:C:2012:716, paragraph 49.

Second, when dealing with the relation between neutrality and equality, the Court uses words that do not have the same meaning in the various linguistical versions. In *NCC Denmark*, the Court considers that the principle of fiscal neutrality was intended by the Community legislature 'to reflect',[74] in matters relating to VAT, the general principle of equal treatment.[75] Most of the time, for the English word 'reflect', the Court uses the word *traduction* (in French), *traducion* (in Spanish), *traduzione* (in Italian)[76] which mean in English 'translation'. And such 'translation', in common language, implies a kind equivalence or implementation in another legal order. Between a general principle of EU law (non-discrimination) and a principle of interpretation (elimination of distortions of competition), there is no equivalence. Between neutrality (absence of distortion of competition) and equality (i.e., non-discrimination) there are similarities but also major differences. The German *zum Ausdruck gebracht* and the Dutch *uitdrukking gegeven* means rather 'transposition into another legal order'.[77] However, in *Solleveld*, the French version of the published case uses the word 'refléter' and not 'traduire'[78] and this is much closer to both the English version and the way the Court has interpreted the concept of neutrality in the case law. Interestingly, the Court refers to the Cases *Dornier*[79] and *Kingscrest*[80] regarding equal treatment. In *Turn- und Sportunion Waldburg*, the Court considers that the principle of fiscal neutrality precludes, in particular, treating similar supplies of services, which are thus in competition with each other, differently for VAT purposes:[81] from the question raised by the national Courts and from the wording of the Court of Justice, this is clearly an issue of equal treatment.

Third, the Court has admitted in *Zimmerman*,[82] that the concept of neutrality is used in different meanings, while it still refers to 'the' principle of neutrality:

74. In CJEU, 10 November 2011, Case C-259/10, *Rank Group*, ECLI:EU:C:2011:719, paragraph 61, the Court uses the word 'intended to reflect'.
75. CJEU, 29 October 2009, Case C-174/08, *NCC Construction Danmark*, ECLI:EU:C:2009:669, paragraph 41, referring to *Marks & Spencer, supra* n. 58, paragraph 49, and the case-law cited there.
76. In CJEU, 8 June 2006, Case C-106/05, *L.u.P*, ECLI:EU:C:2006:380, paragraph 48, the Court uses the expression *égalité de traitement, en matière de TVA, se traduit par neutralité*, while the English version does not even refer to neutrality but only to equal treatment.
77. Interestingly, it has been observed that neutrality is the transposition of the general principle of equal treatment to VAT terms by the EU legislature. However, while this last principle has constitutional status, the principle of VAT neutrality requires the legislative framework to be prepared through EU secondary legislation, *see* Teresa Famulska and Beata Rogowska-Rajda, *Principle of VAT Neutrality and the Reverse Charge Mechanism* (14)(3) e-Finanse: Financial Internet Quarterly (2018), 87.
78. CJEU, 27 April 2006, Joined Cases C-443/04 and C-444/04, *Solleveld and van den Hout-Eijnsbergen*, ECLI:EU:C:2006:257, paragraph 35; *see also* CJEU, 6 November 2003, Case C-45/01, *Christoph-Dornier-Stiftung für Klinische Psychologier*, ECLI:EU:C:2003:595, paragraphs 42 and 69.
79. *Dornier-Stiftung, supra* n. 78, paragraph 69.
80. CJEU, 26 May 2005, Case C-498/03 *Kingscrest Associates and Montecello*, ECLI:EU:C:2005:322, paragraphs 29 and 52.
81. CJEU, 12 January 2006, Case C-246/04, *Turn- und Sportunion Waldburg*, ECLI:EU:C:2006:22, paragraphs 44 to 46 referring to CJEU, 11 October 2001, Case C-267/99, *Adam*, ECLI: EU:C:2001:534, paragraph 36; CJEU, 23 October 2003, Case C-109/02, *Commission v. Germany*, ECLI:EU:C:2003:586, paragraph 20; and *Kingscrest, supra* n. 80, paragraph 41.
82. *Zimmerman, supra* n. 73.

- On the one hand, recalling that the deduction is intended to relieve the trader entirely of the burden of the VAT payable or paid in the course of all his economic activities, the Court has held that the common system of VAT seeks to ensure neutrality of taxation of all economic activities, provided that those activities are themselves subject in principle to VAT;[83]
- On the other hand, according to settled case-law, the principle of fiscal neutrality means that supplies of goods or services which are similar, and which are accordingly in competition with each other, may not be treated differently for VAT purposes.[84]

When in *Zimmerman,* the Court considers that supplies of goods or services which are similar may not be treated differently, it actually refers to the principle of equality and not of neutrality. Equality is included in neutrality in such a way that the scope of equality is narrower than neutrality, even if for a breach of principle of equality, it is not necessary to bring evidence that some supplies of goods and services are in competition with the other.

Fourth, the Court considers that the principle of fiscal neutrality includes the principles of VAT uniformity and of elimination of distortion in competition.[85]

But at the same time, neutrality is limited to those activities that are subject to VAT with right of deduction of input VAT.[86] In other words, transactions that are out of the VAT scope[87] or VAT exempt without right of deduction of input VAT,[88] but subject to VAT, are excluded from the concept of VAT neutrality.

Therefore, one may wonder whether it is still useful to refer before the courts to the principle of neutrality, except when there are no VAT exemptions or when specific provisions of the Directive mention the obligation of Member States to implement the Directive in the national rules without distortions of competition. Actually, the VAT Directive contains 18 provisions in that way.[89]

Another point is that the Court of Justice has sometimes fundamentally changed its interpretation.

The contribution of Javier Sánchez Gallardo and Amparo Sanchis Sierra[90] is of a great help. Firstly, because the large number of the cases analysed. Second, because

83. *See, inter alia,* to that effect, *NCC Construction Danmark, supra* n. 75, paragraph 27, and CJEU, 22 December 2010, Case C-277/09, *RBS Deutschland Holdings*, ECLI:EU:C:2010:810, paragraph 38.
84. *See, inter alia,* CJEU, 17 February 2005, Joined Cases C-453/02 and C-462/02, *Linneweber and Akritidis,* ECLI:EU:C:2005:92, paragraph 24; *Rank Group, supra* n. 74, paragraph 32 and the case-law cited.
85. CJEU, 3 May 2001, Case C-481/98, *Commission of the European Communities v. French Republic,* ECLI:EU:C:2001:237, paragraph 22.
86. CJEU, 21 March 2018, Case C-533/16, *Volkswagen,* ECLI:EU:C:2018:204, paragraph 38; CJEU, 21 September 2017, Case C-441/16, *SMS Group,* ECLI:EU:C:2017:712, paragraph 40; CJEU, 22 March 2012, Case C-153/11, *Klub,* ECLI:EU:C:2012:163, paragraph 36.
87. CJEU, 25 July 2018, Case C-140/17, *Gmina Ryjewo,* EU:C:2018:595, paragraph 29.
88. CJEU, 3 July 2019, Case C-316/18, *University of Cambridge,* ECLI:EU:C:2019:559; CJEU, 9 July 2020, Case C-374/19, *HF,* ECLI:EU:C:2020:546, paragraph 18.
89. *See* Directive 2006/112/EC Articles 13(1) second al; 19 second al; 26(2); 27; 34(2); 59a; 72;112; 132(1)(f);132(1)(l); 132(1)(o); 133(d); 134(b); 143(f)bis; 145(2); 151(1); 177; 191; 342;343.
90. Sánchez Gallardo & Sanchis Sierra, *supra* n. 59, 71 to 185.

their analyses is not limited to the 'principle of neutrality' but includes various legal provisions that may have an impact on the distortion of competition, such as the freedoms granted by the Treaties, the general principles of EU Law, specific provisions of the EU VAT Directives, and the prohibition of discrimination or equal treatment.

In the further of this section, we will identify cases in which the CJEU found the absence of neutrality (i.e., distortion of competition) to be unacceptable or acceptable.

[B] Reasons Why the Court of Justice Rejected Claims of Distortion of Competition and Discriminations

[1] The Court Interprets the Existing Rules

The Court is bound by clear political decisions of the Council. According to the Advocate General Jacobs: 'It is inherent in the existence of exceptions to the VAT system that they will interfere to some extent with the application of the principles of neutrality and of equality of treatment. Whatever the merits of the decision to treat public bodies as final consumers, it forms an integral part of the Directive. In that and in comparable situations, the treatment of taxable persons and persons excluded from the VAT system will inevitably be different.'[91]

In *Ideal tourisme*, a Belgian bus transporter considered that he was discriminated by comparison to airlines. International transport of passengers by air was (and is still) zero-rated (with right of deduction) while transport by bus is either taxed, exempted (without right of deduction), or out of the scope, depending on the country where the transport takes place. A single transport between two cities in the EU will be subject to various VAT rules. This was and is still the consequence of a temporary measure granted by the Sixth VAT Directive. The Court considered that in the present state of harmonization of the laws of the Member States relating to the common system of VAT, the principle of equal treatment does not preclude legislation of a Member State which in accordance with the Sixth VAT Directive continues to exempt international passengers by air, and on the other hand taxes international passenger transport by coach.[92] The preferential treatment of airlines is the result of successful lobbying some 30 years ago of the European Commission, convincing her that taxation of air transport would create deflection of traffic in the European Union which, at the time, consisted of only 12 Members.

In the Case C-502/13, *Commission v. Luxembourg*,[93] Luxembourg argued that the reduced VAT rates on books should also be applied to e-books. The Court considered that the principle of fiscal neutrality cannot extend the scope of reduced VAT rate to the supply of electronic books,[94] because point 6 of Annex III to the VAT Directive is not a provision which, unequivocally, extends the scope of reduced rates of VAT to the

91. In his Opinion, 18 November 2004 preceding the Case C-378/02, *Waterschap Zeeuws Vlaanderen*, ECLI:EU:C:2004:726, paragraph 38.
92. CJEU, 13 July 2000, Case C-36/99, *Ideal Tourisme*, ECLI:EU:C:2000:405, paragraph 40.
93. CJEU, 5 March 2015, Case C-502/13, *Commission v. Luxembourg*, ECLI:EU:C:2015:143.
94. *Zimmermann*, *supra* n. 73, paragraph 50, and the case-law cited there.

supply of electronic books. Based on the context and the purpose of the legislation of which that provision forms a part, that point cannot be interpreted as including the supply of electronic books within its scope.

According to the Court, there are objective justifications for not respecting equal treatment:

- between trains and trucks, because these two modes of transport are not generally interchangeable and the situation of undertakings operating in each of those different transport sectors is accordingly not comparable;[95] therefore a VAT exemption could be granted to trucks but not to trains;
- between travel agencies that mediate on their own behalf and those mediating on behalf of third parties was not the same;[96]
- between oxygen concentrators that are for the exclusive personal use of the disabled and those 'which could also be used' in hospitals;[97]
- between reimbursable and non-reimbursable medicinal products; the reduced rate of VAT on reimbursable medicinal products does not have the effect of favouring the sale of such product over the sale of medicinal products that are not reimbursable because the consumer preference remains within the category of those products that are reimbursable and, consequently, the decision to purchase is not triggered by the lower rate of VAT;[98]
- between management services of 'special investment funds' under specific State supervision and others not subject to that regime;[99]
- between transactions by a public or a private postal operator as the former supplies postal services under a legal regime which is substantially different from that under which the latter category provides such services.[100]

According to the case law, such objective justifications have to comply with the EU principle of proportionality, i.e., there is no more suitable alternative. In *Ampafrance and Sanofi,* the Court observed that in order for a EU measure concerning the VAT system to be compatible with the principle of proportionality, the provisions which it embodies must be necessary for the attainment of the specific objective which it pursues and have the least possible effect on the objectives and principles of the Sixth Directive.[101] However, the scope of this principle is limited in that violations must be assessed on the basis of the information available at the time of its adoption.[102]

95. CJEU, 19 July 2012, Case C-250/11, *Lietuvos geležinkeliai AB,* ECLI:EU:C:2012:496, paragraph 46.
96. CJEU, 13 March 2014, Case C-599/12, *Jetair and BTWE Travel4you,* ECLI:EU:C:2014:144.
97. CJEU, 9 March 2017, Case C-573/15, *Oxycure,* ECLI:EU:C:2017:189.
98. *Commission v. France, supra* n. 85, paragraph 27.
99. CJEU, 9 December 2015, Case C-595/13, *Fiscale Eenheid X,* ECLI:EU:C:2015:801.
100. CJEU, 23 April 2009, Case C-357/07, *TNT Post Ltd,* ECLI:EU:C:2009:248, paragraphs 39 and 45.
101. CJEU, 19 September 2000, Joined Cases C-177/99 and C-181/99, *Ampafrance and Sanofi,* ECLI:EU:C:2000:470, paragraph 60.
102. CJEU, 12 July 2001, Case C-189/01, *Jippes,* ECLI:EU:C:2001:420, paragraphs 82-84. But why the evolution of the legal and technological environment since the adoption of a legal provision could not be taken into account by Tribunals? According to the Judge Lenaerts, the President of the Court of Justice, when judges interpret a legal provision, they place

[2] *The Subsidiarity of the EU Rules*

In implementing the provisions of a Directive, the Member States must consider the principle of equal treatment, like other general principles of EU law which have constitutional status. They bind those Member States when they take action in a field covered by EU law.[103] Of course, this is the case only when the Directive itself does not intentionally create discrimination, like in the case of the preferential treatment of the air transport sector. Those who benefit from preferential treatment can rely on the direct effect of the Directive in order to protect a competitive advantage created by the Directive.

[3] *Strict Interpretations of the VAT Exemptions*

Advocate General Sharpston in her Opinion on the *Deutsche Bank*-case observed that if all activities partly in competition with each other had to receive the same VAT treatment, the final result would be - since practically every activity overlaps to some extent with another - to eliminate all differences in VAT treatment entirely. That would (presumably) lead to the elimination of all exemptions since the VAT system exists only to tax transactions.[104]

Based on such interpretation, the Court decided that exemptions for childcare did not apply to Mrs. Bulthuis-Griffioen, who was a private person and, therefore, not a body, or legal entity as required by the Directive.[105] However, the Court of Justice changed its interpretation in later decisions.

From a purposive perspective of a VAT system (and of the Treaties) with limited exemptions, the Court was probably correct in deciding that outsourcing of back-office services in the insurance sector was taxable but not in the banking sector;[106] that the transport of organs was taxable but not the supply of organs;[107] that TV services provided in a hospital room were taxable but not the provision of the room;[108] that the management of a pension fund is taxable but not the management of a fund;[109] that

themselves in the position of the Legislature if the question had been raised before the Legislature at the time of the adoption of a legal provision.

103. *NCC Construction Danmark*, *supra* n. 75, paragraph 45; *see*, to that effect, CJEU, 18 May 2000, Case C 107/97, *Rombi and Arkopharma*, ECLI:EU:C:2000:253, paragraph 65; and CJEU, 8 June 2000, Case C 396/98, *Schloßstraße*, ECLI:EU:C:2000:303, paragraph 44.
104. Conclusion of the AG Sharpston in Case C-44/11, *Deutsche Bank*, ECLI:EU:C:2012:276, paragraph 60.
105. CJEU, 11 August 1995, Case C-453/93, *Bulthuis-Griffioen*, ECLI:EU:C:1995:265.
106. CJEU, 3 March 2005, Case C-472/03, *Arthur Andersen*, ECLI:EU:C:2005:135.
107. CJEU, 3 June 2010, Case C-237/09, *De Fruytier*, ECLI:EU:C:2010:316. However, it is questionable whether this solution is in line with a previous case describing very accurately the legal context of such business, *see* CJEU, 11 January 2001, Case C-76/99, *Commission v. France*, ECLI:EU:C:2001:12.
108. CJEU, 1 December 2005, Case C-394/04, *Ygeia*, ECLI:EU:C:2005:734. It could be interesting to compare this case with the principles referred in CJEU, 12 June 1979, Case 126/78, *Nederlandse Spoorwegen*, ECLI:EU:C:1979:150.
109. CJEU, 7 March 2013, Case C-424/11, *Wheels Common investment Fund Trustees*, ECLI:EU:C:2013:144.

child care provided by an individual is taxable, but VAT exempt when performed by a legal entity,[110] etc. Businesses facing restrictive interpretations of the VAT exemptions will certainly object by arguing that they are discriminated against and should be VAT exempt. However, except in very particular situations, businesses seem not to argue for taxation, unless when facing substantial investments, in which case VAT exempt business will set up the most sophisticated structures in order to recover input VAT. Puzzling is not that the Court decided that such operations are taxable but rather that similar operation are exempt. Moreover, most people no longer understand the rationale of certain distinctions, which may have made sense historically but seem inappropriate in the current economic context.

[C] Reasons Why the Court Accepted Claims of Distortions of Competition and Discriminations

Because of the difficulty of use of the concept of neutrality, other legal bases may be preferable in order prevent the consequences of the lack of neutrality, i.e., distortions of competition.

[1] Direct Effect of Treaty Provisions

Businesses established in another EU Member States may not be penalized in comparison to local suppliers. This is the essence of a common market.

The case *Gaston Schul* concerned the import from France into the Netherlands of a secondhand yacht by a private individual, who had to pay import-VAT while no VAT had been due if he had purchased the yacht in the Netherlands. The Court decided that Article 95 of the Treaty of Rome (Article 110 TFEU) obligated the Netherlands to give a credit for the non-deducted VAT in France,[111] notwithstanding the absence of any provision in the Directive to that extent.

Lease Plan Luxembourg leased out 5 cars to Belgian residents. The European Commission suggested to Belgium that Lease Plan Luxembourg had a fixed establishment in Belgium. When Lease Plan requested a refund of the VAT paid on the fuel purchased by the drivers in Belgium, it appeared that the conditions for the granting of interest to a foreign supplier in case of late refund by the Belgian State where less favourable to foreigners than to Belgians. The Court considered that this constituted discrimination prohibited by Article 59 of the Treaty of Rome (currently Article 65 of the TFEU) and the principle of free movement of capital, services, and persons.[112]

The Société Générale des grandes sources d'eaux minérales françaises received an invoice from a German supplier mentioning German VAT. However, it lost this invoice and replaced it with a duplicate. Referring to the text of the 8th Directive, the German tax authorities refused to grant the deduction because it was a duplicate and

110. *Bulthuis-Griffioen, supra* n. 105.
111. CJEU, 5 May 1982, Case 15/81, *Gaston Schul,* ECLI:EU:C:1982:135.
112. CJEU, 7 May 1998, Case C-390/96, *Lease Plan Luxembourg,* ECLI:EU:C:1998:206.

not an original, even though using a duplicate for this purpose was allowed to taxable persons established in Germany. The Court of justice decided that this was a violation of the Article 7 of the Treaty of Rome (Article 18 TFEU) prohibiting discriminations.[113]

However, EU Member States are not prevented to treat their own residents less favourable than the residents of other EU Member States, as far as discriminations are acceptable according to the national regulations, i.e., based on objective reasons.

[2] The Text of the Directive

Specific provisions of the Directive refer to the obligation of the Member States to adopt provisions in order to avoid distortion of competition. Other provisions allow a broad interpretation.

The VAT Directive specifically excludes distortions of competition for activities of public authorities acting as such, the 'Independent Group of persons' intended to avoid the negative consequences of VAT exemptions, etc.[114] Therefore, the Court considers that there is a distortion of competition by reference to specific provisions of the Directive, but not on the basis of the principle of neutrality.

In *Isle of Wight and others*, the Court refers to the concept of distortion of competition, because this concept is contained in Article 13(1) of the VAT Directive.[115] For this reason, the Court decided that a private person who is in competition with a public body and alleges that that body is treated as a non-taxable person or is undertaxed may rely on the prohibition of distortion of competition specifically mentioned in this provision of the Directive.[116]

However, the rejection of possible distortion of competition may be the consequence of the fact that the text of the Directive as such does not allow a difference in treatment even without any reference to a distortion of competition. For example:

- Preparatory acts must themselves be treated as constituting economic activity.[117] Indeed, the text of the Directive does not allow to make a distinction between business already carrying out taxable activities and other business seeking by investment to commence activities which will in future be a source of taxable transactions.[118]
- The terms 'other duly recognized establishments of a similar nature' and 'other organizations recognized as charitable by the Member State concerned',

113. CJEU, 11 June 1998, Case C-361/96, *Société Générale des grandes sources d'eaux minérales françaises*, ECLI:EU:C:1998:282.
114. *See* Directive 2006/112/EC, Article 13(1) second al; 19 second al; 26(2); 27; 34(2); 59a; 72;112; 132(1)(f);132(1)(l); 132(1)(o); 133(d); 134(b); 143(f)bis; 145(2); 151(1); 177; 191; 342;343.
115. CJEU, 16 September 2008, Case C-288/07, *Isle of Wight Council and others*, ECLI: EU:C:2008:505.
116. CJEU, 8 June 2006, Case C-430/04, *Feuerbestattungsverein Halle*, ECLI:EU:C:2006:374.
117. CJEU, 14 February 1985, Case C-268/83, *Rompelman*, ECLI:EU:C:1985:74.
118. CJEU, 28 February 2018, Case C-672/16, *Imofloresmira*, ECLI:EU:C:2018:134, paragraph 43, referring to CJEU, 29 February 1996, Case C-110/94, *Inzo*, ECLI:EU:C:1996:67, paragraph 22.

do not exclude from that exemption natural persons running a business.[119] The terms 'establishment' and 'organization' are in principle sufficiently broad to include natural persons as well. It may be added that none of the language versions of Article 13(A) of the Sixth Directive include the term 'legal person', which would have been clear and unambiguous, instead of the abovementioned terms. It may be inferred that in employing those terms the Community legislature did not intend to confine the exemptions referred to in that provision to the activities carried on by legal persons but meant to extend the scope of those exemptions to activities carried on by individuals. Therefore, in *Gregg and Gregg*, the Court reversed the interpretation adopted in *Bulthuis-Griffioen*.
- The Directive entails no distinction, as far as exemptions are concerned, between lawful and unlawful exports. When the latter consist of goods which fall within the scope of the Sixth Directive, they must accordingly be treated in the same manner as lawful exports of the same goods.[120]

[3] Equal Treatment

In *Muys' en De Winter Bouw-en aannemingsbedrijf*, the Court considered that the objective of the common system is in particular to secure equal treatment for taxable persons. That objective would be disregarded if the purchaser were to be taxed on credit granted by this supplier, whereas a purchaser seeking credit from a bank or another lender receive credit exempt from tax.[121]

In *JP Morgan* the Court decided that the management of special closed-ended investment funds cannot be excluded from the exemption because they are collective investment undertakings which allow investors to invest in securities and where those funds are in competition with funds exempt from VAT. Indeed, the principle of fiscal neutrality includes the principle of elimination of distortion in competition as a result of differing treatment for VAT purposes. Therefore, distortion is established once it is found that supplies of services are in competition and are *treated unequally* for the purposes of VAT.[122] It is irrelevant, in that connection, whether the distortion is substantial.

In *Ambulanter Pflegedienst Kügler*, the Court considered that the principle of fiscal neutrality precludes, *inter alia*, economic operators carrying on the same activities from being treated differently as far as the levying of VAT is concerned. That

119. CJEU, 7 September 1999, Case C-216/97, *Gregg and Gregg*, ECLI:EU:C:1999:390; *see also* CJEU, 3 April 2003, Case C-144/00, *Matthias Hoffmann*, ECLI:EU:C:2003:192, paragraph 27.
120. CJEU, 2 August 1993, Case C-111/92, *Wilfried Lange*, ECLI:EU:C:1993:345, paragraph 19.
121. CJEU, 27 October 1993, Case C-281/91, *Muys' en De Winter's Bouw- en Aannemingsbedrijf*, ECLI:EU:C:1993:855, paragraph 14.
122. CJEU, 28 June 2007, Case C-363/05, *JP Morgan*, ECLI:EU:C:2007:391, paragraph 47, referring to CJEU, 29 March 2001, Case C-404/99, *Commission v. France*, ECLI:EU:C:2001:192 paragraphs 45-47.

principle would be disregarded if the application of the exemption were dependent on the legal form in which the taxable person carries on his activity.[123]

In *Canterbury Hockey Club* the Court followed the same reasoning and concluded that the neutrality principle would be violated if the possibility of invoking the benefit of an exemption were to depend on the organizational structure particular to the sporting activity practiced.[124]

[4] Others General Principles of EU Law

In the case law about formalities, the principle of neutrality is mentioned, but the Court relies on the general principle of proportionality.

In *EMS Bulgaria,* the Court considered that the principle of fiscal neutrality precludes a penalty consisting in a refusal of the right to deduct if VAT is accounted for belatedly, but does not preclude the payment of default interest, provided that that penalty complies with the principle of proportionality.[125]

In *Ecotrade,* the Court decided that the principle of fiscal neutrality requires deduction of input tax to be allowed if the substantive requirements are satisfied, even if the taxable person has failed to comply with some of the formal requirements.[126]

According to the Court in *Maya Marinova,* the measures which the Member States may adopt under Article 273 of the VAT directive to ensure the correct collection of the tax and to prevent evasion must not go further than is necessary to attain such objectives and must not undermine the neutrality of VAT.[127]

[5] Right of Deduction

It would in fact be contrary to the principle of neutrality of VAT to make a taxable person bear VAT on expenditure incurred for the purposes of his taxable transactions on the sole ground that a third party derives an ancillary benefit.[128]

123. CJEU, 10 September 2002, Case C-141/00, *Ambulanter Pflegedienst Kügler,* ECLI:EU:C:2002:473, paragraph 30, *see, to that effect, Gregg and Gregg, supra* n. 119, paragraph 20.
124. CJEU, 16 October 2008, Case C-253/07, *Canterbury Hockey Club,* ECLI:EU:C:2008:571, paragraph 30.
125. CJEU, 12 July 2012, Case 284/11, *EMS-Bulgaria,* ECLI:EU:C:2012:458, paragraph 77.
126. CJEU, 8 May 2008, Joined Cases C-95/07 and C-96/07, *Ecotrade,* ECLI:EU:C:2008:267, paragraph 63; *see also* CJEU, 27 September 2007, Case C-146/05 *Collée,* ECLI:EU:C:2007:549, paragraph 31; CJEU, 26 January 2012, Case C-588/10, *Kraft Foods Polska,* ECLI:EU:C:2012:40; CJEU, 23 April 2015, Case C-111/14, *Sarviz AG Germania,* ECLI:EU:C:2015:267, paragraph 42; *Volkswagen, supra* n. 86, paragraph 50.
127. CJEU, 5 October 2016, Case C-576/15, *Maya Marinova,* ECLI:EU:C:2016:740, paragraph 44; CJEU, 6 March 2015, Case C-499/13, *Macikowski,* ECLI:EU:C:2015:201, paragraph 37 and the case-law cited.
128. CJEU, 1 October 2020, Case C-405/19, *Vos Aannemingen,* ECLI:EU:C:2020:785, paragraph 29, and CJEU, 18 July 2013, Case C-124/12, *Maritza East,* ECLI:EU:C:2013:488.

§3.05 DISTORTIONS OF COMPETITION AND VAT EXEMPTIONS

The view that VAT neutrality is of little help as legal principle is confirmed by the VAT Directive provisions and the case law regarding VAT exemptions and transactions out of the scope of VAT. VAT neutrality in the sense of absence of distortion of competition is only possible when there is a full right of input VAT deduction at each stage of the chain of production. VAT neutrality is reduced when the right of deduction by a producer of goods and services is limited. The main obstacles to neutrality are the VAT exemptions and out-of-scope transactions, combined with the freedom of an enterprise to determine how and where organize his activity,[129] using whichever possibility offered by the law[130] and whatever the consequences on actual competition.[131] In other words, the only obstacle to the distortions of competition are appropriate rules.

However, some limitations of the right of deduction are actually simplification measures such as the small business exemption aimed at mitigating compliance costs,[132] methods such as self-supplies to tax consumption when business purchases benefit owners or employees, [133] and lump sum imitations of the right to deduct input VAT[134] to circumvent the difficulty of distinguishing between final consumption and business expenses. In addition, the Directive contains various specific provisions to limit the adverse consequences of the VAT exemptions.[135]

The benefit of a concept of neutrality that is restricted in its application to goods and services produced in the ring of taxable transactions (i.e., not exempt and not out of scope),[136] may be demonstrated by taking a look at the consequences of VAT exemptions from the perspective of a business and of a tax practitioner.

[A] Impact of VAT Exemptions within a Tax Jurisdiction

When services, and possibly goods, falls under the scope of an internal exemption, the input VAT is (in principle) not deductible by the supplier.[137] This is a cost on production that will vary between service providers depending, *inter alia*, on their degree of vertical or horizontal integration,[138] method of determination of the deductible input VAT, and the tax planning methods used, etc. Although the amount of

129. *RBS Deutschland Holding, supra* n. 83, paragraph 53; CJEU, 18 July 2013, Case C-26/12, *PPG Holding*, ECLI:EU:C:2013:526, paragraph 28.
130. CJEU, 9 October 2001, Case C-108/99, *Cantor Fitzgerald*, ECLI:EU:C:2001:526, paragraph 33.
131. *RBS Deutschland Holding, supra* n. 83, paragraph 53; *PPG Holding, supra* n. 129, paragraph 28.
132. Articles 281-284 of the VAT Directive.
133. Articles 18, 26 and 27 of the VAT Directive.
134. Articles 176 and 177 of the VAT Directive.
135. Article 132(1)(f) of the VAT Directive (Independent Groups of persons); Article 136(a) of the VAT Directive.
136. CJEU, 6 April 1995, Case C-4/94, *BLP*, ECLI:EU:C:1995:107, paragraph 25; *University of Cambridge, supra* n. 88; *Gmina Ryjewo, supra* n. 87, paragraph 29; *HF, supra* n. 88, paragraph 18.
137. Article 168 of the VAT Directive.
138. Arthur Kerrigan, *Effects of VAT in Financial Services* in *Taxing Banks Fairly* 127, 135 (Sajid M. Chaudhry and Andrew W. Mullineux, eds. Edward Elgar, 2014).

non-deductible input VAT can be determined at aggregate level, it is impossible to determine it for each individual service,[139] unlike for taxable transactions.

In addition, the limitation of the right to deduct input VAT at stages prior to the final consumption is a source of double taxation comparable to what happened under the former cumulative turnover taxes which were replaced by the EU VAT system: the non-deducted VAT on inputs is included in the taxable base for output transactions and, consequently, taxed again. The position that VAT exemptions favour the activities concerned is true, but only under specific circumstances.[140] It is not the case where the exemption applies to business investments, internal acquisition of goods and services, which happens very frequently.[141]

One of the most complex consequences of VAT exemptions is the determination of the right of deduction when a business makes both taxable and out-of-scope supplies.

When no method of deduction can give appropriate results, the Court of Justice admitted that it 'is in the discretion of the Member States which, when exercising that discretion, must have regard to the aims and broad logic of the directive and, on that basis, provide for a method of calculation which objectively reflects the part of the input expenditure actually to be attributed, respectively, to those two types of activity'.[142] In practice, it means that the right of deduction depends on the creativity of a business, the supervisory capabilities of the tax authorities and their ability to find more objective criteria. Despite the existence of corrective measures, this renders extremely difficult the organization of the activities of the health, educational, and cultural sector.

[B] Impact of VAT Exemptions in an International Context

In addition, the Sixth Directive gave Member States considerable discretionary powers to reduce the costs of some VAT exemptions, such as the arrangements for VAT grouping and cost-sharing associations, and the power to allow businesses to opt for taxation of transactions that are in principle exempt from VAT. Also, the scope of the exemptions and the rules for deduction of input VAT are not harmonized at all,[143] and transactions that are exempt from VAT in the Member State of destination may give rise

139. The possibility to determine the precise amount of tax supported on each individual transaction at the time of exports has been the reason why Europe introduced VAT in 1967, *see* Christian Amand, *EU VAT or the Emergence of an Efficient Consumption Tax in an Internal Market* in (*CFE Tax Advisers Europe – 60th Anniversary – Liber Amicorum* 36 Servaas van Thiel et al., eds., IBFD, 2019).
140. *See*, CJEU, 16 October 2008, Case C-253/07, *Canterbury Hockey Club*, *supra* n. 124, paragraph 19.
141. Tax advisers make use of the situation by setting up sophisticated tax reduction schemes. Sometimes, the only difference between an 'abusive practice' and 'the freedom of businesses to structure their activities so as to limit their VAT liability or the burden of VAT' is the approval of the latter schemes by the national tax authorities.
142. CJEU, 6 September 2012, Case C-496/11, *Portugal Telecom*, ECLI:EU:C:2012:557, paragraph 42; CJEU, 13 March 2008, Case C- 437/06, *Securenta*, ECLI:EU:C:2008:166, paragraphs 33 and 39.
143. *See* VAT Survey Financial services – IBFD, December 2006, 13, http://ec.europa.eu/taxation_customs/resources/documents/taxation/vat/how_vat_works/VAT_insurance/VAT_survey_

to the right to deduct input VAT in the Member State where the supplier is established.[144]

[1] Taxation in the Country of the Supplier Combined with Exemption in the Country of the Customer

Distortive consequences of exemptions without right of deduction are multiplied by the absence of international (within and outside of the EU) harmonization of VAT exemptions and tax jurisdiction rules (place of supply rules). From an adviser's point of view, the most interesting are those which combine:

- In the country of the supplier: taxation/exemption with right deduction/no VAT (non-EU)/option to tax.
- In the country of the customer: VAT exemption or out of the VAT scope.

This allows for full deduction of input VAT on the costs while no VAT is incurred by the consumers/VAT exempt producers who are normally supposed to acquire goods and services with VAT. This explains why some businesses are concentrated in certain EU Member States or have moved their back office outside of the EU.[145]

Such kinds of structures are legal and have been confirmed by the CJEU. For example, in *BBL* a Belgian bank supplied advisory services to Luxembourg SICAVs[146] without charging Belgian VAT. BBL had logically considered that the place of supply was in Luxembourg and therefore the reverse charge mechanism was supposed to be applicable in Luxembourg,[147] because a SICAV is a taxable person according to the Belgian VAT Code and the VAT Directive, and advisory services are not VAT exempt according to the Belgian rules that are in line with the Directive. A Belgian tax inspector argued that according to his information, SICAVs were not taxable persons in Luxembourg and, therefore, according to rules regarding the place of supply, the services supplied by BBL from Belgium to Luxembourg should have been subject to VAT in Belgium. The dispute was subject to a preliminary ruling before the CJEU which decided that the purpose of the Sixth Directive, in particular the creation of a common system of VAT upon a uniform definition of 'taxable persons', requires that status to be assessed solely on the basis of the criteria set forth in the Sixth Directive and, therefore,

financial.pdf (accessed on 7 June 2021). The fact that specific activities are concentrated in 3 or 4 Member States is generally an indication of VAT concessions applicable in those Member States.

144. *RBS Deutschland Holding*, *supra* n. 83.

145. In Australia, this issue has been solved by the denial of input tax credits for taxed acquisitions or importations that relate to input taxed supplies, even if those acquisition-supplies relate to making taxable or GST-free supplies, or indeed to other non-input taxed supplies. There is no direct counterpart to this concept in the European VAT, *see* Rebecca Millar, *The Principle of Neutrality in Australian GST* 17 Austl. GST J. 26 (2017).

146. A Société d'investissement à Capital Variable (SICAV) is a publicly traded open-end investment fund structure offered in Europe. SICAV funds are similar to open-end mutual funds in the U.S. Shares in the fund are bought and sold based on the fund's current net asset value.

147. Application of Articles 44 *jo.* 196 of Directive 2006/112/EC.

SICAVs are taxable persons.[148] This case solved the problem of the suppliers concerning the VAT liability in Belgium, but it had no impact on Luxembourg where the services continued to be not taxed. According to Article 169(a) of the VAT Directive, a taxable person has a right to deduct VAT referring to transactions carried out outside the Member State and in respect of which VAT would be deductible if they had been carried out within that Member State.

A similar solution can be found in *RBS Deutschland.*[149] Under that judgment, a lessor established in Germany, whose supplies are deemed to be made in the United Kingdom but not actually taxed there, is entitled to recover UK VAT relating to those transactions.

[2] Exemption in the Country of the Supplier and Taxation in the Country of the Purchaser

Eurodental was established in Luxembourg and was engaged in making dental prostheses for customers based in Germany. This activity was exempted in Luxembourg and therefore it could not deduct input VAT. And since this activity was taxable in Germany, the intra-community supply was taxable again in Germany, and double taxation occurred.[150]

[3] VAT Grouping and Cross-Border VAT Grouping

In *FCE Bank*, the Italian branch of FCE Bank UK supplied exclusively VAT exempt financial services and therefore it had no right of VAT deduction. FCE Bank Italy acquired various services from FCE Bank UK such as consultancy, management, staff training, data processing and the supply and management of application software. The Italian tax authorities argued that the reverse charge mechanism was applicable in Italy on these services, which would be irrecoverable for the branch. The CJEU considered that the Italian branch to which the UK Head Office supplied services, should not be treated as a separate taxable person by reason of the costs imputed to it in respect of those supplies. In other words, the reverse charge mechanism could not be applied in Italy,[151] like it is the case for activities in a single country. In addition, FCE Bank UK was part of the Ford VAT Group which enjoyed a high rate of input VAT deduction in the UK. As a result, the Italian branch could outsource services to the UK for a much lower price than it could purchase the same services from local suppliers in Italy.
Large businesses advocate strongly for VAT grouping and in particular cross-border VAT grouping. This reduces the cost of pre-financing the VAT during the production and distribution process consecutive to the absence of synchronization of the tax liability, the VAT deduction and the actual payment by customers.

148. CJEU, 21 October 2004, Case C-8/03, *BBL*, ECLI:EU:C:2004:650.
149. *RBS Deutschland Holding*, *supra* n. 83.
150. CJEU, 7 December 2006, Case C-240/05, *Eurodental*, ECLI:EU:C:2006:763.
151. CJEU, 23 March 2006, Case C-210/04, *FCE Bank*, ECLI:EU:C:2006:196.

§3.06 INTERNATIONAL VAT/GST GUIDELINES OF THE OECD (2017)

The Guidelines of the OECD set forth a number of principles for the VAT treatment of the most common type of international transactions. They are built on international dialogue among OECD members and partners and other relevant stakeholders, including academia and private institutions. Chapter 2 of the Guidelines 2017 is devoted to neutrality of value added taxes in the context of cross-border trade. It mentions 6 basic neutrality principles. The Guidelines 2.4 and 2.6 do not raise conceptual problems:

- To ensure foreign businesses do not incur irrecoverable VAT, jurisdictions may choose from a number of approaches.
- Where specific administrative requirements for foreign businesses are deemed necessary, they should not create a disproportionate or inappropriate compliance burden for the business.

However, the other points clearly reflect the recent EU interpretation:

- The burden of value added taxes themselves should not lie on taxable businesses, except where explicitly provided for by legislation. Indeed, in the EU VAT, the VAT exemptions are created by explicit legislation.
- Businesses in similar situations carrying out similar transactions should be subject to similar levels of taxation. Indeed, VAT exemptions have as consequence that the level of taxation is not similar and this is increased by sophisticated tax planning structures.
- VAT rules should be framed in such a way that they are not the primary influence on business decisions. Indeed, in case of exemptions, VAT is the primary criterion for business decisions and it is so important, that it prevents any change of structure. It has a major impact on the choice of localization of the production, either in certain EU Member States or outside the EU.
- With respect to the level of taxation, foreign businesses should not be disadvantaged or advantaged compared to domestic businesses in the jurisdiction where the tax may be due or paid. Indeed, foreign business may not be disadvantaged, but because of VAT, some industries migrate to other countries within or, what concern the EU, outside of the EU.

§3.07 ALTERNATIVES TO VAT EXEMPTIONS AND IMPROVEMENTS OF NEUTRALITY

[A] Zero-Rating

Zero rating means that no tax is levied on output supplies, a feature it has in common with the so-called exemptions. However, where zero-rating and exemptions diverge is on the input side. Exempt transactions do not allow for input VAT credits, but under zero rating the full right to deduct input VAT is retained.[152]

From the archives of the negotiation of the Sixth VAT Directive, it appears that in the year 1960, during the negotiation of the Second VAT Directive, Member States were strongly opposed to zero-rating because the tax authorities would have to set up a special service to check and pay refunds. Such repayment would be inconsistent with the principle of a tax applicable to all consumption and would have to be funded by an increase of the tax rate. It would be contrary to Article 99(2) of the VAT Directive.

During the negotiation of the Sixth VAT Directive, the arguments put forward against zero-rating were the following:[153]

- VAT is a general tax on consumption and therefore a zero-rate extensively applied would lead to full remission of tax in a large area of consumption and consequently runs counter to the principles laid down in the First VAT Directive.
- Broad application of zero-rates is liable to create distortion of competition.
- Maintenance in certain countries of zero-rates could give rise to political pressures in countries where such rates are not applied.
- Zero-rates are liable to have an effect upon the determination of the Communities own resources due to the difficulty of checking the basis of assessment of such rates.

As earlier suggested, the zero-rating of B2B financial services would seriously increase the neutrality of the VAT in favour of businesses establishes within the EU and it would not increase the risks of fraud.[154] It would be very easy to implement and not create any additional compliance cost.

In a challenging study, Rita de la Feria and Michael Walpole have highlighted that applying more than one rate gives rise to significant difficulties, creates economic distortions, and it is at best unclear whether it has the social and distributional effect that it aims to achieve.[155] These objections are relevant in the context of discussions of alternatives to the current VAT exemptions, but they may not be decisive.

[B] Extension of the Neutrality to Social Contributions

Social security levies are an important cost component of the price of goods and services produced in Europe. The EU VAT rules do not prevent the Member States to collect these levies intended to finance social funds with the mechanism of the VAT,

152. This is also the solution adopted by Australia where the 'social goods' such as basic foods, education, healthcare, childcare, water and sewage, various religious and charitable activities and cars for disabled people are GST free. i.e., contrary to the VAT exemption in the EU, the tax burden is fully removed by GST Act 1999 subdivs. 38 A, B, C, D, F, G, I and J. *See* Rebecca Millar, *supra* n. 145.
153. Sixth Directive Historical Archives, folder10_1979, T/289/74(fin).
154. Christian Amand, *EU VAT and Financial Services: Which Rules, What Consequences and Which Possible Solutions?* 30 (5) Int'l. VAT Monitor (2019).
155. De la Feria and Walpole, *supra* n. 38; *see also* Chapter 4 of this book.

i.e., on the basis of total annual turnover.[156] This is the case in Denmark, partly in Germany and many other new Member States. This allows for the reduction of export costs and reduces the distortion of competition faced by national production.

§3.08 CONSEQUENCES OF THE DISTINCTION BETWEEN NEUTRALITY AND EQUALITY

A distinction between neutrality and equality has important consequences for practitioners and for the lawmakers, at least in Europe.

For practitioners, to concentrate on the equal treatment may simplify the debate before the courts, as they can present concepts with which the courts are familiar and for which a lot of national and European case law is available.

It has also consequences for the numerous tax planning schemes that utilize the non-taxation caused by the VAT exemptions: as long as the principle of equal treatment is respected, tax authorities have no legal means to challenge distortions of competition.

Large businesses argue that neutrality could be improved by extending the concept of VAT grouping and in particular cross-border VAT grouping, as this would significantly reduce the cash flow cost associated with VAT. This should be examined in the light of the purpose of the VAT system as well the principle of non-discrimination.

The distinction Neutrality /Equality may also explain the major reservations made by some EU Member States against Cross-Border Rulings (CBR). CBR is a pilot exercise organized by the European Commission to avoid double taxation. When the European Commission proposes a mechanism to resolve disputes arising from the interpretation or the application of agreements in order to eliminate double taxation,[157] it does not mention that these situations have been caused by the Directive itself or by a temporary derogation granted by the Directive. Therefore, double taxation or non-taxation are fully in line with the text of the Directive and cannot be challenged before the courts. From the few CBR rulings issued, it appeared that a Member State did not hesitate to agree to two different interpretations of exactly the same facts and related to the same company, active in three Member States.[158] In other cases, they agreed on interpretation contrary to their own legal provisions, which remained in force.[159] These are evident violations of the principle of equality that is supposed to be part of the legal fundamental rules of each EU Member State.

156. CJEU, 27 November 1985, Case 295/84, *Rousseau-Wilmot*, ECLI:EU:C:1985:473.
157. *An Action Plan for Fair and Simple Taxation Supporting the Recovery Strategy*, Communication from the Commission to the European Parliament and the Council, Brussels (15 July 2020), https://ec.europa.eu/taxation_customs/sites/taxation/files/2020_tax_package_tax_action_plan_en.pdf (accessed on 16 February 2021).
158. EU VAT FORUM Cross-Border Rulings 2014/2 and 2015/12, Brussels (22 October 2019), https://ec.europa.eu/taxation_customs/sites/taxation/files/cross-border-rulings.pdf.
159. Refurbishment of vintage cars, Cross-border ruling 2019/22 contrary to the national provisions that are still applicable despite the existence of the cross-border ruling.

As already pointed out, certain provisions of the existing VAT system are discriminatory. Some of them have been accepted by the Courts and others not. For many others, we do not know what the position of the Courts will be, especially in the light of the evolution of technology and the legal system, impacting indirectly on the VAT, such as the administrative cooperation provisions. The principles of equality and non-discrimination, in combination with the other principles of EU Law and in particular the principle of proportionality, are fundamental in order to evaluate proposals submitted by the European Commission.

Finally, it should be observed that pursuant to Article 113 TFEU as it entered into force on December 1, 2009, the European Commission has received the unanimous mandate from the EU Member States to submit proposals in order to eliminate distortions of competition, also when such distortions affect only transactions within a single Member State. It is questionable whether the scope of this obligation has been properly understood by the Commission.

§3.09 CONCLUSIONS

From the history, it appears that neutrality firstly intended to limit the economic negative impact of tax planning and later to make 'single consumption taxes' collected at each stage of production compatible with the international trade rules and common markets. Neutrality is vertical because it includes all the stages of the production and distribution process in order to allow absence of distortion of competition at retailer level. However, neutrality does not grant rights protected by courts, unless a right is specifically mentioned in the text of an EU Directive.

Equality requires that similar situations shall not be treated differently unless differentiation is objectively justified, without any obligation to prove the existence of a distortion of competition. It is a right that is protected by the courts, except when the discrimination has been explicitly authorized by the EU legislature.

Neutrality and equality may sometimes cover identical situations because neutrality is much broader than equality. However, discrimination, i.e., violation of equality, does not require a distortion of competition.

VAT exemptions are the cause of absence of neutrality and business are entitled to adopt the least taxed method or organization contrary to neutrality. Paradoxically, the political discourse that characterizes VAT to be regressive provides shelter for distortive planning schemes adopted by (partially) exempt businesses, mainly in the financial sector, and that position is an obstacle to an optimal organization of the health, educational, cultural, non-profit, and public service activities. Zero-rates, or possibly reduced rates, could be an appropriate and easy solution to the challenges caused by the VAT exemptions.

A clear distinction between neutrality and equality raises questions about the lawfulness of recent initiatives of the European Commission such as those intended to solve issues of double taxation and of non- taxation. While neutrality is an objective to attain, equality is an obligation to respect, even by the legislature, unless there are objective reasons to derogate from it within the parameters set by the principle of proportionality. From a non- EU perspective, this distinction may present itself as rather academic in nature. However, in the EU, where the VAT progressively emerged as a succession of short-term solutions to a never-ending process of creation of an internal market by old and independent countries, the concepts of neutrality and equality are essential from the perspective of the future evolution of the VAT system.

CHAPTER 4

Rate Policy: Evaluating the Arguments for a Single Rate Versus Multiple Rates

Robert F. van Brederode

§4.01 INTRODUCTION

Before discussing policy issues related to the rate structure of VAT, it may make sense to start with taking inventory of the current state of affairs. Of the countries included in our overview in §4.02 just under half (46%) apply a single rate and a small majority (54%) apply a multiple rate structure. This demonstrates the different results of the political decision-making process. The rationale for a multiple rate structure is discussed in §4.03. We identify four main reasons. First, the necessity to give preferential treatment to gain societal support for the tax. Second, to improve distributional equality by combating the alleged regressivity of VAT. Third, to do right to goods and services that produce externalities, which require correction through either Pigouvian taxes or subsidies. Fourth, to help realize certain objectives of economic cyclical policy. The next section, 4.04, addresses a number of practical difficulties associated with a multi-rate system: increased compliance and administrative costs, and—on the basis of case law from the Court of Justice of the European Union (CJEU) and national courts of three European Union (EU) member states—classification problems, and composite supplies. The advantages of a single rate are summarized in §4.05 and our conclusions are found in §4.06.

§4.02 OVERVIEW OF CURRENT GLOBAL VAT RATES APPLIED

Table 4.1 shows the diversity of the 2020 VAT rates applied in 152 countries.

*Table 4.1 Global VAT Rates**

Country	Standard Rate	Reduced Rate	Increased Rate	Country	Standard Rate	Reduced Rate	Increased Rate
Albania	20	6	–	Lao PDR	10	–	–
Algeria	19	9	–	Latvia	21	5, 12	–
Andorra	4.5	0, 1	9.5	Lebanon	11	–	–
Angola	14	–	–	Liechtenstein	7.7	2.5, 3.7	–
Antigua & Barbuda	15	–	–	Lithuania	21	9	–
Argentina	21	10.5	27	Luxembourg	17	3, 8, 14	–
Armenia	20	–	–	Madagascar	20	–	–
Australia	10	–	–	Malawi	16.5	–	–
Austria	20	10, 13	–	Maldives	6	–	12
Azerbaijan	18	–	–	Mali	18	5	–
Bahamas	12	–	–	Malta	18	5, 7	–
Bahrain	5	–	–	Mauritania	16	–	18, 20
Bangladesh	15	1.5, 2.25, 4.5, 5, 7.5, 10		Mauritius	15	–	–
Barbados	17.5	0, 10	22	Mexico	16	0	–
Belarus	20	10	25	Moldova	20	8, 15	–
Belgium	21	6, 12	–	Mongolia	10	–	–
Benin	18	–	–	Montenegro	21	7	
Bolivia	13	–	–	Morocco	20	7, 10, 14	–

Country	Standard Rate	Reduced Rate	Increased Rate	Country	Standard Rate	Reduced Rate	Increased Rate
Bosnia & Herzegovina	17	–	–	Mozambique	17	–	–
Botswana	12	–	–	Namibia	15	–	–
Brazil (IPI)	10-15	–	–	Nepal	15	–	–
(ICMS)	18-20	12	25				
(ISS)	2-5	–	–				
Bulgaria	20	9	–	Nicaragua	15	–	–
Burkino Faso	18	–	–	Niger	19	5	–
Cape Verde	15	6	–	Netherlands	21	9	–
Cambodia	10	–	–	New Zealand	15	–	–
Cameroon	19.25	–	–	Nicaragua	15	–	–
Canada Federal (GST)	5	0	–	Nigeria	7.5	–	–
Combined (HST)	13-15	–	–				
Chad	18	–	–	N. Macedonia	18	5	–
Chili	19	–	–	Norway	25	0, 12, 15	–
China	13	6, 9	–	Pakistan	17	–	–
Colombia	19	0, 5	–	Palestinian Terr.	16	–	–
Congo Dem. Rep.	16	–	–	Panama	7	–	10, 15
Congo Rep.	18 (+ 5% surtax = 18.90)	5	–	Papua New Guinea	10	–	–
Costa Rica	13	5, 10	–	Paraguay	10	5	–
Croatia	25	5, 13	–	Peru	18	–	–
Cyprus	19	5, 9	–	Philippines	12	–	–

Country	Standard Rate	Reduced Rate	Increased Rate	Country	Standard Rate	Reduced Rate	Increased Rate
Czech Rep	21	10	–	Poland	23	5, 8	–
Denmark	25	–	–	Portugal	23	6, 13	–
Dominican Rep.	18	13	–	Romania	19	5, 9	–
Ecuador	12	0	–	Russia	20	10	–
Egypt	14	5	–	Rwanda	18	–	–
El Salvador	13	–	–	Saint Lucia	12.5	0, 10	–
Equatorial Guinea	15	0, 6	–	Samoa	15	–	–
Estonia	20	9	–	Saudi Arabia	15	–	–
Ethiopia	15	–	–	Senegal	18	–	–
Fiji	9	–	–	Serbia	20	10	–
Finland	24	10, 14	–	Singapore	7	–	–
France	20	2.1, 5, 10	–	Slovak Rep	20	10	–
Gabon	18	5, 10	–	Slovenia	22	5, 9.5	–
Georgia	18	–	–	South Africa	15	–	–
Germany	19	7	–	Spain	21	4, 10	–
Ghana	12.5	3	–	Sri Lanka	8	–	–
Greece	24	6, 13	–	Sudan	10	–	–
Guatemala	12	–	–	Swaziland	15	–	–
Guinea	14	–	–	Sweden	25	6, 12	–
Guyana	14	0	–	Switzerland	7.7	2.5, 3.7	–
Haiti	10	–	–	Taiwan	5	–	–
Honduras	15	–	18	Tajikistan	18	–	–
Hungary	27	5, 18	–	Tanzania	18	–	–
Iceland	24	11	–	Thailand	10	–	–

Country	Standard Rate	Reduced Rate	Increased Rate	Country	Standard Rate	Reduced Rate	Increased Rate
India	18	0, 5, 12	28	Togo	18	–	–
Indonesia	10	–	–	Trinidad & Tobago	12.5	0	–
Ireland	23	0, 9, 13.5	–	Tunisia	19	7, 13	–
Isle of Man	20	0, 5	–	Turkey	18	1, 8	–
Israel	17	–	–	Turkmenistan	15	–	–
Italy	22	4, 5, 10	–	Uganda	18	–	–
Ivory Coast	18	9	–	Ukraine	20	7	–
Jamaica	15	10	25	United Arab Emirates	5	–	–
Japan	10	8	–	United Kingdom	20	0, 5	–
Jersey	5	–	–	Uruguay	22	10	–
Jordan	16	8	–	Uzbekistan	15	–	–
Kazakhstan	12	–	–	Vanuatu	15	–	–
Kenya	14	0, 8	–	Venezuela**	16	15	5-25
Korea South	10	–	–	Vietnam	10	5	15
Kosovo	18	8	–	Zambia	16	–	–
Kyrgyzstan	12	–	–	Zimbabwe	14.5	–	–

Source: PwC, https://taxsummaries.pwc.com/quick-charts/value-added-tax-vat-rates#:~:text=Combined%20federal%20and%20provincial%2Fterritorial,from%205%25%20to%2015%25.&text=The%20rate%20of%20GST%20varies,rate%20of%20tax%20being%2018%25.

* Rates per July 2020. Temporary rate reduction to combat the economic downturn caused by the COVID-19 pandemic are not taken into account.
** Additional tax on certain purchases in foreign or crypto currency.

In addition to the standard rate, 78 countries apply reduced rates, and 13 countries apply increased rates. Of the countries with increased rates, 9 combine the standard rate with reduced and increased rates, and 4 countries combine a standard rate with 1 or 2 increased rates and apply no reduced rates. Of the countries with reduced rates, 38 countries apply a single reduced rate, while 40 apply 2 or 3 reduced rates. A minority of countries, 70 applies only the standard rate. This indicates potentially different economic prioritizations, but most certainly different outcomes of the political decision-making process (*see* §4.03[A]).

Of the reviewed jurisdictions, only 5 countries in Asia/Pacific apply reduced rates, 14 in Africa/ Middle East, 15 in the Americas/Caribbean, and the remaining 43 are all in Europe. The spread confirms the history of the proliferation of VAT as described in Chapter 1. The multi-rate design is of European origin and logically widely applied there with a following in a number of countries with which Europe has old colonial ties. The small number of countries in Asia seems in line with the geographical origin of the Modern VAT and the dates of introduction of VAT in Asian countries, mostly after the New Zealand VAT was recognized as the preferred model.

§4.03 RATIONALE FOR MULTIPLE RATE STRUCTURE

[A] Political Feasibility Rationale

When VAT is proposed, political leadership needs to ensure that they secure sufficient buy-in from both the general public and the business community, which is charged with collecting the tax. This is true regardless of whether the VAT is the first consumption tax to be levied in a country or is a replacement of an existing consumption tax. A positive public perception of the VAT is essential as demonstrated by the re-call of VAT through a referendum in British Columbia (*see* Chapter 1). Without a high degree of voluntary compliance by the business community, tax collection is illusionary. For these reasons, political decision makers may not be able to avoid granting concessionary treatment to certain industries or certain supplies of goods and services. The introduction of VAT in what is now the EU is a good illustration of this point. European policy makers applied a dual strategy. On the one hand they portrayed the VAT as a continuation of the existing turnover taxes,[1] in that businesses would continue collecting tax on all their sales but, unlike under the turnover tax, they would be allowed to recuperate all tax paid on their procurement—a clear and attractive improvement. On the other hand, they recognized the necessity to replicate, at least to some extent, the variable impact of the multiple rate structure of the turnover tax by conceding to exemptions and a multiple rate system.[2]

1. To the extent that in many official documents VAT is still referred to as a turnover tax and two of the founding member states, the Netherlands and Germany, kept the name "turnover tax" in the title of the Act imposing the VAT (Wet op de omzetbelasting and Umsatzsteuergesetz, respectively).
2. Richard Krever, *Designing and Drafting VAT Laws for Africa*, in *VAT in Africa* 16 (Richard Krever, ed., Pretoria University Law Press, 2008).

David Child hits the nail on its head where he states that taxes are political in nature.

> [Taxes] have to satisfy political needs as well as economic ones and politics tends to complicate where theory would argue for simplicity. It is the nature of politics and electoral considerations (in democracies) for favour the status quo (or the award of further concessions) rather than simplify taxes.[3]

[B] Combating Regressivity

It is generally accepted that VAT is regressive, i.e., that the portion of income used for consumption expenditure declines with rising incomes and, thus, relative to income the effective tax rate would decline as well. In other words, as a percentage of income the tax falls as income rises. A regressive distributional effect is used as an argument against introducing a VAT or other consumption tax or is at best accepted as the price to be paid for the advantage of tax efficiency. The conclusion that VAT is regressive purely on the basis of a declining C/Y ratio as income increases may be premature, or at least paints an incomplete picture. Prima facie there is truth in the assumption. Assume we have Mary with a disposable income of 30,000 monetary units, spending all her money on consumption. With a tax rate of 10%, she will pay 3,000 in tax. Compare Mary to Jane making 100,000 and spending 70,000, saving 30,000, and paying 7,000 in tax. Obviously, Jane pays more tax in absolute terms,[4] but her tax burden relative to income is 7% while Mary's is 10%. Saving remain untaxed because it is not used for consumptive expenditure. The degree of VAT's regressivity has a direct correlation with the saving ratio, i.e., a VAT is regressive to the extent that the saving ratio increases with income.[5] Where *t* is the tax rate, this is demonstrated by the following equation:[6] $\frac{tC}{Y} = t(1 - \frac{S}{Y})$.

Regressivity is generally measured on an annual basis as we have done above, and Mary seems worse off than Jane. However, Mary is at the beginning of her

3. David Child, *VAT Administration: Addressing Private Sector Concerns*, in *VAT in Africa* 129 (Richard Krever, ed., Pretoria University Law Press, 2008).
4. That is generally the case, *see* Ian Crawford et al., *Value Added Tax and Excises*, in *Dimensions of Tax Design: The Mirrlees Review* 275 (James Mirrlees et al., eds., Oxford University Press, 2010).
5. Robert F. van Brederode, *VAT's Regressivity: Empirical Truth or Political Correctness*, 18(2) Int'l VAT Monitor 86 (2007).
6. Since income (Y) is consumed (C) or saved (S), Y = C + S or C = Y – S. The total amount of consumption tax is: tC, which means that tC = t (Y – S). The amount of consumption tax relative to income is $\frac{tC}{Y}$. Consequently, $\frac{tC}{Y} = t\left(\frac{Y}{Y} - \frac{S}{Y}\right) = t\left(1 - \frac{S}{Y}\right)$.

professional endeavors and ten years later she reaches the top of her career, making 150,000, while Jane has retired enjoying her golden years on a fixed income of 50,000. Their positions from the perspective of regressivity have reversed. That observation alone indicates that taking a time capsule (of one year) to assess the incidence of a consumption tax for people who enjoy different incomes during their life is inaccurate and misleading.

VAT appears to be regressive because increase of income allows for increase of saving. Saving, however, is a rational undertaking. People save for the purpose of repair and replacement of durable goods, or to create funding for retirement as Jane uses her saving to complement her social security benefits. In other words, saving is postponed consumption,[7] and saving is taxed not when put in reserve but at the future time when utilized for consumption expenditure. Except for the highest income groups, households generally consume all their saving over lifetime.[8] As a result, and confirmed by a number of studies,[9] for most income groups[10] measured over lifetime the VAT will be more or less proportional in terms of incidence. That is what you would expect if you measure VAT payments as a percentage of expenditure, i.e., consumption, instead of income. In countries that apply a multiple rate structure the VAT may then be slightly progressive but only for the highest disposable income decile,[11] insignificant an effect to justify the economic distortions caused by rate variation. It is generally held that VAT is an inadequate instrument to realize distributional objectives; income tax exemptions and income subsidies are better suited for reaching these purposes, because they can be targeted more effectively at low income groups.[12]

Nevertheless, the perception of regressivity and the higher effective tax rate that lower income groups as a result incur, is one of the reasons policymakers decide to apply rate differentiation as an instrument to combat the regressivity of VAT, sometimes along broader distributional objectives.[13] Generally, this takes the form of introducing additional rates above and below the standard rate. Reduced rates are applied to goods and services for which lower income groups spend a larger portion of

7. Clara K. Sullivan, *The Tax on Value Added* (Columbia University Press, 1965).
8. Franco Modigliani, *The Role of Intergenerational Transfer and Life Cycle Saving in the Accumulation of Wealth*, 2(2) J. Econ. Persp. 15 (1988).
9. For example, Paul Menchik and Martin David, *The Incidence of a Lifetime Consumption Tax*, 35 Nat'l Tax J. 189 (1982); James M. Poterba, *Lifetime Incidence and the Distributional Burden of Excise Taxes*, 79(2) Am. Econ. Rev. 325 (1989); Donald Fullerton and Diane L. Rogers, *Lifetime versus Annual Perspectives on Tax Incidence*, 44 Nat'l Tax J. 277 (1991); Erik Caspersen and Gilbert Metcalf, *Is A Value Added Tax Regressive? Annual versus Lifetime Incidence Measures*, 47(4) Nat'l Tax J. 731 (1994).
10. Except for the so-called one-percenters and the lowest income group without prospect of socio-economic mobility. Both these groups represent an a-typical situation and their respective consumption patterns are of marginal importance at best when assessing the regressivity or even the fairness of VAT, and deciding on general tax policy, *see* Brederode, *supra* n. 5, 92.
11. Because they spend a higher proportion of the expenditure on standard rated goods and services, *see* Francesco Figari and Alari Paulus, *The Impact of Indirect Taxes and Imputed Rent on Inequality: A Comparison with Cash Transfers and Direct Taxes in Five EU Countries*, GINI Discussion Paper No. 28, 29-31 (Amsterdam: AIAS, 2012), available at www.gini-research.org. (accessed on October 5, 2020).
12. Figari and Paulus, *supra* n. 11, 30.
13. Krever, *supra* n. 2, 18-20.

their income, such as basic necessities, and higher rates to luxury items. However, determining which goods and services are predominantly acquired by the relatively poor and which by the better off is not a straightforward exercise, as consumption patterns of high and low-income categories tend to converge and, as a result, the impact of rate variations may be much less than expected. Moreover, rate variation fails to accomplish its goal. Reduced rated commodities are not exclusively procured by lower income groups. Although it is true that they will allocate a larger portion of their income for basic necessities than higher income groups,[14] in absolute terms higher income groups spend more on those goods and services. Also, expenditure on reduced-rated goods and services, measured as a percentage of total expenditure, increases as income increases. The better off benefit sometimes as much and often more from lower rates.[15] For example, a lower rate on public transportation benefits bankers traveling to the City of London as much as commuting local blue-collar workers; a lower rate on utilities benefits most those living in the largest houses; a lower rate on water allows millionaires in the suburbs to fill their swimming pool at preferred rates. Irish research from 1984 shows that in absolute terms the better off spend twice as much on food than lower income groups, because they buy more expensive varieties, more frequently eat out, and more easily throw food away, providing the better off with twice the tax relief accosted to the relatively poor.[16] It is unimaginable that reduced rates are successful in addressing regressivity, were effectively, although unintentionally, they result in large subsidies for the better off. Nonetheless, reduced rates may have some effects on the purchasing power of different household groups, particularly in countries with the highest dispersions in real incomes, and much less in countries with a relatively even income distribution.[17] Measuring the distributive effectiveness of a reduced rate across different income groups is difficult and, as a result, the measure lacks transparency which, in turn, makes it an ineffective tool for restoring equity.[18] The revenue lost on sales of concessionally taxed commodities to the better off is larger than the tax saved by lower income groups. Thus, if the reduced rates would be abolished, the government could use the additional revenue to finance a direct income subsidy to the relatively poor, and still enjoy a positive result for the treasury.[19]

Reduced rates violate the principle of economic neutrality in terms of consumer choices in that final consumers may substitute standard-rated goods and services for those subject to a reduced rate. Since the revenue lost because of these tax concessions can only be offset within the VAT system by increasing the standard rate, exacerbation of the distortion will be the result.

14. Copenhagen Report, *infra*, n. 24, at 73, Table 31, found (for the EU 15 and year 1999) that the household incomes in the bottom 20% range spent 21.3% of their income on food against 11.7% for the highest quintile of income, and 3.1% on utilities against 1.8%.
15. *See* Stuart Adam et al., *A Retrospective Evaluation of Elements of the EU VAT System*, Full Report (Institute for Fiscal Studies, 2011).
16. *Third Report of the Irish Commission on Taxation: Indirect Taxation*, Dublin, June 1984, 71, and Appendix 9.
17. Copenhagen Report, *infra* n. 24, 74.
18. Akama S. Penda and Bande G.M. Tarh, *The Buoyancy of the Value Added Tax on Economic Development: Its Drifts and Challenges in Cameroon*, 7(2) Int'l J. Adv'd Rsrch 80, 92 (2019).
19. Richard Krever, *supra* n. 2, 19.

[C] Merit and Demerit Goods and Services

Even if you underwrite the benchmark position that from an optimal tax position all goods and services at final consumption should be taxed equally,[20] i.e., at the same rate, an exception is generally made for goods and services that produce externalities, which require correction through either Pigouvian[21] subsidies or taxes. A Pigouvian tax serves to redistribute back costs borne by society of adverse side effects created by producers but not included in the market price of the product. For example, environmental pollution caused by the production process, public healthcare costs related to the use of alcohol and tobacco products, deforestation as the result of the use of paper products. Pigouvian levies generally take the form of excise type of taxes, such as the carbon emission tax, or specific taxes on alcoholic beverages and tobacco, plastic and paper shopping bags, plastic straws or drinking cups, etc. The objective of the tax is to ensure that the externalized costs are ultimately borne by the users or consumers of the products. As such, Pigouvian taxes must be equal to the social marginal costs generated by the production for the purpose of realizing a more efficient allocation of resources. This is precisely the problem as governments do simply not have the information to accurately calculate the externality cost and the correct price and output for a particular market. Over or underestimation of the costs means that the redistribution will be inaccurate and, thus, as before the introduction of the Pigouvian tax, the market economy remains unable to reach equilibrium.

The same problems arise when VAT is transformed into a Pigouvian tax by levying an increased rate on certain demerit goods or services. VAT could be the only such tax, or work in tandem with a specific excise tax on that product, but without accurate calculation of the externalized costs the tax will be unable to fulfill its purpose.

A Pigouvian subsidy is appropriate when a good or service, as the result of positive externalities, is under-consumed in the free market. The subsidy should be equal to the marginal external benefit of the good or service. Making selections of goods and services eligible for the status of bearing merit and, as such, rewarded with a reduced VAT rate, renders the risk of being found paternalistic and elitist where policy makers decide which goods should more frequently be enjoyed by the masses. Moreover, in reality, their choices, often for cultural icons such as museums, opera, and ballet, generally benefit the better off more.

[D] Economic Policy

The end of the 19th century gave birth to the idea of using taxation as an instrument of social policy, including redistribution of income and wealth.[22] John Keynes was a

20. Anthony Atkinson and Joseph E. Stiglitz, *The Design of Tax Structure: Direct Versus Indirect Taxation* 6(1-2) J. Pub. Econ. 55 (1976).
21. After Arthur C. Pigou, an English economist and important contributor to externality theory, *see The Economics of Welfare* (Palgrave Macmillan [1920] 2013).
22. Adolph D. Wagner, *Finanzwißenschaft*, Vol. 2 (C.F. Winter, 1880), 288.

dominant influence for using taxation as a tool of economic cyclical policy[23] where economic conditions determine tax revenue and rates. VAT is generally not perceived as an adequate tool for social policy, but rate variation has been used and is still used for realizing non-fiscal purposes. Apart from encouraging or discouraging the consumption and use of merit and demerit goods and services, discussed in the previous section, temporary rate variation can be used to realize economic policy, for example by reducing rates (to increase demand) to counter the effects of an economic downturn or by increasing rates (to lower demand) in times of an overheated economy. Another economic argument for applying reduced rates is the contribution to increased productivity or reduced structural unemployment. Reduced rates are used to lower the cost of services that are commonly substituted by household production (tax free do-it-yourself) or by the informal economy, such as the services of lawn care, gardening, hairdressing, house painting, plumbing, cleaning, food preparation, because they are essentially too expensive to attract sufficient demand. A lower tax rate would lead to a lower consumer price which, in turn, would generate an increase of demand, thus also improve demand for low skill labor and production efficiency in general.[24] To seriously contemplate VAT rate variation, the increased economic efficiency must outweigh the distortionary cost.

Whether rate variation is an effective tool to accomplish these purposes will entirely depend on the degree of forward shifting of the tax burden which, in turn, is linked to the demand elasticity of a good and the substitution effect of a price increase. To the extent a VAT rate change is not passed through, the policy will be ineffective.[25] One would expect that there exists a correlation between forward shifting and the relative size of the tax base to which the rate change applies; the broader the base, the smaller the substitution effect, and the higher the rate of pass through. Empirical studies confirm that reduced rates on in-elastic goods, such as basic foods, produce a consumer demand disproportionate to the reduction: a 1 % rate reduction triggers only an 0.5 % increase of consumption. Increased rates have a stronger and faster response than rate reductions. Rate reductions create a stronger production and employment response for labor-intensive industries compared to capital-intensive industries.[26] The pass through of a rate change will also depend on the intensity of competition in a given market sector. Limited competition will likely result in a less than full forward shifting. Where businesses tend to achieve price maximization, prices set at high monopolistic levels will not be fully adjusted downward in case of a rate reduction; rather prices will be re-optimized to maximize profits.[27] Unless introduced stealthy, temporary rate variations will trigger anticipative consumer response. For example, a temporary rate

23. John Maynard Keynes, *The General Theory of Employment, Interest and Money* (Macmillan, 1936).
24. Copenhagen Report, *Study on Reduced VAT Applied to Goods and Services in the Member States of the European Union* (Copenhagen Economics, 2007), 4.
25. In that case, producers effectively absorb the tax increase, wholly or partially, and accept a lower margin, effectively shifting the tax increase not forward but backward to the labor and capital factors.
26. Copenhagen Report, *supra* n. 24, 9, 10.
27. Copenhagen Report, *supra* n. 24, 10.

reduction will lead to shrinking demand from the date of announcement to the date of effect, followed by strong increase in demand during the period the reduced rate applies due to hoarding behavior by consumers, then followed by a stark decrease in demand after the rate is re-set at its prior level. Several studies show asymmetry in the pass-through of VAT rates changes, i.e., the pass through is larger for rate increases than for rate decreases. The lack of downward price adjustments indicates that VAT rate reductions are not an adequate measure to raise consumer demand.[28]

If consumer choices do not depend on ability to pay, optimal consumption taxation is uniform when a fully non-linear income tax is available.[29] The disincentive effects of achieving optimal distribution of after-tax income are minimized if individual consumption choices are left undistorted.[30] The most efficient VAT system affects consumer choices as little as possible, which depends on the price elasticity of the taxed goods and services. Higher VAT rates could be levied on price inelastic goods and services and lower rates on price elastic goods and services.[31] It is practically infeasible to implement such an efficient VAT because it would require policy makers to estimate the price elasticity of every product and service on the market, and to do so frequently as elasticities change with changes in consumer preferences and the entry of new products and services in the marketplace.[32]

§4.04 PRACTICAL PROBLEMS OF MULTIPLE RATES

Multiple rates lead to classification problems for goods and services on or close to the dividing line of definition (*see* §4.04[A] below), and they may result in a significant increase of the compliance costs for businesses and administrative costs for the government (*see* §4.04[C]). Multiple rates also cause technical problems where goods and/or services, individually subject to different rates, are bundled and sold for a single price (*see* §4.04[B]). If tax concessions in the form of reduced rates cannot be avoided, it is important to minimize the negative impact on the neutrality of the VAT. Krever proposes to cap the concession for utilities, i.e., to apply the reduced rate up to a certain threshold of liters of water or kilowatts of electricity, and apply the standard rate to

28. Youssef Benzarti and Dorian Carloni, *Who Really Benefits from Consumption Tax Cuts? Evidence from a Large VAT Reform in France*, NBER, Working Paper No. 23848 (2017); Youssef Benzarti et al., *What Goes Up May Not Come Down: Asymmetric Incidence of Value-Added Taxes*, Working Paper No. 23849 (NBER 2017, revised 2018); Clement Carbonnier, *Who Pays Sales Taxes? Evidence from French VAT Reforms, 1987–1999*, 91(5-6) J. Pub. Econ. 1219 (2007); Tuomas Kosonen, *More and Cheaper Haircuts After VAT Cut? On the Efficiency and Incidence of Service Sector Consumption Taxes*, 131 J. Pub. Econ. 87 (2015); Ricardo B. Politi, and Enlinson Mattos, *Ad-valorem Tax Incidence and After-Tax Price Adjustments: Evidence from Brazilian Basic Basket Food*, 44(4) Can. J. Econ. 1438 (2011).
29. Atkinson and Stiglitz, *supra* n. 20.
30. Gregory N. Mankiw, Matthew C. Weinzierl, and Danny F. Yagan, *Optimal Taxation in Theory and Practice*, 23(4) J. Econ. Persp. 147, 165 (2009).
31. Based on the insight of Frank P. Ramsey, *A Contribution to the Theory of Taxation*, 37(145) Econ. J. 47 (1927) that to minimize dead weight loss, the tax rate on a good or service should be inversely proportional to its demand elasticity, implying rates to be differentiated across different groups of goods and services of various demand elasticities.
32. Copenhagen Report, *supra* n. 24, 8.

supplies over the threshold.[33] It is a practical approach but limited in its application as it cannot be used for many other goods and services that often receive preferential treatment, such as healthcare, education or food products.

Based on the guidance provided by de CJEU to the national judiciary, this section will demonstrate through a selection of national court cases from Germany, the Netherlands, and the UK,[34] the intricacy of the problems arising from the application of multiple rates as regards classification and composite supplies. They serve as an illustration of the complexity only and it is not the aim of this section to provide a comprehensive treatise of classification and composite supplies for VAT purposes.

[A] Classification

Rate differentiation, especially when applied to products and services within the same broad category, leads to delineation problems. The courts or tax agencies may develop guidelines and criteria for arriving at distinctions that enable classification, but this does not prevent disputes over many remaining borderline cases between taxpayers and tax agencies. In reality, clarifications often just move the definition problems to a narrower concept and the outcome can be quite nuanced as demonstrated by the *Harrier* case.

Harrier is a high-tech digital printing, photo-processing and personalized gift manufacturing company. Customers upload photos at third party retail stores, choose the preferred page layout and format of a so-called photobook to celebrate birthdays, newborn babies, or other special occasions, insert text, and finally order the desired quantity. Initially Harrier accounted for VAT on its supplies, but subsequently it submitted a repayment claim on the basis that it was making supplies of books or booklets which qualified for zero-rating. HMRC rejected the claim on the basis that Harrier was making supplies of photographic services which did not qualify for zero-rating. Harrier appealed. The tribunal allowed the appeal in part. Judge Berner held that "looking at the objective characteristics of the supplies that (Harrier) makes, the principal supply is clearly that of the photobooks themselves, a supply of goods. The services that surround that supply, including the making available of the production process, are ancillary to the supply of the goods. Those supplies are so closely linked that, viewed objectively, they form a single, indivisible supply, and that is, in this case, a supply of goods." On the evidence, most of Harrier's "photobooks" qualified for zero-rating, but two types of "photobook" failed to qualify on the basis that they did not "satisfy the minimum characteristics for the external appearance of a book or booklet," and that their leaves had "the quality and appearance of individual photographic prints, and not pages of a book."[35]

A German company is focused on the marketing and sale of scientific research. To that end, it contracts with authors to include their theses, research papers, or other

33. Krever, *supra* n. 2, 20.
34. I am grateful to Georg Eder, Jeroen Bijl, and Colin Woodward for their assistance with selecting these cases.
35. *Harrier LLC v. Commissioners for HMRC*, [2011] UKFTT 725 (TC).

scientific products into an online catalogue, to digitalize and convert the work into PDF format, and market the work. The work can be purchased either as a book, or as a CD-ROM or PDF file by download. At issue was whether the downloads and CD-ROM versions should share the reduced rate applicable to the printed version of the works. The taxpayer argued that downloading and CD burning is equivalent to classical printing. The medium used to produce the works on should not matter for the application of the reduced rate. The process of burning a CD-ROM is comparable to photocopying and it seemed unreasonable to apply different treatment depending on the medium used to provide the same data. The taxpayer, essentially, relied on an equal treatment argument. Indeed, one could argue that where the same information or date is being provided, the medium used to carry that information should not lead to different tax treatment. However, the court felt bound by the text of the law and the corresponding tariff classification provision of the Combined Nomenclature, which limits the application of the reduced rate to paper products.[36] This case demonstrates the need to regularly update legislative definitions to prevent the disadvantaging of technological innovation and, thus, violation of the neutrality principle of VAT.

Many classification issues arise in the context of health-related services. In a German case the court ruled that the services of a so-called Floating Center, where customers could enjoy the therapeutic and relaxation benefits of a saltwater bath were not subject to the reduced rate because they did not qualify as a medicinal bath. That would only be the case if the bath were administered within the context of medical treatment for the protection of human health and the curation of a disease.[37] Similarly, a salt bath was denied the application of the reduced rate because it did not meet the criteria to be recognized as a medical bath.[38] In a Dutch case the question was raised under which circumstances toothpaste and sun cream could qualify as pharmaceuticals, subject to the reduced rate. Although these products were not registered as pharmaceuticals under the Netherlands pharma products law,[39] the Supreme Court found, with reference to the Netherlands law and EU pharmaceutical directive,[40] that the products met the requirements of a pharmaceutical product both in terms of presentation and of therapeutical effect. This approach is valuable in that it demonstrates how legal certainty can be served by referencing to known quantities in existing laws (*see also* Chapter 6) for the purpose of defining concessionary categories under VAT.

[B] Composite Supplies

A composite supply occurs when two or more goods and/or services that individually are subject to different taxability rules (such as different positive rates, or a positive rate combined with exemption) are sold as a package for a single price. The issue with

36. FG Hamburg, 23 March 2007, 2 K 79/06, Juris.
37. BFH, 28 August 2014, V R 24/13, BFHE 247, 354; BStBl II 2015, 194.
38. Hessisches FG, 16 March 2017, 1 K 1488/15, Juris.
39. Geneesmiddelenwet of 8 Feb. 2007, Stsbl. 20 March 2007.
40. Directive 2001/83/EC of 6 Nov. 2001, OJ L 311/67.

composite supplies is the determination of how it should be taxed. Theoretically, there are three possibilities. One of the elements of the composite supply is dominant, while the others are ancillary, and the VAT treatment of the package follows the treatment of the dominant element. Thus, if the dominant element is standard rated, the whole composite supply will be subject to the standard rate, regardless of the treatment of the individual elements. Alternatively, the bundle could be split into its components and each is taxed according to its own regime. Lastly, the bundled supply could be regarded as a supply sui generis and taxation determined according to its combined characteristics. The guidance from the Court of Justice of the European Union (CJEU) follows this theoretical model.[41] However, it made splitting the composite supply into its elements the main rule[42] with the caveat that a composite supply should not be artificially split.[43] Absorption by the dominant supply was considered an exception, requiring the feasibility of distinguishing between principle supplies and ancillary supplies, where the latter serve to enhance the enjoyment of the principle supply and their acquisition is not a separate aim of the customer.[44] However, a sui generis supply occurs when the bundled supply forms a unitary complex from the economic perspective of the typical customer. The principle of neutrality requires that similar goods and services be treated, and thus rated, the same to avoid economic distortions. Obviously, if a supply is included in a composite supply, it leads to a treatment different from the one that the supply would receive if supplied separately. However, according to the CJEU that does not constitute a violation of the neutrality principle, simply because "a complex supply of services consisting of several elements is not automatically similar to the supply of those elements separately."[45] In other words, fiscal neutrality is not a consideration when determining whether or not a composite supply exist. The CJEU recognizes that the diversity of commercial operations will make it impossible to provide "exhaustive guidance on how to approach the problem correctly in all cases."[46] According to the CJEU "there is no absolute rule for determining the extent of a supply from the point of view of VAT, and consequently, to determine the extent of a supply, all the circumstances must be taken into consideration."[47] In other words, a single fact by itself cannot be taken as decisive; rather, the complex of all facts and circumstances in their interrelationship should be the basis for determining whether a single supply of multiple supplies is rendered. Therefore, it will not come as a surprise that court rulings are driven by the facts and may seem not always to be consistent. In *BGZ* the CJEU

41. *See*, e.g., CJEU, 25 February 1999, Case C-349/96, *Card Protection Plan Ltd v. Commissioners of Customs & Excise* ECLI:EU:C:1999:93, and CJEU 22 October 1998, Joined Cases C-308/96 and C-94/97, *Commissioners of Customs & Excise v. T.P. Madgett, R.M. Baldwin and The Howden Court Hotel*, ECLI:EU:C:1998:496.
42. *Card Protection Plan*, *supra*, paragraph 29.
43. CJEU, 27 October 2005, Case C-41/04, *Levob Verzekeringen BV and OV Bank NV v. Staatssecretaris van Financiën*, ECLI:EU:C:2005:649, paragraph 22.
44. *Card Protection Plan*, *supra*, n. 35, paragraph 30; and *Madgett & Baldwin*, *supra* n. 41, paragraph 24.
45. CJEU, 19 January 2012, Case C-117/11, *Purple Parking Ltd and Airparks Services Ltd v. Commissioners for Her Majesty's Revenue & Customs*, ECLI:EU:C:2012:29, paragraph 39.
46. *Card Protection Plan*, *supra*, n. 35, paragraph 27.
47. CJEU, 27 September 2012, Case C-392/11, *Field Fisher Waterhouse LLP v. Commissioners for Her Majesty's Revenue and Customs*, ECLI:EU:C:2012:597, paragraph 19.

made clear that the existence of a relation between two supplies not automatically means that one supply is ancillary to the other. In the particular case, lessees of moveable property were offered insurance of the property through the lessor. The CJEU held "*Although such insurance supplied to the lessee through the lessor facilitates the enjoyment of the leasing service ..., it must be held that constitutes essentially an end in itself for the lessee and not only the means to enjoy that service under the best conditions.*"[48] The lessees were not obligated to take insurance through the lessor and remained free to obtain insurance from another supplier, which indicated that splitting the supplies was feasible. Moreover, the decision to obtain the insurance through the lessor was made independently of the decision to lease the property. This element was important in the following British case.

An UK association of trial lawyers (barristers) leased out office space (the Inn) to its members which was subject to the standard rate of VAT.[49] The association also owned a network of underground pipes through which cold water was supplied to the building by a local water company. The building had a single meter, the offices did not have separate meters. The water company charged the association for the supply of water. In turn, the association charged the individual renters on the basis of the size of the rented space. The supply of cold water was zero rated. The issue arose whether the association made a single supply of the leasing of immovable property, which incorporated the provision of cold water, or two independent supplies of property and water. The appeals court reasoned: "*We acknowledge that the two elements supplied by the Middle Temple to the tenants may be provided separately in other circumstances. A tenant of a landlord ... outside the Inn may obtain a supply of water directly from the water company. However, the tenants of premises in the Inn have no choice but to obtain water from the Middle Temple. As both accommodation and water are essential if they are to occupy and use the premises, the tenants must be assumed to require a combination of those two elements if the premises are to fulfil their economic purpose. We consider that the leasing of the premises and the supply of the water to those premises under the lease form a single economic supply which it would be artificial to split because, from the point of view of the typical tenant, both the premises and the water are equally indispensable and inseparable. It cannot be disputed that the right to occupy the premises is an indispensable part of the supply to the tenants.*"[50]

British Telecom purchased new cars directly from the manufacturers. The contracts were for sale and delivery of the cars, and ownership of a car passed only on or after delivery. An identifiable separate charge was made for delivery of the cars. The input VAT on the purchase of cars was excluded under UK law, but the tax agency also denied the deduction of the input VAT on the delivery charges. At issue was whether the delivery services qualified as a separate service, in which case input VAT recovery would be allowed, or whether the delivery was an integral part of the supply of the car,

48. CJEU, 17 January 2013, Case C-224/11, *BGZ Leasing sp. z o.o. v. Dyrektor Izby Skarbowej w Warszawie*, ECLI:EU:C:2013:15, paragraph 42.
49. The lessor made use of the option to tax the real estate lease under Schedule 10, paragraph 2, of the VAT Act 1994.
50. *Revenue and Customs Commissioners v. The Honourable Society of Middle Temple*, [2013] UKUT 0250 (TCC), paragraph 69.

and the related input VAT therewith banned from recovery. The final court considered that it was artificial to split the various parts of the transaction into different supplies for VAT purposes, because what British Telecom wanted was a delivered car. Therefore, the delivery was incidental or ancillary to the supply of the car and it was only on or after delivery that property in the car passed. Accordingly, if the transaction was looked at as a matter of commercial reality, there was one contract for a delivered car and one supply for VAT purposes. BT was not therefore entitled to deduct input tax on the delivery charges.[51]

A German hotel and restaurant provide lodging services with breakfast and calculates VAT at the reduced rate over the total consideration received under the assumption that the supply of breakfast is absorbed by the supply of lodging services. The court rejects this, arguing that breakfast services are a distinct supply, which forms an end in itself for the customer and does not solely serve to optimize the enjoyment of the lodging service. Thus, they are subject to the standard rate.[52]

A German publisher sells a computer magazine with a CD-ROM. The title page of the magazine refers to the CD-ROM, which was dedicated to the content of the magazine. The court concludes to a single supply, subject to the reduced rate as the supply of the magazine is the dominant component.[53]

It seems logical to assume that all elements of a composite supply would follow the same rate regime applicable to the dominant supply. However, in *Commission v. France* (Undertakers)[54] and in *Talacre Beach*[55] the CJEU seems to have left the door open to the possibility that a single supply can be taxed at two separate rates, in particular when one element can still be separated as a concrete and specific element on the condition that the dual rate application does not negatively influence the proper functioning of the VAT system. The *Card Protection Plan* criteria serve to establishing the nature of transactions for the purpose of determining whether there exists only a single, composite supply or multiple independent supplies. *Commission v. France* concerns whether and, if so, to what extent a member state is allowed to identify elements within a composite supply and treat them as falling within or without the scope of a reduced rate. The issue of applying dual rates to elements of a single supply was raised in, e.g., *Colaingrove*.[56] Colaingrove provided serviced chalets and static caravans at holiday parks. In respect of certain promotional supplies, a fixed charge was made for electricity, which was collected separately from the customer at the time when the customer made the reservation. Although electricity supplied to the static caravans and chalets was metered, to save the burden and expense of separate metered charges, Colaingrove simply charged a fixed daily fee for electricity. There was no

51. House of Lords, 1 July 1999, *Customs and Excise Commissioners v. British Telecommunications plc*, [1999] STC 758.
52. BFH, 24 April 2013, XI R 3/11, BFHE 242, 410, BStBl II 2014, 86.
53. FG Hamburg, 30 June 2005, VI 323/03, juris., and FG München, 30 January 2003, 14 K 3152/00, juris.
54. CJEU, 8 May 2003, Case C-384/01, *Commission v. France*, ECLI:EU:C:2003:264.
55. CJEU, 6 July 2006, Case C-251/05, *Talacre Beach Caravan Sales Ltd v. Customs and Excise Commissioners*, ECLI:EU:C:2006:451.
56. *Revenue and Customs Commissioners v. Colaingrove Ltd.*, [2015] UKUT 80 (TCC).

correlation between the fixed fee and the actual consumption of electricity by the customer. On appeal there was no dispute that Colaingrove made a single supply. The remaining dispute was whether the supply of electricity should be taxed at a reduced rate, notwithstanding that the charge for electricity is an element of a single composite supply of serviced accommodation, which as such is taxed at the standard rate. In other words, if the national legislator has specified a reduced rate for an independent supply, should that reduced rate also be applied if the supply is a relevant element of the composite supply? Otherwise, Colaingrove reasoned, a metered supply of electricity within the context of a wider supply of services accommodation would be treated differently from an unmeasured supply of electricity rendered within the same context. For the court, the answer depended on whether the literal text of the law provides room for such an extension and on the legislative intent of Parliament, neither of which supported Colaingrove's position.

In a Dutch case, Stadion Amsterdam owns a multi-purpose facility consisting mainly of a football stadium and a museum of the local, professional football club, AFC Ajax. The stadium is leased out to the football club for sports competitions and incidentally to others for music concerts. When no such events take place, Stadion Amsterdam organizes guided tours of the stadium, included unguided access to the museum. It is not in dispute that the tours and the museum visit constitute a single supply. Stadion Amsterdam takes the position that the consideration should be split, with application of the standard to the part received for the tour, and application of the reduced rate to the part of the consideration received for access to the museum. The CJEU first explains the limited scope of the *Talacre Beach* and *Commission v. France* cases and makes clear that from the latter case "*no conclusion can be drawn …regarding any possibility of applying a separate rate of VAT to separate elements of a single supply.*"[57] Thus, removing any doubt as to the specific scope of the case. As to Stadion Amsterdam, the CJEU advises "*a single supply, such as that at issue in the main proceedings, comprised of two distinct elements, one principal, the other ancillary, which, if they were supplied separately, would be subject to different rates of VAT, must be taxed solely at the rate of VAT applicable to that single supply, that rate being determined according to the principal element, even if the price of each element forming the full price paid by a consumer in order to be able to receive that supply can be identified.*"[58]

[C] Compliance and Administrative Costs

Obviously, the simpler the tax system, the less effort it takes for businesses to comply with the provisions of the law and the lower the associate costs. A simpler tax will also lead to comparatively lower cost for tax agencies to administer the tax and monitor and audit taxpayer compliance. Exemptions and multiple rates lead to an increase in both

57. CJEU, 18 January 2018, Case C 463/16, *Stadion Amsterdam C.V. v. Staatssecretaris van Financiën*, ECLI:EU:C:2018:22, paragraph 31.
58. *Supra*, paragraph 36.

compliance and administration costs, especially in relation to industry sectors characterized by a multitude of products, such as the food industry. Sections 4.04[A] and [B] above illustrate with concrete examples the technical complexities caused by multiple rates and any conflict between tax agency and taxpayer triggers additional costs of legal counsel and regularly litigation. Multiple rates require businesses to keep records of sales and purchases based on the applicable VAT rate. If we take a VAT with a single rate, a zero rate for exports, and minimal exemptions, a business must keep track of the total value of domestic sales, the total value of exports, the total value of exempt sales (if applicable), the total value of domestic purchases, the total value of purchases used for making exempt sales (non-deductible input-VAT) and the total value of imported goods. Each additional rate would require two additional recordings, one on the input and one on the output side. Multiple rates also complicate the application by the taxpayer of self-supply, reverse charge, and postponed accounting rules. Auditing becomes more complex and time consuming as well with multiple rates because more records need to be checked, and product classification for rate application must be assessed on correctness.

The costs associated with taxation are threefold: the tax itself, the deadweight losses caused by tax-induced market distortions, and the operating costs, divided in administrative costs for government and compliance cost for businesses. Generally, more complex VAT legislation triggers both higher administrative and compliance costs, but their burden does not move in tandem and may differ depending on economic sector, rate structure, thresholds, etc. In a literature overview study, it was concluded that VAT compliance costs are high and significant, they are regressive, and do not fall over time.[59] A detailed study into the compliance cost of VAT is beyond the scope of this chapter, but Chapter 6 of this volume provides a more substantive analysis of these costs. However, the compliance costs associated with a multiple rate VAT system is particularly regressive as smaller businesses lack economies of scale and must spread the cost over fewer sales than larger enterprises, and generally are unable to apply automated inventory and sales tracking systems. It is clear that a multi-rate system creates higher compliance and administration costs than a single rate VAT system.

§4.05 RATIONALE FOR A SINGLE RATE STRUCTURE

The rationale for a single rate VAT system is rather straightforward. It is relatively simple and avoids the technical problems of classification and composite supplies. Thus, it also avoids the deadweight losses associated with the additional cost of compliance and conflict resolution. Moreover, a single rate preserves the economic neutrality of VAT as it does not distort consumer choices and the allocation of factor inputs.

59. Luca Barbone et al., *The Costs of VAT: A Review of the Literature*, Working Paper 12 (International Center for Public Policy, 2012), 18.

Apart from the strength of the arguments supporting a single rate, the rationale for a multiple rate structure is not convincing. VAT is not regressive and as a tool for income redistribution or to realize other economic objectives it is ineffective. In terms of efficiency it costs less using income taxes to redistribute income.[60]

§4.06 CONCLUSIONS

A single rate VAT system is obviously simpler than a multi-rate system and, therefore, the associated compliance costs for the business sector and administration costs for tax agencies will be lower. The deadweight loss caused by disputes over classification and rate application for composite supplies do not occur under a single rate VAT. Applying a single rate blocks the use of VAT for socio-economic purposes but, as we discussed in §4.03[C], VAT is not the appropriate vehicle to accomplish these goals. As we suggested that VAT is a proportional rather than a regressive tax, rate variation for the purpose of countering such regressivity logically has lost its rationale. If merit goods and services indeed need a financial incentive to boost sales, a direct price subsidy is as effective, more transparent, and easier to administer. Discouraging the purchase of demerit goods and services can be realized through a targeted excise tax. That leaves political feasibility as a reason for rate variation, i.e., the need to create facilities for certain stake holders whose support is indispensable for the successful introduction of a VAT, or to accommodate public objections. This situation may more likely occur when VAT replaces another consumption tax that already included preferential treatment of certain industry sectors (as was the case in Europe), but will less likely arise or to a lesser degree in countries where a preexisting consumption tax is absent. Nevertheless, pressure from special interest groups seeking preferential treatment and the need to cope with a negative perception of public opinion on certain aspects of the proposed tax may still require a degree of accommodation in order to get the law passed. As the Japanese experiment demonstrates (*see* Chapter 21), political pressure may even end a successful single rate consumption tax system.

60. Gregory N. Mankiw et al., *supra*, n. 30, 166.

CHAPTER 5

Exemptions in VAT: A Theoretical Overview of Traditional and Modern VAT Systems

Christian Knotzer & Sebastian Pfeiffer

§5.01 GENERAL CONSIDERATIONS

[A] Exemptions: A Fallacy of VAT

The purpose of a VAT is to impose a broad-based tax on final consumption.[1] Therefore, the tax should be neutral for businesses supplying goods and services, and should ultimately be borne by final consumers. In the fractioned collection process—which is a core design feature of a VAT system and differentiates it from a single-stage tax[2]—neutrality is (usually) achieved by applying the invoice-credit method.[3] The business is able to credit input VAT, paid on procurements, against output VAT, which is invoiced to the customer. Only the (final) consumer has no possibility to claim an input tax credit. Consequently, even though the tax is collected and remitted by

1. OECD, *International VAT/GST guidelines* (OECD Publishing, 2017), m.no. 1.2. In the EU VAT Directive (2006/112/EC) this principle is stipulated in Article 1 (2): "The principle of the common system of VAT entails the application to goods and services of a general tax on consumption exactly proportional to the price of the goods and services, however many transactions take place in the production and distribution process before the stage at which the tax is charged."
2. For example, Retail Sales Tax (RST). *See* Ben Terra, *Sales Taxation: The Case of Value Added Tax in the European Community* 21 et seq. (Kluwer Law Int., 1988).
3. As compared to the subtraction method. *See* OECD, *supra* n. 1, m.no. 1.6, and Robert F. van Brederode, *Systems of General Sales Taxation: Theory, Policy and Practice* (Kluwer Law Int., 2009), 99 et seq.

economic operators, it is intended that only final consumers bear the burden of the VAT.[4]

This book is a treatise on the virtues and fallacies of the VAT. Exemptions[5] clearly must be assigned to the latter category. There is widespread consensus in academic literature that exemptions should be avoided in a VAT system as they represent a significant and fundamental design imperfection of VAT systems, detrimental to both the efficiency and neutrality of a VAT and violating its logic and functionality.[6] In his opinion regarding the *Kingscrest* case, Advocate General Colomer described exemptions as "the original sin of Community VAT."[7] In the European Union VAT, at least, it is also apparent that exemptions are an ever-recurring issue in case law and are regularly scrutinized by European institutions.[8]

The approach to exemptions is far from uniform among global VAT systems. Whereas the EU VAT, commonly referred to as the traditional VAT system, contains a high number of exemptions, modern VAT systems (e.g., the VAT of New Zealand)[9] provide for only few.[10] This chapter first provides a general overview of exemptions and their consequences in VAT systems, and then discusses the similarities and differences of those varying approaches to VAT exemptions.

[B] How Do Exemptions in VAT Work?

In Black's Law Dictionary, the term "exemption" is defined as the "[f]reedom from a duty, liability or other requirement."[11] VAT exemptions do not fulfill this definition. Under VAT, an exemption means that the supplier does not have to charge VAT on the exempt supply but is precluded from deducting the VAT incurred on purchases related to the exempt supply. In other words, exempt supplies are taxed on their inputs.[12]

---

4. Joachim Englisch, *The EU Perspective on VAT Exemptions* in *VAT Exemptions: Consequences and Design Alternatives*, 37, 39 (Rita de La Feria. ed., Wolters Kluwer, 2013).
5. Exemptions may have very different backgrounds and policy objectives. One can distinguish between exemptions designed to ensure the proper functioning of the destination principle in international transactions (e.g., exemption for exports) and exemptions that serve other objectives (e.g., exemptions for activities in the public interest). This contribution focuses only on the latter category.
6. *See*, e.g., Rita de La Feria and Richard Krever, *Ending VAT Exemptions: Towards a Post-Modern VAT*, in *VAT Exemptions: Consequences and Design Alternatives* 3, 4 (Rita de La Feria. ed., Wolters Kluwer, 2013); Sijbren Cnossen, *Is the VAT's Sixth Directive Becoming an Anachronism?* 43(12) Bul. Int'l Fisc. Doc. 434 (2003); Veronique Lenoir, *April 1954 – April 2004 VAT Exemptions: The Original Misunderstanding*, 44(10) Eur. Tax'n 456, 459 (2004).
7. Opinion of AG Colomer, CJEU, 26 May 2005, Case C-498/03, *Kingscrest*, section V.A. ECLI: EU:C:2005:322.
8. Most recently in its Action plan for fair and simple taxation (COM (2020) 312 final) the European Commission envisages to amend the "outdated provisions" for the exemptions of financial services in the VAT Directive.
9. For a close analysis, *see* the contribution of White in this book.
10. Most non-EU countries follow the modern approach (e.g., Canada, South Africa, Singapore or Australia; *see* van Brederode, *supra* n. 3, 8). Few of those, however, are as strict with exemptions as the VAT system in New Zealand (*see* De la Feria and Krever, *supra* n. 6, 10 et seq.).
11. Bryan A. Garner, *Black's Law Dictionary* 717 (2019).
12. *See* van Brederode, *supra* n. 3, 127; Ian Crawford et al., *Value Added Tax and Excises*, in *Dimensions of Tax Design: The Mirrlees Review* 275, 292 (James Mirrlees et al., eds., Oxford

Thus, the exemption "breaks the chain of credit and refund, leading to an element of production taxation."[13] The input tax becomes a cost factor for the business, which likely leads to tax cascading.[14] This violates the general purpose of a VAT, being a tax on final consumption that should be neutral amongst businesses. There are no systematic but only fiscal reasons for the refusal of the input tax credit.[15] Only if the output is tax exempt and the business is eligible for an input tax credit, is the transaction truly free of VAT.[16] Such exemptions with deduction are commonly referred to as "zero-rating."[17] They are usually (only) applied for cross-border transactions, to ensure compatibility with the destination principle.

The term exemption in VAT is not devoid of irony. For businesses, exempt supplies lead to burdens of unrecoverable input VAT and therefore to costs. In contrast, supplies subject to VAT trigger the right to deduct input VAT, thus providing the supplier with full tax relief and reducing the VAT to accounting entries. To put it short and aptly: Businesses subject to VAT are exempt; and exempted businesses are actually subject to VAT.[18]

[C] Classifications of VAT Exemptions

The use of exemptions in VAT systems is widespread and diverse.[19] For a precise classification and analysis of the respective exemptions, a detailed knowledge of domestic and possibly transnational VAT (case) law is necessary. Nevertheless, in general, exemptions can be classified using two differing systems: One the one hand

University Press, 2010). The effects of the tax exemption are therefore very similar to the situation when a transaction or business does not fall within the scope of the VAT system at all (out-of-scope supplies or out-of-scope suppliers; *see* De la Feria and Krever, *supra* n. 6, 12 et seq., and Holger Stadie, *Befreiungen und Ermäßigungen - Chaos, System oder Konglomerat?* in *Umsatzsteuer im Europäischen Binnenmarkt* 143, 146 (Roman Seer, ed., Schmidt, 2009)).

13. Crawford et al., *supra* n. 12, 305.
14. Aptly, some countries (e.g., Portugal and Brazil) use the term "input taxed supplies" instead of exemption (*see* OECD, *Consumption Tax Trends: VAT/GST and Excise Rates, Trends and Policy Issues* (OECD Publishing, 2020), 84, and Rita de La Feria and Herman van Kesteren, *Introduction to This Special Issue – VAT Exemptions: Consequences and Design Alternatives*, 22(5) Int'l VAT Monitor 300 (2011)). In Austria, although the law does not include this term, these transactions are referred to as false or fake exemptions.
15. Hans G. Ruppe, *System und Rechtfertigung unechter Steuerbefreiungen*, in *Unechte Steuerbefreiungen*, 23, 27 (Markus Achatz and Michael Tumpel, eds., Linde Verlag, 2010); Marianna Steurer, *VAT and Direct Tax Policy on Exemptions*, in *Global Trends in VAT/GST and Direct Taxes* 89, 95 et seq. (Sebastian Pfeiffer & Marlies Ursprung-Steindl, eds., Linde Verlag, 2015)
16. OECD, *supra* n. 1, m.no. 1.9.
17. However, although this term is also quite inaccurate, as an exemption has to be distinguished from the tax rate that would be applicable, were the transaction not exempt. However, the effects are identical. As zero-rating is the term commonly used to describe an exemption with the right to deduct input VAT, we will use the term accordingly in this chapter. For exemptions without the right to deduct input VAT, the term exemption is used.
18. *See* De la Feria & van Kesteren, *supra* n. 14, 300; De la Feria & Krever, *supra* n. 6, 11; van Brederode, *supra* n. 3, 127; and earlier J. Reugebrink, *The Sixth Directive for the Harmonisation of the Value Added Tax*, 15(3) C. M.t L. Rev. 309, 317 (1978), who refers to this effect as the VAT paradox.
19. For an overview of exemptions used in VAT systems of OECD countries, *see* OECD, *supra* n. 14, 79 et seq.

VAT exemptions can be divided into exemptions for goods and services in the public interest and technical exemptions. [20] On the other hand, exemptions can be classified as being either subjective or objective in nature.

Exemptions in the public interest are usually justified by the political objective to either reduce or mitigate VAT's regressivity, or to subsidize positive externalities.[21] Typical examples include exemptions for hospital and medical care, charitable work, or education. The justification for technical exemptions is based on the perceived difficulty to tax certain transactions, in particular the inability to accurately determine the tax base. Examples of such transactions are financial services, the use, letting and transfer of immovable property, and gambling and betting services.[22] The objective/subjective distinction separates exemptions for a specific transaction (objective exemption) from those targeting a specific taxpayer (subjective exemption).[23] The exemption for small enterprises is the most prominent example of a subjective exemption.[24] The rationale of the exemption for small enterprises, in general, is that the administrative and compliance costs associated with the registration of such taxpayers preclude their inclusion in a VAT system.[25] Occasionally, mixed forms can be observed as well (e.g., medical care services are exempt when provided by professionals).[26] Objective exemptions are generally preferable over subjective exemptions. Subjective exemptions that are too far-reaching inevitably represent a distortion of competition and (further) violate the neutrality of a VAT.[27]

20. However, historically exemptions in EU VAT were not based on clear policy considerations but served to satisfy stakeholders who benefitted from exemptions under the previous turnover tax systems (*see* De la Feria & Krever, *supra* n. 6, 22; and De la Feria & van Kesteren, *supra* n. 14, 300). The history of the exemptions of the EU VAT Directive will be analysed in § 5.02[B][2] of this contribution.
21. De la Feria & Krever, *supra* n. 6, 22 et seq.
22. De la Feria & Krever, *supra* n. 6, 25.
23. *See* Ruppe, *supra* n. 15, 30; Steurer, *supra* n. 15, 98; Herman van Kesteren and Mandy Gabriël, *Value Added Tax Exemptions in Europe: Recent Developments,* in *The Future of Indirect Taxation—Recent Trends in VAT and GST Systems Around the World* 607, 608 et seq. (Thomas Ecker et al:, eds., Wolters Kluwer, 2011).
24. *See* Englisch, *supra* n. 4, 42. In that context is has to be noted, that in some VAT systems small enterprises are not in the scope of the VAT system at all because they fall below a certain registration threshold. However, the VAT treatment of such out-of-scope suppliers are to a great extent identical (exempted output, taxed input). Another example would be public bodies that are sometimes deemed to be outside the scope of the VAT system. Other examples of subjective exemptions include exemptions for blind persons (this exemption is applied by Austria and Germany, for example, *see* Ingrid Rattinger, *§ 6,* in *Umsatzsteuergesetz – Kommentar,* 2. Auflage (Stefan Melhardt and Michael Tumpel, eds., Linde Verlag, 2015), m.no. 382 et seq.) or members of supervisory boards (*see* Hans G. Ruppe, *"Unechte" Umsatzsteuerbefreiungen* in *Die Steuerrechtsordnung in der Diskussion: Festschrift für Klaus Tipke zum 70. Geburtstag* 457, 468 et seq. (Joachim Lang and Klaus Tipke eds., Schmidt, 1995)).
25. Liam P. Ebrill et al., *The Modern VAT* (International Monetary Fund, 2001).
26. Ad van Doesum et al., *Fundamentals of EU VAT law* (Kluwer Law International, 2020), at 307 and 314, Englisch, *supra* n. 4, 40 et seq.
27. *See* van Doesum et al., *supra* n. 26, 307; Ruppe, *supra* n. 15, 30.

[D] The Rationale and Economic Effects of VAT Exemptions

In fact, there are only few arguments in favor of exemptions in a VAT system:

- Exemptions serve to *alleviate the regressivity* of a VAT.[28] VAT is perceived to be regressive in that low-income earners pay a higher percentage of their disposable income in tax than higher income groups on consumption expenditure. In other words, the more a person earns, the less, relatively, s/he is burdened by the VAT. However, the goal of mitigating regressivity can only be reached roughly through VAT exemptions,[29] as it is impossible to align exemptions precisely with the consumption patterns of low-income groups.[30] Income taxes are much better equipped to take differences in income into consideration.[31]
- Exemptions *reduce the price* of certain necessities, or of goods and services of public interest, and thus incentivize their consumption.[32]
- Exemptions are often intended to *avoid the technical difficulties* of applying the VAT (e.g., determination of the tax base for certain financial services).[33]
- For tax administrations, exemptions may be a *less costly and more convenient alternative to reduced rates* and avoid the difficulties associated with refunding the input tax.[34]
- Lastly, exemptions can simply function as a means to *create VAT revenue*.[35]

The distortive effects of VAT exemptions outnumber their benefits by far. The denial of input tax credit leads to the taxation of business procurement, rather than of private consumption. This violates the main purpose of the tax.[36] In further consequence, exemptions may also violate the destination principle, because the non-deductible input VAT (hidden/embedded tax, *see* below) incurred at a stage in the supply chain before exportation has become part of the cost price of a product and cannot be refunded upon exportation.[37] Thus, taxation takes place in the state of origin. Recent global developments, such as intensified competition between public and

28. van Brederode, *supra* n. 3, p. 127; De la Feria & van Kesteren, *supra* n. 14, 300.
29. Ruppe, *supra* n. 15, 31.
30. Cnossen, *supra* n. 6, 438.
31. Sijbren Cnossen, *What Rate Structure for a Value-Added Tax?* 35 Nat'l Tax J. 205, 209 (1982).
32. van Brederode, *supra* n. 3, p. 127; De la Feria & van Kesteren, *supra* n. 14, 300.
33. van Brederode, *supra* n. 3, p. 127; Ebrill et al., *supra* n. 25, 90.
34. Ebrill et al., *supra* n. 25, 91.
35. *See* the Austrian restrictions of the option for taxation with regard to renting out immovable property (1. Stabilitätsgesetz 2012, RB EB 1680), justified as "relief of the public budget." Indeed, enlarging the scope of an exemption can lead to additional VAT revenue (as it further limits input tax credits), especially where the exemption applies to transactions between taxable entities in an industry that cannot avoid making these purchases, e.g., the construction businesses.
36. OECD, *supra* n. 14, 44.
37. Ebrill et al., *supra* n. 25, 88.

private suppliers, the continuous progress and adoption of e-commerce, and outsourcing, have increased the significance of distortions caused by VAT exemptions.[38] The distortive effects are listed below:

- If the exemption is applied at a stage in the supply chain prior to the retail stage sale (B2C), tax *cascading* occurs[39] which, ironically, VAT systems are supposed to avoid. As an exempt business cannot deduct input VAT, the tax represents a cost to the business, which will likely, depending on demand elasticities, be shifted forward in the price and eventually passed on to the final customer. This *hidden* or *embedded* VAT cannot be deducted by the (non-exempt) business customer, although, in general, this business would be allowed to an input VAT credit.[40] If the exemption is applied at an intermediate stage (B2B), it leads to an effective tax rate paid by the final consumer, which is higher than the statutory tax rate.[41] If the exemption is applied at the retail stage, the VAT revenue actually decreases because the value added, the margin, of the retailer escapes taxation.[42] As a result, the retail stage exemption translates into a lower effective tax rate for the consumer.
- As the input VAT is not creditable for the exempt businesses, exemptions create incentives for *vertical integration* and create a bias for *insourcing* over outsourcing activities.[43] As a result, economic inefficiencies arise.[44] This already was a problem with the turnover tax systems, that the VAT was intended to replace.[45] However, in some cases, insourcing may not be economically feasible because of economies-of-scale, or the specialized nature of the goods or services. Therefore, activities that require less specialization are more susceptible to insourcing (e.g., providing security services in-house rather than to commission a specialized firm).[46]
- Exemptions *distort input choices*. On the one hand, they are distortive because exempt businesses have an incentive to acquire inputs with a lower or no VAT burden. Consequently, exempt businesses may be inclined to lobby for further sectors to be subject to exemptions (*exemption creep*),[47] in an effort to remove

38. De la Feria & van Kesteren, *supra* n. 14, 301.
39. van Doesum et al., *supra* n. 26, 306; Christian Amand, *Treaty of Lisbon and B2B VAT Exemptions*, 23(4) Int'l VAT Monitor 242, 246 (2012). For illustrative numerical examples of the cascading effect, *see* van Brederode, *supra* n. 3, 129.
40. *See* van Doesum et al., *supra* n. 26, 306 et seq.; Lenoir, *supra* n. 6, 458; OECD, *supra* n. 15, 44 et seq.
41. Wolfgang Berger et al., *Titel IX: Steuerbefreiungen* in *Kommentar zur Mehrwertsteuer – Mehrwertsteuersystemrichtlinie* (Thomas Ecker et al., eds., LexisNexis), m.no. 1.
42. Ebrill et al., *supra* n. 25, 85.
43. Englisch, *supra* n. 4, 48.
44. OECD, *supra* n. 15, 45; van Brederode, *supra* n. 3, 130; Lenoir, *supra* n. 6, 458; Crawford et al., *supra* n. 12, 305; Donato Raponi & Arthur Kerrigan, *Introduction: The Growth in VAT Cases*, in Michael Lang et al., eds., *ECJ: Recent Developments in Value Added Tax* 1, 7 (Linde Verlag, 2014).
45. Cnossen, *supra* n. 6, 434. To counteract such incentives, some VAT systems deem a fictitious (self-)supply, *see* van Brederode, *supra* n. 3, 131 et seq.
46. Ebrill et al., *supra* n. 25, 86 et seq.
47. OECD, *supra* n. 14, 45.

(otherwise non-deductible) VAT charges at previous stages.[48] On the other hand, exempt businesses have a competitive disadvantage insofar the input choices of their (business) customers are distorted by the hidden VAT embedded in their sales price, which may create a bias for purchasing from taxable suppliers.[49]

- Exemptions lead to *issues of classification and delimitation*. It is not always an easy task for taxpayers or administrations to determine whether a transaction or a taxpayer falls within the scope of a given exemption or not, leading to an increase in compliance and administrative costs.[50] An ever-increasing number of exemption-related EU VAT cases referred to the Court of Justice of the EU bears witness to these issues.[51]
- Likewise, for businesses making both taxable and exempt supplies, the *allocation of input VAT* to exempt (not deductible) and taxable (deductible) transactions can be complex and might lead to higher administrative and compliance costs.[52] Furthermore, the complex allocation also creates an incentive to only produce and supply taxable goods and services.[53]
- Considering the abovementioned negative effects of VAT exemptions, states commonly implement additional provisions in order to eliminate or alleviate those effects.[54] However, such countermeasures often add to the complexity of the VAT system in question and thus lead to further uncertainties and disputes.[55]
- Furthermore, due to these distortive effects, exemptions are sometimes exploited for tax planning purposes.[56] They create incentives for tax avoidance or

48. For example, in some countries the exemption for basic foods has led to increased pressure to exempt agricultural inputs (*see* Ebrill et al., *supra* n. 25, 89).
49. Ebrill et al., *supra* n. 25, 86.
50. van Brederode, *supra* n. 3, 132; OECD, *supra* n. 14, 45.
51. De la Feria & Krever, *supra* n. 6, 24; Amand, *supra* n. 39, 246. Recent examples include CJEU, 25 March 2021, Case C-907/19, *Q-GmbH*, ECLI:EU:C:2021:237, CJEU, 10 December 2020, Case C-488/18, *Golfclub Schloss Igling*, ECLI:EU:C:2020:1013, CJEU, 2 July 2020, Case C-231/19, *BlackRock Investment Management*, ECLI:EU:C:2020:513 and CJEU, 18 September 2019, Case C-700/17, *Wolf-Henning Peters*, ECLI:EU:C:2019:753.
52. *See* Lenoir, *supra* n. 6, 458 and Crawford et al., *supra* n. 12, 305. Such higher administrative costs are borne both by the business as well as the tax administration, as in audit procedures, the determination of whether the attribution of input tax was done correctly is time consuming and prone to arguments between the tax administration and the business. However, it has to be acknowledged that this issue is not unique to the distinction between taxable and exempt transactions/businesses. Such classification issues might also arise in the context of the delimitation between taxable and out-of-scope supplies and suppliers, one prominent example being holding companies (*see* the contribution of Herbain in this book).
53. Ebrill et al., *supra* n. 25, 88 et seq.
54. One example would be the exemption for cost-sharing groups in Article 132(1)(f) of the VAT Directive (*see* van Doesum et al., *supra* n. 26, 317 et seq.).
55. *See*, e.g., CJEU, 18 November 2020, Case C-77/19, *Kaplan International Colleges UK*, ECLI: EU:C:2020:934.
56. Englisch, *supra* n. 4, 38; De la Feria & Krever, *supra* n. 6, 24. *See also* Amand, *supra* n. 39 in footnote 38.

even tax evasion practices (e.g., purposeful misclassification of goods or services to secure the input VAT credit).[57]

What can be done to alleviate or even eliminate those distortions? Three different approaches can be found in academic literature:

(1) The *abolishment* of exemptions: the previously exempted transactions or businesses should be subject to a zero-rate.[58]
(2) The *abolishment* of exemptions: the previously exempted transactions should be subject to VAT (either at the standard or a reduced rate).[59]
(3) As a compromise solution, businesses could be allowed the *option* to treat exempt transactions as supplies subject to VAT.[60]

§5.02 COMPARISON OF TRADITIONAL AND MODERN VAT SYSTEMS

[A] General Remarks

Arriving at the conclusion that exemptions as such are—in an overall view—a deviation from the intention of a neutral VAT system, it has merit to have closer look at how different VAT systems around the world deal with exemptions. To that end, §5.02[B] and [C] below compare the approach taken under a traditional VAT system, the EU VAT, with that of modern VAT systems, i.e., the Australian GST system and the new kid on the VAT block—the VAT system of the Gulf Cooperation Council (GCC).

[B] Traditional VAT System: The EU VAT Directive

[1] Introduction: More Exemptions than Elsewhere

The VAT system of the EU, commonly referred to as the "traditional VAT," is rather old relative to other VAT/GST systems. The EU system contains more exemptions than most other VAT/GST systems around the globe.[61] As the adoption of the common VAT system is a prerequisite for EU membership,[62] the Member States cannot avoid

57. Ebrill et al., *supra* n. 25, 89 et seq.
58. Lenoir, *supra* n. 6, 459. Effectively, this would replicate the effects of an exemption with the right to deduct input VAT.
59. For illustrative numerical examples *see* van Brederode, *supra* n. 3, 114 et seq. and 129 et seq.
60. Ruppe, *supra* n. 15, 26; Lenoir, *supra* n. 6, 459. For examples of such options, *see* Article 137 or 290 of the EU VAT Directive. The former contains options for certain technical exemptions (e.g., financial exemptions). The latter allows small enterprises to opt for the application of the normal VAT arrangements. However, such options might lead to further complexity, as well as increased administrative and compliance costs.
61. De la Feria & Krever, *supra* n. 6, 7.
62. Moreover, also third states that enter into association treaties with the EU in many cases have to adhere to the EU VAT rules in order to facilitate cross-border trade. *See* further, for example the

implementing the wide range of mandatory exemptions contained in the EU VAT Directive.[63]

It is settled case law of the CJEU that exemptions constitute independent concepts of EU Law whose purpose is to avoid divergences in the application of the common VAT system amongst Member States.[64] Therefore, in general, exemptions must be given an EU definition and cannot depend on its classification in domestic law.[65] Furthermore, as exemptions deviate from the general principle that VAT is to be levied on all goods and services supplied for consideration by a taxable person, they have to be interpreted strictly.[66] However, strict does not mean restrictive, as of deprived of their meaning.[67]

This chapter focuses on the explicitly mentioned exemptions in the VAT Directive, namely "*Exemptions for certain activities in the public interest*" (Article 132 of the VAT Directive) and "*Exemptions for other activities*" (Article 135 of the VAT Directive), as well as on the exemptions within the special scheme for small enterprises (Articles 281-294 of the VAT Directive) and public bodies.[68] All those exemptions are characterized by the denial of input VAT deduction (*see* Article 168 of the VAT Directive). Consequently, all of the disadvantages and distortive effects mentioned above obviously apply to the exemptions created by the EU VAT Directive. As the directive contains a high number of exemptions, these issues are particularly prevalent in the EU VAT system. According to the OECD, contrary to the EU practice, the standard advice for VAT design is to (only) have a short list of exemptions.[69]

At the level of the EU, there has been dissatisfaction for some time with the current state of VAT exemptions. This is clear from the repeated efforts to abolish or fundamentally reform individual exemptions.[70] In 2010, the European Commission

---

Association Agreement between the European Union and the European Atomic Energy Community and their Member States, of the one part, and Georgia, of the other part, available at https://eur-lex.europa.eu/legal-content/EN/TXT/?uri=CELEX:02014A0830(02)-20180601; especially Annex XXII, Taxation.

63. Council Directive 2006/112/EC of 28 Nov. 2006, on the common system of value added tax, OJ L 347 of 11 Dec. 2006. This, however, is not true for reduced rates. According to Article 98 of the VAT Directive, it is optional for Member States to apply either one or two reduced rates. For a closer analysis of the rate structure, *see* the contribution of van Brederode in this book (Chapter 4).
64. *See*, e.g., *BlackRock Investment Management*, *supra* n. 51, m.no. 21; and *Golfclub Schloss Igling*, *supra* n. 51, m.no. 46.
65. van Doesum et al., *supra* n. 26, 307 et seq.
66. *See*, e.g., *BlackRock Investment Management*, *supra* n. 51, m.no. 22; and *Kaplan International Colleges*, *supra* n. 55, m.no. 37.
67. Ben Terra et al., *Commentary on European VAT Directives, Chapter 9—Exemptions* (IBFD ed. 2019), section 9.1. *See also* CJEU, 14 June 2007, Case C-434/05, *Horizon College*, ECLI: EU:C:2007:343, m.no. 16.
68. Public bodies are, in principle, deemed to be out of scope of the EU VAT system according to Article 13 of the VAT Directive. Therefore, those bodies are treated as non-taxable persons. Accordingly, the VAT treatment is—economically—the same as for exempt taxpayers without the right to deduct input VAT. For a closer analysis of public bodies, *see* below.
69. OECD, *supra* n. 14, 44.
70. *See*, e.g., *Amended proposal for a Council Directive amending Directive 77/388/EEC as regards value added tax on services provided in the postal sector*, COM (2004) 468 final, that envisaged the abolition of the exemption for postal services (Article 132(1)(a) of the VAT Directive). However, the proposal ultimately failed at attracting sufficient political support and was

made a more fundamental effort at reconsidering the VAT exemptions.[71] It noted that "[t]he continued relevance of many of the existing exemptions is questionable" and there would be a "need to review these exemptions, notably in the light of economic and technological changes."[72] However, these ambitious plans have not (yet) materialized in legislative adjustments. Therefore, all the exemptions that were already part of the Sixth Directive of 1977[73] still exist today. Consequently, it is worthwhile to have a look at the historical roots of exemptions in the EU VAT Directive.

[2] The Historical Roots of Exemptions in the EU VAT Directive

To understand the exemption system of the EU VAT Directive and its rationale, one has to be aware of its historical roots, which lie in France where the VAT was gradually introduced after WW2.[74] In 1954, France changed its tax on production into a tax on the value added, including the right for businesses to deduct input VAT paid on procurements.[75] However, the French system did not move into a full VAT until 1968, when the retail sector was included into the system. A year earlier, Denmark enacted the first full VAT in Europe.[76] However, the work on what later would become the common EU VAT system already started in the late 1950s, when the Commission, acting on the mandate provided by Article 99 of the Treaty of Rome, set up several working groups to study the harmonization of turnover taxes of the Member States.[77] One of the reports of these working groups, the Neumark Report, concluded that the Member States should replace their turnover taxes with value added taxes.[78] In light of these recommendations, the Commission proposed a directive that envisaged the introduction of a common system of VAT. After some time of consultation and discussion, the first two VAT Directives were adopted on 11 April 1967.[79]

withdrawn in 2013. Another (more recent) example is the *Action plan for fair and simple taxation* (COM (2020) 312 final) of the European Commission where the amendment of the "outdated provisions" for the exemptions of financial services in the VAT Directive is intended for the period of 2020/2021.

71. *See* European Commission, *Green Paper on the future of VAT* (2010), COM (2010) 695 final.
72. European Commission, *supra* n. 71, 10 et seq.
73. *See* Council of the European Communities, *Sixth Council Directive 77/388/EEC of 17 May 1977 on the harmonization of the laws of the Member States relating to turnover taxes - Common system of value added tax: uniform basis of assessment* OJ L 145/1 of 13 June 1977 (Article 13).
74. De la Feria & Krever, *supra* n. 6, 3 et seq.
75. Amand, *supra* n. 39, 243.
76. Kathryn James, *Exploring the Origins and Global Rise of VAT, in The VAT Reader* 16 (Tax Analysts, 2011); van Brederode, *supra* n. 3, 7.
77. For a detailed discussion of the origins of the common EU VAT system, *see* Rita de La Feria, *The EU VAT system and the internal market* (IBFD, Academic Council 2009), 48 et seq.
78. *See* De la Feria, *supra* n. 77, 49, Lenoir, *supra* n. 6, 457, Christian Amand, *Are VAT Exemptions Compatible with Primary EU Law?* 21 (6) Int'l VAT Monitor 411 (2010), and Amand, *supra* n. 39, 243 et seq. The roots of the EU VAT in turnover taxes of its Member States can be seen in the German *Umsatzsteuergesetz*, which literally translated would mean "turnover tax act."
79. *See* Council of the European Economic Community, *First Council Directive 67/227/EEC of 11 April 1967 on the harmonisation of legislation of Member States concerning turnover taxes* and Council of the European Economic Community, OJ of 14 April 1967, No. 71/1301 *Second Council Directive 67/228/EEC of 11 April 1967 on the harmonisation of legislation of Member States*

The First Directive required Member States to "replace their present system of turnover taxes by the common system of a value added tax [...]" by the beginning of 1970 at the latest (Article 1). Where the First Directive functioned as an explanatory memorandum, the Second Directive contained the modalities of the tax, i.e., more detailed rules "concerning the structure of, and the procedure for applying, the common system of a value added tax."[80] The Second Directive envisaged rules concerning exemptions as it mentioned in the recitals that it would be "highly desirable to limit strictly the number of exemptions [...]." However, besides certain exemptions for international trade in Article 10 (1) and (2) of the Second Directive, Article 10 (3) left the Member States considerable leeway in determining further exemptions.[81] Article 10 (3) stated that "[e]ach member state may ... determine the other exemptions which it considers necessary." Therefore, it can be concluded that neither the number nor the nature of exemptions were harmonized from the outset. Nevertheless, the denial of the deduction of input VAT for exempt transactions was already stipulated (*see* Article 11 (2) of the Second Directive) and kept ever since.

Not only with regard to exemptions, but also for other design options, the Second Directive left Member States a considerable amount of autonomy.[82] This resulted in national VAT systems that were substantially different from each other. This lack of determination and the resulting differences led to the adoption of the Sixth Directive[83] that contained more detailed rules and gave Member States much less room for autonomous action.[84] This also held true for exemptions, meaning that the Sixth Directive, for the first time, contained a detailed list of goods and services to be exempt by Member States (Title X).[85] The recitals of the Sixth Directive mentioned that "a common list of exemptions should be drawn up so that the Communities' own resources may be collected in a uniform manner in all the Member States."[86] In the proposal for the Sixth Directive of the Commission, the recitals also expressed that "the number of exemptions must be as small as possible, so that value added tax may remain a general tax on consumption."[87] Obviously, the Commission was already

concerning turnover taxes - Structure and procedures for application of the common system of value added tax, OJ of 14 April 1967, No. 71/1303.

80. *See* Article 3 of the first directive.
81. *See* also Englisch, *supra* n. 4, 37 or De la Feria, *supra* n. 77, 52 et seq.
82. For examples, *see* De la Feria, *supra* n. 77, 53. Indeed, with the Second Directive, also the VAT grouping mechanism was first introduced in EU VAT legislation. *See* Sebastian Pfeiffer, *EU VAT Grouping – Past, Present Future*, in Karina Elgaard et al. (eds) *Anthology on VAT Grouping and Cost-Sharing* (Copenhagen, 2020) in print with further references.
83. The third, fourth and fifth directives were enacted to accommodate Member States that had difficulties meeting the initial implementation deadline of January 1, 1970.
84. De la Feria, *supra* n. 77, 53 et seq.
85. Terra et al., *supra* n. 67 argue that the harmonization of exemptions might have been the main reason for the introduction of the sixth directive (*see* section 9.1.). As the list of exemptions provided for in the sixth directive largely corresponds to the exemptions in place on the VAT Directive today, we refer to the subsequent chapters.
86. *See* OJ L 145/13.6.77, 2. This corresponds to recital 35 of the EU VAT Directive.
87. *See* Commission of the European Communities, *Proposal for a Sixth Council Directive on the harmonization of legislation of Member States concerning turnover taxes. Common system of value added tax: uniform basis of assessment*, COM (73) 950, 42.

aware of the disadvantageous effects of exemptions. However, this consideration did not make it into the final Sixth Directive.

The "Exemptions within the territory of the country" in the Sixth Directive (Article 13) were divided into "Exemptions for certain activities in the public interest" (Part A of Article 13) and "Other exemptions" (Part B of Article 13). These exemptions correspond to the exemptions to be found in Articles 132 and 135 of the VAT Directive (*see* below). The explanatory memorandum attached to the proposal of the Commission for the Sixth Directive, provides information on the reasons of the individual exemptions.[88] The exemptions of Part A were "those already existing in the majority of Member States." Therefore, it can be concluded that the exemptions in this part were not the result of clearly articulated policy objectives but rather stem from the leeway given to Member States within the First and Second Directive. Therefore, the exemptions in the Sixth Directive correspond to those already existing in the turnover tax systems of the Member States, which actually should be replaced by the VAT system.[89] It seems that the EU was not prepared to engage in discussions with Member States and previously advantaged (highly integrated) sectors were unwilling to waive their (alleged) preferential treatment.[90] The exemptions of Part B were "justified for reasons of general policy common to all Member States." For some of the exemptions in this part, the explanatory memorandum offers a more specific explanation: The exemption for letting of immovable property (Article 13(B)(b)) was justified on "technical, economic and social grounds." The exemption of betting, lotteries, and other forms of gambling (Article 13(B)(f)) was based "on purely practical considerations." It was mentioned that such activities would be better dealt with by means of special taxes. For all other exemptions, there is no (further) explanation.[91]

Since then, not much has changed in terms of exemptions in the EU VAT system. Despite small alterations in the wording of the exemptions[92] or their order in the respective provisions,[93] all of the exemptions already introduced by the Sixth Directive are also part of the current EU VAT Directive.

[3] The Exemptions in the VAT Directive

[a] General Remarks

This section provides an overview of the exemptions of the EU VAT Directive, as defined for the purposes of this chapter. Furthermore, it will deal with public bodies,

88. *See* Commission of the European Communities, *supra* n. 87, 15 et seq.
89. Englisch, *supra* n. 4, 38; Lenoir, *supra* n. 6, 457; Amand, *supra* n. 78, 413 or De la Feria & Krever, *supra* n. 6, 8 et seq. Amand, *supra* n. 39, 245, argues that these exemptions particularly stem from prior German and French legislation.
90. van Brederode, *supra* n. 3, 8.
91. *See* Commission of the European Communities, *supra* n. 87, 16.
92. For example, the wording of the exemption for services by dental technicians and dental prostheses has slightly changed.
93. In comparison to the sixth directive the arrangement of the "Exemptions for other activities" has changed.

which are—under certain circumstances—deemed non-taxable persons (Article 13 of the VAT Directive). Their inclusion in this subchapter is justified as the consequences of being out of the scope of the VAT resemble the effects of an exempt transaction without the right to an input VAT deduction.

According to Article 131 of the VAT Directive Member States shall apply the exemptions in Title IX of the Directive "in accordance with conditions which the Member States shall lay down for the purposes of ensuring the correct and straightforward application of those exemptions and of preventing any possible evasion, avoidance or abuse." Such a provision is of course not conducive to the idea of harmonization of VAT in the EU. However, the scope of application of this provision is not all too broad. While, for example, Article 131 of the VAT Directive can be used to require taxpayers to provide evidence of the fulfillment of the requirements for the application of an exemption,[94] the conditions that Member States introduce by means of this provision cannot affect the definition of the subject-matter of exemptions itself.[95] Exemptions are independent EU concepts, not affected by definitions in domestic laws.[96] However, it has to be acknowledged that the wording of several of the exemptions stipulated in Articles 132 and 135 of the VAT Directive leaves the Member States with a considerable amount of leeway (e.g., some provisions require Member States to exempt "certain" supplies of goods or services, without determining the specific scope of application of the exemption).

[b] Exemptions in the Public Interest (Article 132 of the VAT Directive)

Article 132 of the VAT Directive contains an exhaustive list of mandatory exemptions of *certain* activities in the public interest. That means that other activities, perceived as being in the public interest, are not exempt.[97] The rationale of these exemptions is to incentivize the consumption of goods and services with positive externalities, and to make those goods and services more accessible to low-income consumers.[98] Commonly those exemptions are referred to as merit or concessional exemptions. The exemptions of Article 132 (1) of the VAT Directive include:

94. However, when exercising the powers conferred to them by Article 131 of the VAT Directive, Member States must respect the general principles of law within the EU, including, in particular, the principles of legal certainty and proportionality and the principle of protection of legitimate expectations (*see*, e.g., CJEU, 28 February 2018, Case C-307/16, *Pieńkowski*, ECLI: EU:C:2018:124, m.no. 33 and other cases of the CJEU cited therein).
95. *See Kingscrest, supra* n. 7, m.no. 24. *See also* van Doesum et al., *supra* n. 26, 310.
96. *See* for example *BlackRock Investment Management, supra* n. 51, m.no. 21; and *Golfclub Schloss Igling, supra* n. 51, m.no. 46 and other cases of the CJEU cited therein.
97. *See also* van Doesum et al., *supra* n. 26, 315.
98. *See* Kyriaki Yiallourou, *CJEU: Developments on VAT Exemptions in 2019*, 47(6/7) Intertax 678 (2020). For example, with regard to the exemption provided for certain services closely linked to sport or physical education by non-profit-making organizations the CJEU held that this exemption is intended to encourage those types of activities (*see* CJEU, 16 October 2008, Case C-253/07, *Canterbury Hockey Club und Canterbury Ladies Hockey Club*, ECLI:EU:C:2008:571, m.no. 19).

- Public postal services (other than passenger transport and telecommunications services) and goods incidental thereto under point (a).[99]
- Medical care under points (b), (c), (e) and (p). Whereas Article 132(1)(b) exempts such services in a hospital environment by bodies governed by public law or, under social conditions comparable with those applicable to bodies governed by public law, by hospitals, centers for medical treatment or diagnosis and other duly recognized establishments of a similar nature, Article 132(1)(c) provides for an exemption of activities outside hospitals (e.g., at the home of the patient) in the exercise of the medical and paramedical professions as defined by the Member State concerned. The exemptions for dental care services and dental prostheses by dentists or dental technicians (e) as well as for transport services for sick and injured persons in vehicles specially designed for that purpose, by authorized bodies (p) belong to this category as well.
- Human organs, blood and milk under point (d). Interestingly, this is one of the few exemptions solely for goods.
- Cost-sharing groups under point (f). The goal of this exemption is actually to alleviate the consequences of VAT exemptions without the right to deduct input VAT. The tax shall not become a distortive factor when a group of persons find it necessary to engage in cooperation.[100]
- Services and goods closely linked to welfare and social security work by bodies governed by public law or by other bodies recognized by the Member State concerned as being devoted to social wellbeing under point (g).
- Services and goods closely linked to the protection of children and young persons by bodies governed by public law or by other bodies recognized by the Member State concerned as being devoted to social wellbeing under point (h).
- Education services by bodies governed by public law having such as their aim or by other organizations recognized by the Member State concerned as having similar objects under point (i) and tuition given privately by teachers and covering school or university education under point (j).
- Supply of staff by religious or philosophical institutions for the purposes of the activities mentioned under points (b), (g), (h) and (i) with a view to spiritual welfare under point (k).
- Services and goods closely linked thereto, to their members in their common interest in return for a subscription fixed in accordance with their rules by non-profit-making organizations with aims of a political, trade-union, religious, patriotic, philosophical, philanthropic or civic nature, provided that this exemption is not likely to distort competition under point (l).

---

99. However, this exemption only covers public or operators who undertake universal postal services as defined by Directive 97/67/EC on the common rules for the development of the internal market of Community postal services. The exemption does not apply to supplies of services or of goods incidental thereto for which the terms have been individually negotiated. *See further* CJEU, 23 April 2009, Case C-357/07, *TNT Post UK Ltd.* ECLI:EU:C:2009:248.
100. van Doesum et al., *supra* n. 26, 318.

- Certain services closely linked to sport or physical education by non-profit-making organizations to persons taking part in such education under point (m).[101]
- Certain cultural services and the supply of goods closely linked thereto by bodies governed by public law or by other cultural bodies recognized by the Member States concerned under point (n).
- Services and goods, by organizations whose activities are exempt under points (b), (g), (h), (i), (l), (m) or (n) in connection with fund-raising events organized exclusively for their own benefit, provided that the exemption is not likely to distort competition under point (o).
- Activities, other than those of a commercial nature, carried out by public radio and television bodies under point (q).

Articles 133 and 134 of the VAT Directive contain further provisions for the exemptions envisaged by Article 132(1)(b), (g), (h), (i), (l), (m) and (n). According to Article 133 of the VAT Directive, Member States may make the granting of these exemptions to bodies other than those governed by public law subject to one or more specifically defined conditions (e.g., that they must be managed and administered on an essentially voluntary basis). Article 134 of the VAT Directive provides that these exemptions shall not be granted where the supply is not essential to the exempt transaction (*see* point (a))[102] or where the basic purpose of the supply is to obtain additional income through transactions, which are in direct competition with those of commercial enterprises subject to VAT (*see* point (b)).

[c] Exemptions for Other Activities (Article 135 of the VAT Directive)

Article 135 of the VAT Directive lists "*Exemptions for other activities.*" The rationales of the exemptions of Article 135 are diverse. Most of these exemptions could be labelled as technical exemptions, meaning that pragmatic (e.g., the difficulty to accurately define the tax base) rather than policy reasons are the grounds for the exemption.[103] Furthermore, some individual exemptions may be explained by more specific reasons. Where appropriate, the reason is mentioned in the list below. The exemptions of Article 135 include:

- Insurance and Reinsurance transactions, including related services performed by insurance brokers and insurance agents under point (a).

---

101. The wording of *certain* services to be exempted led to uncertainties in the recent past. According to the CJEU, this wording leaves the Member States with discretion, on which activities to exempt (*see Golfclub Schloss Igling, supra* n. 51, m.no. 31).
102. For a closer analysis of what is "essential to the transactions exempted," *see* Panagiotis Dodos, *Die Bestimmung des Kernbereichs von Mehrwertsteuerbefreiungen,* 1 MwStR 9 (2017).
103. *See*, e.g., Yiallourou, *supra* n. 98, 678.

- Financial services (found in Article 135(b)-(g)).[104] One prominent example is the exemption of granting and the negotiation of credit (b). The explanatory memorandum to the proposal of the Sixth Directive does not include an explanation for this exemption. In academic literature and the case law of the CJEU,[105] various views have been expressed: Administrative reasons, as the intermediation charge, which should be taxed, cannot be separated from interest, premiums or rate of returns, which should not be taxed;[106] credits do not proxy consumption but are rather a shifting of money;[107] VAT shall not increase the prices for consumer credits.[108] Other examples of exempt financial services include negotiation of or any dealings in credit guarantees under point (c), transactions concerning deposit and current accounts, payments, transfers, debts, cheques and other negotiable instruments under point (d) or the management of special investment funds as defined by Member States under point (g).
- Postage stamps valid for use for postal services, fiscal stamps and other similar stamps under point (h).
- Betting, lotteries, and other forms of gambling, subject to the conditions and limitations laid down by each Member State under point (i). The reason for this exemption is, despite the difficulties in determining the accurate tax base, that Member States often already levy specific taxes for such activities.[109]
- The supply of a building or parts thereof and the land on which it stands under point (j). However, supplies before first occupation (Article 12(1)(a) of the VAT Directive) are not covered by the exemption. Furthermore, the supply of land is exempt as well under point (k) but the supply of building land (Article 12 (1)(b) of the VAT Directive) is not covered by the exemption and therefore subject to VAT.
- Leasing and letting of immovable property under point (l). According to Article 135(2) of the VAT Directive, this exemption does not include accommodation in the hotel sector or similar, the letting of premises and sites for the parking of vehicles, the letting of permanently installed equipment and machinery and the hire of safes.[110]

---

104. For comprehensive study of the VAT treatment of financial services, *see* Robert F. van Brederode and Richard Krever, *VAT and Financial Services: Comparative Law and Economic Perspectives* (Springer, 2017).
105. *See*, e.g., CJEU, 19 April 2007, Case C-455/05, *Velvet & Steel Immobilien*, ECLI:EU:C:2007:232, m.no. 24.
106. Cnossen, *supra* n. 6, 436.
107. Stadie, *supra* n. 12, 149 et seq.
108. Stadie, *supra* n. 12, 149 et seq. *See also* Opinion of AG Sharpston in Case C-44/11, *Deutsche Bank*, ECLI:EU:C:2012:276, m.no. 36.
109. van Doesum et al., *supra* n. 26, 345.
110. Despite the general objective of a harmonized application of the exemptions, especially those for buildings and parts thereof and the land on which it stands and for the leasing and letting of immovable property are transposed very differently in the Member States. It is, for example, possible for Member States to add additional exceptions to the exemption for the leasing and letting of immovable property or even to treat such services generally subject to VAT and to, by way of an exception, only exempt lettings of immovable property to be used for dwelling

In respect of certain exempt supplies, namely financial services, buildings, or parts thereof and the land on which it stands, land which has not been built on and the leasing and letting of immovable property, Article 137 of the VAT Directive grants Member States the right, to allow taxable persons to opt for taxation. It has to be noted, that these options are only available for certain exemptions mentioned in Article 135 of the VAT Directive. Therefore, Member States are prohibited from granting the right to opt for taxation in regard of exemptions covered by Article 132 of the VAT Directive.

[d] Exemption for Small Enterprises

The VAT Directive contains a number of special schemes,[111] including one for small enterprises (Chapter 1 of Title XII of the VAT Directive, Articles 281-294). Under this special scheme, Member States are entitled (but not obliged) to exempt taxable persons whose annual turnover is below a certain threshold (*see* Articles 284-287 of the VAT Directive). The reason for this option is that small enterprises often face relatively high administrative costs relative to their turnover.[112]

The threshold for the exemption of small enterprises varies significantly among Member States with a current maximum of EUR 88,500 in Romania.[113] However, in comparison to modern VAT systems, this range of thresholds is relatively low.[114] Furthermore, some Member States even introduced more than one threshold for different sectors.[115] These differences result in a lack of uniformity in the exemption for small enterprises across EU Member States. Although at EU level amending legislation has passed to improve this facility,[116] these changes still allow for a number of domestic

purposes (*see* CJEU, 3 February 2000, Case C-12/98, *Amengual Far*, ECLI:EU:C:2000:62, m.no. 15). Moreover, the VAT Directive itself contains derogations from the exemptions (*see*, e.g., Article 117(2) of the VAT Directive that allows Austria to apply a reduced rate to the letting of immovable property for residential use).

111. Beside the special scheme for small enterprises (Chapter 1 of Title XII of the VAT Directive), the VAT provides special schemes for farmers (Chapter 2 of Title XII), travel agents (Chapter 3 of Title XII) and investment gold (Chapter 5 of Title XII) for example.
112. *See* Cnossen, *supra* n. 6, 437 and Proposal for a Council Directive amending Directive 2006/112/EC on the common system of value added tax as regards the special scheme for small enterprises, COM/2018/21 final, 1.
113. Small traders are not automatically relieved from all VAT obligations because of the exemption. In Belgium, France, Greece, and Malta, for example, small enterprises must be registered under a special procedure (*see* Fabiola Annacondia, *VAT Registration Thresholds in Europe*, 31(6) Int'l VAT Monitor 343(2020)).
114. Ine Lejeune, *The EU VAT Experience: What Are the Lessons?* In *The VAT Reader* 271 (Tax Analysts, 2011).
115. This for example is the case in France or Malta (*see* Annacondia, *supra* n. 113).
116. *See further* Council Directive (EU) 2020/285 amending Directive 2006/112/EC on the common system of value added tax as regards the special scheme for small enterprises and Regulation (EU) No 904/2010 as regards the administrative cooperation and exchange of information for the purpose of monitoring the correct application of the special scheme for small enterprises.

options for Member States and non-harmonized SME thresholds.[117] The new rules will apply from the beginning of 2025.[118]

According to Article 289 of the VAT Directive, taxable persons exempt from VAT are not entitled to an input tax credit. However, those small enterprises have the right to opt for normal VAT arrangements (Article 290 of the VAT Directive). By exercising that option, small enterprises must register and collect VAT on their outputs. On the other hand, they obtain the right to deduct input VAT (when providing output supplies subject to VAT), thus escaping the detrimental effects of exemptions in VAT.

[e] Out-of-Scope Suppliers: Public Bodies

According to Article 13 of the VAT Directive, public bodies ("States, regional or local government authorities and other bodies governed by public law") shall not be regarded as taxable persons in respect of activities or transactions in which they engage as public authorities. Effectively, those bodies are treated in the same way as consumers, and the consequences of the exclusion resemble those of activities exempted without the right of an input tax credit.[119] However, insofar their exclusion would lead to significant distortions of competition, the respective activities and transactions of public bodies shall be subject to VAT. This is stipulated in the second sentence of Article 13 and is aimed at addressing one of the core criticisms of the "exemption" for public bodies, namely that, apart from pure government services, they compete with the private sector.[120] The "exemption" leads to legal uncertainties[121] and higher administrative costs as a delimitation between "out-of-scope supplies" and taxable supplies has to be made. Therefore, a wider or even full inclusion of public bodies into the VAT system[122] would not only alleviate possible distortions of competition with private actors but would also obviate the necessity to delineate between "exempt" and taxable transactions that might be subject to VAT.[123] Furthermore, their inclusion would also be more in line with the nature of a VAT as a broad-based tax on final consumption.[124] In any event, for some activities carried out by public bodies, Article 13 jo. Annex I of the VAT Directive stipulates that those should be treated as

117. *See further* Sebastian Pfeiffer and Karoline Spies, *CJEU Case Law on Taxable Persons and Related Issues* in 2019, in Georg Kofler et al. (eds.) *CJEU—Recent Developments in Value Added Tax 2019* (Linde, 2020) Chapter 4.
118. For further information on the new regime *see* van Doesum et al., *supra* n. 26, 679 et seq.
119. Sometimes, the treatment of public bodies is even referred to as an exemption (*see* van Doesum et al., *supra* n. 26, 108).
120. Cnossen, *supra* n. 6, 437.
121. *See*, e.g., the case law of the CJEU with further discussions Karoline Spies, *CJEU Case Law on Taxable Persons in 2018*, in Michael Lang et al. (eds), *CJEU—Recent Developments in Value Added Tax 2018* (Linde, 2019); Sebastian Pfeiffer, *Recent CJEU Case Law on Taxable Persons and Public Bodies*, in Michael Lang et al (eds), *CJEU—Recent Developments in Value Added Tax 2015* (Linde, 2016); Oskar Henkow, *When is a Public Activity an Economic Activity?* in Michael Lang et al. (eds), *CJEU— Recent Developments in Value Added Tax 2016* (Linde, 2017).
122. As proposed by numerous authors, *see*, e.g., Alan A. Tait, *Value Added Tax: International Practice and Problems* (IMF, 1988), 77 or Crawford et al., *supra* n. 12, 305 et seq.
123. Cnossen, *supra* n. 6, 437,
124. van Doesum et al., *supra* n. 26, 109.

subject to VAT, provided that they are not carried out on a negligible scale. Those activities include telecommunication services, supply of water, gas, electricity, and thermal energy, transport of goods, port and airport services or passenger transport, for example. The scope of application of Article 13 is thus significantly narrowed. Whether public bodies must be regarded as taxable persons in respect of supplied goods or services must be determined in a case-by-case assessment.[125]

[C] Modern VAT Systems

[1] Australia

[a] General Remarks

The Australian GST system is a modern, broad-based value added tax system.[126] The Australian GST system is characterized—especially when looked at from a purely domestic perspective—as very neutral: a very limited number of exempt supplies[127] is paired with a broad entitlement to deduct input tax.[128] Where exemptions exist, neutrality enhancing measures have been adopted, such as a reduced input tax credit regime for a limited category of financial supplies in order to prevent the cascading of irrecoverable input tax.[129]

[b] Exemptions under the Australian GST

Exempt supplies or input taxed supplies as they are called in Australia, are financial supplies and supplies regarding residential premises.[130] The main rationale behind the exemption for financial services is the difficulty of determining the taxable base.[131] However, in effect, these exempt financial supplies only cover domestic Australian B2B and B2C financial services as the zero-rating of exported supplies takes precedence

125. For the relevant criteria in this assessment, *see* van Doesum et al., *supra* n. 26, 108 et seq. One example, where the CJEU held, that a body governed by public law is not engaged in competition with private operators, is CJEU, 19 January 2017, Case C-344/15, *National Roads Authority*, ECLI:EU:C:2017:28, where the public body carried out an activity consisting in providing access to a road on payment of a toll.
126. *See* Rebecca Millar & Lorenna Moon, *Australia*, in, *Improving VAT/GST: Designing a Simple and Fraud-Proof Tax System* 23 (Michael Lang and Ine Lejeune, eds., IBFD, 2014).
127. The term exempt supplies shall refer to supplies exempt without input VAT credit.
128. Miller & Moon, *supra* n. 126, 26.
129. *See further* Ross Sitt, *Financial Supplies: Bundling & unbundling*, 9(2) eJ. Tax Rsrch 194, 195 (2011).
130. Residential premises is defined as land or a building that: (a) is occupied as a residence or for residential accommodation; or (b) is intended to be occupied, and is capable of being occupied, as a residence or for residential accommodation. The term of occupation or intended occupation is irrelevant. Residential premises also include floating homes. *See* further A New Tax System (Goods and Services Tax) Act 1999, Division 195-1.
131. Millar & Moon, *supra* n. 126, 62.

over the exempt character of exported supplies.[132] Financial supplies in Australia are defined as the provision, acquisition or disposal of an interest in or under:[133]

- an account made available by an authorized Australian deposit-taking institution;
- a debt, credit arrangement, right to credit, or letter of credit;
- a charge or mortgage over property;
- a superannuation fund;
- an annuity or pension;
- life insurance;
- a guarantee or indemnity;
- Australian or foreign currency; and
- securities or derivatives.

When implementing the GST system, the Australian legislator was aware of the evident problems of creating exemptions.[134] Particularly the distortion caused if large financial institutions are able to access in-house resources to provide inputs that smaller institutions would have to source from outside suppliers. To prevent any market distortions caused by non-recoverable input tax by institutions using outside providers, a partial input tax credit was introduced.[135] The reduced input tax credit (RITC) functions in a way that allows eligible financial institutions a reduced input tax credit for acquisitions that otherwise would not be entitled to any input tax credit. As the name indicates, the tax credit is reduced to 75% of a full credit and available for specified purchases, so called "reduced credit acquisitions."[136]

The goods and services, for which the RITC is allowed, are listed in the Australian legislation. This list of qualifying taxable supplies used by financial institutions comprises more items than the number of input-taxed financial supplies.[137]

132. Millar & Moon, *supra* n. 126, 60.
133. *See* Millar & Moon, *supra* n. 126, 60; *see also A New Tax System (Goods and Service Tax) Regulations 2019*, reg. 40-5.09.
134. *See* Ross Sitt (2011), *supra* n. 129, 195. Namely that financial suppliers insource many of the activities that they had previously acquired from third party service providers.
135. *See further* Senate Furthers Supplementary Explanatory Memorandum to the New Tax System (Goods and Services Tax) Bill 1998, paragraphs 5.1 and 5.2.
136. The types of services encompassed by the list include transaction banking and cash management services, payment and fund transfer services, securities transaction services, loan services, debt collection services, insurance services, services remunerated by commission and franchise fees, funds management services and trustee and custodial services. *See further* Sitt, *supra* n. 129, 196.
137. The following groups of acquisitions attract the input tax credit: Transaction banking and cash management services; Payment and fund transfer services; Securities transactions services; Loans services; Credit union services; Debt collection services; Asset based finance services; Trade finance services; Capital markets and financial instruments services; Funds management services; Insurance services; Services remunerated by commission and franchise fees; Trustee and custodial services; Supplies to recognized trust schemes; Monitoring service. *See, A New Tax System (Goods and Service Tax) Regulations 2019*, reg. 70-5.02.

[c] Public Bodies

The GST treatment of public bodies is quite different from the treatment under the traditional VAT of the EU. Supplies for consideration by governments and government bodies in Australia are taxable supplies.[138] GST does not apply to federal, state, or local taxes.[139] Supplies to the public for which no charge is made such as police, parks, etc. are out of scope supplies, as they do not involve consideration.[140] Transfer payments between governments are also treated as out of scope supplies. Registered governments and government agencies can claim input tax credits for out-of-scope supplies in the same manner as private businesses.[141]

[2] GCC VAT System

[a] General Remarks

The Gulf Cooperation Council (GCC) is a regional, intergovernmental, political, and economic alliance of six countries, Bahrain, Kuwait, the Kingdom of Saudi Arabia (KSA), Oman, Qatar, and the United Arab Emirates (UAE). Since 1 January 2018, they are committed to implementing a VAT based on the VAT Framework Agreement (VFA), which is a supranational instrument comparable to an EU Directive. The provisions of the VFA, therefore, need to be transposed into the national legislation of each Member State. The GCC is a Customs union and common market to some degree comparable to the EU, and the VFA, as may be expected, mimics the EU rules as regards cross-border transactions within the GCC.[142] The VFA contains mandatory provisions that are absolute in character, mandatory provision that still leave a large degree of discretion to the Member States, and optional provisions. The VFA is broad-based and has a narrow scope of exemptions.[143]

The main rationale for the introduction of VAT in the GCC was the need to ensure more stable government revenue for the individual Member States, which were to a large extent dependent on rather volatile revenue from oil production.[144]

138. *See* A New Tax System (Goods and Services Tax) Act 1999, Division 9-5, where taxable supplies (amongst others) are defined as supplies for consideration in the course or furtherance of an enterprise. An "enterprise" is defined as an activity by the Commonwealth, a State or a Territory, or by a body corporate, or corporation sole, established for a public purpose by or under a law of the Commonwealth, a State or a Territory. *See* A New Tax System (Goods and Services Tax) Act 1999, Division 9-20(1)(g).
139. With further references to Australian law, *see* Rebecca Millar, *Smoke and Mirrors: Applying the Full Taxation Model to Government under the Australian and New Zealand GST Laws*, in *VAT Exemptions: Consequences and Design Alternatives* 143 (Rita de la Feria, ed., Wolters Kluwer, 2013).
140. With further references to Australian law, *see* Millar, *supra* n. 139, 157.
141. *See* Millar, *supra* n. 139, 143.
142. *See* Robert F. van Brederode and Marcus Susilo, *The VAT in the Arab Countries of the Gulf Cooperation Council*, 28(6) Int'l VAT Monitor 435 (2017).
143. *See* van Brederode & Susilo, *supra* n. 142, 437.
144. *See* van Brederode & Susilo, *supra* n. 142, 437.

[b] Exemptions in the GCC VAT Framework Agreement

Article 29 of the VFA[145] allows Member States to either exempt or zero-rate the sectors of education, health, real estate and local transport.[146] Financial services performed by banks and financial institutions licensed under the Member States' laws, are exempt from VAT.[147] The restriction of the exemption to services rendered by locally licensed institutions, means that financial services provided by non-licensed entities, such as a special purpose vehicle within a group of companies, are taxed.[148]

Even though exempt, the VFA allows financial institutions to recover input VAT "based on refund rates determined by each Member State."[149] Prima facie, this seems contradictory, as input-VAT related to exempt supplies is unrecoverable.[150] However, academic literature argues that these refund rates constitute a pro-rata rule for input VAT deduction in case financial institutions also render services abroad.[151] The VFA does not contain a definition of financial services, which is left to the Member States. The absence of a GCC-wide definition bears the risk of different treatment of essentially similar services.

Member States can choose to exclude certain categories of recipients from paying VAT when receiving goods and services or allow them to reclaim VAT paid. These recipients include government bodies and charities as designated by the Member State, exempt companies under international event hosting agreements, citizens of Member States when constructing their homes for private use, and farmers and fishermen that are not registered for tax.[152] As the aforementioned categories of recipients do not have taxable outputs, this provision is equivalent to zero-rating and provides full relief from VAT.[153]

[c] Implementation of the GCC Rules

Under the VFA, all 6 Member States were required to implement the VAT as of January 1, 2018. In reality, only the KSA and UAE were able to do so. Bahrain postponed until January 2019, and at the time of writing of this chapter Oman and Kuwait are scheduled to introduce VAT per April 2021, and the introduction date of VAT in Qatar is still uncertain. Below we will compare the legislation of the three GCC countries

145. *See* an English translation of the GCC VAT framework at https://www2.deloitte.com/content/dam/Deloitte/xe/Documents/tax/me_Deloitte-english-GCC-VAT-Treaty-translation-May-7.pdf (accessed October 21, 2020).
146. *See* Article 29(1)(a)-(d) GCC VAT framework Agreement.
147. *See* Article 36 GCC VAT framework Agreement.
148. *See* van Brederode & Susilo, *supra* n. 142, 446. In contrast, under EU VAT, the status of the service provider is irrelevant for the application of the exemption. *See*, e.g., CJEU, 25 July 2018, Case C-5/17, *DPAS*, ECLI:EU:C:2018:592. This in turn leads to unwanted situations and structures to ease the unrecoverable VAT burden.
149. *See* Article 36(1) of the GCC VAT framework Agreement.
150. *See also* Article 44(1) of the GCC VAT framework Agreement.
151. *See* van Brederode & Susilo, *supra* n. 142, 446.
152. *See* Article 30 of the GCC VAT framework Agreement.
153. *See* van Brederode & Susilo, *supra* n. 142, 446.

where VAT is in force, and of Oman that published its laws, on their rules for the exemptions identified above in subsection [b].

Table 5.1 Comparison of VAT Exemptions Applied in Bahrain, KSA, and the UAE

	KSA	UAE	Bahrain	Oman
Education	Zero-rated (Saudi citizens) / taxed (non-citizens)	Zero-rated	Zero-rated	Exempt
Health	Zero-rated	Zero-rated	Zero-rated	Exempt/ zero-rated
Real estate	Exempt	Zero-rated/ exempt	Zero-rated/ exempt	exempt
Local transport	Taxed	Exempt	Zero-rated	Exempt
Financial services	Exempt	Exempt	Exempt	Exempt
Governmental bodies	Refund mechanism	Recovery mechanism	Taxed/recovery mechanism	Recovery mechanism

Source: Author's own work.

From a purely technical point of view, the VFA is rather straightforward as to exemptions. Only financial services are exempt from VAT without input VAT deduction. For other supplies, which are in traditional VAT systems also exempt, the VFA provides for an option to either implement exemptions or zero-rates. When looking at the actual implementation of the VFA in the Member States, differences can be identified. While the VFA gives the option to either exempt or zero-rate education and health services, the Member States discussed mainly zero-rate these supplies. Indeed, certain peculiarities can be found. Education services in the KSA are zero-rated only when supplied to Saudi nationals,[154] otherwise they are taxed. The UAE zero-rates the following educational services:[155] (a) the supply of educational services when provided in accordance with the curriculum recognized by the federal or local competent government entity regulating the education sector where the course is delivered; (b) educational services provided by an educational institution which is recognized by the federal or local competent government entity regulating the education sector where the course is delivered; and (c) educational services provided by a higher education institution, which is either owned by the federal or local government or receives more

154. Pursuant to Royal Decree No (A/86).
155. *See* Article 45(13) of the UAE VAT Law (Federal Decree-Law No. 8 of 2017 on Value Added Tax), available at https://www.tax.gov.ae/-/media/Files/FTA/links/Legislation/VAT/01-VAT-Decree-Law-No-8-of-2017.pdf.

than 50% of its annual funding directly from the federal or local government.[156] Thus, zero-rating depends on the status of the institution or the curriculum. Bahrain also zero-rates education services[157] under the condition that the institution is licensed by a competent authority,[158] while Oman chose to exempt them.[159]

Public healthcare services in the KSA are out-of-scope of VAT as they are carried out by a public body. Public healthcare institutions can recover VAT via a refund in their public capacity (*see* below). The supply of certain medicines, vitamins and medical goods are zero-rated.[160] Health services provided by private health institutions in the KSA are neither exempt nor zero-rated, but taxed. Healthcare services are zero-rated in the UAE,[161] and in Bahrain,[162] while Oman either applies the zero-rate to the supply of medicines and medical equipment [163] and exempts heath related services.[164]

The VFA allows Member States to exempt or zero-rate real estate transactions. The Member States that implemented the VFA, decided on varying paths. The KSA exempts the lease and license of residential real estate. While on the outset this seems to lower the costs on lessees, the lessors input VAT will be non-deductible. The UAE takes a more sophisticated approach by zero-rating the first supply (within three years) of residential buildings, either through sale or lease in whole or in part,[165] while exempting the subsequent sales or rents, and the supply of bare land.[166] In Bahrain, the zero-rate applies to the construction of new buildings,[167] and the exemption applies to the supply of bare land and buildings by way of sale or rental.[168] In Oman the exemption regards the supply of undeveloped land (bare land), the resale of residential properties and the renting of properties for residential purposes.[169]

---

156. *See* Article 40 of the UAE Executive Regulation of the Federal Decree-Law No. 8 of 2017 on Value Added Tax, available at https://www.tax.gov.ae/-/media/Files/FTA/links/Legislation/VAT/Executive-Regulation-of-Federal-Decree-Law-No-8-of-2017---Publish.pdf.
157. *See* Article 53(12) of the Bahrain VAT Law (Decree (48) of 2018 Regarding Value Added Tax, available at https://www.nbr.gov.bh/pdf/81129_Bahrain_VAT_Law.pdf).
158. *See* Kingdom of Bahrain VAT General Guide (2018) p. 44 (available at https://www.nbr.gov.bh/pdf/20190116_VAT_General_Guide_v1_3.pdf).
159. *See* Article 47(3) of the Oman VAT Law (Royal Decree 121/2020), an unofficial translation is available at https://assets.kpmg/content/dam/kpmg/om/pdf-2020/10/kpmgs-unofficial-english-translation-of-the-oman-vat-law.pdf.
160. Article 33 KSA VAT Law.
161. *See* Article 45(14) of the UAE VAT Law (Federal Decree-Law No. 8 of 2017 on Value Added Tax).
162. *See* Article 53(4) of the Bahrain VAT Law (Decree (48) of 2018 Regarding Value Added Tax.
163. *See* Article 51(2) of the Oman VAT Law (Royal Decree 121/2020).
164. *See* Article 47(2) of the Oman VAT Law (Royal Decree 121/2020).
165. Article 45(9) of the UAE VAT Law (Federal Decree-Law No. 8 of 2017 on Value Added Tax). *See further* Article 37 of the Executive Regulation, which lays down further rules on the interpretation of residential buildings, available at https://www.tax.gov.ae/-/media/Files/FTA/links/Legislation/VAT/Executive-Regulation-of-Federal-Decree-Law-No-8-of-2017---Publish.pdf.
166. *See* Article 46(2) and (3) of the UAE VAT Law (Federal Decree-Law No. 8 of 2017 on Value Added Tax).
167. *See* Article 53(11) of the Bahrain VAT Law (Decree (48) of 2018 Regarding Value Added Tax.
168. *See* Article 55 of the Bahrain VAT Law (Decree (48) of 2018 Regarding Value Added Tax.
169. *See* Article 47(4), (5) and (7) of the Oman VAT Law (Royal Decree 121/2020).

The treatment of local transportation services is diverse. They are exempt in the UAE[170] and Oman,[171] zero-rated in Bahrain,[172] and taxed in the KSA.[173]

Following the European example, financial services are exempt without the right to deduct input tax in all four countries.[174] However, the definition of what constitutes financial services is different and laid down in additional regulations. Pursuant to the Saudi Arabian implementation, financial services comprise—amongst others—the provision of credits,[175] money and security transfers[176] or other financial instruments.[177] However, the exemption for financial services is not applicable in cases "where the consideration payable in respect of the Service is by way of an explicit fee, commission or commercial discount."[178] It stands to reason to assume that such supplies are to be taxed. Similarly, while the UAE VAT Law exempts financial services, further guidance given by the Executive Regulation states that certain services (connected to dealings in money, and the provision of credit) are only exempt where they are not conducted in return for an explicit fee, discount, commission, and rebate or similar,[179] otherwise they are subject to VAT.[180] Similar rules can also be found in the Bahrain VAT system.[181]

Government services as such are not considered to constitute economic activities,[182] and are, thus, out of scope of the VAT. All four countries provide for relief from input tax for governmental bodies by allowing a refund of VAT incurred in their official capacity, explicitly excluding input tax related to commercial activities.[183] Bahrain, the UAE and Oman limit the refund to foreign governments, international organizations,

170. *See* Article 46(4) of the UAE VAT Law (Federal Decree-Law No. 8 of 2017 on Value Added Tax).
171. *See* Article 47(6) of the Oman VAT Law (Royal Decree 121/2020).
172. *See* Article 53(13) of the Bahrain VAT Law (Decree (48) of 2018 Regarding Value Added Tax). This includes the supply of goods and passengers transport services by land, water or air with certain exceptions.
173. As there is no special exemption or zero-rate laid down in the KSA VAT Law. *See also* keypoint, VAT briefs (2018) p. 1, available at https://www.keypoint.com/media/files/VAT-brief-Logistics.pdf.
174. *See* Article 27 of the KSA VAT Law; Article 46(1) of the UAE VAT Law (Federal Decree-Law No. 8 of 2017 on Value Added Tax), as further defined in Article 42 of the Executive Regulation of the Federal Decree-Law No. 8 of 2017 on Value Added Tax; Article 54 of the Bahrain VAT Law (Decree (48) of 2018 Regarding Value Added Tax; and Article 47(1) of the Oman VAT Law (Royal Decree 121/2020).
175. *See* Article 27(2)(b) KSA VAT Law.
176. *See* Article 27(2)(a) KSA VAT Law.
177. *See* Article 27(2)(c) KSA VAT Law. This includes derivatives, options, swaps, credit default swaps and futures.
178. *See* Article 27(1) last sentence.
179. *See* Article 42(3) of the Executive Regulation of the Federal Decree-Law No. 8 of 2017 on Value Added Tax, available at https://www.tax.gov.ae/-/media/Files/FTA/links/Legislation/VAT/Executive-Regulation-of-Federal-Decree-Law-No-8-of-2017---Publish.pdf.
180. *See* Article 42(4) of the Executive Regulation of the Federal Decree-Law No. 8 of 2017 on Value Added Tax,
181. *See* Bahrain VAT General Guide (2018) p. 115 (available at https://www.nbr.gov.bh/pdf/20190116_VAT_General_Guide_v1_3.pdf).
182. *See*, e.g., Article 9(5) of the KSA VAT Law.
183. Article 74(7) of the KSA VAT Law; Article 57 of the UAE VAT Law (Federal Decree-Law No. 8 of 2017 on Value Added Tax); Article 57(2) of the Bahrain VAT Law (Decree (48) of 2018 Regarding Value Added Tax; and Article 87(2) of the Oman VAT Law.

diplomatic bodies, and missions. However, Oman's VAT Law provides for a blanket delegation clause that allows for the refund of VAT in "any other cases specified by decision of the head,"[184] but regulations have not been published yet.

Overall, the implementation of the Member States—as far as they are available—shows that where the GCC VAT framework allows for options to either exempt or zero-rate, Member States have mostly taken the route of zero-rating these supplies. Similarly, the possibility for (partial) refunds of public bodies when carrying out non-taxable activities will lead to a better VAT neutrality.

§5.03 CONCLUSIONS

The OECD regularly measures the performance of VAT systems on the basis of their respective VAT Revenue Ratio (VRR),[185] which compares actual VAT revenues under current law with potential VAT revenue that would be raised if all supplies were taxed at the standard rate with perfect enforcement. Therefore, a VRR of 1 would mean that all potential VAT revenue is actually collected. The VRR provides policy makers with valuable insights into the revenue loss caused by policy choices, such as the concessionary treatment of certain sectors through exemptions and reduced rates, or by non-compliance in terms of mistakes, tax avoidance and fraud. The VRR ratio tends to be significantly higher for modern VAT systems than for older ones, with New Zealand at the top with a VRR of 0.99 for the year 2018 and an OECD average of 0.56. The unweighted average VRR for the EU in 2018 is 0.56, which means that the EU actually collects 44% less than what would be possible under a benchmark VAT regime. Although not the only factor, exemptions play a significant role in the constitution of the low VRR ration for the EU.[186]

As pointed out by many scholars before us, exemptions should be avoided to the farthest extent possible when designing a VAT for all the economic reasons explained above, as well as to mitigate dead weight costs created by administrative and compliance difficulties associated with exemptions and disputes between tax administrations and taxpayers. Tax planning to avoid the denial of input VAT credits is quite common—and from a business perspective rational as the VAT should not be a business cost—and often leads to conflicts where tax administrations feel obliged to protect the revenue base. Statistics show that nearly a third of all cases referred to the CJEU deal with exemptions,[187] which only represent the tip of the iceberg as it can fairly be assumed that the number of cases handled by domestic courts must be much higher.

If exemptions lead to so many known problems, the final question is why the problems remain unresolved? The answer lies largely in the political difficulty in

184. Article 87(6) Oman VAT Law.
185. OECD, *supra* n. 14, 49 et seq.
186. *See also* De la Feria & van Kesteren, *supra* n. 14, 300.
187. *See* Ine Lejeune and Liesbeth Vermeire, *50 Years of Case Law in VAT: In What Direction Is the CJEU Going?* in Georg Kofler et al. (eds), *CJEU—Recent Developments in Value Added Tax 2019* (Linde Verlag, 2020).

removing tax concessions once granted. Moreover, in the EU the political decision-making process is burdensome in that for the area of taxation unanimous decisions by all Member States are required. Finding a "one-size-fits-all solution" for 27 Member States is problematic and progress often requires compromise where legislative changes are accepted while providing more leeway for Member States in the form of options.[188] It remains to be seen whether the Commission's proposed change to Qualified Majority Voting[189] will prevail.

188. *See* further Sebastian Pfeiffer and Karoline Spies, *supra* n. 117, Chapter 4 with regard to the legislative changes of the SME scheme in the EU.
189. *See* European Commission, *Towards a More Efficient and Democratic Decision Making in EU Tax Policy* (2019), COM (2019) 8 final.

CHAPTER 6

Counting the Costs of VAT Compliance

Chris Evans & Richard Krever

§6.01 INTRODUCTION

The reasons for the widespread adoption of the VAT in developed and developing countries are dealt with elsewhere in this volume, where the virtues of the tax are considered in detail. The benefits of the tax do not come without costs, however. The purpose of this chapter is to consider one specific set of the costs that necessarily accompany the VAT for those business taxpayers obliged to comply with its requirements. Those costs are typically referred to as *tax compliance costs*,[1] although, as noted later in this Introduction, there is also a growing literature that considers the slightly different concept of the *tax compliance burden*. A number of studies have suggested that the VAT is the most burdensome of all business taxes,[2] and that its compliance costs are disproportionately high, constituting a major disadvantage to set against its significant merits.[3]

Tax compliance costs are those costs 'incurred by taxpayers, or third parties such as businesses, in meeting the requirements laid upon them in complying with a given

1. Tax compliance costs are one component of the operating costs of the tax system. Operating costs typically comprise the costs expended by taxpayers in complying (or sometimes not complying) with their tax obligations (usually referred to as 'compliance costs'); and the costs to the government (ultimately borne by taxpayers) of administering and collecting the taxes (usually referred to as 'administrative costs').
2. *See*, e.g., Luca Barbone, Richard Bird, and Jaime Vazquez-Caro, *The Costs of VAT: A Review of the Literature* 8 (CASE Network Reports No. 106/2012, Warsaw, 2012); Sebastian Eichfelder and François Vaillancourt, *Tax Compliance Costs: A Review of Cost Burdens and Cost Structures*, 210 Hacienda Pública Española/Rev. Pub. Econ 111, 125-126 (2014); and Chris Evans, Ann Hansford, John Hasseldine, Philip Lignier, Sharon Smulders, and François Vaillancourt, *Small Business and Tax Compliance Costs: A Cross-Country Study of Managerial Benefits and Tax Concessions*, 12(2) eJ. Tax Rsrch. 453, 463 and 474 (2014).
3. Cedric Sandford, *Minimising the Compliance Costs of a GST*, 14 Austl. Tax F. 125, 125 (1998).

structure and level of tax'.[4] While this is an area in which there will always be debate, it is possible to identify a 'hard core' of costs that are indisputably part of the costs of complying with tax requirements.

These costs will include:

- the costs of labour/time consumed in completion of tax activities such as the time taken by a business person to acquire appropriate knowledge to deal with the tax obligations imposed by a tax or tax system or the in-house time taken in compiling receipts and recording data in order to be able to complete a tax return;
- the costs of expertise purchased to assist with completion of tax activities (typically, the fees paid to professional tax advisers for assistance with tax compliance, the provision of tax advice or assistance with tax litigation); and
- incidental expenses incurred in completion of tax activities, including the costs of computer hardware and software, postage, travel, etc.

This definition suggests that it is relatively simple to identify tax compliance costs and that estimates of such costs can be made with some level of precision and certainty. This is, however, far from the case. An extensive literature reveals that there is some degree of imprecision and uncertainty about what is meant by tax compliance costs, and the manner in which they are identified and expressed for comparative purposes.[5] As Sandford, Godwin and Hardwick note, 'complexities and inter-relationships make it difficult if not impossible to define the various costs with absolute precision or in a neat, mutually exclusive way ...'.[6]

There is, for example, a perfectly reasonable view that any measure of tax compliance costs ought to take into account non-monetary costs such as the psychological costs that may arise as a result of dealing with taxes: the stress, anxiety and frustration that inevitably occurs in attempts to comply with legal and administrative obligations imposed by taxes. However, although there have been one or two brave attempts to identify and measure the psychological costs of tax compliance,[7] such costs are very rarely factored into tax compliance cost studies.

Other social and non-monetary costs that may well be a part of the costs of tax compliance are also usually ignored because they are difficult to measure. For example, a tax change, such as the introduction of a higher rate of VAT on a particular range of goods, which causes a trader to cease to stock those goods (in order to keep tax affairs

---

4. Cedric Sandford, Michael Godwin, and Peter Hardwick, *Administrative and Compliance Costs of Taxation* 10 (Fiscal Publications, 1989).
5. This literature is reviewed in Chris Evans, *Taxation Compliance and Administrative Costs: An Overview*, in *Tax Compliance Costs for Companies in an Enlarged European Community* 447 (Michael Lang, Christine Obermair, Josef Schuch, Claus Staringer, and Patrick Weninger eds, Kluwer Law International, 2008), and more recently in Eichfelder and Vaillancourt, *supra* n. 2, at 125-126.
6. Sandford, Godwin, and Hardwick, *supra* n. 4, at 3.
7. *See*, e.g., Robin Woellner, Cynthia Coleman, Margaret McKerchar, Michael Walpole, and Julie Zetler, *Taxation or Vexation – Measuring the Psychological Costs of Tax Compliance*, in *Tax Compliance Costs: A Festschrift for Cedric Sandford* 35 (Chris Evans, Jeff Pope & John Hasseldine, eds., Prospect, 2001).

simple), thereby inconveniencing customers who have to travel further to continue to buy those goods and possibly have to pay more because of the reduction in competition, may arguably give rise to a cost of tax compliance for the consumer. But once again, such costs are rarely, if ever, included in the costs of tax compliance.

There are also other conceptual difficulties that compound any precise definition of tax compliance costs. Sometimes tax compliance costs are divided into unavoidable/involuntary costs and avoidable/voluntary costs: the former comprising those costs that have to be incurred by taxpayers (such as completing and submitting tax returns), while the latter include those discretionary costs that relate to tax planning and the like. The argument is then made that the former should be included in any definition of tax compliance costs, but the latter should not. However most major studies have not distinguished computational and tax planning costs in their estimates of compliance costs – if only for the obvious reason that it is often almost impossible to disentangle the one from the other. Nevertheless, 'both kinds of costs are real resource costs of collecting the taxes'.[8] Similar problems of disentanglement account for the inclusion of both 'commencement' (or once-only) and 'recurrent' (or on-going or regular) costs in most estimates of compliance costs.

There is also another problem of disentanglement. Despite careful attempts to quarantine tax compliance costs from the underlying costs of being in business – core business or accounting costs – there is almost certainly some overlap between business or accounting costs and tax compliance costs. Such 'joint cost problems'[9] relating to the extent of overlap add to the imprecision and uncertainty in the identification and estimation of tax compliance costs and confirm the conclusion that there is no definitional certainty and that most estimates of taxation compliance costs can only be indicative at best.

A penultimate conceptual issue relating to definitional aspects has arisen in the literature more recently. There has been a growing distinction between what might be referred to as tax compliance *costs* and a broader concept of the tax compliance *burden*. Although tax compliance costs generally represent the economist's attempt to quantify or measure the imposition of tax compliance obligations in monetary terms, the tax compliance burden is a somewhat broader, more multidimensional and qualitative concept. It is not a single numerical estimate of costs, but a vector of many qualitative and quantitative factors. This subtle difference is not, however, developed any further in this chapter and the terms are used interchangeably.[10]

Finally, there is a conceptual issue about the appropriate characterization of compliance costs related to concessional measures in the VAT including zero-rates for some domestic supplies, reduced rates, and exempt supplies. The traditional VAT regimes in Europe, evolved from multiple turnover tax systems, inherited many of the

8. Joel Slemrod and Nikki Sorum, *The Compliance Cost of the US Individual Income Tax System*, 37(4) Nat'l Tax J. 461 (1984).
9. Maarten Allers, *Administrative and Compliance Costs of Taxation and Public Transfers in the Netherlands* 31 (Wolters-Noordhoff 1994).
10. The distinction between tax compliance costs and tax burden is explored in more detail in Yige Zu, Chris Evans, and Richard Krever, *The VAT Compliance Burden in the UK: A Comparative Assessment* [2020] 3 Brit. Tax Rev. 356.

concessions found in the predecessor laws and while some were pared back in the mandated common models for VAT in the European Union,[11] political considerations led to many jurisdictions seeking derogations from the common rules to adopt a wide range of additional concessions. Many modern VAT systems are also replete with concessions. The Australian and Canadian GST regimes, for example, were relatively pure tax systems as initially proposed but as they worked through the parliamentary process, both acquired complex and far reaching concessions.

For tax and budget purposes, concessional rules in the VAT are generally not considered tax measures. Rather, they are treated as substitutes for direct spending measures located in tax laws and the cost of the concessions are recorded in tax expenditure budgets that measure the effect of the concessions as if the revenue lost due to the concessions had been collected and paid to the persons enjoying the benefits of reduced taxation.

As will be seen, concessional measures in VAT regimes, particularly multiple rates, exemptions and zero-rating, generate significant compliance costs for businesses, particularly small businesses with far less capacity to use economies of scale to absorb compliance costs. The budget treatment of concessions as spending programs, usually with social-welfare objectives, raises the question as to whether associated compliance costs should be regarded as tax compliance costs or costs incurred to enjoy the benefit of indirect government spending programs. Complicating the analysis is the disconnect between the cost of compliance related to concessions and the benefit of those concessions. This link is easy to see in the case of income tax concessions that flow directly to taxpayers but in the case of VAT concessions, the compliance costs are borne by registered enterprises while the benefits of the concessions are assumed to be passed on, at least partially, to final consumers.

However the conceptual question of whether compliance costs related to VAT concessions should be regarded as tax compliance costs or benefit compliance costs is resolved, registered enterprises encounter the costs when completing VAT returns and consider them as consequences of their VAT obligations. From the perspective of the registered businesses assessed for VAT, the conceptual nature of concessions as tax measures or spending measures and the consequent characterization of these expenses as tax or benefit compliance costs is a secondary issue. The concern of these businesses are the costs of compliance, whatever their cause or theoretical character and, accordingly, as this chapter investigates compliance costs from the perspective of affected businesses, costs associated with compliance are reviewed without consideration of their conceptual nature.

This chapter provides an overview of the research into tax compliance costs generally and of the VAT more particularly (Part §6.02), explaining how and where the research has taken place and what the research has shown. Part §6.03 then identifies

11. Originally in Council Directive 77/388/EEC of 17 May 1977 on the Harmonization of the Laws of the Member States Relating to Turnover Taxes – Common System of Value Added Tax: Uniform Basis of Assessment, OJ [1977] L 145/1-40 (commonly referred to as the 'Sixth Directive'), replaced by Council Directive 2006/112/EC of 28 November 2006 on the Common System of Value Added Tax, OJ [2006] L347/1-117 (commonly referred to as the 'VAT Directive').

the key drivers of the VAT compliance burden. Policy options that may help to mitigate the VAT compliance burden are considered in Part §6.04, and emerging compliance cost challenges and opportunities are considered in Part §6.05 prior to concluding remarks in Part §6.06.

§6.02 REVIEW OF THE RESEARCH

Research into tax compliance costs by academic and public policy researchers commenced in the first half of the 20th century,[12] but has only gained traction and momentum in the last 50 years or so.[13] Most of the more significant research efforts from the 1970s through to the 1990s were concentrated in Europe,[14] and in particular in the United Kingdom (UK).[15] The European wave dominated the research for the next twenty years or so, before research in the 'New World' began to flourish, evidenced by major research projects in North America[16] and Australasia.[17] Subsequently research into tax compliance costs has taken place throughout the world, predominantly in the more developed countries but increasingly in transitional and developing countries.[18]

A variety of approaches has been used to identify the nature of tax compliance costs and to attempt to measure their size. These have involved both quantitative and qualitative research paradigms. Initially, far greater emphasis was placed on quantitative techniques. Postal surveys of a random selection of businesses were frequently the main source of data in the earlier years, with an estimated two-thirds of all studies up to 2003 using this methodology.[19] Increasingly electronic and digital surveys have come to replace postal surveys, and other more qualitative techniques - such as interview-based methodologies, diary and case study approaches and documentary analysis - have also been utilized.

---

12. Robert M. Haig, *The Cost to Business Concerns of Compliance with Tax Laws*, 24 Mgmt. Rev. 323 (1935) is identified as one of the earliest studies into tax compliance costs.
13. *See* Chris Evans, *Studying the Studies: An Overview of Recent Research into Taxation Operating Costs*, 1(1) eJ. Tax Rsrch. 64 (2003).
14. Burkhard Strumpel, *The Disguised Tax Burden Compliance Costs of German Businessmen and Professionals*, 19(1) Nat'l Tax J. 70 (1966).
15. Cedric Sandford, *Hidden Costs of Taxation* (Institute for Fiscal Studies 1973).
16. *See*, e.g., François Vaillancourt, *The Administrative and Compliance Costs of the Personal Income Tax and Payroll Tax System in Canada* (Canadian Tax Foundation 1986); Martha Blumenthal and Joel Slemrod, *The Compliance Costs of the US Individual Income Tax System: A Second Look after Tax Reform*, 45(2) Nat'l Tax J. 461 (1992); and Robert Plamondon, *GST Compliance Costs for Small Business in Canada* (Department of Finance 1993).
17. *See*, e.g., Jeff Pope, Richard Fayle, and Michael Duncanson, *The Compliance Costs of Personal Income Taxation in Australia, 1986/87* (Australian Tax Research Foundation 1990); and Chris Evans, Katherine Ritchie, Binh Tran-Nam, and Michael Walpole, *A Report into Taxpayer Costs of Compliance* (Commonwealth of Australia 1997).
18. Eichfelder and Vaillancourt, *supra*, n. 2; and Sharon Smulders and Chris Evans, *Mitigating VAT Compliance Costs – A Developing Country Perspective*, 32(2) Austl. Tax F. 283 (2017). *See also, e.g.*, Nahida Faridy, Brett Freudenberg and Tapan Sarker, *The Devil is in the Detail: An Analysis of VAT Compliance Costs for SMEs in a Developing Nation*, 23(2) N.Z. J. Tax'n L. & Pol'y 176 (2017) (focusing on Bangladesh).
19. Chris Evans, John Hasseldine, Andy Lymer, Robert Ricketts, and Cedric Sandford, *Comparative Taxation: Why Tax Systems Differ* 218 (Fiscal Publications 2017).

However, surveys require considerable effort and time and the results are not always conclusive given the low response rates sometimes achieved. Other quantitative and qualitative approaches have often proved to be just as time consuming and just as inconclusive. As a result, more recent efforts to better understand the burden of tax regulations have largely entailed the use of estimation and simulation techniques, including the Standard Cost Model widely used by the European Commission[20] and the PricewaterhouseCoopers (PwC) Paying Taxes annual survey[21] which is part of the World Bank's Doing Business (DB) series.[22] While each of these methodologies has a number of useful features, they also present their own set of conceptual and practical limitations.[23]

Studies into tax compliance costs over the last 50 years have considered most of the different types of tax and most of the different persons who carry or otherwise have an impact upon the costs of tax compliance. The diverse taxes and related topics under review have ranged from personal and corporate income taxes, through specific and general indirect taxes, to tax expenditures, petroleum revenue taxes and road tolls. The subjects of the research have included taxpayers of all kinds (such as the employed, employers, the retired, investors, those in business, and road users) as well as those who have an impact upon those costs (such as tax practitioners).[24]

Three major conclusions have emerged from the studies: compliance costs are high and significant; compliance costs are regressive; and compliance costs are not reducing over time.[25]

Compliance costs are high and significant for the main taxes typically levied by national governments, such as the personal income tax, the corporate income tax and the VAT. They are high however measured, whether in absolute money terms or relative to tax yield, gross domestic product (GDP) or administration costs. For example, empirical studies suggest that compliance costs of such taxes are typically anywhere between 2% and 10% of the revenue yield from those taxes, up to 2.5% of GDP, and usually a multiple (of between two and six) of administration costs.[26] A survey of six industry sectors and four types of enterprise conducted in 20 European countries in 2016 identified that tax compliance was a significant burden for European enterprises: its results suggested that the average enterprise incurred tax compliance

20. *See* International Working Group on Administrative Burdens, *The Standard Cost Model: A Framework for Defining and Quantifying Administrative Burdens for Businesses* (August 2004), https://ec.europa.eu/eurostat/documents/64157/4374310/11-STANDARD-COST-MODEL-DK-SE-NO-BE-UK-NL-2004-EN-1.pdf/e703a6d8-42b8-48c8-bdd9-572ab4484dd3 (accessed 12 Oct. 2020).
21. *See* World Bank Group and PwC, *Paying Taxes 2020* (2019), https://www.pwc.com/gx/en/services/tax/publications/paying-taxes-2020.html (accessed 19 Oct. 2020).
22. *See* World Bank, *Doing Business 2020*, https://www.doingbusiness.org/ (accessed 12 Oct. 2020).
23. Richard Highfield, Michael Walpole, and Chris Evans, *A Proposal for the Development and Testing of a Diagnostic Tool for Assessing VAT Compliance Costs*, 28(3) Int'l VAT Monitor 228 (2017).
24. Evans et al., *Comparative Taxation: Why Tax Systems Differ*, *supra* n. 19, at 217.
25. Chris Evans, *The Compliance Costs of Taxing Capital Gains: Implications for New Zealand*, 25(4) N.Z. J. Tax'n L. & Pol'y 381 (2019).
26. Evans, *Taxation Compliance and Administrative Costs: An Overview*, *supra* n. 5, at 457.

costs of just under EUR 7,000 in meeting its tax obligations which comprised 2.5% of its turnover and up to 52% of its total tax liability. VAT, corporate income tax, and wage-related taxes and contributions were rated as the most burdensome taxes, in that order.[27] In contrast, compliance costs for property taxes are low in absolute and relative terms, as are compliance costs of some excise duties in developed countries (for example, tobacco and petrol) where the sales are high and the number of business taxpayers involved are low.

The research also points strongly to the regressive nature of compliance costs of such taxes. The size of the business is a key factor in determining compliance costs, and most of the studies confirm that smaller businesses carry disproportionately higher compliance costs.[28] There are two major reasons for this. First, there are large diseconomies of scale involved in complying with tax requirements, and small firms have to carry the high fixed costs of compliance regardless of the fact that the particular activity or transaction that gives rise to the compliance costs may only occur once or infrequently. Associated with this, there is a learning curve effect that militates strongly against small firms - they may have to commit resources to identify the tax implications of a one-off transaction, compared to a larger business able to amortize that learning cost against a large number of similar transactions. The second reason for the regressive nature of tax compliance costs relates to the indivisibility of factors or inputs used in tax compliance; for example, a taxpayer cannot purchase half a computer in order to deal with tax compliance.

The evidence from the studies also points to the fact that compliance costs are seen to be an ongoing cause for concern. The problem is not perceived as diminishing over time, despite attempts by governments (ostensibly) to reduce the burden faced by taxpayers. Recent Australian studies into the compliance costs faced by small and medium enterprises[29] and by large corporations[30] confirm that tax compliance costs have increased, rather than declined, in constant dollar terms over time. This outcome is confirmed in an extensive 2018 study undertaken by the European Commission, which noted that 'the burden of tax compliance is not significantly reducing over time'.[31]

These three general conclusions that derive from the broader review of the literature that relates to tax compliance costs - that they are high, that they are regressive, and that they are not reducing over time - hold particularly true for the VAT. Indeed, it is not entirely coincidental that the rise of interest in, and research into, tax compliance costs has accompanied the introduction of VAT regimes around the

27. European Commission, *Study on Tax Compliance Costs for SMEs: Final Report* xv (2018).
28. *Ibid.*, xvi. In that report it was noted, at xvi, that, 'on average, SMEs spend 2.5% of their turnover on compliance with tax obligations whereas, [larger enterprises] spend only 0.7% of turnover on tax compliance obligations'.
29. Philip Lignier, Chris Evans, and Binh Tran-Nam, *Tangled Up in Tape: The Continuing Tax Compliance Plight of the Small and Medium Enterprise Business Sector,* 29(2) Austl. Tax F. 217 (2014).
30. Chris Evans, Philip Lignier, and Binh Tran-Nam, *The Tax Compliance Costs of Large Corporations: An Empirical Enquiry and Comparative Analysis,* 64(4) Can. Tax J. 751 (2016).
31. European Commission, *Study on Tax Compliance Costs for SMEs: Final Report, supra* n. 27, at xvi.

world, given the significant and disproportionately high compliance costs often associated with the VAT in both developed and developing countries.

Initial empirical studies focusing on the compliance costs of the VAT were primarily conducted in developed countries.[32] As with the research into other forms of taxation, this research has indicated that these costs are high and significant, as well as severely regressive – even more so than for other business taxes – and not reducing over time.[33] Research into VAT compliance costs in developing countries has also started to surface with much the same outcome. This includes research by the World Bank Group, which, between 2006 and 2011, conducted tax compliance cost studies for businesses in developing and transition countries in Africa, Asia, Latin America and the Middle East.[34] Other VAT compliance cost studies have subsequently been conducted in countries such as Algeria, Botswana, Croatia, Czech Republic, Mauritius, Nepal, Slovakia, Slovenia, South Africa, and Ukraine, with much the same results: all have found that VAT compliance costs are high and, in most cases, regressive.[35] The studies find VAT to be usually the tax with the highest, or second highest, compliance costs out of all the taxes for most of these countries, and confirm in all countries the regressive nature of the compliance costs.

A review of the literature on VAT compliance costs thus leads to the overwhelming conclusion that VAT compliance costs are significant and high for all businesses in both developed and developing countries, but that they fall particularly heavily on the small business sector given the highly regressive nature of their impact. This latter outcome may be of particular concern given the predominance and significance of the small business sector in both developed and developing countries. Most of the relevant evidence also points to the fact that compliance costs in all jurisdictions are not reducing over time,[36] though that evidence is, as yet, somewhat thin in developing countries given the relatively recent nature of the empirical work conducted in those countries.

§6.03 DRIVERS OF THE COMPLIANCE BURDEN

This chapter has already noted that business size is a very strong determinant of the tax compliance burden, with smaller businesses bearing disproportionately higher tax compliance costs. In addition to enterprise size, many other factors also help to account for the compliance burden. These include the industry sector and country in which the business operates, the nature of the business structure, the existence of cross-country

32. Smulders and Evans, *Mitigating VAT Compliance Costs*, *supra* n. 18, at 288.
33. Chris Evans and Michael Walpole, *The Hidden Costs of a GST – An International Perspective*, 12(4) Pol'y 3 (1996-97); Barbone et al., *supra* n. 2, at 8.
34. Jacqueline Coolidge, *Findings of Tax Compliance Cost Surveys in Developing Countries*, 10(2) eJ. Tax Rsrch. 250, 253 (2012).
35. Smulders and Evans, *Mitigating VAT Compliance Costs*, *supra* n. 18, at 289.
36. *See*, e.g., European Commission, *Study on Tax Compliance Costs for SMEs: Final Report*, *supra* n. 27, at xviii, where it is noted that 'overall, the survey respondents almost unanimously reported that tax compliance [in 2016] has become more burdensome than in 2010'.

trade and the extent of out-sourcing of the tax function to professional intermediaries.[37] Other research has indicated that in addition to these factors, the number and nature of taxes that a business has to deal with, international exposure, legal uncertainty and risk profile all drive the compliance costs of larger businesses,[38] while tax law complexity and administrative requirements, in addition to business size, have featured very prominently as key factors in driving tax compliance costs for the SME sector.[39]

In broad terms, all these factors and others can be considered by reference to three overarching determinants of the burden imposed by tax compliance: complexity, change and choice.

[A] Complexity

Complexity is clearly a major determinant of the compliance burden. The more complex the tax system is, the higher the compliance costs are likely to be. But it is important to recognize that there may be different forms of complexity at work in driving tax compliance costs. McCaffery identifies three types, or layers, of complexity.[40]

In the first place there is 'technical complexity', which relates to the level of understanding or comprehensibility of a particular legislative provision in isolation. The second form of complexity is 'structural complexity' (sometimes referred to as transactional or procedural complexity), which relates to the way in which laws are interpreted and applied, and which can affect the certainty and manipulability of legislative provisions.

These two layers of complexity - the technical and the structural - are closely related to the statutory provisions and refer, overall, to the difficulty by which a tax law can be read, understood, applied and resolved (in cases of disputes at court) in various practical situations. Often, this statutory complexity is a product of the policy considerations underlying the particular provision.

The third layer of complexity is labelled 'compliance complexity' by McCaffery and relates to the variety of administrative requirements, such as record-keeping and form-completing tasks, that a taxpayer must perform to comply with the tax laws. This final layer of complexity is neatly described as 'grit in the system' - the way that the taxpayer interacts with the revenue authority at the operational, day-to-day, level.[41]

In its benchmark form, the VAT is, in theory, a remarkably simple tax - registered businesses simply keep a running tally of purchases and sales, deduct the input tax on the former from the output tax on the latter and remit the difference or receive a refund if inputs exceed outputs in a tax period. The only small compliance burden businesses incur is the need to distinguish purchases from registered and unregistered smaller

37. *Ibid.*, xv.
38. Evans et al., *The Tax Compliance Costs of Large Corporations*, *supra* n. 30.
39. Lignier et al., *Tangled Up in Tape*, *supra* n. 29, at 247.
40. Edward J. McCaffery, *The Holy Grail of Tax Simplification* [1990] 5 Wisc. L. Rev. 1267.
41. KPMG, *Administrative Burdens - HMRC Measurement Project* 6 (KPMG LLP 2006).

businesses. In practice, as noted, however, the VAT has proved to be a terribly complex tax with high compliance burdens.

The explanation for the dichotomy between theory and practice lies in the vast array of deviations from a benchmark in practice, a consequence of both history and politics. Inheriting many design features from predecessor turnover taxes, the traditional (European) VAT ended up with multiple rates, requiring businesses to track separately every purchase, and an array of concessional exempt supplies. The first draft of most modern VATs often appeared close to a simpler benchmark VAT but inevitably as the legislation passed through the legislative process, almost all ended up with a host of concessions and special regimes that added layers of complexity to the laws. Compounding the resulting technical and structural complexity was the adoption of multiple concessional rules intended to reduce the compliance burden of the tax but more often than not enhancing with new administrative complexity as businesses were required to navigate the consequential optional or compulsory alternative rules.

While in theory many of these causes of compliance burdens can be addressed through reform, other features of the VAT are intrinsically burdensome. The most significant aspects in this regard are the frequency of tax periods and the segregation of changes into different time periods. In an annual tax such as an income tax, with final filing many months after the end of the tax year, taxpayers may have up to a year and a half to resolve questions or uncertainties. In a VAT, issues must be resolved completely each month for many taxpayers and many times a year for most others. If circumstances change for income tax purposes, taxpayers can often address the issue with a simple amendment of a return. The segmentation of the VAT into separate tax periods means all changes must be addressed by way of adjustment events and evidenced by new documentation in the form of adjustment notes, creating additional tasks for all parties.

[B] Change

Frequent change in legislation, or the introduction of new legislation, can significantly impact upon the compliance burden, and it does not matter whether that change is as a result of the introduction of a relieving provision or the introduction of an integrity measure designed to protect the revenue base. In this sense, 'an old tax is a good tax'. The notion is that change interferes with the smooth operation of the tax administrative machinery that facilitates the interactions that necessarily occur between taxpayer and revenue authority, which takes time to settle down to cope with change.

Compared to the income tax, which is often in a state of almost continual amendment, the VAT seems remarkably stable in most jurisdictions. The apparent stability masks the impact of the less regular changes, however. The most common changes to the VAT are new concessions, creating new borderlines and new uncertainty. This, in turn, leads to new ruling requests and litigation as the VAT structure becomes 'littered with privileges and exemptions that minimise its revenue impact and make it difficult to manage'.[42] Few governments or revenue authorities pay much attention to the compliance costs they impose on taxpayers as they move ever further away from the design ideal.

[C] Choice

A final key determinant of tax compliance costs or burden is - somewhat surprisingly - optionality or choice. It is ironic that often tax complexity (and the consequent taxpayer compliance costs) is the product of tax policy and tax law designed specifically to offer taxpayers choice. Choice can certainly help to reduce the burden of the tax itself and provide a more equitable tax system than would otherwise be the case; but these outcomes often come at the price of a higher compliance burden. Too much choice can be less than optimal.

The compliance cost of optionality is directly tied to the flexibility of business, the attribute that allows enterprises to survive and prosper as the economy continuously evolves. There are no enduring certainties for a business in an ever-changing business environment and as circumstances change, the tax consequences of different options may also change. If an option is available and businesses can freely move between alternative calculations, they will double their compliance costs each tax period to determine their liability for that period under each option and then avail themselves of the system that offers the greatest tax savings. The 'simplification' options described further below illustrate the phenomenon.

§6.04 POLICY OPTIONS TO MITIGATE COMPLIANCE BURDEN

The significant research to date on VAT compliance costs and ongoing concern over both the economic consequences of deadweight compliance costs and the personal costs to businesspersons, particularly proprietors of small businesses, have led to adoption of a wide range of mitigation measures in different jurisdictions. Experience has shown some responses to be very effective while others are problematic both in terms of their impact on compliance costs and the behavioural responses to which they have led. Mitigation measures fall into two broad groupings: changes to the VAT laws; and changes to administrative practices.

[A] Changes in VAT law

Three statutory responses are commonly considered as responses to the high cost of complying with the VAT law, and in particular its regressive impact on small business:

42. Richard Bird and Pierre-Pascal Gendron, *Is VAT the Best Way to Impose a General Consumption Tax in Developing Countries?* 33 (International Studies Program Working Paper 06-18, Andrew Young School of Policy Studies, Georgia State University, May 2006). *See also*, in relation to the EU, Sijbren Cnossen, *Modernizing the European VAT* (CESifo Working Paper No. 8279, May 2020).

high registration thresholds to remove small businesses from the VAT system; clearer borderlines between different types of supplies subject to different treatment under the VAT; and the use of different simplification regimes for small business that may involve modest retreats from pure VAT norms for what are hoped to be comparatively larger reductions in compliance costs for small businesses.

[1] A High Registration Threshold

The most common response to the impact of VAT compliance burdens, in particular the regressive impact on smaller businesses, is the adoption of a high registration threshold, leaving enterprises below the threshold out of the VAT system, meaning they are not required to remit VAT on sales and are not able to claim input tax credits on acquisitions. From a compliance burden perspective, the optimal threshold is the point at which increased revenue from VAT remitted exceeds business' cost of compliance and the tax authority's cost of administration.[43] Translating the theory into practice is challenging, however - best guesses can be made but a truly accurate measurement of VAT compliance costs remains elusive.

Registration thresholds vary widely across jurisdictions but generally it is assumed that higher registration thresholds are more effective at reducing compliance costs. It can be assumed with some confidence that the potential revenue lost may not be that great. An unregistered business is the equivalent of a business that is registered and makes exempt supplies. There is thus no revenue cost to a higher threshold in terms of business making mostly exempt supplies. At the same time, businesses making primarily zero-rated supplies will voluntarily register if the registration threshold is higher than their turnover so the threshold level will not affect the absence of tax revenue from these enterprises. To the extent a business makes what would otherwise be taxable supplies, a high threshold only means the final retail mark-up remains untaxed.[44]

Raising the registration threshold as a means of mitigating compliance burdens is not without its drawbacks, however. A widely recognized problem with any registration threshold is the 'bunching' phenomenon - the large number of enterprises with turnovers just below the registration threshold. The phenomenon is attributed to three factors: enterprises with turnovers above the threshold that split operations into different businesses to remain below the threshold, illegal underreporting of sales, and holding back, or deliberately slowing business output to remain below the threshold.[45]

43. Michael Keen and Jack Mintz, *The Optimal Threshold for a Value-Added Tax*, 88(3-4) J. Pub. Econ. 559 (2004).
44. Cedric Sandford, long regarded as the one of the globe's foremost experts on compliance costs, argues this factor, plus the possibility of higher returns on administrative costs possible if resources are deployed elsewhere in the tax administration, suggest the threshold should be higher than might have been first thought optimal. *See* Cedric Sandford, *Minimising the Compliance Costs of a GST*, in *Tax Administration: Facing the Challenges* 129 (Chris Evans & Abe Greenbaum, eds., Prospect 1998).
45. A comprehensive account of the threshold conundrum and possible solutions can be found in Yige Zu, *VAT/GST Thresholds and Small Businesses: Where To Draw the Line?* 66(2) Can. Tax J.

The first two causes can be countered to a large extent with conventional tax administration tools aimed at avoidance or evasion. The concern of businesses in the third group, however, can only be addressed if compliance costs by a business entering the VAT system are kept to a level below the point at which they more than offset revenues from increased sales above the threshold. If this cannot be achieved, businesses have every incentive to reduce business output and be in the same net profit position.

The economic costs of this behaviour could be significant and some jurisdictions have attempted to address the problem through the use of 'transitioning' measurements that provide tapering credits that allow firms that cross the registration threshold to keep some of the VAT they collect as compensation for the compliance costs they encounter. The compensation reduces gradually as turnover above the registration threshold rises.[46]

[2] Clarifying the Borderlines

A feature of VAT law regularly identified as a driver of VAT compliance burdens is the existence of indistinct borderlines in laws with different rates, exempt supplies or domestic zero-rated supplies. Unless the terms used to describe supplies falling on one side of a borderline or the other are precise and unambiguous, taxable persons and revenue authorities can spend inordinate efforts trying to ascertain the character of particular supplies. In a self-assessment environment in which penalties can apply for what turn out to be incorrect characterizations, the cost of ensuring compliance can be particularly high with reliance on professional firms or costly ruling processes.

The cost of characterizing supplies near borderlines tends to be particularly regressive for two reasons. In the first place, and quite simply, there is the mitigating effect of economies of scale. Even if the costs were the same for large integrated enterprises and small business, those costs can be amortized over far more sales by the larger businesses. The larger businesses are also far more likely to use sophisticated stock and price labelling processes that automatically identify goods by bar code and record the correct VAT character of the supply while small businesses may have to distinguish supplies manually.

A second feature is the likelihood of small businesses carrying stock that does not fit obviously into existing and known categories. Retailers of ethnic foods, for example, will stock items that may be unknown in the general community or even unique to the shop.[47] Limited circulation supplies of this sort will not be addressed in general rulings or guidance and must be decided on a case-by-case basis.

---

309 (2018). *See also*, on potential fairness considerations in favour of a higher threshold, Emily Ann Satterthwaite, *On the Threshold: Smallness and the Value-Added Tax*, 9 Colum. J. Tax L. 177 (2018).

46. *See further* Zu, *supra* n. 45, at 332-334.
47. Compliance queries in Australia include, for example, the nature of mini ciabatta (*see Lansell House Pty Ltd v. Federal Commissioner of Taxation* [2011] FCAFC 6) and semi-dried biltong (*see* ATO GST Industry Issue Ruling 10 (14 October 2020): biltong – semi-dried, soft).

General concepts such as 'food', 'medical' and 'education' can be particularly problematic, and a review of case law from litigated disagreements reveals an almost never-ending list of ambiguities from the characterization of 'books'[48] to the nature of 'new residential premises'.[49] Compounding the compliance cost of characterizing supplies in the face of multiple rates, exemptions or domestic zero-rating is the difficulty of dealing with mixed supplies comprising elements from different VAT groups.[50] Taxpayers have found it particularly challenging to distinguish mixed supplies that can be separated into parts for tax purposes[51] from composite supplies that retain a single tax character despite comprising parts that are subject to separate tax rules on their own.[52]

One effective way of removing or at least largely reducing the costs of characterizing supplies near borderlines is to remove or greatly reduce uncertainty by drawing on definitions from specialized external legislation rather than attempting to develop new definitions in tax law consistent with the policy objectives of concessional rates, exemptions or zero-rating. Thus, for example, the definition of concessionally taxed medical supplies can simply cross reference to items enumerated as medical supplies for the purpose of a national health insurance program[53] and concessionally taxed education supplies can cross reference to definitions used for education spending programs.[54] The borders of these concepts are likely to be very clearly defined in spending legislation, and ambiguities and interpretations have been considered and resolved by experts in the ministries responsible for the related spending programs.

It is far more logical to rely on experts in the spending portfolios to make decisions on the boundaries of tax expenditure spending programs than to delegate this to experts in fiscal law with no knowledge of the policy objectives behind the concessions. Most importantly, the clearer borderlines can greatly reduce the compliance costs associated with the characterization of supplies.

48. *See*, e.g., the UK decision in *Customs and Excise Commissioners v. Colour Offset Ltd* [1995] STC 85, considering whether blank diaries and address books were books for VAT purposes.
49. *See*, e.g., the Australian decision in *Marana Holdings Pty Ltd v. Commissioner of Taxation* [2004] FCAFC 307, considering whether the sale of separately titled motel units for residential occupation constituted sales of new residential premises.
50. *See*, e.g., the Australian case of *Commissioner of Taxation v. Luxottica Retail Australia Pty Ltd* [2011] FCAFC concerning the sale of glass frames and lens, each of which has a different character for Australian GST purposes.
51. For example, *Sea Containers Services Ltd v. Customs and Excise Commissioners* [1999] EWHC Admin 853; [2000] STC 82 (train travel that included provision of a meal).
52. *British Airways plc v. Customs and Excise Commissioners* [1990] STC 643 (air travel that included provision of a meal).
53. *See*, e.g., the Australian GST law which defines zero-rated (GST-free in Australian terminology) medical services as 'a service for which medicare benefit is payable under Part II of the *Health Insurance Act 1973*' (A New Tax System (Goods and Services Tax) Act 1999 (Cth) sections 38-7, 195-1).
54. For example, the definition of a 'tertiary course' comprising an 'education course' for the supply of which GST-free classification may be available relevantly includes 'a course of study or instruction that is a tertiary course determined by the [Education Minister] under subsection 5D(1) of the *Student Assistance Act 1973* for the purposes of that Act' (A New Tax System (Goods and Services Tax) Act 1999 (Cth) sections 38-85, 195-1).

[3] Simplification Measures

Aware of both the deadweight economic costs of VAT compliance burdens and their impact on business acceptance of, and compliance with, the tax law, but unwilling to bear the possible political cost of addressing the fundamental drivers of the burdens, governments have sought ways to mitigate those costs through a range of 'simplification' measures. Notionally intended to reduce time and effort by eliminating some steps, including those caused by complexity drivers such as borderlines caused by concessional rates or exemptions, the measures are often counter-productive, particularly if they are optional.

A common 'simplification' measure is the optional use of cash accounting for small or small and medium businesses. The measure rests on two assumptions: first that it is easier for businesses to record transactions when they receive payment rather than when they make a sale; and second, that there is a cash flow benefit to a small business if taxes are not remitted until payment is in hand. Both are questionable but in any event the assumption may largely be moot as few small businesses make sales on credit, particularly those dealing with final consumers. They are, however, likely to encounter credit arrangements on acquisitions if they are supplied by large businesses, in which case it is to their advantage to use ordinary accrual accounting and claim credits at the time of supply, not when the account is settled.

If the use of cash accounting is optional, businesses may incur additional compliance costs in calculating tax liability twice, with each method tested, to determine the relative benefit of cash or accrual recognition in their circumstances. The businesses that then opt to use cash accounting do so recognizing that it results in greater complexity but will yield a financial benefit in terms of tax savings or the time value of money.[55]

The optional use of cash accounting also raises the risk of avoidance schemes by taxpayers structuring transactions between related parties using different accounting rules in order to receive refunds of claimed input credits on one side of the transaction while output tax liability on the other is deferred indefinitely. To counter whipsaw transactions, further and more complex exceptions to the cash accounting rules are needed.[56]

A less common small business simplification rule, intended to reduce the cost of compliance arising from the tedious and complex task of tracking all inputs where a small business uses inputs that may be subject to different rates or that may include exempt or zero-rated inputs, is the use of 'presumptive' input tax credits. Under a presumptive input tax credit regime, the tax authority determines an average credit entitlement for businesses making particular types of supplies, commonly expressed as a percentage of turnover, and then allows all small businesses making the same type of

55. Rebecca Klahr, Lucy Joyce, Rory Donaldson, Graham Keilloh, and Cheryl Salmon, *Behaviours and Experience in Relation to VAT Registration: Final Report* (HM Revenue and Customs Research Report No. 446, 2017).

56. Yige Zu and Richard Krever, *GST Cash and Accrual Mismatches: Avoiding the Avoidance*, 46(4) Austl. Tax Rev. 27 (2017).

supplies to claim credits using the same presumptive entitlement rate, without having to track each input. In some cases, broad categories are used while in others finer distinctions between different types of businesses are used to provide greater accuracy on the average entitlement.[57]

As 'simplification' measures, the presumptive input tax credit regimes suffer from a number of inherent problems. To begin with, both the broad band and narrower category variants are inconsistent with the actual business operations of many firms, which may straddle different categories of input tax entitlement. Special rules to accommodate straddlers add new levels of complexity to the 'simplification' regimes while if the use of presumptive input tax credits is optional, businesses are likely once again to calculate their rules using actual entitlements and presumptive entitlements so the perceived benefit - not requiring enterprises to track every input - is necessarily lost.

The additional burdens associated with optionality can be removed if presumptive rules are made compulsory. An example is the mandatory use of a margin scheme for travel agents in the EU.[58] As a presumptive scheme is based on averages rather than actual inputs for each business, the simplification benefits for the industry as a whole come at the cost of some over-taxation and some under-taxation for particular enterprises. Also, however discrete the industry may appear to be, there will inevitably be transactions that appear to fall outside the boundaries of the supplies covered by any presumptive regime.[59]

In summary, it appears that in practice simplification regimes intended to offset the additional costs resulting from primary drivers of compliance burdens such as multiple rates or exempt inputs may add new layers of complexity and compliance burdens to the VAT system. A more effective tactic might be to tackle the underlying drivers.

[B] Changes in Administrative Practices

Changes in administrative practices can have a strong impact upon tax compliance costs in a variety of ways.

Often the relationship between compliance costs and administrative costs will be direct - they both move in the same direction. A poorly designed and administered legislative provision will cause both sets of costs to increase. Equally important, however, is that well-designed and administered provisions can considerably reduce the compliance burden faced by businesses in dealing with the VAT.

The relationship between tax compliance costs and tax administrative costs is not, of course, always direct. On many occasions the two sets of costs will move in

57. The Canadian regime, for example, has two broad categories; the UK regime has 55 different presumptive input tax categories.
58. VAT Directive, Articles 306-310.
59. *See*, e.g., *Travel Incentives Meetings Exhibitions Ltd v. HMRC* [2016] UKFTT 24 (TC) where the question arose whether conference organization and services, including travel arrangements for participants, was a single supply of conference arrangements or a mixed supply including travel that fell in the mandatory margin scheme system.

opposite directions - measures designed to make life easier, or save costs, for the revenue authority may well impose a higher burden on business. A self-assessment regime is the obvious example of this inverse relationship, where the compliance burden falls on the taxpayer rather than the tax authority. But other examples can be found. Spending cuts to the revenue workforce, perhaps in the form of less available customer support, may well translate to higher compliance costs for business. Conversely, a decision to 'socialise' tax operating costs by requiring the revenue authority to take on more of the administrative burden of a particular tax can have beneficial effects for the business community in the form of lower tax compliance costs. This has often been the case when new taxes or major changes are in prospect. For example, when the Australian GST was introduced at the beginning of this century, the Australian Taxation Office was given responsibility for (and was funded for) many administrative aspects of the compliance regime of the new tax that would typically have fallen upon the business community.

Aside from this key relationship between the revenue authority and business, much contemporary research indicates that administrative factors are important drivers of compliance costs and therefore that changes to the way that the VAT is administered can significantly mitigate (or exacerbate) those costs.[60] Hence factors such as the frequency of reporting and filing of the tax return, the level of other documentation required to be submitted, technological solutions adopted (for example with pre-filled tax returns and e-filing) as well as the costs of audits, appeals and litigation are critical. Carefully considered measures designed to improve any of these factors can reduce compliance costs. Conversely, a defect anywhere in the VAT administrative system, starting at registration and ending at deregistration and the ease with which it can be done, can bring down the best designed VAT system.[61] Thus, the registration and reporting processes, the rate at which refunds are paid, audit practices and the availability of helpful guidance from the revenue authority all need careful consideration as they impact directly on VAT compliance costs.[62]

[1] The Registration Process

The importance of setting the registration threshold at the appropriate level has already been identified as a key feature of legislative design. It is also critically important, given that 'the taxpayer registry is the backbone of all tax administrations',[63] to ensure that the administrative process of registration is as straightforward and painless as possible.

60. Eichfelder and Vaillancourt, *supra*, n. 2, at 134; Smulders and Evans, *Mitigating VAT Compliance Costs*, *supra* n. 18, at 290; and Chris Evans, Richard Highfield, Binh Tran-Nam, and Michael Walpole, *Diagnosing the VAT Compliance Burden: A Cross-Country Assessment*, 31(2) Int'l VAT Monitor 228 (2020).
61. Richard Bird and Pierre-Pascal Gendron, *The VAT in Developing and Transitional Countries*, 161-192 (Cambridge University Press, 2007).
62. Kathrin Bain, Michael Walpole, Ann Hansford, and Chris Evans, *The Internal Costs of VAT Compliance Costs: Evidence from Australia and the United Kingdom and Suggestions for Mitigation*, 13(1) eJ. Tax Rsrch. 158 (2015).
63. Mark Gallagher, *Benchmarking Tax Systems*, 25(2) Pub. Admin. & Dev. 125, 139 (2005).

A primary cause of lengthy and complex (and hence costly) VAT registration processes is the verification process adopted by the tax administration to prevent fraudulent activity. As procedures for registration evolved in developed countries, revenue authorities shifted to more systematic and specialized risk-based processes to validate the integrity of VAT registrations. These were paralleled by the use of internal and/or external data sources to identify businesses that should be, but are not, registered for VAT.[64] Although the position is not as clear-cut in developing countries, there are signs that the importance of finding solutions to ease the VAT registration burden, including the use of automated and on-line taxpayer registries with standardized databases across different taxes and harmonized administrative procedures, is being recognized. A survey of the compliance burden of 47 Forum on Tax Administration (FTA) countries conducted in 2017 found that roughly two-thirds of the revenue bodies surveyed offered an electronic registration service, and that this helped to reduce the burden in those countries with the facility available.[65]

[2] Frequency and Length of Reporting and Remittance

VAT compliance costs are heavily influenced by the number of times a business must report information, or make payments, and also by the amount of information that has to be reported each time. Most developed countries are not only conscious of the need to keep reporting and remitting requirements to the minimum possible, but also actively pursue policies and administrative procedures that achieve this outcome. Hence just over two-thirds of the 47 FTA countries surveyed in 2017 sought to ease the compliance burden for small businesses by allowing VAT returns and payments on a quarterly or less frequent basis for this group, with only nine countries out of the 47 requiring monthly filing and payment for small businesses.[66] The outcomes were not quite as positive in terms of the length or volume of information required in periodic reports, however. Only eight revenue bodies were reported as having relatively streamlined VAT return information requirements, with no more than 10 boxes or fields requiring completion in a typical VAT return, compared to more than half of the 47 countries which required the completion of 21 or more boxes or fields.[67] Many developing countries share this disappointing outcome, both in terms of the volume of information requirements. Many also often require returns and payments to be made on a monthly basis.[68]

Clearly, therefore, steps taken to reduce both the frequency of reporting and the volume of information that has to be reported (sometimes with accompanying

64. OECD, *Developments in VAT Compliance Management in Selected Countries* 36 (OECD Publishing 2009).
65. Richard Highfield, Chris Evans, Binh Tran-Nam, and Michael Walpole, *Diagnosing the VAT Compliance Burden: A Cross-Country Assessment* 15 (Amended Final Report, 21 October 2019), https://www.unsworks.unsw.edu.au/primo-explore/fulldisplay?vid=UNSWORKS&docid=unsworks_modsunsworks_59518&context=L (accessed 20 Oct. 2020).
66. *Ibid.*
67. *Ibid.*
68. Smulders and Evans, *Mitigating VAT Compliance Costs*, *supra*, n. 18, at 306.

documentation) can go a considerable way to mitigate the compliance burden. There are numerous examples of countries around the world that have significantly reduced the compliance burden by switching from monthly to quarterly reporting and remitting schedules, including Azerbaijan, Macedonia, Rwanda, South Africa, Ukraine and Vietnam in the last few years.[69] Often, and as considered in more detail later in this chapter, this switch has been accompanied and facilitated by changes in the use of technology to file the reports and make the payments, including the use of electronic and on-line filing and payment mechanisms.

[3] Refund Procedures

The underlying rationale and mechanics of VAT systems often lead to an outcome where much of the VAT that is initially collected by businesses and handed over to revenue authorities subsequently falls to be repaid to those same businesses. Refunds are particularly prevalent when a large proportion of supplies are exported or when the jurisdiction has generous zero-rated concessions for domestic supplies such as food, health or education. The need for refunds to be made, combined with the timeliness of those refunds and the payment of interest on delayed refunds, can have a significant impact on the compliance burden of the business community. The survey of the 47 countries of the FTA with a VAT in place in 2017 found that revenue authorities in just over half the countries involved (24) refunded in excess of 30% of gross annual VAT collections, and this included 11 countries where the refunded amounts constituted over 40% of collections. Those countries with high levels of VAT refunds often had lengthy VAT refund claim processing periods (in some cases in excess of 3 months) and limits on the payment of interest on delayed refunds.[70]

The impact upon the compliance burden caused by refund procedures can be compounded where the refund claim requires the submission of additional supporting documentation, including copies of invoices, financial statements or contracts with suppliers. While this is often considered necessary to combat fraudulent claims or other criminal activity, it nonetheless can prove a costly exercise for those businesses affected.

Mitigation of this aspect of the compliance burden involves a careful balancing of the need to design administrative systems that can detect and prevent fraud - using sophisticated data and risk analysis techniques - and operating the system in such a way that it permits refunds to be made within acceptable time limits and without imposing onerous documentation requirements. In the event that legitimate refunds are not made expeditiously, businesses that are affected should be financially compensated for the delay, with interest paid on delayed repayments.

Following this path, countries as diverse as Egypt, Côte d'Ivoire, Senegal, Armenia, Israel and Mauritius were all able to show reductions in the VAT compliance burden in 2020 as a result of the introduction of faster refund procedures and on-line

69. *Ibid.*
70. Highfield et al., *Diagnosing the VAT Compliance Burden: A Cross-Country Assessment* (Amended Final Report, 21 October 2019), *supra* n. 65, at 15.

case management systems for processing VAT refunds.[71] Elsewhere, other design features have been built into systems to expedite the refund process. For example, in Romania, businesses have been allowed since 2014 to claim refunds below EUR 10,000 (to be paid within 45 days) by simply ticking the relevant box on the VAT return. Although they may then be subject to a post-approval inspection, this simple measure permitted over 50% of those businesses impacted by the change to receive their refunds - and hence incur lower compliance costs - more expeditiously than had been the case before the change.[72]

[4] Audit Practices

The modern trend towards risk-based approaches to tax administration is usually underpinned by an effective audit strategy on the part of the revenue authority. Audit and investigation can take many different forms, ranging from low profile queries resulting in no further action through to full-scale investigation resulting in prosecution for fraud.[73] The scale of audit and investigation activity can also vary considerably across different countries.

Inevitably any audit activity has the capacity to impose significant compliance costs on businesses affected by the activity. This will be particularly true if the administrative costs of the audit incurred by the revenue authority are also be charged back to the business.[74]

As is the case with many other aspects of the compliance burden, the capacity for mitigation of the potentially significant compliance costs that can arise when post-filing audits take place lies principally with the revenue authority. A well-balanced and well-targeted audit program based upon clearly articulated risk factors is the foundation stone for ensuring that unnecessary compliance costs are not inflicted on the business community. This can be accompanied by other strategies designed to improve the effectiveness of the audit process including the introduction of specialized VAT audit divisions and the upskilling of audit staff, as well as the use of technology that can provide the revenue with enhanced intelligence that can therefore avoid unnecessary and often futile and costly investigation and examination.[75] An example is the use of electronic invoicing systems that generate easily confirmed business invoices when required.

71. World Bank Group and PwC, *Paying Taxes 2020*, *supra* n. 21, at 45-46.
72. Joe Stanley-Smith, *How Prepared Are Taxpayers and Authorities in GCC Countries for VAT?* 27(3) Int'l Tax Rev. 8 (2016).
73. Margaret McKerchar and Chris Evans, *Sustaining Growth in Developing Economies through Improved Taxpayer Compliance: Challenges for Policy Makers and Revenue Authorities*, 7(2) eJ. Tax Rsrch 171 (2009).
74. Salman Shaheen, *A New Age Dawns for Indirect Tax*, 23(10) Int'l Tax Rev. 22 (2012-13).
75. Smulders and Evans, *Mitigating VAT Compliance Costs*, *supra* n. 18, at 309-310.

[5] Revenue Authority Capacity and Guidance

The level of VAT compliance costs or burden will inevitably be strongly influenced by the capacity and capability of the revenue authority to be able to meet the service and compliance needs of business - effectively the extent to which it is able to assist taxpayers to comply with their obligations so far as the operation of the VAT regime is concerned. VAT compliance costs can be minimized if taxpayers are fully informed about the consequences of VAT by tax officials trained to correctly answer any questions posed to them.[76] Conversely, the lack of appropriate guidance from the relevant revenue authority may result in increased compliance costs for businesses.[77]

Once again, empirical evidence gathered from a survey of 47 FTA countries in 2017 suggests that the level of support is highly variable, and that particular problems arise in relation to inadequate or poorly designed services and programs for newly registered businesses, and in weaknesses in revenue authority phone enquiry services.[78]

There are many examples around the world of good practice in revenue authorities designed to foster compliance, provide guidance and minimise VAT compliance costs. These include: the development of centralized taxpayer educational units; adherence to quality management systems designed to impose international standards for organizational service delivery; taxpayer awareness campaigns to promote voluntary compliance; provision of an array of guidance documents which present, clearly and concisely, the revenue authority view and interpretation of legislative provisions; the availability of easy to reach and well-informed revenue authority staff to answer business taxpayer queries; and the extensive use of on-line and interactive tools designed to assist the taxpayer in resolving VAT issues.[79]

[6] The Role of Technology

It was noted by the Organisation for Economic Co-operation and Development (OECD) nearly 20 years ago that advances in the fields of information and related technology, together with the spread of internet communications, have opened up many opportunities to transform traditionally paper-based interactions between business and government into paperless interactions, providing greater opportunities for the automation of tasks such as the collation of information, the calculation of taxes and lodgement of tax reports.[80] Since then, even more significant reductions in the compliance burden have been made possible as a result of technological developments, and this is particularly the case so far as the administration of the VAT is concerned.

76. Sandford, *Minimising the Compliance Costs of a GST*, *supra* n. 3, at 127.
77. Bain et al., *supra* n. 62, at 181.
78. Highfield et al., *Diagnosing the VAT Compliance Burden: A Cross-Country Assessment* (Amended Final Report, 21 October 2019), *supra* n. 65, at 23.
79. Smulders and Evans, *Mitigating VAT Compliance Costs*, *supra* n. 18, at 313-315.
80. OECD, *From Red Tape to Smart Tape: Administrative Simplifications in OECD Countries* (OECD Publishing 2003).

There are four broad stages that have been identified in the adoption of technology for the administration of VAT.[81] Progression through each of these stages has usually – though not inevitably – led to a reduction in the compliance burden facing businesses.

In the first stage, minimal use is made of technology and most recording, reporting and transactions are paper based. The largely manual processes inevitably lead to relatively high compliance burdens for businesses in countries that are identified as being at this stage of technological development. It has been suggested that countries such as Venezuela, Bolivia and Gabon are still at this stage of technological development so far as the administration of their VAT systems is concerned, and that as a consequence they suffer relatively high VAT compliance burdens.[82]

The second stage of technological development for VAT administration typically involves some form of on-line filing and payment which generally leads to a reduction in the compliance burden for business taxpayers. Countries at this stage of development, according to the PwC Paying Taxes report, include the Ivory Coast, the Kyrgyz Republic and Indonesia.

The third stage of technological advance in VAT administration entails a move to real-time systems, involving close integration of taxpayers' and tax administrations' technology solutions. This advance in technology can include real-time or near real-time filing together with mandated e-invoicing and payment systems. This can provide benefits in the form of lower compliance costs for businesses, largely achieved as a result of the high volume of transactions and the removal or reduction of archiving and ancillary reporting requirements; and enhanced fraud prevention and greater control over data for the revenue authority. Notable examples include Spain (real-time invoicing), Italy (mandatory business-to-government, business-to-business and business-to-consumer invoicing through a government-run portal) and Hungary (reporting of e-invoice information by way of its KOBAK system).[83]

The fourth level of cutting-edge technology – which includes the use of blockchain, artificial intelligence and big data – is, as yet, in its infancy, but is nonetheless being assessed and piloted in many countries and further benefits (in the form of lower compliance costs for businesses and enhanced efficiency and transparency for revenue authorities) are anticipated. There are already examples of countries adopting this next level of technology. For example, in Kazakhstan blockchain is already in use in the administration of some VAT receipts and is showing promising results. In the UK, HM Revenue and Customs is still evaluating the technology as a part of its comprehensive VAT digitization programme.[84] China's Tax Administration Information System-3 currently being piloted builds on earlier initiatives to digitize VAT invoicing and uses 'big data' to integrate VAT enforcement with that of other taxes.[85]

81. World Bank Group and PwC, *Paying Taxes 2020*, *supra* n. 21, at 20-23.
82. *Ibid.*, 20.
83. *Ibid.*, 20-23.
84. *Ibid.*
85. *See* Chengrui Xiao and Yuchen Shao, *Information System and Corporate Income Tax Enforcement: Evidence from China*, J. Acct. Pub. Pol'y 106772 (2020). The VAT invoice information obtained has collateral benefits in terms of national statistics and economic modelling: Yuning

Whichever stage a country finds itself at, there is little doubt that technological advances have the capacity to help reduce the compliance costs encountered by the business community as a result of the operation of the VAT. But some caution is also needed. There are often short-term costs associated with the adoption of new technologies. To some extent these can be mitigated, as evidenced in Australia in the lead up to the introduction of its GST in 2000 when the Government provided vouchers for businesses which could be used to purchase appropriate software. But compliance costs do not inevitably fall as a result of advances in technology. A 2016 study of SMEs conducted by KPMG on behalf of the European Commission and based on over 3,000 telephone interviews noted that even though 93% of enterprises filed either the corporate tax return or the VAT return electronically (and 75% filed both returns electronically), the data did not show that this development alone had led to a significantly lower relative compliance burden: 'e-filing is prevalent but does not necessarily reduce the compliance burden'.[86] The same may also be true of other advances in technology.

§6.05 EMERGING COMPLIANCE COST CHALLENGES AND OPPORTUNITIES

The rise of the digital economy, and in particular the growth of cross-border commerce built on the internet, has posed new VAT compliance cost challenges for businesses and tax administrators, falling into five broad groups.

One of the first issues confronting tax administrations was the growth of offshore platforms that could be used by tens of thousands of small retailers to reach customers across the globe.[87] The resulting flood of imports arriving in the mail or by courier threatened to overwhelm local customs authorities. An initial response was to provide an exemption for low value goods but vigorous campaigns by local retailers unable to compete with tax-free imported goods led to what is emerging as a common response, a requirement that retail platforms register and collect VAT when sales into a jurisdiction exceed the registration threshold. Compliance costs from this route are unlikely to be high. Digital platforms are highly automated and can easily cope with automatic inclusions of VAT on sales with delivery addresses in a jurisdiction that has legislated a VAT liability on foreign sales platforms.

Gao, Meng Li and Yufeng Lu, *What Can Be Learned from Billions of Invoices? The Construction and Application of China's Multiregional Input-Output Table Based on Big Data from the Value-Added Tax*, 56(9) Em. Mrkts & Trd. 1925 (2020). For a discussion of proposals in the New Zealand context, *see also* Peter Scott, *Thirty Years on: GST at a Crossroads: GST and Technology*, 23 N.Z. J. Tax'n L. & Pol'y 146.

86. European Commission, *Study on Tax Compliance Costs for SMEs: Final Report*, *supra*, n. 27, at xvi. *See also*, in relation to compliance costs of HMRC's application of the Making Tax Digital to VAT, House of Commons Public Accounts Committee, United Kingdom, *Tackling the Tax Gap* 14 (Twentieth Report of Session 2019-21, HC650, 16 October 2020).

87. For a discussion of the developing role of platforms in VAT/GST enforcement and collection, *see*, e.g., Luisa Scarcella, *E-Commerce and Effective VAT/GST Enforcement: Can Online Platforms Play a Valuable Role?* 36 Comp. L. & Sec. Rev. 105371.

The platforms will face additional compliance costs when selling into jurisdictions with multiple rates or exempt goods, comparable to the additional costs incurred by local retailers in those jurisdictions. The problem in this case is not one of new retailers or digitalization but rather the fundamental complexity of the VAT regime in these jurisdictions.

A second and somewhat similar issue is the rule now found in many jurisdictions that requires foreign suppliers of digital services delivered over the internet such as media streaming services to register in the jurisdiction and remit VAT if sales to the jurisdiction exceed the registration threshold. Once again, the firms in question rely on sophisticated computerized and automatic billing and payment systems and adding VAT to invoices to customers with IP addresses in a jurisdiction is not difficult. The cost may be marginally lower for the firms if a clearing house for multiple jurisdictions is available such as the digital clearing house (the 'mini one-stop shop') in the EU.[88]

The third, and possibly most significant, issue for small business presented by the rise of digital commerce is the creation of new compliance obligations for local businesses able for the first time to import digital services from providers who may fall below registration and remittance rules for foreign digital suppliers. VAT systems commonly provide for registered importers of untaxed digital supplies to account for tax on the supplies on a reverse charge basis if the importer will use them to make exempt supplies or imports them for personal use. Many jurisdictions extend the reverse charge rule to all untaxed imports of digital services, even if the reverse charge tax liability is simultaneously offset by an input tax credit obligation.

While not overly onerous, reverse charge rules can create a burden for small business, particularly for those that have previously not encountered a reverse charge obligation. The burden can be reduced significantly if the reverse charge is limited to those instances in which the charge only applies if the importer will use the services for reasons other than in the course of a business to make taxable supplies.[89]

A fourth VAT compliance issue arising out of the digital economy concerns participants in the sharing economy such as drivers for passenger services or for delivery services and hosts for home accommodation. These new roles in the economy raise a number of issues and there has been legislation and litigation in many jurisdictions over the status of individuals (are they employees or independent contractors) and the nature of their businesses (for example, are passenger drivers subject to general business registration thresholds or possibly lower thresholds for taxis). The resolution of the issues may differ across jurisdictions depending on local considerations including labour laws and VAT design objectives.

In one sense, in terms of the VAT outcome, the issue is analogous to the question in the traditional economy whether services are provided by individual hairdressers or

88. *See* Martha Papis-Almansa, *VAT and Electronic Commerce: The New Rules as a Means for Simplification, Combatting Fraud and Creating a More Level Playing Field*, 20(2) ERA Forum. 201 (2019).
89. This is the rule, for example, in Australia.

the hair salon in which they operate[90] or whether prostitutes offer individual services or services in the context of a brothel's business (or, as the services and business are euphemistically referred to practice in some jurisdictions, masseuses providing services in massage parlours).[91] In the traditional economy, these questions are laboriously resolved on a case-by-case basis looking at a range of facts including customers' perceptions of the arrangements. In contrast, however, in the digital sharing economy, the platform is the sole business entity known to the customer and all communication with the individual service provider is through the platform. From a policy perspective, a strong case may be made for using the same approach for shared economy providers that has been adopted for online retail platforms for goods, measuring registration thresholds at the platform level rather than the individual supplier level.

Whether registration thresholds are applied at the platform level or individual provider level, compliance burdens can be kept very low as a consequence of the fully automated and computerized nature of the transaction.[92]

A fifth area of compliance burden issues related to the digital economy concerns the many small businesses that have taken advantage of the internet to promote sales to international customers. These enterprises for the first time must deal with any rules that are in place for zero-rated exports. In many jurisdictions, zero-rated sales abroad entail no additional compliance costs; enterprises simply record sales abroad as export sales and sell for a non-tax inclusive price. Additional costs are encountered in jurisdictions that have other rules for export sales. Eliminating unnecessary record-keeping or other administrative requirements in these jurisdictions would be a desirable reform not connected with the fact that the internet has facilitated export sales by businesses that had previously only served domestic customers.

§6.06 CONCLUSION

VAT is an important revenue source for all governments levying the tax. The collections fund important public goods and services that enhance the lives of those persons whose consumption triggers the tax and who ultimately bear the burden of the tax. Along the supply chain to that final consumption, however, a chain of intermediary businesses often incurs substantial compliance burdens. These costs, both monetary and in kind, contribute nothing to the public revenue or to the businesses that incur them. They are, moreover, more often than not very regressive, impacting small business far more severely than the largest enterprises in the economy. Businesses and the larger economy and society stand to gain if policy, design or administrative practice reforms can reduce the dead-weight losses from these burdens.

---

90. *See*, for example, *Commissioners of Revenue and Customs v. Denyer* [2007] EWHC 2750; *Customs and Excise Commissioners v. MacHenrys (Hairdressers) Ltd and MacHenrys II (a firm)* [1993] BVC 43 and *Kieran Mullin Ltd. v. Customs and Excise Commissioners* [2003] STC 274; [2003] EWHC 4 (Ch).
91. *See*, for example, *Byrom, Kane & Kane (t/a Salon 24) v. Commissioners of Revenue & Customs* [2006] EWHC 111 (Ch).
92. *See* further Michael Walpole, *The Australian GST Cross-Border Rules in a Global Context*, eJ. Tax Rsrch. forthcoming (2020).

While recognition of the level of compliance burdens, their regressive nature, and their causes has increased significantly in recent years, little has been done to address the underlying issues that lead to compliance burdens. The rapid rise of the digital economy has both created some new compliance issues and solutions to those issues and offered the means, through digital records and processing of both digital and traditional supplies, of reducing some compliance costs to negligible amounts. Unfortunately, the source of compliance burdens lies not so much in the mechanics of calculation or remittance of tax as in the costly and time-consuming process of determining the base in the first place, particularly making judgments about the character of supplies in systems with multiple borderlines between concessionally-taxed and ordinary supplies. The burdens are compounded by the double calculations caused by optional regimes and the web of administrative practices of differing degrees of complexity in many jurisdictions.

Almost no VAT compliance burdens are inherent to the tax and the differences in compliance burden levels across jurisdictions are significant. Among other things, those differences provide useful guides to reforms that can reduce compliance burdens, often substantially. In almost every case, the key to reform is political will and skill. What is needed are politically viable packages that trade the removal of concessions and systems popular for particular groups for gains that benefit the entire community. The challenge is great.

CHAPTER 7

VAT Gaps in Developing Countries: Measurement, Administration and Politics*

Pierre-Pascal Gendron & Richard M. Bird

§7.01 INTRODUCTION

The economic devastation from COVID-19 will undoubtedly force many governments to seek enhanced revenue mobilization opportunities to finance the extraordinary expenditures due to the pandemic and to compensate for the fall in revenues from core taxes that resulted from the economic slowdown. Because the impact is severe, ongoing, and may be long-lived, it will be necessary to focus on solutions that provide long-term answers.

The value-added tax (VAT) seems particularly well suited for this revenue mobilization challenge. The VAT is the mainstay of revenue systems in many countries, particularly less developed countries, and an important source of revenue in over 160 countries around the world.[1] Countries have adopted VATs for many reasons. The principal reason is simply that it is a major revenue producer. In contrast to alternatives or complementary policies such as income taxes, import duties or selective excise taxes, a broad-based consumption tax like VAT is a relatively efficient way to raise significant amounts of revenue from an economic perspective because it is less distorting and hence less likely to discourage investment and growth. Finally, because consumption is a more stable revenue source than other tax bases, VAT revenues

* This is a revised version of a chapter presented at the Webinar O que podemos aprender com a experiência internacional do IVA/IBS, Série Reforma Tributária, FGV Direito SP, São Paulo, Brazil, 30 July 2020. We thank our discussants Rita de la Feria and Cornelius Fleischhaker for their insightful comments, and Melina Rocha Lukic for helpful discussions and resources on the ongoing consumption tax reform in Brazil. We also thank Sijbren Cnossen for his comments on a subsequent draft.

1. The discussion draws on Richard M. Bird, *VAT During and After the Pandemic*, Tax N. Int'l 6 (28 September 2020).

generally should grow more or less at the same rate as the entire economy, unlike other taxes and notably those on business income, whose revenues usually expand more rapidly when the economy grows but tend to contract rapidly when growth slows down.

Many developing countries have engaged in sustained efforts to enhance revenue mobilization through the VAT. A few without a VAT have considered adopting one. The central focus of most reforms is the revenue that an enhanced or new VAT system might produce, an issue that supersedes the alleged superior efficiency of VAT for most stakeholders. How can one assess the potential revenue? In recent years, several methodologies to calculate the so-called VAT gap have been developed and implemented. Loosely speaking (for now), the VAT gap is the difference between the potential revenue of a VAT and the actual revenue, that is, the revenue that could be collected but is not for a number of reasons.

This chapter explores why it is desirable to measure the VAT gap, how to do so, and some of the potential uses and challenges presented by such measures. Section 7.02 outlines the background and justification for focusing on the VAT gap. Section 7.03 briefly describes the main approaches to measuring the gap. Section 7.04 explores some interpretations and limitations of VAT gap estimates, and §7.05 considers their implications for tax policy and tax administration. Section 7.06 examines the political economy of VAT gap estimates. Section 7.07 concludes.

§7.02 VAT REVENUE: MIND THE GAP

A relatively large and growing literature on VAT gaps has emerged over the last decade. This section reviews the reasons and motivations for that growth, explains the anatomy of VAT gaps (several versions exist), and provides a brief overview of how these gaps may be measured.

[A] Beyond Simple Ratios

Until about a decade ago, the standard macro analysis of VAT revenue performance relied on simple ratios such as:

- VAT revenues to total tax revenues;
- VAT revenues to consumption;
- VAT revenues to GDP; and
- VAT buoyancy.[2]

2. VAT buoyancy equals (Percent change in VAT revenue) / (Percent change in GDP). The ratio tracks the total response of VAT revenues to changes in national income and to discretionary changes in tax policy over time. For further discussion of this and other performance indicators, *see* International Monetary Fund, *Tax Policy Assessment Framework: VAT Module*, available at https://www.imf.org/en/Data/TPAF (last accessed 25 July 2020).

- VAT elasticity.[3]
- VAT tax expenditures.[4]

For example, Figure 7.1 illustrates the relative importance of VAT revenues by region in terms of the usual measures of VAT revenue as a percent of revenue and GDP, and total tax revenue as a percent of GDP. The data show interesting patterns. VAT tends to be a relatively important component of revenue systems not only in regions with relatively low overall tax revenue mobilization (Sub-Saharan Africa, Latin America and the Caribbean) but also in revenues with high overall tax ratios (Europe and Central Asia). North America is an outlier with strong revenue mobilization and a very low weight for VAT in total tax revenues, largely because the United States does not have a VAT.

Figure 7.1 VAT as a Source of Revenue, 2019

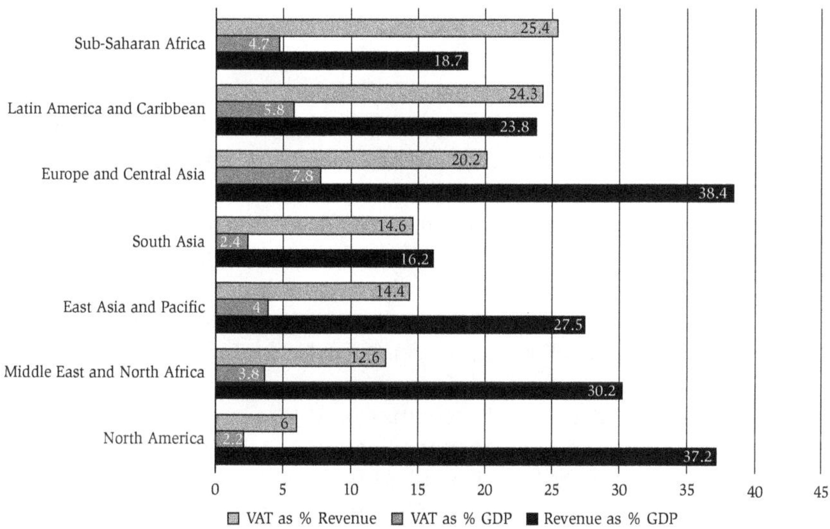

Source: Bird, *supra* note 1, Table 1, at 41.

While measures like these provide useful and necessary starting points to understand revenue performance, they do not provide insight on the reasons for poor

3. Elasticity of VAT revenue with respect to gross income or household expenditure, or the responsiveness of VAT revenues to changes in gross income or expenditures. *See* Jean Acheson, Yota Deli, Edgar Morgenroth, Derek Lambert, and Martin Murphy, *VAT Revenue Elasticities: An Analytical Approach*, ESRI Working Paper No. 596 (Dublin: The Economic and Social Research Institute, 2018).
4. Tax expenditures reflect the cost of certain policies in terms of revenue foregone. *See* Pierre-Pascal Gendron, *Canada's GST at 21: A Tax Expenditure View of Reform*, 1 W. J. VAT/GST L. 125 (2012).

(perceived or real) revenue performance.[5] Governments (and outside technical advisers) seeking to uncover the reasons for poor performance also have access to much more detailed data from tax administrations, albeit often in a relatively unstructured (quantitatively speaking) and qualitative way.[6]

Under the intellectual leadership of the Fiscal Affairs Department (FAD) of the International Monetary Fund (IMF), a new performance measure was born: the C-efficiency ratio.[7] Write VAT revenue (denoted by *V*) as a percentage of GDP (*Y*) as:

$$(1) \qquad \frac{V}{Y} = \tau_s E^C \left(\frac{C}{Y}\right)$$

where τ_s denotes the standard VAT rate, *C* denotes consumption (valued at VAT-exclusive prices), and E^C denotes C-efficiency.

Further, define C-efficiency as:

$$(2) \qquad E^C \equiv \frac{V}{\tau_s C}$$

The C-efficiency ratio compares the revenue an actual VAT raises with the revenue it would raise if perfectly enforced and levied at a uniform rate (equal to the standard rate) on all consumption with no exemptions. A C-efficiency close to 100% suggests strong revenue performance while one close to zero suggests a very poor performance. VAT-Revenue-Ratio or VRR in the OECD's terminology is essentially another name for C-efficiency, defined as in the formula, but measured a bit differently as the ratio of actual VAT revenue to the potential revenue if the standard VAT rate were applied to final (including public) consumption in the national accounts less actual VAT revenue.[8]

Table 7.1 lists VRR for OECD countries in 2017 along with the evolution of standard VAT rates over time and the year of inception of the VAT. These ratios range from a low of 0.33 for Mexico to a high of 1.04 for New Zealand, with an unweighted average of 0.60. On average, VATs reach 60% of consumption in OECD countries, on an unweighted basis. A significant share of consumption goes untaxed. This simple conclusion obscures the fact that the presence of reduced rates in some VATs will reduce revenues and make the standard rate overestimate the true potential. On the other hand, exemptions that affect the retail stage will not only reduce revenues but

5. For a detailed recent analysis of African VATs using similar indicators and additional micro indicators, *see* Sijbren Cnossen, *Modernizing VATs in Africa* (Oxford University Press, 2019), Table 6.1, at 63.
6. For one account of technical assistance experience, *see* Pierre-Pascal Gendron, *Real VATs vs the Good VAT: Reflections from a Decade of Technical Assistance*, 32 Austl Tax F. 257 (2017).
7. *See* Liam Ebrill, Michael Keen, Jean-Paul Bodin, and Victoria Summers, *The Modern VAT* (Washington, DC: IMF, 2001); and Michael Keen, *The Anatomy of VAT*, 66 Nat'l Tax J. 423 (2013). The discussion in this section draws more closely on the latter.
8. *See* Hannah Simon and Michelle Harding, *What Drives Consumption Tax Revenues? Disentangling Policy and Macroeconomic Drivers*, OECD Taxation Working Papers No. 47, Annex B (Paris: OECD, 2020).

also increase taxation of intermediate goods. A high C-efficiency number (or VRR) thus does not necessarily indicate good performance because a 'bad' VAT that taxes investment through heavy taxation of intermediate goods due to exemptions would raise the numerator of E^C in equation (2). The unwillingness or inability of tax administrations to provide VAT refunds would have a similar impact. Although many have nonetheless used the C-efficiency ratio, rightly or wrongly, to compare the VATs of different countries, static comparisons of such numbers do not reveal much.

Because VAT revenue, standard VAT rate and consumption are all interdependent, understanding why the C-efficiency indicator changes over time requires decomposing it further, as we next discuss.

Table 7.1 VAT-Revenue-Ratios (C-Efficiencies) and Standard VAT Rates, OECD Countries (2017)

	Implemented	1995	2005	2007	2009	2011	2013	2015	2017	VRR 2017
Australia	2000	-	10	10	10	10	10	10	10	0.51
Austria*	1973	20	20	20	20	20	20	20	20	0.64
Belgium	1971	20.5	21	21	21	21	21	21	21	0.50
Canada*	1991	7	7	6	5	5	5	5	5	0.51
Chile	1975	18	19	19	19	19	19	19	19	0.67
Czech Republic	1993	22	19	19	19	20	21	21	21	0.66
Denmark	1967	25	25	25	25	25	25	25	25	0.67
Estonia	1991	18	18	18	20	20	20	20	20	0.80
Finland	1994	22	22	22	22	23	24	24	24	0.61
France*	1968	20.6	19.6	19.6	19.6	19.6	19.6	20	20	0.53
Germany	1968	15	16	19	19	19	19	19	19	0.59
Greece*	1987	18	19	19	19	23	23	23	24	0.46
Hungary	1988	25	25	20	25	25	27	27	27	0.64
Iceland	1990	24.5	24.5	24.5	24.5	25.5	25.5	24	24	0.61
Ireland	1972	21	21	21	21.5	21	23	23	23	0.52
Israel*	1976	17	16.5	15.5	16.5	16	18	17	17	0.66
Italy	1973	19	20	20	20	21	22	22	22	0.42
Japan	1989	3	5	5	5	5	5	8	8	0.74
Korea	1977	10	10	10	10	10	10	10	10	0.72
Latvia	1995	18	18	18	21	22	21	21	21	0.60
Lithuania	1994	18	18	18	19.7	21	21	21	21	0.56
Luxembourg	1970	15	15	15	15	15	15	17	17	0.95
Mexico	1980	15	15	15	15	16	16	16	16	0.33
Netherlands	1969	17.5	19	19	19	19	21	21	21	0.56
New Zealand	1986	12.5	12.5	12.5	12.5	15	15	15	15	1.04
Norway	1970	23	25	25	25	25	25	25	25	0.61
Poland	1993	22	22	22	22	23	23	23	23	0.53
Portugal*	1986	17	21	21	20	23	23	23	23	0.55
Slovak Republic	1993	25	19	19	19	20	20	20	20	0.55
Slovenia	1999	-	20	20	20	20	22	22	22	0.65
Spain*	1986	16	16	16	16	18	21	21	21	0.46
Sweden	1969	25	25	25	25	25	25	25	25	0.63
Switzerland	1995	6.5	7.6	7.6	7.6	8	8	8	8	0.71
Turkey	1985	15	18	18	18	18	18	18	18	0.44
United Kingdom	1973	17.5	17.5	17.5	15	20	20	20	20	0.47
Unweighted average		17.8	17.9	17.8	18.0	18.7	19.2	19.3	19.3	0.60

Source: Simon and Harding, *supra* n. 8, Table B.1, at 42.

[B] What Are VAT Gaps?

Departures from 100% C-efficiency can arise for two reasons. First, they may reflect the extent to which VAT design differs from a uniform tax on all consumption (and only consumption, with no exemptions and no indirect taxes on production). This is what the literature calls the *policy gap*: it is zero if the VAT applies at a single rate to all (but only) consumption. Second, the implementation and administrative operation of the tax may be less than perfect. This is what the literature calls the *compliance gap*: it is zero only if implementation and operation of the VAT are perfect, that is, if the full potential revenue from applying the statutory VAT rate(s) to the statutory tax base is realized.

The policy gap – which assumes full compliance – represents the impact of tax expenditures implemented through the VAT system through the provision of concessions and special treatments in pursuance of policy goals. The policy gap arises for two reasons: the *rate gap*, reflecting the impact of differentiation in statutory VAT rates (reduced rates or the zero rate on domestic consumption), and the *exemption gap*, reflecting the impact of exemptions. The policy gap thus reflects two conflicting factors. On the one hand, to the extent that exempting consumption reduces the size of potential VAT 'recoveries' (offsets of VAT on inputs), net VAT revenues are increased so the revenue loss from this component of the policy gap is overstated. On the other hand, since in principle pure public goods should not be subject to VAT, the inclusion of such goods and services in the *C* variable in the formula for C-efficiency in equation (2) tends to overstate the potential revenue cost of the gap. This raises an important question we cannot discuss in detail here: whether and to what extent activities financed by the public sector should be included in any estimate of the potential VAT base.[9]

The compliance gap is conceptually quite different. It measures the difference between the VAT that should be payable not from a (hypothetical) tax on all potentially taxable consumption (*see* later discussion) but from the actual VAT law in place and the VAT revenues actually received by the authorities. Further decomposition of the compliance gap yields further insights. The compliance gap arises for two reasons also: the *collections gap* and the *assessment gap*.[10] The collections gap measures the difference between what taxpayers have declared as being due, or have had assessed as being due, and the amount of VAT collected. The assessment gap measures the difference between the total amounts declared as assessed or being due, and the total potential amount of VAT that should have been declared or assessed. Some studies, notably in the United Kingdom (UK), have broken down the assessment gap into such components as numerical errors, evasion and avoidance, although the distinction

9. We mention only two problems. First, in many countries a substantial share of public spending – an item often measured in the national accounts largely by the size of the public wage bill – does not provide pure public goods; second, in many countries many activities are called 'public' and largely financed and provided by public sector agencies and enterprises that are provided privately in other countries. Further exploration of this issue lies beyond the scope of this chapter.
10. Eric Hutton, *The Revenue Administration-Gap Analysis Program: Model and Methodology for Value-Added Tax Gap Estimation*, Technical Notes and Manuals (IMF, 2017).

between the latter two categories is controversial and handled differently in different countries.

Unlike the policy gap, which is measured with reference to an 'ideal' or 'reference' VAT at a uniform rate on all consumption without exemptions, the compliance gap is measured with reference to the revenues that should be collected based on the existing policy design. Generally, the compliance gap is expressed as a proportion of the amount of VAT that should be payable, that is, as a ratio less than 1.0 and not a monetary amount.

Much of the discussion about VAT gaps in the literature really refers only to the compliance gap. One reason for this emphasis may be simply that estimating the compliance gap is more difficult and hence technically more challenging. Another reason, however, is perhaps that the policy gap may be interpreted as a criticism of policy decisions. Although the compliance gap may also be interpreted as a criticism of policy, it focuses on possible deficiencies in tax administration, a less politically sensitive issue for most governments. The compliance gap also appears to provide governments a way to assess the performance of tax administrations on the one hand, and an indication of the extent of tax evasion on the other. We return to these interpretations below.

Strictly speaking, however, as mentioned earlier, the total VAT gap combines both compliance and policy gaps. Based on the above decomposition into policy and compliance gaps, we can now write C-efficiency as:

$$(3) \qquad E^C = (1 - P)(1 - \Gamma)$$

where P is the policy gap and Γ is the compliance gap. Section 7.03 discusses the relation between these two principal components of the VAT gap in a little more detail.

[C] Why Measure VAT Gaps?

Interest in measuring tax gaps (not just VAT gaps) has been driven by two quite different factors, both of which focus on the compliance gap. The first factor, as evidenced by the recent popular pressure for increased taxation of the 'one percent' and multinational enterprises, is the perception many now seem to hold that revenues need to be increased especially in developing countries and raised more equitably in almost all countries.[11] The size of the tax gap (however measured) may not provide an accurate picture of the potential revenue that may realistically be raised, as we discuss later, but measuring it may both provide motivation for greater tax effort and perhaps also suggest where such effort is most needed.

A second motivation for estimating tax gaps comes from the increasing attention paid recently to benchmarking various dimensions of governance including fiscal

11. For an extended discussion of those perceptions, *see* Mick Moore, Wilson Prichard, and Odd-Helge Fjeldstad, *Taxing Africa: Coercion, Reform and Development* (Zed Books, 2018).

performance,[12] and particularly the performance of tax administrations.[13] Benchmarking is essentially a systematic process of identifying and measuring 'performance gaps' – the difference between how well a given unit (a state, a revenue administration) does with respect to a particular activity when its performance is compared to some standard. The standard may be some hypothetical ideal, its own past performance, or, often, the performance of other comparable units, especially those recognized as leaders in the field. The core rationale for benchmarking performance is not to provide input into the old political game of praising winners and berating losers – though the results of such studies may sometimes be used for this purpose – but because by identifying and measuring such gaps one can better understand not only why gaps exist but how they may be reduced.

Comparing tax gaps across time or countries very rarely yields direct inferences about causality or provides novel or important insights into how to resolve the factors that give rise to the measured discrepancy – the gap – between reality and the benchmark standard. However, even incomplete and partial benchmarking using, for example, compliance gap measures may encourage revenue administrations to collect and analyse some of the data that they need to understand if they want to know what they are doing and to do it better. Similarly, policy gap measures may push countries towards such policy changes as broadening the VAT base. Tax gap analysis may thus be helpful in identifying areas of weakness and in providing some guidance to how to improve both tax policy and tax administration.

Gap analysis may thus be useful both for those who make tax policy – the government – and the agencies that implement it – the revenue administration and customs. Much of the drive for more and better estimates of tax gaps, however, has come from international institutions concerned about ensuring that countries are taxing themselves adequately by international standards and from outsiders such as civil society groups concerned with highlighting the scale of potential tax abuses by multinational enterprises or the wealthy and international interests. International organizations and civil society stakeholders have not only exerted pressure to improve and extend tax gap analysis but have also contributed significantly to the literature on this subject. Although these considerations apply to tax gaps in general, they are perhaps most clearly relevant with respect to VAT gaps, given the substantial importance of this tax in many countries and the relatively greater ease with which moderately reliable data can be obtained.

[D] Overview of the Main Approaches to Measurement

The two main ways to estimate VAT gaps are *top-down* and *bottom-up* approaches. Both approaches estimate the theoretical VAT liability and compare it with actual revenues to calculate the compliance gap. Once that gap is calculated, the policy gap

12. Michael Gallagher, *Benchmarking Tax Systems*, 25 Pub. Admin. & Dev. 125 (2005).
13. Jaime Vázquez-Caro and Richard M. Bird, *Benchmarking Tax Administrations in Developing Countries: A Systemic Approach*, 9 eJ. Tax Rsrch. 5 (2011).

arises as a residual. Separate VAT tax expenditure estimates may then be made to validate the residual policy gap, as discussed further below.

The top-down approach aims to estimate potential VAT revenue directly by using information on consumption from such sources as national accounts, supply-use (input-output) tables, expenditure surveys, and the tax code. This approach has two main advantages. First, the estimate should cover all compliance losses, whether they are separately identified or not. Second, the results can be compared to the costs of tax expenditures and reliefs. The top-down approach is data-intensive and computationally demanding and requires various assumptions and adjustments.

In contrast, the bottom-up approach uses operational information and taxpayer files from the various activities of tax administrations (registration, filing, payment, enforcement, and audit) to estimate VAT due but unpaid. While in many countries considerable work may be required to assemble the data in usable form, in principle any country operating any tax should have all the needed information at hand. The main advantage of the bottom-up approach is that it enables the individual estimation of each behavioural component of the compliance gap and may therefore facilitate identifying drivers of non-compliance and suggesting ways in which tax administration may perhaps be improved. In addition, when available, a bottom-up approach also provides a way to validate and check the reasonableness of top-down estimates.

§7.03 MEASUREMENT AND ESTIMATION

This section reviews how the components of VAT gaps and the various components of policy and compliance gaps are estimated, focusing on two widely accepted top-down approaches and describing more briefly bottom-up and complementary approaches.

[A] Top-Down Approach I: European Union

Although a number of earlier country studies reported various estimates of VAT gaps with different base and rate structures, the first major comparative study employing a top-down approach to estimating VAT gaps was a 2009 study conducted for the European Union.[14] A few years later, this work was picked up and further developed by the Center for Social and Economic Research (CASE).[15] Since 2013, CASE has produced more or less comparable annual VAT gap estimates for European Union countries, with the most recent one for 2019. These reports estimate the potential VAT base as the sum of the amount of VAT theoretically liable on final consumption and the non-deductible

---

14. Reckon LLP, *Study to Quantity and Analyse the VAT GAP in the EU-25 Member States* (Reckon LLP, 2009). For instances of earlier work in this direction, *see* Carlos Aguirre and Partho Shome, *The Mexican Value-Added Tax*, Working Paper 87/21 (International Monetary Fund, 1987) and Richard M. Bird, *The Reform of Indirect Taxes in Jamaica*, Jamaica Tax Structure Examination Project Staff Paper No. 24 (Metropolitan Studies Program, Maxwell School, Syracuse University, 1989).
15. Luca Barbone, Misha Belkindas, Leon Bettendorf, Richard Bird, Mikhail Bonch-Osmolovskiy, and Michael Smart, *Study to Quantify and Analyse the VAT Gap in EU-27 Countries*, CASE Network Reports No. 116/2013 (Warsaw: CASE, 2013).

VAT imposed on intermediate consumption (including capital formation and inventories) due to exemptions, as well as on domestic purchases by non-residents. In effect, the approach estimates the potential VAT liability as the sum of VAT on final consumption (*C*) and *G* (where *G* is a measure of the amount of non-deductible VAT imposed on public, non-profit and other non-taxable inputs). Hence, CASE labels its work as a 'consumption side' approach. These reports focus on the compliance gap first, but then derive estimates of the policy gap, broken down between rate gap and exemption gap. The most recent reports introduce the concept of 'actionable gap', the difference between the total policy gap and exemptions on services that either should not be taxed in principle (e.g., government-provided pure public goods), or for technical or other reasons (e.g., financial services and insurance).[16] A more detailed discussion of these and other base issues lies beyond the scope of this chapter.[17]

[B] Top-Down Approach II: IMF's RA-GAP

The second top-down estimation method comes from the IMF's Revenue Administration GAP (RA-GAP) methodology.[18] Technical assistance teams have applied this methodology in a significant number of countries under the Revenue Administration Gap Analysis Program.[19] With reference to Figure 7.2, this process begins the estimation of the policy gap in 3 steps:

(1) Step 1: Estimate the potential reference revenue (RPR), equal to box ACHE.
(2) Step 2: Calculate actual revenue (AR), equal to box ABFD.
(3) Step 3: Compute the tax gap = RPR – AR.

The estimation of the compliance gap follows a similar logic, noting that the potential revenue against which actual revenue is compared reflects the current statutory framework rather than the reference framework. This estimation also comprises 3 steps:

(1) Step 1: Estimate potential revenue under current policy (CPR), equal to box ACGD.
(2) Step 2: Calculate actual revenue (AR), equal to box ABFD.
(3) Step 3: Compute the tax gap = CPR – AR.

Once the compliance gap is calculated, the policy gap arises as the difference between the estimated potential reference revenue (RPR) and current potential revenue (CPR).

16. For a recent example, *see* CASE, *Study and Reports on the VAT Gap in EU-28 Member States: 2019 Final Report* (Center for Social and Economic Research, 2019).
17. For a useful recent discussion, *see* Sijbren Cnossen, *Modernizing the European VAT*, CESifo Working Papers 8279 (Munich: CESifo, 2020).
18. This exposition of the methodology draws on Hutton, *supra* n. 10.
19. For a recent example, *see* Mick Thackray and Kanar Ahmed, *Poland: Revenue Administration Gap Analysis Program—The Value-Added Tax Gap*, IMF Country Report No. 18/357 (IMF, 2018).

Figure 7.2 Components of the Tax Gap

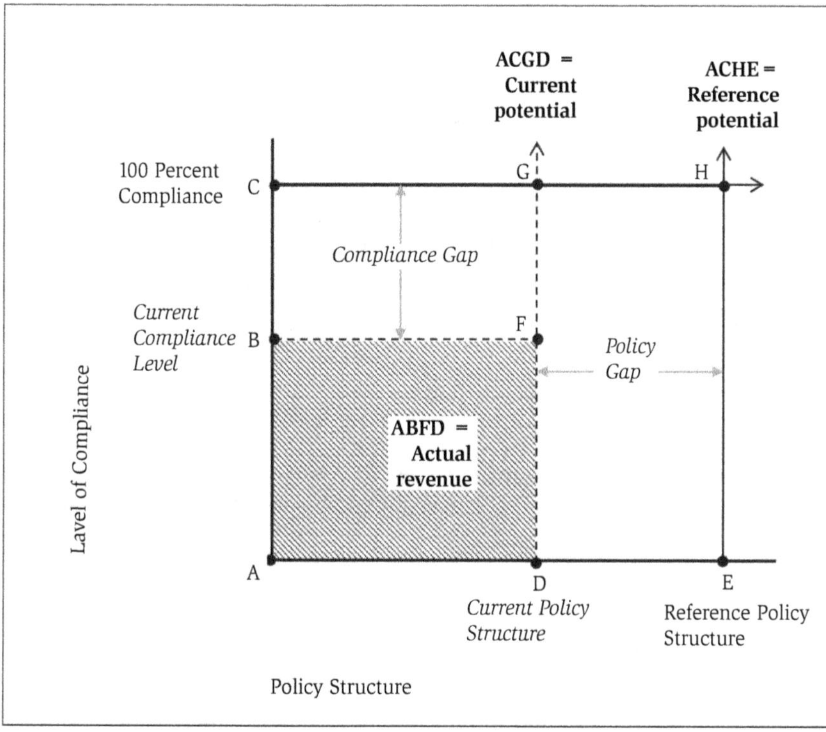

Source: Hutton, *supra* n. 10.

The RA-GAP model estimates directly the amount of taxable output in each sector and the input tax credits in each economic sector in order to determine the potential net VAT for each sector. Its estimation follows the mechanical logic of the VAT as applied to value-added (outputs minus inputs) as opposed to its base (final consumption). The RA-GAP approach is more data and computationally intensive than the CASE method and other top-down approaches. Like those approaches, it requires multiple adjustments to data.[20] On the other hand, this approach produces sectoral estimates of compliance gaps which potentially useful for prospective enforcement and other compliance enhancing activities.

[C] Other Top-Down Approaches

Other top-down gap estimates do not neatly fall under the RA-GAP or CASE approaches. Some World Bank studies, for example, have produced estimates of the VAT

20. Hutton, *supra* n. 10, describes the data, adjustments, assumptions and equations.

gap following a 'consumption approach' (related to the CASE methodology), that relies on national accounts data and household expenditure survey data.[21]

The Inter-American Center of Tax Administrations (CIAT) has produced estimates for Latin America that follow similar, although not identical, methodologies. The purpose of the work was to explore VAT revenue, tax expenditures and various sources of inefficiency.[22] The work resembles CASE reports in that it calculates indicators for a group of countries based on a common methodology. It uses the following three indicators related to earlier discussion:

C-efficiency: E^C in equation (2).

G-inefficiency: inefficiency due to tax expenditure (the policy gap).

X-inefficiency: inefficiency in compliance due to tax administration (an indicator of the compliance gap).

In the CIAT model:

$$C\text{-}efficiency + G\text{-}inefficiency + X\text{-}inefficiency = 100\% \quad (4)$$

where G-inefficiency is estimated directly via VAT tax expenditure evaluation and X-inefficiency arises as a residual after C-efficiency and G-inefficiency are summed together and subtracted from 100%.

[D] Bottom-Up Approaches

Bottom-up approaches include any gap estimation methodology that begins with data produced by the tax administration in the course of its core operations: registration, filing, payment, enforcement, and audit. This expands to include technical details of administration such as risk profiling and the management of arrears, collections, and refunds. Estimates arise from a variety of numerical and statistical methods, and micro-simulations. Typical analysis includes the random sampling of taxpayers for audit, evaluations of preliminary and final assessments, compliance risk analysis and the evaluation of intervention results.

Bottom-up estimates provide insights on compliance behaviours and risks that top-down estimates cannot deliver. They can also test or validate top-down estimates. Bottom-up estimates can only cover specifically identified sources of compliance gap, not the total compliance gap. In addition, bottom-up estimation is more labour intensive and requires good internal IT systems to be conducted effectively. Australia

21. For example, *see* World Bank, *Republic of Kosovo Public Sector Revenues: Tax Policies, Tax Evasion and Tax Gap*, Report No. 89195-XK, Poverty Reduction and Economic Management Unit, Europe and Central Asia Region, 2014.
22. Santiago Díaz de Sarralde Miguez, *Value-Added Tax: Revenue, Efficiency, Tax Expenditure and Inefficiencies in Latin America*, Working Papers No. 5, Tax Studies and Research Directorate (Panama: CIAT, 2017).

is known to supplement top-down VAT/GST gap estimates with detailed bottom-up gap estimates. The UK uses bottom-up approaches for other indirect taxes also.[23]

[E] Top-Down Versus Bottom-Up: Summing Up

Table 7.2 summarizes the advantages and disadvantages of both approaches and provides a preference ranking. When resources allow it, a combination of both top-down and bottom-up approaches, as in the UK, is preferred. The next best alternative would be the bottom up approach, although it is unlikely that some tax administrations in developing countries could produce the required estimates. Finally, the top-down approach is both simpler to apply and remains the only one currently accessible in a (roughly) comparable form across countries.

Table 7.2 Information Sources for Compliance Gap Estimation Approaches

Rank	Approach	Description	Advantages	Disadvantages
3	Top-down	Use aggregate (external) data that is compiled externally and independently of the revenue administration, that can be applied directly or indirectly to estimate the taxable base for a tax. Statistical calculations based on broad observations e.g. Australian Bureau of Statistics (ABS) data.	Simple Independent Macro approach (from the general to the specific)	Data weaknesses aggregate approach circularity
2	Bottom-up	Management Information from normal operational programs: Data warehouse and risk engine Data matching (internal and external sources) Random audit enquiries to complement management information Illustrative data from operational experts	Disaggregation to the taxpayer level Micro approach (from the specific to the general)	Endogeneity- Data does not look beyond knowns uplift factors for unknowns
1	Combination (Ideal)	Utilising a combination of top-down and bottom-up approaches	Enables verification	May not be able to match approaches

Source: Warren, *supra* n. 23.

[F] Complementary Approaches

Other approaches may of course contribute to understanding the VAT gap although they do not produce an estimate of the gap. Statistical and econometric analyses can be useful to understand correlations between a host of variables that represent economic and administrative characteristics and the size of the VAT gap. In a recent CASE econometric analysis of VAT gap determinants, for example, explanatory variables of interest included the scale of the tax administration, information technology expenditure, and the size of the public deficit.[24] In addition, the model included variables that

23. *See* Neil Warren, *Estimating Tax Gap Is Everything to an Informed Response to the Digital Era*, 16 eJ. Tax Rsrch. 536 (2019); and HM Revenue and Customs, *Measuring Tax Gaps 2020 Edition: Tax Gaps Estimates for 2018 to 2019* (London: HMRC, 2020).
24. CASE, *supra* n. 16.

represent macroeconomic characteristics, sectoral characteristics, rate dispersion, the age of the VAT, government effectiveness, and population. The size of the VAT gap is the dependent variable.

This study found that information technology expenditures and the size of the public deficit are associated with a lower VAT gap, while a larger tax administration is associated with a larger VAT gap. Given the ad hoc nature of the model (and its inherent data mining) and potential sources of omitted-variable bias and endogeneity, the results are only indicative of correlations and cannot be interpreted as representing causality in any way. The World Bank has also conducted occasional econometric analyses of the determinants of tax gaps.[25] Econometric analysis may be useful in understanding VAT gaps but it does not help in estimating gaps and the relative infrequency of changes in VAT system parameters suggests that the statistical precision of estimates based on such analyses is questionable.

§7.04 INTERPRETATION, LIMITATIONS, AND OPPORTUNITIES

This section discusses the interpretation of gap estimates, their limitations, and opportunities they present beyond policy and administration.

[A] Interpreting Gap Estimates: Some Comparisons

VAT gap results come in different versions, and either in absolute or relative numbers. The RA-GAP top-down methodology expresses the compliance gap (Γ) from equation (3) as:

$$(5) \qquad \Gamma = \frac{\textit{Current potential revenues} - \textit{Actual collections}}{\textit{Current potential revenues}}$$

The model produces a raw monetary measure of the compliance gap equal to the difference between current potential revenues and actual collections. Such an absolute number means little taken by itself, especially when comparing gaps between different countries. The relative measure in equation (5) expresses the compliance gap as a percentage of current potential revenues.

The CASE methodology expresses VAT compliance gaps both as absolute gap figures (the difference between actual revenues (*revenues*) and potential revenues, or *VAT Total Tax Liability* (VTTL) and as a percentage of the total gap.[26] Table 7.3

25. *See*, for instance, Munawer Sultan Khwaja and Indira Iyer, *Revenue Potential, Tax Space, and Tax Gap: A Comparative Analysis*, Policy Research Working Paper 6868, Poverty Reduction and Economic Management Department, Europe and Central Asia Region (World Bank, 2014). For a useful analysis emphasizing the cyclical behaviour of gap estimates, *see* Junji Ueda, *The Evolution of Potential VAT Revenues and C-Efficiency in Advanced Economies*, Working Paper WP/17/158, FAD (IMF, 2017).
26. CASE, *supra* n. 16.

summarizes the results from the latest CASE report. Based on 2017 data, the compliance gap ranged from a low of 0.7% in Luxembourg (LU) to a high of 33.6% in Greece (EL), with an average of 11.2% and a median of 10.1%.

Table 7.4 shows the comparative policy gap numbers for the same group of countries for the year 2017. The policy gap is broken down between different additive components: rate gap versus exemption. The total policy gap figures range from a low of 29.47% in Bulgaria (BG) to a high of 59.42% in Spain (ES), with an average of 44.52%. The wide range reflects both the structural differences between different countries and the fact that despite the requirement that all EU member states adhere to the common EU VAT directive, when it comes to ex post performance VAT harmonization is apparently not that tight a concept in the EU.

The actionable gap attempts to measure the gap that could be closed with policy decisions. Actionable gaps in the EU are small as measured in the CASE study owing largely to the Sixth Directive's arguable requirements with respect to the treatment of public and financial services.[27] As noted earlier, any sensible VAT should exclude public goods that cannot be sold for consideration. In fact, however, a substantial section of the policy gap in EU countries reflects the extent to which private goods and services that could be sold by governments for consideration or that compete with private sector supplies are exempted and considered non-actionable. Moreover, in principle there exist viable methods to impose VAT on at least fee-based and most intermediation-based financial services.[28]

27. For a strong critique of the EU's Sixth Directive on these (and other) grounds, *see* Cnossen, *supra* n. 17.
28. *See* Pierre-Pascal Gendron, *Canada's GST and Financial Services: Where Are We Now and Where Could We Be?* 64 Can. Tax J. 401 (2016). We do not discuss the always controversial treatment of housing (including imputed rent) here: *see*, for instance, Cnossen, *supra* n. 17, and Michael Smart, *Departures from Neutrality in Canada's Goods and Services Tax*, in Jack Mintz and Stephen Richardson, *After Twenty Years: The Future of the Goods and Services Tax* (Toronto: Canadian Tax Foundation, 2014) 105-108.

Table 7.3 Comparative EU-28 Compliance Gap Results 2016-2017 (EUR Million)

	2016				2017				VAT Gap Change (pp)
MS	Revenues	VTTL	VAT Gap	VAT Gap (%)	Revenues	VTTL	VAT Gap	VAT Gap (%)	
BE	28,750	32,615	2,865	11.9%	29,763	33,759	3,996	11.8%	0.0
BG	4,417	5,020	603	12.0%	4,664	5,289	625	11.8%	-0.2
CZ	13,091	12,355	2,264	14.7%	14,721	16,803	2,082	12.4%	-2.3
DK	26,735	29,113	2,378	8.2%	27,931	30,166	2,235	7.4%	-0.8
DE	218,779	242,441	23,662	9.8%	226,582	251,598	25,016	9.9%	0.2
EE	1,974	2,101	126	6.0%	2,148	2,270	122	5.4%	-0.7
IE	12,826	14,767	1,941	13.1%	13,278	15,215	1,938	12.7%	-0.4
EL	14,333	20,769	6,436	31.0%	14,642	22,041	7,399	33.6%	2.6
ES	70,705	72,769	2,024	2.8%	74,107	75,913	1,806	2.4%	-0.4
FR	154,490	169,784	15,294	9.0%	161,932	173,962	12,030	6.9%	-2.1
HR	6,016	6,519	503	7.7%	6,485	6,944	459	6.6%	-1.1
IT	102,378	139,422	37,044	26.6%	107,901	141,530	33,629	23.8%	-2.8
CY	1,664	1,750	87	5.0%	1,851	1,862	11	0.6%	-4.4
LV	2,032	2,342	310	13.2%	2,164	2,549	385	15.1%	1.9
LT	3,026	4,054	1,027	25.3%	3,310	4,429	1,119	25.3%	-0.1
LU	3,436	3,554	119	3.3%	3,469	3,492	23	0.7%	-2.7
HU	10,587	12,400	1,813	14.6%	11,725	13,617	1,893	13.9%	-0.7
MT	712	783	71	9.1%	810	823	13	1.6%	-7.5
NL	47,849	50,755	2,906	5.7%	49,900	52,644	2,744	5.2%	-0.5

MS	2016				2017				VAT Gap Change (pp)
	Revenues	VTTL	VAT Gap	VAT Gap (%)	Revenues	VTTL	VAT Gap	VAT Gap (%)	
AT	27,301	29,685	2,384	8.0%	28,304	30,748	2,444	7.9%	-0.1
PL	30,838	38,599	7,761	20.1%	36,330	42,094	5,764	13.7%	-6.4
PT	15,767	18,069	2,301	12.7%	16,809	18,738	1,929	10.3%	-2.4
RO	10,968	17,169	6,201	36.1%	11,650	18,063	6,413	35.5%	-0.6
SI	3,316	3,555	239	6.7%	3,479	3,606	128	3.5%	-3.2
SK	5,420	7,294	1,874	25.7%	5,917	7,708	1,791	23.2%	-2.5
FI	19,694	21,293	1,599	7.5%	20,404	22,026	1,622	7.4%	-0.1
SE	42,770	43,484	714	1.6%	44,115	44,769	654	1.5%	-0.2
UK	163,344	183,224	19,880	10.9%	161,509	180,708	19,199	10.6%	-0.2
Total EU-28	1,043,219	1,188,647	145,428	12.2%	1,085,899	1,223,369	137,470	11.2%	-1.0
Median				10.3%				10.1%	

Source: CASE, *supra* n. 16, Table 2.1, at 19.

Table 7.4 Comparative EU-28 Policy Gap Results 2017 (EUR Million)

	Policy Gap (%)	Rate Gap (%)	Exemption Gap (%)	o/w Imputed Rents (%)	o/w Public Services (%)	o/w Financial Services (%)	Actionable Exemption Gap (C - D - E - F) (%)	Actionable Policy Gap (G + B) (%)
BE	51.50	10.20	41.30	7.12	27.43	3.45	3.30	13.50
BG	29.47	3.88	25.59	10.05	16.66	2.56	-3.68	0.20
CZ	37.96	5.77	32.19	8.31	19.40	2.50	1.99	7.76
DK	41.59	0.77	40.82	7.48	27.94	5.23	0.18	0.95
DE	44.26	7.35	36.91	6.71	22.47	3.24	4.50	11.85
EE	35.01	2.91	32.10	7.00	19.96	2.57	2.57	5.48
IE	47.91	14.00	33.91	10.20	26.01	-0.89	-1.41	12.59
EL	46.03	8.20	37.83	9.20	18.91	1.90	7.82	16.02
ES	59.42	13.07	46.35	9.81	19.59	2.53	14.42	27.49
FR	53.78	11.84	41.94	9.37	25.15	3.61	3.81	15.65
HR	33.90	8.44	25.47	7.59	14.43	2.06	1.40	9.83
IT	53.81	12.75	41.06	10.87	20.44	1.35	8.40	21.15
CY	45.41	29.55	15.86	8.55	20.66	-5.66	-7.69	21.86
LV	40.29	3.12	37.17	9.90	19.62	1.98	5.66	8.78
LT	33.48	4.20	29.28	5.21	17.28	1.65	5.13	9.33
LU	39.49	12.14	27.35	8.78	4.71	2.59	11.27	23.41
HU	43.48	5.75	37.73	7.48	22.87	3.59	3.79	9.54
MT	43.70	16.46	27.23	4.31	19.72	2.84	0.37	16.83
NL	51.84	11.19	40.65	7.28	27.56	7.00	-1.19	10.00
AT	45.85	10.40	35.45	7.22	21.97	2.93	3.32	13.73
PL	48.36	14.61	33.74	3.82	18.40	3.81	7.71	22.32
PT	51.21	11.95	39.27	8.38	21.22	3.21	6.45	18.40
RO	34.00	8.37	25.63	9.75	15.07	0.12	0.70	9.07
SI	47.78	11.29	36.49	7.87	20.79	2.95	4.89	16.18
SK	38.29	2.44	35.85	6.71	20.83	3.79	4.52	6.96
FI	48.86	9.89	38.97	10.09	23.75	2.83	2.30	12.19
SE	46.45	7.95	38.50	5.42	30.59	3.94	-1.45	6.50
UK	53.50	9.18	44.32	11.72	21.23	4.00	7.37	16.56
EU-28	44.52	9.56	34.96	8.08	20.88	2.56	3.44	13.00

Source: CASE, *supra* n. 16, Table 4.1, at 53.

Application of the IMF RA-GAP methodology produces a range of indicators. Table 7.5 shows estimates of equation (5) and other indicators for countries that requested technical assistance under this program and agreed to make the results public: Denmark, Estonia, Finland, Jamaica, Poland, South Africa, and Uganda. Each country features multiple years of data. The first three data columns show the compliance gap, the policy gap and the total gap (the sum of compliance and policy gaps) as a percent of GDP. The next two columns show the compliance and policy gaps as a percent of potential VAT revenue. The next two columns show the collection and assessment gaps (the two components of the compliance gap) as a percent of GDP, while the next two show the same numbers as a percent of the compliance gap. The last two columns show the collection and assessment gaps as a percent of potential VAT revenue. Although the range in gap estimates (and in the importance of different components across countries) is large, there is also a noticeable variation from year to year in the estimates for most countries. In detailed work, it is important to consider the composition and mix of expenditure components of GDP as well as the composition of consumption itself. Time series estimates would be ideal because they allow for calculation of averages and size of deviations from averages.[29] In contrast to the case of most EU countries, Table 7.5 shows that the policy gap exceeds the compliance gap in all countries except Uganda, where the pattern is reversed.

In §7.03[C], we discussed the CIAT top-down estimation methodology. That study also reports comparative numbers for Latin American Countries.[30] Table 7.6

29. Along the lines discussed by Simon and Harding, *supra* n. 8.
30. Díaz de Sarralde Miguez, *supra* n. 22, Table 3, at 25.

shows a number of VAT ratios for 16 Latin-American countries: VAT tax expenditures to GDP (GT/GDP), VAT tax expenditures to actual VAT revenue (GT/VAT), and VAT tax expenditures to actual VAT revenue (GT/VATpot).

Although the CIAT methodology differs from RA-GAP and CASE, the results are of interest. Excluding negative values, the compliance gap (X-inefficiency) ranges from a minimum of 5.1% in Chile to a maximum of 57.9% in Mexico. Although Ecuador, Paraguay and Panama show compliance gaps of -5.7, -6.1, and -31.3% respectively, the negative numbers obviously do not indicate that compliance is excessive. They result from the inevitable reality that all variables are measured with error, the residual nature of the compliance gap in the model, and the fact that, as mentioned earlier, C-efficiency can be increased in undesirable ways (e.g., by taxing intermediate goods).

Table 7.5 RA-GAP Compliance Gap Estimates from Selected Country Reports

Country	Year	Compliance Gap (% GDP)	Policy Gap (% GDP)	Total Gap (% GDP)	Compliance Gap (% potential VAT revenue)	Policy Gap (% potential VAT revenue)	Collection Gap (% GDP)	Assessment Gap (% GDP)	Collection Gap (% compliance gap)	Assessment Gap (% compliance gap)	Collection Gap (% potential VAT revenue)	Assessment Gap (% potential VAT revenue)
Denmark	2008	1.08	5.02	6.09	10.00	-	0.03	1.05	2.59	97.41	-	-
Denmark	2009	0.69	6.44	7.13	7.00	-	0.05	0.64	7.31	92.69	-	-
Denmark	2010	0.55	6.47	7.02	6.00	-	0.05	0.50	8.87	91.13		
Denmark	2011	0.57	6.11	6.68	6.00	-	0.07	0.50	11.69	88.31	-	-
Denmark	2012	0.55	6.28	6.83	5.00	-	0.10	0.45	18.23	81.77	-	-
Estonia	2007	-	-	-	9.58	12.44	-	-	-	-	-	-
Estonia	2008	-	-	-	8.26	19.42	-	-	-	-	-	-
Estonia	2009	-	-	-	10.45	22.44	-	-	-	-	-	-
Estonia	2010	-	-	-	12.14	23.17	-	-	-	-	-	-
Estonia	2011	-	-	-	17.84	18.27	-	-	-	-	-	-
Estonia	2012	-	-	-	14.78	17.65	-	-	-	-	-	-
Finland	2008	0.83	5.36	6.19	9.65	-	0.30	0.58	36.00	64.20	-	-
Finland	2009	0.70	6.08	6.78	7.84	-	0.20	0.50	30.00	69.60	-	-
Finland	2010	0.44	6.71	7.15	4.91	-	0.10	0.30	23.00	76.50	-	-
Finland	2011	0.63	6.51	7.14	6.70	-	0.10	0.50	22.00	78.10	-	-
Finland	2012	0.42	6.89	7.32	4.48	-	0.10	0.30	32.00	68.40	-	-
Finland	2013	0.47	7.32	7.79	4.81	-	0.20	0.30	39.00	61.40	-	-
Finland	2014	0.47	7.40	7.87	4.82	-	0.20	0.30	36.00	63.90	-	-
Jamaica	2008	3.54	6.12	9.66	31.00	-	-	-	-	-	2.00	29.00
Jamaica	2009	3.30	5.75	9.05	33.00	-	-	-	-	-	2.00	31.00
Jamaica	2010	3.38	5.73	9.11	31.00	-	-	-	-	-	1.00	29.00
Jamaica	2011	2.95	6.68	9.63	28.00	-	-	-	-	-	2.00	26.00
Jamaica	2012	2.34	6.33	8.67	23.00	-	-	-	-	-	2.00	21.00
Jamaica	2013	2.47	5.79	8.25	23.00	-	-	-	-	-	2.00	21.00
Poland	2010	1.98	8.10	10.08	20.51	-	0.04	1.94	1.77	98.23	-	-
Poland	2011	1.71	8.29	10.00	18.09	-	(0.05)	1.76	(2.80)	102.80	-	-
Poland	2012	2.38	8.22	10.60	24.50	-	(0.00)	2.38	(0.05)	100.05	-	-
Poland	2013	2.59	8.39	10.98	26.86	-	0.02	2.57	0.77	99.23	-	-
Poland	2014	1.69	8.39	10.09	18.62	-	(0.02)	1.71	(1.19)	101.19	-	-
Poland	2015	2.18	8.07	10.24	24.16	-	0.01	2.16	0.61	99.39	-	-
Poland	2016	1.83	8.20	10.03	20.64	-	(0.03)	1.85	(1.41)	101.41	-	-
South Africa	2007	0.39	2.45	2.84	5.20	27.40	-	-	-	-	-	5.00
South Africa	2008	0.61	2.62	3.23	8.30	28.40	-	-	-	-	1.00	8.00
South Africa	2009	0.69	3.74	4.43	9.50	31.40	-	-	-	-	1.00	9.00
South Africa	2010	0.45	3.06	3.51	6.50	33.40	-	-	-	-	1.00	5.00
South Africa	2011	0.38	3.08	3.46	5.60	33.40	-	-	-	-	2.00	4.00
South Africa	2012	0.40	3.89	4.29	5.60	33.10	-	-	-	-	3.00	3.00
Uganda	2004	4.80	0.52	5.31	54.79	-	-	-	-	-	-	-
Uganda	2005	5.03	0.55	5.58	57.26	-	-	-	-	-	-	-
Uganda	2006	5.70	0.69	6.39	58.06	-	-	-	-	-	-	-
Uganda	2007	6.09	0.57	6.66	59.95	-	-	-	-	-	-	-
Uganda	2008	5.69	0.29	5.98	56.25	-	-	-	-	-	-	-
Uganda	2009	6.18	0.62	6.80	60.11	-	-	-	-	-	-	-
Uganda	2010	6.18	0.62	6.80	60.11	-	-	-	-	-	-	-
Uganda	2011	6.88	0.68	7.56	62.32	-	-	-	-	-	-	-
Uganda	2012	6.36	1.03	7.39	61.69	-	-	-	-	-	-	-
Uganda	2013	6.09	0.22	6.31	57.82	-	-	-	-	-	-	-

Notes: Symbol "-" stands for not available; some figures may not add up exactly due to rounding.

Source: Authors' compilation based on data provided by the Revenue Administration Gap Analysis Program (RA-GAP) of the Fiscal Affairs Department, IMF.

Table 7.6 VAT Indicators and Gaps for Latin-American Countries (Percent)

Country	GT/GDP	GT/VAT	GT/VATpot	C-EFFIC	G-INEF	X-INEF
Ar	1.2	16.1	13.9	46.1	7.4	46.5
Bo	1.0	13.0	11.5	78.8	10.2	11.0
Ch	0.7	8.0	7.4	64.1	5.1	30.8
Co	1.7	31.8	24.1	44.4	14.1	41.5
CR	3.0	62.9	38.6	46.7	29.4	23.9
Ec	2.1	33.7	25.2	79.1	26.6	-5.7
ES	1.5	21.5	17.7	55.4	11.9	32.7
Gu	1.5	31.2	23.8	43.9	13.7	42.5
Mx	1.3	33.5	25.1	31.5	10.6	57.9
Ni	4.2	67.8	40.4	48.3	32.7	19.0
Psn	2.7	91.0	47.6	68.7	62.6	-31.3
Par	1.1	16.5	14.1	91.1	15.0	-6.1
Pe	1.6	23.7	19.2	60.7	14.4	24.9
DR	3.2	65.4	39.6	39.0	25.5	35.4
Ur	3.4	35.5	26.2	55.2	19.6	25.2
Md	2.0	36.8	24.5	56.9	19.9	23.2

Source: Díaz de Sarralde Miguez, *supra* n. 22, Table 3, at 25.

Finally, various country studies have reported other results that are often not directly comparable with the cross-country studies mentioned. For example, a recent study of Bolivia estimated that its C-efficiency ratio rose from only 28% in 1990 to 80% in 2012, with the compliance gap declining over the same period from 60% to only 9%.[31] A World Bank study mentioned earlier reported a VAT gap of approximately 34% of potential VAT revenues in Kosovo based on 2011 data.[32] Another recent country study for Togo reported a total VAT gap of 45% of potential revenues and 8.3% of GDP for 2015, while a study of Benin and Burkina Faso found Benin to have a total VAT gap of 50% with about 80% due to compliance issues and Burkina Faso to have a total VAT gap of 60% but a compliance gap of less than 10% (compared to 50% a decade earlier).[33]

31. Matteo Godin, Romain Houssa, and Kelbesa Megersa, *The Performance of VAT in DGD-partner Countries*, Working Paper 16 (University of Namur, Belgian Policy Research Group on Financing for Development, 2017).
32. World Bank, *supra* n. 21.
33. Adama Combey, *Evaluation of the VAT Gap in Togo*, 27 Revue Economique et Monétaire 44, June 2020; Romain Houssa, Kelbesa Megersa, and Roukiatou Nikiema, *The Sources of VAT Gaps in WAEMU: Case Studies on Benin and Burkina Faso*, BeFinD Working Papers 22 (CRED, University of Namur, 2017).

[B] Limitations

VAT gap estimations like those just mentioned are of course always subject to data and related limitations at several levels in the estimation process. For instance:

- The lack of data may preclude the estimation of VAT gaps using methodologies like the data-intensive top-down approach.
- The definitions of economic sectors in national accounts may differ across some countries.
- Some information, such as supply-use (input-output) tables and household expenditure surveys, may not be available or sufficiently up to date to ensure sensible matching with other economic statistics such as the components of expenditure-based GDP.
- The lack of data may preclude the calculation of the adjustments necessary to harmonize national accounts data to operational tax data or to convert collections from a cash basis to an accrual basis.
- Information systems may not be sophisticated enough to allow for extraction and manipulation of data at a reasonable cost.
- Information systems between different administrations (domestic tax administration, customs, and national statistics) may be unable to communicate with one another.[34]
- GAP estimation, especially annual estimates, data sampling and model maintenance all require specialized labour inputs and computational power and may compete with other important administrative functions.
- Validating top-down estimates using bottom-up estimates is even more resource intensive and difficult.

Of course, the lack of data in one or more areas does not mean one cannot produce a useful gap analysis. A clearly documented estimate or range of estimates – based on sensitivity analyses – is much better than no estimate at all, not least because the mere exercise of making such estimates forces analysts – and (one can always hope) even administrators and policy-makers – to ask more questions and to find the data needed to answer them.

Gap estimates, however well done, must in any case always be interpreted in a broader context than just monetary gap amounts or percentage gap ratios. Proper interpretation requires prior investment in understanding macroeconomic indicators that relate to the VAT system (GDP, consumption, revenues, sectoral composition of consumption and GDP, household expenditures, and so on). It also requires a proper understanding of the operational data that tax administrations produce – but do not always use – notably audit rates, filing and payment delinquency rates, reassessments, arrears, excess credit positions, refunds, de-registrations, and so on.

34. For a discussion of the problem of data integration between administrations, *see* Gendron, *supra* n. 6.

Despite such problems, however, VAT gaps and their various components (exemption gap and rate gap in the policy gap, collections gap and assessment gap in the compliance gap) are all relevant when it comes to improving tax policy and tax administration. The CASE reports mentioned above have done an excellent job on the macroeconomic side. Although the more detailed IMF RA-GAP country reports tend to show less work along these lines, other IMF studies (headquarters data consolidation, area missions, Title IV missions, and tax policy or tax administration technical assistance missions), though not always publicly available – in part because their release is subject to country vetoes – presumably cover these matters in detail.

Of course, even the best gap analysis may be unable to uncover certain variations in revenue performance and may be of limited use as an indicator of fraud. As an example, some recent research suggests that small and medium enterprises located in rural areas may be more prone to fraud for a host of reasons.[35] Such factors cannot be captured in a top-down analysis that relies on national accounts. A bottom-up analysis that segments businesses by size and/or tax administration unit (e.g., large taxpayer unit versus small and medium taxpayers) could presumably address this problem.

[C] Opportunities

The fact that even the best gap studies are inevitably limited does not mean they are not worthwhile. They are. Carrying out and disseminating such studies both improves transparency in policy objectives and broadens the range of stakeholders beyond ministries of finance and tax administrations, thus perhaps making a bit more smooth the difficult road to the sort of modernization of tax systems needed to fund the state and economic development in general.[36] The growing number of countries where such studies are available perhaps provides some grounds for optimism in this respect. In the next section, we discuss a few more implications of gap analysis for tax policy and tax administration.

§7.05 IMPLICATIONS FOR TAX POLICY AND ADMINISTRATION

We first discuss the implications of gap analysis for VAT policy and administration and highlight the interdependence between the two. We then explore the role of other core taxes and discuss other policy options that may arise when considering other taxes.

---

35. *See* Kiriaki Yiallourou, *The Limitations of the VAT Gap Measurement*, 2019/4 EC Tax Rev. 196 (2019).
36. For examples, *see* Warren, *supra* n. 23, and Pierre-Pascal Gendron, *Tear Down and Rebuild, or Retrofit?-A Critical Review of Sijbren Cnossen's Modernizing VATs in Africa*, 35 Austl. Tax F. 430 (2020).

[A] VAT Policy

As an input to policy, gap analysis is clearly most meaningful and useful at the country level. The comparison of VAT gaps across countries, although common practice, raises a host of questions about comparability of key features of the economic environment such as: income level and distribution, household expenditure level and distribution, sectoral composition of GDP, growth, inflation rates, the size and nature of the informal sector, governance conditions, and so on. Those indicators must be understood properly and thoroughly in order to put gap estimates in proper context. Cross-country 'top-down' gap comparisons like those in the CASE studies are always interesting. They may sometimes even be inspirational, motivating 'low-ranking' countries to do better. But what is likely to be much more useful for any particular country is a disaggregated gap estimate which focuses on its particular circumstances and needs.

In this regard, it is critical to acknowledge the interdependence between policy and administration decisions. At a conceptual level, delivering good policy decisions may seem to be both more important and more straightforward than improving tax administration. The oft-repeated mantra in the policy literature about getting key VAT policy parameters (rate, base, registration threshold) right when launching a new VAT or reforming one in depth because these things are so hard to change thereafter definitely has some validity. Of course, it is equally true that good policy can only be good if administered well.[37] One of the most important lessons from the literature on the VAT gap is that it is much easier to measure the policy gap than the compliance gap. This does not mean, of course, that it will be easier to change 'bad' policy than to improve 'bad' administration so in any country. Rather, it means that no matter what the size of their policy gaps may be, countries need to have as good an estimate as possible of the compliance gap.

Since in any country much (though not all) of the information needed for estimating tax gaps must be provided by the tax administration, it is more likely to provide good information if it is clearly in its interest to do so, for example because the results are directly useful to the tasks with which it is charged. The RA-GAP's focus on understanding and assessing the effectiveness of tax administration in securing compliance is thus probably a realistic approach in a world in which politicians find it much easier to at least pretend to be improving tax administration than they do to face the political storm likely to be stirred up by any substantial attempt to change VAT policy. Still, estimating the cost of the policy gap, especially that attributable to incentives and reliefs supposedly designed primarily to reduce the regressivity of the VAT may perhaps help deflate some of the politics surrounding tax reforms by clarifying the effect on revenues. This may be particularly useful if some of the recent literature on VAT 'regressivity' (noted briefly below) begins to enter the public discussion.

37. Gendron, *supra* n. 36.

[B] VAT Administration

Most tax administrations would likely perform better with more resources. In the real world, however, they need to operate with the resources they have as well as whatever tax law they are required to enforce. This is the 'iron law', so to speak, of tax administration.[38] Of course, all too often administrations - sometimes responding to explicit directions from above - manage to waste many of the resources they have especially if the law is not as good as it should be. As an astute observer of the VAT recently remarked:

> VAT administration is at best misdirected and becomes at worse dysfunctional if, as a result of VAT policy, scarce administrative resources are diverted to settling refunds (of input VAT on zero-rated domestically consumed goods and services), monitoring lower rates (on 'deserving products'), imposing turnover taxes on small firms (whose inputs are already subject to VAT), or spending time in court (because of litigation), rather than being directed towards basic taxpayer education and compliance control processes, such as audit.[39]

Sadly, this quote describes much of the day-to-day experience of VAT administration in many developing countries, especially if one adds spending significant amounts of time on taxpayer premises (which is never a good idea). Unfortunately, it also describes the experience in some advanced countries with respect to litigation and other wasteful activities, especially because of overly complex or poorly designed VATs. Tax administrations that have had to wrestle with badly designed VATs and policies that are counter-productive often seem to find it very hard to improve matters, as considerable experience in the field with tax administration and tax policy technical assistance to governments suggests.[40] Indeed, in some countries, years after the introduction of a 'new' VAT, administrations have been found to follow (generally bad and unnecessary) practices that reflect the vestiges of taxes that preceded the VAT.

It is hard to conceive of a successful policy reform process that would not be accompanied by a through reform of tax administration processes and mindsets. A reformed VAT with fewer exemptions and exclusions and a reasonably high threshold should be easier to administer on a fixed budget although close attention must be paid to reshaping the administration to ensure that the promise of added revenue materializes. To help in doing so, international organizations sponsor initiatives for tax administration and benchmarking, in addition to technical assistance. One example is the Tax Administration Diagnostic Assessment Tool (TADAT).[41] Anyone who looks, even casually, at this tool will quickly realize that improving the administration of a VAT - a task that cannot be accomplished in isolation from general administrative improvement - is a significant undertaking that requires resources, direction, and political will.

38. *Ibid.*
39. Cnossen, *supra* n. 5, at 289.
40. For a summary of such experience and sources on the experiences of others, *see* again Gendron, *supra* n. 6.
41. International Monetary Fund and the World Bank, *TADAT – Tax administration diagnostic assessment tool*, available at https://www.tadat.org/home (last accessed 26 July 2020).

As a rule, tax administrations are judged by their political masters almost entirely on their ability to collect more revenues. From this perspective, their performance with respect to the VAT (or any other tax for which 'gaps' can be estimated) will usually be judged in terms of the extent to which they are seen to close the compliance gap. The general public often does not distinguish between the (inevitably rather rough) estimates of the size of the 'shadow' or 'underground' economy that are sometimes reported, the frequent headline articles about tax evasion (especially by the rich), and estimates of the compliance gap.[42] Despite the intuitive appeal of the argument above about the degree of endogeneity between the policy gap and the compliance gap, it is hard to demonstrate empirically. The argument to introduce a clean policy design – one which the present authors have often made – thus relies more on common sense (and considerable anecdotal experience) than on hard data.

[C] Other Core Taxes

Tax gap frameworks have been developed for all other core taxes: corporate income tax, personal income tax, international variants of income taxes, and pay as you earn (PAYE) or social security contributions. The tax administration in Canada has produced studies on some of these topics in the past five years.[43] The UK has done so for a longer period, and more regularly and publicly. Other countries like the US and Australia have also been active. The UK and Australia estimate tax gaps for excise taxes, the poor child of indirect taxation but an important revenue source for many developing countries, not least because coordinating with excises is important with respect to import duties and the VAT. Extending tax gap assessments beyond the VAT provides useful information when it comes to making tax policy decisions with a view to the entire tax system and may take some pressure off the VAT.

§7.06 POLITICAL ECONOMY AND GAP ANALYSIS

'Clearly, fiscal modernization, the VAT included, is also a political question.'[44] VAT reform, like any significant tax reform, is primarily a political process. As noted earlier, there are good reasons for modernizing and improving VATs and no shortage of

42. Although the variance in estimates of the hidden economy may be so large as to swamp the apparent changes over time in some countries (Norman Gemell and John Hasseldine, *The Tax Gap: A Methodological Review*, Working Paper 09/2012 (Chair in Public Finance, Victoria University, Wellington)), some literature suggests a strong association between taxes and the size of the hidden economy. *See*, e.g., Friedrich Schneider, *The Shadow Economy and Tax Evasion: What Do We (Not) Know*, 13 CESifo Forum 2 (2012).
43. On income tax gaps, *see* Canada Revenue Agency, *Tax Gap and Compliance Results for the Federal Corporate Income Tax System*, available at https://www.canada.ca/en/revenue-agency/corporate/about-canada-revenue-agency-cra/tax-canada-a-conceptual-study/taxgap-compliance-results.html (last accessed 26 July 2020).
44. Cnossen, *supra* n. 5, at 289.

suggestions of how to do. Tax reform, however, is not simply a technocratic process: it is fundamentally a political process and often a very challenging one.[45]

[A] General Considerations

First, because VAT is transactional, consumers are reminded of its existence with every taxable purchase just as businesses are reminded of its burden every time they file a return or interact with the tax administration. In some countries with VAT-inclusive pricing, the VAT is shown separately on invoices. The salience of the tax offers many opportunities for groups to seek concessions and for politicians to score points. Since VAT is usually considered to be regressive, consumer groups often press for concessions of various sorts, whether reduced rates or full exemption of 'necessities' (e.g., food, housing, utilities). Similarly, firms often argue that VAT concessions (on what they sell or what they buy) will lead them to invest more or are necessary to keep them competitive (and providing jobs). As many countries have shown recently in reaction to the pandemic,[46] and many others have shown over the years, politicians frequently give in to such pressures – and are usually praised for doing so, whether the change is intended to be permanent or, as in the recent crisis, is supposedly only temporary. Experience suggests that no matter why any tax preference is given, regardless of its effectiveness in achieving the declared objective, it is difficult to reverse it. All too soon, concessions quickly come to be seen as entitlements.

Second, the technocratic route to VAT reform seems to have reached a plateau. Numerous developing countries have benefited from periodic technical assistance on tax policy and tax administration from international organizations. The Fiscal Affairs Department (IMF) has invested heavily in the process of promoting the VAT and improvements to existing VATs consistent with best practices.[47] Yet, VATs in developing countries continue to suffer from very similar problems that seem to abate only incrementally here and there.[48] Major overhauls of VAT in the right direction almost never occur although some recently adopted VATs in developing countries (in Southern African Customs Union (SACU) countries in Africa, for example) show better designs. While there is much to be said for Cnossen's recent recommendation to review standard exemptions and exclusions (governments and agencies; healthcare, education and social services; immovable property; and financial services), even substantial moves in this direction would be unlikely to enlarge the VAT base much even in the medium term without significant governance and regulatory improvements in areas well beyond the VAT.[49] Other IMF-recommended macro technocratic processes such as the estimation of VAT tax expenditures to motivate reform have also met with limited success. Many countries do not produce such estimates or produce only rudimentary

45. For a thorough discussion of the political dimension of taxation in Africa, with a probing discussion of the VAT, *see* Moore et al., *supra* n. 11, especially at Chapters 6 and 9. The discussion that follows draws largely on Gendron, *supra*, n. 36.
46. *See* Bird, *supra* n. 1.
47. International Monetary Fund, *supra* n. 2.
48. For a discussion of such experience, *see* Gendron, *supra* n. 6.
49. Cnossen, *supra* n. 5, at chapter 18.

ones.[50] Even though the size of revenues foregone by such estimates may shock some, there is almost no evidence that tax expenditure estimation has been a persuasive factor leading to tax reform anywhere. The details involved in a more micro approach to analysing VAT gaps seldom seem to grab the attention of the media or high-ranking civil servants and politicians.

Third, many stakeholders tend to focus on the VAT without consideration for other taxes and expenditure policies. Given the importance of VAT as a revenue source in developing countries, concern with its distributional impact is understandable. Unfortunately, the obsessive focus on the burden distribution of VAT and its alleged regressivity obscures two important points. One is that there is increasing evidence that VATs actually are not all that regressive, especially in developing countries, although we cannot expand further on this here.[51] More importantly, it is clear that expenditure policies are far more critical than the marginal effects of any one tax. As recently noted by an eminent commentator:

> Efficient regressive taxes (such as the VAT) when combined with generous well-targeted transfers can result in a net fiscal system that is equalizing. Even more because a net fiscal system with a regressive tax could be more equalizing than without it ... policy recommendations—such as eliminating [or undermining with exemptions] the regressive tax—based on piecemeal analysis could be flatly wrong.[52]

High quality and well-targeted pro-poor policies require political commitment and processes to come to life, just as quality expenditure policies exert much more influence in achieving development and any desired distributional outcome.[53] When it comes to VAT reliefs and 'incentives', there is little or no evidence that the desired objectives are sufficiently attained to make it sensible to mess up a major revenue source like VAT.

Fourth, VAT is never the only problem or often *the* main revenue problem. Tax systems in Africa, for example, suffer from under-performing personal income taxes, widespread tax preferences and exemptions, corruption, and the underuse of information technology. Personal income taxes that under-perform from a revenue perspective

---

50. For a discussion of VAT/GST tax expenditures based on state-of-the art estimation models, *see* Gendron, *supra* n. 4.
51. *See* Pierre Bachas, Lucie, Gadenne, and Anders Jensen, *Informality, Consumption Taxes and Redistribution*, NBER Working Paper No. 27429 (June 2020), and Alastair Thomas, *Reassessing the Regressivity of the VAT*, OECD Taxation Working Papers No. 49 (2020). For another recent discussion of the regressivity of supposedly 'progressive' exemptions and domestic zero-rating, *see* Rita de la Feria and Michael Walpole, *The Impact of Public Perceptions on General Consumption Taxes*, Paper presented in the Webinar Série Reforma Tributária, O que podemos aprender com a experiência internacional do IVA/IBS, FGV Direito SP, São Paulo, Brazil (21 July 2020).
52. Cnossen, *supra* n. 6, at 101, quoting Nora Lustig, *Fiscal Policy, Inequality, and the Poor in the Developing World*, WIDER Working Paper 2016/164 (2016), United Nations University World Institute for Development Economics Research.
53. For extended discussions supporting this argument, *see* Peter H. Lindert, *Growing Public: Social Spending and Economic Growth since the Eighteenth Century* (Cambridge University Press, 2004), and Sven Steinmo (ed.) *The Leap of Faith: The Fiscal Foundations of Successful Government in Europe and America* (Oxford University Press, 2018).

place a tremendous burden on the VAT to produce revenues. Taxes on income from property and investments, professional self-employment, and wealthy individual could all be better structured and implemented.[54] In many countries, more revenue could and should also be raised from excises on tobacco and alcohol, and probably personal motor vehicles as well as from immovable property.

Finally, much of the impetus for VAT reform in many developing countries has come from international organizations, sometimes upon request for technical assistance from the host country or donor organizations. This model has arguably worked fairly well in at least some countries in recent decades, but it seems increasingly unlikely to succeed on its own in the future. As a recent analysis of taxation in Africa concluded: 'if it is to be implemented effectively, a tax reform agenda for developing countries needs to be "locally owned": that is, designed in that country, for its inhabitants, in line with local conditions. It needs to transcend the disadvantages of the colonial inheritance and a history of over-reliance on external advice.'[55] We agree.

[B] Considerations Specific to VAT Gaps

A major value of gap analysis is to increase transparency and accountability. Some countries have chosen to make the results of their VAT gap analyses publicly available (*see* Table 7.5 for a non-exhaustive list). One of the advantages of transparency is that it provides evidence of an honest effort to improve government institutions and may promote enhanced buy-in for reforms from some stakeholders. Tax administrations and ministries have used this strategy in various contexts to promote better compliance from taxpayers.[56]

A VAT gap analysis also clarifies who is accountable for what. It is often assumed that tax administrations are directly responsible for the compliance gap and that ministries of finance are directly responsible for the policy gap. This is too simple: tax administrations have to work with the resources, VAT law, and directions they are given. Finance ministers also face many constraints in deciding tax policy issues, not least the usual desire of governments to retain power. VAT gap analysis may shed unwelcome light on matters that those responsible may not wish to have revealed, which may in some cases make them unwilling to engage in such an analysis in the first place.

In some cases, another problem may be that revenue administrations may sometimes – perhaps in response to pressures from above – seek to maximize revenues rather than to aim at simply collecting the taxes that are due, consistent with the law. In such cases, they may give preference to enforcement measures that maximize revenue gains rather than combat tax fraud, and prioritizing tax fraud *management*

54. Moore et al., *supra* n. 11, at Chapter 6; and Michael Keen, *Taxation and Development – Again*, in Clemens Fuest and George Zodrow (eds.), *Critical Issues in Taxation and Development* (MIT Press, 2013), at chapter 2.
55. Moore et al., *supra* n. 11, at 214.
56. For example, a recent proposal for consumption tax reform in Brazil suggests that when all pay, all pay less. *See* Ministério da Economia, *Reforma Tributária: Quando todos pagam, todos pagam menos*, Government of Brazil (21 July 2020).

over tax fraud *suppression* can lead to selective enforcement.[57] Of course, given resource constraints, an administration behaving this way may be reacting quite rationally, not least because eliminating fraud often requires policy responses that extend beyond the purview of the domestic tax administration.[58] As with tax reform in general, administrative reform frequently requires changes to a host of other institutions, a process that, like renovating an old house, will almost always take much more time and effort than anyone thinks.

§7.07 CONCLUSION

While refinements to the conduct of top-down estimations and more systematic conduct of bottom-up estimations are always possible, VAT gap estimations can provide countries and would-be reformers with deep insights into potential improvements in existing VAT/GST systems or the potential of new ones. The tax gap framework has much to offer governments and interested stakeholders in understanding and analysing VAT reform proposals. Although it is not particularly appropriate as a tool to assess the effectiveness and efficiency of a tax administration, or to establish tax inspector compensation, the bottom-up (and sectoral) approach to gap analysis can also assist tax administrations in developing better approaches to doing their job. Even if only a top-down analysis is possible, the emergence of a few (and relatively consistent from the point of view of results) top-down methods applied to an increasing number of countries has clearly improved comparability across countries and perhaps provided some with an aspirational target indicating how much better they may be able to do.

What remains on the task list is to move to producing gap estimates using a common methodology in a wide variety of countries, just as the calculation of C-efficiency (or VRR) is now the norm for high-level comparisons of revenue efficiency. To achieve this aim, many countries will need assistance to develop the inputs (national statistics, up-to-date supply-use tables and household expenditure surveys, easily extractible administrative and operational tax data, and so on). Most importantly, they need to conduct their own tax gap estimations and to determine how best to utilize this information to improve both tax policy and tax administration. Analysts also need to continue work, in particular on developing useful bottom-up approaches and exploring in more depth (e.g., through case studies) the politics and political economy of VAT gaps and tax gaps in general.

57. Rita De La Feria, *Tax Fraud and Selective Law Enforcement*, 47 J. L. & Soc'y 240 (2020).
58. For example, on the role of imports and customs administrations, *see* the research paper by Peter Morrow, Michael Smart, and Artur Swistak, *VAT Compliance, Trade and Institutions* (June 2020). The authors exploit the variation in the share of imports to consumption to make inferences about domestic non-compliance and tax gaps.

CHAPTER 8
Susceptibility to Fraud

Robert F. van Brederode

§8.01 INTRODUCTION

Value added tax (VAT) and the retail sales tax (RST) have the same economic objective: taxing private consumption expenditure. They differ in how tax relief is provided for business consumption transactions (*see* §8.02). Governments that decide to introduce a general consumption tax have the choice between these two models with VAT, given its global proliferation, being the preferred model. i.e., the consumption tax of choice. This chapter makes a comparison between a benchmark VAT and a benchmark RST with a focus on their respective susceptibility to fraud. Scholars generally agree that VAT and RST are on a par in terms of potential revenue collection (assuming same tax base and same tax rate), neutrality, and facilitation of cross-border transactions (although RST has an advantage here as it requires no refunds).[1] The orthodox view is that VAT has the upper hand regarding compliance rate and fraud mitigation (*see* §8.03), and we will examine empirical data to determine whether and, if so, to what extent this is true. Thus, we may establish whether from a fraud resistance perspective the one tax is more suitable than the other for modern, economically developed societies that are technologically advanced and are characterized by well-organized governments with competent tax agencies.[2] Although very important, fraud resistance is, of course, only one of a number of factors to be compared when assessing the superiority of the one consumption tax over the other. The European Commission is considering modifying the current VAT system by introducing a general reverse charge, which would make the VAT almost identical to

1. Robert F. van Brederode & Sebastian Pfeiffer, *VAT's Superiority: Is the Emperor Dressed Like Adam?* 26(4) Int'l VAT Monitor 226, 233 (2015).
2. In developing countries, the retail sector operates mainly in the informal economy which makes RST less feasible in our view.

RST. Unsurprisingly, criticism of the reverse charge mimics the traditional objections against RST. Logically, the feasibility of the reverse charge VAT system is identical to that of RST in comparison to the traditional VAT. Whether a benchmark RST and its twin sister the reverse charge VAT are feasible alternatives for the traditional credit-invoice method VAT depends on the validity of the arguments against RST and pro VAT, not in its historical but in its contemporary socio-economic context. After a comparison between a benchmark VAT and RST (§8.02), we evaluate the historical rationale for preferring VAT over RST (§8.03). Section 8.04 takes a closer look at the reality of the so-called fractioned collection system of VAT, followed by an assessment of its effectiveness in reducing retail stage fraud (§8.05), and an analysis of whether the retail sector, in the contemporary economic context, is indeed the weakest link in the supply chain from the perspective of tax compliance (§8.05[C]). Section 8.06 discusses different types of VAT fraud, and §8.07 tries to measure the size of the respective types of VAT fraud and compares to data of RST fraud established in California (§8.08). We summarize and conclude in §8.09.

§8.02 DESCRIPTION OF THE BENCHMARK VAT AND RST

Both RST and VAT aim to only tax private consumption expenditure. RST accomplishes this by only taxing sales made by businesses directly to consumers (B2C), i.e., retail sales, and exempting business-to-business (B2B) sales as shown in Figure 8.1.

Figure 8.1 Application of Sales Tax Through the Supply Chain

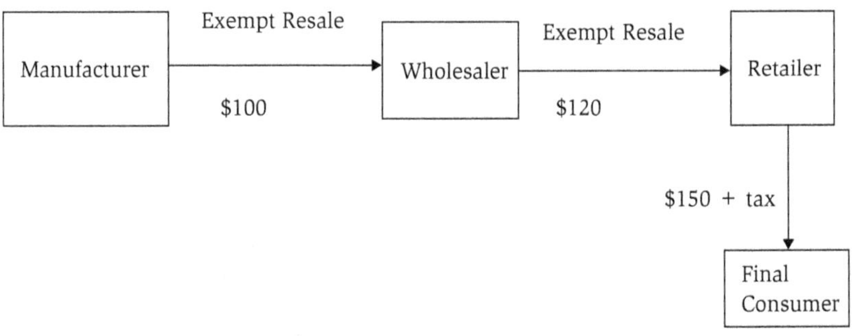

Source: Author's own work.

Under VAT, all transactions in the supply chain are taxed, but businesses receive relief through a credit of the VAT paid on procurement (input-VAT) to off-set against VAT collected on sales (output-VAT): Output-VAT -/- input-VAT = VAT payable. The final consumer, of course, is not allowed any input-VAT credit. Thus, the VAT sticks at the retail stage, just as the RST. This is shown in Figure 8.2.

Figure 8.2 Application of VAT Through the Supply Chain

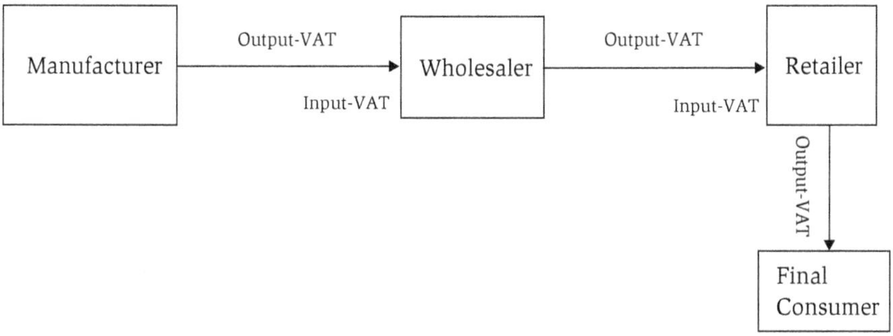

Source: Author's own work.

The crucial difference between RST and VAT is the manner in which they provide tax relief to intermediate business transactions.[3] To arrive at the proper consumption tax base, either business inputs remain untaxed (RST), or a credit is given for taxes paid on inputs to relieve businesses from the tax (VAT).

In reality, the functions of manufacturer, wholesaler and retailer are not strictly separated in the sense that some manufacturers and/or wholesalers may also sell directly to consumers; and a retailer may occasionally make supplies to a business. Establishing the status of the customer is, therefore, relevant for the seller under RST, as this determines whether to charge the tax. In the US, the buyer issues an exemption certificate as proof of his business status, allowing the seller to refrain from charging RST. Alternatively, the tax agency could allocate a unique RST ID number that the seller can verify in a database. Under VAT, the seller will always charge the tax irrespective of the status of the customer. The customer must make the input-VAT claim in his tax return, but the seller, in principle, does not have to verify status.[4] VAT may have a slight advantage over RST in this respect.

A benchmark indirect consumption tax should be broad-based including all supplies of goods and services. VAT applies such a broad base, generally but, due to policy choices made by the national legislatures to give preferential treatment to certain economic sectors, to varying degrees and, as a result, the C-efficiency ratio of VAT for OECD countries averages only about 50% (*see* further §8.07). The RST currently in place in the US and Canada at the subnational level is applied almost exclusively to the sale of goods and only to a limited number of services.[5] A benchmark RST would broaden that base to include all services to the extent possible. The RST, as applied in

3. Richard Krever, *Designing and Drafting VAT Laws for Africa*, in *VAT in Africa* 11 (Richard Krever, ed., Pretoria University Law Press, 2008).
4. The exception in the EU is that the seller must verify the purchaser's VAT registration number to justify the application of the 0% VAT rate on intra-Community, cross-border transactions.
5. RST-bases cover on average 22% of total personal consumption expenditures (*see* John Mikesell, *State Sales Tax in Fiscal 2007: More Slow Growth*, 48 St. Tax N. (May 26, 2008)), much less than the EU VAT-base that covers on average 67%; *see* Sijbren Cnossen, *Evaluating the National Retail*

the US and Canada, has a rather narrow scope of exemptions for intermediate stage transactions[6] with the result that 40% of the tax is actually paid by businesses.[7] In essence, the subnational RST is a hybrid tax, partially gross receipt tax and partially retail sales tax, and as such it disqualifies as a suitable comparable to VAT.[8]

There are some difficult policy issues to resolve under any consumption tax, whether RST or VAT. The ideal consumption tax would be levied on all sectors at a single rate. In practice, lawmakers may give preferential treatment through exemptions or reduced rates for certain supplies of goods or services, either to reduce the effect of the alleged regressivity of VAT/RST, or as a response to the technical difficulty to effectively tax a certain economic sector, such as the financial sector. Full exemption under VAT occurs when a business does not have to charge VAT on its outputs while retaining its right to deduct all input-VAT. Partial exemption occurs when the output is not taxed but the related input-VAT cannot be deducted; in other words, the business is treated like a consumer. Such a business is input-taxed and effectively only its margin remains untaxed. Under RST full exemption can be achieved by allowing a business to register and thus make purchases without incurring RST while at the same time not requiring it to collect RST on its sales of goods and/or services. Partial exemption can be implemented by simply not allowing it to register, in which case the business would not be required to collect RST from its customers but also could not make exempt purchases; similar as under VAT, the business would be treated as a final consumer and only the margin would escape taxation. These issues and policy choices are the same under VAT and RST, so no advantage or disadvantage will arise between the two taxes from this perspective.

To achieve external neutrality, export must be relieved from the tax, which VAT realized through the application of the 0% rate and RST by simply not taxing exports. At importation, tax should be levied to create a level playing field with domestically produced goods and services. Under VAT, imports are taxed but a taxable business can recuperate the import-VAT by deducting it as input-VAT in its periodical VAT return. Thus, only private consumers and the partially exempt businesses would effectively pay VAT at importation. RST should also be collected upon importation by the Customs agency unless the importer presents its registration number as proof of status. As a safety net, the law should include a refund procedure in case at the time of importation proof of business status of the importer of record cannot be provided or verified.

Sales Tax from a VAT Perspective, in *United States Tax Reform in the 21st Century* (George R. Zodrow & Peter Mieszkowski, eds., Cambridge University Press 2002).

6. The most important exemptions are for goods sold for resale by the buyer; and sales of components or ingredients of property produced for sale. Thus, many capital goods such as delivery trucks and computers are taxed as they are not perceived as part of the product sold and the business is seen as the consumer of these items. Many states have introduced additional exemptions to reduce taxation of business procurement, such as sales of property consumed in the manufacture or production of goods for sale; sales of machinery and equipment directly used in the manufacturing of tangible goods; and sales of containers and packaging.
7. *See* Raymond J. Ring, *Consumer's Share and Producer's Share of the General Sales Tax*, 52(1) Nat'l Tax J. 79 (1999).
8. Studies comparing VAT to RST generally use the sales as applied in the US at subnational level to argue VAT's superiority, the exception being Brederode and Pfeiffer, *supra* n. 1.

§8.03 WHY VAT WAS HELD TO BE THE SUPERIOR CONSUMPTION TAX

When considering the introduction of an indirect tax aimed at targeting the consumptive expenditure of private individuals, destination-based RST and VAT are theoretically suitable candidates, both for single state application or in a federal or common market. Where VAT and RST are economically equivalent in taxing final consumption, provided they are levied at the same rate and share the same tax base, it is necessary to determine what the main reasons are for a preference of VAT over RST. The EEC (now EU) accepted that a single point retail tax would be ideal from the perspective of neutrality and eliminating internal borders, but rejected it because it would have put the whole turnover tax burden on the retailer, economically the weakest link in the chain of distribution and at the most difficult point of collection.[9]

The general consensus of the virtues of VAT is well-documented in textbooks[10] and journal articles.[11] [12] Recently, the general reverse charge VAT was opposed on the main argument that it would effectively transform the VAT into a RST,[13] perceived to be more susceptible to fraud. Logically, fraud in this context must mean fraud at the retail stage as this is the only stage where RST is levied. In other words, under a VAT, the fraud at the retail stage is held to be relatively smaller than under RST, and significantly enough to justify pulling all stages of the supply chain into the scope of VAT.

In the context of fraud mitigation, the following virtues are generally attributed to VAT vis-à-vis RST:

- Under a VAT, the collection weight is not put on the weakest link, i.e., the retail sector, but is equally distributed over the supply and distribution chain; instead of collecting the full tax from the retailer, as under RST, there is a fractioned collection system where part of the tax is collected upstream from traders and producers prior to the retail stage.
- VAT creates a paper trail of invoices through the supply chain from manufacturer to retailer, allowing the authorities to effectively audit and cross-check compliance.

9. Johannes Jansen, *Tax Harmonization in the European Community*. Community Topics 29. (European Community Information Service, 1968), 6. This argument is still maintained, e.g., Cnossen, *Three VAT Studies* (CPB, 2010) at 25 states: "[R]etailers are less likely to default on the VAT invoiced to them by their suppliers than on the tax they would have had to pay in full to the tax authorities if, instead, an equivalent retail sales tax had been imposed."
10. *See*, e.g., Alan A. Tait, *Value Added Tax: International Practice and Problems* (IMF, 1988); Ben Terra, *Sales Taxation. The Case of Value Added Tax in the European Community* (Kluwer Law International, 1989).
11. Sijbren Cnossen, *The Technical Superiority of VAT Over RST*, 4 Austl. Tax F. 419 (1987); Sijbren Cnossen, *Broad-Based Consumption Taxes: VAT, RST or BTT?* 6 Austl. Tax F. 392 (1989).
12. Majority or consensus view is not fact. If delegates at the United Nations by majority or even unanimously declare that the earth is flat, the shape of our planet is not actually changing to comply with their statement. Likewise, the majority view that VAT is the superior consumption tax does not make it so.
13. Rita de la Feria, *The New VAT General Reverse-Charge Mechanism*, Editorial, 2019-4 EC Tax Rev. 172, 173 (2019).

- VAT creates a self-policing effect because input-tax credits need to be supported by invoices.

However, as a single stage tax, under RST the risk of fraud is also limited to that single, retail stage. Under VAT, tax collection and thus the risk of fraud is extended to all stages of the supply chain.[14] Fraud prior to the retail stage does simply not occur under RST; intermediate stage fraud is the direct result of the operational mechanism of VAT.

The self-policing effect seems to have two functions. First, it helps facilitating the actual creation of the paper trail. Second, it is a deterrence to VAT fraud in the supply chain. Under RST a paper trail will also exist as in advanced economies transactions do not take place between legitimate businesses without compliance to often automated administrative processes. A Purchase Order from the buyer followed by a sales invoice created by the Accounts Receivable department of the seller is required to produce a shipping document without which the logistics department will not initiate delivery. The buyer's Accounts Payable department will not process payment without an underlying invoice issued by the seller.

The European Commission argues that the "self-policing character of the VAT system is linked to the need for each customer to pay the VAT to its supplier and to hold an invoice to be allowed to deduct the VAT paid to its supplier who, in turn, is discouraged from evading taxes (as it has issued an invoice)."[15] The reasoning is not convincing in a policy assessment comparing VAT to RST. The VAT is not superior to RST because it creates a self-policing mechanism of B2B transactions that is simply not required under RST where these transactions are not taxed in the first place. Indeed, under a VAT, a buyer likely will insist on receiving a purchase invoice as such an invoice is the documentary proof for claiming the corresponding input-VAT credit. However, traders have no reason to monitor whether the seller actually remits the VAT to the tax agency.[16] At best, self-policing encourages the seller to report the VAT it has collected, while under RST there is no tax to report and potential fraud in the chain of B2B transactions cannot occur, so no mechanism to encourage honesty is required. The only advantage of self-policing is that it encourages the actual issuing of invoices and, thus, the creation of an auditable paper trail. Indeed, the need for an input-tax credit being absent, there is no tax induced reason for buyers to insist on the issuing of invoices under RST, so paper trail compliance may be somewhat weaker. On the other hand, the fraud deterrence function of self-policing is irrelevant under RST at intermediate stages in the supply chain.

The further assumption is that the existence of a paper trail would also deter fraud at the retail stage because underreporting of output VAT on the re-sale of goods of which the corresponding input-VAT had been deducted could easily be detected through cross-checking purchase accounts with sales accounts and inventory.

14. Brederode and Pfeiffer, *supra* n. 1, 235.
15. European Commission, Commission Staff Working Document, *Impact Assessment General Reverse Charge Mechanism*, SWD (2016) 457, Brussels, 21 December 2016, 7 (2016).
16. Richard Hemming & John Kay, *The United Kingdom*, in *The Value Added Tax: Lessons from Europe* 75-89 (Henry J. Aaron ed., Brookings Institution, 1981).

Policymakers at the time must have felt that the self-policing character of VAT would vastly reduce or marginalize—if not totally prevent—fraud in the intermediate, B2B chain of transactions. Whether this assumption is true in practice is immediately relevant for evaluating the superiority of VAT. If the pre-retail stage fraud is found to be of quantitative importance, the question arises whether the reduction in retail stage fraud triggered by the paper trail is larger than the B2B-stage fraud created by including the pre-retail stage transactions into the scope of the consumption tax.

In the remainder of this chapter we concentrate on two aspects. First, we analyze the reality of the fractioned collection system which is hailed as an important advantage offered by VAT over RST, as it suggests that there is less retail stage fraud under VAT to the extent that part of the total tax burden of the consumption sale has been collected at earlier stages in the supply chain (§8.04). Second, we compare the size of fraud under RST and VAT, respectively. Section 8.05 is focused on retail stage fraud and seeks to establish whether we can confirm the orthodox view that VAT is less susceptible to this type of fraud than RST. If there is, indeed, a difference, we need to determine whether it is significant enough to justify a policy choice for the one tax over the other. In §8.06, we will look at intermediate stage fraud, which is unique to VAT and cannot arise under RST. It is relevant, nevertheless, in the context of a comparative evaluation of the susceptibility to fraud of both taxes. If VAT has an advantage as to retail stage fraud and RST has an advantage as to intermediate stage fraud, a quantitative assessment of the fraud in each stage is helpful in determining the overall susceptibility to fraud of the two types of consumption tax. Intermediate stage fraud consists of B2B reporting fraud (§8.06[B]) and carousel fraud, exploiting the zero-rate applied to cross-border transactions (§8.06[C]). The core of our study is a general assessment of the size of all types of VAT fraud, based on VAT gap studies (§8.7), compared to RST based on data for the state of California (§8.8). We summarize and conclude in §8.9.

§8.04 VAT COLLECTION IN THE SUPPLY CHAIN: CONFUSION VERSUS REALITY

As long as transactions remain within the ring of business transactions, effectively, no VAT will accrue to the treasury due to the input-VAT credit system. In a typical B2B transaction, the seller collects VAT from the purchaser and remits the VAT amount to the tax agency which, in turn, restitutes the same VAT to the purchaser either through a refund or through allowing the purchaser to credit the VAT amount paid against VAT collected on the purchaser's output. Clearly, B2B transactions do not lead to any net gain for the treasury. The portrayal of VAT as a fractioned collection system whereby slices of the amount of tax on the final consumption of a product are collected at each stage of the supply chain, is incorrect. It is an optical illusion,[17] created by the actual reporting of tax due by each vendor over its value added, i.e., the positive difference

17. *See* Brederode and Pfeiffer, *supra* n. 1, who compare the VAT collection system to the illusion portrayed in M.C. Escher's "The Waterfall" (lithograph 1961), where the waterfall keeps driving the waterwheel, which keeps recycling the water to create the waterfall.

between output-VAT minus input-VAT. This is shown in Table 8.1 and Figure 8.3, which provide generally utilized models to demonstrate VAT collection in the supply chain.

Table 8.1 VAT Collection in the Supply Chain

Tax Rate 10%	Price	Tax on Sales	Credit	To Revenue
Producer 1	1,000	100	–	100
Producer 2	2,000	200	100	100
Producer 3	3,000	300	200	100
Wholesaler	4,000	400	300	100
Retailer	5,000	500	400	100
Total				**500**

Source: Author's own work.

Table 8.1 seems to show that an amount of VAT is collected at each stage of the supply chain, equal to the tax rate applied to the value added of each stage.

Figure 8.3 VAT Flow Chart

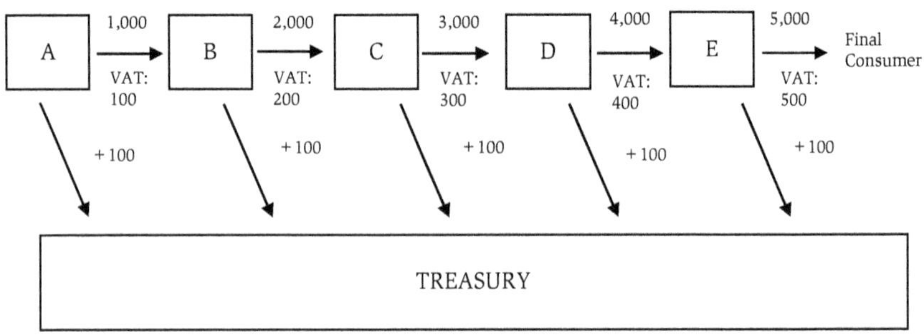

Source: Author's own work.

A through E are all businesses in a supply chain where E is the retailer making the sale to the final consumer. A sells goods to B for 1,000 and charges 100 VAT which is paid over to the Treasury. B supplies these goods for a total amount of 2,200 (including 200 VAT) to C. B deducts its input VAT of 100 from the 200 received from C and pays the difference of 100 to the Treasury. C sells these goods on for 3,300 (including 300 VAT) to D. C deducts its input VAT of 200 from the 300 received from D and pays the difference of 100 to the Treasury. D sells to E for 4,400 (including 400 VAT) and deducts the input VAT of 300 from the 400 VAT received from E, paying over the difference of 100. Finally, E sells the goods for 5,500 (including 500 VAT) to a final consumer. D deducts its input VAT of 400 from the 500 received and pays the difference of 100 to the Treasury.

The European Commission concludes when describing a similar supply chain that at each stage, "VAT is paid to the Treasury on the added-value; i.e., the difference between the VAT received from the buyer and the price paid to the supplier." That is in itself true, but payment should not be confused with actual revenue collection. Indeed, VAT results in a *fractioned payment* system but there is no actual *fractioned collection* of VAT, because until the final retail sale no tax actually accrues to the Treasury.[18] What remains somewhat hidden in the preceding table and figure, is that the VAT collected at each stage automatically becomes an input-VAT credit of the next stage; this is caused by the linking of the credit to the subsequent sale of the buyer and not to the sale of the supplier. However, the input-VAT credit is not dependent on the resale of a good or service. Under VAT, a business can deduct all VAT incurred in the tax period, regardless of whether the corresponding inputs have been used or been resold. VAT on capital goods[19] and overhead cost, on parts and raw materials is deductible and so is the VAT paid for goods intended for resale but still in inventory. Table 8.1 and Figure 8.3, meant to provide a simple demonstration of how VAT moves through the supply chain, create an optical illusion that VAT is actually collected on each B2B transaction. This becomes clear when we show the tax collection outcome per transaction in Table 8.2.

Table 8.2 VAT Collection per Transaction

Tax Rate 10%	Price	Tax on Sales	Credit to Purchaser	Revenue Collected on Transaction
Producer 1	1,000	100	100	0
Producer 2	2,000	200	200	0
Producer 3	3,000	300	300	0
Wholesaler	4,000	400	400	0
Retailer	5,000	500	0	500
Total				**500**

Source: Author's own work.

Because of the credit system, any output-VAT charged by each vendor becomes the input-VAT credit of the purchaser at the next stage of the supply chain. The purchaser pays the VAT to the supplier, who remits the VAT to the Treasury, and receives a credit in the same amount against the Treasury. Thus, the B2B transactions do not lead to any accrual of VAT-revenue to the Treasury. Therefore, no actual VAT amount is collected until the good or service reaches the final consumer; in other words, only the retail sale leads to an accrual of tax to the Treasury. This is also demonstrated in Figure 8.4.

18. The exception is non-deductible input-VAT incurred by exempt businesses.
19. Some jurisdictions apply a so-called Capital Goods Scheme to align VAT deductions with the longer lifecycle of capital goods, *see* Robert F. van Brederode, *Systems of General Sales Taxation: Theory, Policy and Practice*, section 8.2.7 (Kluwer Law International, 2009).

Figure 8.4 The Movement of VAT Through the Supply Chain

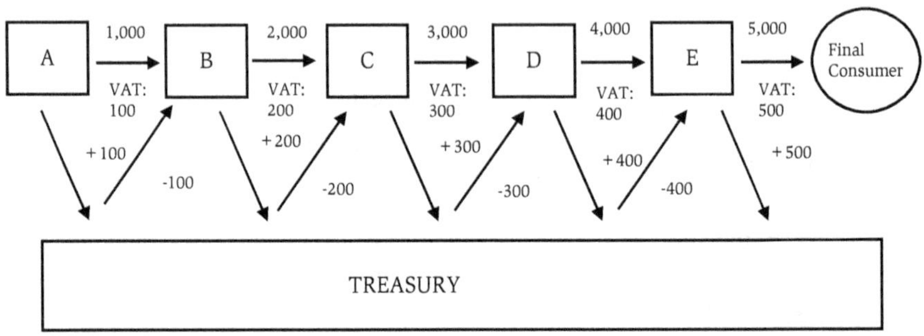

Source: Author's own work.

Within the ring of business transactions each payment of VAT is off-set by an equal amount of input-VAT credit. From Table 8.2 and Figure 8.4 it follows that only the retail transaction generates tax revenue; all previous transactions within the supply chain are neutral in terms of tax collection, i.e., any tax remitted to the revenue by a seller is off-set by an equal amount of tax credited to the purchaser. In other words, levying VAT at each stage within the ring of B2B transactions is meaningless from a revenue accrual perspective; it only serves the creation of a paper trail.

§8.05 REDUCTION OF RETAIL STAGE FRAUD

The rationale for VAT as a tax less susceptible to fraud than comparable consumption taxes can be traced in history, but it is the premise of this chapter that the historical justification is no longer valid today. When the EU was deciding on what consumption tax to introduce, it concluded that a retail sales tax (which economically has the same result as VAT in taxing private consumption expenditure) was too sensitive to fraud as tax collection would be entrusted to hundreds of thousands small, privately owned, and often family-managed retail stores. VAT would do two things: first it would create a paper trail of invoices allowing the tax authorities to effectively audit transactions through the supply chain, which would reduce fraud at the retail stage (§8.05[A]); second, fraud at the retail level would be limited to the tax calculated over the retailer's value added or margin (§8.05[B]). If these assumptions are all true, retail stage fraud should be lower under VAT than under RST. It is our position that the retail industry is no longer the weakest link in terms of tax compliance due to significant changes in the scale of the retailers and the modern operational dynamics of the industry. We describe the retail industry changes in §8.05[C].

[A] Effectiveness of Paper Trail for Audit Purposes

Governments must be able to observe economic transactions if they want to tax those transactions. Therefore, paper trails and third-party reporting are crucial tax compliance enforcement tools. One of the advantages contributed to VAT is the incentive to issue invoices imbedded in the self-policing effect, thus creating a verifiable paper trail (*see* §8.03). This incentive is absent in regard of B2C transactions.

Although, prima facie, the existence of the paper trail appears to be helpful in the compliance-auditing process, in practice, auditors do not check invoices upstream and/or downstream the supply chain, unless there is a suspicion of fraud. In other words, auditors, generally, rely on the books of the business under audit and cross-check invoices with suppliers and customers only in exceptional cases, which reflects the notion that it is practically impossible to cross-check every invoice against evidence that earlier VAT has been paid.[20] It seems, therefore, that the existence of a paper trail primarily creates a preventive deterrence effect on fraud. This is confirmed by Pomeranz[21] who conducted an empirical research project evaluating the existence of the self-policing properties of VAT. She tested the effect of an increase of audit probability on VAT payment through an audit preannouncement experiment in Chili. As the response was less in relation to transactions covered by a paper trail, this strongly suggest that the existence of the paper trail, indeed, has a preventive deterrence effect. She also found that firms with a larger share of retail sales responded stronger to the increase in audit probability, suggesting that non-compliance is higher in the retail sector than in the pre-retail stages of the supply chain. However, this could also be caused by the average retail firm being relatively small as the experiment also confirmed that larger firms tend to be less involved in tax evasion than small firms. She also found a strong relation between tax compliance and audit probability. The existence of the paper trail is, in itself, not self-enforcing but creates this effect in correlation with the probability of cross-checks by the tax authority. Without enforcement, the paper trail has little value. The integrity of the tax agency plays a role as well; although the existence of a paper trail would reduce the margin of discretion of an auditor, enforcement could still be avoided to the extent auditors are susceptible to bribery.

We conclude that the existence of a paper trail is, indeed, effective for audit purposes, provided however that the audit probability is both real and sufficiently high. This conclusion does not provide a clear advantage for VAT over RST as in advanced economies the audit trail, required for effective auditing, exists independent of the institution of a VAT or RST.

20. Michael Keen and Stephen Smith, *VAT Fraud and Evasion: What Do We Know, and What Can be Done?* 59 Nat'l Tax J. 861 (2006).
21. Dina Pomeranz, *No Taxation without Information: Deterrence and Self-Enforcement in the Value Added Tax*, 105(8) Am. Econ. Rev. 2539 (2015).

[B] Limitation of Fraud to Retailer's Margin

The reasoning here is that if a retailer would commit fraud by not reporting some of the output-VAT collected, likely that retailer would also keep the corresponding purchases out of the books and not deduct the input-VAT incurred. As a result, VAT would still accrue to the Treasury in the amount of the non-deducted input-VAT and, effectively, only the margin of the retailer would have escaped tax. Thus, in monetary terms, under a retail sales tax, the treasury would lose an amount equal to the statutory rate (let us say 10%) times the full retail price (assume 100), thus 10% x 100 = 10; under a VAT levied at the same rate, the loss would be limited to the tax on the retail price minus the not-deducted input VAT on the purchase price (assume 40), thus 10% x 100 -/- (10% x 40) = 6. It appears that VAT holds an advantage on this point. However, as explained above, tax collection within the circle of business transaction only occurs if input-VAT is not deducted. The conclusion that VAT compared to RST has a lower effective fraud level because the Treasury would only forgo the VAT over the retailer's margin is based on the *assumption* that a fraudulent retailer would keep the corresponding purchase out of the books and, thus, not deduct the related input-VAT. In many cases that will, indeed, be the case, but it is not necessarily so. A retailer may choose to deduct the input-VAT while not reporting the sale and retaining the sold products in his accounts as part of his inventory.[22] As a result, the accounting entries all match, and the only way for an auditor to identify the tax mischief is by counting the physical inventory of the retailer. In practice, given the high number of inventory items, without any suspicion of fraud that will likely not happen, at best the auditor will make a random check. Contemplating the structure of his fraud, a retailer weighs the risk of detection based on the frequency and thoroughness of audits. i.e., the chances: 1) of being audited at all; 2) that the auditor will count all physical inventory; 3) if a random check on inventory is performed, the sample will include the type of products to be used in the fraudulent sales. Not all fraudsters may seek to take this gamble and, therefore, prefer to up their chances by not reporting the purchase; others may make a different assessment of those probabilities. In the latter case, the fraud would not be limited to the tax due on the retailer's margin but would extend to the tax due on the full retail price (as with RST). Our conclusion is that VAT has, indeed, an advantage over RST in limiting the fraud to the retailer's margin, if all fraudsters refrain from claiming input-VAT credit related to the corresponding purchases. The advantage is absent to the extent that fraudsters do claim input-VAT deduction of purchases corresponding to unreported sales. To our knowledge there exist no statistical data that could assist in determining what choices fraudsters have made in this regard. VAT still retains somewhat of an advantage as it reduces large-scale fraud, because firms that make input tax credits that are high relative to their reported output will raise a red flag with the tax authorities.[23]

---

22. Even when a small retailer uses an automated accounting and inventory management system, if the barcode of a sold item is not scanned at the cash register, it remains part of inventory.
23. George R. Zodrow, *The Sales Tax, the VAT, and Taxes in Between – Or, Is the Only Good NRST a "VAT in Drag"?* 52(3) Nat'l Tax J. 429 (1999).

[C] The Development of the Retail Industry: Is It still the Weakest Link for Tax Compliance Purposes?

One of the main reasons for recommending the EEC (now EU) to adopt VAT over RST was that for collection purposes the latter would depend on a large number of small retailers unable to maintain precise bookkeeping.[24] Indeed, research has shown that tax evasion declines with increase of firm size or, from the opposite perspective, voluntary tax compliance improves with the increase of firm size.[25] In other words, this argument against RST and pro VAT may have held true in the 1960s when the EU was discussing which type of consumption tax to choose. However, our position is that the retail industry, at least in developed countries, has changed significantly since then and has now, *mutatis mutandis*, a positive tax compliance profile. While the retail industry, traditionally, was dominated by often family owned and managed, small traders, the composite of the industry has changed and is now concentrated in large conglomerate entities with annual sales in the billions of dollars. Although the first department stores in the US and Europe emerged in the mid to late 19th century,[26] they catered to affluent clientele in urban centers. Small pop-and-mom convenience stores, however, served rural areas and dominated the retail sector. The self-service supermarket concept started in the 1930s with the King Kullen supermarket on Long Island[27] and A&P in the mid-West,[28] gradually replacing groups of small stores. The largest national supermarkets chains in the US measured in 2018 revenue and number of stores are displayed below in Table 8.3.

24. Neumark Report. *Report of the Fiscal and Financial Committee*, in *The EEC Reports on Tax Harmonization*, 93-156, 124 (IBFD, 1968).
25. Peter Mieszkowski & Michael Palumbo, *Is a National Retail Sales Tax Administrable? A Proposal for a Hybrid NRST*. Working Paper, Rice University (1998); Henrik J. Kleven et al., *Why Can Modern Governments Tax So Much? An Agency Model of Firms as Fiscal Intermediaries*, Working Paper 15218 (National Bureau of Economic Research, 2009), available at http://www.nber.org/papers/w15218; Pomeranz, *supra* n. 21.
26. Aristide Boucicaut opened *Le Bon Marché* in Paris in 1852, *Printemps* opened in 1865 and *Galeries Lafayette* in 1895; *Harrods* of London can be traced back to 1834; in de US, *Hudson's* opened in Chicago in 1891, *Marshall Field's* in Chicago in 1852, *the Marble Palace* opened in New York in 1846 and *Macy's* in 1878, *Gimbels* in Vincennes, Indiana in 1842, *Neiman-Marcus* in Dallas in 1907; *Tietz* opened as the first department store in Germany in 1882 and *Karstadt* opened in 1881; in the Netherlands the oldest store is the Winkel van Sinkel which opened in Utrecht in 1839, *De Bijenkorf* was founded in 1870; the first department store in Spain was *Almacenes el Siglo* which opened in 1881 in Barcelona.
27. King Kullen Grocery Co., Inc. was acquired late 2019 by Ahold Delhaize USA's Stop & Shop chain.
28. A&P was the largest grocery store chain from 1915-1975. After bankruptcy, the supermarkets were either sold or closed in 2015.

Table 8.3 Largest US Supermarkets in 2018 based on Retail Sales (in USD Billions)

Name	Sales in USD Billions	No. of Stores
Kroger	110.60	2,764
Albertson	60.53	2,260
Ahold Delhaize	44.17	1,961
Publix	36.10	1,239
Aldi	28.78	1,800
H-E-B	24.02	340
Neighborhood Market/Marketside (Walmart)	18.73	699
Wakefern/Shoprite	16.57	352
Whole Foods (Amazon)	15.95	476

Source: Statista 2020 and Annual Reports 2018.

In addition, there exist dozens of independent, i.e., not owned by any of the national conglomerates, regional supermarket chains.

Supermarkets in the US are also big in size with the median store measuring 41,561 square feet. The average store carries more than 33,000 individual items. There are about 26,000 conventional supermarkets in the US, carrying a full line of groceries, meat and produce.[29] In addition, there are warehouse stores, such as Costco with 533 stores in the US in 2018 and US operations revenue of USD 102.28 billion,[30] Sam's Club with 597 stores and USD 59.2 billion in 2018 revenue,[31] and BJ's with 216 stores and 2018 revenue of USD 12,75 billion.[32]

It was not until the 1960s that the first Walmart, K-Mart and Target stores opened, and the next several decades they expanded strategically across the US.[33] Walmart is the world's largest retailer and has 3,961 supercenters and discount stores in the US with sales of USD 299.75 billion for 2018.[34] Target has 1,844 stores in the US with 2018 sales of USD 74.43 billion. The largest home improvement store chains are Home Depot with 1,981 stores in the US and with 2018 US revenue of USD 99.39,[35] and Lowes with 2,002 stores in the US and Canada and 2018 revenue of USD 71.30,[36] controlling a combined 90% of the market. The restaurant industry is also important as it sells

29. Colman Andrews, *Kroger, Publix and Hy-Vee on list of best grocery store chains in every state.* USA Today, December 16, 2019.
30. Source: Costco Wholesale Corporation, Annual Report 2018.
31. Source: Walmart, Inc., Annual Report 2018.
32. Source: BJ's Wholesale Club, Inc., Annual Report 2018.
33. Thomas O. Graff & Dub Ashton, *Spatial Diffusion of Wal-Mart: Contagious and Reverse Hierarchical Elements*, 46 The Professional Geographer 19 (1994).
34. Source: Walmart, Inc., Annual Report 2018. This revenue is for Walmart US minus the revenue generated by the Neighborhood Market chain; and it does not include Sam's Club, and Walmart International.
35. Source: The Home Depot, Inc., Annual report 2018.
36. Source: Lowe's Companies, Inc., Annual report 2018.

directly to consumers and has 2018 sales of USD 767.8 billion.[37] It is a diverse industry composed of kiosks, quick service restaurants, such as Starbucks, Dunkin Donuts, McDonalds, KFC, Chick-fil-A, Panera Bread, and full-service restaurants, such as Ruth's Chris Steakhouse or Olive Garden. The industry breakdown of market share per type of restaurant, measured in revenue is shown in Table 8.4.

Table 8.4 Restaurant Industry 2018 Sales per Sector

Type of Business	2018 Sales (USD Billions)	% of Total Industry Sales
Total industry sales	767.8	100.00
Full-service restaurants	274.8	35.79
Quick-service restaurants	239.1	31.14
Cafeterias, buffets	6.1	0.79
Snack & non-alcoholic bars	41.8	5.44
Social caterers	9.0	1.17
Bars & taverns	21.2	2.76
Other	175.8	22.89

Source: Nation's Restaurant News, April 5, 2019.

Restaurants are either independent or corporation owned, and many chains operate as a franchise and are subject to strict financial and inventory oversight by the franchisor. Independent restaurants dominate and number 480,900 or 68% of the industry total, compared to 231,400 chain restaurants, representing 32% of the industry total. Of the independent restaurants, 68% classify as full-service restaurants and 32% as limited service restaurants. Chain restaurants, generally, tend to fall more within the quick service category. However, sales volume of independent operators is generally less than sales volume of chain restaurants. About 40% of independent full-service restaurants have annual sales less than USD 500,000, and 47% generate sales between USD 500,000 and USD 1 million. Among independent limited service restaurants, 79% has less than USD 500,000 in annual sales and 18% between USD 500,000 and USD 1 million. In comparison, only 2% of full-service chain restaurants and 24% of limited service chain restaurants have less than USD 500,000 in annual sales.[38]

Most retail companies are still small with 99% employing 50 or less employees and 95% have just one location. Earlier research confirms that small enterprises tend to be concentrated in the retail trade and services, but that the majority of sales is made by large corporations.[39] For the year 1994, 15.94% of all sole proprietors were located in the retail industry,[40] generating together with partnerships only 8% of all retail sales

37. Excluding non-commercial restaurant services and military restaurant services. Source: Nation's Restaurant News, April 5, 2019.
38. Source: https://www.chd-expert.com/blog/press_release/independent-restaurant-market/. Numbers refer to 2017.
39. Mieszkowski and Palumbo, *supra* n. 25, 6-7.
40. IRS, SOI, Bulletin, Fall 1996 as produced by Mieszkowski and Palumbo, *supra* n. 25, 6.

while corporations with sales over USD 1 million generate 87% of all retail sales.[41] IRS data shows that for the year 2016, 9.12% of sole proprietorships were active in the retail trade, generating gross revenue of USD 174.6 billion,[42] or 3.6% of total 2016 US retail sales of USD 4.852 trillion.[43] In developing markets, the emergence of retail chains started in the 1980s and reached a market share as a percentage of total retail between 20%-40% in Brazil, China, Indonesia, Malaysia, Philippines, Singapore and Thailand, but India is still quite behind in the trend with chains accounting for only 5% market share.[44]

In the US, small firms, however, have a large presence in the service industry and create 30%-45% of sales in that sector while 55% of sales in services accrue to corporations with revenues exceeding USD 1 million. However, 70% of all sales are made by corporations and only 30% by sole proprietorships and partnerships. Professional services in the medical, legal, engineering and accounting professions, are less prone to tax-induced entry due to licensing and higher education requirements. Fraud opportunities are further limited in the medical sector as a result of third-party payments (insurers) which create an auditable paper trail.

This shift in the composition of the retail sector is relevant, not only because such a change would indicate a lower degree of tax evasion, but also because the tax base usually is concentrated in the largest companies.[45] The data above show that in the US the share of retail sector sales made by larger corporations has grown from 87% in 1994 to about 94% in 2016. Large companies are subject to stockholder control, public scrutiny, extensive government regulation and reporting obligations, requiring the creation of effective financial and inventory control frameworks. Based on Mieszkowski and Palumbo's findings, *grosso modo,* tax evasion can be expected to be concentrated in the 8% for 1994 and 3.6% for 2016 sales made by small, non-corporate enterprises, where capital, management and most of labor are in one hand.

§8.06 FRAUD IN THE SUPPLY CHAIN PRIOR TO THE RETAIL STAGE

[A] Introduction

What EU policymakers did not fully realize was that the preferred invoice-credit VAT system, while likely reducing fraud at the retail stage, would also create a huge opportunity to commit fraud at stages prior to the retail stage. Some fraud was likely anticipated but it was expected to be sufficiently countered by the self-policing system under which issuing invoices would be a demand of any business purchaser. The volume of VAT that moves through a business' accounting system—the VAT "throughput" or the VAT a business must manage on both the input and output side—amounts

41. Mieszkowski and Palumbo, *supra* n. 25, 7.
42. IRS, SOI, Bulletin, Spring 2019.
43. US Census Bureau, *Annual Retail Trade Survey: 2017*, available at https://www.census.gov/data/tables/2017/econ/arts/annual-report.html (accessed September 14, 2020).
44. Subidita Pattanaik and Bidhu B. Mishra, *Evolution of Retail Industry in India*, 2(4) J. Res'ch Innov. & Mgmt Sc. 51 (2016).
45. Keen and Smith, *supra* n. 20, 869.

to 30%-35% of its annual turnover. To put that into perspective, a business with annual sales of USD 1 billion, manages up to USD 350 million in VAT. Attractive amounts for those operating in the shadows of respectability and honesty.

Intermediate-stage VAT fraud can be distinguished into two main groups: underreporting of tax collected and/or claiming non-existent input-tax credits[46] (we will refer to this type as B2B reporting fraud); and the so-called carousel fraud, abusing the zero rate applied to cross-border transactions.

[B] B2B Reporting Fraud

The first type of fraud, typically, either underreports output-VAT (pocketing the difference between output-VAT actually collected from customers and the VAT reported and remitted to the tax agency), or overclaims input-VAT credit (claiming more than charged by suppliers or claiming input-tax for imaginary purchases). Both types of fraudulent actions may be supported by counterfeit invoices, but not necessarily so. The fraudsters may issue a correct invoice to B2B customers, allowing them to take correct credit for input-tax actually paid, while recording a counterfeit invoice, showing a lower sales price and VAT amount than actual. The customer may be unaware of this. Input-tax fraud may be supported by counterfeit invoices showing more tax than actually paid or suggesting purchases that were actually never made. In most cases, the supplier will be unaware of the abuse.

Tait reports an estimation in the Netherlands showing that 44% of all VAT fraud consisted of false input tax credit claims,[47] which is a significant portion. However, this number cannot be used as an indication of the present size of this type of fraud relative to the other types of VAT fraud, because it dates from before the EU-wide emergence of the carousel fraud scheme.[48]

[C] Carousel Fraud

A special category of intermediate stage VAT fraud exploits the zero rate of exported goods in conjunction with the system of refunds of excess input-tax credits. After the introduction of the so-called transitional VAT system per 1993, which introduced 0% VAT rates on cross-border B2B transactions, organized crime has developed a lucrative scheme of defrauding governments generally referred to as carousel fraud or Missing Trader fraud. In simplified form the scheme operates as displayed in Figure 8.5.[49]

46. Including fraudulent registration of "businesses" for VAT in an attempt to claim illegitimate input tax credits.
47. Tait, *supra* n. 10, 307. Unfortunately, he provides neither a source nor explains the methodology of the calculation.
48. Carousel fraud took a flight after the EU-wide zero-rating of inter-state, cross-border transactions with the introduction of the transitional VAT system per 1993. Prior to that, only the Benelux countries applied zero-rating to cross-border transactions within their jurisdiction and carousel fraud was logically limited to these three countries.
49. On the carousel fraud, *see* Robert F. van Brederode, *Third Party Risks and Liabilities in Case of VAT Fraud in the EU*, 34(1) Int'l Tax J. 31 (2008); and Sebastian Pfeiffer and Pavel Semerád,

Figure 8.5 Carousel Fraud

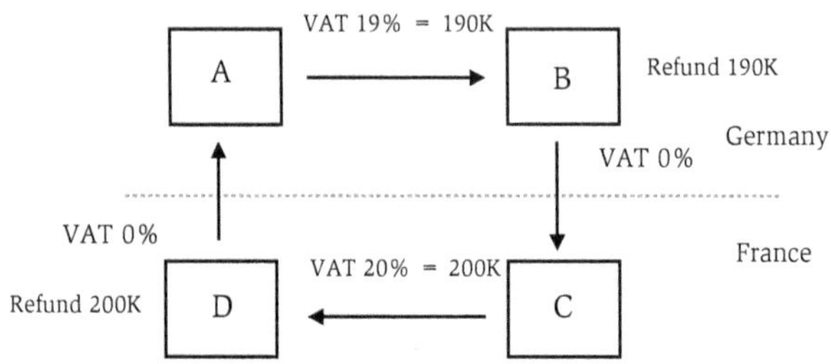

Source: Author's own work.

All parties participating in the scheme are registered as taxable persons, A and B in this example in Germany and C and D in France. All four companies are controlled by the same criminal organization. A imports a certain quantity, let us assume 10,000, electronic devices from the United States. The VAT paid upon importation is subsequently deductible as input VAT in A's monthly VAT return in Germany. A sells the devices to company B, also in Germany, for EUR 100 each and charges 19% VAT as the transaction constitutes a domestic supply. A charges EUR 1,000.000 plus EUR 190,000 in VAT. A does not remit the VAT to the tax authorities. In turn, B sells the tablets to company C in France also for EUR 100 each and charges 0% VAT as this qualifies as a cross-border, so-called intra-Community supply. B receives a refund of EUR 190,000 from the German tax authorities for the VAT paid to A. C needs to account for the intra-Community acquisition in France, but the VAT due in that respect is immediately, and in the same return, deductible as input VAT. Next, C sells the tablets to company D, again for EUR 100 each, or a total of EUR 1,000,000. This constitutes a domestic supply in France in relation to which C must charge French VAT at 20%, i.e., EUR 200,000. Company C does not remit this VAT to the tax authorities, but D who in turn sells the tablets back to A in Germany with VAT at 0%, files a claim for refund of the EUR 200,000 input VAT invoiced to him by C. Thus, a circular chain of transactions (carousel) has been created whereby the goods start and end up with the same trader. The carousel is repeated several times, each time leading to a combined VAT refund claim of EUR 390,000, after which the tablets are sold in bulk for cost price on the local German market, and this in fact the only real sale to a third party. The companies are dissolved, and new companies are set up and the fraud scheme will be repeated. As the tax authorities became more aggressive in investigating this type of fraud, the carousel schemes have become more and more sophisticated. Smokescreens have been created to make it more difficult for the authorities to discover the fraud, e.g., by mixing low-volume legitimate transactions with high-volume artificial ones, by expanding the chain with bona fide unrelated traders, so-called buffers, and by increasing the chain's geographical complexity, i.e., adding more cross-border transactions, spread over

Missing Trader Fraud in European VAT. MENDELU Working Papers in Business and Economics 41/2013 (Mendel University, 2013), available at http://ideas.repec.org/s/men/wpaper.html.

more jurisdictions, including jurisdictions located outside the EU, such as Switzerland and Dubai.[50] Originally the fraud schemes involved high-value electronics but more recently they also include intangibles such as carbon credits and green energy certificates.

This type of fraud is essentially caused by the mechanics of the tax-from-tax method VAT, characterized by fractioned payments and deductions system. The fraudsters, as demonstrated above, exploit the deduction mechanism of the tax, realizing that the invoice not only is proof required for exercising the right to deduct input-VAT, but in essence is a "bearer note" on the government.[51] The level of VAT refunds as a proportion of gross VAT receipts is quite high in the EU at 38.1%.[52]

The European Commission estimates the amount of VAT carousel fraud for 2014 to be EUR 50 billion.[53] Carousel fraud is not equivalent to deliberate underpayment of tax, i.e., Revenue receives less than it should; rather, this type of fraud constitutes a cash payout from the Treasury to the fraudster.

[D] Fraud Counter Measures

The most important proposals to combat carousel fraud are presented below. As the carousel fraud hinges on the exploitation of the 0% rate to cross-border transactions within the EU, most solutions are focused on replacing the 0% rate with an actual VAT charge (§8.06[D][1]) either at origin or at destination, or via an additional "central" tax on cross-border, interstate transactions; by securing payment in combination with the use of certified software (§8.06[D][2]); in requiring direct payment by the purchasers to the tax agency or special bank account (§8.06[D][3]); shifting the tax liability to the purchaser (§8.06[D][4]); removing charges on all B2B transactions (§8.06.[D][5]); and finally, by requiring clearing of VAT invoices prior to the sale through life reporting (§8.06[D][6]).

[1] Actual VAT Charge on Inter-State Sales

Taxation at Origin with Clearing

The European Commission in the 1990s proposed the definite VAT system under which cross-border supplies within the EU would be taxed at the rates applicable in the

50. Brederode, *supra* n. 49.
51. Richard M. Bird, *Review of "Principles and Practices of Value Added Taxation: Lessons from Developing Countries."* 41(6) Can. Tax J. 1222, 1224 (1993).
52. Graham Harrison & Russell Krelove, *VAT Refunds: A Review of Country Experience*. IMF Working Paper WP/05/218 (2005), at 8. Luca Barbone, Richard M. Bird, and Jaime Vazquez-Caro, *The Cost of VAT: A Review of the Literature*. Working Paper 12-22, at 26 (International Center for Public Policy, 2012).
53. European Commission, Commission Staff Working Document, *Impact Assessment General Reverse Charge Mechanism*, SWD (2016) 457, Brussels, 21 December 2016, at 6(2016).

country of origin.[54] In B2B transactions, the buyer would be allowed to deduct the foreign VAT incurred on the cross-border procurement from the output VAT due in his Member State of establishment. As a result, the Member State of establishment would provide a credit for input-tax collected by another Member State, which would give an advantage to net-exporting countries. A clearing house was proposed to periodically reallocate revenues among the Member States to ensure revenue would accrue to the country of destination.[55] Each cross-border transaction leads either to a payment obligation or to a refund claim for a Member State. Under this system, cross-border supplies within the EU would no longer be zero rated, which would remove an important incentive for carousel or missing trader fraud. With billions of inter-state transactions, the origin system with clearing would involve a complex and perhaps overwhelming administrative exercise. Moreover, as long as significant rate differences exist between the Member States, it remains lucrative to remit false purchase invoices to suggest transactions in high tax jurisdictions, while in fact the goods were bought locally, and cash in the VAT difference. Moreover, all Member States would be required to coherently and reliably collect VAT.[56]

Taxation at Origin at the VAT Rate of Country of Destination without Clearing

Another proposal was to tax all cross-border transactions at the rate of the country of destination.[57] To prevent suppliers from having to register in all Member States, the tax authorities of the destination country would be required to establish tax offices in the country of origin to accept payments and deal with all VAT matters in relation to cross-border transactions. Since VAT is not fully harmonized in the EU and significant differences exist between the Member States in practical rules and in how the VAT is administered, exporters would nevertheless be required to comply with the diverse VAT rules of potentially all other Member States outside their home state. Tax authorities of individual Member States would potentially set up an office (and perhaps more than one depending on the export volume) in each of the other Member States. For reasons of complexity and cost of administration and compliance, this proposal was never seriously considered.

54. International supplies, i.e., transactions with third countries, would remain subject to zero-rating.
55. Thus, also neutralizing the advantage of net-exporting countries.
56. As the Member States' motivation to collect VAT could decrease where the VAT belongs to a different state. *See* for that issue also Alexander Hagen & Wolfram Reiß, *Die Zukunft der Umsatzsteuer als EG-Steuer*, Umsatzsteuer-Rundschau 109 (2000), and Christian Weber, *Der lange Weg zum Ursprungslandprinzip*, Umsatzsteuer-Rundschau 424 (2003).
57. Frans Vanistendael, *A Proposal for a Definitive VAT System Taxation in the Country of Origin at the Rate of the Country of Destination, Without Clearing* 1 EC Tax Rev. 45 (1995).

VIVAT

The VIVAT model has been developed for cross-border trade within the EU[58] but can be applied by any federal system where the states levy consumption taxes.[59]

Under the VIVAT proposal, international transactions will be relieved from tax through zero rating, but inter-state supplies would be taxed at a uniform rate. That same uniform rate would also apply to domestic transactions between taxable persons, but each state would retain full autonomy to determine the tax rates for domestic supplies to final consumers. In essence, this system combines a uniform VAT with a sub-national retail sales tax. Under the current VAT system in the EU, suppliers must administratively distinguish between domestic, inter-state and export supplies. Under VIVAT, a supplier must distinguish between export supplies, supplies to registered customers (B2B) and supplies to final consumers (B2C).

The VIVAT retains the audit and collection trail and relies on a clearing system to allocate the tax to the destination country. VIVAT shares strong similarities with the C-VAT, discussed in the next section.

C-VAT

The compensating VAT or C-VAT is focused on ensuring the actual taxation of interstate supplies within a federal state where both the central government and the each of the states levy a consumption tax.[60] At the state level, independent rates can be imposed, and intra-state transactions are subject to both de federal and state tax. Individual states would zero rate inter-state supplies, but the latter would be subject to both federal consumption tax and the C-VAT. Registered customers in the state of arrival would be eligible to a credit for C-VAT paid against the federal consumption tax. The subsequent domestic supply would be subject to the tax in the state of arrival.

Dual VAT

The dual VAT system has been proposed to especially cope with cross-border supplies in a system that consists of both a federal and a sub-national consumption tax, imposed at different rates, and without internal border controls.[61] For that reason, it could apply

58. Michael Keen & Stephen Smith, *Viva VIVAT!* 7(6) Int'l Tax & Pub. Fin. 741 (2000); Michael Keen, *VIVAT, C-VAT and All That: New Forms of Value-Added Tax for Federal Systems* 48(2) Canadian Tax J. 409 (2000).
59. According to Richard Bird & Pierre-Pascal Gendron, *The VAT in Developing and Transitional Countries* (Cambridge University Press, 2007), 125, n. 28, the VIVAT system is not very appropriate in developing countries.
60. Charles E. McLure, *Implementing Subnational VATs on Internal Trade: The Compensating VAT (C-VAT)* 6(7) Int'l Tax & Pub. Finance 723 (2000); Ricardo Varsano, *Subnational Taxation and Treatment of Interstate Trade in Brazil: Problems and Proposed Solution*, in *Decentralization and Accountability of the Public Sector* (Shahid J. Burki & Guillermo Perry, eds., Annual World Bank Conference on Development in Latin America and the Caribbean, World Bank, 2000).
61. Richard M. Bird & Pierre-Pascal Gendron, *Dual VATs and Cross-Border Trade: Two Problems, One Solution?* 5 Int'l Tax & Pub. Finance 429 (1998); Richard M. Bird & Pierre-Pascal Gendron, *C-VAT, VIVAT, and Dual VAT: Vertical "Sharing" and Interstate Trade*, 7 Int'l Trade & Pub. Finance 753 (2000).

not only in Canada, for which it was designed, but also in the United States if and when a federal consumption tax is introduced, or in the EU. It is based on the Quebec model where both the federal GST and the provincial GST are combined and administered at the sub-national level. Under the dual VAT system all inter-state supplies are zero-rated. Imports from another state within the federation or common market will be taxed when the importer resells the goods. We demonstrate how the dual VAT system works on the basis of the same transaction flow used to describe the C-VAT.

Company A sells goods for USD 100 to company B located in the same state Y. The dual VAT rate in state Y is 25%, consisting of a 10% state component and a 15% federal component. Therefore, A must charge USD 125 to B, the VAT component (25) of which the latter can deduct as an input VAT. B exports the goods for USD 200 to C in state Z, which is a zero-rated supply. As a result, B will receive a refund of the VAT paid to A because the VAT due on the outputs is zero. As a registered business, C does not have to account for any VAT regarding his purchase from B nor is he eligible for any input VAT because the purchase was zero-rated. The subsequent sale of goods by C to D in state Z for USD 300 is subject to the dual VAT rate in his state Z, which is 27%, consisting of a federal component of 15% and a state component of 12%. C will be charging USD 300 + USD 81 VAT = USD 381. In turn, D will be able to recover the VAT paid to C as input VAT because he is making a domestic supply to a final consumer P for USD 400 + USD 108 = USD 508. State Z receives 108-81 = 27 in VAT and the federal government collects 60.

[2] Certified Software and Third-Party Payment

This proposal envisions requiring a business to purchase and use certified VAT software as a build-on to its ERP system to determine its VAT compliance in combination with certified third-party payment collection.[62] In regard of intra-state, cross-border B2B transactions the seller will not be allowed to apply the zero-rate unless the certified software is used and, on the flipside of the coin, if the purchaser fails to use the software, input tax credit will be denied. However, fraud, by not reporting and remitting VAT collected on the subsequent domestic supply, would remain possible. To counter this, the proposal includes the mandatory use of certified third-party payment agents. It would be required that all payments for all transactions throughout the supply chain be handled by a third party who would also be responsible for the remittance of VAT to the tax authorities. Under the common VAT system, a business deducts input tax from output tax and remits the difference to the authorities. That would no longer be possible as the output tax would already be remitted to the tax authorities by the payment agent. As a result, this system would require the actual pay out of refunds on input tax incurred, which create a negative cash flow effect on all businesses. The scope of this proposal is limited to B2B transaction; including B2C

62. Richard T. Ainsworth, *The Digital VAT (D-VAT)* 25 Virg. Tax Rev. 875 (2006); Richard T. Ainsworth, *Carousel Fraud in the EU: A Digital VAT Solution* Tax Notes Int'l 443 (2006).

transaction is theoretical feasible but would require a legal mandate for the use of electronic payments for B2C transactions and the prohibition of cash transactions.

[3] Direct Payment (Withholding) by Purchasers (Split Payments)

The current system relies on seller-based collection of VAT, which gives rise to the opportunity for the supplier to disappear without reporting the tax collected. A potential solution is found in the application of a split payment mechanism, which would effectively remove the supplier from collecting the tax. Purchasers would be required to withhold the VAT amount included in an invoice and remit the tax either directly to the tax authorities or to a blocked VAT account of the supplier and pay the net amount of the invoice to the supplier. The problem is the same as with the system of payment agents discussed in the previous section. As all output VAT is remitted to the tax authorities by the purchaser, the seller can no longer off-set his input tax credits against it and actual refunds must be given, causing cash flow disadvantages for all businesses in the ring of B2B transactions. Only retailers would be able to deduct input tax from output tax. A study on behalf of the European Commission, found no evidence that the benefits of split payments (reduction of fraud) would outweigh the associated administrative and compliance costs.[63] Depending on the scope of the application of the split payment system, the VAT gap could be reduced by 27%-56%. However, negative business cash flow would amount to EURO 16.9 billion to 39 billion; and administrative and compliance cost would increase by 33%-58% or EUR 98.4 billion to EUR 117 billion.

[4] Shifting the VAT Liability to Purchasers (General Reverse Charge)

Under the reverse charge mechanism, the VAT liability is shifted from the supplier to the customer. The customer accounts for the VAT on the purchase in his VAT return as output VAT and deducts the same as input VAT. No actual tax payment would be made to the tax authorities in relation to this supply if the customer has the full right to deduct input VAT. The VAT would be reduced to making two accounting entries, one for input tax and one for output tax, which in the aggregate would be reported in the periodical return, but no payments would be due. Only a retailer would actually collect and remit tax. This would remove the opportunity for intermediate stage VAT fraud as well as carousel fraud. The general reverse charge VAT would ironically constitute a de facto metamorphosis of VAT into a retail sales tax.[64]

63. Deloitte, *Analysis of the Impact of the Split Payment Mechanism as an Alternative VAT Collection Method*, Final Report, (Publication Office of the European Union, 2017).
64. Robert F. Brederode & Sebastian Pfeiffer, *Combating Carousel Fraud: The General Reverse Charge VAT* 26(3) Int'l VAT Monitor 146 (2015).

[5] *Removing VAT Charges on B2B Transactions (Zero-Rating)*

Under zero rating arrangements, the seller must charge zero-percent VAT and, thus, does not collect any tax, removing the risk of non-reporting, and the purchaser's inputs are effectively tax free, thus removing the need for credits and refunds. Because B2B transactions between fully taxable persons do not lead to any accrual of tax to the Treasury due to the input tax credit system, applying the zero rate in these instances is revenue neutral, while it removes the opportunity for intermediate stage and carousel fraud. Tax would need to be charged in case of B2C and B2G(overnment) transactions. There is a minor issue with B2B transactions where the purchaser is a (partially) exempt person. Due to the zero rate the purchaser's inputs would be fully tax free where he should be input-taxed to the extent purchases are used for generating exempt sales. This can be resolved by introducing a self-supply for zero-rated inputs used for making exempt supplies. This would increase compliance and tax auditing efforts, though, but not to any extent that would jeopardize its implementation.

Zero rating would, indeed, solve fraud within the ring of B2B transactions but can, obviously, not be applied to the retail stage. Although the tax would legally remain a VAT because a tax rate would apply to all transactions in the supply chain, from a material perspective the VAT would undergo a metamorphosis into an RST with a paper trail of reporting de facto untaxed sales. If serious consideration is given to zero-rating B2B transactions under VAT, its replacement with a benchmark RST would deserve equal consideration.

[6] *Life Reporting*

Under life reporting a business would be required to first submit draft sales invoices to the tax authorities for checking and approval, after which they can be issued to customers for settlement. Thus, tax authorities are enabled to digitally verify and reconcile all sales and purchase invoices. The life reporting or e-invoicing arrangements are not identical and differ considerably in detail among the limited but growing number of countries that have introduced it. For example, in Brazil, a seller needs to issue an electronic invoice in a predetermined format with the tax authorities. When authorized, a unique code is provided which must be included on the invoice to the customer. Only then may goods be shipped to the customer and a paper version of the approved invoice must accompany the shipment. In Italy, resident companies must submit their domestic B2B and B2C invoices to the tax authorities via the so-called Sdl portal for real time approval. Sdl forwards the invoice to the customer for settlement and input-tax recovery. In Mexico, vendors are issued a unique electronic signature key and a digital sales certificate by the tax authorities. All vendors must appoint a government approved e-invoicing company to validate and stamp invoices as they are issued with the digital sales certificate. A vendor issues an invoice through the e-invoicing company which must validate and stamp the invoice and then send it to the tax authorities. The system is only partially successful in South Korea. Although it has decreased compliance costs, it has had limited success with identifying false invoices and preventing false claims of input tax credits. In particular, the system is unable to timely identify cases where output and input invoices match, but no output tax was actually paid to the tax agency.[65] In China, registered businesses must issue invoices using the government-owned Golden Tax System, which allows the tax authorities to automatically verify the information with data from banks, industry, and Customs.[66]

[7] Evaluating the Anti-fraud Measures

VAT carousel fraud causes the tax administration to pay out amounts of tax that has not been collected. The anti-fraud measures listed above are, essentially, bandages to stop or reduce the revenue bleeding caused by VAT fraud; they do not increase VAT revenue collection but only reduce fraud related losses. Even if one of the solutions would fully neutralize the fraud, still net VAT revenue would be zero due to the input-tax credit applied in the ring of B2B transactions. Only if a fraud countermeasure includes the retail stage, which is the case in some countries with e-invoicing, would net VAT revenue increase. But, as most of these countermeasures are designed to combat carousel fraud and intermediate stage fraud, their focus is on inter-state B2B transactions. One has to wonder whether it is rational tax policy to implement complex fraud counter-measures that increase administrative and compliance cost significantly, create economic inefficiencies, and potentially infringe on civil liberties all for the purpose of safeguarding a tax collection system that does not generate any real revenue in net terms. The problem with these anti-fraud measures is that they fight the symptoms and not the disease. Life reporting has the benefit that it could be extended to the retail stage. In that case, it may secure actual revenue by preventing fraud where it matters, although it is difficult to comprehend how to apply that system to over the counter sales. However, under life reporting, the whole supply chain is subjected to an Orwellian surveillance system for the purpose of preventing fraud either at stages where no net revenue will be realized (B2B transactions) or at the retail stage where fraud seems to be rather limited in scope and size (*see* §8.05[C], 8.07, and 8.08). In addition, if all invoices must be submitted to a government database, serious privacy and civil liberty concerns arise.[67] Moreover, such a system may trigger the unwelcome response of moving transactions to the shadow economy. Before introducing a life reporting system, a cost-benefit analysis should be undertaken, that includes both financial and ethical desiderata, to determine whether this is desirable, i.e., whether the cure is not more harmful than the disease.

The cause of B2B and carousel fraud is found in the mechanics of VAT itself, i.e., the fractioned "collection" system that does not lead to any true gain in revenue but introduces tax charges into the chain of transactions down the supply chain, which are

65. Richard Krever, *Combating VAT Fraud: Lessons from Korea*, 3 British Tax Rev. 303 (2014).
66. Charlene A. Herbain, *Fighting VAT Fraud and Enhancing VAT Collection in a Digitalized Environment* 46(6/7) Intertax 579 (2018).
67. In the US, e.g., North Carolina tried to mandate that e-commerce companies report detailed customer purchase records as a means to verify use tax compliance by consumers, which was successfully challenged as unconstitutional in court: *Amazon.com LLC v. Lay*, No. C10-664-MJP, 2010 WL 4262266 (WD Wash October 25, 2010).

exploited, either opportunistically or premeditatedly, by unscrupulous operators. The only true solution, obviously, is to eliminate those charges within the ring of B2B transactions. This would fully mitigate these two types of fraud and no revenue would be lost as net revenue arises only from B2C transactions.

There are two options within the VAT system to achieve this, application of the general reverse charge mechanism or of zero-rating to all B2B transactions. Under either of these options, the tax system would de iure remain a VAT since VAT charges would apply to intermediate transactions in the supply chain, but de facto a metamorphosis would occur changing the VAT into a retail tax. Instead of applying either of these two options, a true RST could replace the VAT, removing administrative and compliance cost from the supply chain prior to the retail stage.

§8.07 THE VAT GAP AND THE GENERAL SIZE OF THE FRAUD

Revenue efficiency refers to the revenue performance of a tax, i.e., the ability to raise revenue with the least distortion to incentives and therefore the least loss of real incomes. VAT collection efficiency can be measured relative to Gross Domestic Product (GDP) or to consumption. The GDP efficiency ratio [to avoid confusion, Bird and Gendron 2007, 62 call that one VAT productivity] is targeted toward an income type VAT and the C-efficiency ratio toward a consumption type VAT. The latter is, therefore, the most adequate.[68]

The C-efficiency ratio is the quotient of the actual VAT revenue (AR) of a country to the theoretical or potential revenue (PR), or $e^c = \frac{AR}{PR}$, where the PR is derived from the product of aggregate final consumption (exclusive of tax) and the standard VAT rate,[69] or PR = $\tau^s(C{-}t)$. The C-efficiency ratio reflects, economically, the ability of government to collect VAT revenue, and the lower the ratio is, the higher the difference between the theoretical amount of revenue and the actual amount collected. This difference is generally referred to as the VAT gap.

The benchmark is a uniform tax on all consumption, which would give a C-efficiency ratio of 100. Higher or lower values indicate deviation from the single rate tax on all consumption. Reduced or zero rates would drive the ratio below 100%. Tax cascading or incomplete functioning of the input-tax credit system would result in a ratio greater than 100 %. An OECD study of 2006 covering 29 developed countries, using 2003 data, found an average C-efficiency rate of 52.9%. New Zealand's VAT had the highest rate with 96.4% and Mexico had the lowest rate with 30.4%.[70] The average C-efficiency ratio for developed countries in 2014 is 56%, a slight improvement, with New Zealand again leading with a ratio of 97%.[71]

68. Liam Ebrill et al., *The Modern VAT* (IMF, 2001).
69. Michael Keen, *The Anatomy of VAT* 66 Nat'l Tax J. 423 (2013).
70. OECD, *Consumption Tax Trends* (OECD, 2006).
71. OECD, *Consumption Tax Trends* (OECD, 2016).

For 15 Latin-America countries, using data from 2012-2015, a C-efficiency spread of 31.5 % (Mexico) to 91.1% (Paraguay) was established with an average rate of 56.9%.[72]

The VAT gap is to a large extent caused by policy choices made by the legislative branch (policy gap), i.e., preferential treatment of certain economic sectors, or certain goods and services, through exemptions and lower tax rates. As such, these reductions in VAT revenue are anticipated and in accordance with the law. The policy gap represents the difference between revenues under the current policy and those under benchmark VAT policy. To the remaining extent, the revenue shortfall is caused by the compliance gap, i.e., the difference between VAT collection with perfect compliance and actual collection. This difference, i.e., the underpayment of taxes is due to a combination of errors, mismanagement, taxpayer insolvency, and tax evasion.

A recent study observed both upward and downward trends in C-efficiency for 26 European countries and Japan over a period of 15 years (2000-2015). It concluded that large cumulative changes in C-efficiency were caused by changes in policy gaps, which suggests, for advanced economies, that "trends in C-efficiency are explained less by changes in tax compliance than by changes in the effects of tax policy."[73]

The Latin-American study, referred to above, found an average policy gap of 19.9% and an average compliance gap of 23.2%. The lowest compliance gap was calculated for Bolivia with 11% and the highest for Mexico with 57.9%.[74] The study does not provide further analysis into the components of the compliance gap, such as the size of fraud due to lack of data.[75] Indeed, quantitative data on fraud, generally, and for particular types of fraud, specifically, is hard to obtain. For instance, regarding Lebanon, researches used personal interviews with government administrators to gain insight in types and methodology of VAT fraud, but they were unable to obtain any quantitative data, allowing them to measure the size of the fraud.[76]

For the year 2017, the total VAT gap in the EU was 11.2% of PR,[77] or EUR 137.5 billion. The smallest gaps were observed in Cyprus (0.6%), Luxembourg (0.7%), and Sweden (1.5%). The largest gaps were registered in Romania (35.5%), Greece (33.6%), and Lithuania (25.3%). Overall, half of the 28 Member States recorded a gap exceeding 10.1%. In nominal terms, the largest gaps were recorded in Italy, Germany, and the United Kingdom with EUR 33.6 billion, EUR 25 billion, and EUR 19.2 billion respectively.[78] Table 8.5 provides an overview of the actual VAT revenue collected, the theoretical or potential revenue and the size of the VAT gap of each of the then 28 EU member states and for the EU as a total.

72. Santiago Díaz de Sarralde Miguez, *Value Added Tax: Revenue, Efficiency, Tax Expenditures and Inefficiencies in Latin America* (Inter-American Center of Tax Administrations - CIAT, 2017).
73. Junji Ueda, *The Evolution of Potential VAT Revenues and C-Efficiency in Advanced Economies*, IMF Working Paper WP/17/158 (IMF, 2017).
74. Díaz de Sarralde Miguez, *supra* n. 72, 39.
75. Díaz de Sarralde Miguez, *supra* n. 72, 29, n. 18.
76. Rana Ismail et al., *Value Added Tax Evasion and Illegal Recovery Cases in Lebanon*, 109 Procedia-Social and Behavioral Sciences 527, 528 (2014).
77. Referred to as VAT Total Tax Liability or VTTL in the CASE report.
78. CASE (Center for Social and Economic Research), *Study and Reports on the VAT Gap in the EU-28 Member States* (CASE, 2019).

Table 8.5 2017 VAT Revenue, Potential Revenue and VAT Gap

Country	A VAT Revenue (EUR Million)	B PR	C VAT-Gap % of PR
Austria	28,304	30,748	8
Belgium	29,763	33,759	12
Bulgaria	4,664	5,289	12
Croatia	6,485	6,944	7
Cyprus	1,851	1,862	1
Czech Rep	14,721	16,803	12
Denmark	27,931	30,166	7
Estonia	2,148	2,270	5
Finland	20,404	22,026	7
France	161,932	173,962	7
Germany	226,582	251,598	10
Greece	14,642	22,041	34
Hungary	11,725	13,617	14
Ireland	13,278	15,215	13
Italy	107,901	141,530	24
Latvia	2,164	2,549	15
Lithuania	3,310	4,429	25
Luxembourg	3,469	3,492	1
Malta	810	823	2
Netherlands	49,900	52,644	5
Poland	36,330	42,094	14
Portugal	16,809	18,738	10
Romania	11,650	18,063	36
Slovakia	5,917	7,708	23
Slovenia	3,479	3,606	4
Spain	74,107	75,913	2
Sweden	44,115	44,769	1
UK	161,509	180,708	11
EU Total	1,085,899	1,223,369	11

Source: CASE, VAT Gap report 2019.

Table 8.6, using data from the 2019 CASE report, analyzes the VAT-gap and measures the size of its components: the policy gap and the compliance gap, the latter being the VAT loss due to fraud, insolvency, etc. Table 8.5 provides data on the actual amount of VAT collected of each country and the theoretical size of VAT revenue (PR), the difference constituting the Euro amount of the VAT gaps (Table 8.6, column B). Column C is generated by deducting the policy gap percentage from the total VAT gap, which must be 100%. Column D calculates the VAT compliance gap in Euros by applying the VAT non-compliance percentage of column C to the VAT gap amount of column B. Column E shows the compliance gap as a percentage of the actual VAT collected for each country (as shown in Table 8.5, column A).

Table 8.6 Gap Analysis 2017

Country	A Policy gap as % of Total VAT-Gap	B VAT Gap in EUR Millions (PR-AR)	C Compl. Gap as % of Total VAT-Gap	D Compl. Gap in EUR	E Compl. Gap as % of Actual Revenue
Austria	45.85	2,444	54.15	1,323	4.67
Belgium	51.50	3,996	48.50	1,938	6.51
Bulgaria	29.47	625	70.53	441	9.46
Croatia*		459			
Cyprus	45.41	11	54.59	6	0.32
Czech Rep	37.96	2,082	62.04	1,292	8.78
Denmark	41.59	2,235	58.41	1,305	4.67
Estonia	35.01	122	64.99	79	3.68
Finland	48.86	1,622	51.14	829	4.06
France	53.78	12,030	46.22	5,560	3.43
Germany	44.26	25,016	55.74	13,944	6.15
Greece	46.03	7,399	53.97	3,993	27.27
Hungary	33.90	1,892	66.10	1,251	10.67
Ireland	47.91	1,937	52.09	1,009	7.60
Italy	53.81	33,629	46.19	15,533	14.40
Latvia	40.29	385	59.71	230	10.63
Lithuania	33.48	1,119	66.52	744	22.48
Luxembourg	39.49	23	60.51	14	0.40
Malta	43.70	13	56.30	7	0.86
Netherlands	51.84	2,744	48.16	1,322	2.65
Poland	48.36	5,764	51.64	2,977	8.19
Portugal	51.21	1,929	48.79	941	5.60
Romania	34.00	6,413	66.00	4,233	36.33
Slovakia	38.29	1,791	61.71	1,105	18.67
Slovenia	47.78	127	52.22	66	1.90
Spain	59.42	1,806	40.58	733	0.99
Sweden	46.45	654	53.55	350	0.79
UK	53.50	19,199	46.50	8,928	5.53
EU Total	44.52	137,470	55.48	76,268	7.02

Source: CASE, VAT Gap report 2019 and our calculations.

*The CASE report did not provide policy gap information for Croatia, which disallowed us to make the calculations for columns C, D, and E for that country.

The total VAT gap is roughly EUR 137.5 billion, of which just over EUR 76 billion can be attributed to the compliance gap. Column E demonstrates the significance of the compliance gap relative to actual VAT collected. The highest relative compliance gaps occur in Romania (36.33%), Greece (27.27%), Lithuania (22.48%), Slovakia (18.67%) and Italy (14.40%); i.e., these countries have the lowest rate of compliance. The smallest gaps are found in Cyprus (0.32%), Luxembourg (0.40%), Sweden (0.79%), Malta (0.86%), Spain (0.99%), and Slovenia (1.99%); therefore, these are the countries with the highest rate of compliance.

Australia starting point for the VAT gap is not the PR but the theoretical revenue under current policy and the VAT actually collected, so the policy gap is already eliminated from their estimations and they arrive directly at the compliance gap. Table 8.7 shows the Australian Tax Office data for the fiscal years 2012-2013 through 2017-2018.

Table 8.7 Australian GST Gap from 2012-2013 to 2017-2018

Year	2012-2013	2013-2014	2014-2015	2015-2016	2016-2017	2017-2018
Gross gap*	6,567	6,556	6,789	7,435	7,064	7,276
Amendments*	2,509	2,497	2,550	2,279	2,351	2,282
Net gap*	4,058	4,059	4,239	5,156	4,712	4,995
Tax paid*, or AR	48,805	51,840	55,134	57,511	60,950	63,560
Theoretical liability*	52,864	55,899	59,373	62,667	65,662	68,555
Gross gap %	12.4	11.7	11.4	11.9	10.8	10.6
Net gap %	7.7	7.3	7.1	8.2	7.2	7.3

Source: Author's own work.

* in AUD million

The net compliance gap, calculated as a percentage of the theoretical revenue fluctuated between 7.1% and 8.2% with an average of 7.47%.[79] If we calculate the net gap as a percentage of actual revenue, it fluctuates from 7.69% to 8.97% with an average of 8.06%, just over 1% higher than the EU average for 2017 in Table 8.6.

In a report for the European Commission, based on responses from nine member states, fraud was estimated to be responsible for 36% of the VAT gap. On average, 20% of the overall VAT gap was considered to be caused by carousel fraud, while the

79. https://www.ato.gov.au/About-ATO/Research-and-statistics/In-detail/Tax-gap/Goods-and-services-tax-gap/. Table 1.

estimated weighted average (based on overall VAT gap proportion) is 24%.[80] If we apply these findings to the numbers compiled in Table 8.6, then fraud at 36% of the total 2017 VAT gap would amount to EUR 49.5 billion. Carousel fraud would create a leakage of EUR 33 billion. The other forms of VAT fraud, i.e., intermediate stage fraud (excluding carousel fraud) and the retail stage fraud combined is then 12%.

Table 8.8 Components of 2017 EU VAT Gap

a. Total VAT gap in Euros	137.5
b. Policy gap, 44.52%	61.2
c. Compliance gap, 55.48%	76.3
d. Fraud general, 36%	49.5
e. Carousel fraud, 24%	33.0
f. Retail and intermediate stage fraud, ex carousel (d -/- e), 12%	16.5
g. Other causes of VAT loss (errors, insolvency) (c -/- d), 19.48%	26.8

Source: Author's own work.

As to category f, the study does not further distinguish between the size of retail stage fraud and the size of intermediate stage fraud. Obviously, together they are only half the size of the carousel fraud. Logically, that also raises doubts whether the rationale for the VAT is still valid. The numbers do not show that the retail stage is more vulnerable to fraud than the earlier stages in the supply chain.

Retail stage fraud is generally committed by small enterprises and with a small number of transactions relative to total number of sales transactions; it is small-scale and opportunistic in nature. In contrast, carousel fraud is designed to accommodate fraud and the schemes are operated by professional crime organizations. This type of fraud is unique to VAT and absent under RST. Through applying the credit-invoice system, VAT sadly gave birth to the carousel fraud. The invoice system, perceived as a strength in its ability to reduce retail stage fraud, is at the same time VAT's Achilles' heel. The numbers in Table 8.7 show a much higher degree of fraud in the pre-retail stages. If we conveniently assume that the rate of fraud in category f can be evenly split between retail and intermediate stages, retail fraud would only account for 6% of the VAT gap, or EUR 8.25 billion, whereas all fraud committed in the B2B chain would amount to 30% of the VAT gap, or EUR 41.25 billion.

§8.08 RST FRAUD IN THE STATE OF CALIFORNIA

In the US, sales and use taxes are not levied at the federal but only at the state and sometimes local level. The states do not undertake any sales tax gap studies to gain

80. Ernst & Young LLP, *Implementing the "Destination Principle" to Intra-EU B2B supplies of Goods*, Feasibility and Economic Evaluation Study (European Commission, 2015).

insight in the size of fraud. Moreover, most states do not maintain statistics on fraud, which makes it hard to estimate the size of fraud generally. However, the state of California[81] was able to share information in respect of fraud audits conducted from 2007 through 2018.

Table 8.9 California Sales Tax Fraud Data[82]

A Fiscal Year	B No. of Cases	C Tax Fraud Amount (in USD)	D % Fraud to Total Audits	E Sales Tax Revenue (in USD)	F % Fraud to Total Sales Tax Revenue
2007-2008	48	19,900,000	10.50%	44,416,478,000	0.04%
2008-2009	45	18,000,000	4.50%	39,924,935,000	0.05%
2009-2010	31	9,800,000	3.70%	42,165,819,000	0.02%
2010-2011	30	10,200,000	4.10%	42,517,662,000	0.02%
2011-2012	45	23,400,000	9.70%	41,196,804,000	0.06%
2012-2013	37	15,300,000	3.90%	44,679,961,000	0.03%
2013-2014	41	16,700,000	4.90%	48,006,801,000	0.03%
2014-2015	59	17,400,000	5.30%	50,600,175,000	0.03%
2015-2016	49	19,900,000	6.70%	52,407,325,000	0.04%
2016-2017	27	11,700,000	4.00%	$53,436,672,000	0.02%
2017-2018	44	19,500,000	7.70%	$56,999,020,000	0.03%

Source: Author's own work.

Column B gives the number of sales tax fraud conducted for each fiscal year listed in column A. Column C shows the total amount of tax assessed related to the fraud and column D measures the size of the fraud as a percentage of total audits conducted in the fiscal year in dollars. Column E shows the total sales tax revenue for the fiscal year and that allows to calculate the size of fraud as a percentage of total sales tax revenue in dollars, shown in column F.

Due to the absence of a sales tax gap study, a complete comparison with the EU data will not be possible. The average of fraud in California as a percentage of total sales tax revenue is 0.03%. For the EU, taking the data displayed in Tables 8.6 and 8.8, the retail and intermediate stage fraud is 12% of the VAT gap and 21.62% of the compliance gap. Where the compliance gap is 7.02% of actual revenue, the combined retail and intermediary stage fraud would be 1.52% of actual revenue. There is no data to further separate retail stage fraud from intermediate stage fraud. If we split in evenly, the retail stage fraud under EU VAT would amount to 0.76%, which is 25 times higher

81. California offers a viable comparison to EU countries given the size of its economy. Using 2019 data, as a separate state, California would have been the 5th largest economy in the world with an economic output of USD 3.13 trillion, surpassing the UK (USD 2.74 trillion), France (USD 2.70 trillion), Italy (USD 1.98 trillion), Spain (USD 1.39 trillion) and behind Germany (USD 3.86 trillion).
82. Courtesy California Department of Tax and Fee Administration; data received January 31, 2020.

than the retail fraud in California. The fraud data for California is likely deflated as it is based on audit results and not on a gap study, and the actual number must be higher, but the California fraud numbers strongly indicate that likely retail stage fraud in the EU is significantly less than half of the combined retail and intermediate stage fraud. The California number on retail stage fraud shows that it is relatively insignificant. If we apply the California fraud size of 0.03 % of total revenue to the EU, the revenue loss for 2017 due to retail stage fraud would amount to EUR 326 million. We realize that the California fraud percentage cannot simply be extrapolated to the EU, and this number may be too low. However, the comparison indicates that the real problem in the EU is not retail stage fraud but, indeed, intermediate stage and carousel fraud which, we repeat, is triggered by the VAT system itself with the introduction of tax levies at all stages of the supply chain notwithstanding that only the retail stage transactions would lead to an accrual of revenue.

§8.09 EVALUATION AND CONCLUSIONS

From a tax policy perspective, it is important to establish whether a benchmark RST could be a valid alternative for a credit-invoice VAT. Where a reverse charge VAT is materially identical to RST our findings are also directly relevant for the feasibility of such a VAT. This link between reverse charge VAT and RST is exemplified by remarks of Rita de la Feria of Durham University commenting on the European Commission's plan for the general reverse charge. She concluded, correctly as we have shown, that such a mechanism would transform the VAT effectively into RST.[83] Given that result, she then opposes the general reverse charge on the ground that RST would be inferior to VAT because of the paper trail the latter creates and the underlying fractioned collection system.[84] It seems that she is suggesting that the reverse charge would lead to an increase in fraud at the retail stage due to the disappearance of the paper trail and the fractioned collection system. If that is true, then the assessment needs to be made whether the monetary impact of retail stage fraud is larger than the carousel fraud. Our findings do not confirm that. In the contrary, intermediate stage fraud is significantly larger as a percentage of the VAT gap in the EU than retail stage fraud.

VAT was preferred over RST because of the latter's vulnerability to retail stage tax fraud. The paper trail would allow the tax authorities to follow a good or service downstream through the supply chain, which would increase the likelihood of detection of fraud and, therewith, would increase voluntary compliance at the retail sector. The levying of VAT on all transactions in the supply chain creates opposing positions for seller and buyer, as the latter would insist on receiving an invoice for purchases made because the invoice is the evidentiary basis for the input-VAT credit. Thus, the B2B VAT charge strengthens compliance with the invoice requirement and supports the actual creation of the paper trail. In addition, the insistence of buyers to receiving an invoice would reduce the appetite for sellers to underreport collected

83. *See also* Robert F. van Brederode and Sebastian Pfeiffer, *supra* n. 64, 156.
84. Rita de la Feria, *supra* n. 13, 172.

output-VAT. Under RST and the reverse charge VAT a paper trail would still exist. Invoicing is a requirement under the commercial law in most countries and, where not, can simply be introduced in the tax law. Moreover, in advanced economies, invoicing is standard business practice. The reverse charge VAT requires buyers to account for their purchases and report these in the periodical VAT return. Indeed, compliance with reporting and recording requirements may be weaker as the incentive for buyers to insist on receiving an invoice would no longer exist. On the other hand, the function of the invoice and the opposing positions of buyer and seller in preventing or reducing fraud on the seller's side by underreporting output-VAT is obsolete under RST and reverse charge VAT, because VAT charges and payments do simply not occur in the B2B circle of transactions.

RST and reverse charge VAT have an advantage over the traditional invoice credit VAT, because B2B fraud in the supply chain prior to the retail stage would no longer be feasible and, moreover, the carousel fraud scheme would be fully mitigated. The final question is whether RST and the reverse charge VAT are likely to be more vulnerable to retail stage fraud than the tradition credit-invoice method VAT. Although we have no way of determining whether the paper trail can be fully credited for it, we have established that the retail stage fraud is relatively small in the EU at 6% or, if we extrapolate our findings for California, much less of the VAT gap. In contrast, intermediate stage fraud (including carousel schemes) account for at least 30% but up to 35% of the VAT gap. It seems safe to say that VAT has created a larger fraud problem at the intermediate stage than it was designed to prevent or reduce at the retail stage. There is no reason to believe that retail stage VAT fraud would more than marginally increase if the credit invoice system VAT were to be replaced with a general reverse charge VAT of RST, because the paper trail would be maintained and the sector risk factors would remain unchanged.

Where fraud is more prominent under small traders, a benchmark RST could copy the practice of VAT by excluding businesses with gross sales below a certain ceiling from registration and, thus, from collecting the RST. This would have three advantages: a) fraud would be significantly reduced as traders posing the highest risks are removed from the tax system; b) the cost-benefit balance would be restored as administrative costs related to small traders generally exceed the revenue they generate; c) it would relieve small traders from compliance costs, which tend to be regressive,[85] and for that reason may be perceived as unfair. Because these exempt small traders are not registered for RST, their inputs would be taxed (as under VAT) and the revenue loss would be limited to the product of the tax rate and their profit margin, while much higher administrative and compliance cost are being avoided.

85. Sijbren Cnossen, *Administrative and Compliance Costs of the VAT: A Review of the Evidence*, 43 Tax N. Int'l 1649 (1994); Helena Blažić, *Tax Compliance Costs of Small Business in Croatia*. Occasional Paper No. 22 (Institute of Public Finance, 2004); Chris Evans, *Taxation Compliance and Administrative Costs: An Overview*, in *Tax Compliance Costs for Companies in an Enlarged European Community* 447 (Michael Lang et al., eds., Linde Verlag, 2008).

In summary, we have reached the following conclusions:

- There exists no fractioned collection system under VAT, only a fractioned tax payment system; no VAT accrues to the Treasury until the final sale to the consumer.
- Only if a fraudulent retailer does not deduct input-VAT related to the not-reported sales, has VAT an advantage over RST in that the tax loss would be limited to the product of the tax rate and the retailer's margin on the not-reported sales. There exists no data to determine whether, or to what extent, fraudulent retailers deduct the related input-VAT or not.
- Historically, VAT was preferred over RST in the EU, because of the fraud risk associated with the retail sector, at the time dominated by often family owned and managed, small traders. The composition of the retail sector has changed and is now concentrated in large conglomerate entities with annual sales in the billions of dollars, which pose a significantly lower risk of fraud. Moreover, the tax base is concentrated in larger firms. This argument against RST is likely no longer valid for developed economies.
- Under VAT, tax collection and thus the risk of fraud is extended to all stages of the supply chain.
- The fraud committed in the stages prior to the retail stage is much larger in the EU than the retail stage fraud.
- VAT has created a larger fraud problem at the intermediate stage than it was designed to prevent or reduce at the retail stage.
- The counter measures taken or proposed to combat carousel fraud are cumbersome, increase administrative and compliance costs, may negatively impact on civil liberties, and do not pass any reasonable cost/benefit test.
- For developed economies, a benchmark RST or its twin, the generally reverse charge VAT, seem to offer superior alternatives to the traditional VAT from a fraud prevention perspective.

CHAPTER 9

Value-Added Tax Adjustments*

Kathryn James & Karoline Spies

§9.01 INTRODUCTION

Although the economic goal of most Value-Added Taxes (VATs) or Goods and Services Taxes (GSTs)[1] is to tax final consumption, in practice VATs seek to tax expenditure on items of final consumption or more specifically, the transactions that give rise to that expenditure, as a proxy for consumption. The VAT is therefore predictive in that by taxing expenditure on transactions it seeks to tax consumption before it occurs. This contrasts to the income tax or a post-paid direct expenditure tax which are reactive, intended to be levied on a person's actual income or expenditure after it has been derived or spent.[2]

By using expenditure on consumption as a proxy for consumption itself, the VAT can mostly avoid the difficult task of measuring the value of consumption - itself an economic concept with a contested meaning - which would require authorities to possess accurate and up to date information about the location and timing of an individual's consumption patterns including the use of the things they consume.[3] The

* This research was partially supported by the Australian Government through the Australian Research Council's Discovery Projects funding scheme (project DE190100346). The views expressed herein are those of the authors and are not necessarily those of the Australian Government or the Australian Research Council. Our thanks to Rick Krever and Andy Ditchfield for their input on the Australian portion. Our thanks to Peter Mellor and Markus Mittendorfer, LL.M. (WU), for excellent research assistance. All mistakes are our own.

1. For ease of reading, the terms Value-Added Tax or VAT are used in this chapter to refer to any national tax that embodies the basic features of a value-added tax, by whatever name or acronym it is known; however, the terms Goods and Services Tax and GST are used in the discussion of Australia.
2. Ben Terra & Julie Kajus, *A Guide to the European VAT Directives* 7.2.2 [IBFD online] (15 April 2011).
3. Terra & Kajus, *supra* n. 2, at 7.2.2; Kathryn James, *The Rise of the Value-Added Tax* 41-42 (Cambridge University Press, 2015).

VAT therefore makes predictions as to where, when and in what amount consumption is likely to take place.[4] In most VAT systems, transactions consisting of a supply of goods or services on the market between the seller and purchaser serve as this reference point. The intellectual work in most VAT systems is therefore devoted to identifying those transactions that trigger the expenditure on consumption and the liability to pay VAT (paid by the retailer on behalf of the consumer) as well as a complementary inquiry to assess whether non-final consumers, i.e., eligible and registered entities such as businesses, can receive credit for the VAT paid on their purchases of these taxable transactions that go toward making their own supplies.

Although taxing expenditure on consumption on a transactional basis eliminates some measurement difficulties, it does not eliminate all issues. VAT adjustments deal with events that arise after a transaction occurs which have the effect of altering the VAT liability or liabilities of the parties to that transaction. An example might be a lawyer supplying legal services to a client who does not pay the bill.[5] The need to provide an adjustment is a product of the predictive nature of VATs which, by focusing on liability at a particular point in time (e.g., the supply of legal services or the issue of an invoice thereof), also requires revision when subsequent events change that liability (e.g., the non-payment of the invoice). An adjustment is necessary to reflect the economic value of the consumption - which is measured at zero in the case of a service for which no fee has been paid - and to ensure that the lawyer (or their paying clients if the lawyer can pass on the cost in the form of higher fees) is not penalized by paying VAT on the fees never received. However, the need to revisit transactions in light of subsequent events that change economic realities must be balanced against the need for certainty and faithfulness to the transactional and predictive nature of the VAT which suggests a need to limit the time by which transactions will be revisited so as to avoid lengthy inquiries as to changing liabilities over time.

Despite the importance of the topic of VAT adjustments at a policy and practical level, it is difficult to find any substantive discussion of the topic as a whole - at best there is piecemeal discussion of various aspects of the issues involved.[6] This chapter seeks to remedy this gap and explores these issues broadly in three pars under five sections. The first of these (§9.02) contextualizes VAT adjustments and provides a typology of adjustments that commonly arise in VAT systems. Next, §9.03 explores the VAT design issues that arise in dealing with such events and emphasises the importance of domestic context in shaping jurisdictional responses to VAT adjustments. This makes comparative analysis a fraught task. The final part (§9.04-§9.06) attempts such a task by exploring how these challenges are dealt with in Australia and the European Union (and its Member States as more specific examples). Australia is included as it provides an example of what most experts label a modern VAT - that being a VAT with

4. Rebecca Millar, *Jurisdictional Reach of VAT*, in *VAT in Africa*, 175, 178-179 (Richard Krever, ed., Pretoria University Law Press, 2008); *see also* Organisation for Economic Co-operation and Development (OECD), *Ottawa Taxation Framework* 25-26 (2001).
5. The example assumes a taxpayer reporting on an accounts/accrual rather than cash basis.
6. *See, e.g.*, the references cited in relation to the issues of cancelled transactions and third-party rebates.

a relatively broad base of domestic consumption with minimal rate variation.[7] The EU, included because of its continued prominence in VAT policy, is a more traditional VAT model relying to a greater degree on exemptions and rate variations.[8] The approach of each jurisdiction is analysed according to the relevant responses to the types of VAT adjustments outlined in §9.03. The respective analyses demonstrate how the common challenge of being both faithful to the predictive nature of the VAT and trying to capture relevant subsequent variations gives rise to broadly similar policy responses but with important variations influenced by the respective local and regional contexts. Section 9.07 concludes.

§9.02 VAT ADJUSTMENTS: CONTEXT AND TYPOLOGY

A VAT adjustment can only arise if a transaction has already taken place with VAT consequences. An analysis of VAT adjustments therefore depends on the underlying rules that give rise to taxable transactions and VAT refunds, and the rules that determine when such transactions crystallize into VAT obligations or entitlements. Therefore, a number of preliminary questions need to be addressed to establish whether and what type of adjustment is required including: (i) whether a taxable (or other) transaction has taken place (such as a taxable event in the EU) (with a corresponding analysis of the right to input-tax credits/VAT deductions on the recipient side); and (ii) whether (or when) VAT has fallen due (but not necessarily become payable) (such as a 'chargeable event' in the EU) (and whether and when the right to a VAT deduction arises).[9]

Analysis can therefore be complicated by: the fact that taxable events can be defined differently; that a taxable event and chargeable event might not necessarily coincide (as might be the case with some advance payment scenarios);[10] that chargeable events might differ between taxpayers (such as between those taxpayers reporting on a cash or accounts/accruals basis);[11] or that taxable events might occur over a period of time (e.g., the continuing observation of leasehold covenants under a lease) which require rules for defining the chargeable event (e.g., the EU and Australia treat

7. Liam Ebrill, Michael Keen, Jean-Paul Bodin & Victoria Summers, *The Modern VAT* (International Monetary Fund, 2001). *Cf.* James, *Rise of the Value-Added Tax, supra* n. 3, 12, Chapter 6.
8. Ian Crawford, Michael Keen & Stephen Smith, Value Added Tax and Excises, in Dimensions of Tax Design: The *Mirrlees Review* 275, 279, 305 (Stuart Adam et al. eds. for the Institute for Fiscal Studies, Oxford University Press, 2010).
9. *See* Council Directive 2006/112/EC of 28 November 2006 on the Common System of Value Added Tax [2006] OJ L 347/1 ('EU VAT Directive'), Article 62, that refers to 'chargeable event and chargeability of VAT'. On the difference between 'taxable event' and 'chargeable event', *see* Ad van Doesum et al., *Fundamentals of EU VAT Law* 230 et seq. (2nd ed., Wolters Kluwer 2020).
10. The time of tax payment may again be a different point in time, commonly depending on the taxable period and linked to the time limit to submit (advance) VAT returns.
11. *See* on both methods Alan Schenk, Victor Thuronyi & Wei Cui, *Value Added Tax: A Comparative Approach* 172 (2nd ed., Cambridge University Press, 2015), 226-235.

each successive period as a separate taxable event attributable to each period for VAT purposes).[12]

The variations in approach to these preliminary issues determining VAT liability mean that VAT adjustments necessary in one jurisdiction (as the taxable and chargeable event have already occurred in an earlier tax period) might not be necessary in another (as the taxable event and/or chargeable event has yet to occur).

With these important caveats noted, post-transaction events which might affect the VAT liability of parties to a transaction can generally be grouped into two types. The first includes those events that affect the *quantum* or the price of the transaction which may result in a higher or lower price than originally agreed and therefore require a revision of the parties' VAT liabilities. The second includes those events which change the *character* of the transaction so that, although the total amount paid remains the same, a subsequent event, such as a change in the use of the thing supplied from a creditable to a non-creditable purpose, has the effect of altering one or more of the parties' VAT liabilities in a transaction.

[A] Changes in Quantum

The price of a transaction might be subsequently (i.e., subsequent to the taxable and/or chargeable event) varied for a number of reasons – each of which might give rise to discrete issues and different VAT outcomes. Five common scenarios demonstrate the issues and will be used to guide analysis of the rules throughout this chapter.

[1] The Parties Agree to Change the Price

Parties might agree to change the price of a supply for a number of reasons: to reduce a price when the goods supplied might not be of satisfactory quality; to correct errors including VAT-related errors; to offer (and accept) payment on terms that provide for various discounts (for early payment) or penalties (for late payment); to adjust a previously agreed price between related parties triggered by the requirements of other fields of law (such as a transfer pricing adjustment for direct tax law purposes).[13] Key characterization issues commonly include whether there is a change in the price of the original transaction (thus giving rise of a VAT adjustment) or a new price for a further transaction (thus possibly giving rise to VAT obligations for a new supply).

12. *See, e.g.*, EU VAT Directive Article 64; A New Tax System (Goods and Services Tax) Act 1999 (Cth.) Div. 156 (ANTS Act 1999).
13. *See* chapter 10 of this volume for an analysis of the specific issues that arise when a transfer pricing adjustment by the taxpayer for income tax purposes might trigger a corresponding VAT adjustment to reflect the change in consideration.

[2] An Incentive or Rebate Payment Is Made Affecting the Total Price Paid

Rebates might be considered a special class of discount but also raise additional issues depending on from whom and to whom they are provided and in what form. At its most simple the payment of a cash rebate from a retailer to a consumer upon purchase of a good or service is generally treated as consideration for the supply (and liable to an adjustment depending on the timing). Further complications are added when the rebate is made in a form other than cash such as a voucher, including one acquired through loyalty programs.

Rebates might be paid to or received from a third party. A rebate might be provided by a third party or to a party other than an end user. An example of the first scenario might be a manufacturer providing a cash rebate to a consumer after they have purchased a certain brand of appliance from a retailer. An example of the second scenario might be a manufacturer who offers general incentives to a retailer who makes certain sales to end users but who acquires the stock from another party. In the first scenario, the absence of a direct contractual relationship between the provider of the rebate and the beneficiary of the rebate complicates the application of the adjustment rules. In the second scenario, the manufacturer's entitlement to offset the rebate against their VAT liability turns on the sufficiency of the link to a taxable supply. This give rise to issues around whether, in the absence of a contractual relationship between the third-party supplier of the rebate and the recipient of the original supply, such rebates are sufficiently connected to the original supply to warrant a revision in the price. In addition, an issue might arise as to whether the provider of the rebate can claim an input credit so that the VAT collected does not exceed the value of consumption or impose additional VAT costs on the business providing the rebate (*see* §9.05[A][3] for the Australian approach and §9.06[A][3] for the CJEU case law).

[3] Cancelled Transactions and Early Termination

Most VAT systems recognize that a cancelled transaction can give rise to a VAT adjustment. However, different contracts can be cancelled or terminated for a variety of reasons (e.g., breach of an essential term including non-payment, failure to complete) with a variety of different consequences (e.g., issuing of refunds, payment of damages, forfeiture of deposits or payment of cancellation fees) which affects the VAT treatment.

A cancellation might: require an adjustment of the taxable amount for a previously executed supply (if, for example, the cancellation/termination of the contract alters the consideration paid and occurs in a subsequent tax period to the taxable (or chargeable) event (e.g., a refund); or be included in the assessment of the consideration for the initial supply (*see* below); or be something else.

The answer depends on the nature of the contractual provisions giving rise to the supply, the nature of the termination and the consequences ascribed under the general law and the relevant VAT law. This is demonstrated by contracts that are paid for (in part or full) in advance and which, in the event of cancellation or early termination, the payer forfeits their deposit and/or the whole consideration. This might be treated as the consideration for an initial supply (and therefore not an adjustment event) or as compensation or a penalty for cancellation or early termination (therefore potentially giving rise to an adjustment). Such contracts have been the subject of extensive judicial consideration in Australia (§9.05[B]) and the EU (§9.06[B]).

[4] The Price Is Not Paid Resulting in a Bad Debt

As the example in the introduction demonstrated, when VAT liability is determined on an accruals/accounts basis rather than a cash basis there is a need for adjustment provisions to allow for debts that might never be paid.[14] The rationale for allowing adjustments in the case of bad debts (beyond the general need to reflect the economic value of the consumption) is that to deny a VAT adjustment would force the seller to either absorb the VAT component of the debt or pass it on to paying customers (through higher prices).[15] The risks in allowing adjustments for bad debts is the potential for abuse; for example, in the absence of sufficient proof of non-payment of the debt a taxpayer might falsely claim a decreasing adjustment to reduce VAT liability. This has led some developing countries to simply deny adjustments for bad debts.[16]

[5] Court Orders and Third-Party Adjustments

In the absence of an agreement between the parties, the price paid for a good or service might be subsequently varied by a court order or some other award, such as a transfer pricing adjustment issued by revenue authorities. This gives rise to discrete issues and clear differences in approach between jurisdictions. For example, in Australia it is generally accepted that a court order can lead to a VAT adjustment provided it sufficiently relates to an earlier supply (*see* §9.05[D]). In Europe the position is not yet settled with a competing view being that such variation by an external body should not have any effect on the VAT amount, since the taxable base for VAT purposes is commonly understood as the subjective value (i.e., the price agreed between the parties) (*see* §9.06[D]).[17]

Further issues arise over the nature of the variation. For example, a court order might consist of damages independent of any supply (and have no VAT consequences), or might itself create new rights and obligations that give rise to a new supply (with its own VAT consequences), or might be sufficiently connected with the original

14. The issue does not arise under cash accounting methods as VAT liability does not arise until payment is made whereas VAT liability arises when the debt is incurred (or invoice issued) under an accrual method: *see, e.g.*, ANTS Act 1999, *supra* n. 12, section 21-5(2).
15. Schenk, Thuronyi & Cui, *supra* n. 11, 172.
16. Schenk, Thuronyi & Cui, *supra* n. 11, 172.
17. *See*, amongst others, CJEU, 24 October 1996, Case C-317/94, *Elida Gibbs*, ECLI:EU:C:1996:400, paragraph 27 and the case law cited; van Doesum et al., *Fundamentals of EU VAT Law*, *supra* n. 9, 252.

supply to affect the VAT liability on that earlier supply and lead to a corresponding obligation to make a VAT adjustment.

How a given jurisdiction treats variations by external bodies (e.g., court orders, tribunal awards, or assessments by revenue authorities) will have implications for how the jurisdiction manages transfer pricing adjustments by revenue authorities. For a full discussion of this issue *see* Chapter 10 of this volume.

[B] Changes in Character

A VAT adjustment might be necessary when a buyer purchases a good or service for a particular purpose (e.g., a car is purchased for business use – i.e., VAT deductible) but later changes the purpose or use to which the good or service is put with the effect that the VAT payable or their entitlement to input credits is altered (e.g., the car is then used for a private purpose and no longer VAT deductible). The VAT (and adjustment) consequences of these changes can differ according to: the sphere of taxable activity (e.g., taxed/input taxed or exempt activities, business use/private use, economic/non-economic use); the point in time when the change takes place; and the intention of the taxpayer and the actual use to which an acquisition is put.

The change in character might happen *at the time* of the transaction or *after* the transaction has occurred and the chargeable event has arisen. The first scenario, for example, might occur if a buyer asks for the goods to be shipped from the manufacturer in France to its store in Canada but, before the items are shipped, changes the place of shipment to its store in Marseille, which is low on stock (changing the character of the transaction from a VAT-free or zero-rated export to a taxable domestic supply). Alternatively, it might occur if a buyer purchases a computer for its retail arm but then realizes it needs it for its financial services business before the computer arrives (changing the character of the transaction from a taxable to an exempt or input taxed supply). Such changes might affect the VAT payable and entitlement to input credits, but depending on the timing, might simply result in a change to the chargeable event (or the reporting of VAT liability) or result in an adjustment (if, for example, the issue was not picked up during the relevant reporting period).

The change in use might be *intended* or *unintended* with such intention potentially affecting VAT outcomes. As an example of the former, a property developer might build new residential premises with the intention of leasing the premises (as an input-taxed/exempt supply) and then, after some years, selling those premises (as a taxable supply of new residential property with right to input credits – assuming that the relevant VAT system treats such a supply as taxable). As an example of the latter, a property developer might construct new residential premises with a view to selling those premises (as a taxable supply with right to input credits) but then decide to lease those premises due to a downturn in market conditions (as an input taxed supply without right to input credits). Such changes are more likely to happen with long life goods and assets. Adjustments might also be necessary because of a change in the taxpayer's circumstances such as when a good is purchased while a business is in operation and registered (and entitled to input credits on eligible transactions) but the business is later wound up and de-registered (with the good later used for private purposes).

These adjustment rules perhaps best demonstrate the tension between the transactional or slice-in-time nature of the VAT and the need to accommodate subsequent events in a manner that alters previous liabilities.

§9.03 DESIGN AND POLICY ISSUES

In striking the balance between the predictive and transactional nature of the VAT against the need to ensure the VAT correctly reflects a taxpayer's actual economic position, policymakers need to take account of a range of considerations, such as:

- whether the design of the rules will be holistic and articulate broad criteria by which a VAT adjustment might arise or specify detailed conditions for VAT adjustments;
- whether and how to impose time-limits on adjustment periods;
- integrity considerations such as the proof required to obtain an adjustment and whether to link such claims to the VAT position of the other party/ies to the transaction;
- how to treat adjustments that arise in the context of related party dealings in which prices can be manipulated to maximize VAT outcomes (*see* chapter 10 of this volume for a discussion of these risks in the context of transfer pricing).

Despite facing similar issues, the response of each particular jurisdiction is affected by a number of factors. These include global or regional influences such as the approach of the Organisation for Economic Co-operation (OECD) and, particularly in the context of EU jurisdictions, the role of the EU VAT Directive and jurisprudence of the Court of Justice of the European Union (CJEU). The response is further mediated by the domestic context - by policymakers, draftspersons, administrators, tribunals, courts and taxpayers and the institutional constraints within which they operate. These constraints include the drafting of domestic legislation including VAT and other taxes such as the income tax (for example, in defining key terms such as what constitutes a bad debt in Australia or in providing methods to ascertain market value) and the manner in which the underlying legal system defines the rights and liabilities of parties to a transaction such as the laws of contract and property which might define key terms such as 'consideration' or specify the consequences of a variation, breach or termination of contract.[18] These laws and principles will in turn affect the approach of taxpayers to structuring their affairs, administrators to administering the rules and courts and tribunals and courts to applying the rules in the resolution of disputes.

A simple example suffices to demonstrate the point. The term 'consideration' might make intuitive sense to a common lawyer who understands that the exchange of

18. Andrew Sommer, *The Application of the GST Law to Complex Transactions*, in *GST in Australia: Looking Forward from the First Decade* 97, 97-98 (Christine Peacock ed., Thomson Reuters, 2011); *see also* Hon. William Gummow, *The Law of Contracts, Trusts and Corporations as Criteria of Tax Liability*, 37(3) Melb. U. L. Rev. 834, 835, 838 (2014).

consideration between the parties to a contract is one of a number of legal requirements to produce a valid and legally binding contract. However, the concept has no direct equivalent in the law of obligations in many civil law systems. Under German and Austrian contract law, for example, a valid offer and acceptance suffices to bind the parties to a contract.[19] And yet, the EU VAT Directive uses the criterion of a supply of goods or services 'for consideration' as a necessary component of a taxable transaction.[20] Moreover, the CJEU has stated that the term 'consideration' forms part of EU law with the consequence that Member States are not free to ignore the impact of EU law on the domestic treatment of the term.[21] However, localised rules and interpretive approaches matter when the resolution of a VAT dispute turns on those domestic laws - such as the laws of contract in determining the consequences of a breach.[22] As a result the notion of 'consideration' is overlaid by differing legal traditions and approaches to interpretation which can account for differences in approach between jurisdictions. Outcomes will be further influenced by the judicial approach to interpreting legislation, for example, the primacy accorded to the principle of neutrality in EU VAT jurisprudence is not a feature of the Australian approach to interpretation of the VAT.[23]

Awareness of these influences calls for a degree of caution in generalisations and in assuming the transferability of terms, rules and decisions from one jurisdiction to another.[24] With these points in mind, the next section provides a comparative overview of the EU VAT and the Australian GST as context to the treatment of VAT adjustments in each of the sections that follow thereafter.

---

19. For the requirement of consideration as an essential element of a valid and binding contract in common law systems such as Australia: *see* J. W. Carter, *Carter on Contract* [06-001] (LexisNexis online, last updated December 2014) and references there cited. In Germany, the rule that a valid offer and acceptance suffices to bind the parties is to be found in section 151 of the Civil Code (*Bürgerliches Gesetzbuch*) according to which '[t]he contract is concluded by the acceptance of the offer'. In Austria, a similar rule is to be found in section 861 of the General Civil Code (Allgemeines Bürgerliches Gesetzbuch).
20. EU VAT Directive, Articles 2, 2(1).
21. *See*, e.g., CJEU, 5 February 1981, Case C-154/80, *Coöperatieve Aardappelenbewaarplaats*, ECLI:EU:C:1981:38, paragraph 9; Emanuela Santoro, *Transfer Pricing and Value Added Tax in the European Community: Is There Room for Inaction and, If So, Where?* 14(3) Int'l Transfer Pricing J. 147, 159, 161 (2007).
22. *See*, e.g., Yige Zu & Richard Krever, *The United Kingdom Has Spoken: The Receding Impact of European Jurisprudence on the UK Interpretation of the Common VAT System*, 49(1) Comm. L. World Rev. 75, 76-78, 81 (2020).
23. *See infra* §9.04. For the EU, *see, inter alia*, CJEU 23 November 2017, Case C-246/16, *Enzo Di Maura*, ECLI:EU:C:2017:887, paragraphs 23 and 27. For Australia, *see Re Electrical Goods Importer* [2009] AATA 854, 996, 998, [62]-[64]; *cf.* Rebecca Millar, *The Principle of Neutrality in Australian GST*, 17 Austl. GST J. 26, 28, 33-34, 41 (2017).
24. Australian courts and tribunals have been reluctant to rely too heavily on overseas authority for this reason: *Re Electrical Goods Importer* [2009] AATA 854, 996, [60].

§9.04 AN OVERVIEW OF THE EU VAT AND AUSTRALIAN GST

[A] An Overview of the Australian GST

The Australian GST is generally considered a modern VAT levied on a base of domestic consumption through the invoice-credit method. Introduced in 2000, the GST was drafted with the benefits of lessons learned from almost half a century of European and other experience. As a result, the rules governing tax liability and access to credits/refunds tend to be broader than those of the EU. Unlike the EU, the GST applies to government and public enterprises as well as charities, and the list of exempt supplies (without credit) is generally constrained.[25] However, in other respects the Australian GST is narrower than its European counterpart as it contains a large number of zero-rated domestic supplies (termed 'GST-free' in Australia, i.e., exempt supplies with credit) in place of rate variations or exemptions, most notably excluding basic food as GST-free in this way.[26]

The primary legislative criteria that give shape to the GST are *taxable supplies* (equivalent to EU taxable transactions)[27] and *taxable importations* as well as *creditable acquisitions* and *creditable importations*. This discussion will primarily focus on the rules for domestic supplies. The legislative criteria are broadly drafted in a way that is generally consistent with an intention that the final consumer (rather than business) bears the economic burden of the GST. However, this is not stated as an express purpose of the Act and Australia's ultimate appellate court, the High Court, has made it clear that the proper subject of judicial analysis is the legal rules, not any broader economic ideas of final consumption, or any applicable equivalent to the EU principle of neutrality, that might inform those rules.[28]

GST is payable at 10% of the *value* of a taxable supply with value calculated as either the *price* paid for a supply (if consideration is expressed as an amount of money) or the *GST inclusive market value* for consideration expressed as something other than an amount of money.[29] Liability to remit the GST generally falls on the supplier.[30] Generally GST liabilities reflect the value agreed by the parties; however, similar to the

25. ANTS Act 1999, *supra* n. 12, Div. 40.
26. ANTS Act 1999, *supra* n. 12, Div. 38; James, *Rise of the Value-Added Tax, supra* n. 3, at 12, Chapter 6; Richard Krever & Peter Mellor, *Legal Interpretation of Tax Law: Australia*, in *Legal Interpretation of Tax Law* 15, 35 (2nd ed., Robert F. van Brederode & Richard Krever eds., Kluwer, 2017).
27. ANTS Act 1999, *supra* n. 12, sections 9-5 and 9-40.
28. *Commissioner of Taxation v. Reliance Carpet Co. Pty Ltd* (2008) 236 CLR 342, 346, [3] quoting *Sterling Guardian v. Federal Commissioner of Taxation* (2006) 228 ALR 712, 258, [15]; *Commissioner of Taxation v. Qantas Airways Ltd* (2012) 247 CLR 286, 292-295, [14]-[22]; *Travelex Ltd v. Commissioner of Taxation* (2010) 241 CLR 510, 1, [2], 8, [24], 11, [36] per French C.J. and Hayne J., 16, [54] per Heydon J., 19, [64], 23-24, [82] per Crennan and Bell JJ.; *Commissioner of Taxation v. Unit Trend Services Pty Ltd* (2013) 250 CLR 523, 539, [47] per French C.J., Hayne, Crennan, Bell and Gageler JJ.; *Commissioner of Taxation v. MBI Properties Pty Ltd* (2014) 254 CLR 376, 383-385, [3]-[14], 390-392, [34]-[41].
29. ANTS Act 1999, *supra* n. 12, sections 9-70 and 9-75.
30. ANTS Act 1999, *supra* n. 12, sections 9-40 and 13-15. For exceptions, *see* Divs. 83 and 84 outlining voluntary and compulsory reverse charge mechanisms: *ibid*.

EU, a specific anti-avoidance rule imposes an open market value on certain supplies that are made 'without consideration' or for 'inadequate consideration' between associates when the recipient of the supply is not in a position to obtain full input credits.[31]

For a *supply* to be a taxable supply it must be made *for consideration* in the course or furtherance of an *enterprise* that the *registered* supplier carries on and be connected with Australia.[32] A supply is not a taxable supply to the extent that it is[33] 'GST-free' (the equivalent of EU *zero-rated or exempt with credit*);[34] or 'input taxed' (the equivalent of EU *exempt without credit*).[35] The *enterprise*[36] and *registration*[37] requirements, the respective equivalents of *economic activity* and *taxable person* in the EU, are designed to ensure, as far as possible, that the GST applies to market-based consumption.

The individual components of the term 'taxable supply' have been broadly defined and interpreted. Therefore a *supply*, defined as 'any form of supply whatsoever',[38] includes voluntary and involuntary supplies, legal and illegal supplies, and positive supplies and negative supplies (when the supplier refrains from doing an act).[39] *Consideration* is likewise broadly defined to include 'any payment, or any act or forbearance, *in connection with* a supply of anything' or 'in response to or for the

31. ANTS Act 1999, *supra* n. 12, Div. 72; *see also* section 84-20.
32. ANTS Act 1999, *supra* n. 12, sections 9-5, 9-10, 9-15, 9-20, 9-25 and 23-5; A New Tax System (Goods and Services Tax) Regulations 1999 (Cth) ('ANTS Regulations 1999'), Regulations 23-15.01 and 23-15.02. *See* ANTS Act 1999, *supra* n. 12, section 9-40 for 'taxable importations'.
33. ANTS Act 1999, *supra* n. 12, sections 9-5 and 9-30, Divs. 38, 40. A supply which could be classified as both input taxed and GST free will generally be treated as a GST-free supply: section 9-30(3).
34. ANTS Act 1999, *supra* n. 12, section 9-5, Div. 38.
35. ANTS Act 1999, *supra* n. 12, section 9-5, Div. 40.
36. *Enterprise* is broadly defined to include business, charities, religious institutions and government entities (*cf.* the EU which excludes the activities of government and charities as 'non-economic'). An enterprise can be constituted by a single activity or series of activities and relevant to the inquiry is the nature of the activity as being business-like or trade-like (excluding the charitable and government inclusions) rather than being 'for private recreational pursuit or hobby' or by an individual or partnership of individuals 'without a reasonable expectation of profit or gain' (*cf.* the EU which includes such unprofitable activities of individuals and partnerships): ANTS Act 1999, *supra* n. 12, sections 9-20 and 195-1 – 'enterprise', 'business'; Australian Taxation Office (ATO), Miscellaneous Taxation Ruling MT 2006/1, The New Tax System: The Meaning of Entity Carrying On an Enterprise for the Purposes of Entitlement to an Australian Business Number (5 February 2020); *Russell v. Federal Commissioner of Taxation* (2011) 190 FCR 449; Millar, *The Principle of Neutrality in Australia*, *supra* n. 23, 27-28.
37. Only registered entities (or entities required to be registered) are capable of making a taxable supply and only insofar as the supply relates to carrying on an enterprise. This excludes from taxation supplies made by a registered person in a personal capacity. Registration is compulsory for entities with annual (current and/or projected) turnover exceeding AUD 75,000 for entities other than non-profit entities and AUD 150,000 for non-profit entities: ANTS Act 1999, *supra* n. 12, section 23-5; ANTS Regulations 1999, *supra* n. 32, Regulations 23-15.01 and 23-15.02. Registration is voluntary for entities below this threshold: ANTS Act 1999, section 23-10.
38. ANTS Act 1999, *supra* n. 12, section 9-10(1).
39. ANTS Act 1999, *supra* n. 12, section 9-10; *Saga Holidays Ltd v. Commissioner of Taxation (Cth) and others* (2006) 156 FCR 256, 265, [35]; *Commissioner of Taxation v. Reliance Carpet Co. Pty Ltd* (2008) 236 CLR 342, 346, [4], 352, [28]; *Commissioner of Taxation v. Qantas Airways Ltd* (2012) 247 CLR 286, 292, [14], 299, [33]; *Commissioner of Taxation v. MBI Properties Pty Ltd* (2014) 254 CLR 376, 390, [34].

inducement of a supply of anything'.[40] It does not matter whether the 'payment, act or forbearance' was voluntary, provided by the recipient of the supply (or someone else), or done in compliance with the order of a court, tribunal or similarly empowered body or with a settlement relating to such proceedings.[41] The Australian rules are therefore broader than the EU requirements - for example, there is no requirement of a direct link, such as a legal relationship, between the recipient of a good or service and the consideration received (cf. §9.04[B]).

Much of the existing appellate case law has focused on the nexus requirement that there be a supply '*for* consideration' to constitute a 'taxable supply'.[42] The High Court has ruled that the link need not be a narrow, contractual one but that it has some 'connection or relationship between the supply and the consideration'.[43] While a transaction or series of transactions might give rise to more than one 'supply' and more than one criterion of 'consideration' which itself might be received for more than one supply, there will only ever be one 'taxable supply', i.e., a 'supply for consideration' on which GST is payable and this will be attributed to the first tax period in which consideration is either received or an invoice issued (*see* below).[44]

Place of taxation rules require that a supply must be 'connected with' Australia to constitute a taxable supply. The test for connection varies according to the thing supplied and broadly conforms to the destination principle.[45]

The term *creditable acquisition* permits registered entities to claim an input tax credit (the equivalent of an EU *input VAT deduction*) for the GST incurred on eligible

40. ANTS Act 1999, *supra* n. 12, section 9-15(1). This positive definition is qualified by negative exceptions which are not relevant for this chapter: section 9-17. Note the use of the term 'thing' (and its variants). 'Thing' is a basic term defined (somewhat circularly) to mean 'anything that can be supplied or imported': section 3-5(3) - Item 13, section 195-1 - 'thing'. Thing is often but not always used when describing services or intangibles (e.g., sections 9-17(1), 9-25(5) (for taxable supplies); 11-5, 11-15(1) (for creditable acquisitions)). For adjustments: section 19-10(2)(a) refers to the return to a supplier of a thing, or part of a thing, supplied (whether or not the return involves a change of ownership of the thing) (clearly referring to goods); section 21-15(c) - supplier of a thing you acquired writes off a bad debt; section 21-20(b) (decreasing adjustment for a bad debt). *See also* ATO, Goods and Services Tax Ruling GSTR 2009/4, New Residential Premises and Adjustments for Changes in Extent of Creditable Purpose, [62]-[64] (31 October 2012, as amended).
41. ANTS Act 1999, *supra* n. 12, sections 9-15(2) and 9-15(2A).
42. The terms 'in connection with' complements the requirement that a supply be 'for' consideration: *Commissioner of Taxation v. Reliance Carpet Co. Pty Ltd* (2008) 236 CLR 342, 346, [4], 352, [28]; *Commissioner of Taxation v. Qantas Airways Ltd* (2012) 247 CLR 286, 292, [14], 299, [33].
43. *Commissioner of Taxation v. Qantas Airways Ltd* (2012) 247 CLR 286, 292, [14].
44. *Commissioner of Taxation v. Reliance Carpet Co. Pty Ltd* (2008) 236 CLR 342, 347, [1], 349-350, [22], 355-356, [39], [42]; *Commissioner of Taxation v. Qantas Airways Ltd* (2012) 247 CLR 286, 293-294, [19]; *Commissioner of Taxation v. MBI Properties Pty Ltd* (2014) 254 CLR 376, 392, [43]: 'The general operation of the GST Act avoids double taxation not by establishing an exclusive connection between a particular amount of consideration and a particular supply but rather by establishing an exclusive connection between a particular amount of consideration and a particular tax period.'
45. ANTS Act 1999, *supra* n. 12, section 9-25, div 84, div 85. The legislative term adopted is 'indirect tax zone' which means Australia excluding the external territories and some offshore petroleum and gas developments: section 195-1. For ease of reading the indirect tax zone will be referred to as Australia.

inputs used in the production of goods and/or services.[46] A creditable acquisition requires that the acquisition is solely or partly for a *creditable purpose* which, in essence, permits input tax credits 'to the extent that' the acquisition is made in 'carrying on' an 'enterprise', but denies relief to the extent that the acquisition relates to making input taxed supplies or is of a private or domestic nature.[47] In contrast to the EU which generally permits a refund if it relates to the making of an equivalent taxable or GST-free supply,[48] the *creditable purpose* concept is designed to provide a broad starting position that brings all acquisitions made in the carrying on of an enterprise into the net but then excludes those acquisitions that relate to input taxed supplies or those of a private or domestic nature.[49]

Registered entities (i.e., taxpayers) are required to file GST returns and remit GST in quarterly or, in certain circumstances, monthly or annual *tax periods*.[50] For taxpayers reporting on an accounts or accruals basis, the GST payable on a taxable supply or an input credit for a creditable acquisition is *attributable* to the tax period during which the earlier of two events occurs – the receipt of consideration for a taxable supply (or the provision of consideration for a creditable acquisition) or, if an invoice is issued relating to a supply or acquisition before any consideration is received or provided, the date the invoice is issued.[51] There are specific attribution rules for more complex supplies such as progressive or periodic supplies (which are treated as separate supplies attributable to the relevant tax period).[52] These attribution rules broadly equate to *time of supply* or *chargeable event* rules in the EU.[53] Apportionment rules apply to composite supplies or acquisitions (e.g., such as a car used for both business and private purposes) that enable GST liabilities to be allocated accordingly.[54]

46. *Ibid.*, sections 11-5 and 11-10. For the highest appellate consideration of the term 'creditable acquisition' to date, *see Rio Tinto Services Ltd v. Federal Commissioner of Taxation* (2015) 235 FCR 159.
47. ANTS Act 1999, *supra* n. 12, sections 11-5, 11-10, 11-15 and 11-20. The terms 'to the extent that' allows for apportionment of input credits for inputs used in making composite supplies (i.e., both input taxed and taxable/GST-free supplies): at sections 11-15(1), 11-25 and 11-30; *HP Mercantile Pty Ltd v. Commissioner of Taxation* [2005] FCR 553, 560, [21] (Hill J.). The other three requirements for a creditable acquisition are that: (1) the supply of the acquisition was a taxable supply; (2) the entity provided or was liable to provide consideration for the acquisition; and (3) the entity is registered or required to be registered under the Act: at section 11-5.
48. *Cf* EU VAT Directive, Article 168 (§9.04[B]).
49. Ross Stitt, *Uncertainties Surrounding Input Tax Credit Entitlement in Australia*, in *GST in Australia: Looking Forward from the First Decade* 115, 117 (Christine Peacock ed., Thomson Reuters, 2011); Explanatory Memorandum to the A New Tax System (Goods and Services Tax) Bill 1998, 1.1.27, 3.2.6. As §9.04[B] demonstrates the broad interpretation of the right to deduct rules in the EU reduces the gap between both approaches.
50. ANTS Act 1999, *supra* n. 12, Divs. 27, 151.
51. ANTS Act 1999, *supra* n. 12, sections 29-5(1) and 29-10(1). Eligible small business entities (with an annual turnover of less than AUD 10 million) who elect to report on a cash basis are required to attribute GST to when consideration is received for taxable supplies and attribute input credits to when consideration is provided on creditable acquisitions: sections 29-5(2) and 29-10(2).
52. ANTS Act 1999, *supra* n. 12, Div. 156, sections 156-1 and 156-22.
53. Rebecca Millar & Lorenna Moon, *Australia*, in *Improving VAT/GST – Designing a Simple and Fraud-Proof Tax System* 23, [2.2.1], fn. 1 (Michael Lang & Ine Lejeune eds., Kluwer Law International, 2014).
54. *See, e.g.*, ANTS Act 1999, *supra* n. 12, sections 9-80, 11-30 and 13-25.

Depending on timing, a change in the GST status of a transaction might be dealt with under these attribution/apportionment rules rather than as an adjustment.

When the GST charged on supplies exceeds the total input tax credits that the taxpayer is entitled to claim over a *tax period*, the taxpayer remits a net amount to the Australian Taxation Office (ATO) (Australia's national revenue collection agency headed by the Federal Commissioner of Taxation).[55] When the input tax credits exceed the tax charged on supplies over a *tax period*, the taxpayer is entitled to a refund or to offset the amount against other outstanding tax liabilities.[56]

Generally, a taxpayer has four years from the tax period in which the credit/refund was first reported/attributed to, to claim an input credit or refund for overpaid GST. The Commissioner has four years from issuing an assessment to amend it (and in turn recover any unpaid GST or wrongly paid refunds).[57] Taxpayers generally have four years to challenge an assessment.[58] Taxpayers wishing to challenge a decision of the Commissioner, including an assessment, can do so internally within the ATO and externally to the Administrative Appeals Tribunal or to the Federal Court (or ultimately the High Court) on a question of law.[59] Adjustments are not subject to this limitation period as they are generally attributed to the tax period in which a taxpayer becomes *aware* of the adjustment or, for a decreasing adjustment above a certain amount, when the taxpayer holds the requisite documentary proof.[60]

[B] Overview of the EU VAT System

The EU VAT is a traditional invoice-credit VAT levied on a destination basis albeit tailored to the single economic zone. The VAT system in the EU Member States is harmonized by the EU VAT Directive which is binding on all EU Member States and sets a legal framework for the domestic VAT systems of all EU Member States.[61] However, the Directive must be implemented into national law in order to be fully effective. A division of labor exists whereby matters forming part of EU law are subject to oversight by the CJEU but matters which turn on domestic law are determined by the

55. ANTS Act 1999, *supra* n. 12, sections 17-5, 33-3 and 33-5.
56. ANTS Act 1999, *supra* n. 12, section 35-5; Taxation Administration Act 1953 (Cth.) sections 8AAZL-8AAZLB and 8AAZLE.
57. The four-year rule is subject to a number of exceptions; for example, there is no time limit on amending assessments in cases of fraud, evasion or in certain instances of avoidance: ANTS Act 1999, *supra* n. 12, sections 93-5 and 93-15; Taxation Administration Act 1953 (Cth) sections 155-35, 155-55 and 155-60.
58. Taxation Administration Act 1953 (Cth) section 155-35.
59. Taxation Administration Act 1953 (Cth) Pt. IVC. Taxpayers can also apply directly to the original jurisdiction of State Supreme Courts or the Federal Court for a declaration of the relevant law applicable to them: Administrative Decisions (Judicial Review) Act 1977 (Cth); Commonwealth of Australia Constitution sections 75(v) and 78; Judiciary Act 1903 (Cth) sections 39B, 60 and 64. For an overview *see* Millar & Moon, *supra* n. 53, at [2.5.5].
60. ANTS Act 1999, *supra* n. 12, section 29-20(1).
61. Council Directive 2006/112/EC of 28 November 2006 on the Common System of Value Added Tax [2006] OJ L 347/1 (EU VAT Directive).

courts in Member States.[62] Member States are not free to ignore the impact of EU law and the domestic VAT law of each Member State should, as far as possible, be interpreted in line with the Directive and its object and purpose.[63] The principle of neutrality, which broadly attempts to bring about the outcome that the Directive is interpreted so as to ensure that the amount of VAT payable is strictly proportional to the consideration actually received by a taxable person, has a significant impact on VAT jurisprudence and can often counteract some of the narrowness of the EU VAT Directive.[64]

Although the EU VAT Directive leads to comprehensive harmonization between EU Member States (regarding the scope of VAT) and should prevent double taxation (by harmonizing place of taxation rules), there are still many areas where EU Member States enjoy discretion. Differences in domestic VAT law still exist, particularly when it comes to tax rates and procedural requirements (e.g., filing of VAT returns). In addition, a large number of provisions in the Directive are optional,[65] or give discretion to Member States,[66] and many Member States also apply special derogations in some areas[67] including for adjustments.

Outside of special rules for imports[68] and self-supplies,[69] a supply of goods or services is subject to EU VAT as a *taxable transaction* if the supply is 'for consideration', takes place 'within the territory of a Member State' and is carried out 'by a taxable person acting as such'.[70]

On the one hand, the scope of the Directive is broad in that every person conducting an economic activity is treated as a *taxable person*.[71] The Directive does not permit high registration thresholds (technically implemented as exemption without credit) and thresholds vary from between EUR 0 (Netherlands, Spain) to approximately EUR 47,000 (Poland, Romania) in sales per taxable period.[72] On the other hand, the exclusion of out-of-scope supplies or 'non-economic'[73] supplies or uses (i.e., those supplies that are neither private nor economic) narrows the scope of the EU VAT

62. *See, e.g.*, *Coöperatieve Aardappelenbewaarplaats*, *supra* n. 21, paragraph 9; Santoro, *supra* n. 21, 159, 161; Zu & Krever, *supra* n. 22, 76-77.
63. *See, e.g.*, CJEU, 18 December 2014, Joined Cases C-131/13, C-163/13 and C-164/13, *Italmoda*, ECLI:EU:C:2014:2455, paragraph 52.
64. *Elida Gibbs*, *supra* n. 17, paragraphs 28-30; confirmed, amongst others, in CJEU, 26 January 2012, Case C-588/10, *Kraft Foods Polska*, ECLI:EU:C:2012:40, paragraphs 26-27; *see*, in more detail, van Doesum et al., *Fundamentals of EU VAT Law*, *supra* n. 9, 277-278.
65. *See*, *inter alia*, EU VAT Directive, Articles 11, 12, 18, 27, 59a, 66 (and many more).
66. *See*, *inter alia*, EU VAT Directive, Articles 90, 132(g)-(i) ('other bodies recognised by the Member State concerned'), 133, and 273.
67. *See* EU VAT Directive, Title XIII on Derogations (Articles 370 et seq.).
68. EU VAT Directive, Article 2(1)(b) and (d).
69. EU VAT Directive, Articles 16, 18 and 26.
70. EU VAT Directive, Article 2.
71. EU VAT Directive, Article 9.
72. As of 1 July 2019. A list of the applicable threshold is available at: https://ec.europa.eu/taxation_customs/sites/taxation/files/resources/documents/taxation/vat/traders/vat_community/vat_in_ec_annexi.pdf (accessed 1 December 2020).
73. A non-economic use (out-of-scope) use under the EU VAT rules is the use of a good or service for an activity that does not qualify as 'private' or as 'economic' for VAT purposes; it is a third sphere of a taxable person consisting of an activity which does not involve taxable transactions: van Doesum et al., *Fundamentals of EU VAT Law*, *supra* n. 9, 84-86.

compared to the Australian GST (which has no equivalent concept). The distinction, developed by CJEU case law rather than stated in the Directive,[74] treats as non-economic certain activities including those done by a public body as a public authority,[75] the activity of a pure holding company (mere passive ownership),[76] and charitable activities.[77] The scope of the EU Directive is further narrowed in comparison with Australia's GST by the extensive use of exemption without credit for certain activities considered in the public interest (e.g., health care, education) which go beyond the limited exemptions (also recognised in Australia) of financial services and certain supplies connected with real estate.[78]

The EU rules around taxable transactions are narrower in scope than in Australia. According to settled case law, a supply of goods or services is taxable only if there is a 'legal relationship' between the supplier and the recipient including a 'reciprocal performance'; this includes that the 'remuneration received by the provider of the service [constitutes] the value actually given in return for the service supplied to the recipient'[79] (also referred to as 'direct link').[80] This requirement, amongst others, meant that a street musician who received 'donations' did not carry out a taxable supply.[81]

Whether a supply takes place 'within the territory of a Member State' is defined in several place of taxation rules for goods and services which, in general, follow the destination principle.[82] The EU VAT system defines its jurisdictional reach by allocating taxing rights to Member (or third) States according to different categories of supply that are allocated by general and specific place of taxation rules using different proxies for the place of destination.[83] The location of the supplier does not play a role for purposes of the scope of the EU VAT,[84] but is relevant when identifying the person liable to pay VAT on certain supplies (e.g., reverse charge rules).[85]

The taxable amount for purposes of a taxable transaction is defined as 'everything which constitutes consideration obtained or to be obtained by the supplier, in

74. *See* CJEU, 13 March 2008, Case C-437/06, *Securenta*, ECLI:EU:C:2008:166, paragraph 26.
75. *See* EU VAT Directive, Article 13; CJEU, 25 July 2018, Case C-140/17, *Szef Krajowej Administracji Skarbowej*, ECLI:EU:C:2018:595.
76. CJEU, 16 July 2015, Joined Cases C-108/14 and C-109/14, *Larentia + Minerva mbH & Co. KG*, ECLI:EU:C:2015:496, paragraph 19 and the case law cited.
77. CJEU, 3 July 2019, Case C-316/18, *The Chancellor, Masters and Scholars of the University of Cambridge*, ECLI:EU:C:2019:559, paragraph 30.
78. *See* EU VAT Directive, Articles 132-137.
79. This formula was developed in the famous *Tolsma* case in 1994 (CJEU, 3 March 1994, C-16/93, *Tolsma*, ECLI:EU:C:1994:80, paragraph 14); since then this formula has been constantly repeated by the Court (*see, inter alia*, CJEU, 22 June 2016, C-11/15, *Český rozhlas*, ECLI: EU:C:2016:470, paragraph 21).
80. *See, inter alia*, CJEU, 27 September 2001, C-16/00, *CIBO Participations*, ECLI:EU:C:2001:495, paragraph 43.
81. *Tolsma, supra* n. 79.
82. Van Doesum et al., Fundamentals of EU VAT Law, *supra* n. 9, 181.
83. *See* in more detail on the different design techniques Rebecca Millar, *Echoes of Source and Residence in VAT Jurisdictional Rules* section III (University of Sydney Law School Research Paper 09/44, 2009). *Also see* OECD, *International VAT/GST Guidelines* paragraph 3.4 (2015).
84. Except when applying the place of supply rule in Article 45, where the supplier location serves as proxy for consumption.
85. *See* reverse charge rules in EU VAT Directive, Articles 192a-196.

return for the supply, from the customer or a third party, including subsidies directly linked to the price of the supply'.[86] According to settled CJEU case law, the taxable amount is a 'subjective value, since the basis of assessment for the provision of services is the consideration actually received and not a value assessed according to objective criteria'.[87] Against this background, the fact that the price paid for an economic transaction is 'higher or lower than the cost price [...] is irrelevant'.[88] However, an optional anti-avoidance rule[89] allows Member States, who have implemented the rule into domestic law, to levy VAT on an 'open market value' in circumstances when the transaction is between closely related parties such as family members or entities in a corporate group and one of those parties does not have a full right to input VAT deduction.[90]

As a general rule, the EU VAT is chargeable 'when the goods or the services are supplied' (chargeable event).[91] There are special rules for certain transactions including for progressive and periodic supplies which, as in Australia, are treated as separate supplies chargeable and complete upon each relevant period,[92] and for advance payments, i.e., payments that are made before the goods or services are supplied, whereby VAT becomes chargeable on receipt of the payment and on the amount received.[93] These special rules impact the issue of adjustments. Whether or not the taxable event has already occurred, and a (subsequent) adjustment might be needed, or whether the matter can be dealt with under these special rules, depends on the specific services and contracts and administrative practice in the relevant Member State.

As in Australia, Member States may offer the option of cash accounting methods for certain transactions or certain categories of persons so that VAT is chargeable no later than the time the payment is received.[94]

For VAT to be deductible (*input VAT deduction*),[95] the input transactions must have a 'direct and immediate link with the output transactions giving rise to a right of deduction'.[96] However, established case law has also held that a taxable person may also have a right to deduct even where there is no such 'direct and immediate link' between a particular input transaction and a particular taxed output transaction, when

86. EU VAT Directive, Article 73.
87. *Coöperatieve Aardappelenbewaarplaats, supra* n. 21, paragraph 13; CJEU, 2 June 1994, Case C-33/93, *Empire Stores*, ECLI:EU:C:1994:225, paragraph 18.
88. CJEU, 20 January 2005, Case C-412/03, *Hotel Scandic Gåsabäck*, ECLI:EU:C:2005:47, paragraph 22; CJEU, 9 June 2011, Case C-285/10, *Campsa Estaciones de Servicio*, ECLI:EU:C:2011:381, paragraph 25.
89. EU VAT Directive, Articles 80, 72.
90. *See*, on this rule, *Campsa, supra* n. 88, paragraphs 27-40; CJEU, 26 April 2012, Joined Cases C-621/10 and C-129/11, *Balkan and Sea Properties*, ECLI:EU:C:2012:248, paragraphs 44-62.
91. EU VAT Directive, Article 63.
92. EU VAT Directive, Article 64.
93. EU VAT Directive, Article 65.
94. EU VAT Directive, Article 66.
95. Within the EU the term 'input VAT deduction' is more commonly used (*see* EU VAT Directive, Article 167).
96. EU VAT Directive, Articles 167 et seq.; *see*, amongst others, CJEU, 6 September 2012, Case C-496/11, *Portugal Telecom*, ECLI:EU:C:2012:557, paragraph 36 and the case law cited.

the costs of the assets or services in question 'are part of his general costs and are, as such, components of the price of the goods or services which he supplies'.[97] That is, an input VAT deduction may be available if the costs have a direct and immediate link 'with the taxable person's economic activity as a whole'.[98] Whether input VAT on overhead costs (e.g., consultancy services, costs for fundraising) are deductible is determined on a case-by-case basis taking all relevant circumstances into account and CJEU jurisprudence has not been consistent on this issue.[99] Furthermore, deduction of input tax paid by the taxable person must correspond as precisely as possible to the actual use of the goods and services purchased by the taxable person; consequently, the actual use of goods and services takes precedence over any initial intention.[100]

The tax periods, VAT returns and the timing of payment are not comprehensively harmonized by the EU VAT Directive and so can vary between Member States.[101] The EU VAT Directive does also not harmonize limitation periods or sets time limits to challenge an assessment. Member States can therefore determine such rules provided they are in line with the general principles of effectiveness and equivalence.[102]

§9.05 THE AUSTRALIAN APPROACH TO GST ADJUSTMENTS

The Australian approach to GST adjustments is relatively detailed and prescriptive with the legislation listing events that can trigger obligations to adjust GST liabilities. The documentary obligations differ according to each category of adjustment and most adjustments (other than those relating to a change in use of a creditable acquisition) are not subject to limitation periods.

The Australian GST legislation contains three broad categories of adjustment scenarios which this chapter labels 'Category 1', 'Category 2' or 'Category 3' adjustments. Most are contained in 'Category 1' which specifically enumerates *adjustment events*.

An *adjustment event* is defined to include any event which has the effect of: (a) cancelling a supply or acquisition; or (b) changing the consideration for a supply or acquisition; or (c) causing a supply or acquisition to become, or stop being, a taxable supply or creditable acquisition.[103] Categories (a) and (b) relate to changes in quantum and category (c) to changes in character. Further instances of 'adjustment events' are then provided without limiting the scope of the definition and these include: (a) the return to a supplier of a thing, or part of a thing, supplied (whether or not the return involves a change of ownership of the thing); or (b) a change to the previously agreed consideration for a supply or acquisition, whether due to the offer of a discount or otherwise; or (c) a change in the extent to which an entity that makes an acquisition

97. *The Chancellor, Masters and Scholars of the University of Cambridge*, *supra* n. 77, paragraph 26.
98. CJEU, 22 October 2015, Case C-126/14, *Sveda*, ECLI:EU:C:2015:712, paragraph 28.
99. *See* further *Portugal Telecom*, *supra* n. 96, paragraph 37 and the case law cited.
100. CJEU, 12 November 2020, Case C-42/19, *Sonaecom*, ECLI:EU:C:2020:913, paragraphs 58-59.
101. *See*, *inter alia*, EU VAT Directive, Articles 206-207 and 250.
102. *See* on these two principles, *inter alia*, CJEU, 19 July 2012, Case C-591/10, *Littlewoods Retail Ltd and Others*, ECLI:EU:C:2012:478, paragraphs 27 et seq.
103. ANTS Act 1999, *supra* n. 12, sections 19-10(1) and 195-1.

provides, or is liable to provide, consideration for the acquisition.[104] As the breadth of this definition suggests, 'adjustment events' include most of the common adjustment triggers under our two broad types, i.e., changes in the quantum of consideration (including cancelled transactions, changes by agreement, supplier-issued rebates) and changes in character.

A Category 1 adjustment only arises when an adjustment event occurs in a later tax period which changes the GST payable or the amount of input tax credit available that was, or would have been, attributable to an *earlier* tax period.[105] As a result not all adjustment events will require an adjustment. An 'adjustment event' arising in the *same* tax period to which the GST or an input credit is attributed is not treated as such but is accounted for in calculating the GST payable or input tax credits for that period.[106]

The Act provides instructions for calculating the *corrected adjustment amounts*.[107] For GST payable on taxable supplies, the amount of the adjustment is the difference between the *previously attributed GST amount* (taking into account other relevant prior adjustments)[108] and the *corrected GST amount*.[109] For input tax credits on creditable acquisitions, the amount of the adjustment (referred to as the *corrected input tax credit amount*)[110] is the difference between the *previously attributed input tax credit amount* (taking into account relevant prior adjustments)[111] and the *corrected input tax credit amount*.[112] This corrected adjusted amount is either added to or subtracted from the taxpayer's net liability for that tax period.[113] If the difference increases the GST payable by a taxpayer or reduces their input credits an *increasing adjustment* occurs;[114] if the difference results in a decrease in the GST payable or an increase in input tax credits then a *decreasing adjustment* occurs.[115]

104. ANTS Act 1999, *supra* n. 12, section 19-10(2).
105. ANTS Act 1999, *supra* n. 12, sections 19-40(b) and 19-70(1)(b). ATO, Goods and Services Tax Ruling GSTR 2000/19, *Making Adjustments Under Division 19 for Adjustment Events*, 4, [15] (21 June 2000) ('GSTR 2000/19').
106. GSTR 2000/19, *supra* n. 105, 4, [15].
107. ANTS Act 1999, *supra* n. 12, section 19-40(c).
108. Relevant prior adjustments include previous adjustments made under Div. 19 as well as Category 2 adjustment events for bad debts under Div. 21 and third-party payment adjustments under Div. 134: ANTS Act 1999, *supra* n. 12, sections 19-40(c) and 19-45.
109. ANTS Act 1999, *supra* n. 12, sections 19-40 and 19-45; ATO, GSTR 2000/19, *supra* n. 105, 22, [84].
110. ANTS Act 1999, *supra* n. 12, section 19-70(1)(c).
111. Relevant prior adjustments include previous adjustments made under Div. 19 (Category 1 adjustments), Category 2 adjustments for bad debts (Div. 21), or third party adjustments (Div. 134) and Category 3 adjustments relating to changes in creditable purpose (Div. 129), adjustments arising from gross-up clauses (Div. 133) and taking special account of rules that allow for annual apportionment of input tax credits relating to acquisitions for a partly creditable (Div. 131): ANTS Act 1999, *supra* n. 12, sections 19-70(2) and 19-75.
112. ATO, GSTR 2000/19, *supra* n. 105, at 29, [100].
113. ANTS Act 1999, *supra* n. 12, section 17-10; GSTR 2000/19 offers a simplified option for calculating adjustments for wholly taxable supplies or wholly creditable acquisitions is to multiply the amount of the adjustment by 1/11: GSTR 2000/19, *supra* n. 105, at 23, [86]-[87], 30-31, [102]-[103A].
114. ANTS Act 1999, *supra* n. 12, sections 19-50 and 19-80.
115. ANTS Act 1999, *supra* n. 12, sections 19-55 and 19-85.

Category 1 claims that might result in a decreasing adjustment require documentary proof, usually in the form of an *adjustment note* for adjustments with a value of more than AUD 75 (which matches the value at which an invoice is required to support a refund of input GST).[116] Such adjustment notes should contain certain information (e.g., the identity of the supplier, and the amount, reason for and effect of the adjustment)[117] and should generally be provided within 28 days (of either the recipient of the supply requesting it or the supplier becoming aware of the adjustment).[118] In keeping with the general design of the Australian GST there is generally no need for an adjustment to be linked to a corresponding increase or decrease in the GST liability of the other parties to the transaction. However, the identity of the recipient of the supply is required for adjustment notes relating to original supplies in excess of AUD 1,000.[119]

Category 2 deals with adjustments that arise from bad debts (*see* §9.05[C]).

Category 3 contains a number of special rules that alter the basic adjustment rules[120] and includes specific adjustment rules for insurance,[121] deceased estates,[122] supplies of going concerns,[123] the beginning and cessation of business activity,[124] the treatment of third-party rebates,[125] gross-up clauses,[126] and further rules relating to changes of character.[127] Reference to these rules will only be made when relevant to the discussion of adjustments in the categories identified at §9.02 and include special rules for third-party rebates (§9.05[A][3]) and changes in creditable purpose (§9.05[E]).

116. ANTS Act 1999, *supra* n. 12, section 29-75(1)(d); A New Tax System (Goods and Services Tax) Adjustment Note Information Requirements Determination 2012 (Cth) cl. 5(1); ATO, Goods and Services Tax Ruling GSTR 2013/2, Adjustment Notes, 6-13, [17], [25]-[26] (21 August 2013). Increasing adjustments and decreasing adjustments with a value less than AUD 75 can be attributed to a tax period when the taxpayer became *aware* of the adjustment (irrespective of whether they have an adjustment note): ANTS Act 1999, *supra* n. 12, sections 29-20(1), 29-20(3) and 29-80(2); A New Tax System (Goods and Services Tax) Regulations 1999 (Cth), Regulation 29-80.02.
117. ANTS Act 1999, *supra* n. 12, section 29-75(1); A New Tax System (Goods and Services Tax) Adjustment Note Information Requirements Determination 2012 (Cth); ATO, GSTR 2013/2, *supra* n. 116, at 3-5, 12 [53]-[56]. The Commissioner of Taxation has the discretion to treat a document that does not satisfy the legislative requirements for an adjustment note as an adjustment note on a case-by-case basis: ANTS Act 1999, section 29-75(1); ATO, Law Administration Practice Statement PSLA 2004/11, The Commissioner's Discretions to Treat a Particular Document as A Tax Invoice or Adjustment Note (7 November 2004). *See also Vadasz v. FCT* 2006 63 ATR 1236 (taxpayer failed to provide adequate documentary evidence to amount to an adjustment note).
118. If the supplier did not issue a tax invoice and was not requested to issue a tax invoice there is no requirement to issue an adjustment note unless the recipient requests it: ANTS Act 1999, *supra* n. 12, sections 29-75(2) and 29-80(1); GSTR 2013/2, *supra* n. 116, 3, [8].
119. ANTS Act 1999, *supra* n. 12, section 29-70(1)(c)(ii).
120. ANTS Act 1999, *supra* n. 12, Pt. 4.4.
121. ANTS Act 1999, *supra* n. 12, Divs. 78, 79, 80.
122. ANTS Act 1999, *supra* n. 12, Div. 139.
123. ANTS Act 1999, *supra* n. 12, Div. 135.
124. ANTS Act 1999, *supra* n. 12, Div. 137-138.
125. ANTS Act 1999, *supra* n. 12, Div. 134.
126. ANTS Act 1999, *supra* n. 12, Div. 138.
127. ANTS Act 1999, *supra* n. 12, Divs. 129-132.

[A] The Parties Agree to a Change in Price

Parties agreeing to a change in price is a Category 1 adjustment event. The provisions are generally broad in scope and include the many different scenarios which might lead the parties to agree to a change in the consideration for a supply including discounts and penalties, rebates and correcting errors that affect the quantum of consideration.[128]

Generally, these changes can be located in one of three categories: first, as a change in consideration sufficiently linked to the original transaction and thus an adjustment event (i.e., the equivalent of Article 90 of the EU VAT Directive); second, as consideration for a further/separate supply (i.e., the equivalent of Article 73 of the EU VAT Directive applying to that new supply); third, as consideration for the original supply (i.e., the equivalent of Articles 73 and 79 of the EU VAT Directive) (or a combination of all three).[129] The appropriate treatment turns on the drafting and interpretation of contractual terms and factual characterization. This makes it difficult to generalize, but the following analysis draws out the main issues.

[1] Discounts and Penalties

The legislation makes it clear that 'a change to the previously agreed consideration for a supply or acquisition, whether due to the offer of a discount or otherwise' is an adjustment event.[130] However, whether or not a discount or penalty counts as an adjustment event or consideration for a new supply depends on the nature of the discount/penalty and the circumstances in which it is given.

For example, a prompt payment discount made to encourage early payment of an amount owing on a supply might be considered a change in consideration if the discount is sufficiently linked to the original supply to constitute an adjustment event and provided payment is made according to the discount terms.[131] However, the discount could also be classified as consideration for a financial supply – the early repayment of credit within a specified period.[132] The ATO has ruled that a discount offered in arriving at, or negotiating, the initial consideration for the supply would not constitute an adjustment event but simply form part of the consideration for the original supply.[133] If a discount is routinely applied over a period of time between two parties then it might be regarded as simply part of the consideration for the initial supply and not an adjustment event.[134] Discounts offered for damaged goods and other failures to meet terms might, depending on the facts, be treated as akin to a payment

128. ANTS Act 1999, *supra* n. 12, sections 19-10(1)(b) and 19-10(2)(b).
129. Payments made with more than one purpose (e.g., that both change consideration *and* constitute a new (financial) supply) need to be apportioned to each purpose accordingly: ATO, GSTR 2000/19, *supra* n. 105, 5, [19], ANTS Act 1999, *supra* n. 12, section 29-70(2).
130. ANTS Act 1999, *supra* n. 12, section 19-10(2)(b).
131. ATO, GSTR 2000/19, *supra* n. 105, at 5, [20]. By extension the ATO applies the same classification to tiered settlement discounts which offer discounts that decrease as payment time increases: at 6, [22].
132. ANTS Act 1999, *supra* n. 12, 6, [22].
133. ANTS Act 1999, *supra* n. 12, 5, [21].
134. ANTS Act 1999, *supra* n. 12, 6, [23]; *Ballarat Brewing Co. v. FCT* (1951) 82 CLR 364, 369-371.

by the supplier to the recipient to surrender a right (such as a right to repair or to a replacement) and therefore consideration for a separate supply.[135] By contrast, a discount for defective performance offered above and beyond any contractual or other legal obligations but sufficiently connected to the original supply might constitute an adjustment event.

The importance of characterization can be seen by the ATO's contrasting treatment of late payment charges, which it classifies as consideration for the supply of an interest in a credit arrangement and therefore consideration for a separate financial supply rather than a change in the consideration for the original supply.[136] Compromising or settling a debt, however, is treated as an adjustment event because it has the effect of reducing the consideration paid.[137]

It is worth noting in passing the existence of a specific anti-abuse[138] rule which imposes an open market value on certain supplies that are made 'without consideration' or for 'inadequate consideration'[139] between associates when the recipient of the supply is not in a position to obtain full input credits (having acquired the thing supplied 'otherwise than solely for a creditable purpose').[140] This is designed to preclude parties from manipulating prices to affect GST outcomes by, for example, colluding to reduce prices to reduce non-refundable GST. The provisions have potential relevance to all non-arm's length dealings (including adjustments) and are discussed in chapter 10 of this volume in relation to the issue of transfer pricing.

[2] Correcting Errors

Beyond deficiencies in the actual good or service supplied other errors might arise which, if they have the effect of changing the previously agreed consideration for a supply, might constitute an adjustment event.

Errors might occur in invoicing or reporting. The effect of mistakes on GST treatment depends on the type of mistake made.[141] Generally errors will not result in an adjustment event unless 'the parties treat the mistake as a change to the previously agreed consideration for the supply' (provided the adjustment occurs in a subsequent tax period).[142] If the mistake is in the invoice or reporting only and has no impact on the 'previously agreed consideration' then no adjustment event occurs, but there would be

135. ATO, GSTR 2000/19, *supra* n. 105, 15, [53]-[55].
136. ATO, GSTR 2000/19, *supra* n. 105, 7-8, [29]-[33].
137. ATO, GSTR 2000/19, *supra* n. 105, 14, [50]. *Cf.* §9.05[C].
138. Although labelled an anti-avoidance or anti-abuse rule, the rule applies irrespective of abuse or avoidance. The associate rules apply in addition to the general anti-avoidance rule in Div. 165: ANTS Act 1999, *supra* n. 12, Divs. 72, 165; Millar & Moon, *supra* n. 53, at [2.4.2].
139. ANTS Act 1999, *supra* n. 12, section 72-70(1).
140. ANTS Act 1999, *supra* n. 12, section 72-25(1)(b).
141. For example, GST-inclusive pricing means that the GST is calculated as a percentage of the invoiced price: *ibid.*, section 9-75. Therefore, errors relating to the calculation of GST on the invoice are errors on the invoice itself and do not affect the consideration and GST payable. *See further* Millar & Moon, *supra* n. 53, at [2.1.3.9].
142. ATO, GSTR 2000/19, *supra* n. 105, at 6-7, [25]-[26].

a need to correct the GST error.[143] Similarly, wrongly classifying a supply as taxable when it is in fact a GST-free supply is not an adjustment event unless it affects the consideration paid (but rather an error that requires correcting).[144] A reimbursement of the wrongly charged GST *would* constitute an adjustment event[145] and the supplier would likely have a decreasing adjustment[146] and the recipient an increasing adjustment.[147]

[3] Rebates

Generally, a rebate provided by a supplier to an end user, such as a cash-back offer, is treated much like a discount – if it has the effect of reducing the previously agreed consideration for the supply then an adjustment event occurs (provided all the other criteria are met).[148] However, even in this simple scenario much can depend on factual characterization, contractual drafting and interpretation, especially as it relates to the intention of the parties to the transaction(s). So, for example, a rebate provided on condition of the performance of an obligation (e.g., conducting a product review) might instead be treated as consideration for a separate supply provided the requisite conditions are met.[149] By contrast, a truly unconditional incentive payment made to a customer, such as a gift given to encourage the customer to purchase from the supplier but with no obligations attached, might be considered neither an adjustment event nor consideration for a separate supply.[150]

The position with third-party rebates has not been straightforward. Despite the broad drafting of the GST legislation, Australian courts (and tribunals) have interpreted the provisions quite narrowly at times resulting in a more restrictive approach than that in the EU. This narrow approach has been partly mitigated by legislative amendment specifically permitting adjustments for third-party rebates and might also not survive a more expansive approach taken to the interpretation of the GST by Australia's ultimate appellate court – the High Court of Australia.

---

143. The difference between an adjustment and an error is that a 'GST adjustment relates to a reported sale or purchase that was correct at the time of lodgment, whereas a GST error relates to an amount that was incorrect at the time of lodgement': ATO, 'Definition of a GST Error' (6 June 2017), https://www.ato.gov.au/Business/GST/In-detail/Managing-GST-in-your-business/Reporting,-paying-and-activity-statements/Correcting-GST-errors/?page=2#Definition_of_a_GST_error (accessed 20 December 2020); ANTS Act 1999, *supra* n. 12, section 17-20(1); Goods and Services Tax: Correcting GST Errors Determination 2013 (Cth); ATO, GSTR 2000/19, *supra* n. 105, at 19, [70]-[71].
144. ATO, GSTR 2000/19, *supra* n. 105, at 19, [70].
145. ANTS Act 1999, *supra* n. 12, sections 19-10(1)(b) or (c) and 142-10 – Note 1.
146. ANTS Act 1999, *supra* n. 12, sections 19-55 and 142-10 – Note 1. A supplier is generally not able to claim a refund for wrongly charged GST unless they reimburse the recipient of the supply (or amend an assessment): Div. 142-A; Taxation Administration Act 1953, Sch 1, section 155-75.
147. ANTS Act 1999, *supra* n. 12, sections 19-80 and 142-10 – Note 1; ATO, GSTR 2000/19, *supra* n. 105, at 19, [70].
148. ANTS Act 1999, *supra* n. 12, sections 19-10(1)(b) and 19-10(2)(b); ATO, GSTR 2000/19, *supra* n. 105, at 6, [23].
149. ATO, GSTR 2000/19, *supra* n. 105, at 16, [56]-[57].
150. ATO, GSTR 2000/19, *supra* n. 105, 16, [58]. *Cf.* such a promotional gift would likely be deemed a self-supply (and taxable as such) under EU rules: EU VAT Directive, Articles 16, 26.

In *Electrical Goods Importer*, a third-party rebate provided by a wholesaler to a consumer who upon purchasing certain electrical goods was entitled to claim cash-back, was found neither to constitute third party consideration for a supply (from either the wholesaler to the retailer or from the retailer to the consumer) nor an adjustment event (if made in a subsequent tax period).[151] The Tribunal found that the payment made to the consumer by the wholesaler lacked a sufficient nexus to either the supply from the wholesaler to the retailer or from the retailer to the consumer.[152] Although there was *some* link to the other supplies it was not found to be *sufficient* to amount to consideration 'for' or 'in connection with' those supplies.[153]

In *AP Group* a variety of third-party rebates provided by various car manufacturers to car dealers were found to only amount to consideration if the payments could be *directly* linked to a reduction in the price for the final consumer.[154] Consequently, general incentive payments based on the dealer reaching a certain level of sales or orders were found to be insufficiently connected to a particular supply to constitute consideration as they 'did not depend on the sale of any particular car in any particular way' and were therefore treated as akin to gifts.[155] Naturally the effect of *all* the various payments was to reduce the costs of vehicles to the retailers with the savings passed on to consumers. Therefore, to enable the retailer to claim full credits for such rebates but ignore their effect on the final sale amounted to an under-taxation of the final sale.[156] Although the case did not concern adjustments,[157] the ATO subsequently ruled that,

151. *Electrical Goods Importer and FCT* [2009] AATA 854, 985, [6]; ANTS Act 1999, *supra* n. 12, sections 9-5 and 19-10(b).
152. *Electrical Goods Importer and FCT* [2009] AATA 854, 996, [59]; 998, [63].
153. 'There is, it might be said, a link between the payment of the cash-back and the transactions which preceded it, but it is not made in consideration of either of them': *Electrical Goods Importer and FCT* [2009] AATA 854, 996, [59].
154. Under the arrangement cars were sold by the manufacturers to interposed finance companies who entered into various bailment arrangements with the dealers who only acquired title to stock in their possession immediately prior to a final sale: *AP Group Ltd v. Federal Commissioner of Taxation* (2013) 214 FCR 301, 305-306, [12]-[20], 313-314, [44], [46]. Those sufficiently connected payments (fleet-rebate and runout support payments) amounted to consideration even if the customer did not know of the rebate or if it was not passed on in the price to the consumer.
155. *AP Group Ltd v. Federal Commissioner of Taxation* (2013) 214 FCR 301, 315, [48]. *See* further ATO, Goods and Services Tax Ruling GSTR 2014/1, Motor Vehicle Incentive Payments, 3-10, [13]-[46] (1 October 2014). But note the obiter of Bromberg J. who expressed reservations about the finding that these general incentive payments were not consideration for a supply and noted that the 'relevant question is not whether the conduct was for consideration but whether the particular supply which arose from the conduct was for consideration': 319-321, [65]-[66],[76]-[77]. However, because the Commissioner had not challenged this finding, the issue was not pursued further: 321-322, [74]-[81]. For further criticism of this aspect of the Full Federal Court's reasoning including questioning its validity in light of High Court authority, *see* Richard Krever & Jonathan Teoh, *Justice Edmonds and Interpretation of Australia's GST Legislation*, 45(2) Austl. Tax Rev. 121, 127-130 (2016).
156. Krever & Teoh, *supra* n. 155, 128.
157. *AP Group Ltd v. Federal Commissioner of Taxation* (2013) 214 FCR 301; Kevin O'Rourke, *Incentives, Rebates and Third-Party Adjustments after the AP Group Decision*, 13 Austl. GST J. 64, 74 (2013).

following *Electrical Goods Importer*, such payments would *not* amount to an adjustment event.[158]

Both decisions have been criticized for ignoring the commercial realities of these arrangements (i.e., that money is always paid for something) in favour of a narrow or overly contractual focus that consideration be for a specific supply.[159] Two developments have offset this narrow approach.

The first and most direct was legislative reform, taking effect from 1 July 2010, which, subject to certain conditions, enables a third party, such as a manufacturer of whitegoods who provides a cash-back rebate to a consumer, to make a decreasing adjustment as if the consideration for the manufacturer's taxable supply of the whitegoods to the retailer had been reduced by the amount of the third-party payment (the cash-back rebate).[160] A corresponding increasing adjustment is required for an end-user registered for the GST (as if the consideration for their acquisition had been reduced by the amount of the rebate).[161] A decreasing adjustment arises irrespective of whether GST is payable (e.g., on the supply to the consumer) in a current or previous tax period.[162] Relevant conditions include that the payment 'is made in connection with, in response to or for the inducement of the payee's acquisition of the thing', and that the payment is not consideration for a supply to the payee (i.e., thus giving rise to a separate taxable supply).[163] Division 134 would apply to all the incentive payments in the *Electrical Goods Importer* and *AP Group* arrangements.[164] However, Division 134 does not solve all the third-party rebate issues and arguably creates a number of its own such as reconciling the potential overlap of the broad definition of consideration as payment 'in response to or for the *inducement* of a supply of anything'[165] with the requirement that the third-party rebate payment 'is made in connection with, in

158. ATO, Goods and Services Tax Ruling GSTR 2019/1, Supply of Anything Other Than Goods or Real Property Connected With the Indirect Tax Zone (Australia), 10-13, [40]-[42B] (11 December 2019).
159. The Tribunal in *Electrical Goods Importer* was not moved to depart from its conclusion despite: previous Federal Court authority recognizing third party consideration when a discount was provided at point of sale (with a material difference being the existence of two supplies in this case rather than one); the breadth of the definition of consideration and the nexus with a supply (which still required a stronger link to constitute payment for either supply than existed here); policy arguments that the supplier should bear no greater GST liability than the reality of their economic position allows; and rejected the importation concepts such as the European principle of fiscal neutrality: *Electrical Goods Importer v. FCT* [2009] AATA 854, 991-992, [40]-[52], 996, [58]-[59]; *TT Line v. FCT* (2009) 72 ATR 982 (*per* Stone J.); *TT Line Company Pty Ltd v. Federal Commissioner of Taxation* (2009) 181 FCR 400, 404, [16]-[18] (*per* Emmett J.), 410 [50]-[51] (*per* Edmonds J.). For criticisms of the *AP Group* approach for ignoring commercial reality, *see* Krever & Teoh, *supra* n. 155, at 128-130; O'Rourke, *supra* n. 157, 76.
160. ANTS Act 1999, *supra* n. 12, section 134-5(2).
161. ANTS Act 1999, *supra* n. 12, section 134-10.
162. ANTS Act 1999, *supra* n. 12, section 134-5(20). A third-party adjustment note is required for decreasing adjustments (above AUD 75): section 134-20.
163. ANTS Act 1999, *supra* n. 12, sections 134-5(1) and 134-10(1).
164. ATO, GSTR 2014/1, *supra* n. 155, at 10-18, [47]-[85] – *see esp.* 16, [71].
165. ANTS Act 1999, *supra* n. 12, sections 9-15(1)(a)(b) (emphasis added) and 9-75(b).

response to or for the inducement of the payee's acquisition of the thing'.[166] Division 134 also does not extend the Australian provisions as far as those of the EU.[167]

The second development has been the subsequent emergence of a line of High Court and appellate court authority that has rejected a narrow contractual approach to interpreting the requirement that a supply be 'for consideration' and emphasizing instead that this 'requires a connection of relationship between the supply and consideration' and not the adoption of 'contractual principles'.[168]

This more expansive approach was referred to in a recent Federal Court decision which held that casino operators were allowed to offset payments (including rebates and discounts) made to gambling junket operators (for organizing gambling junkets) as part of the *total prizes paid* to be deducted from the *total amounts wagered* under special rules that use a profit/loss margin to calculate GST liability on gambling supplies.[169] The effect of including these payments in the global GST amount rather than accounting for such payments as consideration for a separate supply of services was to reduce the GST liability of the casino operator.[170] Like *Electrical Goods Importer* the case concerned two separate supplies: (1) the services provided to the Casino by the junket tour operator in arranging the junket; and (2) the gambling supplies provided by the Casino to gamblers under the junket arrangement.[171] However, unlike, *Electrical Goods Importer* the court found that a contractual relationship existed between all three parties - the casino, junket operators and gamblers[172] with the consequence 'that commission and rebates are not separate and distinct amounts to be disintegrated from the collective win/loss results'.[173]

166. For this and other issues *see* O'Rourke, *supra* n. 157, 78.
167. *Cf.* Millar & Moon, *supra* n. 53, at [2.1.3.5] - contend that the Div. 134 rules effectively legislate the European case law approach established in cases such as *Elida Gibbs*. However, the wholesalers in that case would not be able to deduct the full amount that applied prior to the rebate: ANTS Act 1999, *supra* n. 12, section 134-10.
168. *See*, e.g., *Commissioner of Taxation v. Qantas Airways Ltd* (2012) 247 CLR 286, 292. [14] *per* Gummow, Hayne, Kiefel and Bell JJ. O'Rourke attempts to suggest that the subsequent High Court decision of *Qantas Airways* 286, 292, [14] which held that the link to a supply can be established beyond merely a contractual link casts doubts over the *Electrical Goods Importer* authority. AAT decisions are not binding on the Courts, but the decision has not been disturbed: O'Rourke, *supra* n. 157, at 76.
169. ANTS Act 1999, *supra* n. 12, Div. 126, section 126-10; *Crown Melbourne Ltd v. Federal Commissioner of Taxation* [2020] FCA 1295, [52]-[54], [65], [71].
170. Liability of the casino operator is calculated as follows: Global GST amount + Other GST - Input tax credits: ANTS Act 1999, *supra* n. 12, section 126-5(1). In a line similar to the *Electrical Goods Importer* decision, the Commissioner unsuccessfully contended that the consideration paid to junket tour operators was neither '"consideration" for or in connection with the applicants' gambling supplies or "monetary prizes" that the applicants are liable to pay on the outcome of gambling events': *Crown Melbourne Ltd v. Federal Commissioner of Taxation* [2020] FCA 1295, [45]; ANTS Act 1999, section 126-10.
171. *Crown Melbourne Ltd v. Federal Commissioner of Taxation* [2020] FCA 1295, [68].
172. The 'terms agreed by the casino with the junket tour operator with respect to the conduct of a junket at the casino constitute an offer by the casino to make gambling supplies to junket participants on the terms agreed, and the commencement of gambling by the junket players constitutes acceptance of that offer': *Crown Melbourne Ltd v. Federal Commissioner of Taxation* [2020] FCA 1295, [69].
173. *Crown Melbourne Ltd v. Federal Commissioner of Taxation* [2020] FCA 1295, [70], [71].

Although the decision might be limited to the different nature of the contractual relationships and the specific provisions for gambling supplies, the court noted two relevant points. First, the 'word 'consideration' has the same meaning in the context of' the special rules for gambling supplies as it did for basic rules for taxable supplies and so the 'same reasoning is apt with respect to the use of the word "for" in the phrase "consideration for all of your gambling supplies" [as it is for "you make the supply for consideration"] which informs the nature and degree of the connection required'.[174] Second, following the High Court decision of *Qantas*, the operation of these provisions 'does not depend on the characterisation of the commission and rebates as "consideration" as a matter of strict contractual principle' but rather by reference to the relevant provisions of the Act.[175] The extent to which this case will be applied to a third party rebate scenario will depend on the extent to which the rules in Division 134 cover the issue.[176]

The appropriate treatment of supplier-customer rebates might be further complicated when the rebate takes other forms such as a loyalty reward or voucher. The issue has not been the subject of judicial consideration, but vouchers are dealt with separately under special legislative provisions[177] and both vouchers and loyalty programs have been the subject of extensive rulings by the ATO.[178]

In brief, whether the provision of a rebate in the form of a voucher would give rise to an adjustment depends on the voucher. A face-value voucher (i.e., with a dollar amount limited to the value on the voucher) redeemable anywhere is subject to special rules and is likely to be treated as akin to cash provided it meets the requirements of the special rules (with GST consequences (including adjustments) only once the voucher is redeemed).[179] For a price discount or refund voucher entitling the consumer to further reduced price or 'free' purchases at the same (or another) retailer it is likely that, from the perspective of the final consumer, the price paid for the initial supply (and any discounted price on the subsequent supply) captures the value of both that initial supply and the subsequent supply (and so no adjustment arises).[180]

The position is complicated with loyalty programs. The ATO has ruled that the redemption of a loyalty reward by a final consumer is a supply but not a taxable supply unless further consideration is paid.[181] However, the redemption of the reward is also

174. *Crown Melbourne Ltd v. Federal Commissioner of Taxation* [2020] FCA 1295, [54].
175. *Crown Melbourne Ltd v. Federal Commissioner of Taxation* [2020] FCA 1295, [68], [71]. *See* above (§9.04[A]).
176. For potential gaps which might arise *see* O'Rourke, *supra* n. 168, 77-78.
177. ANTS Act 1999, *supra* n. 12, Div. 100.
178. ATO, GSTR 2003/5 - Goods and Services Tax: Vouchers (28 May 2003); ATO, GSTR 2012/1 - Goods and Services Tax: Loyalty Programs (14 August 2013, consolidated version) - for the types of loyalty programs covered by the Ruling *see* 4-6 [7]-[15].
179. ATO, GSTR 2003/5, *supra* n. 178, 3-4, [9], 33-36, [139]-[154] (third-party vouchers). The third-party provider of the voucher should be able to claim an input credit for GST incurred (if any) in providing the benefit provided that they can show the input was for a creditable purpose and does not relate to an input taxed or GST-free supply: 33-36, [139]-[154]. *Cf.* the more complex treatment in the EU: Zu & Krever, *supra* n. 22.
180. ATO, GSTR 2003/5, *supra* n. 178, 42-43 [182]-[190]; ATO, GSTR 2012/1, *supra* n. 178, 7 [16], 8 [24].
181. ATO, GSTR 2012/1, *supra* n. 178, 8 [23]-[27], 22 [100]-[103].

treated as a possible taxable supply (of the underlying reward to a member) by the participating retailer to the loyalty program operator.[182] The question of whether the supply is taxable (and whether the loyalty program operator can obtain input credits for the consideration paid for the supply) ultimately depends on the taxable status of the underlying rewards supplied - e.g., if the redeemed products or services are taxable supplies then input credits are available, if they are input-taxed supplies then input credits are not available.[183] This treatment of loyalty rewards limits the scope for adjustment issues to arise. The Ruling seeks to overcome many of the issues experienced in the CJEU case law (*see* §9.06[A][3]) but has not been subject to judicial scrutiny and has been subject to many revisions and remains open to challenge.[184]

[B] Cancelled Transactions and Early Termination

The legislation makes it clear that 'cancelling a supply or acquisition' is a Category 1 adjustment event.[185] This includes 'the return to a supplier of a thing, or part of a thing, supplied (whether or not the return involves a change of ownership of the thing)'.[186] However, if the return does not have the effect of cancelling the supply or changing the consideration for the supply, such as returning goods for repair or exchange, it would not constitute an adjustment event. As usual, much depends on the factual circumstances and contractual arrangements.[187]

The amount of a decreasing adjustment available to a supplier for a cancelled supply is linked to the reimbursement of any GST passed on to the recipient of the initial supply. This prevents suppliers from double-dipping (i.e., keeping the GST charged on the original supply and then offsetting that GST component against their net GST liability).[188]

As discussed at §9.02[A][3], a contract that is paid for (in part or full) in advance and for which the payer forfeits their deposit and/or the whole consideration can produce different GST outcomes (including whether or not an adjustment is required). This issue has dominated Australian appellate case law - with three of the five cases decided by the High Court on the GST concerning the appropriate treatment of consideration received and/or forfeited under an executory contract (a contract which requires subsequent performance of obligations by either party at a later date in order

182. ATO, GSTR 2012/1, *supra* n. 178, 8 [25]-[27].
183. ATO, GSTR 2012/1, *supra* n. 178, 8 [26].
184. *See, e.g.*, ATO, GSTR 2012/1, *supra* n. 178, 12, [44]-[47B]; ATO, Ruling Compendium - ER 2012/1. The ATO has further ruled that the provision of a loyalty program by the loyalty program operator to a retailer is a (potential) taxable supply and input credits are likewise (potentially) available for *points fees* paid by retailers to participate in the program (the amount generally calculated by reference to the number of points allocated to the retailer's customers). The taxable status of the *points fees* paid by participating retailers to the loyalty program operator is based on estimating the likely composition of supplies (as taxable, GST-free or input taxed): GSTR 2012/1, *supra* n. 178, 7 [17]-[22], 18-19 [75]-[83].
185. ANTS Act 1999, *supra* n. 12, section 19-10(1)(a).
186. ANTS Act 1999, *supra* n. 12, section 19-10(2)(a).
187. ATO, GSTR 2000/19, *supra* n. 105, at 4, [16].
188. ANTS Act 1999, *supra* n. 12, section 142-20.

for the contract to be executed).[189] All three involved the High Court correcting the misinterpretation by the Federal Court of the underlying executory contract giving rise to the alleged supply as well as the legislative scheme.[190] Two are discussed here.

In the first High Court case on the GST, *Reliance Carpet*, a vendor was held liable to pay GST on a deposit that had been forfeited under a contract for the sale of land which was terminated due to a default by the purchaser.[191] The taxpayer argued that no supply had occurred (because of the failure of the principal supply - the sale of land) and that therefore the deposit received could not be consideration for any supply arguing, consistent with French authority (*Société Thermale d'Eugenie les Bains*), that the deposit instead acted as a form of (non-taxable) damages or compensation unrelated to any supply.[192] The High Court rejected the argument and decided in favour of the Commissioner that the deposit constituted consideration for a supply being 'security for the performance of the obligation of the purchaser to complete the Contract'.[193] Therefore GST was payable on the resulting taxable supply in the relevant tax period during which the forfeiture occurred.[194] The High Court distinguished the French authority on two bases. First, the EU VAT Directive required a specific connection between the services provided (in that case, provision of a hotel room) and what was received for them, which was not required in the Australian legislation.[195] Second, in contrast to French contract law, the common law does not regard a deposit as fixed compensation independent of the obligations it attaches to.[196]

The subsequent High Court case of *Qantas* concerned a distinct but related issue of whether payment for a fare made to an airline for a flight that was neither taken nor refunded represented consideration for a taxable supply.[197] As the High Court made clear (and as was accepted by the parties) the issue did not concern a Category 1

189. *See, e.g., Commissioner of Taxation v. Reliance Carpet Co. Pty Ltd* (2008) 236 CLR 342; *Commissioner of Taxation v. Qantas Airways Ltd* (2012) 247 CLR 286; *Commissioner of Taxation v. MBI Properties Pty Ltd* (2014) 254 CLR 376, 390-392, [32]-[41], 393, [46]; Gummow, *supra* n. 18, at 843-844.
190. *See further* the High Court's criticism of the Full Federal Court's misapplication of the term 'rescission' in the context of the executory contract: *Commissioner of Taxation v. Reliance Carpet Co. Pty Ltd* (2008) 236 CLR 342, 345, [2], 348, [13], 350, [24]. *See also* the influence of contract and property law in the High Court's treatment of the deposit: 349-353, [22]-[29], [30].
191. *Commissioner of Taxation v. Reliance Carpet Co. Pty Ltd* (2008) 236 CLR 342, 353-357.
192. *Commissioner of Taxation v. Reliance Carpet Co. Pty Ltd* (2008) 236 CLR 342, 352-353 [29]-[30]; CJEU, 18 July 2007, Case C-277/05, *Société Thermale d'Eugénie-les-Bains*, ECLI:EU:C:2007:440.
193. *Commissioner of Taxation v. Reliance Carpet Co Pty Ltd* (2008) 236 CLR 342, 352, [28].
194. The Court found that the deposit operated as security for the supply of obligations under the contract, which included not just the obligation to transfer title to the land on payment of the balance of the purchase price, but obligations to refrain from accepting offers from other prospective purchasers, obligations to maintain the land in its current condition, etc. By virtue of special provisions in the Australian GST legislation, a deposit was not consideration for a supply unless forfeited or applied as all or part of the consideration for supply: *Commissioner of Taxation v. Reliance Carpet Co. Pty Ltd* (2008) 236 CLR 342, 355-356, [38]-[42]; ANTS Act 1999, *supra* n. 12, Div. 99, sections 99-5 and 99-10.
195. *Commissioner of Taxation v. Reliance Carpet Co. Pty Ltd* (2008) 236 CLR 342, 352-353, [29]-[30]; ANTS Act 1999, *supra* n. 12, section 99-10; EU VAT Directive, Articles 2(1), 6(1), 11A(1)(a).
196. *Commissioner of Taxation v. Reliance Carpet Co. Pty Ltd* (2008) 236 CLR 342, 352-353, [29] to [30] considering *Société Thermale d'Eugénie-les-Bains, supra* n. 192, paragraph 26.
197. ANTS Act 1999, *supra* n. 12, sections 9-5 and 9-15.

adjustment because there was no change in consideration by reason of a refund of the fare, but rather concerned instances in which a refund was either not available or not claimed.[198] The High Court held that a proper construction of the executory contract showed that Qantas had not made an unconditional promise to carry the passenger and their baggage on a particular flight but had made a qualified promise to use best endeavours to carry the passenger and their baggage in the circumstances.[199] This promise rather than the flight itself constituted the *taxable supply* and payment of the fare therefore constituted *consideration* for the *supply*, with Qantas liable to remit GST at the time of entering the contract (even if the passenger failed to take that flight and the contract was not executed).[200]

In both decisions, any concerns around double taxation (i.e., by taxing the initial supply of rights and subsequent supply) could be dealt with by attribution rules which allocated the consideration received for the taxable supply to the relevant tax period in which the consideration for the fare was received (for Qantas) or when the deposit was forfeited (for Reliance).[201]

These High Court decisions therefore align the Australian jurisprudence much more closely to the *MEO*, *Vodafone Portugal* and *Air France KLM* series of cases in the EU, rather than the *Societe-Thermal* approach (*see* §9.06[B]).

[C] Bad Debts

An unpaid debt will not constitute a Category 1 adjustment because it involves no change to the previously agreed consideration for a supply or acquisition.[202] However, given that a bad debt might involve a de facto change in consideration for taxpayers reporting on an accounts basis (when it is either not paid or received), Division 21 provides a means for recognizing changes in GST payable or input tax credits available for bad debts (thus constituting a Category 2 adjustment event).[203]

A decreasing adjustment (of 1/11th of the outstanding amount) applies to the whole or part of an unpaid debt that is either written off as bad or is outstanding for

198. *Commissioner of Taxation v. Qantas Airways Ltd* (2012) 247 CLR 286, 290 [3]. The airline had contended that the failure to take the flight meant that there was no supply and therefore no 'supply for consideration' and thus no taxable supply giving rise to a liability to remit GST: at 288-289.
199. *Commissioner of Taxation v. Qantas Airways Ltd* (2012) 247 CLR 286, 299 [33].
200. *Commissioner of Taxation v. Qantas Airways Ltd* (2012) 247 CLR 286, 299 [33].
201. *Commissioner of Taxation v. Qantas Airways Ltd* (2012) 247 CLR 286, 290, [4]-[5] – the Court accepted the Commissioner's argument that 'GST on the consideration received is not payable in each of the tax periods in which a series of events occur in performance of an executory contract; the GST is payable once, in the tax period of the first payment or invoice': 294 [19], 299 [34]; *Commissioner of Taxation v. Reliance Carpet Co. Pty Ltd* (2008) 236 CLR 342, 356, [39].
202. ANTS Act 1999, *supra* n. 12, section 19-10(1)(b).
203. ANTS Act 1999, *supra* n. 12, Div. 21, section 21-5(2). Div. 136 contains special rules for transactions that are not taxable or creditable to the fullest extent – for example, an adjustment will need to be apportioned to reflect the extent to which an acquisition was only partly for a creditable purpose: section 136-10; ATO, Goods and Services Tax Ruling GSTR 2000/2, Adjustments for Bad Debts, 15-19 (29 March 2000).

more than 12 months (and the debtor is aware of this).[204] Bad debts are not an adjustment event and so there is no requirement to issue adjustment notes.[205] Adjustments arise if the GST payable on a taxable supply (or input credits claimed) was attributable to a previous tax period or to an earlier supply (or acquisition) in the same tax period.[206]

Mirror provisions apply for increasing adjustments for taxpayers (debtors) who owe an unpaid debt for which they have claimed an input credit when they become *aware* that a debt has been written off as bad or has been overdue for 12 months or more.[207] There is, however, no requirement for suppliers to notify the recipient of a supply that the debt has been written off.[208]

If a taxpayer subsequently recovers (or pays) a debt, then this is attributed to the period in which the debt is recovered (or paid) and a corresponding increasing adjustment (of 1/11th of the amount recovered) is required for the creditor and a decreasing adjustment for the debtor.[209]

Taxpayers wanting to make an adjustment for a debt *less than* twelve months old must show first that the debt is bad and secondly that the debt has been written off (i.e., some form of written record evidencing a decision to write the debt from an account such as a journal entry in a book of account).[210] Taxpayers wanting to make an adjustment for a debt more than 12 months old need only show that the debt has been *overdue* for 12 months or more, which offers greater certainty than the EU approach.[211]

'Bad debt' is an undefined term and question of fact which turns on an objective consideration of all the relevant circumstances.[212] The ATO has ruled that it will generally accept a debt is bad if a taxpayer makes a 'bona fide commercial decision that the debt is unlikely to be recovered',[213] but has also indicated that such a decision must be based on 'sound commercial considerations'[214] which is not satisfied if there is a 'real and continuing dispute in relation to the sum owed'.[215] The debt must be 'more

204. ANTS Act 1999, *supra* n. 12, section 21-5(1)(c), 29-20(1), 21-5(1); ATO, GSTR 2000/2, *supra* n. 203, at 4 [16].
205. ATO, GSTR 2000/2, *supra* n. 203, at 5, [18]; 11, [50].
206. By contrast, Category 1 adjustment events are only available for subsequent tax periods. Amounts claimed in the same tax period must be separately accounted for and not merely offset against the other: *ibid.*, 4, [15], 5, [21], 7, [34]. Mirror rules exist for entities making creditable acquisitions needing to make increasing adjustments: at 5, [21].
207. ANTS Act 1999, *supra* n. 12, sections 29-20(1) and 21-15; ATO, GSTR 2000/2, *supra* n. 203, at 5, [22].
208. ATO, GSTR 2000/2, *supra* n. 203, at 11, [51].
209. ANTS Act 1999, *supra* n. 12, sections 21-10 and 21-20; ATO, GSTR 2000/2, *supra* n. 203, at 4, [17]; 5, [23].
210. ATO, GSTR 2000/2, *supra* n. 203, 6 [28], 8-10, [37]-[47].
211. ANTS Act 1999, *supra* n. 12, sections 21-5(1)(c) and 195-1 – 'overdue' – 'a debt is overdue if there has been a failure to discharge the debt, and that failure is a breach of the debtor's obligations in relation to the debt'; ATO, GSTR 2000/2, *supra* n. 203, 8, [36].
212. ATO, GSTR 2000/2, *supra* n. 203, 6, [27], 8-9, [39]-[42]. The Commissioner defers to a ruling on the treatment of bad debts for the purposes of the income tax to outline the factors relevant to the classification of a debt as bad: ATO, Taxation Ruling TR 92/18, Income Tax: Bad Debts, 5-8, [26]-[33] (17 December 1992).
213. ATO, GSTR 2000/2, *supra* n. 203, 6 [27]; *cf.* ATO, TR 92/18, *supra* n. 212, 5-6, [26].
214. ATO, GSTR 2000/2, *supra* n. 203, 8, [37].
215. ATO, GSTR 2000/2, *supra* n. 203, 8, [38].

than merely doubtful'[216] and there must be 'little to no likelihood of recovering the debt'[217] which might be evidenced by the debtor being in liquidation with insufficient funds to pay the debt and the supplier being unable to trace the debtor (having taken appropriate steps to recover the debt).[218]

Much of the compliance activity and case law on bad debts reflects the inherent risks in providing for adjustments for bad debts. These include that individuals might seek to fabricate or over-inflate claims and, relatedly, a lack of sufficient supporting evidence of either the debt or the writing off.[219]

As with all categories of adjustment, timing and characterization matter. If, for example, a creditor forgives or settles a debt then such a settlement amounts to a Category 1 adjustment event because the parties have agreed to a change in consideration (either a partial or full reduction).[220] Once settled, the debt no longer exists and cannot be written off.[221] If the debt is assigned, Division 21 does not operate because only the entity that makes the underlying taxable supply (subject of the debt) can make the adjustment for the bad debt related to that supply.[222] This precludes the assignee from relying on Division 21, but would not preclude the assignor from doing so prior to the assignment.[223] The assignment of the debt itself is a separate input taxed financial supply (and imposes no obligation on the assignor to make an increasing adjustment).[224] By contrast, recovering money from a guarantor under a guarantee for a written off debt will constitute an increasing adjustment even though the debt is recovered from someone other than the debtor.[225]

[D] Court Orders and Third-Party Adjustments

As §9.02[A][5] detailed, the notions of supply and consideration are broad enough to encompass court orders and out of court settlements. However, whether or not such

216. ATO, GSTR 2000/2, *supra* n. 203, 9, [42]; ATO, TR 92/18, *supra* n. 212, 1, [2], 6, [30].
217. ATO, GSTR 2000/2, *supra* n. 203, 8, [41].
218. ATO, GSTR 2000/2, *supra* n. 203, 8, [40].
219. *See, e.g.*, *Vadasz v. FCT* 2006 63 ATR 1236, 1247, [40], 1248, [42] (unreliable and deficient records did not support the taxpayer's claims to adjustments under Div. 19 and Div. 21 bad debts); *Re QFP Professional Tomato Project and Others v. FCT* [2010] AATA 864 (taxpayers failed to make an increasing adjustment for unpaid debts of more than 12 months for which earlier input credits were claimed; the taxpayers failed to provide sufficient proof that the debts had been paid. The taxpayer therefore failed to show that the Commissioner's assessment was excessive. The failure to make an increasing adjustment amounted to misleading conduct with the continuing failure constituting recklessness and penalties (of 50% of the amount owed) applied).
220. ANTS Act 1999, *supra* n. 12, section 19-10(1)(b); ATO, GSTR 2000/2, *supra* n. 203, 9, [46].
221. ATO, GSTR 2000/2, *supra* n. 203, at 9, [45].
222. ANTS Act 1999, *supra* n. 12, sections 21-5(1) and 21-10(a)(b); ATO, GSTR 2000/2, *supra* n. 203, 10, [47].
223. *See, e.g.*, ATO, TR 92/18, *supra* n. 212, 10, [38]-[39].
224. ANTS Act 1999, *supra* n. 12, section 40-5; ANTS Regulations 1999, *supra* n. 32, Regulation 40-5.09(3) – item 3; ATO, Interpretive Decision ID 2005/201, GST and Increasing Adjustment Where Previously Written Off Bad Debts Are Sold to a Debt Factor (21 October 2004), https://www.ato.gov.au/law/view/document?DocID=AID/AID2005201/00001.
225. ANTS Act 1999, *supra* n. 12, section 21-10; *Apple Computer Australia Pty Ltd v. Mekrizis and Ors* (2003) 54 ATR 383, 385-386, [205]-[208] (NSWSC).

orders or settlements have GST consequences depends on satisfying the nexus requirement for a taxable supply that the supply be for consideration[226] and/or the nexus requirement for an adjustment that such an order or settlement is sufficiently connected to an earlier (taxable) supply.

Although the discussion here concerns court orders, the broad principles discussed should also generally apply to decisions or actions taken by the Commissioner including those undertaken as a result of a Tribunal decision. It is clear that such actions, such as an assessment following an audit, can have different effects depending on whether or not the changes made sufficiently relate to the underlying supply (to give rise to an adjustment) or create new rights and obligations in relation to a new supply. Australia does not share the apparent reluctance in the EU to recognize these variations initiated outside those changes agreed by the parties to the initial supply. This in turn affects the discrete issue of the treatment of transfer pricing adjustments by revenue authorities which is discussed in chapter 10 of this volume.

In its Public Ruling on the issue, the ATO distinguishes the various GST consequences of out of court settlements or court orders in three different contexts. First, court orders or settlements that *do not* relate to any underlying supply such as an award for damages arising from a successful claim in negligence. A court order will generally have no GST consequences as either a taxable supply (as there is no underlying supply for which the payment ('consideration') is received) or as a subsequent adjustment (as there was no earlier supply to which the payment relates).[227] A court order does not involve parties creating or surrendering new rights because the resolution of the dispute stems from the court order.[228] By contrast, an out-of-court settlement might involve one or both parties making a (taxable) supply by surrendering a right to pursue further legal action,[229] entering into an obligation to refrain from legal action or releasing another party from further obligations in the dispute.[230] However, the ATO takes the view that, if the amount paid relates to the original damages claim, it is generally not possible or desirable to ascribe a separate value to this discontinuance supply.[231] To the extent that this view might be challenged, it should only affect the issue of whether a new taxable supply exists rather than affect an earlier supply and therefore the issue of adjustments.[232]

226. ANTS Act 1999, *supra* n. 12, sections 9-5 (a), 9-10(2), 9-15(1), 9-15(2) and 9-15(2A).
227. ATO, Goods and Services Tax Ruling GSTR 2001/4, GST Consequences of Court Orders and Out-of-Court Settlements, 11-13, [60]-[73], 26-28, [145]-[155] (20 June 2001 – last updated 15 July 2020); ANTS Act 1999, *supra* n. 12, section 9-10(4); *Walter Construction Group Limited v. Walker Corporation Ltd & Ors* [2001] NSWSC 283; *Gagner Pty Ltd (trading as Indochine Café) v. Canturi Corp Pty Ltd* [2009] NSWCA 413 (NSW CA) (Aust.); *Osric Investments Pty Ltd v. Woburn Downs Pastoral Pty Ltd* (2001) 48 ATR 184 (Fed. Ct.) (Aust.); *Interchase Corporation Ltd v. ACN 010 087 573 Pty Ltd* (2000) 45 ATR 445 (QSC) (Aust.). Orders for costs are not taxable supplies and so will not give rise to an adjustment: Christopher Sievers, *GST on Judgments and Out of Court Settlements: Is GSTR 2001/4 Still Relevant?* 12 Austl. GST J. 16, 20-25 (2013).
228. ATO, GSTR 2001/4, *supra* n. 227, at 12, [69]-[70].
229. ANTS Act 1999, *supra* n. 12, section 9-10(2)(e).
230. ANTS Act 1999, *supra* n. 12 s, 9-10(2)(g); ATO, GSTR 2001/4, *supra* n. 227, at 7 [37], 10, [54].
231. ATO, GSTR 2001/4, *supra* n. 227, at 19, [106]-[111].
232. For a contrary view, *see* Sievers, *supra* n. 227, 26-31.

Second, court orders or settlements might require action that itself constitutes a new (potentially) taxable supply provided there is sufficient nexus between the payment and the supply, as might be the case with an obligation to pay a licensing fee arising from a dispute over a breach of trademark.[233] Given that this taxable supply arises from the court order itself or settlement agreement it should not result in any adjustment events, unless part of the order also relates to an earlier supply (e.g., damages for breach of contract) in which case apportionment might be required and a possible adjustment in relation to the damages component only.[234]

Third, a settlement or court order might arise from a dispute relating to an earlier taxable supply, such as an order to pay damages for breach of an earlier contract to provide goods or for payment of a debt.[235] An order relating to an earlier supply that is GST-free or input taxed will not give rise to a GST liability.[236] However, a Category 1 adjustment event can occur when an out of court settlement or court order changes the consideration that was the subject of the initial supply provided the other relevant requirements are met.[237] Attribution to the relevant tax period rather than an adjustment suffices in circumstances where the payment constitutes the consideration provided for an earlier or current supply (rather than alters consideration previously provided) or if the supplier or recipient attributes on a cash basis or if no invoice was issued for the supply and no part of the consideration for the supply was provided or received in any previous tax period.[238] If the order or settlement relates to a debt previously subject to a decreasing adjustment under the bad debt provisions, an increasing adjustment will be required (i.e., a Category 2 adjustment).[239]

[E] Changes in Character

As §9.02[B] explained, a VAT adjustment might be necessary when a buyer purchases a good or service for a particular purpose but later changes the *purpose or use* to which the good or service is put in a way that changes the VAT payable or their entitlement to input credits. As that section explained, these changes might occur at the time of the supply or afterwards with different rules applying to each.

[1] Change in Character at the Time of Supply

A change occurring at the time of the supply including the redirecting of a good previously bound for export (as a GST-free supply) to a domestic location (as a taxable supply) would be considered a Category 1 adjustment event because it has the effect of

233. ATO, GSTR 2001/4, *supra* n. 227, 9, [48]-[49], 12, [68], 19, [105].
234. ATO, GSTR 2001/4, *supra* n. 227, 20, [115], 21, [120]-[122], 21-22, [123]-[125].
235. ATO, GSTR 2001/4, *supra* n. 227, 8-9, [45]-[47], 18, [101].
236. ATO, GSTR 2001/4, *supra* n. 227, 32 – 'Appendix 1'.
237. These requirements include that the entity reports on an accruals basis and that the adjustment event occurs in a subsequent tax period: *see* §9.04[A]; ANTS Act 1999, *supra* n. 12, section 19-10(1); ATO, GSTR 2001/4, *supra* n. 227, at 18, [103], 22-24, [127]-[136].
238. ATO, GSTR 2001/4, *supra* n. 227, at 22, [127].
239. ATO, GSTR 2001/4, *supra* n. 227, 23, [130]-[131]. *See* §9.05[C].

'causing a supply or acquisition to become, or stop being, a taxable supply or creditable acquisition'.[240] If the adjustment event arose in a subsequent tax period, either an increasing adjustment arises (as would be required under the example) or a decreasing adjustment (with mirror obligations for the recipient of the supply in relation to the relevant creditable acquisitions). If the adjustment event arose in the *same* tax period in which the GST or an input credit is attributed, this is accounted for in calculating the GST payable or input tax credits for that period (and no adjustment is required).[241]

By contrast, a subsequent change in the extent to which a taxpayer uses an acquisition for a creditable purpose (thereby affecting a purchaser's ability to claim input tax credits on that acquisition) is not a Category 1 adjustment event because such a change does not cause the acquisition to become (or stop it from being) a creditable acquisition.[242] Such scenarios are instead dealt with as Category 3 adjustments under various special rules.

[2] Subsequent Changes in Character Affecting Creditable Purpose and Entitlement to Input Tax Credits

Most rules are contained in Division 129 of the *ANTS Act 1999*. Others rules, some of which have already been discussed,[243] are not further addressed in this section (unless specifically relevant).[244] These include special rules that permit a decreasing adjustment for stock on hand that was purchased prior to registration (for which input credits have not already been claimed)[245] as well as rules requiring an increasing adjustment when an entity ceases its registration, thereby losing its (remaining) entitlement to input tax credits on all items previously received (including goods, services, real property whether or not held on capital account).[246]

An adjustment under Division 129 can arise for an acquisition or importation in respect of any *adjustment period*, whether or not such an acquisition or importation was initially treated as a creditable acquisition or creditable importation.[247] An adjustment arises when the *actual application of a thing* differs from its *intended*

240. ANTS Act 1999, *supra* n. 12, section 19-10(1)(c) including the example to the section which states that: 'If goods that are supplied for export are not exported within the time provided in section 38-185, the supply is likely to become a taxable supply after originally being a supply that was GST-free'; GSTR 2000/19, *supra* n. 105, at 17, [62]-[63].
241. ATO, GSTR 2000/19, *supra* n. 105, at 4, [15].
242. ATO, GSTR 2000/19, *supra* n. 105, 17, [64].
243. *See, e.g.*, third party payments (ANTS Act 1999, *supra* n. 12, Div. 134), *see supra* §9.05[A][3]), bad debts (Div. 136, *see supra* §9.05[C]), adjustments from cancelled supplies (Div. 142-B, *see supra* §9.05[B]).
244. *See, e.g.*, rules relating to adjustments arising from: entities that elect for annual apportionment for input tax credits used for partly creditable purpose (ANTS Act 1999, *supra* n. 12, Div. 131), providing additional consideration under a gross-up clause (Div. 133), distributions from deceased estates (Div. 139), Tradex scheme goods (Div. 141).
245. ANTS Act 1999, *supra* n. 12, section 11-5(d), Div. 137; *Re GOL-HUT Pty Ltd as trustee for the Helensvale Unit Trust v. FCT* [2013] AATA 199, [21], [25]. Note that Div. 60 also permits input tax credits for eligible pre-incorporation expenses incurred up to six months prior to registration: ANTS Act 1999, Div. 60.
246. ANTS Act 1999, *supra* n. 12, Div. 138 (note exceptions in section 138-17).
247. ANTS Act 1999, *supra* n. 12, Div. 129.

application or, in the event of a previous adjustment having been made, from the *former application of the thing* in a manner that affects the creditable purpose for which the thing is used.[248] The legislation outlines a number of steps necessary to calculate a Division 129 adjustment; however, the bulk of the work lies in a comparison of the 'extent (if any)' to which the actual *application*[249] (or use) of a *thing*[250] for a *creditable purpose*[251] (i.e., the extent to which the thing is applied in carrying on the taxpayer's enterprise) has differed from the *intended* or *former* application of the thing for a creditable purpose.[252] Establishing (and comparing) intention and application (or use) is therefore crucial.

The rules enable an adjustment to be made when, for example, a car previously purchased for personal use (with no entitlement to input-tax credits) is later used for a registered business (with entitlement to input tax credits to the extent of the new creditable purpose).[253] Division 129 can also apply to the reverse situation whereby a good originally acquired as a creditable acquisition is subsequently applied solely or partly to private or domestic use with a corresponding need for an increasing adjustment by virtue of a reduced entitlement to an input tax credit.[254]

As the examples in §9.02[B] demonstrated, changes in use might be *intended* or *unintended* and both use and intention can change over time. Intention is objectively ascertained and, therefore, factual characterization and supporting evidence is crucial.[255] The legislative text in Division 129 accommodates dual (or multiple) concurrent intentions, dual (or multiple) applications, dual (or multiple) consecutive intentions or applications or a combination of both.[256] The application of the Division 129 rules has

248. ANTS Act 1999, *supra* n. 12, section 129-40(1).
249. Apply is broadly and inclusively defined in the legislation and has been broadly interpreted by the ATO to include sale, disposal, destruction, use or even holding an asset (or allowing another to do these things): *ibid.*, sections 129-55 and 195-1 – 'apply'; ATO, GSTR 2009/4, *supra* n. 40, at 8-9, [34]-[35], 8, [33] – the ordinary meaning of apply relevantly includes 'to put to use, employ', 'to devote to some specific purpose' and 'make use of as relevant or suitable; employ': *Macquarie Dictionary* (4th ed., 2005).
250. *See supra* n. 40 for discussion of the term "thing".
251. A thing is applied for a creditable purpose to the extent it is applied in *carrying on* an *enterprise* but not to the extent that the application relates to making supplies that are input taxed or of a private or domestic nature. Creditable purpose in the context of Div. 129 has a similar meaning to creditable acquisitions: ANTS Act 1999, *supra* n. 12, sections 129-50, and 195-1 'carrying on', *cf.* sections 11-15 and 15-10; ATO, GSTR 2009/4, *supra* n. 40, at 21-22, [62]-[66].
252. ANTS Act 1999, *supra* n. 12, section 129-40(1) – Step 1, – Step 2.
253. ANTS Act 1999, *supra* n. 12, sections 11-15(1) and 11-15(2); ATO, Goods and Services Tax Ruling GSTR 2000/24, Div. 129 – Making Adjustments for Changes in Extent of Creditable Purpose, 5, [14] (28 June 2000).
254. Alternatively, Div. 130 can apply to this scenario although it is narrower in scope – only applying to goods (i.e., tangible personal property but not services and real property) and only applying from solely creditable acquisitions to solely non-creditable acquisitions. The application of Div. 130 precludes that of Div. 129 and vice versa: ANTS Act, *supra* n. 12, sections 129-15, 130-5(1), 130-5(3) and 195-5 – 'goods'. *See* Austl. GST Guide Commentary [¶17-580] (CCH Australia, online).
255. ATO, GSTR 2009/4, *supra* n. 40, at 6, [23]-[24], 12, [45].
256. ANTS Act 1999, *supra* n. 12, sections 129-50(1) and 129-50(2). The ATO expressly acknowledges this: ATO, GSTR 2009/4, *supra* n. 40, at 16-17, [48]-[53].

been prominent in the real property sector particularly in relation to various build-to-rent schemes.[257]

Changes (to intention and use) can result in different tax treatment. Consider the following example: two different developers separately construct residential premises, hold those premises (without more) for two years, and then sell those premises. Developer 1 does so with the intention of selling and is therefore entitled to full input tax credits. Developer 2 holds the residential premises with the intention of leasing and so is denied input credits (for the period for which they held the residential premises with the requisite intent).[258] There is an obvious incentive for Developer 2 to characterize their intention as one to sell rather than lease the said premises. However, their ability to do so is constrained by the objective ascertainment of that intention and by the two-step test which relies both on (objective) intention and application/use.

In relation to intention, the ATO states in a Ruling that a 'preponderance of relevant factors to support a conclusion that premises are being held for the purposes of sale' would be required such as marketing of the premises for sale, business plans, financial documents, and the length of time the asset is held (the shorter the length the more likely an intention to sell rather than hold as an investment).[259] In the only High Court case to concern the application of a Category 3 adjustment provision,[260] the Court held that a taxpayer was liable to pay additional GST under an increasing adjustment provision that required the recipient of the sale of a going concern (ordinarily a GST-free supply)[261] to do so if they *intend* that some or all of the supplies made through the going concern will be input-taxed supplies.[262] The going concern consisted entirely of the transfer of the leasehold reversion on three serviced apartments and the taxpayer had expressly assumed the ongoing rights and obligations under the lease (i.e., input taxed residential supplies) in the contract of sale.[263] This objective intent to make input-taxed supplies was established by the contracts and the proper characterization of the rights subject of the supply and could not be circumvented by claims that the taxpayer subjectively intended otherwise.

The AAT decision in *GXCX* shows that the two-step test which requires a comparison of intention to the actual *application* of the thing means that intention

257. ATO, 'Build-to-Rent Property Developments', https://www.ato.gov.au/Business/GST/In-detail/Your-industry/Property/GST-and-residential-property/?page=4#Build_to_rent_property_developments.

258. ATO, GSTR 2009/4, *supra* n. 40, at 9, [37]; ANTS Act 1999, *supra* n. 12, section 129-50(2).

259. ATO, GSTR 2009/4, *supra* n. 40, at 12-13, [44]-[47].

260. The case concerned ANTS Act 1999, *supra* n. 12, section 135-5 which requires an initial adjustment by the recipient of a supply of a GST-free going concern (section 38-325) when the recipient intends that some or all of the supplies made through the enterprise to which the supply relates will be supplies that are neither taxable supplies nor GST-free supplies. Section 135-10 also incorporates Div. 129 to require adjustments when the recipient of a GST-free supply of a going concern subsequently changes the application of a thing in a manner affecting creditable purpose.

261. *Commissioner of Taxation v. MBI Properties Pty Ltd* (2014) 254 CLR 376, 390, [32]; ANTS Act 1999, *supra* n. 12, section 38-325.

262. *Commissioner of Taxation v. MBI Properties Pty Ltd* (2014) 254 CLR 376, 384-385, [13]-[14], 393, [46]; ANTS Act 1999, *supra* n. 12, sections 135-5(1)(b), 40-35 and 156-5.

263. *Commissioner of Taxation v. MBI Properties Pty Ltd* (2014) 254 CLR 376, 385, [17], 390-392, [32], [35]-[41], 3939 [46]; ANTS Act 1999, *supra* n. 12, section 38-325.

alone will not be determinative. In that case a developer intended to sell newly constructed residential apartments – it sold some but retained others and leased them for a number of years with an intention to sell in the future.[264] Although the Tribunal accepted that a taxpayer can have different but contemporaneous purposes (e.g., an intention to lease and intention to sell),[265] it found that, for the leased residential apartments, the 'application during this period was entirely for a non-creditable purpose' and the apartments 'were not *applied* for the creditable purpose of selling merely because the holding company had an intention to sell at some time in the future'.[266]

An adjustment is only required under the rules, if the acquisition or importation exceeds a certain threshold calculated on a GST-exclusive value of the thing acquired.[267] This threshold is AUD 10,000 for acquisitions or importations that relate to business finance (mostly relevant to financial services entities)[268] and AUD 1,000 for all other acquisitions/importations.[269]

These actual and intended or former applications are calculated as percentages.[270] If the actual application of a thing for a creditable purpose is *less than* its intended or former use then an *increasing adjustment* is required (corresponding with a reduced entitlement to an input tax credit over the period); if the actual application is *more than* its intended or previous use then a *decreasing adjustment* results (corresponding with an increased entitlement to an input tax credit over the period).[271]

The ATO expects that taxpayers use a fair and reasonable method for apportioning use of a thing between creditable and non-creditable purposes.[272] There is much guidance on the methodologies available as well as dispute over acceptable methods.[273]

Unlike a Category 1 adjustment which is attributable to the tax period when a taxpayer becomes *aware* of an adjustment, a Division 129 adjustment is attributable to

264. *Re GXCX* [2009] AATA 569; 2009 ATC 1-012; (2009) 73 ATR 380, [1]-[2], [20]; ATO, GSTR 2009/4, *supra* n. 40, at 11, [42]-[43] – Example 2.
265. *Re GXCX* [2009] AATA 569, [23]-[27], [32].
266. *Re GXCX* [2009] AATA 569, [34], [35].
267. An adjustment is not required when a thing acquired for a creditable purpose is subsequently gifted to certain charities unless specific conditions are met: ANTS Act 1999, *supra* n. 12, section 129-45; ATO, GSTR 2000/24, *supra* n. 253, at 8-9, [26]-[27].
268. ANTS Act 1999, *supra* n. 12, sections 129-5(2), 129-10(1) and 129-10(3). An acquisition can only relate to business finance for an entity that exceeds the financial acquisitions threshold, which is exceeded when an entity makes (or is likely to make) sufficient financial acquisitions over a 12 month period (excluding borrowings for non-input-taxed supplies) so that the *entitlement* to input-tax credits on such acquisitions exceeds either the lesser of AUD 150,000 or 10% of the total amount of input tax credits to which the entity would be entitled: at 11-15(4); Div. 189; ATO, Goods and Services Tax Ruling 2003/9, Financial Acquisitions Threshold (14 May 2003).
269. ANTS Act 1999, *supra* n. 12, section 129-10(2).
270. ANTS Act 1999, *supra* n. 12, section 129-40(2).
271. ANTS Act 1999, *supra* n. 12, section 129-40 (1) – Steps 3 and 4.
272. ATO, GSTR 2000/24, *supra* n. 253, at 14-15, [48]-[55]; ATO, GSTR 2009/4, *supra* n. 40, at 25-38, [81]-[144]; ATO, Goods and Services Tax Ruling GSTR 2006/4, Goods and Services Tax: Determining the Extent of Creditable Purpose for Claiming Input Tax Credits and for Making Adjustments for Changes in Extent of Creditable Purpose (12 April 2006).
273. *See*, e.g., *A Taxpayer v. Commissioner of Taxation* [2011] AATA 160; 2011 ATC 1-029.

the relevant tax period that is the *adjustment period* established under the relevant rules.[274] An *adjustment period* is a *tax period* (varying according to whether the taxpayer reports monthly, quarterly or yearly) commencing at least 12 months after the end of the tax period to which the acquisition or importation is attributable[275] and ending on or as near to 30 June as possible in any year.[276]

The legislation provides time limits on the amount of adjustment periods that apply depending on the type of acquisition/importation and its value. These range from one adjustment period for acquisitions from AUD 10,001-50,000 that relate to business finance or up to 10 adjustment periods for any acquisition more than AUD 500,000.[277] Otherwise the type of acquisition (i.e., good, service or real property on capital or revenue account) is irrelevant.[278] The number of adjustment periods can be shortened in particular circumstances.[279]

The Commissioner states that the GST-exclusive value on an acquisition is determined on a per-item basis. Although this avoids pushing an entity into a higher number of adjustment periods, it can mean that an entity needs to keep track of multiple acquisitions across multiple different adjustment periods.[280] This creates additional complexity for progressive or periodic supplies such as construction services performed and paid in instalments.[281] With each period treated as a separate supply attributable to the relevant tax period[282] and the provisions of Division 129 applying to periodic supplies,[283] numerous overlapping adjustment periods might arise which presents significant complexity and compliance risks especially in the property sector.[284]

274. ANTS Act 1999, *supra* n. 12, section 129-90.
275. Or would be attributable if it were a creditable acquisition or creditable importation: ANTS Act 1999, *supra* n. 12, section 129-20(1)(a).
276. ANTS Act 1999, *supra* n. 12, section 129-20(1)(b) – the 'as near to' requirement is for those entities whose tax period does not end on 30 June. The 'in any year' requirement is presumably read to mean from the commencement of the tax period until 30 June in any given year by which time the adjustment period ends.
277. ANTS Act 1999, *supra* n. 12, section 129-20.
278. Millar & Moon, *supra* n. 53, at [2.1.3.3].
279. Circumstances include: by determination of the Commissioner (relevant only to acquisitions/importations that do not relate to business finance): ANTS Act 1999, *supra* n. 12, section 129-20(3); if the relevant entity dies (if an individual), is wound up (if a company) or has their registration cancelled: at sections 27-40 and 129-20(1); or by virtue of special rules that apply if a thing acquired is disposed of, destroyed or only acquired for a particular period: at section 129-25; ATO, GSTR 2000/24, *supra* n. 253, at 10-13 [33]-[44].
280. ATO, GSTR 2000/24, *supra* n. 253, at 7, [18].
281. *Commissioner of Taxation v. MBI Properties Pty Ltd* (2014) 254 CLR 376, 383-384, [10], 391, [36].
282. ANTS Act 1999, *supra* n. 12, sections 156-1 and 156-22.
283. ANTS Act 1999, *supra* n. 12, section 156-20.
284. *See further* ATO, GSTR 2009/4, *supra* n. 40, at 21-22, [64]-[66]; ATO, GSTR 2000/24, *supra* n. 253, at 7, [20]. For a preliminary exploration of the issues involved, *see* Austl. GST Guide Commentary [¶17-520] (CCH Australia, online).

Generally, a taxpayer must keep records that are sufficient for GST liability to be readily ascertained for five years after making a creditable acquisition or importation.[285] For acquisitions/importations subject to Division 129 adjustments, sufficient records or a reasonable estimate of the changes in the extent of the use of the acquisition/importation for a creditable purpose might be required over a longer period of time.[286]

§9.06 THE EU VAT APPROACH TO VAT ADJUSTMENTS

The EU VAT Directive provides separate adjustment rules for the supplier and the recipient of a supply. Member States have the right to determine conditions and details for both sets of adjustment rules.[287]

Article 90 of the EU VAT Directive is the key provision for adjustments to the taxable amount for the supplier. Three main categories of adjustment are identified: (1) cancellation and refusal;[288] (2) total or partial non-payment, and (3) situations where the price is reduced after the supply takes place (price reductions). Member States must provide in their national law that one of these three events will reduce the taxable amount accordingly. Category 1 and 3 are the equivalent of a Category 1 adjustment in the Australian GST rules; Category 2 on 'non-payment' is the equivalent of bad debts (also Category 2). The EU VAT Directive also contains a number of special rules for specific adjustment questions (e.g., regarding currency issues upon importation,[289] and costs of returnable packing material[290]), which are not further addressed in this chapter.

Established CJEU case law recognizes that Article 90 of the EU VAT Directive implements the principle of neutrality (since it ensures that the amount of VAT payable is strictly proportional to the consideration actually received by the taxable person).[291] Therefore the CJEU tends to interpret Article 90 broadly to require Member States to

285. Taxation Administration Act 1953 (Cth) Sch. 1, section 382-5; ATO, GSTR 2000/24, *supra* n. 253, at 24, [89].
286. Taxation Administration Act 1953 (Cth) Sch. 1, section 382-5(1)(4); ATO, GSTR 2000/24, *supra* n. 253, at 25, [91].
287. EU VAT Directive, Articles 90 and 184-192, *See* also CJEU, 28 May 2020, Case C-684/18, *World Comm Trading*, ECLI:EU:C:2020:403, paragraphs 27-29.
288. Article 90(1) lists cancellation and refusal with a comma in between ('cancellation, refusal or total or partial non-payment') which indicates that these are two different adjustment events. Moreover, some language versions of the Directive even list 'termination' as a fifth category. In the authors' opinion, however, the three terms cancellation, refusal and termination have no substantially different meaning for VAT purposes; all three terms refer to the scenario that a contract is terminated based on civil law by one of the parties and not fully performed (as initially agreed). The Court distinguishes between 'cancellation' and 'refusal' by referring to their different legal consequences as regards temporal effects: 'cancellation with retroactive effect' (*ex tunc*) and 'refusal with effect for the future' (*ex nunc*); *see* CJEU, 12 October 2017, Case C-404/16, *Lombard*, ECLI:EU:C:2017:759, paragraph 31.
289. EU VAT Directive, Article 91.
290. EU VAT Directive, Article 92.
291. *Elida Gibbs*, *supra* n. 17, paragraphs 28-30; confirmed, amongst others, in *Kraft Foods Polska*, *supra* n. 64, paragraph 27; *see* in more detail van Doesum et al., *Fundamentals of EU VAT Law*, *supra* n. 9, at 227-228.

reduce the taxable amount and, consequently, the amount of VAT payable by the taxable person whenever, after a transaction has been concluded, part or all of the consideration has not been received by the taxable person.[292] Although Member States can in theory derogate from the rules relating to total or partial non-payment (Category 2), CJEU case law has significantly constrained the scope of this optional derogation (*see* in more detail §9.06[C]).

Articles 185-192 provide the adjustment rules for the recipient of a supply. Under these provisions, an initial deduction shall be adjusted when it is higher or lower than that to which the taxable person was entitled. In particular, adjustments shall be made when some change occurs in the factors used to determine the amount to be deducted after the VAT return is submitted. The provision lists the same three examples for adjustment events: (1) cancellation;[293] (2) total or partial non-payment; and (3) price reductions.[294] Based on the wording, Member States have some leeway with respect to adjustments for total or partial non-payment because they are not obliged to implement an adjustment mechanism but merely 'may' require adjustment of input VAT to be made.

All three categories explicitly listed in both adjustment provisions relate to changes in quantum. In contrast to the Australian GST rules, the EU VAT Directive does not provide a list of more detailed examples (e.g., return of a good supplied, discount, agreed change in the price, etc.). However, it is generally understood that these scenarios are covered by the adjustment rules. Whereas the list of adjustment events in the provision from the perspective of the supplier (Article 90) is exhaustive, the list in the adjustment provisions from the perspective of the recipient is not. The phrase 'some change occurs in the factors used to determine the amount to be deducted' in Article 185, therefore, also includes changes in character (i.e., the equivalent of a Category 3 adjustment event in Australia).

EU Member States' legislators have implemented these adjustment rules in different ways into their national VAT law. For example, the *Umsatzsteuergesetz 1994* (Austrian VAT Code, or UStG) provides one adjustment rule for both supplier and recipient, requiring either to adjust the VAT payable or the amount of input tax credit if the taxable base of the taxable supply has changed.[295] A similar legal technique appears in the German *Umsatzsteuergesetz* (German VAT Code, or UStG).[296] The Austrian VAT Code (UStG) further specifies that an adjustment is to be made in the following three scenarios: first, if consideration for a supply has become irrecoverable; second, if the supply has not been performed; and third, if the supply has been reversed. The Austrian VAT Guidelines (UStR 2000) list some frequent examples as including: the return of consideration (e.g., in the event of partial reversal of the legal transaction), reduction in consideration (e.g., discounts, rebates), increases in consideration (e.g., due to a value assurance clause), the irrecoverability of the consideration,

292. CJEU, 3 July 1997, Case C-330/95, *Goldsmiths*, ECLI:EU:C:1997:339, paragraph 16; *Kraft Foods Polska, supra* n. 64, paragraph 26.
293. The term 'refusal' is not separately mentioned in EU VAT Directive, Article 185.
294. EU VAT Directive, Article 185.
295. Umsatzsteuergesetz 1994 ('Austrian VAT Code (UStG)'), section 16.
296. Umsatzsteuergesetz ('German VAT Code (UStG)'), section 17.

and the waiver of receivables (debts).[297] Although the wording of the Austrian VAT rules on adjustments is slightly different from that in the EU VAT Directive, it is generally understood that there are no material differences from the EU VAT Directive.[298] However, one notable difference is that the Austrian rules limit the obligation to adjust the taxable amount to 'taxed supplies' which seems to exclude exempt supplies.[299]

Neither the EU VAT Directive nor the Austrian VAT Code (UStG) provide details on how the adjustment should be calculated and are therefore less prescriptive than the Australian legislation.

Member States are also left to determine the relevant criteria and proof in support of an adjustment subject to the requirement that such measures comply with the principle of proportionality and not undermine VAT neutrality, i.e., they should not make it impossible or excessively difficult to reduce the taxable amount.[300] Neither the EU VAT Directive nor the Austrian VAT Code (UStG) require specific documentary proof (such as an adjustment note) for an adjustment to occur. The EU VAT Directive does not require that an adjustment on the side of the supplier is automatically and systematically linked with an adjustment on the side of the recipient. In fact, the CJEU held in the *FIRIN* case that the fact that the VAT payable by the supplier had not itself been adjusted did not affect the right of the tax authority to obtain repayment of the VAT deducted by the purchaser.[301] The *Kraft Foods Polsksa* case indicates that Member States are permitted (but not obliged) to link the adjustment of VAT liabilities at the level of the supplier to the receipt of a correcting invoice by the recipient which is justified by ensuring the integrity of VAT collection and seems similar to the Australian approach of an 'adjustment note'[302] (*see* §9.05). However, the CJEU also ruled in that case that Poland could not insist on this receipt being in a specific format that made it practically impossible to force the purchaser to comply with.[303]

The EU VAT Directive does not provide any time limit for an adjustment relating to changes in quantum but leaves this to the discretion by Member States (for time limits on adjustments relating to changes in character/use on the input VAT side, *see* § 9.06[E][2][c]). The Austrian VAT Code (UStG) also does not specify a time limit for VAT adjustments relating to changes in quantum.[304] According to prevailing opinion in

297. Umsatzsteuerrichtlinien 2000 ('Austrian VAT Guidelines (UStR 2000)'), as of 28 November 2019, marginal number 2382.
298. Hans Georg Ruppe & Markus Achatz, *Umsatzsteuergesetz* §16 paragraph 10 (5th ed., LexisNexis, 2017).
299. Austrian VAT Code (UStG), section 16(1).
300. CJEU, 15 May 2014, Case C-337/13, *Almos Agrárkülkereskedelmi kft*, ECLI:EU:C:2014:328, paragraphs 37-38; *Enzo Di Maura, supra* n. 23, paragraphs 23-29.
301. CJEU, 13 March 2014, Case C-107/13, *FIRIN*, ECLI:EU:C:2014:151, paragraph 57.
302. *See* Rebecca Millar, *Taxable Amount: Fiscal Neutrality in Action*, in ECJ – *Recent Developments in Value Added Tax* 221, 237 (Michael Lang et al., eds., Linde, 2014).
303. *Kraft Foods Polska, supra* n. 64, paragraph 33, 38-42; confirmed in CJEU, 6 December 2018, Case C-672/17, *Tratave*, ECLI:EU:C:2018:989, paragraphs 36-42.
304. In general, there is a five-year limitation period (extendable up to 10 years in cases of suspected tax evasion) in Austria beginning from the end of the year in which the tax claim first arose: Bundesabgabenordnung ('Austrian Federal Fiscal Code (BAO)'), sections 207(2) and 208(1)(a). However, prevailing opinion considers that this rule does not apply to consideration

Austria, the supplier may (in the case of a reduction of the taxable amount) or must (in the case of an increase of the taxable amount) therefore make an adjustment of the VAT payable and a correction of invoices without any time limitation if a change in the consideration occurs subsequent to the transaction.[305] The EU VAT Directive does not specify whether an adjustment has *ex tunc* or *ex nunc* effect. The Austrian VAT Code (UStG) provides that the correction is to be made for the tax period in which the change in consideration occurred (*ex nunc*).[306]

[A] The Parties Agree to a Change in Price

[1] Price Reductions

Article 90 of the EU VAT Directive requires an adjustment for 'price reductions' (e.g., a rebate, discount, etc.) that occur *after* a supply takes place.[307] This covers any reduction in the price irrespective of whether the reduction has been agreed between both parties to the supply (e.g., correcting errors) or is granted unilaterally by the supplier (e.g., discount, rebate). The EU VAT Directive includes a separate rule for discounts and rebates in Article 79 which provides that the taxable amount shall not include price reductions by way of discount for early payment and price discounts and rebates granted to the customer and obtained by them at the time of the supply.[308] Article 79 of the EU VAT Directive is the equivalent rule (of Article 90) for any rebate or discount granted *prior to* or *at the time of* the supply which is taken into account when calculating the taxable amount from the outset and will therefore not require a consideration adjustment.

[2] Discounts

The VAT treatment of discounts for early payment has not yet been addressed by the CJEU. According to prevailing Austrian opinion, the granting of a discount is to be seen as a commitment by the supplier to grant a certain price reduction if payment is made within a certain period, therefore a consideration adjustment only occurs when the recipient of a supply takes advantage of the discount (i.e., pays within the agreed time period). If the recipient does not make use of the cash discount, there is no change in the tax base.[309]

---

adjustments as section 16(10) is *lex specialis* and 'is not subject to a time limit and continues to exist even if the underlying tax liability is already statute-barred': Ruppe & Achatz, *supra* n. 298, at §16, paragraph 67.

305. Ruppe & Achatz, *supra* n. 298, §16, paragraph 67.
306. Austrian VAT Code (UStG), section 16(1)(2) (last sentence).
307. EU VAT Directive, Article 90(1).
308. The definition in Article 79, referring to discounts and rebates, is regarded as mostly redundant, since these amounts should be excluded from the taxable amount as defined in Article 73 EU VAT Directive in the first place (as they are not paid 'in return for the supply'): *see* van Doesum et al., *Fundamentals of EU VAT Law*, *supra* n. 9, 275.
309. *See*, amongst others, Ruppe & Achatz, *supra* n. 298, §16, paragraph 43.

According to the *Umsatzsteuerrichtlinien 2000* ('Austrian VAT Guidelines (UStR 2000)'), a discount may have different VAT effects depending on whether the cash discount is deducted from the total price including VAT (gross method) or only from the payment (net method). If the discount is calculated from the gross amount, the amount after deduction of the discount and the discount amount itself contain VAT. Only the cash discount amount minus the VAT included represents the amount of the adjustment.[310] This is the most commonly used procedure in Austria.

Some German scholars argue that a discount could, alternatively, be seen as remuneration for an independent service provided by the purchaser, namely the pre-financing of the purchase price. On this view, the consideration for the underlying supply of the good would always be the price after deduction of the discount (cash price). If the discount is not used by the purchaser, the amount of the discount would qualify as consideration for the supply of credit (exempt from VAT) granted by the supplier.[311] However, this seems to be a minority view.

[3] Rebates

The term 'rebate' covers situations where a partial reduction of the total price occurs after the supply has taken place; reductions covering 100% of the price are not considered to be 'rebates' or 'price reductions' within the meaning of the EU VAT rules.[312] If the price is reduced by 100%, the transaction may qualify as a supply free of charge and, consequently, trigger a taxable self-supply.[313]

A consideration adjustment resulting from a rebate is only available for the supplier when the rebate is actually used by the recipient, the mere possibility of use is insufficient for a reduction of the taxable amount by the supplier of that rebate.[314] The recipient is obliged to make an adjustment of input VAT deduction upon use of a rebate, even if she does not have a separate invoice relating to the discounts granted.[315]

The CJEU has ruled on the VAT treatment of rebates in multiple party transactions and third-party rebates in several cases and, in direct contrast to the Australian case law, has held that rebates granted to or by a third party who is not in a direct supply relationship with the respective taxable person can lead to a reduction of the taxable amount and the VAT payable.

310. Austrian VAT Guidelines (UStR 2000), as of 28 November 2019, marginal number 2383.
311. Holger Stadie, in *Umsatzsteuergesetz* §17, paragraph 282 (Günter Rau & Erich Dürrwächter, eds., loose-leaf, Otto Schmidt, 176th suppl., March 2018).
312. CJEU, 27 April 1999, Case C-48/97, *Kuwait Petroleum*, ECLI:EU:C:1999:203, paragraphs 16-17.
313. *Kuwait Petroleum*, *supra* n. 312, paragraphs 16 et seq.
314. CJEU, 29 May 2001, Case C-86/99, *Freemans plc.*, ECLI:EU:C:2001:291 – a mail order company can only claim credit for the discount given to the agent for their own purchases at the time the agent actually uses the accumulated commission (e.g., by reduction against their balance) and not when the commission is posted to the agent's commission account.
315. *World Comm Trading*, *supra* n. 287, paragraphs 33-38.

The leading case is the 1996 decision in *Elida Gibbs*[316] concerning a toiletries manufacturer who sold goods to wholesalers and also reimbursed retailers for discounts claimed by final consumers via money-off or cash back coupons (i.e., a third-party payment). The CJEU ruled that the manufacturer was entitled to a reduction of the taxable amount on the supply to the wholesaler equal to the amount of the reimbursement paid out to the retailer, even though the manufacturer was not in a direct legal relationship with, nor had made a direct supply to, the retailer. The CJEU decided this despite the requirement in Article 73 of the EU VAT Directive that the taxable amount 'shall include everything which constitutes consideration obtained or to be obtained by the supplier, *in return for the supply*' which suggests that there should be a direct and close link between a specific payment (and a corresponding rebate) to a specific supply.[317] The Court justified the decision by reference to the principle of neutrality, i.e., tax authorities should not receive more VAT than was actually paid by the final consumer, at the expense of the taxable person who should not have to pay VAT on a sum exceeding the sum it finally received.[318] The *Elida Gibbs* approach has been confirmed in subsequent CJEU decisions.[319]

Interestingly, the CJEU also ruled that, notwithstanding the reduction of the taxable amount for Elida Gibbs, the wholesalers would still be entitled to their initial deduction of input VAT (instead of on the reduced taxable amount) because 'there is no need to readjust the taxable amount for the intermediate transactions'.[320] The taxable amount of the retailers, for example, consists of the price paid by the consumers and the amount reimbursed by the manufacturer (as third-party consideration).[321] Scholars have criticized this result from a policy perspective because the tax authorities in essence finance the difference between the VAT payable by Elida Gibbs and the VAT deductible by the wholesaler.[322] The Austrian tax authorities have addressed this issue by requiring that the last customer in the chain, who has a right to input VAT deduction, correct the amount of input tax deduction.[323]

The ruling in *Elida Gibbs* was confirmed and extended in the *Boehringer* case in 2017.[324] The case concerned a rather complicated discount structure applied outside the supply chain. A pharmaceutical company offered discount via two streams: first,

316. *See* Ad van Doesum and Frank Nellen, *Taxable Amount and VAT Rates*, in *CJEU – Recent Developments in Value Added Tax 2017* 251, 264-274 (Michael Lang et al., eds., Linde, 2018).
317. *Cf.* Opinion of AG Fennelly in C-317/94, *Elida Gibbs*, ECLI:EU:C:1996:255, paragraphs 35-37.
318. *Elida Gibbs, supra* n. 17, paragraphs 29-31. On the principle of neutrality as a principle of interpretation, *see* CJEU, 19 July 2012, Case C-44/11, *Deutsche Bank AG*, ECLI:EU:C:2012:484, paragraph 45. Van Doesum & Nellen, *supra* n. 316, at 265; *contra* Jeroen Bijl, *VAT: 'Money Off Vouchers' and 'Cash Back Schemes' – What Are The Problems and How Can They Be Solved?* 21(5) EC Tax Rev. 262, 266 (2012).
319. CJEU, 15 October 2002, Case C-427/98, *Commission v. Germany*, ECLI:EU:C:2002:581; CJEU, 16 January 2003, Case C-398/99, *Yorkshire Co-operatives Ltd.*, ECLI:EU:C:2003:20.
320. *Elida Gibbs, supra* n. 17, paragraph 33.
321. *Yorkshire Co-operatives Ltd, supra* n. 319, paragraph 21.
322. Van Doesum & Nellen, *supra* n. 316, at 267.
323. Austrian VAT Guidelines (UStR 2000), as of 28 November 2019, marginal numbers 2382 and 2396.
324. CJEU, 20 December 2017, Case C-462/16, *Boehringer Ingelheim Pharma GmbH & Co. KG*, ECLI:EU:C:2017:1006.

pharmacies sold medicines to public health insurance funds at a discount and were reimbursed by Boehringer (i.e., a third-party payment); second, pharmacies sold medicines direct to end consumers at full price who could then claim a discount from their private insurers (who were reimbursed by Boehringer). German revenue authorities allowed the first discount to reduce the taxable amount but not the second discount (because the private insurer was not in the supply chain, having neither acquired nor sold the medicinal products). The CJEU ruled that Boehringer was permitted to reduce its taxable amount by the amount it paid in reimbursements for both the first and second discount streams. This reflected the economic reality that either discount method reduced the consideration received by Boehringer and so there had in fact been a reduction in price after the time at which the supply took place in accordance with Article 90(1) of the EU VAT Directive.[325]

The *Boehringer* ruling led to some confusion and possible contradictions with earlier case law which had previously held that discounts or rebates provided by a party outside the supply chain would not affect the taxable amount.[326] If *Boehringer* does extend the *Elida Gibbs* ruling, then it appears that a crucial condition for an adjustment to occur in these multiple party transactions is for the existence of an *enforceable* obligation to grant a rebate and that the supplier of the rebate actually bears the cost of the rebate. In doing so, the Court appears willing to look to the economic substance of the arrangement. However, in taking account of these complex discount structures and going beyond the supply chain for the relevant goods and services there is a risk of disparity between taxable amounts and deductions which needs to be addressed by revenue authorities. Beyond this, some Member States try to ensure the integrity of the *Elida Gibbs* doctrine by requiring taxpayers to satisfy conditions and proof (of the existence of the rebate and its payment) in order for a taxpayer to make VAT adjustments for rebates/vouchers.[327]

The *Elida Gibbs* line of case law does not lead to the result that any third-party rebate leads to a VAT adjustment. A reduction of the taxable base still requires a direct link of the rebate/voucher to a certain supply of goods or services. Therefore, a reduction of the tax base will not arise if the expenditure associated with the redeemed voucher is for general promotional purposes and cannot be allocated to a specific supply of a good or service. For example, the Austrian VAT Guidelines (UStR 2000)

325. The principle of equal treatment influenced the Court's approach: *Boehringer, supra* n. 324, paragraphs 38-42, 46.
326. For criticism *see* van Doesum & Nellen, *supra* n. 316, 271-273; CJEU, 16 January 2014, Case C-300/12, *Ibero Tours GmbH*, ECLI:EU:C:2014:8, paragraphs 28-33 – the CJEU held that the *Elida Gibbs* principles did not apply when a travel agent, acting as an intermediary, granted at his 'own initiative and at his own expense', a price reduction on the principal service provided by the tour operator to the final consumer. Such a discount would not lead to a reduction of the taxable amount, either for the mediated transaction or for the service provided by the travel agency. Key to the decision was that the travel agent was not part of a supply chain leading from the tour operator to the final consumer. This case might be distinguished from *Boehringer* on the basis that the obligation to discount was legally enforceable in *Boehringer* but only volunteered in *Ibero*, but this has not been settled by the case law.
327. For an example of the conditions imposed for a manufacturer to claim an adjustment for a rebate paid to an end-user *see* Austrian VAT Guidelines (UStR 2000), marginal numbers 2397, 2399.

state that if a shopping centre distributed vouchers entitling final consumers to free or discounted supplies at participating retailers in the centre to encourage patronage within the centre, the shopping centre cannot reduce the taxable amount of its supplies by the value of those redeemed vouchers because the redeemed vouchers cannot be linked to a specific supply of good or service made by it.[328]

When rebates take the form of different types of vouchers or rewards then further complications arise. Elida Gibbs concerned third party provided discount and price refund vouchers ('money-off coupons' and 'cash-back coupons'). There are special rules for vouchers in the VAT Directive (applying to vouchers issued after 31 December 2018) dealing with the time of supply for certain vouchers, which do not apply to discount and price refund vouchers.[329] When the discount is offered through a loyalty or rewards program further complications arise as the CJEU case law remains unsettled. The CJEU has addressed some aspects of the VAT treatment of loyalty programs in decisions such as *Kuwait Petroleum* and *Loyalty Management UK*.[330] However, these judgments still leave unresolved issues, have been subject to major criticism, and are also not applied in a consistent way in Member States.[331]

In a recent 2020 decision, the German Federal Fiscal Court held that only the actual use of such bonus points by the customer in a *second* supply leads to a price reduction/reduction of the taxable amount in the *first* supply.[332] The Court reasoned that the same treatment would apply in multiple party transactions, e.g., if the 'point clearing' is outsourced to a third party that makes a monthly settlement on all issued bonus points with the businesses involved in the bonus points scheme. The German Federal Fiscal Court reached this conclusion with reference to the authorities of *Freemans*, *Elida Gibbs* and *Boehringer*. This results in administrative difficulties for the businesses involved, since the supplier who provided the first supply to the customer

328. *See*, Austrian VAT Guidelines (UStR 2000), marginal number 2394.
329. EU VAT Directive, Article 30a-30b. Each transfer of a single-purpose voucher made by a taxable person acting in his/her own name shall be regarded as a supply of the goods or services to which the voucher relates. By contrast, the taxable event for multi-purpose vouchers only occurs at the point in time when the actual handing over of the goods or the actual provision of the services in return for a multi-purpose voucher takes place (the preceding transfer of that multi-purpose voucher shall not be subject to VAT): Recital 4 of the Council Directive (EU) 2016/1065 of 27 June 2016 Amending Directive 2006/112/EC as Regards the Treatment of Vouchers: 'instruments entitling the holder to a discount upon purchase of goods or services but carrying no right to receive such goods or services should not be targeted by these rules'; *see also* Austrian VAT Guidelines (UStR 2000), marginal number 4. For criticism of the limited scope of the voucher rules and a (failed) proposal to amend the VAT Directive to include a rule to treat such discount/refund vouchers as consideration for a separate supply of services from the redeemer to the issuer, *see* European Commission, Working Paper No. 983 – *Questions Raised Following Implementation of the Voucher Directive*, taxud.c.1(2019)7743273, 4 and 24 (13 November 2019); European Commission, *Proposal for a Council Directive Amending Directive 2006/112/EC on the Common System of Value Added Tax, As Regards the Treatment of Vouchers*, COM(2012) 206, 3.
330. Kuwait Petroleum, *supra* n. 312; CJEU, 7 October 2010, Joined Cases C-53/09 and C-55/09, *Loyalty Management UK and Baxi Group*, ECLI:EU:C:2010:590.
331. John Watson & Kate Garcia, *Babylonian Confusion Following the ECJ's Decision on Loyalty Rewards*, 22(1) Int'l VAT Monitor 12, 12 et seq. (2011); Zu & Krever, *supra* n. 22, 80-90.
332. Judgment of the German Federal Fiscal Court (*Bundesfinanzhof*, BFH), 16 January 2020, V R 42/17, BStBl 2020 II, 361.

needs to find out when and how many points the customer used in the subsequent second supply (which might be made at a different retailer). The German court decided the case without referring preliminary questions to the CJEU despite the unsettled CJEU jurisprudence on bonus schemes and loyalty programs. This is regrettable given the inconsistent state of CJEU authority and it risks Member States' courts and authorities developing divergent VAT approaches to an increasingly important issue.

[B] Cancelled Transactions and Early Termination

Article 90(1) of the EU VAT Directive requires Member States to provide a VAT adjustment in the event of 'cancellation' or 'refusal' of a contract. According to CJEU case law, irrespective of the reason for the cancellation or refusal (non-payment or something else), the termination of a contract falls within 'cancellation' or 'refusal' if two prerequisites are met:[333] (i) the termination based on national civil law restores the parties to their original position; and (ii) it is certain that the supplier will not receive the (full) consideration due to the termination.[334]

The EU VAT adjustments rules are dependent on domestic civil law (contract law) to some extent (e.g., to define under what circumstances a party has the right to cancel a contract having the effect of restoring both parties to the original situation). However, in dealing with questions on the VAT treatment of cancellation, early termination and related compensation payments, the Court tends to apply an economic, substance-over-form, approach when analysing the nature and qualification of a specific payment. This reflects a certain division of labour whereby the circumstances giving rise to a 'cancellation' or 'refusal' and the respective consequences turn on domestic civil law, but the concept of consideration for a supply is given its content autonomously as part of EU law.[335] Arguably this EU law, substance-over-form understanding of consideration helps prevent tax planning which might otherwise resort to careful contractual drafting and reliance on technical civil law arguments to favourably characterize the nature and qualification of a payment for VAT purposes.

The 2018 decision of *MEO* concerned the status of the payment of a predetermined amount by a consumer for telecommunications services supplied under a contract with a minimum commitment period, which was received by MEO when the contract was terminated early by a customer or for a reason attributable to the customer. The predetermined amount corresponded to the amount that the operator would have received for the remainder of that period. The CJEU held that the payment was consideration akin to payment of a service charge for the supply of those services.[336] In reasoning similar to the Australian High Court in *Qantas*, the Court stated that the service received by the customer consisted of 'the customer's *right* to

333. *Lombard, supra* n. 288, paragraphs 29-34.
334. *See also* Karoline Spies, *CJEU Case Law on Taxable Amount and Tax Rates 2017 – Comments*, in *CJEU – Recent Developments in Value Added Tax 2017* 281, 282-283 (Michael Lang et al., eds., Linde, 2018); van Doesum & Nellen, *supra* n. 316, 261-263.
335. *See Coöperatieve Aardappelenbewaarplaats, supra* n. 21, paragraph 9.
336. CJEU, 22 November 2018, Case C-295/17, *MEO – Serviços de Comunicações e Multimédia*, ECLI:EU:C:2018:942, paragraph 44.

benefit from the fulfilment, by MEO, of the obligations under the services contract, even if the customer does not wish to avail himself or cannot avail himself of that right for a reason attributable to him'.[337]

In the *Vodafone Portugal* case in 2020, the CJEU extended this reasoning to agreed 'compensation payments' arising from early termination which did not fully correspond to the agreed amount of consideration. The Court highlighted that 'from the perspective of economic reality, which constitutes a fundamental criterion for the application of the common system of VAT, the amount due upon the early termination of the contract seeks to guarantee the operator a minimum contractual remuneration for the service provided'.[338]

These cases rely on reasoning similar to the 2013 decision of *Air France KLM*, whereby the CJEU held that prepaid airfares that, in the event of a 'no show', were non-refundable attracted VAT because:[339]

> [T]he consideration for the price paid when the ticket was purchased consists of the passenger's right to benefit from the performance of obligations arising from the transport contract, regardless of whether the passenger exercises that right, since the airline company fulfils the service by enabling the passenger to benefit from those services.

These cases show that payments in the case of non-use of a service (with or without cancellation/termination) can be subject to EU VAT and do not allow for a consideration adjustment. In all these cases the CJEU has characterized such payments as consideration for the service in terms of the *right* (or the promise) to use something (the assets, the flight, the telecommunication network, etc.) rather than for the actual use. The Court has not found that the payments in question constitute specific damages as opposed to a minimum contractual remuneration for the supplier.

In individual cases, it might be difficult to distinguish such types of consideration for the *right* to use a service from non-taxable cancellation fees/compensation payments. For example, the CJEU held in the *Société Thermale d'Eugénie-les-Bains* case in 2007 that cancellation fees (in the form of the retention of a deposit) in the hotel industry qualify as non-taxable damages, since 'it is regarded as compensation for the loss suffered as a result of client default and [...] has no direct link with the supply of any service for consideration'.[340] The Court in *Air France* distinguished the issue from the treatment of the deposit in *Société Thermale*[341] stating that the forfeited fares did not constitute compensation in the form a contractual indemnity 'for possible harm suffered ... as a result of a passenger's "no-show", but constitutes remuneration, even where the passenger did not benefit from the transport'.[342] In *Société Thermale*, the customer had the right to use the service (hotel) and merely decided not to use it; it is

337. *MEO*, *supra* n. 336, paragraph 45.
338. CJEU, 11 June 2020, Case C-43/19, *Vodafone Portugal*, ECLI:EU:C:2020:465, paragraph 40.
339. CJEU, 23 December 2015, Case C-250/14, *Air France-KLM*, ECLI:EU:C:2015:841, paragraph 28.
340. *Société Thermale d'Eugénie-les-Bains*, *supra* n. 192, paragraph 26.
341. *Air France-KLM*, *supra* n. 339, paragraph 33.
342. *Air France-KLM*, *supra* n. 339, paragraphs 34 and 50.

therefore not clear how this case can be distinguished from the other cases other than perhaps on the contractual terms and their treatment in French contract law.

Whether *Société Thermale* can be confined to its specific facts (or contractual terms/treatment) or might no longer be considered good law remains to be seen. The resolution of the issue will depend on a case-by-case analysis of the amount of the agreed compensation, the reasons for the cancellation and the contractual terms. For example, if a payment by the customer due to cancellation or early termination of the contract aims at compensating specific damages of the supplier and does not correspond to the agreed consideration (but is considerably lower or higher), this payment might qualify as non-taxable and be excluded from the taxable amount (thus potentially resulting in an adjustment event).

[C] Bad Debts

The scenario of partial or total non-payment is one of the three adjustment events explicitly mentioned in Article 90 of the VAT Directive (Category 2). Unlike the Australian GST law, the EU VAT Directive does not provide rules detailing under which conditions adjustments for a bad debt can be made. It has therefore fallen to the CJEU to answer this question. Even though Article 90(2) of the EU VAT Directive grants some leeway to the Member States when defining 'partial or total non-payment' and the conditions for bad debt adjustments, the CJEU has limited this discretion to a minimum.

The CJEU referenced the principles of neutrality[343] and proportionality when it ruled in the famous *Enzo Di Maura* case in 2017 that the discretion of Member States extends only to imposing requirements to prove non-payment to a 'reasonable probability that the debt will not be honoured',[344] but cannot extend to an outright denial of an adjustment for non-payment.[345] The CJEU has applied an autonomous interpretation of 'non-payment' so as to ensure uniformity in interpretation and establish a minimum standard necessary for bad debt adjustments that applies to all Member States.[346] In determining the evidentiary requirements to prove the irrecoverability of the debt, Member States must satisfy the proportionality standard – that is,

343. *Enzo Di Maura, supra* n. 23, paragraph 23; confirmed amongst others in CJEU, 15 October 2020, Case C-335/19, *E. sp. z o.o. sp. K*, ECLI:EU:C:2020:829; slightly different in the earlier case: *Almos Agrárkülkereskedelmi kft, supra* n. 300; this case seems to have been implicitly overruled by the *Enzo Di Maura* case.

344. *Enzo Di Maura, supra* n. 23, paragraph 27.

345. *Enzo Di Maura, supra* n. 23, paragraph 22. Advocate General Kokott even argued that the fundamental right of equal treatment, included in the EU Charter of Fundamental Rights, would require such an interpretation of the VAT Directive and 'call for a possibility of prompt correction' because 'pre-financing of VAT over periods of several years [by the taxable person] is out of the question': Opinion of 8 June 2017 by AG Kokott, C-246/16, *Enzo Di Maura*, ECLI:EU:C:2017:440, paragraphs 56 and 69.

346. *See* on the objective of uniform interpretation of the terms mentioned in Article 90 EU VAT Directive: *Lombard, supra* n. 288, paragraph 21.

they 'must be appropriate to achieve the objectives stated in that measure [of the EU VAT Directive] and must not go beyond what is necessary in order to attain them'.[347]

The CJEU has disallowed the following national measures related to bad-debt adjustments as disproportionate to the EU VAT Directive: (1) a requirement to prove that the insolvency proceedings of the debtor have been unsuccessful (when such proceedings may last longer than 10 years) (Italy);[348] (2) denying an adjustment solely because the debtor is no longer a taxable person for the purposes of VAT (Czech Republic)[349] or no longer registered for VAT (Poland) or is subject to insolvency or winding up proceedings (Poland);[350] (3) requiring creditors to lodge a claim in insolvency proceedings against the debtor even if it is evident that such a claim would not be recoverable (Slovenia).[351] By contrast, the CJEU upheld a requirement that the creditor give prior notice of its intention to cancel all or part of the VAT to the purchaser of goods or services (if that purchaser is a taxable person) as long as the condition was not too burdensome (Romania).[352]

The Austrian VAT Code (UStG) lists the irrecoverability of a claim as one of three exemplary adjustment events,[353] but there are no legislative conditions or formalities for bad debt adjustments. The law provides that if the payment is received subsequently, the tax amount and input tax deduction must be corrected again. The Austrian Supreme Administrative Court has ruled that the assessment of whether and when a debt can be considered uncollectable or irrecoverable must be made on a case-by-case basis, but the collectability of a receivable must be more than merely doubtful.[354] For example, a devaluation in a balance sheet does not automatically give rise to a VAT adjustment because, according to Austrian accounting principles, doubtfulness alone can trigger a devaluation.[355] By contrast, illiquidity of the debtor can lead to 'irrecoverability' within the meaning of the law.[356] The Austrian VAT Guidelines (UStR 2000) generally follow this approach and further state that, in case of doubt, the tax authority will have to demand proof that a claim is irrecoverable (e.g., evidence of recovery attempts).[357] The Guidelines also stipulate, in favour of the taxable person, that an adjustment can be made prior to the end of insolvency proceedings based on the expected quota the creditor might receive.[358]

Neither the Austrian VAT Code (UStG) nor the Austrian VAT Guidelines (UStR 2000) require an exchange of documents between the creditor and debtor for a bad debt

347. *Enzo Di Maura*, *supra* n. 23, paragraph 25.
348. *Enzo Di Maura*, *supra* n. 23.
349. CJEU, 8 May 2019, Case C-127/18, *A-PACK CZ s.r.o.*, ECLI:EU:C:2019:377.
350. *E. sp. z o.o. sp. k.*, *supra* n. 343.
351. CJEU, 11 June 2020, Case C-146/19, *SCT d.d.*, ECLI:EU:C:2020:464.
352. Tratave, *supra* n. 303.
353. *See* Austrian VAT Code (UStG), section 16(3)(1).
354. Judgment by the Austrian Supreme Administrative Court (*Verwaltungsgerichtshof*, or VwGH) of 3 September 2008, ECLI:AT:VWGH:2008:2003130109.X00.
355. Judgment by the Austrian Supreme Administrative Court of 20 October 2004, ECLI:AT:VWGH:2004:2001140128.X00.
356. Judgment by the Austrian Supreme Administrative Court of 29 January 2015, ECLI:AT:VWGH:2015:2012150012.X00.
357. Austrian VAT Guidelines (UStR 2000), as of 28 November 2019, marginal number 2388.
358. Austrian VAT Guidelines (UStR 2000), as of 28 November 2019, marginal number 2405.

adjustment. The taxable person whose claim has become wholly or partially irrecoverable can therefore reduce the payment by the amount of the loss without having to notify the debtor of this. However, the tax authority of the correcting taxable person (creditor) will, in practice, inform the tax authority of the insolvent taxable person (debtor) of the irrecoverability of the claim by means of a control notification.[359] The adjustment of VAT payable at the level of the supplier in Austria is not systematically linked to and dependent on a corresponding adjustment of the amount of input VAT deduction at the level of the debtor. The creditor can therefore also make an adjustment of its VAT liability if the tax authorities are unable to collect the correction of input VAT at the level of the debtor (e.g., due to insolvency).

[D] Court Orders and Third-Party Adjustments

Whether adjustments of the agreed price by an external body (e.g., a court) can lead to a consideration adjustment under EU VAT law is neither clearly regulated nor decided (or even greatly discussed). In the 1982 decision of *Bausystem*, the CJEU held that the award of interest by a court for an outstanding debt was not a 'supplementary payment' connected to the taxable amount (for the underlying supply) but rather was separate consideration for a grant of credit occasioned by the delay in payment that was fixed by law and therefore only 'remotely connected to the main services provided'.[360] Some have inferred from this that consideration adjustments decided by a third party (e.g., court) do not, in general, have an impact on the VAT base, and refer to policy arguments that the taxable amount is in general defined as the subjective value agreed to by the parties in support of such claims (*see* §9.06).[361] However, others have argued that *Bausystem* should be limited to its facts (i.e., that the ruling specifically turned on the nature of an interest charge on a late payment) and should not be understood as authority for the broader proposition that a court or third party alteration can *never* have VAT consequences.[362] This position would leave open the possibility of the EU adopting the more inclusive Australian approach whereby court orders can lead to VAT adjustments if sufficiently related to the initial supply (*see* above §9.05[D]).

The uncertainty around the effects of court orders and third-party variations affects the EU position on the VAT consequences of a transfer pricing adjustment by a revenue authority (*see* chapter 10 of this volume).

359. Austrian VAT Guidelines (UStR 2000), as of 28 November 2019, marginal number 2389.
360. CJEU, 1 July 1982, Case C-222/81, *B.A.Z. Bausystem*, ECLI:EU:C:1982:256, paragraph 10.
361. Santoro, *supra* n. 21, 161; Alexandra Martins, *VAT Transfer-Pricing Rules: A Portuguese Perspective*, 37(5) Intertax 322, 328 (2009); European Commission, VAT Committee, Working Paper 923, *Possible VAT Implications of Transfer Pricing*, taxud.c1 (2016) 1280928 – EN, 20-21 (28 February 2017).
362. European Commission, VAT Committee, Working Paper 923, *supra* n. 361, at 21.

[E] Changes in Character

[1] *Change in Character at the Time of Supply*

The EU VAT Directive does not include any specific rules for changes that occur *at the time* of the initial transaction as with the example at §9.02[B] of a good manufactured in France and intended to be shipped to Canada (exempt with input credit) but redirected to the recipient's store in Marseille which is low in stock (taxable). Member States are therefore left to address the issue subject to the proportionality principle.

Under Austrian law, at the level of the supplier such a change would not be covered by the adjustment rules relating to a change in taxable amount[363] or change in use,[364] but might require correction of the invoice and VAT return according to the general domestic procedural rules applying to all taxes.[365] However, the position of the supplier is also affected by documentary and proof requirements linked to exports within the EU and to states outside the EU. As a general rule, an export can only be zero-rated under EU law if the supplier has proof of the cross-border transport.[366] In the absence of such proof, a supplier should not treat the supply as exempt (with input credit) - hence any necessary change should be prevented from the outset. Any subsequent effects on entitlements to VAT deductions at the level of the recipient resulting from a change of use should be dealt with under the rules discussed at (§9.06[E][2][c]) if the change occurs in a taxable period subsequent to the chargeable event (after the initial VAT return is made).[367] If it is in the same period, there is no need for any correction, but this should be taken into account when declaring the original supply.

For the reversed scenario where a taxable person treats the supply as a taxed supply, even though it should be exempt (e.g., export) and issues an invoice with VAT, a correction of the invoice given to the recipient of the supply is required. The taxable person remains liable for VAT until the invoice is corrected and the recipient has no right to input VAT deduction of the wrongly invoiced VAT.[368] A corrected invoice has *ex nunc* effect.[369] The EU VAT Directive does not contain any provisions on the correction of unduly invoiced VAT, so it falls on Member States to provide for the modalities of the correction.[370]

---

363. Austrian VAT Code (UStG), section 16.
364. Austrian VAT Code (UStG), section 12 (10)-(13).
365. *See, e.g.*, Austrian Federal Fiscal Code (BAO), sections 293-307.
366. For the proof of transport related to exports to Member States (intra-Community supplies) *see* Implementing Regulation (EU) No 282/2011 as regards certain exemptions for intra-Community transactions, Article 45a; for proof of transport related to exports to non-Member States: *see* Austrian VAT Code (UStG), section 7(4); EU VAT Directive, Article 131; CJEU, 19 December 2013, Case C-563/12, *BDV Hungary Trading Kft.*, ECLI:EU:C:2013:854, paragraph 34.
367. Austrian VAT Code (UStG), section 12(10)-(13); EU VAT Directive, Articles 184 et seq.
368. *See* CJEU 13 December 1989, Case C-342/87, *Genius*, ECLI:EU:C:1989:635, paragraphs 13-19.
369. Austrian VAT Code (UStG), section 16(1).
370. CJEU, 15 March 2007, Case C-35/05, *Reemtsma*, ECLI:EU:C:2007:167.

[2] *Subsequent Change in Character*

Under EU VAT law, a *subsequent* change in character, potentially leading to an adjustment of input credits of a taxable person, can take place in three different scenarios: first, a change from business to private use (and vice versa); second, a change from economic to non-economic use (and vice-versa); and third, a change from taxable to exempt (and vice versa). Each is regulated by three different sets of rules which replicate the greater variety and complexity of rules that apply to different supplies in the EU.

[a] *Business Versus Private*

A change in the use of a good or service from a business purpose to a private purpose will trigger a deemed taxable transaction for self-consumption[371] with the taxable amount either the purchase price of the goods or of similar goods or, in the absence of a purchase price, the cost price, determined at the time when the application takes place.[372] The provision only applies if the taxable person has already deducted input VAT on the respective good/service and will result in a correction of the initial input VAT credit.[373] However, because the taxable amount is not limited to the amount of the initial deducted input VAT, the VAT liability may exceed the amount of the initial input VAT deduction if the value of the good has increased since the acquisition.

The EU VAT Directive makes no allowance for an adjustment when an asset initially acquired for private purposes is later used for business purposes.[374]

[b] *Economic Versus Non-economic*

As the non-economic sphere concept is developed by the CJEU rather than by the EU legislature,[375] the EU VAT Directive does not include specific apportionment or adjustment rules for changes in use of assets for economic and non-economic activities.[376] The CJEU has ruled that Member States can establish methods and criteria to do so, provided that they are consistent with the principles underlying the common system of VAT and the principle of neutrality (i.e., the result should objectively reflect

371. EU VAT Directive, Articles 16, 18 and 26.
372. EU VAT Directive, Article 74. In the case of the (time-limited) use of a good or service allocated to the business sphere for private purposes, the taxable amount of such deemed supply of services shall be the full cost to the taxable person of providing the services: at Article 75.
373. Van Doesum et al., *Fundamentals of EU VAT Law*, *supra* n. 9, 134.
374. *See* on this issue *inter alia*, CJEU, 11 July 1991, Case C-97/90, *Lennartz*, ECLI:EU:C:1991:315.
375. *See Securenta*, *supra* n. 74, paragraph 26.
376. The CJEU has held that Articles 184-192 only apply to these changes in limited instances: CJEU, 25 July 2018, Case C-140/17, *Szef Krajowej Administracji Skarbowej*, *supra* n. 75; *Securenta*, *supra* n. 74, paragraph 33; *Portugal Telecom*, *supra* n. 96, paragraphs 42 and 47.

the part of the input expenditure actually to be attributed, respectively, to those two types of activity).[377]

Member States could, but do not have to, apply the same adjustment and apportionment rules that apply to taxable/exempt acquisitions. The Austrian legislator has not implemented any specific set of rules for a change in character between the economic and non-economic sphere, but prevailing opinion considers that the adjustment rules for taxable/exempt activities can apply.[378]

[c] Taxable Versus Input Taxed (Exempt) Activity

A change in use between taxed and exempt activities (and vice versa) or a change in the proportion of use for mixed/composite acquisitions will trigger a decreasing or increasing adjustment for the recipient of a supply when the deduction is 'higher or lower than that to which the taxable person was entitled'.[379] Adjustments are required when some 'change occurs in the factors used to determine the amount to be deducted'.[380] These adjustment rules, for example, might apply when a computer originally purchased for the purposes of the portfolio management of a bank (right to input VAT deduction) is later used for the credit business of a bank (no right to input VAT deduction),[381] or when the computer is used exclusively for portfolio management then equally for both portfolio management and the credit business (e.g., from 100% to 50/50). EU Member States enjoy a rather broad discretion when implementing these rules in their national law.

Unlike the prescriptive formula in the Australian GST legislation requiring a comparison of intended and actual use, the EU VAT Directive does not provide any definition of when a change in factors occurs.[382] According to Austrian jurisprudence, the decisive factor is an actual change in *use*.[383] Mere intention to change the use is generally insufficient, however, the intention to change the use of an asset or service from taxed to exempt activities (or vice versa) is relevant if there is a binding agreement in place (e.g., with a future tenant or buyer) which provides clear evidence on the future change.[384] In other words, similar to Australia, the intention must be objectively evident, clearly defined and binding.

377. *Securenta, supra* n. 74, paragraphs 34-37. Member States have discretion to apply appropriate formulas in doing so without being required to restrict themselves to only one of those methods: *Securenta, supra* n. 74, paragraph 38.
378. Austrian VAT Code (UStG), section 12(10); Ruppe & Achatz, *Umsatzsteuergesetz, supra* n. 298, at §12, paragraphs 294-295.
379. EU VAT Directive, Article 184, Articles 182-189. On the scope of the rules, *see* van Doesum et al., *Fundamentals of EU VAT Law, supra* n. 9, 449.
380. EU VAT Directive, Article 185.
381. *See* with a similar example Doesum et al., *Fundamentals of EU VAT Law, supra* n. 9, 450.
382. EU VAT Directive, Article 185(1).
383. Judgment by the Austrian Supreme Administrative Court of 20 April 2006, ECLI:AT:VWGH:2006:2006150020.X02.
384. Judgment by the Austrian Supreme Administrative Court of 11 November 2008, ECLI:AT:VWGH:2008:2006130070.X00: the conclusion of rental agreements for flats intended for sale may lead to an adjustment.

The EU VAT Directive provides the general legal framework for adjustments with the technical details left to Member States to implement.[385] Unlike Australia, there are specific rules for adjustments for capital goods[386] and immovable property[387] which, among other things, impose time limits on the adjustment period. Corrections are not made retroactively, but for the year of the change. These adjustment rules lead to the apparently incongruous outcome that adjustments for a change in use are time limited whereas adjustments made for output VAT are not time limited.[388] However, this is similar to Australia and most likely reflects the fact that the practical need to time limit adjustments on the input VAT deduction side is greater than on the taxable amount side.

The adjustment rules seem to be primarily addressed at *unintended* changes in character. The right to input VAT credit for *intended* changes in character (i.e., known at the time of acquisition) should be limited at the time of acquisition by applying a recovery ratio. There are no specific rules in the EU VAT Directive or the Austrian VAT Code (UStG) as to how such a recovery ratio for input VAT deduction could be calculated at the time of acquisition. In general, input VAT should be directly allocated to output activities in an economic way. Any method that ensures an appropriate allocation of input tax to the output transactions to which they economically relate could be permissible. As a result, the applicable recovery ratio might lead to extensive discussions with the tax authorities in practice.

The Austrian legislator has implemented the adjustment rules without material deviations. The main adjustment rule applies to 'fixed assets', i.e., objects which are intended to serve the business permanently (Austrian implementation of 'capital goods').[389] Adjustments are required over four calendar years from the first year of use when the circumstances decisive for the deduction of input tax change (this extends to subsequent expenses relating to the asset which must be capitalized from the adjustment period beginning in the following year after such an expense first arose). The adjustment period for immovable property (including the expenses to be capitalized and the costs of major repairs) is 20 calendar years. Consistent with the Directive, annual adjustments are limited to one-fifth of the VAT charged or, if the adjustment period has been extended, in respect of the corresponding fraction thereof which, in the case of immovable property, is 1/20th of the total input VAT. Adjustments are only required if the amount to be adjusted exceeds EUR 60 for the calendar year.[390]

385. EU VAT Directive, Article 186.

386. For example, adjustments for capital goods are spread over five years (generally from the date of acquisition or manufacture or in some cases use) with annual adjustments limited to one-fifth of the VAT charged in respect of the corresponding fraction thereof: EU VAT Directive, Articles 187-188.

387. For example, with extensions of up to 20 years for adjustments for immovable property acquired as capital goods: EU VAT Directive, Articles 187. Member States also have the power to make further modifications – e.g., define capital goods: at Articles 189-192. *See generally* van Doesum et al., *Fundamentals of EU VAT Law, supra* n. 9, 451.

388. EU VAT Directive, Article 90.

389. Austrian VAT Code (UStG), section 12(10); Ruppe & Achatz, *Umsatzsteuergesetz, supra* n. 298, §12, paragraph 308.

390. Austrian VAT Code (UStG), section 12(13).

The method to calculate yearly adjustments is not clearly specified by the EU VAT Directive, CJEU case law or the Austrian VAT Code (UStG). According to prevailing opinion, the adjustment is not calculated based on the total input tax credit, but based on the input VAT difference, i.e., the amount that at the later time appears deductible or no longer deductible as a result of the change in circumstances compared with the original amount of input tax credit.[391] This is broadly consistent with the Australian approach (§9.05[E][2]).

Example: *unintended change in use, negative adjustment based on the EU VAT Directive*[392]

In January 2018, a taxable person purchases a new building with the intention (supported by objective evidence) of using the building for providing legal services (transactions subject to VAT and giving right to input VAT credit); the VAT charged amounts to EUR 100,000. For 2018, the taxable person has a 100% right to input VAT deduction; there is no need for an input VAT adjustment as the building is used as originally intended.

In January 2019, she begins to provide (exempt) insurance services which amount to 25% of the overall turnover for 2019. A change of the factors from taxed to exempt activities triggers an adjustment of the deduction 'in respect of one-fifth of the VAT charged on the capital good' (Article 187(2) of the EU VAT Directive), i.e., 1/5 of EUR 100,000 = EUR 20,000. The change in use of the building from taxable to exempt activities amounts to 25%; therefore, the negative yearly adjustment in 2019 is EUR 5,000 (25% of EUR 20,000).

§9.07 CONCLUSION

VAT adjustments create tension between the transactional nature of the VAT and the need to ensure that VAT liabilities reflect the economic reality of the parties to a transaction when subsequent events change those liabilities. The responses can be relatively straightforward, e.g., when parties clearly agree to reduce the price for a taxable supply, or they can be very complex. This complexity might arise for various reasons, as was evident in the discussion of third-party rebates (due to the difficulties in accounting for transactions outside the VAT chain), cancelled transactions (due to the complexity in the differing legal treatment of the underlying transactions) and changes in creditable purpose (due to the need to monitor use and/or compare intention over an extended period).

The analysis of the Australian and EU responses to these issues shows that the same issues tend to generate complexity. The responses can differ in substance (as was shown in the treatment of court orders) and in form - such as in the different legal institution that provides the response (with third-party rebates addressed in case law in the EU but through legislative reform in Australia). In general, the Australian legislation takes a more prescriptive approach to the issue and demonstrates the benefits of

391. Van Doesum et al., *Fundamentals of EU VAT Law*, *supra* n. 9, at 452; for the Austrian view, Ruppe & Achatz, *Umsatzsteuergesetz*, *supra* n. 298, §12, paragraph 311.
392. Van Doesum et al., *Fundamentals of EU VAT Law*, *supra* n. 9, 452.

some policy learning from the EU experience. The EU approach is more general – in keeping with the nature of a Directive – which leaves much of the technical detail to be specified by Member States and/or CJEU case law. This difference was evident in the treatment of bad debts. Despite the issues and responses being broadly similar, domestic context matters in shaping responses – as evidenced by the discussion of cancelled transactions and the treatment of consideration. The issue of VAT adjustments shows that a proper review of the virtues of the VAT is incomplete if it begins and ends at the level of a transaction.

CHAPTER 10
VAT and Transfer Pricing*

Kathryn James & Karoline Spies

§10.01 INTRODUCTION

Estimates suggest that anywhere between 30% and 60% of global trade consists of related party dealings within multinational enterprises (MNEs).[1] The rules around how tax liabilities are incurred, allocated and enforced is of great interest to those MNEs, to their domestic competitors, to revenue authorities and to the governments and citizens of all nation states who rely on an appropriate level of revenue to fund the essential functions and services of their respective states.

Cross-border trade affects, and is in turn primarily affected by, three main areas of revenue law: first, direct tax obligations, namely the corporate income tax (as well as the personal income tax); secondly, indirect tax obligations consisting of customs duties (for cross-border supplies of tangible goods) and, thirdly, the value-added tax (VAT) (for cross-border supplies of all goods and services).[2]

* This research was partially supported by the Australian Government through the Australian Research Council's Discovery Projects funding scheme (project DE190100346). The views expressed herein are those of the authors and are not necessarily those of the Australian Government or Australian Research Council. Our thanks to Rick Krever, Andy Ditchfield, Peter Mellor and Markus Mittendorfer for their assistance. All errors are our own. Law current until 31 January 2021.

1. Liu Ping & Caroline Silberztein, *Transfer Pricing, Customs Duties and VAT Rules: Can We Bridge the Gap?* 1(1) World Com. Rev. 36, 36 (2007). Despite the regular quoting of this 60% figure the data in support is unclear. The Tax Justice Network explains the proportion is likely to be at least one-third: Nick Shaxson, *Over a Third of World Trade Happens Inside Multinational Corporations*, Tax Justice Network (9 April 2019), https://www.taxjustice.net/2019/04/09/over-a-third-or-more-of-world-trade-happens-inside-multinational-corporations/.
2. Naturally, other taxes can affect cross-border trade including recent innovations such as a digital services tax (which, depending on the design might be classified as a type of income or consumption tax) or a carbon tax (a form of excise), but this chapter focuses on the 3 main revenue types specified.

Much attention has been paid to the direct tax implications of the cross-border related party dealings within MNEs, especially in relation to the base-erosion and profit shifting (BEPS) framework that followed the 2008 global financial crisis.[3] Harmful transfer pricing practices have been an important contributor to BEPS. *Transfer pricing* is the criteria by which income generated by an MNE is allocated to different jurisdictions according to various methods designed to give effect to the *arm's length standard* (ALS) which attempts, in various ways, to value related-party dealings as if they had been effected by non-related parties in similar circumstances.[4] The nature and value of these related-party transactions affect the corporate income tax liability of MNEs. *Harmful* transfer pricing practices consist of those techniques that exploit intra-group cross-border dealings to allocate corporate profit to low or no tax jurisdictions and corporate expenses to high tax jurisdictions in a manner that results 'in outcomes in which the allocation of profits is not aligned with the economic activity that produced the profits'.[5] Although reliable estimates are hard to come by, up to USD 183 billion or 9.2% of corporate income tax revenue may be lost to harmful transfer-pricing practices (including such practices relating to interest on intra-group financial transactions).[6] Reforming those transfer pricing rules to minimize abuse has therefore constituted one important component of the BEPS response.[7] The Organisation for Economic Co-operation and Development (OECD) has also undertaken significant work on the treatment of cross-border supplies of services and intangibles for VAT purposes (including some cross-border related party dealings) in its *International*

3. *See, e.g.*, Organisation for Economic Co-operation and Development (OECD), *Action Plan on Base Erosion and Profit Shifting* (OECD Publishing 2013); OECD, *OECD Secretary-General Tax Report to G20 Finance Ministers and Central Bank Governors – October 2019* (OECD, October 2019).
4. *See, e.g.*, OECD, *Model Tax Convention on Income and on Capital* (2017) Article 9(1) (*Model Tax Convention*) – 'Where ... conditions are made or imposed between the two [associated] enterprises in their commercial or financial relations which differ from those which would be made between independent enterprises, then any profits which would, but for those conditions, have accrued to one of the enterprises, but, by reason of those conditions, have not so accrued, may be included in the profits of that enterprise and taxed accordingly'; OECD, *Transfer Pricing Guidelines for Multinational Enterprises and Tax Administrations* Chapter 1, [1.6]; glossary, 24-25, 31 (2017) (*Transfer Pricing Guidelines*).
5. European Commission, *Question Concerning the Application of EU VAT Provisions – Possible VAT Implications of Transfer Pricing* 3 (Value Added Tax Committee (Article 398 of Directive 2006/112/EC) Working Paper No. 923, taxud.c.1(2016)1280928, 28 February 2017); with reference to OECD, *Aligning Transfer Pricing Outcomes with Value Creation: Actions 8-10 – 2015 Final Reports*, OECD/G20 Base Erosion and Profit Shifting Project 9 (OECD Publishing 2015).
6. *See, e.g.*, Thomas Tørsløv, Ludvig Wier & Gabriel Zucman, *The Missing Profits of Nations* (National Bureau of Economic Research Working Paper, 22 April 2020): this study finds that lost tax revenue broadly related to transfer mispricing of services through tax havens ('excessive' payments for high-risk services and 'excessive' receipts of interest on foreign direct investment) is significant at approximately USD 183 billion (or 9.2% of CIT revenue) for all OECD and the main developing countries in 2015 (Online Appendix, 32-33 and Table C4d); however, corresponding lost revenue on transfer mispricing of goods from several studies cited is generally much lower with estimates of between 0.38% and 2.01% (Online Appendix, 37-38 and Table D2).
7. *See, e.g.*, OECD, *Aligning Transfer Pricing Outcomes with Value Creation*, *supra* n. 5; OECD, *Transfer Pricing Documentation and Country-by-Country Reporting: Action 13 – 2015 Final Report*, OECD/G20 Base Erosion and Profit Shifting Project (OECD Publishing 2015). Cf. OECD, *OECD Secretary-General Tax Report to G20 Finance Ministers and Central Bank Governors – October 2019*, *supra* n. 3.

VAT/GST Guidelines.[8] Significant work has also been undertaken on efforts to coordinate the administration of direct tax obligations and customs duties.[9]

However, comparatively little work has been undertaken on the relationship between the VAT and transfer pricing despite the topic giving rise to a number of complex and important issues and potentially involving significant revenue risks. This chapter addresses that gap. Tax arbitrage is of course the product of a number of aspects of international taxation.[10] Transfer pricing need not occur across borders and related-party dealings need not be restricted to members of a corporate group. However, the significance of these issues (in value and risk) is most pronounced in the context of cross-border related-party dealings within an MNE. It is important to examine the interaction between these two aspects of the direct and indirect tax base because tax liability under both depends on the *value* ascribed to transactions but that value is generally ascertained through different methods with different underlying purposes which can amplify revenue and compliance risks. Apropos these risks, there are some important policy observations to make at the outset.

The goal of the VAT is to tax consumption by private households in a given jurisdiction according to the market-based expenditure of the recipient (commonly referred to as taxing on a destination basis).[11] In doing so, the VAT (and customs law) is generally faithful to the value ascribed by the parties to that transaction and aims for neutrality in its treatment of business-to-business (B2B) supplies.[12] By contrast, the goal of the corporate income tax, and transfer pricing rules, is to allocate taxable profits among jurisdictions by imposing a notional value (an arm's length value) on intra-group transactions for the purposes of determining corporate income tax liability.[13] As the EU Advocate-General noted in the case of *FCE Bank*:[14]

> [T]he 'arm's length' principle ... is based on a legal fiction ... A fundamental criterion of the common VAT system, however, is that it is the actual economic situation that matters. It is as a consequence of this principle, in particular, that the taxable amount for VAT purposes is the value actually received in consideration of the service supplied and not a value determined according to objective criteria. It would therefore be contrary to the system to apply a legal fiction and to treat an internal transaction as if it had taken place between two independent entities.

8. *See, e.g.*, OECD, *International VAT/GST Guidelines* (2017).
9. *See, e.g.*, World Customs Organization (WCO), *Guide to Customs Valuation and Transfer Pricing* (WCO 2018).
10. *See, e.g.*, OECD, *Action Plan on Base Erosion and Profit Shifting*, *supra* n. 3: action items 8-10 and 13 relate to transfer pricing (of a total of 15 action items).
11. Folkert Idsinga, Bart-Jan Kalshoven & Monique van Herksen, *Let's Go Tango! The Dance between VAT, Customs and Transfer Pricing* 9(10) Int'l Transfer Pricing J. 199, 202 (2005).
12. European Commission, *Question Concerning the Application of EU VAT Provisions*, *supra* n. 5, at 15.
13. European Commission, *Question Concerning the Application of EU VAT Provisions*, *supra* n. 5, 16-17.
14. The comment was made with reference to the fictional notion that a permanent establishment is a separate entity but is equally apt to transfer pricing between associated entities generally: Opinion of Advocate-General Léger of 29 September 2005, *FCE Bank*, C-210/04, EU:C:2005:582, paragraph 64. The decision of the European Court of Justice was consistent with the opinion of the Advocate-General in this case: Judgment of 23 March 2006, *FCE Bank*, C-210/04, EU:C:2006:196.

It is customary (at least within the EU) to refer to these different values as 'subjective' (for customs and VAT) and 'objective' (for transfer pricing).[15] However, the terms are apt to mislead as the values involved in transfer pricing are more properly described as criteria-based rather than objective. They are vulnerable to manipulation by taxpayers which suggests a degree of subjectivity in the sense that tax liability is contingent on the manner in which the taxpayer has chosen to structure their affairs. The real difference is that, whereas the VAT in most instances accepts the price agreed on by the parties as the basis for measuring liability, the price agreed by the related parties is simply one of a number of factors taken into account for transfer pricing purposes.

As the quote from the EU Advocate-General suggests, some commentators question whether there *should* be any overlap between the two taxes at all.[16] However, the reality is that, whether or not one desires it otherwise, increasingly there *are* points of overlap between the VAT and transfer pricing which require a principled and considered policy response that is alive to the different purposes of the two taxes among other things including the risks to revenue.[17]

Section 10.02 provides an overview of the issues that arise with cross-border related-party dealings across all three tax bases including an analysis of how the bases interact, before focusing on the specific issues that arise in relation to transfer pricing and the VAT. These issues include: to what extent should direct and indirect tax rules overlap (if at all) especially in relation to the valuation of intra-group transactions (for example, should transfer pricing methodologies influence VAT valuation and vice versa); what administrative coordination (i.e., between customs and revenue authorities) is required to ensure that tax leakage is minimized across VAT, income tax and customs duties; and, in what circumstances might a transfer pricing adjustment give rise to a corresponding VAT adjustment (and vice versa). The analysis reveals that broadly two approaches might be applied to determining the relationship between the VAT and transfer pricing: the first being to treat both areas as completely separate; the second, to treat both areas as related, which then entails further issues such as to what degree the two areas are related – completely or only in part.

As with any tax policy issue, the implementation of approaches requires jurisdictions to legislate, administer and coordinate their responses. This in turn brings to bear domestic, regional and international influences that shape the response. Sections 10.03 and 10.04 provide an overview of how these issues are dealt with in Australia and the European Union. The analysis reveals that Australia and the EU jurisdictions acknowledge that VAT and transfer pricing can overlap, but not completely. It further demonstrates that the points of overlap recognized by different jurisdictions can vary in both substance and degree. The analysis shows that much work remains to be done on both determining and coordinating the most appropriate approach to govern the

15. European Commission, *Question Concerning the Application of EU VAT Provisions*, *supra* n. 5, at 15. This also derives from CJEU case law (*see*, e.g., CJEU 23 November 1988, C-230/87, *Naturally Yours*, ECLI:EU:C:1988:508, paragraph 16).
16. Emanuela Santoro, *Transfer Pricing and Value Added Tax in the European Community: Is There Room for Interaction and, If So, Where?* 14(3) Int'l Transfer Pricing J. 147, 155 (2007).
17. Ping & Silberztein, *supra* n. 1, 37-38.

relationship between transfer pricing and the VAT. Such work should also be cognisant of possible future changes to the taxation of cross-border income so as to determine the best method to approach the relationship, if any, between the rules that apply to the taxation of cross-border income and the VAT rules that apply to cross-border supplies of goods and services.

§10.02 AN OVERVIEW OF THE REVENUE TREATMENT OF CROSS-BORDER RELATED PARTY DEALINGS

This section provides an overview of the way in which cross-border trade by MNEs is affected by (and in turn affects) the corporate income tax, customs duties and the VAT. Each is examined in turn before the relationship between all three is outlined. The section concludes with an overview of the various issues and approaches that arise in relation to the question of whether a transfer pricing adjustment can and should have VAT implications which gives a practical focus to the theoretical concerns about the relationship between the various tax bases.

[A] Corporate Income Tax and Transfer Pricing

MNEs can choose to structure their corporate groups in various ways with the chosen structures influencing the application of the rules to the taxation of cross-border income (as well as to other taxes and charges: *see*, e.g., §10.02[C]).

Depending on the corporate structure, an MNE might engage in: (i) intra-group transactions between entities that are legally independent but part of the same corporate group (e.g., parent-subsidiary relationship); and/or (ii) intra-entity transactions between different establishments of the same legal entity (e.g., head office-permanent establishment relationship).

Under the OECD *Model Tax Convention*, which although non-binding is considered the global standard on the treatment of cross-border income, the rules differ depending on whether a transaction is an intra-group or intra-entity transaction.[18] Nevertheless, both sets of rules apply the arm's length standard and, consequently, taxation will ultimately depend on the domestic implementation of the arm's length standard in the relevant jurisdictions. For intra-group transactions, generally two separate enterprises are taxed separately in their resident jurisdictions unless one is sufficiently associated with, or controlled by, the other which then permits the taxing jurisdiction of one to tax the income of the associated company in another jurisdiction according to the arm's length standard, i.e., profits that would have been made but for the association are attributed to the associated entity.[19] For intra-entity transactions,

18. The OECD *Model Tax Convention*, *supra* n. 4, and OECD *Transfer Pricing Guidelines*, *supra* n. 4, are not binding but are very influential and are frequently adhered to by taxpayers and revenue authorities (particularly within OECD Member States) and in many respects reflect a global standard on the issues. *See also* United Nations, *Model Double Taxation Convention between Developed and Developing Countries* (2017).
19. OECD, *Model Tax Convention*, *supra* n. 4, Article 9.

tax is generally imposed on a residence basis unless profit is derived through a permanent establishment in another jurisdiction with the corresponding profits attributable to that source jurisdiction calculated according to the relevant arms-length standard (i.e., those that would be attributed as if the permanent establishment was operating as a separate independent enterprise).[20]

The various transfer-pricing methods designed to value transactions according to an arm's length standard (ALS) apply irrespective of whether or not taxpayers have engaged in tax abuse or evasion. The selection of a valuation method to identify the arm's length price is based on the 'most appropriate method in the circumstances of the case'[21] and each method differs according to the factors examined (e.g., price, profits, costs) or its ability to apply on a transactional or global basis.[22] Importantly, the value of these related-party transactions is not determined simply by the price agreed upon by the parties but rather by consideration of the various factors that each ALS method entails (prominent factors include the allocation of risk and functions in the corporate group).[23]

The first group are labelled 'traditional transactional methods' and, as their name implies, are able to be disaggregated to a transactional level with the first two focused on price and thus more readily transferable to the VAT context.[24] The first method, the *comparable uncontrolled price (CUP) method*, compares the *price* charged for property or services transferred in a controlled transaction to the price charged for property or services transferred in a comparable uncontrolled transaction in comparable circumstances. The difficulty lies in finding 'a transaction between independent enterprises that is similar enough to a controlled transaction such that no differences have a material effect on price'.[25] The second, the *resale price method (RPM)*, takes as its starting point the price at which a product that has been purchased from an associate is resold to an independent entity. This resale price (agreed with an independent party) is then reduced by a gross margin (the 'resale price margin') representing the amount out of which the reseller would seek to cover its relevant expenses (e.g., marketing expenses) – with what is left (after taking into account other costs such as customs duties) the appropriate arm's length price. This method might be used to value services offered by a subsidiary acting as a wholesale or resale distributor including the marketing expenses related to the resale of such products (which in turn affects the 'resale price margin' and the appropriateness of the RPM method to value such transactions in the first place).[26] The third, the *cost-plus method*, takes the costs incurred in a particular related-party transaction (for example, to produce a particular good) and then adds an appropriate mark-up with the amount representing the appropriate profit relevant to the functions performed and market conditions. The

20. OECD, *Model Tax Convention*, *supra* n. 4, Articles 5, 7.
21. OECD, *Transfer Pricing Guidelines*, *supra* n. 4, [1.9].
22. OECD, *Transfer Pricing Guidelines*, *supra* n. 4, Chapter 2.
23. OECD, *Transfer Pricing Guidelines*, *supra* n. 4, Chapter 2.
24. Isabelle Rouberol, *Interactions between Transfer Pricing and VAT Adjustments in the European Union* 27(5) International VAT Monitor 316, 317 (2016).
25. OECD, *Transfer Pricing Guidelines*, *supra* n. 4, [2.16], [2.14].
26. OECD, *Transfer Pricing Guidelines*, *supra* n. 4, [2.27], [2.38].

OECD states that this method is most useful when semi-finished goods are sold between associated parties, when associated parties have concluded joint facility agreements or long-term buy-and-supply arrangements, or for valuing the provision of services.[27] However, the use of cost rather than price as the basis for valuation makes it less-well aligned to VAT methods.[28]

Alternative 'transactional profit methods' include the 'transactional net margin method' which attributes a net profit from a related-party transaction(s) to an appropriate base such as costs, sales and assets (rather than price).[29] The 'transactional profit split method' identifies the profits to be attributed to a controlled transaction and then attempts to split those profits between the associated enterprises on an 'economically valid basis that approximates the division of profits that would have been anticipated and reflected in an agreement made at arm's length'.[30] Such methods tend to be less compatible with VAT rules because they split profits across associated enterprises on a global (rather than transactional) basis according to factors other than price alone.[31]

The nature of the question asked in determining a transfer pricing value (i.e., to value a transaction which in reality has no true comparable) combined with the degree of flexibility in the choice and application of each method means that the process tends to generate a range of potential prices rather than one clearly correct price and is vulnerable to disagreement and dispute. Even after having agreed upon a method, revenue authorities and taxpayers might produce a range of ambit values under a particular method before settling on an acceptable price.[32] This might occur in advance, through the use of advance pricing arrangements (APAs), or as the result of a settlement after an assessment, audit or adjustment.[33]

When a revenue authority (or a taxpayer in anticipation of that authority) establishes that a transaction/s does/do not properly align with the relevant ALS, then an adjustment might arise to more closely value that transaction/s according to the ALS (and re-allocate corporate income tax liabilities accordingly).[34] The obligation to adjust

27. OECD, *Transfer Pricing Guidelines*, *supra* n. 4, [2.45].
28. *Cf.* §10.02 [B] for the discussion of the suggested use of cost-allocation methods in the application of the VAT-recharge method under the OECD *International VAT/GST Guidelines*, *supra* n. 8.
29. OECD, *Transfer Pricing Guidelines*, *supra* n. 4, [2.64].
30. OECD, *Transfer Pricing Guidelines*, *supra* n. 4, [2.114].
31. Rouberol notes that profit split methods are not well aligned to VAT principles as there is 'no direct link between the good or service and the consideration received': Rouberol, *supra* n. 24, at 316-317; *see also* Madeleine Merkx, *Should EU VAT Apply the Recharge Method in the Place of Supply Rules for B2B Services?* 22(6) EC Tax Rev. 282, 286-287 (2013).
32. Massimo Fabio, *Customs Value and Transfer Pricing: WCO and ICC Solutions to Be Adopted by Customs Authorities* 15(6) Global Trade and Customs J. 273, 275 (2020).
33. OECD, *Transfer Pricing Guidelines*, *supra* n. 4, 23 – the glossary defines an 'advance pricing arrangement' as 'an arrangement that determines, in advance of controlled transactions, an appropriate set of criteria (e.g., method, comparables and appropriate adjustments thereto, critical assumptions as to future events) for the determination of the transfer pricing for those transactions over a fixed period of time'. Such arrangements generally last from 3-5 years: WCO, *Guide to Customs Valuation and Transfer Pricing*, *supra* n. 9, at 47, [3.5.1].
34. European Commission, *Question Concerning the Application of EU VAT Provisions*, *supra* n. 5, 16-17, [3.2.2].

arises independently of the contractual obligations entered into by the parties and independently of their intent (to minimize tax or otherwise).[35]

A compensating adjustment is one initiated by the taxpayer generally at year's end but before filing a return.[36] Such adjustments serve to protect the taxpayer's position *vis-à-vis* the relevant revenue authorities by altering the value of related-party transactions over the course of the year to more closely align with the arm's length method values.[37] Such a compensating adjustment does not necessarily lead to a change of the payment obligations and amounts actually charged between the associated enterprises.[38] The OECD Transfer Pricing Guidelines note that most of its member states do not recognize compensating adjustments 'on the grounds that the tax return should reflect the actual transactions'.[39]

Adjustments by revenue authorities can take the form of a primary adjustment (an adjustment made by a tax administration in a first jurisdiction to a company's taxable profits as a result of applying the arm's length principle to transactions involving an associated enterprise in a second tax jurisdiction),[40] a corresponding adjustment (made by the revenue authority in the second jurisdiction where the related party is located to correspond with the primary adjustment and ensure a consistent allocation of profits (i.e., avoid double-taxation))[41] or a secondary adjustment (an adjustment to complement a primary adjustment that imposes tax on a secondary constructive transaction (such as a constructive dividend, constructive equity contribution, or constructive loan) to ensure that the taxpayer's taxable profit matches their accounting profit).[42]

As previously indicated, the obvious issue that besets all transfer pricing methods is the artificiality and ultimate futility of the underlying premise – that the transactions available to a corporate group have an appropriate arm's length comparator when, without the existence of the corporate group, many of those transactions would not be available in the first place.[43] Despite the increased attention to multinational profit shifting that followed the global financial crisis, including through transfer pricing

35. European Commission, *supra* n. 5, 6 [2.15]; OECD, *Transfer Pricing Guidelines, supra* n. 4, [1.2].
36. The OECD defines such as adjustment as one 'in which the taxpayer reports a transfer price for tax purposes that is, in the taxpayer's opinion, an arm's length price for a controlled transaction, even though this price differs from the amount actually charged between the associated enterprises. This adjustment would be made before the tax return is filed.' OECD, *Transfer Pricing Guidelines, supra* n. 4, 25.
37. Santoro, *supra* n. 16, 162.
38. OECD, *Transfer Pricing Guidelines, supra* n. 4, 184, [4.38].
39. OECD, *Transfer Pricing Guidelines, supra* n. 4, 184, [4.39].
40. OECD, *Transfer Pricing Guidelines, supra* n. 4, 28.
41. OECD, *Transfer Pricing Guidelines, supra* n. 4, 25.
42. OECD, *Transfer Pricing Guidelines, supra* n. 4, 30; European Commission, *Question Concerning the Application of EU VAT Provisions, supra* n. 5, 8-10.
43. European Commission, *Question Concerning the Application of EU VAT Provisions, supra* n. 5; Kerrie Sadiq & Richard Krever, *Anatomy of Transfer Pricing: Lessons from Australia* 100(5) Tax Notes Int'l 679, 680 (2020) – 'There are no comparable providers in the market place for internal group intangible supplies'; Ping & Silberztein, *supra* n. 1, 36; WCO, *Guide to Customs Valuation and Transfer Pricing, supra* n. 9, 14, [3.1]; Independent Commission for the Reform of Corporate Taxation (ICRICT), *International Corporate Tax Reform: Towards a Fair and Sustainable Base* 4-5 (October 2019).

techniques, reforms have so far only been made to the relevant transfer-pricing rules rather than abandoning the standard as the method to allocate corporate income tax liabilities. There are ongoing discussions at the G20/OECD level as to whether a global formulary apportionment approach (instead of, or in addition to, transfer pricing) would be a better way forward to distribute the profits of an MNE and to allocate tax revenues among jurisdictions. Recent announcements by the G7 suggest a cautious move towards shifting the international consensus on these reform options.[44] The shifting nature of the policy responses should be taken into account when determining the best approach for reconciling the relationship between direct and indirect tax obligations including the VAT.

[B] Customs Duties

Related-party cross-border supplies give rise to indirect tax liabilities incurred under relevant customs laws including duty payable on imported goods. Customs duties will *only* affect cross-border supplies of tangible goods (including any related intellectual property attached to those goods). The tax treatment of cross-border supplies of services and intangible goods (wherein much of the MNE tax arbitrage focuses) affects

44. *See, e.g.*, G7 Finance Minister and Central Bank Governors, *Communique* (5 June 2021) [16]; OECD, *Aligning Transfer Pricing Outcomes with Value Creation, supra* n. 5; OECD, *Transfer Pricing Documentation and Country-by-Country Reporting, supra* n. 7. Cf. OECD, *OECD Secretary-General Tax Report to G20 Finance Ministers and Central Bank Governors – October 2019, supra* n. 3, which recommended two pillars for reform of corporate taxation. The first attempts to allocate a greater share of taxing rights to jurisdictions which provide the market for digital products and services and certain consumer goods. It does so by proposing two variations on the ALS complemented by an alternative formula-based approach which allocates 'residual' corporate profits to jurisdictions based on certain (limited) criteria such as sales (for digital supplies) and other indicators of market presence (for consumer goods) to that jurisdiction: OECD, *Tax Challenges Arising from Digitalisation – Report on Pillar One Blueprint: Inclusive Framework on BEPS*, OECD/G20 Base Erosion and Profit Shifting Project (OECD Publishing, October 2020). The second attempts to develop an alternative minimum corporate tax that is designed to apply in circumstances where other jurisdictions have either failed to tax the corporate profit or taxed the profit at low effective rates: OECD, *Tax Challenges Arising from Digitalisation – Report on Pillar Two Blueprint: Inclusive Framework on BEPS*, OECD/G20 Base Erosion and Profit Shifting Project (OECD Publishing, October 2020). For criticism of transfer pricing and the arm's length standard, the twin pillars approach and advocacy for the alternative standard of global formulary apportionment, *see* ICRICT, *supra* n. 43, 4-8; Tax Justice Network, 'G7 take big steps to recover tax but just for themselves' (press release, 5 June 2021) https://taxjustice.net/press/g7-take-big-step-to-recover-tax-but-just-for-themselves/. For a more detailed discussion of formulary apportionment and its practical operation in the most significant contexts in which it is currently found, that of the subnational state income taxes in the United States and provincial income taxes in Canada, *see, respectively*, Shirley Sicilian & Joe Huddleston, *The US States' Experience with Formulary Apportionment*, in *The Allocation of Multinational Business Income: Reassessing the Formulary Apportionment Option* 39, 41, 42, §2.02 (Richard Krever & François Vaillancourt, eds., Kluwer Law International, 2020) and, also in that volume (at 71, 75), Michael Smart & François Vaillancourt, *Formulary Apportionment in Canada and Taxation of Corporate Income in 2019: Current Practice, Origins and Evaluation*; further criticisms of the arm's length standard, and the formulary apportionment alternative, are also set out in that volume (at 163, 169, §6.01 and at 176, §6.03 and references there cited, respectively), in J. Clifton Fleming, Jr., Robert J. Peroni & Stephen E. Shay, *Is Unilateral Formulary Apportionment Better than the Status Quo?*.

income tax and VAT liabilities only.[45] Whereas the OECD *Model Tax Convention*, the OECD Commentary to the Model and the OECD *Transfer Pricing Guidelines* are non-binding but highly influential,[46] international customs law is governed by a binding and widely-implemented multilateral instrument.[47] Discrepancies between national approaches are therefore less likely.

Duty is generally calculated on a transactional basis using the transaction value method.[48] This means that the price actually paid or payable for the goods when sold for export to the country of importation serves as the basis for calculating customs duties; this usually corresponds to the price declared by the importer. This price is adjusted by certain costs such as those that might need to be added to the transaction value (e.g., commissions and brokerage, packing expenses, cost of containers).[49] This transaction value method applies *unless* such a method is not appropriate. This includes situations in which there are fairly strong grounds to consider abuse (i.e., the transaction is a related party dealing *and* in the 'circumstances surrounding the sale' that relationship may have influenced the price).[50] Both Australia and the EU follow this approach. For example, when interpreting the Union Customs Code, the Court of Justice of the European Union (CJEU) has held that 'as a general rule the price actually paid or payable for the goods forms the basis for calculating the customs value, that price is a factor that potentially must be adjusted where necessary in order to avoid the setting of an arbitrary or fictitious customs value'.[51]

Much of the compliance work is therefore focused on ascertaining whether the relationship of the parties has influenced the price of the transaction. If customs authorities form this opinion, the importer is invited to make submissions as to why the price is justifiable, which entails considerations sufficiently proximate to what might be considered an arm's length market value (determined by one of three alternative methods that are distinct from, albeit not entirely alien to, the transfer pricing methods).[52] This transaction value must be accepted if it 'closely approximates' what might be considered an arm's length market value.[53]

There has been much work at the international and national level to determine two issues in connection with the relationship between transfer pricing and customs

45. OECD, *Aligning Transfer Pricing Outcomes with Value Creation*, *supra* n. 5, 63-139; OECD, *Transfer Pricing Guidelines*, *supra* n. 4, 36, [1.9].
46. *See supra* n. 18.
47. The Customs Valuation Agreement offers an example of a binding and widely implemented international agreement: *Agreement on Implementation of Article VII of the General Agreement on Tariffs and Trade 1994*, signed 15 April 1994, 1868 UNTS 279 (entered into force 1 January 1995) (*Customs Valuation Agreement*); Fabio, *supra* n. 32, 273-274; WCO, *Guide to Customs Valuation and Transfer Pricing*, *supra* n. 9, 19-24, [3.3].
48. *Customs Valuation Agreement*, *supra* n. 47, Articles 1 and 8 (adjustments).
49. *Customs Valuation Agreement*, *supra* n. 47, Article 8.
50. *Customs Valuation Agreement*, *supra* n. 47, Articles 2(a), 15(4).
51. CJEU, 20 December 2017, Case C-529/16, *Hamamatsu Photonics Deutschland GmbH*, ECLI: EU:C:2017:984, paragraph 27 with reference to further case law.
52. *Customs Valuation Agreement*, *supra* n. 47, Article 2(b). The customs and transfer pricing valuation methods both share a similar goal to ensure 'that the price is set as if the parties were not related and had been negotiated under normal business conditions': WCO, *Guide to Customs Valuation and Transfer Pricing*, *supra* n. 9, 57, [4.1].
53. *Customs Valuation Agreement*, *supra* n. 47, Articles 2(b), 5, 6.

duties: first, what is the relevance of each set of rules to appropriately value transactions, and secondly, how should an adjustment in one area be treated in the other.[54]

On the valuation issue, it is generally acknowledged that both valuations might be relevant albeit that they are determined on different bases and for different purposes.[55] This has involved addressing questions such as whether customs can rely on transfer pricing documentation for customs valuation purposes (in general, yes, on a case-by-case basis).[56] The World Customs Organization (WCO) further recommends that: 'Customs and tax administrations ... verify the duty/tax liability of MNEs ... via compliance-based audit, selected on the basis of risk criteria.'[57]

On the adjustment issue, as a general principle, despite approaches varying between jurisdictions, the WCO suggests that a transfer pricing adjustment should at least be considered by customs authorities. Different consequences might flow depending on who initiated the adjustment (the taxpayer or revenue authorities), the type of adjustment (a tax-only or price-inclusive adjustment) and the timing of the adjustment (prior or post-importation) and whether the adjustment is reflected in the taxpayer's accounts.[58] In general terms, the WCO suggests that a transfer pricing adjustment be taken into account for customs purposes if the adjustment influences the actual price paid for the goods (i.e., a price-inclusive adjustment) such as by increasing the price (therefore requiring the payment of additional duty) or decreasing the price (therefore entailing a refund of duty). A transfer pricing adjustment might also be relevant if it indicates that the relationship of the parties influenced the price which is more likely if the transfer pricing adjustment is price-inclusive but still potentially relevant for a tax-only adjustment as it might indicate something about how the relationship of the parties might have influenced the price of the transaction.[59] In practice, approaches vary between jurisdictions.[60]

As for the converse situation, the WCO regards it as 'good practice' for revenue authorities and customs to have established avenues for exchange of information including how the value of goods has been arrived at (by either the taxpayer or customs authority).[61] To the extent that an adjustment by customs authorities indicates a lack of arm's length price, such information should be relevant to, but not determinative of,

54. WCO, *Guide to Customs Valuation and Transfer Pricing*, *supra* n. 9, 59, [4.2].
55. OECD, *Transfer Pricing Guidelines*, *supra* n. 4, [1.137].
56. WCO, *Guide to Customs Valuation and Transfer Pricing*, *supra* n. 9, 63, [5.1] – in particular, of relevance is 'what particular information typically found in a transfer pricing study may be useful to Customs in order to demonstrate that the price had not been influenced by the relationship'. As for the converse situation, it was recognized that the '"test values" option in Article 1.2(b) and (c) for examining related party transactions was not likely to be useful for MNEs which typically sell unique goods': 59, [4.3]; Technical Committee on Customs Valuation, Commentary 23.1 (Examination of the Expression 'Circumstances Surrounding The Sale' under Article 1.2 (a) in relation to the Use of Transfer Pricing Studies) cited in WCO, *Guide to Customs Valuation and Transfer Pricing*, *supra* n. 9, 60, [4.4]; Fabio, *supra* n. 32, 282.
57. WCO, *Guide to Customs Valuation and Transfer Pricing*, *supra* n. 9, 59, [4.2].
58. WCO, *Guide to Customs Valuation and Transfer Pricing*, *supra* n. 9, 69-70, [5.3.2].
59. No one factor is determinative. Further work would need to be undertaken to determine the appropriate price using the established customs methodologies: WCO, *Guide to Customs Valuation and Transfer Pricing*, *supra* n. 9, 69-70, [5.3.2].
60. WCO, *Guide to Customs Valuation and Transfer Pricing*, *supra* n. 9, 69, [5.3.1].
61. WCO, *Guide to Customs Valuation and Transfer Pricing*, *supra* n. 9, 73-74, [6.4].

the issue of the appropriateness of the transfer pricing values and whether or not a transfer pricing adjustment might be necessary (which considers more factors than just price alone and through different methods).[62]

Recently there has been a push by some within the business sector, notably the International Chamber of Commerce (ICC), to apply transfer pricing methods to customs valuations (and by implication VAT for jurisdictions which link VAT liability to dutiable value). This has also entailed a push to have customs authorities recognize an upwards or downwards post-transaction transfer pricing adjustment (whether made by revenue authorities or the taxpayer/importer).[63] This suggests a desire to streamline documentary and administrative requirements as well as a perceived advantage in being able to use transfer pricing methods in these other areas. In essence, the perceived advantage stems from a business being able to rely on their transfer pricing methods and documentation (accepted by a revenue authority) to, by extension, show that the relationship of the parties has not influenced the price (for customs purposes) or, by extension, that the price satisfies an equivalent open market value (in the context of objectively related party transactions for the VAT in instances of suspected avoidance or abuse).[64] There is a notable push to be able to use advance pricing arrangements (APAs) or similar arrangements to determine inter-related liabilities for all three revenue bases in advance.[65] The approach between jurisdictions differs. One can see the benefits in such arrangements offering a degree of certainty (for revenue authorities and taxpayers) as well as efficiency. However, there is an obvious need for revenue authorities to be cautious in doing so because of the obvious policy tension that arises from the need for valuations and adjustments to reflect the economic reality of the parties' position especially when that reality might be distorted by tax gaming. There is an additional need to guard against regulatory capture in making, relying upon and extending such agreements.

62. *See, e.g.*, Australian Taxation Office (ATO), Taxation Ruling TR 97/20, Income Tax: Arm's Length Transfer Pricing Methodologies for International Dealings, 35-36, [2.119]-[2.122] (5 November 1997).
63. International Chamber of Commerce (ICC): ICC, *Policy Statement – Transfer Pricing and Customs Valuation – 2015*, 1-2 (Document No. 180/104-536, 2015), 2-6 – Proposals 1-6.
64. ICC, *Policy Statement, supra* n. 63.
65. OECD, *Transfer Pricing Guidelines, supra* n. 4, 23; WCO, *Guide to Customs Valuation and Transfer Pricing, supra* n. 9, at 47, 67-68 – the WCO encourages customs administrations to enter into similar advance valuation agreements for customs purposes. The ICC does not formally endorse such a solution because they label APAs as 'often very rigid, time- and cost-consuming, and not appropriate for businesses that continually evolve': ICC, *Policy Statement – Transfer Pricing and Customs Valuation, supra* n. 63, 2. There is no VAT equivalent of an APA in either the EU or Australia, although there is a pilot-project in the EU on advance cross-border rulings (which do not concern price or valuation per se but rather attempt to offer some degree of certainty on the interpretation of the relevant rules): *see* European Commission, *VAT Cross Border Rulings (CBR): EU Pilot Project*, https://ec.europa.eu/taxation_customs/business/vat/vat-cross-border-rulings-cbr_en (accessed 1 February 2021).

[C] VAT

As the introduction explained, similar to the valuation of customs duties, VAT liability is generally assessed according to the consideration agreed upon by the parties.[66] However, not all transactions involving consideration are treated as within the scope of a VAT system and would, by extension, not be affected by a transfer pricing adjustment.

In general, VAT law builds on domestic civil law and the legal capacity of the entities and persons created therein.[67] Therefore, as a general rule any person or entity that has legal capacity under domestic civil law will be treated as a separate taxable person for VAT purposes and transactions between such persons are potentially subject to VAT (exceptions include the VAT grouping rules and recharge method discussed below). The VAT consequences ascribed by a given jurisdiction to a given transaction within an MNE (including a transfer pricing adjustment) can in turn depend on the structure of the MNE and whether the transaction is an intra-group or intra-entity transaction. For example, in jurisdictions that do *not* recognize intra-entity transactions for VAT purposes and that do not have any form of anti-abuse rule, any arm's length test and transfer pricing adjustment applied to these types of transactions for corporate tax purposes will not affect VAT outcomes.

As a tax on final consumption expenditure, the VAT is generally neutral in its treatment of B2B supplies, at least in relation to those entities which can claim full input credits. Many VAT systems have VAT grouping rules which allow eligible corporate (or other)[68] groups to form a VAT group and be treated as one single taxable entity. So rather than one related entity charging VAT to another group member, remitting that VAT to revenue and the other group member being refunded the same VAT paid, the transactions between entities that are part of the group are effectively ignored or treated as out-of-scope of VAT (on Australia *see* §10.03[A]; on the EU approach *see* §10.04[A]).[69] As a result, whether or not the prices on those B2B transactions are too high or too low for income tax purposes is of no relevance for VAT purposes. This approach offers administrative convenience for the taxpayer (and tax authorities) but can produce revenue and compliance risks when parts of the VAT group are input taxed, i.e., carry out transactions that are exempt without the right for

66. *See* Chapter 9, §9.02[A][5], §9.04[B], and Chapter 16, §16.01 and §16.06 of this volume.
67. *See* Karoline Spies, *Permanent Establishments in Value Added Tax* 278-279 (IBFD Publications, 2020); Ad van Doesum, Herman van Kesteren & Gert-Jan van Norden, *Fundamentals of EU VAT Law* 62-64 (2nd ed., Wolters Kluwer, 2020).
68. *See, e.g.*, Australia which permits grouping for not-for profit and government entities and which has special grouping rules for religious organizations: *see infra* n. 123.
69. On VAT grouping in general and its implementation in various jurisdictions *see* Karina Kim Egholm Elgaard, *A Comparative Analysis of VAT Grouping Schemes from a Nordic Perspective – Aspects of Tax Avoidance and Fiscal Competition*, [2017] 1 Nordic Tax J. 1; Sebastian Pfeiffer, *VAT Grouping from a European Perspective* (IBFD Publications, 2015). *See, e.g.*, A New Tax System (Goods and Services Tax) Act 1999 (Cth.), Div. 48 (ANTS Act 1999); European Commission, Council Directive 2006/112/EC of 28 November 2006 on the Common System of Value Added Tax, OJ L 347, 11 December 2006, Article 11 (EU VAT Directive).

deduction of input VAT as might be the case when one or more group members are financial-service providers.

Besides VAT grouping, another instance of VAT rules applying to supplies and acquisitions made *within* an entity is found in jurisdictions, such as Australia and Singapore, which have special rules in place for the import of services by domestic branches which aim to prevent the distortion of competition that occurs when an entity acquires services (e.g., human resource support) via an offshore branch in order to avoid VAT (which would apply if such services were acquired domestically).[70] Based on such rules, the (internal) recharge of costs from an offshore establishment to a domestic establishment of the same legal entity is subject to VAT (via a reverse-charge). Often, the scope of such rules is limited to entities that have no full right to input credit, since offshoring is more attractive to such entities (*see* §10.03[B] for an example of the Australian rules).

The latter approach also finds some equivalent in the OECD *International VAT/GST Guidelines* ('the Guidelines') which outline principles for the VAT treatment of international trade in services and intangibles. The Guidelines build on the neutrality and destination principles and aim to reduce the uncertainty and risks of double taxation and unintended non-taxation that result from inconsistencies in the application of VAT in a cross-border context.[71] Among other things, the Guidelines discuss how to achieve the destination principle for B2B supplies of services and intangibles when the recipient is a 'multiple location entity', i.e., a legal entity that has establishments in more than one jurisdiction.[72] According to the Guidelines, the taxing rights should accrue to the jurisdiction(s) where the establishment(s) using the service or intangible is (are) located.[73] This result can be achieved either by directly attributing the services to the establishment that uses the service ('direct use method') or by requiring multiple location entities to internally recharge the cost of an externally acquired service to their establishments that use this service, as supported by internal recharge arrangements, and treating these recharges as subject to VAT ('recharge method').[74] Whereas under the direct use method, intra-entity supplies are commonly treated as out-of-scope (*see*, e.g., the EU system § 10.04[A]), under the recharge method, inbound cross-border intra-entity supplies of services are within the scope of VAT (*see*, e.g., the Australian system §10.03[B]).

70. On the BEPS issues connected to remote supplies to a multi-location enterprise in the area of VAT, *see* OECD, *Addressing the Tax Challenges of the Digital Economy: BEPS Action 1 – 2015 Final Report*, Ch. 5.3.2, paragraphs 201-203 (OECD Publishing 2015); for such tax planning structures within the EU VAT system *see* Joep Swinkels, *Fixed Establishments and VAT-Saving Schemes* 17(6) Intl. VAT Monitor 415 (2006); Madeleine Merkx, *Fixed Establishments in European Value Added Tax: Base Erosion and Profit Shifting's Side Effects?* 26(1) EC Tax Rev. 36 (2017).
71. OECD, *International VAT/GST Guidelines*, *supra* n. 8, paragraph 5. The Guidelines were adopted as recommendation by the Council of the OECD in September 2016.
72. OECD, *International VAT/GST Guidelines*, *supra* n. 8, Chs. B.3 and B.5.
73. OECD, *International VAT/GST Guidelines*, *supra* n. 8, guideline 3.4.
74. OECD, *International VAT/GST Guidelines*, *supra* n. 8, paragraph 3.24. The Guidelines propose the 'direct delivery method' as a third alternative approach. This method focuses on the establishment to which the service or intangible is delivered and can only be applied for a certain category of services (on-the-spot-supplies): at paragraph 3.31.

However, the Guidelines only deal with externally acquired services that are then passed on. They currently do not (explicitly) deal with the complex question of how to value inter-company transactions (internal value created)[75] and so offer limited guidance on how to address the VAT consequences of transfer pricing adjustments.[76] The significance of this gap is greatest when dealing with businesses that are (partially) input taxed, i.e., exempt without the right for the deduction of input VAT. However, the Guidelines and instances of their domestic implementation do offer some indications of possible approaches. For example, the Guidelines recommend that the allocation of taxing rights on *externally* acquired services by multiple location entities to the jurisdiction where the services are actually used should be done by tracing the external cost elements within the in-house supply chain of the multiple location entity and by allocating the costs to the business units to which they effectively contribute.[77] Against this background, the OECD recommends limiting the taxable amount of the internal recharges to the costs of the *externally* purchased service.[78] Hence, internal costs (personnel) should not be part of the taxable amount of the recharge and no arm's length test or mark-up should be applied.[79] In this context, any transfer pricing adjustment on the intra-entity supply made for corporate tax purposes should not have any VAT effect.[80] However, not all jurisdictions which adopt the recharge method follow this recommendation by the OECD with some jurisdictions (including Australia: §10.03[B]) applying an open market value to the internal recharge in certain circumstances[81] which may (or may not) incorporate transfer pricing approaches to valuation or adjustments.

The Guidelines do discuss some possible interaction between transfer pricing and the internal recharges based on the recharge method. The Guidelines mention that the attribution of the external cost elements to the establishments of use could be done by applying cost allocation or apportionment methods (allocation keys). In order to

75. *See*, on this question in more detail, Kathryn James & Thomas Ecker, *Relevance of the OECD International VAT/GST Guidelines for Non-OECD Countries* 32(2) Austl. Tax F. 317, 354-355 (2017).
76. Examples of the types of inter-company transactions not covered by the Guidelines include a supply wholly self-created by one establishment and supplied cross-border to another establishment or cases where an establishment transforms input into a new output with increased value which it supplies cross-border to another establishment of the same business: James & Ecker, *Relevance of the OECD International VAT/GST Guidelines for Non-OECD Countries, supra* n. 75, 355.
77. *See* Spies, *Permanent Establishments in Value Added Tax, supra* n. 67, 479.
78. OECD, *International VAT/GST Guidelines, supra* n. 8, 3.99 ('the taxable amount would in principle be the amount of the recharge that corresponds to the purchase price of the service or intangible'), paragraph 3.106 ('In cases where the separation of external costs from other costs within an internal recharge would be necessary *to ensure that the recharge method is applied only on the cost of the externally purchased service* or intangible...'), paragraphs 3.101-3.102 (emphasis added).
79. *See* further Spies, *Permanent Establishments in Value Added Tax, supra* n. 67, 471-474.
80. *See* Spies, *Permanent Establishments in Value Added Tax, supra* n. 67, 474.
81. *See*, for Singapore, Karoline Spies, *International Trade in B2B Services under VAT/GST Law and the Role of Permanent/Fixed Establishments – A Comparison of EU VAT and Singaporean GST Law in the Light of the OECD VAT/GST Guidelines* 25(3) Asia-Pacific Tax Bull. (2019).

establish reasonable methods, businesses should be allowed to make use of information that is already available for accounting or tax purposes,[82] which may also include information and data collected for transfer pricing purposes.[83] However, against the fundamental difference of transfer pricing in corporate tax (allocation of profits to business units) and the recharge method in VAT (allocation of external cost elements to the establishments of use), the potential relevance of transfer pricing methods for the recharge method might be limited.[84]

If an (intra-group or intra-entity) transaction is treated as taxable (within the scope of VAT), the next question that arises is how to define the taxable base for this transaction. Although VAT liability is generally assessed according to the consideration agreed upon by the parties, many VAT systems include an important exception in the form of anti-abuse rules directed at related-party transactions, such as those between family members or associated entities (corporate groups). The rules generally apply when the *recipient* of a supply is not entitled to full input credits and an incentive therefore exists for the related parties to agree to artificially inflate or reduce a price to manipulate the right to input VAT deduction which in turn affects tax revenues.[85] Similar anti-abuse rules may also apply if the *supplier* is not entitled to full input credits because there might be an incentive for the related parties to agree to artificially increase the price of a taxed output transaction of the supplier and minimize the price of an input-taxed or exempt transaction in order to manipulate the recovery ratio for input VAT deduction of the supplier (e.g., applied on overheads) which in turn also could affect tax revenues.[86] Such rules usually require the use of an objective or open market value for determining the price of a transaction rather than the usual 'subjective' standard of the price agreed to by the parties. These anti-abuse rules give rise to issues such as to what extent should transfer pricing methods be relevant to the determination of the relevant open market or arm's length value for VAT purposes and whether or not the parties are sufficiently related to trigger the application of the rules (*see* §10.03[C] and §10.04[C]).[87]

[D] Interaction of the Tax Bases and Administrative Issues

It is important to note the interaction between the three different taxes.[88] As a general rule, a party importing goods will want to declare a *low* value to minimize customs duty

82. OECD, *International VAT/GST Guidelines, supra* n. 8, paragraph 3.93.
83. *See*, in more detail, Spies, *Permanent Establishments in Value Added Tax, supra* n. 67, 475-481.
84. *See also* Merkx, *Should EU VAT Apply the Recharge Method in the Place of Supply Rules for B2B Services?, supra* n. 31, 286-287.
85. *See, e.g.*, EU VAT Directive, *supra* n. 69, Article 80(1)(a); ANTS Act 1999, *supra* n. 69, Div. 72. *See infra* §§10.03[B] and 10.04[B].
86. *See, e.g.*, EU VAT Directive, *supra* n. 69, Article 80(1)(b)-(c).
87. European Commission, *Question Concerning the Application of EU VAT Provisions, supra* n. 5, 13-14, 17; Rouberol, *supra* n. 24, 318; Fernando Matesanz, *Transfer Pricing Adjustments and VAT* 29(1) Int'l VAT Monitor 6, 8 (2018).
88. WCO, *Guide to Customs Valuation and Transfer Pricing, supra* n. 9, 57; the WCO states that '[a]lthough congruence is theoretically desirable, different transfer prices may be recorded or reported for different purposes' (at 16).

and a customs authority will be focused on assessing whether such an amount is an *under-estimation* designed to minimize duties and related taxes. By contrast, for income tax purposes the importer/taxpayer will want a *high* value for transfer pricing purposes (especially if the importer is in a high tax jurisdiction) and tax authorities will be focused on assessing whether such a value is *overestimated* so as to artificially increase income tax deductions.[89] In theory, a taxpayer who can claim full input credits will be indifferent to the VAT treatment (given that a higher price will result in higher input credits) but the interactions become significant for taxpayers who cannot claim full input credits (such as an import of furniture equipment by a financial services firm). In this case, the importer has an interest in minimizing the VAT amount.[90]

Institutionalized approaches to tax collection and enforcement will inform approaches to the issues such as the degree of integration between income tax and VAT collection within revenue authorities as well as the degree of coordination and information sharing between customs and revenue authorities. For example, in jurisdictions where the customs value of imported goods serves as the basis for the assessment of (import) VAT and other taxes (e.g., excise), the final determination of these amounts might affect these other liabilities.[91] Therefore, if the VAT law of a certain jurisdiction links the taxable base for import VAT to the customs value[92] and customs chooses to take account of a transfer pricing adjustment, then this should, in theory, also affect VAT liability. However, in jurisdictions with separate customs and VAT administrations or in which customs values do not inform VAT liability, revenue authorities are less likely to be bound by (or possibly even have information on) the decision of customs authorities.

There are therefore also important administrative questions around the degree of coordination required between revenue authorities and customs authorities (if both are separate) to improve collection and compliance.[93] For example, it is important for revenue authorities and customs authorities to have appropriate information exchange and be sufficiently coordinated to cross-check what information taxpayers are declaring for transfer pricing purposes and for customs/VAT purposes.[94] This is especially so when the incentives act in different directions for each tax base and so each acts as a

89. European Commission, *Question Concerning the Application of EU VAT Provisions, supra* n. 5, 23; Ping & Silberztein, *supra* n. 1, 36; Gina Lazanas, Paul Welch & Fletch Heinemann, *Interaction between Customs Duty, GST/VAT and Transfer Pricing in Australia*, Tax Planning International Indirect Taxes 1 (1 August 2008); OECD, *Transfer Pricing Guidelines, supra* n. 4, [1.138]; Fabio, *supra* n. 32, 274.
90. European Commission, *Question Concerning the Application of EU VAT Provisions, supra* n. 5, 11, n. 40; Rouberol, *supra* n. 24, 317-319.
91. *See*, for the European Union: European Commission, *Question Concerning the Application of EU VAT Provisions, supra* n. 5, 15-16, 23.
92. *See* EU VAT Directive, *supra* n. 69, Article 85: 'In respect of the importation of goods, the taxable amount shall be the value for customs purposes, determined in accordance with the Community provisions in force.'
93. WCO, *Guide to Customs Valuation and Transfer Pricing, supra* n. 9, Chapter 6; Sachin Dave & Vinod Mahanta, *Government to Vet GST, Income Tax and Transfer Pricing Filings to Find Leakage*, The Economic Times (New Delhi) (28 August 2018).
94. WCO, *Guide to Customs Valuation and Transfer Pricing, supra* n. 9, 73-74, [6.4]. Within the EU tax authorities can exchange information with customs authorities on importations subject to VAT and customs fraud (*see* Council Regulation (EU) 2018/1541 of 2 October 2018 amending

natural check and balance on the other (i.e., a high price might reduce income tax payable but also increase duty or VAT payable). If the interactions are not sufficiently monitored and coordinated by revenue and customs authorities then significant revenue loss or potential inconsistencies can arise. For example, if a taxpayer has over-inflated prices for transfer pricing purposes but under-declared values for customs/VAT purposes this results in a win/win for the taxpayer and a lose/lose for revenue authorities in a way that cannot wholly be justified (given the values on one side must be either over- or undervalued presuming a degree of overlap in the definition of the taxable or dutiable amount). Likewise, sufficient coordination might be required so that a taxpayer does not lose/lose with an assessment that imposes a very high valuation for customs/VAT purposes but a very low value for transfer pricing purposes (even after taking account the different methods to achieve those values).[95]

At a practical level the issue of the potential interaction between the three bases is likely to arise at the point when an adjustment is made for the purposes of one tax giving rise to the question of whether this should have any effect on another tax. For jurisdictions where the duty value affects VAT liability, any customs adjustments will likely have VAT implications. The relationship between transfer pricing adjustments and customs was addressed at §10.02[B]. As was discussed in the context of an adjustment by customs, an adjustment for VAT purposes, particularly one that might arise as a result of an anti-abuse provision using an open market value instead of the subjective value (agreed price), which could indicate a lack of arm's length price, *should* be relevant to the issue of transfer pricing. However, such a VAT adjustment is unlikely to be *wholly determinative* of either an assessment of transfer pricing values or whether a transfer pricing adjustment is required at all because of the different valuation methods (and resultant values) which, in the context of transfer pricing, are often the product of more factors than just price alone.[96] The next section therefore focuses on the more prevalent issue of whether a transfer pricing adjustment made for income tax purposes should have VAT consequences.

[E] The Relevance of Transfer Pricing Adjustments to VAT Liability

A number of views have been expressed as to whether and in what circumstances a transfer pricing adjustment imposed for income tax purposes should give rise to a corresponding obligation to adjust VAT liabilities.[97] A 2017 European Commission

Regulations (EU) No. 904/2010 and (EU) No. 2017/2454 as regards measures to strengthen administrative cooperation in the field of value added tax, OJ L 259, 16.10.2018, 1-11).

95. *See, e.g.*, the concerns expressed by the International Chamber of Commerce (ICC): ICC, *Policy Statement – Transfer Pricing and Customs Valuation – 2015*, *supra* n. 63, 1-2.

96. *See supra* § 10.02 [A]. For the best analysis of when a VAT adjustment might have consequences for transfer pricing including adjustments (albeit in a primarily European context) *see* Rouberol, *supra* n. 24, 318-319.

97. *See, e.g.*, European Commission, *Question Concerning the Application of EU VAT Provisions – Possible VAT Implications of Transfer Pricing – The Point of View of the VAT Expert Group 2* (Value Added Tax Committee (Article 398 of Directive 2006/112/EC) Working Paper No. 945Rev, taxud.c.1(2018)2329129, 19 April 2018) (transfer-pricing adjustments should be considered out of scope for VAT purposes – with a possible exception made in the context of abuse

Working Paper contains a comprehensive assessment of the issue, but has not resulted in any formal resolutions.[98]

As outlined in the introduction to this chapter, there are two broad opinions on the relationship between transfer pricing and the VAT. The first (minority view) treats the two areas as entirely separate,[99] the second (majority view) treats the two areas as related. The second approach then gives rise to the question of the degree to which the two approaches are integrated. No one suggests they are entirely integrated for the reasons already outlined, i.e., they are different taxes with different bases. In relation to the issue of the VAT consequences of a transfer pricing adjustment, such an adjustment might result in one of four VAT outcomes in a given case depending on the circumstances: (1) none; (2) VAT consequences due to specific anti-abuse or avoidance rules; (3) a new taxable supply under the VAT; or (4) a VAT adjustment. Each is briefly discussed in turn.

The first outcome in a given case could be that the transfer pricing adjustment does not trigger any VAT consequences. This might result if a VAT system did not recognize the specific transaction to which the transfer pricing adjustment is applied for VAT purposes. To return to an earlier example given at §10.02[C], a VAT system that does not recognize intra-entity supplies will similarly not ascribe VAT consequences to an intra-entity transfer pricing adjustment. In some jurisdictions no consequences will occur if the transfer pricing adjustment is merely reflected/deemed for corporate tax purposes (and not reflected in the books and payments), or when the transfer pricing adjustment for corporate tax is based on a profit split method and hence cannot be linked to any specific transaction (*see* further below).

---

for taxpayers for whom full input credits are not available); Matesanz, *supra* n. 87, 9 (only taxpayer (cf. revenue authority) initiated compensatory adjustments that are sufficiently linked to the original supply should give rise to a VAT adjustment); Idsinga, Kalshoven & van Herksen, *supra* n. 11, 207-208 (whether a compensatory adjustment gives rise to a VAT adjustment depends on the connection to the original supply); Santoro, *supra* n. 16, 157-163 (limited scope for a transfer pricing adjustment to result in a VAT adjustment – primarily limited to situations when the adjustment arises by agreement between the parties and is reflected in their cash accounts); Rouberol, *supra* n. 24 (VAT consequences depend on the type of transfer pricing adjustment (i.e., if it is effected on a transactional or global basis) and whether or not the adjustment satisfies the criteria for VAT liability whether it be a VAT adjustment or VAT liability for a new supply).

98. European Commission, *Question Concerning the Application of EU VAT Provisions*, *supra* n. 5; European Commission, *Minutes of 110th Meeting of the Value Added Tax Committee*, item 4, 4.1 (Value Added Tax Committee (Article 398 Directive 2006/112/EC) Working Paper No. 952, 13 April 2018) – 'The Commission services concluded that the issue is complex and that it will likely be impossible to agree on a general rule. The drafting of guidelines, as suggested by a few delegations, would be considered but could be difficult.'

99. The underlying rationale is the neutrality of the VAT towards B2B transactions: European Commission, *Question Concerning the Application of EU VAT Provisions – Possible VAT Implications of Transfer Pricing – The Point of View of the VAT Expert Group*, *supra* n. 97, 2 *cf.* Matesanz, *supra* n. 87, 9. Such an approach was favoured by some business interests in response to the EC Paper (at least when both parties have a full right of to recover input-VAT) but met with some scepticism by EC delegates: European Commission, *Question Concerning the Application of EU VAT Provisions – Possible VAT Implications of Transfer Pricing – The Point of View of the VAT Expert Group*, *supra* n. 97, 2, 8; European Commission, *Minutes of 110th Meeting of the Value Added Tax Committee*, *supra* n. 98, item 4, 4.1.

Secondly, jurisdictions might generally ignore intra-group and/or intra-entity transactions and/or generally apply the agreed price as the taxable base, except when the recipient of a supply is unable to claim full input credits or in cases of suspected avoidance and abuse.[100] This is most readily satisfied when a jurisdiction has a special anti-abuse rule in place for certain related-party transactions which applies the 'open market value' as the taxable amount. In these circumstances, a transfer pricing adjustment made by a revenue authority in order to establish the correct arm's length price might also indicate that an adjustment of the 'open market value' for VAT purposes is necessary.[101] In addition, there is a further question around the relevance, if any, of transfer pricing methods to determining arm's length or open market value for VAT purposes.[102]

Thirdly, the transfer pricing adjustment might constitute consideration for a new (subsequent) supply (e.g., of rights, obligations or services) as might occur if an additional payment arising from a transfer pricing adjustment is construed as consideration paid for a separate supply or in jurisdictions which might attribute VAT consequences to constructive transactions that result from a secondary adjustment.[103]

Fourthly, a transfer pricing adjustment can result in a VAT adjustment for a previous supply. This will require that the transfer pricing adjustment is sufficiently linked to the consideration of the previous supply as, for example, might be the case if the parties to the original transaction agree to change the consideration payable.[104]

The appropriate treatment of a specific transfer pricing adjustment (i.e., which of the four possible outcomes applies) will depend on factors such as: factual characterization; the manner in which the parties have structured their dealings; the manner in which the underlying general law characterizes the transaction; the legislative criteria including the underlying criteria giving rise to the initial supply (or creditable acquisition) and any obligation to adjust; the definition of the taxable amount within the VAT

100. European Commission, *Question Concerning the Application of EU VAT Provisions*, *supra* n. 5, 17 – notes the policy implications if all transfer pricing adjustments resulted in a VAT adjustment which would undermine the notion of 'subjective consideration' as stipulated by Article 73 of the VAT Directive, *supra* n. 67, and effectively apply an arm's length/open market value; European Commission, *Question Concerning the Application of EU VAT Provisions – Possible VAT Implications of Transfer Pricing – The Point of View of the VAT Expert Group*, *supra* n. 97, 2.

101. Santoro, *supra* n. 16, 162; Alexandra Martins, *VAT Transfer-Pricing Rules: A Portuguese Perspective* 37(5) Intertax 322, 328 (2009); Rouberol, *supra* n. 24, 318.

102. Rouberol, *supra* n. 24, 318, suggests that Articles 80 and 72 of the EU VAT Directive, *supra* n. 69, are drafted to at least be consistent with transfer pricing methods in the OECD *Transfer Pricing Guidelines*, *supra* n. 4; European Commission, *Question Concerning the Application of EU VAT Provisions – Possible VAT Implications of Transfer Pricing – The Point of View of the VAT Expert Group*, *supra* n. 97, 2.

103. European Commission, *Question Concerning the Application of EU VAT Provisions*, *supra* n. 5, 15 (n. 53); European Commission, *Question Concerning the Application of EU VAT Provisions – Possible VAT Implications of Transfer Pricing – The Point of View of the VAT Expert Group*, *supra* n. 97, 3; Idsinga, Kalshoven & van Herksen, *supra* n. 11, 207; Ronald van den Brekel, Ad van Doesum & Herman van Kesteren, *VAT Effects of Year-End Transfer Pricing Adjustments* 26(4) EC Tax Rev. 182, 191-192 (2017); Santoro, *supra* n. 16, 161-163.

104. European Commission, *Question Concerning the Application of EU VAT Provisions*, *supra* n. 5, 15; Rouberol, *supra* n. 24, 317; van den Brekel, van Doesum & van Kesteren, *supra* n. 103, 192. *See* Chapter 9 including §9.2[A] of this volume for when VAT adjustments might apply.

system; judicial approaches to interpretation; the method of transfer pricing applied (e.g., transaction-based or profit split); the type of transfer pricing adjustment undertaken (tax only or reflected in the taxpayer's accounts)[105] and which party made it (the taxpayer or revenue authority).[106]

For example, a primary adjustment achieved through a transaction-based method (such as the comparable uncontrolled price method) applied to identifiable previous transactions is *more likely* to have VAT consequences than an adjustment changing the global remuneration of a company (i.e., based on profit split or comparable profit methods).[107] A transfer pricing adjustment that is not exclusively made in the tax accounts, but is also reflected in the commercial books and payments (in money or in kind) and that can be disaggregated and linked to a previous transaction, is *more likely* to have VAT consequences.[108] Moreover, the likelihood of any effect on the VAT might also depend on the extent to which it affects revenue in a given jurisdiction (which in turn depends on whether or not the recipient or supplier of the original supplies can claim full input tax credits and how the jurisdiction deals with the resulting revenue risks in the context of transactions within a corporation or group).[109]

Some argue that a 'compensating adjustment' initiated by the parties to the original transaction, which leads to balancing payments, should warrant a corresponding VAT adjustment provided that it is sufficiently linked to a previous supply because it is a change in consideration.[110] A number of European scholars and advocates have argued that transfer pricing adjustments at the initiative of the tax authorities should not have any VAT implications, since such adjustments do not constitute a form of consideration agreed to between the parties.[111] However, this conclusion also depends on how a given jurisdiction treats variations of prices or consideration by external bodies (e.g., court orders, tribunal awards, or assessments by revenue authorities). To the extent that such a conclusion presumes the inapplicability of these external variations to VAT valuations and adjustments, it is unlikely to represent a universal

105. The European Commission states that for a transfer pricing adjustment to amount to a change of consideration it must be reflected in the taxpayers' accounts: European Commission, *Question Concerning the Application of EU VAT Provisions*, *supra* n. 5, 18.
106. European Commission, *Question Concerning the Application of EU VAT Provisions*, *supra* n. 5, 20-21.
107. Rouberol, *supra* n. 24, 316-317.
108. *Cf.* European Commission, *Question Concerning the Application of EU VAT Provisions*, *supra* n. 5, 16-18; van Doesum, van Kesteren & van Norden, *supra* n. 67, 290. When no direct link to a previous supply can be established, it might be argued that the adjustment leads to a separate taxable supply (Santoro, *supra* n. 16, 162).
109. Rouberol offers a good analysis of the likely scenarios with revenue implications: Rouberol, *supra* n. 24, 319 – for an overview of how the VAT and transfer pricing might overlap and interact in the EU *see* examples 1-6: 317-319.
110. The general consensus is that such an adjustment can result in a corresponding VAT adjustment if sufficiently linked to the original transaction and if reflected in the accounts of the taxpayer: Santoro, *supra* n. 16, 162-163; Matesanz, *supra* n. 87, 9; van Doesum, van Kesteren & van Norden, *supra* n. 67, 290.
111. Santoro, *supra* n. 16, 161; Martins, *supra* n. 101, 328; van den Brekel, van Doesum & van Kesteren, *supra* n. 103, 185; Matesanz, *supra* n. 87, 8-9; van Doesum, van Kesteren & van Norden, *supra* n. 67, 290; European Commission, *Question Concerning the Application of EU VAT Provisions – Possible VAT Implications of Transfer Pricing – The Point of View of the VAT Expert Group*, *supra* n. 97, 2.

position because such a presumption is not universally shared (even within the EU: *see* § 10.04[E])[112] and elsewhere explicitly rejected (as in Australia: *see* §10.03[E]).

As the above analysis suggests, the approach of different jurisdictions varies – even in the EU where an effort by the EC to initiate some discussion around the issue has resulted neither in concrete proposals nor recommendations to coordinate approaches. In broad terms, there is, increasingly, an appetite not to ignore the interaction between all three areas of revenue law. Sections 10.03 and 10.04 provide an overview of the respective approaches of Australia and the EU.

§10.03 THE AUSTRALIAN APPROACH TO TRANSFER PRICING AND THE GST

The Australian approach to the relationship between the GST and transfer pricing offers MNEs the choice of very generous GST treatment of intra-entity and intra-group dealings but with some restrictions. The Australian approach generally takes the second approach outlined in §10.02[E] of ignoring intra-entity and intra-group transactions[113] except in limited circumstances when the recipient of a supply is unable to claim full input credits and/or in cases of suspected avoidance and abuse. The Australian Taxation Office (ATO) headed by the Federal Commissioner of Taxation administers income tax and the GST except on imported goods which is administered by the Australian customs authority, known currently as the Australian Border Force, which administers customs duties and other related taxes on imported goods including the GST.

It is also worth briefly mentioning the place of taxation rules that are relevant to the question of the treatment of cross-border supplies within an MNE. Place of taxation rules generally require that a supply must be 'connected with' Australia to constitute a taxable supply.[114] The test for connection varies according to the thing supplied: for goods this includes delivery to, importation into, or removal from Australia;[115] for real property this includes the land to which the supply relates being located in Australia;[116] and for supplies of 'anything else', commonly understood as things other than goods and real property such as services and intangibles, this includes supplies done in Australia, or made through an enterprise in Australia, or, made to a recipient of a supply (of an intangible or service provided by a non-resident) who is an Australian

112. European Commission, *Question Concerning the Application of EU VAT Provisions*, *supra* n. 5, 20-21. *See further* Chapter 9 of this volume (§§ 9.2[A][5], 9.5[D] and 9.6[D]).
113. *See, e.g.*, the grouping provisions in ANTS Act 1999, *supra* n. 69, Div. 48.
114. ANTS Act 1999, *supra* n. 69, section 9-25. This concerns the application the destination principle. The legislative term adopted is 'indirect tax zone' which means Australia excluding the external territories and some offshore petroleum and gas developments: section 195-1. For ease of reading, the indirect tax zone will be referred to as Australia.
115. ANTS Act 1999, *supra* n. 69, sections 9-25(1)-9-25(3A).
116. ANTS Act 1999, *supra* n. 69, section 9-25(4).

consumer.[117] Further special rules provide place of taxation rules for other supplies such as imports of low value goods provided by non-resident entities.[118]

[A] Taxability of Intra-Group and Intra-Entity Transactions

Under the Australian GST, an MNE has a number of choices relevant to its GST treatment. It might first choose to form a GST-group (taking internal supplies between members (including non-residents) of the group outside the scope of the GST, i.e., the equivalent of intra-entity dealings, subject to the possible exceptions discussed at §10.03[B]-[C]). It might secondly choose to form GST-branches (which recognizes internal supplies and offers consolidated accounting and reporting requirements). It might thirdly choose to appoint a resident agent to act in relation to the GST obligations of the non-resident principal(s).[119] Or it might choose nothing.[120] If none of the first three options are chosen, then the GST treatment should follow the specific structure of the MNE and the application of the place of taxation rules. So, for example, if a single corporate entity (resident or non-resident) is registered for GST, then any supplies and acquisitions made between branches of that company (whether those branches are located in Australia or elsewhere) are ignored for GST purposes (subject to the possible application of the reverse charge provisions at §10.03[B]). Alternatively, a group of separate but related entities would be treated as separate entities which are subject to the standard registration, reporting, refund and remittance requirements.

One notable feature of the Australian approach which distinguishes it from the EU approach is that, for the most part, the GST rules for dealings within an MNE do not heavily depend on income tax or related concepts such as permanent or fixed establishment.[121] So, for example, the place of taxation rules outlined above will determine the taxing obligations for supplies between separate members of a corporate group (who do not avail themselves of the GST-grouping or branching provisions). Indeed, the terminology used within the Australian legislation can be fuzzy at times. For example, the legislation offers MNEs the options of forming a GST-group or GST-branches, but these options do not directly map on to the intra-group and intra-entity distinctions of the income tax.

---

117. ANTS Act 1999, *supra* n. 69, section 9-25(5), sub-Div. 84-B.
118. ANTS Act 1999, *supra* n. 69, Div. 84: including offshore supplies of low value goods: sub-Div. 84-C; Div. 85 (telecommunication supplies); sections 9-25(3A) and 9-25(5)(d).
119. ANTS Act 1999, *supra* n. 69, Div. 57. The rules act as a de facto anti-avoidance provision and make the resident agent liable for the GST obligations of a non-resident principal (including entitlements to credits/refunds) subject to some exceptions, e.g., if the GST liability arises because of an enterprise that the non-resident principal carries on in Australia: section 57-5(3). The rules do not apply to non-residents who are part of a GST group: section 57-50. Due to their more limited scope, the rules are not further discussed in this chapter.
120. Specific rules also permit limited pooling of GST obligations for parties in eligible joint venture projects, rules which were designed specifically for mining projects but can extend to any eligible joint venture. Due to their project-specific nature and more limited scope, these rules are not further discussed: *ibid.*, Div. 51.
121. For an exception, *see* the discussion of the associate provisions in §10.03[C] which rely on the income tax definition of associate for GST purposes.

Millar and Moon note that:[122]

> It is a basic principle of GST that an entity cannot make a supply to itself. Therefore, the Australian GST generally does not recognize internal dealings as transactions, whether they occur domestically or across borders.

This statement is true for intra-entity supplies and for intra-group supplies between members of a GST group. For MNEs which choose to register as a GST group,[123] then, once registered, the group is for the most part treated as a single entity with the representative member responsible for filing, remitting GST, claiming/apportioning input credits, and adjustments etc. on behalf of the group.[124] Supplies between group members are for the most part excluded – they are not treated as taxable supplies (but are supplies)[125] and an acquisition made from another member of the group is not a creditable acquisition *unless* the supply of the thing acquired by the entity was a taxable supply by virtue of the reverse-charge rules.[126] As a result, intra-group transfer pricing arrangements are for the most part ignored (other than the exceptions discussed below).[127] Members of a GST group are jointly and severally liable for the GST liability of the representative member.[128] Anecdotally, GST grouping is more common across large corporate groups.

The grouping rules were reformed in 2010 following a review by the Board of Taxation with input from business representatives, and since then have offered very generous grouping treatment for groups that meet the eligibility criteria – this discussion covers groups formed after the reforms took effect on 1 July 2010.[129] Members must each meet the relevant requirements for registering as a GST group (e.g., companies must have 90% common ownership) and the representative member must

122. Rebecca Millar & Lorenna Moon, *Australia*, in *Improving VAT/GST – Designing a Simple and Fraud-Proof Tax System* 23, 54, [2.2.2] (Michael Lang & Ine Lejeune eds., Kluwer Law International 2014); ATO, Goods and Services Tax Ruling GSTR 2006/9, Goods and Services Tax: Supplies, 27, [95]-[98] (12 December 2018) – 'Proposition 7: An entity cannot make a supply to itself'.
123. The grouping and branching provisions can extend beyond members of a corporate group. Group membership includes companies, individuals, trusts, partnerships and government organizations subject to each group member meeting the requisite criteria for membership: ANTS Act 1999, *supra* n. 69, sections 48-10, 48-15 and 149-25. Additional provisions permit grouping for religious organizations (Div. 49) and an additional branching option exists for not-for-profit entities (who can also access the general branching provisions) (Div. 63). These additional provisions are not further discussed in this chapter.
124. Importations are the responsibility of individual group members: ANTS Act 1999, *supra* n. 69, sections 48-40, 48-45(1) and 48-50.
125. ANTS Act 1999, *supra* n. 69, section 48-40(2).
126. ANTS Act 1999, *supra* n. 69, section 48-45(3), div 84. *See* §10.03[B].
127. ANTS Act 1999, *supra* n. 69, section 48-40(2). Further exceptions include things acquired within a GST joint venture which are subject to separate rules: section 48-20(2)(ii), Div. 51 and when the individual group member is liable for GST on taxable importations on a different basis to the representative member: section 48-40(2)(b).
128. *Taxation Administration Act 1953* (Cth), Sch. 1, section 444-90; ANTS Act 1999, *supra* n. 69, sections 48-40(1) and (1A).
129. Board of Taxation, *Review of the Legal Framework for the Administration of the Goods and Services Tax: A Report to the Assistant Treasurer and Minister for Competition Policy and Consumer Affairs*, Chapter 7 (December 2008); *Tax Laws Amendment (2010 GST Administration Measures No. 2) Act 2010* (Cth).

be resident in Australia but other members of the GST group can include resident and non-resident members (this option offers a much more generous treatment than in the EU and reflects a permissive approach, i.e., one that ignores intra-groups dealings even across borders subject to the possible exceptions outlined below).[130] The entity who nominates the GST group (and who will later be the representative member) self-assesses the group's eligibility to form a GST group. The formation of the GST group generally takes effect from the date specified by the nominated representative member in the requisite notice given to the Commissioner.[131]

Alternatively, should an MNE elect for branch registration then, provided that the registration requirements are satisfied (e.g., by establishing the requisite independence of the relevant branches through demonstrating separate accounting systems, locations/activities), the GST branch rules will recognize internal supplies between branches (and between a branch and parent) but consolidate reporting requirements.[132] Unlike the self-assessed grouping provisions, applications for GST branches need to be approved by the Commissioner and generally take effect on a date specified by the Commissioner.[133] An election to form a GST group precludes the formation of a GST branch and vice versa.[134]

Should the GST branch registration commence, the GST legislation then effectively treats internal supplies and acquisitions between branches as taxable supplies (or GST-free or input-taxed) or creditable acquisitions.[135] Each branch accounts for the GST separately; however, the parent remains responsible for the GST liabilities of the branches. Liability is calculated after a process of netting the GST payable, taking into account any additional net amount payable for each branch for each tax period and the parent entity's own net amount after attributing certain transactions to the branch and parent (including transactions between the branch and parent as well as adjustments).[136] Some have expressed doubt that the disaggregation of transactions between parent and branch extends to a treatment that is the exact equivalent of supplies and acquisitions between two independent entities, but such concerns extend beyond the

130. ANTS Act 1999, *supra* n. 69, sections 48-5(1)(e) and 48-10. Cf. §10.04[A]. Allowing non-residents to join as members of the GST-group was *not* a feature of the original ANTS package, but was introduced in the spate of amendments made between the release of the package and the passage of the reforms: Government amendments (Senate) to Clause 48 of the A New Tax System (Goods and Services Tax) Bill 1998, made on 25 June 1999 (Senate Journal pp. 1273-1275); Amendments explained in Supplementary Explanatory Memorandum to the A New Tax System (Goods and Services Tax) Bill 1998, tabled in the Senate, 28 April 1999, Senate Hansard, p. 4406.
131. ANTS Act 1999, *supra* n. 69, sections 48-5(1) and (3)-(4). Prior to the 2010 reforms, applications for GST groups needed to be approved by the Commissioner and could only take effect from the beginning of a tax period.
132. ANTS Act 1999, *supra* n. 69, section 54-5(1). The Commissioner must also be satisfied that the parent entity is carrying on an enterprise (or intends to) through the branch: section 54-5(1)(c).
133. ANTS Act 1999, *supra* n. 69, section 54-10.
134. ANTS Act 1999, *supra* n. 69, sections 54-5(3) and 48-10(1)(g).
135. ANTS Act 1999, *supra* n. 69. sections 54-40 and 54-45.
136. ANTS Act 1999, *supra* n. 69, sections 54-40 and 54-45.

scope of this chapter.[137] Anecdotally, branching is a less common choice among corporate groups.

It might be noted in passing that the language for the GST branch provisions slips from discussing the relationship of a branch to parent (rather than parent-subsidiary or head office-branch as these terms are more commonly understood) thus demonstrating the way in which the GST rules are not obviously drafted in a manner reflecting key income tax distinctions (cf. §10.03[C]).

MNEs are potentially subject to two anti-abuse rules, which might apply to intra-group and intra-entity supplies in certain circumstances.

[B] Compulsory Reverse Charge on Selected Supplies

The first exception applies a compulsory reverse charge to certain supplies of services or intangibles by an offshore supplier that do not satisfy the place of taxation rules (i.e., are not connected with Australia). The reverse-charge applies when the recipient of the supply is registered or required to be registered and acquires the thing partly or solely for the purpose of their Australian enterprise but is not entitled to full input credits (having not acquired the thing solely for a creditable purpose).[138] The reverse-charge provisions are a version of the recharge method discussed at §10.02[C].

The provisions aim to ensure that things acquired for use in Australia, such as intellectual property rights or services, are taxable in Australia despite not otherwise meeting the place of taxation rules in circumstances where the recipient was not using the thing solely for a creditable purpose.[139] The provisions serve to prevent the offshoring of these services to avoid the GST.[140] The provisions apply irrespective of the form of the entity/ies and so apply to intra-entity and intra-group dealings as well as to unrelated entities.[141] This has the slightly anomalous result that for intra-entity

137. For example, in calculating the net amount owed by the parent entity or attributed to the branch the taxpayer must account for 'all *transfers* of anything' made by the branch (or any other branch) to the parent entity and vice versa 'that would have been supplies [or acquisitions] made' by the branch or parent if it were an entity as 'supplies [or acquisitions] made by the separate entity'. Some contend that the term 'transfer' might entail a higher threshold requiring some transfer of proprietary interest and thus excluding the provision of services between branch and parent. However, such an argument must be offset against the requirement that such transfers 'would have been supplies' or acquisitions: CCH Australia, *Australian GST Guide Commentary* (online), [44-580]; ANTS Act 1999, *supra* n. 69, sections 54-40(2)(c)-(e) and 54-45(1)(c)-(e).

138. ANTS Act 1999, *supra* n. 69, Div. 84, section 84-5. *See* Chapter 9 (§9.4[A]) of this book for an overview of the creditable purpose requirement as a core component of accessing input credits in Australia.

139. Explanatory Memorandum to the A New Tax System (Goods and Services Tax) Bill 1998, [6.126]: '[u]nder these [place of taxation] rules a supply of a thing that is not goods or real property, such as an intellectual property right, could be made from outside of Australia when the thing is for consumption in Australia, such as an intellectual property right that is to be exercised in Australia, and the supply would not be connected with Australia'; furthermore, '[t]here should be GST on the supply if the thing is going to be used in Australia other than solely for a creditable purpose': [6.128].

140. Millar & Moon, *supra* n. 122, [2.2.2.2].

141. ANTS Act 1999, *supra* n. 69, sections 48-40(2) and 84-15.

dealings and dealings within a GST group, such supplies will be taxed if acquired from overseas but not if acquired domestically (from another domestic branch of the domestic entity or a domestic member of the GST group).[142] In keeping with the intent of the provisions, the reverse-charge requirement only applies to taxable supplies (not input-taxed or GST-free supplies) or, in other words, when GST revenue is at stake.[143]

In order to be a taxable supply under the rules, the supply must be for consideration.[144] The recipient is required to pay GST on '10% of the price of the supply' which is reduced by any input tax credits (to the extent that the acquisition was partly for a creditable purpose).[145] *Price* is defined to incorporate the term 'consideration' which, when expressed in monetary terms, is taken as the agreed price (or subjective consideration) and when not expressed as an amount of money is the 'GST inclusive market value of that consideration'.[146] Millar and Moon note that, in the context of transfer pricing, given the breadth of the definition of consideration so as to include 'any payment, act or forbearance' given for a supply, an internal transfer of funds could amount to consideration for such a deemed supply with GST applying at 10% of the amount paid. They then state:[147]

> Thus, if there is an actual allocation of costs or an actual payment made in response to a transfer pricing adjustment for income tax, GST consequences may flow from that payment, provided of course that it can be clearly identified as being consideration for a particular supply of inbound services. This is more likely to be the case where the company allocates costs for particular activities than when a retrospective adjustment is made as a result of an ATO transfer pricing audit. Typically, a non-resident parent company will charge a resident subsidiary management and administrative fees, which might include an allocation of centralized costs (such as IT costs). The ATO has been very active in examining such arrangements from a GST perspective.

However, if the consideration is not expressed as a monetary amount then the 'GST inclusive market value' rule applies. In addition, the provisions incorporate their own anti-abuse rules (similar to Division 72 below) which apply a 'GST inclusive market value'[148] as the price of a supply from a recipient's associate that is 'without consideration' or 'for consideration that is less than the GST inclusive market value'.[149] This has the effect of deeming consideration for these supplies. Supplies between associates 'without consideration' are attributed to the tax period 'in which the thing supplied starts to be done'.[150]

---

142. Millar & Moon, *supra* n. 122, [2.2.2.2].
143. ANTS Act 1999, *supra* n. 69, section 84-5(1).
144. ANTS Act 1999, *supra* n. 69, section 84-5(1)(a).
145. ANTS Act 1999, *supra* n. 69, sections 84-12(1) and 84-13(1).
146. ANTS Act 1999, *supra* n. 69, sections 9-75, 84-12(1), 84-20 and 195-1 – 'price'.
147. Millar & Moon, *supra* n. 122, [2.2.2.2].
148. ANTS Act 1999, *supra* n. 69, section 195-1 – 'GST inclusive market value' of 'consideration in connection with a supply' or 'a thing, or a supply or acquisition of a thing … means the market value of the consideration or thing, without any discount for any amount of GST or luxury car tax payable on the supply'.
149. ANTS Act 1999, *supra* n. 69, section 84-20(1). The definition of associate is the same as that used in Div. 72: at section 195-1 – 'associate'; *see infra* §10.03 [C].
150. ANTS Act 1999, *supra* n. 69, section 84-25.

These rules in effect operate as an exception to the protection or quarantining that would normally apply to supplies between members of a GST group (or different branches of a single entity) by including as taxable supplies (or creditable acquisitions) those supplies to which Division 84 applies. The rules, in effect, deem the value of consideration for supplies made without consideration between associates (thus preserving their status as taxable supplies) or deem the value of under-valued supplies between associates (both at GST inclusive market value).[151] The scope of the reverse-charge rules is much broader than those in the EU (*see* §10.04[B]-[C]).

[C] Supplies Between Associates

The second exception is an example of the type of anti-abuse[152] rule discussed in §10.02[C] which includes certain supplies between associates as taxable supplies even if such supplies are made 'without consideration' or for 'inadequate consideration'[153] in circumstances when the recipient of the supply is not in a position to obtain full input credits (either not being registered (or required to be so) or having acquired the thing supplied 'otherwise than solely for a creditable purpose').[154] The rules then impose an open market value (the 'GST exclusive market value') on such supplies. Whereas the reverse-charge rules require a taxable supply (but effectively deems consideration by imposing a market-value price on supplies between associates made for no or low consideration), the associate rules expressly state that the fact that a supply is 'without consideration' does not stop it from being a taxable supply in certain circumstances.[155] The rules appear broader in scope in this respect.

Although Division 84 applies to supplies of services and intangibles, Division 72 can apply to supplies of anything including tangible or intangible goods and services. The provisions apply to supplies that would otherwise be taxable supplies, GST-free or input taxed supplies (including financial supplies) if made for consideration and so are broader in scope than the Division 84 rules which only apply to taxable supplies.[156] However, in a situation in which Division 84 applies, the Division 84 rules generally take precedence and so, for example, valuation would occur on the basis of the 'GST inclusive market value' of the supply.[157]

Although the Commissioner has no public position on the issue, it is conceivable that, in establishing either a GST inclusive market value (for Div. 84 purposes) or a GST

151. ANTS Act 1999, *supra* n. 69, sections 48-40(2), 48-45(3), 84-13 and 84-20.
152. Although labelled an anti-avoidance or anti-abuse rule the rule applies irrespective of abuse or avoidance. The associate rules also apply in addition to the general anti-avoidance rule in Div. 165: Millar & Moon, *supra* n. 122, [2.4.2].
153. The trigger for taxable supplies made for inadequate consideration is if a supply is made to an associate for 'consideration that is less than the GST inclusive market value'. In such circumstances, the value of the taxable supply 'is the GST exclusive market value of the supply'. Presumably the trigger for input taxed or GST-free supplies is simply the market value of the supply although this is not stated: ANTS Act 1999, *supra* n. 69, section 72-70(1).
154. ANTS Act 1999, *supra* n. 69, section 72-25(1)(b).
155. ANTS Act 1999, *supra* n. 69, section 72-5(1).
156. ANTS Act 1999, *supra* n. 69, section 72-25.
157. ANTS Act 1999, *supra* n. 69, section 72-10(3); *cf. infra* n. 168.

exclusive market value (for Div. 72 purposes), in addition to having reference to an independent valuation of the respective goods or services, the Commissioner might exercise a discretion to have reference to transfer pricing documentation as might be appropriate or required (i.e., in a similar manner to that exercised by Customs as discussed at §10.03[D]).

The provisions contain mirror rules that enable an acquisition from an associate 'without consideration' to remain a 'creditable acquisition' (which would otherwise require a creditable acquisition to be for consideration) to the extent of the recipient's relevant creditable purpose.[158]

In a clear instance of the influence of income tax and transfer pricing terminology, the term 'associate' takes its meaning from the legislative definition used for income tax purposes.[159] Specific legislative criteria details what constitutes an associate for natural persons (e.g., relatives),[160] companies (e.g., when a company is controlled by or sufficiently *influenced* by another entity/ies),[161] trustees (e.g., any entity that benefits under the trust)[162] and partnerships (e.g., a partner in the partnership).[163]

Division 72 explicitly states that the associate rules apply to GST branches.[164] It is also apparent that the definition of associate is broad enough to include members of a GST group.[165] However, whereas the GST group rules are specifically made subject to the Division 84 rules (so that intra-group transactions are ignored unless there is an eligible offshore supply of services or intangibles for which the recipient is not entitled to an input tax credit),[166] they are not made subject to the Division 72 rules and there is nothing within Division 72 that suggests an obvious intention to override the general proviso that intra-group transactions are generally ignored.[167] There is therefore an

158. ANTS Act 1999, *supra* n. 69, sections 72-40 and 72-45.
159. ANTS Act 1999, *supra* n. 69, section 195-1 – 'associate'; *Income Tax Assessment Act 1936* (Cth), section 318 (ITAA 1936).
160. ITAA 1936, *supra* n. 159, section 318(1).
161. ITAA 1936, *supra* n. 159, section 318(2). *See*, *BHP Billiton Ltd v. Federal Commissioner of Taxation* (2020) 94 ALJR 326 in which the High Court held that, in the context of related companies (engaged in transfer pricing) the associate rules were satisfied by establishing sufficient influence (which requires less than control: at 328, [7]) and which requires showing that the company, or its directors, are accustomed to, or under an obligation (whether formal or informal) to, or might reasonably be expected to, act in accordance with the directions, instructions or wishes of the entity/ entities: ITAA 1936, *supra* n. 159, section 318(6)(b). This was satisfied on the facts in that case because both companies were in effect a 'single unified economic entity' sharing common ownership, common directors obliged to act in the interest of both entities and with complementary voting and dividend rights: at 329, [9]-[11], 330, [15]-[19], 331, [24], 334-345, [46].
162. ITAA 1936, *supra* n. 159, section 318(3); *see* section 318(5) for associates of trustees of public unit trusts.
163. ITAA 1936, *supra* n. 159, section 318(4).
164. ANTS Act 1999, *supra* n. 69, section 72-90.
165. ANTS Act 1999, *supra* n. 69, sections 48-10 and 48-15.
166. ANTS Act 1999, *supra* n. 69, sections 48-45(3) and 84-5.
167. Monk argues that Div. 72 should only have a residual application to deem a market value for otherwise taxable supplies under the Act rather than to transform supplies that are not taxable (by virtue of the group rules) into taxable supplies: Andrew Monk, *The Associate Rules and their Interaction with Other Provisions of the GST Act*, 4(3) Austl. GST J. 34, 46-47 (2004).

argument to suggest that the Division 72 associate rules do not include intra-group transactions (even those made for no or inadequate consideration to an entity who cannot claim full input credits) unless the requirements of Division 84 are satisfied. This reading is supported from a policy perspective because if intra-group supplies are ignored then there is no need to manipulate the value of intra-group transactions for VAT purposes (i.e., there is no mischief to address).

On the other hand, the mere absence of a stated intention to override the grouping provisions is not alone determinative. Without delving too deeply into the specific arguments available, there might be legislative scope for a broad interpretation of the Division 72 rules including for them apply to a situation not covered by the reverse-charge provisions but which involves members of a GST-group (one of whom is input-taxed) structuring transactions to avoid or minimize GST liability.[168] However, whether there is a *need* to apply Division 72 in this manner remains to be seen. Examples occurring in a domestic context suggest that the need to apply the associate provisions might arise when the grouping rules are used to access some additional GST benefit in a way that was not necessarily intended. For example, there have been a number of schemes which have sought to use GST groups to obtain (unintended) benefits in relation to domestic real property transactions. Such a scheme could include a situation where a member of a GST group (G1) purchases lands for a residential property development which it sells to another group member (G2) (G1 claims input tax credits on the construction and acquisition costs but charges no GST on the intra-group sale). G2 then sells the residential development to a third party as an input taxed supply of an existing residential property (no GST is applied on the basis that the

168. This reading is supported by ANTS Act 1999, *supra* n. 69, section 48-55, the heading of which states that 'GST groups treated as single entities for *certain purposes*' (emphasis added). These purposes are primarily stated as working out the amount of input tax credits of the representative member or determining whether that member has any adjustments to make and the value of any such adjustments. Additionally, the wording of both sets of provisions is different – the reverse-charge rules apply to supplies for consideration but with specific provision to deem a supply at the GST inclusive market value if made for no consideration. By contrast, Div. 72 applies to a supply for no (or inadequate) consideration and is arguably broader in scope. Moreover, the interpretive maxim *generalia specialibus non derogant* although not determinative suggests that the specific associate rules might override the grouping rules in instances of avoidance/abuse and supports a residual application of the associate rules (i.e., in an instance of potential abuse to which Div. 84 did not apply). The general anti-avoidance provisions might also apply: Div. 165. Section 72-5(1) further states that the fact that a supply is without consideration does not stop it from being a taxable supply and is said to apply even though section 84-5(1)(a) requires that a taxable supply be for consideration. This suggests an intention to override that part of the Div. 84 rules. By comparison the *value* of such supplies is made subject to the Div. 84 rules suggesting that Div. 84 will override only on the question of value but not on the issue of whether a taxable supply exists without consideration. *See also* section 72-20 which states that if a supply to, or acquisition from, an associate 'would be a sale or some other kind of supply' apart from a lack of consideration then the supply or acquisition is taken to be a supply of that kind or through that means respectively. *See also* section 72-25; section 72-70 which applies to under-valued supplies and is made subject to the Div. 84 rules. The wording of the provisions suggests there might be residual scope for Div. 72 to apply at least to supplies made *without* consideration.

previous intra-group sale constituted the first otherwise taxable supply of new residential premises, meaning that the subsequent sale to a third party is an input taxed supply of residential premises). The group therefore obtains input tax credits and pays no GST when, without the interposed group transaction, input tax credits should be obtained but GST should also be payable.[169] The risks within these domestic transactions were not dealt with by the Division 72 rules but rather by specific legislative reform (to disregard intra-group supplies in determining whether a property is new residential premises) and the use of the general anti-avoidance provisions.[170] It is conceivable that there might be scope for similar schemes to arise most likely in the context of the financial services sector if GST grouping is used to avail the group of an additional advantage not intended by the Act; however, the application of Division 72 to GST groups has not been publicly addressed by the Commissioner in any rulings or by the tribunals or courts.

Generally, Division 72 and Division 84 appear broader in scope than Articles 80 and 72 of the EU VAT Directive. However, a further difference which narrows their comparative scope is that, unlike Article 80(1)(c) of the EU VAT Directive, the provisions only apply to supplies made *without* or for *inadequate* consideration. As a consequence, supplies made at or *higher* than market value consideration would not be caught by the valuation rules in either Division 72 or Division 84 and so would *not* apply to the more common situation of a taxpayer having artificially inflated the price on imported goods or services to maximize deductions in Australia for transfer pricing purposes. *See* §10.03[E] for some possible implications of this.

[D] Interaction with Customs

Australian customs authorities follow the WCO approach of relying on the stated value (the transaction value method) unless the relationship of the parties is shown to have influenced the price.[171] Customs authorities *may* have reference to transfer pricing documentation to assist in either or both of valuing the relevant goods and in establishing whether or not the relationship of the parties influenced the price.[172] There

169. ANTS Act 1999, *supra* n. 69, sections 40-65(2)(b) and 40-75(1)(a). The schemes were many and varied and exploited various special rules; for an overview, *see*, e.g., ATO, GSTR 2005/4, Goods and Services Tax: Arrangements of the Kind Described in Taxpayer Alerts TA 2004/6 and TA 2004/7: Use of the Grouping or Margin Scheme Provisions of the GST Act to Avoid or Reduce the Goods and Services Tax on the Sale of New Residential Premises (14 September 2005); Stephen Jones & Umberto Torresi, *Clever GST Transactions – Are the Anti-Avoidance Provisions Cleverer?* 40(5) Taxation in Australia 243, 243-248 (2005).
170. *See, e.g.*, ANTS Act 1999, *supra* n. 69, section 40-75(2A).
171. *Customs Act 1901* (Cth), sections 159 and 161-161H.
172. Australian Customs and Border Protection Services, Practice Statement B_IND08 – Valuation – Transfer Pricing Policy, [1.2], [1.3], [1.6] (12 April 2013).

is also provision to adjust customs values either up (requiring payment of additional duty) or down (requiring a refund) following a transfer pricing adjustment provided that the relevant criteria are met (e.g., the adjustments must not be merely notional but reflected in the actual priced paid/transfer of funds and relate to specific goods imported) as well as provision to make corresponding adjustments in GST payable when customs value change.[173]

However, the ATO has confirmed in a Practice Statement that when a transfer pricing adjustment affects customs values then, upon request by the taxpayer, the ATO should provide further information to disaggregate values to a transactional level or, if this is not possible, to provide an explanation of how the transfer pricing adjustment affects global values (for example, based on the profit split method). This suggests that transfer-pricing adjustments on these broader bases (i.e., on global values derived through the profit-split method) *might* be taken into account for customs purposes.[174]

For exports (which, in a transfer pricing context, might give rise to an incentive to overstate the value of goods exported to a low-tax jurisdiction) the effect on the GST is neutral as no GST is collected.

Consistent with the discussion at §10.02[B], the Commissioner of Taxation has stated in a public ruling that '[c]ustoms values are often indicative of an arm's length outcome'.[175] However, the Commissioner then notes the different manner in which the rules operate, for example, in the recourse to global or aggregate values over transactional valuation methods in transfer pricing that is not shared by customs or in the presumption in favour of the price declared by the importer by customs which is not the starting point for transfer pricing purposes.[176] The ATO therefore states that 'conformity of transfer prices with customs values does not of itself prove that the standard in Australia's transfer pricing rules has been satisfied'.[177]

[E] The Impact of Transfer Pricing Adjustments on GST Liabilities

A transfer pricing adjustment can occur in a number of different contexts – initiated by the taxpayer (as is generally required under the transfer pricing rules),[178] by agreement

173. Australian Customs and Border Protection Services, Practice Statement, *supra* n. 172, [1.1.2], [1.1.3], [1.7]; Deloitte, *The Link Between Transfer Pricing and Customs Valuation: Country Guide* 8 (2018).
174. ATO, Practice Statement Law Administration PS LA 2016/1, Transfer Pricing Adjustments with Potential Customs Implications (14 April 2016), [7], [4] – notes the context for the Practice Statement and identifies that the need for an approach reconciling transfer pricing adjustments with customs values arose from a requirement contained in reforms introduced to address multi-national profit-shifting through harmful transfer-pricing that 'the arm's length conditions must be attributed to the value of individual components that form part of the tax equation even if a profit based method is used'.
175. ATO, Federal Commissioner of Taxation, Taxation Ruling TR 97/20, *supra* n. 62, at [2.119].
176. ATO, TR 97/20, *supra* n. 62, [2.120]-[2.121].
177. ATO, TR 97/20, *supra* n. 62, [2.122].
178. *Income Tax Assessment Act 1997* (Cth.), Sub-div. 815-B.

between the taxpayer and the Commissioner of Taxation,[179] imposed by the ATO (as a result of an assessment or audit) and/or confirmed by Court order.[180]

There is very little publicly available information on how such adjustments are treated for GST purposes. There is an argument that a transfer pricing adjustment undertaken by a taxpayer that has the effect of altering the consideration for a previous supply (and is reflected in real accounts) should give rise to a Category 1 adjustment (*see* Chapter 9 of this book (§9.05)). Millar and Moon state that this requirement is likely to be satisfied by a taxpayer-initiated transfer pricing adjustment.[181] However, by analogy with the treatment of court orders, to the extent that a transfer pricing adjustment initiated by a revenue authority is sufficiently related to a previous supply and affects the consideration payable (in a real rather than notional way) then there is no reason in principle why this should not trigger a GST adjustment. As chapter 10 detailed, the broad drafting of the GST provisions – applying as they do to a broad range of supplies and acquisitions and by extension adjustments – suggests greater potential for a transfer pricing adjustment to have GST consequences (including resulting in a GST adjustment) in Australia than in the EU. For example, there is no requirement of a direct link, such as a legal relationship, between the recipient of a good or service and the consideration received for a supply to be a taxable supply.[182] Therefore, unlike the EU, there might be a real question as to whether a secondary transfer pricing adjustment involving a constructed transaction has GST consequences.

An impact on GST liabilities is arguably more likely if the transfer pricing adjustment is more than a mere requirement to pay a global sum but is instead disaggregated to a level that has an impact on the value of transactions and results in an actual transfer of funds. This might be contrasted against the potentially more expansive approach for customs purposes implied by the Practice Statement above which, although not specifically addressing the impact on GST liabilities, might be relevant to the extent that GST liability relies on customs values. In practical terms, a transfer pricing adjustment is only likely to have GST consequences if it also enlivens the exceptions discussed above at §10.03[B] and §10.03[C] because this will affect revenue. However, the fact that Division 84 and Division 72 require an *undervaluation* to apply, which is less likely to arise in a transfer pricing context, might explain the lack of publicly available information on the issue. It might be that reform is required to expand the application of Division 84 and Division 72 to include over-inflated valuations in the event that the need arises. However, from a GST perspective this will likely only arise in limited contexts[183] and the application of the general anti-avoidance rule should also be considered.[184]

179. This might be as the result of a settlement or due to an advance pricing agreement (APA): *see, e.g.*, ATO, Practice Statement Law Administration PS LA 2015/4, Advance Pricing Agreements (16 March 2017).

180. ATO, Practice Statement Law Administration PS LA 2016/1, *supra*, n. 174 [2].

181. Millar & Moon, *supra* n. 122, [2.2.2.2] – *see* text accompanying *supra* n. 147.

182. *Cf.* §10.04[E]; Chapter 9 of this book (§§ 9.4-9.5).

183. This might apply to supplies made to an input taxed recipient (e.g., a financial services provider) that are overvalued but for which the recipient is entitled to a reduced input tax credit (of up to 75%), e.g., funds management services and loan services or marketing and human resources services. In such a situation one can envisage a risk to revenue from artificially

§10.04 THE EU APPROACH TO TRANSFER PRICING AND THE VAT

The EU VAT system follows the second approach described in §10.02[E] which recognizes that the VAT and transfer pricing can overlap in limited circumstances albeit in ways different to the Australian approach.

[A] Taxability of Intra-Group and Intra-Entity Transactions

As in Australia, intra-entity supplies are generally considered out-of-scope for VAT purposes, irrespective of whether they take place domestically or across borders.

The EU VAT Directive does not contain any special rules for inter-company transactions (e.g., head office-branch), but generally holds that only a 'person who, independently' carries out an economic activity can provide and receive taxable transactions.[185] It is commonly understood that a branch or permanent establishment is neither a 'person' nor acts 'independently' and therefore taxable transactions within one legal entity do not seem to be possible under EU VAT law.[186] This understanding was confirmed by the CJEU in the *FCE Bank* case of 2006 when it held that the recharge of costs from one establishment to another establishment of the same taxable person is, in principle, not subject to VAT. The Court found that the fixed establishment was 'dependent upon' the head office because it did not bear any economic risk[187] and so 'with it, constitutes a single taxable person'.[188] That is, the lack of independence meant that the fixed establishment did not fulfil the criteria for a 'taxable person'[189] and as a consequence it could not conduct any taxable transactions.[190] Due to the lack of reverse charge rules comparable to the Australian system, this result applies for inbound and outbound supplies. The *FCE Bank* ruling has been confirmed in subsequent judgments and is considered settled case law.[191] It is conceivable that a fixed establishment might be considered a separate taxable person for VAT purposes in the exceptional case it enjoys substantial independence from a head office. However, the authors are not

---

inflated values – a loss of income tax revenue from an overvalued supply (thus increasing the deduction of the Australian resident) and the ability for the recipient of that supply to claim a GST credit of up to 70% of the value of that supply: ANTS Act 1999, *supra* n. 69, Div. 70; *A New Tax System (Goods and Services Tax) Regulations 1999* (Cth.), Div. 70, rr. 70-5.01A, 70-5.02, 70-5.02A (specific rules for reduced input tax credits for related party dealings affected by section 84-5), 70-5.03.

184. ANTS Act 1999, *supra* n. 67, Div. 165 – the general anti-avoidance rule will only apply to prevent a GST benefit (rather than an income tax benefit) which would properly be the subject of the anti-avoidance provisions in the income tax legislation: *Income Tax Assessment Act 1936* (Cth), Pt. IVA.
185. EU VAT Directive, *supra* n. 69, Article 9 in conjunction with Article 2.
186. Spies, *Permanent Establishments in Value Added Tax, supra* n. 67, 274-296.
187. *FCE Bank, supra* n. 14, paragraphs 35-36.
188. *FCE Bank, supra* n. 14, paragraph 37.
189. EU VAT Directive, *supra* n. 69, Article 9.
190. EU VAT Directive, *supra* n. 69, Article 2.
191. *See* among others CJEU, 16 July 2009, Case C-244/08, *Commission v. Italy*, ECLI: EU:C:2009:478, paragraph 38; CJEU, 12 Sept. 2013, Case C-388/11, *Le Crédit Lyonnais*, ECLI:EU:C:2013:541, paragraph 34; CJEU, 7 August 2018, Case C-16/17, *TGE Gas Engineering*, ECLI:EU:C:2018:647, paragraph 41.

aware of any individual case where the CJEU or a domestic court has reached this conclusion. Section 10.04[C] below outlines two other possible exceptions to the general rule of ignoring intra-entity transactions.[192]

The approach to intra-group supplies is different. Supplies between legally independent entities within a corporate group (MNE) can be treated as out-of-scope for domestic groups (depending on the VAT law of the specific Member State, as described below). However, these supplies are taxable if they take place between related companies that are resident in different (Member or third) states because the EU VAT grouping rules limit membership of a VAT group to members who are established in the territory of the one Member State.[193]

According to Article 11 of the EU VAT Directive, after consulting the VAT Committee, each Member State may regard as a single taxable person any persons 'established in the territory of that Member State' who, while legally independent, are closely bound to one another by 'financial, economic and organisational links'.[194] Should a Member State choose to use this option,[195] all transactions between the entities of the group will be treated as out-of-scope for VAT purposes.[196]

The effect of the VAT grouping rules is limited by several conditions. The CJEU has ruled that Member States must define the substantive requirements of 'financial, economic and organisational links' in more detail[197] but they can exercise discretion when doing so.[198] The result is great variation between Member States on the scope of their VAT grouping rules.[199] Similar to Australia, some Member States permit VAT

192. Note that the *Skandia* ruling (discussed at §10.04[B]) was not based on a finding of the independence of the fixed establishment and as a result is not an example of a court making such a finding. A third exception also applies to the cross-border transfer of goods. Under Article 17 of the EU VAT Directive, *supra* n. 69, the physical cross-border transfer of goods from one Member State to another Member State (e.g., from one warehouse to another warehouse) is treated as a fictitious supply for VAT purposes and triggers a reporting obligation. This deemed supply is triggered by the cross-border transfer of goods and so applies irrespective of whether there is any transaction or recharging of costs or fixed establishment involved.
193. EU VAT Directive, *supra* n. 69, Article 11.
194. EU VAT Directive, *supra* n. 69, Article 11.
195. The option in Article 11 is not exercised by, e.g., Poland, Portugal, and Spain.
196. The aim of these rules is indicated by the Explanatory Memorandum to the Proposal for a Sixth Council Directive on the Harmonisation of Legislation of Member States Concerning Turnover Taxes, Common System of Value Added Tax: Uniform Basis of Assessment, COM(1973) 950 final, 8 (20 June 1973): '[I]n the interests of simplifying administration or of combating abuses (e.g., the splitting up of one undertaking among several taxable persons so that each may benefit from a special scheme) Member States will not be obliged to treat as taxable persons those whose "independence" is purely a legal technicality.'
197. CJEU, 16 July 2015, Joined Cases C-108/14 and C-109/14, *Larentia + Minerva*, ECLI: EU:C:2015:496, paragraph 50.
198. For example, the Austrian tax authorities in general require a shareholding size of 75% (financial link), reasonable business interdependence between the group members meaning that their activities must be interrelated and complement each other (economic link), and that the majority of persons acting as legal representatives/managing directors is identical across the related companies (organizational link): *see* Austrian VAT Guidelines (UStR), as of 18 November 2019, paragraphs 236-239 (Austrian VAT Guidelines).
199. Moreover, Article 11(2) EU VAT Directive, *supra* n. 69, provides that Member States that implement VAT grouping 'may adopt any measures needed to prevent tax evasion or avoidance'. According to CJEU case law this enables Member States to limit the scope of VAT grouping to specific categories of persons or industries if this is necessary to combat abusive

grouping as a voluntary regime (upon request of the MNE), while others apply automatically if the requisite conditions are met.[200]

Unlike Australia, Article 11 of the EU VAT Directive permits VAT grouping only for persons who are 'established in the territory of that Member State'.[201] EU VAT law therefore prevents the inclusion of subsidiaries or other related entities that are resident abroad (i.e., in another Member State or third country) into a VAT group. Although some scholars have argued that this territorial limitation could be in conflict with the (higher ranking) freedom of establishment enshrined in Article 49 of the Treaty on the Functioning of the European Union,[202] the lawfulness of the territorial limitation has not yet been referred to the CJEU (with the exception of the *Skandia* case discussed below). The European Commission justifies this territorial limitation of the EU VAT grouping rules by the need to avoid the same legal entity simultaneously being part of two (or more) VAT groups, which would be incompatible with the basic principles of the common VAT system (e.g., conflicts of tax sovereignty, administrative difficulties).[203]

Given that transfer pricing issues more commonly arise in a cross-border context, the limited scope of the VAT grouping rules means that they cannot prevent a transfer pricing adjustment from having a potential effect on VAT, as §10.04[E] below explains.

[B] Exceptions to the Non-Taxability of Intra-Entity Supplies

The EU VAT Directive includes reverse charge rules.[204] However, in contrast to the Australian reverse charge rules, these rules *do not* effectively deem consideration to establish a taxable supply (which would otherwise be out-of-scope), but rather only define the person liable for VAT on transactions that are within the (substantive and territorial) scope of the EU VAT. As a result, the rules do not alter the general rules

structures: CJEU, 25 April 2013, Case C-480/10, *Commission v. Sweden*, ECLI:EU:C:2013:263, paragraphs 38-39; *Larentia + Minerva*, *supra* n. 197, paragraph 41. On the different implementation of the VAT grouping rules in Member States, *see* van Doesum, van Kesteren & van Norden, *supra* n. 67, 97-103.

200. In Austria, VAT grouping applies automatically if the conditions are met. By contrast, in Sweden VAT grouping only applies upon request of the taxable persons.

201. EU VAT Directive, *supra* n. 69, Article 11.

202. *Treaty on the Functioning of the European Union*, opened for signature 7 February 1992, [2009] OJ C 115/199 (entered into force 1 November 1993) (TFEU). *See*, among others, Ad van Doesum, Herman van Kesteren & Gert-Jan van Norden, *The Internal Market and VAT: Intra-Group Transactions of Branches, Subsidiaries and VAT Groups* 16(1) EC Tax Rev. 34, 37-41 (2007); Casper Bjerregaard Eskildsen, *VAT Grouping versus Freedom of Establishment* 20(3) EC Tax Rev. 114 (2011); Pfeiffer, *VAT Grouping from a European Perspective*, *supra* n. 69, section 4.

203. European Commission, Communication from the Commission to the Council and the European Parliament on the VAT Group Option Provided for in Article 11 of Council Directive 2006/112/EC on the Common System of Value Added Tax, COM(2009) 325 final, 7-8 (2 July 2009): 'national VAT grouping schemes should preclude taxable persons from joining more than one VAT group at a time. This is also essential from a tax monitoring perspective'. The Australian approach to this risk is to specifically prohibit an entity from being a member of more than one VAT group, which may be more difficult to coordinate and monitor across the Member States of the EU (§10.03[A]).

204. EU VAT Directive, *supra* n. 69, Articles 194-199.

described in §10.04[A] above.[205] Therefore, unlike the Australian GST system, imported (intra-entity) services from offshore branches are, as a general rule, not subject to VAT including a situation in which the recipient has no full right to input credit. In this context, the EU VAT Directive does not contain any specific rules for inbound intra-entity supplies (cross-border branch-branch or head office-branch transactions) which could prevent tax planning structures (offshoring/channeling services through branches in preferential jurisdictions).[206] In other words, the EU VAT law system does not follow the 'recharge method' as outlined in the OECD *International VAT/GST Guidelines*, but rather the 'direct use method' (*see* §10.02[C]).

However, the EU VAT Directive might offer interested Member States two possible options to tax certain intra-entity supplies of services (recharging between establishments of one entity), which are discussed in turn.[207] The first option would apply the *Skandia* (and *Danske Bank*) ruling to the domestic VAT grouping rules. The second option would be to tax in-house supplies of services by using the optional rule in Article 27 of the EU VAT Directive.[208]

Key to the first exception is the highly controversial and much discussed *Skandia* case of 2014 in which the CJEU held that a domestic (Swedish) branch of an entity with its main place of business in the United States could be part of the domestic Swedish VAT group regime on a stand-alone basis.[209] In such a scenario, the Swedish branch forms part of a different taxable person than the head office, namely the Swedish VAT group consisting of the domestic branch and other closely related domestic companies. The Court ruled that, based on this fiction, services provided by the foreign US-based head office (which had previously been acquired from an external third party) to the local branch were potentially subject to VAT as both the head office and branch were effectively separate taxable persons.[210]

205. The reverse charge rules do not have any effect on the scope of the EU VAT and the taxable base. The taxable amount of a supply is assessed based on the same rules (Articles 72 et seq. EU VAT Directive, *supra* n. 69) irrespective of whether the supplier or recipient is liable for VAT. Against this background, the reverse charge rules do not raise any specific (additional) issues with respect to the taxable amount and transfer pricing adjustments.

206. An attempt at reform based on a 2003 proposal by the Commission failed to reach sufficient agreement in the Council: Proposal for a Council Directive amending Directive 77/388/EEC as Regards the Place of Supply of Services, COM(2003) 822 final) (23 December 2003) and the corresponding, Interinstitutional File, FISC 150 (2004), p. 4; *see*, in more detail, Spies, *Permanent Establishments and Value Added Tax*, *supra* n. 67, 349-352.

207. *See also* Rasa Mikutiene, *The Preferred Treatment of the Fixed Establishment in European VAT* 3(3) World J. VAT/GST L. 166, 186-190 (2015).

208. *See*, in more detail, Spies, *Permanent Establishments and Value Added Tax*, *supra* n. 67, 308-332.

209. CJEU, 17 Sept. 2014, Case C-7/13, *Skandia*, ECLI:EU:C:2014:2225. For discussions of the case and the controversy caused, *see* European Commission, VAT Committee, *CJEU Case C-7/13 Skandia America: VAT Group*, Working Paper No. 845, taxud.c.1(2015)747072 (17 February 2015); Simon Cornielje & Ivan Bondarev, *Scanning the Scope of Skandia* 26(1) Int'l VAT Monitor 17 (2015); Odile Courjon, *New Rules for Head Office to Branch Scenarios – Comments on the* Skandia *Case* 26(1) Int'l VAT Monitor 22 (2015); Rahiela Abdoelkariem & Frank Prinsen, *The Interaction between Head Office, Branch and VAT Grouping: New Challenges Ahead for the European Union* 26(4) Int'l VAT Monitor 205 (2015).

210. *Skandia*, *supra* n. 209, paragraphs 31-32.

The CJEU so ruled without detailed reasons for this result and without explaining how this interpretation was consistent with Article 11 of the EU VAT Directive. The scope of the *Skandia* doctrine is disputed and there is significant uncertainty around issues such as: whether the same reasoning applies to internal services charged to a domestic *head office* (rather than a domestic branch);[211] whether such reasoning applies to *in-house* created services (rather than externally acquired services which are subsequently recharged);[212] whether one Member State is obliged to recognize that a foreign establishment is part of the VAT group of *another* Member State;[213] and under what circumstances the supply provided by the foreign head office to the local branch (cost allocation by internal invoices) qualifies as a 'supply *for consideration*' which, based on established case law, requires a legal relationship and direct link.[214] The answers to all of these questions all impact upon the potential impact of transfer pricing rules and adjustments on VAT outcomes. To the surprise of some commentators, according to the follow-up ruling in the *Danske Bank* case (Case C-812/19), published in March 2021, the *Skandia* approach seems to have a very general scope of application. However, it yet remains to be seen how Member States' legislators and authorities will implement the *Danske Bank* judgment in practice.

The second option might be to rely on Article 27 of the EU VAT Directive which allows Member States to 'treat as a supply of services for consideration the supply by a taxable person of a service for the purposes of his business' (often referred to as an 'internal' supply)[215] if the taxable person has no full right to input credit.[216] Some scholars argue that this provision might be interpreted so that cross-border supplies of services from one establishment to another establishment of the same taxable person could be made subject to VAT.[217] The taxable amount for supplies covered by Article 27 is defined as the open market value.[218] This rule could potentially be used to address the off-shore outsourcing risk which the Australian reverse charge rules are designed to prevent.

However, both Articles 11 and 27 have limitations which restrict their possible scope and effect. Both are optional rules which have not been broadly implemented by Member States (this is especially true of Article 27).[219] As optional rules they include a

211. *See* van Doesum, van Kesteren & van Norden, *supra* n. 67, 103-106.
212. Courjon, *supra* n. 209, 23.
213. The obligation of a Member State to recognize that a foreign establishment is part of the VAT group of another Member State was confirmed in the *Dankse Bank* case (CJEU 11 March 2021, Case C-812/19, *Danske Bank*, ECLI:EU:C:2021:196).
214. European Commission, VAT Committee, *CJEU Case C-7/13 Skandia America: VAT Group*, *supra* n. 209, 11-14.
215. *See* van Doesum, van Kesteren & van Norden, *supra* n. 67, 147.
216. EU VAT Directive, *supra* n. 69, Article 27.
217. *See*, among others, Mikutiene, *supra* n. 207, 186-190.
218. EU VAT Directive, *supra* n. 69, Article 77.
219. Less than 10 Member States have applied for authorization to use Article 27 of the EU VAT Directive, *supra* n. 69: *see* Consultations of the VAT Committee as at 1 January 2020, available at: https://ec.europa.eu/taxation_customs/business/vat/vat-committee-0_en (accessed 23 January 2021); *see also* Mikutiene, *supra* n. 207, 186 who contends that only Belgium has effectively implemented Article 27 into national law.

relatively large margin of discretion for Member States,[220] which is constrained by the requirement that a Member State seek approval by the VAT Committee before implementing the rules domestically.[221] Although Articles 11 and 27 might not have been specifically designed with the purpose of taxing *cross-border intra-entity* services and/or implementing the 'recharge method',[222] this does not prevent Member States from using the rules to tax such supplies. However, the optional character of both rules means that the unilateral application of these rules to *cross-border* intra-company supplies by some Member States could lead to conflicts with the objective of an internal market and the common VAT system because it might result in double- or non-taxation. Take the example of multiple use services (i.e., services acquired under one contract centrally by one establishment, but effectively used by different establishments). One Member State by implementing Article 27 (recharge method) might apply VAT in the hands of the domestic establishment of use upon the internal recharge. Another Member State, following the general rule in Article 44 (direct use method) might tax the same supply of services in the hands of the contracting establishment or the head office (which in cases of doubt is deemed to be the establishment of use).[223] The resulting double-taxation suggests the risks in using these unilateral approaches in the absence of a coordinated response.

Despite these constraints, there might be limited scope for either approach to be used as a tool in combating tax planning and abuse by taxing cross-border intra-company transactions. *See* § 10.04[E] below for the consequent impact on the relevance of transfer pricing adjustments for VAT purposes.

220. *See*, *Le Crédit Lyonnais*, *supra* n. 191, paragraph 39; *Larentia + Minerva*, *supra* n. 197, paragraphs 39, 41 and 50.
221. The VAT Committee was established to promote the uniform application of the EU VAT Directive through offering (non-binding) guidance on the application of the Directive. It consists of representatives of Member States and of the Commission. Some optional provisions of the EU VAT Directive require Member States to consult the VAT Committee before they implement options provided by the Directive into their national law: https://ec.europa.eu/taxation_customs/business/vat/vat-committee-0_en; EU VAT Directive, *supra* n. 69, Article 398.
222. Article 27 of the VAT Directive has the aim of achieving neutrality between insourcing and outsourcing by making insourcing subject to VAT. On the comparable rules for the supply of goods in Article 18(a) EU VAT Directive, *see* Annex A, Point 7 of the Second Council Directive 67/228/EEC of 11 April 1967 on the Harmonisation of Legislation of Member States Concerning Turnover Taxes; CJEU, 8 Nov. 2012, Case C-299/11, *Gemeente Vlaardingen*, ECLI: EU:C:2012:698, paragraph 27; Spies, *Permanent Establishments in Value Added Tax*, *supra* n. 67, 319-332. In light of this context, Article 27 arguably is primarily targeted at domestic scenarios and is not specifically addressed to tax cross-border and branch-branch/head office-branch transactions. The EU VAT grouping rules in Article 11 clearly also do not have the aim of implementing the recharge method, as they do not deal with cross-border or branch scenarios at all.
223. EU VAT Directive, *supra* n. 69, Articles 27, 44; Article 22 Council Implementing Regulation (EU) No 282/2011 of 15 March 2011 laying down implementing measures for Directive 2006/112/EC on the common system of value added tax, OJ L 77, 23 March 2011, p. 1-22; Spies, *Permanent Establishments in Value Added Tax*, *supra* n. 67, 352-354, 414.

[C] Supplies Between Associates

A special anti-avoidance rule might apply to those related party transactions, which are within the scope of the EU VAT (in particular cross-border intra-group transactions). Article 80 of the EU VAT Directive contains an optional anti-avoidance rule according to which Member States may levy VAT on a supply of goods or services based on its 'open market value' rather than the consideration actually paid.[224] The aim of this rule is to 'prevent loss of tax revenues through the use of connected parties to derive tax benefits'.[225] Although generally labelled an anti-avoidance or anti-abuse rule, the rule applies irrespective of any intention of abuse or avoidance. The rule only applies if three conditions are met: first, that there is a supply of goods or services between persons with close ties; second, that one of those persons does not have a full right to input credits; and, third, that the consideration agreed is lower or higher than the open market value.

Article 80 is part of the section in the EU VAT Directive on the taxable amount[226] and so requires a taxable transaction before it can operate. That is, the provision does not itself create or deem a taxable transaction in the absence of a pre-existing taxable transaction, but rather defines the value of a pre-existing taxable transaction. Therefore, Article 80 does not apply to transactions that are not already within the scope of the EU VAT such as intra-entity transactions. Consequently, if a transaction is *without consideration* Article 80 would not apply because the Directive provides that only a supply 'for consideration' is a taxable transaction.[227] However, any supply made free of charge could potentially be subject to the self-supply rules and, thereby, trigger VAT on the purchase price for a similar good at the time of the transaction or on the full costs in case of services.[228]

Article 80 has been implemented by about 20 Member States, including Austria, Belgium, Germany, Italy, Luxembourg, Poland, Portugal and Spain.[229] The rule has only been the subject of limited consideration by the CJEU which has so far applied a relatively restrictive interpretation of the scope of the rule in favour of business. In particular, the Court has held that Article 80 is 'an exception to the general rule [...] which must as such be interpreted strictly'[230] and that the scope of Article 80 is

224. EU VAT Directive, *supra* n. 69, Article 80.
225. Recital 26 in the preamble to the EU VAT Directive, *supra* n. 69.
226. EU VAT Directive, *supra* n. 69, Title VII – Taxable Amount.
227. EU VAT Directive, *supra* n. 69, Article 2.
228. EU VAT Directive, *supra* n. 69, Articles 16 and 26 in connection with Articles 74-75. This is the prevailing opinion in Austria: Austrian Transfer Pricing Guidelines (VPR), as of 28 October 2010, paragraph 346; Hans Georg Ruppe & Markus Achatz, UStG, §4, paragraph 182 (5th ed., 2017). A self-supply is triggered if goods or services are used 'for purposes other than those of his business', which, for example, includes promotional gifts: CJEU, 27 April 1999, Case C-48/97, *Kuwait Petroleum*, ECLI:EU:C:1999:203.
229. *See* EU, *Notifications of the VAT Committee, State-of-Play on 1 February 2020*, available at: https://ec.europa.eu/taxation_customs/sites/taxation/files/notifications.pdf (accessed 13 December 2020).
230. CJEU, 26 April 2012, case C-621/10, *Balkan and Sea Properties*, ECLI:EU:C:2012:248, paragraph 45.

'exhaustive'.[231] Consequently, Member States cannot use the open market value as a taxable amount in cases other than those listed in that provision such as when the supplier and/or acquirer has a full right to input credit.[232] It further follows that a Member State cannot apply Article 80 to an under-valued related party transaction if it has not properly implemented the option in Article 80 in its domestic law.[233]

The first condition for Article 80 to apply requires close ties, which includes when 'the supply of goods or services involve[es] family or other close personal ties, management, ownership, membership, financial or legal ties as defined by the Member State'.[234] Legal ties may include the relationship between an employer and employee or the employee's family or any other closely connected persons (e.g., shareholders). Member States have discretion to define the scope of the ties including any condition of shareholding size to qualify as an associated enterprise for the purposes of the rule. There is therefore scope for variation between Member States. It is possible that in a certain transaction the parties might fall within the definition of 'related parties' of a Member State's transfer pricing rules for income tax purposes, but not within the domestic implementation rules for Article 80 and vice versa. It is also possible that the transaction may be covered by the domestic implementation of Article 80 in one Member State but not in another.[235] Not all Member States provide clear definitions, which can add to uncertainty. For example, neither the Austrian VAT Code nor the Austrian VAT Guidelines provide an explanation on the degree of association (e.g., shareholding size) necessary to apply this rule.

Article 80 lists three scenarios covered by the second and third requirements referred to at the outset of this section; they include that:

(1) the consideration is *lower* than the open market value and the *recipient* of the supply does not have a full right of deduction;
(2) the consideration is *lower* than the open market value and the *supplier* does not have a full right of deduction;
(3) the consideration is *higher* than the open market value and the *supplier* does not have a full right of deduction.

Scenario (1) addresses cases where related parties agree to artificially deflate the price to reduce the input VAT costs for the recipient, which in turn affects tax revenues. Scenarios (2) and (3) target situations in which the supplier tries to manipulate the recovery ratio for input VAT deductions on mixed used goods and services (e.g., overheads) by artificially setting a high price for taxed output transactions (for which input tax deductions are available) and/or a low price for exempt output transactions

231. *Balkan and Sea Properties, supra* n. 230, paragraph 51.
232. *Balkan and Sea Properties, supra* n. 230, paragraph 51.
233. *Balkan and Sea Properties, supra* n. 230, paragraphs 53-62; similarly previously, CJEU, 9 June 2011, Case C-285/10, *Campsa*, ECLI:EU:C:2011:381, paragraphs 24-27.
234. EU VAT Directive, *supra* n. 69, Article 80(1).
235. For criticism of this flexibility, *see* Eline Polak & Mayra O. Lucas Mas, *Transfer Pricing – Global Topics, Value Added Tax*, section 6.2.3.2, IBFD Online (accessed 14 December 2020).

(for which input tax deductions are not available).[236] According to Article 80(2), Members State have the right to restrict the categories of suppliers or recipients to whom the measures shall apply.

According to Article 72 of the EU VAT Directive, the 'open market value' is defined as the:[237]

> ...full amount that, in order to obtain the goods or services in question at that time, a customer at the same marketing stage at which the supply of goods or services takes place, would have to pay, *under conditions of fair competition*, to a supplier at *arm's length* within the territory of the Member State in which the supply is subject to tax.

In a case for which no comparable supply of goods or services 'can be ascertained', i.e., as a second-best option, the 'open market value' should be the full costs to the taxable person of providing those services or, in the case of goods, the purchase price or, as a last resort, the cost price of those goods.[238]

The concept of 'open market value' has been criticized for leading to uncertainty because there is a lack of guidance on the methods relevant to determining the open market value.[239] Some scholars argue that the preference for a comparability test and the term 'arm's length' indicate an intention to be consistent with corporate transfer pricing guidelines.[240] However there is no legislative material or CJEU judgment which confirms this understanding. As the CJEU has so far been reluctant to interpret terms in the VAT Directive with reference to direct tax terminology,[241] it is questionable whether the Court would regard Article 80 as an implementation of corporate tax principles.[242] From a practical perspective, an interpretation in line with the corporate tax terminology might ease compliance burdens but runs the risk of muddying the VAT

236. *See, e.g.*, EU VAT Directive, *supra* n. 69, Article 174.
237. EU VAT Directive, *supra* n. 69, Article 72 (emphasis added).
238. EU VAT Directive, *supra* n. 69, Article 72(1)-(2).
239. European Union, Opinion of the European Economic and Social Committee on the Proposal for a Council Directive Amending Directive 77/388/EEC as Regards Certain Measures to Simplify the Procedure for Charging Value Added Tax and to Assist in Countering Tax Evasion and Avoidance, and Repealing Certain Decisions Granting Derogations, COM(2005) 89 final, 2005/0019 (CNS) (16 March 2005), point 3.5: 'Difficulties may arise in practice, however, in determining a significant difference between the value of the transaction and the open market value, as there is no clear definition of either open market value, which depends on the assessment of the parties involved, or of a significant difference of value.' *See also* Polak & Lucas Mas, *supra* n. 235, at section 6.2.3.3.
240. *See* Rouberol, *supra* n. 24, 318.
241. *See, FCE Bank*, *supra* n. 14, paragraph 39: '[i]t should be noted that the OECD Convention is irrelevant since it concerns direct taxation whereas VAT is an indirect tax'.
242. In a similar vein, *see* European Commission, *Question Concerning the Application of EU VAT Provisions – Possible VAT Implications of Transfer Pricing*, *supra* n. 5, 16-17.

with the uncertainty, risks and gaming that occurs in the corporate tax transfer pricing context.

According to prevailing opinion in Austria, the primary method to identify the 'open market value' is a 'direct price comparison'.[243] This method can be applied if the supplier also carries out comparable transactions with recipients with whom it does not have a close relationship. Alternative methods to assess market prices, such as those determined from stock exchange quotations or financial statements customary in the industry or obtained from price overviews of associations, should only be used as a subsidiary basis for comparison.[244] Additionally, the Austrian VAT Guidelines hold that in cross-border situations an arm's length price identified for income tax purposes by using a *transaction based method* may also be used as the open market value for VAT purposes.[245] There are other instances of Member States prescribing valuation methods that similarly align with income tax principles.[246] This suggests some scope for transfer pricing adjustments to have VAT consequences which is discussed further at §10.04[E] below.

Overall, the concept of the open market value in Article 80 of the EU VAT Directive is different from the arm's length concept in corporate income tax law. It is narrower in scope in some aspects, but broader in others. While the arm's length principle in corporate tax law must be generally observed in *all* cross-border intra-group and intra-entity transactions under the OECD transfer pricing rules, Article 80 of the EU VAT Directive is optional for Member States and can only be used for transactions involving taxable persons who do not have a full right to an input VAT credit. Article 80 can apply to both cross-border transactions and purely domestic transactions, which is not the case for the OECD transfer pricing rules which are limited to cross-border transactions (although domestic laws might address the risk of domestic transfer pricing). Moreover, the open market value rule in Article 80 is much more underdeveloped and uncertain than the corporate tax equivalent as it lacks guidance regarding the relevant methods available to ascertain values and grants leeway to Member States to fill in this gap. It might be that, despite the different scope and purpose of transfer pricing and VAT rules, this gap is filled by transfer pricing methods for valuation purposes at least.

243. Austrian VAT Guidelines (UStR), *supra* n. 198, paragraph 682.
244. Austrian VAT Guidelines (UStR), *supra* n. 198, paragraph 682; Ruppe & Achatz, *supra* n. 228, §4, paragraph 192.
245. Austrian VAT Guidelines (UStR), *supra* n. 198, paragraph 682.
246. *See* Polak & Lucas Mas, *supra* n. 235, section 6.2.3.3; in more general terms, Rouberol, *supra* n. 24, 318. On the UK rules, *see* HM Revenue and Customs, *Transfer Pricing: Operational Guidance: Interaction with Indirect Taxes: Interaction with VAT*, Internal Manual INTM486010 (9 April 2016, updated 20 October 2020), available at: https://www.gov.uk/hmrc-internal-manuals/international-manual/intm486010.

[D] Interaction with Customs

Customs law is harmonized within the EU by the Union Customs Code (UCC)[247] (formerly the Community Customs Code (CCC)).[248] Following the WCO approach, Article 70 of the UCC provides that the primary basis for determining the customs value of imported goods is the transaction value, that is, the price actually paid or payable for the goods, unless (among other exceptions) the relationship between the buyer and seller has influenced the price setting.[249] The CJEU has also held that, for the purposes of customs valuation, the 'price actually paid or payable for the goods [...] is a factor that potentially must be adjusted where necessary in order to avoid the setting of an arbitrary or fictitious customs value'.[250]

Whether the relationship of the parties has influenced the price (i.e., the acceptability of a price agreed upon between related parties) must be examined by the customs authorities by taking account of the circumstances surrounding the sale. Alternatively, the declarant has the option of submitting certain 'test values' in order to demonstrate that the declared transaction value closely approximates to a transaction value in a sale between unrelated parties.[251] When the customs value of goods cannot be determined based on Article 70 of the UCC (i.e., the price *has* been influenced by the relationship), the customs value should be determined according to a range of ranked criteria beginning with the transactional value of 'identical' goods, then the transactional value of 'similar' goods and then by reference to the costs of materials plus an adequate profit margin.[252]

There is no specific rule in EU legislation which clarifies whether transfer pricing adjustments for corporate tax can have an influence on customs valuation. In the leading case of *Hamamatsu* of 2017 (the facts of which fell within the previous CCC regime),[253] the decision of the CJEU suggests that the link between transfer pricing and EU customs law is not a strong one.[254] In that case, transfer prices for the sale of goods within a group of companies were initially set according to an Advanced Pricing Agreement (APA) and were later adjusted at the end of the year by a lump sum for all shipments taken together in the relevant year. In the disputed year, this led to a downward adjustment (i.e., resulting in a possible refund of duty to the importer). The

247. Council Regulation (EU) No. 952/2013 of the European Parliament and of the Council of 9 October 2013 Laying Down the Union Customs Code, OJ L 269, 1-101, as amended by Regulation 2019/632 (UCC).
248. Council Regulation (EEC) No. 2913/92 of 12 October 1992 Establishing the Community Customs Code (OJ 1992 L 302, 1), as amended by Regulation (EC) No. 82/97 of the European Parliament and of the Council of 19 December 1996 (OJ 1997 L 17, 1)(CCC).
249. UCC, *supra* n. 247, Article 70(3)(d).
250. *Hamamatsu, supra* n. 51, paragraph 27 with reference to further case law.
251. UCC Implementing Regulation (EU) 2015/2447 of 24 November 2015 Laying Down Detailed Rules for Implementing Certain Provisions of Regulation (EU) No 952/2013 of the European Parliament and of the Council laying down the Union Customs Code, Article 134 (former Article 29(2)(a) and (b) Community Customs Code).
252. UCC, *supra* n. 247, Article 73.
253. *Hamamatsu, supra* n. 51.
254. Juha Tuominen, *The Link between Transfer Pricing and EU Customs Valuation Law: Is There Any and How Could It Be Strengthened?* 25(6) Int'l Transfer Pricing J. 436, 449-452 (2018).

German customs authority rejected the global correction of the total price, since the adjustment amount was not broken down by product and import transactions. The CJEU was asked whether the transaction value could be adjusted by retrospective correction of the actual price payable. The Court came to the rather general conclusion that there is no legal basis for valuation structures that are based on transfer pricing principles with potential year-end adjustments. According to the CJEU, the subsequent adjustment of the transaction value for customs purposes 'is limited to specific situations' (e.g., defect in the goods discovered).[255] The Court emphasized that:[256]

> [I]n the version in force, the Customs Code does not impose any obligation on importer companies to apply for adjustment of the transaction value where it is adjusted subsequently upwards and it does not contain any provision enabling the customs authorities to safeguard against the risk that those undertakings only apply for downward adjustments.

Some scholars infer from these general statements that a corporate tax-driven APA and any retroactive adjustment deriving from it does not affect customs valuation.[257] The judgment has been criticized for being 'cryptic' and not aligning with international practice.[258] The judgment is certainly unclear on whether the reasoning applies to all transfer pricing methods (including transactional-based methods)[259] and whether the result might be different under the new UCC, which has been in force since 1 May 2016.[260] Despite the judgment, some Member States' customs authorities still require that a price increase resulting from a transfer pricing adjustment be retroactively included in the customs value, by, for example, arguing that the price has been influenced by the relationship of the parties.[261]

Customs values are also relevant for VAT purposes because the EU VAT Directive provides that the taxable amount for imported goods shall be the value for customs purposes determined in accordance with the Community provisions in force.[262] As the taxable amount for import VAT is heavily dependent on the customs value, any arm's length test applied for the purposes of customs valuation and any change in the

255. *Hamamatsu, supra* n. 51, paragraph 30.
256. *Hamamatsu, supra* n. 51, paragraph 33.
257. *See* Enrico De Angelis & Theo Elshof, *The Interplay between Transfer Pricing and Customs Valuation in Case of Retroactive Profit Adjustments: The Position of the ECJ in the Case Hamamatsu Photonics Deutschland GmbH (C-529/16)*, 25(4) Int'l Transfer Pricing J. 300, 304 (2018).
258. *See* Johannes Schimmer, *Transfer Pricing & Customs Valuation, Country Tax Guides – Germany*, section 2, IBFD Online (accessed on 14 December 2020).
259. For the view that the *Hamamatsu* reasoning applies to all transfer pricing methods, *see* De Angelis & Elshof, *supra* n. 257, 304; for the view that the judgment is limited to the residual profit split method, *see* Tuominen, *supra* n. 254, 446-448.
260. *See* De Angelis & Elshof, *supra* n. 257, 304.
261. *See* examples mentioned by Tuominen, *supra* n. 254, 448. On Germany, *see* Schimmer, *supra* n. 258, section 2.1.
262. EU VAT Directive, *supra* n. 69, Article 85(1); Article 86 lists certain factors which should be added to the customs value if they are not already included (e.g., taxes and charges due outside the Member State of importation, incidental expenses such as commission and packaging incurred up to the first place of destination within the territory of the Member State of importation). Article 87 clarifies that the taxable amount should not include price reductions and discounts.

customs value based on a revaluation for customs purposes may therefore also affect the taxable amount for import VAT.[263] For exports to non-EU Member States (where in a transfer pricing context the incentive might be to overstate the value of goods exported to a low-tax jurisdiction) the effect on the VAT is neutral as no VAT is collected.

[E] The Impact of Transfer Pricing Adjustments on VAT Liabilities

Recently there has been much discussion on the interaction between transfer pricing rules and VAT in the academic literature[264] and at the European Commission.[265] Despite the discussion, there is neither clear consensus nor any CJEU judgment determinative of the issues.

Whether a transfer pricing adjustment has an effect on VAT will depend on various factors. Many EU scholars consider that transfer pricing adjustments can have VAT implications in limited circumstances.[266] As Rouberol contends, it could never be stated as a general rule that a transfer pricing adjustment always leads to an adjustment of the VAT taxable amount for a supply of goods or services. Instead all the relevant conditions for the VAT Directive to apply would need to be satisfied, such as: identifying a specific transaction and the consideration provided for that transaction; and, determining where the supply takes place and whether the chargeable event has occurred.[267] The European Commission similarly concluded in a 2017 working paper that the impact of transfer pricing rules on the EU VAT should be considered on a case-by-case basis according to the general VAT rules, particularly because transfer pricing rules deviate from the subjective value laid down as the taxable base for the purposes of EU VAT.[268]

From a policy perspective, a transfer pricing adjustment might have VAT consequences under EU VAT law in four main instances: firstly, it might constitute an adjustment of the taxable amount of a previous supply under the general rules or qualify as a new supply under the general rules; secondly, it might be a situation to

263. European Commission, *Question Concerning the Application of EU VAT Provisions – Possible VAT Implications of Transfer Pricing*, *supra* n. 5, 23.
264. *See*, in particular, Santoro, *supra* n. 16, 162-163; Martins, *supra* n. 101, 328; Matesanz, *supra* n. 87, 9; van Doesum, van Kesteren & van Norden, *supra* n. 67, 290; Rouberol, *supra* n. 23, at 316; van den Brekel, van Doesum & van Kesteren, *supra* n. 103; Karol Dziwinski, *Transfer Pricing and VAT: An Analysis of Two Overlapping Disciplines*, 25 Transfer Pricing Int'l 28 (2020).
265. European Commission, *Question Concerning the Application of EU VAT Provisions – Possible VAT Implications of Transfer Pricing*, *supra* n. 5, at 16-17; European Union, VAT Expert Group, *Paper on Topic for Discussion: Possible VAT Implications of Transfer Pricing*, VEG No. 071 REV2, taxud.c.1(2018)2326098 (18 April 2018).
266. *See supra* n. 97 and n. 264.
267. Rouberol, *supra* n. 24, 317.
268. European Commission, *Question Concerning the Application of EU VAT Provisions – Possible VAT Implications of Transfer Pricing*, *supra* n. 5, 16-17; *see also* the conclusion by the chair at the VAT Committee meeting of 27 and 28 March 2017: '[t]ransfer pricing could have an impact in some concrete cases, but those would be subject to a case-by-case assessment' (European Union, VAT Committee, Minutes to the 108th Meeting, 27 and 28 March 2017, taxud.c.1(2017)3063070, 9).

which Article 80 applies (i.e., for intra-group supplies); thirdly, it might be a situation to which the *Skandia* exception applies (i.e., for intra-entity supplies); and fourthly, it might be a situation to which Article 27 applies (i.e., for intra-entity supplies). Each possibility is discussed in turn before concluding with a final reflection on how the outcome is likely to be affected by the approach of individual Member States.

[1] Adjustment for a Previous Supply or Qualification as a New Supply under the General VAT Rules

As §10.02[E] explained, a transfer pricing adjustment may only have an effect for VAT purposes based on the general rules if it can be sufficiently linked to a previous taxable supply (adjustment of the taxable amount) *or* be regarded as consideration for a new supply of goods or services.[269] According to settled case law, a supply of goods or services is taxable only if there is a 'legal relationship' between the supplier and the recipient, which includes the notion of 'reciprocal performance', which is met if the 'remuneration received by the provider of the service [constitutes] the value actually given in return for the service supplied to the recipient' (also referred to as 'direct link').[270] This formula was developed in the famous *Tolsma* case in 1994 when the CJEU denied the existence of a taxable supply when a street musician received 'donations' for his performance. [271] Since then, this formula has been consistently reaffirmed by the Court.[272] Against this background, a secondary adjustment that takes the form of dividend distributions or capital contributions should not have any VAT effect, as there is no reciprocal performance involved in such cases and no direct link given between the payment (in money or in kind) and a supply.[273] Such reciprocal performance between the adjustment and a specific supply is more likely to exist in the case of transactional-based methods, but will be more difficult to establish for profit-split methods.[274] Contracts could be used as evidence of a connection between an adjustment to an initial pricing of a prior supply particularly when they provide for price adjustment clauses which subject prices to periodic modifications under certain circumstances.[275]

Relevant to the assessment of whether a direct link to an earlier supply exists is who initiated the adjustment: the taxpayer or the authorities/court. A transfer pricing

269. *See, e.g.*, EU VAT Directive, *supra* n. 69, Articles 2, 90; van den Brekel, van Doesum & van Kesteren, *supra* n. 103, 185-187; Polak & Lucas Mas, *supra* n. 235, sections 6.3.1 and 6.3.2. *See* Chapter 9 (§9.06) of this book for a discussion of the general requirements for VAT adjustments in the EU.
270. *See, inter alia*, CJEU, 27 Sept. 2001, Case C-16/00, *CIBO Participations*, ECLI:EU:C:2001:495, paragraph 43.
271. CJEU, 3 March 1994, Case C-16/93, *Tolsma*, ECLI:EU:C:1994:80, paragraph 14.
272. *See, inter alia*, CJEU, 22 June 2016, Case C-11/15, *Český rozhlas*, ECLI:EU:C:2016:470, paragraph 21.
273. *CIBO Participations*, *supra* n. 270, paragraph 43; CJEU, 26 June 2003, Case C-442/01, *KapHag*, ECLI:EU:C:2003:381; Polak & Lucas Mas, *supra* n. 235, section 6.3.4.
274. Rouberol, *supra* n. 24, 316-317; Polak & Lucas Mas, *supra* n. 235, section 6.3.1.
275. Polak & Lucas Mas, *supra* n. 235, section 6.3.2; European Commission, *Question Concerning the Application of EU VAT Provisions – Possible VAT Implications of Transfer Pricing*, *supra* n. 5, 21.

adjustment that has been agreed to by the parties to the supply themselves (e.g., compensating adjustment) is more likely to have VAT effects[276] because, from a policy perspective, EU VAT law is usually based on the price agreed between the parties (subjective value) which serves as the taxable amount.[277] However, as chapter 9 of this volume (§9.06[D]) explained, it is not yet settled whether an adjustment to the agreed price by an external body (e.g., an authority or a court) can constitute a consideration adjustment under EU VAT law with opinion divided on whether transfer pricing adjustments undertaken by a third party can impact the VAT base.[278]

A transfer pricing adjustment is more likely to have an effect on VAT if it is recognized in the balance sheet and/or leads to an additional payment by the parties.[279] If a transfer pricing adjustment has a 'direct tax effect' only, i.e., merely leads to an adjustment of the taxable profit for corporate tax purposes, this adjustment as a general rule will not qualify as 'consideration' for VAT purposes and, hence, can neither affect a previous taxable supply nor establish a new taxable supply.[280]

In light of these considerations, a majority of EU scholars consider that *compensatory adjustments* based on *transactional-based methods* can lead to an adjustment of the VAT base provided that they are recognized in the commercial books (balancing payments) and that they can be directly linked to a previous supply or a new supply of goods or services.[281]

These general considerations are separate from, and in addition to, the potential application of the special rules discussed at §§10.04[B] and [C] which are separately addressed in the remaining discussion.

[2] Transactions Covered by Domestic Implementation Rules to Article 80 (Open Market Value Rule)

As §10.04[C] demonstrated, a transfer pricing adjustment could potentially play a role under EU VAT law for transactions between two legally independent entities that are associated, i.e., transactions within a group of companies (e.g., parent-subsidiary relationship).

If a Member State has implemented Article 80 of the EU VAT Directive and uses the open market value as the taxable amount for certain related party transactions, the

---

276. Van den Brekel, van Doesum & van Kesteren, *supra* n. 103, 185.
277. *See* EU VAT Directive, *supra* n. 6, Article 73.
278. CJEU, 1 July 1982, Case C-222/81, *B.A.Z. Bausystem*, ECLI:EU:C:1982:256, paragraph 10. For the view that a third-party change to consideration cannot constitute an adjustment, *see* Santoro, *supra* n. 16, 161; Martins, *supra* n. 101, 328. For the view that a third-party variation might constitute an adjustment, *see* European Commission, *Question Concerning the Application of EU VAT Provisions – Possible VAT Implications of Transfer Pricing, supra* n. 5, 21; *see generally* Rouberol, *supra* n. 24.
279. Santoro, *supra* n. 16, 162-163; Matesanz, *supra* n. 87, 9; van Doesum, van Kesteren & van Norden, *supra* n. 67, 290.
280. *See* van den Brekel, van Doesum & van Kesteren, *supra* n. 103, 185; Dziwinski, *supra* n. 264, 29.
281. Santoro, *supra* n. 16, 162-163; Matesanz, *supra* n. 87, 9; van Doesum, van Kesteren & van Norden, *supra* n. 67, 290.

effect of a transfer pricing adjustment might trigger the application of Article 80. For example, a transfer pricing adjustment based on a transaction-based method might lead a Member State's revenue authority to consider whether the 'open market value' is satisfied for VAT purposes.[282] Whether this is the case will depend on the specific Member State's implementation of Article 80, the scope of the rule and the domestic understanding of 'open market value'. Since Article 80 of the EU VAT Directive does not link to any price agreement by the parties, it will be irrelevant in these cases whether the adjustment is recognized in the balance sheet or as a balancing payment and/or was initiated by the parties to the transaction. However, a transfer pricing adjustment is not likely to be relevant for VAT purposes under the scope of Article 80 if the profit allocation for corporate income tax is made by applying profit split methods (rather than transaction-based methods).

It is also conceivable that there might be no need for Article 80 to apply in a situation involving a transfer pricing adjustment that results in an adjustment of the actual consideration for a particular transaction to be paid between the parties (e.g., a compensatory adjustment) that has a direct link to a previous supply. Such a transfer pricing adjustment might already trigger an adjustment of the taxable amount for VAT purposes based on the general adjustment rules discussed above. In this case, the remuneration after the adjustment should correspond to the open market value in any event, which means that an adjustment based on the domestic rule implementing Article 80 might no longer be necessary.[283] This presumes a degree of alignment between the valuation methods used for transfer pricing and VAT purposes in the relevant Member States.

[3] Application of the Skandia Ruling

As §10.04[A] explained, the general rule under the EU VAT is that cross-border supplies of services (including recharging of costs) between one establishment and another establishment of the same legal entity (e.g., in a branch-branch or head office-branch relationship) are not subject to VAT. Consequently, transfer pricing adjustments for purposes of Articles 7 and 5 in a specific double tax treaty for corporate income tax based on the OECD *Model Tax Convention* (i.e., profit allocation between head office and permanent establishment) would, generally speaking, not be relevant under EU VAT law.

However, a practical relevant exception potentially applies to those Member States which have implemented VAT grouping following the *Skandia* and *Danske Bank* rulings. If a Member State following these rulings treats inbound intra-company transactions as taxable, a transfer pricing adjustment might have VAT consequences. Whether it does will depend on the administrative practice and the relevant understanding of the *Skandia* and *Danske Bank* rulings in the individual Member State. An

282. For the Austrian view, *see, e.g.*, Thomas Ecker in Thomas Ecker, Thomas Epply, Ferdinand Rößler & Dietlind Schwab (eds.), *Umsatzsteuergesetz*, 46, §4, paragraphs 473-475 (Supplement 2015).
283. *See* Thomas Ecker, *supra* n. 282, §4, paragraph 474.

effect on VAT would be more likely if the taxable person did not have a full right to input VAT deduction and the Member State has implemented the option in Article 80 to use the 'open market value' as the taxable amount. As a general rule, transactions between two establishments of the same legal entity would likely satisfy the association requirement in Article 80. If the Member State does not use Article 80, a transfer pricing adjustment is more likely to affect VAT outcomes if a transaction-based method was used. However, a case-by-case approach will be required.

[4] Transactions Falling Within the Domestic Implementation Rules of Article 27

Should a Member State use Article 27 to tax cross-border intra entity supplies (the authors are not aware of any Member State currently doing so), a transfer pricing adjustment will have a similar effect as under Article 80 of the EU VAT Directive because the taxable amount for transactions covered by Article 27 is also defined as the open market value.[284]

Despite these four theoretical possibilities, the approach by Member States to the effects of transfer pricing adjustments on VAT liabilities is unclear.[285] For example, the Austrian Ministry of Finance only provides very general guidelines that provide that a transfer pricing adjustment can lead to a consideration adjustment for VAT purposes if it involves a recognition of receivables and payables. However, the Guidelines state that such consideration adjustments may not be necessary if they have no effect on the tax revenue in Austria, i.e., if the persons involved have a full right to input credit in Austria.[286] This limitation seems coherent in light of the fact that Austria has implemented Article 80 of the VAT Directive, according to which the open market value can be applied if a transaction between related parties takes place and one of the parties does not have a full right to input credits. However, the Austrian Guidelines do not distinguish between primary and compensating adjustments and the transfer pricing methods applied and give no indication of the circumstances under which a direct link of an adjustment to a taxable supply is given.

§10.05 CONCLUSION

The understanding of the relationship between transfer pricing for income tax purposes and the rules for VAT is nascent and the approaches taken by the various jurisdictions are also continuing to develop. Further work and reform will likely be required. On the one hand, it makes sense to keep the two areas separate given the different purpose of the VAT and the income tax and manner in which they operate. It makes additional sense to insulate the VAT from the gaming that inheres in transfer pricing and from being too heavily affected by future reforms which might change the basis for assessing

284. EU VAT Directive, *supra* n. 69, Articles 27, 77 and 80.
285. Polak & Lucas Mas, *supra* n. 235, section 6.3.1.
286. Austrian Transfer Pricing Guidelines (VPR) as of 28 October 2010, *supra* n. 226, marginal numbers 338-343.

the income tax liability of MNEs. On the other hand, there are certain areas where a degree of overlap is inevitable such as when a party to a cross-border supply within an MNE is not entitled to full input tax deductions and an incentive to game also exists for VAT purposes. The analysis has shown the diversity of responses to the issue within Australia and the EU and emphasized the need to at least coordinate administration of VAT, customs and income tax so that the risks are appropriately identified even if the responses still require further co-ordination.

CHAPTER 11
Vouchers and VAT

Jeroen Bijl

§11.01 INTRODUCTION

This chapter examines the value added tax (VAT) treatment of vouchers[1] with focus on face-value vouchers and cash back or rebate vouchers. Rebate vouchers are issued by the manufacturer to the end consumer who is not the original customer of the manufacturer of the goods. Face-value vouchers are of interest because their treatment has only recently been (partly) harmonized in the European Union (EU).[2] The Court of Justice of the EU (CJEU) has issued several rulings on rebate voucher transactions, which seem not to correspond with some of the basic principles of VAT, reason to examine these transactions in more detail. Central to this study is the VAT treatment of vouchers, as defined above, in the EU but I will make comparisons to the treatment of the same in New Zealand, Australia and South Africa insofar as these jurisdictions have implemented or use different rules or methods of taxing these instruments and/or connected transactions.

Finally, I will use the (EU VAT) principle of neutrality and 'economic reality' as basic tests to compare the different treatments of the selected voucher transactions and to determine which treatment is preferable. VAT neutrality for this purpose does not only mean that VAT should be exactly proportional to the price of the goods and

1. This chapter is, to a large extend, based on my PhD thesis (Jeroen Bijl, *The EU VAT Treatment of Vouchers in the* Context of Promotional Activities, Wolters Kluwer, 2019), but I have added a number of potential VAT treatments of voucher transactions as well as a comparison to the VAT or GST treatment of these scenarios under the relevant rules in New Zealand, Australia and South Africa.
2. Before 2019, EU Member States applied different VAT treatments to transactions involving vouchers. From 1 January 2019, Council Directive (EU) 2016/1065 of 27 June 2016 amending Directive 2006/112/EC as regards the treatment of vouchers, OJ L 177/9 of 1 July 2016, came into force. From that date, all EU Member States apply uniform rules for the VAT treatment of face value vouchers.

services,[3] but also implies the equal treatment of similar goods and services to prevent distortion of competition.[4] The principle of legal certainty, and consequently the protection of legitimate expectations, requires that rules of law must be clear and precise and their application be foreseeable by those subject to them.[5] For this purpose, I use the term 'economic reality' as a means to determine the objective nature of a transaction which, in turn, should determine the correct VAT treatment. In that sense, 'economic reality' is a manifestation of the concept of 'substance over form'.[6]

The term 'voucher' is a blanket term for many different instruments: gift cards, book tokens, food stamps, phone cards, admission tickets and discount coupons, just to mention a few. Vouchers are described as embodying rights.[7] The Cambridge online dictionary describes a voucher as 'a piece of paper that can be used to pay for particular goods or services or that allows you to pay less than the usual price for them'.[8] The right embodied in a voucher would, under this specific definition, be the right to use the voucher as means of (partial) payment, instead of payment in legal tender, or as proof of (pre)payment for certain supplies of goods or services, as well as proof of entitlement to a discount on certain transactions.

Businesses that use vouchers usually do this for several different reasons, some of which are:[9]

- Some of the voucher business models are partially based on the foreseeable fact that not all vouchers will be redeemed ('breakage revenue', a cash advantage) – this advantage only applies to vouchers that are supplied for consideration.
- The business issuing the voucher has money at its disposition before any supply is made (cash flow advantage) – this advantage only applies to vouchers that are supplied for consideration,
- Voucher schemes increase customer loyalty.
- Voucher schemes increase the sales of specific products.

3. This is referred to as 'the principle of the common system of VAT' in Article 1(2) of the EU VAT Directive.
4. CJEU, 10 April 2008, Case C-309/06, *Marks & Spencer plc v. Commissioners of Customs & Excise*, ECLI:EU:C:2008:211, paragraph 49.
5. *See*, e.g., CJEU, 22 February 2018, Case C-396/16, T-2, *družba za ustvarjanje, razvoj in trženje elektronskih komunikacij in opreme, d.o.o. (sedaj v stečaju) v. Republika Slovenija*, ECLI: EU:C:2018:109, paragraph 52; and CJEU, 9 October 2014, Case C-492/13, *Traum EOOD v. Direktor na Direktsia 'Obzhalvane idanachno-osiguritelna praktika' Varna pri Tsentralno upravlenie na Natsionalnata agentsia za prihodite*, ECLI:EU:C:2014:2267, paragraph 28.
6. For more on VAT and economic reality, I refer to Ad J. van Doesum & Frank J.G. Nellen, *Economic Reality in EU VAT* 29(5) EC Tax Review (2020).
7. *See* the Proposal for a Council Directive, amending Directive 2006/112/EC on the common system of value added tax, as regards the treatment of vouchers, COM(2012)206, not published in the Official Journal, available at: http://eur-lex.europa.eu/LexUriServ/LexUriServ.do?uri=COM:2012:0206:FIN:EN:PDF (last visited on 12 March 2019).
8. Cambridge Dictionaries Online, Definition of voucher (noun) from the Cambridge Advanced Learner's Dictionary & Thesaurus © Cambridge University Press, accessed on 12 December 2020.
9. Some of these advantages are described by Jon Hart and Melanie Hill, *Fighting Over the Balance Left on Unused Gift Cards*, The Wall Street Journal Online, accountant, at: http://online.wsj.com/public/resources/documents/SB107219160756934900.htm (last accessed on 28 December 2020).

- Voucher schemes get people to come to a shop to redeem the voucher, thereby increasing sales overall, because research shows that the average consumer spends considerably more than the value of the voucher.
- Vouchers remove the 'risk' associated with certain goods or services that are often given as presents, such as books, music, and beauty products, increasing the sale of such products as gifts – this advantage only applies to vouchers that are supplied for consideration.
- Some issuers of vouchers require the holders to provide them with information that can be of value for marketing purposes, e.g., by linking consumer data to specific transactions or trends in purchasing behaviour.
- Vouchers can create tax advantages (e.g., an employer providing its employees luncheon vouchers as part of their salary (in kind). Under certain circumstances, these benefits are excluded from the personal income tax base).[10]

Vouchers that are issued or sold for consideration create a separation between a payment and a (subsequent) supply, thereby creating the possibility of breakage revenue, where a company recognizes into revenue a portion of a liability that will not be redeemed by the customer.

Because of the limited scope of this chapter, the focus is limited to the VAT treatment of two types of voucher transactions. First, I will focus on transactions involving vouchers with a face value, that are sold or given away free of charge and which can be used as (part) consideration for the supply of goods and services. These face value vouchers can be redeemed with either the business that issued them or with other businesses which, in turn, will be reimbursed by the issuer of the vouchers. In this chapter, these types of vouchers are referred to as 'face value vouchers'. From 1 January 2019, all EU Member States apply uniform rules for the VAT treatment of face value vouchers.[11] This means that it is possible to compare the EU VAT treatment of face value vouchers with their treatment in other jurisdictions that operate a comparable VAT or Goods and Services Tax (GST) system. The European Commission's attempt at harmonising the VAT treatment of other types of vouchers, such as discount coupons and money off vouchers, was unsuccessful due to a lack of agreement between the EU Member States.[12] That is why comparing the VAT treatment of transactions involving these other types of vouchers is far more cumbersome. I will, however, focus on one other type of voucher transaction: businesses that grant money off or cash back on their products that are sold down a distribution chain, to the end consumers of these products. The CJEU has issued several rulings in regard of this type

10. From the facts of a referral to the CJEU by a Luxembourg court, Case C-395/12, *État du Grand-duché de Luxembourg, Administration de l'enregistrement et des domaines v. Edenred Luxembourg SA*, OJ C 366 of 24 November 2012, 24; removed from the register on 9 November 2012, OJ C 108 of 13 April 2013, 19.
11. On that date, Council Directive (EU) 2016/1065 of 27 June 2016 amending Directive 2006/112/EC as regards the treatment of vouchers, OJ L 177/9 of 1 July 2016, came into force.
12. *See* the Proposal for a Council Directive, amending Directive 2006/112/EC on the common system of value added tax, as regards the treatment of vouchers, COM(2012)206, not published in the Official Journal, available at: http://eur-lex.europa.eu/LexUriServ/LexUriServ.do?uri=COM:2012:0206:FIN:EN:PDF, last visited on 21 December 2020.

of voucher or promotion scheme, allowing for a comparison between the rules as laid down by the CJEU with the VAT/GST treatment of such transactions in other jurisdictions.

§11.02 FACE VALUE VOUCHERS AND VAT

Transactions involving face value vouchers (FVVs) can be treated in a number of different ways from a VAT perspective:

(1) It can be argued that FVVs are similar to currency, deposits or negotiable instruments as mentioned in Article 135(1)(d) and (e) of the EU VAT Directive.
(2) It can be argued that the issuance of an FVV constitutes the transfer of a right, which is a supply of a service that should be taxed.
(3) If the VAT treatment of the transaction that is to be performed upon redemption of the FVV is known at the time of issuing the FVV, the issuing and sale of the FVV can be considered as a prepayment for the underlying transaction.
(4) If the VAT treatment of the transaction that is to be performed upon redemption of the FVV is known at the time of issuing the FVV, the issuing and sale of the FVV can be considered as performing the underlying transaction for which the FVV can be redeemed.
(5) The issuing and sale of the FVV can be considered making a deposit for a future, unknown transaction.

[A] Should FVVs Be Treated Similar to Currency, Deposits or Negotiable Instruments?

Money are bearer notes, generally issued by the central bank of a state, with a specific face value expressed in the state's currency. It is value paper guaranteed by the state and used as an intermediary in exchanges of goods and services.

Face value vouchers have some use elements in common with money but that does not make vouchers equivalent to money or legal tender. Vouchers often have a face value, expressed in legal tender. If I want to give my friend, an avid reader, a book but I am not sure which particular one would please her most, I can, instead, give her a gift card for $50, which she can redeem at any bookstore belonging to the chain or the organization issuing the voucher. A gift card does not have to be for a particular type of product, like a book, but could be more general, i.e., a gift card to be redeemed when purchasing any good or service within the range offered by the issuer. The gift card has a monetary value equivalent to the amount of legal tender I handed over to purchase the card, and the value is stated in the gift card. Essentially, the gift card is documentation that embodies the following: the obligation of the redeemer to supply any good or service from the range covered by the gift card; a right of the holder of the gift card to be supplied with her choice of good or service from the range offered by the redeemer; proof of pre-payment. A gift card contains, thus, elements of a contract between the issuer or affiliate and the bearer of the gift card, who is unknown at the time of issuance, for the supply of an undetermined good or service at an unspecified time in the future but before the expiration date of the gift card (if any).

The contractual elements are absent in money and that sets vouchers clearly apart in function. Moreover, vouchers have limited use as they can only be redeemed within a specific network of suppliers and only for the purchase of goods and services within the range offered by the ring of associated suppliers; whereas state issued money, legal tender, is generally accepted as means of payment, i.e., for all and any transaction within the jurisdiction of the state, and through currency exchange also beyond borders.

Therefore, my conclusion is that vouchers, although they may carry a monetary value, cannot be regarded as money because of the difference in both function and scope of use.

The principle of neutrality dictates that similar transactions should be treated the same for VAT purposes. In the EU context, it is irrelevant in that respect whether there actually exists competition between the identical supplies; nor is it required that the different treatment would actually cause distortion of existing competition.[13] In order to assess whether, in the light of the principle of fiscal neutrality, two types of services are similar and require the same VAT treatment it must be established whether the use of those types of services is comparable from the point of view of the average consumer and meets the same needs of that consumer.[14] This leads to the question whether vouchers are sufficiently similar to credit/debit cards or cheques to allot them the same, i.e., exempt treatment.

Support for the view that transactions regarding some vouchers are similar to VAT exempt payment services can be found in CJEU case law and in comments on this topic from various parties involved in these types of transactions. For example, the CJEU has pointed out that services provided by a credit card company do not only consist of guaranteeing payment for the goods purchased by means of the card, but also serve the promotion of the supplier's business by enabling him to acquire new customers, possible publicity on his behalf or the like.[15] Therefore, 'means of payment' may have more than just a financial component. Besides that, it can also be argued that credit cards can also only be used to pay for transactions within a limited network of

13. CJEU, 10 November 2011, Joined Cases C-259/10 and C-260/10, *Commissioners for Her Majesty's Revenue and Customs v. The Rank Group plc*, ECLI:EU:C:2011:719.
14. More examples of CJEU case law on the requirement of fiscal neutrality for transactions similar to VAT exempt transactions to also be treated as VAT exempt, unless the transaction is absolutely prohibited, are: CJEU, 6 December 1990, Case C-343/89, *Max Witzemann v. Hauptzollamt München-Mitte*, ECLI:EU:C:1990:445; CJEU, 11 June 1998, Case C-283/95, *Karl-heinz Fischer v. Finanzamt Donaueschingen*, ECLI:EU:C:1998:276; and CJEU, 7 July 2010, *Gennaro Curia v. Ministero dell'Economia e delle Finanze et Agenzia delle Entrate*, ECLI: EU:C2010:406.
15. CJEU, 25 May 1993, Case C-18/92, *Chaussures Bally SA v. Belgian State*, ECLI:EU:C:1993:212.

suppliers,[16] because not all businesses accept payment by credit card and if they do, they do not always accept all credit cards.

Also, various businesses that are involved in transactions regarding vouchers responded to the European Commission's Consultation Paper on modernising the VAT treatment of vouchers and related issues in support of treating transactions regarding 'payment vouchers' the same as payment services. Moreover, two parties representing financial services providers submitted the view that (certain) vouchers should qualify as means of payment,[17] and the only body representing accounting organisations agreed with that position.[18]

In my view, vouchers are not sufficiently similar to financial instruments such as credit cards, debit cards, or checks for two main reasons. First, because of the contractual elements, vouchers are linked to a supply, even if yet unspecified. Second, the primary use of charge cards and cheques is the transfer of monetary units from one person to another. The core business of the issuer of vouchers is the underlying supply of goods and services for which the voucher can be used as (partial) payment. For the issuers of credit cards, etc., the core business is the intermediary payment service itself for which they are paid through a flat rate per transaction and/or a percentage of the purchase price made with the card. Again, in terms of function and use vouchers and charge cards are insufficiently similar to justify the same VAT treatment.

In December 2006, Directorate General for Taxation and the Customs Union of the European Commission undertook a public consultation to assist with the formulation of a proposal on the VAT treatment of vouchers.[19] In the Introduction, it is stated that 'vouchers continue to evolve in their scope, in some cases taking a role indistinguishable from a general payment vehicle'. Most of the responses defined certain types of vouchers as means of payment or a 'money exchange for a substitute for money', i.e., as a financial service.[20] In the Impact Assessment accompanying the Proposal, only transactions regarding certain prepaid telephone cards are identified as possibly

16. Services based on instruments that can be used to acquire goods and services only under a commercial agreement with the issuer within a limited network of suppliers are excluded from the application of the Directive on payment services within the internal market, Directive 2007/64/EC of the European Parliament and of the Council of 13 November 2007 on payment services in the internal market amending Directives 97/7/EC, 2002/65/EC, 2005/60/EC and 2006/48/EC and repealing Directive 97/5/EC, OJ L 319, of 5 December 2007, 1-36, Article 3(k).
17. The European Banking Federation's response stated: 'The payments rather than the MPV should be the centre of the debate', and the British Bankers Association's response positioned: 'There is therefore a very fine line between what can be construed as actual legal tender and what essentially "equates" to being legal tender.'
18. The Tax Faculty of the Chartered Institute of Chartered Accountants of England and Wales submitted a memorandum to the Commission, stating: 'All other vouchers (i.e., all vouchers except "Single-purpose Vouchers", JB) for which consideration has been given should be treated as means of payment … .'
19. European Commission, *Consultation Paper on Modernizing the Value Added Tax Treatment of Vouchers and Related Issues*, December 2006, available at: http://ec.europa.eu/taxation_customs/resources/documents/common/consultations/tax/consultation_paper_vouchers_en.pdf.
20. European Commission, Working Party 1, *Harmonisation of Turnover Taxes, Summary of Results*. Public Consultation on 'Modernising the Value Added Tax Treatment of Vouchers and Related Issues', TAXUD/2131/07 rev 1- EN, p. 8.

qualifying as financial services.[21] In the Proposal itself a distinction was made between vouchers and payment instruments (i.e., means of payment). According to the Commission, it is necessary to look closely at the essential nature of the operation of a method of payment. Vouchers should always lead to the supply of goods or services and are often issued to promote the sales of a particular supplier or group of suppliers or to facilitate purchases. These characteristics, when combined with the entitlement to receive goods or services (corresponding to an obligation to supply these goods or services) play a role in distinguishing vouchers from mere general payment instruments (that do not contain such specific elements). According to the Commission, the distinction between a voucher and a payment service hinges on the existence of a right to receive goods or services.[22]

In the EU Directive on Payment Services, paper based vouchers and services based on instruments that can be used to acquire goods or services only in the premises used by the issuer or under a commercial agreement with the issuer either within a limited network of service providers or for a limited range of goods or services, are explicitly excluded from the application of that Directive.[23] It is clear from this that the European Commission does not consider services based on vouchers to be 'payment services'. The Commission does not qualify vouchers as 'electronic money' either. The EU Directive on the taking up, pursuit and prudential supervision of the business of electronic money institutions[24] does not apply to monetary value stored on specific pre-paid instruments, designed to address precise needs that can be used only in a limited way, because they allow the electronic money holder to purchase goods or services only in the premises of the electronic money issuer or within a limited network of service providers under direct commercial agreement with a professional issuer, or because they can be used only to acquire a limited range of goods or services. An instrument should be considered to be used within such a limited network if it can be used only either for the purchase of goods and services in a specific store or chain of stores, or for a limited range of goods or services, regardless of the geographical location of the point of sale. Such instruments could include store cards, petrol cards, membership cards, public transport cards, meal vouchers or vouchers for services (such as vouchers for childcare, or vouchers for social or services schemes which subsidise the employment of staff to carry out household tasks such as cleaning, ironing or gardening), which are sometimes subject to a specific tax or labour legal framework designed to promote the use of such instruments to meet the objectives laid

21. European Commission, Staff working document, Impact Assessment accompanying the Proposal for a Council Directive amending Directive 2006/112/EC on the common system of value added tax, as regards the treatment of vouchers, SWD (2012) 127 final, section 2.5) p. 21/2.
22. *See* the original Voucher Proposal, *infra* n. 38.
23. Directive 2007/64/EC of the European Parliament and of the Council of 13 November 2007 on payment services in the internal market amending Directives 97/7/EC, 2002/65/EC, 2005/60/EC and 2006/48/EC and repealing Directive 97/5/EC, OJ L 319, 5.12.2007, pp. 1-36, Articles 3(g)(v) and 3(k).
24. 5th Preamble to Directive 2009/110/EC of the European Parliament and of the Council of 16 September 2009 on the taking up, pursuit and prudential supervision of the business of electronic money institutions amending Directives 2005/60/EC and 2006/48/EC and repealing Directive 2000/46/EC (Text with EEA relevance), OJ L 267, 10.10.2009, pp. 7-17.

down in social legislation. Where such a specific-purpose instrument develops into a general-purpose instrument, the exemption from the scope of this Directive should no longer apply. Instruments which can be used for purchases in stores of listed merchants should not be exempted from the scope of this Directive as such instruments are typically designed for a network of service providers which is continuously growing. This means that voucher transactions are not considered payment services nor services concerning electronic money, which are typically VAT exempt.

Some businesses issue FVVs for consideration and these FVVs can be redeemed at a large number of participating businesses but not at the business issuing the vouchers. The issuer will reimburse the businesses that accept the FVVs, usually charging or withholding a commission or other payment for its services. At first sight, these FVVs closely resemble 'cheques' or other means of payment. Examples of these types of FVVs are film vouchers, book tokens and luncheon vouchers. Some countries, such as the Netherlands, used to treat transactions concerning these vouchers as VAT exempt.[25] Be that as it may, in my view, the main purpose of issuing these FVVs is either to promote certain lines of business (e.g., cinemas, book shops or participating restaurants) or to provide (often tax friendly) employee benefits, expense management or loyalty schemes. Even though they are 'as good as money', they can only be 'spent' at participating businesses. They cannot be compared to credit cards because no credit is granted by the businesses issuing the vouchers. In my view, they are not 'cheques' as referred to in Article 135(1)(d) of the EU VAT Directive either, because the purpose of the issuers of the voucher is not the provision of a financial service.

If FVVs are issued at a discount (i.e., a price lower than the face value), treating the FVVs as money or negotiable instruments could lead to issues when determining the taxable amount for the supplies of goods and services made upon redemption of the FVVs. I will elaborate on that in the section where I describe the VAT treatment of vouchers in South Africa.

[B] Is the Supply of a Voucher the Supply of a Right or Does It Embody the Right to a Supply?

From an EU VAT perspective, the supply of a right (for consideration) can be a taxable transaction: any transaction that does not constitute a supply of goods is a supply of services.[26] In the EU VAT Directive, even the supply of goods is defined as the transfer of a right (the 'right to dispose of tangible property as owner').[27] Other examples of taxable transactions regarding rights are the conferring by a landlord on a tenant, for an agreed period and in return for payment, of the *right* to occupy property as if that person were the owner and to exclude any other person from enjoyment of such a

25. Decree on the VAT treatment of gift cards of 30 December 1999, Ref. No. VB1999/2649, repealed from 1 January 2019.
26. *See* Article 24(1) of the EU VAT Directive.
27. *See* Article 14(1) of the EU VAT Directive.

right,[28] the supply of the exclusive *right* to install and operate cigarette machines for a specific period of time on the premises of someone else,[29] the supply of a *right* to make use of a golf club's facilities in exchange for a membership fee[30] and the supply of the *right*, against payment, to catch fish in a specific part of a river.[31] Other examples of rights are intellectual property right and trademarks. It can also be argued that admission tickets (e.g., to concerts or museums) and travel tickets (e.g., a train ticket or a boarding card for an air journey) embody rights: the right to enter the designated premises (at, during or before a certain time) or the right to be transported (at during or before a certain time).

With regard to the supply of a right 'as such', even if the 'underlying goods or services' are not used, the right (to something) is actually transferred to the purchaser. Examples of a 'rights as such' are intellectual property rights (e.g., a patent), certain subscriptions and memberships, fishing rights/permits and the lease of moveable and immoveable property. Because the transfer of the right 'as such' is the object, or aim, of a transaction, the supply of that right is a VAT taxable transaction.[32] The person that obtains these rights, pays for these 'rights as such', and not for (based on the above examples) the actual number of patented products made and sold,[33] the time he actually makes use of the facilities of the golf course at the golf club that he is a member of, the (number of) fish that he actually catches or the time that he actually uses the (relevant part of) the building. These types of rights can also be worded as follows: having the right to use goods and/or services and/or intellectual property rights (or the right to disallow the use of goods and/or services and/or intellectual property by others) during an agreed period of time.

This is different from the right to a future supply. In that case, the 'right' is not the object of the transaction. The transaction embodies the promise that the recipient will receive an agreed supply in the future. Payment and supply are separated in time. Therefore, it is also possible to supply the right to the future supply of a right, e.g., the lease of an apartment that commences in six months' time. A cinema ticket embodies the right to be admitted to the cinema, often at a specific date and time to see a certain film. A book token embodies the right for the holder to use it as (part) payment for the purchase of a specific good to be supplied by (a) specific supplier(s). The actual (future) supplies are the admission to the cinema and the supply of the book. If a person buys a cinema ticket at the cinema for a film that will play shortly, and he subsequently enters the building to see that film, the temporal separation between payment and supply is minimized, making it even more clear that the payment is made

28. CJEU, 18 November 2004, Case C-284/03, *Belgian State v. Temco Europe SA*, ECLI:EU:C:2004:730, paragraph 19 and case law cited there.
29. CJEU, 12 June 2003, Case C-275/01, *Sinclair Collis Ltd v. Commissioners of Customs & Excise*, ECLI:EU:C:2003:341.
30. *See*, CJEU, 21 March 2002, Case C-174/00, *Kennemer Golf & Country Club v. Staatssecretaris van Financiën*, ECLI:EU:C:2002:200.
31. *See*, CJEU, 6 December 2007, Case C-451/06, *Gabriele Walderdorff v. Finanzamt Waldviertel*, ECLI:EU:C:2007:761.
32. If made for consideration by a taxable person acting as such.
33. It is also possible to pay for an intellectual property right by calculating the 'actual use' of the right.

for the actual admission to the film. Buying that same ticket online two days in advance does not change that.

The difference between the supply of a 'right as such' and other rights to obtain or use goods or services in the future can be further explained as follows. A gym membership fee or the lease of a car costs a certain amount, which can be paid in advance. The (residual) value of this membership or the use of the car does not depend on the actual use, but on the time elapsed between the beginning and the end of the period in which the right can be exercised.[34] By this I mean that if it would be possible to transfer the membership or the lease half way the contractually agreed period, the price for the remaining time is not dependent on the actual use so far[35] or the foreseen future use of the transferred right (in and by itself). This is different for, e.g., a right to come to the gym and use the facilities for a fixed number of times (e.g., during a month) or the right to catch a specific number of fish (per year). The (residual) value of these rights depends on the actual use or consumption of those rights until the moment of the agreed transfer of that right.[36] With regard to the latter type(s), if these rights are transferred, the object of that supply is not the right 'as such', but the (remaining) actual (or possible) use or the actually agreed predetermined 'units'[37] that are to be supplied.

Support for my view that a voucher is not the aim or purpose of a transaction can be found in the European Commission's original proposal for the VAT treatment of vouchers.[38] In this original proposal, the Commission proposed to include the following provisions in the EU VAT Directive: 'The supply of a voucher carrying a right to receive a supply of goods or services and the subsequent supply of these goods or services shall be regarded as a single transaction. This single transaction shall be treated in the same way as a supply of goods or services had the goods or services not been supplied through the use of a voucher'[39] and 'Where a single transaction as referred to in Article 30b consists in the supply of a multi-purpose voucher and a subsequent supply of goods or services, the redeemer shall be regarded as having carried out the taxable supply.'[40]

34. Assuming that the value of the car, e.g., through depreciation, is irrelevant for calculating the lease instalments.
35. By this I mean the number of times or the duration of the actual use of the right during the period for which the right is granted, e.g., how often a car is actually driven during the lease period or how often the person holding the membership actually went to the gym. The taxable transaction consists of the goods or services being at the disposal of the customer during the agreed period of time.
36. Use can, of course, also be measured in time. For example, an agreement that allows a customer to use the Internet for 5 hours each month for a fixed price is not the supply of a right 'as such', even though the (residual) value is determined by time, because in this case 'time' is a measure for use/consumption.
37. Units meaning measures for use or consumption.
38. Proposal for a Council Directive, amending Directive 2006/112/EC on the common system of value added tax, as regards the treatment of vouchers, COM(2012)206 (the Voucher Proposal), not published on the OJ, but available at: http://eur lex.europa.eu/LexUriServ/LexUriServ.do?uri=COM:2012:0206FIN:EN:PDF) last visited on 14 March 2019).
39. Proposed Article 30b from the original Voucher Proposal, *supra* n. 38.
40. Proposed addition to Article 193 of the original Voucher Proposal, *supra* n. 38.

The Commission explained its reason for proposing these provisions as follows: 'Under the terms of this article, where a voucher bears a right to a supply of goods or services, the supply of this right and the subsequent supply of goods or services are linked and shall be regarded as a single transaction. Since the tax treatment of this single transaction shall be the same as that which would have been applied had the goods or services not been supplied through the use of a voucher, the place of supply and the applicable rate should be determined by the goods or services supplied' and 'The paragraph to be included in this article, clarifies that it is always the redeemer (...) who carries out the taxable supply of goods or services and is therefore the person liable for payment of VAT. This is significant where the issuer and the redeemer of the voucher are not the same person. Only the redeemer knows what has been supplied and where and when that supply took place.'[41]

Also, if issuing an FVV by itself would be considered a taxable service, i.e., the supply of a right, this could create some specific VAT issues and potentially lead to double taxation. For example, under the current Dutch VAT rules, granting access to a cinema is subject to the lower VAT rate. However, the supply of a right to access to a cinema is not included in the enumeration of reduced rated items. The lower rate can only apply when the right to access would be equated with the access itself, basically admitting that the right itself is, in fact, not a separate 'thing' that is supplied.

If issuing an FVV is a supply that is subject to VAT, how to treat the supply of the goods or services upon redemption of the FVV? Insofar a consideration was paid for the issuing of the FVV, this consideration can no longer be allocated to the (subsequent) supply of the goods or services upon redemption of the FVV. This does not only create potential VAT rate issues, as described above, but also other issues. Are the goods and services then supplied for no consideration? As a consequence, legal provisions dealing with supplies free charge may need to be applied, which may actually lead to double taxation. Or is the right, that is embodied in the FVV, bartered for the goods and services, creating another taxable supply? How to determine the taxable amount for these supplies? And in the end, from an economic and commercial perspective as well as from the viewpoint of the average customer, only the goods and services that are obtained upon redemption of the FVVs are 'consumed'. Should not only these supplies be taxed?

Based on the above, in my view, a voucher does not embody a right as such.

[C] Treating the Issuing and Sale of FVVs as a Prepayment for the Underlying Transaction

Prepayment means that the consideration is paid prior to the actual supply of the underlying goods or services Treating the consideration paid for a FVV as prepayment

41. *See* the original Voucher proposal, *supra* n. 38, section 5 (Detailed Explanation of the Proposal), Articles 30b and 193.

for the underlying, future supply would avoid the potential issues created by considering a FVV to constitute the transfer of a right as such. Accordingly, the FVV would function as proof of the prepayment made.

However, under EU VAT, prepayments trigger specific consequences and that has been the subject of litigation before the CJEU.[42] Under the relevant provision in the EU VAT Directive, receiving a prepayment causes the VAT on a future supply to become chargeable (payable to the tax authorities) when that prepayment for the future supply is received.[43] Determining the correct VAT treatment is only possible if that future supply can be effectively characterized (in terms of good or service) and classified (in terms of standard rated, reduced rated, exempt, or zero rated) at the time of the prepayment.[44] This means that, at least from an EU VAT perspective, not all payments that are received before the actual supply is made can qualify as 'prepayments' for EU VAT purposes. Businesses that issue FVVs that the holder can redeem for the purchase from a large range of products or even in multiple jurisdictions would not be able to determine the VAT treatment in advance, i.e., before the underlying supply is actually made, in terms of tax jurisdiction and applicable rate. Therefore, treating the issuance of FVVs as prepayments for the underlying transactions, taxable at the time the prepayment is received, is only possible, realistically, in the situation that all particulars of the future supply are known at the time of issuance.

If VAT is due at the time of issuance of a FVV, the actual fulfilment of the underlying transaction at a later time should not be taxed, or only taxed insofar the final sales price exceeds the face value of the voucher, otherwise double taxation would occur.

Based on CJEU case law, a service is deemed to be performed when the business that is to accept a voucher as payment for its service fulfils the service by enabling the holder of the voucher to benefit from the service, through fulfilling his contractual obligations by putting the holder of the voucher in a position to claim his rights to the services provided for by that business.[45] This implies that as soon as the holder of a voucher is put in a position to benefit from the agreed service, but decides not to redeem the voucher, the underlying service is deemed to be supplied and no breakage revenue could arise. This can, in my view, only apply in cases where the service to be obtained by redeeming the voucher is sufficiently well defined and, arguably, where that service will be performed irrespective of whether the holder of the voucher decides to redeem it.[46]

Another potential issue that could arise when considering the payment for an FVV to be a prepayment for the future supply of the goods or services, is the VAT

42. *See, inter alia*, CJEU, 21 February 2006, Case C-419/02, *BUPA Hospitals Ltd and Goldsborough Developments Ltd v. Commissioners of Customs & Excise*, ECLI:EU:C:2006:122; CJEU, 16 December 2010, Case C-270/09, *MacDonald Resorts Ltd v. The Commissioner for Her Majesty's Revenue & Customs*, ECLI:EU:C:2010:780; and CJEU, 23 Dec. 2015, Joined Cases C-250/14 and C-289/14, *Air France-KLM and Hop!-Brit Air SAS v. Ministère des Finances et des Comptes publics*, ECLI:EU:C:2015:841.
43. Article 65 of the EU VAT Directive.
44. BUPA, *supra* n. 42.
45. *Air France-KLM and Hop!-Brit Air SAS*, *supra* n. 42.
46. *See* Bijl, *supra* n. 1, paragraph 9.5.2.3.

treatment of the transfer of the FVV in a chain of subsequent suppliers. If the business that (first) issues the FVV can determine the VAT treatment of the future supplies that the FVV can be redeemed for, he will have to treat the consideration received for the FVV as a prepayment and pay VAT to the tax authorities. Should the subsequent seller of that same FVV also treat the money it receives as a prepayment? As an example, assuming that a phone card that can only be used for actual phone calls within a single jurisdiction qualifies as an FVV, should the shop that purchases this phone card from the issuing telecommunications company and sells it to its customer, also consider the payment received from its customer as a prepayment? If so, and under the definition of 'prepayment' in the EU VAT Directive this is possible, it should also be allowed to deduct the VAT on the purchase of the FVV. VAT Deduction is only allowed by businesses that are recipient of the goods or services they purchase ('supplies *to him* of goods or services').[47] Is that shop the recipient of the underlying telecommunication services? If not, this could possibly lead to double taxation, unless it is argued that prepayments, in the EU VAT sense, can only be received by the businesses that will actually perform the future supplies for which the prepayments are received.

The above also means that for businesses that accept these FVVs, it should be clear whether VAT was paid upon issuing or selling the FVVs in order to avoid possible double taxation. This issue can be avoided if it is argued that prepayments can only be received by the businesses that will actually perform the future supplies for which the prepayments are received.

[D] Treating the Issuance and Sale of FVVs as Performing the Underlying Transaction for which the FVVs Can Be Redeemed

Treating the issuance and supply of a voucher as the supply of a right as such, i.e., as a service, ensures that the full amount paid by the end consumer for the voucher is taxed. However, as described above, this option could lead to double taxation as well as the application of a VAT rate that may not be applicable to the supply of the goods or services for which the voucher is redeemed.

If the issue and supply of a voucher is treated as a prepayment, VAT will become chargeable upon receipt of the prepayment, to the amount received (or rather from the amount received, since that amount will be a VAT inclusive amount). If these vouchers are never redeemed or not fully redeemed, it can be argued that the VAT included in the breakage revenue and remitted to the tax agency should be repaid to the issuer, since he never performed the underlying transaction for which payment was received. VAT is only due where a business performs a taxable supply for consideration: no taxable supply - no VAT amount due. It could, however, be argued that VAT should be chargeable on the full prepayment, because VAT is not levied on consumption itself but on the expenditure made for it as a proxy for consumption. Under this approach, breakage revenue should be taxed.

47. Article 168(a) of the EU VAT Directive.

The potential issues created by treating the issuance of a voucher as the supply of a right, i.e., double taxation and applying an incorrect VAT rate, may be avoided by treating the issue of vouchers as the supply of the transactions for which they can be redeemed, at the time of issuance of the voucher. Also, the discussion about VAT refunds in case of breakage revenue would be avoided since there would be no breakage revenue: the underlying transaction is deemed to be performed, eliminating the possibility of a VAT refund caused by lack of a taxable transaction.

Treating the issuance of a voucher as the actual supply, is only possible if the relevant characteristics of the goods or services for which the FVV can be redeemed are known at the time of issuance. This means that at least the place of the (intended) supply as well as the applicable VAT rate should be known. If that treatment would be extended to FVVs issued for no consideration,[48] in addition to the place of supply and the applicable VAT rate there must be certainty as to the purchase price of the goods or of similar goods or, in the absence of a purchase price, the cost price of the goods (in case of goods)[49] or the full cost to the taxable person of providing the service (in case of services).[50] Otherwise, the taxable amount, and therefore the amount of VAT due, cannot be determined at the time of issuance of the FVV. In practice, this will probably not occur very often.

A significant drawback of treating the issuance and supply of a FVV as the supply of the underlying goods or services is that if the FVV is never redeemed, VAT is remitted anyway. As mentioned above, it can be argued that this would be correct in relation to (certain) services, but it goes against the EU VAT concept of 'supply of goods'. Under the EU VAT Directive, a supply of goods is defined as the transfer of the right to dispose of tangible property as owner.[51] Where FVVs that can be redeemed for goods are not redeemed, the right to dispose of those goods will not effectively be transferred. There is no consumption in reality. Therefore, this should in my view not actually be taxed. Obviously, being able to avoid discussions about taxation of breakage revenue has its advantages, but in my view achieving that by treating the issuance and supply of FVVs as the supply of the underlying goods is too high a cost for that.

Another practical issue can arise under this approach when, upon redemption of the FVV, goods or services are supplied with a greater value than the face value of the redeemed vouchers. The part of the (single) supply for which an additional (cash) payment is received, cannot be 'ignored' and should be taxed. As a result, part of the 'physical' supply is taxed at the moment of the additional cash payment, where the other part is considered to have already been supplied or is 'ignored' since taxation of the service, i.e., granting the right to goods or services, already occurred.

48. Articles 16 and 26 of the EU VAT Directive.
49. Article 74 of the EU VAT Directive.
50. Article 75 of the EU VAT Directive.
51. Article 14 of the EU VAT Directive.

[E] The FVV as Proof of a Deposit for a Future Transaction

This approach is the same as the approach where vouchers are not considered the aim or purpose of a transaction, but just a medium that embodies the step between the payment for a future supply and the actual performance of that supply. This would imply that issuing and selling vouchers is not subject to VAT (albeit, in many cases, an 'economic activity'). VAT only becomes chargeable upon redemption.

Under this rationale, the FVVs are merely an intermediary step between a (pre)payment and a (subsequent) supply of goods or services, providing the holder of the FVV proof of payment for these (future) supplies. In situations where FVVs can be redeemed for a large variety of goods and services, and even in different jurisdictions, taxing the supply of the goods or services for which the FVV is redeemed is the most practical way of ensuring that the aim of VAT is reached: taxation of expenditure for local consumption.

Even though this approach ensures no VAT becomes chargeable where there is no (actual) consumption and that the appropriate VAT rate is applied to the actual supplies made, it can lead to problems. For example, if the vouchers are not issued or supplied for their face value, because it may prove difficult to establish the taxable amount for the transaction where the voucher is redeemed. Also, breakage revenue will remain untaxed, even in cases where it can be argued that the underlying supply was effectively made based on local case law, e.g., in the EU in certain cases of 'no shows' as described earlier.[52]

[F] What Treatment is Most in Line with the Aim and Purpose of the EU VAT System?

In my view, issuing and transferring FVVs should not be subject to VAT. An FVV, in my view, is never the actual 'purpose' or 'object' of a transaction. The issuance or transfer of an FVV should not be considered a 'separate' transaction 'in its own right', but rather a step in or towards the supply of goods or services for which it can be redeemed.

Only the supply of goods and services are subject to VAT.[53] Goods are tangible objects, which means that, if anything, the supply of a vouchers as such would be considered the supply of a service.[54] Indeed, the CJEU has ruled, in a single case, that the supply of a voucher was a taxable supply of a service;[55] however, in a number of

52. *See* Jeroen Bijl, *Air France-KLM: The SAFE Equivalent for Services?* 27(2) Int'l VAT Monitor 95-97 (2016).
53. Also, the intra-Community acquisition of goods and the importation of goods are subject to VAT, provided that certain other requirements are met.
54. Although many vouchers have a physical form, this is not a characteristic of a voucher and electronic vouchers serve the exact same purpose. The value of the 'carrier medium' that is a voucher does not correspond with the actual face value (or other value) that the voucher 'represents'.
55. CJEU, 29 July 2010, Case C-40/09, *Astra Zeneca UK Ltd v. Commissioners for Her Majesty's Revenue and Customs*, ECLI:EU:C:2010:450, paragraphs 26-27.

other cases the CJEU ruled that the supply of voucher is actually not a taxable supply at all.[56]

In my view, an FVV is an instrument that embodies or evidences the right of the holder to be the (future) recipient of a supply of goods or services. Above, I described the reasons why the supply of a voucher should not be considered the supply of a service (i.e., the transfer of a right). Basically, this can be traced back to the fact that the supply of a voucher is not the actual 'object' of the transaction. This in contrast to the supply of intellectual property rights or the right to use a good for a specified period of time, which are purchased in their own right[57] and result in actual 'consumption'.

VAT is a general tax on consumption,[58] and the supply of a voucher for consideration is not a transaction that embodies consumption. As said, it is a 'step towards consumption' or 'a narrowing of the spending possibilities of the holder of the voucher'. From a VAT perspective, a complete taxable transaction has taken place only when the voucher is redeemed for actual goods or services. In other words, from a 'consumption' perspective, the supply of a voucher is only part of a (chain of) transaction(s) that lead(s) to a supply of consumable goods and services[59] A transaction that does not entail any benefit that would qualify the recipient as a consumer of goods or services should not be subject to VAT.[60]

The fact that, for various reasons, transactions are divided into elements that separate payment from supply, or the granting of the right to a discount from the underlying supply, does not make that these parts or elements of the (total) transaction should be subject to VAT, because there is no consumption (yet). The term 'consumption' should be interpreted as 'the supply of goods or services to an identifiable consumer or any benefit capable of being regarded as a cost component of the activity of another person in the commercial chain'.[61] The issuance or supply of the voucher is only a part of or a step in that total transaction.

This view is supported by the CJEU in the *Argos*-case[62] where it decided that the taxable amount for a supply (of goods or services) in return for a voucher is the 'actual money equivalent' of that voucher, which is the money actually received for (issuing, supplying or accepting) that voucher.[63] This can only be the case if a direct link exists between the payment of that money (equivalent) and the underlying supply of goods

56. In the same sense, *see* Walter van der Corput, *Astra Zeneca – The VAT Treatment of Vouchers* 21(5) Int'l VAT Monitor 365 (2011).
57. Patrick Gallagher, and Roderick Cordara, *Supply of Rights and Rights to a Supply* 22(1) Int'l VAT Monitor 161 (2001).
58. *See* Article 1(2) of the EU VAT Directive.
59. This is different from, e.g., the supply of shares, because shares are the aim or object of the supply. Shares give the holder certain powers and/or rights, such as the right to vote in shareholders meetings, the right to receive dividend, etc. The supply of shares (for consideration and by a taxable person acting as such) is a (VAT exempt) taxable transaction.
60. CJEU, 29 February 1996, Case C-215/94, *Jürgen Mohr v. Finanzamt Bad Segeberg*, ECLI: EU:C:1996:72, paragraph 22.
61. CJEU, 18 December 1997, Case C-384/95, *Landboden-Agrardienste GmbH & Co. KG v. Finanzamt Calau*, ECLI:EU:C:1997:627, paragraph 23.
62. CJEU, 24 October 1996, Case C-288/94, *Argos Distributors Limited v. Commissioners of Customs and Excise*, ECLI:EU:C:1996:398.
63. *Argos, supra* n. 62, paragraph 21.

or services. Under the current EU VAT rules, for a payment to be a consideration for a supply, there must be a direct link between the supply and the payment. Otherwise, two supplies should have been identified: one supply of a voucher for money, the taxable amount being the money received for the voucher, and one supply of goods in return for a voucher, which must be considered a barter transaction because no money is involved, and for barter transactions, the taxable amount is the cost or purchase price of the supply.

Even though issuing a voucher should not be considered a taxable transaction, it should in my view be considered an economic activity within the scope of VAT.[64] After all, it cannot be denied that issuing vouchers is a business activity, albeit that the payment should be attributed to the subsequent or underlying transaction, which means that, from a VAT perspective, issuing vouchers is not a supply for consideration.[65] It is possible that this is (one of) the reason(s) that the European legislator decided to consider the supply of a voucher and the subsequent redemption of the voucher (for goods and/or services) as one single transaction in its original proposal for the VAT treatment of voucher transactions.

[G] The EU VAT Treatment of FVVs

In the EU, a combination of two of the approaches described above applies. Under the relevant provisions of the EU VAT Directive, a distinction is made between the VAT treatment of transactions involving 'single-purpose vouchers' and 'multi-purpose vouchers'.[66] A single-purpose voucher is defined as a voucher where the place of supply of the goods or services to which the voucher relates, and the VAT due on those goods or services, are known at the time of issuance of the voucher.[67] Multi-purpose vouchers are all vouchers that are not single-purpose vouchers.[68] Under the EU VAT rules, a voucher is defined as an instrument where there is an obligation to accept it as consideration or part consideration for a supply of goods or services and where the goods or services to be supplied or the identities of their potential suppliers are either indicated on the instrument itself or in related documentation, including the terms and conditions of use of such instrument.[69] This basically excludes discount vouchers and the like.

The issuance and supply of a single-purpose voucher is regarded as a supply of the goods or services to which the voucher relates and the actual handing over of the goods or the actual provision of the services in return for the single-purpose voucher accepted as consideration or part consideration by the supplier shall not be regarded as an independent transaction from a VAT perspective.[70] If the business that accepts a single-purpose voucher as (part) consideration for the (actual, physical) supply of

64. *See* Article 9 of the EU VAT Directive.
65. This is, of course, different if a (separate) fee is charged for issuing the voucher.
66. *See* Article 30a-30b of the EU VAT Directive.
67. Article 30a(2) of the EU VAT Directive.
68. Article 30a(3) of the EU VAT Directive.
69. Article 30a(1) of the EU VAT Directive.
70. Article 30b(1) of the EU VAT Directive.

goods or services is not the taxable person that issued that single-purpose voucher, he is deemed to have made the (part of the) supply of the good or service for which he accepted the voucher to the taxable person that issued the single-purpose voucher.[71] For the same supply, where the other part of the consideration is not paid using a single-purpose voucher, that part of the supply is covered by the 'normal' EU VAT rules, meaning that that part of the supply is made to the person obtaining the goods or services for that part of the consideration. This can lead to situations where the business accepting the single-purpose voucher as part payment will have to issue two invoices for that supply: one to the issuer of the single-purpose voucher (covering the part supply paid for with the voucher) and one to the purchaser of the goods or services (for the remainder of the total supply).

Another potential drawback of the EU VAT treatment of single-purpose vouchers is that breakage revenue is always taxed. Based on CJEU case law, this can be acceptable for services because it is sufficient for constituting a taxable service that the supplier puts the holder of the single-purpose voucher in a position to claim his rights to the service in return for the voucher.[72] However, the supply of goods as a taxable transaction is clearly defined in the EU VAT Directive. A 'supply of goods' shall mean the transfer of the right to dispose of tangible property as owner.[73] Issuing or selling a single-purpose voucher does, by itself, not transfer the right to dispose of tangible property as owner. Therefore, the provision under which the issuance or sale of a single-purpose voucher that entitles the holder to a specific good is treated as the supply of that good for VAT purposes, contradicts the definition of a supply of a good in that same Directive.

Under the relevant EU VAT rules, each transfer of a multi-purpose voucher preceding the redemption of that voucher shall not be subject to VAT. The actual handing over of the goods or the actual provision of the services in return for a multi-purpose voucher shall be subject to VAT under the applicable general VAT rules.[74] Breakage revenue is not taxed this way. However, where multi-purpose vouchers are sold through a distribution chain at a (decreasing) discount, even though from an economic perspective the discount could be considered payment for the distribution service, this service remains untaxed unless the parties involved explicitly agree to the provision of distribution or promotion services for an agreed upon consideration.[75]

Also, under the relevant EU VAT Directive, the taxable amount of the supply of goods or services provided in respect of a multi-purpose voucher shall be equal to the consideration paid for the voucher or, in the absence of information on that consideration, the monetary value indicated on the multi-purpose voucher itself or in the related documentation, less the amount of VAT relating to the goods or services

71. Article 30b(1) of the EU VAT Directive.
72. *Air France, supra* n. 42, paragraphs 28 and 42.
73. Article 14(1) of the EU VAT Directive.
74. Article 30b(2) of the EU VAT Directive.
75. *Supra* n. 74.

supplied.[76] This could be interpreted as meaning that if a business accepts a multi-purpose voucher as consideration for a supply but is reimbursed by the issuer less than the face value of the multi-purpose voucher (or the amount paid for the multi-purpose voucher), will still have to remit VAT based on the face value of that voucher, basically requiring that business to remit VAT on an amount that is higher than the amount effectively received for his supply of goods or services.[77] In practice, this happens when the issuer of the FVVs withholds an amount for operating the scheme or for the promotion of the business that accepts the FVV, without making this sufficiently explicit for the amount withheld to constitute a consideration for VAT purposes.[78] This is not in line with CJEU case law about determining the taxable amount in such situations, under which VAT is paid based on the amount actually received in return for a supply.[79]

Considering the above, in my view, the appropriate VAT treatment of transactions involving single-purpose vouchers is to consider payments for such vouchers to be prepayments for the underlying, future supplies. The current VAT treatment of multi-purpose transactions (no taxation on issuing or transferring the MPVs, taxation upon redemption of the MPVs) is already appropriate. Upon redemption, the taxable amount for the supply for which a multi-purpose voucher is used as (part) consideration should be the amount actually received by the supplier in return for the supply.

[H] The New Zealand GST Treatment of FVVs

In 1986, New Zealand introduced a broad-based consumption tax called GST. The Goods and Services Tax Act 1985 (New Zealand GST Act) imposes GST on taxable supplies of goods and services made in New Zealand by a GST-registered person in the course or furtherance of a taxable activity.[80] It is designed in a similar way to the EU VAT Directive, meaning that it is a broad-based tax on final consumption' and the 'central design feature of a VAT' is the staged collection process.[81]

New Zealand has twice modified its rules on vouchers.[82] Under the current rules, the issuance or supply of face value vouchers is taxed, except where it is impractical.[83] A situation in which it may not be practical to treat the issuance or sale of a voucher as a supply of goods and services includes one in which the issuer or seller of a voucher

76. Article 73a of the EU VAT Directive.
77. Bijl, *supra* n. 1, Chapter 9.5.2.11, pp. 288-289.
78. Something along this line can be observed in CJEU 7 October 2010, Joined Cases C-53/09 and C-55/09, *Commissioners for Her Majesty's Revenue and Customs v. Loyalty Management UK Ltd (C-53/09) and Baxi Group Ltd (C-55/09)*, ECLI:EU:C:2010:590; and CJEU 12 June 2014, Case C-461/12, *Granton Advertising BV v. Inspecteur van de Belastingdienst Haaglanden/kantoor Den Haag*, ECLI:EU:C:2014:1745.
79. *Argos Distributors, supra* n. 62.
80. Graeme Olding, Robert Grignon and Alexandra Bensemann, *New Zealand – Goods and Services Tax*, in Panos Thliveros, Zsolt Szatmari, Jordi Sol (eds.) *VAT Worldwide* (IBFD, 2020).
81. OECD, International VAT/GST Guidelines 14-15 (OECD Publishing, 2017).
82. Rebecca M. Millar, *The Vouchers Problem: An Insoluble Conflict or an Illustration of the Nature of Consideration in the 'Complex Parallel Universe' of GST?* 18 Austl Tax F. 107(2003).
83. Goods and Services Tax Act 1985 (NZ), sections 5(11D)-(11I) and 9(2A) and (2B).

and the supplier of the goods and services for which the voucher is redeemed are different persons.[84] Further guidance on the GST treatment of vouchers is provided in a Special Report from the Inland Revenue, which – among other things – contains further clarification on the concept of 'impractical'.[85]

I have briefly described the potential disadvantages of upfront taxation of vouchers above.

[I] The Australian GST Treatment of FVVs

The Australian GST is effectively a tax on final private consumption in Australia.[86] It came into effect on 1 July 2000.[87] The Australian GST Act has been amended many times since its introduction. Australian GST is a tax on the supply of most goods, services, rights, real property, and intangibles. Its purpose and design resemble the EU VAT Directive.

The GST treatment of face value voucher is explicitly included in the Australian GST legislation.[88] Under the relevant rules, the supply of a face value voucher is not a taxable supply if on redemption of the voucher, the holder of the voucher is entitled to supplies up to the face value of the voucher and the consideration for supply of the voucher does not exceed the face value of the voucher.[89] Where the consideration for supply of the voucher exceeds its face value, the consideration is treated as if it were reduced by that face value.

The act of redeeming a face value voucher is not a supply. A supply for which the voucher is redeemed is a taxable supply.[90] The consideration for a taxable supply acquired by fully or partly redeeming a face value voucher is the sum of the face value of the voucher, reduced by any amount of that value refunded to the holder of the voucher in respect of the supply; and any additional consideration provided for the supply.[91] Specific rules apply for taxing breakage revenue.[92]

It is held that problems arise with regard to the Australian approach to the GST treatment of vouchers, in particular when the transactions are complicated by the interposition of other parties, because of the underlying presumption that all transactions are reciprocal bilateral events, an assumption that simply does not hold true for

84. *Supra*, n. 83, section 5(11GA).
85. Special report from the Policy Advice Division of Inland Revenue of 9 April 2001, *GST treatment of tokens, stamps and vouchers – amendments to sections 5(11D) to 5(11I) of the Goods and Services Tax Act 1985*.
86. Andrew Ditchfield, *Australia – Goods and Services Tax*, in Panos Thliveros, Zsolt Szatmari, Jordi Sol (eds.) *VAT Worldwide* (IBFD, 2020).
87. A New Tax System (Goods and Services Tax) Bill 1998, The Parliament of the Commonwealth of Australia, House of Representatives, A New Tax System (Goods and Services Tax) Bill 1998, Explanatory Memorandum, to be found online at *A New Tax System (Goods and Services Tax) Bill 1998* (legislation.gov.au) (last accessed on 29 December 2020).
88. A New Tax System (Goods and Services Tax) Act 1999, *supra* n. 87, Division 100 (Vouchers).
89. *Supra* n. 87, Division 100-5(1).
90. *Supra* n. 87, Division 100-10(1).
91. *Supra* n. 87, Division 100-12 (1).
92. *Supra* n. 87, Division 100-15.

many multi-party and/or multi-step transactions.[93] It is argued that reform of the legislation is required to ensure GST applies as intended. Any change should aim to ensure that the basic GST principles are complied with.[94] However, in my view, the Australian approach, which is similar to the EU VAT treatment of multi-purpose vouchers, does ensure that taxation only occurs when consumption takes place. This does not hold true for the taxation of breakage revenue, which does not occur under the EU VAT treatment of multi-purpose vouchers.

[J] The South African VAT Treatment of FVVs

VAT was introduced in South Africa in 1991, replacing the sales tax system that was introduced in 1978. The South African VAT is a broad-based, multi-stage indirect tax on consumption.[95] VAT is levied on nearly all supplies of goods and services. This VAT closely resembles the EU VAT system.

As a general rule, the issuance of a voucher does not amount to a supply of goods or services, but merely constitutes the issuing of a payment method that can be utilised by the recipient when he chooses.[96] The South African VAT rules make a similar distinction between two types of vouchers as the EU VAT rules, based on whether the vouchers entitle the holder to specified goods and services.[97]

Under the relevant rules, where a face value voucher entitles the holder to a supply of goods or services in the amount stated on the voucher, VAT must be accounted for when the holder redeems the voucher for goods or services.[98] However, where the amount initially paid for the voucher exceeds its monetary value, VAT must be accounted for when it is purchased.[99]

Where a voucher entitles the bearer to the future supply of specified goods or services, the issuance of the voucher itself attracts VAT.[100] The subsequent redemption of the voucher attracts no further VAT.[101] In these cases, the voucher, although still a payment method, cannot be equated with cash or a similar payment instrument. Since the voucher can only be redeemed for specific pre-determined goods or services from pre-determined suppliers, possible double taxation of the voucher can be avoided.[102]

The supply of vouchers which allow the holder a choice from a range of goods and services, is not a taxable supply, but is regarded as a medium of exchange similar to money.[103] VAT is not levied on the intrinsic value of the voucher, but rather on the

---

93. Millar, *supra* n. 82.
94. Millar, *supra* n. 82.
95. Marlene Botes, *South Africa – Value Added Tax*, in Panos Thliveros, Zsolt Szatmari, Jordi Sol (eds.) *VAT Worldwide* (IBFD, 2020).
96. S.P. van Zyl, *The VAT treatment of vouchers: a comparative study between South Africa and the European Union* 46(2) Comp. & Int'l L. J. S. Afr. 234, 236 (2013).
97. South African Value-Added Tax Act 89 of 1991, section 10(18).
98. *Supra* n. 97.
99. *Supra* n. 97.
100. South African Value-Added Tax Act 89 of 1991, section 10(19).
101. *Supra* n. 100.
102. Van Zyl, *supra* n. 96, 239.
103. SARS Draft Interpretation Note: Vouchers supplied at a discount (2012) at 2.

monetary value of the goods or services for which the voucher may be redeemed. However, where the voucher was issued for consideration exceeding the face value of the voucher, the issuing vendor must account for VAT on the consideration that exceeds the face value of the voucher.[104] This is in accordance with the principle of VAT as a tax on value added.[105]

Where vendors issue vouchers at a discounted price, i.e., a price lower than the face value for which they can be redeemed, specific rules apply. In the case of vouchers for unspecified goods, the vendor should account for VAT on the value of the goods or services supplied upon redemption of the voucher, and not on the consideration paid for the voucher. This potentially leaves the issuing vendor out of pocket.[106]

Generally, the VAT Act provides that where an unconditional discount has been granted, the supplier needs to only account for VAT on the gross amount of the supplies less discount (i.e., the amount in money received).[107] However, as the voucher is regarded as a payment method rather than a supply, the vendor must account for VAT on the intrinsic monetary value of the voucher and not the amount in consideration that was paid for the voucher.[108]

The South African Revenue Service notes that the part of the monetary value of the voucher that was not redeemed, but has either been paid out in cash or forfeited, does not attract VAT.[109]

§11.03 VOUCHERS USED FOR 'LEAPFROG' CASHBACKS AND REBATES

[A] Introduction

Temporarily lowering the price of a product is a proven method of enticing consumers to try a product and eventually grow the customer base. Most manufacturers do not sell directly to consumers and there is no guarantee that a discount given to a wholesaler or retailer will be passed on to the final consumer. For that reason, many manufacturers apply promotional campaigns that bypass the downstream supply chain (leapfrogging, in the words of an advocate-general to the CJEU[110]) and offer the product at the discounted price to the end-consumer via either a cashback or a money-off voucher.

Cashback schemes are rebates (i.e., retroactive discounts) that are settled directly between manufacturer and consumer. For example, a customer may have to scan and upload a barcode printed on the packaging of the product and a picture of the purchase

104. *Supra* n. 97.
105. Van Zyl, *supra* n. 96, 240.
106. Van Zyl, *supra* n. 96, 241.
107. South African Value-Added Tax Act 89 of 1991, section 10(3)(a).
108. Van Zyl, *supra* n. 96, 241.
109. SARS Draft Interpretation Note: Vouchers supplied at a discount (2012) at 3.
110. Advocate-general Jacobs on 20 September 2001 in Case C-427/98, *Commission of the European Communities v. Federal Republic of Germany*, ECLI:EU:C:2001:457, paragraph 31. According to the Advocate General, the nature of 'leapfrogging' schemes is such that they almost inevitably apply only to goods and only when the goods concerned are not noticeably transformed by the transactions in the chain – the aim of the business granting the discount is to promote the sale of his own goods, not of goods (or services) incorporating his supply.

receipt to the manufacturer's website to initiate pay out of the discount. Money-off promotion schemes use printed vouchers distributed generally through the mail which are redeemed with the retailer at the time of purchase. Essentially, the voucher is accepted by the retailer as part payment, and the manufacturer reimburses the retailer for the face value amount of the voucher.

[B] Possible Treatments

Granting a discount essentially means that a business will receive a lower consideration for certain supplies that the 'standard selling price'. If a discount is given at the time of the supply, the discount is simply deducted from the advertised price and the discounted amount is the consideration for the supply. If the consideration is a VAT inclusive amount, the VAT has to be excluded to determine the taxable amount for this supply.

Where a discount is granted retroactively (i.e., a rebate), the original consideration is lowered. If the discount is granted in a different taxable period than the original supply, questions can arise about the time of the adjustment, especially if VAT rules, e.g., the VAT rate applicable to the supply, have changed between these taxable periods.

For leapfrog discounts, the above is less straightforward. Because the discount is granted by a manufacturer to a consumer who is not the party to which the manufacturer sold its product initially (as that would be the wholesaler or the retailer), it may seem counterintuitive to adjust the transaction price between the manufacturer and the original purchaser. However, this is the approach taken by the CJEU in the *Elida Gibbs*-case[111] as further explained below and in the next section (§12.03[C]), and also applied in Australia (*see* §11.03[D]).

Both Wittock[112] and Bijl[113] have described the technical and practical issues of the adjustment method applied in *Elida Gibbs*. First of all, it may prove hard to actually allocate the cash back payment made by the manufacturer to the consumer upon the redemption of the voucher to a specific output for which the taxable amount should be decreased if more than one VAT rate applies to the various outputs of the manufacturer. This is, however, often a minor practical issue. Also, in some countries, manufacturers are not allowed to adjust their taxable base in all cases, which may affect the calculation of their deductible proportion (pro rata) if this is turnover based.[114] Then there are 'gross-net-issues', created by the fact that under this approach leapfrog discounts are to be used as (partial) payment of the gross value of a transaction between a retailer and its customer, as well as to serve as the basis for a

111. CJEU, 24 October 1996, Case C-317/94, *Elida Gibbs Ltd v. Commissioners of Customs and Excise*, ECLI:EU:C:1996:400.
112. Nathalie Wittock, *Sales Promotion Techniques and VAT – A Search for Neutrality for the Sales Promoter, also Asking into Account the Other Key Features and Principles of the VAT System*, 211-243 (Kluwer, 2019).
113. Bijl, *supra* n. 1, 130-174.
114. This is also explicitly ruled by the CJEU, 15 October 2002, Case C-427/98, *Commission of the European Communities v. Federal Republic of Germany*, ECLI:EU:C:2002:581, paragraph 64.

deduction of the taxable amount, which is by definition a net amount, by the manufacturer, and by the fact that the payment by the manufacturer can be made to partially pay for a net price charged by the retailer (in case of a transaction subject to the reverse charge mechanism or cross-border supplies of goods) but are meant to fund the total VAT inclusive price paid by the final customer.

Lowering the original manufacturer sales price of the product does, however, have its practical advantages and it follows the 'economic purpose' of these transactions in the sense that in the end, the manufacturer will end up with a smaller amount of money in relation to the sale that he made.[115] Considering that the taxable amount is defined in the EU VAT Directive as *'everything which constitutes consideration obtained or to be obtained by the supplier, in return for the supply, from the customer or a third party'*,[116] in the end, it could perhaps be argued that the rebate paid to the end-consumer constitutes a 'negative consideration obtained', or 'an amount paid' in connection to the supply to a third party.

The other way of treating these rebates is to consider them as third-party payments, which was the position taken by the tax authorities in the *Elida Gibbs*-case These rebates are paid to persons (private individuals or legal persons) that were not party to the original transaction. It can be argued that the manufacturer granting the rebate effectively funds part of the final purchase of his own product on behalf of the end-consumer. The manufacturer is neither the purchaser of those goods, nor the seller. From a VAT perspective, there would be no need for any adjustments as the retail price remains unchanged and all parties in the supply chain prior to the retail stage have been relieved from the tax through the credit system. However, this view was not accepted by the CJEU as further explained in the next section.

[C] The EU Treatment of Leapfrog Discounts

In the EU, the VAT treatment of leapfrog discounts is not prescribed by law. The CJEU has clarified the interpretation of the relevant concepts of EU VAT underlying this issue.[117] In the *Elida Gibbs*-case,[118] the CJEU confirmed that the relevant provision in the Directive about VAT adjustment (in case of discounts) refers to the normal case of contractual relations entered into directly between two contracting parties, which are modified subsequently. The fact remains, however, that the provision is an expression of the principle that the position of taxable persons must be neutral. According to the CJEU, it follows therefore from that provision that, in order to ensure observance of the principle of neutrality, account should be taken, when calculating the taxable amount for VAT, of situations where a taxable person who, having no contractual relationship with the final consumer but being the first link in a chain of transactions which ends

115. *Elida Gibbs, supra* n. 111, paragraph 28.
116. Article 73 of the EU VAT Directive.
117. *See*, e.g., *Elida Gibbs, supra* n. 111; *Commission v. Germany, supra* n. 112; CJEU, 16 January 2014, Case C-300/12, *Finanzamt Düsseldorf-Mitte v. Ibero Tours GmbH*, ECLI:EU:C:2014:8; and CJEU, 20 December 2017, Case C-462/16, *Finanzamt Bingen-Alzey v. Boehringer Ingelheim Pharma GmbH & Co. KG*, ECLI:EU:C:2017:1006.
118. *Elida Gibbs, supra* n. 111.

with the final consumer, grants the consumer a reduction through retailers or by direct repayment of the value of the coupons. Otherwise, the tax authorities would receive by way of VAT a sum greater than that actually paid by the final consumer, at the expense of the taxable person.[119] This means that leapfrog discounts lower the taxable amount of the original supply, even though that was made to a different person than the person receiving the discount.

As mentioned above, Both Wittock[120] and Bijl[121] have described the technical and practical problems and issues of this adjustment method. It goes beyond the scope of this contribution to describe the objections to this adjustment systems in depth. Both authors describe an alternative system for treating the leapfrog discount, that is more in line with the principles underlying the EU VAT system, while avoiding the issues created by the Elida Gibbs-method. The alternative would be to consider the amount of the discount paid as a third-party payment rather than a discount, and to consider the business making that payment as the recipient of the supply insofar as he has paid for it, therefore allowing him a (possible) VAT deduction. Under the current EU VAT rules, this is not possible, as only the recipient of a supply can deduct the VAT on the costs of the supply.[122] However, a recent CJEU case might offer an opening.[123] The case deals with a business that purchases goods and services for the furtherance of its own taxed business, but that are also used by others, that also benefit from these supplies. The referring court wanted to understand whether the relevant EU VAT provisions on VAT deduction would allow the formal recipient of these goods and services to fully deduct the VAT on these purchases. The CJEU held that '(f)or the purposes of determining the scope of the taxable person's right to deduct, it is for the referring court to determine the extent to which the services concerned were actually supplied in order to allow the taxable person to carry out his taxable transactions. It is only to that extent that the input VAT paid will be regarded as chargeable on the *services supplied to the taxable person*'[124] (emphasis by the author). This seems to suggest that for a part, the services are considered not to be supplied to the taxable person. In my view, this can only mean that they were supplied to someone else. Could it be possible that that other recipient can deduct the VAT on the part of the services that is deemed to be supplied to him? This will hopefully be the topic of future litigation.

[D] The Australian GST Treatment of Leapfrog Discounts

I have not found specific rules for the GST or VAT treatment of leapfrog discounts in either New Zealand or South African legislation or case law. However, the Australian

119. *Elida Gibbs, supra* n. 111, paragraph 31.
120. Wittock, *supra* n. 112, 211-243.
121. Bijl, *supra* n. 1, 130-174.
122. Also, *see* Jeroen Bijl, *VAT Deduction: The Relevance of Being 'The Recipient' of a Supply and the Use of the Supply*, 29(5) EC Tax Review 227 (2020).
123. CJEU, 1 October 2020, Case C-405/19, *Vos Aannemingen BVBA v. Belgische Staat*, ECLI: EU:C:2020:785.
124. *Vos Aannemingen, supra* n. 123, paragraph 40.

GST Act specifically contains a division on the GST treatment of third-party payments.[125]

Under the relevant Australian GST rules, a business is allowed to decrease the VAT amount paid on an initial supply if it makes a payment to an entity (the payee) that acquires a thing that the business supplied to another entity and the original supply was a taxable supply subject to Australian GST.[126] The Australian rules are similar to the adjustment method developed by the CJEU. This implies that the Australian adjustment method has the same shortcomings as the EU VAT system.

§11.04 CLOSING REMARKS

In this chapter, I have looked at the EU VAT treatment of transactions involving FVVs and leapfrog discounts, and compared these, where possible, to the VAT or GST treatment in other jurisdictions. I have come to the conclusion that the current EU VAT treatment of transactions involving FVVs, albeit harmonized, still raises some fundamental issues that need to be addressed. Neither the EU nor the New Zealand, Australia and South Africa VAT systems achieve full neutrality or are in line with all relevant principles VAT.

The issuance and sale of FVVs should be treated as the payment of a deposit for future transactions. In case of payments for vouchers that entitle the holder to obtain (sufficiently) specific goods or services, the payment for these vouchers should be treated as prepayment, shifting the moment that VAT becomes payable forward to the time that the prepayment is received. However, if the face value vouchers are not redeemed, the VAT remitted should be repaid, unless it can be argued, as is the case for some services, that the agreed supply has been made even without the holder of the voucher having actually used or received that service.

Also, the current EU VAT treatment of leapfrog discounts should be replaced by a system of 'joint payment and shared deduction'. Under this system, the business granting the discount or rebate would be allowed to claim VAT on the supply that it has funded from the local tax authorities of the jurisdiction where that supply takes place. The VAT paid on the remaining part of the consideration can be deducted by the customer, insofar as he has the right to deduct VAT. This solution reflects the economic and commercial reality under which businesses should be entitled to take these 'leapfrog' discounts and rebates into account for VAT purposes. Also, the purpose of VAT, i.e., the taxation of expenditure for local private consumption, is left intact by this solution.

There are many more types of transactions involving vouchers than the transactions involving FVVs. One of the issues within the EU is that only the VAT treatment of

125. A New Tax System (Goods and Services Tax) Act 1999, Division 134 – Third party payments. These rules are further explained by the Australian Taxation Office in a document from 10 April 2017, GST and Rebates, QC 16694.
126. *Supra* n. 125, Division 134-5 - Decreasing adjustments for payments made to third parties.

the latter transactions is harmonized. There are no harmonized rules for, e.g., the VAT treatment of discount vouchers or for points saved in promotional activities. This inevitably leads to different VAT treatments in different Member States, which, in turn, can lead to double taxation or non-taxation of such transactions. In that respect, the EU still has a long way to go.

CHAPTER 12

The Evolving Concept of Fixed Establishment in EU VAT Law

Aleksandra Bal

§12.01 INTRODUCTION

Fixed establishment (FE) is an important concept in EU VAT law.[1] It plays a crucial role in determining the place of the supply of services, the person liable to charge VAT in the context of the reverse charge mechanism, and the right to a VAT refund. It is less relevant for cross-border supplies of goods for which the place of supply is identified on the basis of the physical location or movement of goods. The fiscal connection that the supplier has with a country is generally irrelevant. There are, however, some exceptions to this rule.[2]

Despite its importance, neither the Sixth VAT Directive[3] nor its successor, the VAT Directive, defined FE and the concept of FE is essentially a creation of the judiciary, i.e., the Court of Justice of the European Union (CJEU). The CJEU formulated an FE definition in its landmark judgment in the *Berkholz* (168/84) case,[4] and this

1. The EU VAT system is based on *Council Directive 2006/112/EC of 28 November 2006 on the common system of value added tax* (hereinafter: VAT Directive).
2. For example, the term 'fixed establishment' is relevant to identify the place of supply of electricity, gas, heat and cooling energy (which are considered goods for EU VAT purposes) under Articles 38 and 39 of the VAT Directive and to determine the existence of a call-off stock arrangement under Article 17a of the VAT Directive.
3. *Sixth Council Directive 77/388/EEC of 17 May 1977 on the harmonization of the laws of the Member States relating to turnover taxes – Common system of VAT: uniform basis of assessment* (hereinafter: Sixth VAT Directive).
4. CJEU, 4 July 1985, Case 168/84, *Gunter Berkholz v. Finanzamt Hamburg-Mitte-Altstadt*, ECLI: EU:C:1985:299.

definition was subsequently included into the VAT Implementing Regulation.[5] Although the FE concept has been discussed in numerous subsequent CJEU judgments, it is still far from clear. This is evidenced by a continuous stream of referrals from national courts requesting more clarity on the FE criteria.

The purpose of the FE concept is to safeguard the neutrality principle and to allocate taxing rights among jurisdictions. In the EU VAT system, the place-of-supply rules seek to ensure that the Member States do not use different proxies for the place of actual consumption, thus preventing the creation of a multitude of overlapping and competing taxing jurisdictions. The FE concept plays an important role in determining the taxing jurisdiction for services, and thus to allocate the taxing rights between countries.[6]

The principle of neutrality states that domestic and foreign taxable persons performing the same business activities in a Member State and with a similar organizational structure should be treated in a similar way. This is reflected in the provision stating that foreign businesses having a local FE that intervenes in the performance of supplies of goods or services should be subject to local VAT compliance obligations.[7]

Although the FE concept pursues a similar objective and shares some characteristics with the permanent establishment (PE) in direct taxation, both terms are independent of each other. The FE is an autonomous concept of EU VAT law, whereas the PE has been shaped by international tax treaty law. The PE concept is much older: it can be traced back to the Industrial Code of Prussia (1845) and to the treaty between the Governments of Austria-Hungary and Prussia (1899), which is recognized as the first international tax treaty.[8] In contrast, the FE traces its origin to the Sixth VAT Directive, which was enacted in 1977.

The purpose of this chapter is to explore the meaning and significance of the FE concept for VAT purposes. It first discusses the FE definitions in the EU VAT legislation, §12.02, and jurisprudence of the CJEU, §12.03. Next, §12.04 compares the FE concept with that of PE to establish similarities and differences between the two. Section 12.05 addresses the relationship between the head office and an FE. Finally, §12.06 comments on the evolution of the FE concept, trying to predict the direction in which it may or should be heading.

---

5. *Council Implementing Regulation (EU) 282/2011 of 15 March 2011 laying down implementing measures for Directive 2006/112/EC on the common system of value added tax* (hereinafter: VAT Implementing Regulation).
6. The concept of a purchase PE (Article 44 of the VAT Directive) also serves to ensure that services provided to business customers are taxed in the country of their use. Thus, it seeks to implement the principle of taxation at destination. For the definition of a purchase PE, *see* §12.02.
7. The principle of neutrality is implemented by the concepts of sales FE (Article 45 of the VAT Directive) and intervention PE (Article 192a of the VAT Directive). For the definitions of both terms, *see* §12.02.
8. Arvid A. Skaar, *Permanent Establishment: Erosion of a Tax Treaty Principle* (Kluwer Law Int'l, 1991), 75.

§12.02 FEs IN EU VAT LEGISLATION

The VAT Directive uses the term 'FE' in several provisions but does not define it. The most important provisions where the FE concept is used are Articles 44 and 45 (the default rules for the place of supply of services) and Article 192a (liability to remit value added tax (VAT) in the context of the reverse charge mechanism).[9] Each of these 3 articles has its own FE definition in the VAT Implementing Regulation.[10] The FE concept also plays an important role in the VAT refund rules of Directive (2008/9/EC), which applies to refund applicants from other EU Member States, and the Thirteenth VAT Directive (86/560/EEC), which governs the VAT refund for applicants from third countries.[11]

[A] Place of Supply Rules

The FE concept is of particular importance in the place-of-supply rules, which serve to allocate tax jurisdiction. The ultimate aim of the place-of-supply rules is to determine a location that could serve as the best proxy for the actual place of consumption. Article 44 of the VAT Directive lays down the main rule for the taxation of services in a business-to-business (B2B) scenario: a supply of services to a taxable person takes place in the country where the customer has established his business. However, if services are provided to an FE of the taxable person in another country, the place of

9. Other provisions of the VAT Directive that mention the FE concept are Article 17a (call-off stock arrangements), Articles 38 and 39 (supply of electricity, gas, heat and cooling energy), Article 56 (hiring of means of transport), Articles 219a and 221 (invoicing obligations), Article 307 (special scheme for travel agents), Articles 358a and 361 (special scheme for telecommunications, broadcasting or electronic services supplied by taxable persons not established within the European Union) and Articles 369a and 369g (special scheme for telecommunications, broadcasting or electronic services supplied by taxable persons established within the European Union but not in the Member State of consumption).
10. The VAT Committee takes the view that there is a single FE definition: 'These two requirements [*added by the author: i.e., to receive and use services and to provide services*] should not be seen as creating two different definitions of the concept of fixed establishment for "purchasing" and "supplying" fixed establishments. There is only one single definition of the concept of fixed establishment requiring on the one hand a sufficient degree of permanence and, on the other hand, a suitable structure in terms of human and technical resources which however has to be assessed on a case-by-case basis with regard to the circumstances at stake.' *See* VAT Committee, Working Paper No. 857 (6 May 2015), taxud.c.1(2015)2177802.
11. Article 3 of Directive (2008/9/EC) states that 'This Directive shall apply to any taxable person not established in the Member State of refund who meets the following conditions: (a) during the refund period, he has not had in the Member State of refund, the seat of his economic activity, or a fixed establishment from which business transactions were effected.' According to Article 1 of the Thirteenth VAT Directive (86/560/EEC), 'A taxable person not established in the territory of the Community [...] shall mean a taxable person who [...] has had in that territory neither his business nor a fixed establishment from which business transactions are effected.' The definition of an FE for the purposes of the VAT refund rules is not provided in the VAT legislation. However, as the wording of both refund directives mentions 'fixed establishment from which business transactions are effected', it seems reasonable to assume that reference is made to the concept of a sales FE defined in Article 11(2) of the VAT Implementing Regulation, which mentions an establishment that needs a suitable structure in terms of human and technical resources to enable it to provide services.

supply of those services switches to the place where the FE is located. According to the general rule for business-to-consumer (B2C) supplies of services (Article 45 of the VAT Directive), the taxing right belongs to the state where the supplier has established his business or, alternatively, to the state hosting the FE from which the services are provided.

The wording of Articles 44 and 45 of the VAT Directive could imply that the place of business establishment and the FE are equivalent alternatives to determine the place of supply, or even that the location of the FE acts as a *lex specialis* to the general rule (the place of business). However, the CJEU rejected this view. In *Berkholz*, the Court held that the place where the supplier has established its business should act as the 'primary point of reference' for determining the place of supply of services. If 'the reference to the place where the supplier has established his business does not lead to a rational result for tax purposes or creates a conflict with another Member State',[12] another establishment may come under consideration as the place of supply. Shortly afterwards, the Court applied the 'rational result' test in the *DFDS* case[13] to conclude that a UK subsidiary constituted an FE of the Danish parent. If it had ruled that the Danish company was the primary point of reference, the services provided to UK consumers would have been taxable in Denmark. As the Danish law applied a VAT exemption for the services in question, the services would escape taxation. The CJEU held that: 'Systematic reliance on the place where the supplier has established his business could in fact lead to distortions of competition, in that it might encourage undertakings trading in one Member State to establish their business, in order to avoid taxation, in another Member State which has availed itself of the possibility of maintaining the VAT exemption for the services in question.'[14]

By introducing the 'rational result' test, the CJEU sought to provide a simple and clear rule: the place of the business is the primary criterion that taxable persons can rely upon. Only if the use of this criterion does not lead to a rational result or creates a conflict with another Member State, the FE concept can be used. However, the term 'rational result' is vague and subjective, giving rise to legal uncertainty. It is also not supported by the wording of the VAT Directive. It would seem more appropriate to consider the FE as a primary criterion.[15] Only if there is no FE, or the FE has not been involved in the transaction, the place of business should be used. Giving priority to the place of business implies taxation at origin, which is contrary to the main principle of the VAT system stating that supplies should be taxed in the country where they are likely to be consumed. Strengthening the role of the FE would be closer to the spirit of the destination principle.

The definition of the FE for the purposes of Articles 44 and 45 of the VAT Directive is provided in the VAT Implementing Regulation (1042/2013). Article 11(1) of the Implementing Regulation defines the FE for the purposes of Article 44 of the VAT

12. *Berkholz, supra* n. 4, pt. 17.
13. CJEU, 20 Feb. 1997, Case C-260/95, *Commissioners of Customs and Excise v. DFDS A/S*, ECLI:EU:C:1997:77.
14. *DFDS, supra* n. 13, pt. 23.
15. Pasquale Pistone, *Fixed Establishment and Permanent Establishment*, 10(3) Int'l VAT Monitor 101, 103 (1999).

Directive (hereinafter referred to as 'purchase FE' or 'receiving FE') as any establishment, other than the place of establishment of a business, characterized by a sufficient degree of permanence and a suitable structure in terms of human and technical resources to enable it to receive and use the services supplied to it for its own needs. An FE for the purposes of Article 45 of the VAT Directive (hereinafter referred to as 'sales FE' or 'supplying FE') is defined in Article 11(2) of the VAT Implementing Regulation (1042/2013) as any establishment, other than the head office, characterized by a sufficient degree of permanency and a suitable structure in terms of human and technical resources to enable it to provide the services that it supplies.

The purchase FE contains an additional criterion that is absent in the definition of the sales FE; namely, the FE must use the services for its own needs. This additional criterion was not mentioned in the CJEU case law and, as such, gives rise to legal uncertainty. Does this mean that the FE must be the end user (i.e., consumer) of the services or can it subsequently sell them? Should 'use for one's own needs' be interpreted in the sense of the use and enjoyment criterion? The case law has not clarified this issue yet.

[B] Reverse Charge Mechanism

Another important reference to the FE concept is made in the rules on the reverse charge mechanism. Article 196 of the VAT Directive provides that, by way of derogation from the principle that suppliers of goods and services must account for VAT on supplies made by them, registered recipients of specific services must account for the VAT due under the reverse charge mechanism, if the services are supplied to them by service providers not established within the territory of the Member State where the VAT is due. In this context, Article 192a provides that a taxable person who has an FE within the territory of the Member State where the tax is due shall be regarded as a taxable person who is not established within that country provided the FE 'does not intervene in the supply' ('intervention FE').

Article 53 of the VAT Implementing Regulation clarifies the conditions under which an FE is presumed to have intervened in the supply for the purpose of Article 192a of the VAT Directive. It first defines an FE as an establishment characterized by a sufficient degree of permanence and a suitable structure in terms of human and technical resources to enable it to make the supply of goods or services in which it intervenes (a similar definition to the one of the sales FE in Article 11 of the VAT Implementing Regulation). Next it explains that an FE does not intervene in the supply of goods or services, unless the technical and human resources of that FE are used in the fulfilment of the taxable supply of those goods or services made within that Member State, before or during this fulfilment. However, if the resources of the FE are only used for administrative support tasks, such as accounting, invoicing and collection of debt-claims, they shall not be regarded as being used for the fulfilment of the supply of goods or services. Finally, if an invoice is issued under the VAT identification number attributed by the Member State to the FE, that FE shall be regarded as having intervened in the supply of goods or services made in that Member State unless there is proof to the contrary.

The purpose of Article 192a was to put an end to the principle of force of attraction that some Member States applied: they considered suppliers of goods or services established outside the customer's Member State to be established in that Member State on the mere ground that they had an FE in that Member State, even if that establishment was not involved in making the supply. Under those circumstances, the transaction was excluded from the reverse charge mechanism in the Member State concerned and the non-resident supplier's FE was required to issue an invoice and to remit the VAT to the authorities of the customer's Member State.

Article 192a was not entirely successful in eliminating the force of attraction: the criterion of 'intervention' has emerged as a new problematic concept in EU VAT law. Some Member States saw a minimal involvement of the FE in making the supply as 'intervention' that excludes the application of the reverse charge mechanism.[16]

§12.03 FEs IN CJEU JURISPRUDENCE

The FE concept first appeared in the Sixth VAT Directive, which took effect on 1 January 1979. The Sixth VAT Directive only mentioned this term in Article 9 (the place-of-supply rules) but did not provide any definition. This omission may be explained by the limited relevance of the FE due to the low volume of cross-border supplies of services in the 1980s. As the volume of cross-border services increased, so did the importance of the FE concept.

The fact that the English version of the Sixth VAT Directive used a term for FE different from the one used for PE in the OECD Model Convention may indicate that the intention was to have different concepts for both direct taxes and VAT. However, in the French and Dutch versions, the same expression was used for VAT and income taxes ('établissement permanent', respectively 'vaste inrichting'). A strange situation occurred in Germany: domestic VAT legislation did not refer to the FE using the term contained in the Sixth VAT Directive (*feste Niederlassung*) but used the term applied in direct taxation (*Betriebstätte*).

In 1984, in the proposal for a Nineteenth VAT Directive,[17] the EU Commission proposed a definition of the FE that would be aligned with the PE definition contained in Article 5 of the OECD Model. Under the proposed Article 9(4), 'the expression "fixed establishment" ... means any fixed installation of a taxable person, even if no taxable transaction can be carried out there'. If this proposal had been approved, there would be similar concepts for both VAT and direct tax purposes. However, the proposal did not gain enough support among the Member States and was withdrawn.

16. For a detailed discussion of the concept of intervention, *see* Peter Schilling & Deirdre Hogan, *Intervention – A Problematic New Concept in EU VAT Law*, 21(3) Int'l. VAT Monitor 187 (2010), Gorka Echevarría Zubeldia, *Abolition of the Force of Attraction of the Fixed Establishment?*, 27(6) Int'l. VAT Monitor 405 (2016).
17. Final Proposal for a Nineteenth Council Directive on the Harmonization of the Laws of the Member States relating to Turnover Taxes amending Directive 77/388/EEC – Common System of VAT, COM 84/648, 5 Dec. 1984.

In the absence of an FE definition in the VAT legislation, the CJEU was asked to provide guidance. On 4 July 1985, the CJEU decided its first case concerning the interpretation of the FE concept. The *Berkholz* judgment shaped the approach to the FE concept for many years to come and became determinative for the FE definition introduced into the VAT Implementing Regulation in 2011. The cases referred to the CJEU can be divided into 2 groups: those concerning the place-of-supply rules and those dealing with the right to a VAT refund.[18]

[A] *Berkholz*

The first case in which the CJEU considered the FE concept was the *Berkholz* case. Berkholz installed gaming machines onboard two ferries that traveled regularly between Germany and Denmark. Although these machines were maintained, repaired, and replaced at regular intervals by Berkholz employees, Berkholz did not maintain any permanent staff on the ferry boats.

The question referred to the CJEU was whether the gaming machines onboard the ferryboats should be regarded as an FE of Berkholz for the purposes of Article 9 of the Sixth VAT Directive.[19] The CJEU answered this question in the negative, stating that the operation of gaming machines may be regarded as an FE only if the establishment entails the permanent presence of both the human and technical resources necessary for the provision of services and it is not appropriate to deem those services to have been provided at the place where the supplier has established his business (the 'rational result' test).

The *Berkholz* judgment is still considered the leading case on the FE concept, and the definition that the CJEU provided in that case served as a basis for the FE concept introduced into the VAT Implementing Regulation in 2011.

[B] *DFDS*

Nearly ten years after the *Berkholz* judgment, the CJEU was again asked to provide guidance on the FE concept – this time for the purposes of Article 26 of the Sixth VAT Directive (special scheme for travel agents). In the *DFDS* case, the Court was specifically asked whether a separate legal entity (a subsidiary in another Member State) could constitute an FE.

DFDS A/S was a Danish tour operator that sold package tours to passengers and travel agents in the United Kingdom (UK) through a wholly owned subsidiary, DFDS Ltd, pursuant to an agency agreement. The UK tax authorities took the view that the UK subsidiary was an FE of the Danish company. Consequently, services supplied by an FE in the United Kingdom had to be taxed in the United Kingdom. DFDS claimed that the

18. Cases concerning the relationship between the FE and head office are discussed in §12.05.
19. Article 9(1) of the Sixth VAT Directive reads as follows: 'The place where a service is supplied shall be deemed to be the place where the supplier has established his business or has a fixed establishment from which the service is supplied or, in the absence of such a place of business or fixed establishment, the place where he has his permanent address or usually resides.'

supplies were taxable in Denmark, where the tour operator had its headquarters, in line with the previous CJEU case law concerning the primary point of reference.

The CJEU observed that reliance on the place of business as the primary point of reference would not lead to a rational result in this case as this approach would take no account of the place where the services would actually be consumed. The Court then proceeded to examine whether the Danish company had an FE in the United Kingdom by investigating whether the subsidiary had an independent status in relation to the parent company. The fact that the subsidiary was a separate legal person with its own business premises was not sufficient to establish an independent status. Instead, all factual circumstances had to be examined. As the parent company owned the entire share capital of the subsidiary and imposed several contractual restrictions on it, the subsidiary was found to be an auxiliary organ of the parent company and therefore an FE. Finally, the CJEU ruled that given the organizational structure of DFDS Ltd, DFDS A/S had a minimum level of human and technical resources permanently present in the United Kingdom. To summarize, based on the DFDS judgment, a subsidiary may be regarded as an FE of the parent company if it acts as a mere auxiliary organ of the parent and has the human and technical resources characteristic of an FE.

[C] *ARO Lease* and *Lease Plan Luxembourg*

Five months after the *DFDS* judgment, the CJEU ruled on the FE concept for the purposes of Article 9 of the Sixth VAT Directive in the *ARO Lease* case (C-190/95).[20] ARO Lease BV was a Dutch company that leased passenger cars to Dutch and Belgian customers. It did not have any premises in Belgium. Belgian customers were introduced to ARO by self-employed Belgian intermediaries, and the contracts were drawn in the ARO Dutch offices. According to the Belgian tax authorities, the presence of a fleet of cars in Belgium constituted an FE of ARO Lease.

The CJEU did not agree with this interpretation. It first observed that the place where the supplier had established his business served as the primary point of reference. However, if this criterion did not lead to a rational result, another establishment possessing a sufficient degree of permanence and a structure adequate, in terms of human and technical resources, to supply the services in question on an independent basis might be referred to. The Court held that the leasing of vehicles consists principally in negotiating, drawing up, signing, and administering the relevant agreements and in making the vehicles physically available to customers. Consequently, if a leasing company did not possess in a Member State either its own staff or a structure which has a sufficient degree of permanence to provide a framework in which agreements may be drawn up or management decisions taken, it could not be regarded as having an FE in that country. The existence of other factors ancillary and supplementary to the leasing services (the fact that the vehicles are registered in Belgium where road tax is also payable, or the fact that customers choose their vehicles

20. CJEU, 17 July 1997, Case C-190/95, *ARO Lease BV v. Inspecteur van de Belastingdienst Grote Ondernemingen te Amsterdam*, ECLI:EU:C:1997:374.

themselves at the premises of self-employed Belgian dealers) could not invalidate that conclusion.

In the *ARO Lease* decision, the CJEU maintained the *Berkholz* criteria (a minimum degree of stability derived from the permanent presence of both the human and technical resources) but introduced 2 new requirements: (1) an adequate structure that allows (2) to supply the services on an independent basis. The latter criterion has not been incorporated into the FE definitions of the VAT Implementing Regulation but has been repeated in subsequent CJEU decisions.

The *Lease Plan Luxembourg* case involved a similar situation: the lease of passenger cars by a Luxembourg company to Belgian customers.[21] The CJEU merely repeated its position, expressly referring to the ARO Lease judgment.

[D] *RAL (Channel Islands)*

The *RAL (Channel Islands)* case concerned the exploitation of gaming machines.[22] The RAL Group operated gaming machines in the United Kingdom from premises which it owned or leased. Following a restructuring, the principal purpose of which was to ensure that the place of supply of the gaming machine services would be deemed to be outside the territory of the EU for VAT purposes, a group company was established in Guernsey and given a license to install and operate machines on premises leased by the RAL Group. The RAL Group claimed that the gaming machines were supplied by its Guernsey entity, which did not have any human and technical resources in the UK and thus did not meet the criteria established in *Berkholz* and *ARO Lease* to be considered an FE.

Unfortunately, the CJEU failed to comment on the FE issue in its judgment. Instead, it chose to apply what is now Article 53 of the VAT Directive, concluding that the gaming services supplied by the Guernsey entity should be regarded as 'entertainment and similar activities'. An interesting point was mentioned in the Opinion of Advocate General Maduro, who considered that in *Berkholz* and *ARO Lease*, the Court 'did not make the permanent presence of all possible human and technical resources, possessed by the supplier himself, in a certain place, a precondition for concluding that the supplier has a fixed establishment there'.[23] In his opinion, the RAL Group's gaming machines in the United Kingdom satisfied the 'minimum-requirements test' for the existence of an FE.

---

21. CJEU, 7 May 1998, Case C-390/96, *Lease Plan Luxembourg SA v. Belgian State*, ECLI: EU:C:1998:206.
22. CJEU, 12 May 2005, Case C-452/03, *RAL (Channel Islands) Ltd, RAL Ltd, RAL Services Ltd, RAL Machines Ltd v. Commissioners of Customs and Excise*, ECLI:EU:C:2005:289.
23. AG Opinion, 27 Jan. 2005, C-452/03, *RAL (Channel Islands) Ltd, RAL Ltd, RAL Services Ltd, RAL Machines Ltd v. Commissioners of Customs and Excise*, ECLI:EU:C:2005:65, paragraph 41.

[E] *Planzer Luxembourg*

The *Planzer Luxembourg* case concerned a dispute between Planzer Luxembourg Sàrl, a company incorporated under Luxembourg law, and the *Bundeszentralamt für Steuern* (the German Federal Central Tax Office) about the rejection of applications for refund of VAT paid by the company on fuel supplies in Germany.[24] Planzer Luxembourg was wholly owned by a Swiss company and had limited human resources in Luxembourg. Having established that Planzer did not have any equipment or other property at the address stated in its refund application, the German tax authority took the view that the applicant's business was managed in Switzerland rather than in Luxembourg. In the course of the court proceedings, it was further established that certain business decisions (such as the purchase of vehicles, staff recruitment) were taken in Luxembourg by the directors who were present there for a few days per week and that the company's administration was also located there. Business operations were nevertheless carried out from Switzerland.

The CJEU was asked to provide guidance on the concept of place of business and FE for the purposes of the Thirteenth Council Directive (86/560/EEC). The CJEU made an explicit reference to *Berkholz* and *ARO Lease*, repeating that 'the term fixed establishment implies a minimum degree of stability derived from the permanent presence of both the human and technical resources necessary for the provision of given. It thus requires a sufficient degree of permanence and a structure adequate, in terms of human and technical resources, to supply the services in question on an independent basis.' Furthermore, the CJEU made it clear that the performance of preparatory and auxiliary activities does not give rise to an FE. It ruled that: 'A fixed installation used by the undertaking only for preparatory or auxiliary activities, such as recruitment of staff or purchase of the technical means needed for carrying out the undertaking's tasks, does not constitute a fixed establishment.'[25] This CJEU's conclusion is not surprising as the mere performance of auxiliary activities would not allow an establishment to perform services on an independent basis as required by the Court in the *ARO Lease* decision. Finally, the CJEU ruled that a fictitious presence, such as that of a 'letter box' company, could not constitute a place of business for the purposes of Article 1(1) of the Thirteenth Directive.[26]

24. CJEU, 28 June 2007, Case C-73/06, *Planzer Luxembourg Sàrl v. Bundeszentralamt für Steuern*, ECLI:EU:C:2007:397.
25. *Planzer Luxembourg, supra* n. 24, pt. 56.
26. According to the CJEU, the determination of a company's place of business requires a number of factors to be taken into consideration, the most important of which are: the registered office, the place of central administration, the place where directors meet and the place where the general policy of the company is determined. Other factors, such as the place of residence of the main directors, the place where general meetings are held, the place where administrative and accounting documents are kept, and the place where the company's financial, and particularly banking, transactions mainly take place, may also need to be taken into account.

[F] *Daimler* and *Widex*

In the joined cases *Daimler* and *Widex*, the CJEU was asked whether a taxable person carrying out technical testing or research work in another Member State could be regarded as having in that other Member State a 'fixed establishment from which business transactions are effected' within the meaning of Directive 2008/9 and whether the presence of a wholly owned subsidiary in that Member State was relevant for this evaluation.[27]

Daimler AG, a company established in Germany, carried out winter testing of cars at some locations in Northern Sweden. It had no permanent staff and neither did it perform any taxable activities in Sweden. All testing staff and technical equipment were flown in for the test periods. Daimler had a wholly owned subsidiary in Sweden which provided premises, test tracks and services connected with the testing activities. The staff of the Swedish subsidiary consisted of four seasonal employees and a director.

Widex A/S, a company established in Denmark, had a research division in Stockholm. No sales, marketing or other services were performed in Stockholm other than pure research. Widex also had a subsidiary in Malmö which sold and distributed its goods in Sweden. However, the research division was independent of the subsidiary. The Swedish tax authorities refused to grant a VAT refund to Daimler and Widex on the ground that the companies had an FE in Sweden.

The CJEU ruled that a wholly owned subsidiary is a taxable legal person on its own account: the *DFDS* judgment should not be generalized and must be viewed in the context of the specific circumstances of that case. The Court also held that for the purposes of exclusion of a right to refund, 2 conditions must be cumulatively present: (1) the presence of an FE and (2) taxable transactions be carried out by the FE. Since no output transactions were performed by Daimler and Widex in Sweden, the right to refund could not be excluded irrespective of whether or not they had an FE in that State.

[G] *E.ON Global Commodities SE*

In the *E.ON Global Commodities SE* case,[28] the CJEU considered the question whether a tax representative may constitute an FE for the purposes of the Eighth Council Directive (79/1072/EEC).[29] E.ON Global Commodities (formerly E.ON Energy Trading), a company established in Germany, carried out supplies of electricity in Romania.

27. CJEU, 25 Oct. 2012, Joined Cases C-318/11 & C-31/11, *Daimler AG v. Skatteverket, & Widex A/S v. Skatteverket*, ECLI:EU:C:2012:666.
28. CJEU, 6 Feb. 2014, Case C-323/12, *E.ON Global Commodities SE v. Agenția Nationala de Administrare Fiscala, Direcția Generala a Finanțelor Publice a Municipiului București – Serviciul de administrare a contribuabililor nerezidenți*, ECLI:EU:C:2014:53.
29. The Eighth Directive was repealed as from 1 January 2010 by *Council Directive 2008/9/EC of 12 February 2008 laying down detailed rules for the refund of value added tax, provided for in Directive 2006/112, to taxable persons not established in the Member State of refund but established in another Member State.*

E.ON did not have any physical presence in Romania, but it had designated a tax representative there. The tax representative carried out business activities (supplying electricity and re-invoicing transport services) in the name of E.ON.

The Romanian tax authorities claimed that the presence of a tax representative was sufficient to prevent E.ON Global Commodities from relying on the Eighth Council Directive (79/1072/EEC) to obtain a refund of input VAT incurred in Romania.[30] However, the CJEU concluded that 'the mere designation of a tax representative does not suffice to permit the taxable person concerned to be regarded as having available a structure possessing a sufficient degree of permanence and his own staff who are responsible for the management of his economic activities'.[31]

[H] *Welmory*

The *Welmory* case was the first one where the CJEU was asked to interpret the concept of a purchase FE (Article 44 of the VAT Directive).[32] The CJEU acknowledged that its previous case law, regardless that it concerned sale FEs or FEs for the purposes of the VAT refund rules, can also be applied to determine the existence of a purchase FE.[33]

Welmory Ltd, a company established in Cyprus (Welmory CY), entered into a cooperation agreement with Welmory sp. z o.o., a company established in Poland (Welmory PL). Based on this contract, Welmory CY operated an auction website through which Welmory PL sold goods in its own name and on its own account to Polish customers. To operate the website, Welmory CY used personnel and technical resources belonging to Welmory PL. Welmory CY held 100% of the shares of Welmory PL. Welmory PL provided several services to Welmory CY, such as advertising, data processing and the provision of information, but charged no VAT on those services, as it believed that they were taxable in Cyprus where the recipient had established its business (the default rule for B2B services). The Polish tax authorities, however, took the view that the services were provided to an FE of Welmory CY in Poland and should be subject to Polish VAT.

The Polish Regional Administrative Court agreed with the tax administration by concluding that the activities of the two companies formed an economically indivisible

30. Article 1 of the Eighth Directive provided two cumulative conditions which had to be satisfied before a taxable person could be regarded as not being established in the territory of the country, and therefore entitled to a refund under Article 2 of that directive. First, the taxable person could not possess any establishment in the Member State where it was seeking to claim VAT refund. Second, it could not have made any supplies of goods or services in respect of which the place of supply was deemed to be in that Member State, with the exception of certain supplies of specified services.
31. *E.ON Global Commodities SE*, *supra* n. 28, pt. 47.
32. CJEU, 16 Oct. 2014, Case C-605/12, *Welmory sp. z o.o. v. Dyrektor Izby Skarbowej w Gdańsku*, ECLI:EU:C:2014:2298.
33. The CJEU held that 'The wording of Article 44 of the VAT Directive is similar to that of Article 9(1) of the Sixth Directive. Furthermore, both Article 44 of the VAT Directive and Article 9(1) of the Sixth Directive are provisions determining the point of reference for tax purposes of supplies of services and pursue the same objective, so that the Court's case-law on the interpretation of Article 9(1) of the Sixth Directive can in principle be applied mutatis mutandis to the interpretation of Article 44 of the VAT Directive.' *Welmory*, pt. 43.

whole and the object of their entire business could be achieved in Poland only through cooperation between the two companies. As Welmory CY was making use of the Polish company's technical and human resources, the Polish company was to be treated as an FE of the Cypriot company in Poland.

The CJEU was asked to determine whether the recipient of the services supplied by Welmory PL was Welmory CY or an FE of the Cypriot company in Poland (provided that one existed). In other words, the issue was whether by using the infrastructure of the supplier (Welmory PL) the customer (Welmory CY) had an FE in the Member State of the supplier.

The CJEU did not provide a clear answer as to whether or not the structure in the case in question could give rise to an FE. Instead, it asked the referring court to determine whether Welmory CY had the necessary human and technical resources to receive and use the supplied services in Poland. If the necessary technical resources were not in Poland, no Polish FE could be deemed to exist. The referring court was also asked to ascertain the extent of the independent business of Welmory CY in Poland and whether or not it had control comparable to that of an owner over the human and technical resources. The CJEU ruled that 'the fact that a business such as that carried on by the Cypriot company (...) can be carried on without requiring an effective human and material structure in Polish territory is not determinative. Despite its particular character, such a business requires at least a structure that is appropriate in terms especially of human and technical resources, such as appropriate computer equipment, servers and software.'[34]

The CJEU did not expressly negate the possibility of recognizing the supplier's resources as forming the FE of the recipient of the service. It can be inferred from the CJEU decision that an FE may exist even in the absence of own human and technical resources. However, by referring the case to the national court, the CJEU failed to explain under which circumstances external resources are sufficient to create an FE.

The *Welmory* case only concerned the question of whether a purchase FE (within the meaning of Article 44) was deemed to exist. If, however, an FE for receiving the services was found to exist, there could also be a sales FE in the same jurisdiction. If the customer was found to have a sales FE in the Member State of the supplier and supplied services from that FE, it would have to register for VAT purposes in the supplier's country, fulfil local VAT compliance obligations and apply local bookkeeping and invoicing requirements.

The *Welmory* decision created the risk that tax authorities more easily would assume the existence of an FE. This could have an impact on groups of companies where technical and human resources are jointly used by several group entities. A non-EU entity, relying on the resources of an EU group entity, may find that it has an FE in the European Union and, therefore, is subject to the extensive EU VAT compliance obligations.

34. *Welmory*, *supra* n. 32, pt. 60.

[I] *WebMindLicences*

The *WebMindLicences* case did not focus on the concept of an FE, but rather on the activities which must be performed by an FE in order for these services to be considered to have been supplied from there.[35]

WebMindLicences, a company registered in Hungary, acquired know-how enabling the operation of an erotic website and made it available by a licensing agreement to a company established in Madeira. The Hungarian tax authorities claimed that the transfer of know-how was abusive and the place of supply of services by WebMindLicences to its customers was in Hungary. WebMindLicences argued that there were commercial, technical, and legal reasons for the involvement of the Madeira company and, therefore, the place of supply was Portugal.

The CJEU ruled that, in order to determine whether the licensing agreement constituted a wholly artificial arrangement, it had to be determined whether the FE (the Madeira company) engaged in the economic activity in its own name and on its own behalf, under its own responsibility and at its own risk.

[J] *Dong Yang Electronics*

In a recently decided case, *Dong Yang Electronics*, the CJEU was asked whether an EU subsidiary may be regarded as an FE of a parent company established outside the European Union.[36]

Dong Yang Electronics sp. z o. o., a company established in Poland, concluded with LG Display Co. Ltd. (LG Korea), established in the Republic of Korea, a contract to provide services consisting in the assembly of printed circuit boards from certain components. These components were provided to Dong Yang by LG Display Polska sp. z o.o. (LG Poland), a subsidiary of LG Korea established in Poland. LG Korea assured Dong Yang that it did not have an FE in Poland and that it did not employ staff, own immovable property, or have technical resources there. Consequently, Dong Yang invoiced the assembly services to LG Korea, treating those services as not subject to Polish VAT. The Polish tax administration took the view that Dong Yang had supplied assembly services in Poland as LG Poland constituted an FE of LG Korea. Furthermore, Dong Yang should not have relied solely on the statement of LG Korea that it did not have any FE in Poland; rather it should have examined who the actual beneficiary of the services was.

The CJEU was asked whether it could be inferred that an FE existed in Poland from the mere fact that a company established outside the European Union had a subsidiary in the territory of Poland and whether a third party was required to examine contractual relationships between a company established outside the European Union

35. CJEU, 17 Dec. 2015, Case C-419/14, *WebMindLicences Kft. v. Nemzeti Adó- és Vámhivatal Kiemelt Adó- és Vám Főigazgatóság*, ECLI:EU:C:2015:832.
36. CJEU, 7 May 2020, Case C-547/18, *Dong Yang Electronics Sp. z o.o. v. Dyrektor Izby Administracji Skarbowej we Wrocławiu*, ECLI:EU:C:2020:350.

and its subsidiary in order to determine whether the former company had an FE in Poland.

The CJEU observed that a subsidiary might constitute an FE of its parent company. However, the Court noted that the mere fact that LG Korea had a subsidiary in the EU did not mean that there was indeed an FE. The qualification as an FE did not depend on the legal form, but on the material conditions that must be assessed in the light of economic and commercial reality.

The CJEU noted that Article 22 of the VAT Implementing Regulation contains criteria that a supplier must consider when determining whether it provides services to an FE of the customer. First, the nature and use of the service by the customer must be examined. If the nature and use of the services do not permit the supplier to identify the FE to which the service is provided, it should pay attention to whether the contract, the order form and the VAT identification number communicated by the customer identify the FE as the recipient of the service. What must also be considered is whether the FE is the entity paying for the service. If based on the above criteria it is not possible to denote the FE as the service recipient, the supplier may legitimately assume that the services are provided to the main place of business. The CJEU also concluded that a supplier does not need to investigate contractual relationships between the customer and its subsidiaries to determine whether a subsidiary may be regarded as an FE for VAT purposes. By doing so, the CJEU avoided an unreasonably heavy burden of proof and additional costs for service providers who generally have no insight into contractual relationships within the customer's group.

[K] *Titanium v. Austria*

In 2020, the CJEU was asked by the Austrian Federal Financial Court (*Bundesfinanzgericht*) whether the criteria of human and technical resources must be met cumulatively or whether there can also be an FE without the deployment of its own personnel. In *Titanium v. Austria*,[37] a Jersey-based company (Titanium) owned immovable property in Austria that was rented out to 2 local taxable persons (the option for taxation was exercised). Titanium engaged a local company to perform property management activities; however, it remained competent to make fundamental decisions, such as concluding or terminating renting agreements, making investments or carrying out repairs. Titanium did not charge any Austrian VAT on the rent received. As it did not have an FE in Austria, the Austrian tenants had to account for VAT under the reverse charge mechanism.

According to the Austrian tax authorities, the immovable property constituted an FE of Titanium, which should therefore calculate VAT on the rental services provided. However, Titanium considered that the immovable property was not an FE because of the lack of own personnel.

37. Request for a preliminary ruling from the Bundesfinanzgericht (Austria), 20 December 2019, Case C-931/19, OJ 16 March 2020, C 87/10.

At the time of the writing of this chapter, the CJEU has not decided the case yet. The Court decision case may have huge practical consequences if the CJEU concludes that it is sufficient for the existence of an FE to use personnel of another, contracted business and the deployment of own personnel is not necessary.[38]

[L] *Berlin Chemie*

In July 2020, a Romanian court asked the CJEU whether a sub-subsidiary may constitute an FE of the parent company in the *Berlin Chemie* case.[39]

Berlin Chemie, a company established in Germany, sold pharmaceutical products in Romania. It was registered for VAT purposes in Romania and had a fiscal representative there. Berlin Chemie concluded a contract for marketing and advertising services with its Romanian sub-subsidiary BCAM. The Romanian BCAM employees were not authorized to conclude contracts on behalf of Berlin Chemie. BCAM issued invoices to Berlin Chemie without Romanian VAT and the latter accounted for VAT under the reverse charge mechanism. However, the Romanian tax authorities took the view that BCAM was an FE of Berlin Chemie and the marketing services were taxable in Romania.

The Romanian referring court asked the CJEU to clarify whether a sub-subsidiary can be regarded as an FE of the parent company if it operates under the control of the parent and performs its activities entirely for business purposes of the parent company.

§12.04 PERMANENT VERSUS FIXED ESTABLISHMENTS

The PE concept is used to determine when a state has the right to tax business profits of a company resident in another state. According to Article 7 of the OECD Model,[40] business profits are taxable in the state where the company is located unless it carries out its activity in the other state through a PE situated therein. The profits attributable to such PE may be taxed in the state where the PE is located.

The PE definition remained quite stable over the years since it first appeared in the OECD Draft (1963), but recently its scope has been expended as a result of the OECD Base Erosion and Profit Shifting (BEPS) project, which sought to curb abusive practices allowing to avoid a PE in other jurisdictions. Action 7 of the BEPS Project recommended numerous changes to the PE concept that were included in Articles

38. In a similar case in the Netherlands, the Dutch Supreme Court (*Hoge Raad*) confirmed that a holiday home of a foreign owner cannot be regarded as an FE. According to the Supreme Court, an FE would exist if the landlord had the personnel and technical resources in the Netherlands to draw up rental contracts or to take management board decisions. The landlord however used an independent intermediary to manage the property. Hoge Raad, 8 Feb. 2019, Zaaknummer 17/04018, ECLI:NL:GHSHE:2017:3230.
39. Request for a preliminary ruling from the Curtea de Apel Bucureşti (Romania), 22 July 2020, *Berlin Chemie A. Menarini SRL v. Administraţia Fiscala pentru Contribuabili Mijlocii Bucureşti — Direcţia Generala Regionala a Finanţelor Publice Bucureşti*, Case C 333/20, OJ 12 Oct. 2020, C 339/2.
40. OECD, *Model Tax Convention on Income and on Capital 2017 (Full Version)*, OECD Publishing, 2019).

12-16 of the OECD Multilateral Convention to Implement Tax Treaty Related Measures to Prevent Base Erosion and Profit Shifting (MLI). The changes to the PE definition were also incorporated in the OECD Model and the Commentary as part of the 2017 update.

Although the concepts of FE and PE are similar, the CJEU has explicitly ruled that the PE concept is irrelevant in the interpretation of the VAT Directive.[41] The Commentary on the OECD Model also clarifies that the VAT treatment of transactions is irrelevant for the purposes of the interpretation and application of the PE definition in the OECD Model.[42] In the past, there were however attempts to align both terms: the proposal for a Nineteenth VAT Directive contained a definition of FE that aligned with the PE definition contained in Article 5 of the OECD Model.

[A] Basic Rule PE

Article 5(1) of the OECD Model defines the term 'permanent establishment' as a fixed place of business through which the business of an enterprise is wholly or partly carried on (the 'basic rule' PE). Article 5(2) of the OECD Model includes a list of examples that constitute a PE: a place of management, a branch, an office, a factory, a workshop, a mine, an oil or gas well, a quarry, or any other place of extraction of natural resources. The 'basic rule' PE has the following characteristics: (1) a tangible place of business at the disposal of the enterprise, (2) fixed in a geographical and temporal sense (permanence), and (3) the business is carried on through that place.

[1] Tangible Place at the Disposal of the Enterprise

The term 'place of business' covers any facilities or installations used for carrying on the business of the enterprise whether or not they are used exclusively for that purpose. It is immaterial whether those facilities are owned, rented, or situated on the premises of another company. No formal legal right to use a particular place is required for that place to constitute a PE. It is sufficient that the enterprise can access and use the resources.[43]

The CJEU has adopted a similar approach to premises that may constitute an FE for VAT purposes. In *DFDS*, it ruled that premises legally owned by one person can give rise to an FE of another person. The organizational structure of the UK subsidiary was considered an FE of the Danish parent company. In *Welmory*, the Advocate General said that in order to attribute humans or technical resources to a person other than the owner, that person must 'have comparable control over the human and technical resources (...) as if they were his own'.[44] This can be interpreted to mean that the CJEU

41. CJEU, 23 March 2006, Case C-210/04, *Ministero dell'Economia e delle Finanze and Agenzia delle Entrate v. FCE Bank plc.*, ECLI:EU:C:2006:196, paragraph 39.
42. OECD Model Commentary, *supra* n. 40, Article 5, paragraph 5.
43. OECD Model Commentary, *supra* n. 40, Article 5, paragraphs 10 and 11.
44. AG Opinion, *Welmory*, Case C-605/12, ECLI:EU:C:2014:340, pt. 51, *see also*, *supra* n. 32.

follows an economic approach and the actual power to dispose over certain facilities is decisive.

[2] Geographical and Temporal Permanence

The place of business is 'fixed' (i.e., has a certain degree of permanency) if it is not of a purely temporary nature and there is a link between the place of business and a specific geographical point.[45] If the nature of the business activities carried on by an enterprise is such that these activities are often moved between neighboring locations, these neighboring locations may constitute a PE if they form a coherent whole, commercially and geographically.[46] If a particular place of business is used for only very short periods of time but such usage takes place regularly over long periods of time, the place of business should not be considered to be of a purely temporary nature.[47]

An FE must also be characterized by a sufficient degree of permanence: this criterion can be found in all the FE definition in Articles 11(1), 11(2) and 53 of the VAT Implementing Regulation. Permanence refers to the presence of both human and technical resources. Temporary or occasional activities cannot give rise to an FE. In *Berkholz*, the Advocate General interpreted the term 'fixed' as equivalent to 'lasting' or 'continuous' and the opposite of 'temporary' or 'occasional'.[48] In the *ARO Lease* case, the CJEU ruled that an FE requires a 'minimum degree of stability derived from the permanent presence of both the human and technical resources'.[49] By reference to a 'minimum degree of stability', the CJEU confirmed the need for a minimum duration.

The CJEU has never explicitly clarified whether an FE must be fixed at a certain geographical location. Although it rejected an FE consisting of a fleet of cars or gaming machines onboard a ferry, it did not use the argument of lack of geographical coherence to do so. Treating movable objects as FEs would contradict the purpose of the FE concept, which is to allocate taxing rights among the Member States. If an object could move easily from one country to another, the place of supply would change as well. Therefore, geographical coherence, similar to that required for direct tax purposes, should also apply in the area of VAT.

[3] Human and Technical Resources

For a PE to exist, the business of an enterprise must be wholly or partly carried on through the PE. The business of an enterprise is carried on mainly by the entrepreneur or persons who are in a paid-employment relationship with the enterprise (personnel). A PE may exist, however, even if the business of the enterprise is carried on through

45. OECD Model Commentary, *supra* n. 40, Article 5, paragraphs 21 and 28.
46. OECD Model Commentary, *supra* n. 40, Article 5, paragraph 22.
47. OECD Model Commentary, *supra* n. 40, Article 5, paragraph 28.
48. AG Opinion, *Berkholz*, Case C-168/84, ECLI:EU:C:1985:244, pt. 2, *see also, supra* n. 4.
49. *ARO Lease, supra* n. 20, pt. 15.

automatic equipment and the activities of the personnel are restricted to setting up, operating, controlling, and maintaining such equipment.[50]

According to the CJEU case law, stand-alone technical resources cannot not give rise to an FE. The CJEU established the presence of human resources as a necessary condition for an FE in *Berkholz* and kept repeating the *Berkholz* criteria, which were ultimately included in the VAT Implementing Regulation, in all its subsequent judgments. In *RAL (Channel Islands)*, the Advocate General Maduro did not consider the permanent presence of human and technical resources to be a precondition for the constitution of an FE.[51] However, the CJEU did not refer to this statement in its judgment. In *Welmory*, the CJEU had an opportunity to reconsider its position on the necessity of own human resources but unfortunately the Court did not answer this question.

Intangible assets should not give rise to a PE within the meaning of the OECD Model. According to the Commentary on Article 5 of the OECD Model, a website or software does not result in a 'physical presence at that location' and, therefore, cannot constitute a PE.[52] The concept of a 'virtual PE' was discussed in the context of Action 1 of the BEPS project but ultimately rejected.

The CJEU has not had an opportunity to discuss the question whether the required technical resources may entirely consist of intangible assets. However, in *Welmory*, the Court made a reference to software as one of the factors to evaluate in examining the existence of an FE: 'despite its particular character, such a business requires at least a structure that is appropriate in terms especially of human and technical resources, such as appropriate computer equipment, servers and software'.[53] Despite this statement, it seems appropriate to disregard intangible assets (software, website) as criteria relevant for the FE concept given the inherent problems resulting from their nature.[54]

The question of the nature and quantity of human and technical resources that are required for an FE to exist requires a case-by-case analysis of the specific transactions and business models. Some business models require hardly any human resources for their operation. Therefore, it should be possible to establish an FE if only one person is present at the business premises. The fact that no criteria on the resource requirements and their permanence are available in the VAT legislation or non-binding guidance creates a significant grey area and may give rise to disputes. This is

50. OECD Model Commentary, *supra* n. 40, Article 5, paragraph 41.
51. AG Opinion, *RAL (Channel Islands)*, *supra* n. 23, paragraph 41.
52. OECD Model Commentary, *supra* n. 40, Article 5, paragraph 123.
53. *Welmory*, *supra* n. 32, pt. 60.
54. Intangible assets can be easily transferred and quickly reproduced. Although the creation of digital goods may require high fixed costs, they can be subsequently replicated at no cost and transferred without delay to almost everywhere. Thus, it is difficult to define their location. Intangibles are also transmutable meaning that the content of digital products can be changed instantly. For more information on the characteristics of intangible assets, *see* Aleksandra Bal, *Taxing the Consumption of Digital Goods* in *Tax Sovereignty in the BEPS Era*, 143 (Sergio A. Rocha and Allison Christians, eds., Wolters Kluwer, 2017).

exacerbated by the fact that some domestic courts consider the presence of technical resources enough to create an FE.[55]

[B] Construction Site PE

Article 5(3) of the OECD Model contains a special rule for building and construction sites, which constitute a PE only if they lasts more than twelve months. From a VAT perspective, supplies related to immovable property (Article 47 of the VAT Directive) or installation and assembly projects (Article 36 of the VAT Directive) take place in the country where the property is located, or a project carried out. A building site could constitute an FE if it has a sufficient degree of permanence as well as the human and technical resources necessary to perform or receive services. The duration of a building site has no impact on the existence of an FE.

[C] Auxiliary Activities

Article 5(4) of the OECD Model contains an anti-fragmentation rule[56] and lists exceptions to the 'basic rule' PE laid down in Article 5(1), which include the use of a facility for storage, display, purchase and delivery of goods, public relations, invoicing or collection of information. Following the recommendations of BEPS Action 7, these exceptions are limited to activities that have a preparatory or auxiliary nature. What constitutes core functions of a particular enterprise clearly depends on the nature of the business carried on by that enterprise.[57] The reason why preparatory activities are excluded from the PE definition is that they are too remote from the actual generation of profits.

From a VAT perspective, the question of whether auxiliary and preparatory activities can give rise to an FE depends on the type of an FE to be considered as there are different conditions of the existence of a sales and purchase FE.

All the exceptions mentioned in Article 5(4) of the OECD Model can give rise to a sales FE if the facilities have a structure adequate in terms of human and technical resources to supply services in an independent manner. However, if no output transactions are performed from the facilities in question, no sales PE will exist. In the sales FE context, the CJEU dealt with auxiliary activities in *ARO Lease*. The Court observed that the company did not perform any core activities in the other Member

55. The German *Finanzgericht* (Tax Court) Nordrhein-Westfalen (Münster) considered windmills to be FEs even if there was no personnel present to operate them. The lack of human resources was compensated by the importance of technical resources (judgment of 5 Sept. 2013, 5 K 1768/10 U).
56. The anti-fragmentation rule was added following the recommendations of BEPS Action 7. It states that an enterprise cannot segment a cohesive operating business into several small operations in order to argue that each part is engaged in preparatory or auxiliary activities and hence that there is no PE. The EU VAT law does not know a similar anti-fragmentation rule.
57. For instance, for Internet providers who operate servers for the purpose of hosting websites or other applications for their clients, the operation of servers is an essential part of their commercial activity and cannot be considered as preparatory or auxiliary.

State so it could not have an FE there. The mere performance of auxiliary activities would not allow an establishment to perform services on an independent basis as required by the CJEU case law.

Business premises that are used to perform preparatory or auxiliary activities within the meaning of Article 5(4) of the OECD Model could constitute a purchase PE if an adequate structure to receive and use services is present. In such a case, the fact that no output transactions are performed is irrelevant.

In *Planzer Luxembourg*, the CJEU considered the existence of an FE in the context of the VAT refund rules. The CJEU made it clear that the performance of preparatory and auxiliary activities did not give rise to an FE by ruling that 'a fixed installation used by the undertaking only for preparatory or auxiliary activities, such as recruitment of staff or purchase of the technical means needed for carrying out the undertaking's tasks, does not constitute a fixed establishment'.[58]

In the context of the 'intervention FE' used for the purposes of the reverse charge rules, Article 53 of the VAT Implementing Regulation clarifies that resources of an FE that are only used for administrative support tasks such as accounting, invoicing and collection of debt-claims, shall not be regarded as being used for the fulfilment of the supply of goods or services and therefore do not result in the existence of an FE.

[D] Agency PE

Under Article 5(5) of the OECD Model, a PE is deemed to exist, even without a fixed place of business, where a dependent agent is acting on behalf of an enterprise and has, and habitually exercises, an authority to conclude contracts in the name of the enterprise (the agency PE). The recommendations of BEPS Action 7 expanded the scope of the agency PE: it will now exist if a person 'habitually plays the principal role leading to the conclusion of contracts that are routinely concluded without material modification by the enterprise'. Under the recommended new rules, Intermediaries who do not conclude contracts but negotiate them to a large extent or whose intervention appears to be useful in concluding contracts for another group entity could qualify as a PE for direct tax purposes under the new rules.

The EU VAT law does not recognize the concept of an agency FE. A stand-alone person cannot be considered to constitute an FE. According to the CJEU case law and the FE definition in the VAT Implementing Regulation, the presence of technical resources is required.

According to Article 5(6) of the OECD Model, independent agents are excluded from the agency PE rule if they act in their ordinary course of business. The BEPS project has narrowed the scope of the independent agent exception: companies that are closely related, i.e., with more than a 50% shareholding, and which are almost exclusively acting for the parent company cannot be considered to act as independent agents.

58. *Planzer Luxembourg*, *supra* n. 24, pt. 56.

In the *ARO Lease* case, the CJEU did not regard independent agents who merely brought potential clients into contact with the principal without becoming involved in the drawing up or the performance of the contracts as human resources needed to establish an FE. Therefore, due to the increased scope of the independent agent provision, intermediaries may result in a PE for direct tax purposes but there will be no FE for VAT purposes.

[E] Subsidiary PE

Article 5(7) of the OECD Model clarifies that a subsidiary company does not, in itself, constitute a PE of its parent. A subsidiary company can be a PE of its parent, however, if it makes its space or premises available to its parent company and the parent company carries on its own business through that place, or if it habitually exercises the authority to conclude contracts in the name of its parent company and does not act as an independent agent.

In the VAT context, a subsidiary may be regarded as an FE of the parent company if it acts as a mere auxiliary organ of the parent and has the human and technical resources characteristic of an FE. However, the principle established by the CJEU in the *DFDS* case should be regarded as an exception and must be viewed in the context of the specific circumstances of that case. If the CJEU had denied the existence of an FE of DFDS A/S in the United Kingdom, the services in question would escape taxation. Thus, the CJEU was guided by the 'rational result' test when acknowledging the existence of a UK FE of the Danish company. In *Daimler* and *Widex*, the Court emphasized that a 'wholly-owned subsidiary' is 'a taxable legal person on its own account' and in *Welmory*, the Advocate General observed that 'the judgment in DFDS is not ... capable of general application ... it serves the purpose of legal certainty in regard to the person liable for tax if a legal person with its own legal personality cannot at the same time be the fixed establishment of a different legal person'.[59]

§12.05 RELATIONSHIP BETWEEN HEAD OFFICE AND PE

The CJEU commented on the relationship between the head office and its FE in the *FCE Bank* case.[60] The Court was asked to answer the question whether VAT should be levied on services provided by the UK head office to its Italian FE. It ruled that this should be the case only if there is a legal relationship between both parties. Such a relationship may exist if the FE independently performs an economic activity and bears the economic risk arising from its business.[61] In the *FCE Bank* case, the Italian branch

59. AG Opinion, *Welmory*, *supra* n. 34, pt. 36.
60. *FCE Bank*, *supra* n. 41. In its decision, the CJEU used the terms 'fixed establishment' and 'branch' interchangeably.
61. In contrast, for the purposes of corporate tax, profits are attributed to a PE on the basis of a separate entity approach and the arm's length principle. According to the authorized OECD approach, profits to be attributed to a PE are the profits that the PE would have earned at arm's length, in particular in its dealings with other parts of the enterprise, if it were a separate and

did not bear any risk as it had no endowment capital. Therefore, the CJEU concluded that the services in question were not subject to VAT.[62]

In *Skandia America Corporation*, the CJEU considered the taxability of supplies of services between an American head office and a Swedish branch that formed part of a Swedish VAT group.[63] The Swedish branch was of the opinion that the services were not taxable as they were performed within the same legal entity. The CJEU confirmed that since the Swedish branch did not operate independently and did not have any capital of its own, it could not be regarded as a taxable person. However, the CJEU took the view that the supplies of services made by a third party to a member of a VAT group must be considered to have been made not to that member but to the VAT group to which that member belongs.[64] Thus, the US head office supplied services to the Swedish VAT group and the group should account for VAT under the reverse charge mechanism.

The *Skandia* judgment may give rise to double taxation if applied to situations involving countries that use VAT groups and those that have not implemented this concept yet. For example, a French head office supplying services to its Swedish FE that is part of a Swedish VAT group would consider the services as being outside the scope of VAT based on the FCE judgment.[65] The Swedish VAT group would account for VAT under the reverse charge mechanism following the *Skandia* decision. If the group is not entitled to input VAT deduction, double taxation would arise (as VAT would be paid to the Swedish tax administration without a corresponding deduction).[66]

Another related question is the right to deduct input VAT incurred by the FE. In the case *Le Crédit Lyonnais*, concerning a French bank with foreign FEs, the CJEU ruled that the bank was not allowed to take account of its foreign branches' turnover when

independent enterprise engaged in the same or similar activities under the same or similar conditions, taking into account the functions performed, assets used and risks assumed by the enterprise through the permanent establishment and through the other parts of the enterprise. *See* OECD, *2010 Report on the Attribution of Profits to Permanent Establishments* (22 July 2010).

62. This conclusion was not undermined by Article 9(1) of the Sixth Directive (the place-of-supply rule) as that provision concerned the determination of the taxable person in transactions between a branch and third parties and was irrelevant as far as transactions between a company resident in a Member State and its branch established in another Member State.
63. CJEU, 17 Sept. 2014, Case C-7/13, *Skandia America Corp. (USA), filial Sverige v. Skatteverket*, ECLI:EU:C:2014:2225.
64. In the *FCE Bank* case, the head office of the FCE Bank was part of a VAT group in the United Kingdom but the judgment did not mention this when establishing the facts of the case. Christian Amand, *Cross-Border Entities and EU VAT: A Contradictory Concept?* 21(1) Int'l. VAT Monitor 20, 21 (2010).
65. At the time of the writing of this chapter, France has not implemented the concept of VAT group. However, the draft Finance Bill for 2021 includes measures to introduce a VAT group regime. Article 45 of the draft Finance Bill will transpose Article 11 of the EU VAT directive into French law.
66. On 4 November 2019, the Swedish Supreme Court asked the CJEU for a preliminary ruling in *Danske Bank* (C-812/19) on whether services provided by a Danish head office – which is a member of a local VAT group – to an FE in Sweden should be subject to Swedish VAT. In other words, the question is whether the branch should be considered an independent taxable person when receiving a service from the head office because the latter belongs to a VAT group. This is a 'reverse Skandia' scenario. At the time of the writing of this chapter, the CJEU has not rendered its judgment yet.

calculating the portion of deductible VAT but the right of deduction should be determined independently for each jurisdiction. If the head office were permitted to include the turnover of its branches in calculating the deductible proportion, the laws of the FE countries would be seriously jeopardized.[67] The *Le Crédit Lyonnais* judgment can lead to irrecoverable VAT in situations where the FE does not perform any taxable transactions, but the head office does. It also seems to contradict the FCE Bank decision where the FE and head office were considered a single taxable person.

The issue of the input VAT deductibility in FE/head-office relationships became even more complex after the CJEU decision in *Morgan Stanley*.[68] This case concerned the scope of input VAT deduction of a French FE that performed taxed financial services for its French clients and non-taxable internal activities for the UK head office, which carried out both taxable and exempt supplies. The FE fully recovered VAT on the costs it incurred believing that, in line with the *Le Crédit Lyonnais* decision, only the taxed French-sourced turnover was relevant for the calculation of the input VAT deduction. However, the CJEU held that the turnover of the foreign head office also needed to be taken into account and determined the rules for calculating the pro-rata for input VAT incurred on expenses used solely by the head office and those used jointly by the FE and head office. The Court also ruled that the *Le Crédit Lyonnais* judgment did not prevent this conclusion as in that case the relationship between the costs of the head office and the turnover of the FE was not certain.[69]

Based on the above-mentioned judgments, an FE may qualify as independent taxable person if it acts autonomously and bears the economic risks arising from its business. In such a case, supplies of services between the FE and head office may be subject to VAT.[70] However, if the FE joins a VAT group, supplies of services between the FE and head office (remaining outside of the group) will be subject to VAT. The CJEU also ruled that a single taxable person (i.e., the head office and its FEs) should not be considered a single entity for the purposes of VAT deduction: if the FE carries out its own economic activities in its country of establishment, its turnover is subject to the laws of that country and not to the laws of the head office. However, if the FE incurs costs that are used by the foreign head office to perform its transactions, the turnover of the head office needs to be taken into account in calculating the deductible proportion.

67. CJEU, 12 Sep. 2013, Case C-388/11, *Le Crédit Lyonnais v. Ministre du Budget, des Comptes publics et de la Réforme de l'État*, ECLI:EU:C:2013:541, paragraphs 24 and 35.
68. CJEU, 24 Jan. 2019, Case C-165/17, *Morgan Stanley & Co International plc v. Ministre de l'Économie et des Finances*, ECLI:EU:C:2019:58.
69. On 7 October 2019, a French administrative court asked the CJEU for a preliminary ruling in the case *Bank of China* (C-737/19) to determine whether the *Morgan Stanley* judgment also applies if the head office is established outside the European Union. If this question is answered in the affirmative, the referring court would like to know under which conditions banking transactions carried out by the head office established in a third country may be regarded as giving rise to a right to input VAT deduction in the Member State of the FE.
70. In contrast, a supply of goods between a head office and branch is a taxable transaction as the VAT consequences depend on the movement/location of the goods and not on the status of the parties.

§12.06 FE OF THE FUTURE

[A] One FE Concept for VAT Purposes

Despite the VAT Committee's claim that there is only one FE concept, the term 'FE' has a different meaning depending on whether the establishment is supplying or receiving services. The existence of 2 different FE definitions may result in a situation in which one establishment will be considered a purchase FE but not a sales FE. Representative offices performing marketing or sales-enablement functions that have a permanent presence but lack the capability to provide services will not be regarded as sales FEs. However, they are capable of receiving and using services (for example, legal advice) for their own needs. On the other hand, a sales FE will nearly always constitute a purchase FE as well: a structure that has the capacity to supply services to third parties is generally able to receive and use services for its own needs.

As the VAT Directive uses only one FE concept, it remains unclear why the VAT Implementing Regulation contains two such concepts. Implementing provisions should not go beyond the wording of the VAT Directive and supplement it with additional criteria. The aim of any implementing regulations is to bring clarity and uniformity and not to create additional legal uncertainty. Therefore, the author advocates unifying the different FE definitions into one concept.

[B] (No) Need for Human Resources

One of the main differences between the PE and FE is that the latter still requires the presence of human resources. This requirement first appeared in the *Berkholz* judgment in 1985 and kept being repeated by the CJEU ever since. It may seem questionable whether the reliance on the human resources component is still desirable, given the technological developments that allow automated service provision. The FE definition in the proposed but withdrawn 19th Directive made no reference to the availability of personnel: an FE was defined as any fixed installation of a taxable person even if no taxable transaction could be carried out there. On the other hand, if the presence of human resources were not considered necessary, the mere ownership of real estate or equipment (e.g., windmill) that is involved in a business transaction would give rise to an FE. This would significantly increase the number of FEs that taxable persons have in other Member States and would expose these taxable persons to additional VAT obligations. The CJEU will have an opportunity to provide its views on this matter in this future judgment in the *Titanium* case.

[C] FE and Head Office: One of Two Persons?

The relationship between the FE and its head office is another grey area. An FE and its head office may be treated as a single entity when they engage in transactions with one another; however, for the purposes of input VAT deduction, they should be considered as two separate entities. Things get even more complicated when one of them joins a

VAT group as the VAT group regimes vary significantly among Member States. It would be recommendable to consider whether the corporate tax approach (i.e., treating FE as a separate entity) could be used for VAT purposes as well. The EU VAT law often refers to 'economic reality' which would support treating an FE in another country as a separate taxable person.

[D] More Alignment Between PE and FE?

Both the FE and the PE concepts pursue the same objective, which is the allocation of taxing rights to a particular jurisdiction. In line with the destination principle, the FE concept should allocate the taxing rights to the country of consumption, whereas the PE concept allocates taxing rights to the country where profits are actually generated. Having one term for secondary establishments in both direct and indirect tax law would promote consistency and conceptual coherence. However, developing such a unified concept would require significant changes to the EU VAT law and a careful review of the place of supply rules. If the current PE concept were used for indirect tax purposes, double taxation would inevitably arise due to the mismatch and overlap between the PE criteria and the current place of supply rules. The PE concept has a broader scope of application than the FE. This is understandable as Article 5 of the OECD Model covers more types of economic activity carried out by a wide variety of persons. In contrast, the FE concept in the VAT Directive is mainly used in connection with the supply of certain services.

The PE concept is defined in much greater detail than that of the FE. The Commentary on Article 5 of the OECD Model provides a significant amount of interpretative guidance. In contrast, guidance on the FE concept is limited as this concept has been mainly developed by the CJEU case law. The disadvantage of this approach is that only questions that are explicitly asked by the referring courts are clarified. The CJEU is bound by the facts presented in the case in question and cannot develop general theories. As a result, important points remain unanswered until they reach the CJEU in another case. It is very unfortunate that the legislator did not provide more detailed guidance on the FE concept. For the sake of legal certainty and consistency in the interpretation of the EU law, interpretative guidelines would be very much welcome. While it is true that the FE concept is rapidly evolving, it is not clear in what direction it is heading. Given the significant uncertainty surrounding the FE concept, it is too early to talk about aligning FE with PE. All the pieces of the FE puzzle must first align with one another.

CHAPTER 13

How Are Holdings Holding Up with VAT?

*Charlène Herbain & Christopher Thompson**

§13.01 INTRODUCTION

Holding companies are commonly used to structure large enterprises with multiple business units spread throughout the territory of many countries. They are also favoured as investment vehicles in international transitions of private equity houses and as acquisition vehicles for mergers and acquisitions.

At a basic level, a holding company is a company which owns assets. In most cases these assets will consist of equity, i.e., shares of stock in other corporations, but in fact, holding companies can own anything ranging from real estate to patents to movies rights to copyrights to trademarks, etc. Holding companies exist for the purpose of owning assets. As such, holding companies do not engage in operating activities. Therefore, in principle, they merely oversee the assets they own. In practice, however, there are, different types of holding companies. On the one hand, there are pure holding companies, which only hold assets and on the other hand, mixed holding companies which hold assets and perform certain operational activities. Overall, a large scope of activities is performed by holding companies and this has value added tax (VAT) implications.

The VAT regime of the European Union (EU) applicable to holding companies and their activities is not supported by dedicated provisions in Directive 2006/112/EC (the 'VAT Directive') but instead by a series of judgments of the Court of Justice of the EU (CJEU). This situation obviously renders the matter complex to grasp in that it is almost constantly evolving and at times rather unclear.

* The opinions expressed in this chapter are those of the authors only and are not necessarily shared by the institutions with which they are associated.

The case law of the CJEU has developed around the particulars of holding companies and the sophisticated structures that businesses have built around them in attempts to alleviate VAT costs and administrative obligations.

This chapter will look at the VAT concepts applicable to holding companies and the developments of the EU VAT case law in relation with their status of taxable persons and their right to deduct input VAT, which both have evolved significantly over the years.

§13.02 THE QUALIFICATION OF TAXABLE PERSON

Those who qualify as taxable persons in the EU VAT system are charged with the responsibility of collecting VAT. That notion deserves to be defined broadly to ensure the proper collection of VAT.[1]

The determination of the status of taxable person is laid down in Article 9 of the VAT Directive: 'any person who independently carries out in any place any economic activity, whatever the purpose or results of that activity'. This definition revolves around 4 elements: (1) any person, (2) independently (3), in any place and last (4) economic activity. When businesses perform commercial or industrial activities, even just occasionally, then, obviously, they meet the criteria set out in the legal definition and qualify as taxable person. However, despite the broad scope of the definition, the particulars of the activities performed by holding companies render their VAT status difficult to determine. The first 3 elements of the definition of VAT taxable person do not stir much controversy. It is the last one, the economic activity, that is not crystal clear in the context of holding companies. Even though the concept of 'economic activity' is broadly defined by the Directive, the activities in which holding companies engage raise questions as to whether they constitute economic activities under the Directive. The Directive states: 'Any activity of producers, traders or persons supplying services, including mining and agricultural activities and activities of the professions, shall be regarded as "economic activity". The exploitation of tangible or intangible property for the purposes of obtaining income therefrom on a continuing basis shall in particular be regarded as an economic activity.'[2] Based on this wording, a taxable person is one who produces, trades or supplies services. To determine the VAT status of holding companies, their activities need to be examined to assess whether they qualify as economic activities. Based on their activities, different kinds of holding companies can be distinguished. The Commission identified the following 3:

(1) 'type 1: a holding company whose sole task is to receive dividends from its subsidiaries and pay them out to its own shareholders;
(2) type 2: a holding company which also carries on investment activities connected with the holding of shares in other companies;

1. Ad van Doesum et al., *Fundamentals of EU VAT Law*, 2nd ed., 60 (Wolters Kluwer, 2020).
2. Article 9 of Directive 2006/112/EC.

(3) type 3: a holding company which, apart from financial activities, supplies other services to its subsidiaries in return for charging the costs to them.'[3]

In this section, we will consider in turn whether pure holding companies of type 1 and active holding companies of types 2 and 3 constitute taxable persons. After that, we will briefly focus on the specific situation of mixed holding companies, i.e., those which combine an active and passive status in respect of different shareholdings or a passive status with other separate taxable activities.

[A] Pure Holding Companies

Holding companies do not produce or trade. As indicated by their name, they 'hold' assets. The question is therefore whether the holding activity translates into supplying a service for VAT purposes. The VAT Directive defines the supply of services as 'any transaction which does not constitute a supply of goods'.[4] Prima facie, it may appear that holding companies could be involved in supplying services. But although the definition of supply of services is effectively broad, it nonetheless comes with the requirement that the supply is of an economic nature. This is the question that remains to be answered: whether the 'holding service' sufficiently aligns with what the directive considers to be an economic activity.

[1] Holding of Shares

The CJEU performed this analysis in the case *Polysar*[5] which concerned a Dutch company, Polysar Investments Netherlands BV (Polysar BV), whose activities solely consisted in the holding of shares in subsidiary companies.[6] Accordingly, Polysar BV's activities were limited to exercising its rights as shareholder. The issue raised before the CJEU was whether Polysar BV was entitled to recover the VAT incurred on a number of professional expenses. The CJEU addressed this issue by considering first the status of taxable person of Polysar BV.

The CJEU considered that the income yield from that holding (i.e., the dividends received) could not be economic, since it merely resulted from the ownership of said holding. The property acquired would need to be made available to a third party for consideration in order for it to be an economic activity. Holding assets does not equate to exploiting them and to the Court it is the same as being a private investor.

3. CJEU, 20 June 1991, Case C-60/90, *Polysar Investments Netherlands v. Inspecteur der Invoerrechten en Accijnzen*, Report for the Hearing of case, ECR I-311 2 [1993]; ECLI:EU:C:1991:268, point 17.
4. Article 24 of Directive 2006/112/EC.
5. *Polysar, supra* n. 3.
6. *Polysar, supra* n. 3, opinion of Mr Advocate General Van Gerven, paragraph 5.

It is clear from this ruling and the following cases,[7] that the acquisition and holding of shares and the subsequent exercise of shareholder's rights do not constitute economic activities in the view of the CJEU. However, it is questionable whether a holding company which holds equity in its subsidiaries is really acting in the same way as a private investor.[8] The observation is especially relevant in the situation of a controlling holding, which has significant influence over the corporate actions of its subsidiaries, actions and, therewith over year-end profit and the amount of the dividend.[9] When the CJEU considered that the holding of an asset could not be seen as an economic activity, it also based its analysis on the view that the revenue yield from the ownership of the asset did not constitute a consideration for VAT purposes. Yet, the holding of assets, such as shares, so as to receive dividend income, is definitely utilization of assets for profit. The CJEU is of the opinion that dividend distribution by a corporation to its shareholders should be excluded from the scope of VAT.[10] The main argument is that there is no direct link between the receipt of a dividend and any supplies of goods or services provided by the shareholder. The shareholder's dividend is dependent on the types of shares it owns, and on the profit available for distribution. However, the type of shares owned does not impact on the involvement of the shareholder in corporate activities. Because the amount of dividend paid out is determined by both available profits and the types of shares held, there is no relation between dividends and any supply of goods or services made by the shareholder to the enterprise. All that leads to the conclusion that a dividend constitutes a return on the investment made in an undertaking and is not a consideration for a supply. That said, the above is only true to a certain extent since a holding company can have an impact on the year-end profit of the subsidiary even if only by exercising its shareholders' rights. For instance, a shareholder may participate and vote in general meetings, possibly influencing company policy and, at times, where appropriate, be involved in the appointment of the company's directors or officers and/or in apportioning the subsidiary's profits, as well as the receipt of any dividends declared by the subsidiary or the exercise of shareholders' preferential rights or options.[11]

Despite its somewhat flawed basis, this case law is written in stone. Some have read in it an attempt to avoid the risk spotted by the Advocate General of a misplaced extension of the VAT net to people not intended to be included: 'If a different view were

7. In particular CJEU, 20 June 1996, Case C-155/94, *Wellcome Trust v. Commissioners of Customs & Excise*, ECLI:EU:C:1996:243 and CJEU, 29 April 2004, Case C-77/01, *Empresa de Desenvolvimento Mineiro SGPS SA (EDM) v. Fazenda Pública*, ECLI:EU:C:2004:243.
8. For further arguments as to why it is not self-explanatory that the acquisition and holding of financial holdings in other undertakings does not amount to an economic activity, *see* Ad van Doesum et al., *supra* n. 1, 469 et seq.
9. The question was raised in May 2020 by Advocate General Kokott in her conclusions for CJEU, 12 November 2020, Case C-42/19, *Sonaecom SGPS SA v. Autoridade Tributária e Aduaneira*, ECLI:EU:C:2020:378.
10. *See*, e.g., CJEU, 14 November 2000, Case C-142/99, *Floridienne SA and Berginvest SA v. Belgian State*, ECLI:EU:C:2000:623, paragraph 22; CJEU, 27 September 2001, Case C-16/00, *Cibo Participations SA v. Directeur régional des impôts du Nord-Pas-de-Calais*, ECLI:EU:C:2001:495, paragraph 42.
11. *Polysar, supra* n. 3, opinion of Advocate General Van Gerven, paragraph 6.

taken, any holder of shares or securities would have to be regarded as a taxable person ... for example mum and dad shareholders.'[12]

[2] Holding of Debt or Other Securities

A holding company may be used to own real estate, intellectual property rights, stock and other assets. If the holding of shares does not constitute an economic activity from a VAT standpoint, the question arises as to whether the same conclusion must be reached when other types of assets are held?

In the *Harnas and Helm* case, the CJEU was asked whether the acquisition and holding of bonds should also be regarded as non-economic activities. A bond is a debt security in that bondholders have a creditor stake in the company. The holder of the bond is entitled to interest. The Court determined that bondholding, even thought it was remunerated by interest, was not different from shareholding. The court observed that bondholding is a form of investment which does not extend further than straightforward asset management, and that the interest derived from bondholding derives from the mere ownership of the bonds.[13]

Likewise, the Court in the case *EDM*, ruled that the mere acquisition of negotiable securities, such as holdings in investment funds, not carried out in the course of a business of trading in securities, did not amount to exploitation of an asset intended to produce revenue on a continuing basis, as the yield, like the dividend for shares, does not constitute direct consideration for making capital available for the benefit of a third party. The yield cannot be regarded as the effective exchange for services rendered. Consequently, those investments do not constitute supplies of services 'effected for consideration'.[14]

[3] Selling the Assets

A holding company can sell the shares it owns. This is not comparable to a company that holds shares as stock and operates commercially the trade of these shares. Such a company is not a holding company but a business trading in securities, a broker-dealer. A holding company can sell shares, but it cannot be a recurring activity in the sense that the purpose of holding the shares must not be generating a profit from their subsequent sale.

As a pure holding's sole revenue is supposed to be dividends, the question was raised whether the profit potentially realized in the case of a sale could trigger a change in its VAT position.

The *Wellcome Trust* case concerned the sale of numerous shares by a limited-liability trust corporation. The Advocate General observed that the trust corporation

12. Paul Stacey and William Brown, *GST Treatment of Debt & Equity Income Streams: An Australian View*, 14(3) Inter'l VAT Monitor, 295, 297 (2003).
13. CJEU, 6 February 1997, Case C-80/95, *Harnas & Helm v. Staatssecretaris van Financiën*, ECLI:EU:C:1997:56.
14. *EDM, supra* n. 7, paragraphs 57-63.

did not endeavour to make profits through buying and selling shares it had held for several decades and did not engage in risky investments and speculation like a dealer would. Instead, the trust corporation was primarily concerned with managing its assets and ensuring the highest possible dividends.[15] The CJEU concurred that the Trust corporation confined its activities to managing its investment portfolio in the same way as a private investor and considered that since the mere acquisition of financial holdings in other undertakings does not amount to an economic activity for VAT purposes, the same must be true of activities consisting in the sale of such holdings.[16]

The same conclusion was reached in regard of other transactions amounting to a sale. In *EDM,* which was concerned with a range of financial transactions, including the sale of negotiable securities, the CJEU held that the mere sale of negotiable securities could not amount to exploitation of an asset intended to produce revenue on a continuing basis when the only consideration for those transactions consisted in a possible profit on the sale of those securities.[17]

From this settled case law, it is clear that holding companies are non-taxable persons for VAT (type 1) whenever their activities revolve around acquiring assets for long-term investment, holding these assets, receiving dividends or interest, and disposing of the assets in a non-commercial manner. This said, it is nonetheless not a simple matter as holding companies may perform some of the above-mentioned activities in a context that lies within the scope of VAT.

[B] Holdings with Investment Activities

The CJEU has provided guidance in respect of the activities that could constitute economic activities and thus confer the status of taxable person to holding companies. The most usual activities that holding companies perform in addition to the mere holding of assets relate to the management of their assets,[18] but other related activities may constitute economic activities granting them the status of taxable person.[19]

[1] 'Involvement' in the Management of Subsidiaries

A holding company can be involved in the management of its subsidiaries which, as per the CJEU, may constitute an economic activity:

> [the mere acquisition and holding of shares in a company is not to be regarded as an economic activity]. It is otherwise where the holding is accompanied by direct or indirect involvement in the management of the companies in which the holding

15. *Wellcome Trust, supra* n. 7, Advocate General, ECLI:EU:C:1995:426, paragraph 19.
16. *Wellcome Trust, supra* n. 7, paragraphs 33 and 36.
17. *EDM, supra* n. 7, paragraph 58.
18. This could be put in parallel to the type 2 holding companies identified by the Commission in *Polysar, supra* n. 3, Report for the Hearing of the case, paragraph 1.
19. *Ibid.*, this could be put in parallel to the type 3 holding companies identified by the Commission, or such other activities may lead holding companies to become mixed (*see* further).

has been acquired, without prejudice to the rights held by the holding company as shareholder.[20]

If that criterion is not new, until recently, uncertainty existed about whether it introduced a 'special form of economic activity, namely to be involved in the management of subsidiaries'[21] or if it required that services are supplied for consideration. Hints were provided in *Welthgrove,* in which the CJEU disregarded the active guidance provided by a holding company to its subsidiaries because said guidance was rendered for no consideration.[22] In the *EDM* case, where the holding company's principal activity was the management of its shareholdings, the CJEU did not refer to the requirement that the holding is accompanied by direct or indirect involvement to rule on the VAT taxable status of the holding company.[23]

All in all, until recently, the scope of the 'involvement' criterion remained unclear. Is it necessary for the holding company to actually 'manage' the subsidiary? Is it sufficient that the holding company supplies the subsidiary with services for consideration such as administrative, accounting, financial, commercial, information technology and technical services? In practice, the question of involvement was often ignored. National tax authorities and businesses operators focussed directly on the supply of taxable services instead. Some submitted that 'involvement' was not meant to be a special form of economic activity for the determination of the taxable status of holding companies at all, but that the statement of the CJEU in *Polysar* was solely directed towards the Commission's classification of holding companies.[24] They were correct in their assumption. In a recent case, the CJEU elaborated: 'the term "involvement of a holding company in the management of its subsidiary" must, accordingly, be understood as covering all transactions constituting an economic activity, within the meaning of the VAT Directive, performed by the holding company for the benefit of its subsidiary'.[25]

[2] Financing Activities

Intra-group financing often relies on loans to fund subsidiaries. In its case law, the CJEU held that where a holding company makes capital available to its subsidiaries, that activity may be considered an economic activity, conveying the status of taxable person upon the holding company, if certain criteria are met.

20. *Polysar, supra* n. 3, paragraph 14.
21. Oskar Henkow, *Financial Activities in European VAT: A Theoretical and Legal research of the European VAT System and the Actual and Preferred Treatment of Financial Activities* 158 (Kluwer Law International, 2008).
22. CJEU, 12 July 2001, Case C-102/00, *Welthgrove BV v. Staatssecretaris van Financiën,* ECLI: EU:C:2001:416, paragraph 17.
23. *EDM, supra* n. 7.
24. Henkow, *supra* n. 21, 159.
25. CJEU, 5 July 2018, Case C-320/17, *Marle Participations SARL v. Ministre de l'Économie et des Finances,* EU:C:2018:537, paragraph 32. Several authors have raised doubts in respect the guidance provided by this judgement, *see* van Doesum et al., *supra* n. 1, 479; and Leoni de Boer, *VAT and Holding Companies' Involvement: Benefit of the Doubt?* IBFD 15/8/2018, http://link.library.ibfd.org/portal/VAT-and-holding-companies-involvement--benefit/zZqhkGCtv6s/.

First, it shall not be carried out merely on an occasional basis.[26] This condition seems easily fulfilled since even one single interest-bearing loan is aimed at generating a continuing payoff for the lender. Second, the activity shall not be confined to managing an investment portfolio in the same way as a private investor.[27] This distinction seems hard to make, because it can be inferred from the CJEU's own case law that a private investor may act with the view to maximizing his or her return[28] but that is a feature shared by private and commercial investors. To the knowledge of the authors, the Court has not provided positive guidance in that respect. It is consequently a question open for debate. We would argue that a private investor likely will seek to maximize his or her return while managing the risk level, whereas a holding company may take a broader view putting group interests above its own, and for that reason issue lower-interest bearing loans (subject to transfer-pricing considerations of course). However, the CJEU does not follow this approach. On the contrary, the Court has indicated that the financing activity shall consist in exploiting the capital lent out with a view to obtaining income by way of interest therefrom on a continuing basis and be carried out with a business or commercial purpose characterized by, in particular, a concern to maximize returns on capital investment.[29] This leaves open the uncertainty as to the distinction to be made between a financing granted as a private investor and that made as a business. The CJEU also indicated that whether those loans are granted as economic support to the subsidiaries or as placements of treasury surpluses or for other reasons has no impact, as long as the business or commercial purpose is present.[30]

To the contrary, as per the case law where a holding company reinvests dividends received from its subsidiaries in loans to those subsidiaries, this financing does not constitute a taxable activity to the extent the interest collected on the loans must be considered, by extension, the result of ownership of the assets.[31] This distinction seems to come from the applicants in the case *Floridienne* who contended '*that in lending they merely reinvest, in a manner akin to a private investor, sums received by way of dividend*'.[32] This is rather unfathomable. The fact that the return on equity (dividend) and the return on debt (interest) are treated differently from a VAT standpoint is to a certain extent understandable as it relies on the dichotomy between absence and presence of the right to remuneration. The distinction made between the way the debt is funded is on the other hand circumvoluted to say the least. It is common ground that the term 'economic activity' for VAT purposes is objective in character. It is therefore necessary to consider an activity objectively and per se to identify its characteristic features for the purpose of deciding whether its nature is that of an

26. *Floridienne*, *supra* n. 10, paragraph 28.
27. *Floridienne*, *supra* n. 10, paragraph 28.
28. *Wellcome Trust*, *supra* n. 7, paragraph 34.
29. *Floridienne*, *supra* n. 10, paragraph 28 and case law quoted.
30. *EDM*, *supra* n. 7, paragraph 58.
31. *Floridienne*, *supra* n. 10, paragraph 30.
32. *Floridienne*, *supra* n. 10, Opinion of Advocate General, ECLI:EU:C:2000:186, paragraph 32.

economic activity.[33] An interest-bearing loan shall be evaluated as per its own features: does it provide a maximum return to the lender? Is it in line with market terms? To adhere significance to the origin of the investment funds can only arise from a misunderstanding of the VAT system. For example, if that reasoning were applied consistently, all the return received from economic activities that are funded with savings from the salary received by the entrepreneur in his other capacity as employee should be deemed out of the scope of VAT too, and so on.

The justification of applying different treatment to equity and loan financing is based on the legal entitlement of receiving a return. This is a legal distinction; economically these forms of financing are equivalent. While it is uncertain whether dividends will be paid out as this will depend on circumstances normally out of control of the financier, interest payments are based on an enforceable contractual stipulation. Both forms of financing carry a degree of risk, but loans are often secured to protect against borrower default, which is not possible for equity financing. The distinction the Court seems to be making is that loan financing is obviously an activity within the scope of VAT, while that is only conditionally the case with equity financing.

[3] Extension of the Taxable Activity of the Person

Under the extension doctrine, an activity which on itself is uneconomical can be drawn into the scope of VAT because it is subordinate to, or an extension of, an existing taxable economic activity. In the *Régie Dauphinoise* case[34] the Court reasoned that the financial investments by a property manager were the consequence of the monetary advances made by the owners and the lessees of the properties and were economic as they were 'the direct, permanent and necessary extension of the taxable activity of property management companies'.[35]

In the context of a holding company, the extension doctrine has been applied in the *SKF* and *C&D Foods* cases which both concerned a sale of shares by an active holding company.[36]

In the *SKF* case, a holding company actively managed its subsidiaries and supplied various services to them for consideration. SKF subsequently sold some of its holdings, and the CJEU was asked whether such sale was economic from a VAT standpoint. The CJEU held that the sale constituted an economic activity because it was the direct, permanent, and necessary extension of the taxable activity of SKF. The

33. This is an established principle in the case law. *See* notably CJEU, 26 March 1987, Case C-235/85, *Commission of the European Communities v. Kingdom of the Netherlands*, ECLI: EU:C:1987:161, paragraph 8; CJEU, 12 September 2000, Case C-408/97 *Commission of the European Communities v. Kingdom of the Netherlands*, ECLI:EU:C:2000:427, paragraph 25; CJEU, 8 March 2001, Case C-260/98 *Commission of the European Communities v. Hellenic Republic*, ECLI:EU:C:2000:429, paragraph 26.
34. CJEU, 11 July 1996, Case C-306/94, *Régie dauphinoise – Cabinet A. Forest SARL v. Ministre du Budget*, ECLI:EU:C:1996:290, paragraphs 18-22.
35. *Ibid.* paragraph 22.
36. CJEU, 29 October 2009, Case C-29/08, *Skatteverket v. AB SKF*, ECLI:EU:C:2009:665; CJEU, 8 November 2018, Case C-502/17, *C&D Foods Acquisition ApS v. Skatteministerie*, ECLI: EU:C:2018:888.

taxable activity draws the sale of shares into the economic sphere. The CJEU considered that: 'In the present case, the sale of shares by SKF is more than a mere sale of securities because it constitutes an involvement by SKF in the management of the [companies whose shares it was selling].'[37] Such a transaction consequently falls within the scope of VAT.

In the *C&D Foods* case, the CJEU developed the extension doctrine further. The Court took the use of the proceeds of the sale of shares into consideration for determining whether the sale qualified as the direct, permanent, and necessary extension of the taxable economic activity of the holding. Such a sale is economic if the proceeds are allocated 'directly to the taxable economic activity of the parent company in question or to the economic activity carried out by the group of which it is the parent company'.[38]

In *SKF*, the holding qualified already as a taxable person due to its primary management activities, and the sale of shares was a 'direct, permanent and necessary extension' of these taxable activities.

C&D Foods shows that even in the absence of primary taxable activities, a sale of shares may bestow the status of taxable person onto a holding company, if the sale funds the economic activity of group companies and not of the holding company itself. In other words, a pure holding company may undergo a metamorphosis when it sells shares and the proceeds are used to fund the economic activities of group companies. One can only concur with Van Doesum when he notes appositely 'this implies that the economic activities of other persons (i.e., the group members) are determinative of the holding companies' economic activities. Although this matches well with the idea of a group of companies being a unit from an economic perspective, it goes against the idea set out in Polysar that each group member must be evaluated on its own merits, unless a VAT group exists.'[39]

[C] The Janusian Nature of Mixed Holding Companies

Although holding companies were found a long time ago to be either 'pure holding companies' or 'active holding companies', one matter relating to their VAT treatment remained partly unresolved until 2008. The major sticking point was related to the treatment of active holding companies in the context of services supplied from a different country (so-called cross-border services). In the case of a mixed holding company that combined pure holding activities with taxable supplies, an issue arose in regard of the proper application of tax jurisdiction rules in case services were received from a supplier located in another country. Under the rules in place at the time the issue reached the courts, the tax jurisdiction for cross-border services depended on the status of the recipient. If the recipient was a non-taxable person, the services were taxable in the country of the supplier; if the recipient, however, was a taxable person, the services

37. *AB SKF*, *supra* n. 36, paragraph 33.
38. *C&D Foods*, *supra* n. 36, paragraph 38.
39. *See* Van Doesum et al., *supra* n. 1, 491.

were taxable in the country of the recipient.[40] It was therefore necessary to know how to classify a holding company receiving such a service. If the holding company received the service in connection to its non-taxable holding activity, should the service be taxable in the country of the supplier? Or did the economic character of its other activities take precedence and require the service to be taxable in the resident country of the holding company? The debate could be boiled down to whether a holding company had single or dual status for VAT purposes, i.e., taxable person for its commercial activities and non-taxable person in relation to its holding activities. Member States held different positions as to this question, which gave rise to cases of double taxation or non-taxation.

This matter was settled by the CJEU in the *TRR* case.[41] A Swedish foundation (TRR) combined out of scope activities with taxable activities (the former accounted for approximately 5% of its income). TRR purchased consultancy services from Denmark solely for the purpose of its out-of-scope activities and sought a ruling from its national authorities to ascertain whether it was to be treated as a taxable person for tax jurisdiction purposes in the context of its purchase with the result that VAT would be due in Sweden. The Court observed that the applicable place of supply rule in the Directive did not make express reference to the purpose for which the taxable person was using the supply, nor did it require that the taxable person be acting as such. Therefore, TRR was a taxable person for the purpose of its purchase even if the service acquired was for its non-taxable activities. This ruling was not limited to foundations but was applicable to mixed holding companies too. In 2010 this court ruling was codified in the Directive via the implementation of Article 43(1) which provides that 'a taxable person who also carries out activities or transactions that are not considered to be taxable supplies [...] shall be regarded as a taxable person in respect of all services rendered to him'.

Since the TRR case and its codification by Article 43(1) it is clear that the activities of a mixed holding are not to be split for the purpose of determining tax jurisdiction in case of cross-border services. On paper, this provides a fair amount of simplification but in practice, it has induced certain businesses (i.e., conglomerates) to divide their activities over different holding companies to avoid incurring a VAT liability on services supplied from non-EU suppliers, thereby eliminating any simplification gain.

The conclusion of this section is that the determination of the VAT status of holding companies is a difficult task requiring a deep and up to date knowledge of the CJEU case law and a thorough examination of the facts at hand. Moreover, once the

40. We refer to the tax jurisdiction rules in force before 1 January 2010 and in particular the rule provided by Article 56(1) of the VAT Directive which stated: ' The place of supply of the following services to customers established outside the Community, or to taxable persons established in the Community but not in the same country as the supplier, shall be the place where the customer has established his business or has a fixed establishment for which the service is supplied, or, in the absence of such a place, the place where he has his permanent address or usually resides ... .'

41. CJEU, 6 November 2008, Case C-291/07, *Kollektivavtalsstiftelsen TRR Trygghetsrådet v. Skatteverke*, ECLI:EU:C:2008:609.

VAT status is determined, the next step is to establish the extent to which input tax can be deducted.

§13.03 VAT DEDUCTION RIGHT OF HOLDING COMPANIES

Just like for determining the taxable status of holding companies, the VAT Directive is of limited assistance for determining their VAT recovery rights.

At a basic level, one must therefore refer to the general VAT deduction rules as interpreted in the CJEU's case law. Recently, the CJEU summarized these rules based on its earlier case law:[42]

- The existence of a direct and immediate link between a particular input transaction and a particular output transaction or transactions giving rise to the right to deduct is necessary, in principle, before the taxable person is entitled to deduct input VAT and in order to determine the extent of such entitlement. The right to deduct VAT charged on the acquisition of input goods or services presupposes that the expenditure incurred in acquiring those goods or services was a component of the cost.
- A taxable person, however, also has a right to deduct even where there is no direct and immediate link between a particular input transaction and an output transaction or transactions giving rise to the right to deduct where the costs of the transactions in question are part of his general costs and are, as such, components of the price of the goods or services which he supplies. Such costs do have a direct and immediate link with the taxable person's economic activity as a whole.
- In the context of the direct-link test, one should consider all the circumstances surrounding the transactions concerned and take account only of the transactions that are objectively linked to the taxable person's taxable activity.
- Where goods or services acquired by a taxable person are used for purposes of transactions that are exempt or do not come within the scope of VAT, no output tax can be collected or input tax deducted. In both cases, the direct and immediate link between the input expenditure incurred and the economic activities subsequently carried out by the taxable is severed.

It would be a mistake to assume that determining the extent of the right to input VAT credits for holdings is a straightforward affair. Once one drills down to the treatment applicable to various types of concrete input costs, it quickly becomes apparent that there is no 'one size fits all' approach possible, a point aptly illustrated by

42. CJEU, 16 September 2020, Case C-528/19, *Mitteldeutsche Hartstein-Industrie AG v. Finanzamt Y*, ECLI:EU:C:2020:712, paragraphs 26-28 and 36.

the fact that the guidance issued by the Irish Revenue Commissioners in this respect spans a full 18 pages (admittedly including a series of citations).[43]

The complexity is further exacerbated by the long period (over 30 years) during which the CJEU has issued its guidance in this respect. As a result, it is sometimes difficult to determine to what extent older decisions are still valid in light of the more recent evolution of the Court's (general) case law.

In this section, we aim to establish, based on CJEU case law, for which type of expenditure input tax credit is, or is not, available for each of the different types of holding companies identified afore. In addition, we will where appropriate also draw a link with more recent case law covering other situations faced by holding companies or setting out principles of broader relevance.

[A] Pure Holding Companies

Pursuant to Article 168 of the VAT Directive and the CJEU's general case law with respect to input VAT recovery as summarized above, only taxable persons have a right to recover input VAT.

Since we established in §13.02[A] that pure holding companies constitute non-taxable persons for VAT purposes, we can immediately conclude that this type of holding does not have any right to VAT recovery.

This situation generates VAT leakage for the holdings concerned where they receive supplies of goods (including importations) and intra-EU supplies of services, which generally attract EU VAT. However, it is clearly justified under the CJEU's interpretation of the proper working of the EU VAT system.

It is worth noting that there is normally no need for non-taxable persons to be identified for VAT purposes as services received from abroad are taxed in the resident country of the supplier. If these services are received from outside the EU, they may be zero rated in the origin country as exported services and, thus do not carry any VAT. This puts EU suppliers of services to EU passive holding companies at a competitive disadvantage compared with non-EU suppliers. Holding companies may be presented with a planning opportunity by sourcing services from outside the EU. However, given the difficulty of determining the status of a holding, they would do well to monitor their activities on a continuous basis (e.g., financing/lending transactions), lest a small change should lead them to unwittingly acquire taxable status at some point and become liable for significant amounts of back tax.

43. Irish Revenue Commissioners, *VAT Deductibility for Holding Companies, Tax and Duty Manual*, available on https://www.revenue.ie/en/tax-professionals/tdm/value-added-tax/part03-taxable-transactions-goods-ica-services/Financial-Services/vat-deductibility-for-holding-companies.pdf (last viewed on 30 November 2020).

[B] Active Holding Companies

Insofar as an active holding company qualifies as a taxable person, it can have a right of deduction, depending on the input transaction involved and on the activities to which it is linked.

There are a whole range of situations to consider in this respect, and we will examine these per type of expenditure (which inevitably means that we will not encounter the various situations in exactly the same order as the CJEU and will occasionally need to cross-reference case law which we will encounter further on in our article).

[1] Acquisition of Shares

In the *Cibo Participations* case,[44] the CJEU was asked to rule on the VAT recovery available to a holding company in respect of VAT incurred in connection with the acquisition of shares in three subsidiaries, to which it subsequently provided administrative, financial, commercial, and technical services for consideration.

With reference to its general case law in terms of VAT recovery (*see* above), the Court found that:

> [T]here is no direct and immediate link between the various services purchased by a holding company in connection with its acquisition of a shareholding in a subsidiary and any output transaction or transactions in respect of which VAT is deductible. The amount of VAT paid by the holding company on the expenditure incurred for those services does not directly burden the various cost components of its output transactions in respect of which VAT is deductible. That expenditure does not form part of the costs of the output transactions which use the services.
>
> On the other hand, the costs of those services are part of the taxable person's general costs and are, as such, cost components of an undertaking's products. Such services therefore do, in principle, have a direct and immediate link with the taxable person's business as a whole.[45]

Pursuant to Article 173 of the VAT Directive, in the case of goods or services used by a taxable person both for transactions in respect of which VAT is deductible and for transactions in respect of which VAT is not deductible, only such proportion of the VAT as is attributable to the former transactions shall be deductible. Specifically, with regard to recovery of such input VAT under the deductible proportion method, the Court therefore recalled its findings in *Floridienne and Berginvest* (*see* further §13.03[B][2]), according to which, since the receipt of dividends does not fall within the scope of VAT, dividends paid by subsidiaries to their holding company which is a taxable person in respect of other activities, and which supplies management services to those subsidiaries must be excluded from the denominator of the fraction.[46]

44. *Cibo Participations*, *supra* n. 10.
45. *Cibo Participations*, *supra* n. 10, paragraphs 32 and 33.
46. *Cibo Participations*, *supra* n. 10, paragraph 44.

This ruling left open the possibility of active holding companies achieving a deductible proportion of 100%, even if the input VAT they incurred significantly exceeds the output VAT chargeable on their taxable management and/or other activities. A number of decisions make this questionable, though, and we will discuss these in §13.03[C] dealing with mixed holdings. Indeed, if the input VAT significantly exceeds the output VAT chargeable on the economic activity of a holding, this might suggest that the holding also has non-economic activity to which part of the inputs are connected, in which case part of the input VAT should not be deductible.

In the *Larentia and Minerva* case, the CJEU reconfirmed that to the extent holding companies involve themselves in the management of the subsidiaries (for consideration) and carry out an economic activity on that basis, the related input VAT will be fully deductible as a general cost. Of course, if the economic activity of the holding includes any exempt transactions, a deductible proportion would again need to be determined.[47]

In the *Marle* case, the CJEU had to opine about a holding company which incurred expenditure (amongst other things) for the purpose of acquiring subsidiaries, to which the only services provided thereafter were the taxable letting of buildings. This allowed the Court to clarify that such expenditure should be regarded as incurred in connection with economic activity in the form of involvement in the management of the subsidiaries and hence belonging to the holding's general expenditure, such that the related input VAT must, in principle, be capable of being deducted in full.[48]

Crucially, the Court went on to indicate that no account could be taken of the turnover achieved by that company from the letting services supplied to those subsidiaries and the income that it draws from its stake in the capital of those subsidiaries, in order to prevent that right from being invoked for fraudulent or abusive ends. Indeed, the right to deduct VAT must be guaranteed, without it being subjected to a criterion relating, *inter alia*, to the result of the economic activity of the taxable person.[49]

It is perhaps remarkable that the Court arrived at this far going reaching without requesting that the Advocate General deliver an opinion. However, it should be noted that Advocate General Kokott had addressed the same issue in some detail in the *Ryanair* case, which was pending before the CJEU at around the same time,[50] and which we will consider next.

Advocate General Kokott considered the position of the European Commission that input tax deduction should be permitted in connection with the acquisition of

47. CJEU, 16 July 2015, Joined cases C-108/14 and C-109/14, *Beteiligungsgesellschaft Larentia and Minerva mbH & Co. KG v. Finanzamt Nordenham and Finanzamt Hamburg-Mitte v. Marenave Schiffahrts AG*, ECLI:EU:C:2015:496, paragraphs 25-28.
48. *Marle Participations*, *supra* n. 25, paragraph 36.
49. *Marle Participations*, *supra* n. 25, paragraphs 40 and 44.
50. As a matter of principle, the opinion of an Advocate General is sought in every case tried by the Court of Justice, unless the latter decides that there is no new point of law. This happens in roughly 30% of the cases each year. Advocates General present their views on the cases, advising the Court of Justice on how it should decide on them. The Court is not bound by the opinions of the Advocates General, although they are commonly regarded as influential.

shares only if proportionate to the output transactions generated by management services. She rebuffed the Commission's proposal, on the following grounds:

> A simple comparison of the values of the turnover from management services and from dividends neglects the fact that the holding of shares does not give rise to recurrent costs. Furthermore, the input tax surplus described above also exists only in the taxation period in which the acquisition of shares of a company occurs. If the management services are supplied for remuneration over a number of years, the situation is different. In addition, the problems of calculation are compounded in a case like this one, where the acquisition is merely planned. In these circumstances, a rough estimate at best could be made of potential dividend income.
>
> Moreover, not every holding of shares in the case of a taxable person can necessarily lead to a non-economic activity alongside the operating business, as this is not compatible with the principle that VAT should be neutral. On the basis of the Commission's approach, any taxable person who also holds shares could claim only proportionate input tax deduction in respect of its general management costs even if it is clear that those costs are incurred in connection with its economic activity, as the holding of a share as such generates at most low costs and the amount of dividend income likewise does not depend on the other general costs.[51]

At the level of tax authorities, the Irish Revenue for example has confirmed its position that where the level of management fees charged by a holding company to a subsidiary is less than input costs incurred in relation to the acquisition of the shares, this does not impact the general principles of deductibility.[52]

The *Ryanair* case concerned costs of consultancy services and other services incurred by Ryanair in connection with the planned acquisition of Aer Lingus to which it intended to provide taxable management services after the takeover. However, for competition law reasons, Ryanair was unable to acquire the full share capital of its target and was ultimately also not able to supply the latter with any taxable services.

With reference to its case law relating to preparatory activities, the Court found that Ryanair acted as a taxable person at the time it incurred the relevant expenditure and that the related input VAT could be fully deducted as a general cost, provided that the exclusive reason for that expenditure was to be found in the intended economic activity consisting in the provision of management services subject to VAT.[53]

Interestingly, the Court did not follow the alternative take on things suggested by Advocate General Kokott to sidestep the issue of disproportion between inputs incurred and management services provided by a holding: 'The expenditure made in connection with acquiring the shares of Aer Lingus undoubtedly constitutes components of the cost of the (intended) output transactions from the airline business following the takeover of Aer Lingus. These costs will also have to be factored into airfares somehow, if Ryanair is to operate profitably. Gaining control of Aer Lingus would have been the condition for improving overall business performance and thus for generating the intended output transactions with the parent company and the subsidiary. Such

51. CJEU, 17 October 2018, Case C-249/17, *Ryanair Ltd v. The Revenue Commissioners*, ECLI: EU:C:2018:834, opinion of Advocate General Kokott, paragraphs 29-31.
52. Irish Revenue Commissioners, *supra* n. 43, section 4.2.1.
53. *Ryanair*, *supra* n. 51, paragraph 31.

influence on the management of a competitor is possible only if the acquiring company holds the majority of the company's shares.'[54]

In other words, the Court granted the deduction right based on the intention of Ryanair to carry on an economic activity consisting in providing management services subject to VAT to Aer Lingus. This approach is in line with the Court's long standing case law that the preparatory acts must themselves be treated as constituting economic activity for deduction purposes.[55] Advocate General Kokott's opinion on the other hand also accepted input VAT recovery based on the intention of Ryanair to perform taxable activities but proposed as an alternative basis the link between the acquisition of Aer Lingus and the development of Ryanair's own taxable activity (i.e., to consider the takeover as a direct, permanent and necessary extension of its pre-existing taxable activity consisting in the provision of air passenger transport services). Whilst the Court and the Advocate General agreed on the end result in this particular case, we see more prospect in the Advocate General's approach for separating artificial and legitimate VAT recovery by active holding companies in general.

[2] Ongoing Costs of a Holding Company

Once a holding company has acquired one or several subsidiaries, it will typically continue to incur costs in connection with these participations. To the extent one is dealing with an active holding company, these costs will generally be at least partly deductible, along the lines of the case law already cited with respect to share purchases.

In the *Floridienne* case, the CJEU was asked to provide guidance on the calculation of the deductible proportion of an active holding company. The Court found that the denominator of the deductible proportion should exclude both dividends received by a holding company and, *to the extent the relevant loan transactions do not constitute an economic activity of the holding company*, the interest paid by the subsidiaries on these loans (emphasis added).[56]

This position may seem a little surprising considering Article 174 of the VAT Directive, which excludes financial transactions from the calculation of the deductible proportion where these transactions are *incidental* to the taxable person's other activities.

The explanation is arguably that in the *Floridienne* case, the Court had already concluded that the loans granted by the holding were in any event not the direct, permanent and necessary extension of general management services, but either constituted a separate economic activity, which could then hardly be considered as incidental, or did not constitute an economic activity at all, which was for the referring court to determine.

54. *Ryanair*, *supra* n. 51, opinion of Advocate General Kokott, paragraph 41.
55. CJEU, 14 February 1985, Case C-268/83, *D.A. Rompelman and E.A. Rompelman-Van Deelen v. Minister van Financiën*, ECLI:EU:C:1985:74.
56. *Floridienne*, *supra* n. 10, paragraph 32.

The Court returned to the concept of incidental financial transactions in the *EDM* case, clarifying that the respective amount of income generated by the main activity and by financial transactions was not a relevant criterion for classifying the latter as incidental. Instead, it put forward as a criterion, whether the transactions involved only very limited use of assets or services subject to VAT.[57]

In conclusion, the input tax deduction related to general costs of a holding is not affected by incidental financial transactions performed by an active holding. It is important to remember, however, that strictly speaking a deductible proportion only applies to mixed use costs. In other words, input costs relating specifically to exempt financing transactions should remain non-deductible. Several Member States enforce this rule strictly, where the deductible proportion has been determined with the exclusion of the turnover from such financing transactions on the basis that they are incidental.[58]

In the *Kretztechnik* case, the CJEU held that costs for the admission of a company to a stock exchange constituted part of its general costs and could therefore be either fully deducted - provided that the company's economic activity comprised of only taxed transactions or deducted in accordance with its deductible proportion otherwise.[59]

The *Sonaecom* case concerned a bond loan, initially intended to provide subsidiaries with the necessary means to make investments, but ultimately made available to the holding's parent company in the form of a loan.[60]

The case gave the Court the opportunity to (re)clarify that an actual use of goods and services takes precedence over the initial intention. To decide otherwise would give certain taxable persons a competitive advantage over other taxable persons having carried out similar transactions, based solely on a difference in their initial intention.[61] Further, the Court agreed with the Advocate General that there was a direct and immediate link between the purchased input services and the loan to the parent company. Accordingly, the holding was not entitled to deduct the relevant input VAT as intermediate loan services are exempt.[62]

[3] Sale of Shares

In the *BLP* case, the CJEU considered whether an active holding company, which sold off 95% of the shares in a subsidiary and used the proceeds to pay off its debts, could deduct the corresponding input tax. The Court noted that in the case at hand, the services acquired were used for an exempt transaction and accordingly held that the

57. *EDM, supra* n. 7, paragraphs 77 and 78.
58. *See*, e.g., the *VAT commentary* of the Belgian VAT authorities, Chapter 11 *Deductions*, section 15.3.c, available at https://eservices.minfin.fgov.be/myminfin-web/pages/fisconet#!/ (last viewed on 30 November 2020).
59. CJEU, 26 May 2005, Case C-465/03, *Kretztechnik AG v. Finanzamt Linz* ECLI:EU:C:2005:320.
60. *Sonaecom, supra* n. 9.
61. *Sonaecom, supra* n. 9, paragraphs 59 and 65.
62. *Sonaecom, supra* n. 9, paragraphs 68 and 71.

holding was not entitled to deduct the input VAT paid.[63] Indeed, to give the right to deduct, expenditures must have a direct and immediate link with taxable transactions, and the ultimate aim pursued by the taxable person is irrelevant in this respect.[64]

The *SKF* case, which we have already discussed in §13.02[B][3], also concerned share sales.[65] As discussed above, the Court found that the transaction fell within the scope of VAT. Accordingly, it was an exempt transaction.

Regarding the deductibility of the related input VAT, the Court recalled earlier case law, stating that 'there is a right to deduct when the input transaction subject to VAT has a direct and immediate link with one or more output transactions giving rise to the right to deduct. If that is not the case, it is necessary to examine whether the costs incurred to acquire the input goods or services are part of the general costs linked to the taxable person's overall economic activity.'

It then went on to affirm that 'in either case, whether there is a direct and immediate link will depend on whether the cost of the input services is incorporated either in the cost of particular output transactions or in the cost of goods or services supplied by the taxable person as part of his economic activities'.[66]

The Court pointed out that it had no jurisdiction to assess or characterize the factual circumstances in the framework of preliminary ruling requests; and it is for the referring court to apply the direct and immediate-link test. Nevertheless, 'in order to give a useful answer', it recalled that in several cases it had allowed the deduction of input VAT in respect of costs relating to a disposal of shares which was outside the scope of VAT on the ground that those costs constituted general costs of the taxable person.

It is fair to say that applying the distinction between expenditure incorporated in the cost of particular output transactions and expenditure incorporated in the general costs of a taxable person is not an easy task in practice.

As pointed out by Advocate General Kokott, for example, the share price of public listed companies is usually determined based on the market price and not through negotiation between parties. This led her to suggest that 'the Court's formulation should be construed as meaning that the expenditure must have an immediate negative impact on the profit from a specific transaction involving a holding or shares and not solely on the overall profit of the company'.

Some practical support can also be found in the guidelines of the Irish Revenue, according to which advice in relation to the appropriateness and consequences of selling shares, valuing and marketing the shares and transferring ownership of the shares are all examples of costs having a direct and immediate link with a share sale and which are hence non-deductible.[67]

---

63. CJEU, 6 April 1995, Case C-4/94, *BLP Group plc v. Commissioners of Customs and Excise*, ECLI:EU:C:1995:107.
64. *BLP Group*, *supra* n. 63, paragraph 19.
65. *Skatteverket v. AB SKF*, *supra* n. 36.
66. *Skatteverket v. AB SKF*, *supra* n. 36, paragraph 60.
67. Irish Revenue, *supra* n. 43, section 6.2.

At this juncture, it is perhaps appropriate to point out that at a more general level, the CJEU has recently ruled that the fact that a taxable person decided to include input costs not in the price of its taxable transactions, but solely in the price of its exempt transactions, has no effect whatsoever on the finding that these costs have a direct and immediate link with its activities as a whole. [68] As regards share sales by active holding companies, the Court reaffirmed its approach in *X BV*.[69]

The final case we will consider in this respect is *C&D Foods*, a case we discussed afore in §13.02[B][3].[70]

In that case, the objective of the share sale of a sub-subsidiary was to settle debts owed by the active holding to a creditor bank. For that reason, the transaction was not made in the direct and exclusive context of the taxable activity of the holding; nor did the transaction constitute the direct, permanent and necessary extension of its taxable economic activity. Accordingly, the share sale was outside the scope of VAT and the related input VAT not deductible.[71]

The Court specifically remarked that the sale could not be related to the termination of the management and IT services provided to the sub-subsidiary by the active holding, because the creditor bank in any case intended to sell the shares. It also pointed out that the fact the intended sale was not completed had no relevance, since if it had been completed no right to deduct would have arisen.[72]

It is interesting to note that off the back of the *SKF* and *C&D Foods* decisions, the Irish Revenue considers that even an active holding company may incur certain costs unrelated to its economic activity, in which case the related input VAT is not deductible. The examples given are share issues or sales, where the proceeds are not used for the company's taxable activity, and restructurings that seek to create shareholder value but do not relate to the company's taxable activity.[73]

[C] Mixed Holding Companies

A mixed holding company qualifies as a taxable person because it combines both activities within the scope of VAT and activities outside the scope of VAT.

Accordingly, it may have a right to recover input VAT depending on whether the expenditure is connected to its economic activities, its non-economic activities or even both. We will discuss this, using the same distinction in categories of expenditure as used before in relation to active holding companies, highlighting relevant differences.

68. CJEU, 18 October 2018, Case C-153/17, *Commissioners for Her Majesty's Revenue and Customs v. Volkswagen Financial Services* (UK) Ltd., ECLI:EU:C:2018:845.
69. CJEU, 30 May 2013, Case C-651/11, *Staatssecretaris van Financiën v. X BV*, ECLI:EU:C:2013:346.
70. *C&D Foods Acquisition ApS*, *supra* n. 36.
71. *C&D Foods Acquisition ApS*, *supra* n. 36, paragraph 39.
72. *C&D Foods Acquisition ApS*, *supra* n. 36, paragraphs 40-41.
73. Irish Revenue Commissioners, *supra* n. 43, section 5.2.

[1] Acquisition of Shares

In *Larentia and Minerva*, which we already discussed in §13.03[B][1], the CJEU specified that before determining the deductible proportion of input VAT,[74] an apportionment of the input VAT would need to be made between the economic and non-economic activities of the holdings. [75]

For the determination of such an apportionment, the Member States have the right to apply an investment formula, a transaction formula, or any other appropriate formula. Indeed, Article 173 of the VAT Directive does not cover this situation, and the Court did not want to substitute itself either for the EU legislature or for the national authorities to determine an appropriate method in this respect.[76] This position was also confirmed in the *Marle* case.[77]

18 months after *Larentia and Minerva*, the CJEU ruled in the case of *MVM*, a holding company which had incurred input VAT (amongst other things) for the acquisition of shareholdings in subsidiaries in whose management it was involved without receiving any consideration.[78]

The main point of interest of this decision from a VAT recovery perspective is the Court's warning that although alongside its passive holding activity MVM also had a taxable economic activity, being the leasing of power plants and fibre optic networks, it appeared difficult to imagine that business-management services relating to the acquisition of shareholdings, may have a direct and immediate link with that leasing activity (although this was a matter for the referring court to determine).[79]

Indirectly, the Court here indicates that the business-management services were used for purposes outside the scope of VAT, thus severing their link with the company's economic activities. Otherwise, if a mixed holding performs management services for no consideration, the related expenditure could only be incorporated in its general costs.

Finally, in the *Sonaecom* case, the Court in a sense combined the principles of the *Larentia and Minerva* and *Ryanair* decisions. The Court ruled that the input VAT related to an aborted acquisition would be deductible on a proportional basis if, and to the extent, that Sonaecom provided taxed management services to only some of its subsidiaries.[80]

74. In case the acquisition cost of the shares would relate both to subsidiaries in whose management the holding was involves and subsidiaries in whose management the holding was not involved.
75. *Larentia and Miverva, supra* n. 47, paragraph 29. *See* also *Securenta, infra* n. 80 and *Portugal Telecom, infra* n. 81.
76. *Larentia and Miverva, supra* n. 47, paragraphs 30-32.
77. *Marle Participations, supra* n. 25.
78. CJEU, 12 January 2017, Case C-28/16, *MVM Magyar Villamos Mǘvek Zrt. v. Nemzeti Adó- és Vámhivatal Fellebbviteli Igazgatóság*, ECLI:EU:C:2017:7.
79. *MVM, supra* n. 77, paragraph 40.
80. *Sonaecom, supra* n. 9, paragraph 47.

[2] *Ongoing Costs of a Holding Company*

It was in the *Securenta* case that the CJEU first clarified that the deductible proportion applies only to inputs connected with a taxable person's activities falling within the scope of VAT. As a prior step, input VAT needs to be apportioned between the economic activities and non-economic activities of a holding, with input VAT related to the latter being non-deductible.[81] The case related to costs incurred by an active holding company for raising capital for its various economic and non-economic activities.

The Court reconfirmed the same position in *Portugal Telecom*, a case in which an active holding company re-invoiced services acquired from consultants to its subsidiaries. The Portuguese tax authorities had sought to impose a pro rata method of deduction because they considered that the re-invoiced services were indissociable from the management of the shareholdings, which was apparently an out-of-scope activity.[82]

As a passing remark, we note that whilst conceptually this two-step approach makes a lot of sense, from a practical perspective application would be easier if the distinction between exempt transactions and out-of-scope transactions were clearer for certain types of activities (e.g., financing, as already discussed).

[3] *Sale of Shares*

Finally, as regards the disposal of shares, mixed holdings are treated the same as active holdings.

§13.04 OVERALL CONCLUSION

As is the case for many areas of VAT, in the absence of any specific rules in the VAT Directive, the regime applicable to holding companies has been shaped by the ever-evolving case law of the CJEU. With the economic stakes high, the debates have been particularly fierce and intricate, delighting academics, but often leaving taxable persons with the feeling that the determination of their VAT position is something of a lottery.

In this chapter, we looked through a number of selected CJEU cases at the VAT status of holding companies and at their right to deduct input VAT. We highlighted that determining the VAT status of different types of holding companies is not straightforward; neither is the position of holding companies clear in respect of VAT recovery.

81. CJEU, 13 March 2008, Case C-437/06, *Securenta Göttinger Immobilienanlagen und Vermögensmanagement AG v. Finanzamt Göttingen*, ECLI:EU:C:2008:166.
82. CJEU, 6 September 2012, Case C-496/11, *Portugal Telecom SGPS SA v. Fazenda Pública*, ECLI:EU:C:2012:557.

The allocation of input costs to output activities remains a real headache when a shareholding activity is present. Although there is logic in allowing holding companies, under circumstances, to recover all their input VAT when they charge limited fees to subsidiaries, this latitude will likely also encourage tax planning and controversy. It does not take a psychic to predict that questions will continue to be submitted to CJEU in the coming years.

CHAPTER 14
VAT Refunds in Developing Countries

*Marius van Oordt**

§14.01 INTRODUCTION

One reason for the widespread adoption of Value Added Tax (VAT)[1] is the theoretical strengths of its collection mechanism.[2] This mechanism allows for the tax to be on consumption, but not only collected at the point of sale to consumers. The tax is collected wherever value is added in the supply chain. Collecting a consumption tax in this manner provides various benefits. One benefit is that the identity of a buyer is irrelevant; firms always charge the tax. Another benefit is that tax is collected by and from larger businesses. Larger businesses tend to keep proper accounting records and appoint specialized tax accountants.

This same collection mechanism also has a major weakness; it requires refunds by governments. Refunds arise where the VAT invoiced by suppliers (input VAT) exceeds the VAT charged by sellers (output VAT). To some extent, governments can reduce refund claims through tax design; adopt a single rate VAT with no domestic supplies charged at another rate. But most VAT refund claims are unavoidable.

Refunds occur often. European countries, where the data is perhaps most reliable and refunds are generally paid, refund about 35 cents for every Euro of VAT collected.[3] Admittedly, the highly integrated European economies, together with VAT designs that

* I wish to thank the International Tax and Investment Center (ITIC) for funding and assistance in conducting this study. Further, Sansia Blackmore, Sijbren Cnossen, Jim Robertson, members of the United Nations Sub-committee on Extractive Industries Taxation in Developing Countries, and multiple firms for informing this paper by sharing their views and experiences.

1. The VAT is also referred to as the Goods and Services Tax (GST) in some jurisdictions.
2. Liam P. Ebrill, Michael Keen, Jean-Paul Bodin, & Victoria P. Summers. *The Modern VAT*. (International Monetary Fund, 2001); Kathryn James, *The Rise of the Value-Added Tax* (Cambridge University Press, 2015).
3. Graham Harrison & Russell Krelove, *VAT Refunds: A Review of Country Experience*, IMF Working Paper WP/05/218 (2005).

result in avoidable refunds contribute to this high statistic. Nevertheless, a contrasting picture emerges in developing countries. Here, governments generally do not refund VAT promptly and sometimes not at all. Other poor tax practices then surround these failures.

One such poor practice is to reduce refund claims by requiring firms to set off VAT credits against future output VAT, rather than paying the refund. This practice is popular among Latin America countries, for instance, Argentina, Colombia, and Mexico, but also in other countries such as Kenya, Ethiopia, Tanzania, and Turkey.[4] By not allowing VAT refund claims, businesses incur inflation and cash flow-related costs.

Another poor practice – common in African countries but also, for instance, in Kazakhstan and Indonesia – is to conduct in-depth audits of all taxes of firms that submit a VAT refund claim. Administrations conduct these audits in an attempt to offset the VAT refund with other tax assessments or to delay refunds. Firms are often audited multiple times in a single year. Some firms forego the refund, rather than undergo the audit for an (unlikely) VAT refund. Other disincentives to claim VAT refunds or tactics to delay refunds, such as excessive compliance requirements, monthly VAT verifications, or limits on the bank account that can receive refunds are also frequently instituted. The result is that in African countries, it takes on average 28 hours to comply with a refund claim - 89 hours in Egypt – and 38.6 weeks to obtain a refund – 109.9 weeks in Tanzania.[5] These failures to pay VAT refunds result in a tax on investment;[6] a tax few developing countries can afford.

There are, however, potential solutions to the VAT refund challenges faced by developing countries. The most extreme solution is to follow Zambia and try to get rid of the VAT altogether. Is this the way to go for developing countries?

This question is considered in §14.02. Section 14.03 discusses policy options to VAT refunds. Administrative options to VAT refunds follow in §14.04. Section 14.05 considers why it is in the interest of developing countries to promptly pay VAT refunds and §14.06 concludes.

§14.02 IS THE VAT THE RIGHT CHOICE FOR DEVELOPING COUNTRIES?

One way to deal with VAT refunds is to replace the VAT with an alternative broad-based consumption tax. The most likely alternative to the VAT is the Retail Sales

4. Regarding Tanzania, there are some exceptions to this general rule as provided in section 82 of Value Added Tax Act No. 10 of 2014 that allow refunds under certain circumstances.
5. *Paying Taxes, Global and Regional Findings: Africa,* World Bank Group and PwC (20 November 2018), available at https://www.doingbusiness.org/en/reports/thematic-reports/paying-taxes-2019.
6. This can be understood with reference to the accounting identity of the VAT. The base of the VAT is $W + (R - I)$, where W is wages, R is normal plus above-normal returns and I is investment. Firms, therefore, receive a full deduction of the tax paid on investment under the VAT (the only difference to an income tax where I is spread over a number of years). Where firms do not have any outputs, the base of the VAT is reduced to I, meaning that failures to pay VAT refunds result in a tax on, and only on investment.

Tax (RST).[7] The turnover tax is generally not recommended due to its cascading and distortionary nature, together with the ease of evading the tax.[8] It is, therefore, of interest to compare the VAT and RST to assess which may generally be preferred in a developing country context.

To compare the VAT and RST, it makes little sense to compare how they are applied in practice. The same forces that turned a VAT into a poor tax will be present if a country adopts the RST; we do not have a counterfactual to assist the comparison. Both taxes do, however, have certain features that are unavoidable in practice. I, therefore, consider these unavoidable features and ask how these two taxes *can feasibly be* applied to obtain the best economic theoretical tax and the implication hereof. I assume that the only aim of a broad-based consumption tax is to obtain revenues in the most economically efficient manner possible, as for instance argued by Cnossen.[9] [10]

The VAT and the RST differ in their collection mechanisms; the invoice-credit method versus exemption/suspension certificates. The purpose of both mechanisms is to suspend the tax in production. Under the VAT, producers deduct the VAT paid on their costs. The same result (zero) is possible by showing exemption certificates (pay nothing, deduct nothing). This is the mechanism of the RST. In theory, both mechanisms only tax consumption. Yet, these mechanisms result in dissimilarities in the feasible base, compliance, administration, and ease of evasion of these two taxes.

Considering the base, the mechanism of the VAT has one primary benefit. Under the VAT, suppliers always charge the tax and hereafter, purchasers account for whether, or to what extent, they will use a good or service in production. Under the RST, whether tax is charged is decided at the point of sale with the purchaser showing an exemption certificate or not. Exemption certificates, in contrast with the invoice-credit method of the VAT, do not allow the consumption part of dual-use goods and services (part production, part consumption) to be taxed. Lack of information by the supplier does not make this workable; the seller does not know how the buyer will actually use the dual-use good or service. Yet, the extent that the tax is charged needs to be decided at the point of sale in a manner that administrations can audit.

Some goods and many services are dual use in nature and cannot feasibly be included in the RST's base; governments collect no tax on these goods and services. In contrast, the base of the VAT can feasibly include all value-added in the formal economy, besides the value-added by small businesses that choose not to register, financial intermediation services and residential accommodation services if there is

7. VAT here refers to the invoice-credit method VAT, rather than the subtraction method VAT. For a detailed discussion comparing the VAT and RST, *see* Sijbren Cnossen, *The Technical Superiority of VAT over RST*, 4 Austl. Tax F. 419 (1987).
8. Richard Bird & Pierre-Pascal Gendron, *The VAT in Developing and Transitional Countries* (Cambridge University Press, 2007).
9. Sijbren Cnossen, *Modernizing VATs in Africa* (Oxford University Press, 2019).
10. This assumption involves that social objectives are better addressed by other taxes and expenditure policy.

real growth in the residence's value.[11] Non-registered businesses, financial intermediation services and residential accommodation are input taxed under the VAT, meaning governments still collect some tax. The feasible base of the VAT is, therefore, broader than the RST.

Moving on to compliance considerations, the VAT and RST have different compliance costs for three reasons. The first reason is that the number of registered firms differ under the two taxes. Retailers and non-retail producers whose supplies exceed the compulsory registration threshold must register and account for VAT, but only retailers must register under the RST. Therefore, more firms will be registered under the VAT than the RST.

The second reason is that the size of the average registered firm will differ. Theoretically, a VAT should have a high compulsory registration threshold that excludes most small businesses, unless they choose to voluntary register.[12] For some of these small businesses, the compliance costs that they would incur if registered may be greater than the benefits of being registered for VAT.[13] Allowing voluntary registration is a benefit of the VATs collection mechanism. If a small business is not registered, governments still collect tax on the value-added up to the small business because of the non-deductibility of input VAT. Further, many small businesses that supply predominantly to producers will voluntarily register.[14] In contrast, the collection mechanism of the RST cannot feasibly allow for voluntary registration. Because RST is only levied on sales to consumers, no small business would voluntarily register because there is no incentive to do so. Small businesses, therefore, must register under an RST if they make sales at retail. The average firm size will, therefore, be greater under the VAT than the RST.

The third reason is that the compliance requirements are different for the two taxes. The collection and issuing of invoices and other documentation that meet the necessary legal requirements to deduct input VAT create legal uncertainty and compliance costs under the VAT.[15] Input tax allocations, required where a purchase relates to an exempt supply (for instance financial services or residential accommodation) and a taxable supply, also raise compliance costs. These costs are not present under the RST. Thus, the VAT is generally regarded as a more complex tax to understand and comply with.[16]

---

11. New Zealand's Goods and Services Tax is an example of such a VAT.
12. Michael Keen & Jack Mintz, *The Optimal Threshold for a Value-Added Tax,* 88 J. Public Econ. 559, 576 (2004).
13. Evidence shows that small firms opt to not register to avoid the VAT's compliance costs, rather than the actual tax burden. *See* Jarkko Harju, Tuomas Matikka & Timo Rauhanen, *Compliance Costs vs. Tax Incentives: Why do Entrepreneurs Respond to Size-Based Regulations?* 173 J. Public Econ. 139, 164 (2019).
14. If an unregistered small business supplies primarily to producers, they will have a competitive disadvantage. This disadvantage relates to the non-deductible VAT on costs that the business passes forward to its clients. There are also reputational benefits if registered for VAT. These benefits will have to be balanced with the compliance costs of being registered for VAT.
15. Marius van Oordt & Richard Krever, *Legal Uncertainty in the South African VAT,* in *Tax Simplification: An African Perspective* 160 (Chris Evans, Riël Franzsen & Elizabeth Stack eds., Pretoria University Law Press, 2019).
16. Bird and Gendron, *supra* n. 8.

From these differences two results are likely. First, the total compliance cost to the economy for the VAT is likely to be greater than the RST. This is so since more firms are required to be registered and the VAT has compliance requirements not present under the RST. Second, the compliance cost distribution of the RST is likely to be more regressive than that of the VAT. This is so since the RST is on average charged on smaller firms who have lower accounting capacity, which increases compliance costs. Further, these smaller firms cannot avoid these compliance costs by opting not to register for the tax as they can under the VAT. The distribution of the compliance costs of the VAT, therefore, benefits small businesses. The distribution of compliance costs of the RST disadvantages small businesses and benefits larger (non-retail) businesses who need not register for the tax.

On administration, both the VAT and RST present their own challenges. Two unique challenges under the VAT are (1) only registering bona fide firms and (2) paying legitimate refunds due. Only registering bona fide firms is important because the deductibility of input VAT opens the door for fraud. VAT refunds, as discussed, are the primary drawback of the VAT's collection mechanism. The RST avoids most administrative challenges by exempting dual-use goods and services. Including these would present administrative challenges that cannot feasibly be overcome. However, one administration challenge that cannot be avoided under the RST is preventing fraud from the use of falsified exemption certificates or the use of legitimate exemption certificates on the purchase of consumer goods and services.

Considering ease of evasion, although both taxes are prone to evasion at the retail stage, the VAT has three advantages over the RST. First, as the average firm size is greater under the VAT, better accounting records to be audited and fewer cash transactions – an easy way to evade a consumption tax – may be present under the VAT. Second, under the VAT, the full tax cannot be as easily evaded. As the tax is partly collected before the retail stage, a VAT refund claim is needed to evade the full tax. Third, before the retail stage, the audit trail left by VAT invoices and opposing incentives of suppliers and purchasers limit the amount of evasion.[17]

Next, I apply the above-discussed policy, compliance, administrative and evasion considerations to the general context of developing countries.

It is well recognized that developing countries need more tax revenues to support sustainable economic development.[18] Because a high-revenue income tax is often administratively out of reach, consumption taxes tend to be the main source of tax revenues.[19] For revenue, the base of the chosen consumption tax should be as broad as possible; a broad base should be an easier sell for politicians than a high rate. Although

17. Dina Pomeranz, *No Taxation Without Information: Deterrence and Self-Enforcement in the Value Added Tax*, 105 Am. Econ. Rev. 2539, 2569 (2015).
18. Major international organizations, including the IMF, OECD, UN, and World Bank have concluded that countries require additional tax revenues to meet the Sustainable Development Goals, *see OECD: Countries Must Strengthen Tax Systems to Meet Sustainable Development Goals* (14 February 2018), available at https://www.oecd.org/tax/countries-must-strengthen-tax-systems-to-meet-sustainable-development-goals.htm.
19. Richard Bird & Eric M. Zolt, *The Limited Role of the Personal Income Tax in Developing Countries*, 16 J. Asian Econ. 928, 946 (2005).

base-broadening may reduce welfare,[20] there are neutrality, including in international trade, and efficiency benefits in broadening the base of consumption taxes. Therefore, limited to revenue and policy considerations, the broader base and greater revenue feasible under a VAT makes it a clear choice for developing countries. As shown by Keen and Lockwood,[21] VAT adoption has generally led to a modest increase in tax revenues, although demand-side factors may be more important to the revenue consequences of the VAT.[22]

The feasible revenue of the VAT may explain, for instance, why India, a developing country, opted for the VAT over its existing sales tax in 2005, but the United States, a developed country, is retaining its RST. The Indian Government Whitepaper on VAT[23] states greater tax revenues as a positive outcome of implementing the VAT.[24] Conversely, some in the United States see the revenue potential of the VAT as a fundamental flaw that, if adopted, will facilitate the expansion of the federal government.[25][26]

Developing countries are also characterized by low taxpayer education and many small businesses with little accounting capacity.[27] Considering taxpayer education, the ease of understanding the RST is preferable to the VAT. However, when considering the number and accounting capacity of small businesses, a VAT that excludes many of these small businesses is preferable to an RST. Whether the VAT or the RST is preferable based on compliance considerations likely depends on the importance of small businesses' production and growth in an economy. In the least developed countries, small businesses are essential to the economy. Here, the VAT appears to be the preferred choice. In developed economies, larger businesses may drive the economy and the total compliance cost to the economy increases in importance. Abstaining from equity considerations, the compliance costs of the RST may then be preferred.

The low administrative capacity of many developing countries provides challenges for any tax.[28] Collecting taxes from larger businesses and before the retail stage under the VAT, and the audit trail left by tax invoices has administrative benefits, especially when administrative resources are limited. But paying legitimate VAT

20. John Piggott & John Whalley, *VAT Base Broadening, Self Supply, and the Informal Sector*, 91 Am. Econ. Rev. 1084, 1094 (2001).
21. Michael Keen & Ben Lockwood, *The Value Added Tax: Its Causes and Consequences*, 92 J. Dev. Econ. 138, 151 (2010).
22. Dongwon Lee, Dongil Kim & Thomas E. Borcherding, *Tax Structure and Government Spending: Does the Value-Added Tax Increase the Size of Government?* 66 Nat'l. Tax J. 541, 570 (2013).
23. *A White Paper on State-Level Value Added Tax* (17 January 2005), available at https://www.finmin.nic.in/sites/default/files/whitepapervat.pdf.
24. Other outcomes mentioned are less tax cascading by freeing inputs from tax, replacement of various smaller taxes, and improved tax compliance.
25. Michael Keen and Ben Lockwood, *Is the VAT a Money Machine?* 59 Nat'l. Tax J. 905, 928 (2006).
26. A further reason may be that a federal consumption tax will intrude on the tax domain of the States with an RST.
27. Lewis I. Baurer, *Tax Administrations and Small and Medium Enterprises (SMEs) in Developing Countries* (The World Bank, 2005).
28. Deborah Brautigam, Odd-Helge Fjeldstad, and Mick Moore, *Taxation and State-Building in Developing Countries: Capacity and Consent* (Cambridge University Press, 2008).

refunds and limiting VAT refund fraud has proven to be a significant challenge.[29] One could expect that limiting exemption certificate fraud could be equally challenging. Although the VAT may be more difficult to evade, limited to administrative concerns neither tax appears clearly preferable.

In conclusion, for developing countries, the VAT appears to be the consumption tax of choice. The policy and revenue benefits of the VAT's potential base, together with the importance of small businesses in many developing countries, gives it the edge. The solution to VAT refund challenges is, therefore, not to abolish the VAT. Solutions should rather be found within the VAT.

§14.03 POLICY OPTIONS FOR VAT REFUNDS[30]

There are three reasons for VAT refunds. The first reason is exports. Under the destination principle, which is applied in nearly all VATs, the VAT charged in an origin country is, at least in theory, removed when goods or services are exported.[31] This is done by zero-rating exports, meaning exporters of goods or services are entitled to deduct input VAT but do not receive output VAT on their exports. So, exporters may require VAT refunds.

Since the destination principle is essential to trade neutrality, not much can be done to reduce VAT refund claims because of exports. Some countries do, however, exacerbate refund challenges due to exports by zero-rating indirect exports. Kenya, for instance, zero-rates the supply of coffee and tea to auction centres to be exported. Ethiopia has a similar scheme for farmers. Without such a zero-rate, exporters – who tend to be fewer than the supplying farmers and keep better accounting records – will be in a refund position. With the zero-rate on the indirect exports, the refund claim is shifted from these exporters to a large number of farmers who tend to keep poor accounting records. Therefore, to keep the number of VAT refund claims to a minimum and ease administration of these refunds, zero-rated indirect export should generally be avoided.

The second reason for refunds is domestic zero-rated supplies. Especially Sub-Saharan African countries often implement domestic zero-rates for equity reasons on goods such as foodstuffs and medicines. As a result, the suppliers of these goods will often be in a refund position. In countries that struggle to pay VAT refunds promptly, opting to ideally standard rate or alternatively exempt domestic supplies that are zero-rated may be a preferred policy.

The third reason for refunds is due to capital acquisitions and the timing differences between these investments and sufficient supplies to offset input VAT. This is, for instance, typical in the extractive industries where capital is primarily imported

29. Harrison and Krelove, *supra* n. 3.
30. Note that the discussion in this section does not pertain to an ideal VAT as was required in the previous section. Rather, the VAT considered reflects those often found in developing countries; governments institute non-essential exemptions and zero rates, refunds are often not paid promptly or at all, and poor administrative practices surround refund claims.
31. VAT exemptions as well as the registration threshold result that in practice some VAT is collected on exports in the country of origin.

into a developing country during the contract negotiation, exploration, and development phases of a project. It can, however, take more than a decade for the production phase of a project to start and supplies be made. So, input VAT builds up through investment, but firms cannot set off this VAT through supplies (no supplies are made) and, so, refunds remain. This situation will be similar for capital costs of other firms. Although the delay between investment and sufficient supplies will generally be less for these firms, their economic viability is still negatively impacted by delayed refunds.

In less developed economies, capital goods are often not domestically produced and, therefore, imported. [32] That capital is imported provides policy opportunities less feasible for domestic supplies. The reason is that imported goods are subject to customs verification, and tax administrations charge VAT, not a supplier. A customs receipt, already in the tax administrations' possession, reflects the flow of goods. That the customs receipt is in the tax administrations' possession provides an administrative benefit compared to domestic supplies, where firms account for the flow of goods in their books.

There are some policy options frequently applied in developing countries that do not take advantage of this administrative benefit. Imported goods are often statutorily exempt (or equivalently zero-rated) or exempt through certificates; customs do not charge VAT so that no VAT deduction applies and there is no VAT to be refunded.

Removing the VAT on imported goods in this manner result in several negative consequences. First, exempting inputs removes the incentive for firms to register to claim input VAT. The exemption, therefore, contributes to the size of the informal sector and firms may prefer to remain informal and supply without charging VAT, substantively reducing VAT revenues. Second, consumers can also purchase some exempt goods. Countries will often exempt imported consumer goods such as printers and computer parts and this reduces VAT revenues. Third, exempting imported goods results in import bias.[33] New domestic investors, therefore, cannot competitively

32. Services are also often imported. However, allowing the recipient of imported services to reverse charge VAT alleviates refunds. Reverse charge involves the recipient of the service charging VAT on itself and immediately deducting the amount of VAT it would have been entitled to if a third party charged VAT on the service. For business to consumer supplies, the reverse charge provides difficulties. The difficulties arise because consumers do not complete VAT returns; they should remit the VAT on imported services through another channel. Many consumers are unaware of this obligation and avoidance is easy. A partial solution is to require large international suppliers of services to register for and charge VAT in all countries they supply, even though their services would otherwise be imported. South Africa adopted this solution with success in the view of tax officials.

33. The import bias is there whether the domestic supply of the type of good imported is exempt from VAT or not. If the domestic supply of the good is exempt (or the supplier is not registered) domestic suppliers cannot deduct input VAT, their marginal costs increase by the VAT rate, and they will include a part or all of this irrecoverable VAT in prices. The price of imported goods, which does not include irrecoverable VAT, will, all else equal, be lower. It seems unlikely that domestic suppliers will be able to reduce their marginal costs to a competitive level through wage reductions, especially in the presence of labour unions. This only seems plausible if the VAT rate is low, which it is not in most developing countries. If the domestic supply of the type of good imported is not exempt but made subject to VAT, firms will be in a refund position for domestic purchases, but not for imports. Hence, firms may prefer imported goods to avoid the need to seek (often unlikely or delayed) refunds and the costs associated with refund claims.

produce goods of which the importation is exempt from VAT. Last, not charging VAT on imported goods create opportunities for abuse and may result in demands for other supplies to become exempt, known as exemption creep. All these unintended consequences from exempting imported goods may contribute to significant revenue losses.

In practice, the exemption of imported goods and the use of exemption certificates will also often come with excessive compliance requirements. For instance, some countries require that firms issue a VAT invoice, that the revenue authority stamp this invoice to show that the exemption applies and that firms then issue a new invoice that shows that the supply is exempt. Other countries require that all documentary evidence be in hard copy. Such requirements create unnecessary costs in the compliance and administration of the VAT. Thus, not charging VAT on imported goods, whether domestic supplies of the good imported are standard-rated, exempt, or zero-rated,[34] is generally not recommended to address refund challenges.[35]

A recommendable option, at least in the short run, is to take advantage of the administrative benefit (i.e., customs verification) of imported goods and allow selected, likely large firms to defer VAT on imported goods. Deferral involves customs not charging VAT when releasing the goods, but that firms account for VAT in their next tax return with a copy of the return sent to customs. When accounting for VAT, firms declare the VAT that customs would have charged and deduct the amount of VAT as if charged by customs. For firms who do not make exempt supplies, this deduction is equal to the VAT declared; the net VAT is zero and no refund claim emerges.

However, this option is not perfect: VAT deferral also results in import bias and incentivizes vertical integration. Since firms require refunds on domestic purchases (or domestic prices are higher due to an alternative policy implemented) but not on imported goods, they will, all else equal, prefer imported goods to avoid VAT refunds and its associated costs. They may also vertically integrate with domestic suppliers to avoid the VAT refund.[36] The only way to remove these unwanted incentives is to pay refunds immediately. But if tax administrations can do this, the reason for implementing the deferral disappears.

We have seen that, besides compliance and administration costs, all alternative policy options to full taxation of imported goods lead to import bias. One may argue that where the imported good is not locally produced, import bias should not be a concern (as for many capital goods in less developed economies). But this argument is only valid in the short-term. In the long-term, import bias hampers the development of

34. Import bias will also be present if the imported goods are exempt from VAT and the domestic supply of the type of good imported is zero-rated. This policy only shifts the VAT refund problem from the importing firm to its many suppliers. A greater number of refund claims to an already resource-limited administration can be expected. Besides the additional compliance costs for the suppliers to the importing firm, if governments do not pay refunds promptly to these suppliers, cash flow and cost inflation considerations will drive prices upwards. If governments do not pay refunds at all, the consequences are the same as when the domestic supply of the type of good imported is exempt. Further, domestic zero rates create an opportunity for misclassification fraud: classifying standard-rated supplies as zero-rated supplies.
35. Interested readers can refer to Chapter 9 of United Nations, *Handbook on Selected Issues for Taxation of the Extractive Industries by Developing Countries* (United Nations, 2017).
36. This is especially relevant for the use of sub-contractors in the extractive industries.

the local economy and the establishment of businesses that domestically produce goods previously imported. Even if the imported goods are not locally produced at current, this does not mean that, without policies that favour large international competitors, they cannot be locally produced in the future.

In the interest of sustainable development, alternative policy options to full taxation of imported goods should, therefore, be short-term solutions. If adopted, a compensatory trade tax may be in order. Yet, even with this combination and avoiding domestic zero-rates, only part of the refund problem is addressed as refund claims due to exports will persist. Therefore, in the long-term, VAT refunds pose an administrative challenge that, ideally, should be met with administrative solutions.

§14.04 ADMINISTRATIVE OPTIONS FOR VAT REFUNDS

The VAT is complex to understand. The difficulty lies in understanding its collection mechanism and the revenue consequences thereof. We should view the collection mechanism as a tool to postpone the tax to the point of consumption. With this view, it is clear that the consumer pays the full amount of VAT. This should not be confused with when governments receive the VAT. Governments receive the VAT from firms when they file their returns, not necessarily when consumers pay the full amount of VAT.[37] Note the reference to 'VAT' as opposed to 'VAT revenue'. From the perspective of administrators, *VAT revenue should only be viewed as the amount of tax received that remains after all VAT refunds have been paid;* the amount of tax paid by the consumer.

Unfortunately, governments often misunderstand the VAT and consider VAT received from firms as VAT revenue and, consequently, VAT refunds as an expenditure item. This results in refunds competing with other expenditure items and potentially insufficient funds to pay refunds when they become due. Unrealistic tax revenue targets on tax administrations may exacerbate this. In my experience, this distorted view of the VAT, together with the attitudes and practices that accompany this view and pressures because of revenue targets, lies at the core of the refund challenges experienced by developing countries.

If governments understand VAT revenues as a net rather than a gross concept, the first and largest practical administrative challenge is to secure enough funds to pay VAT refunds. One option to overcome this challenge is to implement a VAT refund forecasting and monitoring system. The idea of this system is to estimate the percentage of VAT received that a government would have to refund. Tax administrators then set aside this percentage when receiving VAT from firms and it is paid into a separate account. Administrators then pay VAT refunds from this VAT refunds account. The remaining tax is VAT revenues. The recently introduced VAT of Angola, for instance, contains such a system.[38] Although the draft law provided that 50% of daily VAT

37. A single good can take longer than an accounting period to move through the supply chain to the point of sale to a consumer. Further, consumers often purchase on credit, but accounting is generally done on the invoice basis (as opposed to the payment basis).
38. *See* sections 64 and 65 of the Value Added Tax Code 17/19.

collections would be transferred to a refund account, this amount was reduced to 30% in the promulgated law.

Besides a forecasting and monitoring system, there are some other options to fund VAT refunds. One option is to allow firms to offset VAT refunds against liabilities arising from other taxes, for instance, the income tax. Offsetting VAT refunds require a taxpayer debt management system that shows the total tax liability for all taxes. A debt management system may, however, be administratively challenging for many developing countries. This will especially be the case where firms do not file their taxes electronically. But, if administrators limit the practice to the largest firms, it may be feasible to allow the offset of VAT refunds.

Another option is to issue tradable bonds equal to the amount of VAT refunds due. Although investors may prefer a tradable bond to not receiving a VAT refund, this approach risks that governments force investors into accepting tradable bonds. Governments may also become reliant on issuing tradable bonds as VAT refunds. Thus, a forecasting and monitoring system and offsetting of VAT refunds against other taxes by the largest firms are the recommended options for most developing countries.

The second administrative challenge is identifying VAT fraud. In practice, this challenge is overshadowed by the first challenge, which is not having funds to pay refunds. Nevertheless, even with sufficient funds, administrators may delay refunds because of difficulties in identifying fraud. Inefficiencies in tax administration and increased compliance costs then surround these difficulties.

Popular VAT fraud schemes take advantage of open borders between countries, as in the European Union. Since most developing countries do not have open borders, these schemes are less pronounced. Most VAT fraud in developing countries likely relates to false claims of input credits and refunds using forged or falsified invoices and export documentation.[39] This type of fraud takes advantage of the difficulty for tax administrations to cross-check purchasers' and suppliers' invoices and determine whether goods are exported.[40]

To combat VAT fraud, it is important for administrations to identify and focus on high-risk firms by relying on risk-indicating factors. Administrations can incorporate these risk-indicating factors into a green-red channel VAT refund system. It is required to include all firms in this system to use administrative resources efficiently and focus where the risks of fraud are greatest in the entire economy.

A firm in the green channel presents a low risk of refund fraud. Administrations should pay VAT refunds to these firms before auditing them, or without an audit. These firms may also be required to submit less documentary evidence for a refund claim. Red-channel firms present a high risk of refund fraud. Administrations should delay VAT refunds to these firms until an audit is completed. If not, some of these firms may disappear after receiving the refund. Firms should also be able to move from the red

39. *See* Michael Keen & Stephen Smith, *VAT Fraud and Evasion: What Do We Know and What Can Be Done?* 59 Natl. Tax J 861, 887 (2006), for an extensive discussion on VAT fraud.

40. It is likely that the major source of evasion relates to supplies made to consumers without issuing an invoice. Generally, these supplies are made for cash making the evasion difficult to uncover.

channel to the green channel by being tax compliant and vice versa for non-compliance. Being able to change channels provides incentives for firms to start or continue to comply with taxes. The system should also adjust refunds not paid within the statutory period with the rate of interest. Ideally, interest should accrue even if audits are being conducted. Not paying interest incentivizes governments to delay VAT refunds and increases the costs of delayed refunds for firms.

Indicative risk factors for such a VAT refund system may be (1) the date of registration of the claiming firm since certain firms register only to claim fraudulent refunds, (2) the size of the claiming firm since large firms tend to hold substantial reputational value, (3) the business structure of the claiming firm since private companies, for instance, protect their owners and can disappear with relative ease, (4) the sector that the claiming firm operates in since small, common, valuable goods are more suspect to export refund fraud, and (5) the history of tax compliance of the claiming firm.

Refund fraud can also be common for domestically supplied zero-rated goods and services; the supplier misclassifies the supply as a zero-rated good and claims the refund without charging VAT. The preferred option to combat this type of fraud is not administrative but through policy. The zero-rated good or service can be standard-rated, and its aim met through expenditure policies. Overwhelmingly, expenditure policy can better meet equity and merit good (e.g., education, newspapers) aims than VAT policy.[41]

§14.05 WHY SHOULD DEVELOPING COUNTRIES PAY VAT REFUNDS?

In the introduction to this chapter, I mentioned that the non-payment of VAT refunds results in a tax on investment. The policy and administration options discussed should provide attainable solutions for developing countries to not tax investment in this manner. But, without the willingness to improve their refund practice, the options discussed may fall on deaf ears. In this section, I discuss why it is in developing countries' best interest to pay refunds promptly. As we will see, developing countries most likely lose more by not paying refunds promptly, than they gain by regarding VAT refunds as VAT revenues.

The first observation is that the prompt payment of refunds stimulates investment. When foreign investors conduct their financial forecasts of a project, the VAT refund practices of a host country is an important consideration and compared to other countries' practices. This is done since delayed refunds impact investors' cash flows and can result in a direct cost where interest on refunds is not paid or paid at a rate lower than inflation. The non-payment of refunds is always a direct cost to investors. These costs are large enough for investors to forego an investment opportunity, as with a $1.5 billion copper mine expansion project in Zambia.[42] If not foregone, investment

41. Ian Crawford, Michael Keen & Stephen Smith, *Value Added Tax and Excises*, in *Dimensions of Tax Design: The Mirrlees Review* 275 (James Mirrlees et al., eds., Oxford University Press 2010); Marius van Oordt, Zero *Rating Versus Cash Transfers under the VAT* 39 Fisc. Stud. 489 (2018).
42. This statement is based on personal discussions with the relevant firm.

is often reduced or delayed. This means less employment in the local economy and a decrease in governments' fiscal take.

However, the issue extends beyond these monetary considerations. In making investment decisions, investors look for predictability and need to be confident in their investment decisions. Delayed or non-payment of VAT refunds signals unpredictability for investors and creates greater uncertainty in their investment decisions. This uncertainty and accompanying reputational harm to a country can decrease investment over the long run, negatively affecting the local economy and hampering economic development. Thus, the delayed or non-payment of VAT refunds by a government may decrease the welfare of its own citizens.

The second observation is that as outstanding VAT refunds grow, tax administrations tend to target large VAT refund claims for in-depth pre-refund audits (often of all taxes), mostly ignoring other high-risk firms. Tax administrations also create other barriers to refund claims, such as excessive documentation. These inefficiencies in tax administration and tax compliance often result in firms not filing a refund claim, rather absorbing the direct cost to avoid the compliance costs associated with the refund claim and potential audit.[43] A portion of this additional cost will be shifted to the firm's factors of production and another portion to consumers. The cost of this behaviour, therefore, falls on the local economy through less employment, higher consumer prices and dampened economic growth.

The third observation is that failing to pay VAT refunds promptly creates a disincentive for small businesses to enter the formal economy through VAT registration or remain voluntary registered. In general, businesses that supply to producers would benefit from voluntary VAT registration; the VAT provides an incentive to formalize for such suppliers. But delayed or non-payment of VAT refunds may overshadow this benefit, leaving these businesses out of the VAT net. Additional informal supply chains can then develop in the economy.[44] This means lower VAT revenues and a larger informal economy, which is difficult to tax under alternative taxes.

The final observation is that delayed, or the non-payment of, VAT refunds starts a cycle that can decrease future tax revenues, further limiting countries' ability to pay outstanding VAT refunds. First, the tax base shrinks because of decreased investment. Second, revenue from the still existing tax base decrease due to less voluntary registration and a larger informal economy. Third, tax administrators adopt less efficient practices by unduly targeting audits on firms who submitted a VAT refund claim, potentially increasing tax fraud. In combination, total tax revenues diminish. The credit rating of the country also becomes compromised. Countries may then be tempted to hike tax rates but, doing so, may exacerbate the cycle through lower investment and a larger informal sector. Countries can, therefore, find themselves in a refund trap: failure to pay refunds makes it more difficult to pay future refunds. The trap may well end in intentions to abolishment of the VAT, replacing it with a less suitable and lower revenue-generating tax.

43. This statement is based on personal discussions with foreign investing firms.
44. Aureo De Paula & Jose A. Scheinkman, *Value-Added Taxes, Chain Effects, and Informality*, 2 Am. Econ. J. Macroecon. 195, 221 (2010).

The short-term revenue benefits of not paying refunds promptly are overshadowed by its long-run costs.

§14.06 CONCLUSION

Unpaid and delayed VAT refunds are epidemic in developing countries. But it need not be endemic. South Africa, for instance, after an extended period of not paying VAT refunds, reprioritized and some investors now regard it as the developing country with the best VAT refund practice. [45] This suggests that with the necessary political and administrative will, it is possible to pay VAT refunds promptly in a developing-country context.

Paying VAT refunds promptly will benefit investors. But it is also in host countries' best interest to pay VAT refunds promptly. Prompt payment of refunds can incentivize formalization through VAT registration and lead to greater efficiency in tax compliance and administration. Further, paying refunds promptly could increase investment by lowering investor uncertainty. Investment follows certain, consistent, good tax practices.

45. This statement is based on personal discussions with foreign investing firms.

CHAPTER 15

Digital Cross-Border Supplies

Simon Thang & Nicholas Shatalow

§15.01 INTRODUCTION

This chapter focuses on digital cross-border supplies, or e-commerce. These terms can be used to encompass a range of business activities that involve some element of the internet.[1] They exist on a spectrum from brick-and-mortar businesses that simply advertise the sale of goods online or that sell goods online as an additional channel, to businesses whose sales are effected solely online and whose products themselves are digitized and delivered electronically (familiar examples include Netflix, Spotify, Twitter, YouTube, Google Play, and iTunes). For clarity, the use of these terms here is limited to supplies closer to the latter end of the spectrum, that is, supplies that are sold and delivered electronically. Sales of goods effected electronically are an important part of the e-commerce story, but the mechanism for collecting applicable VAT, border controls at the fiscal frontier, are well-established.[2] This chapter will, however, include some discussion of e-commerce involving goods that currently escape taxation under 'low value shipment' or de minimis rules.[3] This chapter will also discuss certain distinctions between business-to-business ('B2B') sales and business-to-consumer ('B2C') sales that have arisen because of their differential treatment under a typical VAT (in particular, the availability of deductions for input VAT for the former but not the latter).

1. For example, *see* Jinyan Li, *Consumption Taxation of Electronic Commerce: Problems, Policy Implications, and Proposals for Reform*, 38 (3) Can. Bus. L. J., 426 (2003).
2. *See* OECD, *Taxation and Electronic Commerce*, 202-205 (2001); David R. Agrawal and William F. Fox, *Taxes in an e-commerce generation*, 24(5) Int'l Tax and Pub. Fin. 903 (2017).
3. We also discuss a 2020 Canadian proposal directed at goods sold directly by non-residents or through certain platforms and fulfilled from within Canada.

The disruptive effect of e-commerce to taxation is nothing new. It has been the subject of study, discussion, consternation for fiscal authorities since its emergence over 25 years ago.[4] As of writing, the international direct tax community continues to grapple with serious challenges posed by e-commerce to the integrity of its tax base.[5] This has been given the moniker 'base erosion and profit shifting' or 'BEPS'. The 'base erosion' aspect of this issue arises because tax jurisdiction in international tax is premised on the benefits concept, which in turn looks at the 'source'. A taxing jurisdiction is considered to have sufficient claim as the 'source' if the relevant business has a permanent establishment in that jurisdiction. The concept of 'permanent establishment' as a prerequisite to taxing jurisdiction has been entrenched in the over 3,500 bilateral direct tax treaties that follow the OECD or UN models:[6]

> The permanent establishment concept is a central element in determining taxation rights under tax treaties and is defined in the OECD Model Tax Convention as, essentially, a 'fixed place of business through which the business of an enterprise is wholly or partly carried on'.[7]

As many have observed, e-commerce has disrupted this core concept because businesses can now generate profits with little or no physical presence in a jurisdiction and, thus, no clear permanent establishment as traditionally defined. Digitization has facilitated this upending of the source concept, or so-called base erosion:[8]

> At the centre of the debate is whether international income tax rules, developed in a 'brick-and-mortar' economic environment more than a century ago, remain fit for purpose in the modern global economy. The fundamental elements of the global tax system which determined where taxes should be paid ('nexus' rules based on physical presence) and what portion of profits should be taxed ('profit allocation' rules based on the arm's length principle), have served their purpose well. Namely, they have enshrined tax certainty and helped to eliminate double taxation stimulating global trade.
>
> Today, however, three important phenomena facilitated by digitalisation – scale without mass, reliance on intangible assets, and the centrality of data – pose serious challenges to elements of the foundations of the global tax system.

To illustrate the struggle to adapt the international direct tax system to e-commerce, consider the OECD's initial focus on attempting to adapt the permanent

4. OECD, report by the Committee on Fiscal Affairs, *Electronic commerce: Taxation framework conditions* (1998); OECD, *Taxation and Electronic Commerce* (2001); OECD, *Implementation of the Ottawa Taxation Framework* (2003); Li, *supra*, n. 1; Jenny E. Ligthart, *Consumption Taxation in a Digital World: A Primer*, 52(4) Can. Tax J. 1076 (2004).
5. Jinyan Li et al., *BEPS and the Emerging Global Approach to Taxing Multinational Enterprises*, Presented at Re-Imagining Tax Policy for the 21st Century: Inspired by Tim Edgar's Scholarship February 8-9, 2019, Toronto, Canada, SSRN Elec. J. (Sept. 14, 2019).
6. BEPS Action 1, paragraph 242.
7. OECD, *Taxation and Electronic Commerce* (2001).
8. https://www.oecd.org/tax/beps/beps-actions/action1/.

establishment concept to computer servers.[9] Should servers constitute a permanent establishment? Should the answer depend on the functions carried out through the server? Is a server alone sufficient, or is human intervention required? While OECD members were debating these questions, technology was already moving towards fully automated e-commerce run through third-party decentralized hosting on 'the cloud'.[10] Server location became meaningless. The global efforts in responding to the challenges of base erosion (and the companion issue of profit shifting) to international income tax have continued to present in the form of the recent OECD BEPS Action Plans.[11] Some jurisdictions have been unwilling to await multilateral consensus. In the interim, some of these jurisdictions imposed or proposed a new unilateral tax called the digital services tax (DST). The DST is designed as a turnover style consumption tax and is intended to help jurisdictions make up for the foregone revenue that has resulted from the digital economy's subversion of the traditional rules of income taxation.[12]

While VAT has not emerged unscathed by e-commerce, it has not faced the same existential reckoning. In this regard, it is telling that of the 15 OECD Action Items developed in response to BEPs, VAT is only included in the latter half of Action 1, *Tax Challenges Arising from Digitalisation*.

This chapter suggests some reasons for VAT's relative durability in the face of e-commerce. First, it is suggested that VATs have a broad tax base encompassing all supplies, whether tangibles, services and intangibles, and are largely technically-agnostic. This broad base helps, in principle, to minimize the distortive effects of 'characterization problems'. Second, near unanimous adoption of the destination principle, which focuses on the *situs* of consumption, renders physical presence of the supplier theoretically irrelevant.

Behind some of VAT's virtues, however, lie challenges that cannot be ignored. First, there are currently no VAT-specific international treaties. This absence of treaties may make enforcement against foreign-based businesses difficult. It may also make it difficult for tax jurisdictions to respond in a coordinated fashion if significant ambiguities in situsing or place of supply rules emerge. Finally, there are forms of digital consumption that have emerged that, while significant, are not adequately captured by a transactional VAT.

---

9. Described in Cockfield, *infra* n. 28, 144-145.
10. For the concept of cloud computing in tax, *see* Orly Mazur, *Taxing the Cloud*, 103(1) Calif. Tax Rev. 1 (2015).
11. The 15 Actions 'equip governments with domestic and international rules and instruments to address tax avoidance, ensuring that profits are taxed where economic activities generating the profits are performed and where value is created'; https://www.oecd.org/tax/beps/beps-actions/.
12. The DST is discussed below in the last section.

§15.02 PROLIFERATION OF GLOBAL VATS

Currently, over 160 countries have adopted some form of VAT.[13] Amongst OECD countries, VAT accounts for approximately 30% of total tax revenues:[14]

> The VAT has been the most pervasive tax reform throughout the world during the second half of the twentieth century (with stragglers following on thereafter) and has proved to be a major source of government revenue. The VAT is widely used in both developed and developing countries, at local, subnational, national, and even supranational (e.g., the European Union) levels of government.[15]

While the tax base is theoretically private consumption,[16] the VAT is typically implemented under the invoice-credit method.[17] Under this form, the VAT applies upon an observable event such as a supply made for consideration.[18] As a result, the VAT can fairly be described as a 'transactional tax', at least in legal form.

[A] Broad Base

The VAT is intended to be a tax on a broad base at a relatively low rate, thereby reducing distortive effects on consumption patterns.[19] However, deviations from the tax base are common for various reasons such as: distributive concerns regarding regressivity, promoting consumption of merit goods, and pre-existing tax preferences. These variances in VAT bases exacerbate compliance obligations for vendors selling into multiple jurisdictions, as discussed below. In general, however, a properly designed VAT should be technology-agnostic; so long as there is taxable event such as a supply, VAT should apply regardless of the medium for delivery or the form of the supply itself.[20]

---

13. The notable exception is the US, which lacks a federal sales tax let alone VAT. *See*, e.g., Robert F. van Brederode, *Introduction to the U.S. State Retail Sales and Use Taxes*, 18(4) Int'l VAT Monitor 270 (2007); Robert F. van Brederode, *Towards a Federal Sales Tax in the U.S.?* 19{2) Int'l VAT Monitor 114-120 (2008); Robert F. van Brederode, *Revenue Distribution under a Combined Federal and State Consumption Tax*, 121(8) Tax Notes, 953 (2008). One implication of this, at least for the subject matter of this chapter, is what reciprocal benefit the US would receive under cooperative agreements on enforcement and information exchange. This is discussed below.
14. OECD, Consumption Tax Trends 2018, VAT/GST and Excise Rates, Trends and Policy Issues. For an explanation of factors behind the proliferation of VAT, *see* Alan Schenk et al., *Value Added Tax, A Comparative Approach*, 2nd ed. (Cambridge Univ. Press, 2015), Chapter 1.
15. Schenk, *supra* n. 14, 23.
16. James Mirrlees, *Tax by Design*, 1st ed., 149 (Institute for Fiscal Studies, 2010) (The Mirrlees Review).
17. Sijbren Cnossen, *A VAT Primer for Lawyers, Economists, and Accountants*, in *VAT Reader* (Tax Analysts, 2011).
18. Excise Tax Act, R.S.C., 1985, c. E-15 (Canada) at 165.
19. James Mirrlees, *supra* n. 16, 154.
20. There are, of course, exceptions. For example, some jurisdictions such as Luxembourg have reduced rates for books. This was applied by Luxembourg to electronic books (which, coupled with an origin-basis rule for electronic services, attracted the likes of Amazon Kindle to locate within the Grand Duchy), until the Court of Justice of the European Union (CJEU) ruled the

> In general, of course, there is an initial presumption in favour of uniformity to avoid distortion of consumption decisions. It is costly in welfare terms if the tax system results in me buying a different set of goods from the ones that I would have bought had all goods been treated the same.[21]

For example, the Canadian *Excise Tax Act* applies to, among other things, taxable supplies made in Canada for consideration.[22] 'Supply' is defined broadly to mean the provision of property or a service in any manner, including sale, transfer, barter, exchange, licence, rental, lease, gift or disposition. 'Property' is turn defined broadly to mean any property, whether real or personal, movable or immovable, tangible or intangible, corporeal or incorporeal. Finally, 'service' means anything other than property, money, or employee labour.[23]

Thus, it is irrelevant whether one purchases goods from a brick-or-mortar store rather than an online vendor, watches a movie in the local theatre rather than on an at-home streaming service, or consults with a tax lawyer in person rather than remotely. All supplies, regardless whether classified as tangibles, services or intangibles, whether delivered remotely or wholly digitally, are subject to VAT in principle.[24] In this sense, VATs are designed to be technology-agnostic, unlike excise duties, Pigouvian taxes, or manufacturer sales taxes, which are designed to impose tax more heavily on some supplies than others.[25]

In contrast, the predecessor taxes that VAT sometimes replaced – such as single-stage retail sales taxes or manufacturer sales taxes – typically applied to a limited base of tangible goods or a limited group of services. As e-commerce grew, it became apparent that existing rules based on tangibles would not adequately capture digital supplies. Efforts were made to bring additional items into the tax base by creating new categories or by expanding existing categories beyond their normal meaning. For example, the former Ontario *Retail Sales Tax Act* widely taxed tangible personal property, certain services, but not intangibles. To address software, 'tangible personal property' was amended to include 'computer programs' retained or transferred in any manner including by electronic means.

The technical agnosticism of VAT extends to its instantiation in the value chain. VAT is designed to apply to all stages of the value chain. Deductions for input VAT, or input tax credits, are available to qualifying suppliers. The effect of these deductions is to ensure that the net tax burden on each stage of the value chain is limited to each suppliers' respective value-add. No deduction is available upon the final sale for

reduced rate only applies to physical books. *See* Judgment of 5 March 2015, Joined Cases C-479/13, *Commission v. France,* and C-502/13, *Commission v. Luxembourg,* ECLI: EU:C:2015:141.

21. James Mirrlees, *supra* n. 16, 154.
22. Excise Tax Act, section 165.
23. Preceding definitions, Excise Tax Act, sections 123(1).
24. In the Canadian example, VAT should apply one way or another even to wholly digitized supplies rendered from outside Canada. The vendor will either be required to collect the VAT, or the consumer will be subject to self-assessment or reverse charge. As discussed below, digitization can make characterization of supplies difficult and this may be relevant to situsing or place of supply rules.
25. James Mirrlees, *supra* n. 16, 169-171, & 231.

private consumption. RSTs or MSTs, in contrast, are limited to a single stage in the value chain (i.e., retail sale or manufacture) and, accordingly, offer no input deductions.[26]

[B] Convergence on the Destination Principle

Conceptually, VAT can be imposed on either an origin basis or a destination basis.[27] An origin basis assigns taxing rights to the location of the supplier - the place of production. Under an origin-based VAT, exports bear the origin country's VAT and imports enter tax-free. In contrast, a destination basis gives taxing rights to the location of the recipient - the place of consumption. Imports are taxed by the consumption jurisdiction, while exports are relieved of the origin jurisdiction's tax. Upon import into the consumption jurisdiction, the staged collection of VAT starts anew.

One of the remarkable aspects of the global proliferation of VATs is the near unanimous adoption of the destination principle. Unlike the network of approximately 3,500 bilateral international tax treaties, there is no specific legal treaty for VAT, let alone one that mandates the destination principle. Instead, this can be described as a form of convergence encouraged through 'soft law' in the form of OECD guidelines.[28] The influence of the EU and compatibility with international obligations under the GATT should also be acknowledged:[29]

> In 1998, however, the OECD members agreed through the Ottawa Taxation Framework to consider VAT reform efforts in the context of global e-commerce. Importantly, the Ottawa Taxation Framework resolved an ongoing debate among OECD Member States surrounding the appropriate tax jurisdiction for cross-border VAT purposes: the OECD countries agreed that for business-to-consumer (B2C) supplies the place of consumption should be the jurisdiction in which the recipient has his or her usual residence and for business-to-business (B2B) supplies tax should apply in the jurisdiction in which the recipient has located its business presence. This development helped to legitimize the European Union efforts, discussed subsequently, to impose collection and remittance obligations on non-European Union consumers who have engaged in B2C transactions with European businesses.

There are other factors to which convergence around the destination principle can be attributed, including encouraging development of exports. There may also be a form of network effect. With early adopters, such as the EU, implementing the destination principle for supplies from the outside, subsequent joiners to the VAT 'network' had little incentive to deviate and adopt the origin basis; otherwise, their exporters could potentially face double taxation.

26. James Mirrlees, *supra* n. 16, 169-171.
27. James Mirrlees, *supra* n. 16, 182.
28. *See* Arthur J. Cockfield, *The Rise of The OECD as Informal World Tax Organization through National Responses to E-Commerce Tax Challenges*, 8 (1) Yale J.L. & Tech (2006).
29. Cockfield, *supra* n. 28, paragraph 148.

The destination principle ultimately gives import jurisdictions significant flexibility to tax consumption, whether through vendor-registration, reverse-charge, or withholding tax measures. This flexibility is a consequence of the fact that suppliers are ultimately more mobile than consumers, particularly in the e-commerce era. For this reason, 'consumption' under a destination-basis is a preferable tax base to 'production' under an origin-basis for jurisdictions seeking to tax e-commerce with VAT instruments.[30]

The adoption of the destination principle has three implications that are relevant in this chapter. First, it requires collection or some form of accounting for VAT in the consumption jurisdiction regardless where the supplier is established. Second, it requires rules to determine the situs of consumption. Third, it identifies consumption, rather than production, as the tax base. These implications are discussed further below, in the same order.

[C] Exception to the Destination Principle: Nexus Requirements

It should be noted that some jurisdictions have special rules that exclude non-residents from VAT obligations unless they cross a nexus or 'carrying on business' threshold. These rules suffer from the same issues described above in the international income tax context, although common law courts may be liberating them from the constraints of PE requirements on a case-by-case basis.

As of writing, in Canada, for example, the GST obligations of non-resident suppliers hinge partly on whether those suppliers 'carry on business' in Canada. Non-resident suppliers who make taxable supplies in Canada but do not carry on business in Canada are not required to register for, collect, and remit GST. (This will change under broad new rules recently proposed.[31] As noted below, non-resident suppliers who exceed a certain sales threshold would be required to register under a simplified regime similar to that endorsed by the OECD. While the focus appears to be on B2C sales of services and intangibles, the proposals also apply to certain sales of tangible goods. They proposals also cover digital platform operators, below.)

This 'carrying on business' concept is a common law concept that originated in 19th century British jurisprudence. It is relevant to other areas of law, such as private international law and income tax law. At a high level, the concept is premised on the 'broad distinction between trading *with* a country and carrying on a trade *within* a country' (emphasis added).[32]

Recent Canadian jurisprudence in the private international law context suggests that non-residents with no physical presence in Canada may be able to carry on business in Canada through wholly digital activities in the Canadian market.[33] Whether these developments at common law will, in principle, subject non-resident suppliers

30. James Mirrlees, *supra* n. 16, 182.
31. 2020 Government of Canada Fall Economic Statement.
32. *Grainger & Son v. Gough* [1896] AC 325 HL.
33. Sophie Stoyan, *Just a Click Away? Jurisdiction and Virtually Carrying On Business in Canada*, 13(3) J. Priv. Int'l L. 602 – 32, 616 (2017) https://doi.org/10.1080/17441048.2017.1387681.

with no physical presence in Canada to the GST's administrative requirements is unclear and contested.[34] At present, however, the administrative policy of the Canada Revenue Agency (CRA) states that non-resident suppliers with no physical presence in Canada are not subject to these requirements in practice.[35]

Canada's nexus rules are deficient in the e-commerce era. On the one hand, they expose non-resident suppliers to a great deal of risk and uncertainty. Even if recent jurisprudence brings supplies made by non-resident e-commerce firms within the ambit of Canada's GST regime, it will likely do so on a fact-specific, case-by-case basis. On the other hand, Canada's rules allow supplies of e-commerce made by non-residents to escape taxation.

In Australia, by contrast, the GST obligations of non-resident suppliers do not hinge exclusively on whether the suppliers carry on business in Australia. Rather, Australia deems supplies to be taxable if (among other things) they are 'connected with the indirect tax zone'.[36] Although certain supplies will be deemed to be connected to Australia if the supplier making those supplies carries on business in Australia, supplies can also be connected to Australia in various other ways.

For example, '[a] supply of goods is connected with the indirect tax zone if the goods are delivered, or made available, in the indirect tax zone to the recipient of the supply'. Regarding supplies of anything other than goods or real property ('inbound intangible consumer supplies'), a supply will be deemed to be connected with the Australia if 'the recipient of the supply is an Australian consumer'. In general, an entity is an Australian consumer if the entity is an Australian resident and is not registered for the GST (or is registered but 'does not acquire the thing supplied solely or partly for the purpose of an enterprise that the entity carries on').[37]

A non-resident who makes supplies of anything other than goods or real property to Australian consumers in the course of a business that the non-resident carries on is, therefore, required to pay the GST on those supplies, assuming the non-resident meets the $75,000 AUD registration threshold, and the market facilitator rules (discussed below) do not apply.[38]

These 'Australian consumer' rules assign nexus to Australia in a manner more consistent with the destination principle than Canada's 'carrying on business' rules. More precisely, the rules are a better proxy for the destination principle because a supply made to an Australian consumer is precisely the taxable event with which a destination-based VAT should be concerned.

34. *See* Nicholas Shatalow, Nicholas, *Policy Forum: The GST/HST Obligations of Non-Resident E-Commerce Firms—Jurisprudence and Policy*, 68(4) Can. Tax J. 1 (2020); Zvi Halpern-Shavim, *Carrying on About Carrying on Business: A Response to 'The GST/HST Treatment of Non-resident E-commerce Firms'*, 68(4) Can. Tax J. (2020).
35. Canada Revenue Agency, GST/HST Policy Statement P-051R2, *Carrying on Business in Canada*.
36. A New Tax System (Goods and Services Tax) Act 1999 (Australia) at 9-5(c). Note that the 'indirect tax zone' is roughly coextensive with Australia.
37. A New Tax System (Goods and Services Tax) Act 1999 (Australia) at 9-25(7).
38. A New Tax System (Goods and Services Tax) Regulations 2019, 23-15.01. Note that the prescribed threshold of AUD 75,000 differs from the statutory default threshold of AUD 50,000 listed in paragraph 23-15(1)(a) of the GST Act.

Australia's rules raise an important question. Namely, what happens if a supplier fails to realize that a customer is an Australian consumer? The *GST Act* foresees this question and relieves suppliers of their obligation to pay GST on supplies to Australian consumers in certain circumstances.

Where a supplier takes reasonable steps to obtain information about whether or not the recipient of its supply is an Australian consumer and that supplier, after taking those steps, reasonably believes that the recipient is not an Australian consumer, the *GST Act* treats the supply as if the recipient was not an Australian consumer.[39] In other words, this provision forgives suppliers of GST payment liability when they reasonably believe (objectively and subjectively) that the recipient of their supply is not an Australian consumer. Similar rules apply when a supplier's usual business systems and processes provide the supplier with a reasonable belief that the recipient is not an Australian consumer.[40] There is also a comparable exception for situations where a supplier reasonably believes a recipient is not an Australian consumer because that recipient is GST registered.[41]

Interestingly, Australia has precluded the use of its 'carrying on business' nexus rules for non-residents with no physical presence in Australia. Whereas Canada has entrusted the judiciary with defining the meaning of 'carrying on business', Australia has limited its 'carrying on business' concept for GST purposes. In particular, Australia's rules only consider a non-resident to be carrying on business in Australia for GST purposes if the non-resident 'is in' (or intends to be in) Australia through one or more fixed places of business.[42] In other words, Australia has embedded its 'carrying on business' concept with an explicit physical presence (or PE) requirement for GST purposes.

There is no inherent reason under a destination basis for these requirements to exist. Historically, they may have addressed the concern of unduly burdening trading partners' businesses with registration requirements, lest those trading partners reciprocally impose similar burdens.[43] These requirements may also have been designed to minimize any deadweight loss generated from discouraging entry into the local market with excess compliance barriers. However, these requirements seem difficult to justify now. First, the revenue loss and competitive inequity resulting from the under-taxation of supplies by non-residents can no longer be ignored. Second, such requirements are a blunt tool. Jurisdictions can design clearer thresholds for screening out smaller businesses-based sales or transaction volumes.

That said, for countries with existing 'carrying on business' nexus rules, there may be some value in retaining these rules as a residual nexus category. Although it is apparent that clear de minimis standards with greater conformity to the destination principle offer a simpler and fairer way of subjecting non-residents to the administrative requirements of a VAT regime, a residual common law category may help to

39. A New Tax System (Goods and Services Tax) Act 1999 (Australia) at 84-100(1).
40. A New Tax System (Goods and Services Tax) Act 1999 (Australia) at 84-100(2).
41. A New Tax System (Goods and Services Tax) Act 1999 (Australia) at 84-105.
42. A New Tax System (Goods and Services Tax) Act 1999 (Australia) at 9-27(1).
43. *See* Li, *supra* n. 1, and van Zyl, *infra* n. 46.

'future-proof' VAT systems. To the extent that future technological developments allow suppliers access to markets while bypassing de minimis sales standards, a residual nexus category may help to safeguard VAT revenues by providing another tool through which jurisdictions may require those suppliers to charge VAT. Of course, retaining 'carrying on business' nexus rules confronts non-resident suppliers with uncertainty and the risk of potential exposure. Policymakers should consider these trade-offs when contemplating the future of such nexus rules.

[D] Alternative De Minimis Standards

De minimis thresholds have arisen as an alternative to the nexus threshold in the e-commerce context. In the United States, for example, states have premised the sales tax liabilities of out-of-state remote sellers on whether the sellers exceed certain de minimis sales standards. These standards have taken two forms: gross sales revenue thresholds and total transaction volume thresholds. In many states, both thresholds are used.[44] Such thresholds provide greater certainty for suppliers than fact-specific, common law standards.

§15.03 COLLECTION OF TAX UNDER THE DESTINATION PRINCIPLE

Since the destination-principle assigns taxing rights based on location of consumption, it should not be relevant where the supplier is established or performs its profit-making activities. If consumption occurs in a jurisdiction, the destination-principle demands that VAT should apply there. There are fewer opportunities for systematic exploitation of BEPS with a destination VAT, in contrast with an origin VAT or direct tax.[45] The main concerns identified by the OECD are 'offshoring' inputs by exempt businesses to suppliers in low or no VAT jurisdictions, and the acquisition of supplies by a business establishment in a low or no VAT jurisdiction for use across establishments in higher VAT jurisdictions. However, both of these issues can be addressed by sufficiently robust domestic rules for B2B self-assessment. B2C is not mentioned at all.

The collection question is instead a technical one. How does the tax apply? Is the customer to self-assess (or reverse-charge) the VAT? Should there be some form of third-party withholding? Or is the VAT to be collected by the vendor? While not as existential, this is a significant challenge: 'The principal deficiency in modern VAT systems is their inability to levy VAT on affected transactions through a simplified

44. Jared Walczak and Janelle Cammenga, State Sales Taxes in the Post-Wayfair Era, 5 Tax Foundation Fiscal Fact No. 680 (December 2019); Robert F. van Brederode, *The Future of the Economic Nexus Standard for U.S. Sales & Use Tax Collection*, 47(10) Intertax 885 (2019).
45. With an origin, VAT, which effectively taxes production, suppliers are incentivized to locate to low-VAT jurisdictions. This occurred, for example, with digital e-books which were taxed in the EU on an origin-basis until 2015. *See* David D. Stewart, *EU Takes on VAT Treatment of E-Book Sales*, Tax Notes Int'l (July 16, 2012).

collection mechanism that does not overburden taxable entities charged with VAT collection, or is not inefficient from an economic point of view.'[46]

Each of these approaches is reviewed below. It has been clear since the rise of e-commerce that the effective collection of VAT on supplies from foreign vendors poses difficulties. The hope, expressed since at least the Ottawa Framework in 1998, has been that technology would play a key role in meeting the challenge. Vendor registration and collection was recommended as an interim solution pending development of a technology-based solution.

As discussed below, technology has yet to deliver a widely applicable solution that does not rely on vendor collection. The interim solution has become the current consensus among countries that impose foreign-vendor registration requirements, at least for B2C sales. While the deficiencies of this approach are recognized, there are presently no better alternatives.[47] As more and more jurisdictions adopt this approach, and as compliance burdens diminish, the case to replace this 'interim' solution with something better becomes less pressing. In other words, vendor registration, while not perfect, may be 'good enough' (especially when combined with the marketplace facilitator rules discussed below).

§15.04 SELF-ASSESSMENT/REVERSE CHARGE

While theoretically possible, self-assessment of VAT by consumers on B2C sales is generally accepted as unfeasible. Compliance is low, even when self-assessment is legally mandated and required to be declared on income tax returns. This approach requires compliance from a multitude of unsophisticated consumers, who are too numerous to realistically audit.[48]

A destination-based VAT is supposed to be neutral as between domestic and imported sales. In other words, consumers should not have a preference for imports based on tax because imports should bear the same VAT burden as domestic sales. This objective fails when imports escape taxation. The consequences are revenue loss and inequity between domestic and imported supplies.[49]

For B2B sales, requiring self-assessment is considered feasible. It is in fact the recommended approach by the OECD. There are several reasons for the OECD's preference for self-assessment in the B2B context. First, businesses in the consumption jurisdiction typically have a tax registration and are subject to audit for compliance by the tax authorities. Second, in the case of businesses entitled to claim input tax credits

46. S.P. van Zyl, *The Collection of Value Added Tax on Cross-Border Digital Trade – Part 1: Registration of Foreign Vendors*, 47 (2) Comp. & Int'l L. J. S. Afr. 154 (2014).
47. We discuss platform or marketplace facilitator registration rules below. In our view, these are effectively a form of third-party withholding and has potential.
48. As demonstrated by the U.S. experience with Use Tax collection, *see* Robert F. van Brederode, *The American Debate on Taxing Distance Sales and E-Commerce*, 18(5) Int'l VAT Monitor 352 (2007).
49. Rosalie Wyonch, *Bits, Bytes, and Taxes: VAT and the Digital Economy in Canada*, C.D. Howe institute, Commentary No. 487 (August 2017), available at https://www.cdhowe.org/sites/default/files/attachments/research_papers/mixed/Commentary_487.pdf.

(i.e., deduct input VAT), there would no net revenue forgone. Finally, requiring local businesses to self-assess is thought to reduce the amount of VAT paid over to foreign vendors, therefore reducing the risk of non-remittance.

§15.05 THIRD-PARTY WITHHOLDING

Various forms of third-party withholding have been considered as a way of ensuring that supplies by non-resident suppliers bear VAT, but this approach does not appear to be widely adopted.[50] One form of third-party withholding involves enlisting a 'trusted third party', such as financial intermediary in the consumption jurisdiction, to withhold the applicable VAT from payment to the supplier. Under this approach, '[n]either the supplier nor the customer is required to register with the relevant revenue authority. Involving financial institutions in the VAT collection process, is an attempt to move VAT closer to a return-free system through the increased use of electronic payment instruments.'[51]

Another form contemplates collection at source by the local tax authority and subsequent transfer to the consumption jurisdiction. While technically feasible, the main obstacles to these approaches are concerns about undue imposition of compliance burden and heavy reliance on inter-governmental cooperation, respectively. Specifically, the absence of VAT-specific tax treaties (discussed above) creates problems for withholding tax measures that require inter-governmental cooperation and revenue sharing.

From an administrative point of view, one of the benefits of a tax on consumption over a tax on production is the fact that consumers are, generally speaking, not highly mobile.[52] This dynamic gives jurisdictions significant flexibility to levy taxes on consumption. Although the OECD has identified vendor registration as the preferred method for addressing supplies of cross-border e-commerce in the interim, it is important to note that jurisdictions have other tax instruments at their disposal if non-resident vendors refuse to comply.

Where a vendor refuses to register, a jurisdiction could, in principle, levy a withholding tax on a domestic third party related to the vendor or transaction. Although withholding taxes have not been widely adopted in this context, they 'are found in practically all tax systems and are widely used in respect of dividends, interest, royalties, and similar tax payments'.[53] In the e-commerce context, a domestic intermediary, such as a bank or credit card company, could be required to collect VAT for supplies where non-resident vendors refuse to register.[54] This approach is clearly

50. *See* OECD 2001 report, *supra* n. 2.
51. S.P. van Zyl and W.G. Schulze, *The Collection of Value Added Tax on Cross-Border Digital Trade – Part 2: VAT Collection by Banks*, 47 (3) Comp. & Int'l L. J. S. Afr. 316 (2014).
52. Michael J. Trebilcock, *The International Movement of People: The Fourth Economic Freedom* (Max Planck Working Paper 2018), 12.
53. OECD, Centre for Tax Policy and Administration, Glossary of Tax Terms, available at (https://www.oecd.org/ctp/glossaryoftaxterms.htm).
54. EY, Argentina, Global Tax Guides (https://assets.ey.com/content/dam/ey-sites/ey-com/en_gl/topics/tax/tax-pdfs/ey-worldwide-vat-gst-and-sales-tax-guide.pdf#page=41?download).

heavy-handed, but it should calm fears that e-commerce has rendered impotent the ability of jurisdictions to tax domestic consumption in respect of supplies made by non-residents.

It appears that only a handful of jurisdictions have attempted to employ a third-party withholding strategy. Policymakers have expressed reluctance about requiring payment intermediaries, such as banks and credit card companies, to collect VAT. Their concerns focus on whether the intermediaries are well-positioned to determine and apply VAT obligations, and whether it is appropriate to require them to bear the administrative cost of implementing such systems. There is also the question of the extent to which these intermediaries would be subject to liability.[55]

Third-party withholding may still play an important role, however. As discussed below, new rules for marketplace facilitators may essentially represent a step in this direction to the extent such facilitators are required to collect and remit applicable VAT to the tax authorities. In addition, withholding is a strong 'stick' in the enforcement arsenal. It could be adopted as a residual approach or 'last resort' for dealing with recalcitrant vendors who do not comply with registration and collection obligations.[56]

§15.06 VENDOR COLLECTION

After the other options are ruled out, the tax authorities are left with relying on foreign vendors to register, remit applicable VAT on supplies, and comply with other requirements. The normal method under a multi-stage invoice-credit VAT is for the vendor to register with the applicable taxation authority and to collect and remit the VAT on every taxable transaction in the supply chain. This staged or fractioned collection system is thought to spread the risk of non-collection on any particular supply. It also creates an auditable paper trail.[57]

There are two distinct challenges with this approach: a multiplicity of compliance obligations for vendors and effective enforcement of those obligations by tax authorities.

[A] Compliance in Multiple Jurisdictions

With over 160 countries around the world employing some form of consumption tax (some of which also have subnational consumption taxes), it has long been noted that e-commerce businesses will face significant compliance burdens if they are required to collect tax of the consumption jurisdiction. Many jurisdictions have attempted to simplify compliance obligations through a streamlined, online registration process that keeps the supplier's information requirements to a minimum. Under these simplified registration schemes, input VAT deduction is not permitted. Vendors still register

55. This issue is discussed below in the context of marketplace facilitators.
56. Richard Doernberg & Luc Hinnekens, *Electronic Commerce and International Taxation* (Kluwer Law International, 1999), as cited in S.P. van Zyl and W.G. Schulze, *supra* n. 51.
57. *See* Schenk, *supra* n. 14, Chapters 1-3.

under the normal process if they pay local VAT on inputs and wish to deduct input VAT.

A number of jurisdictions around the world have implemented some form of simplified registration for non-residents, including: the EU,[58] Australia (discussed below), and the Canadian province of Quebec (discussed below). Under recent proposals, Canada would also adopt a simplified registration regime for non-residents for the federal GST/HST.[59] These rules would apply to supplies of services and intangibles, which are the chief concerns for most jurisdictions with respect to e-commerce. Notably, however, a related set of rules would require non-resident suppliers and certain marketplace facilitators to register under the normal rules if they make certain sales of goods (discussed below).

While helpful, simplified registration is 'low hanging fruit'. The real burden for vendors is determining which jurisdiction's taxes to collect, which rates apply where there are multiple rates, whether exemptions apply, and how to report. The hope, expressed since at least the Ottawa Framework in 1998, has been that technology would develop to reduce this burden. The OECD's current recommendation of vendor registration in fact was originally recommended as an interim solution pending technological innovation:

> There is little doubt that the most difficult issue for the application of consumption taxes to electronic commerce is the collection of tax on digitized products sold from a vendor in one country to a consumer in another. As noted above the 2001 Report recommended an interim approach of simplified registration that would allow a relatively easy registration and reporting system. But the reality is that as sales of these products develop (as they are forecast to) no matter how simple a registration and reporting system may be, the potential requirement for a business to deal with a large number of countries in which it has no physical presence is unlikely to be a sustainable solution. As work has progressed on this subject it has emerged that technology could play the key role, and tax administrations should consider the steps to create the legal and administrative environment which will enable the development of business-driven technological solutions.

Where do these technological solutions currently stand? It is safe to say that no *panacea* has emerged. Many of today's dominant e-commerce players were in their infancy or non-existent in 1998.[60] Yet nearly 25 years later, vendor registration remains the consensus approach. The OECD has also tempered its hopes, recognizing the current reality that technology is more likely to support compliance rather function as a central agent of compliance:

> While it is apparent that automated systems and other technology-based systems have a potentially central role to play in facilitating tax collection on cross-border supplies of services and intangibles from foreign suppliers, at the present time

58. Effective July 2003, the European Union's directive on electronic communications requires all non-EU companies selling digital goods and services online to consumers within the EU to register with an EU tax authority and charge, collect and remit VAT.
59. The 2020 Canadian federal Fall Economic Statement.
60. Amazon was founded in 1994, Netflix in 1997, Google in 1998, Facebook in 2004, and Uber in 2009.

> such systems are more realistically viewed as tools that can be usefully employed, in appropriate circumstances, to support existing collection regimes. As technology and business models continue to evolve, automated systems and other technology-based systems are likely to play an increasingly important role in facilitating cross-border tax collection of services and intangibles from foreign suppliers.

That said, a *market* solution to the compliance problem may have arisen in the form of marketplace facilitators.

§15.07 E-COMMERCE PLATFORMS

Although a technological solution to the compliance concerns raised by cross-border e-commerce has not materialized, recent developments indicate that a market solution may have arisen. Marketplace facilitators, who have come to play a prominent role in the digital economy, may be well-positioned to assume the role of registering for, collecting, and remitting VAT in respect of e-commerce supplies. In effect, marketplace facilitators, rather than financial institutions, may have emerged as the third-party upon whom withholding tax obligations have been placed.

Before proceeding further, it is prudent to offer some clarity on the meaning of 'marketplace facilitators'. The OECD has advised against the imposition of a rigid definition of marketplace facilitators (in their terminology, 'digital platforms'), 'as it is a concept that is likely to evolve over time'.[61] In general, however, marketplace facilitators can be described functionally as follows:

> These can generally be described as the platforms that enable groups of customers (typically buyers and sellers) to interact directly and to enter into transactions, through the use of information technology. These actors have been at the heart of the explosive growth of online trade over recent years.[62]

This section will consider the rationale for imposing VAT obligations on marketplace facilitators and consider existing marketplace facilitator rules.

[A] E-Commerce Portals & Marketplace Facilitators

In this regard, the emergence of platforms merits discussion. We identify two kinds of platforms that should be distinguished.

First, there are portals which provide offer 'all-in-one' e-commerce solutions, such as Shopify and Woo Commerce.[63] Businesses can adopt these platforms for executing various point-of-sale e-commerce functions, such as invoicing and payment processing. These services run in the background of the business's own websites. As transaction processor, they are well-suited to facilitate tax compliance as part of their

61. OECD, Roles of Digital Platforms (March 2019) at p. 6, http://www.oecd.org/tax/consumption/the-role-of-digital-platforms-in-the-collection-of-vat-gst-on-online-sales.pdf.
62. OECD (2019), *supra* n. 61, 26.
63. Shopify.com; WooCommerce.com.

value-add. Shopify's basic service, for example, enables automatic tax collection and offers specific guidance on US sales tax and Canadian, EU, and Indian VAT. For an additional fee, Shopify appears to integrate with Avalara Tax, 'sales tax software that automates tax calculations and the tax filing process. Avalara provides real-time tax rates from more than 12,000 taxing jurisdictions.' Similarly, Woo Commerce states that it 'is fully integrated with Avalara, an automated tax software that provides you with the most current tax rates for every transaction, worldwide'. (Marketplace facilitators are discussed separately below. It should be noted that some leading platform operators such as Amazon offer tax compliance services. However, they appear to be limited.)[64]

Further research should be conducted to determine how accurate this software is, for example, in complying with exemptions without need for local tax advisors. But these services offer a glimpse of what a simple, accessible technological solution could look like for facilitating compliance. They are particularly relevant to smaller vendors who lack the resources to develop their own e-commerce infrastructure. These are the same vendors that are more likely to be sensitive to compliance burdens in multiple jurisdictions. These vendors already appear to be adopting these platforms as a cost-effective alternative to developing their own online point-of-sale infrastructure. They now have access to integrated tax compliance software. The logical progression of these developments would be towards automatic, direct reporting and remittance to the relevant tax authority.

Second, there are intermediary portal or marketplace facilitators that enable buyers and sellers to meet; in effect, they are online markets. Examples of marketplace facilitators include Amazon, Google Play, the Apple AppStore, Airbnb, and Patreon. The potential roles for these platforms in VAT compliance are discussed separately below.

[B] Extant Rules for Marketplace Facilitators

Numerous jurisdictions have enacted marketplace facilitator rules that shift the onus of registering for, collecting, and remitting VAT from the supplier to the marketplace facilitator through which the supply is made.[65] At a high level, marketplace facilitator rules can vary meaningfully in scope:

> These liability obligations may include, without being limited to, treating the digital platform as fully and solely liable for the VAT/GST due on the online sales it facilitates; or as liable for facilitating the VAT/GST collection and payment in the name and on behalf of the underlying supplier that uses this platform to carry out

64. For example, Amazon Canada can calculate Canadian sales taxes, but the service relies on the seller to correctly assign product tax codes and jurisdiction configurations to accommodate exemption, zero-rating and differences in subnational rates. Furthermore, 'no other taxes, regulatory fees, duties, or fees of any kind are calculated as part of the Tax Calculation Services'. *See* Tax Calculation Service Terms, https://sellercentral.amazon.ca/gp/help/external/200787220?language=en_CA&ref=efph_200787220_cont_G521.
65. The marketplace facilitator rules of the Canadian province of Quebec are discussed further below.

its online sales; or as jointly and severally liable for the VAT/GST due on online sales together with the underlying supplier.[66]

Clearly, there is a broad range of ways that a marketplace facilitator could be enlisted into the VAT collection process.

In our view, the structure of a jurisdiction's marketplace facilitator rules will hinge on two issues. First, it will be necessary to determine the scope of supplies covered under the marketplace facilitator rules. Will the rules be limited to supplies of services and intangibles, which are acknowledged to be more difficult to tax when supplied by non-residents? Or will they also include supplies of goods? Will they apply to B2B supplies as well as B2C supplies? Will they apply both to resident and non-resident suppliers? Second, it will be necessary to determine the extent to which marketplace facilitators are responsible for collection and remittance under the marketplace facilitator rules. Will marketplace facilitators chiefly be responsible for providing information to the supplier or facilitating compliance by the supplier? Or will they be directly responsible and liable for those obligations themselves? Will that liability be full and exclusive, or joint and several with the supplier? Similarly, will marketplace facilitator's involvement be voluntary or mandatory? A jurisdiction's answers to these questions will inform the ultimate design of its marketplace facilitator rules.

For example, Australia's marketplace facilitator rules state that a service (such as a website, internet portal, gateway, store, or marketplace) is a marketplace facilitator (or 'electronic distribution platform') if: it allows entities to make supplies available to end users; it is delivered by means of electronic communication; and any inbound intangible consumer supplies are to be made by means of electronic communication.[67] In these cases, the marketplace facilitator, rather than the supplier, is deemed: 'as being the supplier of, and as making, the supply'; 'as having made the supply for the consideration for which it was made'; and 'as having made the supply in the course or furtherance of an enterprise that the operator carries on'.[68] In other words, Australia's marketplace facilitator rules shift the obligations to collect and remit GST in respect of certain supplies from the supplier to the marketplace facilitator.

This arrangement may be altered by written agreement between the marketplace facilitator and the supplier, under certain circumstances.[69]

Although Australia's marketplace facilitator rules apply primarily to supplies of services and intangible personal property (collectively termed 'inbound intangible consumer supplies'), they can be extended to cover supplies of tangible personal property as well. Where a registrant marketplace facilitator agrees with a supplier in writing to treat a supply as if it were an inbound intangible supply for GST purposes, the supply will fall within the marketplace facilitator rules.[70]

66. OECD (2019), *supra* n. 61, 22.
67. A New Tax System (Goods and Services Tax) Act 1999 (Australia) at 84-70(1).
68. A New Tax System (Goods and Services Tax) Act 1999 (Australia) at 84-55(1).
69. A New Tax System (Goods and Services Tax) Act 1999 (Australia) at 84-55(4).
70. A New Tax System (Goods and Services Tax) Act 1999 (Australia) at 84-60.

Canada has recently proposed new GST/HST registration and collection rules for certain 'digital platform operators' through whom supplies are made into Canada.[71] Digital platform operator is defined to mean a person who controls or sets the essential elements of the transaction, or is involved, directly in collecting, receiving or charging the consideration for the supply and transmitting all or part of the consideration to the supplier. The platform operator would be required to register under a simplified regime, even if it does not carry on business in Canada, and would be required to collect GST/HST in respect of B2C supplies of services and intangibles (tangible goods are discussed below) made by unregistered non-resident suppliers.[72]

The proposed rules are what the OECD refers to as a 'full VAT/GST liability regime': the platform operator itself is deemed to make the relevant supply, and not the unregistered non-resident supplier. Thus, the platform operator is the only person liable for the applicable tax and other compliance obligations.[73] Notably, unlike the Australian rules, there does not appear to be statutory mechanism through which the supplier and platform operator can reallocate the compliance obligations, for example, by written agreement.

Various US States have also implemented marketplace facilitator rules in respect of their state sales taxes. Interestingly, these rules often apply to both tangible personal property, which is often defined to accommodate software, and services. In this case, the inclusion of tangible personal property may reflect the fact that inter-state supplies of goods do not cross a 'hard' border where sales tax could be levied.

Marketplace facilitator rules have additional benefits in the domestic context. VAT regimes will often forgive 'small suppliers' of their administrative VAT obligations if those suppliers' sales fall below de minimis sales thresholds. In Canada, for example, GST is not payable on supplies made by non-registrant 'small suppliers'.[74] By design, these small supplier rules introduce leakage into VAT regimes. This leakage may have been justified on the basis that the compliance costs for small suppliers outweighed the revenue generated from VAT on their supplies. However, marketplace facilitators raise the potential for many small suppliers to access consumers in a jurisdiction's market without their supplies being subject to VAT. Requiring marketplace facilitators to collect VAT in these instances will increase VAT coverage as the threshold can be based on all sales through the platform, without imposing an undue compliance burden on small, unsophisticated suppliers. For example, under recently proposed Canadian federal GST/HST rules, certain distribution platform operators would be required to register and collect tax if the total of all B2C sales made by unregistered non-residents through the platform exceeds a CAD 30,000 threshold.[75]

71. Canada 2020 Fall Economic Statement. The proposed rules would generally come into effect starting on July 1, 2021.
72. If registered under the normal rules, the platform operator would also be required to collect GST/HST in respect of B2B sales made by unregistered non-resident suppliers.
73. Sections 211.12 and 211.13 of the Excise Tax Act, as proposed in the 2020 Fall Economic Statement.
74. Excise Tax Act, R.S.C., 1985, c. E-15 (Canada) at 166.
75. Section 211.12 of the Excise Tax Act, as proposed in the 2020 Fall Economic Statement.

Finally, it should be noted that marketplace facilitator rules could be employed to address a different form of tax leakage: imports of goods under a de minimis threshold for VAT (and duty) collection by customs or 'low value shipments'. Imports of goods under these thresholds currently escape taxation, as the view among tax authorities has been that the administrative resources required to collect on them outweigh the revenue benefit. This view may no longer be tenable as e-commerce has led to significant growth of cross-border sales of low value goods.[76] Under legislation in the Australia and the EU,[77] it is contemplated that marketplace facilitators will be liable for collection of VAT on supplies of low value goods.

Interestingly, the Canadian proposals discussed above include ambitious rules that go beyond the low value shipments which are identified by the OECD as the chief concern for e-commerce and goods (given there are extant border collection mechanisms for taxable goods above the de minimis threshold).[78] In fact, the proposals appear to ignore low value imports altogether. They only apply to goods above the de minimis threshold.[79]

The motivation for these rules appears to be a desire to adequately tax the sale of imported goods by unregistered non-resident suppliers that are fulfilled from domestic warehouses.[80] While such goods may have been subject to tax upon import, the tax may only have applied to the declared value, which could be the supplier's wholesale cost and not the final resale price in Canada. Under these rules, the non-resident supplier or the platform operator would be required to collect tax on the price payable by the Canadian customer.

Under these proposals, non-resident suppliers and digital platform operators would be required to register under the *normal rules* (as opposed to a simplified regime) and collect GST/HST on all sales of goods to Canadians other than goods sent by mail or courier from outside Canada once the total of B2C sales exceeds $30,000 over a 12-month period. Similar to the platform operator rules for services and intangibles, the platform operator would bear full liability for the tax.

Since the proposals apply to goods above the de minimis threshold, the goods would have been subject to tax upon importation. As registration is required under the normal rules, this should pose no significant issue in the case where the non-resident supplier is required to collect tax upon the domestic sale. The supplier would simply

76. OECD (2019), *supra* n. 61. There may also be goods that are above de minimis thresholds, but which escape taxation simply because not all imports are adequately screened by customs. It may be difficult to address VAT leakage on these goods through marketplace facilitator rules unless there is strong coordination between customs and tax authorities. For example, if the platform has already collected VAT on the supply the customs authorities will need access to this information to allow the goods to enter without imposing further VAT. There may also be risk of clearance delays unless there is near instantaneous exchange information. However, VAT reporting on supplies is typically at pre-determined intervals, e.g., month, quarterly, annually. This may not be realistic with current technology.
77. OECD (2019), *supra* n. 61, 17. *See* also BEPS Action 1 Report 8.1.1.
78. *See* BEPS Action 1 Report 8.1.1.1.
79. The threshold in Canada is generally CAD 20. A CAD 40 threshold applies to imports from Mexico or the United States, *see* sections 7 and 7.01, Schedule VII, Excise Tax Act.
80. 2020 Fall Economic Statement, 4.8.1.2 Fair Taxation of Goods Supplied through Fulfillment Warehouses.

claim a deduction for the tax paid to import the goods. However, in the case where the platform operator is required to collect the tax, the person who paid tax to import the goods (e.g., the non-resident supplier) and the person required to account for tax on the domestic sale (the platform operator) are different persons. The rules contemplate that the operator would be entitled to deduction for the tax paid by the non-resident supplier to import the goods provided the non-resident supplier furnishes adequate evidence that the tax was paid.[81] One can imagine a variety of scenarios where it may be challenging for operators to obtain such evidence. For example, providing the operator with evidence of the tax paid on import would effectively divulge the supplier's margin to the operator. This may be commercially sensitive information, especially where the platform operator itself sells competitive products.

Other notable aspects of these proposals include information reporting requirements for platform operators and for warehouses which provide the service of storing goods in Canada ordered by sale by non-residents.[82] Marketplace facilitator rules have numerous benefits. From a compliance perspective, they have the benefit of imposing registration requirements upon a smaller number of entities. For domestic tax authorities, this means fewer entities to audit. Indeed, marketplace facilitators may be a market solution to the compliance problems long associated with VAT on cross-border e-commerce. Beyond e-commerce, marketplace facilitator rules may have additional benefits with respect to domestic small suppliers and supplies of low value goods.

[C] Concerns

For rules that shift the onus of registering for, collecting, and remitting VAT away from the supplier to another entity, there is the concern that these rules may fail to properly allocate responsibility. In such a situation, both over-taxation – where VAT is levied by both the supplier and the marketplace facilitator – and under-taxation – where neither the supplier nor the marketplace facilitator charge VAT – are possibilities. Well-drafted marketplace facilitator provisions can limit over-taxation and under-taxation by clearly delineating VAT responsibilities between the supplier and marketplace facilitator. As mentioned above, in Australia, the relationship between marketplace facilitators and suppliers is typically governed by written agreement. Provisions like Australia's should help to minimize concerns that marketplace facilitator rules will necessarily result in over- and under-taxation.

There is also a concern with systems that impose full liability on the platform which could be grounded on fairness. As the OECD notes, full liability regimes should be predicated on the platform reasonably being capable of compliance.[83] This required, for example, availability to a platform of sufficient information to determine the correct application of tax. A platform is essentially software and algorithms designed to facilitate sales made by someone else. The platform itself may know little if anything at all about the potentially thousands of items being transacted. Correctly applying

81. Section 211.22.
82. Section 211.23.
83. OECD (2019), *supra* n. 61, 45 and 2.2.4.

exemptions and preferences, differential rates based on sub-national jurisdictions, and rules based on compound versus multiple supply can be difficult even for sophisticated domestic suppliers. It often depends on the characterization of the particular product and the circumstances of its sale. The necessary information is mostly in the domain of and is best evaluated by the seller, not the platform. Moreover, a platform may not be able to sufficiently indemnify themselves through the seller, who may be in another jurisdiction. Thus, before full liability is countenanced, serious consideration should be given to alternatives and to appropriate 'safe habours', such as due diligence and reasonable reliance.[84]

Finally, although the rise of marketplace facilitators may be cause for optimism from a VAT compliance perspective, the phenomenon may be undesirable in other ways. Recent scholarship has begun to explore e-commerce platforms from the perspective of competition policy and anti-trust law. Anti-trust scholar Lina M. Khan has tracked the growth and power of e-commerce platform Amazon. She writes:

> [T]here is growing public awareness that Amazon has established itself as an essential part of the internet economy, and a gnawing sense that its dominance – its sheer scale and breadth – may pose hazards.[85]

Indeed, the desirability of the present market concentration around e-commerce platforms from these perspectives is contested. Without dismissing these concerns, we note that marketplace facilitators can play a convenient role in simplifying and enhancing compliance for supplies of cross-border e-commerce in the VAT context.

§15.08 EFFECTIVE ENFORCEMENT

Once the practical reality of non-resident vendor registration is accepted, the central issue becomes how to effectively enforce consumption jurisdiction tax obligations. The remarkable proliferation and convergence on a destination-basis VAT in the absence of treaties also means there is no specific legal mechanism for enforcement. In this absence of treaties, how is the tax authority of the consumption jurisdiction to ensure that a foreign vendor properly remits all the VAT it collects, assuming it chooses to register? Apart from questions of legal jurisdiction under applicable domestic law, as a practical matter, how will that authority subject a vendor to audit and levy assessments for tax, interest, and penalties when the vendor has no assets or physical presence in its jurisdiction?

[A] Existing Treaties and Agreements

Enforcement has the potential to be the Achilles Heel of mandatory vendor registration. Recognizing this challenge, various solutions have been considered. One enforcement

84. The OECD also notes alternative potential roles for platforms, such as information sharing, voluntarily intermediary, and joint and several liability with the supplier.
85. Lina M. Khan, *Amazon's Antitrust Paradox*, 126 (3) Yale L. J. 710 (2017).

mechanism would have a vendor collect the consumption jurisdiction's VAT and remit the VAT to its local tax authority. The local authority would then transfer the funds to its counterpart in the consumption jurisdiction. Technologically, this was deemed feasible in 2001, but the OECD recognized the slim likelihood that there would be sufficient intergovernmental cooperation:

> The significant increase in the cost of administration, in addition to the need for international agreements regarding enforcement, collection and revenue transfers, places the feasibility of this option in question, at least in the short to medium term.

This approach does not appear to have been seriously considered since. Instead, the focus has shifted to adapting existing provisions for mutual assistance in bilateral tax treaties and information exchange agreements. Since these instruments are already in existence and are being examined to support a coordinated response to BEPS in international tax, this shift in focus makes sense. That said, there appears to be little research to date on the effectiveness of these instruments in facilitating enforcement of VAT obligations. A potential problem with these instruments is that existing tax agreements mostly focus on direct taxes. Indeed, indirect taxes were not necessarily foremost in the minds of the negotiators of bilateral treaties.

For example, Article 26 of the model OECD bilateral treaty deals with exchange of information. This provision applies to 'such information as is foreseeably relevant ... to the administration or enforcement of the domestic laws concerning taxes of every kind and description imposed on behalf of the Contracting States'.[86] Its application is not restricted to taxes covered by the Convention, and the provision therefore applies as well to the exchange of information with respect to VAT.[87]

In practice, however, the scope and effectiveness of these agreements may be more limited (of course, a consumption jurisdiction would need to have a treaty or information exchange agreement with the supplier's jurisdiction before even entertaining the possibility of seeking recourse to a treaty).[88]

Canada illustrates this point. Canada's largest trading partner is the US. Article XXVII, which pertains to the exchange of information, does indeed apply broadly to all taxes.[89] Article XXVI A of the *Canada-United States Convention with Respect to Taxes on Income and on Capital*, which pertains to assistance in collection, is potentially robust and includes enforcement of assessments of one state by the other as if they were assessments under domestic tax rules. It also applies to 'all categories of taxes collected by or on behalf of the Government of a Contracting State'.[90] However, they are also discretionary and couched in the non-committal language of treaties: the parties 'undertake to *lend assistance*' and '[a] revenue claim of the applicant State that has

86. OECD Model Tax Convention, Article 26.
87. OECD, *International VAT/GST Guidelines* (OECD Publishing, 2017) 105-107, available at http://dx.doi.org/10.1787/9789264271401-en.
88. This raises the interesting possibility of whether suppliers would purposefully locate to jurisdictions that lack treaties and tax information exchange agreements.
89. Canada-United States Convention with Respect to Taxes on Income and on Capital, Article XXVII.
90. Canada-United States Convention with Respect to Taxes on Income and on Capital, Article XXVI.

been finally determined *may* be accepted for collection by the competent authority of the requested State'. A review of Canada's other conventions with several other major trading partners reveals that the relevant Exchange of Information provisions of some partners are limited to the income taxes (the UK, Australia, and China). The Canada-Mexico treaty is sufficiently broad to cover VAT but lacks an assistance in collection provision.[91] Thus, while the convention could assist with providing information necessary for detection of non-compliance by the consumption jurisdiction, it does not provide for any legal consequences in the supplier's home jurisdiction.

A similar critique can be made regarding the tax information exchange agreements that many countries have also entered. As their name suggests, these agreements are more modest in scope and mainly provide for the mutual exchange of information pertaining to the administration and enforcement of domestic tax laws. The OECD TIEA model agreement contemplates that indirect taxes could be covered.[92] The model agreement also has provisions for tax examinations conducted abroad.[93] Canada has entered over 24 TIEA currently in force, largely with smaller trading partners. Many appear capable of covering VAT. While the ability to obtain information is no doubt useful, the model agreement suffers from two notable deficiencies. First, Article 6, which contemplates tax audits abroad, is weak: the other tax authority is not obligated to allow an audit to occur on their soil, and written consent of the person being audited is required. While an audit could quite likely be conducted entirely remotely with sufficient information, the more significant defect is that the model TIEA does not include any legal consequences from an audit in the supplier's home jurisdiction. In contrast, for example, Article XXVI A of the Canada-US treaty has very robust Assistance in Collection obligations, assuming the request is accepted.

To the extent that these agreements, as negotiated, do not cover VAT or do not extent to assistance in enforcement, they do not live up to their potential. While it is possible that the agreements could be amended to better support mutual VAT enforcement, such amendments would likely require sufficient alignment of incentives. It is not evident such an alignment can be easily achieved.

Consider the United States, for example. It can be observed that many of the prominent e-commerce businesses (such as Google, Facebook, Amazon, Apple, and Netflix) are based in the United States. It can be inferred from this that the US is likely a net exporter of e-commerce. The United States is also the only OECD country without a federal VAT. What incentive would the United States have to cooperate under an agreement that covers VAT, such as Article XXVI A of the Convention with Canada? It gains no reciprocal benefit in acceding to information or enforcement requests of the other jurisdiction since there is no federal VAT for the other jurisdiction to assist in collecting. Even if there were, the magnitude of the benefit to the other jurisdiction is likely to be far greater than what the US would receive. It is possible that the US could be incentivized to cooperate with another jurisdiction under an agreement that covers

91. Convention Between the Government of Canada and the Government of the United Mexican States, Article 2.
92. OECD Model TIEA, Article 3.
93. OECD Model TIEA, Article 6.

VAT if the other jurisdiction made concessions that were beneficial to the US in some other area.

Overall, while bilateral tax agreements are potentially applicable and could be made robust, more research is needed to determine the extent to which they are capable of including VAT. Further study is also needed to determine, empirically, how successful consumption jurisdictions have been in accessing these mechanisms in light of imbalanced incentives for cooperation.

Ultimately, the OECD concedes that '[c]ompliance with these requirements is essentially voluntary as the consumers' jurisdictions have limited means to enforce compliance by non-resident non-established suppliers'.[94] But it also notes that the experience to in some jurisdictions indicates that a significant number of suppliers are nonetheless complying. This observation is discussed below.

[B] Are Enforcement Concerns Overstated?

Notwithstanding the critiques above, it is possible that concerns about effective enforcement are speculative and overstated. The Canadian province of Quebec offers an interesting example of why this may be the case. At the very least, Quebec illustrates that there is more at play than bare enforceability.

Quebec imposes and administers a subnational destination-basis VAT, the Quebec Sales Tax (QST). Prior to January 1, 2019, the QST rules were largely similar to the federal GST/HST rules, in that QST applied to supplied 'made in Quebec' and non-residents who did not 'carry on business' in Quebec were generally not required to register for QST, even if they made supplies to consumers in Quebec. In the case of services and intangibles, such as Netflix and Spotify, consumers were generally supposed to self-assess any applicable QST. Of course, self-assessment did not happen:

> First, since consumer self-assessment compliance is practically non-existent, the Québec government sustains substantial tax revenue losses. Second, since the QST is not paid by consumers, suppliers outside Québec have a competitive advantage over Québec businesses, given that the latter are generally required to collect and remit the QST on their supplies in Québec.
>
> The Québec government recognizes the difficulties posed by the application of tax measures in the context of the digital economy, and considers that the status quo is no longer possible. The time has come to adapt the QST system to the realities of the 21st century.[95]

Starting 1 January 2019, Quebec abandoned the 'carrying on business' threshold for non-resident registration. It began requiring non-residents to register and file quarterly returns simply if they exceeded CAD 30,000 in sales to Quebec consumers in the prior year. These rules provide no exclusion for non-residents who do not carry on business in Quebec or have no physical presence in the province. The rules present two

94. OECD, *Addressing the Tax Challenges of the Digital Economy, Action 1* – 2015 Final Report, OECD/G20 Base Erosion and Profit Shifting Project (OECD Publishing, 2015) 122, http://dx.doi.org/10.1787/9789264241046-en.
95. Quebec Economic Plan, March 2018.

options for registration – a simplified approach, which would not permit any input tax refunds, and 'normal' registration.

In addition, Quebec introduced rules for online platforms which enable transactions and 'control key elements of transactions' such as billing, transaction terms and conditions, and delivery.[96] Although not identified by name in the Budget, it appears the rules are intended to address concerns about supplies provided by individuals through online platforms, such as Airbnb and Uber. The proposals force the platform to register and collect applicable tax, even if it is individual users who make the underlying sale.

Early indications appear to be that the new rules are a success. In the two quarters immediately following the new rule, the Quebec government collected CAD 38 million in additional QST revenue.[97] They had estimated revenue loss of CAD 270 million in 2017 as a result of the previous rules. Quebec publishes an online list of registered businesses. Approximately 750 businesses have registered, although not all of them are non-residents of Canada. Notably, they include major e-commerce businesses, including Netflix, Facebook, Google, and Amazon. Anecdotally, businesses that have registered review the list and are apparently informing the Quebec government of competitors who are not listed. Soon after Quebec introduced its registration requirements, the provinces of Saskatchewan and British Columbia introduced similar rules for their respective provincial retail sales taxes. Canada is now in the unusual situation where three subnational jurisdictions have broader non-resident consumption tax registration requirements than the federal government.

It is worth noting that Quebec, as a subnational jurisdiction, does not have direct access to state-to-state level tax treaties and information exchange agreements. Moreover, Quebec's taxation powers are more limited than those of a nation-state. Yet, these factors did not prevent the province from implementing its mandatory registration requirements. The Quebec example therefore suggests there may be other factors at play beyond the brute 'enforceability' mandatory obligations. What those factors are and how compliance regimes can be designed to take advantage of them, deserves further study. What roles do compliance simplification, reputational concerns, or concerns regarding disclosure of liabilities in financial statements play?

It has been suggested that larger, high-profile firms may wish to be seen as tax-compliant for reputational reasons. But this assertion deserves scrutiny. For example, if consumers are nearly universally unwilling to self-assess tax, will they truly be concerned with the compliance reputation of suppliers who do not charge VAT? Research in the US state tax context suggests the non-collection of sales tax on inter-state e-commerce (under the former *Quill* doctrine) in fact shifts consumer

96. 'Specified digital platform' means a digital platform for the distribution of property or services through which a particular person enables another person who is a specified supplier to make a taxable supply in Québec of incorporeal movable property or a service to a recipient, provided the particular person controls the essential elements of the transaction between the specified supplier and the recipient such as billing, the terms and conditions of the transaction and the terms of delivery.

97. Revenu Quebec presentation at the 53rd Tax Executives Institute Annual Conference.

towards purchasing tax-free from out-of-state vendors.[98] It is suggested that there is likely more at play than the vague notion of 'reputation'.

Perhaps the mere possibility of a jurisdiction using the 'stick' of third-party withholding or other heavy-handed measures (discussed above) is a sufficient incentive for some firms to register voluntarily. Simply put, a destination-based VAT offers suppliers fewer avoidance opportunities and equips jurisdictions with more tools to induce compliance than an origin-based VAT would. The apparent success of Quebec's rules in garnering compliance may partly reflect firms' recognition of this fact.

Whatever the reasons, the Quebec example suggests that perfect compliance is not required for vendor registration to be an acceptable solution. It has been noted that e-commerce is dominated by a relatively small number of very large players.[99] If a sufficient number of these businesses register, the tax authorities may be satisfied that tax revenue and competitive equity concerns are adequately addressed.

[C] Risk of Fraud?

As more jurisdictions implement some form of simplified registration for non-residents, fraud is a concern that may become increasingly important. The information requirements under these simplified registration regimes are intentionally kept low. The non-residents to whom these regimes are available generally do not have a physical presence in the taxing jurisdiction. As noted above, the available enforcement mechanisms in bilateral instruments may be weak. The VAT has proven to be susceptible to fraud,[100] and there is no reason why this would not be the case with foreign registrations.[101]

To be clear, the risk of fraud should be limited to non-remittance, and not fraudulent input tax credits or refunds (since these simplified regimes do not provide for such deducts). The latter is more severe as involves direct loss paid out of government coffers, while the former does not. The risk is also mitigated by limiting mandatory foreign registration to B2C sales (as noted above, VAT on B2Bs sales is to be self-assessed). The risk of non-remittance may be deemed acceptable when measured against the benefits of assumed general compliance. There have also been various proposals to deploy technology such as blockchain to combat fraud.[102] As more

98. Liran Einav, Dan Knoepfle, Jonathan Levin and Neel Sundaresa, *Sales Taxes and Internet Commerce*, 104(1) Am. Econ. Rev. 1 (2014); Mark A. Scanlan, *Tax Sensitivity in Electronic Commerce*, 28(4) Fisc. Stud. 417 (2007).

99. *See* Khan, *supra* n. 84, and Kim, *infra* n. 111.

100. For example, *see* Michael Keen and Stephen Smith, *VAT Fraud and Evasion: What Do We Know, and What Can be Done?* 59 (4) Nat'l Tax J. 861 (2006).

101. The risk is likely higher as there would be delays in obtaining information from other jurisdictions relevant to detecting fraud. To mitigate this risk, Canada requires non-residents without any permanent establishment to provide security (such as a bond) as a requirement for registration.

102. Richard T. Ainsworth, & Andrew Shact, *Blockchain (Distributed Ledger Technology) Solves VAT Fraud*, Boston University School of Law, Law & Economics Working Paper No. 16-41. Richard T. Ainsworth, Musaad Alwohaibi, and Mike Cheetham. *VATCoin: The GCC's Cryptotaxcurrency*, Boston University School of Law, Law & Economics Working Paper No. 17-04.

experience accumulates, it may be necessary to make adjustments to the registration regime in order to strike the appropriate balance between simplifying compliance and safeguarding revenues.

§15.09 PLACE OF SUPPLY RULES

A destination-based VAT, which awards taxing rights to the jurisdiction of consumption, inherently requires determining the place consumption. This determination is made through place of taxation or place of supply rules, generally based on proxies for the location of actual consumption. Without adequate international coordination, one could, in theory, have instances of under-taxation or double taxation. For example, a supplier's jurisdiction may consider a supply to be an export and, therefore, zero-rated. Conversely, the consumer's jurisdiction's role may consider that same supply made outside its jurisdiction and therefore not subject to collection by the vendor (instead, it may be subject to a reverse-charge). Moreover, to the extent that these rules are based on classification of supplies into discrete, mutually exclusive categories, e-commerce blurring the line, the potential for inconsistency could be increased.

In practice, nations have implemented different place of supply rules for different kinds of supplies. This is also true for recent cross-border e-commerce regimes, like Australia's, which generally apply to inbound intangible consumer supplies rather than supplies of tangible personal property.

For example, Canada has different place of supply rules for supplies of tangible personal property, intangible personal property, and services. The latter two categories are particularly relevant in the e-commerce context, as they subsume most digital products. For intangible personal property, supplies are deemed to be made in Canada if the property 'may be used in whole or in part in Canada'.[103] For services, in contrast, supplies are deemed to be made in Canada if the service is or is to be 'performed in whole or in part in Canada'.[104] Thus, there are radically different rules depending on characterization of the supply.

In light of these place of supply rules, two related concerns can be identified. First, the rule for services is focused on the place of performance by the supplier not the location of consumption per se. Historically, these rules were not particularly problematic – when services were largely performed in the presence of the customer, there may have been little material distinction. Now that e-commerce has allowed for the radical separation of the consumption of services from service providers, however, these place of supply rules are poor proxies for the destination principle.

In the e-commerce context, these rules may be problematic. To the extent that a service is 'performed' wholly outside of Canada, for example, the supply of that service will be deemed to have been made outside of Canada. This is true regardless of whether the service is consumed by a Canadian recipient. These rules likely shelter non-resident remote service-providers from the GST's administrative requirements, thereby giving

103. Excise Tax Act, R.S.C., 1985, c. E-15 (Canada) at 142(1)(c)(i).
104. Excise Tax Act, R.S.C., 1985, c. E-15 (Canada) at 142(1)(g).

their supplies a price advantage over domestic service-providers and suppliers of intangible personal property.

Second, the rules require suppliers and tax authorities to distinguish whether a supply constitutes property or a service. For many e-commerce supplies, it may not be immediately clear whether the supply constitutes intangible personal property or a service because e-commerce 'blurs the lines between categories'.[105] For example, consider the concept of 'software as a service' or SaaS. This refers generally to software accessed remotely through the internet.[106] Is this intangible personal property?[107] Or has its mode of delivery rendered it a service? This categorization problem creates a perverse incentive for non-residents to recharacterize their supplies as services to achieve the aforementioned price advantage. For this reason, Canada's place of supply rules are not well-positioned to account for e-commerce supplies made by non-resident suppliers.

That said, it is not clear how prevalent such issues actually are. At present, there appears to be sufficient consensus about how these place of taxation rules should be applied. Once again, the remarkable convergence of the VAT around common principles deserves mention. The efforts of the OECD to promulgate a common set of widely adopted guidelines appears to have been successful. Starting in the late 1990s, 'the OECD developed guidelines for tax collection mechanisms for cross-border VAT purchases and began to publish a "Consumption Tax Guidance Series" to promote consensus on the application of VATs with respect to international transactions'.[108] This effort has continued during the BEPS era. The OECD's 2015 Guidelines on International VAT ('OECD Guidelines') were developed with the buy-in of 105 members and institutions. It was adopted as a formal 'Recommendation' in 2016 as 'the first OECD legal instrument in the area of VAT and the first internationally agreed framework for the application of VAT to cross-border trade which aspires to a global coverage'.

The OECD Guidelines, while very detailed, are nonetheless based on general principles. Therefore, they should have the ability to adapt and evolve as required. For example, they endorse business address as the general rule for locating consumption for B2B supplies. There are special rules if an enterprise has multiple locations where the supplies could be considered to be consumed. In the case of B2C supplies, the starting point is place of usual residence with specific guidelines for making that determination based on available information such as billing address and IP address.

105. Mike Nienhuis, *Tax Implications for Non-Residents Conducting E-Commerce in Tax Implications for Non-Residents Conducting E-Commerce in Canada*, 9(1) CJLT 235, 257 (2011).
106. *See*, e.g., Martin Campbell-Kelly and Daniel D. Garcia-Swartz, *From Products to Services: The Software Industry in the Internet Era*, 81(4) Bus. Hist. Rev. 735 (2007). The authors note at p. 738: 'Whereas software was once sold as bits-in-a box, increasingly it is being delivered as a service over the Internet blurring the once sharp boundaries between software products and services.'
107. Note that software was traditionally considered intangible personal property when purchased or licenced. It may even have been considered a tangible good once, when it was sold on a tangible medium.
108. Cockfield, *supra* n. 28, 148.

The OECD is careful to point out that the Guidelines are not intended to be rigid prescriptions:

> 3.37 These Guidelines do not aim to set out which approach should be preferred or to rule out alternatives: each approach is likely to have specific merits in particular circumstances. These approaches are not mutually exclusive and could be combined according to the information that is available to the supplier and the customer. It is for jurisdictions to adopt the approach or approaches that they consider appropriate, taking into account their legal and administrative framework and practices.[109]

However, it is telling that, in the next breadth, it states that '[t]he more jurisdictions adopt the same approach, the greater the reduction in complexity, uncertainty and risks of double taxation and unintended non-taxation'.[110] Ultimately, the success of the Guidelines depends on wide-spread and sufficiently consistent application of the place of supply rules. Clearly it would be preferable to have a binding multilateral instrument to harmonize the place of taxation rules.[111] Since the Guidelines are not legal instruments, however, they are not binding. For the same reason, there are no formal dispute resolution mechanisms to arbitrate inconsistencies or disputes about their application. Nonetheless, the 'soft' nature of the Guidelines and their flexibility should prove to be a virtue. Technology has consistently defied efforts to apply prescriptive rules. Acknowledging this, the flexibility afforded through adoption of broader principles should be more of a virtue than a fallacy. Especially given that the Guidelines are the result of fairly broad consensus, it appears that a workable form of harmonization is achievable – at least until the next technological innovation disrupts the status quo.

§15.10 CONSUMPTION WITHOUT EXPENDITURE: LIMITS OF TRANSACTIONAL VAT

To conclude this chapter on digital cross-border supplies, we look at the implications for VAT of what have been called multi-sided platforms ('MSP').[112] MSPs essentially involve an electronic intermediary that brings together distinct user groups. One user group could be consumers ('user-consumers'), another could be businesses ('user-businesses'). These groups of users may be in different tax jurisdictions from one another and, indeed, from the MSP. The platform benefits from network effects in that

109. OECD (2015), *supra* n. 94, 229.
110. OECD (2015), *supra* n. 94, 229.
111. For example, the government of Quebec signed memorandum of understanding with the government of Canada whereby Quebec will undertake to mirror, under the QST legislation, the place of supply rules under the GST/HST legislation to avoid instances of non-taxation and double taxation.
112. The description of these platforms draws heavily on: Young Ran (Christine) Kim, *Digital Services Tax: A Cross-Border Variation of the Consumption Tax Debate*, 72 Ala L. Rev. 131 (2020). Any errors with the mis-description of the technology and terminology are of this chapter's authors.

the more users there are of one group, the more benefit there is to the other, and vice versa.

Familiar examples of MSPs include the Google search engine and Facebook. Other examples include Twitter, and the free version of Youtube. In the case of Google, user-consumers conduct searches for free. In the case of Facebook, users-consumers access and create content for free. User-businesses pay Google and Facebook for advertising. A user-consumer may, as a result of the interaction make a purchase but not necessarily. Google and Facebook, for their part, improve their algorithms based on these interactions. Consider, for example, a UK user-consumer searching for an automobile through Google. A German automobile manufacturer, the user-business, pays for the advertising viewed by the user-consumer:[113]

> Multisided platforms serve two or more distinct groups of customers or users who value each other's participation. Users on one side of the market are charged little to nothing to participate, while the users on the other side are charged all or the majority of the profits. In the above example, Google does not charge fees to retail users. Instead, it operates other business lines, such as online advertising services, that connect different types of user groups— user-sellers and user-buyers. Most of the profits do not come from the consumers in the UK. Technically, while Google's revenue in this example is relevant to the UK market because it collects and uses UK consumers' data, the profits are paid by German manufacturing companies. Thus, it is more challenging for the UK to exercise tax jurisdiction if the business is located in a different country and the group paying for the services—user-advertisers or user-sellers—is located in a third country.

The current debate with MSPs in direct taxation is tied to the source issue described in the introduction. While MSPs derive benefit from user-consumers located in a putative source jurisdiction, they lack the physical presence traditionally required to allocate taxing jurisdiction. In response, 'market countries have started imposing a new tax, called the digital services tax ("DST"), on certain digital business models, which has ignited heated debate across the globe. Supporters defend the DST, designed as a turnover style consumption tax, as an effective measure to make up the foregone revenue in the digital economy because it is not bound by the traditional rules of income taxation.'[114]

As a turnover tax, the DST is arguably a form of consumption tax. As the name suggests, the tax base is a business's gross receipts. The rate of the specific DST (e.g., 2%) applies to the gross receipts provided there is sufficient interaction with user-consumers in the local market and/or a local revenue threshold is crossed.[115] Initially proposed by the European Commission in 2018, DSTs have been adopted by numerous countries in Europe and are presently under consideration in other jurisdictions.[116]

113. Kim, *supra* n. 112, 134/5.
114. Kim, *supra* n. 112, 132.
115. Kim, *supra* n. 112, 147/8, describing the UK DST.
116. Ruth Mason and Leopoldo Parada, "The Legality of Digital Taxes in Europe" (2020) 40:1 Virginia Law Review 175-217 at page 177; Annex 7, 2021 Federal Budget Canada. Canada's DST is proposed to become effective January 1, 2022.

The study of the consumption tax aspects of these MSPs is emergent. For present purposes, we simply note that the DST illustrates a deficiency of the widely adopted invoice-based VAT form of consumption tax. The VAT has been referred to as a transaction tax or a consumption expenditure tax rather than a pure consumption tax because it tends to be imposed on transactions. The key feature of the above MSPs is that they are free to one group of users, the user-consumer. So even though there is consumption of digital content by user-consumers, there may not be any corresponding consumption expenditure. There is, therefore, no taxable event under a transactional VAT in the consumption jurisdiction of the user-consumer. While there is a consumption expenditure by the user-business who pays for advertising, the VAT accrues to the user-business's jurisdiction. That may be a different jurisdiction than the user-consumer's. All the VAT revenue accrues to the business' jurisdiction with none to the user-consumers. While it may be possible to allocate tax to the user-consumer's jurisdiction at an aggregate level, as the DST attempts to, this is likely not feasible with a transaction VAT. It would require, at the individual invoice level, imputing consideration to users-consumers in all different jurisdictions in order for user-consumers who are registered businesses to recover input VAT. But imputing an appropriate amount of consideration would essentially be arbitrary. Therefore, to the extent that this form of consumption by user-consumers is to be included in a consumption tax base, it cannot adequately be captured by VAT.

Admittedly, there is significant debate among tax policy scholars about whether the DST ought to be characterized as a consumption tax at all. Some scholars argue that the DST is essentially a disguised income tax. More concretely, they argue that the DST's tax base is a crude proxy for income, designed to bypass "the traditional international [income] tax rules that require physical presence" in the taxing jurisdiction. Arguably, the strongest point in favour of this view is the fact that the European Commission explicitly conceived of the DST a provisional alternative to amending its income tax treaties.

That said, the long-term economic incidence of the DST is not yet known. At present, however, the incidence of the DST appears to be mixed. Following the implementation of DSTs in France and the UK, Amazon and Google announced that they would "pass the tax's cost to user-sellers or user-advertisers in those countries by increasing various fees." In contrast, Facebook and eBay publicly committed to bear the costs of the DST themselves. It is not immediately clear why Amazon and Google decided to pass the tax on while Facebook and eBay did not. This issue merits further study. More crucially, it is not clear whether the incidence of the DST will change over time. In our view, the outcome of the DST characterization debate should hinge on the long-term incidence of the tax.

§15.11 CONCLUSION

E-commerce undeniably presents challenges for VAT systems, but these challenges are neither insurmountable nor existential. Jurisdictions that fail to subject cross-border e-commerce transactions to VAT risk distorting their markets by giving non-residents a price advantage over domestic, brick-and-mortar, or otherwise registrant suppliers. Unlike the PE concept in the income tax context, however, the destination principle offers VAT regimes a framework for taxing e-commerce without significant alteration.

In spite of optimism from the OECD, a technological solution to the compliance problems relating to the VAT treatment of cross-border e-commerce has not arisen. Future innovations may yet reduce the costs of compliance, but policymakers should not wait for these developments.

In the absence of a technological solution, a market solution to VAT compliance in the e-commerce era appears to have emerged. Marketplace facilitator rules can minimize the total compliance burden by dramatically reducing the number of entities with administrative VAT requirements. They can also help to 'level the playing field' in respect of supplies made by domestic small suppliers. Policymakers across the world appear aware of these benefits, and many jurisdictions have already implemented marketplace facilitator rules.

Of course, these rules are not without their complications. Policymakers must be astute to issues of over- or under-taxation when both vendor and marketplace facilitator registration rules are pursued. Good marketplace facilitator rules will clearly delineate the respective roles of suppliers, on the one hand, and marketplace facilitators, on the other. Moreover, the fact that marketplace facilitators make convenient VAT collection agents should not completely distract from other critiques of those facilitators in the context competition policy or antitrust law.

There is reason to believe the concerns about the enforcement of administrative VAT obligations on non-residents have been overstated. As mentioned above, marketplace facilitator rules provide compliance benefits that should make it easier for jurisdictions to enforce their administrative VAT requirements. Additionally, there may be soft incentives encouraging non-resident vendors to voluntarily fulfil their administrative VAT obligations. Further empirical research on this point is necessary to gauge the effectiveness of marketplace facilitator rules as compliance measures.

The convergence around the destination principle is highly fortunate with respect to e-commerce. The destination principle has given taxing jurisdictions access to a less mobile tax base (consumption) than the origin principle would have (production). Indeed, the convergence around the destination principle should allow jurisdictions to collect VAT from e-commerce transactions even if non-resident vendors refuse to register, through second- or third-best policies, like withholding tax or reverse-charge measures. The mere threat of these measures may be a 'stick' in governments' arsenal that helps to encourage non-resident vendors to comply with vendor registration rules.

That said, the destination principle still remains aspirational in some VAT regimes. Regimes with nexus requirements depart from the destination principle in a manner that makes taxing cross-border e-commerce more difficult. Place of supply rules can also serve as an imperfect instantiation of the destination principle. This may be especially problematic when place of supply rules treat intangible personal property differently from services, as these categories have been undermined by novel forms of e-commerce.

Further difficulties are to be anticipated. In particular, transactions where consumption appears to occur in more than one jurisdiction are a challenge for VAT regimes. Conversely, VATs are not well-positioned to tax consumption that is untethered from consideration. For this sort of consumption, different tax instruments may be preferable.

CHAPTER 16

Supplies below Cost Price or Free of Charge

Madeleine Merkx

§16.01 INTRODUCTION

The aim of VAT in the European Union (EU) and elsewhere, is to tax private consumption. The tax is levied on expenditure of consumers and other end users. Businesses are the unpaid tax collectors for the government. As a tax on consumption expenditure, VAT is levied as a percentage of the consideration paid. In case of supplies free of charge, a consideration is missing, and these supplies are not subject to VAT. As a consequence, at least under EU VAT law, the person who provides supplies free of charge has no right to deduct input VAT. For such a person, the VAT is a cost and he or she can be regarded as an end user of that supply.

Unfortunately, the EU VAT life is not that simple. Supplies free of charge may be linked to the business, meaning that input VAT is still (partially) deductible even though there is a corresponding supply free of charge. Or, VAT has been deducted because it was yet unclear whether a good or service would be used for the business, or for a supply free of charge, or for private purposes. The EU VAT Directive has mechanisms in place to ensure that supplies free of charge made for private purposes, will be subject to VAT. This is necessary to uphold the neutrality principle in VAT.

Because EU VAT is levied on the actual consideration received by the business, regardless of whether it makes a profit or not (only an aim for yield is required), in principle, supplies below cost price also fall within the scope of EU VAT. The result of this can be that a business can deduct more VAT than it owes. In such a situation disputes may arise as regards the deductibility of VAT and the genuineness of a business' status as a taxable person. Related parties sometimes take advantage of the fact that supplies below cost price are included in the scope of the tax. This result may be undesirable, and the VAT Directive therefore contains provisions that could put an end to such practices. These types of provisions, however, make the EU VAT system more complicated.

This chapter deals with supplies free of charge and against a consideration below cost price. Section 16.02 first explains the nature of EU VAT and the neutrality principle. Subsequently, in §16.03 the status of a taxable person in case of supplies free of charge and below cost price will be addressed. Section 16.04 addresses the consequences for input VAT deduction in case of supplies free of charge or below cost price. Section 16.05 contains an analysis of the provisions referred to above that deal with supplies free of charge for, e.g., private purposes, that ensure the neutrality of the VAT system. Section 16.06 addresses the taxable amount and the provisions that provide EU Member States with the tools to deal with misuse of the subjective nature of the taxable amount. Last but not least, §16.07 provides a comparative law analysis covering the treatment of free of charge and below cost price supplies in Canada and South Africa.[1] Section 16.08 provides a conclusion. Barter transactions are outside the scope of this chapter. It should however be noted that barter transactions are subject to VAT.

§16.02 VAT AS A CONSUMPTION TAX AND THE NEUTRALITY PRINCIPLE

EU VAT is a general tax on consumption.[2] It is classified as an indirect tax because businesses making taxable supplies of goods and services are liable for the tax which is designed to be ultimately borne by consumers when they make consumptive purchases. In other words, consumers pay the tax indirectly, i.e., via the intermediation of sellers of goods and services, who collect the tax from consumers and then remit it to the government. Neutrality is an important feature of the tax as the VAT was introduced in the EU in the 1960s for its ability to avoid the negative effects of the predecessor turnover taxes, such as tax cascading, artificial business integration, and the inability to determine border tax adjustments accurately. Like the legal character of the tax, the neutrality principle is mentioned in Article 1 of the VAT Directive, where it is stated that: 'The principle of the common system of VAT entails the application to goods and services of a general tax on consumption exactly proportional to the price of the goods and services, however many transactions take place in the production and distribution process before the stage at which the tax is charged.'

Even though the objective of EU VAT is to tax private consumption, a clear definition of this concept is missing. The *Hong Kong* case, which will be discussed more extensively in §16.03, makes it clear that consumption takes place only in the last link of the supply chain where the customer cannot pass on the costs of inputs to another person. To ensure that private consumption is taxed, and the neutrality of the system is maintained, supplies free of charge, including supplies for private purposes should

1. The author would like to thank Simon Thang and Marius van Oordt for providing information on the Canadian GST and South African VAT, respectively.
2. This is stressed by Article 1(2) of the VAT Directive. Council Directive 2006/112/EC of 28 November 2006 on the common system of value added tax, OJ L 347, 11.12.2006, pp. 1-118.

be subject to VAT, or VAT on expenses with a private nature should not be deductible for businesses. Both mechanisms may be in place in EU Member States and will be addressed in §16.05 and §16.04, respectively. In case of supplies below cost price the situation is different because the supplier is still able to shift forward at least part of its production costs. For such a business, VAT paid on inputs may exceed the VAT collected on outputs, which may make questionable its status as taxable person and right to input-VAT deduction as further discussed below in §16.03 and §16.04.

§16.03 THE STATUS OF TAXABLE PERSON IN CASE OF SUPPLIES FREE OF CHARGE OR BELOW COST PRICE

In the *Hong Kong* case,[3] the Court of Justice of the European Union (CJEU) ruled that a person who habitually provides services to traders, free of charge, cannot be regarded as a taxable person for VAT. The CJEU refers in its reasoning to the EU VAT system where VAT is no longer deductible when the chain of transactions has come to an end. The tax is then charged to the final consumer who cannot pass on the amount of tax unless there is a further transaction in which a price is paid. When a person's activity consists exclusively in providing services for no direct consideration, there is no basis of assessment and free services cannot be subject to VAT. The person providing services free of charge is equal to a final consumer because he is at the final stage of the production and distribution chain.

From the *Hong Kong* case it becomes clear that the taxable person status depends on the existence of supplies for a consideration. The CJEU judgment in the *Tolsma* case[4] shows that for an activity to qualify as a supply for consideration, two conditions must be fulfilled. There must exist: (1) a legal relationship between the parties involved and (2) a direct link between the consideration paid and the supply.

The necessity of a direct link emerged early in the case law of the Court of Justice. In the *Coöperatieve Aardappelenbewaarplaats* case,[5] the CJEU ruled that there was no direct link between the storage of potatoes by the cooperative for its members and the reduction in value of the members' share in the cooperative. That reduction in value was caused by the fact that the members did not pay for the storage of potatoes. There is no direct link because it is not possible to establish a determinable countervalue. It is clear also from other case law that there is no direct link in the absence of a determinable supply. For example, in *Apple & Pear Development Council*,[6] the CJEU ruled that there was no service for consideration provided by the council to its members because the members did not benefit directly from the council's activities but only indirectly, because the council's activities benefit the whole sector. It follows from the *Tolsma* case that where the remuneration is arbitrary because it can be determined at the discretion of the 'customer', there is also no direct link between the remuneration

3. CJEU, 1 April 1982, Case C-89/81, *Hong Kong*, ECLI:EU:C:1982:121.
4. CJEU, 3 March 1994, Case C-16/93, *Tolsma*, ECLI:EU:C:1994:80.
5. CJEU, 5 February 1981, Case 154/80, *Coöperatieve Aardappelenbewaarplaats*, ECLI:EU:C:1981:38.
6. CJEU, 8 March 1988, Case 102/86, *Apple & Pear Development Council*, ECLI:EU:C:1988:120.

and the service provided. The same applies where the remuneration to be received is uncertain and depends on the outcome of, for example, a race[7] or a company's profits.[8]

In the *Tolsma* case, the CJEU ruled that there was no legally binding relationship between Mr. Tolsma, an organ grinder, and the passers-by who voluntarily and at their sole discretion paid him money. Nor did they ask Tolsma to make music or did the payment depend on the musical performance. Rather, payment was made for personal motives. The absence of the legal relationship meant that there could be no service for consideration.[9]

If there is a direct link and a legal relationship, a supply for consideration exists regardless of the amount of the remuneration. In particular, the fact that the price paid for an economic transaction is higher or lower than the cost price is irrelevant to the question whether a transaction is to be regarded as a 'transaction effected for consideration'.[10] The seller may even make a loss. In a situation where goods or services are supplied below cost price, the deductible VAT may exceed the VAT due. This reason alone, however, does not justify the conclusion that the supplier disqualifies as taxable person for VAT, or that the right to deduct input VAT is lost. The CJEU dismissed a French restriction to that right, which allowed for only a fractional deduction of input VAT where the annual income from the letting of property was less than one-fifteenth of the property's value.[11] The CJEU distinguished between rents involving a concession (in the French and Dutch language versions the CJEU even speaks of generosity: *une libéralité* and *vrijgevigheid* respectively) and rents constituting economic activities. From the case we can derive that, in the CJEU's view, if a consideration is so low that the related supply must be considered as an act of generosity, there is no economic activity.

The *Gemeente Borsele* case[12] clarifies further that an activity may still not qualify as an economic activity even though a supply against consideration exists. The municipality of Borsele was responsible for student transport within its borders. It contracted with bus companies to transport the students. In 2008, it paid these bus companies €458,231 including VAT. Approximately one third of the students' parents paid a fee to the municipality covering part of the transportation costs, but low-income parents were exempt from payment. In 2008, the municipality received a total of €13,958 in fees, which corresponded to 3% of the actual costs incurred for student transport services. The remainder of the transportation costs were paid from the municipality's general fund. According to the CJEU, one way of determining whether an activity constitutes an economic activity is by comparing the circumstances under which a disputed supply is made with the circumstances usually present for that type of supply. Other factors, such as the number of customers and the amount of earnings,

---

7. CJEU, 10 November 2016, Case C-432/15, *Baštová*, ECLI:EU:C:2016:855.
8. CJEU, 14 November 2000, Case C-142/99, *Floridienne/Berginvest*, ECLI:EU:C:2000:623.
9. For a more extensive analysis the author refers to Madeleine Merkx and Koen Verburg, *22 jaar na Tolsma: weer luisteren zonder btw* 69 MBB (2017/2).
10. CJEU, 12 May 2016, Case C-520/14, *Gemeente Borsele*, ECLI:EU:C:2016:334, paragraph 26, and CJEU, 2 June 2016, Case C-263/15, *Lajvér*, ECLI:EU:C:2016:392, paragraph 45.
11. CJEU, 21 September 1988, Case 50/87, *Commission v. France*, ECLI:EU:C:1988:429.
12. *Gemeente Borsele*, *supra* n. 10.

can also be considered. The CJEU gave the referring Dutch Supreme Court a number of further indications for resolving this issue:

- The contributions received by the municipality cover only a small part of the costs. Such a difference between the operating costs and the sums received in return for the services suggests that the parental contribution must be regarded more than a fee than as consideration. From that lack of symmetry, it follows that there is no genuine link between the amount paid and the services supplied. Hence, according to the CJEU, it does not appear that the link between the transport services provided by the municipality and the payment made by parents is sufficiently direct for that payment to be regarded as consideration for that service and, accordingly, for that service to be regarded as an economic activity within the meaning of Article 9(1) VAT Directive.
- The conditions under which the services are supplied are different from those under which passenger transport services are usually provided, since the municipality of Borsele does not offer services on the general passenger transport market, but rather appears to be a beneficiary and final consumer of transport services which it acquires from transport undertakings with which it deals and which it makes available to parents of students as part of its public service activities.

This market criterion was also applied by the CJEU in the *SPÖ* case. SPÖ is a political party financed by subsidies from public funds in accordance with the Austrian national legislation on the financing of political parties, by various donations, and by subscriptions paid by the members of that party.

The only income obtained by SPÖ on a continuing basis comes from public funding and the party members' contributions, which was raised particularly to cover losses from its political advertising activities. The CJEU concluded that SPÖ carried out a communication exercise in keeping with attainment of its political objectives and which sought to spread its ideas as a political organisation. More specifically, the SPÖ's activity is the development of informed political opinion with a view to participation in the exercise of political power. In carrying out that activity, SPÖ did not participate in any market.[13] Consequently, according to the CJEU the activity of SPÖ cannot constitute an economic activity. In my view, the CJEU's reasoning in this case emphasizes that SPÖ is carrying out its primary activities for its own interest and therefore qualifies as a final consumer.

Last but not least, the CJEU judgment in the *Lajvér*[14] case seems to suggest that a twofold approach must be taken. First, it has to be determined whether the payment received has a direct link with the services supplied in the sense that payment is, indeed, paid for the rendering of services and represents the value actually given in return for the service supplied to the recipient, which is not per se effected by the fact

13. CJEU, 6 October 2009, Case C-267/08, *SPÖ*, ECLI:EU:C:2009:619, paragraph 24.
14. *Lajvér*, *supra* n. 10.

that the fees paid are modest due to government subsidies.[15] Second, it needs to be established whether the fee amount has been determined '*as a result of other possible factors that could, depending on the circumstances, call into question the direct link between the services supplied and the consideration*'.[16] It is not exactly clear what the CJEU means by this. If it has to be established that the remuneration only partly remunerates the services supplied or to be supplied, is it no longer a supply for consideration at all or only for the part which is remunerated? And if there is a single supply, can it be split for VAT purposes into a part which is remunerated and a part which is not? In the *Commission/Finland* case,[17] the CJEU also refers to a part payment. The CJEU however immediately links this to the fact that the amount of the fee depends on income and assets. It is unclear to me whether there are two different criteria or just one.[18] The *Commission/Finland* case does, however, provide guidance on what factors to consider when determining the basis of the remuneration. The CJEU ruled in that case that the remuneration for services provided by legal aid offices must be determined on the basis of the degree of difficulty and the number of hours spent on the case. Since the fees were dependent on the income and assets of the recipients, the Court of Justice concluded that there is no direct link.

§16.04 VAT DEDUCTION IN CASE OF SUPPLIES FREE OF CHARGE OR BELOW COST PRICE

As discussed above, a supply free of charge is not subject to VAT and the person providing this supply will not qualify as a VAT taxable person in relation to that particular supply. As a main rule, VAT on costs related to supplies free of charge will not be deductible. However, as this section will show, it is not that simple. Even when costs are related to supplies free of charge, they may still count as general costs of another, taxable part of the business. One of the landmark cases about this issue is the *Sveda* case.[19] With a subsidy from the government, Sveda created a recreational Baltic mythology discovery path. On the basis of the subsidy conditions, the path had to be opened to the public free of charge for five years. According to the CJEU, the recreational path may be regarded as a means of attracting visitors with a view to providing them with goods and services, such as souvenirs, food, and drinks as well as access to attractions and paid-for bathing. Sveda, therefore, acquired or produced the path with the intention of carrying out an economic activity and did act as a taxable person. That finding cannot be put into question by the fact that Sveda was obliged to provide access to the path free of charge. The fact that the grant agreement prohibited the charging of a fee for access to the recreational path does not preclude Sveda from carrying out the economic activities such as the supply of souvenirs, food, and drinks.

15. *Lajvér, supra* n. 10, paragraph 39.
16. *Lajvér, supra* n. 10, paragraph 49.
17. CJEU, 29 October 2009, Case C-246/08, *Commission v. Finland,* ECLI:EU:C:2009:671.
18. *See also* Madeleine Merkx en Anne M. de Wit, *Schoolmodel in de btw: definitief gezakt?* WFR (2019/64).
19. CJEU, 22 October 2015, Case C-126/14, *Sveda,* ECLI:EU:C:2015:712.

In particular, the CJEU takes into account that the path is intended to attract visitors and to encourage them to buy the goods and services that Sveda offers and which are subject to VAT. Because the subsidy in question did not cover the full costs of the path, the costs for the construction of the path will be covered at least in part by the income from the provision of goods and services by Sveda. The *Sveda* case shows that input VAT related to a supply free of charge is deductible in case that supply is a means to sell other goods or services for consideration. It was not decisive for the Court, in my view, that income from the other supplies partly covered he costs of the recreational path; rather they formed merely an extra reason for the CJEU to conclude that deduction of input tax in the *Sveda* case should be allowed.

In case a business is involved in both economic and non-economic activities, it will need to distinguish between costs related solely to the economic activities, costs solely related to non-economic activities and costs related to both activities. VAT on costs solely related to economic activities is deductible unless those activities include exempt supplies. VAT on cost solely related to non-economic activities is not deductible. VAT on costs related to both activities is deductible to a certain extent. From the *Securenta* case[20] it becomes clear that it is up to EU Member States to provide for rules to determine the deductible amount of VAT in such cases, since such rules are absent in the VAT Directive. These rules must attribute the input VAT accurately, i.e., on a pro rata basis between economic and non-economic activities. Although the taxability of subsidies falls outside the scope of this chapter, it should be noted that subsidies that are not directly linked to the price of supplies of goods or services and may relate to non-economic activities can influence the right to deduct VAT on general costs.[21] Article 174(1) VAT Directive allows EU Member States to include those subsidies in the denominator of the deductible proportion. The result of this is that the deductible proportion will be lower.

Another set of cases deals with the situation where a third party benefits from a purchase of a business, while not paying for it. In both the *Iberdrola*[22] and the recent *Mitteldeutsche Hartstein Industrie* case,[23] the CJEU ruled that VAT could be deducted related to an investment that was provided free of charge to a municipality in case the investment was used by both the municipality and the business making the investment. This however only applies insofar as the investment does not exceed that which is necessary for the taxable person to carry out the taxable transactions and where the cost is included in the price of those transactions. In the *Fillibeck*,[24] *Maritza-East*[25] and *Vos Aannemingen* cases[26] the CJEU used similar reasoning. In those cases, third parties benefited from costs incurred as well: employees and a third-party owner of the land on

20. CJEU, 13 March 2008, Case C-437/06, *Securenta*, ECLI:EU:C:2008:166.
21. *See*, on this topic, Robert F. van Brederode and Simon Thang, *VAT and Subsidies: A Comparative Study of Law and Practice in Canada and the European Union* 67(3) Can. Tax J. 533 (2019).
22. CJEU, 14 September 2017, Case C-132/16, *Iberdrola*, ECLI:EU:C:2017:683.
23. CJEU, 16 September 2020, Case C-528/19, *Mitteldeutsche Hartstein-Industrie*, ECLI:EU:C:2020:712.
24. CJEU, 16 October 1997, Case C-258/95, *Fillibeck*, ECLI:EU:C:1997:491.
25. CJEU, 18 July 2013, Case C-124/12, *Maritza-East*, ECLI:EU:C:2013:488.
26. CJEU, 1 October 2020, Case C-405/19, *Vos Aannemingen*, ECLI:EU:C:2020:785.

which apartments were build. According to the CJEU, VAT can be deducted if a third party benefits from services purchased in case there is a direct and immediate link between those services and the taxable person's economic activity and the benefit to the third party is ancillary to the taxable person's business purposes. In my view, the fact that an expenditure is necessary for the furtherance of the business indicates that the interest of a third party likely is ancillary in nature.[27] It is also my view that the Tax officers should not try sitting in the entrepreneur's seat when answering the question of what is necessary for a business. The nature of the expenditure and not the amount should be decisive. For example, an entrepreneur like Mitteldeutsche Hartstein Industrie is free to choose between two types of asphalt in order to build the road that it supplies to the municipality free of charge. If it opts for a more expensive type of asphalt, VAT should still be fully deductible and not be limited to the VAT amount on the procurement of a cheaper asphalt product.[28]

As a main rule, VAT on costs related to supplies below cost price that qualify as supplies for consideration, will be deductible unless the supply is exempt from VAT. Having that said, the reasoning of the CJEU as regards the deductibility of VAT may still cause some doubt. In particular in the *SKF* case[29] the CJEU ruled that input VAT on costs related to the disposal of shares can only be deductible if there exists a direct and immediate link between the costs and either the disposal of shares or the products of SKF as a whole. To establish this, it is necessary to ascertain whether the costs incurred are likely to be incorporated in the prices of the shares which SKF intends to sell or included in the cost components of SKF's products. In case of a supply below costs price, not all costs will be components of the price charged. The *Volkswagen Financial Services* case[30] shows, however, that it is not always necessary to consider whether costs are actually passed on in the price of a product in order to establish that the right to deduct VAT exists. In that particular case, the CJEU ruled that VAT on cost related to leasing of cars could be partially deducted even though the costs were fully incorporated in the exempt granting of credit. Other criteria have been applied by the Court to determine whether and, if so, to what extent a right to deduct VAT exists,[31] but it appears that the incorporation of costs in the price of products remains an important criterion. In the *Chancellor, Masters and Scholars of the University of Cambridge* case,[32] the CJEU ruled about deduction of VAT on management costs of a fund of the university. This fund was fed by donations and endowments. The CJEU ruled that those donations and endowments were not consideration for a supply of goods or services, because they were essentially made for subjective reasons on charitable grounds and on a random basis. The CJEU also ruled that VAT on management costs

27. *See also*, Nino P. Arzini en Sebastiaan J. Carriere, *Profijt door een derde leidt niet tot profijt voor de fiscus* 7 BtwBrief 2020/80.
28. *See also* Jeroen Bijl, *VAT Deduction: The Relevance of Being 'The Recipient' of a Supply and the Use of the Supply* 2020-5 EC Tax Rev. 227, 232 (2020).
29. CJEU, 29 October 2009, Case C-29/08, *SKF*, ECLI:EU:C:2009:665.
30. CJEU, 18 October 2018, Case C-153/17, *Volkswagen Financial Services*, ECLI:EU:C:2018:845.
31. *See* Ad J. van Doesum en Herman W.M. van Kesteren, *De onlosmakelijke samenhang tussen kosten en belastbare handelingen*, WFR (2012/885).
32. CJEU, 3 July 2019, Case C-316/18, *Chancellor, Masters and Scholars of the University of Cambridge*, ECLI:EU:C:2019:559.

could not be deducted as VAT on general costs. The CJEU took into consideration that costs related to the management of donations and endowments invested in the fund are not incorporated into the price of a particular output transaction. The University of Cambridge is a not-for-profit educational establishment and the costs at issue were incurred in order to generate resources that are used to finance all of that university's output transactions, thus reducing the price of the goods and services provided by the university. Therefore, those costs are not components of those prices and, consequently, do not form part of the university's overhead.

This varying importance which the Court of Justice attaches to the criterion that costs must be reflected in the price of products, makes it necessary to ascertain on a case-by-case basis whether a right to deduct input VAT exists. In the case of supplies for less than cost price, the additional question may arise as to whether a full right to deduct exists. It is necessary to establish whether there is a direct and immediate link between the costs incurred and an economic activity. The incorporation of costs in the price of products is in my view merely an aid to establishing this link. The mere fact that the costs are not passed on in full cannot mean that there is no full right to deduct input tax. The author also questions whether the judgment of the CJEU in the *University of Cambridge* case is correct. In particular, because the donations and endowments are most likely provided because the university carries out certain socially desired activities and are not simply provided to an institution on an arbitrary basis. In addition, the funds are also used to invest in the university. The only reason the author can imagine breaking the direct and immediate link is that money is available and can be invested even without the management of the fund. The consequence of the management of the fund is simply that more money is available. However, this money is still used to invest in the activities of the university.

§16.05 DEEMED SUPPLIES IN CASE OF SUPPLIES FREE OF CHARGE

As becomes clear from both the *Hong Kong* case discussed in §16.02 and the provisions on the taxable amount to be discussed in §16.06, there is no VAT due in case of supplies free of charge. To protect the legal character of EU VAT as a tax on private consumption and the neutrality principle (§16.02), supplies by businesses free of charge should be subject to VAT. Articles 16 and 18 of the VAT Directive therefore deem supplies free of charge as taxable supplies of goods. Article 26 of the VAT Directive contains a similar provision for services.

[A] Deemed Supplies of Goods

Under Article 16 of the VAT Directive, the application of goods forming part of a taxable person's business for private use or for that of his staff or, more generally, their disposal free of charge, or the application for purposes other than those of his business, is deemed a supply of goods for consideration, if the VAT on those goods or the component parts thereof was wholly or partly deductible. According to the CJEU, the purpose of this rule is to ensure equal treatment between a taxable person who applies goods for his own private use or that of his staff and a final consumer who acquires goods of the same type, and to prevent situations in which final consumption is untaxed.[33] The *De Jong*-case shows that this might even require the splitting up of one single supply. In the capacity of a taxable person, De Jong had constructed a building on land that he owned privately. According to the CJEU, when a person acts solely for his private requirements, he is acting in a private capacity and not as a taxable person. Therefore, regardless of whether the land and building are inseparable under national legislation, it is necessary to distinguish between taxation of land (private) and taxation of a building which the taxable person has erected on that land in pursuit of his business. De Jong therefore only needed to report VAT on the supply of the building under Article 5(6) of the Sixth Directive (currently: Article 16 of the VAT Directive). From the *Bakcsi* case it becomes clear that it is up to the taxable person to decide whether it wants to attribute dual use goods (i.e., goods that will be used for both private and business purposes) to its business assets or its private assets.[34] The CJEU has however also made clear that the sale by a taxable person of a good which he had assigned to his private assets is not out of the scope of VAT for that reason alone. It is also necessary that such a sale be made by the taxable person not in the course of his economic activity, but in the course of the management and the administration of his private assets. In that respect, the CJEU has stated that a relevant assessment criterion is whether when marketing of the property, the person in question mobilized resources similar to those deployed by producers, traders or persons supplying services.[35]

The provision of Article 16 of the VAT Directive applies to disposals free of charge regardless of whether their disposal was for business purposes or not. In the *Mitteldeutsche Hartstein-Industrie* case[36] the CJEU, however, stated that in case there is no untaxed final consumption or a breach of the principle of equal treatment, the provision cannot be applied. In that case, a company constructed a road for its own business purposes, which was subsequently transferred to the municipality and used by the public as well. Because the works for the extension of the road benefit the Mitteldeutsche Hartstein-Industrie, have a direct and immediate link with its overall economic activity which gives rise to taxable transactions, and the costs of the input services received and linked to the works for the extension of that road form part of the factors in the cost of the output transactions carried out by Mitteldeutsche Hartstein-Industrie, the CJEU came to the conclusion that no VAT was due on the basis of Article 16 of the VAT Directive.

A supply free of charge requires an act of disposal from the taxable person. When a leasing company terminated leasing contracts but was unable to recover the goods from the lessee, the CJEU concluded there was no disposal free of charge, because the

33. *See*, e.g., CJEU, 6 May 1992, Case C-20/91, *De Jong*, ECLI:EU:C:1992:192, paragraph 15, and CJEU, 30 September 2010, Case C-581/08, *EMI group*, ECLI:EU:C:2010:559.
34. CJEU, 8 March 2001, Case C-415/98, *Bakcsi*, ECLI:EU:C:2001:136.
35. CJEU, 9 July 2015, Case C-331/14, *Trgovina Prizma*, ECLI:EU:C:2015:456, paragraphs 22-24.
36. *Mitteldeutsche Hartstein-Industrie, supra* n. 20.

lessee remained in possession of those goods without providing any form of consideration due to the lessee's allegedly wrongful conduct, and not of the disposal free of charge of those goods by the lessor in favour of the lessee.[37]

The use as samples or gifts of small value is not treated as a supply of goods. In the *EMI group* case, the CJEU stated that this exception does not apply if the objective is to satisfy the consumer's needs in relation to the product in question. However, the exception does apply if the objective is to promote the product of which the sample is a specimen. EU Member States are not allowed to limit this exception based on the number or nature of the specimen provided. In certain cases, specimens can for example be specifically produced as samples, but in other cases the specimen must correspond to the final product. EU Member States are allowed to set a monetary threshold for gifts of small value.[38]

Article 16 of the VAT Directive only applies in case VAT on the goods or the component parts thereof was wholly or partly deductible. The mere fact that VAT has been deducted on maintenance costs, but not on the good itself, does not result in a deemed supply on the basis of Article 16.[39] If VAT has not been deducted on the good, but only on a component part, taxation based on Article 16 is still required. According to the CJEU, 'component parts' refer to tangible, physical objects incorporated into the goods.[40] When goods retain their physical and economic distinctiveness they must not be regarded as component parts.[41] According to the CJEU, it is necessary to distinguish between supplies of goods which merely contribute to maintaining the value of the goods and which as a general rule have been consumed at the time of the allocation, and those which lead to a lasting increase in the value of the goods and have not been completely consumed at the time of the allocation. Only in the latter situation goods qualify as component parts. In case VAT has not been deducted upon acquisition of the goods, but VAT has been deducted on component parts, similar to the *De Jong*-case discussed above, taxation on the basis of Article 16 is limited to the component parts.[42] In case VAT has been deducted on use and maintenance costs, but not on the acquisition of the good, there is no supply based on Article 16 of the VAT Directive.[43]

Under Article 18(b) of the VAT Directive, EU Member States may also treat as a supply of goods for consideration: the application of goods by a taxable person for the purposes of a non-taxable area of activity, where the VAT on such goods became wholly or partly deductible upon their acquisition. Under Article 18(c) of the VAT Directive, EU Member States may also treat the retention of goods by a taxable person or his successors as a taxable supply, when the taxable person or successor has ceased its economy activity, under the condition that the VAT on the goods became wholly or partly deductible upon their acquisition. The main objective of Article 18(c) is to avoid

37. CJEU, 17 July 2014, Case C-438/13, *BCR Leasing*, ECLI:EU:C:2014:2093, paragraph 26.
38. *EMI group, supra* n. 31.
39. *Bakcsi, supra* n. 32.
40. CJEU 17 May 2001, Joined cases C-322/99 and C-323/99, *Fischer and Brandenstein*, ECLI: EU:C:2001:280, paragraph 59.
41. *Fischer and Brandenstein, supra* n. 40, paragraph 64.
42. *Fischer and Brandenstein, supra* n. 40, paragraph 77.
43. CJEU, 27 June 1989, Case C-50/88, *Kühne*, ECLI:EU:C:1989:262, paragraphs 13-15.

a situation where the final consumption of goods on which the VAT became deductible is untaxed following the cessation of the taxable economic activity and to effectively eliminate any inequality for VAT purposes between consumers who acquire their goods from another taxable person and those who acquire their goods in the course of their business, regardless of the causes or circumstances of that cessation.[44] From the *Mateusiak* case, it becomes clear that Article 18(c) applies even after the adjustment period provided by Article 187 of the VAT Directive has ended. Article 18(c) applies in case goods on which VAT became deductible still have a residual value when the taxable economic activity ceases, regardless of the period of time between the date of purchase of those goods and the date on which the activity ceases.[45]

The taxable amount for deemed supplies under Articles 16 and 18 of the VAT Directive shall be the purchase price of the goods or of similar goods or, in the absence of a purchase price, the cost price, determined at the time when the application, disposal or retention takes place pursuant to Article 74 of the VAT Directive.

[B] Deemed Supplies of Services

Article 26 of the VAT Directive contains two provisions on deemed supplies of services. Under Article 26(a) of the VAT Directive, the use of goods forming part of the business assets for the private use of a taxable person or of his staff or, more generally, for purposes other than those of his business, is deemed a supply of services for consideration, under the condition that VAT on those goods was wholly or partly deductible. Under Article 26(b), the supply of services carried out free of charge by a taxable person for his private use or that of his staff or, more generally, for purposes other than those of his business are deemed supplies of services for consideration. Member States are allowed to derogate from the provisions of Article 26 provided that such derogations do not lead to distortion of competition. In the *Cookies World* case,[46] the CJEU clarified that under this provision Member States may refrain from treating certain supplies or uses as services supplied for consideration. On the other hand, that provision in no way authorizes the Member States to provide for chargeable events not referred to in Article 26. It is important to note that under Article 26(b) it is not required that the taxable person has indeed deducted VAT on the goods and services used to provide the services free of charge. However, because the services free of charge are deemed taxable supplies under Article 26(b), the taxable person will be allowed to deduct the VAT on those goods and services, so in general no accumulation of the tax should occur. For the deemed supplies the taxable amount shall be the full cost to the taxable person of providing the services pursuant to Article 75 of the VAT Directive. In case goods are used partially for private purposes a portion of the expenses, proportionate to the ratio between the total duration of actual use of the goods and the

44. CJEU, 8 May 2013, Case C-142/12, *Hristomir Marinov*, ECLI:EU:C:2013:292, paragraph 27, and CJEU, 16 June 2016, Case C-229/15 (*Mateusiak*, ECLI:EU:C:2016:454, paragraph 39.
45. *Mateusiak*, *supra* n. 44, paragraph 39.
46. CJEU, 11 September 2003, Case C-155/01, *Cookies World*, ECLI:EU:C:2003:449.

duration of actual non-business use must be taken into account.[47] In certain cases, requirements of the business may make it necessary for an employer to provide certain services, such as transport, to his employees. When the personal benefit derived by employees from such services is of only secondary importance compared to the needs of the business, there is no service that is being provided for other than business purposes.[48] It should also be noted that following the *VNLTO* case a use for non-economic activities by a legal person will not be considered 'use for purposes other than those of his business' when the non-economic activity constitutes the main corporate purpose of that legal person.[49] VNLTO could therefore only partially deduct VAT on those goods, i.e., in so far they were used for business purposes.

Comparing Articles 26 and 16 of the VAT Directive, it should also be noted that under Article 26 services are only deemed as supplies of services for consideration in case they are provided for private use (of the taxable person or his staff) or for other than business purposes, while under Article 16 a supply free of charge for business purposes is also regarded as a supply of goods for consideration. This explains the exception for samples and or gifts of small value.

To maintain the neutrality of the tax, it is important to stress the correlation between the right to deduct VAT and the taxation of deemed supplies of goods and services. If a business, for example, buys Christmas hampers while it is already clear upon purchase that these hampers will be distributed to the staff free of charge, can the business deduct the VAT and will it be required to report a supply under Article 16, or will the business not be able to deduct the VAT at all, meaning that it will not meet the condition of having deducted VAT on the goods supplied to the staff free of charge and not triggering a supply under Article 16? The *Lennartz* case shows that it is important in what capacity a taxable person purchases a good. If a taxable person acquires goods in his private capacity, no VAT can be deducted.[50] The *X*-case shows that even in case of an initial use for private purposes, a person can be regarded as acting in the capacity of taxable person if use for business purposes following the private use can be demonstrated.[51]

As regards the correlation between VAT deduction and deemed supplies there is a chicken or egg situation. The CJEU's reasoning is that where a taxable person acquires goods which he employs partly for private use, he is deemed to effect for consideration a supply based on Article 26 of the VAT Directive. So, consequently, a person who uses goods partly for the purposes of taxable business transactions and partly for private use and who, upon acquiring the goods, recovered all or part of the input VAT, is deemed to use the goods entirely for the purposes of his taxable transactions. Consequently, such a person is in principle entitled to a right of total and

47. CJEU, 26 September 1996, Case C-230/94, *Enkler*, ECLI:EU:C:1996:352, paragraph 37.
48. *Fillibeck*, *supra* n. 24.
49. CJEU, 12 February 2009, Case C-515/07, *VNLTO*, ECLI:EU:C:2009:88, paragraph 39.
50. CJEU, 11 July 1991, Case C-97/90, *Lennartz*, ECLI:EU:C:1991:315, paragraphs 8 and 9.
51. CJEU, 19 July 2012, Case C-334/10, *X v. Staatssecretaris van Financiën*, ECLI:EU:C:2012:473. Compare CJEU 22 March 2012, Case C-153/11, *Klub OOD*, ECLI:EU:C:2012:163, where the CJEU has clarified that no immediate use for business purposes is required. A similar reasoning can be found in CJEU 25 July 2018, Case C-140/17, *Gmina Ryjewo*, ECLI:EU:C:2018:595.

immediate deduction of the input tax paid on purchasing the goods.[52] To put it short, because the private use of business assets is deemed a supply of services, the asset is used wholly for providing taxable supplies, provided that VAT on the business asset has been deducted either fully or in part. A person using goods both for private and business purposes has the choice of (i) allocating those goods wholly to the assets of his business, (ii) retaining them wholly within his private assets, thereby excluding them entirely from the system of VAT, or (iii) integrating them into his business only to the extent to which they are actually used for business purposes.[53] In the first case, VAT will be deducted in full and the private use will be subject to VAT under Article 26. In the second situation, VAT is not deductible at all. In the third situation, VAT will be deductible to the extent that the good is used for business purposes. In both two latter cases there will be no deemed supply on the basis of Article 26 unless the part that is used for business purposes will be used for private purposes in situation 3. Allocating assets fully to the business provides a financing advantage for taxable persons that use goods both for business and private purposes. Such a financing advantage cannot be obtained by non-taxable persons. In the *Puffer* case the CJEU ruled that this financing advantage that was granted to taxable persons did not infringe the right of equal treatment, simply because taxable persons and non-taxable persons are not in the same position, the first carrying out economic activities while the latter do not.[54] The correlation between the right to deduct VAT and the taxation of private use of a business asset is also demonstrated in the *X*-case. In that case, the CJEU considers that in a situation of private use of an immovable property that has been altered, the taxable amount for private use consists of a part of the costs of acquiring the immovable property and the expenditure in respect of the alterations if the taxable person was charged VAT on the purchase of the immovable property that was considered part of its business assets. If, by contrast, the taxable person was not charged VAT on the purchase of the immovable property, the taxable amount relating to the private use will consist solely of the expenditure in respect of the alterations.[55] In the *X*-case, the CJEU considers the alterations to be separate capital items. In my view, if VAT has only been charged and deducted on maintenance or use costs (and not on the acquisition of the good itself, for example, because it is a second hand good or was acquired through an exempt supply) no supply of services will be deemed to exist under Article 26(1)(a) of the VAT Directive, because the VAT on such goods was not wholly or partly deductible. This would also mean that in that situation VAT on maintenance and use costs can only be deducted to the extent that those costs are made for business purposes.[56]

In respect of the correlation between deemed supplies and the right to deduct VAT, Article 176 of the VAT Directive contains a stand still clause for expenditure without strictly a business purpose. Under this provision, EU Member States are allowed to maintain limitations to deduct VAT that they had in place before the

52. *Lennartz, supra* n. 48, paragraph 26.
53. CJEU, 23 April 2009, Case C-460/07, *Puffer*, ECLI:EU:C:2009:254, paragraph 39.
54. *Puffer, supra* n. 53, paragraph 57.
55. *X v. Staatssecretaris van Financiën, supra* n. 49, paragraph 42.
56. *See also* opinion of Advocate-General Mengozzi 22 December 2008, Case C-515/17, *VNLTO*, ECLI:EU:C:2008:769, paragraph 71.

predecessor of the VAT Directive, the Sixth Directive, applied in 1979, or upon their accession to the EU. Because under this provision EU Member States can fully restrict the VAT deduction, a deemed supply of goods under Article 16 or 18 or a deemed supply of services under Article 26(a) will not apply. In case VAT is partially deductible, VAT may be due on the basis of Article 16, 18 or 26 of the VAT Directive. This may result in double taxation. However, it seems that the CJEU accepts those results as part of the not fully harmonized EU VAT system. As shown by the CJEU judgment in the *Grupa Lotos* case,[57] even a restriction of VAT deduction is accepted in case of use for business purposes where costs are components of taxable supplies provided by the taxable person at a later stage. This also causes accumulation of the tax. Article 26, however, provides EU Member States with the option to abstain from levying VAT on deemed supplies of services. I would defend that Member States could also use this provision to abstain partially from levying VAT, which would be a useful tool in situations of double taxation.

As of 1 January 2011, in case of immovable property that is used both for business and private purposes, VAT can be deducted only up to the proportion of the property's use for business purposes, pursuant to the provision of Article 168a of the VAT Directive. Changes in the proportion of use of immovable property shall be taken into account by the adjustment rules. With these provisions the VAT Directive explicitly derogates from the provision of Article 26 and its consequences for VAT deduction as described above. Article 168a (2) of the VAT Directive allows EU Member States to apply the same rules in relation to VAT on expenditure related to other goods forming part of the business assets as the Member State specifies.

[C] No Deemed Supplies in Case of Supplies below Cost Price

In the *Hotel Scandic* case,[58] the CJEU dealt with supplies of goods and services to staff against a consideration that was below cost price. According to the CJEU, the fact that the price paid for an economic transaction is higher or lower than the cost price is irrelevant to the question whether a transaction is to be regarded as a 'transaction effected for consideration'. Because the staff paid a remuneration that was not symbolic, the CJEU decided that the provisions of Articles 5(6) and 6(2) of the Sixth Directive (the current Articles 16 and 26 of the VAT Directive) do not apply here. It should be noted that a reduction in salary corresponding to the value of the benefit in kind or if a certain part of the work done by the employee can be regarded as a consideration for having the benefit in kind being made available to him, there is a supply against consideration too.[59] The *Fillibeck* case[60] demonstrates that there is no supply for consideration in case the work to be performed and the wages received are independent of the benefit provided by the employer, because in that situation it is not

57. CJEU, 2 May 2019, Case C-225/18, *Grupa Lotos*, ECLI:EU:C:2019:349.
58. CJEU, 20 Jan 2005, Case C-412/03, *Hotel Scandic*, ECLI:EU:C:2005:47.
59. CJEU, 29 July 2010, Case C-40/09, *Astra Zeneca*, ECLI:EU:C:2010:450, and CJEU, 18 July 2013, Joined Cases C-210/11 and C-211/11, *Medicom and Alard*, ECLI:EU:C:2013:479.
60. *Fillibeck*, *supra* n. 24.

possible to regard a proportion of the work performed as consideration for the benefit. In my view, there is a supply against consideration if the employee is allowed to choose from a number of benefits, which includes the use of an asset of the company.[61] This position is also taken by the VAT Committee with a large majority.[62]

[D] Application of Regular VAT Rules on Deemed Supplies

A question is whether deemed supplies are taxed in the same way as regular supplies. As regards the taxable amount, as mentioned in §16.05[A] and [B], there are special provisions in the VAT Directive, because a consideration is missing in case of deemed supplies. The question can be asked whether, for example, exemptions or the special rules on the place of supply of services can apply to deemed supplies as well. In the *Seeling* case,[63] the CJEU ruled that private use of a dwelling cannot be regarded as exempted lease of an immovable property. In particular, the CJEU ruled that the private use does not satisfy the conditions for a lease as defined by the CJEU. It is a feature of such private use not only that no rent is paid but also that there is no genuine agreement on the duration of the right of enjoyment or the right of occupation of the dwelling, or to exclude third parties. The CJEU also refers to this outcome as a desirable outcome. Because the VAT will have been deducted on the property, while the adjustment rules only provide for adjustment of the deductible VAT during a certain period. In the *BLM* case,[64] the CJEU clarified that this is not only the case where a dwelling is used for a taxable person's own private purposes, but also where a dwelling is made available for the private use of an employee free of charge. These cases, in my view, show that, if no special provisions have been included in the VAT Directive, deemed supplies should be treated the same way as regular supplies as regards, for example, exemptions or the place of supply. However, due to their nature, a provision, such as an exemption, that would apply to regular supplies, may not be applicable in case of deemed supplies.

In the pending *QM* case[65] the CJEU will need to address the application of special place of supply rules in a situation where an employer established in Luxembourg provides company cars to two German employees that are allowed to use those cars for private purposes. It should however be noted that one of the employees pays a consideration, which makes the supply a regular supply. While the other employee does not pay a consideration, the company has no right to deduct VAT because of its investment activities. It therefore remains to be seen if the question of the referring court about the place of supply will be answered. As regards the situation where there is a consideration, Advocate-general Szpunar is of the opinion that the place of supply rule for long-term lease of means of transport of Article 5(2) of the VAT Directive is

61. *See also* Madeleine Merkx, *VAT on Private Use of Company Cars in Cross-Border Situations: Double or Non-Taxation?* 24(2) EC Tax Rev. 96 (2015), and Wouter J. Blokland, *Taxing Employee Benefits in Kind under EU VAT* 22(2) Int'l VAT Monitor 98, 102 (2011).
62. Guidelines resulting from the 101st meeting of 20 October 2014, taxud.c.1(2016)1136484 – 832.
63. CJEU, 8 May 2003, Case C-269/00, *Seeling*, ECLI:EU:C:2003:254.
64. CJEU, 29 March 2012, Case C-436/10, *BLM*, ECLI:EU:C:2012:185.
65. C-288/19.

applicable. In case of a payment of consideration there is in his view no doubt that rent is being paid. As regards the duration of the leasing agreement, he opined that the duration does not have to be set at a certain date or a number of units of time, such as days, months, or years. The duration of the leasing agreement may also be determined on the basis of a specific event or condition, for example, the duration of the employment relationship of the employee or the duration of the leasing. The employee has that specific vehicle exclusively at his disposal, a determination which is not altered by the use of the vehicle for fulfilling his professional obligations, or the ability of the employer to give instruction which may include the use of the vehicle. The situation would be different if the employer had a fleet of vehicles at his disposal which could be used by the staff as required (and according to the availability of the vehicles concerned) but none of these vehicles had been permanently allocated to a particular employee. The fact that the vehicle is put at the disposal of the employee on the basis of a labour agreement is in the view of *Szpunar* irrelevant. In his view, the solution should align with the objective of the place of supply rules, i.e., to tax services in the country of consumption.[66]

I concur with *Szpunar* that in case a consideration is paid for the private use by the employee, the special place of supply rule of Article 56(2) applies. The question is whether this is also the case for a deemed supply of services. The only difference is that a rent is absent. In the *Seeling* and *BLM* cases this is one of the reasons why the CJEU reasons that there is no lease of immovable property. In my opinion, the objective of Article 26 of the VAT Directive and its relation to Article 168a(2) of the VAT Directive should also be considered. The objective of Article 26 is, in brief, to prevent tax free consumption. As described in §16.05[B], Article 168a(2) allows EU Member States to apply the same rules applicable for private use of immovable property to movable property. The result of applying Article 168a(2) would be that VAT is only deductible to the extent the movable property is used for business purposes. Changes in the relationship between business and private use are dealt with by the adjustment rules of Articles 184-192 of the VAT Directive. In case the EU Member State has used the option of Article 168a(2), Article 26 does not apply. If an EU Member State has availed itself of this option, the taxable person in question will not be allowed to deduct the VAT on the purchase of movable property in full. However, if the supply of services is subject to VAT in the residence state of the employee and if that state has not availed itself of the option under Article 168a(2), the service will be subject to VAT, because the VAT has been partially deducted (for the part that is used for business purposes). This may result in double taxation. In the reverse situation, when the employer is established in an EU Member State that has not availed itself of the option of Article 168a(2), the VAT on a company car that is used both for business and private purposes is fully deductible. In the employee residence state, however, there will be no deemed supply of services under Article 26(1). It is my position that the special place of supply rules does not apply to Article 26(1); and the services under Article 26(1) should be subject

66. Opinion of Advocate-general Szpunar of 17 September 2020, Case C-288/19, *QM v. Finanzamt Saarbrücken*, ECLI:EU:C:2020:736, paragraphs 49, 50, 63, 64 and 66.

to VAT where the employer is established.[67] The CJEU could use the absence of payment of a lease payment as an argument to rule that Article 56(2) of the VAT Directive does not apply.

§16.06 TAXABLE AMOUNT IN EU VAT

[A] General VAT Rules on Taxable Amount

Private consumption in EU VAT is measured by the price that the consumer pays for a product or service. The taxable amount is subjective in nature, meaning that VAT will be charged on the price that a business has obtained from the consumer, regardless of whether this price is lower or higher than the open market value. The taxable amount includes voluntary payments for the supply, such as tips, and subsidies that have a direct link with the supply.[68] The subjective nature of the taxable amount is demonstrated clearly by the CJEU in its case law on barter transactions. For example, the *Empire Stores* case[69] deals with a situation where a person who presents himself, or a friend, as a new customer to Empire Stores, can choose a free product. The dispute in this case was whether Empire Stores needed to charge VAT on the cost price or selling price of the free product. According to the CJEU, the subjective nature of the taxable amount in VAT requires determining the value based on the amount the beneficiary of a service attributes to that service, i.e., what this person is prepared to spend on this service. In this respect, Empire Stores is prepared to give away a product and the cost price of the product should be regarded as the taxable amount both for the service provided by the person presenting a new customer as well as the supply of the free product. Because the person presenting a new customer does not qualify as a taxable person the service is not subject to VAT.

[B] Open Market Value (Article 80 of the VAT Directive)

Article 80 of the VAT Directive was added to the VAT Directive by Directive 2006/69/EC[70] in 2006. Its objective is, as becomes clear from the first and third recital of the preamble of the directive, to combat tax evasion or avoidance, by allowing Member States to intervene as regards the value of supplies and acquisitions in specific limited circumstances to ensure that there is no loss of tax through the use of connected parties to derive tax benefits. Directive 2006/69/EC provided for a general provision. Until then, EU Member States had to apply for individual derogations. In derogation

67. For a more extensive analysis the author refers to previous work, Madeleine Merkx, *VAT on Private Use of Company Cars in Cross-Border Situations: Double or Non-Taxation?* 24(2) EC Tax Rev. 96 (2015).
68. Article 73. VAT Directive.
69. CJEU, 2 June 1994, Case C-33/93, *Empire Stores*, ECLI:EU:C:1994:225.
70. Council Directive 2006/69/EC of 24 July 2006 amending Directive 77/388/EEC as regards certain measures to simplify the procedure for charging value added tax and to assist in countering tax evasion or avoidance, and repealing certain Decisions granting derogations, OJ L 221, 12.8.2006, pp. 9-14.

from the general subjective nature of the taxable amount in VAT pursuant to Article 80, EU Member States may in certain cases determine that the taxable amount is the open market value. This requires family or other close personal ties, management, ownership, membership, financial or legal ties between the taxable person and its customer and can only be applied in order to prevent tax evasion or avoidance. EU Member States have the option to determine that the taxable amount is the open market value in 3 situations.

Figure 16.1 Where the Consideration Is Lower than the Open Market Value and the Recipient of the Supply Does Not Have a Full Right to Deduct VAT

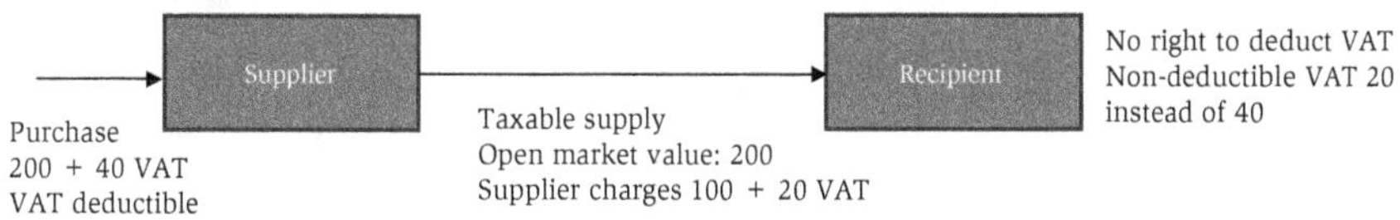

Source: Author's own work.

In this situation the supplier can purchase a good or service and supply it to the recipient for a low price. The supplier can deduct the VAT on the purchase because it supplies the goods or services to the recipient against consideration and needs to apply VAT on that supply. The recipient does not have a (full) right to deduct. However, because the price is lower than the open market value, the non-deductible VAT is smaller than the deductible VAT as shown in the example in Figure 16.1.

Figure 16.2 Where the Consideration Is Lower than the Open Market Value and the Supplier Does Not Have a Full Right of Deduction and the Supply Is Subject to an Exemption

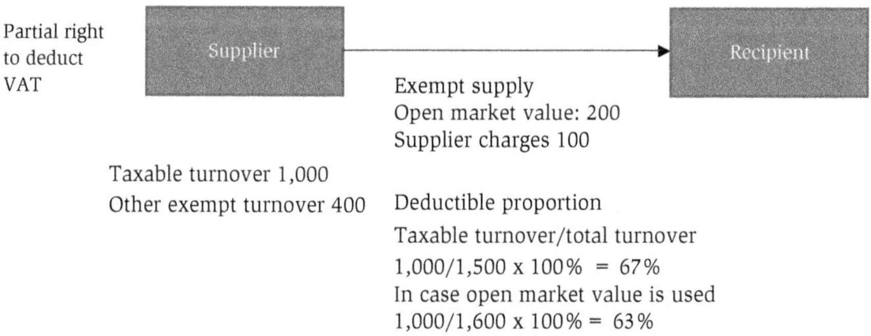

Source: Author's own work.

In this situation the supplier does not have a full right to deduct VAT. This provision appears to deal with artificial boosting of the deductible proportion by the supplier. By charging a low price for exempt supplies, the total turnover is lower, and the deductible proportion will be higher as shown in the example in Figure 16.2.

Figure 16.3 Where the Consideration Is Higher than the Open Market Value and the Supplier Does Not Have a Full Right to Deduct VAT

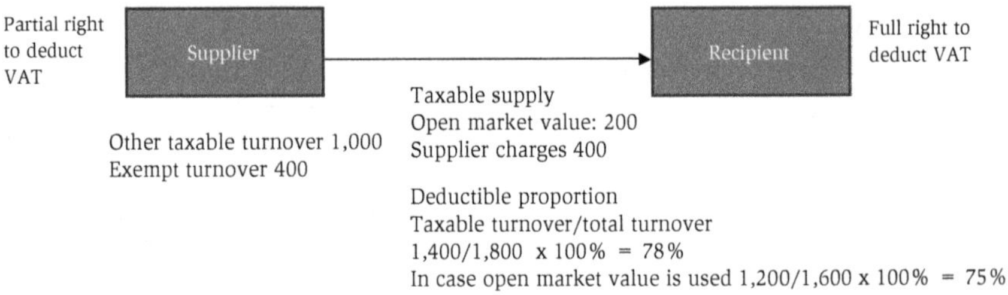

Source: Author's own work.

This provision also deals with boosting the deductible proportion, but by increasing the taxable turnover. If the recipient is able to deduct the VAT, the extra VAT due is not a cost as shown in the example in Figure 16.3.

The VAT Committee must be informed of legislative measures adopted pursuant to Article 80(1) of the VAT Directive. EU Member States may restrict the categories of suppliers or recipients to whom the measures shall apply. As becomes clear from the notifications to the VAT Committee, 19 EU Member States have implemented the provision of Article 80(1) on all types of supplies: Belgium, Bulgaria, Denmark, Estonia, Ireland, Spain, Croatia, Italy, Latvia, Luxembourg, Hungary, Austria, Poland, Portugal, Romania, Slovenia, Slovakia, Finland, and Sweden. The Netherlands and the United Kingdom have limited implementations of Article 80. In the Netherlands, this provision applies to non-business use of a company car or company van (in case a remuneration is paid).[71] In the UK, the provision applies to the supply of fuel.[72] It should be noted that as of 31 January 2020 the UK is no longer an EU Member State, but during a transitional period until and including 31 December 2020, amongst others, EU VAT rules still apply.

From CJEU case law it follows that the provision has an exhaustive nature and cannot be applied in other situations than those mentioned in Article 80(1).[73] In particular, the CJEU has stated that the provision can only be applied in case of a final consumer or a mixed taxable person enjoying only a proportional right of deduction. The provision cannot be applied in case the person concerned enjoys a full right of

71. In case no remuneration is paid there will be a deemed supply under Article 16 or Article 26 VAT Directive.
72. Notifications to the VAT committee – state of play on 1 February 2020, https://ec.europa.eu/taxation_customs/sites/taxation/files/notifications.pdf (accessed on 7 November 2020).
73. CJEU, 26 April 2012, Joined Cases C-621/10 and C-129/11, *Balkan and Sea Properties and Provadinvest*, ECLI:EU:C:2012:248, paragraph 51, and CJEU 21 March 2013, Case C-153/12, *Sani Treyd EOOD*, ECLI:EU:C:2013:201, paragraph 40.

deduction[74] or in case there are no ties as mentioned in Article 80(1).[75] In case of barter transactions, the CJEU has ruled that the taxable amount must be a subjective value and cannot be the open market value in all situations.[76] From the explanatory memorandum of the proposal for Directive 2006/69/EC it becomes clear that the open market value cannot be applied to goods or services sold below cost price as part of a promotion, a sale of damaged stock at a discount or a clearance sale. The explanatory memorandum also shows that both the open market value and the cost price have been considered as taxable amount in situations where there are certain ties. The open market value has been chosen because it allows EU Member States to levy VAT on the added value as well.[77] This also ensures the neutrality of the tax. Regardless of whether a good or service is purchased from or provided to an associated party or a third party, VAT is levied in the same way.

In the *Hotel Scandic* case (addressed in §16.05[C]) it is explained that Article 27 VAT Directive also allows EU Member States to implement a provision to tax low priced services at the open market value (Article 77 of the VAT Directive determines the taxable amount for these services). It is required that the provision prevents distortion of competition and if the service would be supplied by another person the VAT would not be wholly deductible. The VAT Committee must be consulted as well. Different from Article 80, it is not required that there be certain ties between the persons involved. The objective is also different. Article 27 refers to preventing distortion of competition, while Article 80 refers to preventing tax avoidance or evasion.

Last but not least, in my view, the doctrine on abuse of law can be applied here as well. In the *Halifax* case,[78] the CJEU has ruled that when two conditions are met, abuse of law can be established in the area of VAT (1. accrual of a tax advantage the grant of which would be contrary to the purpose of the VAT Directive and 2. the essential aim of the transactions concerned is to obtain that tax advantage). In case abuse of law is established the situation must be re-established to reflect the situation without the abusive transactions. From the *Weald Leasing* case[79] it becomes clear that such an abusive situation can be established in case a price is charged that is unusually low or does not reflect any economic reality. Re-establishing the situation in such a case could require adjustment of the taxable amount.[80] It could however also require a disregarding of an affiliated party that charges the low price if this party is only part of the transaction to obtain the tax advantage.

74. CJEU, *Balkan and Sea Properties and Provadinvest*, *supra* n. 73, paragraphs 46-48.
75. CJEU, 19 December 2012, Case C-549/11, *Orfey Balgaria*, ECLI:EU:C:2012:832, paragraph 48, and CJEU, 7 March 2013, Case C-19/12, *Efir*, ECLI:EU:C:2013:148, paragraph 46.
76. CJEU, *Ofrey Balgaria*, *supra* n. 75 and CJEU, *Sani Treyd*, *supra* n. 73.
77. Proposal for a Council Directive amending Directive 77/388/EEC as regards certain measures to simplify the procedure for charging value added tax and to assist in countering tax evasion and avoidance, and repealing certain Decisions granting derogations, COM/2005/0089 final.
78. CJEU, 21 February 2006, Case C-255/02, *Halifax*, ECLI:EU:C:2006:121.
79. CJEU, 22 December 2010, Case C-103/09, *Weald Leasing*, ECLI:EU:C:2010:804.
80. *See also* Ad J. van Doesum, case law comment, Dutch Supreme Court, 30 March 2012, nr. 09/03079, ECLI:NL:HR:2012:BR4476; FED (2012/69).

§16.07 COMPARATIVE LAW

[A] Introduction

This section contains a legal comparison and briefly compares the EU VAT legislation addressed above to the Canadian GST legislation and the South African VAT legislation. These jurisdictions where chosen because their VAT systems are similar and comparable to the EU VAT system, while at the same time they are located in different regions of the world. The analysis will be done per topic addressed above starting with the status of taxable person (B), followed by VAT deduction (C), deemed supplies (D) and the taxable amount (E).

[B] Status of Taxable Person

Under Canadian GST, supplies that are not made for consideration are generally not subject to the tax. Whether there is a consideration is interpreted similarly to the *Tolsma* case. Supplies below cost price, including supplies against a nominal consideration, are subject to GST. However, there may be limitations as regards the deduction of input VAT (§16.07[C]), or the taxable amount may be adjusted to the fair market value (§16.07[E]). An expectation of profit is required for individuals or partnerships comprised only of individuals. If there is no such expectation, there is no commercial activity, and the supply is non-taxable.

Under South African VAT too, supplies free of charge are not subject to VAT and the taxable amount is nil (Article 10(23) South African VAT Act). This does not apply if these supplies are between connected parties, in which case they are deemed supplies against consideration (§16.07[D]). There are special rules for advantages or benefits granted to employees. There may still be a right to input VAT deduction in case of supplies free of charge (§16.07[C]). Supplies below cost price are subject to VAT.

[C] Deduction of Input Tax

In Canada, as a main rule, there is no deduction of input tax in case of supplies free of charge or if a supply is made for a nominal consideration. However, if the supplies free of charge or for nominal consideration were made for the purpose of facilitating or promoting other taxable activities, there may be a right to input tax deduction. As regards supplies below cost price the input tax deduction may be limited. There is a 'reasonability rule' for input tax deduction,[81] but it is not applied often in practice.

81. An example is provided by GST/HST Memorandum 8-2, *General Restrictions and Limitations* (February 2012), paragraph 21. Mr. X, a registrant, is the owner of a small local chain of pizzerias (XYZ Pizza). Mr. X purchases a USD 5.5 million (including GST) yacht through his company and has a sign advertising 'XYZ Pizza' placed prominently on both sides of the yacht. The yacht is never used to entertain suppliers or customers but is sailed privately by Mr. X throughout the year. Mr. X claims a full ITC on the yacht for the reporting period in which the GST is payable. Given the nature of Mr. X's commercial activities, the cost of the yacht and the

Under South African VAT, if there is a supply free of charge, input VAT can still be deductible in case the supply free of charge is made for the inducement of any supply, such as advertisement goods. The mere fact that supplies are provided below cost price has no impact on VAT deduction.

[D] Deemed Supplies

Under Canadian GST, supplies free of charge or with a consideration less than fair market value can be deemed to be supplies made for fair market value. This applies in case parties are not at arm's length and the recipient is not able to claim a full input tax credit. The same is true for the South African VAT system where supplies that are made free of charge or for a consideration less than open market value between connected persons are deemed to be supplied at open market value if the recipient does not have a full right to input VAT deduction (Article 10(4) of the South African VAT Act).

If input tax has been deducted and goods are taken for private purposes, there is a deemed supply in Canada for GST purposes too. In case purchases are made for private purposes, GST cannot be deducted. If goods are acquired both for private and business purposes, a percentage allocation of deductible input tax is required. There are exceptions, such as capital property, where an 'all or nothing' test is applied based on the primary use. Where the private use results in a taxable benefit for a shareholder or employee for income tax purposes, a full input tax credit is allowed, but there is a deemed supply on which GST is payable. The taxable amount is generally based on the amount of the benefit for income tax purposes.

Under the South African VAT Act, supplies of goods or services to employees as benefit or advantage are deemed a supply of goods or services made by the vendor in the course of his business (Article 18(3) of the South African VAT Act). In that situation, the taxable amount is deemed to be an amount equal to the cash equivalent of the benefit or advantage granted to the employee (Article 10(13) South African VAT Act). In case the advantage includes the right to use a motor vehicle the taxable amount is prescribed by the Minister in the Gazette for the category of motor vehicle used.

[E] Taxable Amount

Under Canadian GST law, as a main rule, VAT is due on the price paid. As mentioned in §16.07[D], supplies free of charge or with a consideration less than fair market value can be deemed supplies made for fair market value. In that situation, GST will be due on the fair market price and the supplier can deduct the input tax. This legislation may also help in mitigating abusive situations that are dealt with in the EU Member States by implementing Article 80 of the VAT Directive or applying the abuse of law doctrine.

---

fact that the yacht is not used for business purposes except inasmuch as the sign could be considered to be advertising, the ITC claimed by Mr. X on the acquisition of the yacht would be denied under subsection 170(2).

The same is true for the reasonability test and the rule that no input tax can be deducted as regards nominal supplies.

In South Africa, VAT is also due on the money paid for a transaction (Article 10(2) and (3)(a) of the South African VAT Act). In case the consideration is not paid in money, but in kind the taxable amount is the open market value of the consideration in kind (Article 10(2) and (3)(b) of the South African VAT Act). In case more consideration is received than has been charged, VAT will be due on the excess, if the excess has not been refunded within four months (Article 8(27) of the South African VAT Act), and VAT will be due on the amount of the excess amount (Article 10(26) of the South African VAT Act).

[F] Conclusions of Comparative Law

As regards the status of the supplier, all three jurisdictions, as a general rule, do not charge VAT on supplies free of charge. Supplies below cost price are subject to VAT, and related input VAT is in principle deductible. Canada applies a reasonability test in some cases, while in the EU the right to deduct VAT might be debated, but as a general rule should be granted.

VAT on supplies made free of charge cannot be deducted in case there is no connection to a supply that is subject to the tax. In Canada, GST can be deducted if the supply free of charge is facilitating or promoting other activities. In South Africa, the test to be applied is whether there is an inducement of another supply. These criteria are similar to the reasoning of the CJEU in the *Sveda* case.

In all three jurisdictions private use needs to be subjected to the tax to ensure the neutrality of the system. VAT or GST on costs made for private purposes only is not deductible.

The taxable amount consists of the amount actually paid in all three jurisdictions. Both Canada and South Africa apply an open or fair market value in case of supplies between connected parties where the recipient cannot deduct the full VAT amount. EU Member States are also allowed to implement such legislation under Article 80 of the VAT Directive, which many EU Member States have done. The Canadian and South-African rules do however not cover the situations discussed in §16.06[B] where the supplier artificially boosts its deductible proportion by charging prices below or above open market value. Article 80 of the VAT Directive, in my view, does not allow for an adjustment of the taxable amount to the open market value in case of supplies free of charge, because it requires a consideration, but a consideration below or above open market value. However, Article 27 of the VAT Directive does allow this. Finally, South Africa deals with payments in kind differently compared to the EU VAT system. Where the *Empire Stores* judgment shows that the taxable amount can be set at cost price, under South African VAT legislation the taxable amount in such situations will be set at sales price.

§16.08 CONCLUSION

This chapter addressed the issue of supplies free of charge and below cost price. Rules dealing with these types of supplies add to the complexity of the EU VAT system but are necessary to uphold the legal character of the tax and the neutrality principle. As the comparative law section shows, these rules are common in the VAT systems discussed in this chapter. However, some modern VAT jurisdictions take a different approach, featuring few restrictions on the input VAT deduction related to free of charge supplies (*see*, e.g., the section on Australia in chapter 17).

Within the EU VAT system, double or non-taxation should be avoided. In that respect, the author made two recommendations:

(1) EU Member States should avail themselves of the option provided by Article 26 of the VAT Directive to abstain from levying VAT on deemed supplies to the extent VAT has not been deducted because of the application of the stand still clause of Article 176 of the VAT Directive.
(2) The special place of supply rules, e.g., for the long-term lease of a means of transport, should not be applied to deemed supplies of services under Article 26(1) of the VAT Directive.

CHAPTER 17

VAT Treatment of Donations in Light of Green Policy Objectives

Bettina Spilker & Benedikt Hoffmann

§17.01 INTRODUCTION

The European Union (EU) Commission, newly elected in 2019, under the presidency of Ursula von der Leyen put an ambitious climate and environmental protection policy on its agenda under the programmatic title *The Green Deal.*[1] A specific project of the EU is the promotion of a circular economy, which aims at a sustainable and careful use of resources by reducing waste and recycling.[2] The Council of the EU believes that indirect taxation can also serve as a policy instrument to achieve the objectives of the Green Deal.[3]

In this context, the value added tax (VAT) also becomes part of current discussions.[4] In recent times, the focus has been on the VAT treatment of donations in kind by businesses. In connection with the waste of resources, companies in the emerging e-commerce sector have come under particular criticism in recent years. According to press reports, returned or defective goods in particular have been destroyed *en masse,* even though they can still be used, e.g., donated to charitable

1. Ursula von der Leyen, *A Union That Strives for More,* accessible on https://ec.europa.eu/commission/sites/beta-political/files/political-guidelines-next-commission_en.pdf (accessed 30 Nov. 2020).
2. Report from the Commission to the European Parliament, the Council, the European Economic and Social Committee and the Committee of Regions on the implementation of the Circular Economy Action Plan as of 4 Mar. 2019.
3. General Secretariat of the Council, Conclusions on fair and effective taxation in times of recovery, on tax challenges linked to digitalisation and on tax good governance in the EU and beyond, 12979/20 as of 20 Nov. 2020.
4. *See,* e.g., for VAT rates, Charlène Herbain, *Should VAT Be the Next Environmental Policy Tool?* 31(2) Int'l VAT Monitor 69 (2020).

organisations.[5] Retailers and online service providers, for their part, blame VAT law, which leads to the paradigm *'destruction is cheaper than donating'*.[6]

This chapter examines the VAT treatment[7] of donations in kind under EU law. We compare the treatment in two EU Member States and benchmark with two-third countries, the United Kingdom (UK) and Australia. The further analysis of the different approaches then leads to a proposal for a uniform EU-wide VAT treatment of donations in kind, taking into consideration the interplay of the system of the EU VAT Directive and the steering objectives of the Green Deal.

§17.02 OUTLINE OF THE PROBLEM

For the purpose of this chapter, a *'donation in kind'* shall be assumed to occur when objects or other goods from the assets of a taxable business are given free of charge and, for example, are donated to a non-profit organisation. *'Free of charge'* in this context means that the donor receives no direct consideration for his donation of business assets.[8]

In the scope of the harmonised EU VAT legislation, the central issue is that donations in kind, which form part of the business assets of a taxable person, are subject to VAT as a deemed supply for consideration or would trigger a correction (loss) of the related input tax deduction. Under circumstances, it may make more economic sense for a business to destroy goods than donate them.[9]

§17.03 QUALIFICATION OF THE DONATION IN KIND IN EU LAW (DE LEGE LATA)

[A] Taxable Donation in Kind Made by a Business

In the case of a donation in kind, goods from the business assets of a taxable person in a Member State are given free of charge, e.g., to a charitable organisation in the same Member State. This is basically a supply of goods within the territory of the Member State.

5. https://www.dailymail.co.uk/news/article-7018955/Exposed-Amazon-destroys-millions-new-items-sell.html (accessed 30 Nov. 2020).
6. https://www.retaildetail.eu/en/news/general/amazon-blames-destruction-goods-vat-rules; https://app.handelsblatt.com/unternehmen/handel-dienstleister/onlinehandel-amazon-deutschlandchef-deutsches-steuerrecht-foerdert-vernichtung-von-retouren/ (accessed 30 Nov. 2020).
7. *See*, in detail for income tax treatment, OECD, Tax Policy Studies, *Taxation and Philanthropy* (OECD Publishing, 2020).
8. The definition shall distinguish the generous donation from sponsorship or other activities where the business of the taxable person receives, e.g., publicity in return for giving money, goods, or other products.
9. *See*, e.g., for Austria for a comparative calculation of overall costs in the case of donation in kind, disposal and release from returning the goods, Silvia Auer and Kristin Resenig, *Sachspende, Entsorgung oder Verzicht auf Rückversand bei Retourwaren* 16-17 SWK 899, 906 (2020).

[1] *Purpose of Generating Income*

The delivery free of charge of goods – as in the case of a donation in kind – does not lead to the loss of the purpose to generate income within the scope of the economic activity of the business of the taxable person. Although the taxable supply of goods under the VAT Directive[10] requires the purpose to generate income by the economic activity (cf. Article 9 paragraph 1 of the VAT Directive), the intention to generate income from an activity of the taxable person is assessed in advance of the subsequent delivery according to the case law of the Court of Justice of the EU (CJEU).[11]

Anyone who acquires, manufactures, or produces goods with the intention of selling them at a later stage for consideration is acting with the purpose of generating income. If the good is not delivered for consideration, this does not mean that the supply is not taxable once the good has become part of the business assets. An unsuccessful entrepreneur who does not generate income remains a taxable person within the meaning of Article 9 of the VAT Directive if the enterprise has acquired or manufactured goods with the intention of selling them on the market as part of a (planned) economic activity but is unable to do so.[12]

[2] *No Taxable Supply Within the Meaning of Article 14 of the VAT Directive*

In principle, however, according to Article 14 of the VAT Directive, only supplies to a customer *for consideration* as defined in Article 2(1)(a) of the VAT Directive are taxable.[13] Only then will there be a legal relationship between the supplier and the customer in which reciprocal supplies are exchanged which are subject to VAT.[14] This is also in line with the requirement of Article 9(1) of the VAT Directive, according to which the taxable person must carry out an economic activity with a view to obtaining sustainable income. Accordingly, a donation in kind, provided out of generosity, is basically outside the scope of the VAT Directive.[15]

10. Council Directive 2006/112/EC of 28 Nov. 2006 on the common system of value added tax (OJ L 347, 11 Dec. 2006, p. 1).
11. Cf. CJEU, 26 Sep. 1996, Case C-230/94, *Enkler*, ECLI:EU:C:1996:352, margin no. 30.
12. CJEU, 8 Jun. 2000, Case C-400/98, *Breitsohl*, ECLI:EU:C:2000:304, margin no. 34; CJEU, 29 Feb. 1996, Case C-110/94, *INZO*, ECLI:EU:C:1996:67, margin nos. 15, 16; CJEU, 14 Feb. 1985, Case C-268/83, *Rompelmann*, ECLI:EU:C:1985:74, margin nos. 22, 23.
13. Cf. CJEU, 11 Mar. 2020, Case C-94/19, *San Domenico Vetraria*, ECLI:EU:C:2020:193, margin no. 20 with citations.
14. *San Domenico Vetraria*, *supra* n. 13, paragraph 21.
15. E-003465/2019 Answer given by Mr. Gentiloni on behalf of the European Commission as of 27 Jan. 2020, https://www.europarl.europa.eu/doceo/document/E-9-2019-003465-ASW_EN.pdf (accessed 30 Nov. 2020).

[3] *Deemed Taxable Supply Within the Meaning of Article 16 of the VAT Directive*

However, Article 16 of the VAT Directive provides for an alternative taxable event. According to this provision, the application of goods by a taxable person forming part of his business assets for his private use or for that of his staff, or their disposal free of charge or, more generally, their application for purposes other than those of his business, are treated as a supply of goods for consideration.[16] The deemed supply for consideration only applies where the VAT on those goods or the component parts thereof was wholly or partly deducted.[17] Thus, donations in kind are also subject to VAT if the input tax on the goods subsequently donated was previously deducted.

The rules laid down in Article 16 of the VAT Directive are therefore of particular importance to the Union's VAT system. On the one hand, they ensure that a taxable person who uses business assets for non-business purposes is treated in the same way[18] as an ordinary consumer who purchases such goods.[19] On the other hand, including supplies free of charge into the scope of VAT through the provision of Article 16 VAT Directive serves to avoid untaxed final consumption.[20]

[B] No Tax Exemption for Donations in Kind

Donations of business assets free of charge are not covered by a tax exemption under the VAT Directive.

The VAT Directive provides in Articles 131 et seq. for tax exemptions for certain activities in the domain of public welfare.[21] Beneficiaries of the exemptions are entities (taxable persons) carrying out the activities referred to in Article 132 of the VAT Directive. For example, services and supplies of goods closely linked to social welfare and social security are exempt (Article 132(1)(g) of the VAT Directive). However, there is no provision in the VAT Directive which exempts the supply of goods free of charge to an entity pursuing the aims of public welfare as defined in Article 131 et seq. Donations in kind to charitable organisations are therefore generally not exempt under the VAT Directive.

Any interpretation beyond the wording of any of the provisions of Articles 131 et seq. to the effect that donations (in kind) to charitable organisations would also be

16. Michael Langer, *Kommentar zu Art. 16 MwStSystRL* in *Kommentar zum Umsatzsteuergesetz*, margin no. 10 (Wolfgang Reiß, Jörg Kraeusel, and Michael Langer, eds., Stollfuss, 2020).
17. This requirement avoids double taxation arising from the taxation of the supply of goods free of charge for which no input tax has previously been deducted; cf. CJEU, 25 May 1993, Case C-193/91, *Mohsche*, ECLI:EU:C:1993:203, margin no. 9.
18. For the importance of the principle of equal treatment in Union law, *see* Juliane Kokott, *Das Steuerrecht der Europäischen Union*, §3 margin nos. 12 et seq. (C.H. Beck Verlag, 2019)
19. Timo Hartman, *Kommentar zu §3 Umsatzsteuergesetz* in *Kommentar zum Europäischen Steuerrecht*, margin no. 18 (Andreas Musil and Heinrich Weber-Grellet, eds., C.H. Beck Verlag, 2019).
20. CJEU, 6 May 1992, Case C-20/91, *De Jong*, ECLI:EU:C:1992:192, margin no. 15; CJEU, 20 Jan. 2005, Case C-412/03, *Hotel Scandic*, ECLI:EU:C:2005:47, margin no. 23; Michael Langer, *supra* n. 16, margin no. 21.
21. *See also* CJEU, 20 Nov. 2019, Case C-400/18, *Infoho*, ECLI:EU:C:2019:992, margin nos. 11, 41-42.

exempt from VAT would not be possible for EU law purposes. The interpretation must take account of the overall context of the common VAT system.[22] The provisions of Articles 131 et seq. contain autonomous Union law concepts designed to avoid different application of the VAT system from one Member State to another. The CJEU has consistently held that tax exemptions must be interpreted narrowly.[23] They are merely exceptions to the general principle that all transactions carried out for consideration by a taxable person are subject to VAT.[24] This also applies to transactions carried out free of charge, which are equivalent to transactions carried out for consideration according to Article 16 VAT Directive.

An exception to the principle of the narrow interpretation of exemptions applies only if it would have the effect of overriding other exemptions under the VAT Directive.[25] Although charitable organisations are covered by an exemption, the obligation of the donor to pay VAT on donations in kind does not override the effect of that exemption. Charitable organisations would benefit from a tax exemption for donations only indirectly through the expected increase in donations in kind. That does not, however, justify an interpretation which generally qualifies donations in kind as tax-exempt. This approach is in line with the CJEU's view that not every activity in the public interest leads to a tax exemption.[26]

[C] Input Tax Deduction

Since the donation in kind is treated as a deemed supply for consideration, a taxable and not-exempted transaction occurs at the time of donation. As a result, the input tax deduction on the donated goods remains unchanged. The question of input tax adjustment does not arise because the taxable deemed supply for consideration is attributable to the business of the taxable person. The output VAT is due at the time when the good is withdrawn from the business assets for donation purposes.

[D] Taxable Amount

Where the consideration received for a supply normally is the tax base for calculating VAT, special provisions for determining the tax base are required when a consideration is absent such as with donations in kind.

For deemed supplies as defined in Article 16 of the VAT Directive, Article 74 of the VAT Directive determines the taxable amount as the purchase price of the goods or of similar goods. If there is no purchase price, the cost price must be applied. The

22. CJEU, 8 Mar. 2001, Case C-240/99, *Försäkringsaktiebolaget Skandia*, ECLI:EU:C:2001:140, margin no. 23.
23. CJEU, 12 Apr. 2014, Case C-461/12, *Granton Advertising*, ECLI:EU:C:2014:1745, margin no. 25; CJEU, 5 Jul. 2012, Case C-259/11, *DTZ Zadelhoff*, ECLI:EU:C:2012:423, margin no. 20, 40; CJEU, 28 Jul. 2011, Case C-350/10, *Nordea*, ECLI:EU:C:2011:532, margin no. 23.
24. CJEU, 3 Jun. 2010, Case C-237/09, *Natalie de Fruytier*, ECLI:EU:C:2010:316, margin no. 19.
25. CJEU, 10 Jun. 2010, Case C-86/09, *Future Health Technologies*, ECLI:EU:C:2010:334, margin no. 30.
26. CJEU, 28 Jan. 2010, Case C-473/08, *Eulitz*, ECLI:EU:C:2010:47, margin no. 26.

relevant price has to be determined at the time when the application, disposal or retention takes place.

The CJEU has clarified that this value corresponds in practice to the residual value of the corresponding goods at the time of the donation.[27] Consequently, the change in the value of the goods between their acquisition and the date of the donation must be accounted for.[28] The provision of Article 74 and the CJEU's interpretation thereof can be directly invoked by taxable persons of the Member States vis-à-vis the national tax authorities as it has direct effect.[29]

The EU Commission applies an approach to food donations similar to that of the CJEU, emphasising that tax rules – such as those of the VAT Directive – should not create obstacles to donating.[30] With regard to food donations, the EU Commission provides *inter alia* guidelines for the determination of the taxable amount in its announcement of 25 October 2017.[31] For example, a lower value than the original purchase price or cost price may be used as the taxable amount if the product is no longer marketable at the time of the donation, which may occur, for example, shortly before the expiration date of food products. In this case, an assessment basis of EUR 0 is possible.[32]

It is unclear, however, whether the above-mentioned principles of the EU Commission are also transferable to donations in kind made by the non-food sector, given that the recommendations only refer to the taxable amount for food donations.

A transfer of these principles to non-food products that are defective and thus no longer marketable, e.g., due to incorrect labelling, colour deviations, content shortfalls or damage to the packaging, would be justified because the motivation for the donation of such goods is comparable. The same applies to seasonal items, items that no longer fit in the product range, returned goods, and surplus due to overproduction. The fact that the alternative to donation would be the disposal of the goods shows that it is appropriate to set the tax base for such items at zero value.

However, the EU Commission has so far not made this explicitly clear. There is thus no clear specification for the determination of the taxable amount in this context. The result is that Member States provide for different treatments. Due to the legal uncertainty and in order to avoid a VAT charge, businesses generally prefer to destroy returned goods rather than donate them.

---

27. CJEU, 8 May 2013, Case C-142/12, *Marinov*, ECLI:EU:C:2013:292, margin no. 35; CJEU, 17 May 2001, Joined Cases C-322 and 323/99, *Fischer and Brandenstein*, ECLI:EU:C:2001:280, margin no. 80.
28. Kokott, *supra* n. 18, §8 margin no. 461.
29. *Marinov, supra* n. 27, margin no. 40.
30. E-006248/2015 Answer given by Mr. Moscovici on behalf of the Commission as of 14 Jul. 2015, https://www.europarl.europa.eu/doceo/document//E-8-2015-006248-ASW_EN.html (accessed 30 Nov. 2020).
31. Commission Notice 2017/C 361/01 on EU guidelines on food donation (OJ C 361/25 25.10.2017); Guidelines resulting from the 97th meeting of the EU VAT Committee of 7. Sep. 2012.
32. Commission Notice 2017/C 361/01, *supra* n. 31, 167.

§17.04 COMPARATIVE LAW ANALYSIS OF PREFERENCE SCHEMES FOR DONATIONS IN KIND FOR VAT PURPOSES

A look at the legal systems of individual countries shows how differently donations in kind in practice are dealt with for VAT purposes. Benefits are partly based on legal regulations, partly on administrative regulations; however, there is no uniform line so far within the EU or other third countries. This is shown by comparing the applicable regulations of the three largest economies in Europe (Germany, UK,[33] France) and of Australia.

[A] Germany (Reduced Taxable Amount)

In Germany, under section 3(1b) of the German VAT Act (*Umsatzsteuergesetz*, UStG), a donation in kind is treated as a deemed supply for consideration if the goods have entitled the taxable person to full or partial deduction of input tax, i.e., a so-called *Entnahme* (withdrawal). The withdrawal of the good from the business assets for donation purposes is therefore basically charged with 19% VAT at the standard tax rate.[34] There is no tax exemption for donations in kind.

At the same time, the input tax deduction for expenditure related to the donated goods is retained – if the other conditions of section 15 UStG are met. If, on the other hand, goods are acquired with the intention of using them as a donation in kind, input tax cannot be deducted because the taxable person lacks the intention at the time of purchase to use them for an economic activity.[35]

The taxable amount for the withdrawal from the business assets within the meaning of section 3, paragraph 1b UStG is the purchase price (plus ancillary expenses) for the good or for a similar good or, in the absence of a purchase price, the cost price at the time of turnover, i.e., a 'fictitious purchase price' or 'fictitious cost price'.[36]

According to the German Federal Finance Administration, the fictitious purchase price corresponds to the replacement costs determined at the relevant intermediary level at the time of the donation as stated in the application decree of the German VAT Act (UStAE) of the German Federal Ministry of Finance (BMF).[37]

The BMF has issued a circular letter of March 2021[38] intended to clarify the requirements and mechanics for a reduction of the taxable amount in relation to donations of food and non-food goods. This uniform federal administrative approach

33. For the purposes of this chapter, the UK's VAT rules on donations in kind are still analysed against the background of the EU VAT Directive, as the Directive remained in force during the transition period following the UK secession from the EU on 1 Jan. 2020.
34. *See* section 12(1) UStG. The exception provided for in the German VAT Act for gifts of low value (to be assumed if the gift does not exceed EUR 35.00 per calendar year) in accordance with section 3(1b) sentence 1 no. 3 UStG is not taken into account here due to its minor impact.
35. Sarah Ryglewski, *Steuerliche Vereinfachung von Sachspenden*, 4 UVR 97 (2020).
36. Section 10, paragraph 4, sentence 1, no. 1 UStG.
37. UStAE no. 10.6 paragraph 1 sentence 2.
38. BMF circular 2021/0251308 as of 18 Mar. 2021 on the assessment of donations in kind for VAT purposes and the tax base for donations in kind.

replaces the isolated and uncoordinated administrative regulations previously issued at state level.[39]

Pursuant to the BMF, the taxable amount shall be reduced according to the limited marketability of a good. Limited marketability is to be assumed if the goods are no longer or only with difficulty marketable due to considerable material or packaging defects or lack of marketability (e.g., goods from the previous season).[40] Material or packaging defects include content shortfalls, incorrect labelling, or damaged returns. On the other hand, there should be no restriction on marketability if new goods without defects are excluded from the business only for economic or logistical reasons.[41]

The principles of the BMF apply to both food and non-food products. According to these principles, if, for example, a shampoo bottle is incorrectly labelled, it can no longer be used for normal retail sales, even though the shampoo itself is not defective. This limits its marketability and, in the case of a donation in kind, results in a correspondingly lower taxable amount. In such cases a price reduction should be applied that corresponds with the reduced marketability of the product. To that end, certain principles are laid down for determining the taxable amount.[42]

The BMF clarifies for food and non-food products that a taxable amount of EUR 0 can only be applied for donations of perishable products which are close to their expiration date, as these are generally qualified as worthless.[43] A taxable amount of EUR 0 cannot be applied in other cases even if new and undamaged goods would otherwise be destroyed, e.g., if clothes were ordered, tried on and returned filthy.[44]

[B] UK (Conditional 0% Tax Rate)

The UK provides for preferential tax treatment for donations in kind (e.g., commercial goods) in that the donor may apply a tax rate of 0% conditioned on the status of the beneficiary and the use it makes of the donated goods.[45] The beneficiary must be a recognized charity or a local amateur sports club (*community amateur sports club*, CASC), and must intend to sell, hire out, or export the donated goods.[46] As the zero rate is a positive VAT rate, it allows for full input tax recovery while no output VAT is payable.[47]

---

39. Higher Finance Authority of Niedersachsen, circular of 27 Mar. 2017, S 7109 – 31 – St 171, UR 2017, 608; circular of 9 Feb. 2016, S 2223 – 324 – St 235; Higher Finance Authority of Sachsen, circular of 18 Sep. 2012, S 7109 – 10/2-213, DStR 2013, 199.
40. UStAE no. 10.6 paragraph 1a sentence 4.
41. UStAE no. 10.6 paragraph 1a sentence 7.
42. UStAE no. 10.6 paragraph 1a sentence 9.
43. UStAE no. 10.6 paragraph 1a sentences 2 and 3.
44. UStAE no. 10.6 paragraph 1a sentence 8.
45. Section 30 paragraph 2 in connection with Schedule 8, Part II Group 15 item 2 UK VAT Act 1994; *see also* https://www.gov.uk/tax-limited-company-gives-to-charity/equipment-and-trading-stock (accessed 30 Nov. 2020).
46. This use of goods by the charity is also zero-rated under certain conditions pursuant to section 30 paragraph 2 in connection with Schedule 8, Part II, Group 15 items 1, 1a and 3 UK VAT Act; VAT Notice 701/1 paragraph 5.5.1.
47. Section 30 paragraph 1 UK VAT Act.

If the conditions cannot be met, the applicable standard or reduced VAT rate must be applied. The compliance with these conditions must, in principle, be proven by a certificate issued by the charity including the necessary information (*eligibility declaration or certificate*).[48]

[C] France (Exception from the Input VAT Correction)

If goods are acquired for the purpose of donating them, the corresponding input VAT cannot be recovered as the expenditure is not made in relation to an economic activity.[49]

However, if goods are initially acquired for business purposes, the corresponding input VAT will of course be deducted and if these goods are later used for non-business purposes, such as a charitable donation, French VAT law as laid down in the French General Tax Code (*Code general des impôts*, CGI) prevents non-taxation through two alternative modes of correction.

If the taxable person deducted input VAT, the donation in kind can be treated as a self-supply pursuant to Article 257 II 1 1⁰ of the CGI[50] (*livraison à soi-même*, corresponding to Article 16 of the VAT Directive). This qualifies as a withdrawal from the business assets. The self-supply is a deemed supply for consideration and thus taxable. A VAT exemption, however, does not exist for donations in kind. Therefore, the input VAT deduction on the donated goods is retained in this scenario, but the donor must remit VAT on the value of the donated item.

Alternatively, pursuant to Article 271 III lit. b of the CGI (*regularisation*), the taxable person could correct the input VAT deducted when the donated good was purchased. In this scenario, the taxation of a self-supply would not apply.

In February 2020, an exception from the above-mentioned requirement to correct the initially deducted input VAT was introduced in relation to donations in kind to recognized charities. Pursuant to Article 273 of the CGI, the taxable person is not required to correct input VAT on goods purchased for business purposes but later

48. *See* https://www.gov.uk/tax-limited-company-gives-to-charity/equipment-and-trading-stock (accessed 30 Nov. 2020).
49. BOI-TVA-CHAMP-10-20-20, TVA – Champ d'application et territorialité – Opérations imposables par disposition expresse de la loi – Livraisons à soi-même de biens et de services as of 26 Aug. 2020, margin no. 80.
50. Article 257 II 1 1⁰ CGI: *'Le prélèvement par un assujetti d'un bien de son entreprise pour ses besoins privés ou ceux de son personnel ou qu'il transmet à titre gratuit ou, plus généralement, qu'il affecte à des fins étrangères à son entreprise, lorsque ce bien ou les éléments le composant ont ouvert droit à une déduction complète ou partielle de la taxe sur la valeur ajoutée. Toutefois, ne sont pas visés les prélèvements effectués pour les besoins de l'entreprise pour donner des cadeaux de faible valeur et des échantillons. Le montant à retenir pour l'imposition des prélèvements correspondant aux cadeaux de faible valeur est fixé par arrêté. Cette limite s'applique par objet et par an pour un même bénéficiaire; […].'*

donated to recognized organisations serving humanitarian, social, or charitable purposes. The relief is not limited to goods that can no longer be sold on the market but also applies to new or as-new goods.[51]

However, this concession is accompanied by strict formal requirements.[52] The beneficiary must provide the donor with a certificate with the following information: the name and address of the donor and the beneficiary; the purpose of the charity and the date and decision number under which it was recognized as a charitable organisation under French law; and a detailed statement indicating the date of the donation and the nature and quantity of the items donated. In the case of a continuous donating by the same donor, it is sufficient for a certificate to be issued for all donations in kind within a maximum of one calendar year. A copy of the relevant certificate must be kept for six years by both the donor and the beneficiary in accordance with the general rules.[53] If the exception of input VAT correction applies, according to the official letter of application from the French tax authorities, there is also no taxation as a self-supply under Article 257 II 1 1^0 of the CGI.[54] As a result, the donation in kind leads to untaxed final consumption.

The purpose of Article 273 of the CGI for donations in kind is to reuse unsold goods with a view to the sustainable use of resources. The introduction of this provision is part of the extensive environmental protection measures which France has implemented with effect from 12 February 2020 by Law No. 2020-105 on the fight against waste and the recycling of resources.[55] The stated objective of the law is in particular the avoidance of waste, which for consumer products translates into encouraging reuse and recycling or – if neither is possible – at least the sensible recovery of the waste.[56] However, the new provision constitutes an exception to the principle laid down by EU law that a deduction of input tax is to be granted only in connection with output transactions subject to VAT. This leads at least from an EU perspective to untaxed final consumption, which is generally not in line with the system and the objective of the VAT Directive.

51. Article 273 septis D: '*Une régularisation de la taxe initialement déduite et grevant un bien n'est pas opérée pour les invendus alimentaires et non alimentaires neufs qui ont été donnés aux associations reconnues d'utilité publique présentant un intérêt général de caractère humanitaire, éducatif, social ou charitable dans des conditions fixées par décret.*'
52. French General Tax Code, Annexe 3, CGIAN3. Article 84 B (V).
53. Article L102 B French Procedural Tax Code (*livre des procédures fiscales*).
54. BOI-TVA-CHAMP-10-20-20, TVA – Champ d'application et territorialité – Opérations imposables par disposition expresse de la loi – Livraisons à soi-même de biens et de services of 26. Aug. 2020, margin no. 130: '*Le bénéfice de cette dispense de régularisation vaut également dispense de taxation de la livraison à soi-même au titre du 1° du 1 du II de l'article 257 du CGI.*'
55. LOI n° 2020-105 du 10 février 2020 relative à la lutte contre le gaspillage et à l'économie circulaire, JORF n° 0035 du 11 février 2020.
56. Article L110-1-1 Environmental Act (*Code d'Environment*): '*La transition vers une économie circulaire vise à atteindre une empreinte écologique neutre dans le cadre du respect des limites planétaires [...], par ordre de priorité, à la prévention de la production de déchets, notamment par le réemploi des produits, et, suivant la hiérarchie des modes de traitement des déchets, à une réutilisation, à un recyclage ou, à défaut, à une valorisation des déchets.*'

[D] Australia (Full Credit for all Input GST)

The Australian *Goods and Services Tax* (GST)[57] is a comprehensive VAT, which is similar to the VAT commonly applied in the EU but bases on a modern VAT model.

Under the GST, a registered enterprise must account for GST on any taxable supplies it makes. A taxable supply is defined as a supply made for consideration, unless the supply is specified to be an input taxed (exempt) supply.[58] A supply provided for no consideration such as donation is an out-of-scope supply, falling outside the definition of a taxable supply so that no GST is payable on a donation.[59]

Australian tax law also provides for the refund of input tax to businesses registered for GST purposes (*input tax credit, GST credit*), which has been incurred on the purchase of goods and services.[60] It is required that the taxable person intends to use all or part of the goods purchased for a creditable purpose which is defined as any acquisition made in the course of carrying on an enterprise unless the acquisition relates to an intended making of an *input-taxed* supply (Australian terminology for an exempt supply)[61] or was of a private or domestic nature.[62] Furthermore, the purchase price must have actually included GST. If the purchase price is higher than AUD 82.50, the taxable person claiming an input tax credit must also provide a tax invoice as proof.[63]

An acquisition that is used to make a supply for no consideration will still give rise to input tax credits provided the supply is made in the course of an enterprise. Thus, an enterprise using acquisitions to make free promotional supplies, samples, prizes, and so forth will be entitled to full input tax credits on the acquisitions.

A special adjustment event rule applies where there is a change in purpose in respect of an acquisition. The rule provides for a pro-rata adjustment event when an acquisition acquired for a purpose other than a creditable purpose is converted to a creditable purpose or an acquisition acquired for a creditable purpose is later applied to a non-creditable purpose. The adjustment value is based on the amount of time the acquisition has been used for one purpose before being applied to another.

A special rule applies to changes of purpose if an acquisition acquired for use in the enterprise is later supplied without consideration to a charity or not-for-profit organization. Provided the supply will be used for a purpose of the receiving entity, the change in purpose adjustment event will not apply and there will be no adjustment

---

57. Introduced by the Australian Federal Government with the A New Tax System (Goods and Services Tax) Act 1999 (GST Act) with effect from 1 Jul. 2000 ('GST Act'), remade and improved by A New Tax System (Goods and Services Tax) Regulations 2019. Prior to the GST, Australia operated a Wholesale Sales Tax which imposed a tax on wholesales of goods.
58. Section 9-5 GST Act.
59. Section 9-17 paragraph 2 GST Act: '[...] Making a gift to a non profit body is not the provision of consideration.'
60. Section 11-20 GST Act.
61. Section 11-15 GST Act.
62. Section 11-15 GST Act. In contrast, the taxable person is entitled to an input GST credit in respect of acquisitions used to make *GST-free sales* (the Australian term for zero-rated supplies).
63. *See*, for details, https://www.ato.gov.au/business/gst/claiming-gst-credits/when-you-can-claim-a-gst-credit/ (accessed 30 Nov. 2020).

event when the donation is made.[64] The rule is intended to avoid any doubt as to whether a gift that was not intended at the time of acquisition is still made in the course of the enterprise. It only applies to donations made to charities and not-for-profit bodies that qualify for preferential treatment under the income tax legislation and satisfy the definitions in that law.

§17.05 EVALUATION OF THE DIFFERENT APPROACHES TO THE TREATMENT OF DONATIONS IN KIND

The analysis of the VAT treatment of donations in kind in the four countries discussed above shows three different approaches: (1) preferential treatment within the taxable amount, (2) the tax rate, or (3) the deduction/correction of input tax.

Looking at the different approaches from the point of view of environmental protection by promoting the circular economy, the legal provisions in the UK, France, and Australia have an excessive steering effect. In these countries, the incentives for donations in kind also apply to new, fully marketable goods and products which could be sold without difficulty. These are not subject to the condition that they would otherwise have to be destroyed or disposed of by traders for economic reasons. At the same time, however, the UK rules are too narrow, as the zero rate is ultimately only applicable if the beneficiary uses the gifted items for specific transactions.

In Germany, on the other hand, the reduction of the taxable amount depends on the lack of marketability of the goods as otherwise no substantial reduction of the taxable amount could be justified. The decisive factor is whether the taxable person can no longer use these goods for the business. If this is the case, the enterprise should not be disadvantaged financially when it decides to donate those goods instead of destroying them. This is in line with the objective of conserving natural resources. In this way, the VAT provision corresponds to the environmental policy objective of promoting the circular economy when determining the taxable amount. However, the German administrative regulation also appears to be too narrow in that it only applies to perishable food and non-food products donated close to their expiration date, i.e., when they have essentially become worthless, thus justifying a taxable amount of EUR 0. Focusing on the expiration date as the authoritative criterion, the scope remains relatively narrow as the use of non-food products rarely depends on an expiration date. The taxable amount of EUR 0 should thus also apply to goods that would otherwise be destroyed subject to proper justification and documentation of this intention.

§17.06 SUMMARY AND OUTLOOK

While the tax authorities in Germany use the taxable amount to treat donations in kind more favourable and under specific circumstances allow a valuation of EUR 0, the UK

64. Section 129-45 GST Act. Gifts to gift deductible entities: '(1) If you are or were entitled to an input tax credit for the creditable acquisition of a thing, an adjustment does not arise under this Subdivision merely because you supply the thing as a gift to an endorsed charity or gift deductible entity. [...].'

uses a zero tax rate. However, both regulations are too narrow: While the German administrative regulation for a tax base of EUR 0 is limited to goods close to their expiration date, in the UK the beneficiary of the donation must meet strict conditions.

The most extensive preferential treatment is provided for in France. There, in the case of a donation in kind, a special legal provision relieves the donor from the obligation to make an input tax adjustment for the donated goods and at the same time waives the tax on the self-supply. The latter approach corresponds to the approach taken in Australia, where the deduction of input tax related to goods which are later donated in kind is also not to be corrected. However, within the scope of the harmonised VAT Directive, donations in kind should, first, be treated in a uniform manner throughout the EU and, second, benefit from VAT relief in line with the EU's efforts to achieve an efficient circular economy and to prevent a waste of resources. This could be realized through legislative amendment of the Directive.

The legal comparison of the countries analysed above could provide guidelines for developing an EU-wide approach for the VAT treatment of donations in kind. The UK (zero rate) approach forms an exception to the VAT system and thus complicates the application of VAT rules, for which reason this option seems less desirable. If one followed the French or Australian preferential treatment by excluding the input tax adjustment, Article 16 of the VAT Directive would have to provide for an exemption from the tax on the deemed self-supply in the case of a donation in kind. Member States would also have to establish appropriate verification procedures, similar to the French verification requirements. In addition, an amendment to Article 185(2) of the VAT Directive would be necessary, to create an exception for the correction of the input VAT deduction in the case of a donation in kind (possibly with language limiting the exception to donations to charitable organisations as defined by national law).[65] However, such a provision would infringe on the systemic correlation between input VAT credits and taxable outputs as applied in the EU.

Within an overall view, a solution on the taxable amount is preferable. This would be the simplest, quickest, and most effective option[66] to encourage donations in kind throughout the EU in the future, in cases where gifted items no longer have any value for the taxable person. This could also be achieved through interpreting existing EU law accordingly. The CJEU has already shown the way forward.[67] This would also remove the need to amend the VAT Directive, which is a politically complicated process due to the requirement of unanimity.

However, the EU Commission's task would be to provide the Member States with an interpretation of the value for the taxable amount to be applied to donations in kind in order to standardise the application of VAT law – going beyond the food sector. For

65. *De lege lata*, Article 185(2) VAT Directive only provides for an exception for the correction in proven cases of destruction, loss or theft as well as in case of gifts of low value and commercial samples.
66. Cf. E-006248/2015, *supra* n. 30.
67. *See Marinov, supra* n. 27, margin no. 35; and *Fischer and Brandenstein, supra* n. 27, margin no. 80.

example, the VAT Committee[68] could draw up appropriate guidelines with the involvement of the relevant interest groups. In our view, a general reduction of the tax base up to a value of EUR 0 for all donations in kind should be considered if the goods no longer have any business value for the taxable person and are therefore considered for donation. According to the case law of the CJEU, the 'residual value' of the gifted item thus appears to be a suitable benchmark for the taxable person. According to national understanding, the residual value comes close to the 'going concern value' of an asset.

68. The VAT Committee was set up under Article 398 VAT Directive as an advisory committee on VAT and is intended to promote the uniform application of the VAT Directive rules. It is composed of representatives of the Member States and the European Commission. In addition to the points which, under the VAT Directive, require consultation of the VAT Committee, the VAT Committee also examines questions relating to the application of Community legislation on VAT. Questions of this kind are submitted to it by the chairman, either on his own initiative or at the request of the representative of a Member State.

PART II Country Treatises

CHAPTER 18

The New Zealand Broad-Based, Uniform-Rate GST: Virtue or Fallacy?

David White

§18.01 INTRODUCTION

The New Zealand Goods and Services Tax (GST) is a modified version of the European Value Added Tax (VAT). While the New Zealand GST uses the same invoice-credit mechanism as the European VAT, it had two key innovations when it was designed in the mid-1980s. First, it had a uniform rate of tax, not multiple rates. Second, its tax base was comprehensive, without exemptions other than those necessary to define the base. In New Zealand, the GST tax instrument was designed to be efficient in practice and collect revenue at least cost, leaving distributional and other social and economic objectives to be achieved by other instruments: the income tax, the social welfare system (especially for working families and children), government expenditure and regulation. For 35 years, these two, and other, innovative features of the New Zealand GST have received favourable comments from international commentators,[1] with some characterising it as a 'second-generation' VAT.[2]

1. James A. Mirrlees et al., *Tax by Design: The Mirrlees Review* 484 (Oxford University Press, 2010); Robert F. van Brederode, *Systems of General Sales Taxation: Theory Policy and Practice* 333-340 (Kluwer Law International, 2009); Sijbren Cnossen, *Evaluating the National Retail Sales Tax from a VAT Perspective*, in *United States Tax Reform in the 21st Century* 215-244, 244 (George R. Zodrow and Peter Mieszkowski, eds., Cambridge University Press, 2002); Richard Krever, *Design and Structure of the VAT* in *VAT in Africa* 18 (Richard Krever, ed., Pretoria University Law Press, 2008). For an example of a specific New Zealand GST regime recommendation, *see* Sijbren Cnossen, *A Proposal to Apply the Kiwi-VAT to Insurance Services in the European Union* 20(5) Int'l Tax & Pub. Fin. 867-883 (2013).
2. With the EU model described as a 'first-generation' VAT. Richard M. Bird, *Commentary on Value Added Tax and Excises*, in *Dimensions of Tax Design: The Mirrlees Review* 363-369, 366 (James Mirrlees et al., eds., Oxford University Press, 2010).

The focus of this country chapter is rate and base policy as I consider it will be the most important issue for the New Zealand GST in the medium term, especially if the uniform GST rate of 15% were increased. Issues such as the optimal trade-offs and innovations in the New Zealand GST treatment of real property, financial services or internet transactions, for example, are important but narrowing the New Zealand GST base or introducing reduced tax rates would have significant implications for revenue generation and both individual and social welfare, as will become clear in this chapter. In addition, there is already sufficient literature on the trade-offs involved in New Zealand's responses on key VAT technical problem issues.[3]

VAT rate policy and VAT base policy have been discussed in general terms in Chapters 4 and 5 respectively. In this part of the book, these issues are discussed in respect of two OECD countries in the Pacific Ocean that both had broad-based, single-rate consumption taxes for many years, with Japan departing from that long-standing policy on increasing its standard rate of consumption tax to 10% in 2019. When New Zealand last raised its standard rate of GST from 12.5% to 15% in 2010, however, it retained its broad-based, uniform-rate policy. While this approach to GST design has been sustained by all New Zealand governments for 35 years now, suggesting a degree of acceptance in the community, it has at times been contested, especially in relation to the tax treatment of food and basic necessities. For some, the comprehensive, uniform-rate approach in the GST is a 'virtue': it is a less costly way of collecting revenue, with other governmental instruments available to achieve distributional, wellbeing and other objectives they seek. For others, it is a 'fallacy': the GST itself should balance efficiency and equity, as there is no guarantee that other governmental instruments will achieve the distributional, wellbeing or other objectives they seek.

The purpose of this chapter, then, is to examine some of the latest research and data about the revenue and economic performance of the New Zealand broad-based, uniform-rate GST and its distributional effects and reflect on some of the implications for New Zealand if the GST base were narrowed or multiple rates of tax were introduced in future. It takes a practical tax policymaking perspective, drawing on my experience, including: being a tax policy analyst in the New Zealand Treasury from 1986 to 2000; co-organising a multi-disciplinary team of 30 experts from eight countries to test the New Zealand GST model in 2006-2007;[4] co-organising a review of the New

3. *See*, e.g., Ian Dickson and David White, *Commentary on Value Added Tax and Excises*, in *Dimensions of Tax Design: The Mirrlees Review* 387-406, 400-403 (James Mirrlees et al., eds., Oxford University Press, 2010); Matt Benge, Marie Pallot, and Hamish Slack, *Possible Lessons for the United States from New Zealand's GST* 66:2 Nat'l Tax J. 479-498, 492-496 (2013).
4. Agreeing with Michael Keen (then Head, Tax Policy Division, IMF) that GST/VAT was 'shamefully under-researched' at the time (Keen speaking at the International Tax Dialogue VAT Conference held in Rome in 2005) and collaborating with Richard Krever (then of Monash University, Melbourne), this 2006-2007 New Zealand GST project: celebrated in the Grand Hall of the New Zealand Parliament the work of 15 major contributors who designed and implemented New Zealand's innovative GST in the mid-1980s; held a conference entitled 'Twenty Years of GST: The Best Path Forward' with 30 speakers from 8 countries, as often as possible organised in multidisciplinary and international panels, each addressing a key issue (142 delegates from 20 countries attended); with support from the IMF, held a workshop where 15 South Pacific tax administrators from 8 countries discussed the relevance of the conference discussions for each of

Zealand tax system and participating as a member of the Victoria University of Wellington Tax Working Group (VUW TWG), which recommended the last increase in the New Zealand standard rate of GST in 2010;[5] and, being a VAT commentator for the book of initial tax studies for the Mirrlees Review of the United Kingdom tax system from 2006-2010, with the final Mirrlees review team recommending a broad-based, almost uniform-rate VAT.[6]

Section 18.02 of this chapter considers the New Zealand GST rate and base recommendations of the 3 reviews of the New Zealand tax system that have taken place over the last 20 years, as well as the rate and base recommendations of recent reviews of the United Kingdom VAT and the Australian GST (and briefly noting the revenue and economic impact of Canada's GST base and rate structure). Section 18.03 examines the latest data on the relative revenue performance, neutrality, and distributional effects of New Zealand's broad-based, uniform-rate GST, mostly in relation to OECD countries, and particularly to the United Kingdom, Australia and Canada. Specifically, it reviews the amount of revenue collected, the level of the standard rate, its distributional effects, the revenue and economic performance of the tax, and its operation in an economic crisis. Section 18.04 concludes.

§18.02 EXPERT REVIEWS OF THE BROAD-BASED, UNIFORM-RATE DESIGN

As noted in the introduction, there has been a degree of acceptance and disapproval of the broad-based, uniform-rate design of GST in New Zealand, especially in relation to the tax treatment of food and basic necessities. Most New Zealand political parties have, at least once while they were in opposition in the last 35 years, taken GST-exemption policies to the electorate but, with insufficient support, the policies have subsequently been dropped from their party platforms.[7] In 2010, a private member's bill to exempt healthy food from GST received insufficient votes in Parliament to be referred to a select committee for consideration.[8] Support for the broad-based, uniform-rate approach has come from policy officials and economists in particular, and even a

their countries; published a book of conference papers on current and future GST/VAT issues in March 2007; and, published 6 journal articles based on conference papers in New Zealand Journal of Taxation Law and Policy in 2007. The book is *GST in Retrospect and Prospect* (Richard Krever and David White, eds, Brookers Ltd, 2007).

5. Victoria University of Wellington Tax Working Group, *A Tax System for New Zealand's Future* (Centre for Accounting, Governance and Taxation Research, Victoria University of Wellington, 2010), available at https://www.victoria.ac.nz/sacl/centres-and-institutes/cagtr/pdf/tax-report-website.pdf (accessed 31 January 2021).
6. Dickson and White, *supra* n. 3, 387-406.
7. For example, the National Party in 1987, the Labour Party from 2010 to 2014, and the Maori and Mana Parties in 2010. The exception is the New Zealand First party, which has had some GST-exemption policy platform for much of its existence since the 1990s.
8. Rahui Katene, MP, Maori Party – Te Tai Tonga, *Goods and Services Tax (Exemption of Healthy Food) Amendment Bill*, available at https://www.parliament.nz/en/pb/hansard-debates/rhr/document/49HansD_20100908_00001000/goods-and-services-tax-exemption-of-healthy-food-amendment (accessed 31 January 2021).

child poverty welfare group,[9] while opposition to it has included some public health academics[10] and a legal academic,[11] mostly arguing their case on equity grounds. A collective with a wide membership of health, consumer and community organisations and academic leaders was established in 2018 to reduce the harm from tobacco, alcohol and unhealthy foods and beverages. Among other things, Health Coalition Aotearoa is promoting further research on removing GST from fruit and vegetables.[12] And, in 2018-2019, the Tax Working Group (TWG) set up by the government to review the New Zealand tax system received 'many public submissions' arguing that the GST rate should be reduced, most arguing that this would increase the progressivity of the tax system. It also received 'a large number of submissions arguing for exceptions to the GST base', such as healthier food and drink or items likely to be purchased by low-income households.[13]

In this section, we examine the assessment by expert reviews in New Zealand, the United Kingdom and Australia of their national VAT or GST systems and their tax base and rate recommendations. An interesting point to bear in mind, which is covered in detail in the next section, is that an OECD measure of VAT performance at least suggests that the New Zealand GST with its broad base and uniform rate has been collecting almost all of the potential New Zealand GST base. By contrast, the GSTs in Australia and in Canada, as well as the VAT in the United Kingdom, have been collecting less than half their respective potential tax bases.

[A] Three New Zealand Tax Reviews

Three reviews of the New Zealand tax system have occurred in the last 20 years: the McLeod Review in 2001; the VUW TWG in 2009-2010; and the TWG in 2018-2019.

In 2001, the government-appointed McLeod Review supported the broad-based, uniform-rate design of the New Zealand GST and did not propose material reform. This group referred to New Zealand studies that 'show that GST is roughly proportional to income for the 80 percent of households in the middle of the income distribution' and concluded that the 'use of multiple rates or exemptions for particular items to address concerns about regressivity would be a backward step. It would serve to create considerable additional costs (including increased taxpayer compliance costs) and

9. Child Poverty Action Group, *Will Removing GST on Fresh Fruit and Vegetables Achieve its Stated Aim?* (CPAG, 2010), available at https://www.cpag.org.nz/will-removing-gst-on-fresh-fruit-and-vegettables/ (accessed 31 January 2021).
10. For example, Moira B. Smith and Louise Signal, *Global Influences on Milk Purchasing in New Zealand – Implications for Health and Inequalities* 5(1) Global Health 9 (2009), available at https://doi.org/10.1186/1744-8603-5-1 (accessed 31 January 2021).
11. Anna Percy, *New Zealand's GST v. Exclusions: A Case for the Exclusion of Basic Food and Menstrual Products from Goods and Services Tax in New Zealand* 25 Auckland Un. Law Rev. 228 (2019).
12. Nick Wilson et al., *Food Taxes and Subsidies to Protect Health: Relevance to Aotearoa New Zealand* 133 NZMJ 71, 73 (2020). More broadly, *see* the coalition website: https://www.healthcoalition.org.nz/about-us/ (accessed 31 January 2021).
13. Tax Working Group, *Future of Tax: Interim Report*, 83-92, 84 and 87 (New Zealand Government, 2018), available at https://taxworkinggroup.govt.nz/resources/future-tax-interim-report (accessed 31 January 2021).

anomalies.'[14] It concluded that New Zealand's tax mix with two main tax bases at the time was broadly right but that as GST distorted economic decisions less than the income tax, any overall increase in tax in future should be implemented through GST and any reduction in tax should be focused on income tax.[15]

In 2009-2010, the VUW TWG was set up to review the tax system with support from the Ministers of Finance and Revenue. This group also supported the broad-based, uniform-rate design of the New Zealand GST. It proposed material tax-mix reform: a shift away from income tax towards GST and tax on immovable property. All members of the VUW TWG supported New Zealand reducing income tax rates to reduce the potential adverse impact of New Zealand's tax structure on economic growth over the short- to-medium term. They disagreed, however, about how to fund those income tax cuts in a fiscally-neutral package. Most VUW TWG members supported increasing the standard GST rate from 12.5% to 15% and increasing taxation of immovable property, with mixed views about 'whether the efficiency benefits from increasing GST would be sufficient to outweigh possible equity effects'.[16] The argument for increasing the GST rate was that it would reduce the tax bias against saving and investment relative to consumption. To compensate people who would be disadvantaged, the group recommended increased benefit levels and reductions in the personal tax scale, not a narrowing of the GST base, for example by excluding food. All of the VUW TWG agreed that such an exclusion from the base would 'substantially reduce' the efficiency of GST, increase compliance and administrative costs and have 'limited impact on equity'. [17]

The government accepted many of the VUW TWG recommendations. From 1 October 2010, the standard GST rate was increased from 12.5% to 15%, all personal income tax rates were reduced, and a GST compensation package for adversely-affected welfare groups was implemented. From 1 April 2011, in most cases, the company income tax rate was reduced (from 30% to 28%). Changes to the way that property was taxed were also implemented largely in the income tax. The tax mix change was meant to be broadly fiscally neutral.

The third and most recent New Zealand tax review was in 2018-2019. The terms of reference of this government-appointed TWG excluded consideration of an increase in the GST rate. This group also supported the broad-based, uniform-rate design of the New Zealand GST, expressing its view that 'the broad base of New Zealand's GST is

---

14. Robert McLeod et al., *Tax Review 2001: Final Report*, 35 (New Zealand Treasury 2001).
15. *Supra* n. 14, 26.
16. Victoria University of Wellington Tax Working Group, *supra* n. 5, 66. Weighing on my equity concerns as we expressed our views in the VUW TWG on increasing the GST uniform rate was my assessment that the group would not express sufficient support for base broadening with respect to the taxation of capital (an essential element in the tax-mix package in my opinion). For my views on that topic, *see* Leonard Burman and David White, *Taxing Capital Gains in New Zealand*, 9 NZ J Tax L & Policy 355 (2003); Leonard E Burman and David I White, *Taxing Capital Gains in New Zealand: Assessment and Recommendations*, Paper commissioned by the New Zealand Treasury for consideration by the VUW TWG, available at www.victoria.ac.nz/sacl/centres-and-institutes/cagtr/twg/twg-papers-index (accessed 31 January 2021).
17. *Supra* n. 16.

one of its greatest strengths'.[18] While acknowledging public concerns about the regressive nature of GST, the Group considered, but did not recommend, either a reduction in the GST rate or the introduction of exceptions, such as food and drink. The group questioned the efficacy of GST exceptions in achieving distributional goals and the degree of pass-through of GST reductions to consumers.[19] They noted the complexity and significant compliance costs of GST exceptions and the dangers of opening up political lobbying. In the group's view, welfare payments or personal income changes were more effective ways to increase progressivity than making changes to the GST. Finally, the group noted that maintaining the 15% rate ensured that GST was collected from people, such as tourists, who would otherwise not be part of the New Zealand tax base.[20]

[B] Review of a First-Generation VAT in United Kingdom: The Mirrlees Review

The Mirrlees Review was a comprehensive review of taxes and transfers chaired by Nobel economics laureate Sir James Mirrlees and undertaken from 2006 to 2011. It involved a multi-disciplinary, international team of 73 experts who had different roles in a two-step process. First, it commissioned studies dealing with different aspects of the tax system and a series of commentaries by different expert authors on those studies, publishing the studies and commentaries in a book. Next, a review team published final conclusions regarding tax design issues for open economies and made policy recommendations for the United Kingdom tax system in a second book.

For the final Mirrlees Review team, the main problem with the United Kingdom VAT was that it applied zero or reduced rates of tax on far too many goods and services, often justifying this as a means of supporting the poor. This policy resulted in large

18. Tax Working Group, *supra* n. 13, 83.
19. Recent Eurozone research supports these pass-through concerns of the Tax Working Group. A group of researchers empirically tested the assumption often made in practical tax policy making and in distributional analyses that VAT reform changes (changes in standard rates, reduced rates and reclassifying commodities across existing rate categories) are fully passed through to consumer prices. The researchers used monthly observations on consumer prices and VAT rates for about 70 commodity groups in 17 Eurozone countries over the period from 1999 to 2013 but, unfortunately, were not able to incorporate some other factors they identified as possibly having a systematic impact on VAT reform pass through (individual VAT reform announcement dates, market structure, trade intensity, the degree of compliance and the business cycle, for example). Their results suggest that the policy-making assumption of 100% pass through of standard VAT rate changes in the long run (before, during and after the standard rate change) is a reasonable starting point. For changes in reduced rates, however, cumulative pass through in the long run was estimated at only 28%. For VAT reclassifications across existing rate categories, 'average pass through seems to be typically close to zero'. The researchers argued that the results 'caution against the ... conventional assumption that the benefits of reduced rates are fully passed on to the poorer households they are generally intended to benefit' but there is more work to be done in the future, hopefully with additional data sets not available at present. Dora Benedek et al., *Varieties of VAT Pass Through* 27 Int'l Tax & Pub. Fin. 890-930, especially 901-906 and 914-916 (2020), available at https://doi.org/10.1007/s10797-019-09566-5 (accessed 31 January 2021).)
20. Tax Working Group, New Zealand Government, *Future of Tax: Final Report Vol. 1*, 104 (New Zealand Government, 2019), available at https://taxworkinggroup.govt.nz/resources/future-tax-final-report (accessed 31 January 2021).

administrative and compliance costs and created distortions between different types of consumption. While there might be arguments for differential taxation to offset work disincentives, most of the potential gains, other than relating to childcare, for example, were not sufficient to outweigh practical problems and the costs of complexity and distorting spending patterns.[21]

The Review pointed out that New Zealand provided a working example of how it was possible to apply the standard rate of VAT to almost all goods and services.[22] Putting the cost of complexity to one side, it estimated the costs of a narrow base in the United Kingdom VAT through the distortion to spending patterns: 'simulations suggest that, if uniformity were optimal, extending VAT at 17.5% to most zero-rated and reduced-rated items would (in principle) allow the government to make each household as well off as it is now and still have around £3 billion of revenue left over. The true figure could be higher or lower than this.' [23]

One of the main themes of the Mirrlees Review was that a tax and transfer system must be considered as a whole. Not every tax needed to achieve all objectives. As the Review considered that VAT was a 'poor choice of tax to use to achieve redistribution', they recommended that the United Kingdom should tax 'virtually all goods and services at the full rate', addressing the distributional and work incentive effects of broadening the VAT base in an 'appropriate package of reforms to the personal tax and benefit system'.[24] Their package was designed to avoid damaging work incentives. In assessing their own tax-and-benefits package, they emphasised the benefits of measuring distributional effects against expenditure and taking a lifetime perspective and the limitations of measuring VAT burdens against income, particularly a snapshot of income over shorter periods (a year, for example).[25]

[C] Review of a Second-Generation GST in Australia: The Thodey Review

The most recent consideration of the Australian GST design by an expert panel was completed in August 2020 by the New South Wales Review of Federal Financial Relations (Thodey Review).[26] While the review was being undertaken, there were two catastrophic events: the unprecedented bushfire season in 2019-2020 with the fire ground in New South Wales covering 7% of the state, and the ongoing COVID-19 pandemic. The financial cost of recovery from these two events is so great it would test the best tax system. The report reviewed the New South Wales current taxes and tax options, finding many areas for substantial improvement, including in the Australian GST.

21. Mirrlees, *supra* n. 1, 484.
22. Research and data about the New Zealand GST experience had been discussed in the VAT commentary by Dickson and White in the first Mirrlees book, *supra* n. 3, 387-406.
23. Mirrlees, *supra* n. 1, 484.
24. Mirrlees, *supra* n. 1, 484.
25. Mirrlees, *supra* n. 1, 485.
26. *See* Chapter 3 of the NSW Review of Federal Financial Relations, *Final Report*, 32-39 (NSW Treasury 2020).

The largest revenue source for New South Wales is the Australian GST, which is collected by the federal government and distributed to the states. The Thodey Review pointed out that the 20-year-old GST was Australia's last major tax reform and that it had meant to be predictable, result in minimal damage to the economy and grow with the economy. But instead of doing that, the GST tax base have been shrinking over the past 20 years, as the share of household spending subject to GST fell from around 60.8% in 2001-2002 to 55.4% in 2018-2019. The escalating cost of exempt services such as health and education were a major part of the problem. Further, as the population aged, more expensive health technologies were introduced and health expectations rose, the problem was likely to be exacerbated.

Prior to the COVID-19 pandemic, the Australian federal government had predicted that the GST exemptions would result in AUD 27.4 billion of revenue foregone in 2019-2020: fresh food (AUD 7.6 billion); health (AUD 7.0 billion); education (AUD 4.9 billion); water, sewerage and drainage (AUD 1.1 billion) and other goods and services.[27] The Thodey Review concluded that broadening the GST base to cover all of these exemptions would improve the existing Australian GST by, among other things:

- tackling the base erosion issue, as the level of GST revenue would reflect the level of consumption, not whether heightened consumer demand is taxed or not taxed;
- stabilising revenues, as more non-discretionary spending, which is typically more consistent, would be taxed; and
- simplifying compliance and administration of the GST.[28]

The Thodey Review identified some difficult transitional issues with base-broadening but recommended that 'State governments, in consultation with the Commonwealth, should assess and agree options for lifting the GST rate and/or expanding the base over the medium to longer term to offset erosion and move away from more harmful Commonwealth and state taxes.'[29] It also noted that credible reform of the GST base or rate would require higher social security payments and lower income tax rates to be used to compensate those on low incomes and ensure that they do not unfairly bear the burden of reform.

27. Commonwealth of Australia, *Tax Benchmarks and Variations Statement 2019* (Canberra, 2020).
28. NSW Review of Federal Financial Relations, *supra* n. 26, 36. Similar concerns with another second-generation GST, the Canadian GST, have been expressed by Canadian public finance scholars: for example, *see* Michael Smart, *Departures from Neutrality in Canada's Goods and Services Tax* in *After Twenty Years: The Future of the Goods and Services Tax* 81-114, 81 (Jack Mintz and Stephen Richardson, eds, Canadian Tax Foundation, 2014). 'In reality, Canada's VATs have large exemptions, rebates, and rate preferences that reduce revenues and hamper productivity. If all these tax preferences were eliminated, government VAT revenues would increase by as much as $39 billion, or more than 50 percent. Moreover, taxing consumer commodities at a single rate reduces opportunities for tax evasion, simplifies tax compliance, and in most cases increases economic productivity. Given the fiscal and productivity challenges currently facing Canadian governments, a new look at VAT design is clearly warranted.' More generally on compliance costs, *see* Chris Evans and Richard Krever in chapter 6 in this book and Chris Evans et al., *Diagnosing the VAT Compliance Burden: A Cross-Country Assessment* 31(2) Int'l VAT Monitor (2020).
29. NSW Review, *supra* n. 26, 39.

§18.03 THE RELATIVE PERFORMANCE OF THE NEW ZEALAND GST DESIGN

Given that New Zealand and international expert reviews have often made favourable comments about the New Zealand 'second-generation' VAT with its broad-based, uniform-rate design, this section now assesses the latest data and research on the relative performance of this New Zealand GST design. The comparisons are sometimes in relation to all OECD countries (OECD), sometimes all OECD countries, except Colombia, and selected other economies: Argentina, China, Indonesia and South Africa ('OECD Plus') and sometimes 3 selected countries: Australia, Canada and the United Kingdom. This section starts by painting the broader OECD picture of 'general consumption taxation' (i.e., VAT/GST, sales taxes and other general taxes on goods and services that are not specific, such as excises). Then, it concentrates on the major type of general consumption tax, the VAT/GST. At all times, the focus is on where New Zealand GST design and practice sits in this wider context. The aggregated percentages in this section are unweighted averages.

This section reviews the OECD data and research about:

(1) The reliance on general consumption tax revenues in OECD countries.
(2) The amount of New Zealand GST collected as a percentage of GDP and total taxation.
(3) The relative reliance on GST revenue by New Zealand.
(4) The relative standard rate of the New Zealand GST and the distributional effects of having a uniform rate of tax on a broad base.
(5) The relative performance of the New Zealand GST using the OECD concept of the VAT Revenue Ratio (VRR), which seeks to measure the neutrality and uniformity of VAT/GST tax systems.
(6) The relative performance of a broad-based, uniform-rate tax, such as the New Zealand GST, in an economic crisis.

First, there is a broad OECD picture of growing reliance on general consumption taxation. From 1975 to 2018, the increased reliance was almost twofold: as a percentage of GDP in OECD countries, the increase was from 4.1% to 7.1%; as a percentage of total tax revenue in OECD member countries, the increase was from 13.4% to 21.2%.[30] And, from 1975 to date, the key general consumption tax development has been the widespread adoption of the VAT or GST system. In 1975, there were just 13 VATs in the current OECD member countries. Today, 36 of the 37 OECD countries have a VAT (the USA being the exception).[31] As a consequence of the wide adoption of this invoice-credit method of consumption taxation, VATs in OECD countries have, from 1975 to

30. OECD, *Consumption Tax Trends 2020: VAT/GST and Excise Rates, Trends and Policy Issues*, 16 (OECD Publishing, 2020), available at https://doi.org/10.1787/152def2d-en (accessed 31 January 2021).
31. OECD, *supra* n. 30, 16.

2018, more than doubled their contribution to tax collection, measured as a percentage of GDP from 3.1% to 6.8%, and as a percentage of total taxation from 8.8% to 20.4%.[32]

Second, New Zealand has followed this OECD trend but New Zealand's increasing reliance on GST revenue over the last 35 years is even more marked, with its predecessor general consumption tax collecting around 10% of total taxation in the mid-1980s and GST collecting around 30% of total taxation today:

- In 1985, a narrow-base wholesale sales tax with many exemptions and 19 rates ranging from 10% to 60%[33] was just 3.2% of GDP and 10.4% of total taxation.
- In 1990, the GST, with its broad base and uniform rate of 12.5%, was 8.4% of GDP and 22.4% of total taxation.
- In 2018, the same broad-based GST, now with a uniform rate of 15%, was 9.7% of GDP and 29.6% of total taxation.[34]

Third, New Zealand's reliance on GST revenue is now high in comparison with other OECD Plus or OECD countries. The results can differ according to the year and measure used. Comparing VAT revenues as a share of GDP by country in 2018, for example, New Zealand ranks the highest and Chile 9th highest (*see* Figure 18.1). Comparing VAT revenues as a percentage of total tax revenues in 2018, however, Chile ranks highest and New Zealand is the second highest.[35]

Figure 18.1 VAT Revenues as a Share of GDP by 'OECD Plus' Country in 2000, 2008 and 2018

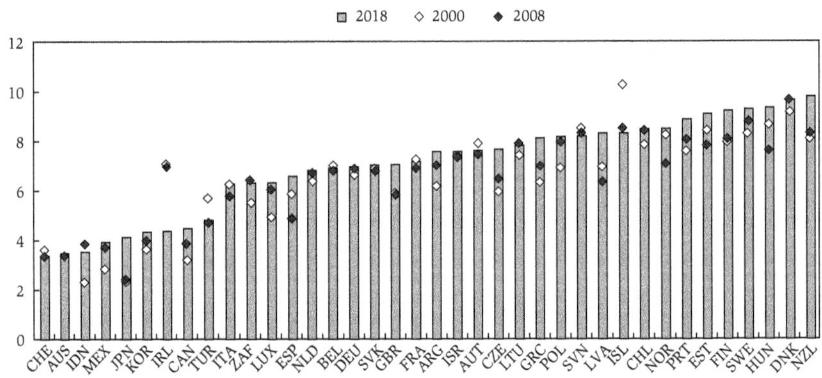

Source: OECD Global Revenue Statistics Database[36]

---

32. OECD, *supra* n. 30, 37.
33. John Due, *The Wholesale Sales Tax in Australia and New Zealand* 31(2) Can. Tax J. 207, 210 and 223 (1983).
34. OECD, *Consumption Tax Trends 2008: VAT/GST and Excise Rates, Trends and Administration Issues*, 41-42 (OECD Publishing, 2008); OECD, *supra* n. 30, 37.
35. OECD, *supra* n. 30, 17. This is a comparison between OECD countries.
36. OECD, *Tax Policy Reforms 2020: OECD and Selected Partner Economies*, 82 (OECD Publishing, 2020) available at https://doi.org/10.1787/7af51916-en (accessed 31 January 2021). As the United States does not have a VAT, it is not in this figure.

Fourth, New Zealand has been able to generate that relatively high level of GST revenue, whether measured as a share of GDP or total taxation, charging a relatively low standard VAT rate across most goods and services expenditure. Figure 18.2 below shows that the standard New Zealand GST rate of 15% is the sixth lowest standard rate among 35 OECD countries with a VAT. Chile with a higher standard rate of 19% on a very wide base has the 11th lowest standard rate.

If a substantial item of household expenditure, such as food, were excluded from the New Zealand GST tax base, a revenue-neutral GST reform, for example, would require taxes to be raised elsewhere. One option would be to impose GST at a higher uniform rate on all other goods and services, which might invite producers, distributors or consumers of those goods and services to seek concessional treatment too. Another option would be to raise the lost revenue by imposing much higher rates of GST on a limited range of specified goods and services. In this case, there would be an even greater incentive for political lobbying by producers, distributors or consumers of the affected goods and services.

New Zealand has long experience from 1933 to 1985 of the many problems posed by consumption taxation with multiple (sometimes very high) rates and exemptions (by 1985, the New Zealand narrow-base wholesale sales tax had 19 rates ranging from 10% to 60%).[37] Other OECD countries have experience of these difficulties in relation to their current VATs. Without the barrier created by New Zealand's 'clean' GST, with its comprehensive base and uniform rate, many OECD countries continue to apply a wide range of reduced rates. From 2018 to 2020, at least 15 OECD countries extended the application of their reduced VAT rates and many OECD countries introduced temporary VAT rate reductions in response to COVID-19.[38] The history of VAT reduced rates or zero-rates often involves movable boundary lines that may have social welfare implications, particularly if the line-drawing distorts production.[39]

A popular rationale for a multiple-rate GST structure is that it is necessary to support the poor. As the New Zealand GST model was being developed in the late 1970s and early 1980s, as well as over the last 35 years, there has been ongoing theoretical and empirical research on the distributional effects of the New Zealand GST. In 2020, Thomas, a senior economist at the OECD, completed his PhD thesis and published a paper in the OECD taxation working paper series on this topic. He has developed insights for VAT policymakers using microsimulation modelling, drawing on household expenditure microdata from household budget surveys in 27 OECD countries. His OECD paper confirms the view that VAT burdens are better measured

37. Due, *supra* n. 33.
38. OECD, *supra* n. 30, 43-44.
39. For a taxonomy of tax policy notches (discontinuous quantity or characteristic jumps in the choice set of individuals and firms), the line drawing that creates them, including in commodity taxation, and their welfare costs, *see* Joel Slemrod, *Buenas Notches: Lines and Notches in Tax System Design* 11(3) eJ. Tax Research 259 (2013).

relative to expenditure rather than income, as this removes the distorting influence of savings behaviour that occurs when an income-based comparison is made. He finds that a broad-based VAT, such as the New Zealand GST with few reduced VAT rates or exemptions, can produce 'a small degree of regressivity'. Further, even roughly proportional VAT/GSTs can have 'significant equity implications for the poor'. The question is how best to ensure progressivity in the whole tax-welfare system to compensate households on low incomes and ensure that they do not unfairly bear the burden of paying VAT.[40]

In part of his recent PhD thesis, Thomas uses behavioural VAT microsimulation models built for 23 OECD countries to investigate whether reduced VAT rates or targeted cash transfers would provide more effective support for poorer households. His microsimulation results vary depending on the specific product receiving the reduced VAT rate, with some reduced rating of products having a progressive effect and other reduced rating having a regressive effect. A reduced VAT rate for food consumed at home, for example, generally had a progressive impact but rich households received a larger aggregate benefit than poor households. The second compensation mechanism he tested with microsimulation models was an income-tested cash transfer. In all 23 OECD countries, these microsimulation results showed that an income-tested cash transfer better targeted support for most poor households then reduced VAT rates. Surprisingly, a universal cash transfer was also better than reduced VAT rates at targeting support to poor households. After comparing the empirical results of these stimulations, Thomas concludes that countries are better advised to use their income tax or benefit system to achieve desired distributional goals than using reduced VAT rates.[41]

Thomas also uses a model that is data and resource demanding to examine the effects of introducing reduced rates to New Zealand's broad-based, uniform-rate GST to provide support for poorer households, taking into account behavioural responses induced by the price changes. Consistent with his other findings, he concludes that the current New Zealand family tax credit provides 'far superior' support to poorer households than reducing GST rates. In his opinion, 'it is clear that New Zealand should maintain its current approach of a broad-based single-rate GST and income-tested tax credits to support poorer households'.[42]

40. Alastair Thomas, *Reassessing the Regressivity of the VAT, OECD Taxation Working Papers No 49*, 23-38 (OECD, 2020).
41. Alastair G.A. Thomas, *The Distributional Effects of Value-Added Taxes in OECD Countries*, PhD thesis, Chapters 5 and 6 in particular (2020), available at http://researcharchive.vuw.ac.nz/handle/10063/9272 (accessed 31 January 2021). The thesis contains rich data and insights for VAT/GST policymakers, who would be well advised to read this thorough, thoughtful and carefully-expressed report of his research.
42. Thomas, *supra* n. 41, 163-196, 196. Again, the description of the setting-up of the model and selection of data, as well as the results of the simulated reforms is well worth reading.

Figure 18.2 Standard Rates of VAT in OECD Countries, 2020

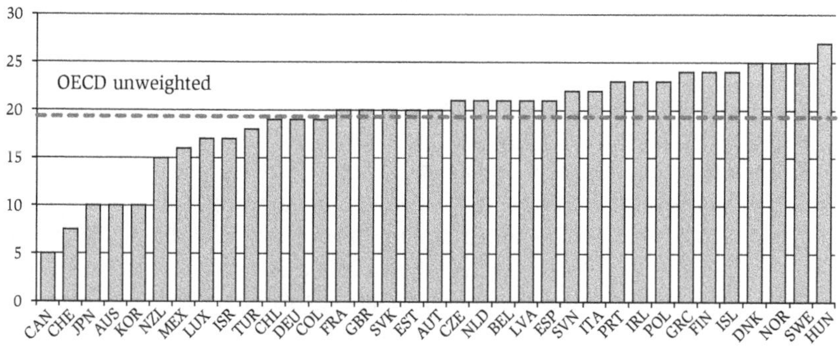

Source: OECD author's work based on country information. [43]

The fifth point concerns the relative revenue-raising performance of New Zealand's broad-based, uniform-rate GST in comparison with other VAT/GSTs. The IMF and OECD have developed VAT performance measures to assist policymakers to assess performance and identify how to raise additional revenue by improving VAT performance. The OECD VRR is the amount of VAT taxation collected as a proportion of the potential VAT base. It is an estimate of the loss of revenue from expenditure exclusions from the tax base and reduced rates of tax, as well as poor compliance through fraud, evasion, or tax planning. In other words, it is an attempt to assess the policy gap and the compliance gap together. If VAT were collected at the standard rate on the entire potential tax base and all revenue was collected, the VRR would be 1.0. There are several methodological difficulties in calculating the VRR, which have been well canvassed by the OECD and others: for example, how do you define the potential VAT base for each country and how do you ensure that comparable data is being used in the cross-country comparisons? [44] Without considering these issues further here, we can at least observe that OECD VRRs are rough guides of VAT system performance, which may be useful if treated with care.

During the global financial crisis of 2008-2009, the unweighted average VRR for OECD countries declined from 0.59 in 2007 to 0.53 in 2009. Since 2010 (to 2018), the OECD average VRR has remained about 0.55, suggesting that, on average, about 45% of potential VAT revenue is not collected as a result of exclusions from the tax base, reduced rates of tax and non-compliance. From a tax revenue collection perspective, that is a vast amount of revenue still on the table, especially while governments face huge fiscal, economic and social challenges.

And what are the VRRs of the 4 OECD countries selected for comparison in this chapter? First, recall that VAT experts sometimes draw a distinction between first-generation VATs from Europe and second-generation VATs that were implemented

43. OECD, *supra* n. 30, 42.
44. OECD, *supra* n. 30, 51-56; Dickson and White, *supra* n. 3, 388-389; Benge et al., *supra* n. 3, 484-485.

later with improvements, putting into practice lessons learned from Europe. The OECD VRRs for 2018 in Figure 18.3, however, at least suggest that the policy-and-compliance gap for the first-generation VAT in the United Kingdom is much the same as that gap in the so-called second-generation VATs in Australia and Canada. Starting from the bottom, the VRR for the United Kingdom is 0.45, for Australia 0.47 and for Canada 0.49. All of them are below the OECD unweighted average of 0.56.

And what of New Zealand? According to the OECD, the VRR in 2018 is 0.99 – if this were so, it is saying that New Zealand as collecting GST at 15% on almost the entire potential tax base and that all the GST revenue is being collected. The OECD commentary lists a number of factors that underlie the high VRR that the New Zealand GST has had since it was first implemented in 1986: a broad base, limited exclusions, limited zero-rates, and the taxation of public services (where there are upward and downward modifying effects on the calculation).

Even if it is necessary to make some downward adjustment to the New Zealand VRR, the VAT performance comparison with the other 3 countries is stark. Using the VRR, the VATs in the 4 selected countries are ranked, best to worst, out of 36 VATs in the OECD: New Zealand No. 1, Canada No. 27, Australia No. 28 and the United Kingdom No. 31. The non-neutralities in the United Kingdom, Australian and Canadian VAT/GSTs are large compared with other countries, especially New Zealand. Given their fiscal, economic, and social imperatives, the question of how the United Kingdom, Australia, and Canada could improve the design of their VAT/GST systems to collect more of this potential revenue is a significant issue in each of these countries, as we saw in §18.02.

Figure 18.3 OECD VAT Revenue Ratios 2018

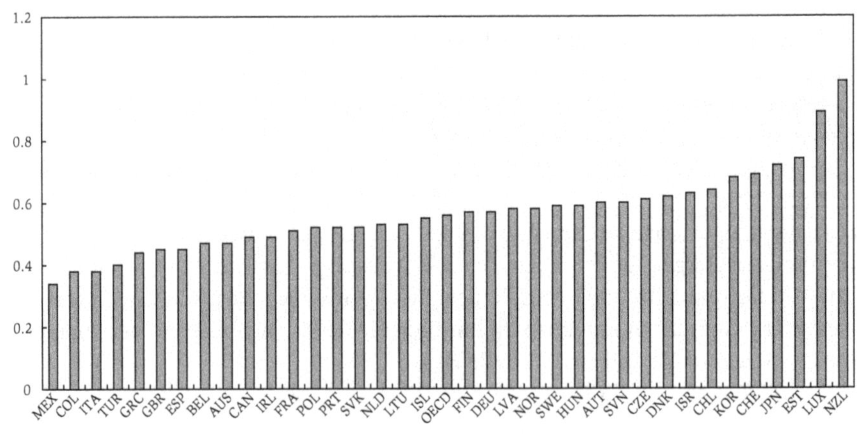

Source: OECD author's own work. OECD is OECD unweighted average.[45]

45. OECD, *supra* n. 30, 53.

Figure 18.4 New Zealand: Retail Sales and Private Consumption

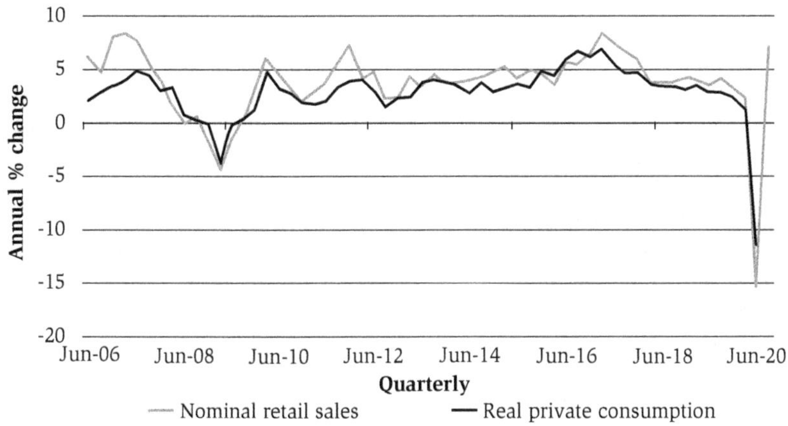

Source: Stats NZ.[46]

A sixth and final point relates to the tax revenue merits of a broad-based, uniform-rate VAT, both in an economic crisis and in the period of adjustment afterwards, while revenues are returning to pre-crisis levels. In the last 13 years there have been two global economic crises when consumption has slumped in New Zealand: in 2007-2009 during the global financial crisis and in 2020 with the COVID-19 pandemic (*see* Figure 18.4 showing annual percentage change in New Zealand nominal retail sales and real private consumption in the period from 2006 to 2020, for example). For New Zealand with a broad-based, uniform-rate GST that includes government consumption, any changes in the pattern of consumption during either of these economic crises and in the period of adjustment afterwards is not likely to be material. For New Zealand GST revenue estimation and collection purposes, it is the level of consumption that is important, not what is being consumed - almost all consumption is part of the tax base and it is taxed at the same uniform rate.

For a country that has a GST/VAT with a narrower base and/or a multiple rate structure, such as Australia, Canada or the United Kingdom, both the level and type of consumption occurring in the economic crisis and the subsequent period of adjustment are relevant, as is the GST/VAT tax treatment of the changing pattern of consumption. For VAT/GST revenue estimation and collection purposes in these countries, it is necessary to estimate the levels of consumption and also whether there has been a

46. New Zealand Treasury, *Half Year Economic and Fiscal Update 2020*, 13 (The Treasury, 16 December 2020), available at https://www.treasury.govt.nz/system/files/2020-12/hyefu20.pdf (accessed 31 January 2021).

change in the pattern of consumption that involves greater expenditure on goods and services that are taxed at lower rates or zero-rates.

Recent research by Simon and Harding examines what drives consumption tax revenues, in part using the 2007-2009 global financial crisis and its aftermath as a case study. During that crisis, revenue from all taxes as a share of GDP fell significantly but consumption tax revenue was typically less affected, largely, it seems, because of the relative stability of total consumption compared to other economic aggregates such as investment. Nevertheless, it took until 2012 for VAT revenues to return to their pre-crisis levels. During the 2007-2009 crisis, the researchers noted changes in consumption patterns, with increases in government spending and in private consumption on 'necessity goods'. As these goods are often taxed less in narrow-base, multiple-rate VAT systems, this adversely affected the performance of these VATs as measured by the OECD VRR (as may changes in taxpayer compliance during the crisis have played a part but, as they note, this was not examined in this research). The research found that even though most OECD countries had increased their VAT rates since 2009, the overall OECD implicit tax rate on consumption (consumption tax revenues as a share of their tax base) in 2017 was only slightly higher than it was before the global economic crisis. [47]

Simon and Harding point out the negative implications from their research for some of these countries with low VRRs:

> These findings imply that in the presence of reduced rates and exemptions in VAT systems, increases in standard rates have not increased the implicit tax rates on consumption as strongly as they did before the crisis. In light of lasting changes in the pattern of consumption post-economic crisis, VAT revenues, particularly in countries with low VRRs and high shares of government consumption, are likely to be more exposed to economic changes, as that part of the tax base that is subject to the standard VAT rate is smaller now than it was prior to the crisis. This is particularly the case if an economic crisis directly affects private consumption, rather than investment, as was the case in the [2007-2009 economic] crisis.[48]

The researchers suggest that, in theory, broadening the VAT base and narrowing the range of reduced rates could help make consumption tax revenues more stable in economic crises, quickly adding, in effect, that any reform and compensation packages need to be adapted to local circumstances.[49]

What can we say in January 2021 about the performance of New Zealand's comprehensive, uniform-rate GST in the COVID-19 pandemic, with New Zealand following an early elimination strategy? In the midst of the pandemic with so much uncertainty ahead, all we can do is report the most up-to-date data. During a 5-month period ending on 30 November 2020, New Zealand core Crown expenses were 17.1% higher than the corresponding period in the previous year, much of the increase relating to the high level of COVID-19 social security, welfare and health expenditure

---

47. Hannah Simon and Michelle Harding, *What Drives Consumption Tax Revenues? Disentangling Policy and Macroeconomic Drivers* OECD Taxation Working Papers No. 47 (OECD, 2020) available at https://dx.doi.org/10.1787/94ed8187-en (accessed 31 January 2021).
48. Simon & Harding, *supra* n. 47, 40.
49. Simon & Harding, *supra* n. 47, 40.

to support individuals and firms through this very difficult time. The revenue collection performance of the broad-based, uniform-rate GST, however, must be reassuring to the New Zealand Minister of Finance. On the basis of numerous activity indicators, the New Zealand Treasury expects that a strong recovery in economic activity had occurred in the September quarter of 2020, but that sales would grow more slowly in coming quarters. As a consequence of New Zealand's strong private consumption after the COVID-19 lockdowns, GST receipts on the comprehensive tax base have also been strong, exceeding year-ago levels (*see* Figure 18.4).[50] It is astonishing that private consumption is so strong and that GST revenue is up 9.8% in the 5 months to the end of November 2020 compared with the corresponding 5-month period a year earlier in 2019 before COVID-19 struck (corporate taxes rose 7.2% using the same 5-month periods of comparison in 2019 and 2020).[51] Of course, the path that the New Zealand economy and consumption follows from here is highly uncertain, with much depending on what happens with the COVID-19 pandemic, and other national and global developments.

§18.04 CONCLUSIONS

This chapter identified GST rate and base policy as the most important issue for the New Zealand GST in the medium term, especially if the uniform GST rate of 15% were increased. It argued that narrowing the New Zealand GST base or introducing reduced tax rates would have significant implications for revenue generation and both individual and social welfare. Taking a practical tax policymaking perspective, it considered expert review analysis of GST/VAT systems in 3 countries and the latest research and data about the relative revenue and economic performance of the New Zealand broad-based, uniform-rate GST and its distributional effects, in an OECD context. This wider context enabled reflections on the implications for New Zealand if the GST comprehensive base were narrowed or multiple rates of tax were introduced in future.

This chapter considered five reviews of national tax systems: three in New Zealand over the last 20 years, a well-resourced one in the United Kingdom from 2006 to 2011 and a recent one in Australia on federal financial relations that reported in August 2020. There were common themes. In practice, all 5 reviews supported a broad-based, uniform-rate design for the VAT/GST. The 3 New Zealand reviews pointed to the revenue and neutrality advantages of the New Zealand GST broad-based and uniform-rate design. The United Kingdom and Australian reviews reported the revenue and neutrality drawbacks with narrower bases and multiple rates in their VAT/GST systems. Each of the 5 reviews emphasised the need to assess the impact of the whole tax and transfer system in their country on households, not expecting each tax or benefit instrument to achieve every objective. They agreed that a distributional

50. New Zealand Treasury, *supra* n. 46, 13-14, 19-20.
51. New Zealand Treasury, *Interim Financial Statements of the Government of New Zealand For the Five Months Ended 30 November 2020*, 4 (New Zealand Treasury, 2021), available at https://www.treasury.govt.nz/system/files/2021-01/fsgnz-5mths-20nov.pdf (accessed 31 January 2021).

objective of supporting poor families, for example, was better achieved through personal income tax and benefit systems, not through VAT/GSTs. Common issues discussed in background papers and/or final reports were: the merits of assessing distributional outcomes of tax-reform packages including VAT/GST proposals on a lifetime basis rather than a 'snapshot' yearly basis, and, if separate parts of packages were being analysed, measuring the burden of VAT/GSTs against expenditure rather than income, thus removing the unhelpful influence of savings.

The chapter then assessed the performance of the New Zealand GST using the latest OECD data and research and, essentially the summary results are:

(1) In the forty-odd years to 2018, OECD countries have more than doubled their reliance on VAT/GST, which is by far the major general consumption tax.
(2) In 35 years, New Zealand has trebled its reliance on general consumption taxation (the predecessor general consumption tax collecting around 10% of total taxation in the mid-1980s and GST collecting around 30% of total taxation today).
(3) New Zealand's reliance on GST revenue is now the highest or second highest in the OECD or an extended OECD group, with the results differing according to the year and measure used.
(4) The New Zealand GST generated that high share of total revenue or GDP charging a relatively low standard VAT rate across most goods and services expenditure (the standard New Zealand GST rate of 15% is the sixth lowest standard rate among 35 OECD countries with a VAT).
(5) Using an OECD rough guide of the neutrality and uniformity of a VAT/GST called the VRR, the New Zealand GST ranked the best among all 35 VAT systems in the OECD with the smallest policy and compliance gap and an unadjusted VRR of 0.99 (since 2010, the OECD unweighted average VRR has remained about 0.55, suggesting that, on average, about 45% of potential VAT revenue is not collected as a result of exclusions from the tax base, reduced rates of tax and non-compliance).
(6) Recent research on consumption tax revenues in and after the global financial crisis of 2007-2009 argues that a broad-based, uniform-rate VAT in an economic crisis and in the period of adjustment afterwards, while revenues are returning to pre-crisis levels, may make VAT revenues more stable through that period of economic downturn, which is of profound importance to governments today in the midst of an economic crisis caused by the global COVID-19 pandemic.

And the implications for New Zealand if the GST comprehensive base were narrowed or multiple rates of tax were introduced in future? To anyone suggesting New Zealand can narrow its base or introduce multiple rates in a better way than other countries, my initial response, as a former New Zealand tax policy official who has experienced intense political lobbying, and on two occasions ugly abuse, is that it is well to remember New Zealand history: from 1933 to 1985 New Zealand had an anaemic and awful general consumption tax with multiple rates and exemptions (by

1985, the New Zealand narrow-base wholesale sales tax had 19 rates ranging from 10% to 60% and raised just 10% of total taxation). My second response is to point to the latest research and international data, some of which we have considered or referred to in this chapter, including the following:

(1) The high compliance and administrative costs of narrow bases that have been a focus of reviews of OECD VAT/GST systems generally and specifically in reviews of the United Kingdom, Australian and Canadian VAT/GST systems.
(2) Without the barrier created by New Zealand's 'clean' GST, with its comprehensive base and uniform rate, many OECD countries continue to apply and extend a wide range of reduced rates (from 2018 to 2020, at least 15 OECD countries extended the application of their reduced VAT rates) and these boundary lines may have social welfare implications for the overall wellbeing of people, particularly if the line-drawing distorts production.
(3) The potential high social cost of a narrow base distorting spending patterns is illustrated by the Mirrlees Review's rough estimation in 2011 that if the United Kingdom extended VAT at 17.5% to most zero-rated and reduced-rated items it would, in principle, allow the United Kingdom government to make each household as well off as it was, leaving around GBP 3 billion of revenue to spend in other ways.
(4) The potential high and ongoing revenue cost of a narrow base is illustrated by the Australian shrinking GST base, where the share of household spending subject to GST fell from around 60.8% in 2001-2002 to 55.4% in 2018-2019 (the escalating cost of exempt services such as health and education were a major part of the problem).
(5) Although the latest in-depth research indicates that a broad-based uniform-rate VAT, such as the New Zealand GST, can produce a small degree of regressivity, using several VAT microsimulation models drawing on household expenditure microdata from household budget surveys in up to 27 OECD countries, the researcher concludes that countries are better advised to use their income tax or benefit system to achieve desired distributional goals than using reduced VAT rates (and, specifically, that the current New Zealand income-tested, family tax credit provides 'far superior' support to poorer households than reducing GST rates).

While the New Zealand GST has never been perfect and regularly requires maintenance, it seems clear that the New Zealand broad-based, uniform-rate design is a 'virtue' that should be retained. It is a less costly way of raising revenue and other government instruments can be used to achieve distributional, wellbeing and other objectives. To take one example, possible government responses to the serious and growing obesity problem in New Zealand that do not compromise the current design of the GST include targeted excise taxes, education and advertising programmes, regulation of food and beverage labelling and marketing, and healthy food vouchers.

CHAPTER 19

Japan's Consumption Tax Experiment: Operating a VAT Without Tax Invoice

Yoshihiro Masui

§19.01 INTRODUCTION

Japan's Consumption Tax ("CT") is unique in that it is a credit-subtraction value added tax (VAT) which operates without a tax invoice, not operated by any other country.[1] Despite its deviation from the standard, credit-invoice VAT, the VAT Revenue Ratio ("VRR") of Japan's CT has been consistently higher than the average among the OECD member countries.[2] What are the structural factors that explain this performance? Does the Japanese experience mean that the tax invoice requirement is not necessarily a significant factor for the proper functioning of VAT?

This chapter evaluates the strengths and weaknesses of Japan's CT which operated without a tax invoice for the past 30 years. It shares lessons to be learned from the Japanese experiment which may be meaningful for the rest of the world. Section 19.02 demonstrates how the unique structure emerged in its original form in 1989. Section 19.03 examines how Japan's CT works in practice, focusing on its structural features and its vulnerability to fraud. The Japanese CT succeeded in mixing a broad base with a single rate structure. Since 1997 the CT increasingly resembles an invoice-credit VAT, although significant differences remain. Section 19.04 discusses why Japan's CT is in the process of degenerating into a traditional VAT by adopting multiple rates in October 2019, with an expected move towards requiring a tax invoice from October 2023. Section 19.05 concludes that the broad tax base combined with a

1. Alan Schenk, Victor Thronyi, and Wei Cui, *Value Added Tax: A Comparative Approach*, 2nd edn, 54 (Cambridge University Press, 2015).
2. OECD, *Consumption Tax Trends 2018: VAT/GST and Excise Rates, Trends and Policy Issues* (2018) 90, Annex Table 2.A.7. From 1992 to 2016, the VRR was in the range of 0.66 and 0.73.

single rate was key to the relative success of Japan's CT, while the lack of tax invoices may not have been detrimental from an enforcement perspective.

References in this chapter are limited to selected materials in English which are readily available for the presumed readers of this book.[3] Materials in Japanese language are referred to only where necessary.[4] Legislative developments are covered up to November 2020.

§19.02 THE EMERGENCE OF A CREDIT-SUBTRACTION VAT WITHOUT INVOICE

In order to understand why Japan's CT was designed without the requirement of a tax invoice, it is necessary to examine its historical context. Immediately after the Second World War, Japan had a brief period of adopting, or at least trying to adopt, broad-based indirect taxes. The turnover tax of 1948-1949 was short-lived. The Shoup Mission recommended an income-type VAT in 1949 as a replacement of the enterprise tax (prefectural and municipal), which was made into law but was never put into practice.[5] During the period of high growth until the 1970s, the Japanese Government relied heavily on personal and corporate income taxes in combination with various excise taxes as main revenue drivers. For most of the second half of the 20th century, income tax was the normative ideal for most Japanese policymakers.

Japan faced fierce public opposition to the introduction of a VAT.[6] According to one comparative study, the amount of time involved in the government's attempt to introduce the VAT was similar to Australia, whereas the intensity of opposition was comparable to that in Canada.[7] Indeed, the first proposal in Japan to introduce the General Consumption Tax, a tax-credit type of VAT without invoice, was defeated in 1979. The second proposal for the Sales Tax, a consumption type VAT with tax credits determined on the basis of an invoice, was withdrawn in 1987. The third proposal for the CT was finally made into law in 1989.

Many of the structural features of CT are attributable to the lessons learned from past failures at introducing a general consumption tax.[8] The aborted Sales Tax proposal had met fierce criticisms because its invoice system was believed to disadvantage small

3. Hiromitsu Ishi, *The Japanese Tax System*, 3rd edn, 268-299 (Oxford University Press, 2001) offers a detailed description of the introduction of CT and its developments until early 1990s.
4. Hideaki Sato, *The Trajectory of Japan's VAT* 70(1) J. Tax Research Inst. (2017, in Japanese) records the legislative changes since the introduction of CT. It forms a part of a joint research program conducted by lawyers and economists in Japan. Yoshihiro Masui, *Quo Vadis Japan's VAT? A Comparative Perspective* 70 Tax Research Inst., 515 (2017, in Japanese) critically examines the merits and demerits of invoice-credit VAT by referring to Robert F. van Brederode and Sebastian Pfeiffer, *VAT's Superiority: Is the Emperor Dressed like Adam?* 26(4) Int'l VAT Monitor 226 (2015).
5. Clara K. Sullivan, *The Tax on Value Added* 126 (Columbia University Press, 1965).
6. Junko Kato, *The Problem of Bureaucratic Rationality: Tax Politics in Japan* (Princeton University Press, 1994).
7. Junko Kato, *Regressive Taxation and the Welfare State: Path Dependence and Policy Diffusion* 170 (Cambridge University Press, 2003).
8. Alan Schenk, *Japanese Consumption Tax: The Japanese Brand VAT* Tax Notes 1625 (March 27, 1989).

businesses by exposing their income with no tax credit breaks. In order to accommodate small traders, who were influential constituents of the Liberal Democratic Party, the CT was designed to operate without a tax invoice. To provide relief for small traders, the CT also had a high registration threshold, and a simplified filing scheme for the computation of the amount of input tax credit. On the other hand, the tax base of CT was made as broad as possible, which was in sharp contrast with the preceding Sales Tax proposal which had as many as 51 tax-exempt items.

§19.03 HOW JAPAN'S CONSUMPTION TAX WORKS

[A] Broad Base, Single Rate

The tax base of CT is relatively broad. When the CT was introduced in 1989, tax exempt goods and services were limited to only a few items. In 1991, the scope of exempt items was widened for the purpose of achieving social policy objectives.[9] Nevertheless, the exempt items remained to be limited to those commonly applied in most OECD countries, including financial services, transfer and letting of land, the letting of residential buildings, plus some social welfare services.[10]

A notable strength of Japan's CT is that it succeeded in maintaining a single rate structure for 30 years. The original CT in 1989 had a single 3% tax rate. As a transition measure to switch from the previous Commodity Tax, passenger vehicles were subject to a special 6% rate, which was reduced to 4.5% in 1991 and was abolished in 1994. This was the only exception to the single rate aside from zero-rating for exports.

From 1997, the CT rate was increased to 5%. This 5% rate was a combination of the 4% national tax and the 1% local tax. Because the administration of the local CT was totally integrated in the national CT and was dependent on the National Tax Agency which was in charge of administering the CT nationwide, businesses and consumers were uninterested in the exact component of the total 5% rate. Fiscal federalism issues were dealt with by using a formula which allocated the local CT revenues among prefectures and municipalities.[11]

Political decisions for the next rate increase were made during the period 2009-2012 when the Democratic Party, which was backed by labor unions, had the majority in the Diet. In August 2012, the Diet passed the bill to increase the CT rate to 8% from April 2014 and further to 10% from October 2015. The CT tax hike was a significant component of a reform package to fund the social welfare programs in a rapidly aging society. In December 2012, the Democratic Party lost the general election, and the Liberal Democratic Party had a landslide victory. Despite the change in

9. Ishi, *supra* n. 3, 296. For the exemption of medical services, *see* Yumi Nishiyama, *Japanese Consumption Tax: Input Tax Deduction and Exemptions* 3(2) W. J. VAT/GST L. 124 (2014).
10. OECD, *supra* n. 2, 76.
11. Nobuki Mochida, *Fiscal Decentralization and Local Public Finance in Japan* (Routledge, 2008) and Nobuki Mochida et al., *The Economics of Subnational Value Added Tax* (Yuhikaku, 2010, in Japanese).

Cabinet, the CT rate was increased in April 2014 from 5% to 8% (6.3% for national tax and 1.7% for local tax), as planned in the 2012 legislation.

Subsequently, the increase to the 10% rate was postponed twice. It was finally implemented from October 2019. The 10% rate was again a combination of national CT (7.8%) and local CT (2.2%). This time, however, the rate increase came at a price. It was accompanied by the adoption of a multiple rate structure for the first time in the history of Japan's CT, as will be discussed in §19.04.

[B] No Tax Invoice

[1] The Account Method

Japan's CT operates without a tax invoice. How is it possible to police the potential overstatement of input tax without a tax invoice? The administrative solution taken by the National Tax Agency in 1989 was to audit the "accounts" which are kept for individual and corporate income purposes, instead of investigating tax invoices on a transactional basis. In other words, the "account method" of input tax credit was adopted rather than the "invoice method." The account method persisted until today.

Before going into details, it is worthwhile to be crystal clear about the meaning of "account method." A famous treatise refers to Japan's CT as adopting the "account method" of VAT, by which a firm's VAT is calculated by subtracting total purchases from total sales and by subjecting the balance to the rate of VAT.[12] Although the correct term "account method" is employed, this description is not entirely accurate. More accurately, a taxable business subtracts the amount of creditable input tax from the amount of output tax. What distinguishes Japan's CT from a standard invoice VAT is the fact that the CT does not require businesses to substantiate the amount of input tax credit with tax invoices which are issued by registered taxable businesses and which list the amount of VAT separately from tax-exclusive price. Tax-inclusive data shown in the "account" are sufficient for purchasers to substantiate their input tax credit.

For this system to work, it is necessary for businesses to keep accurate records in their accounting books in an orderly manner. In 1989, the recordkeeping requirements were limited to "accounts" which identified the supplier's name, the date of purchase, a description of the goods or services purchased, and the price paid. Alternatively, "receipts etc." were admitted for calculating the input tax credit.

Effective from April 1997, in addition to the recordkeeping previously required, taxable businesses must substantiate their claimed input tax credits with evidence of the purchase with "receipts etc." that document the details of the transaction. The required "receipts etc." fall short of a formal tax invoice because it is not mandatory for businesses to itemize VAT separately from the purchase price in an invoice. Moreover, they did not need to be issued by registered taxable businesses for VAT purposes.

12. Ishi, *supra* n. 3, 281.

However, a leading commentator in Japan predicted that this reform was paving a way towards adopting an invoice VAT in the future.[13]

Like most other VAT regimes, Japan's CT has a partial disallowance rule related to tax-exempt sales. When a business's exempt sales exceed 5% of totals sales for the taxable period, the business can credit only the input tax which is attributable to its taxable sales. In order to determine which portion of input tax is attributable, the business may use either the itemized method or the proportional method. Both methods are administrable by employing the data in the accounting records kept by the business. As an exception to this disallowance rule, businesses can claim their input tax credits on their purchases allocable to all sales, when the businesses' exempt sales are no more than 5% of total sales, or, to put the same condition in a different phrase, when the ratio of taxable sales is 95% or less. This exception is called "the 95% rule" and is a simplification measure to reduce compliance costs. The 95% rule was applicable to all businesses when the CT was introduced in 1989. In 2011, the personal scope of the 95% rule was restricted to businesses with the taxable sales amount of JPY 500 million or more. The 95% rule thus is currently one of the special treatments available for small and medium enterprises.

[2] Illustration

Let us examine more closely how CT works without a tax invoice. Unlike invoice-method VATs, Japan's CT does not require businesses to list the amount of VAT separately on sales invoices.[14] Suppose a taxable business (B1) makes a sale of goods to another taxable business (B2) at the tax-exclusive price of JPY 1,000. Supposing further that this sale is not of exempt items and that a single 10% rate applies, B1 calculates its output tax by subjecting the 10% rate to JPY 1,000. The resulting amount of B1's output tax is JPY 100. Turning next to the CT treatment on the B2 side, the tax-inclusive price for the sale of goods is JPY 1,100. B2 can record this cost of purchase and use this tax-inclusive data in the calculation of its input tax credit. Consequently, B2 is able to credit the amount of 100 (= 1,100 * 10 / 110), if other requirements including the 95% rule are met. Note that this calculation is relatively easy to administer because there is only one CT rate and there exist few exempt items.

Because the amount of VAT is not separately listed, the invoice from taxable suppliers and from exempt small businesses appear the same. This is the fundamental reason why inputs from exempt traders are treated in the same manner as the inputs from taxable suppliers. In other words, Japan's CT permits businesses to calculate their input tax credits based on the tax-inclusive account totals regardless of the VAT status of the seller from whom they make a purchase. To explain this with an example, let us suppose that an exempt business (E1) makes a sale of goods to a taxable business (B2) at the tax-inclusive price of JPY 1,100. No output tax is due for E1 because it is an

13. Hiroshi Kaneko, *Tax Law*, 6th edn 437 (Kobundo, 1997, in Japanese).
14. Alan Schenk, *Japanese Consumption Tax After Six Years: A Unique VAT Matures* Tax Notes 899, 905 (Nov. 13, 1995).

exempt entity. However, B2 can take the credit of JPY 100 by applying the same formula to the purchase price of JPY 1,100, based on the records in its accounting book.

One must say that this feature of Japan's CT is one of its weaknesses. An input tax credit is necessary in order to remove the cascading effect of VAT in the transaction chain. It does not make sense to give input tax credits where no output tax is due in the previous stage of the transaction chain. It provides an unfair advantage to taxable businesses that make purchases from exempt businesses. Moreover, giving tax credits for exempt purchases may risk violating the World Trade Organization (WTO) rules which prohibit export subsidies when the purchaser subsequently exports those goods, although its economic effects may vary depending on the adjustments in the exchange rates.[15]

On the other hand, under the CT, exempt businesses face no difficulties in making sales to taxable businesses who are indifferent to the VAT status of sellers. This treatment protects small traders who are exempt and thus relieved from participating in the VAT collection system and from complying with its requirements. Thus, their inability to issue invoice does not put them at a disadvantage even when they do not fulfill the bookkeeping requirements which are mandatory for ordinary businesses. This treatment is politically convenient because exempt traders do not have to comply with the CT and yet they are not excluded from the transaction chain. As a consequence, however, this treatment gives no incentives for small traders to elect to become taxable businesses for CT purposes. Interestingly, one of the concerns among Japanese practitioners is whether exempt traders will be forced to elect to become taxable businesses in order to be able to issue lawful invoices after October 2023, when the invoice method will be introduced (*see* §19.04 *infra*).

The same treatment is applied to purchases from consumers. Therefore, input tax credit is available on purchase of second-hand goods from consumers. Due to this treatment, there is no need to legislate a margin scheme for second-hand goods under Japan's CT.

[3] Administration and Compliance

When the CT was introduced in 1989, the government anticipated the practical difficulties with administering the tax.[16] However, the National Tax Agency was able to rely on the existing human resources as the CT was a replacement of existing excise taxes and would be administered by the same authority. As a result, the CT tax organization was neither understaffed nor overburdened. A standard procedure for field tax auditors was to examine the books for corporate income tax purposes and make conforming adjustments to CT returns whenever they found errors in the corporate income tax returns, including omitted items of sales and overstated amount of purchases. The CT under the account method thus resembled a second corporate income tax in daily tax practice. Meanwhile, anti-tax movements against the CT

15. In fact, the Japanese yen appreciated rapidly against other currencies including US Dollar in the early 1990s mitigating the impact of the subsidies.
16. Ishi, *supra* n. 3, 291.

continued in the form of litigation. Taxpayers alleged that the CT was unconstitutional on various grounds but were consistently rejected by lower courts.[17]

Effective from April 1997, the statutory wording of the recordkeeping requirement was changed from "books *or* receipts etc." to "books *and* receipts etc." Detailed documents became necessary in addition to regular bookkeeping. This change may seem trivial at first sight. In fact, the additional requirement aroused a stir among CT practitioners who were accustomed to keeping only books, but not receipts etc., under the account method.

A number of disputes arose on the issue whether the books and/or receipts etc. were adequately kept and in an orderly manner. In one of such cases, Japan's Supreme Court reinforced the government's push to strengthen the bookkeeping requirements necessary for claiming input tax credits.[18] The Supreme Court Decision of December 16, 2004[19] concerned the fiscal year 1990 when the law previous to the 1997 change applied. At issue was the procedural requirement for claiming an input tax credit to "keep" one's books or receipts etc. In this case, an individual businessman refused to show the required documents when he was audited by tax officials of the National Tax Agency. It was only later, in the litigation stage, that he produced them. He argued that he had in fact secretly "kept" his books and receipts so that the requirement for the input tax credit was fulfilled. The Supreme Court denied his claim, stating that taxpayers must keep their books and receipts in such a manner that they can readily be inspected by tax officers when conducting an audit. This interpretation is considered to apply generally to the bookkeeping requirements before and after the 1997 change.

[C] Special Treatment for Small and Medium-Sized Enterprises

[1] High Threshold

When the CT was introduced in 1989, it had a threshold exemption of taxable sales of JPY 30 million.[20] This was necessary to dampen opposition from small traders. The government estimated that in 1992, around 60% of all businesses were exempt from CT, while sales by these businesses accounted for only 2-3% of total domestic sales. This threshold was exceptionally high by OECD standards. Yet it was lower than the JPY 100 million threshold which had been proposed for the aborted Sales Tax.

Effective from 2004, the threshold was lowered to JPY 10 million,[21] which embodied a significant scale-back of the scope of the exemption. The number of VAT

17. Osaka High Court Decision of February 28, 1990, Zeimu Sosho Shiryo No. 175, 995; Tokyo District Court Decision of March 26, 1990, Hanrei Times No. 722, 222; Osaka District Court Decision of November 26, 1990, Hanrei Jiho No. 1424, 89; Okayama District Court Decision of December 4, 1990, Hanrei Jiho No. 1424, 47.
18. Yoshihiro Masui, *Legal Interpretation of Tax Law: Japan*, in Robert F. van Brederode and Richard Krever eds., *Legal Interpretation of Tax Law*, 2nd edn 307 (Kluwer Law International, 2017).
19. *Suda* case, Minshu Vol. 58, No. 9, 2458. An official English translation is available at http://www.courts.go.jp/app/hanrei_en/detail?id=727.
20. Schenk, *supra* n. 14, 904.
21. Sato, *supra* n. 4, 11.

filings jumped from 2,019,619 in fiscal year 2004 to 3,557,252 in fiscal year 2005, including returns filed for refunds and excluding returns made to a customs office. Notwithstanding this reform, CT's registration threshold is still one of the highest among the OECD member countries.[22]

Three points are worth mentioning with respect to this threshold for full exemption. First, businesses below the threshold can elect to be subject to the CT. Exempt traders do not incur output tax on their sales and cannot claim input tax credits on their purchases. Exporters often elect to be treated as taxable businesses in order to be able to claim refunds of their excess input tax credits.

Second, the Supreme Court Decision of February 1, 2005, made clear that the threshold was defined as a tax-exclusive amount rather than a tax-inclusive amount, rejecting the taxpayer's argument to the contrary.[23]

Third, the base period for judging the exemption threshold is the tax year two years prior to the current taxable period. Various coordination rules of a mechanical nature exist in order to calculate the threshold in cases of inheritance, mergers, and demergers. One of such rules specifically counters artificial formation of small corporations, or the division of a larger company in smaller ones, for the sole purpose of creating the opportunity for multiple use of the exemption threshold. As a consequence of the base period reference rule, newly incorporated businesses do not have any base year until two years after their incorporation. Therefore, they are automatically exempt for the two taxable periods immediately after their establishment. However, large corporations are capable of complying with CT regulations even if they are newly incorporated. Thus, effective from 1997, the threshold exemption was made to apply only to newly formed corporations with stated capital of JPY 10 million or less. This was a necessary but insufficient restriction because the liberalization of minimum capital requirements in the 2006 Company Act rendered this measure toothless by dramatically easing the formation of thinly capitalized companies. The declared number of newly incorporated corporations which were subject to this measure declined significantly.[24]

Incidentally, the CT in 1989 had a partial exemption for taxable businesses with taxable sales exceeding the threshold of JPY 30 million.[25] The exemption phased out when taxable sales reached JPY 50 million. This partial exemption was abolished from 1997, when the CT rate was increased to 5%.

[2] Simplified Filing Scheme

The election for simplified filing is a major concern for small and medium enterprises in Japan. In 1989, taxable businesses whose annual sales were equal to or less than JPY 500 million were allowed to opt for computing the amount of their input tax credits on

22. OECD, *supra* n. 2, 83, Annex Table 2.A.5.
23. Minshu Vol. 59, No.2, 245. English translation is available at https://www.courts.go.jp/app/hanrei_en/detail?id=734.
24. Sato, *supra* n. 4, 13.
25. Schenk, *supra* n. 14, 904.

a proxy basis where inputs are expressed as a fixed ratio of outputs. This measure was intended to reduce compliance costs by deeming the amount of inputs to be equivalent to 90% of taxable sales for wholesalers and 80% of taxable sales for other traders. With the tax rate of 3% in 1989, the resulting tax liability was 0.3% (=3% * (1 - 0.9)) of taxable sales for wholesalers and 0.6% (=3% * (1 - 0.8)) of taxable sales for other traders. The effect of the simplified filing scheme was equivalent to adopting a turnover tax, which is a systematic deviation from a VAT.

The simplified filing scheme was introduced as a concession to small traders who had opposed the introduction of CT vehemently. It was a measure to reduce compliance costs. As such, however, it was overly generous in two respects. First, this measure was applicable if the amount of sales in a base period, which was 2 years prior to the current tax year, was equal or less than JPY 500 million. In 1986, as many as 96.7% of all businesses were statistically eligible for this scheme.[26] This meant that for most businesses electing to file under the simplified scheme, the CT, in effect, was a turnover tax under the disguise of a credit-subtraction VAT. Second, these fixed ratios did not reflect the true costs that firms incurred for inputs. When taxable businesses elect to apply the simplified filing scheme, they were able to claim input tax credits in an amount larger than the actual costs of purchases as recorded in their books. This aspect of the scheme gave unfair cash flow advantages to eligible firms. If a firm is an exporter, this could have been challenged as a prohibited export subsidy under WTO rules, although there are no court cases on this issue.

A rigorous empirical study,[27] comparing the size of corporations before and after the CT introduction of 1989, showed a clustering of corporations just below the threshold as a result of behavioral responses of firms to the benefits of the simplified filing scheme. In other words, the simplified filing scheme gave incentives to large firms to "masquerade" as many small firms by separately incorporating business units.

Over time, the government took legislative measures to cut back the excessive advantages offered by the simplified filing scheme. First, its threshold was gradually reduced to JPY 400 million in 1991, to JPY 200 million in 1994, and to JPY 50 million in 2003. Second, the original distinction of two business categories (wholesale and others) was extended to four categories in 1991. The number of categories was increased to 5 in 1994, and further to 6 in 2014. As a result, the current fixed ratios are: (i) 90% for wholesale, (ii) 80% for retail, (iii) 70% for construction, manufacturing, utilities, agriculture, forestry, fishery, and mining, (iv) 60% for the categories other than those enumerated in (i)-(iii) and (v)-(vi), (v) 50% for transportation, banking, insurance, services other than restaurants, and (vi) 40% for real estate. There is an ordering rule for cases where a taxable entity is engaged in more than two business categories.

By gradually extending the business categories, the scope of the simplified filing scheme has been tightened as demonstrated by filing statistics. When the threshold for full exemption was reduced to JPY 100 million in 2004, this naturally resulted in a

26. Ishi, *supra* n. 3, 282.
27. Kazuki Onji, *The Response of Firms to Eligibility Thresholds: Evidence from the Japanese Value-Added Tax* 93(5-6) J. Pub. Econ. 766 (2009).

significant increase in the number of taxable small and medium enterprises opting for simplified filing: from 880,000 in 2004 to 1,610,000 in 2005. Notwithstanding this rapid increase, the revenue amount collected from the simplified filing showed a consistent and steady decrease since 1997.[28] The concession was successfully contained.

One might argue that the VRR of Japan's CT is potentially inflated by the simplified filing scheme, which acts like a turnover tax. According to this argument, the VRR seems higher merely because the CT suffers from cascading effects to the extent firms cannot credit their input tax amounts properly. This argument, however, is not supported by evidence. Even in 1992, when the scheme applied to most traders, the VRR was 0.68.[29] And it remained above 0.66 until 2016. Thanks to gradual cutbacks, the simplified filing scheme does not pose a threat to the VRR especially because its revenue significance has declined since 1997.

The above observation does not mean that the simplified filing scheme is without problems and challenges. To the contrary, its elective nature is in conflict with its own policy objective. Eligible firms have the option to compute the amount of input tax credits either (a) by using the tax-inclusive data in their account or (b) by applying the fixed ratio proxy to their taxable sales under the simplified scheme. If a business elects the simplified filing, it must use it for at least two years. The choice may be favorable or unfavorable to each taxable business, depending on the actual amount of inputs and on the exact categories applicable to the business in question. The approach of tax advisors is to calculate the creditable amount of input tax on the basis of both methods before advising clients whether or not to elect the simplified scheme. This practice is far from simple, because it requires double procedures and careful comparison of the results of the two calculation methods. It is squarely contrary to the policy objective of reducing compliance costs.

What is worse, tax attorneys in Japan are often sued by their clients who are dissatisfied with the election or non-election of the simplified filing scheme. Indeed, statistics from professional liability insurance companies show that the largest number of claims against tax attorneys in 2015 stemmed from failures to submit the required documents for the election or the non-election of simplified filing scheme in CT.[30]

[D] Cross-Border Aspects

Since 1989 Japan's CT applies the destination principle under which imports of goods are taxable and exports of goods are zero-rated. Customs officers are in charge of the VAT administration related to cross-border transactions of goods.

From 2013 to 2018, there was a remarkable increase in reported cases of gold imports without Customs declaration and, thus without payment of CT.[31] Gold bullion was brought in secretly by airline passengers or shipped in via air freight, mostly from

28. Sato, *supra* n. 4, 16.
29. OECD, *supra* n. 2, 94.
30. Hajime Kanai, *Japan's VAT Treatment of Small and Medium-sized Enterprises* 70 J. Japan Tax Research Inst. 355, 399 (2017, in Japanese).
31. Ministry of Finance, *Guide to 2019 Tax Reform* 827 (Okura Zaimu Kyokai, 2019, in Japanese).

neighboring countries including Hong Kong, South Korea, Mainland China, and Taiwan. As a countermeasure, the 2019 reform specifically required businesses to keep identification documents of their trading partners as a condition for exercising the right to credit the input tax on their purchase of gold and platinum bullion. As a more general measure, the 2019 reform also disallowed the input tax credit if the business was aware of the fact that the purchased items were illegally imported without incurring CT liability. This disallowance rule means that only innocent "buffers" may be able to credit their input taxes in a transaction involving unlawful imports. The existence of this particular rule in Japan shows that a carousel fraud is not a problem unique to the credit invoice VAT, or to a VAT operating in a single market, such as the European Union (EU). It is a more generic pressure point for VATs applying the destination principle in a world where customs control is not perfect.

Starting from October 2015, the destination principle was reinforced with respect to cross-border electronic services.[32] The reform was in line with the international VAT/GST Guidelines. According to the new (and current) rule, the place of taxation is the place of residence of the person who receives the electronic services. Electronic services are defined as services supplied via electronic and telecommunication networks, excluding those which are ancillary to other transactions. It clearly excludes services that mediate communication using a communication facility such as telephone and telegraphs. Examples of services excluded from the definition of electronic services are software development, internet banking, research and analysis abroad, and legal services. Services other than electronic services remain subject to the previous tax jurisdiction rule by which the location of the supplier's office is determinative in cases where it is unclear where the service was rendered.

Electronic services are subject to different tax regimes according to their nature and terms. B2B services are subject to a reverse charge mechanism, whereas B2C services require a registration and a filing by foreign service providers. Significantly, the distinction between the B2B and the B2C electronic services is based on the nature and terms of the services provided, and not directly on the personal status of the parties to the transaction. This is the consequence of the absence of a registration number system for taxable persons as used in the EU VAT system.[33] The B2B electronic services normally include: distribution of advertisement over the internet, intermediating online sales of games and applications, and online hotel and restaurant bookings (fees from hotel and restaurant owners). Examples of the B2C electronic services are the provision of e-books and music, cloud services, and internet shopping/auction (fees from suppliers).

In a cross-border setting, the Achilles heel of tax administration is the enforcement of tax compliance related to B2C electronic services. When the mandatory registration rule was introduced for B2C electronic services, it was disputed whether or

32. Yuki Nishida, *Japan Consumption Tax on Cross-Border Supplies of Services* 26(4) Int'l VAT Monitor 221 (2015). *See* Satoshi Watanabe, *VAT in Japan with a Focus on International Transactions* 61(9/10) Bull. for Int'l Taxation 379 (2007) for previous law.
33. Yumi Nishiyama, *Latest Changes to the Japanese Consumption Tax: Rate Increase and Taxation of Digital Services* 3(2) W. J. VAT/GST L. 108, 113 (2014).

not foreign suppliers would agree to register voluntarily. The arguments in favor of the registration requirement were twofold. First, it was argued that large service providers would face certain reputational risks in the Japanese market if they did not abide by the local rule. Second, enforcement would be supported through international cooperation under the Convention on Mutual Administrative Assistance in Tax Matters, signed by many foreign jurisdictions. Until today, there exists no empirical study measuring the compliance rate with the registration system. In terms of anecdotal evidence, as of November 18, 2020, there are 107 registered foreign businesses including Amazon Web Services, Airbnb Ireland, Slack Technology Limited, and Zoom Video Communications.[34]

§19.04 THE END OF THE EXPERIMENT: TOWARD A CREDIT-INVOICE VAT

The single rate structure of the CT came to an end by the adoption of a reduced rate effective from October 2019. The reduced rate of 8% is applicable to: (i) foods and beverages with the exception of liquors and eating out, and (ii) subscribed newspapers issued twice or more per week. The standard rate is 10%.

The decision to introduce the reduced rate was the result of a tormenting political process during the 2010s. A short description of key political events is essential in order to understand why Japan's CT abandoned its commitment to a single rate structure and its long-standing account method.

The Great Earthquake hit the Eastern part of Japan on 11 March 2011, and the need to recover provided the last electoral support to the ailing administration formed by the Democratic Party. Prime Minister Noda put all his remaining political energy in striking a deal for the CT hike. His plan was to increase the rate to 8% from April 2014 and to 10% from October 2015. In August 2012, when an agreement was reached among the Democratic Party, the Liberal Democratic Party, and Komeito, the CT hike was programmed as a reform package to fund the increasing social security costs. The 2012 law promised to examine various compensating measures for low-income households including: (i) government subsidies for households on an integrated account of medicare, nursing care, childcare, and disability, (ii) refundable tax credits, and (iii) multiple CT rates.

In December 2012, the Liberal Democratic Party won a landslide victory in the election of the Lower House. It formed a coalition with Komeito, whose campaign pledge was the introduction of a reduced rate for CT. In January 2013, immediately after the election, the coalition parties announced that they aimed to introduce a reduced rate at the time the standard rate would be increased to 10%. They established a special committee and held hearings, debating the pros and cons of introducing a reduced rate. In December 2013 they announced their continued support for the reduced rate. The CT rate was increased to 8% from April 2014 as planned.

34. National Tax Agency, *Registered Foreign Businesses List*, November 18, 2020, available at https://www.nta.go.jp/publication/pamph/shohi/cross/touroku.pdf.

In November 2014, Prime Minister Abe announced postponing the tax hike from 8% to 10%. The original effective date of October 2015 was moved to April 2017. He dissolved the Lower House and tested if the postponement was favored by the voters. He won the majority in the election. The work on adopting a reduced rate continued in 2015. A committee consisting of representatives of the coalition parties compared three blueprints for applying a reduced rate to: (i) foods and beverages with the exception of liquors, (ii) fresh food, and (iii) polished rice. On 12 December 2015, the coalition parties agreed to introduce a reduced rate of 8% to foods and beverages with the exception of liquors and dining-out. This agreement formed the basis of legislation in March 2016.

At this stage, the CT rate was scheduled to increase to 10%, effective from April 2017. In June 2016, however, Prime Minister Abe announced that the rate increase would be postponed for another 18 months. As a result, the CT will have a standard rate of 10% and a reduced rate of 8% from October 2019. This announcement was finally implemented in October 2019.

The disadvantages of adopting a multiple rate structure under the VAT were widely known among Japanese practitioners and academics. The demerits were also repeatedly expressed during public hearings, but these voices of reason were effectively ignored in the political process. Prime Minister Abe even rejected the reappointment of a veteran politician, who was rather reluctant to introduce a reduced rate, as chair of the Tax Committee within the Liberal Democratic Party. The Cabinet favored the coalition with Komeito whose election manifesto was the introduction of a reduced rate. The VRR of Japan's CT will likely decrease after fiscal year 2020 when the reduced rate will be fully factored in.

The adoption of the reduced rate will be accompanied by the introduction of a tax invoice. The government explains that a switch to the invoice method is inevitable because sellers and buyers must be able to determine the tax rate applied to a transaction under the multiple rate structure.[35] The change will be applicable to transactions made on and after October 1, 2023, if there is no further postponement.

§19.05 CONCLUSION

CT was born in 1989 as a credit-subtraction VAT without a tax invoice. This unique VAT certainly has its shortcomings. Most notably, input tax credits may be granted even if no CT was paid in the previous stage of the transaction chain. At the same time, however, Japan's CT succeeded in holding on to a relatively broad base with a single rate structure. Moreover, the government made improvements to the operation of the CT over time. For instance, the simplified filing system has been gradually reformed to make its presumptive nature more fit to reflect the real profit ratio among various business sectors. An overly generous exemption threshold has been curtailed. In 1997, procedural requirements for taxable businesses to claim input tax credits were tightened, although the CT was not quite transformed into a tax invoice VAT. These

35. Ministry of Finance, *Guide to 2016 Tax Reform* 808 (Okura Zaimu Kyokai, 2016, in Japanese).

features contributed to the high VRR of Japan's CT. The single rate structure persisted for 30 years, until in October 2019 the standard rate was finally increased to 10%. Overall, it appears that the lack of tax invoices during the period 1989-2019 did not have a detrimental effect on CT compliance enforcement.

CHAPTER 20

The Destination Principle in International Trade in Services: The Chinese Experience

Yan Xu

§20.01 INTRODUCTION

This chapter focuses on the application of the destination principle to international trade in services and intangibles (hereinafter 'services'). The importance of an effective implementation of the destination principle is accentuated by the increasingly greater role of services in international trade in recent decades.

Services exports have grown from around 9% in total exports of goods and services in 1970 to 25% in 2018, and the share of services exports in world GDP has similarly increased from 1% in 1970 to 7% in 2018.[1] World exports of Information, Computer and Telecommunication (ICT) services expanded much faster than any other services sector over the most recent two and a half decades.[2] Even during the global pandemic of 2019 and 2020 that interrupted world trade in services for most sectors, ICT services recorded positive growth.[3] The digital transformation, accelerated by the pandemic crisis, is expected to further boost ICT services.[4] Modern services enabled by ICT, including financial services and intellectual property services, have gained emerging importance in the global economy, in contrast with traditional

1. *See* Prakash Loungani, Saurabh Mishra, Chris Papageorgiou & Ke Wang, *World Trade in Services: Evidence from A New Dataset*, IMF WP/17/77 (March 2017) 8, available at https://www.imf.org/~/media/Files/Publications/WP/2017/wp1777.ashx; UNCTAD, *2019 Handbook of Statistics* (10 December 2019), 34, available at https://unctad.org/webflyer/handbook-statistics-2019.
2. Loungani et al., *supra* n. 1, 8. As shown in the UNCTAD statistics, international trade in these services was expanded the fastest from 2017 to 2018, recording an annual growth of around of 15%. UNCTAD, *supra* n. 1, 39.
3. World Trade Organization (WTO), *World Trade Statistical Review 2020*, 24-25, available at https://www.wto.org/english/res_e/statis_e/wts2020_e/wts2020_e.pdf.
4. WTO, *supra*, n. 3, 31.

services such as transport, travel and retail.[5] The shift to modern services exports has prompted high technology services exports to become one of the fastest growing sectors of the global economy.[6] While information and telecommunication technologies enable modern services to take place without proximity of supplier and customer, they also benefit traditional services in terms of increased tradability network effects.[7] The line between modern and traditional services is becoming blurred and will continue to do so with further utilisation of modern technologies in the services sectors.

The rapid growth of international trade in services, including modern services, has been a phenomenon seen not only in advanced economies but also in developing economies.[8] As the world's largest developing economy, China has emerged from being almost negligible in 1990 to being the 5th largest services exporter in the world services export market today.[9] China has also become one of the world's largest services importers,[10] and has been ranked as the second largest trader for services since 2010.[11] While travel, transport, and other commercial services have been the largest exporting sectors for China during the past few years, computer and information services exports, as well as construction services, have gained notable momentum in the export of services.[12]

The significant development in international trade in services creates numerous opportunities while posing challenges to the implementation of value added tax (VAT), also referred to as goods and services tax (GST). Unlike international trade in goods, international trade in services does not necessarily need to cross physical borders from one jurisdiction in order for the relevant services to be consumed by the customer in the other jurisdiction. While historically and for traditional services currently, services suppliers and customers need to be face-to-face, modern services can be traded across borders almost instantly (and delivered cheaply) through the internet and other network technologies such as smartphones. Indeed, the virtual capabilities of many services have propelled the rapid expansion of international trade in services. However, it is because of such capabilities that the implementation of VAT or GST (hereinafter 'VAT') to cross-border trade in services has become challenging. The destination principle, a widely endorsed principle under VAT for the purpose of

5. Loungani et al., *supra* n. 1, 12. Modern services defined in the article by Loungani et al. as computer, information, business, intellectual property, and financial services, *see* Loungani et al., *supra* n. 1, 13. Although the WTO Review does not label those services as modern services, the Review separates those services from other categories of commercial services, i.e., transport, travel, and goods-related services and classifies those services as other commercial services. WTO, *supra* n. 3, 69-70.
6. Loungani et al., *supra* n .1, 13.
7. Prakash Loungani & Saurabh Mishra, *Not Your Father's Service Sector* 51 Finance Dev 2 (2019).
8. Loungani et al., *supra* n. 1, 9; UNCTAD, *supra* n. 1, 35; WTO, *supra* n. 3, 25.
9. Loungani et al., *supra* n. 1, 11-12; WTO, *supra* n. 3, 11. *See also* World Data Atlas, *Service Exports in Current Prices,* https://knoema.com/atlas/ranks/Service-exports?baseRegion=CN (China is ranked 5th in 2015, 2016, 2017, 2018 and 6th in 2019). In the UNCTAD 2020 e-Handbook of Statistics, China is ranked 5th overall in 2019: UNCTAD, *2020 e-Handbook of Statistics,* available at https://stats.unctad.org/handbook/Services/Total.html.
10. *See* Loungani et al., *supra* n. 1, 12.
11. WTO, *supra* n. 3, 14-15.
12. Loungani et al., *supra* n. 1, 12.

achieving trade neutrality in a cross-border context, has been applied to levy the tax in the place where final consumption occurs.[13] While it is relatively easy to apply to cross-border transactions in goods, the rules designed for such transactions provide no ready answers to cross-border transactions in services, particularly where services are supplied and consumed without passing through physical borders.

The rapid digital transformation of the economy has exacerbated the issue of identifying the place of taxation, i.e., where final consumption of services supplied across borders takes place, and the challenge of effective tax collection. With respect to services, how can VAT rules be designed or developed to implement the destination principle to achieve its objective of international trade neutrality and what implications, if any, will the design have on the enforcement of the destination principle? This chapter considers these questions, focusing on China's experience in implementing the principle. China was chosen not only because of the increasing importance of international trade in services in the economy but because it is home to one of the largest e-commerce markets in the world and is taking the lead in technological advancement for businesses.[14] Design and implementation issues encountered by China, may well arise in other economies. An analysis of these issues in the context of China may inform the development of the rules for applying the destination principle to suit current modes of commerce that are no longer characterised by brick-and-mortar delivery and consumption of services.

Introduced in 1994, China has recently reformed its VAT system by incorporating services and aligning, to a certain degree, its VAT rules on cross-border trade in services more closely with the norms of the destination principle.[15] A number of issues remain, however, in relation to the determination of the place of taxation, the characterisation of services and the collection of VAT from cross-border transactions in services. This chapter examines these issues from a China perspective, considering the impact of the relevant rules on trade neutrality underpinning the destination principle and suggesting ways to develop or improve where the rules fail to achieve such

---

13. OECD, *International VAT/GST Guidelines* (12 April 2017) 16, available at https://www.oecd.org/ctp/international-vat-gst-guidelines-9789264271401-en.htm (hereinafter OECD VAT/GST Guidelines).
14. The World Bank, *China 2030: Building a Modern, Harmonious, and Creative Society,* The World Bank and the Development Research Center of the State Council, the People's Republic of China (2013), available at http://documents1.worldbank.org/curated/en/781101468239669951/pdf/China-2030-building-a-modern-harmonious-and-creative-society.pdf, Part II Supporting Report, 2, 155-187; Hermione Dace, *China's Tech Landscape: A Primer,* Tony Blair Institute for Global Change (9 January 2020), available at https://institute.global/policy/chinas-tech-landscape-primer; Tarun Chhabra, Rush Doshi, Ryan Hass & Emilie Kimball, *Global Technology China,* (Brookings Institute (April 2020), available at https://www.brookings.edu/research/global-china-technology/.
15. The basic law for China's VAT is the Provisional Regulations on VAT (State Council, issued 13 December 1993 and effective 1 January 1994, latest amendment 19 November 2017). Provision of services has become subject to the VAT under a series of tax circulars for the VAT reform, most importantly the Notice on Comprehensively Implementing the Pilot Reform of Replacing Business Tax with VAT (Ministry of Finance (MOF) and State Taxation Administration (STA), issued 23 March 2016 and effective 1 May 2016) (Caishui [2016] 36). Many provisions of Circular 36 have been modified by subsequent tax circulars.

neutrality. While VAT issues that arise in international trade in services may also occur within domestic borders, this is outside the scope of the chapter.

The rest of the chapter is as follows. Section 20.02 provides an overview of the destination principle under VAT and its recent development at the international and national levels. Section 20.03 dissects the implementation of the principle under China's VAT rules, with a focus on the place of taxation rules including general and specific rules. China's distinctive design and implementation features of these rules are noted. Section 20.04 discusses tax collection on cross-border transactions in services and analyses the impact of the characterisation of services on VAT collection. Section 20.05 concludes the chapter. As the China experience shows, the destination principle, as an overarching principle under a VAT/GST, cannot be applied statically and needs to be implemented with rules that are evolved with changing economic conditions and development of business models. Place of taxation rules and collection mechanisms ought to be designed with logical clearness and practicality, taking into consideration that the ultimate purpose of the destination principle is to achieve trade neutrality as opposed to meeting other purposes. Design features of domestic rules that deviate from the destination principle may lead to unintended double taxation or double non-taxation in cross-border trade that is undesirable in a deeply connected and increasingly digitalised global economy.

§20.02 THE DESTINATION PRINCIPLE IN INTERNATIONAL TRADE IN SERVICES

As a tax on consumption, the VAT is designed to ensure that intermediate businesses will not incur irrecoverable VAT in making taxable supplies of goods and services for final consumption.[16] As such, businesses will not be placed at a competitive advantageous nor a disadvantageous position in trade, both domestically *and* internationally. To achieve this trade neutrality and to put supplies in different jurisdictions on as equal footing as possible with regard to exports, the VAT needs to be levied on a destination basis to the extent possible in a cross-border context.[17] This destination-basis taxation is desirable from the neutrality perspective and reflects the nature of the VAT as a consumption tax, not a tax on intermediate businesses. Such destination-basis taxation means the exporting jurisdiction does not tax the export sale while allowing the seller or supplier to recover any VAT included in the purchase for making the export supply, and the importing jurisdiction, as the destination jurisdiction, levies the VAT on the imported supply.[18] This manner of taxation, known as the destination principle, has been enshrined in the OECD *International VAT/GST Guidelines* ('OECD VAT/GST Guidelines') and widely endorsed and adopted by countries and regions beyond the

16. OECD, *VAT/GST Guidelines*, *supra* n. 13, 15; Michael Keen & Walter Hellerstein, *Interjurisdictional Issues in the Design of a VAT* 63(2) Tax Law Rev. 359 (2010).
17. OECD, *VAT/GST Guidelines*, *supra* n. 13, 22-24. The Guidelines discuss neutrality in international trade and related taxation principles, i.e., Guidelines 2.4, 2.5.
18. OECD, *VAT/GST Guidelines*, *supra* n. 13, 15.

OECD members as an appropriate basis to assert substantive jurisdiction to tax.[19] The destination principle is also approved by the World Trade Organization regarding the common measures of zero-rating on exports.[20] The principle is justified in that a person is taxed only if the person consumes with the choice of consumption being at the person's discretion. Thus, taxation occurs in the place of consumption. The principle helps mitigate harmful tax competition and distortion caused to cross-border trade that would otherwise occur if the tax were levied in the country of origin.[21]

The approach to implementing the destination principle varies among different jurisdictions. In terms of recovery of VAT incurred by businesses on their inputs in making export transactions to their customers, some jurisdictions provide direct refunds of domestic input VAT incurred, while others allow foreign businesses to obtain refunds via local VAT registration or require locally registered customers to pay and claim an input refund for VAT paid.[22] Some jurisdictions, particularly those with limited tax collection capacity and a heavy reliance on VAT for revenue needs, might simply not refund for exports or exempt exporting supplies (without credit), recognising the destination principle only symbolically.[23] The design of legal mechanisms for the implementation of the principle is indeed at the discretion of government on the ground of national sovereignty over taxation.

One of the most critical issues in implementing the destination principle is to design legal rules for the determination of the place of taxation so that VAT is levied and collected in the jurisdiction where consumption occurs. The place of taxation rules (or the place of supply rules as an interchangeable term in the EU VAT context)[24] is designed to determine whether a supply is for consumption or business use within a jurisdiction, and thus the VAT being levied in that jurisdiction.

The OECD has recommended both general and specific rules for the determination of the place of taxation in a cross-border context, which distinguish business-to-business (B2B) supplies from business-to-consumer (B2C) supplies of services.[25] Such differentiation is necessary as taxation is not meant to target the former but the latter. In the case of cross-border B2B supplies, the general rule uses the customer location as the proxy to determine the place of taxation. [26] This rule allocates the taxing right to the jurisdiction of the customer location and requires the jurisdiction of the supplier location to provide zero-rating treatment to the supplier so that the supply is taxed only

19. OECD, *VAT/GST Guidelines*, *supra* n. 13, 18. *See also* Arthur Cockfield et al., *Taxing Global Digital Commerce* (Kluwer Law International, 2013), 72-73; Richard Bird & Pierre-Pascal Gendron, *The VAT in Developing and Transitional Countries* (Cambridge University Press, 2007), 15.
20. WTO, *Agreement on Subsides and Countervailing Measures*, footnote 1. Cited in the OECD, *Addressing the Tax Challenges of the Digital Economy, Action 1 – 2015 Final Report* (5 October 2015), 30, paragraph 52, available at https://dx.doi.org/10.1787/9789264241046-en.
21. OECD, *VAT/GST Guidelines*, *supra* n. 13, 22.
22. OECD, *VAT/GST Guidelines*, *supra* n. 13, 23.
23. Rebecca Millar, *Looking Ahead: Potential Solutions and the Framework to Make Them Work*, Sydney Law School Legal Studies Research Paper No. 16/30 (April 2016), 2, available at https://papers.ssrn.com/sol3/papers.cfm?abstract_id=2770847.
24. Millar, *supra* n. 23, 16-17.
25. OECD, *VAT/GST Guidelines*, *supra* n. 13, Chapter 3.
26. OECD, *VAT/GST Guidelines*, *supra* n. 13, 41-42, Guideline 3.2.

once at the place of consumption – which is more precisely the place of business use under B2B supplies. This general rule applies to all types of services.[27]

With respect to B2C supplies, the general rules on place of taxation are further divided into two categories: services that can only be provided in attendance, or on the spot, such as concerts or restaurant catering, and services that can be provided remotely. The place of taxation for the first type of services is the place of performance which coincides with the place at which the customer enjoys the supply.[28] The place of taxation for the second type of services is the location of the customer's usual residence.[29] This proxy for the place of supply is adopted to overcome the difficulty in ascertaining the location where consumption takes place if the service can be supplied without a fixed or identifiable place and time, provided the customer is not registered for VAT purposes.

For those supplies that do not easily fit into the application scope of the general rules on B2B supplies or B2C supplies, there are a few specific rules for place of taxation.[30] The use of various proxies under the general and specific rules are aimed at predicting the place of consumption, thereby providing legal certainty in the taxation of cross-border transactions in services by allocating the taxing right to the jurisdiction where consumption occurs. However, the various proxies are recommendations of the OECD which do not have binding legal effects, and it is ultimately at the discretion of jurisdictions to adopt the suggested proxies or to design their own rules. In practice, the choice of proxies to be used for 'destination' is far from identical, and the proxies can be interpreted differently across jurisdictions.[31] The application of proxies can also be affected when the underlying facts of a transaction are interpreted differently, leading to different characterisations of the relevant supplies.[32] Resultant discrepancies, or even conflicts of the choice and application of proxies, may cause double taxation or double non-taxation.[33]

The difficulty in identifying the place of taxation through use of proxies for cross-border trade in services has become more acute with the rapid growth of the digitalised economy, which has significantly expanded tradability of services within

---

27. OECD, *VAT/GST Guidelines, supra* n. 13, 41-42, Guideline 3.2.
28. OECD, *VAT/GST Guidelines, supra* n. 13, 67-68, Guideline 3.5. There are three features of the on-the-spot supplies: (1) physically performed at an identifiable place; (2) ordinarily consumed at the time and place of performance; and (3) ordinarily require that both the person performing the supply and the person consuming the supply should be physically present at the place of performance. OECD, *VAT/GST Guidelines, supra* n. 13, 67.
29. OECD, *VAT/GST Guidelines, supra* n. 13, 69, Guideline 3.6.
30. OECD, *VAT/GST Guidelines, supra* n. 13, 78-87, Guidelines 3.7 & 3.8.
31. *See* Cockfield et al., *supra* n. 19, 76-79.
32. Cockfield et al., *supra* n. 19, 76-79.
33. Cockfield et al., *supra* n. 19, 76-79 and Chapter 5. For an analysis of double non-taxation, *see* Rebecca Millar, *Intentional and Unintentional Double Non-Taxation*, in *Value Added Tax and Direct Taxation*, 409-442 (Michael Lang, Eleonor Kristoffersson, Peter Melz & Thomas Ecker, eds., IBFD, 2009). For an analysis of double taxation under VAT/GST, *see* Roland Ismer & Katharina Artinger, *International Double Taxation under VAT: Causes and Possible Solutions* 45(10) Intertax 593 (2017). Double taxation of B2C transactions is believed to be genuinely double taxation but it is unclear about its prevalence. *See* Millar, *supra* n. 23, 12.

and across borders.[34] Many services can now be supplied and consumed entirely on the internet or through other network technologies such as smartphones. The boundary that existed in the bricks-and-mortar business model is broken, and the line between 'goods' and 'services', as well as between modern and traditional services, has become increasingly murky too. Challenges related to the collection of VAT on cross-border trade in services, particularly B2C supplies, have caused considerable revenue losses in many jurisdictions.[35]

The OECD's latest VAT/GST Guidelines reflect current practice in many VAT jurisdictions, including those that are not OECD members. In general, the place of taxation rules and the collection mechanisms recommended by the Guidelines, i.e., a reverse charge in B2B supplies and a simplified registration and compliance mechanism in B2C supplies (discussed further in §20.04) are conceived so as to achieve the objective of the destination principle.

At a regional level, the EU is among the first group of jurisdictions to address the issue of applying VAT to cross-border trade in services and to close the loopholes in collecting VAT from transactions supplied electronically.[36] New rules adopted for e-commerce by the European Commission in December 2017 contain a number of proxies or presumptions, such as the internet protocol (IP) address of the device used by the customer or the customer's billing address. This helps to determine the place of taxation in cases where the customer is not required to be present to receive the services or where the supplier cannot ascertain either the location of the customer's

34. David Agrawal & William Fox, *Taxes in an E-Commerce Generation* 24(5) Int'l. Tax & Publ. Fin. 903 (2017); Cristina Trenta, *European VAT and the Digital Economy: Recent Developments* 17(1) eJournal Tax Res. 118 (2019); Karl Russo, *Superiority of the VAT to Turnover Tax as an Indirect Tax on Digital Services* 72(4) Nat'l. Tax J. 857 (2019); Maya Bacache-Beauvallet, *Tax Competition, Tax Coordination, and e-Commerce* 20(1) J. Pub. Econ. Theory 100 (2018).
35. For example, Australian Treasury estimated that imports of services caused around AUD 1 billion of GST revenue foregone. *See* Productivity Commission (Australia), *Economic Structure and Performance of the Australian Retail Industry*, Inquiry Report No. 56 (4 November 2011), XXXVII, Box 6, available at https://www.pc.gov.au/inquiries/completed/retail-industry/report/retail-industry.pdf. The EU claimed that cross-border VAT fraud amounts to EUR 41 billion, and compliance costs for businesses are around EUR 1 billion. European Commission, *On the Follow-up to the Action Plan on VAT towards a Single EU VAT Area – Time to Act* (4 October 2017). Charlène Herbain, *Fighting VAT Fraud and Enhancing VAT Collection in a Digitalized Environment* 46(6/7) Intertax 579 (2018); European Commission, *Study and Reports on the VAT Gap in the EU-28 Member States 2020 Final Report* (September 2020), available at https://ec.europa.eu/taxation_customs/sites/taxation/files/vat-gap-full-report-2020_en.pdf. *See also* Michael Keen & Stephen Smith, *VAT Fraud and Evasion: What Do We Know, and What Can Be Done?* IMF Working Paper (February 2007), available at https://www.imf.org/external/pubs/ft/wp/2007/wp0731.pdf.
36. European Parliament, *Directorate-General for Internal Policies, Simplifying and Modernising VAT in the Digital Single Market* (2012), available at https://www.europarl.europa.eu/RegData/etudes/etudes/join/2012/492432/IPOL-IMCO_ET(2012) 492432_EN.pdf; European Commission, *VAT Aspects of Cross-Border e-Commerce Options for Modernisation: Final Report* (2016), available at https://op.europa.eu/en/publication-detail/-/publication/dbabd711-b799-11e6-9e3c-01aa75ed71a1/language-en; Marta Papis-Almansa, *VAT and Electronic Commerce: The New Rules as a Means for Simplification, Combatting Fraud and Creating a More Level Playing Field?* 20 ERA Forum 201 (2019); Ben Terra, *Levying VAT in the EU Customs Union: Towards a Single Indirect Tax Area? The Ordeal of Indirect Tax Harmonisation* (2019) 12 Erasmus Law Rev. 269 (2019).

registration or their usual residence.[37] The basic principle is that VAT is levied and collected in the jurisdiction of the customer location in cases of both inbound-to-the EU and within-the-EU electronically supplied services, meaning taxation in the place of consumption. Although these proxies can be, to a degree, arbitrary, they provide legal certainty needed for the supplier, the customer, and the tax authority. The EU rules have also simplified administrative procedures for non-EU businesses to register for VAT purposes through one single online portal hosted by a relevant EU Member State tax authority to encourage tax compliance, particularly in the case of tax collection on B2C transactions.[38] The extensive work done by the EU has improved the implementation of the destination principle both within the EU and between EU Member States and third countries.

At national levels, several jurisdictions such as Australia and Singapore have developed VAT or GST rules to ensure cross-border transactions conducted electronically or remotely are taxed on a destination basis.[39] Even in the US, which does not have a VAT/GST but instead state-level retail sales taxes, the US Supreme Court, in *South Dakota v. Wayfair* in 2018,[40] accepted economic and virtual contacts as a substantial nexus in addition to the decades-old physical presence standard and ruled that exclusively applying the physical presence rule was 'unsound and incorrect' in the era of internet services.[41]

The development of responses to cross-border VAT challenges and the approaches devised for the identification of the place of taxation and tax collection at the international, regional, and national levels suggests VAT/GST systems need to evolve in line with the ever-digitalised economy such that international trade neutrality continues to be guaranteed through the implementation of the destination principle. These responses offer reference with which China's enforcement of the principle can be analysed in an international context.

---

37. European Commission, *The Basic EU VAT Rules for Electronically Supplied Services Explained for Micro Businesses* (19 May 2016), available at https://ec.europa.eu/taxation_customs/sites/taxation/files/information_microbusinesses_euvat_2015_en.pdf. *See also* Matthias Weidmann, *The New EU VAT Rules on the Place of Supply of B2C E-Services: Practical Consequences – The German Example* 24(2) EC Tax Rev. 105 (2015).
38. Weidmann, *supra* n. 37, 114; Ana Paula Silva, *VAT Registration in Europe* 30 Publ. Res. Q. 152 (2014).
39. For Australia, *see* Chris Tang, *Australian GST Update – 2015* 5(1) World J. of VAT/GST 32 (2016); Rebecca Millar, *Taxing the Bull by the Horns: Reforming Australia's Cross-Border GST Rules* 24 Aust. Tax Forum 281 (2009). The enacting legislation on applying Australian GST to offshore intangible supplies to Australian consumers is the *Tax and Superannuation Laws Amendment (2016 Measures No1) Bill 2016*. For Singapore, *see* Inland Revenue Authority of Singapore, *GST Payable on Overseas Digital Services from 1 Jan 2020* (9 December 2019), available at https://www.iras.gov.sg/irashome/News-and-Events/Newsroom/Media-Releases-and-Speeches/Media-Releases/2019/GST-payable-on-overseas-digital-services-from-1-Jan-2020/; and Inland Revenue Authority of Singapore, *GST on Imported Services*, available at https://www.iras.gov.sg/irashome/GST/GST-registered-businesses/GST-and-Digital-Economy/GST-on-Imported-Services/#.
40. *South Dakota v. Wayfair Inc.* (US) 138 S.Ct.2080 (2018).
41. Phillip Popkin, *The Effect of the Internet Era and South Dakota v. Wayfair on the Unitary Business Rule* 60(9) B. C. L. Rev. 82 (2019); Eric Miller, *Answering the Call: South Dakota v. Wayfair, Inc. and a Challenge to the Physical Presence Rule* 64(1) S. D. L. Rev. 94 (2019).

§20.03 IMPLEMENTING THE DESTINATION PRINCIPLE IN CHINA

The most recent reform on the VAT system in China has extended the VAT net to services and introduced rules to implement the destination principle as a fundamental basis to assert substantive jurisdiction to tax on cross-border supplies of services. The reformed system, however, contains a number of distinctive design and implementation features, leading to partial or incomplete implementation of the principle. Some features are a legacy inherited from the previous systems, and some are deliberately offered as a way to mitigate any potential increase in tax liability on services suppliers arising from the reform. As elsewhere, the most significant issues for cross-border trade in services are the failure to adhere to trade neutrality for B2B transactions, i.e., exempt exported supplies without affording credit, and non-taxation in the case of B2C transactions.[42] The discussion below provides a brief account of the development of the VAT system relating to services in China before focusing on the design and implementation of the place of taxation rules.

[A] The Services Sector and the Development of VAT in China

Taxation of the supply of services was previously a relatively minor issue under China's VAT system. In the early 1990s, the country relied, to a considerable degree, on production and exportation of goods for economic development. The manufacturing sector was deemed more important than the services sector. Although various types of services existed, the services usually took place on a comparatively small scale with many individual suppliers using cash for transactions. Unsurprisingly, when the VAT was formally introduced in 1994, the tax was primarily applied to the sale of goods, with the supply of services carved out and subject to another tax called Business Tax.[43]

The Business Tax was merely a turnover tax. Unlike the VAT, input tax incurred by the intermediary businesses was not allowed to be credited against output tax. This led to double taxation on businesses and ran counter to the destination principle in the case of cross-border supplies,[44] notwithstanding cross-border trade in services was relatively insignificant in the early 1990s.[45] With the deepening of the domestic economic reform and the expansion of global trade, China's services sector quickly gained momentum, surpassing the industrial sector in 2013 for the first time.[46] The

42. Millar, *supra* n. 23, 19.
43. Provisional Regulations on Business Tax (State Council, issued 13 December 1993 and effective 1 January 1994), Article 1.
44. *See* Wei Cui, *China's Business-Tax-to-VAT Reform: An Interim Assessment,* 5 British Tax Rev. 617 (2014); Daniel Chan, Doris Ho & Tina Xia, *China's Nationwide VAT Reform – Implementation Rules Issued,* Hong Kong Lawyer (10 May 2016).
45. Ministry of Commerce of People's Republic of China, *Statistics on Imports and Exports of Services (Calendar Years),* available at http://data.mofcom.gov.cn/fwmy/overtheyears.shtml.
46. *See* Prableen Bajpai, *China's GDP Examined: A Service-Sector Surge,* Investopedia (22 April 2020), available at https://www.investopedia.com/articles/investing/103114/chinas-gdp-examined-servicesector-surge.asp. This publication also noted China's services sector has doubled in size over the last two decades to account for about 46% of GDP. *See also* Loungani et al., *supra* n. 1, 11-12.

double taxation issue and its associated cascading effects on businesses in the services sector (and those in the industrial sector who incurred unrecoverable input tax from purchases of services), together with the high costs of reliance on manufacturing and exportation of goods for economic growth, became more striking during the global financial crisis around 2008-2009 in face of the deteriorated external economic environment. This prompted the government to consider changes of the country's economic development model so as to be more focused on services. The Business Tax rules were amended in 2008 in response to this policy change, but the amendment failed to address the double taxation issue in general and in cross-border supplies in particular.[47] The amended rules prescribed that the provision of services and the transfer of intangibles within China was subject to the Business Tax and the term 'within China' meant the supplier or recipient of services, or the recipient of intangibles was in China, a provision with very ambiguous regard to the destination principle.[48] The double taxation issue was finally dealt with in the most recent overhaul of the VAT system, which began in 2012 and was completed in May 2016. [49]

The overhaul, known as Business Tax-to-VAT (B2V) reform, unified the previously bifurcated taxes on consumption – the VAT applying to the sale of goods and the Business Tax applying to the supply of services. Services suppliers, registered as general taxpayers if they meet the relevant requirements (discussed in more detail in §20.03[D]), are permitted to deduct input tax from output tax.[50] These changes have helped to mitigate double taxation on businesses' supply of services, which was a significant barrier to the development and improvement of China's services industry, and to make the sector competitive in the global market. Taxable services are the same as those previously covered under the Business Tax and are grouped into several sub-categories.[51] Modern services such as telecommunication, broadcasting, and financial services are included in the scope of taxable services. There is no definition of the term 'services'. While a definition may not be necessary if the same tax treatment, including tax rates and computation method, applies to all types of services supplied by businesses, it is submitted that it would be needed in China's case. This is due to multiple rates for different types of supplies depending on whether the supplies are characterised as goods or services and the type of services provided.[52] The determination can be particularly complex for mixed supplies. Tax rules on place of taxation, export refunds and issues alike can be different between different types of services too.

---

47. Provisional Regulations on Business Tax (State Council, amended 5 November 2008 and effective 1 January 2009, expired 19 November 2017) Articles 1 and 4; Implementation Rules of the Provisional Regulations on Business Tax (MOF, issued 18 December 2008 and effective 1 January 2009, amended 28 October 2011, expired 19 November 2017), Article 4.
48. Implementation Rules of the Provisional Regulations on Business Tax, *supra* n. 47, Article 4.
49. Caishui [2016] 36, *supra* n. 15. *See also* Dezan Shira & Associates, *An Overview of China's VAT Reform*, China Briefing News (30 December 2016), available at http://www.china-briefing.com/news/2016/12/30/overview-chinas-vat-reform.html.
50. Provisional Regulations on VAT (2017), *supra* n. 15, Articles 1, 4 and 13.
51. Caishui [2016] 36, *supra* n. 15, Annex 1, Appendix 'Explanatory Notes on Sales of Services, Intangibles and Immovable Assets' (hereinafter 'Annex 1 Explanatory Notes').
52. Provisional Regulations on VAT (2017), *supra* n. 15, Article 2. The tax rates and input tax deduction policies have been adjusted by subsequent tax circulars with the currently effective

There are no rules that specifically target services supplied through electronic means. Any service, whether supplied in the traditional way or electronically, would be subject to China's VAT insomuch that it is supplied within, or imported into China.[53] Arguably, the challenges arising from cross-border supplies of modern services, particularly those related to information and telecommunication services, appear not to be as significant as in other jurisdictions. The reason lies in the regulatory aspect of foreign service suppliers' provision of digital services in the country, rather than in the technical aspect of the VAT system. Many foreign internet companies and sharing platforms, such as Google, Facebook and YouTube, are prohibited from direct or indirect operation in China. The relevant gap has been effectively filled by Chinese domestic internet companies and sharing platforms owing to the rapid development of e-commerce and mobile pay in the country. This strict regulatory control has mitigated the need to recommend legal provisions to address non-taxation in the case of inbound B2C supplies of services.

[B] Place of Taxation: The General Rule

Determination of the place of taxation is treated as the first and foremost issue under the OECD VAT/GST Guidelines. As noted earlier, the Guidelines include general and specific rules for the determination, with the former serving as a primary norm dealing with general circumstances and the latter as an exception to the general norm applicable only in special circumstances. While there is no explicit labelling of such rules under China's VAT legislation (in a broad sense), the VAT system does contain rules resembling the function of the general and specific rules under the OECD Guidelines.

Article 1 of the amended Regulations on VAT can be seen as the main rule for determining place of taxation in China, which provides that entities or individuals, selling or importing services (as well as goods) within China, are taxable persons liable for the VAT. The VAT liability arises if either the supplier or the recipient of services and intangibles (excluding the rights to use natural resources) is located in China.[54] The location of supplier or recipient/customer is used as a proxy to identify the place of taxation, which is unusual from an international perspective because the satisfaction of either one will, prima facie, lead to taxation in China. It follows that both inbound and outbound supplies of services will be subject to VAT. While taxation of inbound supplies due to the customer receiving the services in China meets the destination principle, taxation of outbound supplies as the services supplier is in China does not. There would be double taxation on the outbound supplies when the importing jurisdiction applies the destination principle to tax the imports.

---

circular, MOF, STA and General Administration of Customs, *Public Notice on Policies of Deepening the VAT Reform* (Gonggao [2019] 39).

53. Provisional Regulations on VAT (2017), *supra* n. 15, Article 1.
54. Caishui [2016] 36, *supra* n. 15, Annex 1, Articles 1 and 12(1).

This general rule using the location of supplier or customer to claim substantive taxing rights is a legacy from the previous rules of the Business Tax.[55] Previously contentious, the meaning of 'place of supply', a term used under the then Regulations on the tax (as well as the Regulations on the VAT), provided that a supply of services would be taxable in China if the 'supply' was effected in China. This suggests that the place of supply determines the place of taxation. There was, however, no explanation on whether the place of 'supply' referred to the place where consumption took place or the place where services were performed by the supplier for the customer to consume (which may occur in another location). The then Regulations seemed to synonymise the two terms, i.e., the 'place of supply' and the 'place of taxation', which was seemingly like the EU approach to the place of taxation rules.[56] The practice in China, at the time, inclined towards the place where services were prepared and effected, indicating application of the origin principle. The effect of this general provision would be that Chinese suppliers of services would be subject to tax *wherever* the supplied services were consumed, and foreign suppliers would be liable to China tax *whenever* they supplied taxable services to Chinese customers.

The B2V reform unfortunately inherited this approach to identifying the place of taxation.[57] However, outbound supplies of services by Chinese businesses are either exempt or zero-rated where the relevant services are consumed 'completely outside China',[58] a rule that was crafted and introduced to avoid double taxation on cross-border supplies of services. The two types of outbound supplies are discussed in detail in § 20.03[C] and [D]. Similarly, services supplied by foreign suppliers to Chinese customers would be excluded from China's VAT if the services are consumed 'completely outside China'.[59] Obviously, the term 'completely outside China' is crucial as it determines the taxability of a supply in China. The term is briefly defined in the context of outbound supplies by Chinese suppliers to mean:[60]

(1) the actual recipient of the services is outside China, and the services are not related to any good or real property located within China;
(2) the intangible assets are used completely outside China and the use is not related to any good or real property located within China; and
(3) any other situations specified by the Ministry of Finance (MOF) and the State Taxation Administration (STA).

This definition can be applied, by analogy, to supplies of services by foreign suppliers that are consumed by Chinese customers overseas as the term 'completely outside China' is not defined in this case under the revised Regulations on VAT, nor under the tax circular on the B2V reform.

55. Provisional Regulations on Business Tax, *supra* n. 47, Article 1; Implementation Rules of the Provisional Regulations on Business Tax, *supra* n. 47, Article 4.
56. Cockfield et al., *supra* n. 19, 244-247.
57. Caishui [2016] 36, *supra* n. 15, Annex 1, Articles 1 and 12.
58. Caishui [2016] 36, *supra* n. 15, Annex 4, Articles, 1, 2 and 7.
59. Caishui [2016] 36, *supra* n. 15, Annex 1, Article 13.
60. Caishui [2016] 36, *supra* n. 15, Annex 4, Article 7.

The definition of 'completely outside China' may be helpful in ascertaining whether services are consumed in China or abroad and thus avoid unduly expanding the scope of tax in China, except that the criterion, i.e., no connection between services supplied and any good or real property in China, is ambiguous. Taxpayers and tax authorities may differ in their assessment as to whether a cross-border supply involves any movable or immovable property in China based on the criterion. For example, where a Chinese business entity provides marketing services to a foreign company in the jurisdiction of the foreign company for the purpose of facilitating the foreign company's sale of goods in China, it is uncertain whether the marketing services will be treated as services that are not related to any goods in China and thereby qualifying as services consumed 'completely outside China'. Even if the services in question do qualify, the supply of the services will be exempt but not zero-rated since exports of consultation services are treated as exempt supplies under China's VAT rules.[61]

Ambiguity also arises in the case of supplies by foreign suppliers to Chinese customers for consumption overseas. Where, for example, a Chinese customer uses roaming cards purchased in China to consume services by Google while traveling in France, it is unclear whether the telecommunication services would be considered as not relating to any good or property in China. Another type of ambiguity relates to cross-border B2B supplies. For example, where a foreign company supplies a Chinese business customer with consulting services in respect of the Chinese customer's expansion plan in a third jurisdiction, would such services be regarded as being consumed completely outside China if the Chinese customer is in China? The exclusion from VAT liability on the grounds of 'completely outside China' does not appear to provide clear guidance for the determination of the place of taxation.

A further complexity is when the foreign company provides the consulting services in both the third jurisdiction and China. If the tax authorities determine the criterion of 'completely outside China' as not being met, the entire supply would be subject to VAT in China.

This relates to another two-part issue. That is, how to determine the place of taxation where a Chinese business entity supplies services to a business customer with multiple establishments located in different jurisdictions or where a Chinese business entity, with multiple establishments in different jurisdictions, acquires services from a foreign business supplier. This situation will require more frequent determination due to the continuing globalisation of the world economy and the further expansion of Chinese multinationals. The OECD VAT/GST Guidelines recommend that the taxing rights accrue to the jurisdiction(s) where the establishment(s) using the service or intangible is(are) located.[62] Where the supply is acquired by one establishment for its own use, or for multiple use by the other establishments located in different jurisdictions, a recharge method can be applied to enable the allocation of the supply of services in more than one jurisdiction.[63] Putting aside potential administration and compliance complexities with the method, the OECD rules clearly adhere to the general

61. Caishui [2016] 36, *supra* n. 15, Annex 4, Article 2(3)-4.
62. OECD, *VAT/GST Guidelines*, *supra* n. 13, 45, Guideline 3.4.
63. OECD, *VAT/GST Guidelines*, *supra* n. 13, 47-48, B.3.3.

principle that the place of taxation should be the location of the customer even for supplies to multiple location enterprises (MLEs). In China's case, this issue has not been clearly or explicitly addressed in the VAT rules. How to determine the place of taxation in MLE settings is ambiguous, especially in light of the requirement of 'completely outside China'. The unclear treatment could cause different outcomes in practice, i.e., double taxation in some cases while no-taxation in others.

[C] Place of Taxation: The Enumeration Approach

To deal with the uncertainties associated with the VAT treatment of outbound supplies of services, China's national tax authority resorts to the enumeration approach by way of defining the scope of exports of services that would be eligible for VAT zero-rating (with credit) or exemption (without credit).[64] This is similar to the previous practice with the Business Tax. The scope of zero-rated outbound supplies, as shown in Table 20.1, is limited to 3 types of services: international transportation services, air transport services, and a few modern services that are consumed by foreign entities completely outside China.[65] The scope of exempt outbound supplies of services seems broader and covers both on-the-spot services and services that can be provided electronically or remotely, such as telecommunications and broadcasting services.

The VAT exemption treatment is explained further below in §20.03[D]. A pertinent observation is that, as most exports are exempt but not zero-rated, Chinese services suppliers will probably be at a disadvantage in the global market. As critiqued in §20.03[D], the already narrow application of zero-rating can be further narrowed due to the deviation options provided to eligible taxpayers to opt out from zero-rating. This peculiar feature is not merely random. It was influenced by historical practices (i.e., no explicit provisions on exports of services under the predecessor Business Tax imposed on the supply of services and accordingly exports being taxed), the turnover nature of the Business Tax, and the concern of the central government over any potential increase in tax liability on businesses from the B2V reform when the businesses had few input taxes to offset against output taxes. A wide application of the VAT exemption would result in an incomplete implementation of the destination principle. However, this would be seen as necessary, at least in the transitional period, from a turnover tax to a genuine VAT.

Following the issuance of a primary circular on the B2V reform in 2016, a further tax circular was issued to facilitate the implementation of the exempt treatment on outbound services.[66] The circular enumerates 19 types of exempt services and further allows taxpayers to elect to have an additional list of supplies that are nominally zero-rated treated as exempt supplies (discussed in detail in §20.03[D]). It also clarifies circumstances under which an export of services would, or would not, be considered

64. Caishui [2016] 36, *supra* n. 15, Annex 4, Articles 1 and 2.
65. Caishui [2016] 36, *supra* n. 15, Annex 4, Article 1.
66. STA, *Public Announcement on Issuing the Measures for the Exemption of VAT on Cross-border Taxable Activities for the B2V Reform* (Gonggao [2016] 29).

as meeting the requirement that the services are consumed 'completely outside China'.[67]

Table 20.1 VAT Zero-Rated Supplies[68]

Types of Zero-Rated Services	**Specific Scope**
International transport services	'International transportation services' means: (1) transporting passengers or cargo from China to abroad; (2) transporting into China passengers or cargo from abroad; and (3) transporting passengers or cargo outside China.
Aerospace transport services	
Services supplied to foreign entities consumed completely outside China	(1) Research and development (R&D) services; (2) Energy management contracting services; (3) Design services; (4) Production and distribution services of radio, film and television programs (or works); (5) Software services; (6) Circuit design and testing services; (7) Information system services; (8) Business process management services; (9) Offshore service outsourcing business; and (10) Transfer of technologies.

Broadly, there are two situations in which services supplied to foreign entities cannot be considered as being consumed completely outside China. The first is where services relate to any good or real property, defined in broad terms, located in China, and the second is where the actual recipient of services is an entity or individual in China. For example, the circular stipulates that authentication and consulting services supplied to foreign entities outside China would be VAT exempt, unless the services are actually received by entities or individuals in China or services relate to goods or real property located in China.[69] Similarly, professional technical services supplied to foreign entities that are consumed entirely outside China would be VAT exempt, but services that are actually received by entities or individuals in China or that relate to

67. *Supra* n. 66, Article 2(1) to Article 2(19).
68. *See* source from Caishui [2016] 36, *supra* n. 15, Annex 4, Article 1(1), 1(2) and 1(3). There is a catch-all category that includes any other services to be specified by the MOF and STA, Article 1(4).
69. Gonggao [2016] 29, *supra* n. 66, Article 2(13).

China's weather, seismology, sea, the environment, ecology, landscape, geology, hydrology, mineral resources, and urban planning cannot be considered as being consumed completely outside China.[70] Also, outbound supplies of intellectual property services would not be eligible for VAT exemption, even if the supplies are made to foreign entities outside China so long as the use and enjoyment of the services took place in China, i.e., the services are actually received by customers in China.[71] In the same vein, supplies of cultural and sports services, as well as educational and medical services, will not be eligible for VAT exemption, even though they are consumed by foreign entities outside China, if the services are supplied through domestic radio stations, television stations, satellite communications, internet networks or other equipment of a similar kind.[72]

Clearly, the place of supply will be considered 'within China' if immovable property or natural resources to which supplies of services relate are located in China.[73] This is similar to the previous rule,[74] and consistent with the OECD VAT/GST Guidelines on services connected with immovable property.[75]

Putting aside issues with VAT exemption (discussed immediately below), the above-mentioned two situations that prevent a supply from being qualified as meeting the requirement of 'completely outside China' appear to be stringent in applying the exemption treatment to outbound supplies of services. The first limitation – eligible VAT exempt supplies must not have a connection with goods or real property in China – aligns with the requirement set up by the major circular on the B2V reform, which has a higher legal authority, as discussed above.[76] The limitation seems to put emphasis on the entirety of services, and thus even services that are only partially used or related to goods or real property in China, but consumed by foreign entities, would be denied VAT exemption. In terms of the second limitation, being the location of actual recipients, the exclusion from VAT exemption may be explained by concerns about tax arbitrage activities. That is, domestic entities or individuals who are actual customers engage in such activities in order to obtain the benefits of no output tax when the customers incurred little input tax. This limitation primarily applies to four types of services: intellectual property services, authentication and consulting services, professional technical services, and business support services. [77] The problem here is to identify who the 'actual' customer or services recipient is and then ascertain such person's whereabouts, particularly when those services can be supplied electronically and received instantly.

The use of the two limitations seems to suggest that the location of actual customers on the one hand and the location of goods, movable and immovable

70. Gonggao [2016] 29, *supra* n. 66, Article 2(14)-2.
71. Gonggao [2016] 29, *supra* n. 66, Article 2(11), paragraph 2.
72. Gonggao [2016] 29, *supra* n. 66, Article 2(8), paragraph 4.
73. Caishui [2016] 36, *supra* n. 15, Annex 1, Article 12(2) and 12(3).
74. Implementation Rules of the Provisional Regulation on Business Tax, *supra* n. 47, Article 4.
75. OECD, *VAT/GST Guideline, supra* n. 13, 84, Guideline 3.8.
76. That is Caishui [2016] 36, *supra* n. 15, which was issued jointly by the MOF and STA. Gonggao [2016] 29, *supra* n. 66, was issued solely by the STA.
77. Gonggao [2016] 29, *supra* n. 66, Articles 2(11), 2(13), 2(14) and 2(15)-4.

properties on the other hand are adopted as proxies to negate the place of taxation as outside China. That said, once the locations are identified as within China, the relevant supplies would not be considered outbound supplies, even if they are supplied to foreign entities (nominal recipients) and received or consumed overseas.

A number of other proxies are adopted in the particular circular on VAT exemption for outbound supplies. Broadly, services covered by the circular can be grouped into four categories: first, services that must be performed with the physical presence of the customer; second, services provided for projects located overseas or services supplied using immovable properties such as warehouses and storages, or event sites such as cinemas and theatres located overseas; third, services that are supplied for activities or events taking place overseas (e.g., organisational and logistics services for participation in scientific and technological activities, cultural activities and competitions, sports competitions and performances, etc.); and fourth, services connected with exported goods. Lastly, services falling into the above-mentioned two limitation situations can be viewed as another category, which is not eligible for VAT exemption as supplies of those services are not consumed completely outside China. Proxies used for the various categories of supplies may be summarised as in Table 20.2.

Table 20.2 VAT Exempt Supplies

Types of Exempt Services	Proxies
On-the-spot supplies	Place of performance (e.g., cultural and sports as well as educational and medical services)
Services connected with projects or events	Location of goods, immovable properties, or event sites (e.g., construction projects or sites, location of mineral resources, conference and exhibition sites, movable property to be leased, cinemas, video halls, radio stations and alike for broadcasting)
Services connected with activities	Location of activities (e.g., scientific and technological activities, cultural activities and competitions, sports competitions and performances)
Services connected with exported goods	Location of goods (e.g., postal services for parcels and mails to be delivered outside China, collection and delivery services for goods to be exported abroad, issuing of postage stamps abroad)
Modern services (e.g., IP services, authentication and consultation services, professional technical services, business support services)	Location of actual customers
Services connected with immovable property	Location of immovable property

As China's VAT rules do not differentiate between B2B and B2C supplies, these specific proxies are applied in both cases. These proxies broadly include the general and specific rules on cross-border B2B and B2C supplies covered by the OECD Guidelines. Unlike the principle-based approach used in the Guidelines, the enumeration approach adopted in China's VAT system has a major shortcoming, even though it may provide legal certainty to some extent. That is, the enumeration cannot exhaust all circumstances that would occur in business practices. Moreover, the enumeration may give rise to disputes in the determination of place of taxation between tax authorities and taxpayers as to ascertaining the facts and circumstances and interpretation of rules. Such enumeration may also lead cross-border supplies of services, that would otherwise have been included into the VAT exemption or zero-rating scope, to be taxable in China. For example, maintenance, repair, and technology services for equipment installation of construction projects outside China are not covered by either the enumerated list on zero-rating or the list on exemption, and thus these services may be subject to China VAT.

[D] VAT Zero-Rating Versus Exemption

The destination principle is adopted to achieve international trade neutrality, and the corollary of this principle is that the exporting jurisdiction does not tax the export supplies while allowing the seller to recover any VAT included in the purchase to make the export supplies, i.e., no output tax with credit. By contrast, exemption does not allow credit for input tax incurred by the seller, although no output tax is charged to the export supplies. This exemption treatment does not entirely meet the destination principle as exported sales contain embedded tax - the uncovered input VAT - which will be taxed again as it is part of the consideration (of services) or Customs value (of goods) in the importing jurisdiction. The VAT levied in the destination country on the embedded input VAT (incurred in the origin country) leads to double- or over-taxation and creates a competitive disadvantage for affected services exporters in the global market. This is one of the reasons why zero-rating is required, and preferred by businesses, for outbound supplies. China has, however, applied VAT exemption to a broader scope of outbound supplies than zero-rating as discussed above.

VAT exemption without credit can be seen as an example of intentional partial taxation.[78] It has been used in a domestic context and usually applied to supplies of financial services and real property.[79] Often, when VAT-exempt services are supplied across borders, they are exempt with credit through zero-rating.[80] Cross-border sales of financial services are not taxed as input tax can be recovered because the place of

78. Rebecca Millar, *Intentional and Unintentional Double Non-Taxation Issues in VAT*, Sydney Law School Legal Studies Research Paper No. 09/45 (June 2009), 10, available at https://papers.ssrn.com/sol3/papers.cfm?abstract_id=1416582.
79. Millar, *supra* n. 78, 10.
80. Millar, *supra* n. 78, 10.

taxation is in the jurisdiction of the customer location, although unintended double non-taxation may occur. In the case of real property, transactions relating to land would be VAT-exempt without credit, whether the recipient is located domestically or in another jurisdiction. This is because the location of land is used as a proxy to determine the place of taxation for supplies of land and supplies of services connected with land. China has also generally followed this practice for supplies within its domestic borders, and for supplies of services related to land in a cross-border context. However, when financial services that are provided for monetary financing and other financial services are exported to entities abroad, the exports are not zero-rated but VAT exempt under China's rules.[81]

Moreover, there are two further deviations from the zero-rating treatment for outbound supplies in China's VAT system. First, there is an 'opting-out' policy, allowing suppliers of those outbound services that are eligible for zero-rating to opt out from zero-rating and, instead, apply exemption or pay VAT.[82] Once opted out, the relevant taxpayers cannot apply for zero-rating for 36 months.[83] This may appear to be counter-intuitive since services exporters would, theoretically, always prefer zero-rating over exemption so as to recover input taxes incurred for making exported sales and to compete with similar services suppliers in the destination market. Nevertheless, Chinese suppliers may choose to relinquish the zero-rating treatment when they incurred little input VAT that can be used as credit in making outbound supplies of services that would otherwise be zero-rated to avoid a separate refund process. While digital administration systems have improved in recent years enabling export refunds to become more efficient, the refunds have been subject to strict regulation by tax authorities and input VAT is often not fully recovered.[84] Thus, the regulation of export refunds may lead Chinese business exporters to bear certain irrecoverable VAT costs, which may resemble the effect of VAT exemption without credit to some degree. Both cases would render China's services exporters at a disadvantage in the global market, and undermines the destination principle, in particular in cases where exporters choose to pay VAT on outbound services.

The second deviation is that a zero-rated outbound supply of services (as shown in Table 20.1) by entities or individuals in China will be treated as a VAT exempt supply

81. Caishui [2016] 36, *supra* n. 15, Appendix 4, Article 2(5); Gonggao [2016] 29, *supra* n. 66, Article 2(18).
82. Caishui [2016] 36, *supra* n. 15, Annex 4, Article 5; Gonggao [2016] 29, *supra* n. 66, Article 2(20).
83. Caishui [2016] 36, *supra* n. 15, Annex 4, Article 5.
84. Michael Ferrantino, Xuepeng Liu & Zhi Wang, *Evasion Behaviors of Exporters and Importers: Evidence from the U.S.–China Trade Data Discrepancy* 86(1) J. Int. Econ. 141 (2012); John Brondolo & Zhiyong Zhang, *Tax Administration Reform in China: Achievements, Challenges, and Reform Priorities*, IMF Working Paper (2016), available at https://www.elibrary.imf.org/doc/IMF001/23295-9781475523614/23295-9781475523614/Other_formats/Source_PDF/23295-9781475547344.pdf; Lachlan Wolfers, *VAT and Technology: The First Fully Automated Tax?* Int. Tax Rev. (2019), available at https://www.internationaltaxreview.com/article/b1j8ydd4qghx0w/vat-and-technology-the-first-fully-automated-tax; Haichao Fan, Yu Liu, Nancy Qian & Jaya Wen, *Computerizing VAT Invoices in China*, National Bureau of Economic Research Working Paper 24414 (March 2018, Revised April 2020), available at https://www.nber.org/papers/w24414.

when a simplified tax computation method is applied to the relevant suppliers.[85] The simplified tax computation method is primarily adopted for small-scale taxpayers, as opposed to general taxpayers, who are determined according to the taxable amount of annual sales and accounting records of the relevant taxpayers.[86] Taxpayers registered as general taxpayers are allowed to offset input VAT against output VAT in calculating their tax liability based on a general computation method.[87] However, the simplified computation method does not allow small-scale taxpayers to apply input tax credits in calculating their tax liability, instead a reduced rate of 3% is applied to their sales.[88] The simplified computation method is a departure from the nature of VAT and suggests that the so-called VAT on small-scale taxpayers is, in essence, a tax on turnover rather than a tax on value added. The lower rate of 3% is probably adopted in order to ameliorate the cascading effects on intermediate businesses. When small-scale taxpayers make outbound supplies of services, the simplified computation method merely prevents them from applying the zero-rating treatment. Thus, the previously unrecovered input tax flows into the price of the services exported to outside China, causing a hidden or implicit tax burden on the exported services. Given that general taxpayers are eligible for zero-rating in relation to those supplies, the policy creates, unnecessarily, unequal tax treatment between the two types of taxpayers when making those outbound supplies of services.

A further complication is that while the tax circular on the B2V reform states that a general taxpayer, once registered, is not permitted to be converted into a small-scale taxpayer, which appears to be consistent with the State Council's Regulations on the VAT (2017 amendment), the circular leaves room for the STA to prescribe otherwise.[89] A later STA circular has done so, allowing general taxpayers to choose to become a small-scale taxpayer provided certain conditions are satisfied.[90] The simplified computation method will be applied once the change of qualification is completed.[91] In addition, general taxpayers may choose to apply the simplified computation method,

85. Caishui [2016] 36, *supra* n. 15, Annex 4, Article 4; Gonggao [2016] 29, *supra* n. 66, Article 2(20). There are two tax computation methods under the VAT Regulations, namely general computation and simplified computation. Provisional Regulations on VAT (2017), *supra* n. 15, Articles 4, 5 and 11.
86. Provisional Regulations on VAT (2017), *supra* n. 15, Article 11; Caishui [2016] 36, *supra* n. 15, Annex 1, Articles 3, 4 and 5.
87. Provisional Regulations on VAT (2017), *supra* n. 15, Articles 4 and 5; Caishui [2016] 36, *supra* n. 15, Annex 1, Articles 4, 5, 18 and 21.
88. Provisional Regulations on VAT (2017), *supra* n. 15, Articles 11 and 12; Caishui [2016] 36, *supra* n. 15, Annex 1, Articles 16, 17, 19 and 34.
89. Caishui [2016] 36, *supra* n. 15, Annex 1, Article 5, paragraph 2. VAT registration usually requires physical presence of a business. The administrative procedures and documentation requirements for VAT registration have been significantly simplified in recent years. Applicants now only need to submit an application form together with a copy of their business certificate showing General Social Security Code to the relevant tax authority for registration. If a VAT-registered taxpayer intends to change into a small-scale taxpayer, it will not be able to do so unless de-registration.
90. STA, *Public Announcement on Unifying Standards for Small-Scale Taxpayers and Other Matters* (Gonggao [2018] 18), Article 1. General taxpayers meeting the relevant prescribed conditions can fill with in-charged tax authority a form on the change of qualification to small-scale taxpayers. *See* Gonggao [2018] 18, Article 2.
91. Gonggao [2018] 18, *supra* n. 90, Article 3.

without converting into small-scale taxpayers, to specific taxable supplies prescribed by the MOF and the STA, subject to a no-change-back period of 36 months.[92] Services that are covered under the 'opting-out' policy would fall into the scope of this policy. There are other types of services to which general taxpayers are allowed to apply the simplified computation method, such as leasing, warehousing and film broadcasting services.[93] These services may be supplied across borders and thus VAT exemption, but not zero-rating, will be applied.

Clearly, the wide application of VAT exemptions on outbound supplies of services under the Chinese VAT system deviates from the destination principle. The differentiation of small-scale taxpayers from general taxpayers and the adoption of the simplified computation method, as well as relevant policies expanding their application, push China's VAT rules further away from the principle.

[E] VAT Rules for Digital Services

Technological advancement has made the cross-border supply of services more available and efficient than ever before. Many modern services can now be supplied electronically and consumed by customers almost instantly. In China, the services sector is the most digitalised among all economic sectors, and digital services, such as software downloading, streaming, and gaming, are widely used and frequently traded within and outside its borders.[94] China's two popular third-party payment applications, *Alipay* and *WeChat Pay*, have quickly established a global reach for sales of a wide range of services and goods,[95] and facilitate the digitalisation of China's economy and the growth of cross-border e-commerce.[96]

The significant development of the digitalised economy has a huge impact on VAT systems. The challenges posed by digital services are potentially much more complex than those associated with supplies of goods, largely owing to the intangibility of services. Broadly, there are two major VAT challenges: identification of the place of taxation of supplies of digital services and tax collection, particularly from cross-border B2C supplies. Many VAT systems have been grappling with the challenges posed by digital services, and some jurisdictions, such as Australia and the EU, have adopted new rules and mechanisms to address the challenges. The recent B2V reform in China

92. Caishui [2016] 36, *supra* n. 15, Annex 1, Article 18, paragraph 2.
93. Caishui [2016] 36, *supra* n. 15, Annex 2, Article 1(6).
94. Information and telecommunication technology contributed to one third of the services sector's value-added in 2017. *See* Longmei Zhang & Sally Chen, *China's Digital Economy: Opportunities and Risks*, IMF Working Paper (17 January 2019), 8, available at https://www.imf.org/en/Publications/WP/Issues/2019/01/17/Chinas-Digital-Economy-Opportunities-and-Risks-46459.
95. Zhang & Chen, *supra* n. 94, 5.
96. Khoonming Ho, Conrad Turley & Sunny Leung, *A Sisyphean Task? – Tax Plays Catch up with China's Rapid Digitalisation*, Int'l Tax Rev. (10 December 2018), available at https://www.internationaltaxreview.com/Article/3848553/A-Sisyphean-taskTax-plays-catch-up-with-Chinas-rapid-digitalisation.html?ArticleId = 3848553.

provided an opportunity for China's policymakers to address the VAT challenges, but no particular rule was introduced in the reform.[97]

With respect to the place of taxation of the supply of digital services, the first issue is to ascertain what would amount to digital services or electronically supplied services. Absent a general definition of services, the tax circular on the B2V reform has attempted to classify services into seven broad categories, defining each category.[98] Telecommunication is a separate category, while broadcasting is included in the category of modern services, which is broadly defined as technical and knowledge-based services for manufacturing, cultural, modern logistics and other industries.[99] This category is further broken down into 9 sub-categories, with many services able to be supplied electronically or remotely, such as R&D and technical services, information technology services, design services, and broadcasting of radio, film and television programs. Services listed in other categories, such as education services under the category of lifestyle services, can also be supplied electronically. The provision of a prescriptive list for services may be helpful for tax administration and compliance, but it risks becoming outdated and creating loopholes for tax avoidance, not least because it is not possible to provide an exhaustive list of services. Moreover, apart from broadcasting and telecommunication services, there is no general description of features of digital services which would prevent those not explicitly mentioned in the category list from escaping the tax net.

As a comparison, in addition to the provision of a prescriptive list, the EU introduced a general definition of electronically supplied services, referring to those that are delivered over the internet or an electronic network as essentially automated, involving minimal human intervention, and impossible without information technology.[100] These services, along with telecommunications and broadcasting, have been subject to taxation in the country of the customer, meaning taxation at destination, since 1 January 2015 under the EU rules. The lacuna of a general definition in China may be offset by the broadly defined category list and by the usual discretionary power left to the tax policy makers in dealing with new developments and change of circumstances.

As services would be subject to China VAT so long as they are supplied within, or imported into, China, the general place of taxation rule will be applied to supplies of digital services. As discussed above, the general rule prescribes that China VAT will be charged if the supplier or purchaser/customer of services is in China. However, services supplied by foreign suppliers to Chinese customers are not taxed if they are

97. However, China's policymakers for taxation have introduced circulars to tax cross-border trade in goods. Import VAT is levied on goods imported by individuals through cross-border e-commerce platforms, and e-commerce companies, or platforms or logistic companies can be a withholding agent on the import VAT. *See* MOF, General Administration of Customs and STA Notice on Tax Policies of Cross-border E-Commerce Retail Imports (Caiguanshui [2016] 18).

98. Caishui [2016] 36, *supra* n. 15, Annex 1 Explanatory Notes. The 7 categories refer to transportation, postal services, telecommunications, construction, financial services, modern services and lifestyle services.

99. Caishui [2016] 36, *supra* n. 15, Annex 1 Explanatory Notes, Category 1(6).

100. Council Implementing Regulation (EU) No 282/2011, Article 7(1).

consumed 'completely outside China'. Similarly, services exported by Chinese suppliers, if consumed 'completely outside China', will be either zero-rated or exempt. Thus, if digital services, such as telecommunications, broadcasting and software services, are supplied to Chinese customers in China, the services will be taxed because the customer location, as a proxy for place of taxation, is in China. Where these services are consumed completely outside China, the services will not be subject to China VAT. This shows the customer location is used as a proxy to determine the place of taxation, which is consistent with the OECD VAT/GST Guidelines. In both cases, however, the use of the customer location as a proxy for the place of taxation is contingent on the criterion of no connection between supply in question and any good or immovable property in China.

The identification of the customer location will be different between B2B supplies and B2C supplies, although China's rules do not explicitly differentiate the two. With regard to B2B supplies, the location of the customer can be determined by the customer's VAT registration number. In China, businesses are required to register for VAT purposes and those who meet the standards for qualifying as general taxpayers will be registered as such, and thus eligible for input tax credits. When general taxpayers import services for business purposes, they are required to pay, through a withholding mechanism, the import VAT, and recover the tax at subsequent sales. For outbound supply, the tax treatment for Chinese business suppliers is affected by the general approach. That is, most services are exempt but not zero-rated. The Chinese suppliers will need to prove that services exported abroad are not connected to any good or immovable property in China, and that the services are actually consumed abroad. The current Regulations on VAT and the circular on the B2V reform are ambiguous regarding evidentiary proof, in particular with respect to digital services. The circular on exempt supplies provides some explanation on circumstances in which services cannot be considered as consumed completely outside China, as discussed above. For broadcasting, the circular provides that where a broadcasting service is supplied by a Chinese entity abroad using domestic radio stations, television stations, satellite communications, internet networks, cable television and other wireless or wired devices, such service is not regarded as consumed entirely overseas and thus not eligible for VAT exemption.[101] For telecommunications, services that are supplied to an overseas customer with payment settled through an overseas telecommunication entity will be considered consumed completely outside China and thus eligible for VAT exemption.[102]

The above rules suggest that the location of the device with which broadcasting services are supplied and the location of the settlement entity regarding telecommunication services are used to grant or deny VAT exemption in outbound B2B supplies, even though the customer location is outside China. There is no specific rule for services delivered over the internet or via an electronic network such as software services and information system services. These services, if consumed by foreign

101. Gonggao [2016] 29, *supra* n. 66, Article 2(7).
102. Gonggao [2016] 29, *supra* n. 66, Article 2(10).

entities completely outside China, will be zero-rated when exporting from China.[103] The determination of whether these services are consumed completely outside China may be made by reference to the location of the server. If the server is in China, software downloads and updates or other information system services consumed by foreign entities overseas may not be eligible for VAT zero-rating. Even if eligible, it is unclear whether VAT zero-rating applies if the foreign entities act as final consumers because only 'foreign entities' are mentioned in the relevant rule on zero-rating.[104]

In the case of B2C supplies, the determination of customer location could be even more difficult as final consumers can receive digital services anywhere. China's VAT rules have not provided explicit proxies to help identify the customer location in cross-border B2C supplies. By comparison, the EU has introduced rules to address this issue. Under the EU rules, the location will be the jurisdiction where the consumer usually lives, has his/her permanent address, or is registered.[105] There are further presumptions or proxies for the supplier to ascertain the customer location in B2C supplies, and these presumptions include the IP address of the device used by the customer, the billing address of the customer, the Mobile Country Code used by the customer, and the location of the customer's fixed land line through which the service is supplied.[106] This approach is helpful in implementing the destination principle because it allows the supplier to predicate the customer location when relevant services are consumed. China could consider adopting a similar approach to improving the implementation of the destination principle in B2C transactions in digital services.

On the other hand, the difficulty in identifying the customer location in inbound B2C supplies may not be too severe since many foreign supplies of digital services are not accessible to Chinese consumers. Foreign internet companies, social and sharing platforms and foreign software suppliers, including Google, Facebook, and YouTube, are also not allowed to have direct local operations in China. In addition, supplies of software as a service (SaaS) or software services cannot be accessed by China's state-owned enterprises, and private firms would have a strong preference to use only China-hosted software for regulatory reasons.[107] Individual consumers cannot usually access many digital services provided by foreign suppliers. However, they may be able to use a Virtual Private Network (VPN)[108] to circumvent China's internet control to consume relevant services, such as accessing video streaming. As VPN technology can

103. Caishui [2016] 36, *supra* n. 15, Annex 4, Article 1(3).
104. Caishui [2016] 36, *supra* n. 15, Annex 4, Articles 1(3)-5 and 1(3)-7.
105. European Commission, Taxation and Customs Union, *Where to Tax?*, available at https://ec.europa.eu/taxation_customs/business/vat/eu-vat-rules-topic/where-tax_en; Taxamo, *EU VAT B2C: Difference between B2B and B2C* (1 November 2017), available at https://blog.taxamo.com/insights/eu-vat-b2c-difference-b2b-b2c-clients.
106. European Commission, *supra* n. 105.
107. Steve Dickinson, *Selling Software as a Service (SaaS) in China: The Foreign Server Option*, Harris Bricken (12 May 2015), available at https://harrisbricken.com/chinalawblog/selling-software-as-a-service-saas-in-china-the-foreign-server-option/.
108. A VPN is a secure tunnel between users' device and the internet. It enables users to send and receive data across shared or public networks as if their computing devices were directly connected to the private network. VPNs can be used to protect users from interference, censorship and snooping. *See* Wikipedia, *Virtual Private Network*, https://en.wikipedia.org/wiki/Virtual_private_network.

help protect personal identity and location for the users to stay anonymous on the internet, the determination of place of consumption can be difficult or inaccurate. Chinese consumers may have to pay VAT in other jurisdictions where consumption is deemed to occur via the VPN route.

§20.04 THE COLLECTION MECHANISM

The implementation of the destination principle hinges upon the collection of VAT, particularly in an inbound B2C context, as outbound supplies are generally zero-rated in most jurisdictions. In China's case, the large number of exported supplies that are treated as exempt supplies, i.e., supplies without input tax credits, will not cause revenue loss to the government but constitutes a fiscal burden on exporters. By contrast, the lack of an effective tax collection mechanism contributes, to a large extent, to the failure to completely implement the destination principle in the inbound context.[109] Often jurisdictions may choose not to tax the full range of inbound transactions in services simply because of the difficulty of collecting VAT from foreign suppliers that do not have any presence in the importing jurisdiction.[110] China faces the same difficulty. While the rapid growth of the digitalised economy has increased services available to Chinese customers and expanded access to global markets, it may have resulted in tax revenue losses and compromised the country's ability to enforce and collect the VAT based on the destination principle.

[A] Characterisation of Services

The classification of supplies for VAT purposes is not a significant issue if a single positive rate applies to all types of services. However, where different rates apply, classification becomes critical. This is the case under China's VAT system. There are currently 3 positive rates, a zero-rate for outbound supplies, and a reduced rate of 3% for supplies by small-scale taxpayers as shown in Table 20.3.[111]

109. Millar, *supra* n. 23, 7.

110. Millar, *supra* n. 23, 7; *see also* Edward Whittle, *A Shift in the EU VAT system: The Proposed Implementation of the 'Destination Principle' to Intra-EU B2B Supplies of Goods* 4(1) World J. of VAT/GST Law 41 (2015).

111. *See* sources from the STA, *The Most Comprehensive and Useful: The Latest VAT Rates 2019* (31 March 2019), available at http://www.chinatax.gov.cn/n810341/n2340339/c4180655/content.html.

Table 20.3 VAT Rates on Services and Intangibles

Tax Rates	Taxable Transactions
13%	Tangible property leasing services
9%	Transportation services, postal services (general, specific, and other), basic telecommunications, construction services (project services, installation, repair, decorating services and other), sale of immovable property, leasing of immovable property, and transfer of land use rights
6%	Value-added telecommunications Financial services Sale of intangible assets Modern services[112] - R&D and technical services - Information technology services - Cultural creative services - Logistics auxiliary services - Authentication and consultation services - Broadcasting, cinematic and television services - Business support services - Other modern services Lifestyle services - Cultural and sports services - Education and medical services - Tourism and entertainment services - Catering and accommodation services - Residents' daily services (e.g., housekeeping, wedding, funeral services, hairdressing & beauty, message, etc.) - Other lifestyle services
0%	Export of services and intangibles as stipulated by the State Council
3% (levy rate)[113]	Services by small-scale taxpayers and services by general taxpayers using the simplified computation method

The use of multiple VAT rates is problematic because similar services could be taxed at different rates, causing unnecessary complexity and tax planning. Multiple rates also impact on businesses claiming input tax credits as different types of expenses generate different levels of credit. Moreover, there may be difficulty in delineating what constitutes 'goods' and what amounts to 'services', as well as what type of services, as the lines between them have become blurred with new business models being used in an increasingly digitalised economy. Classification may be even more difficult in the

112. Leasing services within the category of modern services are taxed at the rates of 13% and 9%, respectively, to tangible property leasing and immovable property leasing.
113. The levy rate is subject to deviations. A separate levy rate of 5% applies to services related to immovable property, land use rights, sale and lease of old real property projects developed by real estate enterprises, eligible finance leasing of immovable property, labour dispatching, security, and human resource outsourcing by general taxpayers. A reduced levy rate of 1.5% applies to individuals on residential leasing. STA, *supra* n. 111.

case of digital services as some 'goods' can now be virtualised or dematerialised. Table 20.4 shows the relevance of classification to tax rates regarding some digital services under China's VAT rules.

A typical example is supply of software. Until a few years ago, China taxed sales of most software products as sales of goods at the standard rate of 17%, though this standard rate has been reduced to 13%.[114] However, few customers nowadays purchase software products in a physical form. The development of digital services, such as SaaS and cloud computing, results in supply of services, which attracts the rate of 6% according to the VAT rules. As many final products are sold with embedded software, it is not uncommon for tax authorities to treat a software license as a sale of goods and levy VAT at the standard rate of 13%. This highlights the difficulty arising from the classification of the supply of software as a good, a license, or a service. The classification may be made by reference to the relevant contract between the supplier and the customer.

The difficulty of classifying software (and many digital products) as goods or services also exists in other jurisdictions such as the EU.[115] The EU rules treat electronically supplied software as a service, but EU Member States may deviate from that characterisation.[116] Some jurisdictions may use a case-by-case approach to determining classifications, which creates uncertainties to businesses.

In a cross-border context, different classifications will impact on credit claims and collection of taxes. For example, under China's rules, if a transaction of software is treated as a technology transfer, the transfer is entitled to VAT exemption, i.e., no VAT charged to the supply, but no credit allowed.[117] When the transfer is made to foreign entities for consumption completely outside China, the transfer is zero-rated.[118] The different treatment of domestic and outbound transfers of technologies may encourage domestic suppliers to engage in some tax arbitrage to claim input tax credits.

114. The standard rate of 17% was first reduced to 16% and then 13%. *See* MOF and STA, *Notice on VAT Rates Adjustment* (Caishui [2018] 32), Article 1; STA Gonggao [2019] 39, *supra* n. 52, Article 1. The new standard rate of 13% has been implemented since 1 April 2019.

115. Richard Westin, *International Taxation of Electronic Commerce* 153 (Kluwer Law International, 2nd ed., 2007).

116. Westin, *supra* n. 115, 154. *See also* European Commission, *The Basic EU VAT Rules for Electronically Supplied Services Explained for Micro Businesses,* available at https://ec.europa.eu/taxation_customs/sites/taxation/files/information_microbusinesses_euvat_2015_en.pdf; European Commission, *Explanatory Notes on the EU VAT Changes to the Place of Supply of Telecommunications, Broadcasting and Electronic Services that Enter into Force in 2015* (3 April 2014), available at https://ec.europa.eu/taxation_customs/sites/taxation/files/resources/documents/taxation/vat/how_vat_works/telecom/explanatory_notes_2015_en.pdf.

117. Caishui [2016] 36, *supra* n. 15, Annex 3, Article 1(26).

118. Caishui [2016] 36, *supra* n. 15, Annex 4, Article 1(3)-10.

Table 20.4 Classification of Supply

Taxable Activity	Characterisation	Tax Rates	Remark
Sales of point card	Commercial retail	13	Game companies sell entity point card.
	Entertainment services	6	Some companies regard the actual income on point card as taxable amount. Others regard the actual number of deeds consumed as taxable amount.
Transfer of virtual goods	Entertainment services	6	Game companies directly sell virtual goods (e.g., glasses, cloths, shoes, or small speakers, etc.); tax on the number of deeds consumed.
Paid download of digitalised products	Radio and television services or cultural and sports services	6	Unclear differentiation between music and video.
	Electronic publications	13	Online use only, or purchased in physical stores, and can be used offline.
	Transfer of copyright	6	Authorized use after purchase also taxed at 6%.
Websites with link (only the link of sale of goods)	Advertisement	6	Tax on advertising revenue.
	Brokerage	6	As a service of intermediary agent.
Online supply of business information (e.g., Weibo, WeChat)	Commercial retail	13	Tax on supply of information online and mixed sale of goods.
	Information technology services	6	Online platforms collect VAT.
	Advertisement	6	Tax on advertising revenue.
	Brokerage	6	As a service of intermediary agent.
Online supply of non-business information	Value-added telecommunications	6	The portal provides ICP services.
	Advertisement		Tax on advertising revenue.
			Not in the scope of tax collection.
Distance education and medical care	Education and medical services	6	
	Information technology services	6	Online platforms collect VAT.
System maintenance	Information technology services	6	Tax on actual service income.

[B] Collection of VAT

While non-taxation of inbound B2C transactions is a legitimate issue, non-taxation of inbound B2B transactions can encourage the outsourcing of services where the customer is a business making exempt supplies or an entity treated as exempt from the tax,[119] as shown in the China example above. However, the issue of potential non-neutrality in the B2B context would not lead to the same difficulty of collecting VAT as that in the B2C context because enforcement mechanisms such as reverse charge or withholding can be applied relatively easily.[120]

The reverse charge and the withholding mechanisms are the two major collection mechanisms used in cross-border B2B supplies. The OECD VAT/GST Guidelines recommend the reverse charge, and jurisdictions have adopted this mechanism more than withholding.[121] Both mechanisms shift the tax collection obligation from the offshore supplier to the registered domestic customer with the aim of alleviating administrative burdens on foreign suppliers. The reverse charge, under the OECD guidelines, may be limited to business customers who are not entitled to full input tax credits on supplies received from foreign suppliers as there will be a positive tax balance to pay. Business customers with full right to input tax credits may not apply the reverse charge given the VAT paid for the imports would be fully credited against output tax on subsequent sales.

Despite the OECD recommendation, China has adopted a withholding mechanism to collect VAT on cross-border B2B transactions. Where the service supplier is located outside China and has no business establishment in China, VAT is collected from the foreign supplier's agent in China, or from the purchaser or customer in China if there is no China agent.[122] This suggests the VAT payment obligation falls first on the foreign supplier's business establishment in the customer location, i.e., China, second on its agent, and third on the customer. This appears similar to the allocation of VAT obligations under a reverse charge system adopted in some jurisdictions such as Australia.[123] Where the VAT is paid by the customer, the Chinese rules generally entitle the customer to claim input tax credits if registered as a general taxpayer.

119. Millar, *supra* n. 78, 18-19.
120. Millar, *supra* n. 23, 10-11.
121. OECD, *VAT/GST Guidelines, supra* n. 13, 17. Reverse charge is used, for example, in Australia, New Zealand and the EU. *See* A New Tax System (Goods and Services Tax) Act 1999 (Australia), Division 84-10; Goods and Services Tax Act 1985 (New Zealand), sections 8(4B) and 5B; Council Directive 2006/112/EC of 28 November 2006 on the Common System of Value Added Tax (EU), Articles 44 and 196. *See also* Cockfield et al., *supra* n. 19, 257-260, 331-347.
122. Provisional Regulations on VAT (2017), *supra* n. 15, Article 18.
123. The Australian GST law stipulates that in cross-border B2B transactions, the foreign supplier's fixed establishment in Australia is responsible for import VAT payment; and where it does not have such establishment, the business customer in Australia uses reverse charge to remit import GST. *See* Australian Government Treasury, *GST Treatment of Cross-Border Transactions*, Consultation Process (6 October 2015-20 October 2015) available at https://treasury.gov.au/consultation/gst-treatment-of-cross-border-transactions; KPMG, *VAT/GST Treatment of*

The withholding mechanism may not be as efficient as a reverse charge for two major reasons. First, the withholding affects the sale price as the VAT liability would remain at the level of the supplier and, unless the supplier grosses up the price for VAT purposes, it will be short paid, while a reverse charge does not affect the price because the collection obligation is shifted to the customer.[124] Second, the withholding may create difficulties in accounting for the supplier if the invoice is short paid.[125] In China, however, the withholding mechanism seems to have worked effectively in cross-border B2B transactions as it operates to meet China's foreign currency controls as a tax clearance certificate is required for any payment made to suppliers outside China. While the currency controls have been loosened in recent years,[126] there is no indication that China will be moving towards a reverse charge system.

A related issue is whether a foreign business making taxable supplies locally in China can register for VAT purposes. The Chinese law allows foreign companies (foreign invested or wholly owned) to register as VAT general taxpayers provided registration requirements are met.[127] These include having a fixed place of business or establishment in China. Thus, those without such place or establishment are precluded from VAT registration, and not allowed to claim VAT credits. In a digitalised world, foreign suppliers do not need to have a fixed establishment to conduct business in China. The current registration rules are ill-suited to the rapidly digitalising economy where services can be delivered remotely at the click of a button.

Another issue is whether a foreign company's permanent establishment in China for enterprise income tax purposes would automatically confer fixed establishment status of the foreign company for VAT purposes. This is not clear under China's VAT rules, but the general practice appears that it would not. This may be justifiable given that the VAT is a completely different tax from the enterprise income tax, but it highlights tax collection challenges arising from the ever-digitalised economy in the country.

VAT collection on inbound B2C transactions has been a common problem in many jurisdictions, particularly in respect of digital services, due to the lack of incentive of final consumers to self-assess VAT on taxable services acquired from an unregistered foreign supplier. Indeed, self-assessing in cross-border B2C transactions is

Cross-Border Services 2017 Survey, 30-31, available at https://assets.kpmg/content/dam/kpmg/xx/pdf/2017/11/ess-survey-13-nov-17.pdf.

124. KPMG, *VAT and the Digital Economy in China* (March 2016), 13, available at https://assets.kpmg/content/dam/kpmg/pdf/2016/05/tnf-china-vat-digital-economy-march-2016.pdf.

125. KPMG, *supra* n. 124.

126. Zhiyuan Wang, Jagdeep Singh-Ladhar & Howard Davey, *Business Tax to Value-Added Tax Reform in China* 31(4) Pacific Acct. Rev. 602 (2019); Jianjun Li & Xuan Wang, *Does VAT Have Higher Tax Compliance than a Turnover Tax? Evidence from China* (2020) 27 Int Tax & Pub. Finance 280 (2020). Robert Staiger & Alan Sykes, *'Currency Manipulation' and World Trade*, 9(4) World Trade Rev. 583 (2010); Weixian Wei, Junling Zhang, Baomin Dong & Huiqing Wang, *Quantifying the Impacts of China's Currency Depreciation and Capital Control: A CGE Analysis* 25(14) Appl. Econ. Lett. 964 (2018).

127. *See supra* n. 86.

widely considered ineffective under either a reverse charge or a withholding mechanism.[128] To overcome the difficulty of VAT collection on inbound B2C supply of services, the OECD recommends a simplified registration and compliance mechanism to balance the need of effective tax collection with reasonable levels of compliance burdens on businesses.[129] The general feature of the recommended simplified registration system is to require foreign suppliers of B2C services to register and remit VAT to the taxing jurisdiction where the final consumer is located. Legal designs of such system entail a delicate balance between what is necessary for the effective tax collection and compliance burdens that are proportional to the revenue collected.[130] The simplified registration system has been adopted by a number of jurisdictions.[131]

The lack of an effective collection mechanism on cross-border B2C supplies of services has resulted in lost tax revenue in China.[132] If the issue is left unresolved, the revenue loss would become worse with the ever-increasing use of digital services in the country. However, as discussed above, there have been strict regulatory controls over the internet and foreign social platforms in China, which may reduce the impact of ineffective collection on taxes from inbound B2C transactions. Where final consumers in China use VPN to purchase digital services from foreign suppliers, the VAT may be collected by those jurisdictions where the private network used by the Chinese consumers is hosted. It is unclear, though, how wide and how often consumers in China use VPN to acquire services from foreign suppliers.

Some solutions to tax collection may be explored within China's regulatory controls. One solution is to require a foreign business to establish an office in China for supplying the services it wishes to sell or appoint a business agent in the country. This would make the foreign business eligible for VAT registration in China and, accordingly, its China establishment or agent can be a withholding agent for tax collection from B2C supplies. This indirect foreign registration could streamline VAT administration and collection on both B2B and B2C transactions in China, and could be compatible with similar kinds of indirect registration used in other jurisdictions such as Japan.[133] Alternatively, China may consider using financial institutions or operators of electronic marketplaces as intermediaries to account for and remit VAT on foreign supplies of digital services to final consumers in China when payment is settled through those institutions or marketplaces.

---

128. OECD, *Mechanisms for the Effective Collection of VAT/GST*, (24 October 2017) (hereinafter OECD VAT/GST Collection Mechanisms), paragraphs 50-56.
129. OECD, *VAT/GST Guidelines*, *supra* n. 13, C.3.3, at 72-77; OECD, *VAT/GST Collection Mechanisms*, *supra* n. 128, Chapter 3.
130. OECD, *VAT/GST Collection Mechanisms*, *supra* n. 128, paragraph 87.
131. Examples include Australia, the EU, Singapore and South Africa. *See* DLA Piper, *Cross-border Supplies of Intangible Services, Digital Content and Rights* (November 2019), 7-8, 12-14, 18, 80, and 81.
132. OECD estimates that about 55% of all VAT revenue is not properly accounted for in China. Bert Brys, Stephen Matthews, Richard Herd & Xiao Wang, *Tax Policy and Tax Reform in the People's Republic of China*, OECD Taxation Working Papers No. 18, OECD Publishing Paris (4 September 2013), available at http://dx.doi.org/10.1787/5k40l4dlmnzw-en.
133. *See* National Tax Agency (Japan), *Revision of Consumption Taxation on Cross-Border Supplies of Services*, May 2015 (Revised December 2016); *see also* Yuki Nishida, *Japan Consumption Tax on Cross-Border Supplies of Services* 26(4) Int'l VAT Monitor (2015).

Lastly, although many jurisdictions do not apply VAT to consumer-to-consumer (C2C) transactions, China does. In a cross-border context, tax collection on such transactions can be extremely challenging with high administrative and compliance costs. China may just forgo taxes on C2C supplies, considering individual trader-consumers may, after all, have less frequent, low value transactions.

§20.05 CONCLUSION

Cross-border trade in services has been growing rapidly in the world economy. The destination principle, a widely accepted principle under a VAT/GST to achieve international trade neutrality, has been relatively effectively applied to international trade in goods. However, it faces challenges in taxation of cross-border supply of services, in particular digital services. The difficulties of identifying the place of taxation and of tax collection, the two key aspects of implementing the destination principle, have led the OECD and some jurisdictions to conceive and develop new VAT rules so as to keep the implementation compatible with a changing economic environment. In China's case, while the most recent reform on VAT has aligned the rules on cross-border transactions in services more closely to the destination principle, the design of the rules has been influenced by historical practices and has not directly addressed the two key issues regarding place of taxation and tax collection. A notable feature of China's place of taxation rules on cross-border trade in services is to enumerate taxable supply of services in detail in order to determine whether the supply is consumed completely outside China. This is as a response to the ambiguous requirement of the main rule on the place of taxation. International double taxation or double non-taxation may be unavoidable with such approach. The use of a withholding mechanism to collect VAT has created accounting and invoicing issues in cross-border B2B supplies and been ineffective in B2C supplies into the country. The various design features of China's rules suggest that the destination principle is not completely enforced.

The Chinese experience shows that the destination principle ought to be developed in correlation with changes in the global economy and business models. Historical practices could be considered in designing and developing rules, but they should not impede the design of rules, particularly the place of taxation rules and collection mechanisms, in a logical, clear, and comprehensive manner with consideration of administrative practicality and compliance costs. International coordination and cooperation will be needed to help avoid unintended double taxation or double non-taxation that is undesirable in a deeply connected and increasingly digitalised global economy.

CHAPTER 21

VAT in Colombia: The Need for a Brand-New Architecture?

Catalina Hoyos-Jiménez

§21.01 INTRODUCTION

The value added tax (VAT) is an important tax from several perspectives. It is a strong source of public revenue for states; it has been designed—at least in theory—to avoid and control tax evasion;[1] it provides the state with important information about the economic activities and the situation of taxpayers; and, if the tax meets international standards, it must serve to ease revenue collection while remaining economically neutral, i.e., the tax should not distort the competitive conditions between products and services. Notwithstanding these international standards, it has been noted that the Colombian VAT has structural design flaws inconsistent with true VAT philosophy, which create distortions negatively affecting the economy, the neutrality toward competition, and revenue collection.

Over the last few years, proposals by the government and economic studies by the Directorate of National Taxes and Customs (DIAN, for the Spanish initials)[2] have

1. Given that it has been structured as a multiphase tax levied on value added, this tax, despite that it is really levied on consumption, must be collected through the entire goods and services production cycles. This design allows tax evasion to be easily detectable, because all the agents that intervene in the entire chain transmit to and receive permanent information from those with whom they interact. Obviously, this information is reported to the State on tax returns or by other formal means.
2. *See* Ministry of Finance, *Marco Fiscal de Mediano Plazo 2020, Colombia* (The Median Term Fiscal Framework in 2020, Colombia). In the same sense, Directorate of National Taxes and Customs, DIAN *Gasto tributario en el impuesto sobre la renta, el impuesto al valor agregado (IVA) y otros impuestos nacionales- año gravable 2019 (Cifras preliminares)* (Tax Expenditure in Income Taxes, Value Added Taxes (VAT) and Other National Taxes—Taxable Year 2019 (Preliminary Figures)), Coordination of Economic Studies, Office of the Subdirector of Management Operating Analysis, Office of the Dir. of Organizational Management; Directorate of National Taxes and

raised expectations that tax reforms are immanent to bring Colombian VAT in line with the highest international standards, particularly those ensuring strict neutrality. Neutrality is a crucial element of VAT, because the tax influences the day-to-day decisions of every economic agent. Moreover, any failures in the design may hinder commercial exchange, give foreign products a competitive advantage in the local market, or raise the cost of doing business for one sector relative to other economic sectors. Regulatory arbitration is undesirable in taxation, especially when taxation is applied to transactions in competitive markets.

§21.02 HISTORY OF VAT IN COLOMBIA

Colombia was one of the very first countries concerned about developing and structuring an indirect VAT.[3] Legislative Decree 3288 of 1963 introduced the sales tax into Colombian legislation. This decree was issued by the President of the Republic based on special powers granted by Law 21 of 1963.

Initially, the tax was conceived as a single stage tax for the manufacturing industry. The standard tax rate was 3%, although there were other differential rates of 5%, 8% and 10%.[4] To avoid tax cascading, the law allowed taxpayers to deduct—from the sales price—the cost of raw materials on which the tax had been paid for any reason (the so-called base-against-base method). Exports were not taxable if the exporter was the last producer or if the exporter was a merchant that had bought the product from the last producer.

Later on, by Regulation 377 of 1965, the *cost-deduction* or *base-against-base* method was replaced by the *tax credit (or tax offset)* or so-called *tax-from-tax* method. In this way, the tax was being shaped as the VAT that we know today.

Later on, Legislative Decree 1595 of 1966 increased the number of taxable events. The tax remained a single stage tax, but where it initially applied only to the manufacturer stage, it could now, alternatively, be levied at another stage in the supply chain. The law allowed taxpayers to claim credits for the taxes paid for the acquisition of raw materials that were related to the finished product. The standard 3% rate was maintained, and the differential rates were increased to 8% and 15%.

In 1971 (Legislative Decree 435), the VAT on services was introduced. However, this was a selective tax targeting only intermediate production services. The rates changed and went up to 4%, 10%, 15% and 25%, replacing the old rates of 3%, 8%, 10% and 15% respectively.

Customs, DIAN, *Elementos para la discusión de una reforma del IVA en Colombia* (Elements for the discussion of a VAT reform in Colombia), Working Paper by Javier Avila and Angela Cruz, Office of the Subdirector of Operating Analysis Management (January 2012).

3. Parthasarathi Shome, Arnold Harberger, and Pedro Kondratiuk, *El impuesto al valor agregado (IVA): estructura del impuesto y eficiencia y mecanismos de la recaudación* (The Value Added Tax (VAT): Structure of the Tax, Efficiency, and Collection Mechanisms) (Fondo Monetario Internacional, Departamento de Finanzas Públicas, 1991), 9.
4. Mauricio Plazas Vega, *El impuesto sobre el valor agregado* (*The Value Added Tax*), 2nd ed., Bogotá (Temis, 1998), 107.

In 1974, tax reform was enacted that changed the structure of the sales-tax, based upon a study made by the Musgrave Commission. Although the tax was maintained as an initial-phase, multiple-phase tax, new taxable events were created, and the taxable base was broadened. The tax rates for taxable goods were set at 15% (the standard rate), 4%, 6%, 10% and 35%; and the tax rates for services were set at 15% and 6%.

Likewise, VAT *zero-rated* rules were extended, new rules were enacted creating VAT *exempt events* (events not subject to the tax), the number of VAT collection agents was increased, and the right to secure VAT refunds was established for producers of zero-rated products, exporters and merchants who exported and did not qualify as VAT collection agents.[5] Likewise, the law designed technical control methods and introduced a series of procedural and penalty related rules.

But it was not until 1983 that the Colombian VAT obtained its current shape and features. Legislative Decree 3541 of 1983 extended the tax to include the retail sector, transforming it into a true multistage VAT. Likewise, the 1983 reform rationalized the tax rates to a certain extent, by consolidating a standard 10% tax rate, including additional service items in the taxable base and improving management and collection of the tax. It did the latter by simplifying the tax return mechanism and by consolidating the related tax information with the income tax return.

Subsequent reforms sought to increase VAT collections and to grant benefits to certain sectors, which impaired substantially the underlying philosophy and the structure of the tax. Law 6 of 1992[6] increased the general VAT rate to 14%, kept other differential rates, established the general tax for services (except for imported services, which were taxable only where specifically determined by the law), and created tax credits for the VAT paid upon the acquisition or importation of capital assets, which were to be used as effective income tax credits.

Law 223 of 1995 increased the rate from 14% to 16%, created changes in the taxable base of the tax and established withholding tax collections of the sales-tax at the rate of 50%. This added a new distortion factor to the already the VAT complex structure.[7] This withholding tax is maintained today, at differential rates that cannot exceed 50% of the tax.[8]

Law 383 of 1997 created criminal penalties for those who failed to deposit any VAT collected with the banks, as payable to the government. Subsequent laws extended these penalties to those who failed to report the tax.[9] Law 488 of 1998 reduced the list of VAT exempt goods and reduced the general rate to 15%, while eliminating, at the same time, the tax credit for VAT paid on the acquisition of capital assets. As a novelty, it created the rule of the "implicit VAT," which was payable by those importers

5. Plazas Vega, *supra* n. 4, 145.
6. In point of tax collection, this reform was actually poor.
7. At that time, the need to serve public expenditure was particularly acute, given the ambitious spending plan created by the government of Pres. Ernesto Samper, the so-called Social Jump.
8. Article 437-1 of the Tax Code.
9. Law 1819 of 2016.

who imported VAT exempt property in cases where domestic supply was sufficient to cover domestic demand.[10]

The tax reforms of the first decade of the 21st century stand out for the attempt to reduce the number of differential rates, increase the taxable base and increase VAT collections.

Law 633 of 2000 established the 16% rate as the general rate once again and increased the withholding collection rate to 75% of the tax accruing on transactions carried out with withholding tax collection agents.

Law 788 of 2002[11] established new differential rates of 7%, 10%, 20% and 2%; it reduced the list of VAT-exempt goods; it changed the status of certain zero-rated property to VAT-exempt property status; it abolished the implicit VAT for imports of VAT exempt goods; and, in a partial and transitory way only, it made the tax a semi-excise-tax type of tax by establishing a VAT credit for industrial machinery imports. This reform attempted to levy a 2% VAT on the entire products of the so-called general household basket, but the relevant rules were declared unconstitutional by the Constitutional Court.[12] It also taxed mobile telephone services at 20%, under the consideration that mobile telephone services qualified as "luxurious" goods.[13]

Law 863 of 2003 set new rates of 3% and 5% and changed the status of certain goods from exempt to taxable. Law 1111 of 2006 changed the applicable tax rate of certain items of property from reduced rated to standard rate.

The second decade of the 21st century has been the most ambitious in terms of VAT reforms. Law 1607 of 2012 repealed almost all the differential rates to maintain just 3, the 0%, the 5% and the 16% rates; it designed mechanisms for collection agents to be able to claim an effective VAT credit where the final taxable good is taxed at rates that are below the general VAT rate that applies to intermediate goods and services; and it reduced the VAT withholding tax collection rate. In the same manner, this reform somehow developed the idea once again (an idea which still has to consolidate) that Colombian VAT laws must allow a tax credit for VAT paid on the acquisition of capital assets. Historically, the rule of Colombian VAT laws has been precisely the opposite.[14]

---

10. In years 1997 and 1998, the country underwent one of its most serious economic crises. The state-owned banking system carried the biggest blow, with a number of financial institutions going bankrupt. This required the government to assume a greater share of public debt.
11. In addition to covering (public) deficit needs, this reform was driven by the so-called democratic-security plan established by President Alvaro Uribe. This is why the government sought to increase collection of public revenue to pay for the expenses of the country's civil war.
12. Constitutional Court of Colombia, Case C-776 of 2003. The Court rejected the inclusion of life necessities into the tax base as a violation of the right to equality and the principles of progressiveness and equity laid down in Articles 13, 95-99 and 363 of the Constitution, *see* Jose M. Castro Arango, *Avances Jurisprudenciales Con La Sentencia C-776 De 2003 (Mínimo Vital Y Justicia Material Del Gasto)* (Advances in Jurisprudence C-776, 2003 (Vital Minimum and Spending Justice)) (2004). Revista de Derecho Fiscal (Universidad Externado de Colombia), No. 2, 2004, available at SSRN: https://ssrn.com/abstract=1522085.
13. Today, these services are taxed at the general rate and are in addition to that subject to excise taxes.
14. The current Article 491 of the Tax Code establishes the rule that no credits are allowed for the VAT paid on the acquisition of fixed assets.

Law 1739 of 2014 increased the general VAT rate from 16% to 19%, and Law 1819 of 2016 extended the scope of the VAT, as a general rule, to all services imports, introduced the reverse charge rule for services provided from abroad, and created withholding tax collection obligations for debit and credit card companies acting as intermediaries in transactions related to certain digital services.

In the 2018 tax reform, the government attempted to "purify" the Colombian VAT, i.e., align the tax better with the benchmark VAT, by proposing that:

(1) VAT would apply generally to all domestically produced and imported goods and services;
(2) the scope of the zero-rate would be narrowed and only apply to exports; and
(3) the principle of a full VAT credit for the acquisition of capital assets was made effective as a rule of law.

Notwithstanding their theoretical correctness, these proposals did not fly in political circles. As a result, the final Law 1943 of 2018 was confined to reducing the list of VAT exempt goods and services, including clearer rules for the provision of digital services, and including a timid rule that provides a tax credit for VAT paid on the acquisition of capital assets.

Finally, Law 2010 of 2019 revived the rules that bar tax credits for VAT paid on the acquisition of capital assets—allowing the credit only in exceptional cases—, and established mechanisms to transfer certain VAT collection percentage to the most vulnerable population so as to make the tax more equitable.[15]

In short, after almost 60 years' worth of tax reforms, we have an all-stage VAT designed to tax only the added value of a business by allowing taxable vendors to offset the tax paid on procurement against the VAT collected on sales, effectively removing the tax burden from all stages of the production and distribution chain prior to the retail stage. The tax is destination-based by taxing imports and relieving exports from the tax through the application of the zero rate.

However, in analysis, the Colombian VAT system remains highly distortive. It does not fully qualify as a general tax on goods and services due—as a result of lobbying—to the almost endless list of nontaxable and zero-rated events. Moreover, the Colombian VAT does not in all cases allow a tax credit for the VAT paid on the acquisition of capital assets; and it establishes elements that make the system more complex, as is the case of withholding tax collections. Lastly, our regulation is one that has been highly influenced by OECD VAT guidelines;[16] in consequence, efforts have

15. There is a program in Colombia under which a portion of VAT collections is paid out to low-income families. They get a monthly transfer of 2 UVTs (about 20 USD). This amount was defined according to household surveys and is channeled through a number of spending programs such as the so-called *Familias en Acción* ("Families in action"), *Protección social al adulto mayor* ("Social protection for the elderly") and *Jóvenes en acción* ("The young in action"). In practice, all these people get their money through the financial system.

16. OECD, *International VAT/GST Guidelines* (2017); OECD, *The Role of Digital Platforms in the Collection of VAT/GST on Online Sales* (2019), available at www.oecd.org/tax/consumption/the-role-of-digital-platforms-in-the-collection-of-vat-gst-on-online-sales.pdf.

been made to implement mechanisms to ensure tax collection on services imports, particularly in B2C digital transactions.

§21.03 STRUCTURE OF THE VAT AND VAT RATES

In Colombia, the VAT is a tax on the supply of goods and services throughout all stages of their economic cycles, effectively taxing the value added of businesses through the input-VAT credit system.

The aim is to tax the final consumption of goods and services. Accordingly, the regulations provide for rules that impose the tax in the destination country, meaning that imports of goods and services are taxed while exports are not. In the same manner, the legislation allows that the cost of the tax is ultimately passed on to the end consumer, but only in an economic sense, given that the end consumer has no direct tax liability whatsoever towards the State.

However, the Colombian VAT is not a "pure" VAT, because the law does not allow a credit for the VAT paid on the acquisition or import of capital assets,[17] except in the following 2 cases: the acquisition of assets that relate to offshore exploration for hydrocarbons[18] and the acquisition, construction, or imports of real productive fixed assets. In the latter case, the VAT credit must be claimed as an income tax credit for income tax purposes.[19]

The taxable events of VAT in Colombia are 4: sales[20] of personal and real property,[21] sales or assignments of intangible property related to industrial property, the provision of services within national territory or from abroad, and imports of tangible personal property. The circulation, operation, or sales of gambling and similar games, except for those offered online, are also taxable events.[22] VAT does not apply to sales of fixed assets, except for a few cases.[23]

The following are the VAT collection agents: for the sale of goods, all merchants, regardless of the production and distribution stage in which they operate, or those who, without being merchants, habitually carry out acts that are similar to those of merchants; for services, those who provide the services; and in relation to imports, the importer of record.[24] However, natural persons who meet the qualifying conditions for small trader, particularly the requirement that annual sales remain below a certain

17. Article 491 of the Tax Code.
18. Article 485-2.
19. Article 258-1.
20. The following qualify as sales: any acts entailing the transfer of ownership for a consideration or gratuitously; the withdrawal of taxable goods made by the VAT collection agent to use them as inventory or fixed assets; the incorporation of personal property into real property or into exempt services, and the transformation of taxable goods into exempt goods, where the goods have been made by the party that makes the incorporation of transformation.
21. Even though under Article 424-12 of the Tax Code, as amended by Law 2010 of 2019, sales of real property are VAT exempt.
22. Article 420 of the Tax Code.
23. Article 420, Subparagraph 1.
24. Article 437 of the Tax Code.

monetary threshold of currently Columbian Peso (COP) 127,078,000[25] (USD 36,000 approximately) are not required to collect the VAT.[26]

The taxable base of the VAT depends on the type of transaction made. As a general rule, for sales of goods and services the taxable base is the total transaction value, with the understanding that sales cannot be invoiced at a price below the market value. For imports, the taxable base is the Customs value plus the duties themselves. There are special rules to determine the taxable base for used vehicles and aircraft, international airfares, national liquors, oil and gas derivatives, etc. Likewise, by way of exception, there are minimum presumptive taxable bases.[27]

Ever since the tax was introduced (by Decree 3288 of 1963), it has stood out as a tax with a general rate, several differential rates, depending on policies established by on-going tax reform measures, and zero-rated and exempt events. The general VAT rate is 19% today, although certain goods and services are taxed at the rates of 5% and 0%.

Despite the numerous reforms that have been made in an attempt to broaden the base on which VAT is applied, there remain ample rules that facilitate certain sectors, in particular zero-rated events and tax-exempt events.

Zero rates create perfect tax exoneration, or full tax relief, because tax collection agents remain entitled to input-tax credits in relation to the zero-rated output supply. The following are treated as zero-rated goods or events in Colombia: exported personal property; services that are exported under certain conditions; tourist services provided to foreign residents that are used in Colombia; goods that are sold to or in a free trade zone, under certain conditions; goods that are sold to international sales company to be exported; and other goods, as certain notebooks and printed material, carburetion alcohol to be mixed with gasoline for motor vehicles, vegetal or animal biofuel to be used in nationally produced diesel motors and to be used in diesel fuel mixtures, beef, eggs, fresh cheese, milk, fish, shrimp, certain kinds of rice, certain medications, certain vitamins, antibiotics, etc.

To the contrary, tax exemptions lead to imperfect exoneration. Indeed, the supplier of the exempt supply does not have to collect VAT on these exempt outputs but is also denied the right to deduct input-VAT related to these exempt outputs. Thus, these taxes end up being an additional production or sales cost.

In many cases, exemptions lead to a competitive advantage for imported goods and services, because they will be fully relieved from VAT in the country of origin and remain untaxed upon importation, while domestically produced goods and services carry the cost of the non-deductible input-VAT.

VAT exemptions cover a large portion of basic consumer articles, including the majority of foods, anti-conception devices for women, low-cost personal computers, low-cost bicycles and electrical motorbikes, certain types of gasoline, electric power, certain medical use articles, certain insurance policies, certain education related goods and services, scientific and technological research, certain types of transportation

25. This is the amount for 2021.
26. Article 437 of the Tax Code.
27. Articles 447 et seq. of the Tax Code.

services, interests and financial costs of credit transactions, residential utilities, tickets to cultural, sports and entertainment events and shows, funeral services, the acquisition of software licenses for the commercial development of digital contents, the provision of webpages, hosting services, cloud computing, certain services for the adaptation of land and farming and fishery production and sales, hotel and tourism services provided in certain areas of the country, foreign exchange purchase and sales transactions, and transactions on/with financial derivatives, commissions for the utilization of debit and credit cards, certain advertising services in newspapers and small, low-income broadcasting stations, etc.[28]

The list of VAT-exempt goods and services in Colombian legislation is quite long and exceeds any definition of popular consumption items. Given that the greater share of the total VAT burden, evidently, is assumed by a small number of economic sectors, exemptions and other preferential VAT treatments have been strongly criticized.[29]

Academic studies have been consistent in their conclusion that more than half of all VAT revenue is collected by just a few sectors of the economy. Estimates for 2019 suggest that preferential VAT treatments have caused a revenue gap of COP 74.9 trillion, representing 7.1 % of GDP. Of this amount, 61.2 trillion can be allocated to VAT exemptions, 10.1 trillion to zero rating, and 3.4 trillion to the application of the reduced 5 % rate.[30]

By way of comparison, in terms of tax expenditures, the preferential VAT treatments represented 5.3 % of GDP in 2011 and reached 7.1 % in 2019. Moreover, estimates by the International Monetary Fund put VAT evasion in Colombia in the vicinity of 40 % of annual VAT collections.[31] As a matter of fact, a general VAT levied at a single flat rate of 8.9 % on all goods and services with no exceptions or exemptions would generate the same revenue as the VAT system in place today with a standard rate of 19 %, multiple reduced rates, exemptions, and its high evasion rate.

In short, the preferential treatment imbedded in Colombian VAT is not based on structural policy but, instead, on short-term collection needs. A wide range of studies corroborate that the fiscal and administrative cost associated with the preferential VAT treatment by far exceeds the expected benefits of such treatment. Moreover, these studies show that most of the preferential treatment is the result of lobbying efforts by influential advocacy groups, and that the design of Colombian VAT is seriously flawed.

Finally, it is worth noting that the actual responsibility for tax collections falls on only a small group of businesses due to the selective withholding obligations of collection agents, who must withhold up to 50 % of the tax accrued on the transactions in which they participate. This situation constitutes another structural problem of the

28. Articles 424 and 476 of the Tax Code.
29. And this is without taking into account the VAT that is shifted forward by building it into the sales price.
30. Ministry of Finance (2020), *supra* n. 2. In the same sense, DIAN (2019), *supra* n. 2.
31. Mauricio López Bejarano, *La evasión equivale al 30% del total de lo que se recauda de impuestos al año* (Tax evasion amounts to 30 % of the total amount of tax collections in a year). (This 30 % figure refers to total tax evasion of all taxes in Colombia, not to VAT only.) Daily La República (November 19, 2019), available at: https://www.larepublica.co/economia/la-evasion-equivale-a-30-del-total-de-lo-que-se-recauda-de-impuestos-al-ano-2945888.

VAT in Colombia. The withholding rate is based on the unrealistic assumption that businesses enjoy fixed profit margins. As a result of the withholding obligation, many businesses face negative cash flows, increasing the cost of doing business (excess VAT withholding may be reimbursed or offset, but this entails cumbersome procedures and paperwork).[32]

By way of conclusion, VAT is not a neutral tax in Colombia for a variety of reasons: the VAT taxes investments; it has multiple distortions due to the many preferential treatments and the requisite withholding; it is used as a protectionist measure; and, in certain cases, it harms Colombian national industry.

§21.04 RULES FOR EXPORTED SERVICES

Generally, countries apply the destination principle, i.e., goods and services are taxed in the country where they are used or consumed. External neutrality requires border tax adjustments to create fair competition between domestically produced goods and services and imports. Neutrality requires the tax levied on importation to be equivalent to the tax imposed on similar domestic products, and the relief provided to exports in the form of input-VAT credits may not exceed the actual domestic tax. This is not fully realized in Colombia because the law allows for the exempt treatment of certain imports and applies a "selective" zero rate to exported services.

Thus, the law creates double tax exoneration because the exempt imports were likely treated as zero-rated exports in the country of origin. Likewise, the law creates double taxation on exports that are denied the zero rate while being taxed upon importation in the country of destination. These practices can have a serious distortive effect on international trade.

Under Article 481(c) of the Tax Code, the application of the zero rate is limited to those exported services that are used abroad exclusively for companies or persons without any businesses or activities in Colombia (in accordance with the requirements set by regulation).

This condition of exclusive use abroad is perpendicular to the current reality of the trade in intangible property and the supply of e-commerce services. For example, if a Colombian entity would sell an intangible to Microsoft which, in turn, would incorporate the intangible into a service supplied globally, the Colombian entity would be barred from applying the zero rate because the Microsoft service would also be available to customers in Colombia.

To address this issue, the subparagraph of Article 481 provides for two exceptions to the rule that the services must be used abroad exclusively: the services that relate to film and TV production and software development, which, after being exported, are disseminated from abroad by the service beneficiary and can be accessed from Colombia by any technological means. This regulation is an answer—albeit timid—to the problem just mentioned above.

---

32. The VAT withholding rate for services provided from abroad in B2B transactions, scrap metal sales and tobacco sales is 100% of the tax.

§21.05 IMPORTED SERVICES AND DIGITAL ECONOMY

Colombia's last three tax reforms (Law 1819 of 2016, Law 1943 of 2018, and Law 2010 of 2019) introduced important changes in the treatment of imported services. As noted above, most relevant was the unrestricted application of the destination principle to services. As a result, all services regardless of whether they are provided "within the territory" or "from abroad" are taxable, obviously except for those that have been expressly exonerated (Article 420(c) of the Tax Code).

According to Professor Plazas-Vega,[33] and confirmed by DIAN policy,[34] this rule is based on the assumption that these services, although originating and being supplied from abroad, are earmarked for Colombia and serve to benefit Colombian users.

In this way, any digital service provided from abroad is subject to VAT—except for those exonerated by law.

[A] VAT Collection Agents in the Provision of Services from Abroad

[1] B2C Transactions

Based on OECD guidelines,[35] paragraph 2 of Article 437 of the Tax Code provides that DIAN will establish (by resolution) the procedure by which those who provide services from abroad will comply with their obligations as VAT collection agents. Among others, these obligations include the obligation to file a VAT return and pay the tax.

DIAN Resolution 051 of October 19, 2018 established a simplified procedure for persons providing services from abroad to comply with their substantive and formal VAT obligations, which include that they must register in the national unified tax register (RUT for the Spanish initials). The regulations clarify that they are to apply where the local service beneficiary is not required to withhold the tax as further explained in §21.5[A][3] below. This procedure is, therefore, typically used in case of Business to Customer (B2C) transactions.

Besides, the new text of Article 437 establishes that any [VAT] returns that these persons file will be made as a form that allows the filer to translate the US dollar denominated obligation into COP at the market representative rate (TRM for the Spanish initials) of the date of the return and payment. The rule adds that any returns that are filed with no payment being made will be ineffective—without an administrative act that declares such ineffectiveness being required.

This means that foreign service providers are forced to deal with DIAN technology, which is not quite state-of-the-art, and, as a result, they encounter serious challenges in their efforts to comply with their obligations effectively. Indeed, several foreign platforms have registered and are paying VAT in Colombia but, not unexpected

33. Mauricio Plazas Vega, *El impuesto sobre el valor agregado* (*The Value Added Tax*), 3rd edn (Temis, 2015).
34. Directorate of National Taxes and Customs. Ruling 64 of February 6, 2018.
35. *Supra* n. 16.

given the observations presented here, many and sizeable tax controversies have arisen.

In any case, it is worth noting that electronic or digital service providers may voluntarily elect to apply the VAT withholding collection mechanism provided for in Article 437-2(8) of the Tax Code. This mechanism requires that the certain financial intermediaries actually collect the withholding tax as explained below in §21.05[A][2].

[2] Payment Intermediaries

The following are also designated as alternative VAT collection agents: institutions that issue credit and debit cards, persons selling prepayment cards, persons collecting cash for the benefit of third parties and any other person designated by DIAN as intermediaries for the making of payments in respect of certain transactions. The use of these intermediaries as VAT collection agents is optional and at the discretion of the foreign digital service supplier. Their obligation to withhold VAT from payments made through their mediation kicks in when the service provider elects to make use of this legal provision.

Withholding by financial intermediaries as an alternative collection mechanism applies only to designated electronic or digital services, which are the following:

(1) audiovisual services such as music, videos, films, and games;
(2) services provided through digital platforms;
(3) the provision of online advertising;
(4) remote and online teaching or training;
(5) rights to use or exploit intangible property; and
(6) any other electronic or digital services earmarked for Colombian users.

DIAN must issue a resolution designating the service providers to which this rule of the law will apply. In any case, this mechanism applies only to those service providers that are exclusively devoted to providing one or more of the aforementioned activities—and provided that they have not elected to file VAT bimonthly returns and the amount invoiced, collected, and demanded corresponds to the statutory VAT base for the electronic or digital services that they provide.

[3] Persons Acquiring the Services in Colombia (B2B Transactions)

Article 437-2 contains what is universally referred to as the reverse charge rule for cross-border business-to-business (B2B) transactions. Instead of the foreign supplier, the domestic recipient of the service is liable for reporting the tax, if the recipient is registered in Colombia for VAT purposes. In that case, this recipient must collect 100% of the tax, i.e., include the VAT due on the service in his VAT return as output-VAT and, to the extent of his eligibility, claim the same as an input-VAT credit.

§21.06 PROSPECTS FOR VAT REFORM IN COLOMBIA: VAT AND THE DILEMMA OF THE POLITICALLY CORRECT

The conventional position follows the tenet that VAT is a regressive tax on the premise that lower income groups pay a relatively greater share of their own income to the tax (*see* on that topic Chapter 4.03[B] of this volume). It has also been argued that VAT may become less regressive and perhaps even progressive if goods and services predominantly used or consumed by low-income earners were excluded from the tax or subject to a reduced tax rate.

However, it is difficult to apply these premises in actual practice. In the first place, because, as we know through household surveys, low-income earners usually manage to make purchases in VAT-less markets, i.e., either informal markets or markets where the sellers do not charge VAT as their total monthly sales remain under the threshold for the small trader exemption, currently set at about USD 3,000.

And in the second place, because eliminating or reducing the tax on goods and services primarily consumed by low-income earners will benefit the well-to-do at least as much but likely more since they generally have higher consumption levels, including for necessities.

Over the last 3 years, Colombia has engaged in a heated debate on this point. The current Minister of Finance is a proponent of generalizing the application of the standard rate, precisely because household surveys show that the current system with reduced rates and exemptions does not effectively counter VAT's regressivity and benefits the richer instead.[36] In the Minister's view, instead of using preferential tax treatment, it will be more effective to support lower income groups through expenditure, i.e., by strengthening mechanisms already in place to use revenue for direct income support to the most vulnerable families.

In my opinion, broadening the application of the standard rate would serve to ensure that higher income groups, who also have a higher consumption ratio, pay more tax in real terms. For as long as the legislation contains income thresholds below which people are exempt from paying tax, the dilemma of the poor ends up being a less important discussion. Regardless the obvious need, it has been very difficult to push tax reform with these characteristics successfully through Congress. The last tax reform bills—in 2018 and 2019—were set to do that, but there was no political consensus. It is expected that a new tax reform will be passed in 2021—a reform that will inherit the entire problems that the global COVID-19 crisis has created for all of us. Actually, we anticipate that the road toward a more benchmark VAT in Colombia will still be a steep, tough road to traverse.

It is incredible that this very reasonable proposal—enacting a single rate, generally applicable, thus, broad-based VAT that is also levied on all imports, zero-rates exports, and provides for full input-VAT credit on the acquisition of capital

36. The current Director of DIAN (José Andrés Romero) and the President of the Colombian Stock Exchange (Juan Pablo Córdoba) support the Minister of Finance (Alberto Carrasquilla). Other members of the current government staff and of Congress as well as certain universities (such as the Universidad Nacional of Colombia) have raised their concerns and voiced their opposition.

assets—is met with astonishment, indignation, and disapproval. Opponents resort to simple rhetoric, claiming that this proposal is unjust, inequitable, and thoughtless—a proposal that includes the goods of the so-called basic basket of every household—, and so the defense of claiming justice for "the neediest" ends up being the most effective weapon to counteract such initiative.

This debate, however, lacks a good deal of depth and presentation of different perspectives. More studies are needed, especially those of an empirical nature that go beyond theoretical presuppositions, and analyze actual numbers, because it seems that VAT becomes less regressive only where it is applied in a consistent and generalized manner on all products and services. The reason for this is quite obvious: where essential or basic household basket products are exonerated, it is the rich who enjoy the greatest share of the benefit. The financially better-off not only consume more but also frequent upscale, more expensive restaurants throw away food more often, or purchase more than they can actually consume. Moreover, the composition of the Colombian VAT exempt, basic household basket is not based on an analysis of the actual consumption patterns of lower income groups, but the result of active lobbying and political pressure by certain special interest groups. The result is a category of exempt products that constitutes an inconsistent amalgamate. For example, in Colombia, sales of shrimp—a food product that can only be found in the diet of the well-to-do—carries full VAT exemption as it is classified as a VAT zero rated good.

The poorest, and even part of the middle-class in Colombia, do not buy in the big supermarkets nor at sophisticated stores. Generally, they make their purchases instead at small markets, or at artisans' markets, or they buy from small merchants. Generally, these sellers qualify for the small trader exemption and do not charge VAT, or they are part of the informal economy. Either way, lower income groups do not incur much VAT on the basic necessities that they purchase, and that would not change if these products would become subject to the standard VAT rate. Therefore, the introduction of a single rate VAT would, indeed, raise the tax rate applicable to basic food and other necessities, but that would not affect lower income groups much. On the contrary, a single rate VAT would remove from the well-to-do an accumulation of unjustifiable privileges.

Colombia has been unsuccessful in taxing the incomes and fortunes of its wealthiest citizens in a meaningful way because it has been unable to track their origin. Especially, Colombia has failed to tax the wealthy at the point when their fortune can be captured and monitored, which is precisely upon consumption. Hence, Colombia may be missing a unique opportunity to collect taxes where this would potentially improve equity—without the enormous wear and tear of a system that for a variety of reasons has serious problems of justice and design.

CHAPTER 22

India: The Challenges of Implementing VAT in a Federal State

Sacchidananda Mukherjee

§22.01 INTRODUCTION

India's quest for a transition to a comprehensive Value Added Tax (VAT) system, encompassing Union as well as State taxes on goods and services, leads scholars to explore alternative designs of VAT. Given the constitutional assignments of taxation power to the Union and States, designing a comprehensive VAT for India was a challenge. Among the alternative designs, a dual VAT system often suggested for India.[1] After three decades of protracted deliberations, India has embraced Goods and Services Tax (GST) system on July 1, 2017. The concept of GST evolved over time in India and successive tax reform committees played an important role in shaping Indian indirect tax system which finally culminated in the introduction of GST. Designing a destination based dual VAT system for federal country like India was a challenge and, in this perspective, Indian GST is unique. In a federal system harmonization of tax system vis-à-vis fiscal autonomy is always contested, given the constitutional assignments of responsibilities of expenditures between the federal and provincial governments. Difficulty in reaching consensus for a dual VAT system with concurrent taxation powers between the Union and State governments has delayed the India's journey to embrace VAT system.

The constitutional assignment of taxation powers in India included a number of stand-alone taxes on goods and services in addition to a few relatively more broad-based taxes, none of which were comprehensive in covering both goods and services. Further, this assignment divided the powers between the Union (federal/Centre)

1. Robin Burgess et al., *Value-Added Tax Options for India* 2(1) Int'l Tax & Pub. Fin. 109 (1995); Amaresh Bagchi, *Towards GST: Choices and Trade-Offs* 41(14) Econ. & Pol. Weekly 1314 (2006).

government and the State (provincial) governments, thereby requiring a considerable degree of cooperation and coordination among governments in order to initiate and establish a new indirect tax regime which could address some of the concerns emanating from the old regime. Given the fiscal autonomy enjoyed by the sub-national governments, complexities involved in bringing consensus among sub-national governments, the evolution of Indian GST provides an interesting example of reforms in indirect taxes for scholars interested in public finance, especially in the case of federal countries. Designing a destination-based tax system for inter-state (or inter-provincial) trade with seamless flow of input tax credit (ITC) across tax jurisdictions was a major challenge for a federal country like India, where a State enjoys constitutional rights to tax consumption within the politico-administrative boundary of the State and tax administration is an integrated part of the State government. In this context, the present chapter critically evaluate India's quest for a suitable indirect tax framework encompassing goods as well as services. This chapter will focus more general on the evolution of the Indian VAT system over last 3 decades, i.e., evaluating its unique features, its strengths and weaknesses in general, and sharing lessons to be learned from the Indian experience.

The Indian Constitution assigns taxation powers according to the principle of separation. The seventh schedule of the Constitution assigns tax powers between the Centre and States. The Centre has the power to levy excise duties on tobacco and other manufactured products produced in India (excluding alcoholic beverages for human consumption, opium, hump, and other narcotics) under Entry 84 of the Union list. Similarly, States have power to levy taxes on the sale and purchase of only goods (other than newspapers) under Entry 54 of the State list. In addition, States have power to tax alcoholic beverages, opium, Indian hump and other narcotics (Entry 51 of the State List). However, the evolution of taxes on goods and services in India is not restricted to only the entries listed above; there are several other entries either from the Union list or State list which empower the respective governments to levy taxes on goods and services. The Union government has power to levy taxes on entries listed in the Union list, e.g., taxes on inter-state trade and commerce (Entry 42), duties of customs including export duties (Entry 83), taxes on the consignments of goods (Entry 92B) and taxes on services (Entry 92C). State governments have power to levy taxes on entries listed in the State list, e.g., taxes on the entry of goods into a local area for consumption, use or sale therein (Entry 52), taxes on the consumption or sale of electricity (Entry 53), Taxes on advertisements other than advertisements published in the newspapers (Entry 55), taxes on goods and passengers carried by road or on inland waterways (Entry 56), taxes on luxuries, including taxes on entertainments, amusements, betting and gambling (Entry 62). The Constitution (One Hundred and First Amendment) Act, 2016 facilitates emergence of a harmonized tax base for GST on which the Union and States levy respective GSTs (Central GST or CGST and State GST or SGST) concurrently.

By introduction of GST in India, two VAT systems (Central VAT and State VAT) are integrated into one with integration of the tax bases of the Union and State governments. The Union taxes on goods and services which are subsumed into GST are Central Excise Duty (CenVAT), Additional Excise Duty (AED), Excise Duty levied under the Medicinal and Toilet Preparations (Excise Duties) Act, 1955, Services Tax, Additional Customs Duty commonly known as CVD, Special Additional Duty of Customs, and Central surcharges and cesses (related to supply of goods and services). The State taxes which are subsumed into GST are State VAT, Entertainment Tax (other than the tax levied by the local bodies), Central Sales Tax (CST) (only for goods subsumed into GST),[2] Entry tax, Purchase Tax, Luxury tax, Taxes on lottery, betting and gambling, and State cesses and surcharges (related to supply of goods and services).

§22.02 EVOLUTION OF THE CENTRAL VAT SYSTEM

In this section, we discuss the evolution of the VAT system in Central (Union) taxes. Prior to the introduction of GST, the tax base of Central taxes used to constitute of tax on manufacturing, tax on inter-state and international trade and services tax. The CST is a tax on inter-state trade, and it has been replaced by Integrated GST (IGST) since 1 July 2017 for goods which are subsumed into GST. CST is still prevalent for goods which are either kept out of the GST system (alcoholic beverages for human consumption) and/or waiting for the GST council's recommendation for a date on which GST will be levied on them (petroleum crude, high speed diesel, motor spirit, natural gas and aviation turbine fuel).[3] Customs duties constitute of Basic Customs Duty (BCD) which is trade tariff, Countervailing Duty (CVD) is a tax on imports in lieu of Union Excise Duties (UED) and Special Additional Duty (SAD) is a tax on imports in lieu of State sales tax/VAT. In the GST regime, imports attract BCD and IGST. CVD and SAD are subsumed into IGST and some specific commodities attract GST compensation cess. This cess is introduced along with GST to generate revenue to provide compensation to States during the GST transition period (first 5 years of GST introduction).[4]

[A] Evolution of Central VAT on Manufacturing

The Central Excise Duty, Customs Duty and Service Tax were the major indirect taxes of the Central Government. Central Excise Duty (along with AEDs, special additional excise duty, cesses and surcharges) is a tax on manufacturing of goods, and the Indian Constitution assigns power to tax manufacturing to the Central government.

Prior to the introduction of GST, the structure of taxes on manufacturing used to constitute of UEDs, special excise duty (SED), additional excise duty in lieu of State sales tax (AED or AD(ST)), additional duty of excise on textiles and textile articles (AD(T&TA)) and cesses and surcharges on specified commodities. The UEDs were broad based tax on manufacturing, whereas SED was commodity specific. The Union

2. Though CST is a central tax, since the introduction of CST from 1957, CST is collected and retained by the States where inter-state trade originates (exporting States).
3. Sacchidananda Mukherjee, *Plugging Loopholes in Taxation of Interstate Sales*, 55(19) Econ. & Pol. Weekly 18-20 (2020).
4. Sacchidananda Mukherjee, *Possible Impact of Withdrawal of GST Compensation Post GST Compensation Period on Indian State Finances*, NIPFP Working Paper No. 291 (NIPFP, 2020).

government was collecting AED (AD(ST)) on tobacco, textiles, and sugar under the Additional Duties of Excise (Goods of Special Importance) Act, 1957 where States rented out their taxation rights (sales tax) to these commodities to the Union government. Cesses are levied on specific commodities, and AD (T&TA) were primarily meant to raise resources for the development of concerned industries. The Department of Revenue, Government of India used to collect the majority of cesses on some specific commodities, but there were some other departments of the Union government that also used to administer some of the cesses and surcharges. Cesses of the Union government are sole revenue source of the central government and not shared with the State governments.[5] In the GST regime, Out-of-GST petroleum products (petrol, diesel and ATF) are attracting UEDs. Similarly, State sales tax is continuing for motor spirit (gasoline), diesel, ATF, crude petroleum, natural gas and alcoholic beverages for human consumption.

The evolution of Union VAT system can be divided into two phases—Modified VAT (MODVAT) system (from 1986-1987) and Central VAT (CENVAT) system (from 2001-2002). In addition, the Union government introduced the services tax from 1994.

[1] MODVAT System

Following the recommendation of the *Indirect Taxation Enquiry Committee* (Chaired by L. K. Jha),[6] India embraced the principle of VAT in 1986 by replacing the UED by MODVAT. Initially, MODVAT was levied on selected commodities but over the years its scope was extended to cover a large number of commodities.[7] The design of MODVAT also shifted from production-type VAT to consumption-type VAT in 1994-1995, as ITCs were no longer limited to expenditure for raw materials but extended to capital goods. In 1995-1996, more capital goods were included under the MODVAT credit scheme and also coverage of MODVAT was extended to select petroleum products (other than high speed diesel oil), yarn component of the textile sector, and cut tobacco used in manufacturing of cigarettes.[8] The introduction of MODVAT resulted in transparency of tax burden, reduction in cascading of taxes, and inculcating a mechanism to check tax evasion through the self-policing nature of the

5. Cesses are not part of divisible pool of taxes (*see* Ashrita P. Kotha et al., *Cesses and Surcharges: Concept, Practice and Reform*, Report to the Fifteenth Finance Commission. (Vidhi Centre for Legal Policy, 2018).
6. Government of India, *Report of the Indirect Taxation Enquiry Committee, Part I* (Ministry of Finance, Government of India, 1977); Government of India, Report of the Indirect Taxation Enquiry Committee, Part II (Ministry of Finance, Government of India, 1978).
7. MODVAT introduced in India with effective from March 1, 1986 and initially it was limited to only commodities listed in 37 chapters out of total 91 chapters. From March 1, 1987 MODVAT extended to all commodities except petroleum products, textiles, tobacco, cinematographic films and matches, as these excluded commodities used to contribute about half of the total collection of UEDs.
8. Pawan K. Aggarwal, *Modified Value Added Tax (MODVAT): Structure and Resource Mobilisation.* A Paper, prepared for the Working Group on Tax Policy of the Steering Group on Financial Resources for the Ninth Five Year Plan (1997-1998 to 2001-2002) (NIPFP, 1996).

VAT system.[9] However, the introduction of MODVAT is also attributed to the fall in UED revenue caused by a narrowing of the tax base, the decline in average tax rate, and allowance of ITC against purchases of raw materials and capital goods. One of the reasons for the smaller tax base could be the separation of value addition beyond manufacturing to the services sector and/or trade sector by outsourcing activities like packaging and marketing to other business entities, which before were vertically integrated for some manufacturing firms. Being first point sale, the manufacturing sector used to attract both the Union tax (MODVAT) and State sales tax (subsequently State VAT after introduction); moreover, there was no provision for ITC adjustment against State sales tax. State sales tax was levied on MODVAT paid price of goods, as a result there was an additional tax burden on taxpayers in terms of cascading of taxes. Until 1994-1995, there was no service tax, so it was attractive for businesses to shift a part of value addition beyond manufacturing to either tax exempt and/or low tax activities. The fall in revenue from UEDs after the introduction of MODVAT is also attributed to the revenue accounting practice where duties levied on imports in lieu of UEDs by the name "CVD" is accounted under customs duties whereas the ITC against CVD is adjusted with MODVAT liability and is accounted under UEDs.

In the MODVAT system, there were large number of rates, e.g., in 1996 there were 9 tax rates ranging between 5% and 50%. Some specified luxury goods used to attract as high as a 225% tax rate and necessities used to attract tax rates ranging between 1% and 8%.[10] Some commodities having price variation, due to transportation costs or owing to problems related to valuation, were attracting specific rates. There was a plethora of exemptions which resulted in increasing complexities of the tax system and were prone to litigation. Several commodities were kept out of the MODVAT system, e.g., cut tobacco, plastic woven sacks, specified textiles and equipment. During the 1990s, the number of rate categories was reduced, rates were rationalized by converting many specific rates to *ad valorem* rates, and the list of exemptions were also pruned down significantly. For example, in the Union budget of 1995-1996, the MODVAT scheme was extended to include cut tobacco, plastic woven sacks, specified textiles and equipment, the conditions of matching raw materials/capital goods with output for allowing MODVAT credit was withdrawn, the scope of Small Scale Industries (SSI) concessions (turnover limit for availing SSI concessions raised from INR 20 million to INR 30 million) enlarged,[11] and the rate structure was rationalized by reducing tax rates.

However, MODVAT is not the first system in India to allow ITC. Prior to MODVAT, the then excise duty regime had a provision under Rule 56-A (Proforma Credit) of allowing set-off against tax paid on inputs. The system used to be based on

9. Aggarwal (1996), *supra* n. 8.
10. Aggarwal (1996), *supra* n. 8.
11. Clearances up to first INR 3 million in a financial year are exempt from excise duty, further clearances up to INR 2 million are charged duty at a rate 10% lower than the normal rate subject to a minimum of 5%, and subsequent clearances up to INR 2.5 million are charged at 5% lower than the normal rate subject to a minimum of 5%. Clearances beyond INR 7.5 million are subjected to normal duty.

physical verification instead of invoice or account-based method of tax credit. Moreover, the proforma credit scheme used to operate on a case-by-case basis where the decision on allowance of credit was subject to satisfaction of the deciding authority. Possibilities of discretionary practices under the system could not be ruled out. The MODVAT scheme was a rule-based system and the problem of classification disputes was expected to be minimum.[12] In the proforma credit system, availing credit was contingent upon the input and output of the manufacturer falling under the same or particular tariff items or sub-items. Under MODVAT, on the other hand, input falls only under tariff items or sub-items. Under the MODVAT system, the concept of input was a much wider connotation than Rule 56-A. However, the regulations corresponding to availing benefit of Rule 56-A were cumbersome and Rule 56-A is omitted since May 20, 1994.

The reforms initiated in the MODVAT toward the second half of 1990s are mostly attributed to the recommendations of the *Tax Reform Committee* (Chaired by Raja J. Chelliah).[13] Though MODVAT was not free from structural shortcomings, it could be seen as a first step toward the introduction of a modern VAT system in India which helped to achieve GST.

Before discussing the evolution of the CenVAT system, it would be important to discuss the two major developments of the Indian indirect tax system during the second half of 1950s, which have impacted the transition to the GST system.

[2] Tax on Declared Goods

Following the recommendation of the *Taxation Enquiry Commission* (Chaired by John Matthai)[14] and to realize a harmonized tax system across States on goods of special importance in inter-state trade, the Central government backed by Article 286(3)(a) of the Constitution of India[15] declared a list of goods as of special importance under section 14 of the CST Act 1956 and placed certain restrictions on States under section 15 of the CST Act (listed below). The list of declared goods was not restricted to only those goods suggested by the Commission but included a large number of goods (listed under section 14 of the CST Act 1956).[16]

Under section 15 of the CST Act, Centre placed following restrictions and conditions in regard to powers of State governments to tax declared goods inside the State.

12. B.N.P. Singh, *Programmes and Policies of Planning in India*, Deep & Deep Publications (1991).
13. Government of India, *Interim Report of the Tax Reforms Committee* (Ministry of Finance, Government of India, 1991).
14. Government of India, *Report of the India Taxation Enquiry Commission*, 1953-1954: Vol. I-III. (Government of India, 1955).
15. Which authorizes the Parliament of India to declare some goods as of "special importance" and to impose restrictions and conditions in regard to power of the States in regard to levy, rates, and other incidence of tax on such goods.
16. Sacchidananda Mukherjee and R. Kavita Rao, *Decades of Indirect Tax Reforms in India: A Journey Towards Good and Services Tax (GST)* in *Evolution of Goods and Services Tax in India* 7-35 (R. Kavita Rao and Sacchidananda Mukherjee, eds., Cambridge University Pres, 2019).

(1) Tax on declared goods not to exceed 4%.
(2) Reimbursement of local tax if declared goods are sold inter-state.
(3) Goods must be sold in the same form to obtain reimbursement—declared goods purchased must be sold in same form, i.e., identical goods must be sold. Thus, if goods sold after processing are different commodity, reimbursement of local sales tax is not available.
(4) Special provisions about paddy and pulses:
   - If paddy is taxed within State and rice (which is produced from paddy) is also taxed, tax paid on paddy should be given set off while levying tax on rice.
   - Each of the pulses whether whole or separated and whether with or without husk, shall be treated as a single commodity for purpose of levy of tax under State tax law, i.e., if tax is paid on raw pulses, no further tax is payable after it is processed.
   - If paddy is purchased on payment of sales tax and rice procured out of such paddy is exported, the paddy and rice will be treated as "same goods" for purpose of section 5(3) of CST Act.
(5) Sales tax rates applicable for sale of declared goods—State governments cannot charge sales tax for sale within the State at the rate which is more than 4%.

[3] Additional Excise Duty (AED) in Lieu of Sales Tax

To achieve uniformity in the sales tax systems of the different States and to reduce cost of tax collection, tax evasion and the compliance burden of taxpayers, the Union government introduced the Additional Duties of Excise (Goods of Special Importance) Act, 1957.[17] Under this act, the States rent out their right to tax (sales tax) on tobacco, textile, and sugar to the Union government. States abstain to collect sales tax from these commodities, and the Union government used to collect AED in addition to UEDs on these 3 commodities. Prior to the recommendations of the Eleventh Finance Commission, the Union government used to distribute the entire proceeds of AED to the States. However, the Eleventh Finance Commission recommended inclusion of the tax proceeds of AEDs into a divisible pool of taxes. However, the system resulted in revenue loss for the States.[18] The Kelkar Task Force Report on Indirect Taxation (in short KTF) recommended for dispensing with the AED on sugar, textiles and tobacco imposed in lieu of sales tax.[19] As a part of Centre's compensation package to States for revenue loss on account of reduction of CST rate to 2% and implementation of State

17. D.R. Singh, *Substitution of Excise Duty for Sales Tax: Its Impact on State Revenues* Econ. Weekly 1127 (July 11, 1964).
18. M. Govinda Rao, *Reform in Central Sales Tax in the Context of VAT* 38(7) Econ. & Pol. Weekly 627 (2003); D.R. Singh (1964), *supra* n. 17.
19. Government of India, *Report of the Task Force on Indirect Taxes* (Ministry of Finance, Government of India, 2002).

VAT, the power to levy tax on tobacco, textiles and sugar is transferred to the States from April 1, 2003. The abolition of AED on these 3 items happened subsequently.

[4] Central VAT (CenVAT) System

Over the years, the coverage of MODVAT was extended, and in the Union budget of 2000-2001 it was replaced by a relatively rationalized and broad-based tax system called CenVAT. The process of modernization of the Indian taxation system initiated with the introduction of MODVAT took a definitive structure with the introduction of CenVAT, which besides improving the transparency in the tax burden, reduced tax cascading by allowing ITC against outputs as well as capital goods,[20] and strengthened the self-policing nature of the VAT system. The introduction of CenVAT resulted in the rationalization of the rate structure, curtailment in the list of exemptions, and replacement of specific rates by *ad valorem* rates.[21] In the CenVAT, there was a single standard rate of 16% with some variations for selected commodities and the coverage extended to all commodities, except high speed diesel (HSD), gasoline and matches. Some specific products were attracting special excise duty (SED) of 8%, 16%, and 24%. There was no provision for ITC adjustment for goods kept out of the CenVAT system and those items continued to attract UEDs. The majority of the commodities attracting SED were final products but some of them were intermediate goods as well.

[B] The Evolution of the Services Tax

> We must ensure that there will be a unified and rational system of taxation of services applicable to the whole country. This means that the services tax must be part of a value added tax in course of time and should be levied at the Central level. A cascading type of services tax should be avoided at all costs. We envisage that as the Union excise on commodities gets gradually transformed into a value added tax at the manufacturing level, the services tax will get woven into that system and therefore tax could be levied also on services that enter into the productive processes.[22]

The service tax was the second important source of indirect tax revenue of the Central government prior to introduction of GST. The Union government invoked residual power of taxation, as bestowed under Article 97 in the Union list of the seventh

20. In the CenVAT regime, ITC adjustment against capital goods is sequenced over two years where the half (50%) of the duty (tax) paid on the capital goods could be adjusted with output tax liability in the first financial year and the second half in the next financial year, provided the goods are in working condition (except for spares and components). There was no provision of claiming compensation against depreciation in the Income Tax Act, 1961 on that part of the value of the capital good which is equal to the duty paid on the good.
21. Mahesh C. Purohit, *National and Sub-National VATs: A Road Map for India* 36(9) Econ. & Pol. Weekly, 757 (2001).
22. Paragraph 9.49, p. 123 Tax Reform Committee Report, *supra* n. 13.

schedule of the Indian Constitution[23] and introduced a tax on value of services supplied.

The liberalization of the Indian economy resulted in structural changes in terms of an increasing GDP share of the services sector along with a rising growth rate of the economy. The Indian economy grew at an average annual growth rate of 6.4% during 1993-2001 as compared to 5.4% during 1980-1992.[24] The average annual growth rate of the services sector increased from 6.4% during 1980-1992 to 8.2% during 1993-2001. Due to the fall in tax collections from the international trade sector, as a result of reforms initiated in India's external sector by reducing trade tariffs on imports, as well as from the domestic manufacturing activities (UEDs or MODVAT), the Union government introduced the services tax in 1994-1995 to boost revenue. Except for a few stand-alone taxes on services, a large segment of value addition in the services sector was lying outside the tax system. Therefore, a broad base tax on services was overdue in India, as several tax reforms committees or commissions recommended it.[25] However, the power to tax services was neither explicitly listed in the Union list nor in the State list in the seventh schedule of the Indian Constitution. In absence of a specific entry in the seventh schedule, the Union government took the help of Entry 97 of the Union list which has empowered the Union government to levy taxes on all items that do not appear in either the Union or State lists.[26] Backed by the reciprocal power of taxation in the Indian Constitution, the central government introduced the services tax from July 1, 1994. However, the 88th Amendment (The Constitution (Eighty-Eighth Amendment) Act, 2003) of the Indian Constitution inserts a new Article 268A, effective from January 15, 2004. This amendment enables inserting an additional entry "92C. Taxes on services" after entry 92B of the Union list in the seventh schedule of the Constitution. The Amendment assigns the power to levy services tax to the Central government, where the proceeds of the tax fall within the divisible pool of taxes.

Following the recommendations of the Tax Reform Committee, initially, the services tax was levied on 3 services (telecommunication, non-life insurance and stockbrokers). Over the years more and more services were included under the services tax net. The total number of services reached 119 in 2012; and since 1 July 2012 taxation of services based on a negative list has been applied.[27] Initially the services tax was a cascading type tax without provision for ITC adjustment. Following the recommendation of the *Expert Group on Taxation of Services* (Chaired by M. Govinda

23. M. Govinda Rao, *Taxing Services: Strategy and Challenges* in *Fiscal Policies and Sustainable Growth in India* (Edgardo M. Favaro and Ashok. K. Lahiri, eds., Oxford University Press, 2004).
24. M. Govinda Rao, *Taxing Services: Issues and Strategy* 36(42) Econ. & Pol. Weekly 3999 (2001).
25. Mukherjee and Rao (2019), *supra* n. 16.
26. Entry 97 of the Union List: Any other matter not enumerated in List II or List III including any tax not mentioned in either of those Lists.
27. In June 2000, an Expert Group headed by Dr. M. Govinda Rao observed that "selective approach to taxation of services is undesirable for this violates neutrality in taxation, leads to inadequate coverage in addition to raising several avoidable procedural and legal complications." The group recommended that the Centre should move toward a "general and comprehensive extension of the tax to cover all services with a small and clearly-defined exemption list." The group identified six categories of services which may be put in the negative list, and that included all public services of governments, all public utility services of essential nature and all school education.

Rao)[28] as well as KTF report on indirect taxes, ITC against service tax was introduced for selective services in 2002-2003 and the scheme was extended to cover all services from 2003-2004. With the introduction of the ITC system, the service tax rate was increased gradually from 8% from May 14, 2003 to 14% from June 1, 2015. The basic rationale for increasing the tax rate on services was to harmonize the tax rate for services with the CenVAT rate. From June 1, 2016 to July 1, 2017, the service tax rate was 15%. Full integration of ITC between service tax and CenVAT was introduced from 2004-2005, which paved the way for the introduction of GST.

However, the services tax was not a comprehensive tax on all services. Some stand-alone taxes on services remained outside the services tax system. Powers to tax these services are listed either in the Union list or State list in the seventh schedule of the Indian Constitution. Items included under the Union list are taxes on goods and passengers carried by railways, sea or air, taxes on railway fares and freights (Entry 80) and expenditure tax on hotels and restaurants.[29] The expenditure tax was basically a tax on services and governs all taxation-related processes associated with the chargeable expenditure that an individual incurs in certain hotels or restaurants.[30] It is levied under the Expenditure Tax Act of 1987, and this tax has been repealed since June 1, 2003. Items included in the State list in the seventh schedule are taxes on consumption of electricity (Entry 53), taxes on advertisement other than those published in the newspapers (Entry 55), taxes on goods and passengers carried by road or inland waterways (Entry 56), taxes on entertainments, amusements, betting and gambling (Entry 62). When Entry 80 from the central list and Entry 55 and 62 from the State list were subsumed into the GST, other taxes on services remained as stand-alone taxes on services.

Neither in the sales tax/State VAT nor in the services tax, there were provisions for cross adjustment of ITC. In other words, sales tax/VAT imbedded into goods utilized to provide services used to cascade with services tax. Similarly, services tax imbedded in services utilized in manufacturing and distribution of goods used to cascade with sales tax/VAT. Prior to 2004-2005, there was also no provision for cross utilization of ITCs between CenVAT and services tax.

[C] The Evolution of the VAT System in International Trade

Customs duty (including Additional Duty of Customs and Special Countervailing Duty (CV)) is a tax on the import of commodities. In addition to BCD (also known as Customs or trade tariff), imports also used to attract Additional Duty of Customs (also known as CVD) in lieu of CenVAT, CV, or (Special Additional Duty or SAD) in lieu of

28. Government of India, *Report of the Expert Group on Taxation of Services* (Ministry of Finance, Government of India, 2001).
29. The Expenditure Tax Act of 1987 is an act that governs all taxation-related processes associated with the chargeable expenditure that an individual incurs in certain hotels or restaurants.
30. M. Govinda Rao (2001), *supra* n. 24.

State taxes.[31] Customs Duty and associated taxes was the third largest source of indirect taxes of the Central Government prior to introduction of GST. Both CVD and SAD are subsumed into GST, and imports attract BCD, IGST (in lieu of Central and State GST) and other trade related duties (Safeguard duty and Anti-dumping duty) specific to commodities and/or source of origin. In 2004-2005, harmonization in CVD rates at the level equivalent to excise duty was achieved. Further, importers were allowed to claim ITC of CVD against subsequent central taxes (CenVAT and services tax) payable. However, given that central taxes did not extend to the sale of goods, at least part of the ITC might not have been claimed. The maximum tax rate of SAD was 4%, whereas the standard State sales tax/VAT rate was higher at 12.5% since the introduction of State VAT. The changes in customs duty were once again a change in the direction of the rationalization of the indirect tax regime toward a level playing field to domestic production vis-à-vis imports.

Reforms initiated during early 1990s to integrate the Indian economy with the rest of the world have profound impacts on the Indian trade sector. The reform in customs duty consists of reducing "peak" rates, removing exemptions and simplifications of the system.[32] To improve competitiveness, customs tariff rates are brought down to international competitive rates since 1991. The "peak" rate was reduced from 150% in 1991-1992 to 40% in 1997-1998. During 1999-2000 to 2008-2009 it was further reduced from 40% to 10%.[33] With gradual reductions of customs tariffs, India's customs duty collection rate declined from about 47% in 1990-1991 to 29% in 1995-1996. It was 23% in 1998-99 and thereafter it declined by about 1% every year and reached 21% in 2000-2001.[34]

In addition, exports of a few goods from India attract export duty. Export tariffs serve to compliment the export-import policy of India which, in turn, forms part of India's foreign trade policy. To discourage exports of certain agricultural commodities for domestic food security (through stabilization of food prices) and to ensure adequate availability of raw materials for domestic manufacturing activities (mainly minerals and ores), export duties are imposed on certain goods in the second schedule of the Customs Tariff Act, 1975.

To make India's "Additional Duty" on customs (CVD) WTO compatible, it is termed as "CVD", and it is imposed in lieu of CenVAT.[35] ITC adjustment against CVD is allowed for any further value addition and/or utilization in the downstream of the

31. In 2005-2006, Special CVD is introduced at the rate of 4% to compensate State level taxes (sales tax, VAT, local tax or any other charges for the time being leviable on a like article on its sale, purchase or transportation in India) on ITA Bound (except IT software) items and their imports. Full credit of this duty is allowed to manufacturers of excisable goods. Special Additional Duty of Customs levied under subsection (5) of section 3 of the Customs Tariff Act, 1975.
32. Arvind Virmani, *Towards a Competitive Economy: VAT and Customs Duty Reform*, Working Paper No. 4/2002-PC (Planning Commission, Government of India, 2002).
33. The "peak" tariff rate also refers to the same "basic" customs tariffs and is the highest general rate applying to a large majority of imports.
34. The customs duty "collection rate" for any year represents the total customs duty collected under all three sub-heads (basic, AD & SAD) divided by the total value of imports during the year.
35. CVD is levied under subsection (1) of section 3 of the Customs Tariff Act, 1975.

value chain. Separation of account of CVD (equivalent to CenVAT) collection from protective customs duty is also achieved.[36] The challenge was also to set the CVD rate on imports at a level equivalent to that of the CenVAT. Though India moved from a complex excise tax system to the MODVAT system in 1986, the number of tax rates was large. Without a standard tax rate, it was difficult to set equivalent CVD rates. The transition from MODVAT to the CenVAT system since 2001 helped in pruning down tax rates with a single standard tax rate of 16% with some variations for selected commodities. It was envisaged that revenue loss on account of bringing down customs duty rates and allowing ITC against CVD would be compensated by equivalent increase in revenue from domestic economic activities and consumptions.

With the introduction of CenVAT, end-use exemptions were eliminated from the Union excise tax system. However, those exemptions were still prevalent in the structure of customs duty. Virmani[37] identifies about 280 specific exemptions of which over 100 are end-use exemptions. Of the 280 exemptions, about 60 exemptions were the result of international commitments made earlier, about 40 were due to administrative reasons and constraints and over 60 were due to social reasons. More than one-third of the exemptions (about 100) were the results of industrial pulls and pressures from user industries. There was no economic justification behind these exemptions except to raise the effective protection provided to user industries and thus to provide them with hidden (non-budgetary) subsidies.[38]

In the GST regime exports are zero rated. The Government of India has also rolled out the Remission of Duties and Taxes on Exported Products (RoDTEP) scheme from January 1, 2020 by replacing the existing Merchandise Exports from India Scheme (MEIS). RoDTEP is a fully automated route for claiming ITC in the GST regime against embedded Central, State and local taxes/duties which are so far not being rebated/refunded.[39]

§22.03 THE EVOLUTION OF THE STATE VAT SYSTEM

[A] State Sales Tax

Prior to the introduction of VAT at State level, there was tax competition between the States[40] and disharmony in tax rates, the number of tax schedules and exempted items, etc. Table 22.1 provides a comprehensive overview of the sales tax system prevalent across States during 1989-1990, much before the process of harmonization was initiated. There was wide variation in the number of rate categories with some States having 7 rate categories (Odisha and West Bengal) and others having as high as 25 rate categories (e.g., Gujarat). The general rate of sales tax varied from 4% to 12%. In

36. Virmani (2002), *supra* n. 32.
37. Virmani (2002), *supra* n. 32.
38. Virmani (2002), *supra* n. 32.
39. https://www.cbic.gov.in/resources//htdocs-cbec/letter-EP-Councils.pdf (last accessed on January 6, 2021).
40. M. Govinda Rao and Francois Vaillancourt, *Interstate Tax Disharmony in India: A Comparative Perspective* 24(9) Publius 99 (1994).

addition, a wide variation in sales tax rate around the general rate was also reported across the States.[41] Under the sales tax system, variations in point of taxation (single point, double point, multiple point) across States resulted in major roadblocks for the introduction of State VAT. Not able to raise tax beyond first point sales, led States to impose additional levies like turnover tax, additional sales tax, surcharges and so on. This resulted in a non-transparent tax system and the incidence of taxes was arbitrary and unpredictable.

Table 22.1 A Brief Description of Rate Structure of Sales Tax: 1989-1990

States	Mode of Levy	Treatment of Goods When Used as Raw Materials	Additional Tax	Tax Rates		
				No.	Range (%)	General Rate
Andhra Pradesh	SP	CR (≤4%)	TT, SC (10%)	8	1-25	6
Assam	SP	E (SED)	-	12	2-50	7
Bihar	SP	CR (≤3%)	TT, SC (10%)	17	2-25	8
Delhi	SP	E	-	9	1-12	7
Goa	SP	E(SRM)[1]	SC (10%)	10	1-15	7
Gujarat	SP, DP	SO (SRM)	TT, SC (20%)	25	0.5-54	4/8
Haryana	SP	SO	SC (10%)	10	0.5-20	10
Himachal Pradesh	SP	SO	SC (10%)	12	0.5-25	8
Karnataka	SP, DP, MP	CR (≤4%)	TT	14	1-150	7
Kerala	SP	CR (≤2%)[2]	TT, SC (25%)	16	2-75	5
Madhya Pradesh	SP	CR (≤4%)	-	18	0.5-50	8
Maharashtra	SP	SO (CR≤4 OR 6%)[3]	TT, SC (12%)	12	1-50	-
Orissa	SP	CR (≤4%)	SC (10%)	7	2-16	12
Punjab	SP	E[4]	SC (10%)	12	1-12	7
Rajasthan	SP	CR (≤ 3%)	-	15	2-30	10
Tamil Nadu	SP, MP[5]	CR (≤3%)	TT, SC (15%)[6]	17	1-50	8

41. Pawan K. Aggarwal, *Incidence of Major Indirect Taxes in India* (NIPFP, 1995).

States	Mode of Levy	Treatment of Goods When Used as Raw Materials	Additional Tax	Tax Rates		
				No	Range (%)	General Rate
Uttar Pradesh	SP	E(SRM), CR (SRM)	SC (25%)	14	2-32.5	8
West Bengal	SP, MP	CR (≤2%)	TT, SC (15%)	7	1-20	8

Source: Aggarwal (1995, Table 2.2, p. 17).

Notes: SP: Single point, DP: Double point, MP: Multi point, TT: Turnover tax, SC: Surcharge, CR: Concessional rate, E: Exempt, SO: Set off, SED: Selected eligible dealers, SRM: Selected raw materials.

1. Raw materials and packing materials i.e., commodities subjected to last point tax, to be used as inputs, can be purchased without payment of tax.
2. The benefit of concessional rate is not available if the finished goods are exported or sent on consignment basis.
3. 6% is applicable when the manufactured goods are sent on branch transfer outside Maharashtra. Set off is given in respect of the rate, to the extent it exceeds the concessional rate.
4. All transactions among the registered dealers are exempt.
5. In Tamil Nadu, SP and MP up to March 03, 1990 and only SP w.e.f. April 01, 1990.
6. An addition surcharge of 5% is payable in the Madras area.

[B] The Evolution of Taxes on Inter-State Trade

[1] Central Sales Tax

> To ensure that taxation does not cause any hindrance to domestic trade, while assigning the power to tax sale or purchase of goods in general to the States, our constitution makers had taken care to hedge the said powers with some restrictions to prevent tax exportation by any State. The States were debarred from taxing any sales or purchase taking place in the course of import/export as also inter-state trade making it clear that only the State where goods were finally delivered for consumption could impose tax on inter-state sales. Presumably, the objective was to make sure that sales taxation by the States was founded on what has come to be known as the "destination principle" and constitutes a key characteristic of the value added tax adopted by the EU to facilitate free flow of trade within the Union.[42]

The indirect tax regime at the time of adoption of the Constitution of India, was a destination-based system. However, the regime did not contain the necessary structure to appropriately deal with inter-state transactions. This caused some problems of compliance for the sellers and problems of administering the tax for the tax

42. Amaresh Bagchi, *Fifty Years of Fiscal federalism in India: An Appraisal*, Kale Memorial Lecture delivered at Gokhale Institute of Politics and Economics, Pune on December 8, 2002 (NIPFP, 2002), 13-14.

administrators. In light of this and other issues that arose from the constitutional assignment of taxation powers, the implementation of recommendations of the *Taxation Enquiry Commission* (Chaired by John Matthai, Government of India 1955) changed the indirect tax regime in India.

Following the recommendation of the Commission, the Union government introduced CST on inter-state sales of goods from 1957 (under the CST Act, 1956). Though the CST Act is a Central Legislation, the power to collect and retain the taxes on inter-state trade was vested in the States where inter-state trade originates. The tax was applicable only on sales but not on consignment or branch transfers across State borders. The main objective behind the introduction of CST was to reduce the compliance burden of taxpayers involved in inter-state trade. Prior to the introduction of CST, the obligation for return filing both in origin and destination State resulted in a considerable compliance burden for those enterprises involved in inter-state trade.

Initially CST was introduced with tax rate of 1% on inter-state sales of goods between registered dealers, as recommended by the Commission. Gradually, the CST rate increased to 2%, then to 3% and with effect from July 1, 1975, it was 4%. The suggested CST rate for transactions between registered dealers in the origin State and unregistered dealers or consumers in the destination State was the prevailing tax rate in the origin State. The Commission also recommended for transfer of tax proceeds to the destination State for any tax collection "in excess of the receipts from the rate normally leviable on inter-state trade between registered dealers." Though, in principle, the recommendation of the Commission supports the destination principle of VAT system, in practice origin (exporting) States retained the entire CST proceeds. In absence of any system of inter-state clearance of ITC, the CST system transformed a hitherto destination-based tax system into an origin-based tax system. Resistance of the States against abolishing CST was strong, especially from States having a large manufacturing base. In absence of any compensation mechanism, States were not in position to withstand the revenue loss on account of the withdrawal of CST. The issue of compensation for reducing the CST rate surfaced time to time, and it was a contentious issue in Indian taxation history. This is also one of the reasons behind the delay in introduction GST in India. The assurance of GST compensation helped to achieve consensus among the States in favor of the introduction of GST. After the introduction of VAT, the CST rate was reduced from 4% to 3% with effect from April 1, 2007 and a further reduction from 3% to 2% was introduced with effect from June 1, 2008. The gradual reduction of CST rate paved the way for the introduction of a destination-based VAT system in India.

Though ITC against CST sales was allowed, withholding of ITC for various reasons was common in many States, especially in case of consignment/branch transfers. The introduction of CST increased the cost of doing business for manufacturers who were sourcing their inputs from other States and/or selling their outputs to other States. The system provided perverse incentives to manufacturers to either locate their branch offices and/or set up their own distribution networks across all the States of their operations, so that they could send the goods as branch/consignment transfers and avoid paying CST. Transaction costs associated with setting up branch office/own distribution networks and compliance costs arising from dealing with multiple tax jurisdictions (with varying rules and regulations) were important factors determining the expansion plans of businesses. The introduction of CST resulted in the division of one Indian market into several State markets (State-specific markets). The system was not conducive for encouraging market efficiency and constrained improving efficiency and productivity of Indian business.

In the CST system there was no provision mandating or encouraging the establishment of an ITC chain between origin and destination States. The origin States retained the CST collected and, in absence of any mechanism of transferring CST collected on inter-state trade to the destination State(s), the ITC chain broke down. With the breaking down of ITC chain (along with corresponding paper trails) and in absence of any universal statutory obligations for taxpayers to report their inter-state procurements (imports) to the tax authority of the destination State, the system was vulnerable to tax evasion.[43] In 2004, the Empowered Committee of State Finance Ministers set up the Tax Information Exchange System (TINXSYS) to provide a common technology platform, connecting the systems of Commercial Tax Departments (CTDs) of 34 States and Union Territories (UTs) of India, excluding Andaman & Nicobar and Lakshadweep. The objective of the TINXSYS was to provide a centralized system of information exchange among CTDs of all States for better administration of inter-state trade. With the introduction of the TINXSYS, various statutory forms came into force to capture the information. Under current law, an enterprise involved in the inter-state sale of goods, is required to obtain a declaration, in Form "C," from the purchaser of goods and submit a copy of the form to the CTD of the origin State.[44] Earlier, one single "C" form could be issued for all sales bills of the selling dealer for all the transactions effected during one financial year. However, with effect from October 1, 2005, the "C" forms are required to be issued one for each calendar quarter.

The TINXSYS system was designed to facilitate verification of information captured through various Statutory Forms by various State CTDs, submitted by the dealers in support of their claim for concession. However, the effectiveness of the system was largely depended on cooperation of CTDs across States in feeding the data into the system for cross verification. Many States did not adopt the TINXSYS system which reduced effectiveness of the system to track inter-state trade.[45]

Enshrining a destination based inter-state tax system by replacing the origin-based CST system was one of the major hurdles of introducing GST in India. It was expected that the introduction of the State VAT system would facilitate the transfer of ITC from the origin (exporting) State(s) to the destination (importing) State(s) so that ITC against CST paid on imports could be adjusted by the destination States with tax liability arising in the downstream of value chain. In addition to revenue implications for the origin States, a lack of consensus in favor of a specific design of a clearing house

43. In absence of any monitoring system, it was feared that exports from one State to another may be diverted to the local market of the origin State, and it is not necessary that inter-state imports will be reported for taxation in the destination State.
44. "F form" is required for stock transfer to branches/consignment agents or vice-versa from one State to another, without attracting charge of CST.
45. M. Govinda Rao, *Feasibility of Introducing GST in April 2010* 44(29) Econ. & Pol. Weekly 10 (2009).

for settlement inter-state ITC flows led scholars to explore various alternative designs.[46] There were at least 9 alternative models proposed to track payments and refunds, e.g., Compensating VAT (CVAT), Viable Integrated VAT (VIVAT), Prepaid VAT (PVAT).[47] However, none of the proposed models was adopted due to lack of consensus among States and the fear that the Union government would take over the CST administration.

[2] Entry Tax

The discussion on State taxes would be incomplete without discussing Entry tax. There are 2 forms of entry tax—(1) the entry tax that replaced the so-called octroi tax and (2) a tax on the entry of goods into a local jurisdiction. The first type of entry tax was introduced after the phasing out of the octroi. Octroi used to be a tax on the entry of goods into an administrative jurisdiction of urban local bodies/municipalities (including Cantonment Boards). It used to be collected at the entry points of a jurisdiction based on the value of the good determined by physical verification. Since revenue from octroi tax was dependent on physical verification requiring intensive monitoring of the inflow of goods, possibilities of leakage of revenue cannot be ruled out. Because of the revenue leakage and requirement of intensive monitoring, an account based "entry tax" was introduced as a replacement of the octroi tax.[48] The octroi tax was repealed on March 31, 2013 and replaced by the Local Body Tax (LBT) from April 1, 2013 which was account based levy imposed by Urban Local Bodies (including some Cantonment Boards). The second type of entry tax is more or less an equalization levy imposed on the entry of goods into a State. The seventh schedule of the Indian Constitution assigns taxation power to the States to levy taxes on the entry of goods into a local area for consumption, use or sale therein (Entry 52 of the State List). The rationale for the imposition of entry tax was the existing difference in tax rates, where the tax rate of the destination State is lower than that of the origin State for a specific good. In some States the entry tax of second type was commodity specific whereas in some other States it was a broad-based levy for all inter-state imports. Some States used to provide ITC against entry tax of the second type whereas in some other States there was no provision for ITC.[49] Prior to the agreement on tax rate harmonization across States, tax competition created opportunities for trade diversion as a result of the difference in tax

46. Richard Bird and Pierre-Pascal Gendron, *VATs in Federal States: International Experience and Emerging Possibilities*, Working Paper No. 01-4, International Studies Program, Andrew Young School of Policy Studies, (Georgia State University, 2001); Sijbren Cnossen, *Preparing the way for a modern GST in India* 20(4) Int'l Tax & Public Finance 715 (2013).
47. Cnossen (2013), *supra* n. 45, 720.
48. "Unlike Octroi, entry tax is not collected at the time of entry of a commodity into the State. It is an account-based levy assessed and collected on the pattern of sales tax, generally from the same set of registered dealers. It is collected along with the sales tax liability of the dealers," Mahesh Purohit, *Is there a case for states carrying on with entry tax?* Financial Express, (January 29, 2015), https://www.financialexpress.com/opinion/isthere-a-case-for-states-carrying-on-with-entry-tax/36247/ (last accessed on December 27, 2020).
49. For example, Maharashtra used to provide ITC set off against entry tax whereas in Bihar there was no such provision.

rates. The second type of entry tax was introduced to address this concern. The system of CST, along with the entry tax, divided the Indian market into several islands of tax jurisdictions. Manufacturers located in a State, irrespective of their productivity and efficiency used to enjoy absolute advantage against manufacturers located in other States. A number of cases were brought before the Supreme Court of India challenging the legal validity of the entry tax imposed by the States. The Supreme Court of India upheld the constitutional validity of the entry tax imposed by States on goods coming in from other States on November 11, 2016.[50]

With the introduction of GST in India, all forms of entry tax were repealed with effect from July 1, 2017 for all goods (including out-of-GST goods). However, for many urban local governments entry tax was a major source of revenue to finance municipal services. In absence of commensurate revenue compensation from the State governments, fiscal space of some urban local governments is expected to shrink.[51]

[C] State VAT

On November 1999, 3 important decisions of the Government of India helped in accelerating the transition from the State sales tax regime to the State VAT system. The journey of transforming States sales tax to a State VAT system started in 1995. Following the recommendation of the Tax Reform Committee, a study conducted by Bagchi et al. provided an outline of the State VAT system.[52] Harmonization of sales tax rates across commodities was necessary to rein in the unhealthy sales tax rate "war" between States, which tried to attract industry and investments through reduced tax rates or direct incentives, leading to economic distortions. The decision was made to discontinue various sales tax related industrial incentives schemes applied by the States and to harmonize sales tax rates, which were both realized by January 2000. The formation of the Empowered Committee of State Finance Ministers (ECSFM) in November 1999 helped in reaching consensus among the States and expedited the implementation process.[53] The ECSFM also played a crucial role in India's transition to GST as it was instrumental in creating consensus among the individual States and the Union government on the design and structure of the GST. The success of the ECSFM demonstrates the importance in a federal government system of utilizing a multi-state vehicle, in which all State Finance Ministers are directly involved, to encourage line bureaucrats (e.g., State Finance Secretaries, Commissioners of State Commercial Taxes) to implement the decisions promptly. The convergence of State sales tax rates and the withdrawal of industrial incentives schemes related to State sales tax paved the way for setting April 1, 2003 as the date of introduction for State VAT in India in an

50. In the Supreme Court of India, Civil Appellate Jurisdiction, Civil Appeal No. 3453/2002 dated November 11, 2016.
51. Sacchidananda Mukherjee, *Compensation to Cantonment Boards for Revenue Loss on Account of GST*, 55(2) Econ. & Pol. Weekly 15-18 (2020).
52. Amaresh Bagchi et al., *Reform of Domestic Trade Taxes in India: Issues and Options* (NIPFP, 1994).
53. The Empowered Committee of State Finance Ministers, *A White Paper on State-Level Value Added Tax* (2005).

October 2002 meeting of Chief Ministers of all States. Haryana was the first State to introduce VAT from April 1, 2003. However due to certain developments, the introduction of VAT in other States was delayed. The revised date for introduction of State VAT was April 1, 2005. The majority of States introduced VAT during 2005-2006.

The ECSFM helped to hammer out a consensus on the design of a VAT at the State level to replace existing State sales taxes. Difficulties arising during the consensus process resulted in considerable delay of the introduction of the State VAT regimes. The most contentious issue was assurance of revenue protection in the VAT regime.

The State VAT was the first coordinated tax reform in India at sub-national (State) level. Its objective was to harmonize the design, rules, regulations and processes and procedures. State VAT provided for uniform minimum rates for different categories of commodities. The variation in standard rates across States was limited to 3%, and the number of tax schedules or rate categories too was limited and uniform across the country to some extent.[54] As a result the cascading effect was minimized.

However, the State VAT was not a destination-based consumption tax, especially because CST remained to be applied on inter-state sales.[55] The introduction of VAT also had a different revenue impact across States.[56]

However, VAT was not free from shortcomings. VAT was characterized by a narrow base, a plethora of exemptions, multiple rate structure (at least four), and tax cascading due to the breakdown of the ITC chain in relation to inter-state sales. Moreover, some existing indirect taxes on goods (e.g., petroleum products) and services (such as luxury tax, entertainment tax, etc.) were not incorporated in the VAT, creating another source of tax cascading. Further, State VAT was applied on a base inclusive of CenVAT, adding again a source of cascading. The system of CST and entry tax also resulted in cascading of taxes and divided the Indian market into several tax jurisdictions.

§22.04 INDIAN GST

> A comprehensive value added tax (VAT) covering sales of most goods (except those by agriculturists) and many services, should be levied at a single rate or at a few rates. Tax theory and international experience indicate that this constitutes the best "neutral" way of raising the bulk of the indirect tax revenue. A single-rate tax is the easiest to administer; a tax with two or three rates would be manageable. The VAT will apply to domestic products as well as imports, but exports will be exempt.[57]

54. Comptroller and Auditor General (CAG) of India, *Implementation of Value Added Tax in India—Lessons for transition to Goods and Services Tax—A Study Report* (CAG of India, June 2010).
55. Arindam Das-Gupta, *Will State VAT Deliver?* 4(36) Econ. & Pol. Weekly 3917 (2005).
56. Arindam Das-Gupta, *An Assessment of the Revenue Impact of State-Level VAT in India* 47(10) Econ. & Pol. Weekly 55 (2012).
57. Paragraph 2.36a, p. 17 of the Tax Reform Committee, *supra* n. 13.

Prior to the *First Discussion Paper on Goods and Services Tax in India* brought out by the ECSFM,[58] policy discussions on possible designs of GST assumed that statuesque of respective taxation powers on goods and services between the Union and State governments would continue in the GST regime. Though the possibility of the emergence of harmonized tax base for GST (or comprehensive VAT/ concurrent VAT) was recognized, it was thought difficult to find consensus in favor of harmonized tax administration due to the question of fiscal autonomy of the government (the Union as well as States). Taking cue from the experience of other federal countries where GST is introduced and the past experience of States with respect to receiving VAT/ CST compensation from the Union government, it was assumed that consensus for the constitutional amendment in favor of a harmonized base for GST would be forthcoming soon. Therefore, keeping in mind the difficulties associated with harmonizing the tax base in a federal state, scholars/tax reform committees proposed the following alternative designs of GST for India: extension of the MODVAT system beyond the manufacturing to wholesale stage where MODVAT at the wholesale stage will be administered by the State tax authorities of the respective State governments,[59] comprehensive VAT with the proceeds shared between all levels of government,[60] independent dual VATs where State VAT was to be restricted to the retail stage and the Central VAT would be levied only on manufacturers,[61] dual VAT with harmonization of the tax base,[62] and concurrent VAT with harmonization in tax administration.[63] The discussion paper of the ECSFM gave a definitive design of the Indian GST with a hope for the emergence of consensus in favor of a harmonized tax base under the GST. However due to some contentious issues, the desired constitutional amendment was delayed and therewith introduction of GST in India.[64]

The constitutional amendment (the Constitution (One Hundred and First Amendment) Act, 2016 (September 8, 2016)) removes the constitutional barriers relating to taxation between the Centre and States by removing definitional differences between goods and services and the manufacturing and distribution of goods.

A comprehensive multistage VAT system, called GST, was introduced in India on July 1, 2017. The GST encompasses various indirect taxes from the Union and State indirect tax bases. In a federal system, harmonization of the tax base is expected to reduce vertical fiscal imbalance.[65] The shift from an origin-based to a destination-based tax system is also expected to reduce horizontal fiscal imbalance among Indian States.

---

58. The Empowered Committee of State Finance Ministers, *First Discussion Paper on Goods and Services Tax in India* (2009).
59. Tax Reform Committee, *supra* n. 13, 121, section 9.40.
60. Bird & Gendron (2001), *supra* n. 46, 25.
61. Bagchi et al. (1994), *supra* n. 52, xxii.
62. Burgess et al. (1995), *supra* n. 1, 123.
63. Bagchi et al. (1994), *supra* n. 52, xxi.
64. M. Govinda Rao. *Goods and Services Tax: A Gorilla, Chimpanzee or a Genus Like "Primates"?* 46(7) Econ. & Pol. Weekly 43 (2011). Puja Mehra, *The Lost Decade (2008-18): How India's Growth Story Devolved into Growth* (Penguin eBury Press, 2019).
65. M. Govinda Rao, *Resolving Fiscal Imbalances: Issues in Tax Sharing* in, *Intergovernmental Fiscal Transfers: Principles and Practice* 319 (Robin Boadway & Anwar Shah, eds., The World Bank, 2007).

It is expected that the States with a larger consumption base will gain from the GST as compared to States with a larger production base. The reductions in vertical as well as horizontal imbalances are expected to reduce the dependence of the States on the inter-governmental fiscal transfer system as the only instrument to achieve fiscal equity in Indian federalism.

The consolidation of various taxes on goods as well as services under the GST system was long overdue in India. Recommendations of various tax reforms committees, constituted since Independence, helped in removing the cascading of taxes as well as enshrining the destination principle in consumption taxes. The implementation of the recommendations of the tax reform committees in different points of time helped in sequencing tax reforms which ultimately culminated in the introduction of GST.[66]

Indian GST is a dual VAT system with concurrent taxation power bestowed on the Union and State governments. In the GST regime every transaction (or value addition) attracts CGST as well as SGST. Inter-state transactions (including branch/consignment transfers) and imports (in addition to BCD) attract IGST. The IGST rate comprises of prevailing CGST and SGST rates. The ITC is allowed against IGST or CGST-cum-SGST liability arising in the downstream of the value chain. The design of IGST gives continuity in the flow of ITC from the origin (exporting) State to destination (importing) State(s). The CGST and IGST are administered by the Central Tax Administration and SGST is administered by the respective State tax departments.

The continuation of the ITC chain across tax jurisdictions under the IGST framework is expected to reduce cascading of taxes, improve tax compliance and reduce transaction costs associated with inter-state transactions.[67] The CGST and the SGST operate as two parallel channels of tax payments and ITC adjustments without any provision for mutual adjustment of ITC between CGST and SGST. However, IGST credit can be offset against CGST as well as SGST liability. Similarly, IGST liabilities can be adjusted with available CGST and SGST credit. States receive IGST settlement on SGST account and the Centre receives IGST settlement on CGST account.[68] By design it was expected that revenue mobilized on account of IGST would be utilized in the settlement of tax liabilities arising in the downstream of the value chain.[69] However, the IGST account actually shows positive revenue. This is caused by the time lag between tax liabilities arising on account of IGST and CGST-cum-SGST respectively, and by the lack of available information to determine the place of supply in case of inter-state supplies of goods, especially in the case of Business-to-Consumer transactions where transaction value is less than INR 0.25 million. After regular settlement of IGST credit on CGST and SGST accounts, the remaining balance of the IGST account is allocated across States on an ad hoc basis.

66. Mukherjee and Rao (2019), *supra* n. 16.
67. Sacchidananda Mukherjee, *Whether States Have Capacity to Sustain Projected Growth in GST Collection During the GST Compensation Period?* 11(1-2) Rev. Market Integration 30-53 (2019).
68. IGST Settlement on SGST Account = SGST Paid by Using IGST Credit - IGST Paid by SGST Credit and IGST Settlement on CGST Account = CGST Paid by Using IGST Credit - IGST Paid by Using CGST Credit.
69. Sacchidananda Mukherjee, *Issues of Compliance in GST—Reflecting on the CAG's Report* 54(47) Econ. & Pol. Weekly 22-24 (2019).

The States receive their respective share of the CGST from the Centre as per the recommendation of the Finance Commission. In addition, States receive GST compensation in case the actual GST collection falls short of the projected GST collection. The projection of State revenue in GST is based on revenue from taxes that are subsumed in GST (also known as revenue under protection in GST), using 2015-2016 as base year and assuming a 14% annual growth rate (year-on-year) of the revenue under protection during the first five years of GST (the GST transition period).

Revenue uncertainty surrounding any tax reform is a contentious issue which raises resistance to tax reform, and this was specially the case for big tax reform like GST in a federal country like India, where on average two-third of indirect tax revenue of provincial governments is subsumed into GST. The assurance of GST compensation has played an important role to win the hearts of State governments and accelerate the underlying processes and procedures to roll out GST in India. Moreover, the assurance of GST compensation gave leverage to the GST Council to experiment with structural changes of GST (e.g., reduction in tax rates for a large number of goods and services, raising the threshold of GST registration) to moderate the impact of GST on the Indian economy as well as facilitate ease-of-tax compliance. Many believe that the GST compensation is the only centripetal force which is binding the States together and helping the GST Council to keep intact the harmonized structure of GST in a federal system. However, taking cue from the experience of Indian tax reform, designing a suitable framework of revenue compensation to sub-national government for a defined time period could help to initiate tax reforms like Indian GST.

The harmonization of tax rules, regulations, rates, processes, and procedures across States is expected to improve tax compliance as well as ease-of-doing business in India. The removal of tax cascading and the reduction in transaction costs associated with inter-state transactions is expected to encourage investment and, therewith, trigger economic growth. Efficiency gains are expected from several provisions under the GST system, for example, the reverse charge mechanism.

By harmonizing design, structure, and administration (to some extent) of taxes, the GST has facilitated the emergence of a nationwide integrated market for goods and services. Prior to GST, the Indian market for goods and services was divided into State-specific markets. Consequently, businesses incurred substantial transaction costs to comply with the different State tax rules and regulations, and different tax rates applicable to the same commodity. Moreover, the State VAT system was origin-based tax. Thus, the exporting State collected the CST on the inter-state sale of goods. However, the destination State would not allow importing businesses to deduct as ITC against the CST paid in the origin State, because there was no system in place to transfer the tax collected by the origin (exporting) State to the destination (importing) State. As a result, the CST paid on inter-state purchases became a cost for those enterprises importing from other States. Since CST applied only to sales but not to consignment or branch transfers across State borders, businesses set up their own distribution network across States in an effort to avoid the CST cost. In some States imports from other States also attracted entry tax (i.e., tax on the entry of goods into a local jurisdiction), but not all States allowed a credit set off against entry tax, especially when the goods were imported for final consumption. The system of CST and entry tax resulted in tax cascading and divided the Indian market into several tax jurisdictions. The tax system had a negative impact on market efficiency and business productivity.

Under GST, it is expected that the harmonization of the indirect tax structure (tax rates and tax base across States), the concurrent taxation power of Centre and States on consumption of goods and services and the joint monitoring of taxpayers by the Central and State tax administrations will lead to improved tax compliance, reduced revenue leakage, and better tax coordination. The reduction of tax cascading and transaction costs associated with inter-State sales of goods could facilitate higher economic growth by attracting investment.[70] It is the additional expectation of the Union government that the introduction of GST will improve India's standing in the World Bank's ease of doing business ranking.[71]

There are some emerging challenges for the Indian GST related to design, structure, tax administration, and compliance, which we will discuss next.

[A] Emerging Challenges in Indian GST

Future GST reforms may consider addressing problems associated with the present design, structure, and complications in rules, procedures, and administration of GST.

[1] Design Issues

[a] Design of IGST and Blocking of Working Capital

Under the GST regime, inter-state supplies attract IGST at a substantially higher rate than the earlier CST rate. Moreover, under the VAT regime inter-state consignment/branch transfers were exempted from CST liability, while these transactions under the GST regime attract IGST. As a result, the new GST regime has a significant negative cash flow impact on businesses, which may explain the reduction in inventory holdings across India. Moreover, frequent changes in tax rates since the introduction of GST may have contributed to a general "uneasiness" for holding larger inventory, especially of high taxed commodities, since a decline in the rates could result in difficulties in recovering the taxes paid through the ITC mechanism. Present design of IGST is blocking cash flows of those businesses where rolling over of stock is slow. Therefore, reforming IGST design may be considered to provide relief to businesses where cash flow is a serious issue.

---

70. Underlying rationale behind attracting additional investment is that proposed GST will remove cascading of taxes (including transaction costs involved in interstate sales of goods) and release working capital, which is currently blocked as unpaid ITC.
71. India's rank in World Bank's ease of doing business is 63 out of 190 countries, as on May 2019 (*see* https://www.doingbusiness.org/en/rankings).

[2] Structural Issues

[a] Looking Beyond Composition/Compounding Scheme

To reduce the tax compliance burden for businesses with annual turnover up to INR 4 million, the GST registration threshold has been increased to INR 4 million from INR 2 million with effect from April 1, 2019. In addition, businesses also may opt for the application of the composition/compounding scheme[72] if their annual turnover is equal or below INR 15 million.[73] As the number of composition taxpayers has not significantly increased, it appears that this policy change has not made much impact. Since composition taxpayers are not eligible to raise tax invoices against their outward supplies and there is no provision to claim ITC, many taxpayers having annual turnover below the threshold are registered as regular taxpayers so that they could be integrated with larger supply chains. Moreover, the reverse charge mechanism for inward supplies of registered entities sourced from unregistered entities and composition taxpayers in the GST regime is also compelling regular taxpayers to avoid sourcing inputs from unregistered entities and/or composition tax payers.[74] Perhaps, acknowledging this and to facilitate ease-of-tax compliance for small taxpayers, the GST council has decided to roll out the Quarterly Return Monthly Payment (QRPM) Scheme from January 1, 2021 for taxpayers with annual turnover up to INR 50 million in the current (2020-2021) and the preceding financial year 2019-2020.[75]

72. Taxpayers registered under the Composition/Compounding scheme have to pay a certain percentage of their turnover as GST and they will be deprived of availing ITC against their inward supplies as well as raising tax invoices against their outward supplies.
73. In the 32nd meeting on January 10, 2019, the GST council decided to increase the GST registration threshold for sales of goods to INR 4 million from INR 2 million for general category States and from INR 1 million to INR 2 million for special category States with effect from April 1, 2019. There was no change in threshold limits for service providers. All general category States (except Telangana) and Himachal Pradesh, Delhi, Jammu & Kashmir, Ladakh, Assam opted for INR 4 million threshold. Puducherry, Meghalaya, Mizoram, Tripura, Manipur, Sikkim, Nagaland, Arunachal Pradesh and Uttarakhand opted for INR 2 million threshold. The threshold of annual turnover for the composition scheme has also increased from INR 7.5 million to INR 15 million with effect from April 1, 2019. The council also decreased the composition rate from 2% to 1% for manufacturers. However, the limit remains unchanged at INR 7.5 million for North Eastern States and Uttarakhand. New scheme was introduced with a fixed GST rate of 6% (3% CGST and 3% SGST) for independent service providers as well as mixed suppliers of goods and services with an annual turnover of up to INR 5 million in the preceding financial year.
74. Sacchidananda Mukherjee, and R. Kavita Rao, *Value Added Tax and Informality: Determinants of Registration of Enterprises under State VAT in India*, 13(1) Margin—The Journal of Applied Economic Research 21-48 (2019).
75. The QRMP Scheme is for eligible taxpayers to file their Form GSTR-1 and Form GSTR-3B returns on quarterly basis, while paying their tax dues on monthly basis through a challan. In this case payment of challan in cash is mandatory.

[3] *Challenges in Tax Administration*

The introduction of the GST brought forth a major change in the nature and scope of tax administration, both at the Centre and the States. For the State governments, the changes can be broadly summarized as follows:

- Tax administration for the GST regime is supported by the GSTN—a network which takes care of registration, filing of returns, documentation of transaction details and payment of tax. These functions used to be performed by the tax authorities and their assumption by the GSTN lessens the administrative burden of the Union as well as State tax administrations. However, for the majority of taxpayers the frequency of tax filing has increased under the GST regime and, consequently, the workload of tax officials has grown correspondingly. In addition, State tax officials now also deal with service providers which were earlier subject to the Central tax jurisdiction. Similarly, Central tax officials have to deal with traders / distributors which were earlier subject State tax jurisdiction.
- The Centre and the States jointly administer the GST. It has been agreed that the audit function would be shared between these two authorities. While within GST the base of taxpayers has expanded for both State and Center tax departments, it has been agreed that for small taxpayers, i.e., those with turnover below INR 15 million, 90% would be administered by the State tax administration. For those with higher turnover, the administration responsibility would be shared equally between the Centre and the States. Taking it further from here, it is to be expected that even the audit selection process will be harmonized to some extent under the new regime.
- Since sales tax and CST on petrol, diesel, and aviation turbine fuel (ATF), natural gas, crude petroleum and alcoholic beverages are out-of- GST at present and the administration for these taxes must be continued in addition to the GST administration.
- Under the GST regime, information of both inter-state and intra-state movements (transportation) of goods is monitored through the E-Way Bill (EWB) system. Information captured through the EWB system forms a rich source of data. For effective GST enforcement, integration of the EWB information with GST information is desirable as it may lead to better revenue monitoring. However, the EWB generates an enormous volume of data every month, and effective analysis of the data requires trained manpower backed by robust Information Technology infrastructure.

[4] *Tax Compliance*

At introduction, the GST regime had rather onerous compliance requirements. All registered businesses were required to file 3 returns every month—one declaring details of individual transactions of outward supplies, the second which would be partially auto-populated would contain a declaration of the transactions of inward supplies and finally, a third document which is the summary of the output (outward) and input (inward) supplies and self-declaration of the tax liability for the month. The initial difficulties that taxpayers faced with complying with these requirements resulted in a rethinking of the structure of returns. To begin with, the returns were reduced to 2, one documenting output supplies and the other summarizing all transactions to arrive at the tax liability due. It is proposed that this format is temporary and would undergo some more changes in times to come. There are a series of changes in the requirements to file returns and in the ITC rules as well. In addition, some provisions have been added while others have been discontinued. On the other hand, a provision for mandatory generation of e-way bills for the transport of goods with a transaction value above INR 0.05 million and beyond a distance of 10 km was introduced to monitor movement of goods from April 1, 2018 across India. These changes reflect the efforts to streamline the procedures taking into account the concerns of both taxpayers and tax administrations. This evolutionary process also means that the GST regime would take some more time to stabilize, in turn suggesting that the taxpayers would continue to face changes in compliance requirements in times to come.

[5] Revenue Protection in the GST Regime

The impact of GST on the States and Union finances is yet to be analyzed with more information available in the public domain.[76] During the first 5 years of GST implementation (i.e., until June 2022), GST revenues of the States are protected under the GST (Compensation to States) Act 2017. States will receive GST compensation if their GST collection falls short of projected GST collection. So far, the experience of overall GST collection is not very encouraging, and there is shortfall in GST collection.[77] Given the shortfall in GST collection, many scholars believe that the liberal GST revenue protection granted under the GST Compensation Act to the States is unjustifiable.[78] However, the GST compensation period will be over by June 2022 and thereafter GST collection of individual States is expected to depend on their tax (GST) capacity as well as enforcement effort. If the GST compensation period is not extended beyond June 2022, it is expected that there will be revenue shock for the majority of Indian States, and the duration of the shock will vary across States depending on their economic growth rate and structural composition of the economy.[79]

---

76. Sacchidananda Mukherjee, *Goods and Services Tax efficiency Across Indian States: Panel Stochastic Frontier Analysis* 55(2) Indian Econ. Rev. 225 (2020); Sacchidananda Mukherjee and R. Kavita Rao, *Fiscal Implications of Introduction of Goods and Services Tax in India*, Report Submitted to the Fifteenth Finance Commission (NIPFP, 2019).
77. Mukherjee (2020), *supra* n. 76.
78. Manish Gupta and Indira Rajaraman, *Is the 14% Revenue Guarantee to States Justified?* 55(47) Econ. & Pol. Weekly 18 (2020).
79. Moreover, the ongoing COVID-19 pandemic has heightened uncertainties surrounding GST collection in financial year 2020-2021, and it is expected that stabilization of GST will be delayed. Acknowledging that a part of GST revenue loss is due to the pandemic, and that the compensation mechanism to fill the revenue shortfall for 2020-2021 and coming years is still evolving in the GST Council, debates are ongoing in India on GST compensation requirements

[6] Moving from GST to Comprehensive GST

Available studies show that the exclusion of certain petroleum products (gasoline, diesel, ATF), natural gas, crude petroleum and electricity from the GST base is causing tax cascading.[80] Petroleum products directly enter as an input into a large number of economic activities (e.g., transportation, electricity generation and fertilizer production). Apart from such direct uses, there are a number of indirect uses as well. For instance, most commodities need to be transported for use by the final consumer, adding petroleum costs (including taxes) to the final consumer price. Tax increases on petroleum products have a significant impact on the economy often concurrently through direct and indirect routes, leading to a cascading price impact at the consumer level.

Moreover, the GST coverage of services is not universal. It is a challenge to bring all financial services and transportation services into the GST base. Except life and non-life insurance premiums, stock brokerage and certain fee-based banking services, a large segment of financial services are excluded from the GST base. The levy of service tax on road transportation services has always been a contentious issue. The approach taken under the service tax is continued under the GST regime. Transportation services of goods by road (except services of the Goods Transport Agency, or GTA) continue to be exempted. In so far as transportation services of goods are provided by the GTA to specified classes of persons, the tax liability is shifted to the recipients of the service under the reverse charge mechanism. At present loading, unloading, storage and warehousing/cargo handling services and other supporting, incidental or ancillary services related to transportation attract GST.

§22.05 CONCLUSIONS

Reform in any tax system is not a onetime event but an ongoing process, and Indian VAT/GST is not an exception. Designing a destination-based dual VAT system for a federal country like India was a challenge. The Indian GST is unique for its structure, design, and administrative framework. The present chapter captures the historical evolution of Indian VAT system since the mid-1980s.

The successive tax reform committees constituted since Independence played an important role in shaping the Indian indirect tax system that finally culminated in the introduction of GST. The recommendations of various tax reform committees helped in sequencing tax reforms and also paved the way for establishing a destination-based Indian indirect tax system. For a federal country like India, having a fairly decentralized system of fiscal jurisdiction, the sequencing of tax reforms played an important role in minimizing the disruption from major tax reforms such as GST.

of States for the year 2020-2021, *see* Sacchidananda Mukherjee, *Pandemic and GST Revenue: An Assessment for Union and States*, NIPFP Working Paper No. 327 (NIPFP, 2020).

80. Sacchidananda Mukherjee and R. Kavita Rao, *Policy Options for including Petroleum, Natural Gas and Electricity in the Goods and Services Tax* 50(9) Econ. & Pol. Weekly 98 (2015).

The mechanism of IGST settlement with States is evolving, and it is expected that the introduction of new GST return system may improve the IGST settlement. It is an important question under the Indian GST system how to ensure that net exporting States (such as those rich in minerals or with a large manufacturing base) receive sufficient revenue. To address this issue, a mechanism may be developed in the context of the intergovernmental fiscal transfer system.

There is need to obtain clarity as to whether the priority of the GST Council will be the harmonization of tax rules and regulations, or the harmonization of tax rates. The withdrawal of the GST compensation after the GST transition period may compel States to change the tax rates to generate revenue to meet their budgetary needs. Therefore, the possibility of deviation from the harmonized structure of tax rates in the GST regime cannot be ruled out completely. Tax harmonization versus fiscal autonomy is an important issue which requires careful deliberation for a federal country like India. In this context the following caution of Sijbren Cnossen on Indian GST may be taken into consideration:

> Identical GSTs might also lock the Centre and the States into a system that would become undesirable over time, but which would de facto be subject to an unanimity requirement like the European Union's (EU's) common VAT directive. The EU's directive has not been changed since 1977 and is in danger of becoming an anachronism.[81]

The GST regime is evolving in many different ways—it is evolving in structure as well as in the associated compliance and administrative regimes. The evolution is desirable and helpful in as much as it addresses the concerns faced by the taxpayers. However, the evolution also implies a long transition before the regime achieves stability, which in turn introduces an element of uncertainty into the regime. The positive gains expected from GST are associated partly with the structure and partly with the stability of the new regime. In other words, the timeline for the economy to enjoy the gains from the GST may need to be extended beyond the initial years.

81. Sijbren Cnossen, *supra* n. 46, 719.

CHAPTER 23

The VAT under Excess Capacity: The Case of Ethiopia

Marius van Oordt

§23.01 INTRODUCTION

To support economic growth, Ethiopia has long relied on a public investment-led development model financed by debt.[1] Using this model, Ethiopia experienced strong economic growth, decreased unemployment, reduced poverty and greater access to education and health care. However, it also contributed to the doubling of external debt in less than a decade, high rates of inflation and a large trade deficit, which is coupled with significant foreign exchange shortages and worsened by a small external sector.[2] Ethiopia's ability to continue financing this model with debt is, therefore, constrained by these macro-economic vulnerabilities. To reduce these vulnerabilities, domestic resource mobilization and, specifically, raising greater revenues from taxes are required. This requires changes in tax policies.

However, tax policy is never one size fits all and in designing tax policies the specific economy under study should be carefully considered.[3] In the Ethiopian economy there is excess labour of about 22% of the population, associated with a lack of capital and infrastructure.[4] Besides the excess capacity due to insufficient capital and

1. Teklu Kassu, Devendra Mishra & Melesse Asfaw, *Public External Debt, Capital Formation and Economic Growth in Ethiopia* 5 JEDS 222, 232 n. 15 (2014).
2. Data from *A Homegrown Economic Reform Agenda: A Pathway to Prosperity*, Federal Democratic Republic of Ethiopia, https://pmo.gov.et/initiatives/. The high inflation environment is likely due to public investment exceeding real resource creation in the economy.
3. Richard Bird, *Tax Challenges Facing Developing Countries*, Institute for International Business Working Paper 9 (2008).
4. Data from *World Development Indicators*, The World Bank, https://databank.worldbank.org/source/world-development-indicators.

unutilized labour, the economy suffers from low levels of effective demand.[5] The demand side of the Ethiopian economy requires separate consideration since wealthy individuals often transfer their wealth to offshore accounts, rather than invest in the economy. Due to cultural reasons, some wealthy Ethiopians are also reluctant to consume their wealth.[6] Thus, supply does not create demand.[7] These factors, together with an unequal income distribution – the Gini coefficient is estimated at 0.60[8] – constrain both supply-led and demand-led economic growth.

Aligning the characteristics of the economy under study with the adopted theoretical perspective is also important. Consider, for instance, the importance of efficiency, which underlies most of tax theory, in an economy such as Ethiopia's with significant excess capacity. In such an economy, how much should we concern ourselves with how efficient the current capacity operates? In other words, if we know the economy is far from its production possibility frontier and scarcity is of lesser concern,[9] is tax policy best aimed at enhancing growth by attempting to limit its impact on the use of *current* productive resources? Or will growth be better served by tax policies aimed at expanding the *stock* of productive resources?

To my mind, the answer is quite clearly the second option; improving how efficient current resources operate can raise growth but adding to the stock of productive resources likely holds much greater growth-enhancing potential. That tax policies can be used to raise the stock of productive resources is seldom discussed, most likely due to the point of departure of mainstream economics that the economy operates at full capacity.[10] If an economy is assumed to operate at full capacity, there is no role for tax policies to correct for excess capacity and the efficiency of the utilized capacity is of primary concern. However, once we acknowledge that significant excess capacity exists, the importance of efficiency takes second-tier to mobilizing this excess capacity.[11]

To mobilize this excess capacity, Ethiopia requires investment. To increase public investment, Ethiopia requires additional tax revenues. Collecting tax revenues means less reliance on debt, which can reduce the volatility in the inflation rate and thereby decrease investor uncertainty. Further, tax revenues can be used to address supply-side considerations for private investment, such as infrastructure and technology. This underscores the importance that tax policies within the Ethiopian context should be able to raise revenues.

5. For instance, 24% of the populations' incomes are below the national poverty line, which means low levels of consumption from at least these individuals (Federal Democratic Republic of Ethiopia, *supra* n. 2).
6. These last two statements are based on the perceptions of Ethiopian officials.
7. For further discussion on why Say's law does not hold in modern economies, *see* Paul Davidson, *Reviving Keynes's Revolution* 6 J. Post Keynesian Ec. 561, 575 n. 4 (1984).
8. The Gini coefficient is estimated using the *Socioeconomic Survey 2015-2016,* The World Bank, https://microdata.worldbank.org/index.php/catalog/2783, the most recent population-wide survey that collects income data.
9. Scarcity is of lesser concern since we have excess capacity.
10. Any move away from full capacity is only temporarily, for instance, when individuals move between employers. If left to its own, the economy returns to full capacity.
11. It should be mentioned that no economy operates at full capacity. One reason is that firms generally do not operate at full capacity, as later discussed.

In addition to conducive supply-side considerations, firms require funds to be able to invest. With limited access to credit and foreign exchange shortages, firms rely heavily on past profits to invest. This indicates that an aim of tax policies should be not to tighten these financial constraints or increase the trade deficit.

But perhaps more important than these previous considerations, there should be sufficient demand for the goods or services that investors supply or wish to supply. Without a strong consumer market, firms may not consider it profitable to invest and will often, due to low profits, not have the financial resources to invest. This indicates that an aim of tax policies in the case of Ethiopia should be to increase effective demand.

To increase effective demand in the Ethiopian context, tax policies (together with expenditure policies) should in theory redistribute profits to wages.[12] As shown empirically in multiple studies, redistributing profits to wages in an economy with a small external sector leads to increased investment and output.[13] This is so, since the propensity to consume of wage earners is greater than profit earners. Increasing the wage share (i.e., the part of national income allocated to wages) should increase total profits of capitalists, albeit off smaller profit margins. This means that although higher taxes on profits - relative to taxes on consumption or wages - will reduce profit margins, total profits should increase since total consumption in the economy increases. This increase in total profits should raise the confidence of firms and reduce their financial constraints, enabling additional investment.

The challenge for Ethiopia, however, is that its instrument collecting the most revenues and with likely the greatest potential for additional revenues, is the value-added tax (VAT), a tax on consumption.[14] On the one hand, the revenue potential of the VAT can allow for much needed non-debt based public investment or increased redistribution to wage earners, thereby supporting growth. But on the other hand, although being an efficient tax, the VAT's burden is on consumption and will decrease the share of wages in national income. Without sufficient redistribution to wages, the VAT may lead to reduced total profits and hence deter investment. [15]

12. Marc Lavoie, *Post-Keynesian Economics: New Foundations* (Edward Elgar Publishing, 2014).
13. *See*, for instance, Özlem Onaran & Giorgos Galanis, *Is Aggregate Demand Wage-Led or Profit-Led: National and Global Effects* 31 ILO CEACR 1, 51 n. 3 (2012); Engelbert Stockhammer & Özlem Onaran, *Wage-Led Growth: Theory, Evidence, Policy* 1 ROKE 61, 78 n. 1 (2013); Robert Blecker, *Wage-Led Versus Profit-Led Demand Regimes: The Long and the Short of It* 4 ROKE 373, 390 n. 4 (2016).
14. Based on data from the Ministry of Finance and Economic Development, about 30% of tax collections are from the VAT.
15. It should be noted that this result is only likely to hold in a country with a small external sector, which are typically developing countries. It can be expected that taxes on profits will have a larger negative growth effect than taxes on consumption in developed countries with larger external sectors. This is so since demand will generally be profit-led in these countries. The empirical evidence also supports this view. *See*, for instance, William McBride, *What is the Evidence on Taxes and Growth* 207 Tax Foundation Special Report (2012) for a summary of empirical results. The European Union is a unique case where raising profit taxes simultaneously at the EU level can be expected to be growth enhancing since most exports in European Union countries are to other European Union countries. *See* Thomas Obst, Özlem Onaran & Maria Nikolaidi, *The Effects of Income Distribution and Fiscal Policy on Aggregate Demand, Investment and the Budget Balance: The Case of Europe* 44 Camb. J. Econ. 1221, 1243 n. 6 (2020).

The question then is: How should a VAT be designed in an economy with excess capacity, low effective demand, a small external sector, investor uncertainty, foreign exchange shortages, and financial constraints if that economy requires significant additional tax revenues to support public investment? This is the question this chapter attempts to answer. I consider the current design of the Ethiopian VAT and consider how it can be amended to be a revenue raising tax, while limiting its negative growth impact in an economy where efficiency is of lesser importance.

Section 23.02 provides an overview of the Ethiopian VAT, covering the aspects of the VAT most relevant to the above question. Section 23.03 considers potential policy changes that can increase revenues while limiting the VATs negative growth impact. Section 23.04 concludes by discussing the strengths and weaknesses of the Ethiopian VAT and providing some lessons to be learned from applying the VAT in an economy with excess capacity.

§23.02 AN OVERVIEW OF THE ETHIOPIAN VAT

The Ethiopian VAT replaced the general sales tax in terms of Proclamation No. 285/2002 (hereinafter 'VAT Proclamation') on 1 January 2003 at an unchanged rate of 15%. The Council of Ministers Regulations No. 79/2002 provides regulations to be read together with the VAT Proclamation. The tax was amended in terms of Proclamation No. 609/2008, primarily to legislate the use of sales register machines, and in terms of Proclamation No. 1157/2019, primarily to change filing periods and decrease the VAT withholding rate to 50%.

The tax is imposed in terms of section 7(1), which provides that VAT is charged on imported goods and services and on every taxable transaction by a registered person.[16] A taxable transaction is defined in terms of section 7(3) and requires that a supply[17] is made in the course or furtherance of a taxable activity. A taxable activity in terms of section 6 means an activity carried on continuously or regularly in Ethiopia or partly in Ethiopia, whether or not for profit, that involves the supply of goods or services to another person for a consideration. Consideration is not defined in the VAT Proclamation and this may lead to uncertainty regarding, for instance, the treatment of supplies made at no charge.

Supplies that are zero-rated in terms of section 7(2) are aimed at adhering to the destination principle and easing cash flow constraints on the supply of a going concern. The only zero-rated supply that is less common is a zero-rate on indirect exports, specifically the supply of goods to the Ethiopian Commodity Exchange (ECE). Coffee, which is standard-rated if supplied domestically, and many grains and beans that are exempt if domestically supplied, are zero-rated when sold at the ECE.

An important aspect of the Ethiopian VAT is that in terms of section 8(4), exemptions can be introduced by a directive issued by the Minister of Finance and

16. A registered person is a person who is registered or required to be registered. This means that failure to register may result in the payment of VAT that should have been charged during the period that the person should have been registered.
17. The definition of supply is narrow and, for instance, excludes involuntary actions.

Economic Development. The VAT proclamation exempts 16 supplies, and the directives add another 68 exempt supplies, many of which are categories of exempt supplies (e.g., medical equipment). The exemptions include the supply of residential accommodation, financial services, religious services, medicines, medical equipment, medical services, education services, electricity, water, fuels, post office supplies, transport services, books, foodstuffs, farming inputs, imported cement, gas cylinders, cotton, and leather products. Many of the customs duty exemptions also extend to the import of goods under the VAT. Most of the exempt categories (e.g., financial services, medicines, medical equipment, medical services, educational services, transport services, etc.) are not defined or further discussed. This lack of definitions may lead to significant legal uncertainty, evasion and avoidance.

The compulsory registration threshold is set in terms of section 16. Any person whose taxable supplies exceed or will exceed Birr 1,000,000 (about USD 26,000) in any period of 12 calendar months is required to register. Persons below this threshold will be exempt from charging VAT unless they register voluntarily. Voluntary registration is, however, only allowed in terms of section 17 if a person supplies at least 75% of his goods or services to registered persons. Thus, it is possible that a legitimate business prefers to be registered but is unable to do so.

In terms of 21(6), a person that registers for VAT will only be allowed a VAT credit for goods on hand purchased or imported within six months of registering. Thus, if a person is not allowed to register voluntarily, or his registration is delayed, significant upfront costs in terms of non-deductible input VAT may be incurred.

In terms of section 27, VAT refunds are only paid within two months if at least 25% of a person's taxable transactions are zero-rated. In any other case, the VAT credit is rolled over for five months and, hereafter, the remainder of the VAT credit is refunded within two months. Also relevant to VAT refunds is the withholding regime, which provides that 50% of VAT payable is withheld by government institutions on supplies to these institutions.

The following section considers changes to the policies outlined above, taking into account the characteristics of the Ethiopian economy.

§23.03 RECONSIDERING CURRENT POLICIES

[A] Reconsidering the VAT Rate

The current VAT rate of 15% is below the African average of 16.68%.[18] It may therefore be feasible to increase the VAT rate to collect additional revenues. The additional revenues can then be used to pay debt, redistribute, and invest in infrastructure and advanced technologies. If this public investment does not remove business opportunities in the private sector, it may support private investment due to improved supply-side considerations.

18. Data from Sijbren Cnossen, *Modernizing VATs in Africa* (Oxford University Press, 2019).

However, increasing the VAT rate will decrease the wage share.[19] It can therefore be expected that consumption and total profits in the economy will decrease. This should hold since the Ethiopian economy has a small external sector and firms are, therefore, reliant on domestic consumption. The reduction in profits can be expected to decrease the confidence of investors and their financial ability to invest.

It seems likely that the negative investment impact due to lower profits will exceed the positive impact from increased public investment or redistribution. This is the case for Ethiopia in particular, due to the financial constraints faced by firms and the subsequent reliance on past profits for investment. It is therefore likely that a VAT rate increase will deter investment and thereby reduce growth by decreasing effective demand.[20]

If taxes on profits and wealth can be sufficiently raised to allow a reduction in the VAT rate, such a reduction can increase investment and growth. However, due to the current revenue requirements, such a decrease does not seem feasible in the short to medium term. Over the short to medium term, it also seems that a rate increase should be avoided. Rather than a rate increase, base changes can be made as they provide economic benefits beyond additional revenues.

[B] Reconsidering Zero-Rated Supplies

The only non-standard zero-rated supply within the Ethiopian VAT is supplies to the ECE. If this zero-rate is not abused by supplying goods to the ECE which are subsequently illegally sold back into the Ethiopian economy, the zero-rate does not impact VAT revenues. The exporters at the ECE would have been entitled to a VAT credit and the goods would have been zero-rated on export.

Without the zero-rate, exporters at the ECE would have paid VAT over to farmers and likely claimed a VAT refund. With the zero-rate, the farmers no longer receive this VAT and may require a VAT refund. The zero-rate therefore increases the cash flow of exporters and decreases the cash flow of farmers. Further, it may result in an increase in refund claims if the number of farmers supplying to the ECE exceeds the number of exporters. These refunds will also be more difficult to audit since farmers likely have weaker accounting records.[21]

The administrative challenges and potential for fraud and evasion are reasons to abolish the zero-rate on supplies to the ECE. With limited administrative capacity and the difficulties that developing countries are experiencing in paying VAT refunds

19. Large redistributions may change this result, but this seems unlikely following a rate increase.
20. Increasing the VAT rate may also have an inflationary effect. This effect can be once-off, or follow an inflationary path depending on, for instance, monetary policy and the strength of labour unions to increase wages.
21. The impact on investment of this zero-rate is difficult to determine. Reducing financial constraints of exporters may enlarge the external market for farmers and, thereby, incentivize investment by farmers. But their increased financial constraints by not receiving output VAT from exporters and potentially waiting an extensive period for a VAT refund will reduce their potential to invest. The Ethiopian VAT refund practice will, therefore, influence the impact on investment.

promptly, policy should aim to limit the amount of VAT refund claims and the potential for fraud and evasion. The zero-rating of supplies to the ECE works against this aim.

[C] Reconsidering Exempt Supplies

To reconsider exempt supplies under the Ethiopian VAT, it is worthwhile to consider the arguments often made against exempt supplies and the extent to which these arguments hold in an economy with significant excess capacity. The arguments follow.

[1] Decreases Efficiency

That VAT exemptions decrease efficiency is likely the most common argument. The argument is built on the assumption that consumers and producers are able to make optimal decisions and generally have all the required information and computational abilities to make these decisions. Any interference in the decisions of consumers or producers would, therefore, move the economy away from its optimal outcome. VAT exemptions interfere by changing relative prices of goods and services. These changes in prices then incentivize consumers and producers to substitute one good or service for another. Since the point of departure is optimal decisions, this substitution leads to less optimal outcomes.

The assumption that underlies this theory requires some discussion. For consumers and producers to make optimal decisions, it is required that they have all necessary information to rely on probability theory to make optimal decisions. Probability theory is required since whether the decision is optimal depends on future outcomes and conditions. However, our world is non-ergodic, meaning that the future cannot be determined through probability theory as the future is not statistically derived from the past.[22] Neither consumers nor producers can therefore make optimal decisions since optimal decisions require perfect information and an ergodic world. Even if economic agents had access to all information at no cost and the world was ergodic, they would lack the computational abilities to factor it all into their decision making.[23]

It is therefore reasonable to expect that consumer and producer decisions are not optimal and generally inefficient. From this point of departure, it is not clear whether a VAT exemption will increase or decrease efficiency. It may for instance distort the decisions of an inefficient producer to be more optimal or the reverse. It may for instance incentivize vertical integration where not being vertically integrated was less efficient. Without a realistic theory of consumer and producer choices, the efficiency consequences of VAT exemptions cannot be determined with certainty.

---

22. For an in-depth discussion on this *see* Paul Davidson, *Reality and Economic Theory* 18 J. Post Keynesian Ec. 479, 508 n. 4 (1996).
23. Further, the theory implicitly assumes a world where there exist worthy substitutes for all goods and services and that any good or service can be substituted for another. This tends not to be the case for many goods or services.

[2] Taxes Production

The taxing production argument is closely tied to the efficiency argument in that taxing production is more distortionary than taxing consumption and hence introduces inefficiencies. Taxing production is believed to be more distortionary since it influences the decision of labour versus leisure while a uniform consumption tax on all goods and services does not create any distortions. This distortion to labour will arise to the extent that the non-deductible input VAT that arises due to a VAT exemption cannot be shifted forward into consumer prices. It is, therefore, worthwhile to consider whether the VAT can be fully shifted forward in an economy with excess capacity.

At the centre of the theory that shows how the burden of a consumption tax is shared between producers and consumers is the upward sloping marginal cost curve. In other words, that average total costs rise with increased sales. Underlying this cost curve is an assumption of how firms operate. It is assumed that firms operate at full capacity. There are, however, convincing reasons and evidence that this is not the case and that in reality firms generally operate at excess capacity.

One reason for firms operating at excess capacity is that they do not know how demand will fluctuate and have reserves of capacity to deal with sudden increases in demand. Further, the extent to which machines are utilized is often determined by engineers and involves regular repairs and maintenance. In addition, the ratio of labour to capital is bound by how capital is designed to be used. Taking these reasons into consideration, it is not surprising that Blinder et al. found that from 200 companies with sales of more than $10 million, only 11% said that marginal costs are upward sloping in their company. The majority of companies indicated that marginal costs are constant (49%) or declining (40%).[24] In another survey conducted by Eiteman and Guthrie, only 5% of companies indicated that marginal costs have an upward slope. The authors conclude that 'it is obvious that short-run marginal price theory should be revised in the light of reality'.[25] This suggests that a more realistic view is that firms operate below full capacity where average total costs are constant or decreasing with sales.

There is, therefore, little reason to expect that Ethiopian firms operate at full capacity and face upward-sloping marginal cost curves. With flat or downward sloping marginal cost curves, firms will want to supply as much as is demanded and determine their own prices. Prices and by extension how VAT is shifted become a strategic decision of the firm. Prices may, for instance, be determined through cost-plus pricing or with reference to the market leaders' pricing.[26] If cost-plus pricing is used, we would expect the non-deductible input VAT to be fully forward shifted. If reference is made to the market leader, we can expect that the market leader fully shifts VAT forward, but

24. Alan Blinder, Elie Canetti, David Lebow & Jeremy Rudd, *Asking About Prices: A New Approach to Understanding Price Stickiness* (Russell Sage Foundation, 1999).
25. Wilford Eiteman & Glenn Guthrie, *The Shape of the Average Cost Curve* 42 Am. Econ. Rev. 832, 838 n. 5 (1952).
26. In Blinder et al., *supra*, n. 24, 2 of the main reasons that prices generally do not respond quickly to changes in the market is that firms use cost-plus pricing and hold back changes in prices to see the response of other firms.

that those with lower sales (and thereby greater average total costs) to shift some of the VAT onto the factors of production to be more competitive. In conclusion, whether VAT exemptions tax production will depend on the market structure of the firm making the exempt supply and the strategic decisions of that firm.

[3] Violates the Destination Principle

Another argument against VAT exemptions is that it violates the destination principle. This is so since exports are zero-rated under the VAT, meaning there is no VAT on exports. However, if there is an exemption in the production-distribution chain prior to exportation, input VAT will not be deductible and this VAT will be shifted either into higher export prices or onto the factors of production. Where VAT is shifted into higher export prices, the destination principle is violated.

Since Ethiopia suffers from a large trade deficit and foreign exchange shortages, together with low levels of effective demand, reducing the competitiveness of exported goods should generally be avoided.[27] Although the exemption of goods or services used in the production and distribution of exported goods may increase VAT revenues and through public investment and redistribution have a positive impact on private investment, the negative impact of higher export prices on private investment will likely be greater.

[4] Creates Import Bias

That VAT exemptions create a bias for imported goods and services is often argued. This bias exists since imported goods and services are zero-rated when exported. The import is exempt if the same supply is domestically exempt. The price of the domestic supply may, however, include non-deductible input VAT that may not be present in the import. To the extent that this imbedded VAT results in the domestic price being higher, the exemption contributes to import bias.

This argument is valid in the context of Ethiopia to the extent that the exemption relates to goods or services that are in fact domestically produced. Also, the amount of imbedded VAT should be sufficient to increase the domestic price to an uncompetitive level. It may be the case that for many imported supplies there are no competing domestic supplies and the argument would, therefore, not be important in the short term.[28] Or it may be that the price difference between the imported and domestically produced supplies are larger than the amount of imbedded VAT, which will also lessen the importance of the argument. Nevertheless, the negative impact on investment in goods or services that can readily be imported likely warrants the removal of the exemption.

27. An exclusion to this is where the wage share will increase as a result. Since the exported good will generally be supplied domestically, it will increase the VAT burden on consumers and decrease the wage share.
28. It can be argued that over the long term, a good or service may have been domestically produced if it was not for the exemption.

[5] *Other Arguments*

There are other, generally smaller, arguments against exemptions. One is that exemption may incentivize misclassification fraud; classifying an exempt output as taxable to deduct related input VAT. It is indeed the case that this type of fraud is incentivized by exemptions; it also seems likely that if a tax administration is unable to detect this type of fraud, they will also fail to detect the fraud that replaces it, e.g., overstating the value of other inputs to reduce VAT payable. Thus, this argument alone may not be sufficient to avoid all exemptions.

Another argument is that exemptions lead to increased compliance and administrative costs due to input VAT allocations. This happens when a supplier makes both exempt and taxable supplies and a specific input is used towards both these types of supplies. It is the case that allocating inputs is an additional compliance requirement. This is, of course, only a concern for firms who make both exempt and taxed supplies. The use of computers can also drastically reduce the compliance and administrative costs involved in allocating VAT inputs.

The last argument is that of exemption creep. It is argued that one exemption provides opportunity for lobbyists to argue for additional exemptions. Although exemptions often increase over time, it is not clear whether the presence of other exemptions is the determining factor. It may, for instance, be that the number of exemptions would have increased irrespective of the current list of exemptions. Without empirical evidence of this phenomenon, it is difficult to gauge the validity of this argument.[29]

[6] *Ethiopia's Exemptions*

From the discussion above, it seems to be the case that Ethiopia should avoid exemptions that significantly increase export prices or result in import bias. To determine whether other exemptions are warranted, it should be considered whether other VAT exemptions will necessarily decrease growth in the Ethiopian context.

With a VAT exemption, the value-added by the supplier of the exempt good or service goes untaxed. If the exemption is on an intermediate good or service used to make a standard-rated supply, the cascaded input VAT will increase the consumption tax burden of consumers.[30] The wage share will, therefore, decrease and this may reduce investment and growth through its dampening effect on effective demand. It is unlikely that the increased public investment and redistribution due to increased

29. It may be noted that I did not specifically address the revenue consequences of exemptions in this section. This is so since obtaining additional revenues from the VAT may or may not be economically beneficial. This would depend on who contributes these additional revenues, how the revenues are used and the state and structure of the economy. Thus, I do not regard a decrease or increase in revenues in itself as an argument against exemptions.
30. It is possible that the burden is fully shifted onto the factors of production, but this seems unlikely. Empirical evidence also does not support this possibility. *See* Dora Benedek, Ruud De Mooij & Philippe Wingender, *Estimating VAT Pass Through*, International Monetary Fund WP/15/214 (2015).

revenues have a stronger influence on private investment. It therefore seems that exemptions on intermediate goods or services that may be used to make taxable supplies should generally be avoided.

It is, however, possible that exemptions on intermediate goods or services used to make exempt supplies, or exemptions on supplies to consumers may be growth enhancing. This will be the case where the tax benefit from the exemption for consumers with high propensities to consume is greater than the redistribution that these consumers would receive if the exempt supply is taxed. This means that exemptions that provide a greater benefit to high-propensity consumers than low-propensity consumers are likely to be growth enhancing. I say so since redistribution policies are often not well-targeted or do not include all high propensity consumers. This conclusion is, therefore, contrary to that of mainstream economics. In an economy with excess capacity, certain VAT exemptions may be growth enhancing.

In practice, as is the case in Ethiopia, exemptions that benefit high-propensity consumers to a greater extent than low-propensity consumers are uncommon. One reason is that high-propensity consumers tend to purchase goods and services more often in the informal economy (i.e., from non-registered firms) than low-propensity consumers. If low-propensity consumers predominantly purchase goods or services in the formal economy, the additional VAT burden from taxing these goods or services will predominantly fall on these consumers. Another reason is that since low-propensity consumers tend to be wealthier, they may consume more of a good or service than high-propensity consumers.

A number of goods and services in Ethiopia are purchased to a greater extent by high-propensity consumers than low-propensity consumers.[31] These are millet, maize, wheat, barley, sorghum, starch, pulses, oil seeds, farming seeds, fertilizer, fungicides, herbicides, pesticides, animal feed, farming animals, salt, kerosene, firewood, books, raw cotton, and transport by boat.[32] If there are not marked differences in where these goods and services are purchased - the formal or informal economy - and their exemption would not significantly increase export prices, or result in import bias, or be on intermediate goods or services used to make taxable supplies, an exemption on these goods or services may be warranted.

Considering the current list of exempt supplies in terms of the VAT Proclamation, it therefore seems to be the case that at least the exemptions on religious services, medicines, medical equipment, medical services, education services, electricity, water, fuels besides kerosene, post office supplies, transport services besides transport by boat, foodstuffs besides those listed above, farming inputs besides those listed above, imported cement, gas cylinders, and leather products likely have a negative growth

31. Data from the World Bank, *supra* n. 8. For this discussion it is assumed that poorer households have high propensities to consume and wealthy households have low propensities to consume. This is a reasonable assumption since wealthy households are able to save while poor households are less able to do so.

32. Since data are not available on where the goods and services are purchased and it is beyond the scope of this chapter to determine the extent that these goods or services are exported, imported, or used as intermediate goods, I do not provide final recommendations on whether the exemption should apply.

impact on the Ethiopian economy. Taxing these goods and services with redistribution to high-propensity consumers should be growth enhancing.

[D] Reconsidering VAT Registration, Refunds, and the Withholding Regime

The Ethiopian VAT has a number of provisions that limit the growth of firms. Firms' growth is limited by these provisions due to the competitive disadvantages and tightened financial constraints that they cause.

The first provision is that in terms of section 17, a person who does not at least supply 75% of goods or services to registered persons may not register voluntarily. Small firms below the registration threshold who may not register will be at a competitive disadvantage on supplies to registered persons. This is so since these firms cannot deduct input VAT, and this will increase their supply price. That they do not charge output VAT is only an advantage when supplying to consumers. Further, not receiving output VAT tightens financial constraints by reducing cash flows.

The second provision is that in terms of section 27, VAT credits for non-exporters are rolled over for five months after which a refund may be paid within two months. For a firm with financial constraints, having to wait at least seven months to get a refund can greatly reduce its ability to invest and grow. VAT refunds should be paid as promptly as possible. If the revenue administration struggles to do this, deferring input VAT on imported capital for selected businesses may be considered.[33]

The third provision is that in terms of 21(6), a person that registers for VAT will only be allowed a VAT credit for goods on hand, purchased or imported within six months of registering. Firms may, therefore, have inputs that are used to make taxable supplies on which no input VAT could be deducted. Besides tightening financial constraints and taxing intermediate goods, this provision removes part of the incentive for firms to register under the VAT. Firms who are unable to deduct input VAT on capital will be at a competitive disadvantage.

The last provisions are those that provide for the withholding regime on supplies to government institutions. Although withholding regimes may potentially reduce evasion, a supplier under such a regime will not receive output VAT, or receive a reduced amount of output VAT. Such a supplier may, therefore, require a refund of input VAT. Again, the cash flow consequences of this may greatly deter investment and firm growth. Further, since government institutions possess the invoices on supplies to them, cross checking these invoices against the declarations of suppliers to government institutions should be fairly easy.

33. Deferral of import VAT involves customs not charging import VAT to VAT registered businesses, but that these businesses declare output VAT and deduct an equivalent amount of input VAT in their next tax return. A copy of the VAT return is then sent to customs.

§23.04 CONCLUSION

The Ethiopian VAT has some strengths. For instance, it only applies a single non-zero rate. Especially in countries with limited administrative capacity, multiple rates under the VAT create unnecessary complexities. The potential efficiency gains from multiple rates are also less relevant in the Ethiopian context. Also, it has a high registration threshold. Not implementing a compliance burden on small firms that opt not to register is important to support the growth of these firms. Further, administrations should focus their attentions on large taxpayers, especially in countries with limited administrative capacity.

Unfortunately, the weaknesses of the Ethiopian VAT dwarf its strengths. As in many African countries, the law lacks definitions of important terms. Without definitions, the application of the VAT can become arbitrary. Where there are definitions, these are often too narrow or too broad to ensure that the VAT works as intended.[34] The definitions are also scattered throughout the Proclamation with many definitions only referring to other definitions.

There are also institutional weaknesses, such as allowing the Minister of Finance and Economic Development to make base changes by directive. Although in terms of the Proclamation this should be limited to exemptions, zero-rated supplies have also been introduced in this manner. That these directives do not need parliamentary approval may have led to excessive lobbying, political influence peddling, and base erosion, as suggested by the 68 exempt supplies provided by directive.

The policy weaknesses are however most concerning. The selection of exempt supplies is broadly not in the interest of economic growth and development. As discussed, in an economy with excess capacity, certain VAT exemptions may increase private investment and enhance growth. However, most of the current exemptions predominantly provide a tax benefit to consumers with low propensities to consume. These exemptions decrease revenues, effective demand, and total profits in the economy. Removing these exemptions and redistributing to consumers with high propensities to consume will likely increase effective demand, total profits, investment, and the utilized capacity of the economy. The bases of other taxes will broaden and provide additional tax revenues. Removing most of the VAT exemptions should, therefore, be central to the Ethiopian domestic resource mobilization strategy.

Reducing financial constraints should also be central to this strategy. The VAT has the ability to improve the cash flows of registered firms. But current provisions, especially those applicable to voluntary registration, claiming VAT refunds, and the withholding regime tighten financial constraints. It is also not the case that firms can easily obtain credit to ease these constraints. To be credit worthy, a firm would require a favourable profit record, which requires past investment and freedom from financial constraints. Firms can therefore be in a financial trap. Further, in an environment of

34. An example of a too narrow definition is that of supply, which limits the meaning to the sale of goods or rendition of services. The definition of export is, for instance, too broad in that any goods taken out of Ethiopia are regarded as exported.

high inflation and consequently increased interest rates, the liquidity preference of banks may be high, leading to strict credit rationing.

It may have been noticed that this chapter does not mention equity. This is so since in an economy with excess capacity, the objectives of growth and equity are generally aligned. In such an economy, the objective of taxes is much greater than obtaining funds for public goods by disturbing the economy as little as possible while avoiding (subjective) unequitable outcomes. The objective of taxes is to enhance growth by reallocating resources, while removing supply side and financial constraints to investment. There is much work to be done to better align countries' VATs with this objective.

Bibliography

Abbott, George M., *The Precarious Politics of Shifting Direction: The Introduction of a Harmonized Sales Tax in British Columbia and Ontario* 186 BC Studies 125 (2015).

Abdoelkariem, Rahiela, and & Frank Prinsen, *The Interaction Between Head Office, Branch and VAT Grouping: New Challenges Ahead for the European Union* 26(4) Int'l VAT Monitor 205 (2015).

Acheson, Jean, Yota Deli, Edgar Morgenroth, Derek Lambert, and Martin Murphy, *VAT Revenue Elasticities: An Analytical Approach*, ESRI Working Paper No. 596 (The Economic and Social Research Institute, 2018).

Adam, Stuart et al., *A Retrospective Evaluation of Elements of the EU VAT System*, Full Report (Institute for Fiscal Studies, 2011).

Adams, Thomas S., *Fundamental Problems of Federal Income Taxation* 35(4) Q. J. Econ. 527 (1921).

Agence Européenne de productivité de l'Organisation Européenne de Coopération Economique, *Le Régime Fiscal du Chiffre d'Affaires et son incidence sur la productivité (The Regime of Turnover Tax and its Effect on Productivity)*, Project No. 315 (November 1957).

Aggarwal, Pawan K., *Incidence of Major Indirect Taxes in India* (NIPFP, 1995).

Aggarwal, Pawan K., *Modified Value Added Tax (MODVAT): Structure and Resource Mobilisation*, Paper prepared for the Working Group on Tax Policy of the Steering Group on Financial Resources for the Ninth Five Year Plan (1997-1998 to 2001-2002) (NIPFP, 1996).

Agrawal, David R., and William F. Fox, *Taxes in an E-commerce Generation* 24(5) Int'l Tax and Pub. Fin. 903 (2017).

Aguirre, Carlos, and Partho Shome, *The Mexican Value-Added Tax*, Working Paper 87/21, (International Monetary Fund, 1987).

Ainsworth, Richard T., and Andrew Shact, *Blockchain (Distributed Ledger Technology) Solves VAT Fraud*, Boston University School of Law, Law & Economics Working Paper No. 16-41.

Ainsworth, Richard T., *Carousel Fraud in the EU: A Digital VAT Solution* Tax Notes Int'l 443 (2006).

Ainsworth, Richard T., Musaad Alwohaibi, and Mike Cheetham, *VATCoin: The GCC's Cryptotaxcurrency*, Boston University School of Law, Law & Economics Working Paper No. 17-04.

Ainsworth, Richard T., *The Digital VAT (D-VAT)* 25 Virg. Tax Rev. 875 (2006).

Alastair Thomas, Alastair, *Reassessing the Regressivity of the VAT, OECD Taxation Working Papers No 49* (OECD, 2020).

Allers, Maarten, *Administrative and Compliance Costs of Taxation and Public Transfers in the Netherlands* (Wolters-Noordhoff 1994).

Amand, Christian, and Veronique Lenoir, *Pro Rata Deduction of VAT by Financial Institutions – Gross Margin or Interest*? 17(1) Int'l VAT Monitor 17 (2006).

Amand, Christian, *Are VAT Exemptions Compatible with Primary EU Law?* 21(6) Int'l VAT Monitor 411 (2010).

Amand, Christian, *Cross-Border Entities and EU VAT: A Contradictory Concept?* 21(1) Int'l. VAT Monitor 20 (2010).

Amand, Christian, *EU VAT and Financial Services: Which Rules, What Consequences and Which Possible Solutions?* 30(5) Int'l. VAT Monitor (2019).

Amand, Christian, *EU VAT or the Emergence of an Efficient Consumption Tax in an Internal Market* in *CFE Tax Advisers Europe – 60th Anniversary – Liber Amicorum* 36 (Servaas van Thiel et al., eds., IBFD, 2019).

Amand, Christian, *Treaty of Lisbon and B2B VAT Exemptions,* 23(4) Int'l VAT Monitor 242, 246 (2012).

Amand, Christian, *VAT Neutrality: A Principle of EU Law or a Principle of the VAT System?* 2(3) W. J. VAT/GST L. 163 (2013).

Andrews, Colman, *Kroger, Publix and Hy-Vee on list of best grocery store chains in every state.* USA Today (16 December 2019).

Annacondia, Fabiola, *VAT Registration Thresholds in Europe,* 31(6) Int'l VAT Monitor (2020).

Arzini, Nino P., and Sebastiaan J. Carriere, *Profijt door een derde leidt niet tot profijt voor de fiscus* 7 BtwBrief 2020/80.

Assibey-Mensah, George O., *The Value Added Tax in Ghana* 19(2) Pub. Budg. & Fin. 76 (1999).

Atkinson, Anthony, and Joseph E. Stiglitz, *The Design of Tax Structure: Direct Versus Indirect Taxation* 6(1-2) J. Pub. Econ. 55 (1976).

Auer, Silvia and Kristin Resenig, *Sachspende, Entsorgung oder Verzicht auf Rückversand bei Retourwaren* 16-17 SWK, 899 (2020).

Austl. GST Guide Commentary (CCH Australia, online).

Australian Customs and Border Protection Services, *Practice Statement B_IND08 – Valuation – Transfer Pricing Policy* (12 April 2013).

Australian Government Treasury, *GST Treatment of Cross-Border Transactions*, Consultation Process (6 October 2015-20 October 2015), available at https://treasury.gov.au/consultation/gst-treatment-of-cross-border-transactions.

Australian Taxation Office (ATO), GSTR 2005/4, *Goods and Services Tax: Arrangements of the Kind Described in Taxpayer Alerts TA 2004/6 and TA 2004/7: Use of the Grouping or Margin Scheme Provisions of the GST Act to Avoid or Reduce the Goods and Services Tax on the Sale of New Residential Premises* (14 September 2005).

Australian Taxation Office (ATO), *Practice Statement Law Administration PS LA 2016/1, Transfer Pricing Adjustments with Potential Customs Implications* (14 April 2016).

Australian Taxation Office (ATO), *Practice Statement Law Administration PS LA 2015/4, Advance Pricing Agreements* (16 March 2017).

Australian Taxation Office (ATO), Taxation Ruling TR 97/20, *Income Tax: Arm's Length Transfer Pricing Methodologies for International Dealings* (5 November 1997).

Avila, Javier, and Angela Cruz, *Elementos para la discusión de una reforma del IVA en Colombia* (Elements for the discussion of a VAT reform in Colombia) (DIAN, Office of the Subdirector of Operating Management, 2012).

Awashti, Rajul, *Forecasting Tax Revenues: An Overview*, Webinar for Parliamentary Budget Offices, Global Tax Team, Europe and Central Asia Lead, World Bank Group (April 2017).

Ayee, Joseph R.A., *Policy Management in Africa: The Case of Value Added Tax* 2(8/9) Afr. J. Pub. Admin. & Mgmt 51 (1997).

Bacache-Beauvallet, Maya, *Tax Competition, Tax Coordination, and e-Commerce* 20(1) J. Pub. Econ. Theory 100 (2018).

Bachas, Pierre, Lucie Gadenne, and Anders Jensen, *Informality, Consumption Taxes and Redistribution*, NBER Working Paper No. 27429 (June 2020).

Bagchi, Amaresh, *Fifty Years of Fiscal Federalism in India: An Appraisal*, Kale Memorial Lecture delivered at the Gokhale Institute of Politics and Economics, Pune on 8 December 2002 (NIPFP, 2002).

Bagchi, Amaresh, Mahesh C. Purohit, S. Venkatarama Iyer, O.P. Gahrotra, Pawan Aggarwal, and A.V.L. Narayana, *Reform of Domestic Trade Taxes in India: Issues and Options*, (NIPFP, 1994).

Bagchi, Amaresh, *Towards GST: Choices and Trade-Offs* 41(14) Econ. & Pol. Weekly 1314 (2006).

Bain, Kathrin, Michael Walpole, Ann Hansford, and Chris Evans, *The Internal Costs of VAT Compliance Costs: Evidence from Australia and the United Kingdom and Suggestions for Mitigation* 13(1) eJ. Tax Rsrch. 158 (2015).

Bajpai, Prableen, *China's GDP Examined: A Service-Sector Surge*, Investopedia (22 April 2020), available at https://www.investopedia.com/articles/investing/103114/chinas-gdp-examined-servicesector-surge.asp.

Bal, Aleksandra, *Taxing the Consumption of Digital Goods*, in *Tax Sovereignty in the BEPS Era* 143 (Sergio A. Rocha and Allison Christians, eds., Wolters Kluwer, 2017).

Barbone, Luca, Misha Belkindas, Leon Bettendorf, Richard Bird, Mikhail Bonch-Osmolovskiy, and Michael Smart, *Study to Quantify and Analyse the VAT Gap in EU-27 Countries*, CASE Network Reports No. 116/2013 (Warsaw: CASE, 2013).

Barbone, Luca, Richard M. Bird, and Jaime Vazquez-Caro, *The Costs of VAT: A Review of the Literature*, Working Paper 12 (International Center for Public Policy, 2012).

Baurer, Lewis I., *Tax Administrations and Small and Medium Enterprises (SMEs) in Developing Countries* (The World Bank, 2005).

Belgian VAT authorities, *VAT commentary*, Chapter 11 *Deductions*, section 15.3.c, available at https://eservices.minfin.fgov.be/myminfin-web/pages/fisconet#!/.

Benedek, Dora et al., *Varieties of VAT Pass Through* 27 Int'l Tax & Pub. Fin. 890 (2020).

Benedek, Dora, Ruud De Mooij, and Philippe Wingender, *Estimating VAT Pass Through*, International Monetary Fund WP/15/214 (2015).

Benge, Matt, Marie Pallot, and Hamish Slack, *Possible Lessons for the United States from New Zealand's GST* 66(2) Nat'l Tax J. 479 (2013).

Benzarti, Youssef, and Dorian Carloni, *Who Really Benefits from Consumption Tax Cuts? Evidence from a Large VAT Reform in France*, NBER, Working Paper No. 23848 (2017).

Benzarti, Youssef, Dorian Carloni, Jarkko Harju and Tuomas Kosonen, *What Goes Up May Not Come Down: Asymmetric Incidence of Value-Added Taxes*, Working Paper No. 23849 (NBER 2017, revised 2018).

Beretta, Giorgio, *European VAT and the Sharing Economy* (Kluwer Law International, 2019).

Berger, Wolfgang et al., *Titel IX: Steuerbefreiungen* in *Kommentar zur Mehrwertsteuer – Mehrwertsteuersystemrichtlinie* (Thomas Ecker et al., eds., LexisNexis).

Bijl, Jeroen, *Air France-KLM: The SAFE Equivalent for Services?* 27(2) Int'l. VAT Monitor 95 (2016).

Bijl, Jeroen, *The EU VAT Treatment of Vouchers in the Context of Promotional Activities* (Wolters Kluwer, 2019).

Bijl, Jeroen, *VAT Deduction: The Relevance of Being 'The Recipient' of a Supply and the Use of the Supply* 29(5) EC Tax Review 227 (2020).

Bijl, Jeroen, *VAT: 'Money Off Vouchers' and 'Cash Back Schemes' – What Are the Problems and How Can They Be Solved?* 21(5) EC Tax Rev. 262 (2012).

Bird, Richard and Pierre-Pascal Gendron, *VATs in Federal States: International Experience and Emerging Possibilities*, Working Paper No. 01-4, International Studies Program, Andrew Young School of Policy Studies (Georgia State University, 2001).

Bird, Richard M., and Pierre-Pascal Gendron, *C-VAT, VIVAT, and Dual VAT: Vertical 'Sharing' and Interstate Trade* 7 Int'l Trade & Pub. Finance 753 (2000).

Bird, Richard M., and Pierre-Pascal Gendron, *Dual VATs and Cross-border Trade: Two Problems, One Solution?* 5 Int'l Tax & Pub. Finance 429 (1998).

Bird, Richard M., and Pierre-Pascal Gendron, *Is VAT the Best Way to Impose a General Consumption Tax in Developing Countries?* 60 Bul. Int'l Taxation 287 (2006).

Bird, Richard M., *Commentary on Value Added Tax and Excises*, in *Dimensions of Tax Design: The Mirrlees Review* 363 (James Mirrlees et al. eds., Oxford University Press, 2010).

Bird, Richard M., *Review of 'Principles and Practices of Value Added Taxation: Lessons from Developing Countries'* 41(6) Can. Tax J. 1222, 1224 (1993).

Bird, Richard M., *The Reform of Indirect Taxes in Jamaica*, Jamaica Tax Structure Examination Project Staff Paper No. 24, Metropolitan Studies Program, Maxwell School, Syracuse University, 1989.

Bird, Richard M., *VAT During and After the Pandemic* 99(13) Tax N. Int'l 1747 (28 September 2020).

Bird, Richard, and Eric M. Zolt, *The Limited Role of the Personal Income Tax in Developing Countries* 16 J. Asian Econ. 928 (2005).

Bird, Richard, and PierrePascal Gendron, *The VAT in Developing and Transitional Countries* (Cambridge University Press, 2007).

Bird, Richard, *Tax Challenges Facing Developing Countries*, Institute for International Business Working Paper 9 (2008).

Bjerregaard Eskildsen, Casper, *VAT Grouping versus Freedom of Establishment* 20(3) EC Tax Rev. 114 (2011).

Blažić, Helena, *Tax Compliance Costs of Small Business in Croatia*, Occasional Paper No. 22. (Institute of Public Finance, 2004).

Blecker, Robert, *Wage-Led Versus Profit-Led Demand Regimes: The Long and the Short of It* 4 ROKE 373 (2016).

Blinder, Alan, Elie Canetti, David Lebow, and Jeremy Rudd, *Asking About Prices: A New Approach to Understanding Price Stickiness* (Russell Sage Foundation, 1999).

Blokland, Wouter J., *Taxing Employee Benefits in Kind under EU VAT* 22(2) Int'l VAT Monitor 98 (2011).

Blumenthal, Martha, and Joel Slemrod, *The Compliance Costs of the US Individual Income Tax System: A Second Look after Tax Reform* 45(2) Nat'l Tax J. 461 (1992).

Board of Taxation (Australia), *Review of the Legal Framework for the Administration of the Goods and Services Tax: A Report to the Assistant Treasurer and Minister for Competition Policy and Consumer Affairs* (December 2008).

Botes, Marlene, *South Africa – Value Added Tax*, in *VAT Worldwide* (Panos Thliveros, Zsolt Szatmari, Jordi Sol, eds., IBFD, 2020).

Brautigam, Deborah, Odd-Helge Fjeldstad, and Mick Moore, *Taxation and State-Building in Developing Countries: Capacity and Consent* (Cambridge University Press, 2008).

British Bankers Association, *Response to the European Commission's Consultation Paper on Modernising the VAT Treatment of Vouchers and Related Issues* (26 January 2007).

Brondolo, John, and Zhiyong Zhang, *Tax Administration Reform in China: Achievements, Challenges, and Reform Priorities*, IMF Working Paper (2016), available at https://www.elibrary.imf.org/doc/IMF001/23295-9781475523614/23295-9781475523614/Other_formats/Source_PDF/23295-9781475547344.pdf.

Brys, Bert, Stephen Matthews, Richard Herd, and Xiao Wang, *Tax Policy and Tax Reform in the People's Republic of China*, OECD Taxation Working Papers No. 18, OECD Publishing Paris (4 September 2013), available at http://dx.doi.org/10.1787/5k40l4dlmnzw-en.

Brysland, Gordon, *Fiscal Neutrality, Foreign ghost in our GST Machine? Where Policy Meets Reality*, available at https://www.business.unsw.edu.au/News-Events-Site/Events-Site/Documents/Gordon-Brysland-Fiscal-neutrality_paper.pdf.

Burges, Robin, Stephen Howes, and Nicholas Stern, *Value-Added Tax Options for India* 2(1) Int'l Tax & Pub. Fin. 109 (1995).

Burman, Leonard, and David White, *Taxing Capital Gains in New Zealand* 9 NZ J. Tax & Policy 355 (2003).

Campbell-Kelly, Martin, and Daniel D. Garcia-Swartz, *From Products to Services: The Software Industry in the Internet Era* 81(4) Bus. Hist. Rev. 735 (2007).

Canada Revenue Agency, GST/HST Policy Statement P-051R2, *Carrying on Business in Canada.*

Canada Revenue Agency, *Tax Gap and Compliance Results for the Federal Corporate Income Tax System*,(2020) available at https://www.canada.ca/en/revenue-agency/corporate/about-canada-revenue-agency-cra/tax-canada-a-conceptual-study/taxgap-compliance-results.html.

Carbonnier, Clement, *Who Pays Sales Taxes? Evidence from French VAT Reforms, 1987–1999* 91(5-6) J. Pub. Econ. 1219 (2007).

Carter, J.W., *Carter on Contract* (LexisNexis online).

CASE, *Study and Reports on the VAT Gap in EU-28 Member States: 2019 Final Report* (Warsaw: Center for Social and Economic Research, 2019).

Caspersen, Erik, and Gilbert Metcalf, *Is A Value Added Tax Regressive? Annual Versus Lifetime Incidence Measures* 47(4) Nat'l Tax J. 731 (1994).

Castro Arango, Jose Manuel, Avances Jurisprudenciales Con La Sentencia C-776 De 2003 (Mínimo Vital Y Justicia Material Del Gasto) (*Advances in Jurisprudence C-776, 2003 (Vital Minimum and Spending Justice)*) (2004), Revista de Derecho Fiscal (Universidad Externado de Colombia), No. 2 (2004), available at SSRN: https://ssrn.com/abstract=1522085.

Chan, Daniel, Doris Ho, and Tina Xia, *China's Nationwide VAT Reform – Implementation Rules Issued*, Hong Kong Lawyer (10 May 2016).

Chartered Institute of Chartered Accountants in England and Wales, Tax Faculty, *Memorandum to the European Commission in Response to an Invitation to Comment on a Consultation Paper published on 13 November 2006* (March 2007).

Chhabra, Tarun, Rush Doshi, Ryan Hass & Emilie Kimball, *Global Technology China,* (Brookings Institute (April 2020), available at https://www.brookings.edu/research/global-china-technology/.

Child Poverty Action Group, *Will Removing GST on Fresh Fruit and Vegetables Achieve its Stated Aim?* (CPAG, 2010), available at https://www.cpag.org.nz/will-removing-gst-on-fresh-fruit-and-vegettables/ (accessed 31 January 2021).

Child, David, *VAT Administration: Addressing Private Sector Concerns*, in *VAT in Africa* 129 (Richard Krever, ed., Pretoria University Law Press, 2008).

Cnossen, Sijbren, *A Proposal to Apply the Kiwi-VAT to Insurance Services in the European Union* 20(5) Int'l Tax & Pub. Fin. 867 (2013).

Cnossen, Sijbren, *A VAT Primer for Lawyers, Economists, and Accountants*, in *VAT Reader* (Tax Analysts, 2011).

Cnossen, Sijbren, *Evaluating the National Retail Sales Tax from a VAT Perspective*, in *United States Tax Reform in the 21st Century* 215 (George R. Zodrow and Peter Mieszkowski, eds., Cambridge University Press, 2002).

Cnossen, Sijbren, *Excise Taxation for Domestic Revenue Mobilization*, CESifo Working Papers 8442 (July 2020).

Cnossen, Sijbren, *Is the VAT's Sixth Directive Becoming an Anachronism?* 43(12) Bul. Int'l Fisc. Doc. 434 (2003).

Cnossen, Sijbren, *Mobilizing VAT Revenues in African Countries*, 22 Int'l Tax & Pub. Fin. 1077 (2015).

Cnossen, Sijbren, *Modernizing the European VAT*, CESifo Working Papers 8279 (Munich: CESifo, 2020).

Cnossen, Sijbren, *Modernizing VATs in Africa* (Oxford University Press, 2019).

Cnossen, Sijbren, *Preparing the Way for a Modern GST in India* 20(4) Int'l Tax & Public Finance 715 (2013).

Cnossen, Sijbren, *The Role and Rationale for Excise Taxes in ASEAN Countries* 59 Bul. Int'l Fiscal Doc. 503 (2005).

Cnossen, Sijbren, *Three VAT Studies* (CPB, 2010).

Cnossen, Sijbren, *What Rate Structure for a Value-Added Tax?* 35 Nat'l Tax J. 205 (1982).

Cnossen, Sijbren, *Administrative and Compliance Costs of the VAT: A Review of the Evidence* 43 Tax N. Int'l 1649 (1994).

Cnossen, Sijbren, *Broad-Based Consumption Taxes: VAT, RST or BTT?* 6 Austl. Tax F. 392 (1989).

Cnossen, Sijbren, *The Technical Superiority of VAT Over RST* 4 Austl. Tax F. 419 (1987).

Cockfield, Arthur J., *The Rise of The OECD as Informal World Tax Organization through National Responses to E-Commerce Tax Challenges* 8(1) Yale J.L. & Tech (2006).

Cockfield, Arthur, Walter Hellerstein, Rebecca Millar & Christophe Waerzeggers, *Taxing Global Digital Commerce* (Kluwer Law International, 2013).

Colombian Ministry of Finance, *Marco Fiscal de Mediano Plazo 2020, Colombia* (The Median Term Fiscal Framework in 2020, Colombia).

Combey, Adama, *Evaluation of the VAT Gap in Togo*, 27 Revue Economique et Monétaire 44, (June 2020), available at https://mpra.ub.uni-muenchen.de/101478/.

Commonwealth of Australia, *Tax Benchmarks and Variations Statement 2019* (Canberra, 2020).

Comptroller and Auditor General (CAG) of India, *Implementation of Value Added Tax in India – Lessons for transition to Goods and Services Tax – A Study Report* (Comptroller and Auditor General (CAG) of India, June 2010).

Constantinesco, Léontin-Jean, *L'applicabilité directe dans le droit de la CEE* (Bruylant, 2006).

Coolidge, Jacqueline, *Findings of Tax Compliance Cost Surveys in Developing Countries* 10(2) eJ. Tax Rsrch 250 (2012).

Cooper, Graeme, and Richard Vann, *A Few Myths About the GST* 23 UNSW L. J. 252 (2000).

Cooper, Graeme, *The Discrete Charm of the VAT*, Legal Studies Research Paper No. 07/65, Sydney Law School, November 2007, available at http://ssrn.com/abstract=1027512 (2007).

Copenhagen Economics and KPMG, *VAT in the Public Sector and Exemptions in the Public Interest* (2013), available at https://ec.europa.eu/taxation_customs/sites/taxation/files/resources/documents/common/publications/studies/vat_public_sector_exemptions_en.pdf.

Copenhagen Report, *Study on Reduced VAT Applied to Goods and Services in the Member States of the European Union* (Copenhagen Economics, 2007).

Cornielje, Simon, and Ivan Bondarev, *Scanning the Scope of Skandia* 26(1) Int'l VAT Monitor 17 (2015).

Council of European Municipalities and Regions, *VAT and Tax Exemptions on Public Bodies: No Taxation without Representation*, CEMR draft response to the European Commission consultation on the review of existing VAT legislation on public bodies and tax exemptions in the public interest (April 2014), available at https://ccre.org/img/uploads/piecesjointe/filename/CEMR_response_to_VAT_consultation_EN.pdf.

Courjon, Odile, *New Rules for Head Office to Branch Scenarios – Comments on the* Skandia *Case* 26(1) Int'l VAT Monitor 22 (2015).

Cramer, Victor, *Waving Goodbye to VAT?* Bloomberg online, Daily Tax Report: International, (20 June 2019).

Crawford, Ian, Michael Keen, and Stephen Smith, *Value Added Tax and Excises*, in *Dimensions of Tax Design: The Mirrlees Review* 275 (James Mirrlees et al., eds., Oxford University Press, 2010).

Cui, Wei, *China's Business-Tax-to-VAT Reform: An Interim Assessment* 5 British Tax Rev. 617 (2014).

Dace, Hermione, *China's Tech Landscape: A Primer*, Tony Blair Institute for Global Change, (9 January 2020), available at https://institute.global/policy/chinas-tech-landscape-primer.

Das-Gupta, Arindam, *An Assessment of the Revenue Impact of State-Level VAT in India* 47(10) Econ. & Pol. Weekly 55 (2012).

Das-Gupta, Arindam, *Will State VAT Deliver?* 4(36) Econ. & Pol. Weekly 3917 (2005).

Dave, Sachin, and Vinod Mahanta, *Government to Vet GST, Income Tax and Transfer Pricing Filings to Find Leakage* (The Economic Times, New Delhi, 28 August 2018).

Davidson, Paul, *Reality and Economic Theory* 18 J. Post Keynesian Ec. 479 (1996).

Davidson, Paul, *Reviving Keynes's Revolution* 6 J. Post Keynesian Ec. 561 (1984).

De Angelis, Enrico, and Theo Elshof, *The Interplay Between Transfer Pricing and Customs Valuation in Case of Retroactive Profit Adjustments: The Position of the ECJ in the Case Hamamatsu Photonics Deutschland GmbH (C-529/16)*, 25(4) International Transfer Pricing J. 300 (2018).

De Boer, Leoni, *VAT and Holding Companies' Involvement: Benefit of the Doubt?* (IBFD, 15 August 2018).

De La Feria, Rita, and Herman van Kesteren, *Introduction to This Special Issue – VAT Exemptions: Consequences and Design Alternatives* 22(5) Int'l VAT Monitor 300 (2011).

De la Feria, Rita, and Michael Walpole, *The Impact of Public Perception on General Consumption Taxes* [2020] 67/5 British Tax Rev. 637.

De La Feria, Rita, and Richard Krever, *Ending VAT Exemptions: Towards a Post-Modern VAT,* In *VAT Exemptions: Consequences and Design Alternatives* 3 (Rita de la Feria, ed., Wolters Kluwer, 2013).

De la Feria, Rita, *EU VAT Principles as Interpretative Aids to EU VAT Rules: The Inherent Paradox*, Oxford University Center for Business Taxation WP 16/03, available at https://jean-monnet-chair-eu-tax-policy-administration.webnode.gr/_files/200000035-57c0f58bfc/VAT%20Rita%20De%20la%20Feria.pdf.

De La Feria, Rita, *Tax Fraud and Selective Law Enforcement* 47 J. L. & Soc'y 240 (2020).

De La Feria, Rita, *The EU VAT system and the internal market* (IBFD, Academic Council 2009).

De la Feria, Rita, *The New VAT General Reverse-Charge Mechanism*, Editorial, 2019-4 EC Tax Rev. 172, 173 (2019).

De la Feria, Rita, *VAT: A New Dawn for the Principle of Fiscal Neutrality?* (Oxford University Centre for Business Taxation, PP 11/04), available at https://core.ac.uk/download/pdf/288286521.pdf.

De Paula, Aureo, and Jose A. Scheinkman, *Value-Added Taxes, Chain Effects, and Informality* 2 Am. Econ. J. Macroecon. 195 (2010).

Deloitte, *Analysis of the Impact of the Split Payment Mechanism as an Alternative VAT Collection Method,* Final Report (Publication Office of the European Union, 2017).

Deloitte, *The Link Between Transfer Pricing and Customs Valuation: Country Guide* 8 (2018).

Dezan Shira & Associates, *An Overview of China's VAT Reform*, China Briefing News (30 December 2016), available at http://www.china-briefing.com/news/2016/12/30/overview-chinas-vat-reform.html.

DIAN, *Gasto tributario en el impuesto sobre la renta, el impuesto al valor agregado (IVA) y otros impuestos nacionales- año gravable 2019 (Cifras preliminares)* (Tax Expenditure in Income Taxes, Value Added Taxes (VAT) and Other National Taxes – Taxable Year 2019 (Preliminary figures)).

Díaz de Sarralde Miguez, Santiago. *Value-Added Tax: Revenue, Efficiency, Tax Expenditure and Inefficiencies in Latin America*, Working Papers No. 5, Tax Studies and Research Directorate (CIAT, 2017).

Dickinson, Steve, *Selling Software as a Service (SaaS) in China: The Foreign Server Option*, Legal News (12 May 2015), available at https://harrisbricken.com/chinalawblog/selling-software-as-a-service-saas-in-china-the-foreign-server-option/.

Dickson, Ian, and David White, *Commentary on Value Added Tax and Excises,* in *Dimensions of Tax Design: The Mirrlees Review* 387 (James Mirrlees et al., eds., Oxford University Press, 2010).

Ditchfield, Andrew, *Australia – Goods and Services Tax*, in *VAT Worldwide* (Panos Thliveros et al., eds., IBFD, 2020).

DLA Piper, *Cross-border Supplies of Intangible Services, Digital Content and Rights* (November 2019).

Dodos, Panagiotis, *Die Bestimmung des Kernbereichs von Mehrwertsteuerbefreiungen* 1 MwStR 9 (2017).

Doernberg, Richard, and Luc Hinnekens, *Electronic Commerce and International Taxation* (Kluwer Law International, 1999).

Due, John, *The Wholesale Sales Tax in Australia and New Zealand* 31(2) Can. Tax J. 207 (1983).

Dziwinski, Karol, *Transfer Pricing and VAT: An Analysis of Two Overlapping Disciplines* 25 Transfer Pricing Int'l 28 (2020).

Ebrill, Liam P., Michael Keen, Jean-Paul Bodin, & Victoria P. Summers. *The Modern VAT.* (IMF, 2001).

Echevarría Zubeldia, Gorka, *Abolition of the Force of Attraction of the Fixed Establishment?* 27(6) Int'l. VAT Monitor 405 (2016).

Ecker, Thomas, Thomas Epply, Ferdinand Rößler, and Dietlind Schwab (eds.), *Umsatzsteuergesetz* (Supplement 2015).

Egholm Elgaard, Karina Kim, *A Comparative Analysis of VAT Grouping Schemes from a Nordic Perspective – Aspects of Tax Avoidance and Fiscal Competition* 1 Nordic Tax J. 1 (2017).

Egret, Georges, *La TVA* (PUF, 1978).

Eichfelder, Sebastian, and François Vaillancourt, *Tax Compliance Costs: A Review of Cost Burdens and Cost Structures*, 210 Hacienda Pública Española/Rev. Pub. Econ. 111 (2014).

Einav, Liran, Dan Knoepfle, Jonathan Levin, and Neel Sundaresa, *Sales Taxes and Internet Commerce* 104(1) Am. Econ. Rev. 1 (2014).

Eiteman, Wilford, and Glenn Guthrie, *The Shape of the Average Cost Curve* 42 Am. Econ. Rev. 832 (1952).

Englisch, Joachim, *The EU Perspective on VAT Exemptions* in *VAT Exemptions: Consequences and Design Alternatives*, 37 (Rita de la Feria, ed., Wolters Kluwer, 2013).

Ernst & Young LLP, *Implementing the 'Destination Principle' to Intra-EU B2B Supplies of Goods*, Feasibility and Economic Evaluation Study (European Commission, 2015).

Ernst & Young, *Strategically Managing Indirect Taxes in Latin America*, EY Global (2017).

European Banking Federation, *Response to the European Commission's Consultation Paper on Modernising the VAT Treatment of Vouchers and Related Issues* (31 March 2007).

European Coal and Steel Community, *Report on the Problem Raised by the Different Turnover Tax Systems Applied within the Common Market (Tinbergen Report)*, Luxembourg, 1953.

European Commission, *An Action Plan for Fair And Simple Taxation Supporting the Recovery Strategy*, Communication from the Commission to the European Parliament and the Council, Brussels (15 July 2020), available at https://ec.europa.eu/taxation_customs/sites/taxation/files/2020_tax_package_tax_action_plan_en.pdf.

European Commission, Commission Staff Working Document, *Impact Assessment General Reverse Charge Mechanism*, SWD (2016) 457, Brussels, 21 December 2016 (2016).

European Commission, *Consultation Paper on Modernizing the Value Added Tax Treatment of Vouchers and Related Issues*, December 2006; available at http://ec.europa.eu/taxation_customs/resources/documents/common/consultations/tax/consultation_paper_vouchers_en.pdf.

European Commission, *Explanatory Notes on the EU VAT Changes to the Place of Supply of Telecommunications, Broadcasting and Electronic Services that Enter into Force in 2015* (3 April 2014), available at https://ec.europa.eu/taxation_customs/sites/taxation/files/resources/documents/taxation/vat/how_vat_works/telecom/explanatory_notes_2015_en.pdf.

European Commission, *General Report of Sub-groups A, B and C, set up to examine the different possibilities for harmonization value added taxes*, 3310/IV/62-F (January 1962).

European Commission, *Green Paper on the Future of VAT* (2010), COM(2010) 695 final.

European Commission, *Minutes of 110th Meeting of the Value Added Tax Committee*, item 4, 4.1 (Value Added Tax Committee (Article 398 Directive 2006/112/EC) Working Paper No. 952, 13 April 2018).

European Commission, *Notice 2017/C 361/01 on EU guidelines on food donation* (OJ C 361/25 25.10.2017).

European Commission, *On the Follow-up to the Action Plan on VAT Towards a Single EU VAT Area – Time to Act* (4 October 2017).

European Commission, *Question Concerning the Application of EU VAT Provisions – Possible VAT Implications of Transfer Pricing* 3 (Value Added Tax Committee (Article 398 of Directive 2006/112/EC) Working Paper No. 923, taxud.c.1(2016)1280928, 28 February 2017).

European Commission, *Question Concerning the Application of EU VAT Provisions – Possible VAT Implications of Transfer Pricing – The Point of View of the VAT Expert Group* 2 (Value Added Tax Committee (Article 398 of Directive 2006/112/EC) Working Paper No. 945Rev, taxud.c.1(2018)2329129, 19 April 2018).

European Commission, Staff working document, Impact Assessment accompanying the Proposal for a Council Directive amending Directive 2006/112/EC on the common system of value added tax, as regards the treatment of vouchers, SWD (2012) 127 final.

European Commission, *Study and Reports on the VAT Gap in the EU-28 Member States 2020 Final Report* (September 2020), available at https://ec.europa.eu/taxation_customs/sites/taxation/files/vat-gap-full-report-2020_en.pdf.

European Commission, *Study on Tax Compliance Costs for SMEs: Final Report* xv (2018).

European Commission, Taxation and Customs Union, *Where to Tax?* https://ec.europa.eu/taxation_customs/business/vat/eu-vat-rules-topic/where-tax_en.

European Commission, *The Basic EU VAT Rules for Electronically Supplied Services Explained for Micro Businesses* (19 May 2016), available at https://ec.europa.eu/taxation_customs/sites/taxation/files/information_microbusinesses_euvat_2015_en.pdf.

European Commission, *VAT Aspects of Cross-Border e-Commerce Options for Modernisation: Final Report* (2016), available at https://op.europa.eu/en/publication-detail/-/publication/dbabd711-b799-11e6-9e3c-01aa75ed71a1/language-en.

European Commission, VAT Committee, *CJEU Case C-7/13 Skandia America: VAT Group*, Working Paper No. 845, taxud.c.1(2015)747072 (17 February 2015).

European Commission, VAT Committee, Working Paper 923, *Possible VAT Implications of Transfer Pricing*, taxud.c1 (2016) 1280928 – EN, 20-21 (28 February 2017).

European Commission, *VAT Cross Border Rulings (CBR): EU Pilot Project*, available at https://ec.europa.eu/taxation_customs/business/vat/vat-cross-border-rulings-cbr_en.

European Commission, Working Party 1, *Harmonisation of Turnover Taxes, Summary of Results*. Public Consultation on 'Modernising the Value Added Tax Treatment of Vouchers and Related Issues', TAXUD/2131/07 rev 1- EN, p. 8.

European Parliament, *Directorate-General for Internal Policies, Simplifying and Modernising VAT in the Digital Single Market* (2012), available at https://www.europarl.europa.eu/RegData/etudes/etudes/join/2012/492432/IPOL-IMCO_ET(2012) 492432_EN.pdf.

European Parliament, *Report of the Committee for the internal market on the Proposal of the Commission to the Council (Doc 121, 1962-1963) concerning a Directive on the harmonization of the legislations of the Member States on turnover taxes ('Deringer Report')* (European Parliament, Documents Session 1963-1964, 20 August 1963, Document 56, August 1963).

European Union, *Notifications of the VAT Committee, State-of-Play on 1 February 2020*, available at https://ec.europa.eu/taxation_customs/sites/taxation/files/notifications.pdf.

European Union, VAT Expert Group, *Paper on Topic for Discussion: Possible VAT Implications of Transfer Pricing*, VEG No. 071 REV2, taxud.c.1(2018)2326098 (18 April 2018).

Evans, Chris et al., *Diagnosing the VAT Compliance Burden: A Cross-Country Assessment* 31(2) Int'l VAT Monitor (2020).

Evans, Chris, and Michael Walpole, *The Hidden Costs of a GST – An International Perspective* 12(4) Pol'y 3-10 (1996-97).

Evans, Chris, Ann Hansford, John Hasseldine, Philip Lignier, Sharon Smulders, and François Vaillancourt, *Small Business and Tax Compliance Costs: A Cross-Country Study of Managerial Benefits and Tax Concessions* 12(2) eJ. Tax Rsrch 453 (2014).

Evans, Chris, John Hasseldine, Andy Lymer, Robert Ricketts, and Cedric Sandford, *Comparative Taxation: Why Tax Systems Differ* (Birmingham: Fiscal Publications 2017).

Evans, Chris, Katherine Ritchie, Binh Tran-Nam, and Michael Walpole, *A Report into Taxpayer Costs of Compliance* (Commonwealth of Australia 1997).

Evans, Chris, Philip Lignier & Binh Tran-Nam, *The Tax Compliance Costs of Large Corporations: An Empirical Enquiry and Comparative Analysis* 64(4) Can. Tax J. 751 (2016).

Evans, Chris, Richard Highfield, Binh Tran-Nam, and Michael Walpole, *Diagnosing the VAT Compliance Burden: A Cross-Country Assessment* 31(2) Int'l VAT Monitor 228 (2020).

Evans, Chris, *Studying the Studies: An Overview of Recent Research into Taxation Operating Costs* 1(1) eJ. Tax Rsrch 64 (2003).

Evans, Chris, *Taxation Compliance and Administrative Costs: An Overview*, in *Tax Compliance Costs for Companies in an Enlarged European Community* 447 (Michael Lang et al., eds., Linde Verlag, 2008).

Evans, Chris, *The Compliance Costs of Taxing Capital Gains: Implications for New Zealand* 25(4) NZ J. Tax & Policy 381 (2019).

EY, Argentina, *Global Tax Guides*, available at https://ey.com/en_gl/tax-guides.

Fabio, Massimo, *Customs Value and Transfer Pricing: WCO and ICC Solutions to Be Adopted by Customs Authorities* 15(6) Global Trade and Customs J. 273 (2020).

Famulska, Teresa, and Beata Rogowska-Rajda, *Principle of VAT Neutrality and the Reverse Charge Mechanism* 14(3) e-Finanse: Financial Internet Quarterly (2018), 87.

Fan, Haichao, Yu Liu, Nancy Qian, and Jaya Wen, *Computerizing VAT Invoices in China*, National Bureau of Economic Research Working Paper 24414 (March 2018, Revised April 2020), available at https://www.nber.org/papers/w24414.

Faridy, Nahida, Brett Freudenberg and Tapan Sarker, *The Devil is in the Detail: An Analysis of VAT Compliance Costs for SMEs in a Developing Nation* 23(2) N.Z. J. Tax'n L. and Pol'y 176 (2017).

Farmer, Paul, and Richard Lyall, *EC Tax Law* (Clarendon Press, 1994).

Federal Democratic Republic of Ethiopia, *A Homegrown Economic Reform Agenda: A Pathway to Prosperity*, available at https://pmo.gov.et/initiatives/.

Ferrantino, Michael, Xuepeng Liu, and Zhi Wang, *Evasion Behaviors of Exporters and Importers: Evidence from the U.S.–China Trade Data Discrepancy* 86(1) J. Int. Econ. 141 (2012).

Figari, Francesco, and Alari Paulus, *The Impact of Indirect Taxes and Imputed Rent on Inequality: A Comparison with Cash Transfers and Direct Taxes in Five EU Countries*, GINI Discussion Paper 28 (Amsterdam: AIAS, 2012).

Fleming, J. Clifton, Robert J. Peroni, and Stephen E. Shay, *Is Unilateral Formulary Apportionment Better than the Status Quo?* in *The Allocation of Multinational Business Income: Reassessing the Formulary Apportionment Option*, Chapter 6 (Richard Krever & François Vaillancourt, eds., Kluwer Law International, 2020).

Frenkel, Alain, *La Genèse de la Taxe sur la Valeur Ajoutée* (Unpublished thesis, University of Paris II, 1976).

Fullerton, Donald, and Diane L. Rogers, *Lifetime Versus Annual Perspectives on Tax Incidence* 44 Nat'l Tax J. 277 (1991).

Gallagher, Michael, *Benchmarking Tax Systems* 25(2) Pub. Admin. & Dev. 125 (2005).

Gallagher, Patrick and Roderick Cordara, *Supply of Rights and Rights to a Supply* 22(1) Int'l VAT Monitor 161 (2001).

Gao, Yuning, Meng Li & Yufeng Lu, *What Can Be Learned from Billions of Invoices? The Construction and Application of China's Multiregional Input-Output Table Based on Big Data from the Value-Added Tax* 56(9) Em. Mrkts & Trd. 1925 (2020).

Garner, Bryan A., *Black's Law Dictionary* (2019).

Gemell, Norman, and John Hasseldine, *The Tax Gap: A Methodological Review*, Working Paper 09/2012, Chair in Public Finance, Victoria University, Wellington.

Gendron, Pierre-Pascal, *Canada's GST and Financial Services: Where Are We Now and Where Could We Be?* 64 Can. Tax J. 401 (2016).

Gendron, Pierre-Pascal, *Canada's GST at 21: A Tax Expenditure View of Reform* 1 World J. of VAT/GST Law 125 (2012).

Gendron, Pierre-Pascal, *Real VATs vs the Good VAT: Reflections from a Decade of Technical Assistance* 32 Austl. Tax F. 257 (2017).

Gendron, Pierre-Pascal, *Tear Down and Rebuild, or Retrofit? – A Critical Review of Sijbren Cnossen's Modernizing VATs in Africa* 35 Austl. Tax F. 430 (2020).

Godin, Matteo, Romain Houssa, and Kelbesa Megersa, *The Performance of VAT in DGD-Partner Countries*, Working Paper 16, University of Namur, Belgian Policy Research Group on Financing for Development (2017).

Gove, Michael, *Scrapping VAT and Introducing a Lower, Simpler Sales Tax Will Help Britain to Prosper*, Op-Ed, Daily Telegraph (8 June 2019).

Government of India, *Interim Report of the Tax Reforms Committee* (Ministry of Finance, Government of India, December 1991).

Government of India, *Report of the Expert Group on Taxation of Services* (Ministry of Finance, Government of India, 2001).

Government of India, *Report of the India Taxation Enquiry Commission, 1953-54: Vol. I-III*, (Government of India, February 1955).

Government of India, *Report of the Indirect Taxation Enquiry Committee, Part I* (Ministry of Finance, Government of India, October 1977).

Government of India, *Report of the Indirect Taxation Enquiry Committee, Part II* (Ministry of Finance, Government of India, New Delhi, January 1978).

Government of India, *Report of the Task Force on Indirect Taxes* (Ministry of Finance, Government of India, 2002).

Government of India, *Tax Reforms Committee: Final Report - Part-I* (Ministry of Finance, Government of India, August 1992).

Government of India, *Tax Reforms Committee: Final Report - Part-II* (Ministry of Finance, Government of India, January 1993).

Graff, Thomas O., and Dub Ashton, *Spatial Diffusion of Wal-Mart: Contagious and Reverse Hierarchical Elements* 46 The Professional Geographer 19 (1994).

Grube, Friederike, *Neutrality and Input Tax Deductibility* 17 Austl. GST J. 8 (2017).

Gummow, William, *The Law of Contracts, Trusts and Corporations as Criteria of Tax Liability* 37(3) Melb. U. L. Rev. 834 (2014).

Gupta, Manish, and Indira Rajaraman, *Is the 14% Revenue Guarantee to States Justified?* 55(47) Econ. & Pol. Weekly 18 (2020).

Hagen, Alexander, and Wolfram Reiß, *Die Zukunft der Umsatzsteuer als EG-Steuer*, Umsatzsteuer-Rundschau 109 (2000).

Haig, Robert M., *The Concept of Income-Economic and Legal Aspects*, in *The Federal Income Tax* 1-28 (Robert M. Haig ed., Columbia University Press, 1921).

Haig, Robert M., *The Cost to Business Concerns of Compliance with Tax Laws*, 24 Mgmt. Rev. 323 (1935)

Halpern-Shavim, Zvi, *Carrying on About Carrying on Business: A Response to 'The GST/HST Treatment of Non-resident E-commerce Firms'* 68(4) Can. Tax J. (2020).

Harju, Jarkko, Tuomas Matikka & Timo Rauhanen, *Compliance Costs vs. Tax Incentives: Why Do Entrepreneurs Respond to Size-Based Regulations?* 173 J. Pub. Econ. 139 (2019).

Harrison, Graham and Russell Krelove, *VAT Refunds: A Review of Country Experience*, IMF Working Paper WP/05/218 (2005).

Hart, Jon and Melanie Hill, *Fighting over the Balance Left on Unused Gift Cards*, 23 December 2003. The Wall Street Journal Online, available at http://online.wsj.com/public/resources/documents/SB107219160756934900.htm.

Hartman, Timo, *Kommentar zu § 3 Umsatzsteuergesetz* in *Kommentar zum Europäischen Steuerrecht* (Andreas Musil and Heinrich Weber-Grellet, eds., C.H. Beck Verlag, 2019).

Heady, Christopher, and Mario Mansour, *Tax Expenditure Reporting and Its Use in Fiscal Management: A Guide for Developing Economies*, How-to Note No. 19/2 (International Monetary Fund, 2019).

Hemming, Richard, and John Kay, *The United Kingdom*, in *The Value Added Tax: Lessons from Europe* 75–89 (Henry J. Aaron, ed., Brookings Institution, 1981).

Henkow, Oskar, *Financial Activities in European VAT: A Theoretical and Legal Research of the European VAT System and the Actual and Preferred Treatment of Financial Activities* (Kluwer Law International, 2008).

Henkow, Oskar, *When Is a Public Activity an Economic Activity?* in *CJEU – Recent Developments in Value Added Tax 2016* (Michael Lang et al., eds., Linde, 2017).

Herbain, Charlène, *Fighting VAT Fraud and Enhancing VAT Collection in a Digitalized Environment* 46(6/7) Intertax 579 (2018).

Herbain, Charlène, *Should VAT Be the Next Environmental Policy Tool?* 31(2) Int'l VAT Monitor 69 (2020).

Herbain, Charlène, *VAT Neutrality* (Larcier, 2015).

Hernu, Rémy, *Le principe d'égalité et le principe de non-discrimination dans la jurisprudence de la CJUE*, Titre VII [en ligne], April 2020, n° 4, available at https://www.conseil-constitutionnel.fr/publications/titre-vii/le-principe-d-egalite-et-le-principe-de-non-discrimination-dans-la-jurisprudence-de-la-cjue.

Highfield, Richard, Chris Evans, Binh Tran-Nam & Michael Walpole, *Diagnosing the VAT Compliance Burden: A Cross-Country Assessment* 15 (Amended Final Report, 21 October 2019), available at https://www.unsworks.unsw.edu.au/primo-explore/fulldisplay?vid = UNSWORKS&docid = unsworks_modsunsworks_59518&context = L

Highfield, Richard, Michael Walpole, and Chris Evans, *A Proposal for the Development and Testing of a Diagnostic Tool for Assessing VAT Compliance Costs* 28(3) Inter'l VAT Monitor 228 (2017).

HM Revenue and Customs, *Measuring Tax Gaps 2020 Edition: Tax Gaps Estimates for 2018 to 2019* (HMRC, 2020).

HM Revenue and Customs, *Transfer Pricing: Operational Guidance: Interaction with Indirect Taxes: Interaction with VAT*, Internal Manual INTM486010 (9 April 2016, updated 20 October 2020), available at https://www.gov.uk/hmrc-internal-manuals/international-manual/intm486010.

Ho, Khoonming, Conrad Turley, and Sunny Leung, *A Sisyphean Task? – Tax Plays Catch up with China's Rapid Digitalisation*, Int'l Tax Rev. (10 December 2018), available at https://www.internationaltaxreview.com/Article/3848553/A-Sisyphean-taskTax-plays-catch-up-with-Chinas-rapid-digitalisation.html?ArticleId=3848553.

House of Commons Public Accounts Committee, United Kingdom, *Tackling the Tax Gap* 14 (Twentieth Report of Session 2019-2021, HC650, 16 October 2020).

Houssa, Romain, Kelbesa Megersa, and Roukiatou Nikiema, *The Sources of VAT Gaps in WAEMU: Case Studies on Benin and Burkina Faso*, BeFinD Working Papers 0122, Department of Economics, University of Namur (2017).

Hutton, Eric, *The Revenue Administration-Gap Analysis Program: Model and Methodology for Value-Added Tax Gap Estimation*, Technical Notes and Manuals (IMF, 2017).

Idsinga, Folkert, Bart-Jan Kalshoven, and Monique van Herksen, *Let's Go Tango! The Dance Between VAT, Customs and Transfer Pricing* 9(10) Int'l Transfer Pricing J. 199 (2005).

Independent Commission for the Reform of Corporate Taxation (ICRICT), *International Corporate Tax Reform: Towards a Fair and Sustainable Base* 4-5 (October 2019).

Inland Revenue Authority of Singapore, *GST Payable on Overseas Digital Services from 1 Jan 2020* (9 December 2019), available at https://www.iras.gov.sg/irashome/News-and-Events/Newsroom/Media-Releases-and-Speeches/Media-Releases/2019/GST-payable-on-overseas-digital-services-from-1-Jan-2020/; and Inland Revenue Authority of Singapore, *GST on Imported Services*, available at https://www.iras.gov.sg/irashome/GST/GST-registered-businesses/GST-and-Digital-Economy/GST-on-Imported-Services/#.

International Chamber of Commerce (ICC): ICC, *Policy Statement – Transfer Pricing and Customs Valuation* (Document No. 180/104-536, 2015).

International Monetary Fund and the World Bank, *TADAT – Tax Administration Diagnostic Assessment Tool*, available at https://www.tadat.org/home.

International Monetary Fund, *Tax Policy Assessment Framework: VAT Module*, available at https://www.imf.org/en/Data/TPAF.

International Working Group on Administrative Burdens, *The Standard Cost Model: A Framework for Defining and Quantifying Administrative Burdens for Businesses* (August 2004), available at https://ec.europa.eu/eurostat/documents/64157/4374310/11-STANDARD-COST-MODEL-DK-SE-NO-BE-UK-NL-2004-EN-1.pdf/e703a6d8-42b8-48c8-bdd9-572ab4484dd3.

Irish Commission on Taxation, Third Report: Indirect Taxation (Dublin, 1984).

Irish Revenue Commissioners, *VAT Deductibility for Holding Companies, Tax and Duty Manual*, available at https://www.revenue.ie/en/tax-professionals/tdm/value-added-tax/part03-taxable-transactions-goods-ica-services/Financial-Services/vat-deductibility-for-holding-companies.pdf.

IRS, SOI, Bulletin, Fall 1996.

IRS, SOI, Bulletin, Spring 2019.

Ishi, Hiromitsu, *The Japanese Tax System*, 3rd ed. (Oxford University Press, 2001).

Ismail, Rana et al., *Value Added Tax Evasion and Illegal Recovery Cases in Lebanon* 109 Procedia- Social and Behavioral Sciences 527, 528 (2014).

Ismer, Roland, and Katharina Artinger, *International Double Taxation under VAT: Causes and Possible Solutions* 45(10) Intertax 593 (2017).

James, Kathryn, and Thomas Ecker, *Relevance of the OECD International VAT/GST Guidelines for Non-OECD Countries* 32(2) Austl. Tax F. 317 (2017).

James, Kathryn, *Exploring the Origins and Global Rise of VAT* in *The VAT Reader* 16 (Tax Analysts, 2011).

James, Kathryn, *The Rise of the Value-Added Tax* (Cambridge University Press, 2015).

Jans, Jan H. et al., *Europeanisation of Public Law*, 1st ed. (Europa Law Publishing, 2007).

Jansen, Johannes, *Tax Harmonization in the European Community*, Community Topics 29. (European Community Information Service, 1968), 6.

Jenkins, Glenn, Chun-Yan Kuo, and Gangadhar Shukla, *Tax Analysis and Revenue Forecasting: Issues and Approaches*, Harvard Institute for International Development, Harvard University (June 2000).

Jones, Stephen, and Umberto Torresi, *Clever GST Transactions – Are the Anti-Avoidance Provisions Cleverer?* 40(5) Taxation in Australia 243 (2005).

Kaldor, Nicholas, *An Expenditure Tax* (George Allen & Unwin, 1955).

Kanai, Hajime, *Japan's VAT Treatment of Small and Medium-sized Enterprises* 70 J. Japan Tax Research Inst. 355 (2017, in Japanese).

Kaneko, Hiroshi, *Tax Law*, 6th ed. (Kobundo, 1997, in Japanese).

Kassu, Teklu, Devendra Mishra, and Melesse Asfaw, *Public External Debt, Capital Formation and Economic Growth in Ethiopia* 5 JEDS 222 (2014).

Katene, Rahui, MP, Māori Party – Te Tai Tonga, *Goods and Services Tax (Exemption of Healthy Food) Amendment Bill*, available at https://www.parliament.nz/en/pb/hansard-debates/rhr/document/49HansD_20100908_00001000/goods-and-services-tax-exemption-of-healthy-food-amendment (accessed 31 January 2021).

Kato, Junko, *Regressive Taxation and the Welfare State: Path Dependence and Policy Diffusion* (Cambridge University Press, 2003).

Kato, Junko, *The Problem of Bureaucratic Rationality: Tax Politics in Japan* (Princeton University Press, 1994).

Keen, Michael and Jack Mintz, *The Optimal Threshold for a Value-Added Tax* 88 J. Pub. Econom. 559 (2004).

Keen, Michael *Taxation and Development – Again*, in *Critical Issues in Taxation and Development* (Clemens Fuest and George Zodrow eds., MIT Press, 2013).

Keen, Michael, and Ben Lockwood, *Is the VAT a Money Machine?* 59 Nat'l Tax J. 905 (2006).

Keen, Michael, and Ben Lockwood, *The Value Added Tax: Its Causes and Consequences* 92 J. Devel. Econ. 138 (2010).

Keen, Michael, and Jack Mintz, *The Optimal Threshold for a Value-Added Tax* 88(3-4) J. Pub. Econ. 559 (2004).

Keen, Michael, and Stephen Smith, *VAT Fraud and Evasion: What Do We Know, and What Can Be Done?* 59 Nat'l Tax J. 861 (2006).

Keen, Michael, and Stephen Smith, *Viva VIVAT!* 7(6) Int'l Tax & Pub. Fin. 741 (2000).

Keen, Michael, and Walter Hellerstein, *Interjurisdictional Issues in the Design of a VAT* 63(2) Tax Law Rev. 359 (2010).

Keen, Michael, *The Anatomy of VAT* 66 Nat'l Tax J. 423 (2013).

Keen, Michael, *VIVAT, C-VAT and All That: New Forms of Value-Added Tax for Federal Systems* 48(2) Canadian Tax J. 409 (2000).

Kerrigan, Arthur, *Effects of VAT in Financial Services* in *Taxing Banks Fairly* 127 (Sajid M. Chaudhry and Andrew W. Mullineux, eds. Edward Elgar, 2014).

Keynes, John M., *The General Theory of Employment, Interest and Money* (Macmillan, 1936).

Khan, Lina M., *Amazon's Antitrust Paradox*, 126(3) Yale L. J. 710 (2017).

Kim, Young Ran, *Digital Services Tax: A Cross-Border Variation of the Consumption Tax Debate*, 72 Ala L. Rev. 131 (2020).

Klahr, Rebecca, Lucy Joyce, Rory Donaldson, Graham Keilloh, and Cheryl Salmon, *Behaviours and Experience in Relation to VAT Registration: Final Report* (HM Revenue and Customs Research Report No. 446, 2017).

Kleven, Henrik J. et al., *Why Can Modern Governments Tax So Much? An Agency Model of Firms as Fiscal Intermediaries*, Working Paper 15218 (National Bureau of Economic Research, 2009), available at http://www.nber.org/papers/w15218.

Kokott, Juliane, *Das Steuerrecht der Europäischen Union* (C.H. Beck Verlag, 2019).

Kolozs, Borbála, *Neutrality in VAT* in *Value Added Tax and Direct Taxation, Similarities and Differences* 203 (Michael Lang, Peter Melz and Eleonor Kristoffersson, eds, IBFD, 2009).

Kosonen, Tuomas, *More and Cheaper Haircuts after VAT Cut? On the Efficiency and Incidence of Service Sector Consumption Taxes* 131 J. Pub. Econ. 87 (2015).

Kotha, Ashrita P. et al., *Cesses and Surcharges: Concept, Practice and Reform*, Report to the Fifteenth Finance Commission (Vidhi Centre for Legal Policy, 2018).

KPMG, *Administrative Burdens – HMRC Measurement Project* 6 (KPMG LLP 2006).

KPMG, *VAT and the Digital Economy in China* 13 (March 2016), available at https://assets.kpmg/content/dam/kpmg/pdf/2016/05/tnf-china-vat-digital-economy-march-2016.pdf.

KPMG, *VAT/GST Treatment of Cross-Border Services 2017 Survey*, available at https://assets.kpmg/content/dam/kpmg/xx/pdf/2017/11/ess-survey-13-nov-17.pdf.

Krever, Richard, and David White (eds.), *GST in Retrospect and Prospect* (Brookers Ltd, 2007).

Krever, Richard, and Jonathan Teoh, *Justice Edmonds and Interpretation of Australia's GST Legislation* 45(2) Austl. Tax Rev. 121 (2016).

Krever, Richard, and Peter Mellor, *Legal Interpretation of Tax Law: Australia*, in *Legal Interpretation of Tax Law* 15 (2nd ed., Robert F. van Brederode and Richard Krever eds., Kluwer, 2017).

Krever, Richard, *Combating VAT Fraud: Lessons from Korea* 3 British Tax Rev. 303 (2014).

Krever, Richard, *Design and Structure of the VAT* in *VAT in Africa* 18 (Richard Krever, ed., Pretoria University Law Press, 2008).

Krever, Richard, *Designing and Drafting VAT Laws for Africa*, in *VAT in Africa* (Richard Krever, ed., Pretoria University Law Press, 2008).

Langer, Michael, *Kommentar zu Art. 16 MwStSystRL* in *Kommentar zum Umsatzsteuergesetz* (Wolfgang Reiß, Jörg Kraeusel, and Michael Langer, eds., Stollfuss, 2020).

Lasok, Karol P.E., *EU Value Added Tax Law* (Edward Elgar Publishing, 2020).

Lauré, Maurice, *Au secours de la TVA* (PUF, 1957).

Lauré, Maurice, *La Taxe sur la Valeur Ajoutée* (Recueil Sirey, 1952).

Lavoie, Marc, *Post-Keynesian Economics: New Foundations* (Edward Elgar Publishing, 2014).

Lazanas, Gina, Paul Welch, and Fletch Heinemann, *Interaction Between Customs Duty, GST/VAT and Transfer Pricing in Australia*, Tax Planning Int'l Indirect Taxes 1 (1 August 2008).

Leccisotti, Mario, and Mauro Marè, *On the Presumed Technical Superiority of VAT* 9 Austl. Tax F. 259 (1992).

Lecourt, Robert, *L'Europe des juges*, (Bruylant [1976], 2008).

Lee, Dongwon, Dongil Kim, and Thomas E. Borcherding, *Tax Structure and Government Spending: Does the Value-Added Tax Increase the Size of Government?* 66 Nat'l Tax J. 541 (2013).

Lefebvre, Francis, *Union Européenne 2008-2009* (Memento Pratique 2007).

Lejeune, Ine and Liesbeth Vermeire, *50 Years of Case Law in VAT: In What Direction is the CJEU Going?*, in *CJEU – Recent Developments in Value Added Tax 2019* (Georg Kofler et al., eds., Linde Verlag, 2020).

Lejeune, Ine, *The EU VAT Experience: What Are the Lessons?* in *The VAT Reader* 271 (Tax Analysts, 2011).

Lenaerts, Koen, *L'égalité de traitement en droit communautaire* (1-2) Cahiers de droit européen 3, 10 (1991).

Li, Jianjun, and Xuan Wang, *Does VAT Have Higher Tax Compliance than a Turnover Tax? Evidence from China* 27 Int Tax & Pub. Finance 280 (2020).

Li, Jinyan et al., *BEPS and the Emerging Global Approach to Taxing Multinational Enterprises*, Presented at Re-Imagining Tax Policy for the 21st Century: Inspired by Tim Edgar's Scholarship, 8-9 February 2019, Toronto, Canada, SSRN Elec. J. (14 September 2019).

Li, Jinyan, *Consumption Taxation of Electronic Commerce: Problems, Policy Implications, and Proposals for Reform* 38(3) Can. Bus. L. J. 426 (2003).

Lignier, Philip, Chris Evans, and Binh Tran-Nam, *Tangled Up in Tape: The Continuing Tax Compliance Plight of the Small and Medium Enterprise Business Sector* 29(2) Austl. Tax F. 217 (2014).

Ligthart, Jenny E., *Consumption Taxation in a Digital World: A Primer* 52(4) Can. Tax J. 1076 (2004).

Lindert, Peter H., *Growing Public: Social Spending and Economic Growth since the Eighteenth Century* (Cambridge University Press, 2004).

Lock, Clarence W., Donovan J. Rau, and Howard D. Hamilton, *The Michigan Value-Added-Tax* 8(4) Nat'l Tax J. 357 (1955).

López Bejarano, Mauricio, *La evasión equivale al 30% del total de lo que se recauda de impuestos al año* (Tax evasion amounts to 30% of the total amount of VAT collections in a year), Daily La República (19 November 2019), available at https://www.larepublica.co/economia/la-evasion-equivale-a-30-del-total-de-lo-que-se-recauda-de-impuestos-al-ano-2945888.

Loungani, Prakash & Saurabh Mishra, *Not Your Father's Service Sector* 51 Finance Dev 2 (2019).

Loungani, Prakash, Saurabh Mishra, Chris Papageorgiou & Ke Wang, *World Trade in Services: Evidence from A New Dataset*, IMF WP/17/77, 8 (March 2017), available at https://www.imf.org/~/media/Files/Publications/WP/2017/wp1777.ashx.

Lusaka Times, *Cabinet Approves Sales Tax, Abolishes VAT* (2 April 2019).

Lustig, Nora, *Fiscal Policy, Inequality, and the Poor in the Developing World*, WIDER Working Paper 2016/164 (2016), United Nations University World Institute for Development Economics Research.

Mankiw, N. Gregory, Matthew C. Weinzierl, and Danny F. Yagan, *Optimal Taxation in Theory and Practice* 23(4) J. Econ. Persp. 147 (2009).

Martins, Alexandra, *VAT Transfer-Pricing Rules: A Portuguese Perspective* 37(5) Intertax 322 (2009).

Masui, Yoshihiro, *Legal Interpretation of Tax Law: Japan*, in *Legal Interpretation of Tax Law*, 2nd ed., 307 (Robert F. van Brederode and Richard Krever eds., Kluwer L. Int'l, 2017).

Masui, Yoshihiro, *Quo Vadis Japan's VAT? A Comparative Perspective* 70 Tax Research Inst., 515 (2017, in Japanese).

Matesanz, Fernando, *Transfer Pricing Adjustments and VAT* 29(1) Int'l VAT Monitor 6 (2018).

Mazur, Orly, *Taxing the Cloud* 103(1) Calif. Tax Rev. 1 (2015).

McBride, William, *What Is the Evidence on Taxes and Growth* 207 Tax Foundation Special Report (2012).

McCaffery, Edward J., *The Holy Grail of Tax Simplification* 5 Wisc. L. Rev. 1267-1322 (1990).

McKerchar, Margaret, and Chris Evans, *Sustaining Growth in Developing Economies through Improved Taxpayer Compliance: Challenges for Policy Makers and Revenue Authorities* 7(2) eJ. Tax Research 171 (2009).

McLeod, Robert et al., *Tax Review 2001: Final Report*, iv (New Zealand Treasury 2001).

McLure, Charles E., *Implementing Subnational VATs on Internal Trade: The Compensating VAT (C-VAT)* 6(7) Int'l Tax & Pub. Finance 723 (2000).

Mehra, Puja, *The Lost Decade (2008-18): How India's Growth Story Devolved into Growth* (Penguin eBury Press, 2019).

Menchik, Paul, and Martin David, *The Incidence of a Lifetime Consumption Tax* 35 Nat'l Tax J. 189 (1982).

Merkx, Madeleine, and Anne M. de Wit, *Schoolmodel in de btw: definitief gezakt?* WFR (2019/64).

Merkx, Madeleine, and Koen Verburg, *22 jaar na Tolsma: weer luisteren zonder btw* 69 MBB (2017/2).

Merkx, Madeleine, *Fixed Establishments in European Value Added Tax: Base Erosion and Profit Shifting's Side Effects?* 26(1) EC Tax Rev. 36 (2017).

Merkx, Madeleine, *Should EU VAT Apply the Recharge Method in the Place of Supply Rules for B2B Services?* 22(6) EC Tax Rev. 282 (2013).

Merkx, Madeleine, *VAT on Private Use of Company Cars in Cross-Border Situations: Double or Non-Taxation?* 24(2) EC Tax Rev. 96 (2015).

Mieszkowski, Peter, and Michael Palumbo, *Is a National Retail Sales Tax Administrable? A Proposal for a Hybrid NRST,* Working Paper, Rice University (1998).

Mikesell, John, *State Sales Tax in Fiscal 2007: More Slow Growth* 48 St. Tax N. (26 May 2008).

Mikutienė, Rasa, *The Preferred Treatment of the Fixed Establishment in European VAT* 3(3) World J. VAT/GST L. 166 (2015).

Millar, Rebecca M., *The Vouchers Problem: An Insoluble Conflict or an Illustration of the Nature of Consideration in the 'Complex Parallel Universe' of GST?* 18 Austl. Tax F. 107 (2003).

Millar, Rebecca, and Lorenna Moon, *Australia,* in *Improving VAT/GST: Designing a Simple and Fraud-Proof Tax System* 23 (Michael Lang and Ine Lejeune, eds., IBFD, 2014).

Millar, Rebecca, *Echoes of Source and Residence in VAT Jurisdictional Rules*, section III (University of Sydney Law School Research Paper 09/44, 2009).

Millar, Rebecca, *Intentional and Unintentional Double Non-Taxation*, in *Value Added Tax and Direct Taxation* 409-442 (Michael Lang, Eleonor Kristoffersson, Peter Melz & Thomas Ecker, eds., IBFD, 2009).

Millar, Rebecca, *Intentional and Unintentional Double Non-Taxation Issues in VAT,* Sydney Law School Legal Studies Research Paper No. 09/45 (June 2009), 10, available at https://papers.ssrn.com/sol3/papers.cfm?abstract_id = 1416582.

Millar, Rebecca, *Jurisdictional Reach of VAT*, in *VAT in Africa*, 175 (Richard Krever ed., Pretoria University Law Press, 2008).

Millar, Rebecca, *Looking Ahead: Potential Solutions and the Framework to Make Them Work,* Sydney Law School Legal Studies Research Paper No. 16/30, 2 (6 October 2016), available at https://papers.ssrn.com/sol3/papers.cfm?abstract_id = 2770 847.

Millar, Rebecca, *Smoke and Mirrors: Applying the Full Taxation Model to Government under the Australian and New Zealand GST Laws*, in *VAT Exemptions: Consequences and Design Alternatives* 143 (Rita de la Feria, ed., Wolters Kluwer, 2013).

Millar, Rebecca, *Taxable Amount: Fiscal Neutrality in Action*, in *ECJ – Recent Developments in Value Added Tax* 221 (Michael Lang et al., eds., Linde, 2014).

Millar, Rebecca, *Taxing the Bull by the Horns: Reforming Australia's Cross-Border GST Rules* 24 Aust. Tax Forum 281 (2009).

Millar, Rebecca, *The Principle of Neutrality in Australian GST* 17 Austl. GST J. 26 (2017).

Miller, Eric, *Answering the Call: South Dakota v. Wayfair, Inc. and a Challenge to the Physical Presence Rule* 64(1) S. D. L. Rev. 94 (2019).

Ministério da Economia, *Reforma Tributária: Quando todos pagam, todos pagam menos*, Government of Brazil (21 July 2020).

Ministry of Commerce of People's Republic of China, *Statistics on Imports and Exports of Services (Calendar Years)*, available at http://data.mofcom.gov.cn/fwmy/overtheyears.shtml.

Ministry of Finance and State Taxation Administration, *Notice on Comprehensively Implementing the Pilot Reform of Replacing Business Tax with VAT* (Ministry of Finance (MOF), 23 March 2016, effective 1 May 2016 (Caishui (2016) 36).

Ministry of Finance and State Taxation Administration, *Notice on VAT Rates Adjustment* (Caishui (2018) 32).

Ministry of Finance, General Administration of Customs and State Taxation Administration, *Notice on Tax Policies of Cross-border E-Commerce Retail Imports* (Caiguanshui (2016) 18).

Ministry of Finance, *Guide to 2016 Tax Reform* (Okura Zaimu Kyokai, 2016, in Japanese).

Ministry of Finance, *Guide to 2019 Tax Reform* (Okura Zaimu Kyokai, 2019, in Japanese).

Ministry of Finance, State Taxation Administration, and General Administration of Customs, *Public Notice on Policies of Deepening the VAT Reform* (Gonggao (2019) 39).

Mirrlees, James A. et al., *Tax by Design: The Mirrlees Review* 484 (Oxford University Press, 2011).

Mirrlees, James. *Tax by Design*, 1st ed. (Institute for Fiscal Studies, 2010).

Mochida, Nobuki et al., *The Economics of Subnational Value Added Tax* (Yuhikaku, 2010, in Japanese).

Mochida, Nobuki, *Fiscal Decentralization and Local Public Finance in Japan* (Routledge, 2008).

Modigliani, Franco, *The Role of Intergenerational Transfer and Life Cycle Saving in the Accumulation of Wealth* 2(2) J. Econ. Persp. 15 (1988).

Monk, Andrew, *The Associate Rules and their Interaction with Other Provisions of the GST Act* 4(3) Austl. GST J. 34 (2004).

Moore, Mick, Wilson Prichard, and Odd-Helge Fjeldstad, *Taxing Africa: Coercion, Reform and Development* (Zed Books, 2018).

Morrow, Peter, Michael Smart, and Artur Swistak, *VAT Compliance, Trade and Institutions* (2019), CESifo Working Paper No. 7780, available at SSRN: https://ssrn.com/abstract=3434836.

Muir, Elise, *The Essence of the Fundamental Right to Equal Treatment: Back to the Origins*, 20(6) German Law J. 817 (2019).

Mukherjee Sacchidananda, *Plugging Loopholes in Taxation of Interstate Sales* 55(19) Econ. & Pol. Weekly 18-20 (2020).

Mukherjee Sacchidananda, *Possible Impact of Withdrawal of GST Compensation Post GST Compensation Period on Indian State Finances*, NIPFP Working Paper No. 291 (NIPFP, 2020).

Mukherjee, Sacchidananda and R. Kavita Rao, *Fiscal Implications of Introduction of Goods and Services Tax in India*, Report Submitted to the Fifteenth Finance Commission, National Institute of Public Finance and Policy (NIPFP, 2019).

Mukherjee, Sacchidananda, and R. Kavita Rao (2019a), *Decades of Indirect Tax Reforms in India: A Journey Towards Goods and Services Tax (GST)* in *Evolution of Goods and Services Tax in India* 7 (Rao, R. Kavita and Sacchidananda Mukherjee, eds., Cambridge University Press).

Mukherjee, Sacchidananda, and R. Kavita Rao, *Policy Options for Including Petroleum, Natural Gas and Electricity in the Goods and Services Tax* 50(9) Econ. & Pol. Weekly 98 (2015).

Mukherjee, Sacchidananda, and R. Kavita Rao, *Value Added Tax and Informality: Determinants of Registration of Enterprises under State VAT in India* 13(1) Margin—The Journal of Applied Economic Research, 21–48 (2019).

Mukherjee, Sacchidananda, *Compensation to Cantonment Boards for Revenue Loss on Account of GST*, 55(2) Econ. & Pol. Weekly 15-18 (2020).

Mukherjee, Sacchidananda, *Goods and Services Tax efficiency across Indian States: Panel Stochastic Frontier Analysis* 55(2) Indian Econ. Rev. 225 (2020).

Mukherjee, Sacchidananda, *Issues of Compliance in GST – Reflecting on the CAG's Report* 54(47) Econ. & Pol. Weekly 22-24 (2019).

Mukherjee, Sacchidananda, *Pandemic and GST Revenue: An Assessment for Union and States*. NIPFP Working Paper No. 327 (NIPFP, 2020).

Mukherjee, Sacchidananda, *Whether States Have Capacity to Sustain Projected Growth in GST Collection During the GST Compensation Period?* 11(1-2) Rev. Market Integration 30-53 (2019).

National Tax Agency (Japan), *Revision of Consumption Taxation on Cross-border Supplies of Services*, May 2015 (Revised December 2016).

National Tax Agency, *Registered Foreign Businesses List* (18 November 2020), available at https://www.nta.go.jp/publication/pamph/shohi/cross/touroku.pdf.

Neumark Report, *Report of the Fiscal and Financial Committee*, in *The EEC Reports on Tax Harmonization*, 93-156, 124 (IBFD, 1968).

New Zealand Government, Tax Working Group, *Future of Tax: Final Report Vol. 1*, 104 (New Zealand Government, 2019), available at https://taxworkinggroup.govt.nz/resources/future-tax-final-report.

New Zealand Government, Tax Working Group, *Future of Tax: Interim Report* (New Zealand Government, 2018), available at https://taxworkinggroup.govt.nz/resources/future-tax-interim-report.

New Zealand Inland Revenue, Special report from the Policy Advice Division of Inland Revenue, *GST Treatment of Tokens, Stamps and Vouchers – Amendments to Sections 5(11D) to 5(11I) of the Goods and Services Tax Act 1985* (9 April 2001).

New Zealand Treasury, *Half Year Economic and Fiscal Update 2020*, 13 (The Treasury, 16 December 2020), available at https://www.treasury.govt.nz/system/files/2020-12/hyefu20.pdf.

New Zealand Treasury, *Interim Financial Statements of the Government of New Zealand For the Five Months Ended 30 November 2020*, 4 (New Zealand Treasury, 2021), available at https://www.treasury.govt.nz/system/files/2021-01/fsgnz-5mths-20nov.pdf.

Nienhuis, Mike, *Tax Implications for Non-Residents Conducting E-Commerce in Tax Implications for Non-Residents Conducting E-Commerce in Canada* 9(1) CJLT 235, 257 (2011).

Nishida, Yuki, *Japan Consumption Tax on Cross-Border Supplies of Services* 26(4) Int'l VAT Monitor 221 (2015).

Nishiyama, Yumi, *Japanese Consumption Tax: Input Tax Deduction and Exemptions* 3(2) W. J. VAT/GST L. 124 (2014).

Nishiyama, Yumi, *Latest Changes to the Japanese Consumption Tax: Rate Increase and Taxation of Digital Services* 3(2) W. J. VAT/GST L. 108 (2014).

NSW Review of Federal Financial Relations, *Final Report*, 32-39 (NSW Treasury 2020).

O'Rourke, Kevin, *Incentives, Rebates and Third-Party Adjustments after the AP Group Decision* 13 Austl. GST J. 64 (2013).

Obst, Thomas, Özlem Onaran, and Maria Nikolaidi, *The Effects of Income Distribution and Fiscal Policy on Aggregate Demand, Investment and the Budget Balance: The Case of Europe* 44 Camb. J. Econ. 1221 (2020).

OECD, *2010 Report on the Attribution of Profits to Permanent Establishments* (22 July 2010).

OECD, *Action Plan on Base Erosion and Profit Shifting* (OECD Publishing, 2013).

OECD, *Addressing the Tax Challenges of the Digital Economy: BEPS Action 1 – 2015 Final Report* (OECD Publishing 2015).

OECD, *Aligning Transfer Pricing Outcomes with Value Creation: Actions 8-10 – 2015 Final Reports*, OECD/G20 Base Erosion and Profit Shifting Project 9 (OECD Publishing 2015).

OECD, Centre for Tax Policy and Administration, *Glossary of Tax Terms*, available at (https://www.oecd.org/ctp/glossaryoftaxterms.htm).

OECD, *Consumption Tax Trends* (OECD, 2006).

OECD, *Consumption Tax Trends* (OECD, 2016).

OECD, *Consumption Tax Trends 2008: VAT/GST and Excise Rates, Trends and Administration Issues* (OECD Publishing, 2008).

OECD, *Consumption Tax Trends 2018, VAT/GST and Excise Rates, Trends and Policy Issues* (OECD Publishing, 2019).

OECD, *Consumption Tax Trends 2020: VAT/GST and Excise Rates, Trends and Policy Issues* (OECD Publishing, 2020).

OECD, *Countries Must Strengthen Tax Systems to Meet Sustainable Development Goals* (14 February 2018), available at https://www.oecd.org/tax/countries-must-strengthen-tax-systems-to-meet-sustainable-development-goals.htm.

OECD, *Developments in VAT Compliance Management in Selected Countries* 36 (OECD Publishing 2009).

OECD, *From Red Tape to Smart Tape: Administrative Simplifications in OECD Countries* (OECD Publishing 2003).

OECD, *Implementation of the Ottawa Taxation Framework* (OECD Publishing, 2003).

OECD, *International VAT/GST Guidelines* (OECD Publishing, 2017).

OECD, *Mechanisms for the Effective Collection of VAT/GST* (OECD, 24 October 2017).

OECD, *OECD Secretary-General Tax Report to G20 Finance Ministers and Central Bank Governors – October 2019* (OECD, October 2019).

OECD, *Ottawa Taxation Framework* (OECD Publishing, 2001).

OECD, Report by the Committee on Fiscal Affairs, *Electronic Commerce: Taxation Framework Conditions* (OECD Publishing, 1998).

OECD, *Tax Challenges Arising from Digitalisation – Report on Pillar One Blueprint: Inclusive Framework on BEPS*, OECD/G20 Base Erosion and Profit Shifting Project (OECD Publishing, October 2020).

OECD, *Tax Policy Reforms 2020: OECD and Selected Partner Economies*, 82 (OECD Publishing, 2020).

OECD, Tax Policy Studies, *Taxation and Philanthropy* (OECD Publishing, 2020).

OECD, *Taxation and Electronic Commerce* (OECD Publishing, 2001).

OECD, *The Role of Digital Platforms in the Collection of VAT/GST on Online Sales*, 2019, available at www.oecd.org/tax/consumption/the-role-of-digital-platforms-in-the-collection-of-vat-gst-on-online-sales.pdf.

OECD, *Transfer Pricing Documentation and Country-by-Country Reporting: Action 13 – 2015 Final Report*, OECD/G20 Base Erosion and Profit Shifting Project (OECD Publishing 2015).

OECD, *Transfer Pricing Guidelines for Multinational Enterprises and Tax Administrations* (OECD Publishing, 2017).

OECD, *Model Tax Convention on Income and on Capital 2017 (Full Version)* (OECD Publishing, 2019).

Olding, Graeme, Robert Grignon and Alexandra Bensemann, *New Zealand – Goods and Services Tax*, in *VAT Worldwide* (Panos Thliveros et al., eds., IBFD, 2020).

Onaran, Özlem, and Giorgos Galanis, *Is Aggregate Demand Wage-Led or Profit-Led: National and Global Effects* 31 ILO CEACR 1 (2012).

Onji, Kazuki, *The Response of Firms to Eligibility Thresholds: Evidence from the Japanese Value-Added Tax* 93(5-6) J. Pub. Econ. 766 (2009).

Osei, Philip D., *Political Liberalisation and the Implementation of Value Added tax in Ghana* 38(2) J. Mod. Afr. Stud. 255 (2000).

Owusu-Afriyie, Emmanuel, *An Assessment of the Impact of Tax Reforms on the Tax System of Ghana*, Monetary Policy Analysis and Financial Stability Department, Bank of Ghana Working Paper WP/BOG-2009-1 (2009).

Papis-Almansa, Martha, *VAT and Electronic Commerce: The New Rules as a Means for Simplification, Combatting Fraud and Creating a More Level Playing Field* 20(2) ERA Forum: J. Acad. Eur. L. 201-223 (2019).

Pattanaik, Subidita, and Bidhu B. Mishra, *Evolution of Retail Industry in India* 2(4) J. Res'ch Innov. & Mgmt Sc. 51 (2016).

Penda, Akama S., and Tarh, Bande G.M., *The Buoyancy of the Value Added Tax on Economic Development: Its Drifts and Challenges in Cameroon* 7(2) Int'l J. Adv. Rsrch. 80 (2019).

Percy, Anna, *New Zealand's GST v. Exclusions: A Case for the Exclusion of Basic Food and Menstrual Products from Goods and Services Tax in New Zealand* 25 Auckland Un. Law Rev. 228 (2019).

Pfeiffer, Sebastian, and Karoline Spies, *CJEU Case Law on Taxable Persons and Related Issues in 2019*, in *CJEU – Recent Developments in Value Added Tax 2019* (Georg Kofler et al., eds., Linde, 2020).

Pfeiffer, Sebastian, and Pavel Semerád, *Missing Trader Fraud in European VAT*, MENDELU Working Papers in Business and Economics 41/2013 (Mendel University, 2013), available at http://ideas.repec.org/s/men/wpaper.html.

Pfeiffer, Sebastian, *EU VAT Grouping – Past, Present Future*, in *Anthology on VAT Grouping and Cost-Sharing* (Karina Elgaard et al., eds., Copenhagen, 2020).

Pfeiffer, Sebastian, *Recent CJEU Case Law on Taxable Persons and Public Bodies*, in *CJEU – Recent Developments in Value Added Tax 2015* (Michael Lang et al., eds., Linde, 2016).

Pfeiffer, Sebastian, *VAT Grouping from a European Perspective* (IBFD Publications, 2015).

Piggot, John, and John Whalley, *VAT Base Broadening, Self Supply, and the Informal Sector* 91 Am. Econ. Rev. 1084 (2001).

Pigou, Arthur C., *The Economics of Welfare* (Palgrave Macmillan, [1920] 2013).

Ping, Liu, and Caroline Silberztein, *Transfer Pricing, Customs Duties and VAT Rules: Can We Bridge the Gap?* 1(1) World Com. Rev. 36 (2007).

Pistone, Pasquale, *Fixed Establishment and Permanent Establishment* 10(3) Int'l VAT Monitor 101(1999).

Plamondon, Robert, *GST Compliance Costs for Small Business in Canada* (Department of Finance 1993).

Plazas Vega, Mauricio, *El impuesto sobre el valor agregado* (The Value Added Tax), 2nd ed. (Temis, 1998).

Plazas Vega, Mauricio, *El impuesto sobre el valor agregado* (The Value Added Tax), 3rd ed. (Temis, 2015).

Polak, Eline, and Mayra O. Lucas Mas, *Transfer Pricing – Global Topics, Value Added Tax* (IBFD Online).

Politi, Ricardo B., and Enlinson Mattos, *Ad-valorem Tax Incidence and After-Tax Price Adjustments: Evidence from Brazilian Basic Basket Food* 44(4) Can. J. Econ. 1438 (2011).

Pomeranz, Dina, *No Taxation Without Information: Deterrence and Self-Enforcement in the Value Added Tax* 105(8) Am. Econ. Rev. 2539 (2015).

Pomerleau, Kyle, *Does Andrew Yang's 'Freedom Dividend' Proposal Add Up?* Tax Foundation (29 July 2019).

Pope, Jeff, Richard Fayle & Michael Duncanson, *The Compliance Costs of Personal Income Taxation in Australia, 1986/87* (Australian Tax Research Foundation 1990).

Popkin, Phillip, *The Effect of the Internet Era and South Dakota v. Wayfair on the Unitary Business Rule* 60(9) B. C. L. Rev. 82 (2019).

Poterba, James M., *Lifetime Incidence and the Distributional Burden of Excise Taxes* 79(2) Am. Econ. Rev. 325-330 (1989).

PricewaterhouseCoopers, *VAT in Africa: Navigating Africa's VAT Landscape*, 2020 Africa VAT Guide, PwC Global.

Productivity Commission (Australia), *Economic Structure and Performance of the Australian Retail Industry*, Inquiry Report No. 56 (4 November 2011), available at https://www.pc.gov.au/inquiries/completed/retail-industry/report/retail-industry.pdf.

Purohit, Mahesh C., *Is There a Case for States Carrying on with Entry Tax?* Financial Express (29 January 2015), available at https://www.financialexpress.com/opinion/isthere-a-case-for-states-carrying-on-with-entry-tax/36247/ (last accessed on 27 December 2020).

Purohit, Mahesh C., *National and Sub-National VATs: A Road Map for India* 36(9) Econ. & Pol. Weekly, 757 (2001).

Ramsey, Frank P., *A Contribution to the Theory of Taxation* 37(145) Econ. J. 47 (1927).

Rao, M. Govinda and Francois Vaillancourt, *Interstate Tax Disharmony in India: A Comparative Perspective* 24(9) Publius 99 (1994).

Rao, M. Govinda, *Feasibility of Introducing GST in April 2010* 44(29) Econ. & Pol. Weekly 10 (2009).

Rao, M. Govinda, *Goods and Services Tax: A Gorilla, Chimpanzee or a Genus Like 'Primates'?* 46(7) Econ. & Pol. Weekly 43 (2011).

Rao, M. Govinda, *Reform in Central Sales Tax in the Context of VAT* 38(7) Econ. & Pol. Weekly 627 (2003).

Rao, M. Govinda, *Resolving Fiscal Imbalances: Issues in Tax Sharing* in *Intergovernmental Fiscal Transfers: Principles and Practice* 319 (Robin Boadway & Anwar Shah, eds., The World Bank, 2007).

Rao, M. Govinda, *Taxing Services: Issues and Strategy* 36(42) Econ. & Pol. Weekly 3999 (2001).

Rao, M. Govinda, *Taxing Services: Strategy and Challenges* in *Fiscal Policies and Sustainable Growth in India* (Edgaro M. Favaro and Ashok. K. Lahiri, eds., Oxford University Press, 2004).

Raponi, Donato, and Arthur Kerrigan, *Introduction: The Growth in VAT Cases*, in *ECJ: Recent Developments in Value Added Tax* 1 (Michael Lang et al., eds., Linde Verlag, 2014).

Rattinger, Ingrid, *§ 6*, in *Umsatzsteuergesetz – Kommentar*, 2. Auflage (Stefan Melhardt and Michael Tumpel, eds., Linde Verlag, 2015).

Reckon LLP, *Study to Quantity and Analyse the VAT GAP in the EU-25 Member States* (Reckon LLP, 2009).

Reugebrink, J., *The Sixth Directive for the Harmonisation of the Value Added Tax* 15(3) C. M.t L. Rev. 309 (1978).

Richards, John, *British Columbia's Unharmonized Referendum: The Problem with Plebiscitary Democracy* 60(1) Can. Tax J. 103 (2012).

Ring, Raymond J., *Consumer's Share and Producer's Share of the General Sales Tax* (52)1 Nat'l Tax J. 79 (1999).

Robertson, David D., *Comparing the Introduction of the HST in British Columbia and Ontario: Lessons from the Political Trenches* 60(1) Can. Tax J. 113 (2012).

Rouberol, Isabelle, *Interactions Between Transfer Pricing and VAT Adjustments in the European Union* 27(5) Int'l VAT Monitor 316 (2016).

Ruppe, Hand G., *'Unechte' Umsatzsteuerbefreiungen* in *Die Steuerrechtsordnung in der Diskussion: Festschrift für Klaus Tipke zum 70. Geburtstag* 457 (Joachim Lang and Klaus Tipke eds., Schmidt, 1995).

Ruppe, Hans G., *System und Rechtfertigung unechter Steuerbefreiungen*, in *Unechte Steuerbefreiungen*, 23 (Markus Achatz and Michael Tumpel, eds., Linde Verlag, 2010).

Ruppe, Hans Georg, and Markus Achatz, *Umsatzsteuergesetz*, 5th ed. (LexisNexis, 2017).

Russo, Karl, *Superiority of the VAT to Turnover Tax as an Indirect Tax on Digital Services* 72(4) Nat'l. Tax J. 857 (2019).

Ryglewski, Sarah, *Steuerliche Vereinfachung von Sachspenden*, 4 UVR 97 (2020).

Sadiq, Kerrie, and Richard Krever, *Anatomy of Transfer Pricing: Lessons from Australia* 100(5) Tax Notes Int'l 679, 680 (2020).

Sánchez Gallardo, Javier, and Amparo Sanchis Sierra, *ECJ Case-Law on VAT* (Manual Francis Lefebvre, 2019).

Sandford, Cedric, *Hidden Costs of Taxation* (Institute for Fiscal Studies, 1973).

Sandford, Cedric, Michael Godwin, and Peter Hardwick, *Administrative and Compliance Costs of Taxation* (Fiscal Publications, 1989).

Sandford, Cedric, *Minimising the Compliance Costs of a GST*, in *Tax Administration: Facing the Challenges* 129 (Evans, Chris, and Abe Greenbaum, eds., Prospect 1998).

Santoro, Emanuela, *Transfer Pricing and Value Added Tax in the European Community: Is There Room for Interaction and, If So, Where?* 14(3) Int'l Transfer Pricing J. 147 (2007).

Sato, Hideaki, *The Trajectory of Japan's VAT* 70(1) J. Tax Research Inst. (2017, in Japanese).

Satterthwaite, Emily Ann, *On the Threshold: Smallness and the Value-Added Tax* 9 Col. J. Tax L. 177 (2018).

Scanlan, Mark A., *Tax Sensitivity in Electronic Commerce* 28(4) Fisc. Stud. 417 (2007).

Scarcella, Luisa, *E-Commerce and Effective VAT/GST Enforcement: Can Online Platforms Play a Valuable Role?* 36 Comp. L. & Sec. Rev. 105371.

Schenk, Alan, *Japanese Consumption Tax After Six Years: A Unique VAT Matures* Tax Notes 899 (13 November 1995).

Schenk, Alan, *Japanese Consumption Tax: The Japanese Brand VAT* Tax Notes 1625 (27 March 1989).

Schenk, Alan, *Prior U.S. Flirtations With VAT*, in *The VAT Reader: What a Federal Consumption Tax Would Mean for America* 52 (Tax Analysts, 2011).

Schenk, Alan, Victor Thronyi, and Wei Cui, *Value Added Tax: A Comparative Approach*, 2nd ed. (Cambridge University Press, 2015).

Schilling, Peter, and Deirdre Hogan, *Intervention – A Problematic New Concept in EU VAT Law* 21(3) Int'l. VAT Monitor 187 (2010).

Schimmer, Johannes, *Transfer Pricing & Customs Valuation, Country Tax Guides – Germany* (IBFD Online).

Schmölders, Günther, *Organische Steuerreform* (Valhen Verlag, 1953).

Schneider, Friedrich, *The Shadow Economy and Tax Evasion: What Do We (Not) Know*, 13 CESifo Forum 2 (2012).

Schulte, Maria Dolores, *The Economic Theory of the Destination Principle and the Origin Principle* in *Comparison and Harmonization of Public Revenue Systems, Especially of Fiscal Systems*, Congrès de Luxembourg, September 1963, XIX Session.

Scott, Peter, *Thirty Years on: GST at a Crossroads: GST and Technology* 23 N.Z. J. Tax'n L. & Pol'y 146.

Shaheen, Salman, *A New Age Dawns for Indirect Tax* 23(10) Int'l Tax Rev. 22 (2012-13).

Shatalow, Nicholas, *Policy Forum: The GST/HST Obligations of Non-Resident E-Commerce Firms – Jurisprudence and Policy* 68(4) Can. Tax J. 1 (2020).

Shaxson, Nick, *Over a Third of World Trade Happens Inside Multinational Corporations*, Tax Justice Network (9 April 2019), available at https://www.taxjustice.net/2019/04/09/over-a-third-or-more-of-world-trade-happens-inside-multinational-corporations/.

Shome, Parthasarathi, Arnold Harberger, and Pedro Kondratiuk, *El impuesto al valor agregado (IVA): estructura del impuesto y eficiencia y mecanismos de la recaudación* (The Value Added Tax (VAT): Structure of the Tax, Efficiency, and Collection Mechanisms) (Fondo Monetario Internacional, Departamento de Finanzas Públicas, 1991).

Shoup, Carl, *The Sales Tax in France* (Columbia University Press, 1930).

Sicilian, Shirley, and Joe Huddleston, *The US States' Experience with Formulary Apportionment*, in *The Allocation of Multinational Business Income: Reassessing the Formulary Apportionment Option* 39 (Richard Krever & François Vaillancourt, eds., Kluwer Law International, 2020).

Sievers, Christopher, *GST on Judgments and Out of Court Settlements: Is GSTR 2001/4 Still Relevant?* 12 Austl. GST J. 16 (2013).

Silva, Ana Paula, *VAT Registration in Europe* 30 Publ. Res. Q. 152 (2014).

Simon, Hannah, and Michelle Harding, *What Drives Consumption Tax Revenues? Disentangling Policy and Macroeconomic Drivers*, OECD Taxation Working Papers No. 47 (OECD, 2020).

Simons, Henry C., *Personal Income Taxation: The Definition of Income as a Problem of Fiscal Policy* (University of Chicago Press, 1938).

Singh, B.N.P., *Programmes and Policies of Planning in India* (Deep & Deep Publications, 1991).

Singh, D.R., *Substitution of Excise Duty for Sales Tax: Its Impact on State Revenues* Econ. Weekly 1127 (11 July 1964).

Sitt, Ross, *Financial Supplies: Bundling & Unbundling* 9(2) eJ. Tax Rsrch194, 195 2011.

Skaar, Arvid A., *Permanent Establishment: Erosion of a Tax Treaty Principle* (Kluwer Law International, 1991).

Slemrod, Joel, and Nikki Sorum, *The Compliance Cost of the US Individual Income Tax System* 37(4) Nat'l Tax J. 461 (1984).

Slemrod, Joel, *Buenas Notches: Lines and Notches in Tax System Design* 11(3) eJ. Tax Research 259 (2013).

Smart, Michael, and François Vaillancourt, *Formulary Apportionment in Canada and Taxation of Corporate Income in 2019: Current Practice, Origins and Evaluation*, in *The Allocation of Multinational Business Income: Reassessing the Formulary Apportionment Option* 9 (Richard Krever & François Vaillancourt, eds., Kluwer Law International, 2020).

Smart, Michael, *Departures from Neutrality in Canada's Goods and Services Tax* in *After Twenty Years: The Future of the Goods and Services Tax* 81 (Jack Mintz and Stephen Richardson, eds, Canadian Tax Foundation, 2014).

Smith, Moira B. and Louise Signal, *Global Influences on Milk Purchasing in New Zealand – Implications for Health and Inequalities* 5(1) Global Health 9 (2009).

Smulders, Sharon, and Chris Evans, *Mitigating VAT Compliance Costs – A Developing Country Perspective* 32(2) Austl. Tax F. 283 (2017).

Sommer, Andrew, *The Application of the GST Law to Complex Transactions*, in *GST in Australia: Looking Forward from the First Decade* 97 (Christine Peacock ed., Thomson Reuters, 2011).

Spies, Karoline, *CJEU Case Law on Taxable Amount and Tax Rates 2017 – Comments*, in *CJEU – Recent Developments in Value Added Tax 2017* 281 (Michael Lang et al., eds., Linde, 2018),

Spies, Karoline, *CJEU Case Law on Taxable Persons in 2018*, in *CJEU – Recent Developments in Value Added Tax 2018* (Michael Lang et al., eds., Linde, 2019).

Spies, Karoline, *International Trade in B2B Services under VAT/GST Law and the Role of Permanent/Fixed Establishments – A Comparison of EU VAT and Singaporean GST Law in the Light of the OECD VAT/GST Guidelines* 25(3) Asia-Pacific Tax Bull. (2019).

Spies, Karoline, *Permanent Establishments in Value Added Tax* (IBFD Publications 2020).

Stacey, Paul, and William Brown, *GST Treatment of Debt & Equity Income Streams: An Australian View* 14(3) Int'l VAT Monitor, 295 (2003).

Stadie, Holger in *Umsatzsteuergesetz* § 17, paragraph 282 (Günter Rau & Erich Dürrwächter, eds., loose-leaf, Otto Schmidt, 176th Suppl., March 2018).

Stadie, Holger, *Befreiungen und Ermäßigungen - Chaos, System oder Konglomerat?*, in *Umsatzsteuer im Europäischen Binnenmarkt* 143 (Roman Seer, ed., Schmidt, 2009).

Staiger, Robert, and Alan Sykes, *'Currency Manipulation' and World Trade* 9(4) World Trade Rev. 583 (2010).

StanleySmith, Joe, *How Prepared Are Taxpayers and Authorities in GCC Countries for VAT?* 27(3) Int'l Tax Rev. 8 (2016).

State Taxation Administration, *Public Announcement on Issuing the Measures for the Exemption of VAT on Cross-border Taxable Activities for the B2V Reform* (Gonggao (2016) 29).

State Taxation Administration, *Public Announcement on Unifying Standards for Small-scale Taxpayers and Other Matters* (Gonggao (2018) 18).

State Taxation Administration, *The Most Comprehensive and Useful: The Latest VAT Rates 2019* (31 March 2019), available at http://www.chinatax.gov.cn/n810341/n2340339/c4180655/content.html.

Steinmo, Sven (ed.), *The Leap of Faith: The Fiscal Foundations of Successful Government in Europe and America* (Oxford University Press, 2018).

Steurer, Marianna, *VAT and Direct Tax Policy on Exemptions*, in *Global Trends in VAT/GST and Direct Taxes*, 89 (Sebastian Pfeiffer & Marlies Ursprung-Steindl, eds., Linde Verlag, 2015)

Stewart, David D., *EU Takes on VAT Treatment of E-Book Sales* 67 Tax Notes Int'l (16 July 2012).

Stitt, Ross, *Uncertanties Surrounding Input Tax Credit Entitlement in Australia*, in *GST in Australia: Looking Forward from the First Decade* 115, 117 (Christine Peacock, ed., Thomson Reuters, 2011).

Stockhammer, Engelbert, and Özlem Onaran, *Wage-Led Growth: Theory, Evidence, Policy* 1 ROKE 61 (2013).

Stoyan, Sophie, *Just a Click Away? Jurisdiction and Virtually Carrying On Business in Canada* 13(3) J. Priv. Int'l L. 602-632, 616 (2017).

Strumpel, Burkhard, *The Disguised Tax Burden Compliance Costs of German Businessmen and Professionals* 19(1) Nat'l Tax J. 70 (1966).

Sullivan, Clara K., *The Tax on Value Added* (Columbia University Press, 1965).

Sultan Khwaja, Munawer, and Indira Iyer, *Revenue Potential, Tax Space, and Tax Gap: A Comparative Analysis*, Policy Research Working Paper 6868, Poverty Reduction and Economic Management Department, Europe and Central Asia Region (World Bank, 2014).

Swinkels, Joep, *Fixed Establishments and VAT-Saving Schemes* 17(6) Int'l. VAT Monitor 415 (2006).

Tait, Alan A., *Value Added Tax: International Practice and Problems* (IMF, 1988).

Tang, Chris, *Australian GST Update – 2015* 5(1) World J. of VAT/GST 32 (2016).

Taxamo, *EU VAT B2C: Difference between B2B and B2C* (1 November 2017), https://blog.taxamo.com/insights/eu-vat-b2c-difference-b2b-b2c-clients.

Terkper, Seth E., *Ghana Reintroduces VAT: Lessons Learned and Progress after a Year* 20(11) Tax N. Int'l 1253 (2000).

Terkper, Seth E., *Ghana: Scope of New VAT Laws* 10(1) Int'l VAT Monitor (1999).

Terkper, Seth E., *VAT in Ghana: Why It Failed* 12(23) Tax N. Int'l 1801 (1996).

Terra, Ben et al., *Commentary on European VAT Directives, Chapter 9 – Exemptions* (IBFD, 2019).

Terra, Ben, and Julie Kajus, *A Guide to the European VAT Directives*. Vol. 1: Introduction to European VAT (IBFD, 2020).

Terra, Ben, and Julie Kajus, *A Guide to the European VAT Directives* (IBFD online).

Terra, Ben, *Levying VAT in the EU Customs Union: Towards a Single Indirect Tax Area? The Ordeal of Indirect Tax Harmonisation* 12 Erasmus Law Rev. 269 (2019).

Terra, Ben, *Sales Taxation. The Case of Value Added Tax in the European Community* (Kluwer Law International, 1988).

Thackray, Mick, and Kanar Ahmed, *Poland: Revenue Administration Gap Analysis Program—The Value-Added Tax Gap*, IMF Country Report No. 18/357 (IMF, 2018).

The Empowered Committee of State Finance Ministers, *A White Paper on State-Level Value Added Tax* (2005).

The Empowered Committee of State Finance Ministers, *First Discussion Paper on Goods and Services Tax in India* (2009).

The World Bank, *China 2030: Building a Modern, Harmonious, and Creative Society*, The World Bank and the Development Research Center of the State Council, the People's Republic of China, (2013), available at http://documents1.worldbank.org/curated/en/781101468239669951/pdf/China-2030-building-a-modern-harmonious-and-creative-society.pdf.

Thomas, Alastair G.A., *The Distributional Effects of Value-Added Taxes in OECD Countries*, PhD thesis, chapters 5 and 6 in particular (2020), available at http://researcharchive.vuw.ac.nz/handle/10063/9272.

Thomas, Alastair, *Reassessing the Regressivity of the VAT*, OECD Taxation Working Papers No. 29 (2020), available at https://www.oecd-ilibrary.org/taxation/reassessing-the-regressivity-of-the-vat_b76ced82-en.

Tørsløv, Thomas, Ludvig Wier, and Gabriel Zucman, *The Missing Profits of Nations* (National Bureau of Economic Research Working Paper, 22 April 2020).

Trebilcock, Michael J., *The International Movement of People: The Fourth Economic Freedom* (Max Planck Working Paper 2018).

Trenta, Cristina, *European VAT and the Digital Economy: Recent Developments* 17(1) eJournal Tax Res. 118 (2019).

Tuominen, Juha, *The Link Between Transfer Pricing and EU Customs Valuation Law: Is There Any and How Could It Be Strengthened?* 25(6) International Transfer Pricing J. 436 (2018).

Ueda, Junji, *The Evolution of Potential VAT Revenues and C-Efficiency in Advanced Economies*, Working Paper WP/17/158, Fiscal Affairs Department (IMF, 2017).

UNCTAD, *2019 Handbook of Statistics* 34 (10 December 2019), available at https://unctad.org/webflyer/handbook-statistics-2019.

UNCTAD, *2020 e-Handbook of Statistics*, available at https://stats.unctad.org/handbook/Services/Total.html.

United Nations, *Handbook on Selected Issues for Taxation of the Extractive Industries by Developing Countries* (United Nations, 2017).

United Nations, *Model Double Taxation Convention Between Developed and Developing Countries* (2017).

US Census Bureau, *Annual Retail Trade Survey: 2017*, available at https://www.census.gov/data/tables/2017/econ/arts/annual-report.html.

Vaillancourt, François, *The Administrative and Compliance Costs of the Personal Income Tax and Payroll Tax System in Canada* (Canadian Tax Foundation 1986).

Van Brederode, Robert F., and Marcus Susilo, *The VAT in the Arab Countries of the Gulf Cooperation Council* 28(6) Int'l VAT Monitor 435 (2017).

Van Brederode, Robert F., and Richard Krever, *VAT and Financial Services: Comparative Law and Economic Perspectives* (Springer, 2017).

Van Brederode, Robert F., and Sebastian Pfeiffer, *Combating Carousel Fraud: The General Reverse Charge VAT* 26(3) Int'l VAT Monitor 146 (2015).

Van Brederode, Robert F., and Sebastian Pfeiffer, *VAT's Superiority: Is the Emperor Dressed Like Adam?* 26(4) Int'l VAT Monitor 226 (2015).

Van Brederode, Robert F., and Simon Thang, *VAT and Subsidies: A Comparative Study of Law and Practice in Canada and the European Union* 67(3) Can. Tax J. 533 (2019).

Van Brederode, Robert F., *Introduction to the U.S. State Retail Sales and Use Taxes* 18(4) Int'l VAT Monitor 270 (2007).

Van Brederode, Robert F., *Revenue Distribution under a Combined Federal and State Consumption Tax* 121(8) Tax Notes, 953 (2008).

Van Brederode, Robert F., *Systems of General Sales Taxation: Theory, Policy and Practice* (Kluwer Law International, 2009).

Van Brederode, Robert F., *The American Debate on Taxing Distance Sales and E-Commerce* 18(5) Int'l VAT Monitor 352 (2007).

Van Brederode, Robert F., *The Future of the Economic Nexus Standard for U.S. Sales & Use Tax Collection* 47(10) Intertax 885 (2019).

Van Brederode, Robert F., *The Morality of Coerced Tax Collection* 9(1) J. Acct., Ethics & Pub. Policy 1 (2008).

Van Brederode, Robert F., *Third Party Risks and Liabilities in Case of VAT Fraud in the EU* 34(1) Int'l Tax J. 31 (2008).

Van Brederode, Robert F., *Towards a Federal Sales Tax in the U.S.?* 19(2) Int'l VAT Monitor 114-120 (2008).

Van Brederode, Robert F., *VAT's Regressivity: Empirical Truth or Political Correctness* 18(2) Int'l VAT Monitor 86 (2007).

Van den Brekel, Ronald, Ad van Doesum, and Herman van Kesteren, *VAT Effects of Year-End Transfer Pricing Adjustments* 26(4) EC Tax Rev. 182 (2017).

Van der Corput, Walter, *AstraZeneca – The VAT Treatment of Vouchers* 21(5) Int'l VAT Monitor 365 (2011).

Van Doesum, Ad J, and Frank J.G. Nellen, *Economic Reality in EU VAT* 29(5) EC Tax Review (2020).

Van Doesum, Ad J., and Herman W.M. van Kesteren, *De onlosmakelijke samenhang tussen kosten en belastbare handelingen*, 141 WFR (2012/885).

Van Doesum, Ad J., Case Law Comment, Dutch Supreme Court, 20 March 2012, nr. 09/03079, FED (2012/69).

Van Doesum, Ad, and Frank Nellen, *Taxable Amount and VAT Rates*, in *CJEU – Recent Developments in Value Added Tax 2017* 251, 264-274 (Michael Lang et al., eds., Linde, 2018).

Van Doesum, Ad, Herman van Kesteren, and Gert-Jan van Norden, *Fundamentals of EU VAT Law*, 2nd ed. (Wolters Kluwer 2020).

Van Doesum, Ad, Herman van Kesteren, and Gert-Jan van Norden, *The Internal Market and VAT: Intra-Group Transactions of Branches, Subsidiaries and VAT Groups* 16(1) EC Tax Rev. 34 (2007).

Van Hilten, Mariken E., *Over Neutraliteit van de Omzetbelasting en Het Hellend Vlak van de Uitzonderingen* (Kluwer, 2010).

Van Kesteren, Herman, and Mandy *Gabriël, Value Added Tax Exemptions in Europe: Recent Developments,* in *The Future of Indirect Taxation – Recent Trends in VAT and GST Systems Around the World* 607 (Thomas Ecker et al., eds., Wolters Kluwer, 2011).

Van Oordt Marius, and Richard Krever, *Legal Uncertainty in the South African VAT*, in *Tax Simplification: An African Perspective* 160 (Chris Evans, Riël Franzsen & Elizabeth Stack eds., Pretoria University Law Press, 2019).

Van Oordt, Marius, Zero *Rating Versus Cash Transfers under the VAT* 39 Fisc. Stud. 489 (2018).

Van Zyl, S.P., and W.G. Schulze, *The Collection of Value Added Tax on Cross-Border Digital Trade – Part 2: VAT Collection by Banks* 47(3) Comp. & Int'l L. J. S. Afr. 316 (2014).

Van Zyl, S.P., *The Collection of Value Added Tax on Cross-Border Digital Trade – Part 1: Registration of Foreign Vendors* 47(2) Comp. & Int'l L. J. S. Afr. 154 (2014).

Van Zyl, S.P., *The VAT treatment of Vouchers: A Comparative Study Between South Africa and the European Union* 46(2) Comp. & Int'l L. J. S. Afr. 234 (2013).

Vanhee, *Oman publishes VAT Law* (2020), available at https://aurifer.tax/news/oman-publishes-vat-law/?lid=482.

Vanistendael, Frans, *A Proposal for a Definitive VAT System Taxation in the Country of Origin at the Rate of the Country of Destination, Without Clearing* 1 EC Tax Rev. 45 (1995).

Varsano, Ricardo, *Subnational Taxation and Treatment of Interstate Trade in Brazil: Problems and Proposed Solution,* in *Decentralization and Accountability of the Public Sector* (Shahid J. Burki & Guillermo Perry, eds., Annual World Bank Conference on Development in Latin America and the Caribbean, World Bank, 2000).

VAT Committee, *Working paper No. 857* (6 May 2015), taxud.c.1(2015)2177802.

Vázquez-Caro, Jaime, and Richard M. Bird, *Benchmarking Tax Administrations in Developing Countries: A Systemic Approach,* 9 eJ. Tax Rsrch. 5 (2011).

Veronique Lenoir, *April 1954 – April 2004 VAT Exemptions: The Original Misunderstanding* 44(10) Eur. Tax'n 456 (2004).

Victoria University of Wellington Tax Working Group, *A Tax System for New Zealand's Future* (Centre for Accounting, Governance and Taxation Research, Victoria University of Wellington, 2010), available at https://www.victoria.ac.nz/sacl/centres-and-institutes/cagtr/pdf/tax-report-website.pdf (accessed 31 January 20 21).

Victoria-Sanchez, Antonio, *The European Court of Justice and VAT: The European Commission's Perspective* in *CJEU – Recent Developments in Value Added Tax 2014*, 17 (Michael Lang et al., eds., Linde Verlag, 2015).

Virmani, Arvind, *Central Value Added Tax: Time to Act* 36(8) Econ. & Pol. Weekly 630 (2001).

Virmani, Arvind, *Towards a Competitive Economy: VAT and Customs Duty Reform*, Working Paper No. 4/2002-PC (Planning Commission, Government of India, 2002).

Von der Leyen, Ursula, *A Union That Strives for More*, available at https://ec.europa.eu/commission/sites/beta-political/files/political-guidelines-next-commission_en.pdf (accessed 30 November 2020).

Von Siemens, Carl Friedrich, *Veredelte Umsatzsteuer*, 2nd ed. (Siemensstadt 1920, 1921).

Wagner, Adolph D., *Finanzwißenschaft*, Vol. 2 (C.F. Winter, 1880).

Walczak, Jared, and Janelle Cammenga, *State Sales Taxes in the Post-Wayfair Era*, Tax Foundation Fiscal Fact No. 680 (December 2019).

Walpole, Michael, *The Australian GST Cross-Border Rules in a Global Context*, 18(1) eJ. Tax Research 302 (2020).

Wang, Zhiyuan, Jagdeep Singh-Ladhar, and Howard Davey, *Business Tax to Value-Added Tax Reform in China* 31(4) Pacific Acct. Rev. 602 (2019).

Warren, Neil, *Estimating Tax Gap Is Everything to an Informed Response to the Digital Era* 16 eJ. Tax Research. 536 (2019).

Watanabe, Satoshi, *VAT in Japan with a Focus on International Transactions*, 61(9/10) Bull. for Int'l Taxation 379 (2007).

Watson, John, and Kate Garcia, *Babylonian Confusion Following the ECJ's Decision on Loyalty Rewards* 22(1) Int'l VAT Monitor 12 (2011).

Weber, Christian, *Der lange Weg zum Ursprungslandprinzip*, Umsatzsteuer-Rundschau 424 (2003).

Wei, Weixian, Junling Zhang, Baomin Dong, and Huiqing Wang, *Quantifying the Impacts of China's Currency Depreciation and Capital Control: A CGE Analysis* 25(14) Appl. Econ. Lett. 964 (2018).

Weidmann, Matthias, *The New EU VAT Rules on the Place of Supply of B2C E-Services: Practical Consequences – The German Example* 24(2) EC Tax Rev. 105 (2015).

Westin, Richard, *International Taxation of Electronic Commerce*, 2nd ed., 153 (Kluwer Law International, 2007).

Whittle, Edward, *A Shift in the EU VAT System: The Proposed Implementation of the 'Destination Principle' to Intra-EU B2B Supplies of Goods* 4(1) World J. of VAT/GST Law 41 (2015).

Wigny, Pierre, *Historique* in *Les Novelles: Droit des Communautés Européennes* 3 (Walter J. Ganshof van der Meersch, ed., Larcier, 1969).

Wikipedia, *Virtual Private Network*, available at https://en.wikipedia.org/wiki/Virtual_private_network.

Wilson, Nick, Lisa Te Morenga, Sally Mackay, Sarah Gerritsen, Christine Cleghorn, Amanda C Jones, and Boyd Swinburn, *Food Taxes and Subsidies to Protect Health: Relevance to Aotearoa New Zealand* 133 *NZMJ* 71, 73 (2020).

Wittock, Nathalie, *Sales Promotion Techniques and VAT – A Search for Neutrality for the Sales Promoter, also Taking into Account the Other Key Features and Principles of the VAT System* (Kluwer, 2019).

Woellner, Robin, Cynthia Coleman, Margaret McKerchar, Michael Walpole, and Julie Zetler, *Taxation or Vexation – Measuring the Psychological Costs of Tax Compliance*, in *Tax Compliance Costs: A Festschrift for Cedric Sandford* (Evans, Chris, Jeff Pope, and John Hasseldine eds, Prospect 2001).

Wolfers, Lachlan, *VAT and Technology: The First Fully Automated Tax?* Int. Tax Rev. (2019), available at https://www.internationaltaxreview.com/article/b1j8ydd4qghx0w/vat-and-technology-the-first-fully-automated-tax.

World Bank Group & PwC, *Paying Taxes 2020* (2019), https://www.pwc.com/gx/en/services/tax/publications/paying-taxes-2020.html.

World Bank, *Doing Business 2020*, available at https://www.doingbusiness.org/.

World Bank, *Paying Taxes, Global and Regional Findings: Africa* (2018), available at https://www.doingbusiness.org/en/reports/thematic-reports/paying-taxes-2019.

World Bank, *Republic of Kosovo Public Sector Revenues: Tax Policies, Tax Evasion and Tax Gap*, Report No. 89195-XK, Poverty Reduction and Economic Management Unit, Europe and Central Asia Region (2014).

World Bank, *World Development Indicators*, The World Bank, available at https://databank.worldbank.org/source/world-development-indicators.

World Customs Organization (WCO), *Guide to Customs Valuation and Transfer Pricing* (WCO 2018).

World Data Atlas, *Service Exports in Current Prices*, available at https://knoema.com/atlas/ranks/Service-exports?baseRegion = CN.

World Trade Organization (WTO), *Agreement on Subsides and Countervailing Measures*, available at https://www.wto.org/english/docs_e/legal_e/24-scm_01_e.htm.

World Trade Organization (WTO), *World Trade Statistical Review 2020*, available at https://www.wto.org/english/res_e/statis_e/wts2020_e/wts2020_e.pdf.

Worstall, Tim, *University Expansion Wasn't A Good Idea- Gove VAT and Sales Tax Edition*, Continental Telegraph (9 June 2019).

Wyonch, Rosalie, *Bits, Bytes, and Taxes: VAT and the Digital Economy in Canada*, C.D. Howe institute, Commentary No. 487 (August 2017), available at https://www.cdhowe.org/sites/default/files/attachments/research_papers/mixed/Commentary_487.pdf.

Xiao, Chengrui, and Yuchen Shao, *Information System and Corporate Income Tax Enforcement: Evidence from China*, 39(6) J. Acct & Pub. Pol'y 106772 (2020).

Yiallourou, Kiriaki *The Limitations of the VAT Gap Measurement* 2019/4 EC Tax Rev. 196 (2019).

Yiallourou, Kyriaki, *CJEU: Developments on VAT Exemptions in 2019* 47(6/7) Intertax 678 (2020).

Zhang, Longmei, and Sally Chen, *China's Digital Economy: Opportunities and Risks*, IMF Working Paper 8 (17 January 2019), available at https://www.imf.org/en/Publications/WP/Issues/2019/01/17/Chinas-Digital-Economy-Opportunities-and-Risks-46459.

Zodrow, George R., *The Sales Tax, the VAT, and Taxes in Between – Or, Is the Only Good NRST a 'VAT in Drag'?* 52(3) Nat'l Tax J. 429 (1999).

Zu, Yige, and Richard Krever, *GST Cash and Accrual Mismatches: Avoiding the Avoidance* 46(4) Austl. Tax Rev. 27 (2017).

Zu, Yige, and Richard Krever, *The United Kingdom Has Spoken: The Receding Impact of European Jurisprudence on the UK Interpretation of the Common VAT System* 49(1) Comm. L. World Rev. 75 (2020).

Zu, Yige, Chris Evans, and Richard Krever, *The VAT Compliance Burden in the UK: A Comparative Assessment* 3 Brit. Tax Rev. 356 (2020).

Zu, Yige, *VAT/GST Thresholds and Small Businesses: Where to Draw the Line?* 66(2) Can. Tax J. 309 (2018).

Table of Cases

Australia

Ballarat Brewing Co. v. FCT (1951) 82 CLR 364, 237
Interchase Corporation Ltd v. ACN 010 087 573 Pty Ltd (2000) 45 ATR 445 (QSC) (Aust.), 249
Osric Investments Pty Ltd v. Woburn Downs Pastoral Pty Ltd (2001) 48 ATR 184 (Fed. Ct.) (Aust.), 249
Walter Construction Group Limited v. Walker Corporation Ltd & Ors [2001] NSWSC 283, 249
Apple Computer Australia Pty Ltd v. Mekrizis and Ors (2003) 54 ATR 383, 248
Marana Holdings Pty Ltd v. Commissioner of Taxation [2004] FCAFC 307, 138
HP Mercantile Pty Ltd v. Commissioner of Taxation [2005] FCR 553, 229
Saga Holidays Ltd v. Commissioner of Taxation (Cth) and others (2006) 156 FCR 256, 227
Sterling Guardian v. Federal Commissioner of Taxation (2006) 228 ALR 712, 226
Vadasz v. FCT 2006 63 ATR 1236, 236, 248
Commissioner of Taxation v. Reliance Carpet Co. Pty Ltd (2008) 236 CLR 342, 226–228, 245, 246
Gagner Pty Ltd (trading as Indochine Café) v. Canturi Corp Pty Ltd [2009] NSWCA 413 (NSW CA) (Aust.), 249
GXCX v. Commissioner of Taxation [2009] AATA 569; 2009 ATC 1-012; (2009) 73 ATR 380, 254
The Electrical Goods Importer v. FCT [2009] AATA 854, 241
TT Line v. FCT (2009) 72 ATR 982, 241
TT Line Company Pty Ltd v. Federal Commissioner of Taxation (2009) 181 FCR 400, 241
QFP Professional Tomato Project and Others v. FCT [2010] AATA 864, 248
Travelex Ltd v. Commissioner of Taxation (2010) 241 CLR 510, 226
A Taxpayer v. Commissioner of Taxation [2011] AATA 160; 2011 ATC 1-029, 254
Commissioner of Taxation v. Luxottica Retail Australia Pty Ltd [2011] FCAFC, 138
Lansell House Pty Ltd v. Federal Commissioner of Taxation [2011] FCAFC 6, 137

Austria

Colombia

EU

CJEU, 11 October 2001, Case C-267/99, *Christiane Adam, épouse Urbing v. Administration de l'enregistrement et des domaines*, ECLI:EU:C:2001:534, 59

CJEU, 21 March 2002, Case C-174/00, *Kennemer Golf & Country Club v. Staatssecretaris van Financiën*, ECLI:EU:C:2002:200, 335

CJEU, 10 September 2002, Case C-141/00, *Ambulanter Pflegedienst Kügler GmbH v. Finanzamt für Körperschaften I in Berlin*, ECLI:EU:C:2002:473, 67

CJEU, 15 October 2002, Case C-427/98, *Commission of the European Communities v. Federal Republic of Germany*, ECLI:EU:C:2002:581; Opinion AG ECLI: EU:C:2001:457, 348

CJEU, 16 January 2003, Case C-398/99, *Yorkshire Co-operatives Ltd. v. Commissioners of Customs & Excise*, ECLI:EU:C:2003:20, 261

CJEU, 3 April 2003, Case C-144/00, *Matthias Hoffmann*, ECLI:EU:C:2003:192, 66

CJEU, 8 May 2003, Case C-269/00, *Wolfgang Seeling v. Finanzamt Starnberg*, ECLI: EU:C:2003:254, 468

CJEU, 8 May 2003, Case C-384/01, *Commission v. France*, ECLI:EU:C:2003:264, 93

CJEU, 12 June 2003, Case C-275/01, *Sinclair Collis Ltd v. Commissioners of Customs & Excise*, ECLI:EU:C:2003:341, 335

CJEU, 26 June 2003, Case C-442/01, *KapHag Renditefonds 35 Spreecenter Berlin-Hellersdorf 3. Tranche GbR v. Finanzamt Charlottenburg*, ECLI:EU:C:2003:381, 321

CJEU, 11 September 2003, Case C-155/01, *Cookies World Vertriebsgesellschaft mbH iL v. Finanzlandesdirektion für Tirol*, ECLI:EU:C:2003:449, 464

CJEU, 23 October 2003, Case C-109/02, *Commission of the European Communities v. Federal Republic of Germany*, ECLI:EU:C:2003:586, 59

CJEU, 6 November 2003, Case C-45/01, *Christoph-Dornier-Stiftung für Klinische Psychologie v. Finanzamt Gießen*, ECLI:EU:C:2003:595, 59

CJEU, 29 April 2004, Case C-77/01, *Empresa de Desenvolvimento Mineiro SGPS SA (EDM) v. Fazenda Pública*, ECLI:EU:C:2004:243, 384

CJEU, 21 October 2004, Case C-8/03, *Banque Bruxelles Lambert SA (BBL) v. Belgian State*, ECLI:EU:C:2004:650, 71

CJEU, 18 November 2004, Case C-284/03, *Belgian State v. Temco Europe SA*, ECLI: EU:C:2004:730, 335

CJEU, 20 January 2005, Case C-412/03, *Hotel Scandic Gåsabäck AB v. Riksskatteverket*, ECLI:EU:C:2005:47, 233, 467, 482

CJEU, 17 February 2005, Joined Cases C-453/02 and C-462/02, *Finanzamt Gladbeck v. Edith Linneweber and Finanzamt Herne-West v. Savvas Akritidis*, ECLI: EU:C:2005:92, 60

CJEU, 3 March 2005, Case C-472/03, *Staatssecretaris van Financiën v. Arthur Andersen & Co. Accountants c.s.*, ECLI:EU:C:2005:135, 63

CJEU, 12 May 2005, Case C-452/03, *RAL (Channel Islands) Ltd, RAL Ltd, RAL Services Ltd, RAL Machines Ltd v. Commissioners of Customs and Excise*, ECLI: EU:C:2005:289, 363

CJEU, 26 May 2005, Case C-465/03, *Kretztechnik AG v. Finanzamt Linz* ECLI: EU:C:2005:320, 398

CJEU, 26 May 2005, Case C-498/03, *Kingscrest Associates Ltd and Montecello Ltd v. Commissioners of Customs & Excise*, ECLI:EU:C:2005:322, 59, 98

CJEU, 2 June 2005, Case C-378/02, *Waterschap Zeeuws Vlaanderen v. Staatssecretaris van Financiën*, Opinion AG, 18 November 2004, ECLI:EU:C:2004:726, 61

CJEU, 27 October 2005, Case C-41/04, *Levob Verzekeringen BV and OV Bank NV v. Staatssecretaris van Financiën*, ECLI:EU:C:2005:649, 91

CJEU, 1 December 2005, Case C-394/04, *Diagnostiko & Therapeftiko Kentro Athinon-Ygeia AE v. Ypourgos Oikonomikon*, ECLI:EU:C:2005:734, 63

CJEU, 12 January 2006, Case C-246/04, *Turn- und Sportunion Waldburg v. Finanzlandesdirektion für Oberösterreich*, ECLI:EU:C:2006:22, 59

CJEU, 21 February 2006, Case C-255/02, *Halifax plc, Leeds Permanent Development Services Ltd and County Wide Property Investments Ltd v. Commissioners of Customs & Excise*, ECLI:EU:C:2006:121, 473

CJEU, 21 February 2006, Case C-419/02, *BUPA Hospitals Ltd and Goldsborough Developments Ltd v. Commissioners of Customs & Excise*, ECLI:EU:C:2006:122, 338

CJEU, 23 March 2006, Case C-210/04, *Ministero dell'Economia e delle Finanze and Agenzia delle Entrate v. FCE Bank plc.*, ECLI:EU:C:2006:196, 71, 371

CJEU, 27 April 2006, Joined Cases C-443/04 and C-444/04, H.A. *Solleveld and E. van den Hout-van Eijnsbergen v. Staatssecretaris van Financiën*, ECLI:EU:C:2006:257, 59

CJEU, 8 June 2006, Case C-106/05, *L.u.P. GmbH v. Finanzamt Bochum-Mitte*, ECLI:EU:C:2006:380, 59

CJEU, 8 June 2006, Case C-430/04, *Finanzamt Eisleben v. Feuerbestattungsverein Halle*, ECLI:EU:C:2006:374, 65

CJEU, 6 July 2006, Case C-251/05, *Talacre Beach Caravan Sales Ltd v. Customs and Excise Commissioners*, ECLI:EU:C:2006:451, 93

CJEU, 7 December 2006, Case C-240/05, *Administration de l'enregistrement et des domaines v. Eurodental Sàrl*, ECLI:EU:C:2006:763, 71

CJEU, 15 March 2007, Case C-35/05, *Reemtsma Cigarettenfabriken GmbH v. Ministero delle Finanze*, ECLI:EU:C:2007:167, 269

CJEU, 19 April 2007, Case C-455/05, *Velvet & Steel Immobilien und Handels GmbH v. Finanzamt Hamburg-Eimsbüttel*, ECLI:EU:C:2007:232, 112

CJEU, 14 June 2007, Case C-434/05, *Stichting Regionaal Opleidingen Centrum Noord-Kennemerland/West-Friesland (Horizon College) v. Staatssecretaris van Financiën*, ECLI:EU:C:2007:343, 105

CJEU, 28 June 2007, Case C-73/06, *Planzer Luxembourg Sàrl v. Bundeszentralamt für Steuern*, ECLI:EU:C:2007:397, 364

CJEU, 28 June 2007, Case C-363/05, *JP Morgan Fleming Claverhouse Investment Trust plc and The Association of Investment Trust Companies v. The Commissioners of HM Revenue and Customs*, ECLI:EU:C:2007:391, 66

CJEU, 18 July 2007, Case C-277/05, *Société Thermale d'Eugénie-les-Bains v. Ministère de l'Économie, des Finances et de l'Industrie*, ECLI:EU:C:2007:440, 245

CJEU, 27 September 2007, Case C 146/05, *Albert Collée v. Finanzamt Limburg an der Lahn*, ECLI:EU:C:2007:549, 67

Germany

Japan

India

The Netherlands

UK

US

Index

H

I

J

K

L

M

N

O